COMPUTER SECURITY HANDBOOK

Fourth Edition

COMPUTER SECURITY HANDBOOK

Fourth Edition

Edited by

SEYMOUR BOSWORTH

M.E. KABAY

JOHN WILEY & SONS, INC.

ISBN 0-471-41258-9

Printed in the United States of America.

10 9 8 7 6 5

PREFACE

Computers are an integral part of our economic, social, professional, governmental, and military infrastructures. They have become necessities in virtually every area of modern life, but their vulnerability is of increasing concern. Computer-based systems are constantly under threats of inadvertent error and acts of nature, as well as those attributable to unethical, immoral, and criminal activities. It is the purpose of this *Computer Security Handbook* to provide guidance in eliminating these threats where possible, and if not, then to lessen any losses attributable to them.

This *Handbook* will be most valuable to those directly responsible for computer, network, or information security, as well as those who must design, install, and maintain secure systems. It will be equally important to those managers whose operating functions can be affected by breaches in security, and to those executives who are responsible for protecting the assets that have been entrusted to them.

With the advent of desktop, laptop, and handheld computers, and with the vast international networks that interconnect them, the nature and extent of threats to computer security have grown almost beyond measure. In order to encompass this unprecedented expansion, the *Computer Security Handbook* has grown apace.

When the first edition of the *Handbook* was published, its entire focus was on mainframe computers, the only type then in widespread use. The second edition recognized the advent of small computers, while the third edition placed increased emphasis on PCs and networks.

Now, this fourth edition of the *Computer Security Handbook,* gives almost equal attention to mainframes and microcomputers. With 54 chapters alone requiring over 1,100 pages, the related tutorials and appendixes have been installed on the Internet at *www.wiley.com/go/securityhandbook.* This electronic supplement has made possible the manageable size and weight of the present hard-copy book, while presenting a greater wealth of material than ever before. The Internet presence has the added advantages of providing hyperlinks to other relevant sites and of making updates feasible.

Edition	Date	Chapters	Text Pages	Pages of Appendices	Total Pages	Internet Supplement
First	1973	12	162	3	165	—
Second	1988	19	298	93	391	—
Third	1995	23	571	365	984	—
Fourth	2002	54	1184	On Internet	1224	*www.wiley.com/go/ securityhandbook*

The Internet has been invaluable in another way. Each of the 54 chapters has made at least seven retransmissions via e-mail among authors, editors, and the publisher. Earlier editions had all of this done by courier or overnight delivery, with attendant delays and significant costs. Not only are PCs and the Internet a major subject of this volume, but they have also been the instruments without which it might never have come into being.

In speaking of the earlier editions, I would like to give grateful recognition to Arthur Hutt and Douglas Hoyt, my previous co-editors. Although both Art and Doug are deceased, their commitment and their competence remain as constant reminders to strive for excellence. Mich Kabay, my new co-editor continues in their tradition. I would not have wanted to undertake this project without him.

Thanks are also due to our colleagues at John Wiley and Sons. Sheck Cho as Executive Editor, Tim Burgard as Associate Editor, Louise Jacobs as Associate Managing Editor, and Debra Manette and John Curley as copyeditors all have performed their duties in exemplary manner.

Finally, although the authors and editors of this *Handbook* have attempted to cover the essential elements of computer security, the disaster of September 11, 2001, demonstrates that new threats may come from unexpected directions. The primary emphasis of the *Computer Security Handbook* has always been on prevention, but should this fail, the fundamental practices described here will help to mitigate the consequences.

SEYMOUR BOSWORTH
Senior Editor
February 2002

A Note from the Co-Editor

I am immeasurably grateful to Sy Bosworth for his leadership in this project. Although we have never met each other in the physical world, I feel that we have become good friends through our constant communication through cyberspace.

Our authors deserve enormous credit for the professional way in which they responded to our requests, outlines, suggestions, corrections, and nagging. I want to express my personal gratitude and appreciation for their courteous, collaborative, and responsive interactions with us.

Finally, as always, I want to thank my beloved wife, Deborah Black, light of my life, for her support and understanding over the many months during which this project has taken away from our time together.

M.E. KABAY
Co-Editor
February 2002

ABOUT THE EDITORS

Seymour Bosworth (e-mail: *sybosworth@aol.com*), MS, CDP, is president of S. Bosworth & Associates, Plainview, New York, a management consulting firm active in computing applications for banking, commerce, and industry. Since 1972, he has been a contributing editor of all four editions of the *Computer Security Handbook,* and he has written many articles and lectured extensively about computer security and other technical and managerial subjects. He has been responsible for design and manufacture, system analysis, programming, and operations, of both digital and analog computers. For his technical contributions, including an error-computing calibrator, a programming aid, and an analog-to-digital converter, he has been granted a number of patents, and is working on several others.

Bosworth is a former president and CEO of Computer Corporation of America, manufacturers of computers for scientific and engineering applications; president of Abbey Electronics Corporation, manufacturers of precision electronic instruments and digital devices; and president of Alpha Data Processing Corporation, a general-purpose computer service bureau. As a vice president at Bankers Trust company, he had overall responsibility for computer operations, including security concerns.

For more than 20 years, Bosworth was an adjunct associate professor of management at the Information Technologies Institute of New York University, where he lectured on computer security and related disciplines. He holds a master's degree from the Graduate School of Business of Columbia University, and the Certificate in Data Processing of the Data Processing Management Association.

M.E. Kabay, Ph.D., CISSP (e-mail: *mkabay@norwich.edu*) began learning assembler at age 15 and had learned FORTRAN IV G at McGill University by 1966. In 1976, he received his Ph.D. from Dartmouth College in applied statistics and invertebrate zoology. He has published over 350 articles in operations management and security in several trade journals. He currently writes two columns a week for *Network World Fusion;* archives are at *www.nwfusion.com/newsletters/sec/.* Kabay was Director of Education for the National Computer Security Association from 1991 to the end of 1999. He was Security Leader for the INFOSEC Group of AtomicTangerine, Inc., from January 2000 to June 2001 and joined the faculty at Norwich University in July 2001 as Associate Professor of Computer Information Systems. In January 2002, he took on additional duties as the director of the graduate program in information assurance at Norwich. He has a Web site at *www2.norwich.edu/mkabay/index.htm.*

ABOUT THE CONTRIBUTORS

Rebecca G. (Becky) Bace (e-mail: *infomom@infidel.net*) is the President/CEO of Infidel, Inc. (*www.infidel.net*), a network security consulting practice. She has been an active force in the intrusion detection community for over a decade: as the director of the National Security Agency's research program for intrusion detection (1989–1996), where she funded much of the early research in intrusion detection; as deputy security officer for the Computing Information, and Communications Division of the Los Alamos National Laboratory (1996–1997); and in her current capacity at Infidel. Bace is author of the National Institute for Standards and Technology's Special Publication on Intrusion Detection (SP 800-31), the book *Intrusion Detection* (Macmillan Technical Publishing, 2000), and a variety of intrusion detection references published over the last five years. She is currently advising a group of security solution startups; working with Trident Capital (*www.tridentcap.com*), where she is responsible for directing network security investment activities; and serving as faculty for the popular Intrusion Detection Forum series for senior information security managers offered by the Institute for Applied Network Security (*www.ianetsec.com*).

Timothy Braithwaite (e-mail: *tim.braithwaite@titan.com*) has more than 30 years of hands-on experience in all aspects of automated information processing and communications. He is currently Deputy Director of Strategic Programs at the Center for Information Assurance of Titan Corporation. Before joining Titan Corporation, he managed most aspects of information technology, including data and communications centers, software development projects, strategic planning and budget organizations, system security programs, and quality improvement initiatives. His pioneering work in computer systems and communications security while with the Department of Defense resulted in his selection to be the first Systems Security Officer for the Social Security Administration in 1980. After developing security policy and establishing a nationwide network of regional security officers, Braithwaite directed the risk assessment of all payment systems for the agency. In 1982, he assumed the duties of Deputy Director, Systems Planning and Control of the SSA, where he performed substantive reviews of all major acquisitions for the Associate Commissioner for Systems and, through a facilitation process, personally led the development of the first Strategic Systems Plan for the Administration. In 1984, he became Director of Information and Communication Services for the Bureau of Alcohol, Tobacco, and Firearms at the Department of Treasury. In the private sector, he worked in senior technical and business development positions for SAGE Federal Systems, a software development company; Validity Corporation, a testing and independent validation and verification company; and J.G. Van Dyke & Associates where he was Director: Y2K Testing Services. He was recruited to join Titan Corporation in December 1999 to assist in establishing and growing the company's

Information Assurance (IA) practice. He recently authored *Securing E-Business: A Guide for Managers and Executives* (John Wiley & Sons, 2002). He can be reached by phone at 301 982 5414.

Paul J. Brusil, Ph.D (e-mail: *brusil@post.harvard.edu*) founded Strategic Management Directions, a security and enterprise management consultancy in Beverly, Massachusetts, He has been working with various industry and government sectors including healthcare, telecommunications, and middleware to improve the specification, implementation, and use of trustworthy, quality, security-related products and systems. He supported strategic planning that led to the National Information Assurance Partnership and other industry forums created to understand, promote, and use the Common Criteria to develop security and assurance requirements and evaluated products. Brusil has organized, convened, and chaired several national workshops, conferences, and international symposia pertinent to management and security. Through these and other efforts to stimulate awareness and cooperation among competing market forces, he spearheaded industry's development of the initial open, secure, convergent, standards-based network and enterprise management solutions. While at the MITRE Corp, Brusil led R&D critical to the commercialization of world's first LAN solutions, Earlier, at Harvard, he pioneered research leading to noninvasive diagnosis of cardio-pulmonary dysfunction. He is a Senior Member of the IEEE, a member of the Editorial Advisory Board of the *Journal of Network and Systems Management* (*JNSM*), and has been Senior Technical Editor for *JNSM*. He has authored nearly over 100 papers and book chapters. He graduated from Harvard University with a joint degree in Engineering and Medicine.

David Brussin, CISSP (e-mail: *dbrussin@pobox.com*), is a leading technical security and privacy expert. His experience architecting robust, efficient, and secure information handling processes and electronic business systems for Fortune 100 organizations led to the creation of unique formal models for information security, including Three Layer Analysis and Successive Compromise Analysis. His techniques, which provide a complete, repeatable methodology for designing and verifying the security of connected infrastructure, are recognized as an industry-leading approach. He is now serving as Chief Technology Officer for ePrivacy Group, a Philadelphia-based privacy consulting, training, and technology company. He was a founding partner of InfoSec Labs, Inc., and then Director of Security Technology for Rainbow Technologies following its acquisition of InfoSec Labs in 1999. Brussin has published numerous articles and is a frequent speaker on security and privacy issues.

Quinn Campbell (e-mail: *qcampbell@hushmail.com*) has worked in the information security field for over six years. He specializes in IT threat analysis and education.

John M. Carroll, LL.B., Dr. Eng. Sci. (e-mail: *jmcarroll7@aol.com*) is a Professor Emeritus in the Department of Computer Science of the University of Western Ontario. He is a registered professional engineer and works in a criminal law practice. His research interests are information technology risk management; cryptography; and microdocumentary analysis. He has been consulted by police and security forces in seven countries.

Santosh Chokhani (e-mail: *chokhani@cygnacom.com*) is the founder and President of CygnaCom Solutions, Inc., an Entrust company specializing in PKI. He has made numerous contributions to PKI technology and related standards including trust models, security, and policy and revocation processing. He is the inventor of the PKI Certificate Policy and Certification Practices Statement Framework. His pioneering work in this area led to the Internet RFC that is used as the Standard for CP and CPS by governments and industry throughout the world. Before starting CygnaCom, he worked for The MITRE Corporation from 1978 to 1994. At MITRE, he was senior technical manager and managed a variety of technology research, development, and engineering projects in the areas of PKI, computer security, expert systems, image processing, and computer graphics. He obtained his Masters (1971) and Ph.D. (1975) in EE/CS from Rutgers University, where he was a Louis Bevior Fellow from 1971–1973.

Chey Cobb, CISSP (e-mail: *chey@patriot.net*) began her career in information security while at the National Computer Security Association (now known as TruSecure/ICSA Labs). During her tenure as the NCSA award-winning Webmaster, she realized that Web servers often created security holes in networks and became an outspoken advocate of systems' security. Later, while developing secure networks for the Air Force in Florida, her work captured the attention of the U.S. intelligence agencies. Chey moved to Virginia and began working for the government as the senior technical security advisor on highly classified projects. Ultimately, she went on to manage the security program at an overseas site. Chey is now semi-retired and writes books and articles on computer security and is a frequent speaker at security conferences.

Stephen Cobb, CISSP (e-mail: *scobb@cobb.com*) has been helping companies, governments, and individuals to secure their computer-based information for more than 15 years. A best-selling author of over 20 computer books, Cobb has presented security seminars and chaired security conferences in Europe, Asia, and America. He is now Senior V.P. of Research & Education for ePrivacy Group, a Philadelphia-based privacy consulting, training and technology company. He served for two years as Director of Special Projects for the National Computer Security Association, launching its award-winning Web site and the Firewall Product Developers' Consortium. He left NCSA to become a founding partner of InfoSec Labs, Inc., which was acquired by Rainbow Technologies in 1999. Frequently quoted by the media as a security expert in the United States, Europe, and Asia, Cobb has published in a wide range of publications. His recent writings can be found on his Web site at *www.cobb.com.*

Bernard Cowens, CISSP (e-mail: *bernie.cowens@infosec.spectria.com*) is Vice President of Security Services for Rainbow-Spectria, a digital security company. He is a security expert with over 15 years' experience in designing, developing, managing, and protecting complex and sensitive information systems and networks. He has extensive experience managing and securing high availability, multisite military and civilian data centers and is therefore uniquely adept at recognizing and balancing security imperatives with operational realities. He has conducted security reviews and analyses which involved extremely sensitive, highly classified national security data and equipment. Cowens has created, trained, and served on a number of computer emergency and incident response teams over the years and has real-world experience responding to disasters, attacks and system failures resulting from a variety of sources. He has served as a member of and an advisor to national-level panels charged with analyzing network and information system threats, assessing associated risks, and recommending both technical and nontechnical risk mitigation policies and procedures.

He holds a Master's degree in Management Information Systems and undergraduate degrees and certificates in data processing and systems management.

Seth Finkelstein (e-mail: *sethf@sethf.com*) is a professional programmer with degrees in Mathematics and in Physics from MIT. He cofounded the Censorware Project, an anti-censorware advocacy group. In 1998, his efforts evaluating the sites blocked by the library's Internet policy in Loudoun County, VA, helped the American Civil Liberties Union win a federal lawsuit challenging the policy. In 2001, he received a Pioneer of the Electronic Frontier Award from the Electronic Frontier Foundation for his groundbreaking work in analyzing content-blocking software.

Robert Gezelter, CDP (e-mail: *gezelter@rlgsc.com*) has over 27 years of experience in computing, starting with programming scientific/technical problems. Shortly thereafter, his focus shifted to operating systems, networks, security, and related matters. He has more than 26 years of experience in systems architecture, programming, and management. He has worked extensively in systems architecture, security, internals, and networks, ranging from high-level strategic issues to the low-level specification, design, and implementation of device protocols and embedded firmware. He is the author of numerous published articles, which have appeared in *Hardcopy, Computer Purchasing Update, Network Computing, Open Systems Today, Digital Systems Journal,* and *Network World.* He is a frequent presenter of conference sessions on operating systems, languages, security, networks, and related topics at local, regional, national, and international conferences; speaking for DECUS, Encompass, IEEE, ISSA, ISACA, and others. He previously authored the "Internet Security" chapters of "*The Computer Security Handbook, 3rd Edition*" (1995) and its supplement (1997).

Anup K. Ghosh, Ph.D. (e-mail: *anup.ghosh@computer.org*) is Vice President of Research at Cigital, Inc., and an expert in e-commerce security. He is the author of *E-Commerce Security: Weak Links, Best Defenses* (Wiley, 1998), a definitive guide to e-commerce security, and *Security and Privacy for E-Business* (John Wiley & Sons, 2001). His areas of research expertise include intrusion detection, mobile code security, software security certification, malicious software detection/tolerance, assessing the robustness of Win32 COTS software, and software vulnerability analysis. He has served as principal investigator on grants from DARPA, NSA, AFRL, and NIST's Advanced Technology Program and has consulted with Fortune 50 companies to assess the security of e-commerce systems. He has written more than 40 peer-reviewed technical publications, is a regular contributor to popular trade publications, and has been interviewed about Internet credit card fraud on CNBC Business News. He recently received an IEEE Third Millennium Medal for Outstanding Contributions to E-Commerce Security. In February 2001, the District of Columbia Council of Engineering and Architectural Societies (DCCEAS) named Ghosh "Young Engineer of the Year." He holds a B.S. in Electrical Engineering from Worcester Polytechnic Institute and a M.S. and Ph.D. in Electrical Engineering from the University of Virginia.

Carl Hallberg (e-mail: *carl_hallberg@yahoo.com*) has been a *nix systems administrator for years, as well as an information security consultant. He has also written training courses for subjects including firewalls, VPNs, and home network security. He has a Bachelor's degree in Psychology.

David Harley (e-mail: *david.harley@nhsia.nhs.uk*) is a senior manager in the United Kingdom's National Health Service Information Authority, where he is responsible for threat assessment, security alert/advisory, and incident report tracking services. He also coordinates virus incident management within the National Health Service. His affiliations include AVIEN, AVAR, EICAR, and Team Anti-Virus. He works with TruSecure and the WildList Organization on Macintosh security issues. He is coauthor of *Viruses Revealed* (Osborne), and has contributed chapters to *Maximum Security* (SAMS) and Robert Vibert's *Enterprise Anti-Virus Book,* and articles to *Virus Bulletin* and other security industry periodicals. He has presented at Virus Bulletin, SANS, and EICAR conferences.

Benjamin Hayes (e-mail: *bhayes@kl.com*) is an attorney with Kirkpatrick & Lockhart, a national U.S. law firm. His practice centers on legal issues related to privacy, including state, federal, international, and transnational regulatory compliance, the development of codes of practice, and compliance with self-regulatory programs. He has advised multinational, high-technology, and traditional business clients in these matters and is the author of numerous articles on the law of privacy. He is the current Vice-Chair of the ABA Cyberspace Law Committee's Electronic Privacy Subcommittee. He is a graduate of the Ohio State University College of Law and the University of Vermont.

Robert Heverly (e-mail: *techlaw@capturedgraphics.com*) is an attorney and has been practicing law in New York state since 1993. From 1992 to 2001, he was at the Government Law Center of Albany Law School, most recently as assistant director. While at the Center, he focused on the law and policy of technology, telecommunications, and the Internet, among other areas related to government and public administration. In August 2001, he returned to his studies, becoming a graduate fellow at Yale Law School, where his research focuses primarily on information technology and telecommunications. He is an honors graduate of Albany Law School and the State University of New York College at Oswego and anticipates receiving his LL.M. (Master of Laws) from Yale Law School in May 2002.

John D. Howard (e-mail: *johnhoward@earthlink.net*) is a former Air Force engineer and test pilot who currently works in the Security and Networking Research Group at the Sandia National Laboratories, Livermore, CA. His projects include development of the SecureLink software for automatic encryption of network connections. He has extensive experience in systems development, including an aircraft ground collision avoidance systems for which he holds a patent. He is a graduate of the Air Force Academy, has Master's degrees in both Aeronautical Engineering and Political Science, and has a Ph.D. in Engineering and Public Policy from Carnegie Mellon University.

Arthur E. Hutt. The late Arthur E. Hutt, CCEP, was an information systems consultant with extensive experience in banking, industry, and government. He was a principle of PAGE Assured Systems, Inc., a consulting group specializing in security and control of information systems and contingency/disaster recovery planning. He was a senior information systems executive for several major banks active in domestic and international banking. His innovative and pioneering development of online banking systems received international recognition. He was also noted for his contributions to computer security and to information systems planning for municipal government. He was on the faculty of the City University of New York and served as a consultant to

CUNY on curriculum and on data processing management. He also served on the mayor's technical advisory panel for the City of New York. Hutt was active in development of national and international technical standards, via ANSI and ISO, for the banking industry. He was senior editor and contributing author to the Third Edition of the *Computer Security Handbook.*

Robert V. Jacobson, CPP, CISSP (e-mail: *jacobson@ist-usa.com*) is the president of International Security Technology, Inc., a New York City-based risk management consulting firm. Jacobson founded IST in 1978 to develop and apply superior risk management systems. Current and past government and industry clients are located in the United States, Europe, Africa, Asia, and the Middle East. Jacobson pioneered many of the basic computer security concepts now in general use. He served as the first Information System Security Officer at Chemical Bank, now known as J P Morgan Chase. He is a frequent lecturer and has written numerous technical articles. Mr. Jacobson holds B.S. and M.S. degrees from Yale University, and is a Certified Information Systems Security Professional (CISSP). He is also a Certified Protection Professional (CPP) of the American Society for Industrial Security. He is a member of the National Fire Protection Association (NFPA) and the Information Systems Security Association (ISSA). In 1991, he received the Fitzgerald Memorial Award for Excellence in Security from the New York Chapter of the ISSA. He developed the Cost-of-Risk Analysis (CORA) program, a risk management decision support system available online at *www.ist-usa.com.*

Henry L. Judy (e-mail: *hjudy@kl.com*) is of counsel to Kirkpatrick & Lockhart, a national U.S. law firm. He advises clients on a wide range of corporate and financial law matters, as well as federal and state securities, legislative, and regulatory matters, with a particular emphasis on financial institutions, housing finance and technology law. He is recognized for his work on the jurisdiction and dispute resolution issues of electronic commerce. He is a graduate of Georgetown University (J.D. and A.B.)

David M. Kennedy, CISSP (e-mail: *david.kennedy@acm.org*) is TruSecure Corporation's Chief of Research. He directs the Research Group to provide expert services to TruSecure Corporation members, clients, and staff. He supervises the Information Security Reconnaissance team (IS/R) who collect security-relevant information, both above and underground in TruSecure Corporation's IS/R data collection. IS/R provides biweekly and special topic reports to IS/ R subscribers. Kennedy is a retired U.S. Army Military Police officer. In his last tour of duty, he was responsible for enterprise security of five LAN's with Internet access and over 3,000 personal computers and workstations. He holds a B.S. in Forensic Science.

Gary C. Kessler (e-mail: *kumquat@sover.net*) is an Associate Professor and program director of the Computer Networking major at Champlain College in Burlington, VT, where he also is the director of the Vermont Information Technology Center security projects. He is also an independent consultant specializing in issues related to computer and network security, Internet and TCP/IP protocols and applications, e-commerce, and telecommunications technologies and applications. He is a frequent speaker at industry conferences, has written two books and over 60 articles on a variety of technology topics, is a frequent contributor to *Information Security Magazine,* is an instructor for the SANS Institute (*www.sans.org*), and is the chair of the Vermont InfraGard chapter (*www.vtinfragard.org*). He holds a B.A. in Mathematics and a M.S. in Computer Science. More information can be found at *www.garykessler.net/*.

Diane ("Dione") E. Levine, CISSP, CFE, FBCI, CPS (e-mail: *managesecurity@ hotmail.com*), is President/CEO of Strategic Systems Management, Ltd., and one of the developers of the Certification for Information Systems Security Professionals. She has had a notable career in information security as both a developer and implementer of enterprise security systems. Levine has held a series of high-level risk management and security positions in major financial institutions, spent many years as an Adjunct Professor at New York University, and is widely published in both the trade and academic press. She splits her time between security and business continuity consulting, writing, and teaching worldwide. She is a frequent public speaker and member of technical panels and regularly contributes articles and columns to *Information Week, Information Security, Internet Week, Planet IT, ST&D, internet.com* and *Smart Computing.* Levine is active in the Information Systems Security Association (ISSA), the Association of Certified Fraud Examiners (ACFE), the Business Continuity Institute (BCI), the Contingency Planning Exchange (CPE), and the Information Security Auditing and Control Association (ISACA) and has devoted many years serving on the Board of Directors of these organizations.

James Linderman, Ph.D. (e-mail: *jlinderman@aol.com*) is an Associate Professor in the Computer Information Systems department at Bentley College, Waltham, Massachusetts. He is a Research Fellow at Bentley's Center for Business Ethics, and past Vice-Chair of the Faculty Senate. A resident of Fitzwilliam, NH, Linderman is a Permanent Deacon in the Roman Catholic Diocese of Worcester, Massachusetts, and a consultant in the area of computer-assisted academic scheduling and timetable construction.

Pascal Meunier, Ph.D. (e-mail: *pmeunier@cerias.purdue.edu*) obtained his Ph.D. in Biophysics in 1990. After taking computer classes at Purdue, where he enjoyed making computers sing passwords, he joined the Center for Education and Research in Information Assurance (CERIAS, *www.cerias.purdue.edu*) in 1998 as a student. He has participated on the Board of Editors of MITRE's Common Vulnerabilities and Exposures (CVE) project since 1999. He obtained his M.Sc. in computer science in 2000 and became staff at CERIAS. He then created Cassandra (*https://cassandra.cerias. purdue.edu*) and the CERIAS Incident Response Database (*https://cirdb.cerias. purdue.edu*).

Michael Miora, CISSP (e-mail: *mmiora@miora.com*), has been evaluating and improving privacy, security, incident response, and disaster recovery plans for government and industry for the past 25 years. He founded InfoSec Labs, which was acquired by Rainbow Technologies in 1999, for whom he then served as Vice President of Security Services. He is Senior Vice President and Managing Director of ePrivacy Group, a company specializing in helping organizations deal with the labyrinth of privacy issues. Miora is a frequent speaker, has written articles, and has been quoted and interviewed for conventional print and video media as well as in Internet publications. He has advised major corporations across the country, the U.S. Departments of Defense and Commerce, the National Computer Security Center (NCSC) and the National Reconnaissance Office (NRO). He holds a Masters degree in Mathematics from the University of California and is a Certified Information Systems Security Professional (CISSP).

Mike Money, CISSP, CISA (e-mail: *mmoney@redsiren.com*) is a senior consultant with RedSiren Technologies. He has 20 years of experience in information security, risk management, and information systems auditing. He specializes in information systems strategy and policies, information security assessments, security awareness and education, work process optimization, application security, operating system security, investigations, risk management, privacy legislation, and network security. His clients have included the Federal Reserve System, Providian Financial, the New York Mercantile Exchange, Boeing, and Bank of America. His technical experience spans firewalls, NT servers, SAP R/3, SecurID, and remote access; and UNIX, AS/400, and ACF-2 for mainframes. Before joining RedSiren, he was manager of Information Security for Union Carbide Corporation, where he was responsible for developing information security strategy, architecture, and policy, including the implementation of SAP R/3. He holds an undergraduate degree from Fairfield University in Connecticut and an MBA from the University of Houston. He is a Certified Information Systems Security Professional (CISSP) and Certified Information Systems Auditor (CISA).

Scott J. Nathan (e-mail: *snathan@mindspring.com*) is affiliated with Gadsby Hannah LLP and an officer of Autolynx, Inc., a supply chain company in the automobile industry. He has focused his legal work in the areas of risk management, especially service and license agreements, insurance coverage, intellectual property and analysis of business risk for Web-based enterprises.

Louis Numkin (e-mail: *LMN@nrc.gov*) is a Senior Computer Security Specialist in the Office of the Chief Information Officer at the U.S. Nuclear Regulatory Commission. His duties relate to computer security awareness/training, anti-virus activities, classified inspections of nuclear plants, disaster recovery planning, computer security plan review and approval, risk assessments, wireless security policy, and the like. Before joining the NRC, he performed computer security for the General Services Administration (GSA) on the FTS2000. He is a retired Army Sergeant Major with 26 years of service in several fields, including ADP and JAG. His Bachelor of Science Degree is in Business Administration and his Masters Degree is in Technology of Management (majoring in Management Information Systems and Computer Systems), both from the American University. Outside of the office, Numkin volunteers his time as an outreach speaker to provide computer security sessions for schools (elementary through high school), senior citizen centers, and local social organizations, especially dealing in the area of Computer Ethics. He has also been invited to provide awareness presentations at other Government agencies and various conferences. He has served several years on the Steering Committee of the Federal Computer Security Program Managers' Forum and on the Executive Board of the Federal Information Systems Security Educators' Association (FISSEA). Louis Numkin edits the *FISSEA Newsletter* and was presented with the coveted FISSEA "Educator of the Year" Award for 1998.

Robert A. Parisi, Jr. (e-mail: *robert.parisi@aig.com*) is the Senior Vice-President and Chief Underwriting Officer of eBusiness Risk Solutions for American International Group, Inc. He joined the AIG group of companies in 1997 and has held several executive and legal positions. Immediately prior to his current position, Parisi was Chief Underwriting Officer for Technology and Professional Liability. Before joining AIG,

Parisi was in private practice, principally as legal counsel to Lloyds of London. He graduated cum laude from Fordham College and received his law degree from Fordham University School of Law. He is admitted to practice in New York and the U.S. District Courts for the Eastern and Southern Districts of NY. Mr. Parisi has spoken before various business, technology, legal, and insurance forums throughout the world, as well as writing, on issues effecting intellectual property, the Internet, e-commerce, and insurance.

Donn B. Parker, CISSP, Fellow of the Association for Computing Machinery (e-mail: *donnlorna@aol.com*) is a retired (1997) senior management consultant at RedSiren Technologies in Menlo Park, CA, who has specialized in information security and computer crime research for 35 of his 50 years in the computer field. He has written numerous books, papers, articles, and reports in his specialty based on interviews with over 200 computer criminals and reviews of the security of many large corporations. He received the 1992 Award for Outstanding Individual Achievement from the Information Systems Security Association, the 1994 National Computer System Security Award from the U.S. NIST/NCSC, the Aerospace Computer Security Associates 1994 Distinguished Lecturer award, and The MIS Training Institute *Infosecurity News* 1996 Lifetime Achievement Award. *Information Security Magazine* identified him as one of the five top Infosecurity Pioneers (1998).

Franklin N. Platt (e-mail: *fplatt@ncia.net*) is president of Office Planning Services, a Wall Street consultancy for 20 years that has been headquartered in Stark, NH, since 1990. His academic background includes business administration, management, and electrical engineering. His company provides security planning services and emergency management assistance nationwide to protect people, property, and profit. Its services include site evaluation and risk analysis, second opinion, due diligence, exercises, and training. Platt is also a sworn public official and an active Emergency Management Director vetted by the State of New Hampshire and the FBI. He is professionally accredited by the State and by FEMA, and has received extensive government training in emergency management, terrorism, weapons of mass destruction, and workplace violence-training mostly unavailable to the public. He can be reached by phone at 603 449 2211.

N. Todd Pritsky (e-mail: *todd@hill.com*) is the Director of E-learning Courseware at Hill Associates, a telecommunications training company in Colchester, VT (*www.hill.com*). He is a Senior Member of Technical Staff and an instructor of online, lecture, and hands-on classes. His teaching and writing specialties include e-commerce, network security, TCP/IP, and the Internet, and he also leads courses on fast packet and network access technologies. He enjoys writing articles on network security and is a contributing author of *Telecommunications: A Beginner's Guide* (McGraw-Hill/Osborne). Previously, he managed a computer center and created multimedia training programs. He holds a BA in Philosophy and Russian/Soviet Studies from Colby College.

Jeffrey Ritter (e-mail: *jritter@kl.com*) is a partner with Kirkpatrick & Lockhart, a national U.S. law firm, practicing law in the areas of Electronic Commerce, Privacy, Information Security, and Technology Licensing/Joint Ventures/ Strategic Alliances. Ritter is recognized as pioneer in defining the emerging law of electronic commerce. He was the founding chair of the American Bar Association Committee on Cyberspace

Law and served as a Rapporteur to the United Nations on the legal aspects of international electronic commerce. His practice emphasizes assisting multinational corporations with privacy, security and compliance implementation efforts.

K Rudolph, CISSP (e-mail: *kaie@nativeintelligence.com*), is President and Chief Inspiration Officer of Native Intelligence, Inc. (*www.NativeIntelligence.com*), a Maryland-based consulting firm focused on providing creative and practical information security awareness solutions. K develops entertaining web-based security awareness courses and posters based on principles of learning. She frequently speaks on security-related topics. K has more than 15 years of experience in information technology security covering a wide range of technologies and systems. Her experience includes performing system security reviews and assisting in systems designs in military and civilian environments. K now focuses on the most effective, proven IT security countermeasure: people. An aware, well-trained staff is frequently the best control to prevent, identify, and respond to potential security incidents. Thus, she now dedicates her talent and experience to developing effective awareness and training courses, materials, and presentations.

Ravi Sandhu (e-mail: *sandhu@ise.gmu.edu*) is Co-Founder and Chief Scientist of SingleSignOn.Net in Reston, VA, and Professor of Information Technology and Engineering at George Mason University in Fairfax, Virginia. An ACM and an IEEE Fellow, he is the founding editor-in-chief of *ACM's Transactions on Information and System Security,* Chairman of ACM's Special Interest Group on Security, Audit and Control, and security editor for *IEEE Internet Computing.* Sandhu has published over 140 technical papers on information security. He is a popular teacher and has lectured all over the world. He has provided high-level consulting services to numerous private and government organizations.

William Stallings, Ph.D. (e-mail: *ws@shore.net*) is a consultant, lecturer, and author of over a dozen professional reference books and textbooks on data communications and computer networking. His clients have included major corporations and government agencies in the United States and Europe. He has received four awards for the Best Computer Science Textbook of the Year from the Text and Academic Authors Association. He has designed and implemented both TCP/IP-based and OSI-based protocol suites on a variety of computers and operating systems, ranging from microcomputers to mainframes. Stallings created and maintains the Computer Science Student Resource Site at *http://WilliamStallings.com/StudentSupport.html.*

Roger Thompson (e-mail: *rogert@mindspring.com*) is the Director of Malware Research for TruSecure Corporation. His career with microcomputers began in 1979 while living in Australia and working as a mainframe systems engineer. He later started a software development company to develop application software for CP/M and TRS DOS based systems. In 1987, Thompson realized there was a need for anti-virus software, and together he and another individual founded the successful Australian company, Leprechaun Software, and a product known as Virus Buster. After moving to the United States, Thompson started a company known as Thompson Network Software, which developed a range of products known as The Doctor. He later sold Thompson Technology to On Technology, remaining on staff for a year as Director of Anti Virus Development, and was responsible for the Virus Track range of products. He now lives in Atlanta, GA, with his wife, four grown biological children, six adopted children, and three poodles and plays guitar in his spare time.

Lee Tien (e-mail: *tien@eff.org*) is a senior staff attorney with the Electronic Frontier Foundation in San Francisco, California. He specializes in free speech and surveillance law and has authored several law review articles. He received his undergraduate degree in psychology from Stanford University and his law degree from Boalt Hall School of Law, UC-Berkeley. He is also a former newspaper reporter.

Peter Tippett, MD, Ph.D. (e-mail: *ptippett@trusecure.com*) is the CTO of TruSecure Corporation, the Chief Scientist at ICSA Labs, and the Executive Publisher of *Information Security Magazine.* He specializes in utilizing large-scale risk models and research to create pragmatic, corporate-wide security. Tippett studied under two different Nobel Prize laureates at Rockefeller University and has both an M.D. and a Ph.D. from Case Western Reserve University. He is widely credited with creating the first commercial anti-virus product, which later became the Norton Anti-virus. Tippett was awarded the Ernst & Young Entrepreneur of the Year in 1998 and led TruSecure/ICSA Labs to the Inc 500 list. He has spoken on all major television and radio networks and has briefed and consulted with Congress, the Senate, the Joint Chiefs of Staff, and numerous large and medium organizations and governments on practical approaches to computer security.

Myles Walsh (e-mail: *mwalsh@orion.ramapo.edu*) is an adjunct professor at three colleges in New Jersey: Ramapo College, County College of Morris, and Passaic County Community. For the past 12 years, he has taught courses in Microsoft Office and Web Page Design. He also implements small Office applications and Web sites. From 1966 until 1989, he worked his way from programmer to director in several positions at CBS, CBS Records, and CBS News. His formal education includes an M.B.A. from the Baruch School of Business and a B.B.A. from St. John's University.

Gale Warshawsky (e-mail: *msgale50@yahoo.com*) worked at Lawrence Livermore National Laboratory (LLNL), and Visa International. She coordinated and managed the Information Security Awareness, Education, and Training programs. She was the recipient of the ISSA Individual Achievement Award in 1994 and was FISSEA's Security Educator of the Year in 1995. She earned her M.S. in Information Systems from Golden Gate University. After moving to Hawaii, she served as the Director of InfoSec Services Hawaii, a division of Computer-Aided Technologies International, Inc. (CATI). Ms. Warshawsky is currently an adjunct professor at Chaminade University of Honolulu, teaching M.B.A. candidates a Management Information Systems course. She is currently pursuing a M.Ed. in elementary education.

Morgan Wright (e-mail: *mworght@va.adelphia.net*) is a former law enforcement officer with over 15 years experience as a police officer, state trooper, and detective. He has testified as an expert witness in computer crime, forensics, and behavioral analysis at the federal and state levels. He sits on the board of directors for the International Association of Computer Investigative Specialists (IACIS), and develops Information Security Solutions for Unisys Corporation in the Federal Government Group at Reston, VA. Currently, he is directing the development of a seized asset management system for the Colombian Government Narcotics Enforcement Directorate on behalf of the U.S. Justice Department, and a national event management system for law enforcement. He has conducted numerous training courses to law enforcement and private industry on computer crime/forensics, interview/interrogation, and insider crime and has been interviewed numerous times by national news media, including CNN, NBC,and ABC. Wright recently lectured at the Police College in Abu Dhabi, United Arab Emirates, on forensic investigation methods, tools, and insider crime. He holds Bachelor degrees in both Human Resource Management and Computer Information Systems.

Noel K. Zakin (e-mail: *ranco212@aol.com*) is President of RANCO Consulting LLC. He has been an Information Technology/Telecommunications industry executive for over 45 years. He has held managerial positions at the Gartner Group, AT&T, the American Institute of CPAs, and Unisys. These positions involved strategic planning, market research, competitive analysis, business analysis, and education and training. His consulting assignments have ranged from the Fortune 500 to small start-ups and involved data security, strategic planning, conference management, market research, and management of corporate operations. He has been active with ACM, IFIP, and AFIPS and currently with ISSA. He holds an M.B.A. from the Wharton School.

William Zucker (e-mail: *wzucker@ghlaw.com*) is a partner at Gadsby Hannah, LLP, located in Boston, MA; a senior consultant for the Cutter Consortium; and a member of the American Arbitration Association's National Technology Panel. He has counseled clients concerning outsourcing, licensing, trademarks, technology transfers, asset transfers, and intellectual property matters, bringing more than 25 years of experience to the task. He has authored or coauthored a number of publications, including *IT Litigation Strategies* and *Outsourcing Do's and Don'ts* for the Cutter Consortium. Zucker is a graduate of Yale University and Harvard Law School. He can be reached at 617 345 7016.

CONTENTS

Appendices and Tutorials for this *Handbook* are online at
www.wiley.com/go/securityhandbook.

PART ONE

FOUNDATIONS OF COMPUTER SECURITY

CHAPTER 1

BRIEF HISTORY AND MISSION OF INFORMATION SYSTEM SECURITY

Seymour Bosworth and Robert V. Jacobson

CONTENTS

1.1 INTRODUCTION TO INFORMATION SYSTEM SECURITY.   The growth of computers and of information technology has been explosive. Never before has an entirely new technology been propagated around the world with such speed and with so great a penetration of virtually every human activity. Computers have brought vast benefits to fields as diverse as human genome studies, space exploration, artificial intelligence, and a host of applications from the trivial to the most life-enhancing.

Unfortunately, there is also a dark side to computers: They are used to design and build weapons of mass destruction as well as military aircraft, nuclear submarines, and reconnaissance space stations. The computer's role in formulating biologic and chemical weapons, and in simulating their deployment, is one of its least auspicious uses.

Of somewhat lesser concern, computers used in financial applications, such as facilitating the purchase and sales of everything from matchsticks to mansions, and transferring trillions of dollars each day in electronic funds, are irresistible to miscreants; many of them see these activities as open invitations to fraud and theft. Computer systems, and their interconnecting networks, are also prey to vandals, malicious egotists, terrorists, and an array of individuals, groups, companies, and governments intent on using them to further their own ends, with total disregard for the effects on innocent victims. Besides these intentional attacks on computer systems, there are innumerable ways in which inadvertent errors can damage or destroy a computer's ability to perform its intended functions.

Because of these security problems, as well as a great many others described in this volume, the growth of information systems security has paralleled that of the computer field itself. Only by a detailed study of the potential problems, and implementation of the suggested solutions, can computers be expected to fulfill their promise, with few of the security lapses that plague less adequately protected systems. This chapter defines a few of the most important terms of information security and includes a very brief history of computers and information systems, as a prelude to the works that follow.

Security can be defined as the state of being free from danger and not exposed to damage from accidents or attack, or it can be defined as the process for achieving that desirable state. The objective of information system security[1] is to optimize the performance of an organization with respect to the risks to which it is exposed.

Risk is defined as the chance of injury, damage, or loss. Thus, risk has two elements: (1) chance—an element of uncertainty, and (2) loss or damage. Except for the possibility of restitution, information system security (ISS) actions taken today work to reduce *future* risk losses. Because of the uncertainty about future risk losses, perfect security, which implies zero losses, would be infinitely expensive. For this reason, ISS risk managers strive to optimize the allocation of resources by minimizing the total cost of ISS measures taken and the risk losses experienced. This optimization process is commonly referred to as risk management.

Risk management in this sense is a three-part process:

1. Identification of material risks,
2. Selection and implementation of measures to mitigate the risks, and
3. Tracking and evaluating of risk losses experienced, in order to validate the first two parts of the process

The purpose of this *Handbook* is to describe ISS risks, the measures available to mitigate these risks, and techniques for managing security risks. (For a more detailed discussion of risk assessment and management, see Chapters 47 and 54.)

Risk management has been a part of business for centuries. Renaissance merchants often used several vessels simultaneously, each carrying a portion of the merchandise, so that the loss of a single ship would not result in loss of the entire lot. At almost the same time, the concept of insurance evolved, first to provide economic protection against the loss of cargo and later to provide protection against the loss of buildings by fire. Fire insurers and municipal authorities began to require adherence to standards intended to reduce the risk of catastrophes like the Great Fire of London in 1666. The Insurance Institute was established in London one year later. With the emergence of corporations, as limited liability stock companies, the concept has developed of the duty of corporate directors to use prudence and due diligence in protecting shareholders' assets. Security risks are among the threats to corporate assets that directors have an obligation to address.

Double-entry bookkeeping, another Renaissance invention, proved to be an excellent tool for measuring and controlling corporate assets. One objective was to make insider fraud more difficult to conceal. The concept of separation of duties emerged, calling for the use of processing procedures that required more than one person to complete a transaction. As the books of account became increasingly important, accounting standards were developed, and they continue to evolve to this day. These standards served to make books of account comparable and to assure outsiders that an organization's books of account presented an accurate picture of its condition and assets. These developments led, in turn, to the requirement that an outside auditor perform an independent review of the books of account and operating procedures.

The transition to automated accounting systems introduced additional security requirements. Some early safeguards, such as the rule against erasures or changes in the books of account, no longer applied. Some computerized accounting systems lacked an audit trail, and others could have the audit trail subverted as easily as actual entries.

Finally, with the advent of the Information Age, intellectual property has become an increasingly important part of corporate and governmental assets. At the same time that intellectual property has grown in importance, threats to intellectual property have become more dangerous, because of Information System (IS) technology itself. When sensitive information was stored on paper and other tangible documents, and rapid copying was limited to photography, protection was relatively straightforward. Nevertheless, document control systems, information classification procedures, and need-to-know access controls were not foolproof, and information compromises occurred with dismaying regularity. Evolution of IS technology has made information access control several orders of magnitude more complex. The evolution and, more important the implementation, of control techniques have not kept pace.

The balance of this chapter describes how the evolution of information systems has caused a parallel evolution of Information System Security and at the same time has increased the importance of anticipating the impact of technical changes yet to come. This overview will clarify the factors leading to today's Information System Security risk environment and mitigation techniques and will serve as a warning to remain alert to the implication of technical innovations as they appear. The remaining chapters of this *Handbook* discuss ISS risks, threats, and vulnerabilities, their prevention and remediation, and many related topics in considerable detail.

1.2   EVOLUTION OF INFORMATION SYSTEMS.   The first electromechanical punched card system for data processing, developed by Herman Hollerith at the end of the nineteenth century, was used to tabulate and total census field reports for the U.S. Bureau of the Census in 1890. The first digital, stored-program computers developed in the 1940s were used for military purposes, primarily cryptanalysis and the calculation and printing of artillery firing tables. At the same time, punched card systems were already being used for accounting applications and were an obvious choice for data input to the new electronic computing machines.

1.2.1   1950s: Punched Card Systems.   In the 1950s, punched card equipment dominated the commercial computer market.[2] These electromechanical devices could perform the full range of accounting and reporting functions. Because they were programmed by an intricate system of plugboards with a great many plug-in cables, and because care had to be exercised in handling and storing punched cards, only experienced persons were permitted near the equipment. Although any of these individuals could have set up the equipment for fraudulent use, or even engaged in sabotage, apparently few, if any, actually did so.

The punched card accounting systems typically used four processing steps. As a preliminary, operators would be given a "batch" of documents, typically with an adding machine tape showing one or more "control totals." The operator keyed the data on each document into a punched card and then added an extra card, the batch control card, which stored the batch totals. Each card consisted of 80 columns, each containing, at most, one character. A complete record of an inventory item, for example, would be contained on a single card. The card was called a unit record, and the machines that processed the cards were called either unit record or punched card machines. It was from the necessity to squeeze as much data as possible into an 80-character card that the later Y2K problem arose. Compressing the year into two characters was a universally used space-saving measure; its consequences 40 years later were not foreseen.

A group of punched cards, also called a "batch," were commonly held in a metal tray, Sometimes a batch would be rekeyed by a second operator, using a "verify-mode" rather than actually punching new holes in the cards, in order to detect keypunch errors before processing the card deck. Each batch of cards would be processed separately, so the processes were referred to as "batch jobs."

The first step would be to run the batch of cards through a simple program, which would calculate the control totals and compare them with the totals on the batch control card. If the batch totals did not reconcile, the batch was sent back to the keypunch area for rekeying. If the totals reconciled, the deck would be sort-merged with other batches of the same transaction type, for example, the current payroll. When this step was complete, the new batch consisted of a punched card for each employee in employee-number order. The payroll program accepted this input data card deck and processed the cards one by one. Each card was matched up with the corresponding employee's card in the payroll master deck to calculate the current net pay and itemized deductions and to punch a new payroll master card including year-to-date totals. The final step was to use the card decks to print payroll checks and management reports. These steps were identical with those used by early, small-scale, electronic computers. The only difference was in the speed at which the actual calculations were made. A complete process was still known as a batch job.

With this process, the potential for abuse was great. The machine operator could control every step of the operation. Although the data were punched into cards and verified by others, there was always a keypunch machine close at hand for use by the machine operator. Theoretically, that person could punch a new payroll card, and a new batch total card to match the change, before printing checks, and again afterward. The low incidence of reported exploits was due to the controls that discouraged such abuse and possibly to the pride that machine operators experienced in their jobs.

1.2.2   Large-Scale Computers.   While these electromechanical punched card machines were sold in large numbers, research laboratories and universities were working to design large-scale computers that would have a revolutionary effect on the entire field. These computers, built around vacuum tubes, are known as the first generation. In March 1951, the first Universal Automatic Computer (UNIVAC) was accepted by the U.S. Census Bureau. Until then, every computer had been a one-off design, but UNIVAC was the first large-scale, mass-produced computer, with a total of 46 built. The word "universal" in its name indicated that UNIVAC was also the first computer designed for both scientific and business applications.[3]

UNIVAC contained 5,200 vacuum tubes, weighed 29,000 pounds, and consumed 125 kilowatts of electrical power. It dispensed with punched cards, receiving input from half-inch-wide metal tape recorded from keyboards, with output either to a similar tape or to a printer. Although not a model for future designs, its memory consisted of 1,000 72-bit words and was fabricated as a mercury delay line. Housed in a cabinet about six feet tall, two feet wide, and two feet deep was a mercury-filled coil running from top to bottom. A transducer at the top propagated slow-moving waves of energy down the coil to a receiving transducer at the bottom. There it was reconverted into electrical energy and passed on to the appropriate circuit, or recirculated if longer storage was required.

In 1956, IBM introduced the RAMAC (Random Access Method of Accounting and Control) magnetic disk system. It consisted of 50 magnetically coated metal disks, each 24 inches in diameter, and mounted on a common spindle. Under servo control, two coupled read/write heads moved to span each side of the required disk and then inward to any one of 100 tracks. In one revolution of the disks, any or all of the information on those two tracks could be read out, or recorded. The entire system was almost the size of a compact car and held what, for that time, was a tremendous amount of data—5 megabytes. The cost was $10,000 per megabyte, or $35,000 per year to lease. This compares with today's magnetic hard drives that measure about 3½ inches wide by 1 inch high, store as much as 80,000 megabytes, and cost less than $300.[4]

These massive computers were housed in large, climate-controlled rooms. Within the room, a few knowledgeable experts, looking highly professional in their white laboratory coats, attended to the operation and maintenance of their million-dollar charges. The concept of a "user" as someone outside the computer room who could interact directly with the actual machine did not exist.

Service interruptions, software errors, and hardware errors were usually not critical. If any of these caused a program to fail or abort, beginning again was a relatively simple matter. Consequently, the primary security concerns were physical protection of the scarce and expensive hardware, and measures to increase their reliability. Another issue, then as now, was human fallibility. Because the earliest computers were programmed in extremely difficult machine languages, consisting solely of ones (1s) and zeros (0s), the incidence of human error was high, and the time to correct errors was excessively long. Only later were assembler and compiler languages developed to increase the number of people able to program the machines and to reduce the incidence of errors and the time to correct them.

Information system security for large-scale computers was not a significant issue then for two reasons. First, only a few programming experts were able to utilize and manipulate computers. Second, there were very few computers in use, each of which was extremely valuable, important to its owners, and consequently, closely guarded.

1.2.3 Medium-Size Computers. In the 1950s, smaller computer systems were developed with a very simple configuration; punched card master files were replaced by punched paper tape and, later, by magnetic tape, and disk storage systems. The electromechanical calculator with its patchboard was replaced by a central processor unit (CPU) that had a small main memory, sometimes as little as 8 kilobytes,[5] and limited processing speed and power. One or two punched card readers could read the data and instructions stored on that medium. Later, programs and data files were stored on magnetic tape. Output data were sent to card punches, for printing on unit record equipment, and later to magnetic tape. There was still no wired connection to the outside world, and there were no online users because no one, besides electronic data processing (EDP) people within the computer room, could interact directly with the system. These systems had very simple operating systems and did not use multi-processing; they could run only one program at a time.

The IBM Model 650, as an example introduced in 1954, measured about 5 feet by 3 feet by 6 feet and weighed almost 2,000 pounds. Its power supply was mounted in a similarly sized cabinet, weighing almost 3,000 pounds. It had 2,000 (10-digit) words of magnetic drum primary memory, with a total price of $500,000 or a rental fee of $3,200 per month. For an additional $1,500 per month, a much faster core memory, of 60 words, could be added. Input and output both utilized read/write punch card machines.[6] The typical 1950s IS hardware was installed in a separate room, often with a viewing window so that visitors could admire the computer. In an early attempt at security, visitors actually within the computer room were often greeted by a printed sign saying:

> Achtung! Alles Lookenspeepers!
>> Das computermachine ist nicht fur gefingerpoken und mittengrabben.
>> Ist easy schnappen der springenwerk, blowenfusen, und poppencorken mit spitzensparken.
>> Ist nicht fur gewerken bei das dumbkopfen.
>> Das rubbernecken sightseeren keepen hans in das pockets muss . . . :
>> Relaxen und watch das blinkenlichten.[7]

Since there were still no online users, there were no user IDs and passwords. Programs processed batches of data, run at a regularly scheduled time—once a day, once a week, and so on, depending on the function. If the data for a program were not available at the scheduled run time, the operators might run some other job instead and wait for the missing data. As the printed output reports became available, they were delivered by hand to their end users (e.g., the accounting department, payroll clerks, etc.). End users did not expect to get a continuous flow of data from the information processing system, and delays of even a day or more were not significant, except perhaps with paycheck production.

Information System Security was hardly thought of as such. The focus was on batch controls for individual programs, physical access controls, and maintaining a proper environment for the reliable operation of the hardware.

1.2.4   1960s: Small-Scale Computers.   During the 1960s, with the introduction of small-scale computers, dumb[8] terminals provided users with a keyboard to send a character stream to the computer and a video screen that could display characters transmitted to it by the computer. Initially, these terminals were used to help computer operators control and monitor the job stream, while replacing banks of switches and indicator lights on the control console. However, it was soon recognized that these terminals could replace card readers and keypunch machines as well. Now users, identified by user IDs, and authenticated with passwords, could enter input data through a CRT terminal into an edit program, which would validate the input and then store it on a hard drive until it was needed for processing. Later, it was realized that users also could directly access data stored in online master files.

1.2.5   Transistors and Core Memory.   The IBM 1401, introduced in 1960, with a core memory of 4,096 characters, was the first all-transistor computer, marking the advent of the second generation. Housed in a cabinet measuring 5 feet by 3 feet, the

1401 required a similar cabinet to add an additional 12 kilobytes of main memory. Just one year later, the first integrated circuits were used in a computer, making possible all future advances in miniaturizing small-scale computers and in reducing the size of mainframes significantly.

1.2.6   Time Sharing.   In 1961, the Compatible Time Sharing System (CTSS) was developed for the IBM 7090/7094. This operating system software, and its associated hardware, was the first to provide simultaneous remote access to a group of online users through multiprogramming.[9] "Multiprogramming" means that more than one program can appear to execute at the same time. A master control program, usually called an operating system (OS), managed execution of the functional applications programs. For example, under the command of the operator, the OS would load and start application 1. After 50 milliseconds, the OS would interrupt the execution of application 1 and store its current state in memory. Then the OS would start application 2 and allow it to run for 50 milliseconds, and so on. Usually, within a second after users had entered keyboard data, the OS would give their applications a time slice to process the input. During each time slice, the computer might execute hundreds of instructions. These techniques enabled the computer to make it appear to each user as if the computer were entirely dedicated to that user's program. This was true only so long as the number of simultaneous users was fairly small. After that, as the number grew, the response to each user slowed down.

1.2.7   Real-Time, Online Systems.   Because of multiprogramming and the ability to store records online and accessible in random order, it became feasible to provide end users with direct access to data. For example, an airline reservation system stores a record of every seat on every flight for the next 12 months. A reservation clerk working at a terminal can answer a telephoned inquiry, search for an available seat on a particular flight, quote the fare, sell a ticket to the caller, and reserve the seat. Similarly, a bank officer can verify an account balance and make an adjusting entry to correct an error. In both cases, each data record can be accessed and modified immediately, rather than having to wait for a batch to be run.

While this advance led to a vast increase in available computing power, it also increased greatly the potential for breaches in computer security. With more complex operating systems, with many users online to sensitive programs, and with databases and other files available to them, protection had to be provided against inadvertent error and intentional abuse.

1.2.8   A Family of Computers.   In 1964, IBM announced the S/360 family of computers, ranging from very small-scale to very large-scale models.[10] All of the six models used integrated circuits, which marked the beginning of the third generation of computers. Where transistorized construction could permit up to 6,000 transistors per cubic foot, 30,000 integrated circuits could occupy the same volume. This lowered the costs substantially, and companies could buy into the family at a price within their means. Because all computers in the series used the same programming language and the same peripherals, companies could upgrade easily when necessary. The 360 family quickly came to dominate the commercial and scientific markets. As these computers proliferated, so did the number of users, knowledgeable programmers, and technicians. Over the years, techniques and processes were developed to provide a high degree of security to these mainframe systems.

The year 1964 also saw the introduction of another computer with far-reaching influence: the Digital Equipment Corp (DEC) PDP-8. The PDP-8 was the first mass-produced true minicomputer. Although its original application was in process control, the PDP-8 and its progeny quickly proved that commercial applications for minicomputers were virtually unlimited. Because these computers were not isolated in secure computer rooms but were distributed throughout many unguarded offices in widely dispersed locations, totally new risks arose, requiring innovative solutions.

1.2.9   1970s: Microprocessors, Networks, and Worms.   The foundations of all current personal computers (PCs) were laid in 1971 when Intel introduced the 4004 computer on a chip. Measuring $\frac{1}{16}$ inch long by $\frac{1}{8}$ inch high, the 4004 contained 2,250 transistors with a clock speed of 108 kiloHertz. The current generation of this earliest programmable microprocessor contains millions of transistors, with speeds over 1 gigaHertz, or more than 10,000 times faster. Introduction of microprocessor chips marked the fourth generation.

1.2.10   The First Personal Computers.   Possibly the first personal computer was advertised in *Scientific American* in 1971. The KENBAK–1, priced at $750, had three programming registers, five addressing modes, and 256 bytes of memory. Although not many were sold, the KENBACK–1 did increase public awareness of the possibility for home computers.

It was the MITS Altair 8800, advertised as a kit on the cover of the January 1975 issue of *Popular Electronics,* that became the first personal computer to sell in substantial quantities. Like the KENBAK–1, the Altair 8800 had only 256 bytes of memory, but it was priced at $375 without keyboard, display, or secondary memory. About one year later, the Apple II, designed by Steve Jobs and Steve Wozniak, was priced at $1,298, including a CRT display and a keyboard.

Because these first personal computers were entirely stand-alone and usually under the control of a single individual, there were few security problems. However, in 1978, the Visicalc spreadsheet program was developed. The advantages of standardized, inexpensive, widely used application programs were unquestionable, but packaged programs, as opposed to custom designs, opened the way for abuse because so many people understood their user interfaces as well as their inner workings.

1.2.11   The First Network.   A national network, conceived in late 1969, was born as ARPANET[11] (Advanced Research Projects Agency Network), a Department of Defense sponsored effort to link a few of the country's important research universities, with two purposes: to develop experience in interconnecting computers and to increase productivity through resource sharing. This earliest connection of independent large-scale computer systems had just four nodes: the University of California at Los Angeles (UCLA), the University of California at Santa Barbara, Stanford Research Institute, and the University of Utah. Because of the inherent security in each leased-line interconnected node and the physically protected mainframe computer rooms, there was no apparent concern for security issues. From this simple network, with no thought of security designed in, there finally evolved today's ubiquitous Internet and the World Wide Web (WWW) with their vast potential for security abuses.

1.2.12   Further Security Considerations.   With the proliferation of remote terminals on commercial computers, physical control over access to the computer room was no longer sufficient. In response to the new vulnerabilities, logical access control systems were developed. An access control system maintains an online table of authorized users. A typical user record would store the user's name, telephone number, employee number, and information about the data the user was authorized to access and the programs the user was authorized to execute. A user might be allowed to view, add, modify, and delete data records in different combinations for different programs.

At the same time, system managers recognized the value of being able to recover from a disaster that destroyed hardware and data. Data centers began to make regular tape copies of online files and software for off-site storage. Data center managers also began to develop and implement off-site disaster recovery plans, often involving the use of commercial disaster-recovery facilities. Even with such a system in place, new vulnerabilities were recognized throughout the following years, and these are the subjects of much of this *Handbook*.

1.2.13   The First "Worm."   A prophetic science fiction novel, *The Shockwave Rider,* by John Brunner[12] (1975), depicted a "worm" that grew continuously throughout a computer network. The worm eventually exceeded a billion bits in length and became impossible to kill without destroying the network. Although actual worms later became real and present menaces to all networked computers, prudent computer security personnel install, and regularly update, antivirus programs that effectively kill viruses and worms without having to kill the network.

1.2.14   1980s: Productivity Enhancements.   The decade of the 1980s might well be termed the era of productivity enhancement. The installation of millions of personal computers in commercial, industrial, and government applications enhanced the efficiency and functionality of vast numbers of users. These advances, which could have been achieved in no other way, were made at costs that virtually any business could afford.

1.2.15   The Personal Computer.   In 1981, IBM introduced a general-purpose small computer it called the "Personal Computer." That model and similar systems became known generically as PCs. Until then, small computers were produced by relatively unknown sources, but IBM, with its worldwide reputation, brought PCs into the mainstream. The fact that IBM had demonstrated a belief in the viability of PCs made them serious contenders for corporate use.

There were many variations on the basic Model 5100 PC, and sales expanded far beyond IBM's estimates. The basic configuration used the Intel 8088, operating at 4.77 megaHertz, with up to two floppy disk drives, each of 160 kilobytes capacity and with a disk-based operating system (DOS) in an open architecture. This open OS architecture, with its available "hooks," made possible the growth of independent software producers, the most important of which was the Microsoft Corporation, formed by Bill Gates and Paul Allen.

IBM had arranged for Gates and Allen to create the DOS operating system. Under the agreement, IBM would not reimburse Gates and Allen for their development costs; rather, all profits from the sale of DOS would accrue to them. IBM did not have an exclusive right to the operating system, and Microsoft began selling it to many other customers as MS-DOS. IBM initially included with its computer the VisiCalc spreadsheet program, but soon, sales of Lotus 1-2-3 surpassed those of VisiCalc. The open architecture not only made it possible for many developers to produce software that would run on the PC, but also enabled anyone to put together purchased components into a computer that would compete with IBM's PC. The rapid growth of compatible application programs, coupled with the ready availability of compatible hardware, soon resulted in sales of more than 1 million units. Many subsequent generations of the original hardware and software are still producing sales measured in millions every year.

Apple took a very different approach with its Macintosh computer. Where IBM's system was wide open, Apple maintained tight control over any hardware or software designed to operate on the Macintosh so as to assure compatibility and ease of installation. The most important Apple innovations were the graphical user interface (GUI) and the mouse, both of which worked together to facilitate ease of use. Microsoft had attempted in 1985 to build these features into the Windows operating system, but early versions were generally rejected as slow, cumbersome, and unreliable. It was not until 1990 that Windows 3.0 overcame many of its problems and provided the foundation for later versions that were almost universally accepted.

1.2.16   Local Area Networks.   During the 1980s, stand-alone desktop computers began to perform word processing, financial analysis, and graphic processing. Although this arrangement was much more convenient for end users than was a centralized facility, it was more difficult to share data with others.

As more powerful PCs were developed, it became practical to interconnect them so that their users could easily share data. These arrangements were commonly referred to as Local Area Networks (LANs) because the hardware units were physically close, usually in the same building or office area. LANs have remained important to this day. Typically, a more powerful PC with a high storage capacity fixed[13] disk was designated as the file server. Other PCs, referred to as workstations, were connected to the file server using network interface cards installed in the workstations with cables between these cards and the file server. Special network software installed on the file server and workstations made it possible for workstations to access defined portions of the file server fixed disk just as if these portions were installed on the workstations. Furthermore, these shared files could be backed up at the file server without depending on individual users. By 1997, it was estimated that worldwide, there were more than 150 million PCs operating as LAN workstations. The most common network operating systems (NOS) were Novell NetWare and later Microsoft Windows NT.

Most LANs were implemented using the Ethernet (IEEE 802.3) protocol.[14] The server and workstations could be equipped with a modem (modulator/demodulator) connected to a dedicated telephone line. The modem enabled remote users, with a matching modem, to dial into the LAN and log on. This was a great convenience to LAN users who were traveling or working away from their offices, but such remote access created yet another new security issue. For the first time, computer systems were exposed in a major way to the outside world. From then on, it was possible to interact with a computer from virtually anywhere and from locations not under the same physical control as the computers themselves.

Typical NOS logical access control software provided for user-IDs and passwords and selective authority to access file server data and program files. A workstation user logged on to the LAN by executing a log-in program resident on the file server. The program prompted the user to enter an ID and password. If the log-in program concluded that the ID and password were valid, it consulted an access-control table to determine which data and programs the user might access. Access modes were defined as read-only, execute-only, create, modify (write or append), lock, and delete, with respect to individual files and groups of files. The LAN administrator maintained the access control table using a utility program. The effectiveness of the controls depended on the care taken by the administrator, and so, in some circumstances, controls could be weak. It was essential to protect the ID and password of the LAN administrator since, if they were compromised, the entire access-control system became vulnerable. Alert ISS officers noted that control over *physical* access to LAN servers was critical in maintaining the logical access controls. Intruders who could physically access a LAN server could easily restart the server using their own version of the NOS, completely by-passing the installed logical access controls.

Superficially, a LAN appears to be the same as a 1970s mainframe with remote dumb terminals. The difference technically is that each LAN workstation user is executing programs on the workstation, not on the centralized file server, while mainframe computers use special software and hardware to run many programs concurrently, one program for each terminal. To the user at a workstation or remote terminal, the two situations appear to be the same, but from a security standpoint, there are significant differences. The mainframe program software stays on the mainframe and cannot, under normal conditions, be altered during execution. A LAN program on a workstation can be altered, for example, by a computer virus, while actually executing. As a rule, mainframe remote terminals cannot download and save files whereas workstations usually have at least a floppy disk drive. Furthermore, a malicious workstation user can easily install a rewritable CD device, which makes it much easier to copy and take away large amounts of data.

Another important difference is the character of the connection between the computer and the terminals. Each dumb terminal has a dedicated connection to its mainframe and receives only that data that is directed to it. A LAN operates more like a set of radio transmitters sharing a common frequency on which the file server and the workstations take turns "broadcasting" messages. Each message includes a "header" block that identifies the intended recipient, but every node (the file server and the workstations) on a LAN receives all messages. Under normal circumstances, each node ignores messages not addressed to it. However, it is technically feasible for a workstation to run a modified version of the NOS that allows it to capture all messages. In this way a workstation could identify all log-in messages and record the user IDs and passwords of all other users on the LAN, giving it complete access to all of the LAN's data and facilities.

Mainframe and LAN security also differ greatly in the operating environment. As noted, the typical mainframe is installed in a separate room and is managed by a staff of skilled technicians. The typical LAN file server, on the other hand, is installed in ordinary office space and is managed by a part-time, remotely located LAN administrator who may not be adequately trained. Consequently, the typical LAN has a higher exposure to tampering, sabotage, and theft. However, if the typical mainframe is disabled by an accident, fire, sabotage, or any other security incident, many business functions will be interrupted, whereas the loss of a LAN file server usually disrupts only a single function.

1.2.17   1990s: Total Interconnection.   With the growing popularity of LANs, the technologies for interconnecting them emerged. These networks of physically interconnected local area networks were called wide area networks, or WANs. Any node on a LAN could access every node on any other interconnected LAN, and in some configurations, those nodes might also be given access to mainframe and minicomputer files and to processing capabilities.

1.2.18   Telecommuting.   Once the WAN technology was in place, it became feasible to link LANs together by means of telecommunications circuits. It had been expensive to do this with the low-speed, online systems of the 1970s because all data had to be transmitted over the network. Now, because processing and most data used by a workstation were on its local LAN, a WAN network was much less expensive. Low-traffic LANs were linked using dial-up access for minimum costs, while major LANs were linked with high-speed dedicated circuits for better performance. Apart from dial-up access, all network traffic typically flowed over nonswitched private networks. Of the two methods, dial-up communications were considerably more vulnerable to security violations, and they remain so to this day.

1.2.19   Internet and the World Wide Web. The Internet, which began life in 1969 as the ARPANET, slowly emerged onto the general computing scene during the 1980s. Initially, access to the Internet was restricted to U.S. Government agencies and their contractors. ARPANET users introduced the concept of e-mail as a convenient way to communicate and exchange documents. Then, in 1989–1990, Tim Berners-Lee conceived of the World Wide Web and the Web browser. This one concept produced a profound change in the Internet, greatly expanding its utility and creating an irresistible demand for access. During the 1990s, the U.S. Government relinquished its control, and the Internet became the gigantic, no-one-is-in-charge network of networks it is today.

The Internet offers several important advantages: The cost is relatively low, connections are available locally in most industrialized countries, and by adopting the Internet protocol, TCP/IP, any computer becomes instantly compatible with all other Internet users.

The World Wide Web technology made it easy for anyone to access remote data. Almost overnight the Internet became the key to global networking. Internet Service Providers (ISPs) operate Internet-compatible computers with both dial-up and dedicated access. A computer may access an ISP directly as a stand-alone ISP client or via a gateway from a LAN or WAN. A large ISP may offer dial-up access at many locations, sometimes called Points of Presence, or POPs, interconnected by its own network. ISPs establish links with one another through the national access points (NAPs) initially set up by the National Science Foundation. With this "backbone" in place, any node with access can communicate with another node, connected to a different ISP, located half way around the globe, without making prior arrangements.

The unrestricted access provided by the Internet created new opportunities for organizations to communicate with clients. A company can implement a Web server with a full-time connection to an ISP and open the Web server, and the WWW pages it hosts, to the public. A potential customer can access a Web site, download product information and software updates, ask questions, and even order products. Commercial Web sites, as they evolved from static "brochure-ware" to online shopping centers, stock brokerages, and travel agencies, to name just a few of the uses, became known as e-businesses.

1.3   ONGOING MISSION FOR INFORMATION SYSTEM SECURITY. There is no end in sight to the continuing proliferation of Internet nodes, to the variety of applications, to the number and value of online transactions, and, in fact, to the rapid integration of computers into virtually every facet of our existence. Nor will there be any restrictions as to time or place. With 24/7/365, always-on operation, and with global expansion even to relatively undeveloped lands, both the beneficial effects and the security violations can be expected to grow apace.

Convergence, which implies computers, televisions, cell phones, and other means of communications combined in one unit, together with continued growth of information technology, will lead to unexpected security risks. Distributed Denial of Service

(DDoS) attacks, copyright infringement, kiddy porn, fraud, and theft of identity are all recent security threats. So far, no perfect defensive measures have been developed. This *Handbook* provides a foundation for understanding and blunting both the existing vulnerabilities and those new threats that will inevitably arise in the future.

Certainly, no one but the perpetrators could have foreseen the use of human-guided missiles to attack the World Trade Center. Besides its symbolic significance, the great concentration of resources within the WTC increased its attractiveness as a target. After 9-11, the importance of physical safety of personnel has become the dominant security issue, with disaster recovery of secondary, but still great, concern. This *Handbook* cannot foresee all possible future emergencies, but it does prescribe some preventative measures, and it does recommend procedures for mitigation and remediation.

1.4 NOTES

1. Many technical specialists tend to use the term "security" to refer to logical access controls. A glance at the contents pages of this volume shows the much broader scope of Information System Security.

2. For further details, see, for example, *www.cs.uiowa.edu/~jones/cards.*

3. See *http://ei.cs.edu/~history/UNIVAC.Weston.html* and *http://inventors.about.com/library/weekly/aa062398.htm.*

4. See *http://sln.fi.edu/tfi/exhibits/johnson.html.*

5. It is notable that the IBM 1401 computer was so named because the initial model had 1,400 bytes of main memory. It was not long before memory size was raised to 8 kilobytes and then later to as much as 32 kilobytes. This compares with today's personal computers equipped with 256 megabytes or more.

6. See *www.users.nwark.com/~rcmahq/jclark/ibm650.htm.*

7. See *www.columbia.edu/acis/history/650.html.*

8. The term dumb" was used because the terminal had no internal storage or processing capability. It could only receive and display characters and accept and transmit keystrokes. Both the received characters and the transmitted ones were displayed on a cathode ray tube (CRT) much like a pre–color television screen. Consequently, these were also called "glass" terminals.

9. "Multiprocessing," "multiprogramming," and "multitasking" are terms that are used almost interchangeably today. Originally, multitasking implied that several modules or subroutines of a single program could execute together. Multiprogramming was designed to execute several different programs, and their subroutines, concurrently. Multiprocessing most often meant that two or more computers worked together to speed program execution by providing more resources.

10. For details of all models, see *www.fee.co.uk/360.htm.*

11. Also known as ARPAnet and Arpanet.

12. First published 1975. Reissued by Mass Market Paperbacks in May 1990.

13. "Fixed," in contrast with the removable disk packs common in large data centers.

14. See *http://standards.ieee.org/getieee802/802.3.html.*

CHAPTER 2

CYBERSPACE LAW AND COMPUTER FORENSICS

Robert Heverly and Morgan Wright

CONTENTS

2.1   INTRODUCTION.   This chapter provides basic information relating to the law and forensics of cyberspace. Other chapters in this text deal with topics addressed in this chapter in greater detail. These include Chapter 12, "Intellectual Property;" Chapter 34, "Working with Law Enforcement;" Chapter 51, "Censorship and Content Filtering on the Internet;" and Chapter 52, "Privacy in Cyberspace." Where this chapter touches on any of these topics, the reader is encouraged to seek greater detail and a different perspective in the related chapters.

The law touches on a great number of areas of cyberspace, and cyberspace touches a great number of areas of the law. This chapter does not cover every possible interaction of the two. Instead, it looks broadly at the most basic questions of law, cyberspace, and electronic communication. Some of these questions revolve around concepts of copyright and privacy and classic concepts of contract and agreement; others concern networking, liability, and responsibility. The material here is intended to provide background information and knowledge to facilitate basic understanding of the issues raised in the cyberspace arena. Specific advice is not intended or provided, and a competent legal advisor should be consulted prior to taking any action with legal implications.

Although this chapter deals primarily with U.S. law and jurisprudence, many of the principles apply to other jurisdictions. However, readers contemplating legal action or analyzing the legal implications of particular courses of action should consult legal authorities who are expert in the applicable laws of their particular geographical location.

2.2   CONTRACTS.   One of the most interesting and difficult areas of cyberspace law is the area involving agreements. Using conventional rules of agreement and contract as a means for reaching conclusions concerning the problems and questions raised in the cyberspace arena often yields unsatisfactory results.

At common law, the creation of a contract requires an offer, acceptance of that offer, and some type of consideration (often money) that serves as the basis of the contract. At any time until an agreement is finalized, the terms can change; contracting is a process, not necessarily a result of actions taken at one specific moment. An offer can be made, which, if rejected, is no longer be available for acceptance. A counterproposal actually extinguishes the original offer and is therefore a new offer. Acceptance can be indicated in a number of ways but always needs to be communicated in some definite manner.

How these principles apply in light of modern-day statutory and common law developments, such as the Uniform Commercial Code and the requirement that certain contracts be in writing with all terms agreed upon at the time the contract is taken up, is the subject of this section of the chapter.

2.2.1   Shrink-Wrap Licenses.   As discussed later in this chapter (see Section 2.3.1, Copyright), consumers do not buy software. Instead, they purchase a license to use the software. The license is a contract that gives the purchaser the right to do certain things, but not others, with the owner's software. How do software producers and consumers enter into licensing agreements?

Generally, consumers purchase the software before they are aware of the terms of the license. (In actuality, most consumers do not understand the theory behind licensing and believe they are buying a product, not a license to use the product.) A software vendor and a potential user cannot "bargain" for contract terms in the traditional sense; do the terms of an agreement that is included within a sealed, shrink-wrapped package control the license provided to the consumer? This question is particularly thorny given the rule that agreements cannot be entered into without the terms' being set beforehand.

The answer is that such agreements *are* binding. The courts have found that in modern times, it is entirely appropriate, even necessary, for a software vendor to offer the terms of a license in a package that the consumer is unaware of prior to opening the package. If the terms of the license are unacceptable, the purchaser must return the product to the vendor. Absent return, and certainly given use, the consumer is required to abide by the terms of the agreement contained within the package. Thus, terms of use, including the number of machines on which the software may be installed, other copies if any that may be made, and related requirements, are enforceable under contract interpretation.

In addition, shrink-wrap concepts apply to license restrictions contained within the software itself and through which a consumer must click to install the application. This may be true even if the consumer being bound is not the person or entity that actually performed the installation, so long as the software was installed with the knowledge and consent of the end consumer.

This principle has been used to resolve a dispute between a consumer and a software development company concerning whether the company's software was appropriately designed and sold. A clause within a "click-through" agreement contained in the installation software required the dispute to be submitted to arbitration, but the consumer claimed that it had not agreed to the terms because a third-party vendor had actually installed the software. "The court finds that Phoenix's acceptance of the software installations, without complaint or rejection, constitutes acquiescence in the terms of the license agreements."[1]

As with other contracts, shrink-wrap and installation licenses cannot contain "unconscionable" terms. A shrink-wrap agreement that, for example, required payments of $100,000 each time the application was used would likely be unconscionable and unenforceable, at least as to that term. Where terms are conscionable, the courts will read the provisions as they are written, and disputes that fall within a provision requiring arbitration will likely be enforced.[2]

2.2.2   Web-Based Click Agreements.   As with shrink-wrap and click agreements based solely within software applications, click-through agreements on Web sites have also been enforced by the courts. Some of the cases within the Web area, however, raise important points in relation to how agreements may or may not be fully enforceable.

Where the terms of an agreement, especially one allegedly entered into on the World Wide Web by "clicking" agreement, are uncertain or mislead the consumer or other party, the courts hesitate to enforce the terms of the agreement. Specifically in the area of adult uses, one provider of "adult materials" promised free tours to viewers who gave credit card numbers as proof of age. At some point during the tour, the site began charging the viewers' credit cards, using a long-distance telephone access line in Madagascar. When sued by the Federal Trade Commission, the site claimed that viewers had agreed to the charges.

The court did not buy the argument and essentially held the agreements null and void on a number of counts. First, the person whose phone line was being charged was not necessarily the person who clicked on the agreement button. Second, the language of the site was misleading to visitors in indicating that the visit was free and not clearly indicating when the free portion ended. Finally, the terms of the agreement were buried within images and other unrelated text, which the court found was further evidence of the site's intent to deceive. These factors led the court to find that the agreement, if there was one, was unconscionable and invalid.[3]

2.2.3   Digital Signatures.   The legal requirement that a document be signed by the person or entity against whom it is sought to be enforced is central to contract theory. The requirement allows us to know who is to be bound and that this person has in fact agreed to be bound.

This requirement has caused consternation among electronic communicators and others who want to be able to negotiate and close deals using electronic, as opposed to written, communication. While negotiation over the Internet certainly has been possible, many deals have had to be closed by mailing or sending final documents by courier for signature or by actually bringing all the parties together for signing.

To enable those interested in pursuing contracts and agreements via electronic communications to do so without resorting to "hard copies" of documents, various government agencies have enacted "digital signature acts." These acts provide that digital signatures, when they follow the requirements of the law, are as binding and "real" as written signatures. The acts, which have been enacted at the federal level[4] and by a variety of states,[5] provide different methods for signature verification and acceptance. All of the laws require that acceptance of electronic signatures be agreed upon by the parties. In addition, states may provide separately that when filing taxes by electronic means, the electronic signature is sufficient to meet legal signature requirements.[6]

Digital signatures have not been authorized in every circumstance. Careful attention must be paid to the requirements of each applicable law.

2.3   INTELLECTUAL PROPERTY.   There are three primary types of property within the U.S. legal system: real property, such as buildings and land; personal property, such as computers, clocks, jewelry, and similar items; and intellectual property, consisting of "works." Intellectual property is defined by the U.S. Constitution, international treaty, and state laws. In certain areas, such as copyright law, U.S. federal law is primary and there is little role for states to play. In other areas of intellectual property, such as trademark law, federal law exists alongside of state law. Thus, the particular type of intellectual property at issue is critical to the treatment it receives under the law.

For more detailed consideration of intellectual property law, see Chapter 12.

2.3.1   Copyright.   One of the primary aspects of intellectual property is copyright, the legal protection given to original creative works. The purpose of copyright protection is to allow creators—artists, authors, and others—to receive the primary benefit of their creative efforts. Absent such protection, the theory goes, artists and scholars will not be able to earn a living with their creative work, thus decreasing the number and quality of such works.

Copyright protection is given to "original works of authorship fixed in any tangible medium of expression, now known or later developed, from which they can be perceived, reproduced, or otherwise communicated, either directly or with the aid of a machine or device."[7] Copyright laws provide protection for various types of works, including literary, musical, and dramatic works; pantomimes and choreographic works: pictorial, graphic, and sculptural works; motion pictures and audiovisual works; sound recordings; architectural works; and computer programs.[8] The extension of copyright law to computer software applications as "literary works" is based on the authorship of the source and the object code, an application of copyright law by adopted Congress and specifically interpreted by the courts.[9]

2.3.1.1   *Inherent Nature of Copyright.* For many years, in order to obtain a copyright on a work, the first step was to make sure that any published version of the work contained certain basic copyright information: the copyright symbol ©, the name of the copyright holder, and the year of creation or publication of the work. Should a work have been published without such notations, it was very possible that the courts would find that the work was in the public domain, outside of the protections of copyright.

Today, copyright is inherent in the creation of the work itself. It takes nothing further than the creation of an original work in a permanent form to invoke copyright protection. Creation of an electronic copy of an original work satisfies the permanency requirement. This fact has fundamental implications for computer and Web-based applications. It means that whatever is found on the Web, or received by e-mail, or sent via File Transfer Protocol (FTP), is *already* copyrighted by the time it is viewed or received. The fact that the works may not contain copyright information does not act to put them in the public domain and subject them to general use without license. This is true for all works created after March 1, 1989.[10]

2.3.1.1.1   U.S. Copyright Law: Framework. The U.S. Constitution provides for the right of the U.S. Congress to create statues protecting creative works.[11] Pursuant to its statutory authority, Congress has enacted provisions that set out what is required for a creative work to achieve copyrighted status.[12] Those requirements are creation of an original work in a tangible medium and coverage under one of the copyrightable works outlined in the statute.

Copyright provides rights to the creator under copyright statutes. These include the rights of reproduction, preparation of derivative works, public distribution, public performance, public display, and public digital performance of a sound recording.[13]

Certain works created by specified persons may belong, for copyright purposes, in whole or in part, to other people based on the concept of a "work-for-hire." This concept most often applies to an employee who creates a work within the scope of his or her employment responsibilities. Agreements also may lead to the creation of works-for-hire where all of the rights of the creator go to the person specified in the agreement.

Creators of original works have been granted the ability to transfer certain (or all) rights by way of a license to specified or general users. Where licenses transfer rights to others, *only* the rights specifically transferred are provided for. All other rights remain with the original copyright holder.

Copyright protection lasts differing lengths of time depending on who created the work and who has the rights to it. Works created after January 1, 1978, have copyright protection until 70 years after the death of the last surviving author, while works-for-hire (works in which copyright ownership belongs initially to someone other than the creator) retain protection for either 125 years after creation or 95 years after publication, whichever is earlier.[14] For works created prior to 1978, a host of time periods are applicable.[15]

2.3.1.1.2 Copyright Violations.   There are three primary categories of copyright violation: (1) direct, (2) contributory, and (3) vicarious. For a direct copyright violation to occur, the violator actually must take direct action. Carrying a copyrighted image to a photocopier, placing the image on the glass, and pressing "copy" would be direct infringement. The copier has taken all the actions necessary for the violation to occur.

Contributory infringement occurs when a person knowingly provides the means for the copyright to be violated. If the "copier" in the above example tells the copy machine owner about plans to make the illegal copy, and the owner knows or has reason to know the image does not belong to the copier, the photocopier owner has "contributed" to the infringement and has violated the copyright holder's rights under the act.

Finally, vicarious liability exists generally (although not exclusively) in employment situations, where one person has control over another and does two things: (1) either authorizes the infringement or requires the infringement to take place; and (2) has some interest (generally monetary) in the infringement taking place.

Whether particular acts constitute infringement is a question often raised in the courts, and the answer is determined based on the activity undertaken. Where a computer or Web-based site both encourages and facilitates the uploading of copyrighted material, the courts have found the site to have directly infringed the copyright of the owner, even where the provider did not actually upload files.[16] Where an Internet provider provided access to Usenet and was notified that a post originating and residing on its server contained copyright-protected information that was being posted in violation of the copyright, the provider's failure to remove the materials left the provider with potential contributory liability for the infringement.[17] The liability of Internet Service Providers (ISPs), however, has been modified by the Digital Millennium Copyright Act.

2.3.1.2 Digital Millennium Copyright Act.   The Digital Millennium Copyright Act regulates when, and under what circumstances, an ISP would be liable for copyright infringement that is accomplished using its computer networks and facilities. The act defines conditions under which the provider will not be held liable for infringing activities. Specifically, the act requires that a provider have a policy regarding noninfringement, that a specific person be on file as the contact for copyright claims, and that, when notified by a copyright holder that infringement is taking place, the infringing material be removed or blocked. These provisions, outlined here only generally, allow an ISP to provide access without attempting to monitor each and every transmission that originates from within or travels across the network.[18]

2.3.1.3 Fair Use.   One of the most often quoted and misused doctrines of copyright is the concept of fair use. An exception to the rights of a creator in his or her work, fair use allows others to perform, show, quote, copy, and otherwise distribute the work of another for certain purposes. The test for determining whether use is covered by the fair use doctrine is fairly narrow, in contradiction to its popular conception as a catchall to validate infringement. The purposes of fair use are to allow comment, debate, and discussion regarding copyrighted works.

Fair use is allowed for purposes including news reporting, scholarship, or research, and is based in part on the amount of the work used: The more material used, the more likely is it that the use is not covered under fair use. In addition, fair use concerns include the nature of the copyrighted work, the purpose and character of the use, and the effect of the use on the market for the copyrighted work.

A misperception often exists that noncommercial or nonprofit uses are protected by the fair use doctrine. This is not automatically the case. Use for commercial purposes may lead a court to find that the use is outside the fair use protections, but even when the use is not commercial, infringement may be found. This was the case when a nonprofit entity used clipart from a CD collection on its Web site, where such use was not allowed under the CD license. This was, according to the court that decided the case, a clear example of direct infringement unprotected by fair use. That it was for a nonprofit purpose did not preclude liability.[19]

In sum, fair use is intended to allow art and creativity to flourish and for discussion to take place, not to avoid the licensing requirements of the Copyright Act.

2.3.1.4 Software, Counterfeits, and Copies. One of the primary copyright concerns in the software application arena is that of copying software and of software counterfeits. (See Chapters 12 and 26.) Both of these problems cause substantial losses of revenue for software developers and producers. For copyright purposes, copying software occurs not only when one copies the software is copied to removable disks, but also when the disks are used to install the software application on a computer or to run it once it is there.

Not all copying infringes the software owner's copyright. Infringement occurs when the copying is in violation of the license, or software agreement, provided by the creator. If the agreement allows installation on one computer, installing it on a second computer while it remains on the first violates the agreement. If the agreement, as many modern software agreements do, allows installation on an "office" PC and on a portable or home-based PC, installing it on two office PCs is a violation of the agreement. The actual, literal, written terms of the agreement control the determinants here, not extrapolations or inferences users may draw from the license terms.

Without question, making copies of disks, diskettes, or tapes that contain software applications and providing them to users in violation of the agreement constitutes copyright infringement in the clearest terms. Where such acts are done on the commercial or mass level, with sales of the infringing disks, the commercial purposes of the infringement make it all the more egregious, subjecting the violators to the potential of "penalty" damages above and beyond the actual losses suffered by the copyright holder. Removing the commercial purposes, however, such as when users make copies of applications for friends or colleagues, is no less illegal and is no less a violation of the law of copyright. Such activities are not only illegal but are moral violations of copyright holders' rights in their works, and must be avoided.

One final note is appropriate on this topic. While businesses and other users may believe that illegal copying of software is worth the small risk of ever being found out, the Business Software Alliance actively pursues and investigates allegations of illegal copying and use of software applications. One of the primary sources from which the alliance learns of infringing activities is former employees who are disillusioned or angry with their former employer. While the reason someone reports a violator is not particularly important, the action taken by the alliance in investigating and prosecuting the infringement certainly is. All users must be aware of the appropriate and licensed use of software applications; in particular, managers must be vigilant in protecting against copyright infringement at all levels.

2.3.1.5 Music and Video Piracy. Napster, the Internet-based application that was designed to allow music lovers to exchange audio files easily and quickly in the MP3 format, created quite a stir in the copyright world in 2000 and 2001. Following lawsuits by various recording artists and music industry companies and associations, Napster agreed to cooperate in preventing music piracy. Napster's case exemplifies the conflicts that have arisen in copyright because of the increased use of computers and the Internet. Much of the conflict is based on the early development of the Internet, along with the culture of "freedom" that predominated in the Net's early development. Specifically, the idea that information, data, and files should be free conflicts directly with the idea that creative works belong unequivocally to their creators.

Napster developed an application that allowed users to exchange files with other users without the files actually being uploaded to the Napster server. Instead, the server connected users and allowed them to see other users and their music collections online. Napster's position was that it was not infringing copyright by providing this service, even where users were trading files by copying them, in violation of copyright restrictions. Napster claimed that the service did not monitor the user transactions and thus had no knowledge of the violations. Furthermore, as the files were never on the Napster server, the service took the position that it had not actually copied any files; all copying was done by users.

These positions were largely rejected by both the recording industry and the courts. The United States Federal District Court for the Southern District of New York found that Napster was liable not only for contributory infringement for providing a service it knew or should have known was largely being used to infringe legitimate copyright but for a commercial purpose, to boot. This now-classic conflict between "free" exchange and continued copyright protection is likely to repeat itself, most likely with similar results in future cases.[20]

2.3.1.6   Technology Designed to Defeat Copyright Protection.

One specific provision of the Digital Millennium Copyright Act provides that Internet service providers, where seeking the protection of the act, not only must abide by the "takedown" and copyright dispute provisions in the act but also must not support or provide technology to others to assist them in defeating the technological copyright protection built in to many copyright protected files (such as protection on DVD disks that prevents them from being copied onto standard VHS videotapes or onto computers using standard video capture devices).[21]

Where support for such devices or technology is found on the part of an ISP, complying with other provisions of the act will not ensure application of the act's protections. In addition, developing, distributing, or otherwise supporting technology designed to defeat technological protection for copyrighted materials is a violation of federal criminal law and may be punished by fines and a prison sentence.[22]

For a more extensive discussion of antipiracy techniques, see Chapter 26.

2.3.1.7   Copyright and Internet Use: Links and Frames.

Interesting copyright questions are raised around the use of frames on the Internet and World Wide Web. Linking to pages on a Web site may itself raise many legal questions, but copyright infringement concerns are most likely to arise where the link is to infringing material. In such cases, the originator of the link may be liable for contributory infringement. An essential element necessary to prove such liability is the knowledge on the part of the linking site that the site being linked to has infringing material on it. Absent such knowledge, the remaining linking issues are more appropriately discussed within the context of market controls and unfair competition claims.

Framing, however, while using links to create a Web page, involves much more clear opportunity for direct infringement of a copyright holder's rights. Framing occurs where the builder of a Web site utilizes frames technology (a method of constructing an HTML document so that a new Web page can appear in a separate scrollable window), and in doing so makes it appear as if material within the frames originates with or belongs to the site builder. Where the material is in fact that of another site, claims for copyright infringement are likely to result.

Two fairly early (in terms of the of the World Wide Web) cases illustrate the dangers inherent in using framing technology to bring content designed and built by others into a Web site without their permission. The first case involved two competing newspapers in England. The first paper created a site with frames and, using the headlines from a competitor's paper, linked to text that was contained in that competitor's paper. When a user clicked on a headline, the text of the article was brought into the site, making it appear as if it belonged to the framing site. When challenged, the framing site stopped making it appear as if content from its competitor's site actually originated on its site.

It seems to make sense that a competitor should not be able to steal content from a business site and claim it as its own. But what about a site that is not actually in the same business as the copyright holder? TotalNews describes itself as "a search engine and directory of news sites designed to increase your access to information." At its inception, the TotalNews Web site would provide a link with the subject of an article or story, and when the link was clicked, the story would load within the frames. Various news sources framed in this way sued, and TotalNews changed its operating method so that when links are clicked, it is clear that the user is leaving the Total-News sites. Links from TotalNews now take users to the actual site belonging to the news source, and the news source is clearly marked on the links page within the Total-News site.

Framing presents interesting opportunities for copyright infringement. Should such framing method be found to be actual infringement, it is possible that the courts could view every single time the framed material is called up by a user as a separate copyright violation for purposes of assessing damages and penalties. With hundreds, thousands, or even hundreds of thousands of hits on a page, damages from such uses could be significant. It is best either to avoid using frames to incorporate nonoriginal material into the home Web site or to have explicit written agreements to cover such framing.

2.3.2   Trademarks.   Trademarks are identifiers that distinguish one product or service from another; they may consist of specific names, images, or combinations of text and specific typefaces and colors.

2.3.2.1   Nature of Trademark Protection.   Unlike copyright, trademark is wholly a creature of the common law and statute. Trademark protection exists both at the federal level and in the laws of many states. Marks may be protected either where they are nondescriptive of the service or product or where they are descriptive but have gained secondary meaning because people associate the mark with the product for which protection is sought. Protection can be gained simply by use, but in order to pursue a court action based on federal statute, the mark must be registered. The registration process involves proving to the trademark examiner that the mark is either nondescriptive or has acquired secondary meaning. Registrations can be challenged, but it is difficult to win a challenge to a long-registered mark.

Trademark protection involves two primary areas. Prohibitions exist against uses that either are shown to cause a "likelihood of confusion" or may dilute the value of the mark through improper use. This second layer of protection is a fairly recent addition to the statute to provide protection against such acts as cybersquatting (registering domain names that rightfully belong to trademark owners or to famous individuals such as actors in the hope of extorting large payments to give up the domains) and operating Web site with domain names similar to those of registered marks, thereby creating confusion.

2.3.2.2   Domain Names and Trademarks.

Early on in the development of today's World Wide Web, it became apparent that trademark and the primary operators of the Web—domain names—were on a path to conflict. Some people who foresaw the development of the Web as a means of communication for the masses registered domain names that were the marks of both major and minor corporations. When Web use began to explode, these "cybersquatters" then either sold or attempted to sell the registered names to the companies that were just beginning to realize the importance of having a presence on the Web. In addition, competitors or others wishing to trade on the reputations of long-established marks used Web sites with domain names similar to those marks to mislead Web users into visiting their sites.

Traditional notions of trademark and "likelihood of confusion" do not deal effectively with cybersquatting, particularly where the squatter takes no action in relation to the site: A potential user typing the registered URL into the address bar of a browser simply receives a "Web site not found" or "unavailable" message. The problems inherent in cybersquatting, the possibilities of confusion, and the analogies regularly drawn between cybersquatting and extortion led Congress to adopt anti-cybersquatting provisions. Where one registers a domain name without a valid intended use for the name, the mark holder may force the squatter to "unregister" the name and allow the mark holder to register it.[23]

In cases in which confusion is likely, based on a registered domain name, the courts have not hesitated to order its use ended. In a number of cases, registered domain-name-holders have been forced to relinquish their claims on the domains in question upon a finding by the court that either there was an intent to cause confusion and benefit from the mark's hard-earned reputation or there was a substantial likelihood that confusion would result. Where, however, confusion is not likely, the registered owner will most probably be able to continue to use the domain name. One of the more striking examples is the site that was, for quite some time, the home to Delta Tools, a major manufacturer of power tools. Today that name is registered to Delta Airlines, not as the result of a legal action, as both companies have rights to the "Delta" name in their own arenas (airlines and power tools). Instead, it resulted from negotiation between the two companies, with the one that most wanted the domain *www.delta. com* willing to pay for it.

2.3.2.3   Embedded Text and Trademark.

Simply because text that may violate a trademark is hidden from the average viewer or receiver does not necessarily insulate it from allegations that the use of the mark may violate trademark rules. Some Web page designers, ostensibly in an attempt to draw Web users into visiting their sites, placed trademarks belonging to others in hidden *metatext* on their Web pages. Search engines and other technologies use metatext to categorize and index Web pages. With these marks in embedded or hidden text, Web pages would be returned as "hits" when searches were conducted for those marks; thus users could be misled into thinking the link they were following was to a site containing a valid use of the trademark.

Where these cases have arisen, the courts have uniformly held that embedded or hidden text, whether metatext or hidden through other technologies, is subject to trademark analysis. If the use is not otherwise permitted by concepts such as fair use (discussed below), the courts have found trademark violations and ordered the use stopped.[24] Decisions in these cases lead us to the conclusion that the courts may review *any* use of a protected mark to determine whether a violation of trademark has occurred.

2.3.2.4 *Fair Use and Trademark.* As with copyright, fair use concepts apply to trademarks. In many countries, for example, direct comparison of products by name is not allowed. Such comparisons are allowed in the United States, but they would be useless if one competitor could stop another from using its name in comparative advertising. Thus, certain areas of use are considered fair when it comes to trademark protection. As with copyright, however, fair use cannot be invoked to violate trademark and cause a likelihood of confusion.

Fair use in trademarks does not permit marks to be used simply to enhance the image of a product or to otherwise ride on the coattails of another's mark. Such actions may spark a lawsuit alleging trademark dilution (the loss of value in a trademark caused by another's unfair use). In addition, any attempt to use a mark that is likely to or does cause confusion as to the source of a product runs directly afoul of trademark protection.

Fair use does protect a person or entity that wishes to be critical of a product, service, or company and in so doing uses the registered mark. It would be difficult, if not impossible, to criticize meaningfully without naming the product. In addition, such use is allowed in direct comparisons, which, if inappropriate or without factual basis, may suffer from other legal liabilities, such as unfair trade and fair competition laws.

2.3.2.5 *Domain Name Disputes: The ICANN Process.* The Internet Corporation for Assigned Names and Numbers (ICANN, *www.icann.org*), a nonprofit international organization, administers the system of issuing Internet addresses. Under the process developed by ICANN for handling disputes over domain names, first a claim is filed and the current domain name user is given the opportunity to respond. ICAAN looks specifically for evidence of bad faith in registration and determines who has the right to the domain name. The determination is binding on the registrant based on the agreement made at the time the registration is accepted. Not all attempts to gain names for the purpose of later selling them are against ICANN policy. For example, ICANN found that "Allocation.com" did not act in bad faith in registering hundreds of generic domain names. In an interesting turn of events, at least one U.S. Federal District Court has found it is not bound by ICANN decisions.[25]

In November 2000, the ICANN board selected seven new top-level domains for discussion and negotiation: .aero, .biz, .coop, .info, .museum, .name, and .pro (see *www.icann.org/tlds/* for details). Of these, .biz and .info were activated at the end of June 2001. The introduction of the new top-level domains involved extensive provisions for trademark holders to register appropriate domain names for themselves and to challenge possible trademark infringement.

2.4 PRIVACY. Because of the transborder nature of electronic communications today, many areas of regulation and control involve international questions. Certainly, privacy is one of those areas, with a host of international actions occurring regularly.

For a more detailed review of privacy issues, see Chapter 52.

2.4.1 International Implications. One of the primary privacy concerns at the time of this writing for worldwide Internet and computer-based companies is the Online Privacy Directive of the European Union (EU). This directive requires that when companies

export personal data from Europe certain steps be taken, including notifying residents of the data use and providing them with an opportunity to limit its use as well as providing access to the information itself. While there are safe harbor provisions existing for companies that abide by certain restrictions, it is probable that companies will be precluded from receiving European data if they fail to abide by the restrictions. Even Canada, the most important trading partner of the United States, has adopted regulations aimed at bringing it within the EU specifications and requirements.

2.4.2 U.S. Constitutional Law.   That privacy is a right guaranteed under the U.S. Constitution is a proposition that is difficult to argue with. Defining the extent of that right, however, raises particularly difficult questions. The U.S. Constitution is a bar only to government action, not private action, and it is unlikely that the U.S. Supreme Court would ever extend such protections to private actions.

In addition to privacy concerns directly, the Fourth Amendment's guarantee against unreasonable searches and seizures has created protection for what the courts refer to as areas within which people have a "reasonable expectation of privacy." Where the reasonable expectation exists, government may not simply invade the areas encompassed within that reasonable expectation. Inclusion of the term "reasonable" is essential to the concept of protection here. It is not simply an expectation of privacy, but one that is reasonable given circumstances and situations. In order to search content or information protected by the Fourth Amendment's guarantee, government officials must obtain a search warrant from an authorized court of law.

2.4.3 U.S. Statutory Protection.   A large number of federal laws relate to privacy for communications that are relevant to the Internet, but understanding them is often complicated. For example, federal statutes prevent unauthorized eavesdropping or recording of various types of communications, referred to as "wiretapping." The statute, however, allows wiretapping in many situations without a warrant, including where all parties are aware of the tap and consent. It also provides a "business communications" exception that allows employers to monitor employees' business-related communications.

Of specific relevance to Internet and computer-based communications is the Electronic Communications Privacy Act (ECPA).[26] Much like the wiretapping statute, the ECPA prohibits unauthorized interception of electronic communications. It does allow, however, that certain persons or entities will not be held liable for receiving or accessing certain electronic communications. Among these are the administrator or operator of a system for purposes of operating the system as well as employers monitoring the e-mail of their employees. Generally, employers have (or should have) a policy detailing that e-mail and electronic communications such as Web browsing are not private; even absent a policy, employers are not prohibited by the act from reviewing employee e-mail.

Congress has also passed various laws relating to children and protection of child activities on the Internet. Congress requires that online information collected from children be limited in nature. Where a site directed either to children or to the general public collects such information, it must comply with the federal statute that requires disclosures regarding information collection and *actual* parental consent before information is collected from children under 13 years of age.[27]

2.4.4 U.S. States' Statutory and Common Law Protection.   The rules of states are also relevant when it comes to privacy concerns. Individual states have a number of statutory provisions relating to privacy, and some of these, such as protection of the HIV status of people or medical records in general, are severely limited in scope. Generally these provisions, and any common law requirements, must be considered based on the state in which a transaction is taking place. If the transaction is interstate or international in nature, the laws of both the sending and the receiving jurisdiction should be consulted and considered. The overall application of jurisdictional law in these circumstances is still under development, but should raise concerns for those involved in communicating information that may be covered by specific provisions in any involved jurisdiction.

2.4.5   Contractual Protection of Privacy and Contractual Enforcement.   In addition to all of the above safeguards, users may insist that sites and providers abide by the privacy policies they have set out on their sites. Subsequent violations of privacy guarantees are a matter of considerable concern for users and privacy advocates. Where an Internet company was involved in a bankruptcy proceeding, the privacy policy the site had maintained was raised in opposition to the trustee's and creditor's attempt to sell the list of users as an asset to satisfy creditor claims. Agreements and policies play an important role in protecting privacy on the Internet.

2.5   DEFAMATION.   Defamation, more commonly referred to as libel and slander, refers to an area of the law concerned with the effect of spoken and written words on the reputation of another. In order for a defamation suit to succeed, the person who feels defamed must meet state-law requirements to prove a case. Most often these laws require proof that the statement was about the person suing, that it was made public (known as the "publication" requirement), and that it was defamatory in that it tended to cause injury to the person's reputation.

Under traditional common law analysis, truth was considered a defense to a defamation action. In modern legal theory, the falsity of the statement is often something the person suing must prove, many times a difficult task. In addition, where the statement does not allege or imply facts but is solely and entirely an expression of opinion, it will not likely be found to be defamatory.[28]

2.5.1   Persons Liable for Defamation.   That any person who actually makes a statement that is defamatory is liable for damages is readily accepted and widely understood. Where, however, a defamatory statement is republished, the republication of the statement is a separate defamatory act in and of itself, and the republisher may be found liable for it. This is true even where the source of the original statement is noted or the republisher states that there is no knowledge of the truth or falsity of the statement. In contrast with publishers, distributors are not liable for defamation contained in statements they merely distribute, unless they have knowledge of the alleged defamation.

The classic example that shows the differences between publishers and distributors is that of a newspaper and a newspaper stand. The newspaper itself has published the statement, following a process of writing and editing, and is assumed to have direct knowledge of the existence of the statement and control over whether it appears on its pages. A newsstand operator, however, simply receives the paper from the newspaper publisher. If the operator was responsible for each and every possible defamatory statement contained in the newspaper, no periodicals or other printed matter could ever be sold. Newsstand operators are therefore not responsible unless they are notified of a potential liability.

With this background, the question for defamation purposes then becomes whether a particular transmission of a statement is a publication or a distribution. Early cases on this matter generally held that where an online ISP simply provided the mechanism for discussion or distribution of statements, and exercised no control over the content of the messages, the provider was not responsible for defamation occurring within the service provided.[29] Where, however, a particular ISP not only provided the distribution but maintained some control over content (in this case solely to remove "objectionable" content), one court held the service liable for defamation, comparing the review of messages for objectionable content to the editorial functions carried on by a newspaper.[30]

In a provision included within the Communications Decency Act, Congress moved to prevent confusion in similar cases.[31] This provision allows providers to review postings for objectionable content, such as indecent material or text, and not risk subjecting themselves to liability for defamation that is not identified and removed by the reviewers. Thus, ISPs are considered distributors and not publishers for purposes of defamation online. Statements made by the ISP, or for which the provider is responsible, are not immune under these provisions. Only statements made by others using the providers' facilities are protected.

2.5.2   U.S. Constitutional Issues.   Because the pursuit of a defamation action involves the courts and also implicates guarantees surrounding freedom of speech and expression, defamation law in the United States has constitutional aspects. Specifically, in addition to the elements outlined above, where a statement relates to a matter of public concern and is made about a public figure, the public figure can recover for defamation only when the statement was made with "actual malice." Actual malice is found where the speaker knew the statement was false at the time of its making or showed gross disregard for its truthfulness. A public figure is generally someone "famous," as that term is understood in the common sense, or an elected or appointed public official.[32]

This additional requirement is imposed by the Constitution, according to the courts, to preclude persons who are in the public eye from attempting to discourage public discussion and comment about them by aggressively pursuing legal action. Where the public figure cannot show fault on the part of the speaker, the lawsuit will be dismissed.

2.6   DUE DILIGENCE AND PRIVATE LIABILITY.   Where one person's actions allegedly cause injury to another, the first person may attempt to bring a legal cause of action to recover for the damages caused. The law recognizes such causes where certain requirements are met, specifically, that one person owes a duty to act reasonably in relation to another, that the person failed to act reasonably, that the failure caused injury to the other, and that actual damages resulted from the injury. The standard applied to determine reasonableness is a subjective one given all the circumstances and is often determined by a jury. Where someone has failed to exercise "due care" in his or her actions, a negligence lawsuit is likely to follow. Specific circumstances that may involve negligence in the online environment are the subject of this section.

For a more extensive discussion of due diligence, see Chapter 45.

2.6.1   Misstatements.   One of the primary questions in the online environment is the provision of wrong or incorrect data. As the Internet contains a tremendous amount of information, does liability arise in circumstances where incorrect information is provided to users? Generally the answer is no. Because of the nature of the "due care" requirements of law, a duty does not generally arise unless there is some relationship between the provider of the information and the user. This relationship may be contractual or arise where a provider knows that only a few people are likely to use the information. A duty does not generally exist between an information provider and the public at large, even where the public relies on the information.[33]

Actions for negligent misstatement, then, are difficult to sustain where information was provided in books, magazines, or in general-use Web site. That injury occurred from reliance on the information does not save the case if a duty to act reasonably in regard to the general public never existed. Where misstatements are intentional, other causes of action may exist, and where they are defamatory, the duty requirement does not preclude a defamation action.

2.6.2 Negligent Network Administration. While a duty does not likely exist between an information provider and the general public, there is a case for arguing that network operators and administrators owe a duty of care to those to whom their computers are connected. As opposed to the world at large, network operators understand and have knowledge that their system is interconnected with those of others, and that without reasonable operation injury to others may occur.

An analogy to a well-settled area of law may help see the boundaries drawn here. Where a person is driving a car, it is clear that that person has a duty to operate the vehicle reasonably. Failure to do so is the primary impetus for personal injury actions based on auto accidents. This is true even if the driver has never met the person involved in the accident. The duty to act reasonably exists for all drivers on the road.

If these analogies are compared to the Internet and computer networks, such networks are more akin to a series of roads, and the operators to drivers on that road, than they are to a publisher of a book distributed to the whole world. Thus, where a network operator does not operate his or her network in a reasonable fashion, and injury to others occurs, liability may ensue. The specter of liability in these circumstances seems to arise most specifically in the area of unauthorized use of computer facilities by another to attack a third person. Such attacks, whether they involve denial of service or other injury, often utilize computer systems that have not been adequately protected against third-party intrusion and utilization.

Although no cases have been reported to date, it is likely that cases will present themselves in the near future where sites attacked using "victimized" computer systems will sue the alleged victim sites for not reasonably protecting against such uses. Computer security, regularly monitoring and installing patches that might prevent participation in Distributed Denial of Service attacks (DDoS) and related actions, are likely to become critical not only to maintaining the integrity of the computer system but also to protecting against potential liability to third party sites. See Chapter 11 for more information on DDoS.

2.7 INDECENCY AND OBSCENITY. Indecency and obscenity present unique issues in the computer environment. While often linked together in law and policy, they are distinct legal concepts, with distinct implications.

For a more extensive discussion of censorship and content filtering, see Chapter 51.

2.7.1 Indecent and Obscene Communications and the U.S. Constitution. Obscenity is a class of expressive materials defined by the U.S. Supreme Court to be without the protection afforded by the First Amendment to expressive conduct generally. As such, it is considered "unprotected." Government regulation of obscene materials therefore does not implicate the Constitution unless nonobscene materials also are regulated under the guise of obscenity. The Supreme Court has defined obscenity as "(a) whether 'the average person, applying contemporary community standards' would find that the work, taken as a whole, appeals to the prurient interest [citation omitted]; (b) whether the work depicts or describes, in a patently offensive way, sexual conduct specifically defined by the applicable state law; and (c) whether the work, taken as a whole, lacks serious literary, artistic, political, or scientific value."[34]

A number of specific elements to this definition deserve at least slightly closer attention. First, the standard is not whether a "prude" would find that the work appeals to prurient interest or invokes thoughts of lust but whether a reasonable person would. A reasonable person is a legal fiction often used in legal tests and rules.

The "community standards" element means the definition may change from place to place. In the computer field, the community used to determine standards appears to be the receiving community, not the sending community.[35] This fact has serious implications for sending potentially obscene materials via the Internet.

The "patently offensive" language means the definition is only to apply to "hard core" pornography. While the community standards element of the definition means that what may appeal to the prurient interest in one place may not in another, the "value" element is intended to "save" works that might otherwise be found to be obscene in some areas of the nation but have important value for the nation as a whole.

Finally, two important concepts in the obscenity arena are vagueness and breadth. Where laws written to prohibit allegedly obscene materials also encompass materials that are not obscene, the law is considered "overbroad" and is invalid in its entirety. An example would be a law prohibiting transmission of all "nude" pictures, as nudity alone is not obscene, Where a law alleges to attack obscene speech but attacks only some specific obscene speech, it may be underinclusive and thus also be invalidated by the courts. Finally, where the law is not clear and specific as to which speech is prohibited, it is said to be "void for vagueness" and invalidated. These concepts are designed to prevent government from stopping or "chilling" protected speech through the use of restrictions aimed or alleged to aim at unprotected speech.

In contrast to obscene materials, whether something is indecent is determined based on a national standard; unlike obscene materials, indecency receives some Constitutional protection, thus making government regulation more difficult to sustain.[36] Primary among regulations aimed at indecent materials are those intended to prevent children from accessing them.

The standard for determining whether materials are indecent is whether the material exposes children to representations that describe, in terms patently offensive as measured by contemporary standards for the medium in question, sexual or excretory activities or organs, at times of day when there is a reasonable risk that children may be in the audience. The only medium in which indecency restrictions have been upheld regularly are those in broadcasting.[37] Similar attempts to impose blanket restrictions on nonbroadcast media have largely been rejected by the courts. However, attempts to require that indecent materials not be available to children have been upheld by the courts.

2.7.2 Communications Decency Act. The Communications Decency Act, part of the Telecommunications Act of 1996,[38] was intended by Congress to address indecent communications over the Internet. Most constitutional scholars did not believe that such a provisions would stand up. As noted, the only medium in which legislation has been successful in regulating indecent communications was over-the-air broadcasting, where broadcasters had a defined and established responsibility to serve the public interest in their broadcasting.[39] While courts in the broadcasting cases also mentioned that broadcasting was pervasive in our culture, there was a substantial question as to whether that justification alone would support regulation of indecent, as opposed to obscene, materials on the Internet. Adding to the confusion were cases in which the courts had refused to uphold congressional attempts to forbid indecent communication by telephone, finding the differences between telephone and broadcasting too great to withstand constitutional review.[40]

That Congress shared these concerns when it passed the Communications Decency Act is apparent from the inclusion of a mechanism for immediate appeal to the U.S. Supreme Court from any district court challenge to the act's provisions. When challenged, the Federal District Court for the District of Columbia found the act's indecency provisions unconstitutional, and the U.S. Supreme Court upheld the district court's determination.[41] While the indecency provisions were invalidated by the courts, the provisions of the act that prohibit the transmission of obscene materials are still in place. It thus remains a violation of U.S. law to transmit obscene materials via the Internet.

2.7.3 Additional Issues Related to Indecent and Obscene Communications or Products.   In addition to the transmission and receipt issues involved with indecent communications, the use of electronic communications has led to the increased availability of obscene and indecent materials in the workplace. In addition, it is "easier" now to sexually harass others in the workplace, through the use of e-mail and the display of obscene images on computer screens within the view of others who are offended by them.

These developments have been offset to a degree by the relative ease of using these new technologies to gather evidence about the very offenses they have enabled. Specifically, there are numerous cases in which e-mail archives have proven that harassment was in fact taking place and that images and other materials were stored on a company's computer in violation of policies and rules relating to such use.

2.8 LITIGATION.   Nearly any kind of litigation has the potential to involve computers, electronic data, and electronic transmissions. How the various technologies play out in the litigation process, their role and function, is one subject of this section. In addition, we review other litigation issues raised in the computer and Internet arena, such as jurisdiction and location for lawsuits.

2.8.1 Gathering Evidence.   One significant role for electronic communications and for data in litigation is in the gathering of evidence. Nearly every case, whether criminal or civil, involves at least some need to gather evidence from computers and networks. In criminal cases, computers and network equipment can be confiscated and taken into custody to be used as evidence, especially where that equipment is the alleged vehicle for a crime. In civil cases, equipment can be subpoenaed and taken for review by experts.

In addition, court ordered "wiretaps" may be directed where a court finds sufficient reason for them. Cooperating with such directives is essential, as refusing or failing to cooperate may result in a finding of contempt against an ISP or network administrator, with its attendant fees or even jail sentence. Wiretaps may require monitoring of network traffic or transmissions. In addition, logs and other records may be required for litigation. When properly served, subpoenas for such data must be obliged. If questions exist about the propriety of providing information to parties in an ongoing legal case, consult an attorney. Failure to comply with court orders and directives carries potentially severe penalties.

2.8.2   Jurisdiction and Venue.   A critical issue that arises when dealing with the Internet, electronic transmission of data, and related questions is whether such actions will lead an individual or business to be sued in another part of the country or the world. These questions raise two separate issues: (1) jurisdiction, or the authority of a court to hear a case based on the substance of the case (substantive jurisdiction) or on the parties involved (personal jurisdiction); and (2) venue, the proper location for hearing the case.

Under traditional analysis of jurisdiction, courts in one part of the country cannot simply allow suits against persons or entities in another part of the country. There typically must be some connection to the location of the lawsuit in order for the court to hear it. The minimum contacts required generally involve an analysis of whether a state's law allows reaching out to and subjecting persons not physically present within a state to the state's jurisdiction through what is known as a "long-arm statute." Any person or entity physically present within a state is subject to the jurisdiction of its courts.

Where a proper long-arm statute exists, the courts will look to see whether the out-of-state party has sufficient contacts with the state to meet U.S. constitutional requirements relating to due process of law. This requires a determination both that there are purposeful minimum contacts by the party with the state and that the exercise of jurisdiction does not violate concepts of fair play and substantial justice.[42]

In the Internet arena, this analysis has lead to the conclusion that a highly interactive World Wide Web site may sustain jurisdiction in another state, while a noninteractive site most likely will not. Where Internet contacts can be combined with other contacts, such as mailing products or advertisements into a state, jurisdiction is more likely to be found. Jurisdiction also can be agreed to by the parties; where this takes, place the courts will likely accept the parties' agreed terms, especially where further contacts support the determination.[43]

In addition to jurisdiction, venue—the location of the court in which the case will be brought—is also an issue. While jurisdiction in a federal court in one state may be supportable under jurisdictional rules, that court may decide that the case is more appropriately heard in a court located in a place more directly linked to the basis of the dispute.

Determinations of jurisdiction and venue, and analysis of provisions of agreements relating to them, are critical when developing Internet content. The expense of defending a lawsuit in a location distant from the business, hiring local counsel and interacting with counsel and court, can be a tremendous burden to the corporate operation. Paying close attention to how these issues are handled is critical for determining potential exposure to lawsuits, and the expenses they impose, in other states and locations.

2.9   CRIMINAL ACTS.   As with any technology, the potential for abuse is inherent within the structures of high-technology systems. The levels of abuse will vary greatly depending on the skills or trusted access of the user. Although many criminal acts can be litigated concurrently in civil court, this section deals with the forensic aspects of criminal conduct in cyberspace. The lack of boundaries has created an exponential increase in the potential for wrongdoing and a corresponding expansion in the number of those engaged in wrongdoing. In response, those charged with investigating computer crime have been required to develop new investigative techniques to deal with electronic media and the Internet.

In terms of investigative techniques, computer forensics, or the gathering and analysis of information for use in legal proceedings, is a relatively new discipline. Rarely are there areas where law enforcement has been consistently ahead of private sector capabilities, but forensics has been one of those. There are two components to this capability: (1) media analysis and (2) network investigations. Currently a very strong analytical capability gives the edge to the forensic examiners. Most computer users are ignorant of the technical aspects of forensic examinations and the types of evidence that can be gleaned from a detailed analysis of the media. As an example, many users believe that deleting a file using operating system functions destroys the content of that file; however, on most computers, such deletion merely erases pointers to the first piece (cluster) of the file and allows all the clusters to be returned to the list of available space. As a consequence, it is usually easy for investigators to recover the content of all or some of the files that an amateur criminal may have erased in a panic.

However, law enforcement lags behind the private sector in technical expertise involving network investigations. Even with the amount of private sector knowledge, daily reports of new and potentially serious network breaches are far too commonplace. The constant onslaught of experienced, and even neophyte, intruders launching attacks and exploits against networks exceeds the capability of many network and system administrators to keep up. Often business requirements take precedence over security requirements, and it is in this neglected space that many successful criminal acts take place.

For a theoretical framework for describing and analyzing computer crime, see Chapter 3; for a review of methodological issues in studying computer crime statistics, see Chapter 4. For a model of fundamental principles in describing breaches of security, see Chapter 5.

2.9.1 Interception of Communications.   Although an apparently broad category, the area of interception of communications can cause significant economic losses without a parallel loss of data. Communications intercepts have long been a fundamental goal in military intelligence; now that goal has transitioned to the corporate environment. The end of the cold war did not in any way stop the intelligence-gathering operations of many nations. In fact, it has accelerated the efforts not only in military spying but in corporate and economic espionage as well.

At a basic level, the interception of communications can be as simple as reading e-mail over a coworker's shoulder. The collection of data in this example leaves no residual trace on the computer that could be analyzed later in a forensic examination. And once the information is released, it is the equivalent of attempting to "unring'" a bell. In cases such as this, the forensic examination will be less useful than the interview of the suspected perpetrator because the human being may reveal evidence that does not exist on the system.

On a higher level, more advanced tactics are employed. Internally, for example, *sniffers* can collect large amounts of data, including user names, passwords, e-mails, and other critical information. These data can be used to further penetrate a compromised system just as easily as they can be used to steal trade secrets or intellectual property. It is not unusual in high-stakes negotiation for one party to attempt to intercept the communications of the other, sometimes with the assistance of the intelligence service of their own country. Critical points such as price, negotiating position, talking points, discounts, and product availability can be gathered, giving one side or the other valuable bargaining tools.

From a forensic standpoint, these types of cases are difficult to solve. Little, if any, evidence can be found on the victim system because the communication is intercepted after it leaves the user, although certain Trojan horse software, such as BackOrifice or NetBus, do establish a footprint on an affected system. Anytime code is introduced onto a system, forensic examination can provide important clues as to the scope of the compromise.

Effective countermeasures to interception, such as encryption, make intercepts more complicated and less successful. Often the rewards do not justify the effort necessary to decrypt communications, particularly those of a tactical nature, which lose their value over time. The more difficult it is to capture the plain text, the more effective the countermeasure.

Forensic efforts at finding the point of compromise necessarily start with the user and flow through the network to the first point outside of the perimeter where outside assistance is required. In the case of a law enforcement investigation, subpoenas or search warrants will be necessary to obtain information that is outside the victim's control. Audit and system logs, file-integrity checkers (such as Tripwire), and other forms of monitoring will play an essential role in determining whether the source of the compromise is internal or external.

In the case of a compromised server that is used to conduct the intercept, forensics can provide the mechanism of compromise. A review of the operating system looks for telltale signs such as a *rootkit* (a program for obtaining supervisory privileges — often known as *root* due to the terminology used under UNIX — on a system) or other modified system files. By design, many rootkits erase all logging of their activities to prevent just this type of discovery. Restoring from a previous backup does not necessarily solve the problem. Depending on when the system was first compromised, previous backups also might be compromised. A complete rebuild of the system may be necessary.

One complicating factor in determining how to proceed is the mission of the affected system. The more mission critical the elements are, the more likely it is that a full forensic examination will not be possible. Balancing the needs of law enforcement with the needs of business continues to be a sticking point in many investigations and is precisely why some incidents are not reported. The more the investigation of the intercept is delayed, the more likely it is that valuable forensic data will be lost or damaged.

2.9.2 Intrusion and Trespass. Computer intrusions constitute the Mount Everest of the digital world. Many attacks and intrusions are launched simply because the network exists. The vast majority of these cases can be solved if adequate resources are available to investigating agencies. Vast amounts of forensic data can be found on the compromised system that will lead to a successful investigative conclusion. However, due to the overwhelming number of intrusions, many businesses prefer to patch the affected system and not report the incident to law enforcement.

Intrusions and trespassing cases are not limited to the corporate world. The U.S. Department of Defense remains a popular target among attackers. The goals of any intrusion depend on the motives of the intruder. Among younger attackers, simply gaining access is the end game. As new exploits are discovered and announced, a corresponding increase in associated activity can be detected.

As the title of this section indicates, there are differences between an intrusion and a trespass. The differences tend to be more a matter of semantics than a legal definition. From a forensic standpoint, evidence is evidence regardless of the motive. However, understanding the motives for an intrusion or trespass can affect the course of the resulting investigation. If a particular exploit is more of a "point-and-click" type of attack and does not grant the attacker root or elevated privileges, a decision must be made as to how in depth the forensic examination needs to be. If it is a well-known attack that has been properly analyzed, it may be reasonable to conclude that no other actions were taken after the initial compromise.

The sophistication of the attack alone should not be the only criterion by which further actions are directed. The lesson of Occam's Razor is just as relevant in computer forensics as it is in other fields of science: When investigating complex network attacks, the simplest explanation that fits all the facts should be adopted, unless clearly refuted.

During the forensic investigation, important evidence will be found in firewall and intrusion detection logs, among others. Examination of the compromised system should yield files that were created in close proximity to the time of the intrusion, if known. Care should be taken to preserve system logs so that an intruder does not erase them and so that they are not damaged or destroyed inadvertently prior to being turned over to law enforcement.

Forensic investigations of intrusions should not be carried out in a vacuum. Reviewing the latest exploit information on pertinent discussion groups and e-mail lists, along with reading what is available on public exploit sites, such as *www.widexs. nl.packetstorm* or *www.hackernews.com,* can provide additional guidance for technical investigators. Understanding how similar intrusions have been investigated, along with the potential capabilities of the exploit, can increase the odds for determining the full extent of damage on the affected system, and possibly minimizing it.

2.9.3 Destruction of Property (Web Defacement). Web defacements are the electronic version of smashing mailboxes. The acts themselves expose security flaws in the system but do not present as much of a serious threat as gaining root access on a compromised system, for example. That is not to say, however, that Web defacement is not a serious matter. The cost of a single compromise usually is not measured in dollars spent to fix the problem but in dollars lost in reputation and future business. There are also political goals to Web defacements that can be readily tracked with current global events.

Although several sites maintain archives of Web defacements, the Attrition Web page (*www.attrition.org*) has gained popularity among the media and security firms as an authoritative source for measuring the problem. Since tracking began in August of 1999, over 12,000 defaced sites have been reported to Attrition—an average of over 20 new sites per day. The availability of precompiled tools, along with the number of current Web sites worldwide, has created an entire new class of criminal acts not contemplated five years ago.

When conducting an investigation into a Web defacement, one of the key pieces of identifying data is the attacker's Internet provider (IP) address. Unlike a Distributed Denial of Service (DDoS), which routinely spoofs IP addresses, defacements require a valid IP address to which the attack data and captured index page are returned. Should the IP address originate from the same country as that in which the defacement occurred, law enforcement stands a reasonable chance of locating the culprit.

If the attack crosses international boundaries, further efforts at investigation usually are reserved for high-profile cases. The crossing of borders also complicates investigative efforts as two law enforcement agencies must now act in concert while at the same time observing local laws that may or may not permit the disclosure of identifying information to foreign nationals. Should the offender reside in a country where there is no formal extradition treaty, further efforts would prove futile and consume valuable investigative resources that could be directed at more solvable crimes.

During the forensic process, the examiner determines the operating system and applicable Web package that the victimized site uses. The method of exploit can then be quickly narrowed down before any actual examination is conducted, saving additional resources. Again, system logs, along with firewall and intrusion detection logs if available, provide the best identifying clues as to the origin of the attacker.

2.9.4   Denial of Service.   February 7, 2000, signaled the public emergence of a new threat—distributed denial of service. This threat created one of the most difficult and extensive types of investigations ever launched. DDoS attacks require compromising many other computers and inserting and concealing the code that launches the denial of service program. Automated scripts (programs for carrying out a number of operations very quickly) have made multiple compromises possible in a shorter amount of time, reducing the amount of actual work that has to be accomplished by one individual.

Repelling a DDoS attack in its initial stages requires tracing the incoming packets back upstream to the previous router. Since time is critical, successful traces require the cooperation of upstream providers as the packets are traced back from hop to hop. Actual physical examination of media is not a factor until one of the compromised systems is found. Even when the compromised "victim" system is found, forensic analysis of the victim computer tends to reveal more about the intended target of the DDoS attack than about the origin of the actual attacker.

The DDoS tools allow for an attack to start after the delivery of control traffic to the compromised agents. Since no reply to the control traffic is required, little evidence is left on the compromised system to help identify the actual attacker. Complete forensic examinations of the compromised agents are part of an overall case requirement should the offender, and the offender's systems, be located.

Successful DDoS investigations require timely response to the initial attack, reasonable steps to preserve the evidence, the availability of qualified personnel to start the trace-back, the rapid response of law enforcement (depending on the desire of the victim), the cooperation of upstream providers back to the source, additional cooperation of the owners of the compromised system, and some good fortune.

For a review of technical details of denial-of-service attacks, see Chapter 11.

2.9.5   Fraud.   One common thread in any type of criminal activity is the aspect of fraud. The pervasiveness of this element transcends all borders and cultures. As new technologies are created, new methods of fraud are just as quickly developed. In response, law enforcement is moving more rapidly to address these problems.

The Internet Fraud Complaint Center (*www.ifccfbi.gov*) is the most recent of these efforts. Sponsored by the FBI (*www.fbi.gov*) and the National White Collar Crime Center (*www.nw3c.org*), the site was opened on May 8, 2000. Additional information concerning Internet fraud statistics, and the report from the first six months of operation, can be found at *www.ifccfbi.gov/strategy/wn030601.asp*. As of March 6, 2001, the site had received over 37.5 million visits and 20,014 complaints, of which 6,087 (more than 30 percent) were referred to law enforcement agencies around the United States; of the referred complaints, 5,273 (more than 86 percent) involved Internet fraud. In a report dated May 2001 (*www.ifccfbi.gov/strategy/AuctionFraudReport.pdf*), auction fraud constituted over 64 percent of all complaints about Internet fraud.

Since this type of crime traditionally is consumer-oriented, law enforcement has been faced with a lack of desire by victims to prosecute such offenses. Usually the fear of embarrassment is the deciding factor. Although there are isolated cases of large losses (in excess of $100,000), criminals take refuge in the fact that most victims decline to initiate law enforcement intervention when faced with a much smaller loss.

From a forensic standpoint, the desired evidence from the victim usually comes in the form of e-mail or some other type of electronic communication. Instant messaging systems rarely capture the actual session by default unless the user so chooses. Savvy fraud artists will make use of as little recorded communications as possible to ensure anonymity. Forensic examinations may capture fragments of instant messages written to the media stored as part of virtual memory, but the odds are against it.

When an investigation does identify a suspected fraud artist, it is extremely important that search warrants and other resources be quickly marshaled. Valuable forensic evidence on the media of the perpetrator can be destroyed quickly if the suspect believes that arrest is imminent or that a subpoena may be issued. When a suspect is caught unaware, the resulting forensic examination usually reveals a treasure trove of incriminating information.

2.9.6   Extortion.   Combining old tactics with modern day techniques, the Internet extortionist can operate safely from behind the protective walls of international boundaries, while carrying out just as effective an attack as one committed in person. The first step in an extortion is the compromise of a targeted system, one that contains sensitive company or personal financial data. Other potential information targets include trade secrets and intellectual property. Once the desired information is obtained, an extortion threat is issued.

A combination of effective police work and the accompanying technical and forensic investigation forms the basis for a successful resolution. Internet extortion is one of the few electronic crimes where personal contact with the victim is a necessary component. This fact increases the likelihood of perpetrator identification.

However, identification does not necessarily mean personal identification. Because of the lack of effective law enforcement and judicial cooperation involving interjurisdictional use of the Internet, law enforcement may be able to trace back the offender only to an e-mail account or to a particular city if enough information is developed. Since payment is almost always an element of extortion (with the possible exception of politically motivated crimes), the transfer of funds provides the most likely opportunity for solving the offense.

If the extortion threat stems from the compromise of a database or financial system, the potential of information disclosure may not be the only avenue available to the intruder. The possibility of a destructive program (a *logic bomb*) planted within the database or financial system could provide a second threat should the first demand be ignored. In this case, a rapid forensic examination (scanning for unauthorized program code) may be necessary to assure the victim that the other alternative is simply an unfounded threat. Because of the nature of extortion and the corresponding press it generates in high-profile cases, many organizations are extremely reluctant to call in law enforcement because of the potential for bad publicity. Having access to a qualified and experienced incident response team during these situations vastly improves the chances for timely resolution.

2.10   INVESTIGATION.   The investigation of cybercrime is a new and rapidly evolving field. Few areas require as much interaction between the public and private sectors or as much specialized expertise as is needed to conduct effective forensic examinations. The fielding of computer crime units has produced increased cooperation among federal, state, and local law enforcement agencies. Unfortunately, the amount of electronic crime has outpaced the efforts of law enforcement and the private sector to keep up with the demand for services. For more details of computer investigations, see Chapter 34, "Working with Law Enforcement."

2.10.1   Computer Forensics.   Forensic examiners may take as long as three years to gain the experience needed to address today's computer crime cases, while the rapidly changing nature of available technology, combined with the limitless possible criminal uses, requires a constant effort to stay abreast of the emerging trends.

During the forensic process, several steps must be taken to ensure that the evidence has been seized properly, stored correctly, and examined reasonably. The failure of any one of these steps in and of itself may not be fatal to the case, but evidence that is irretrievably lost can never provide the potential clues it may have held. The International Association of Computer Investigative Specialists (IACIS) has produced a set of standards that is available to the public at *www.cops.org/forensic_examination_procedures. htm.* Although originally designed for Windows-based computers, the steps contained within the protocol are just as applicable to any forensic examination. One of the contributing authors to this chapter, Morgan Wright, is a member of the Board of Directors for IACIS.

Regardless of the type of operating system or who may eventually handle the evidence, there are common steps to take that will make the recovered evidence more likely to be introduced as valid in a court of law.

2.10.2   Media Seizure.   The most critical part of the forensic examination process is the initial seizure. Untrained personnel attempting to recover and image seized media can unalterably destroy evidence, including both inculpatory and exculpatory data. Creating a duplicate image of the suspected media is not a difficult process. Rather, it is a repeatable and verifiable process that requires an understanding of how hardware and software interact at a low level and controlling unintended results.

Several programs are available that create a valid forensic image of the data area. Many incorporate a cyclic redundancy code (CRC) checking component to address issues of integrity and reliability; CRCs are a cryptographic hash that makes accidental or deliberate changes to data extremely difficult to conceal (see Tutorial 4 for more about CRCs). Regardless of vendor claims, forensic examiners should conduct their own independent verification and validation tests on selected software tools.

2.10.3   Documentation.   A simple but effective criminal defense technique is to create reasonable doubt through the failure of the forensic examiner to document steps taken during the initial seizure and subsequent examination. Many criminal cases have been lost due to the fact that the officer who initially seized the evidence could not account for the chain of custody. The state of the evidence is secondary to the broader issue of control of the evidence. Examiners must be trained to keep notes and documentation necessary for the later introduction of evidence into a criminal proceeding.

If this standard is met, lesser standards, such as those in civil or administrative cases, will generally not be an issue.

2.10.4 Preservation. Even if the seizure and documentation steps are followed correctly, the failure to correctly preserve the seized media can cause the lack of prosecution in a criminal case. Electronic media that has been properly seized and well documented but stored next to the degaussing machine will most likely be no evidence at all. All media have operating and storage restrictions. Forensic examiners must understand the limitations inherent in the media that are being analyzed and the media that are being used to store the results of the seizure and examination.

2.10.5 Restoration. When it comes time to examine the seized media, it may be necessary to restore the image that was created during the initial step. Some forensic examination software creates its own proprietary image, eliminating the need to restore the seized image before conducting an analysis of it. Other imaging software requires complete restoration to another hard drive, or similar medium, before separate analysis tools are used. Improper restoration can flaw the accompanying forensic examination without the examiner's knowledge. Again, independent testing of all software and hardware used in the restoration process adds credibility and confidence to the final report.

2.10.6 Examination. Assuming that all previous steps have been taken and that no errors have been made, the real skill of a forensic examiner is evident in the examination stage. While it is quite possible to train unskilled personnel in the proper seizure, documentation, storage, and restoration of seized media within one to three days, it is highly unlikely that the same personnel could be trained to conduct a thorough forensic examination during that same course. Formal training from a recognized organization or institution should be a prerequisite sometime during the first year of forensic work. Assuming that it may be necessary to testify in the future, attendance at a recognized course helps establish the credibility of the examiner and makes it more likely that the resulting analysis will be admitted as evidence.

2.10.7 Report of Examination. The last step of an investigation requires production of a report detailing all of its findings. Because poor presentation of the facts can negate evidence that is clearly inculpatory, forensic examiners with significant experience will rely on a standard template and checklist to present the evidence. Far from being a "canned" report, the standard template assures the examiner that all relevant steps have been taken and documented, and helps prevent an inadvertent oversight. Additionally, prosecutors who become familiar with standard report forms become much more proficient at reading them and in noticing any potential weaknesses before making legal decisions about the case.

2.11 FURTHER READING

2.11.1 Books and Treatises

Bick, Johnathan. *101 Things You Need to Know About Internet Law.,* New York: Crown Publishing Group, 2000.

Black, Sharon. *Telecommunications Law in the Internet Age,* Morgan Kaufmann Series in Networking. Morgan Kaufman Publishers, 2001.

Brinson, Dianne J., and Mark F. Radcliffe. *Internet Law & Business Handbook: A Practical Guide.* Ladera Press, 2000.

Dara-Abrams, Benay, Dianne Brinson, and Jennifer D. Masek. *Exploring E Commerce, Site Management & Internet Law, Advanced Website Architecture Series.* Prentice Hall PTR, 2001.

Erbschloe, Michael, and John Vacca. *Net Privacy: A Guide to Developing & Implementing a Successful Privacy Plan.* New York: McGraw-Hill, 2001.

Garfinkel, Simson. *Database Nation: The Death of Privacy in the 21st Century.* O'Reilly & Associates, 2001.

Herrington, TyAnna K. *Controlling Voices: Intellectual Property, Humanistic Studies and the Internet.* Southern Illinois University Press, 2001.

Reis, Al, and Laura Reis. *The 11 Immutable Rules of Internet Branding.* HarperBusiness, 2000.

Stuckey, Kent D. *Internet and Online Law.* Law Journal Press, 1996–2001.

2.11.2 Law Review and Journal Articles

Cizek, Adam. "Traditional Personal Jurisdiction and the Internet: Does It Work?" 7 *U. Balt. Intell. Prop. J.* 109 (1999).

Dearing, Mark C. "Personal Jurisdiction and the Internet: Can the Traditional Principles and Landmark Cases Guide the Legal System into the 21st Century?" 4 *J. Tech. L. & Pol'y* 4 (1999).

"Developments in the Law: The Law of Cyberspace," 112 *Harvard L. Rev.* 1574 *et seq.* (1999).

Dieseth, Paul, "The Use of Document Depositories and the Internet in Large Scale and Multi-Jurisdictional Products Liability Litigation," 27 *Wm. Mitchell L. Rev.* 615 (2000).

Fa, Baoding Hsieh. "When Channel Surfers Flip to the Web: Copyright Liability for Internet Broadcasting," 52 *Fed. Comm. L.J.* (2000).

Fuertes, Roberto A. Camara. "Letting the Monster Out of the Closet: An Analysis of Internet Indecency Regulation," 70 *Rev. Jur. U.P.R.* 129 (2001).

Graydon, Scott M. "Much Ado about Spam: Unsolicited Advertising, the Internet, and You," 32 *St. Mary's L.J.* 77 (2000).

Kane, Matthew. "Copyright and the Internet: The Balance Between Protection and Encouragement," 22 *T. Jefferson L. Rev.* 183 (2000).

Kennedy, Leonard J., and Lori A. Zallaps, "If It Ain't Broke . . . The FCC and Internet Regulation," 7 *CommLaw Conspectus* 17 (1999).

Rogers, Amy. "You Got Mail But Your Employer Does Too: Electronic Communication and Privacy in the 21st Century Workplace," 5 *J. Tech. L. & Pol'y* 1 (2000).

Stankey, Robert F. "Internet Payment Systems: Legal Issues Facing Businesses, Consumers and Payment Service Providers," 6 *CommLaw Conspectus* 11 (1998).

2.12 NOTES

1. *Phoenix Renovation Corp. v. Gulf Coast Software, Inc.,* 2000 U.S. Dist. LEXIS 20026 (E.D. Va. 2000).

2. *In re RealNetworks, Inc. Privacy Litigation,* 2000 U.S. Dist. LEXIS 6584 (N.D. Ill. 2000).

3. *FTC v. Crescent Publ'g Group, Inc.,* 2001 U.S. Dist. LEXIS 452 (S.D.N.Y. 2001).

4. *See, e.g.,* 31 U.S.C. § 1501(a)(1).

5. *See,* Alaska Stat. § 09.25.500 *et seq.* (2001); Arizona. Rev. Stat. §§ 41-132, 41-351 *et seq.,* 44-7001 *et seq.,* and 44-7031 *et seq.* (2000); Ark. Stat. Ann. § 25-31-101 *et seq.* (2000); Cal Civ Code § 1633 *et seq.* (2001); Colorado Rev. Stat. 24-71-101 *et seq.* (2000); 6 Delaware Code § 101 *et seq.* (2000); Florida Stat. §§ 668.001 *et seq.* and Fla. Stat. § 668.50 (2000); Official Code of the State of Georgia Annotated § 10-12-1 *et seq.* (2000); Hawaii Revised Stat. § 489E-1 *et seq.;* Idaho Code § 28-50-101 *et seq.* (2000); 5 Illinois Compiled Stat. 175/5-105 *et seq.,* 5 ILCS 175/10-105 *et seq.,* 5 ILCS 175/15-101 *et seq.,* and 5 ILCS 175/25-101 (2000); Burns Indiana Code Ann. §§ 5-24-1-1 *et seq.* and 26-2-8-101 *et seq.;* Iowa Code § 554D.101 *et seq.* (2001); Kansas Statutes Annotated §§ 60-2616 and 369.101 *et seq.* (2000); 10 Maine Revised Stat. §§ 9401 *et seq.* and § 9501 *et seq.* (2000); Maryland Commercial Law Code Ann. §§ 21-101 *et seq.,* 22-101, and Maryland State Government Code Ann. § 8-504 (2000); Minn. Stat. §§ 325K.01 *et seq.* and 325L.02 *et seq.* (2000); Miss. Code Ann. § 25-63-1 *et seq.*

(2000); § 28.600 Rev. Stat. Missouri (1999); Montana Code Anno., §§ 2-20-102 *et seq.* (2000); Revised Stat. of Neb. §§ 86-1701 *et seq.* and 86-2102 *et seq.* (2000); Nevada Rev. Stat. Ann. §§ 720.010 *et seq.* (2000); 27 New Hampshire Rev. Stat. Annotated 294-D:1 *et seq.* (2000); N.M. Stat. Ann. §§ 14-3-15.1 (2001); N.Y. State Technology Law § 101 *et seq.* (McKinney's 2001); N.C. Gen. Stat. § 66-58.1 *et seq.* (2000); Ohio Revised Code Annotated *et seq.* 1306.01 (Anderson 2001); 12A Okl. Stat. §§ 15-101 *et seq.* (2000); Oregon Revised Stat. §§ 192.825 *et seq.* and 709.335 (1999); 73 Pennsylvania Stat. §§ 2260.301 *et seq.* (2000); Rhode Island Gen. Laws §§ 42-127.1-2 (2001); South Carolina Code Ann. §§ 26-5-20 *et seq.* (2000); South Dakota Codified Laws §§ 53-12-1 *et seq.* (2000); Texas Bus. & Com. Code § 2.108 (1999); Utah Code Ann. §§ 46-1-1 *et seq.* (2000); Virginia Code Ann. §§ 59.1-480 *et seq.* (2000); Rev. Code Washington (ARCW) §§ 19.34.010 *et seq.* (2001); West Virginia Code §§ 39-5-1 *et seq.* (2000); Wisconsin. Stat. §§ 137.04 *et seq.* (2000). *Note:* While the previous list of electronic signature and electronic transactions is extensive, it is by no means exclusive, and listings are provided for reference purposes only.

6. *See, e.g.,* Code of Ala. 40-30-5 (2000).

7. 17 U.S.C. § 102(a).

8. Ibid.

9. 17 U.S.C. § 101, *see,* e.g., *Engineering Dynamics, Inc. v. Structural Software, Inc.,* 26 F.3d 1335 (5th Cir. 1994); *see also Computer Management Assistance Co. v. Robert F. DeCastro, Inc.,* 220 F.3d 396 (5th Cir. 2000).

10. 17 U.S.C. § 102 *et seq.*

11. United States Constitution, Article I, § 8, Clause 8 ("To promote the Progress of Science and useful Arts, by securing for limited Times to Authors and Inventors the exclusive Right to their respective Writings and Discoveries").

12. *See* United States Code, Title XVII, Copyrights.

13. 17 U.S.C. § 106.

14. 17 U.S.C. § 302.

15. *See* 17 U.S.C. §§ 302 & 303.

16. *Playboy Enterprises v. Frena,* 839 F. Supp. 1552 (M.D. Fla. 1993); *see also Sega Enterprises v. MAPHIA,* 857 F. Supp. 679 (N.D. Cal. 1994), and, 948 F. Supp. 923 (N.D. Cal. 1996) (providing site for and encouraging uploading of copyrighted games was copyright infringement).

17. *Religious Technology Center v. Netcom On-line Communication Services, Inc.,* 907 F. Supp. 1361 (N.D. Cal. 1995).

18. Public Law No. 105-304, § 202, 17 U.S.C. § 512.

19. *Marobie-fl., Inc. v. National Association of Fire Equipment Distributors,* 2000 U.S. Dist. LEXIS 11022 (E.D. Ill. 2000).

20. *A&M Records, Inc. v. Napster, Inc.,* 2001 U.S. Dist. LEXIS 2186 (N.D. Ca. 2001); *see also A&M Records v. Napster, Inc.,* 239 F.3d 1004 (9th Cir. 2001).

21. Public Law No. 105-304, § 202, 17 U.S.C. § 512.

22. *See* Public Law No. 105-304, § 202, 17 U.S.C. § 512.

23. Public Law No. 106-113, 15 U.S.C. § 1125(d).

24. *Brookfield Communs., Inc. v. West Coast Entertainment Corp.,* 174 F.3d 1036 (9th Cir. 1999) (use of trademark in Web name was infringement where confusion was likely, and also Web embedded text is subject to trademark analysis); *Bihari v. Gross,* 119 F. Supp. 2d 309 (S.D.N.Y. 2000) (designer failed to show likelihood of success on merits and was denied preliminary injunction because use of her name and mark in metatags of disgruntled clients' Web sites was not likely to cause confusion and was protected as a fair use).

25. *Weber-Stephen Prods. Co. v. Armitage Hardware & Bldg. Supply, Inc.,* 2000 U.S. Dist. LEXIS 6335 (N.D. Ill. 2000).

26. Public Law No. 99-508, 18 U.S.C. § 2701 *et seq.*

27. Public Law No. 105-277, 15 U.S.C. § 6501 *et seq.*

28. Statements that imply facts will not be considered opinions under federal law, even if they are labeled opinion. Opinions labeled as such will therefore not necessarily gain protection

if what follows asserts a fact, such as "It is my opinion that John murdered Fred." *See Milkovich v. Lorain Journal Co.,* 11 S. Ct. 2695 (1990).

29. *Cubby, Inc. v. Compuserve, Inc.,* 776 F. Supp. 135 (S.D.N.Y. 1991).

30. *Strattan Oakmont, Inc. v. Prodigy Services Co.* (N.Y. Sup. Ct. 1995).

31. *See Zeran v. America Online,* 129 F.3d 327 (4th Cir. 1997); *see also Blumenthal v. Drudge,* 992 F. Supp. 44 (D.D.C. 1998).

32. *New York Times Co. v. Sullivan,* 376 U.S. 254 (1964).

33. *See Winter v. G.P. Putnam's Sons,* 938 F.2d 1033 (9th Cir. 1991).

34. *Miller v. California,* 413 U.S. 15; 93 S. Ct. 2607; 1973 U.S. LEXIS 149; 37 L. Ed. 2d 419 (1973).

35. *United States v. Thomas,* 74 F.3d 701 (6th Cir. 1996).

36. *FCC v. Pacifica Foundation,* 438 U.S. 726 (1978).

37. *See Dial Information Servs. Corp. of N.Y. v. Thornburgh,* 938 F.2d 1535 (2d Cir. 1991), *cert den.* 502 U.S. 1072 (1992).

38. Public Law 104-104 (1996).

39. *Red Lion Broadcasting v. FCC,* 395 U.S. 367 (1969).

40. *See Dial Information Servs. Corp. of N.Y. v. Thornburgh,* 938 F.2d 1535 (2d Cir. 1991), *cert den.* 502 U.S. 1072 (1992).

41. *ACLU v. Reno,* 117 S. Ct. 2329 (1997).

42. *International Shoe Co. v. Washington,* 326 U.S. 310 (1945).

43. *Sky Tech. Partners, LLC v. Midwest Research Inst.,* 125 F. Supp. 2d 286 (S.D. Ohio 2000) (location for lawsuit based on Web site not influenced by location of Web server or by where work was done, where location of work was unknown at the time the contract was entered into); *Callaway Golf Corp. v. Royal Canadian Golf Ass'n,* 125 F. Supp. 2d 1194 (C.D. Ca. 2000) (interactive Web site alone is not enough to subject defendant to jurisdiction without more); *S. Morantz, Inc. v. Hang & Shine Ultrasonics, Inc.,* 79 F. Supp. 2d 537 (E.D. Pa. 1999) (Web site e-mail link and forms to order advertising materials were not interactive enough to justify exercise of personal jurisdiction since they did not create the minimum contacts required to establish personal jurisdiction).

CHAPTER 3

USING A "COMMON LANGUAGE" FOR COMPUTER SECURITY INCIDENT INFORMATION

John D. Howard and Pascal Meunier

CONTENTS

3.1 INTRODUCTION. A computer security *incident* is some set of events that involves an attack or series of attacks at one or more sites. (See Section 3.4.3 for a more formal definition of incident.) Dealing with these incidents is inevitable for individuals and organizations at all levels of computer security. A major part of dealing with these incidents is recording and receiving incident information, which almost always is in the form of relatively unstructured text files. Over time, these files can end up containing a large quantity of very valuable information. Unfortunately, the unstructured form of the information often makes incident information difficult to manage and use.

This chapter presents the results of several efforts over the last few years to develop and propose a method to handle these unstructured, computer security incident records. Specifically, this chapter presents a *tool* designed to help individuals and organizations record, understand, and share computer security incident information. We call the tool the *common language for computer security incident information*. This common language contains two parts:

1. A set of "high-level" incident-related terms

2. A method of classifying incident information (a taxonomy)

The two parts of the common language (the terms and the taxonomy) are closely related. The taxonomy provides a structure that shows how most common language terms are related. The common language is intended to help investigators improve their ability to:

- Talk more understandably with others about incidents
- Gather, organize, and record incident information
- Extract data from incident information
- Summarize, share, and compare incident information
- Use incident information to evaluate and decide on proper courses of action
- Use incident information to determine effects of actions over time

This chapter begins with a brief overview of why a common language is needed, followed by a summary of how the incident common language was developed. We then present the common language in two parts: (1) incident terms and taxonomy and (2) additional incident information terms. The final section contains information about some practical ways to use the common language.

3.2   WHY A COMMON LANGUAGE IS NEEDED.   When the first edition of this *Handbook* was published less than 30 years ago, computer security was a small, obscure, academic specialty. Because there were only a few people working in the field, the handling of computer security information could largely take place in an ad hoc way. In this environment, individuals and groups developed their own terms to describe computer security information. They also developed, gathered, organized, evaluated, and exchanged their computer security information in largely unique and unstructured ways. This lack of generalization has meant that computer security information typically has not been easy to compare or combine or, sometimes, even to talk about in an understandable way.

Progress over the years in agreeing on a relatively standard set of terms for computer security (a common language) has had mixed results. One problem is that many terms are not yet in widespread use. Another problem is that the terms that are in widespread use often do not have standard meanings. An example of the latter is the term "computer virus." We hear the term frequently, not only in academic forums but in the news media and popular publications. It turns out, however, that even in academic publications, computer virus has no accepted definition.[1] Many authors define a computer virus to be "a code fragment that copies itself into a larger program."[2] They use the term "worm" to describe an independent program that performs a similar invasive function (e.g. the "Internet Worm" in 1988). But other authors use the term computer virus to describe *both* invasive code fragments and independent programs.

Progress in developing methods to gather, organize, evaluate, and exchange computer security information also has had limited success. For example, the original records (1988–1992) of the Computer Emergency Response Team (now the CERT Coordination Center or CERT/CC[3]) are simply a file of e-mail and other files sent to the CERT/CC. These messages and files were archived together in chronological order, without any other organization. After 1992, the CERT/CC and other organizations developed methods to organize and disseminate their information, but the information remains difficult to combine or compare because most of it remains almost completely textual information that is uniquely structured for the CERT/CC.

Such ad hoc terms and ad hoc ways to gather, organize, evaluate, and exchange computer security information are no longer adequate. Far too many people and organizations are involved, and there is far too much information to understand and share. Today computer security is an increasingly important, relevant, and sophisticated field of study. Numerous individuals and organizations now regularly gather and disseminate computer security information. Such information ranges from the security characteristics and vulnerabilities of computers and networks, to the behavior of people and systems during security incidents—far too much information for each individual and organization to have its own unique language.

One of the key elements to making systematic progress in any field of inquiry is the development of a consistent set of terms and taxonomies (principles of classification) that are used in that field.[4] This is a necessary and natural process that leads to a growing common language which enables gathering, exchanging, and comparing information. In other words, as a field of inquiry such as computer security grows, the more a common language is needed to understand and communicate with one another.

3.3   DEVELOPMENT OF THE COMMON LANGUAGE.   Two of the more significant efforts in the process of developing this common language for computer security incident information were (1) a project to classify more than 4,300 Internet security incidents completed in 1997[5]; and (2) a series of workshops in 1997 and 1998, called the *Common Language Project.* Workshop participants primarily included people from the Security and Networking Research Group at the Sandia National Laboratories, Livermore, California, and from the CERT Coordination Center (CERT/CC). Additional participation and review came from people in the Department of Defense (DoD) and the National Institute of Standards and Technology (NIST).

These efforts to develop the common language were *not* efforts to develop a comprehensive dictionary of terms. Instead, the participants were trying to develop both a minimum set of high-level terms to describe computer security attacks and incidents, and a structure and classification scheme for these terms (a taxonomy), which could be used to classify, understand, exchange, and compare computer security attack and incident information..

Participants in the workshops hoped that this common language would gain wide acceptance because of its usefulness. There is already evidence that this acceptance is taking place, particularly at incident response teams and in the DoD.

In order to be complete, logical, and useful, the common language for computer security incident information was based initially and primarily on theory (i.e., it was a priori or nonempirically based).[6] Classification of actual Internet security incident information was then used to refine and expand the language. More specifically, the common language development proceeded in six stages:

1. Records at the CERT/CC for incidents reported to them from 1988 through 1995 were examined to establish a preliminary list of terms used to describe computer security incidents.

2. The terms in this list, and their definitions, were put together into a structure (a preliminary taxonomy).

3. This preliminary taxonomy was used to classify the information in the 1988 through 1995 incident records.

4. The preliminary taxonomy and classification results were published in 1997.[7]

5. A series of workshops was conducted from 1997 through 1998 (the *Common Language Project*) to make improvements to the taxonomy and to add additional terms.

6. The results of the workshops (the "common language for security incidents") were first published in 1998.

A taxonomy is a classification scheme (a structure) that partitions a body of knowledge and defines the relationship of the pieces.[8] Most of the terms in this common language for security incident information are arranged in such a taxonomy, as presented in the next section. *Classification* is the process of using a taxonomy for separating and ordering. As discussed earlier, classification of information using a taxonomy is necessary for computer security incident information because of the rapidly expanding amount of information and the nature of that information (primarily text). Classification using the common-language taxonomy is discussed in the final section of this chapter.

Our experience has shown that satisfactory taxonomies have classification categories with the following characteristics:[9]

- *Mutually exclusive*—classifying in one category excludes all others because categories do not overlap.
- *Exhaustive*—taken together, the categories include all possibilities.
- *Unambiguous*—clear and precise so that classification is not uncertain, regardless of who is doing the classifying.
- *Repeatable*—repeated applications result in the same classification, regardless of who is doing the classifying.
- *Accepted*—logical and intuitive so that categories can become generally approved.
- *Useful*—can be used to gain insight into the field of inquiry.

These characteristics were used to develop and evaluate the common language taxonomy. A taxonomy, however, is merely an approximation of reality and, as such, even the best taxonomy can fall short in some characteristics. This may be especially true when the characteristics of the data being classified are imprecise and uncertain, as is typical of computer security incident information. Nevertheless, classification is an important, useful, and necessary prerequisite for systematic study of incidents.

3.4   COMPUTER SECURITY INCIDENT INFORMATION TAXONOMY.   We have been able to structure most of the terms in the common language for security incident information into a taxonomy. These terms and the taxonomy are presented in this section. Additional terms that describe the more general aspects of incidents are presented in Section 3.5.

3.4.1   Events.   The operation of computers and networks involves innumerable *events*. In a general sense, an event is a discrete change of state or status of a system or device.[10] From a computer security viewpoint, these changes of state result from *actions* that are directed against specific *targets*. An example is a user taking action to log in to the user's account on a computer system. In this case, the action taken by the user is to *authenticate* to the login program by claiming to have a specific identity and then presenting the required verification. The target of this action would be the user's *account*. Other examples include numerous actions that can be targeted toward:

- *Data* (e.g., actions to *read, copy, modify, steal* or *delete*)

- A *process* (e.g., actions to *probe, scan, authenticate, bypass,* or *flood* a running computer process or execution thread)
- A *component, computer, network,* or *internetwork* (e.g., actions to *scan* or *steal*)

Exhibit 3.1 presents a matrix of actions and targets that represent possible computer and network events (although not all of the possible combinations shown are feasible). A computer or network event is defined as follows:

Event—An action directed at a target that is intended to result in a change of state, or status, of the target.[11]

Several aspects of this definition are important to emphasize. First, in order for there to be an event, there must be an action that is taken, and it must be directed against a target, but the action does *not* have to succeed in actually changing the state of the target. For example, if a user enters an incorrect user name and password combination when logging in to an account, an authentication event has taken place, but the event was not successful in verifying that the user has the proper credentials to access that account.

A second important aspect is that an event represents a *practical* linkage between an action and a specific target against which the action is directed. As such, it represents the way people generally conceptualize events on computers and networks, and not all of the individual steps that actually take place during an event. For example, when a user logs in to an account, we classify the action as *authenticate* and the target as *account.* The actual action that takes place is for the user to access a process (e.g., a "login" program) in order to authenticate. Trying to depict all of the individual steps is an unnecessary complication, whereas the higher-level concepts presented here can describe correctly and accurately the event in a form well understood by people. In other words, it makes sense to abstract the language and its structure to the level at which people generally conceptualize the events.

Exhibit 3.1 Computer and Network Events

An Event Consists of One Action and One Target

Action	Target
Probe	Account
Scan	Process
Flood	Data
Authenticate	Component
Bypass	Computer
Spoof	Network
Read	Internetwork
Copy	
Steal	
Modify	
Delete	

By all means, supporting evidence should be presented so the evidence provides a complete idea of what happened. Stated another way, abstraction, conceptualization, and communication should be applied as close to the evidence as possible. For example, if a network switch is the target of an attack, then the target should normally be viewed as a computer or as a component (depending on the nature of the switch), and not the network, because assuming the network is the target may be an inaccurate interpretation of the evidence.

Another aspect of the definition of event is that it does not make a distinction between *authorized* and *unauthorized* actions. Most events that take place on computers or networks are both routine and authorized and, therefore, are not of concern to security professionals. Sometimes, however, an event is part of an attack or is a security concern for some other reason. This definition of event is meant to capture both authorized and unauthorized actions. For example, if a user authenticates properly, by giving the correct user identification and password combination while logging in to an account, that user is given access to that account. It may be the case, however, that this user is masquerading as the actual user, after having obtained the user identification and password from snooping on the network. Either way, this is still considered authentication.

Finally, an important aspect of events is that not all of the possible events (the action–target combinations depicted in Exhibit 3.1) are considered likely or even possible. For example, an action to *authenticate* is generally associated with an *account* or a *process* and not a different target, such as *data* or a *component*. Other examples include *read* and *copy*, which are generally targeted toward *data; flooding*, which is generally targeted at an *account, process,* or *system;* or *stealing,* which is generally targeted against *data*, a *component,* or a *computer.*

We define *action* and *target* by enumeration as follows:

Action—A step taken by a user or process in order to achieve a result,[12] such as to probe, scan, flood, authenticate, bypass, spoof, read, copy, steal, modify, or delete.

Target—A computer or network logical entity (account, process, or data) or a physical entity (component, computer, network, or internetwork)

3.4.1.1   Actions.   The actions depicted in Exhibit 3.1 represent a spectrum of activities that can take place on computers and networks. An action is a step taken by a *user* or a *process* in order to achieve a result. Actions are initiated by accessing a target, where *access* is defined as follows:

Access—Establish logical or physical communication or contact.[13]

Two actions are used to gather information about targets: *probe* and *scan*. A probe is an action to determine one or more characteristics of a specific target. This is unlike a scan, which is an action where a user or process accesses a set of targets systematically, in order to determine which targets have one or more characteristics.

"Probe" and "scan" are terms commonly used by incident response teams. As a result, they have common, accepted definitions. Despite this, there is a logical ambiguity: A scan could be viewed as multiple probes. In other words, if an attacker is testing for one or more characteristics on multiple hosts, this can be (a) multiple attacks (all *probes*), or (b) one attack (a *scan*). This was discussed extensively in the Common Language Project workshops, and the conclusion was that the terms in the common language should match, as much as possible, their common usage. This common usage is illustrated in Exhibit 3.2.

With probes and scans, it is usually obvious what is taking place. The attacker is either "hammering away" at one host (a *probe*), is randomly testing many hosts (multiple *probes*), or is using some "automatic" software to look for the same characteristic(s) systematically across a group of hosts (a *scan*). As a practical matter, incident response teams do not usually have a problem deciding what type of action they are dealing with.

One additional point about *scan* is that the term "systematic" is not meant to specify some specific pattern. The most sophisticated attackers try to disguise the systematic nature of a scan. A scan may, at first, appear to be multiple probes. For example, an attacker may randomize a scan with respect to hosts and with respect to the characteristic(s) being tested. If the attack can be determined to involve testing of one or more characteristics on a group of hosts with some common property (e.g., an IP address range) or if tests on multiple hosts appear to be otherwise related (e.g., having a common origin in location and time), then the multiple probes should be classified as a scan.

Unlike probe or scan, an action taken to *flood* a target is not used to gather information about the target. Instead, the desired result of a flood is to overwhelm or overload the target's capacity by accessing the target repeatedly. An example is repeated requests to open connections to a port over a network, or repeated requests to initiate processes on a computer. Another example is a high volume of e-mail messages, which may exceed the resources available for the targeted account.

Authenticate is an action taken by a user to assume an identity. Authentication starts with a user accessing an authentication process, such as a login program. The user must claim to have a certain identity, such as by entering a user name. Usually verification is also required as the second authentication step. For verification, the user must prove knowledge of some secret (e.g., a password), prove the possession of some token (e.g., a secure identification card), and/or prove to have a certain characteristic (e.g., a retinal scan pattern). Authentication can be used not only to log in to an account but to access other objects, such as to operate a process or to access a file. In other words, the target of an authentication action is the entity (e.g., account, process, or data) that the user is trying to access, and not the authentication process itself.

Two general methods might be used to defeat an authentication process. First, a user could obtain a valid identification and verification pair that could be used to authenticate, even though it does not belong to that user. For example, during an incident an attacker might use a process operating on an Internet host computer that captures user name, password, and Internet Protocol (IP) address combinations that are sent in clear

Exhibit 3.2   *Probe* Compared to *Scan*

	Test for One or More Characteristics
Test a Single Host	Probe
Nonsystematically Test Multiple Hosts	Multiple probes
Systematically Test a Set of Hosts	Scan

text across the Internet. The attacker could then use this captured information to authenticate (log in) to accounts that belong to other users. As mentioned earlier, this action is still considered *authenticate* because the attacker presents valid identification and verification pairs, even though they have been stolen.

The second method that might be used to defeat an authentication process is to exploit a vulnerability in order to bypass the authentication process and access the target. *Bypass* is an action taken to avoid a process by using an alternative method to access a target. For example, some operating systems have vulnerabilities that an attacker could exploit to gain privileges without actually logging in to a privileged account.

As was discussed with respect to *authenticate,* an action to *bypass* does not necessarily indicate that the action is unauthorized. For example, some programmers find it useful to have a shortcut ("back door") method to enter an account or run a process, particularly during development. In such a situation, an action to bypass may be considered authorized.

Authenticate and *bypass* are actions associated with users identifying themselves. In network communications, processes also identify themselves to each other. For example, each packet of information traveling on a network contains addresses identifying both the source and the destination as well as other information. "Correct" information in these communications is assumed, since it is automatically generated. Thus, no action is included in our list to describe this normal situation. On the other hand, incorrect information could be entered into these communications. Supplying such false information is commonly called an action to *spoof.* Examples include IP spoofing, mail spoofing, and Domain Name Service (DNS) spoofing.

> *Spoofing* is an active security attack in which one machine on the network masquerades as a different machine. . . . [I]t disrupts the normal flow of data and may involve injecting data into the communications link between other machines. This masquerade aims to fool other machines on the network into accepting the imposter as an original, either to lure the other machines into sending it data or to allow it to alter data.[14]

Some actions are closely associated with data found on computers or networks, particularly with files: *read, copy, modify, steal,* and *delete.* There has been some confusion over these terms because their common usage in describing the "physical" world sometimes differs from their common usage describing the "electronic" world. For example, if I say that an attacker *stole* a computer, then you can assume I mean the attacker took possession of the target computer and did not leave an identical computer in that location. If I say, however, that the attacker stole a computer *file,* what does that actually mean? It is often taken to mean that the attacker *duplicated* the file and now has a copy of the file, but it also means that the original file is still in its original location. In other words, "steal" sometimes means something different in the physical world than it does in the electronic world.

It is confusing for there to be differences in the meaning of actions in the physical world and the electronic world. Workshop participants, therefore, attempted to reconcile these differences by carefully defining each term (*read, copy, modify, steal,* or *delete*) so it would have a very specific and mutually exclusive meaning that matched the "physical world" meaning as much as possible.

Read is defined as an action to obtain the content of the data contained within a file or other data medium. This action is distinguished conceptually from the actual physical steps that may be required to read. For example, in the process of reading a computer file, the file may be copied from a storage location into the computer's main memory and then displayed on a monitor to be read by a user. These physical steps (copy the file into memory and then onto the monitor) are not part of the abstract concept of read. In other words, to read a target (obtain the content in it), copying of the file is not necessarily required, and it is conceptually not included in our definition of *read*.

The same separation of concepts is included in the definition of the term "copy." In this case, we are referring to acquiring a copy of a target without deleting the original. The term "copy" does not imply that the *content* in the target is obtained, just that a *copy* has been made and obtained. To get the content, the file must be *read*. An example is copying a file from a hard disk to a floppy disk. This copying is done by duplicating the original file while leaving the original file intact. A user would have to open the file and look at the content in order to *read* it.

Copy and read are both different concepts from *steal*, which is an action that results in the attacker taking possession of the target and the target also becoming unavailable to the original owner or user. This definition agrees with our concepts about physical property, specifically that there is only one object that can not be copied. For example, if someone steals a car, then that person has deprived the owner of his or her possession. When dealing with property that is in electronic form, such as a computer file, often the term "steal" is used when what actually is meant is *copy*. The term "steal" specifically means that the original owner or user has been denied access or use of the target. On the other hand, stealing also could mean *physically* taking a floppy disk that has the file located on it, or stealing an entire computer.

Two other actions involve changing the target in some way. The first are actions to *modify* a target. Examples include changing the content of a file, changing the password of an account, sending commands to change the characteristics of an operating process, or adding components to an existing system. If the target is eliminated entirely, the term "delete" is used to describe the action.

As stated earlier, differences in usage of terms between the physical world and the electronic world are undesirable. As such, we tried to be specific and consistent in our usage. The resulting set of terms is exhaustive and mutually exclusive but goes against the grain in some common usage for the "electronic world," particularly with respect to the term "steal." The situation seems unavoidable. Here are some examples that might clarify the terms:

- A user clicks on a link with the browser and sees the content of a Web page on the computer screen. We would classify this as a *read*. Although what actually happens is that the content of the page is stored in volatile memory, copied to the cache on the hard drive, and displayed on the screen, from a *logical* (i.e., user) point of view, the Web page has *not* been copied (nor stolen). Now, if a user copies the content of the Web page to a file or prints it out, then the user *has* copied the Web page. Again, this would be a logical classification of the action, from the user's point of view.

- A user duplicates a file that is encrypted. We would classify this as *copy*, not *read*. In this case, the file was reproduced, but the content not obtained, so it was not read.

- A user deletes several entries in a password or group file. Should this action be described as several *delete* actions or as one action to *modify*? We would describe this action as *modify*, and the target is *data*. There is no ambiguity here because of the definition of data. Data is defined to be either a file or data in transit (see the next section). If a user deletes a line out of the password file, then the file has been modified. The action would be described as *delete* only if the whole file was deleted. If we had defined data to include part of a file, then we would indeed have an ambiguity.

- A user copies a file and deletes the original. We would classify this as *steal.* Although the steps actually include *copy* followed by a *delete,* that is the electronic way of stealing a file, and therefore it is more descriptive to describe the action as *steal.*

In reality, the term "steal" is rarely used correctly, because attackers who copy files usually do not delete the originals. On the other hand, the term "steal" often is used *incorrectly,* such as in "stealing the source code" when in fact, the correct term is *copy.*

The list of actions was hashed over in numerous group discussions, off and on, for several years before being put into the common language. Most people who participated in these discussions were not entirely happy with the list, but it is the best we have seen so far. Specifically, the list seems to capture all of the common terms with their common usage (*probe, scan, flood, spoof, copy, modify* and *delete*), and the other terms are logical, to the people who participated in the discussion groups, and are necessary to make the action category exhaustive (*authenticate, bypass, read* and *steal*). Here is a summary of definitions of the actions shown in Exhibit 3.1:

Probe—Access a target in order to determine one or more of its characteristics.

Scan—Access a set of targets systematically in order to identify which targets have one or more specific characteristics.[15]

Flood—Access a target repeatedly in order to overload the target's capacity.

Authenticate—Present an identity to a process and, if required, verify that identity, in order to access a target.[16]

Bypass—Void a process by using an alternative method to access a target.[17]

Spoof—Masquerade by assuming the appearance of a different entity in network communications.[18]

Read—Obtain the content of data in a storage device or other data medium.[19]

Copy—Reproduce a target leaving the original target unchanged.[20]

Steal—Take possession of a target without leaving a copy in the original location.

Modify—Change the content or characteristics of a target.[21]

Delete—Remove a target or render it irretrievable.[22]

3.4.1.2   Targets.   Actions are considered to be directed toward seven categories of targets. The first three of these are "logical" entities (*account, process,* and *data*), and the other four are "physical" entities (*component, computer, network,* and *internetwork*).

In a multiuser environment, an *account* is the domain of an individual user. This domain includes the files and processes the user is authorized to access and use. A special program that records the user's account name, password, and use restrictions controls access to the user's account. Some accounts have increased or "special" permissions that allow access to system accounts, other user accounts, or system files and processes, and often are called *privileged, superuser, administrator,* or *root* accounts.

Sometimes an action may be directed toward a *process,* which is a program executing on a computer or network. In addition to the program itself, the process includes the program's data and stack, its program counter, stack pointer and other registers, and all other information needed to execute the program.[23] The action may then be to supply information to the process or command the process in some manner.

The target of an action may be *data* that are found on a computer or network. Data are representations of facts, concepts, or instructions in forms that are suitable for use by either users or processes. Data may be found in two forms: files or data in transit. *Files* are data that are designated by name and considered as a unit by the user or by a process. Commonly we think of files as being located on a storage medium, such as a storage disk, but files also may be located in the volatile or nonvolatile memory of a computer. *Data in transit* are data being transmitted across a network or otherwise emanating from some source. Examples of the latter include data transmitted between devices in a computer and data found in the electromagnetic fields that surround computer monitors, storage devices, processors, network transmission media, and the like.

Sometimes we conceptualize the target of an action as not being a *logical* entity (account, process, or data) but rather as a *physical* entity. The smallest of the physical entities is a *component,* which is one of the parts that make up a computer or network. A *network* is an interconnected or interrelated group of computers, along with the appropriate switching elements and interconnecting branches.[24] When a computer is attached to a network, it is sometimes referred to as a *host computer* or *node.* If networks are connected to each other, then they are sometimes referred to as an *internetwork.*

Here is a summary of definitions of the targets shown in Exhibit 3.1.

Account—A domain of user access on a computer or network that is controlled according to a record of information which contains the user's account name, password, and use restrictions.

Process—A program in execution, consisting of the executable program, the program's data and stack, its program counter, stack pointer and other registers, and all other information needed to execute the program.[25]

Data—Representations of facts, concepts, or instructions in a manner suitable for communication, interpretation, or processing by humans or by automatic means.[26] Data can be in the form of *files* in a computer's volatile memory, nonvolatile memory, or in a data storage device, or in the form of *data in transit* across a transmission medium.

Component—One of the parts that make up a computer or network.[27]

Computer—A device that consists of one or more associated components, including processing units and peripheral units, that is controlled by internally stored programs and that can perform substantial computations, including numerous arithmetic operations or logic operations, without human intervention during execution. The device may be stand-alone or may consist of several interconnected units.[28]

Network—An interconnected or interrelated group of host computers, switching elements, and interconnecting branches.[29]

Internetwork—A network of networks.

3.4.2 Attacks. Sometimes an event that occurs on a computer or network is part of a series of steps intended to result in something that is not authorized to happen. This event is then considered part of an *attack.* An attack has three elements.

1. It is made up of a series of steps taken by an *attacker.* Among these steps is an action directed at a target (an *event,* as described in the previous section) as well as the use of some *tool* to exploit a *vulnerability.*

2. An attack is intended to achieve an *unauthorized result* as viewed from the perspective of the owner or administrator of the system involved.

3. An attack is a series of *intentional* steps initiated by the attacker. This differentiates an attack from something that is inadvertent.

We define an attack to be the following.

Attack—A series of steps taken by an attacker to achieve an unauthorized result.

Exhibit 3.3 presents a matrix of possible attacks, based on our experience. Attacks have five parts that depict the logical steps an attacker must take. An attacker uses a (1) *tool* to exploit a (2) *vulnerability* to perform an (3) *action* on a (4) *target* in order to achieve an (5) *unauthorized result*. To be successful, an attacker must find one or more paths that can be connected, perhaps simultaneously or repeatedly. The first two steps in an attack, *tool* and *vulnerability,* are used to cause an *event* (*action* directed at a *target*) on a computer or network. The logical end of a successful attack is an *unauthorized result.* If the logical end of the previous steps is an *authorized* result, then an attack has not taken place.

Exhibit 3.3   Computer and Network Attacks

Tool	Vulnerability	Action	Target	Unauthorized Result
Physical attack	Design	Probe	Account	Increased access
Information exchange	Implementation	Scan	Process	Disclosure of information
User command	Configuration	Flood	Data	Corruption of information
Script or program		Authenticate	Component	Denial of service
Autonomous agent		Bypass	Computer	Theft of resources
Toolkit		Spoof	Network	
Distributed tool		Read	Internetwork	
Data tap		Copy		
		Steal		
		Modify		
		Delete		

Attack →

Event →

The concept of *authorized* versus *unauthorized* is key to understanding what differentiates an attack from the normal events that occur. It is also a system-dependent concept in that what may be authorized on one system may be unauthorized on another. For example, some services, such as anonymous File Transfer Protocol (FTP), may be enabled on some systems and not on others. Even actions that are normally viewed as hostile, such as attempts to bypass access controls to gain entry into a privileged account, may be authorized in special circumstances, such as during an approved test of system security, or in the use of a "back door" during development. System owners or their administrators make the determination of what actions they consider authorized for their systems by establishing a security policy.[30] Here are the definitions for authorized and unauthorized.

Authorized—Approved by the owner or administrator.

Unauthorized—Not approved by the owner or administrator.

The steps *action* and *target* in Exhibit 3.1 are the two parts of an event as discussed in Section 3.4.1. The following sections discuss the other steps (*tool, vulnerability,* and *unauthorized result*).

3.4.2.1   *Tool.* The first step in the sequence that leads attackers to their unauthorized results is the *tool* used in the attack. A tool is some means that can be used to exploit a vulnerability in a computer or network. Sometimes a tool is simple, such as a user command or a physical attack. Other tools can be very sophisticated and elaborate, such as a Trojan horse program, computer virus, or distributed tool. We define *tool* in this way.

Tool—A means of exploiting a computer or network vulnerability

Tool is difficult to define more specifically because of the wide variety of methods available to exploit vulnerabilities in computers and networks. When authors make lists of methods of attack, often they are actually making lists of tools. Our experience indicates the following categories of tools are currently an exhaustive list (see Exhibit 3.3):

Physical attack—A means of physically stealing or damaging a computer, network, its components, or its supporting systems (e.g., air conditioning, electric power, etc.).

Information exchange—A means of obtaining information either from other attackers (e.g., through an electronic bulletin board) or from the people being attacked, commonly called social engineering.

User command—A means of exploiting a vulnerability by entering commands to a process through direct user input at the process interface. An example is entering Unix commands through a telnet connection or commands at a protocol's port.

Script or program—A means of exploiting a vulnerability by entering commands to a process through the execution of a file of commands (script) or a program at the process interface. Examples are a shell script to exploit a software bug, a Trojan horse log-in program, or a password-cracking program.

Autonomous agent—A means of exploiting a vulnerability by using a program or program fragment that operates independently from the user. Examples are computer viruses or worms.

Toolkit—A software package that contains scripts, programs, or autonomous agents that exploit vulnerabilities. An example is the widely available toolkit called *rootkit*.

Distributed tool—A tool that can be distributed to multiple hosts, which then can be coordinated to anonymously perform an attack on the target host simultaneously after some time delay.

Data tap—Means of monitoring the electromagnetic radiation emanating from a computer or network using an external device.

With the exception of the physical attack, information exchange, and data tap categories, each of the tool categories may contain other tool categories *within* itself. For example, toolkits contain scripts, programs, and sometimes autonomous agents. So when a *toolkit* is used, the *script or program* category is also included. *User commands* also must be used for the initiation of scripts, programs, autonomous agents, toolkits, and distributed tools. In other words, there is an order to some of the categories in the tools block, from the simple user command category to the more sophisticated distributed tools category. In describing or classifying an attack, generally a choice must be made among several alternatives within the tools block. We chose to classify according to the *highest* category of tool used, which makes the categories mutually exclusive in practice.

3.4.2.2   Vulnerability.   To reach the desired result, an attacker must take advantage of a computer or network *vulnerability,* which we define as follows:

Vulnerability—A weakness in a system allowing unauthorized action.[31]

A vulnerability in software is an error that arises in different stages of development or use.[32] This definition can be used to give us three categories of vulnerabilities:

Design vulnerability—A vulnerability inherent in the design or specification of hardware or software whereby even a perfect implementation will result in a vulnerability.

Implementation vulnerability—A vulnerability resulting from an error made in the software or hardware implementation of a satisfactory design.

Configuration vulnerability—A vulnerability resulting from an error in the configuration of a system, such as having system accounts with default passwords, having "world write" permission for new files, or having vulnerable services enabled.[33]

3.4.2.3   Unauthorized Result.   As shown in Exhibit 3.3, the logical end of a successful attack is an *unauthorized result*. At this point, an attacker has used a tool to exploit a vulnerability in order to cause an event to take place. We define unauthorized result as follows:

Unauthorized result—An unauthorized consequence of an event.

If successful, an attack will result in one of the following:[34]

Increased access—An unauthorized increase in the domain of access on a computer or network.

Disclosure of information—Dissemination of information to anyone who is not authorized to access that information.

Corruption of information—Unauthorized alteration of data on a computer or network.

Denial of service—Intentional degradation or blocking of computer or network resources.

Theft of resources—Unauthorized use of computer or network resources.

3.4.3   The Full Incident Information Taxonomy.   Often, attacks on computers and networks occur in a distinctive group that we would classify as being part of one *incident*. What makes these attacks a distinctive group is a combination of three factors, about each of which we may only have partial information.

1. There may be one attacker, or there may be several attackers who are related in some way.
2. The attacker(s) may use similar attacks, or they may be trying to achieve a distinctive or similar objective.
3. The sites involved in the attacks and the timing of the attacks may be the same or be related.

We define *incident* as follows:

Incident—A group of attacks that can be distinguished from other attacks because of the distinctiveness of the attackers, attacks, objectives, sites, and timing.

The three parts of an incident are shown in simplified form in Exhibit 3.4, which shows that an attacker, or group of attackers, achieves objectives by performing attacks. An incident may be comprised of one single attack or may be made of multiple attacks, as illustrated by the return "loop" in the Exhibit.

Exhibit 3.5 shows the full incident information taxonomy. It shows the relationship of events to attacks and attacks to incidents, and suggests that preventing attackers from achieving objectives could be accomplished by ensuring that an attacker cannot make any complete connections through the seven steps depicted. For example, investigations could be conducted of suspected terrorist *attackers,* systems could be searched periodically for attacker *tools,* system *vulnerabilities* could be patched, access controls could be strengthened to prevent *actions* by an attacker to access a *targeted* account, files could be encrypted so as not to *result* in disclosure, and a public education program could be initiated to prevent terrorists from achieving an *objective* of political gain.

3.4.3.1   Attackers and Their Objectives.   *People* attack computers. They do so through a variety of methods and for a variety of objectives. What distinguishes the categories of attackers is a combination of who they are and their *objectives* (what they want to accomplish).

Exhibit 3.4   Simplified Computer and Network Incident

Exhibit 3.5   Computer and Network Incident Information Taxonomy

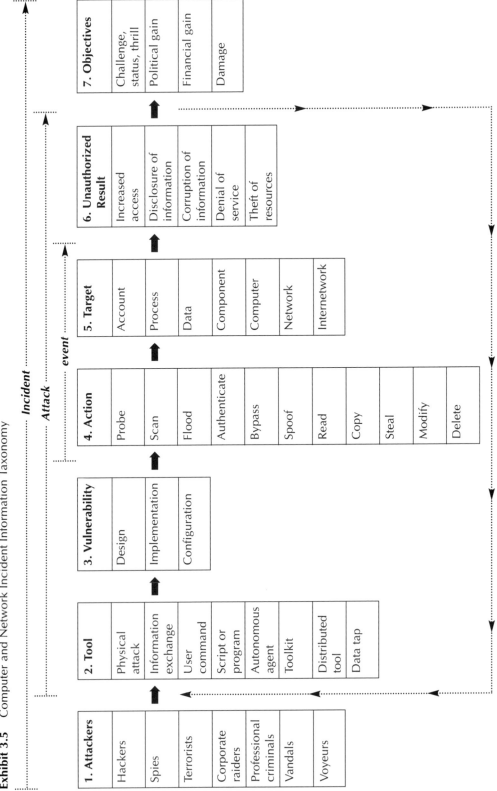

Attacker—An individual who attempts one or more attacks in order to achieve an objective.

Objective—The purpose or end goal of an incident.

Based on their objectives, we have divided attackers into the following categories:

Hackers—Attackers who attack computers for challenge, status, or the thrill of obtaining access. (Note: We have elected to use the term "hacker" because it is common and widely understood. We realize that the term's more positive connotation was once more widely accepted.)

Spies—Attackers who attack computers for information to be used for political gain.

Terrorists—Attackers who attack computers to cause fear for political gain.

Corporate raiders—Employees (attackers) who attack competitor's computers for financial gain.

Professional criminals—Attackers who attack computers for personal financial gain.

Vandals—Attackers who attack computers to cause damage.

Voyeurs—Attackers who attack computers for the thrill of obtaining sensitive information.

These seven categories of attackers and their four categories of objectives are shown in the leftmost and rightmost blocks of Exhibit 3.5. The *Attackers* and *Objectives* categories are fundamental to the difference between *incidents* and *attacks*. This difference is summed up in the phrase "attackers use attacks to achieve objectives."

3.5   ADDITIONAL INCIDENT INFORMATION TERMS.   The taxonomy of the last section presented all of the terms in the common language for computer security that describe how attackers achieve objectives during an incident. However, some other, more general, terms are required in order to fully describe an incident. The next sections discuss these terms.

3.5.1   Success and Failure.   Information on success or failure can be recorded at several levels in the overall taxonomy. In the broadest sense, overall success or failure is an indication of whether one or more attackers have achieved one or more objectives. A narrower focus would be to determine the success or failure of an individual attack by evaluating whether the attack leads to an unauthorized result. Information on success or failure, however, may simply not be known. For example, an attempt to log in to the root or superuser account on a system may be classified as a *success* a *failure*, or as being *unknown*.

3.5.2   Site and Site Name.   "Site" is the common term used to identify Internet organizations as well as physical locations. A "site" is also the organizational level of the site administrator or other authority with responsibility for the computers and networks at that location.

The term "site name" refers to a portion of the fully qualified domain name in the Internet's Domain Name Service (DNS). For sites in the United States, site names generally are at the second level of the DNS tree. Examples would be *cmu.edu* or *widgets.com*. In other countries, the site name is the third or lower level of the DNS tree, such as *widgets.co.uk.* Some site names occur even farther down the DNS tree. For example, a school in Colorado might have a site name of *myschool.k12.co.us.*

Here are the definitions of site and site name.

> **Site**—The organizational level with responsibility for security events; the organizational level of the site administrator or other authority with responsibility for the computers and networks at that location.

> **Site name**—The portion of the fully qualified domain name that corresponds to a site.

Some organizations, such as larger universities and companies, are large enough to be physically divided into more than one location, with separate administration. This separation cannot easily be determined. Therefore, often these different locations must be treated as one site.

3.5.3   Other Incident Terms.   Several additional terms are necessary to fully describe actual Internet incidents. The first of these terms concern dates.

> **Reporting date**—The first date that the incident was reported to a response team or other agency or individuals collecting data.

> **Starting date**—The date of the first known incident activity.

> **Ending date**—The date of the last known incident activity.

Several terms concern the sites involved:

> **Number of sites**—The overall number of sites known to have reported or otherwise to have been involved in an incident.

> **Reporting sites**—The site names of sites known to have reported an incident.

> **Other sites**—The site names of sites known to have been involved in an incident but that did not report the incident.

For most incident response teams, actual site names are considered sensitive information. In our research, in order to protect the identities of the sites associated with an incident, we sanitize the site information by coding the site names prior to public release. An example would be to replace a site name, such as the fictitious *widgets.com,* with numbers and the upper-level domain name, such as *123.com.*

Response teams often use incident numbers to track incidents and to identify incident information.

> **Incident number**—A reference number used to track an incident or identify incident information.

The last term we found to be of use is *corrective action,* which indicates those actions taken in the aftermath of an incident. These actions could include changing passwords, reloading systems files, talking to the intruders, or even criminal prosecution. Information on corrective actions taken during or after an incident is difficult to obtain for incident response teams, since response team involvement generally is limited to the early stages of an incident. CERT/CC records indicate that the variety of corrective actions is extensive, and a taxonomy of corrective actions may be a desirable future expansion of the common language.

Corrective action—An action taken during or after an incident to prevent further attacks, repair damage, or punish offenders.

3.6   HOW TO USE THE COMMON LANGUAGE.   Two things are important to emphasize about using the common language for computer security incident information. First, the common language really is a "high-level" set of terms. As such, it will not settle all the disputes about everything discussed concerning computer security incidents. For example, the common language includes "autonomous agent" as a term (a category of tool). Autonomous agents include *computer viruses, worms,* and the like, regardless of how those specific terms might be defined. In other words, the common language does not try to settle disputes on what should or should not be considered a *computer virus* but rather deals at a higher level of abstraction (autonomous agent) where, it is hoped, there can be more agreement and standardization. Stated another way, participants in the Common Language Project workshops anticipated that individuals and organizations would continue to use their own terms, which may be more specific in both meaning and use. The common language has been designed to enable these "lower-level" terms to be classified *within* the common language structure.

The second point to emphasize is that the common language, even though it presents a taxonomy, does not classify an incident (or individual attacks) as any *one* thing. Classifying computer security *attacks* or *incidents* is difficult because attacks and incidents are a *series of steps* that an attacker must take. In other words, attacks and incidents are not just *one* thing but rather a *series* of things. That is why we say the common language provides a taxonomy for computer security incident *information.*

An example of the problem is found in the popular and simple taxonomies often used to attempt to classify incidents. They appear as a list of single, defined terms. The following 24 terms from Icove, Seger, and VonStorch provide an example.[35]

Covert channels
Data diddling
Degradation of service
Denial-of-service
Dumpster diving
Eavesdropping on emanations
Excess privileges
Harassment
IP spoofing
Logic bombs
Masquerading
Password sniffing
Salamis
Scanning
Session hijacking
Software piracy
Timing attacks
Traffic analysis
Trap doors
Trojan horses

Tunneling

Unauthorized data copying

Viruses and worms

Wiretapping

Lists of terms are *not* satisfactory taxonomies for classifying actual attacks or incidents. They fail to have most of the six characteristics of a satisfactory taxonomy. First, the terms tend not to be mutually exclusive. For example, the terms "virus" and "logic bomb" are generally found on these lists, but a virus may *contain* a logic bomb, so the categories overlap. Actual attackers generally also use multiple methods so their attacks would have to be classified into multiple categories. This makes classification ambiguous and difficult to repeat.

A more fundamental problem is that, assuming that an exhaustive and mutually exclusive list could be developed, the taxonomy would be unmanageably long and difficult to apply. It also would not indicate any relationship between different types of attacks. Finally, none of these lists has become widely accepted, partly because it is difficult to agree on the definition of terms. In fact, many different definitions of terms are in common use.

The fundamental problems with these lists (and their variations) are that most incidents involve multiple attacks, and attacks involve multiple steps. As a result, information about the typical incident must be classified in multiple categories. For example, one of the attacks in an incident might be a flood of a host resulting in a denial of service. But this same incident might involve the exploitation of a vulnerability to compromise the host computer that was the specific origin of the flood. Should this be classified as a flood? As a root compromise? As a denial-of-service attack? In reality, the incident should be classified in all of these categories. In other words, this incident has multiple classifications.

In summary, in developing the common language, we have found that, with respect to *attacks* and *incidents,* we can really *only* hope to (1) present a common set of "high-level" terms that are in general use and have common definitions and (2) present a logical structure to the terms that can be used to classify information *about* an incident or attack *with respect to specific categories.*

Some examples may make this clear. As discussed earlier, most of the information about actual attacks and incidents is in the form of textual records. In a typical incident record at the CERT/CC, three observations might be reported:

1. We found *rootkit* on host xxx.xxx.

2. A flood of e-mail was sent to account *xxx@xxx.xxx*, which crashed the mail server.

3. We traced the attack back to a teenager in *Xyz* city, who said he was not trying to cause any damage, just to see if he could break in.

For observation 1, we would classify *rootkit* in the "toolkit" category under "Tool" and the hostname in the "computer" category under "Target." For observation 2, the "e-mail flood" is a specific instantiation in the "flood" category under "Action" as well as in the "denial-of-service" category under "Unauthorized Result." There is ambiguity as to the target for observation 2: Is it the account or the computer? As a practical matter, the observations would be classified as both, since information is available on both. For observation 3, it could be inferred that this is a "hacker" seeking "challenge, status, or thrill."

What does this taxonomic process provide that is of practical value? First, the taxonomy helps us communicate to others what we have found. When we say that *rootkit* is a type of toolkit, then our common set of terms ("common language") provides us the general understanding of what we mean. When it is said that 22 percent of incidents reported to CERT/CC from 1988 through 1995 involved various problems with passwords (a correct statistic[36]), then the taxonomy has proven useful in communicating valuable information.

The application of the taxonomy, in fact, is a four-step process that can be used to determine the biggest security problems. Specifically, the process is to:

1. Take observations from fragmentary information in incident reports.

2. Classify those observations.

3. Perform statistical studies of these data.

4. Use this information to determine what is the best course(s) of action.

Over time, the same process can be used to determine the effects of these actions.

Two more points are important to emphasize about this taxonomy. First, an *attack* is a process that, with enough information, is *always* classified in multiple categories. For example: in a "Tool" category, in a "Vulnerability" category, in an "Action" category, in a "Target" category, and in an "Unauthorized Result" category. Second, an *incident* can involve multiple, perhaps thousands, of attacks. As such, the information gathered in an incident theoretically could be classified correctly into *all* of the taxonomy categories.

Within these guidelines, the *common language for computer security incidents* has proven to be a useful and increasingly accepted tool to gather, exchange, and compare computer security information. The taxonomy itself has proven to be simple and straightforward to use.

3.7 NOTES

1. E.G. Amoroso, *Fundamentals of Computer Security Technology* (Upper Saddle River, NJ: Prentice-Hall PTR, 1994), p. 2.

2. Deborah Russell and G.T. Gangemi, Sr., *Computer Security Basics* (Sebastopol, CA: O'Reilly & Associates, Inc. 1991), p. 79.

3. The CERT Coordination Center is located at the Software Engineering Institute operated by Carnegie Mellon University. See *www.cert.org.*

4. Bill McKelvey, *Organization Systematics: Taxonomy, Evolution, Classification* (Berkeley: University of California Press, 1982), p. 3.

5. John D. Howard, *An Analysis of Security Incidents on the Internet, 1989–1995,* Ph.D. dissertation, Pittsburgh, PA: Department of Engineering and Public Policy, Carnegie Mellon University, April 1997. Also available online at *www.cert.org/.*

6. Ivan Victor Krsul, *Software Vulnerability Analysis.* Ph.D. dissertation, Lafayette, IN: Computer Sciences Department, Purdue University, May 1998, p. 12.

7. Howard, *Analysis of Security Incidents on the Internet.*

8. John Radatz, ed., *The IEEE Standard Dictionary of Electrical and Electronics Terms,* 6th ed.(New York: Institute of Electrical and Electronics Engineers, 1996), p. 1087.

9. Amoroso, *Fundamentals of Computer Security Technology,* p. 34.

10. Radatz, *IEEE Standard Dictionary,* p. 373.

11. Ibid.

12. Ibid., p. 11.

13. Ibid., p. 5.

14. Derek Atkins et al., *Internet Security Professional Reference* (Indianapolis: New Riders Publishing, 1996), p. 258.

15. Radatz, *IEEE Standard Dictionary,* p. 947, and K.M. Jackson and J. Hruska, eds., *Computer Security Reference Book* (Boca Raton, FL: CRC Press, 1992), p. 916.

16. Merriam-Webster, *Merriam-Webster's Collegiate Dictionary,* 10th ed. (Springfield, MA: Merriam-Webster, 1996), pp. 77, 575, 714, and Radatz, *IEEE Standard Dictionary,* p. 57.

17. *Merriam-Webster's Collegiate Dictionary,* p. 157.

18. Radatz, *IEEE Standard Dictionary,* p. 630, and Atkins et al., *Internet Security,* p. 258.

19. Radatz, *IEEE Standard Dictionary,* p. 877.

20. Ibid., p. 224.

21. Ibid., p. 661.

22. Ibid., p. 268.

23. Andrew S. Tanenbaum, *Modern Operating Systems* (Englewood Cliffs, NJ: Prentice-Hall, 1992), p. 12.

24. Radatz, *IEEE Standard Dictionary,* p. 683.

25. Tanenbaum, *Modern Operating Systems,* p. 12, and Radatz, *IEEE Standard Dictionary,* p. 822.

26. Radatz, *IEEE Standard Dictionary,* p. 250.

27. Ibid., p. 189.

28. Ibid., p. 192.

29. Ibid., p. 683.

30. Krsul, *Software Vulnerability Analysis,* pp. 5–6, and Chapter 28 of the *Handbook.*

31. National Research Council (NRC), *Computers at Risk: Safe Computing in the Information Age* (Washington, DC: National Academy Press, 1991), p. 301; and Amoroso, *Fundamentals of Computer Security Technology,* p. 2.

32. Krsul, *Software Vulnerability Analysis,* pp. 10–11.

33. Atkins et al., *Internet Security,* p. 196.

34. Amoroso, *Fundamentals of Computer Security Technology,* pp. 3–4, 31; Russell and Gangemi, *Computer Security Basics,* pp. 9–10; and Frederick B. Cohen, *Protection and Security on the Information Superhighway* (New York: John Wiley & Sons, 1995), pp. 55–56.

35. David Icove, Karl Seger, and William VonStorch, *Computer Crime: A Crimefighter's Handbook* (Sebastopol, CA: O'Reilly & Associates,1995), pp. 31–52; Cohen, *Protection and Security on the Information Superhighway,* pp. 40–54 (39 terms); and Frederick B. Cohen, "Information System Attacks: A Preliminary Classification Scheme," *Computers and Security,* Vol. 16, No. 1(1997), pp. 29–46 (96 terms).

36. Howard, *Analysis of Security Incidents on the Internet,* p. 100.

CHAPTER 4

STUDIES AND SURVEYS OF COMPUTER CRIME

M.E. Kabay

CONTENTS

4.1 INTRODUCTION. This chapter provides guidance for critical reading of research results about computer crime and alerts research instrument designers to the need for professional support in developing questionnaires and analyzing results. The chapter also reviews well-known studies and surveys of computer crime to give the reader a sense of the current state of the art. Chapter 6 explores the psychology of computer criminals and virus writers in greater detail.

4.1.1   Value of Statistical Knowledge Base.

Security specialists often are asked about computer crime. For example, customers want to know who is attacking which systems how often using what methods. These questions are perceived as important because they bear on the strategies of risk management. To estimate the appropriate level of investment in security, it is useful to have a sound grasp of the probability of different levels of damage. Ideally, one would want to evaluate an organization's level of risk by evaluating the experiences of other organizations with similar system and business characteristics. Such comparisons would be useful in competitive analysis and in litigation over standards of due care and diligence in protecting corporate assets.

4.1.2   Limitations on Knowledge of Computer Crime.

Unfortunately, in the current state of information security, no one can give reliable answers to such questions. Two fundamental difficulties prevent researchers from developing accurate statistics of this kind: difficulties of detection and of reporting. Together these difficulties are known as the problems of ascertainment.

4.1.2.1   Detection.

The first problem is that an unknown number of crimes of all kinds are undetected. For example, even outside the computer crime field, it is not known how many financial frauds are being perpetrated because some of them are not detected. And how can anyone know about crimes that are not detected? Some frauds are discovered long after they have occurred, giving us a sense of the hidden proportion of undetected crimes. Perpetrators provide another source of information about computer crimes that were not detected by their victims; some boast about their depredations or try to use them as the basis for extortion.

In a landmark series of tests at the Department of Defense (DoD), the Defense Information Systems Agency found that very few of the 68,000 penetrations it engineered against unclassified systems within the DoD were detected by system managers. These studies were carried out from 1994 through 1996; about two-thirds of the attacks succeeded, but only 4 percent of the successful attacks were detected.

A commonly held view within the information security community is that only one-tenth or so of all the crimes committed against, and using, computer systems are detected.

4.1.2.2   Reporting.

The second problem of ascertainment is that even if attacks are detected, few are reported in a way that allows systematic data collection. This belief is based in part on the unquantified experience of information security professionals who have interviewed their clients; only about 10 percent of these attacks against computer systems were ever reported to any kind of authority or to the public. The DoD studies were in agreement; of the few penetrations detected, only a fraction of 1 percent were reported to appropriate authorities.

Given these problems of ascertainment, computer crime statistics generally should be treated with skepticism.

4.1.3   Limitations on the Applicability of Computer-Crime Statistics.

Generalizations in this field are difficult to justify; even if we knew more about types of criminals and the methods they use, it still would be difficult to have the kind of actuarial statistic that is commonplace in the insurance field. For example, the establishment of uniform building codes in the 1930s in the United States led to the growth of fire insurance as a viable business. With official records of fires that could be described using a standard typology, statistical information began to provide an actuarial basis for using probabilities of fires and associated costs to calculate reasonable insurance rates.

In contrast, even with access to accurate reports, it would be difficult to make meaningful generalizations about vulnerabilities and incidence of successful attacks for the information technology field. Enterprises use a bewildering variety and versions of processors, operating systems, firewalls, encryption, application software, backup methods and media, communications channels, identification, authentication, authorization, compartmentalization, and operations.

How would someone generalize from data about the risks at (say) a mainframe-based network running MVS in a military installation to the kinds of risks faced by a Unix-based intranet in an industrial corporation or to a Windows NT-based Web server in a university setting? There are so many differences among systems that if one were to establish a multidimensional analytical table where every variable was an axis, many cells would likely contain no, or only a few, examples. Such sparse matrices are notoriously difficult to use in building statistical models for predictive purposes.

4.2   BASIC RESEARCH METHODOLOGY.   This is not a chapter about social science research. However, many discussions of computer crime seem to take published reports as gospel, even though those reports may have no validity whatsoever. This section reviews some fundamentals of research design so that readers will be careful not to base business decisions on computer crime research results without careful thought and judgment.

4.2.1   Some Fundamentals of Statistical Design and Analysis.   More detailed information about the principles to be described can be found in any introductory textbook of applied statistics.

4.2.1.1   *Descriptive Statistics.*   Suppose three companies reported the following losses from penetration of their computer systems: $1 million, $2 million, and $6 million. These results can be described in many ways. For example, the raw data simply can be listed, but such lists could become unacceptably long and it is difficult to make sense of the raw data.

Alternatively, classes could be defined such as "2 million or less" and "more than 2 million," then the number of occurrences in each class could be counted, as shown in Exhibit 4.1. Exhibit 4.2 provides finer granularity.

The definition of the classes affects perception of the results: Exhibit 4.1 gives the impression that the results are clustered around $2 million and gives no information about the upper or lower bounds. Exhibit 4.2 still does not give the exact values

Exhibit 4.1   Crude Categories
of Loss Occurrences

Class	Freq
≤ $2M	2
> $2M	1

Exhibit 4.2   Finer Categories of Loss Occurrences

Class	Freq
≥ $0 & <$1M	0
≥ $1M & <$2M	1
≥ $2M & <$3M	1
≥ $3M & <$4M	0
≥ $4M & <$5M	0
≥ $5M & <$6M	0
≥ $6M & <$7M	1

observed, but it does limit the range to somewhere between $1 million and $7 million and shifts the perceived *central tendency* to around $2 million.

4.2.1.1.1   Location.   One of the most obvious ways to describe data is to say where they lie in a particular dimension. The *central tendency* of the three data can be represented in various ways. For example, two popular measures are:

$$\text{the arithmetic mean or average} = \$(1 + 2 + 6)M/3 = \$3M$$

$$\text{the median (the middle of the sorted list of losses)} = \$2M$$

Note that the mean and the median could not be computed correctly from the summary tables presented in Exhibits 4.1 and 4.2. Such statistics should be computed from the original data, not from summary tables.

4.2.1.1.2   Dispersion.   Another aspect of our data is *dispersion*—that is, variation. The simplest measure of dispersion is the range—the difference between the smallest and the largest value found. In the example, it could be said that the range was from $1 million to $6 million or that it was $5 million. Sometimes the range is expressed as a percentage of the mean; then the range would be stated as 5/3 ≈ 1.67 or ~ 167 percent.

The *variance* (σ^2) of these particular data is the average of the squared deviations from the arithmetic mean; the variance of the three numbers would be $\sigma^2 = [(1-3)^2 + (2-3)^2 + (6-3)^2]/3 = [4+1+9]/3 ≈ 4.67$.

The square root of the variance (σ) is called the *standard deviation* and often is used to describe dispersion. In our example, $\sigma ≈ \sqrt{4.67} ≈ 2.16$.

4.2.1.2   Inference: Sample Statistics versus Population Statistics.   Any data can be described accurately using descriptive statistics; the question is what then is done with those measures.

Usually one expects to extend the findings in a *sample* or subset of a *population* to make generalizations about the population. For example, one might be trying to estimate the losses from computer crime in commercial organizations with offices in the United States and with more than 1,000 employees. The total population of such companies might be 10,000, but one might survey only 5,000, with only 10 percent of their network security staffs willing to respond.

In such cases, one tries to infer the characteristics of the population from the characteristics of the sample. Statisticians describe this inference as *estimating the parametric statistics* from the *sample statistics*.

For example, to estimate the parametric (population) variance (usually designated σ^2), one multiplies the variance of the sample (s^2) by $n/(n-1)$, where n = the number of items in the sample. Thus the estimate (s^2) of the parametric variance (σ^2) in the sample above would be $s^2 = 4.67 * 3/2 \approx 7$. The estimate(s) of the parametric standard deviation (σ) would be $s \approx \sqrt{7} \approx 2.65$.

4.2.1.3 *Hypothesis Testing.*

Another kind of inference from data is hypothesis testing. For example, suppose one was interested in whether there was any association between the presence or absence of firewalls and the occurrence of system penetration. The data about penetrations into systems with or without firewalls shown in Exhibit 4.3 might be collected.

We would frame the hypothesis (the *null hypothesis,* sometimes represented as H_0) that there was *no* relationship between the two independent variables, penetration and firewalls. The sole purpose of this hypothesis is to provide a means for disproving it and therefore to demonstrate the opposite—a relationship between firewalls and penetrations. Accordingly, we can *test* that hypothesis by performing a test of independence of the variables.

One measure of independence is known as the chi-square (χ^2) test, which evaluates the discrepancy between observed and expected occurrences. In our example, a simple chi-square test of independence would give a *test statistic* (a chi-square with one degree of freedom, as indicated by the subscript [1]) of $\chi^2_{[1]} = 2.636$. For details of how to calculate such a test statistic, see any elementary statistics textbook.

If there really was no association between penetration and firewalls in the population of systems under examination, the parametric value of this statistic would be zero. For this example, a table of the distribution of the theoretical chi-square distribution with one degree of freedom shows that such a large value (or larger) of $\chi^2_{[1]}$ would occur in only 10.4 percent of the samples taken from a population where firewalls had no effect on penetration. Put another way, if one took lots of samples from a population where the presence of firewalls was not associated with any change in the rate of penetration, around 10.4 percent of those samples would produce $\chi^2_{[1]}$ statistics as large as or larger than 2.636.

Statisticians have agreed on some conventions for deciding whether a test statistic deviates enough from the value expected under the null hypothesis to warrant inferring that the null hypothesis is wrong. Generally the probability that the null hypothesis is true—often shown as $p(H_0)$—is symbolized as follows:

When $p(H_0) > 0.05$, the results are described as not statistically significant (often designated with the symbols ns).

When $0.05 \geq p(H_0) > 0.01$, the results are described as statistically significant (often designated with the symbol *).

Exhibit 4.3   Contingency Table for Penetrations
with and without Firewalls

| | Penetration | | |
Firewalls	No	Yes	Totals
No	25	75	100
Yes	70	130	200
Totals	95	205	300

When $0.01 \geq p(H_0) > 0.001$, the results are described as highly statistically significant (often designated with the symbols **).

When $p(H_0) \leq 0.001$, the results are described as extremely statistically significant (often designated with the symbols ***).

In other words, if the probability that the null hypothesis is correct is very small, the null hypothesis can be rejected and it can be concluded that there is a relationship between firewalls and penetration.

4.2.1.4   *Random Sampling, Bias, and Confounded Variables.* The most important element of sampling is randomness. A sample is said to be *random* or *randomized* when every member of the population being studied has an equal probability of being selected. When a population is defined one way but the sample is drawn non-randomly, the sample is described as *biased*. For example, if the population being studied were designed to be, say, all companies worldwide with more than 3,000 full-time employees but the researchers sampled mostly from such companies in the United States, the sample could be biased toward U.S. companies and their characteristics. Similarly, in a security study of all companies in the United States with more than 3,000 full-time employees, sampling only from those companies that were willing to respond to a security survey could be a biased sample.

In this last example involving studying only those who respond to a survey, the study is potentially *confounding* variables: The sampling is looking at people who respond to surveys and hoping they are representative of the larger population of people from all companies in the desired population. But what if the people who are *willing* to respond are those who have better security and those who do not respond have terrible security? Then *responding to the survey* is confounded with *quality of security,* and the biased sample could easily mislead us into overestimating the level of security in the desired population. The opposite also could be true—and without further study to tease out the possible biases and confounding variables, no one can be sure what the study means about security.

Another example of how variables can be confounded is comparisons of results from surveys carried out in different years. Unless exactly the same people are interviewed in both years, the study may confound individual variations in responses with changes over time. Furthermore, unless exactly the same companies are represented from year to year, differences among companies may be confounded with changes over time. Similarly, unless similar types of companies are included in the same proportions from year to year, the study may confound differences among industries with changes over time. If external events have led people to be more or less willing to respond truthfully to questions, the study may confound willingness to respond with research groups, the study may be confounding changes in methodology with changes over time.

4.2.1.5   *Confidence Limits.* Because random samples naturally vary around the parametric (population) statistics, it is not very helpful to report a *point estimate* of the parametric value. For example, if the mean damage from computer crimes in a survey is reported as $180,000 per incident, what does that imply about the population mean? What proportion of the computer crimes would be expected to cost between, say, $170,000 and $190,000? Ten percent? Fifty percent?

To express confidence in the sample statistic, statisticians calculate the likelihood of being right if they give an *interval estimate* of the population value. For example, one might find that a 95 percent likelihood of being right in asserting that the mean damage in the example above was between $160,000 and $200,000. In another sample, one might be able to narrow these *95 percent confidence limits* to $175,000 and $185,000.

In general, the larger the sample size, the narrower the confidence limits will be for particular statistics. Exhibit 4.4 shows the confidence limits of percentages for a few representative sample sizes.

For example, a sample of 500 with an observed mean of 50 percent would have 95 percent confidence limits of 45.5 percent to 54.5 percent; that is, based on the sample, there would be a 95 percent probability of correctly estimating the population percentage by claiming that it was somewhere between 45.5 percent and 54.5 percent.

4.2.1.6   Contingency Tables.

One of the most frequent errors in reporting results of studies is to provide only part of the story. For example, a statement may read: "Over 70 percent of the systems without firewalls were penetrated last year." Such a statement may be true, but it cannot be interpreted correctly as meaning that systems with firewalls were necessarily more or less vulnerable to penetration than systems without firewalls. The statement is incomplete; to make sense of it, one needs the other part of the implied *contingency table*—the percentage of systems *with* firewalls that were penetrated last year—before making any assertions about the relationship between firewalls and penetrations.

4.2.1.7   Association versus Causality.

Continuing the example with the firewalls and rates of penetration, another error that untrained people often make when studying statistical information is to mistake *association* for *causality*. Imagine that a study showed that a lower percentage of systems with firewalls were penetrated than systems without firewalls and that this difference was statistically highly significant. Would such a result necessarily mean that firewalls cause the reduction in penetration? No, conceivably the firewalls might be installed in organizations whose security awareness and security policies were more highly developed than in the organizations where no firewalls were installed. In this imaginary example, the firewalls actually might have *no causal effect* whatever on resistance to penetration. This result would illustrate the effect of confounding variables—*presence of a firewall* with *state of security awareness and policies.*

Exhibit 4.4   95 Percent Confidence Limits for Percentages

	Sample Size		
Percentage	100	500	1000
0	0–3.0%	0–0.6%	0–0.3%
10	4.9–17.6%	7.5–13.0%	8.2–12.0%
20	12.7–29.1%	16.6–23.8%	17.6–22.6%
50	40.0–60.1%	45.5–54.5%	46.9–53.1%
80	70.9–87.3%	76.2–83.4%	77.4–82.4%
90	82.4–95.1%	87.0–92.5%	88.0–91.8%
100	97.0–100%	99.4–100%	99.7–100%

4.2.1.8   Control Groups.   Finally, to finish the example of firewalls and penetration, one way to distinguish between association and causality is to *control* for variables. For example, the state of security awareness as well as the presence or absence of firewalls could be measured and comparisons could be made only among groups with the same level of awareness. There are also statistical techniques for mathematically controlling for differences in such variables.

4.2.2   Research Methods Applicable to Computer Crime.   Knowledge of social science research methods is useful in studying computer crime. The following section summarizes the three techniques most suitable for studying computer crime: interviews, focus groups and surveys.

4.2.2.1   Interviews.   Interviewing individuals can be illuminating. In general, interviews provide a wealth of data that are unavailable through any other method. For example, interviewers can learn details of computer crime cases or motivations and techniques used by computer criminals. Interviews can be structured (using precise lists of questions) or unstructured (allowing the interviewer to respond to new information by asking additional questions at will).

Interviewers can take notes or record the interviews for later word-for-word transcription. In unstructured interviewers, skilled interviewers can probe responses to elucidate nuances of meaning that might be lost using cruder techniques such as surveys.

4.2.2.2   Focus Groups.   Focus groups are like group interviews. Generally the facilitator uses a list of predetermined questions and encourages the participants to respond freely and to interact with each other. Often the proceedings are filmed from behind a one-way mirror for later detailed analysis. Such analysis can include nonverbal communications such as facial expressions and other body language as participants speak or listen to others discuss specific topics.

4.2.2.3   Surveys.   Surveys consist of asking people to answer a fixed series of questions with lists of allowable answers. They can be carried out face-to-face or by distributing and retrieving questionnaires by telephone, mail, fax, and e-mail. Some questionnaires have been posted on the Web.

The critical issue when considering the reliability of surveys is *self-selection bias*—the obvious problem that survey results include only the responses of people who agreed to participate. Before basing critical decisions on survey data, it is useful to find out what the response rate was. Although there are no absolutes, in general survey results are more trustworthy when the response rate is high. Unfortunately, response rates for telephone surveys are often less than 10 percent; response rates for mail and e-mail surveys can be less than 1 percent. It is very difficult to make any case for random sampling under such circumstances, and all results from such low-response-rate surveys should be viewed primarily as indicating the range of problems or experiences of the respondents rather than as indicators of population statistics.

From a statistical point of view, there are two types of Web-based surveys: (1) those using strong identification and authentication and (2) those that do not. Those that do not are vulnerable to fraud, such as repeated voting by the same individuals. Those that provide individual URLs to limit voting to one per person nonetheless suffer from the same problems of self-selection bias as any other survey.

4.2.2.4   Validating the Research Methods.   Interviews and other social science research methodologies can suffer from a systematic tendency for respondents to shape their answers to please the interviewer or to express opinions that may be closer to the norm in whatever group they see themselves belonging to. Thus if it is well known that every organization ought to have a business continuity plan, some respondents may misrepresent the state of their business continuity planning to look better than they really are.

In addition, survey instruments may distort responses by phrasing questions in a biased way; for example, the question "Does your business have a completed business continuity plan?" may have a more accurate response rate than the question "Does your business comply with industry standards for having a completed business continuity plan?" The latter question is not neutral and is likely to increase the proportion of "yes" answers.

The sequence of answers may bias responses; exposure to the first possible answers can inadvertently establish a baseline for respondents. For example, a question about the magnitude of virus infections might ask "In the last 12 months, has your organization experienced total losses from virus infections of (a) $1 million or greater; (b) less than $1 million but greater than or equal to $100,000; (c) less than $100,000; (d) none at all?" To test for bias, the designer can create versions of the instrument in which the same information is obtained using the opposite sequence of answers: "In the last 12 months, has your organization experienced total losses from virus infections of (a) none at all; (b) less than $100,000; (c) less than $1 million but greater than or equal to $100,000; (d) $1 million or greater?"

The sequence of questions also can bias responses; having provided a particular response to a question, respondents tend to make answers to subsequent questions about the same topic conform to the first answer in the series. To test for this kind of bias, the interview designer can create versions of the instrument with questions in different sequences.

Some survey designers include questions that mean the same thing but that are phrased in positive and negative terms, respectively. For example, one might ask, "What proportion of your systems have firewalls installed?" and then later ask, "What proportion of your systems do not have firewalls installed?" Inconsistencies between the answers (e.g., "90 percent" for the first question but "50 percent" for the second) would warn the analyst of possible unreliability of other answers.

Another instrument validation technique inserts questions with no valid answers or with meaningless jargon to see if respondents are thinking critically about each question or merely providing any answer that pops into their heads. For example, the nonsensical question "Does your company use steady-state quantum interference methodologies for intrusion detection?" might be inserted into a questionnaire about security. The results of respondents who answer "yes" to this and other diagnostic questions would be invalidated.

Follow-up contacts to repeat certain questions may provide evidence for judging the reliability of previous answers by the same respondents; alternatively, asking some of the same questions to others in the same organization under study may alert the analyst to irregularities in the answers.

Finally, independent verification of answers provides strong evidence of whether respondents are answering truthfully. However, such intrusive follow-up investigations are rare.

4.3   STUDIES OF COMPUTER CRIMINALS.   This section reviews the findings of researchers who have worked with individual computer criminals to build a profile of their psychology and culture.

4.3.1   Donn B. Parker.   Donn B. Parker, formerly of SRI Consulting and later the Senior Security Leader of AtomicTangerine, Inc., has carried out a long series of interviews with hundreds of computer criminals over 28 years. He summarizes his experiences and insights most completely in two chapters of his book *Fighting Computer Crime: A New Framework for Protecting Information.*[1] Chapter 6 of that book is called "Cyberspace Abusers and Misusers" and Chapter 7 is "The Disastrous Hacker Culture." Some highlights of his research are:

- People who commit computer crimes vary widely in skills, knowledge, resources, authority, and motives.

- Computer criminals may have different levels of skill in formal education, social interactions, and use of computer systems.

- There are three classes of computer criminal: tool makers, tool users, and script followers.

- Motives include greed; a need to solve personal problems such as paying gambling debts; an inability to recognize the harm done to others; the personification of computers as adversaries in a game; and the Robin Hood syndrome, which sees corporations as so rich that stealing from them is morally justified.

- Many hackers believe that breaking into systems without theft, vandalism, or obvious breach of confidentiality is a harmless and ethically acceptable hobby.

- Some hackers believe that breaking into systems is a positive good because they think they are contributing to improving security.

- "In today's hacker culture, malicious hackers regularly engage in fabrications, exaggeration, thievery, and fantasy."

- Most active hackers are males ages 12 to 24 years old.

- Many parents of hackers have no idea what their children are doing with the expensive computer equipment they have received as gifts.

- Some hacker sympathizers blame the victims of hackers for having poor security and minimize the ethical issues.

- Some hacker sympathizers describe attacks as justifiable protests or direct action against enemies of the environment or of society in general.

4.3.2   Sarah Gordon.   Sarah Gordon, formerly of IBM Research, has been interviewing virus writers since 1990. In a series of groundbreaking papers, she sketched out the culture and psychology of virus writers.[2] Some of her key findings are:

- There appear to be three categories of active virus writers: (1) young adolescents; (2) college students; and (3) adults, often gainfully employed as professionals.

- Some virus writers stop their harmful hobby and become "mature reformed ex-writers of viruses."

- Virus writers vary widely in their stages of ethical and moral development, and some virus writers fall within the normal ethical-development stages described by psychologists.

- Virus writers also "vary in age, income level, location, social/peer interaction, educational level, likes, dislikes, and manner of communication."

- Some of the older virus writers interviewed seemed to think that society at large qualified as "the Enemy"; however, younger virus writers did not seem to view themselves in an antisocietal battle.

- Virus writers project an antisocial image in their discussion groups, but this image seems to be a posture rather than deep-seated anomie.

- Some recent viruses have been of much higher sophistication than earlier generations of malicious software. This fact suggests that "New Age" virus writers may be creating viruses in the belief that they are contributing to the advance of science and technology by forcing changes in vulnerable products that facilitate virus actions.

- There is no evidence supporting the view that laws making virus-writing illegal would reduce the generation of new viruses; indeed, such laws could conceivably spark an increase in virus writing due to U.S. attitudes toward free speech and antigovernment ideologies around the world.

4.3.3   Popular Books and Journalism.   A number of journalists and security experts have explored the world of criminal hackers and virus writers; the bibliography includes case studies by Stoll (1989), Hafner and Markoff (1991), Sterling (1992), Smith (1994), Slatalla and Quittner (1995), Goodell (1996), Littman (1996), Shimomura and Markoff (1996) and Freedman and Mann (1997). Several of these books deal with Kevin Mitnick, a man who unfortunately became a hero for a generation of criminal hackers and their sympathizers.

4.4.   SURVEYS OF COMPUTER CRIME.   This section summarizes some of the better-known surveys of computer crime incidence and costs.

4.4.1   CSI/FBI Annual Surveys of Computer Crime.   In March 2001, the Computer Security Institute (CSI, *www.gocsi.com*) published the results of its sixth annual *Computer Crime and Security Survey.* The annual study "is conducted by CSI with the participation of the San Francisco Federal Bureau of Investigation's (FBI) Computer Intrusion Squad." The 2000 survey analyzed the responses of "583 computer security practitioners in U.S. corporations, government agencies, financial institutions, medical institutions and universities."[3] The work focuses on the extent and types of computer crime and summarizes the financial estimates of loss from respondents willing to cooperate. Recent studies also included questions about e-commerce problems.

4.4.2   NCSA/ICSA Labs Annual Surveys of Computer Virus Incidence.   ICSA Labs (formerly NCSA and now part of TruSecure Corporation; see *www.trusecure. com* and *www.icsalabs.com*) sponsors an annual survey based on "interviews with technology professionals drawn from 300 corporations and government institutions throughout North America. The survey provides a thorough overview of the state of computer viruses encountered today. The *Computer Virus Prevalence Survey* is funded through sponsorships of anti-virus industry leaders, research organizations, and corporations."[4] The complete survey can be downloaded at no cost by a simple registration process.

4.4.3   CERT-CC Quarterly and Annual Summaries.   The Computer Emergency Response Team Coordination Center (CERT-CC) of the Software Engineering Institute at Carnegie Mellon University (see *www.cert.org*) issues their CERT summary quarterly:

> draw attention to the types of attacks reported to our incident response team during the previous three months, as well as other noteworthy incident and vulnerability information. The summary includes pointers to sources of information for dealing with the problems. CERT summaries are emailed to the CERT mailing list (*www.cert.org/contact_cert/ certmaillist.html*) as soon as they are published. For regular updates of information about the most frequent, high-impact types of security incidents and vulnerabilities currently being reported to the CERT/CC, see the CERT/CC Current Activity webpage, *www.cert. org/current/current_activity.html*.[5]

All these reports are available free of charge.

4.4.4   Other Industry Surveys.   Throughout each year, a variety of organizations publish surveys of computer crime occurrences and costs. Some of these are produced by vendors, others by consulting firms, and some by academic or research institutions. A useful list of pointers to online industry security surveys is available at *www.infowar.com/survey/survey_1.shtml*. However, press reports of the results often leave out crucial information, and anyone wanting to base critical decisions on these data should consult the original, full reports whenever possible, rather than relying on possibly incomplete summaries.

4.5   HISTORICAL REVIEW OF COMPUTER CRIME SURVEYS.   This section briefly summarizes key points from some of the well-publicized surveys reported by the press since 1996. These data are based on the INFOSEC Year in Review research project conducted since 1996 by the author.

4.5.1   Reported in 1996.   At a hearing of the U.S. Senate's Permanent Investigations Subcommittee, participants heard from Dan Gelber, the panel's chief minority counsel, that global losses in the commercial and financial services sector amount to $800 million a year according to a survey by an unnamed research firm. More than half of these losses were attributed to U.S. companies.[6]

Confirming the belief that the Internet can be misused to create a denial of service to employers, a Nielsen Media Research survey published in mid-October suggested that employees from IBM, Apple, and AT&T together spent 13,048 person-hours visiting the Penthouse World Wide Web site in a single month. If we estimate $20 per hour, that makes about $250,000 of wasted pay. At Compaq, in Houston, Texas, about a dozen employees were fired for logging more than 1,000 visits *each* to sex sites while they were at work.[7]

According to Federation of Communication Services chairman Jonathan Clark, fraud costs the phone industry and its customers the equivalent of about $332 million a year in losses in the United Kingdom.[8]

The annual Ernst and Young information security survey results showed that damage from virus infections, insider attacks, and outsider attacks are apparently up, but management support for information security remains abysmal.[9]

USA TODAY reported on a survey of 236 major corporations prepared for a congressional committee. The evidence suggests that more than half the major corporations in the United States have been victimized by computer break-ins. About 58 percent of the companies that responded said they had experienced a break-in in the past year; almost 18 percent said they suffered losses of more than $1 million.

Two-thirds reported losses exceeding $50,000. Respondents claimed that more than 20 percent of the break-ins were industrial espionage or sabotage by competitors. Companies uniformly reported concern over the negative effects of publicizing of any break-ins on public confidence in their firms.[10] On December 18, Dan Farmer, author of SATAN (Security Administrator's Tool for Analyzing Networks), released the results of a preliminary scan of some 2,200 computing systems on the Internet in November to December 1996. He selected what he described as high-profile, commerce-oriented Web sites plus some randomly chosen sites for comparison. Farmer wrote that "using simple, non-intrusive techniques, I determined that nearly two-thirds of these interesting hosts had serious potential security vulnerabilities—a rate about twice that of the randomly selected hosts!"[11]

4.5.2   Reported in 1997.   A survey by Compaq in the financial district of London showed that poor choices are the norm for computer passwords there. A staggering 82 percent of the respondents said they used, in order of preference, "a sexual position or abusive name for the boss" (30 percent), their partner's name or nickname (16 percent), the name of their favorite holiday destination (15 percent), sports team or player (13 percent), and whatever they saw first on their desk (8 percent).[12]

The audit faculty of the Institute of Chartered Accountants of England and Wales, in conjunction with *Accountancy Age* magazine, reported the results of a survey showing that many professionals expect to see an increase in the rate of corporate fraud. Reasons given by the respondents included reduced staffing and increased performance pressure. People thought that legal protection for whistle-blowers and increased vigilance would help fight fraud. The size of the respondent population was not given in the report.[13]

Barclays Bank in England warned shoppers to be on guard against credit card fraud. Although losses have been dropping, theft using cloned (counterfeit) cards are large enough at £23.6 million (about $40 million) to warrant investment in smart cards. In the United Kingdom alone, said a Barclays' spokesman, over half a million retail points of sale will have to be converted to interact with the microchips on the new credit cards.[14] The 1997 Computer Security Institute survey of computer crime revealed that 75 percent of 563 respondents had lost money because of computer crimes in the past year. According to United Press International:

> The institute says 26 respondents reported a total of $24.8 million in losses due to telecommunications fraud; 22 reported $21 million in losses from theft of proprietary information; 26, nearly $4.3 million from sabotage of data or networks; 22, nearly $4 million from unauthorized access by insiders; and 22, $2.9 million from system penetration by outsiders. Computer virus infestations caused nearly $12.5 million in losses for 165 respondents. Laptop theft caused $6.1 million in losses for 160 respondents; employee abuse of Internet privileges caused more than $1 million in losses to 55 organizations."[15]

John D. Howard published his Ph.D. dissertation at Carnegie Mellon University in 1997. He analyzed 4,299 Internet-related security incidents. See Chapter 3 of this Handbook for details of some of his research. The Electronic Privacy Information Center (EPIC) (see *www.epic.org*) released its survey on Web privacy just before an important U.S. government hearing of the Federal Trade Commission. Their research found widespread use of intrusive technology such as cookies without requesting permission from their users. David Kalish, writing for Associated Press, stated that "The survey found that of the Internet's 100 most popular Web sites, about half collect personal information from users who click on their sites or through mailing lists and other means. Only 17 sites even mention the privacy issue, and most of those fell far short of what the group considered adequate disclosure—explaining why information is collected, how it will be used, and what steps will be taken to limit improper use."[16]

A survey of 333 system integrators, value-added resellers, vertical resellers, and consultants was conducted during May 1997 by J. River Inc. and revealed that only about half the companies replying had implemented any network security policies despite widespread plans for intranets and Internet communications. In other sections of the research, there were indications that about half the companies involved used only user IDs and passwords for security and that about a third used no security at all.[17] Christopher D. McDonald, editor of the *Information Systems Update,* wrote:

> Stuart Hanley, a data recovery manager with Ontrack Data International, has an article in the June 1997 edition of *Contingency Planning & Management* entitled "Minimize Loss, Maximize Recovery." He presents a pie-chart for 50,000 hard drives and other data storage devices which Ontrack has examined upon failure since 1987. Again here are REAL numbers to consider for contingency planning. Reasons for failure include: 44% hardware or system malfunction; 32% human error; 14% software program malfunction; 7% computer virus; and 3% natural disasters."[18]

Japanese police asked computer operators to increase security in an attempt to resist increasing attacks by hackers. Reported hacking increased 25 percent in the first six months of 1997. Recommendations included better password management, installation of firewalls, and effective encryption.[19]

Vin McLellan of the Privacy Guild circulated what appears to be a draft letter from the Federal Reserve Bank to all member banks in the United States warning them that they are obliged under law to report all violations of computer security to the FBI.[20]

4.5.3   Reported in 1998.   According to the Australian Computer Emergency Response Team (AusCERT, *www.auscert.org.au*), the number of computer hacker assaults reported in Australia more than doubled in the 12 months to early August 1997. Most of the increase came from "script weenies," unskilled hackers who use automated hacking programs.[21]

According to the Japanese Ministry of Posts and Telecommunications, Japan experienced its worst year of virus infections in July 1997, with 353 reported incidents, of which 66 percent were due to macro viruses.[22] In the United Kingdom, a report from the Audit Commission stated that 45 percent of its respondents reported "computer misuse" such as fraud or use of pirated software in 1997. The reporting rate rose from 36 percent in 1994.[23] The long-standing belief that internal attacks outweigh external threats in computer security may be starting to crumble. Tim Wilson reported in *Communications Week* that "WarRoom Research LLC found that the vast majority of Fortune 1000 companies have experienced a successful break-in by an outsider in the past year. More than half of those companies have experienced more than 30 system penetrations in the past 12 months. Nearly 60 percent said they lost $200,000 or more as a result of each intrusion." In addition, the 1998 Computer Security Institute/FBI survey showed that "520 U.S. companies reported a total loss of $136 million from computer crime and security breaches in 1997—an increase of 36 percent from the year before. The Internet was cited by 54 percent of the respondents as a frequent point of attack—that's about the same percentage of respondents that cited internal systems as a frequent point of attack."[24] The Department of Energy surveyed 64,000 unclassified computer systems and found widespread security vulnerabilities including readable password files, write access through FTP, and the presence of classified and sensitive nuclear weapons information on 1,400 systems open to anyone on the Internet.[25]

Robert Trigaux wrote an extensive review of cases of harassment by criminal hackers. Quoting security expert Ray Weadcock, he wrote: "With the global boom in the Internet and ever-cheaper personal computers, hacking is spreading like online kudzu. Hacking is getting more sophisticated and, in many cases, a lot nastier. And it's chipping away at the ability of government, the military, and the business community to protect proprietary information and preserve individual privacy."[26] Peter G. Neumann, moderator of the RISKS Forum, wrote, "A 1996 survey of 2,000 Japanese companies conducted by an institute affiliated with the Ministry of Industrial Trade and Industry revealed that only 17.1 percent had a security manager in charge of preventing unauthorized access to their computer networks; 14.3 percent offered security education; 7 percent used firewalls. More than half of the respondents said they didn't take necessary protective measures because they don't know what to do."[27] Dr. Virginia Rezmierski of the University of Michigan published a study of the costs incurred in academia by computer incidents, including deliberate attacks as well as accidental downtime. Costs of recovery averaged around $15,000 for the most part but ranged above $100,000 in some severe disruptions.[28]

The Organization for Economic Cooperation and Development (OECD) criticized projections that paint a picture of a world full of e-cash–carrying smart-card users buying products and services online. In fact, the total estimated volume of e-commerce in 1997, $26 billion, was 0.5 percent of the total retail sales (not gross domestic product) in the seven largest economies of the planet.[29] Dana Blankenhorn, writing in *Advertising Age,* reported expert opinions that consumer fears of shopping on the Web were unfounded but that businesses would have to respond anyway to quell the anxiety. One of the mechanisms available for fraud reduction was pattern matching of electronic transactions to detect misuse. The CyberSource company of San Jose, California, was described as providing such a service for Web-based merchants.[30] According to The Knowledge Group, a British consultancy firm, information technology managers largely blame upper management for failing to support efforts at protecting corporate information systems and networks. According to an article by Sylvia Dennis in *Newsbytes,* "For its survey, TKG asked 250 IT [information technology] and network managers to list the contributing factors to network attacks via the Internet. While 33 percent included lack of board-level understanding or commitment to network security as a significant factor, 60 percent said that not enough time or money was invested in access control or risk assessment."[31]

A self-selected sample of 80 security experts answered a survey at the Bellcore/Global Integrity's SecureComm 98 conference in Washington, D.C. The top five information security concerns for 1999 were as follows:

- Ability of current security infrastructure to support electronic commerce activities
- Implementing remote access without compromising the security of the corporate network
- Insider attacks against corporate systems
- The extension of networks to support business partner connections
- Encryption and key management technology for customer-interfacing systems[32]

4.5.4   Reported in 1999.   The official Xinhua news agency reported that computer crime has been exploding in the People's Republic of China (PRC). The annual growth rate of 30 percent led to over 100 recorded cases of computer-related crimes in 1998 with estimates of undetected crime running about 6:1, with a projected rate of

600 crimes in 1998 in the People's Republic. One Chinese estimate guessed that 95 percent of all PRC Web sites have been penetrated by local and overseas criminal hackers because of the relatively weak level of security in the People's Republic. A test of Shanghai and Shenzhen networks showed that almost all of them were vulnerable to penetration. Local software companies are beginning to respond to the need for security software, and in late 1998 an antivirus company announced the release of the first firewall made in the People's Republic.[33]

In Japan, the National Police Agency reported in February that computer crime was up 58 percent in 1998 compared with 1997—a 1,300 percent growth since the first statistics were kept in 1993. Specific crimes increased even more than the aggregate average; for example, forgery and data diddling cases grew 67 percent in 1998. Current Japanese laws do not consider unauthorized penetration of a computer system as a crime; only breaches of data integrity are criminal.[34] Allan Watt, director of forensic operations for computer security specialists S P Bates & Associates of New Zealand, said that his studies strongly support the view that 80 percent of computer crime is perpetrated by insiders. He said that many executives dismiss the consequences of computer crime as malfunctions and warns that it is unwise to allow information technology (IT) staff to investigate suspected crime without supervision by forensic experts outside the department. His research also supports the widespread opinion that 90 percent of detected computer crime is unreported because of fears of embarrassment.[35] The Chinese Department of Public Security announced that it had solved 100 cases of criminal hacking in 1998 but estimated that this was only about 15 percent of the actual level of unauthorized system access. Reported computer crime was growing at an annual rate of 30 percent, the department said. About 95 percent of all Chinese systems on the Internet had been attacked last year, with many banks and other financial institutions the target of Chinese and international criminals.[36] The annual Australian Computer Crime and Security Survey, organized by the Victorian Computer Crime Investigation Squad and Deloitte Touche Tohmatsu, reported on computer crimes in 350 of the largest Australian companies. In brief, about one-third of respondents had suffered one or more attacks on their systems in 1998; of those, 80 percent had experienced insider attacks; 60 percent experienced outsider attacks; and 15 percent of the respondents with any attacks claimed they had been the targets of industrial espionage. Almost three-quarters of all the respondents had no formal policy requiring notification of police authorities in case of attack. More than a fifth of all the respondents had experienced a breach of confidentiality, and almost a fifth reported a breach of data integrity.[37]

The Fourth Annual Computer Security Institute/Federal Bureau of Investigation Computer Crime and Security Survey demonstrated yet again that computer crime is a growing problem for U.S. companies, financial institutions, and government agencies. Losses amounted to hundreds of millions of dollars, much resulting from industrial espionage. The key findings were:

- 26 percent reported theft of proprietary information.
- System penetration by outsiders increased for the third year in a row; 30 percent of respondents reported intrusions.
- Those reporting their Internet connection as a frequent point of attack rose from 37 percent of respondents in 1996 to 57 percent in 1999.
- Unauthorized access by insiders rose for the third straight year; 55 percent reported incidents.

- More companies—32 percent compared with 17 percent in the three prior years—are reporting serious cybercrimes to law enforcement.[38]

M2 Communications (*www.m2.com*) reported in April 1999 that a survey conducted for *Infosecurity '99* and *Government Computing* magazine found serious vulnerabilities among U.K. local authorities (municipal governments):

- 33 percent of local authorities in the United Kingdom were at risk of penetration by hackers.
- 33 percent of British local authorities lacked firewalls.
- 6 percent did not have basic antivirus software installed.
- Many of the systems with firewalls did not successfully enable the firewalls to filter Internet traffic.

A similar survey in 1998 suggested that three-quarters of medium-size accountancy practices, law firms, and public relations and advertising agencies in Britain had no security measures in place at all.[39]

Andrew Darling, writing for *Information Week* in the United Kingdom, penned a dismal litany of management failures to integrate security into their business operations. Interviews with many senior IT staff showed that the same decades-old pattern of ignoring security in favor of a short-term focus on operations and profits makes it impossible for technical staff to do their job adequately.[40]

NTA Monitor Ltd. released a survey of e-mail servers in British government systems that showed that almost half had security vulnerabilities that made it possible for breaches of e-mail confidentiality. "The testing analysed the 689 Internet domains within the gov.uk name space, which includes central government departments, local government and a number of governmental organizations, and after discounting domains where no Internet email systems had been set-up, or which were not reachable during the tests, the survey reported on 345 live email servers." The analysis took place between November 1998 and April 1999.[41]

A poll of 500 households in the United States showed that young people between eight and 18 received minimal parental supervision in their use of the Internet. Some of the key points were:

- 20 percent of parents did not monitor their children's Internet usage.
- 52 percent monitored usage only moderately.
- 18 percent of the children surveyed intended to physically meet someone they met on the Internet.
- 48 percent of parents allowed unlimited frequency of access to the Internet.
- 24 percent of parents placed no restrictions on the length of time their children stay on the Internet.
- 71 percent of parents with children aged 14 years or older did not supervise their children's Internet use at all.[42]

CERT-CC found that malicious software infections increased in the second quarter of 1999, with the Melissa and Chernobyl viruses causing widespread trouble.[43]

The hacking magazine *2600* published letters from victims of Kevin Mitnick that estimated damages from his depredations. Total estimated costs (dismissed as preposterous by the *2600* crew) were $292 million, of which NEC claimed $1.8 million and Nokia reported $135 million.[44]

A study by Georgetown University researchers revealed that about 66 percent of the 7,500 popular Web sites in the review included a privacy policy. Critics claimed that most of these were paying lip service to privacy; EDUPAGE editors wrote, "The FTC [Federal Trade Commission] names five ingredients in its definition of a successful all-encompassing privacy policy, but [the] survey showed that just 10 percent of surveyed sites follow all five steps."[45]

The General Accounting Office (GAO) of the United States reported that some key computer systems at NASA are poorly protected against criminal hackers. "We successfully penetrated several mission-critical systems, including one responsible for calculating detailed positioning data for Earth-orbiting spacecraft and another that processes and distributes the scientific data received from these spacecraft. . . . [W]e could have disrupted NASA's ongoing command and control operations and stolen, modified or destroyed system software and data." Among other findings, the government auditors said that NASA failed to assess risks and evaluate security requirements; 135 of the 155 mission-critical systems reviewed failed the agency's own requirements for risk assessment. NASA provided inadequate computer security training, did not clearly classify information as public or confidential, and was unable to say how mission-critical systems should be protected from known threats from the Internet.[46]

The Business Software Alliance and the Software and Information Industry Association announced a slight fall in piracy in 1998, although worldwide rates of unauthorized use remained at 38 percent (231 million of a total of 615 million new installations). Vietnam, with 97 percent stolen software, and China, with 95 percent, led the pack. Total theoretical losses were around $11 billion worldwide. However, the report also cited evidence that governments were working harder to reduce piracy.[47]

Studies by the Australian government contradicted accepted wisdom about the preponderance of inside attacks on business systems; the results suggested that most attacks were from outsiders rather than from disgruntled or dishonest employees. Apparently 42 percent of businesses said they did not report intrusions, implying that 58 percent did report intrusions. Common agreement among security specialists has been that no more than 10 percent of all detected computer crimes are reported to authorities. Federal Justice Minister Amanda Vanstone asked everyone to stop seeing hackers as "nerdy, pre-pubescent teens with youthful ideals." On the contrary, she said, "Increasingly, organisations around the world are experiencing attacks on their computer systems designed to financially benefit the perpetrator. This is a crime in the old-fashioned sense in that the motivation is greed."[48]

A study by the Computer Economics firm estimated losses to victims of virus and worm infections at around $7.6 billion in the first half of 1999.[49]

In a study of 1,001 respondents selected at random among the general public in the United States, most people expressed suspicion about the security of online transactions. Highlights:

- 58 percent of consumers do not consider any financial transaction online to be safe.

- 67 percent are not confident conducting business with a company that can be reached only online.

- 77 percent think it is unsafe to provide a credit card number over the computer.

- 87 percent want e-commerce transactions confirmed in writing.

The National Technology Readiness Survey was carried out by Rockbridge Associates over a two-year period.[50]

A study of 2,700 information technology professionals in 49 countries was summarized in July in *Information Week*. The Global Security Survey had many interesting findings; highlights include:

- 64 percent of companies fell victim to a virus attack in the past 12 months, up from 53 percent the previous year.

- In the United States alone, viruses hit 69 percent of companies, about four times as many as that of the next-highest category of security breach, unauthorized network entry.

- 22 percent of companies reported no security breaches at all.

- Hackers and terrorists were blamed for 48 percent of the security breaches, compared with 14 percent blaming hackers in 1998.

- 31 percent of respondents blamed contract service providers for breaches (up from 9 percent last year).

- 41 percent blamed authorized users and employees (compared with 58 percent in 1998).[51]

A small group of experts scanned 36 million Internet hosts in three weeks in December 1998, testing for 18 vulnerabilities. They published the results in August 1999. They found 730,213 vulnerabilities on 450,000 hosts. They wrote, "These open points of penetration immediately threaten the security of their affiliated networks, putting many millions of systems in commercial, academic, government and military organizations at a high compromise risk."[52]

According to a study by the Software & Information Industry Association (SIIA), almost half the software sold online in auctions managed by eBay, ExciteAtHome, and ZDNet violates the terms of the software licenses or is frankly pirated. Highlights of the findings covering 221 auction sales:

- 49 percent were illegal software.

- 33 percent were legal.

- 18 percent were of undetermined legality.

The 95 percent confidence limits for percentages in a sample size of 221 are about ±8 percent for the 50 percent mark and decline steadily to about ±2 percent for lower values.[53]

The SANS (System Administration, Networking, and Security) Institute warned in September that the Y2K problem would provide a perfect cover for disgruntled employees to install logic bombs and back doors. In addition, SANS experts warned that most computers have well-known vulnerabilities—Allan Paller estimates from five to 30—that even novice criminal hackers can exploit.[54]

The Business Software Alliance (BSA) released a report showing that the number of Web sites peddling illegal copies of proprietary software grew from 100,000 in 1997 to 900,000 in 1999. Losses are estimated not only at around $11 billion but also in goodwill by customers innocently buying stolen software who are shocked at not receiving support from the publishers of the original software.[55]

The General Accounting Office (GAO) of the U.S. government warned that the nation is increasingly vulnerable to information warfare and that the government is not doing enough to prevent damage. Areas of concern included air-traffic control, law enforcement, national defense, and tax collection among others. As evidence of the rising threat, the GAO report cited statistics from the CERT-CC at Carnegie Mellon University, which handled 1,334 incidents in 1993; in the first half of 1999, the number was 4,398.[56]

The Cutter Consortium reported that about 20 percent of 152 companies they studied had no information security standards at all. About 60 percent claimed they would implement such policies by the end of the year 2000. Only about 25 percent of the respondents said they had used security consulting companies for advice.[57]

Gary Parkinson wrote an extensive review of e-commerce risks for the *Guardian Weekly*. Among his key findings were:

- Some fraud artists trade legitimately online to establish credibility before exploiting online shoppers by withholding products or shipping shoddy substitutes or fake goods.

- Although most credit card companies indemnify victims against losses, online users of debit cards are mostly out of luck if their money is stolen—debit card transactions are equivalent to cash purchases.

- Visa says that half of all credit card disputes are about Internet transactions, even though the Net accounts for only 2 percent of overall business.[58]

Martin Allen-Smith wrote a summary of current studies on internal fraud in British corporations. According to his sources:

- 75 percent of all companies were hit by fraud at least once in the last five years.
- 41 percent were hit five times or more.
- One in four U.K. companies lost more than £600,000 in fraud in the last five years.
- Total U.K. company losses were estimated at 2 percent to 5 percent of annual turnover.
- Only 11 percent of corporate fraud losses are ever recovered.
- Fraud overtook bad debts as the major cause of business failure in the United Kingdom in 1996, according to the Society of Practitioners in Insolvency.
- More than 85 percent of U.K. companies believe that they are more at risk from fraud now than they were five years ago.
- The number of fraud charges made against companies by investors and investigated by the Serious Fraud Office rose by 164 percent from 1993 to 1996. In 10 of the 11 trials conducted in 1995, one or more of the company defendants were convicted.[59]

The e-commerce firm CyberSource commissioned a survey of online merchants; the work was carried out by Mindwave and interviewed over 100 online businesses. The findings showed that 75 percent of the respondents rated credit card fraud as "a concern" but only 59 percent knew that they would be liable for restitution in cases of fraud. About 72 percent of online merchants surveyed believed that sales would increase if online shoppers were not worried about fraud. The 95 percent confidence limits for percentages in a sample of 100 are approximately ±10 percent at worst.[60]

British Telecom released survey results of an unknown sample size about Web security in December 1999. Highlights include:

- 85 percent of "small to medium" businesses that responded had company Web sites.

- 88 percent said they had no idea how to secure those sites.

- 25 percent said they thought better security would hamper online business.

- 12 percent said they offered their Web visitors Secure Sockets Layer (SSL) to secure their sessions.

- 12 percent used a public-key infrastructure (PKI) for digital signatures and encryption.[61]

4.5.5   Reported in 2000.   Internet-related credit card fraud rose 29 percent in 1999, according to the British Home Office's statistics published on the Web.[62] Cybercrime growth accounted for a major part of the rise in total crime, according to Paul Wiles of the Home Office.[63]

The Electronic Privacy Information Center (EPIC; *www.epic.org*) released an interesting survey of the state of privacy on the Web using a sample of 100 prominent sites. The summary was depressing: *Surfer Beware III* found that few high-traffic Web sites offered adequate privacy protection. In fact, not a single one of them fulfilled important elements of Fair Information Practices investigated in the survey. Fair Information Practices serve as basic guidelines for safeguarding personal information. Also alarming was the significant proportion (35 out of 100) of shopping sites that allowed profile-based advertising networks to operate. These advertising networks present a stealthy and invasive way that third parties—companies that display banner advertisements—are tracking online behavior without the knowledge of the Internet user.[64]

A congressional audit report by the General Administration Office included devastating criticisms of the U.S. Environmental Protection Agency (EPA) on February 17, 2000. The EPA had already shut down its public Web site for fear of penetration in the face of observations such as "riddled with security weaknesses" and "a likely target for hackers." The investigators "found serious and pervasive problems that essentially render EPA's agency-wide information security program ineffective. . . . Moreover EPA cannot ensure the protection of sensitive business and financial data maintained by its larger computer systems or supported by its agency-wide network."[65]

A Forrester Research survey of 17,000 households in Germany, France, Sweden, the Netherlands, and the United Kingdom in the summer of 1999 indicates that less than 10 percent of respondents were interested in shopping online. In Sweden, where e-commerce was most popular, 14 percent of households were connected to the Web and 7 percent had ordered goods. At the other end of the scale, only 7 percent of French households were linked to the Net and only 2 percent had bought anything. However, a third of French homes subscribe to Minitel, which has offered shopping and information services for 17 years and presents a strong challenge to Internet-based e-commerce in that country. Most respondents cited privacy concerns and the inability actually to see what they were buying as the major impediments to e-shopping.[66] The Gallup polling organization said that the recent attacks by network vandals on prominent Web sites have left one-third of online consumers less likely to make a purchase via the Internet. The chief executive of At Plan, the online marketing consultancy that sponsored the Gallup poll, says that the attacks were "a cold dose or reality to many people . . . almost like the loss of innocence in first love."[67]

The annual CSI/FBI computer crime survey was released in March 2000. The self-selected response group included 273 organizations and 643 security practitioners in U.S. corporations, government, finance, healthcare, and academia. Total reported losses were $265 million. About 90 percent of the respondents experienced breaches of information security in the preceding 12 months; the top three problems were computer viruses, laptop theft, and employee net abuse. However, 70 percent of the respondents also reported other types of breach: theft of secrets, financial fraud, outsider penetration of security perimeters, denial of service, and sabotage of data or networks. In addition, 74 percent acknowledged financial losses—higher than in the 1998–1999 survey. Some 59 percent of the respondents rated Internet connections as a more frequent point of attack than internal systems (38 percent).[68]

> Ferris Research . . . released the results of a study designed to quantify the costs and benefits of e-mail, and estimates that the overall benefit in terms of increased productivity equals about $9,000 per employee. Rather than treading into the murky area of nonquantifiable benefits, such as improved decision-making, Ferris attempted to focus on items that delivered a tangible benefit, like time not spent on addressing snail mail envelopes, operating postage and fax machines, etc. It derived a 15% to 20% productivity improvement, with an overall increase of 326 hours per employee on the average. Ferris then attempted to quantify those hours, giving them a value of $13,000. Then came the downside: Ferris found that employees waste on an average 115 hours dealing with nonproductive e-mail, translating to a loss of about $4,000 per worker a year. Subtract the loss from the gain, and the result is an overall benefit of $9,000 per employee, or a 15% productivity gain. Ferris says that rate can be raised to 20% by more actively managing company e-mail systems: discouraging personal e-mail, shortening e-mail distribution lists, and helping workers identify and trash spam.[69]
>
> A [highly controversial] study of music sales commissioned by Reciprocal Inc., a digital rights management company, shows that sales of recorded music have declined in the vicinity of college campuses in the last two years, while rising elsewhere. Music sales were up 12% during the first three months of 2000 over the same time period in 1998, but at stores within five miles of a college campus—which account for about half of all music purchased—sales were down 4%. Music industry officials attribute the dip to use of Napster, which has been especially popular among college students. Some colleges have banned the music downloading software from campus computer systems because heavy use was clogging their networks.[70]
>
> Focus groups held . . . [in June] by Greenberg Quinlan, a Washington public policy research firm, . . . [seemed] to indicate a shift in public attitudes about Internet regulation. Whereas two years ago people were more inclined to look to government to regulate pornography and other kinds of activities found on the Internet, they now seem to trust business rather than government. Stanley Greenberg, who directed the research project on behalf of the nonprofit Markle Foundation, says: "People didn't understand the Internet as well. They understand more now about the difficulty of regulation."[71]
>
> A new survey . . . [released in June] by the Digital Media Association, indicates that Internet users who download music to sample are likely to follow up by purchasing CDs in stores or online. The new poll contradicts the findings of previous studies that found digital music downloading via Napster made a significant dent in bricks-and-mortar music store sales, especially in areas around college campuses. This latest survey, conducted by market research firm Yankelovich Partners, says 66% of all consumers said that listening to a song online has at least once prompted them to later buy a CD or cassette featuring that song. Most people who downloaded music (92%) listened to it on their desktop computers, while 10% used a portable device and 14% used their home stereo. More than 60% of them used the Internet to get to music they couldn't find on radio. According to Media Metrix, 22.8 million people visited the top 30 Internet music sites in April, up 19% from November 1999, the most recent number available. Paid digital music downloading is expected to hit $1.1 billion in sales by 2003, according to estimates by Forrester Research.[72]

A study by the Pew Research Institute found:

> There is broad-based concern about privacy being compromised [on the Net]," . . . [said] Lee Rainie, director of the study. Eighty-four percent of respondents reported they were concerned about businesses invading their privacy online, and many were frustrated by their unfamiliarity with the basic mechanics of Internet data collection. For instance, 56% of Internet users surveyed did not know what an Internet "cookie" is. The study attributes this lack of knowledge to the fact that about 35% of the 144 million people who use the Internet in the U.S. came online within the past year. Among more sophisticated Web surfers, only 5% use "anonymizing" software to hide their identities; 10% report using encryption software to protect their e-mail; 20% use a secondary e-mail address when forced to provide information on a Web site; and 25% say they have given a fake name or provided false responses on a Web site information form.[73]

4.6   THE FUTURE OF COMPUTER CRIME RESEARCH.   It is possible that the growth in insurance for computer crime (see Chapter 44) will lead to significant improvements in computer crime statistics. Insurance companies need actuarial information to calculate reasonable costs for coverage of particular systems, so it will be in their interest to keep track of claims. Such information is likely to remain proprietary during the initial phases of development, but companies eventually may agree to allow researchers to have access to anonymized data.

Another possible avenue for better information is mandatory reporting. Perhaps the growing importance of information technology as part of the critical infrastructure of all nations (and especially of technologically advanced nations) will lead to political decisions forcing disclosure of security breaches. Several models of mandatory reporting exist, such as:

- Public health requirements for doctors to report specific kinds of transmissible diseases
- Occupational health and safety reports covering accidents and exposures to toxic substances
- Commercial aviation reports of safety violations to government bodies
- Securities and exchange requirements for notification of financial irregularities

4.7   SUMMARY.   This chapter has reviewed the principles for critical reading of research results published in the popular and technical press and reviews highlights of interview and survey studies of computer crimes and computer criminals. Some of the key points are:

- Computer crime studies suffer from the problems of ascertainment: Some breaches of security are not noticed, and few of those noticed are reported.
- All current studies of computer crime and security incidents are of limited value because of poor response rates that make the samples of respondents nonrepresentative.
- Reports of averages and percentages should be evaluated with respect to sample sizes and variance; interval estimates are more credible than point estimates.
- Association of variables does not necessarily imply causation.
- Study methods should include internal measures of validity.
- A number of surveys of computer crime are carried out yearly and provide some indication of baseline levels of such security incidents.

4.8   BIBLIOGRAPHY AND FURTHER READING

Freedman, D.H., and C.C. Mann. @ *Large: The Strange Case of the World's Biggest Internet Invasion.* New York: Simon & Schuster, 1997.

Goodell, J. *The Cyberthief and the Samurai: The True Story of Kevin Mitnick—and the Man Who Hunted Him Down.* New York: Dell, 1996.

Gordon, S. "Inside the Mind of Dark Avenger" (abridged). Originally published in *Virus News International* (January 1993); *www.research.ibm.com/antivirus/SciPapers/Gordon/Avenger.html.*

Gordon, S. "The Generic Virus Writer I." Paper presented at 4th International Virus Bulletin Conference, 1994; *www.research.ibm.com/antivirus/SciPapers/Gordon/GenericVirus Writer.html.*

Gordon, S. "Technologically Enabled Crime: Shifting Paradigms for the Year 2000." Originally published in *Computers and Security* (1994); *www.research.ibm.com/antivirus/SciPapers/Gordon/Crime.html.*

Gordon, S. "The Anti-Virus Strategy System." Originally published in *Virus Bulletin* (1995); *www.research.ibm.com/antivirus/SciPapers/Gordon/Strategy.html.*

Gordon, S. "The Generic Virus Writer II." Paper presented at the 6th International Virus Bulletin Conference, 1996; *www.research.ibm.com/antivirus/SciPapers/Gordon/GVWII.html.*

Gordon, S. "Virus Writers: The End of Innocence?" Paper presented at the 10th International Virus Bulletin Conference, 2000; *www.research.ibm.com/antivirus/SciPapers/VB2000SG.htm* and *www.research.ibm.com/antivirus/SciPapers/VB2000SG.pdf.*

Hafner, K., and J. Markoff. *Cyberpunk: Outlaws and Hackers on the Computer Frontier.* New York: Touchstone Books, Simon & Schuster, 1991.

Howard, J.D. *An Analysis of Security Incidents on the Internet 1989–1995.* 1997. *www.cert.org/research/JHThesis/Start.html.*

Kabay, M.E. *The InfoSec Year in Review* (annual), 1996–2001. *www.securityportal.com/kfiles/iyir.*

Littman, J. *The Fugitive Game: Online with Kevin Mitnick—The Inside Story of the Great Cyberchase.* Boston: Little, Brown and Company (Boston), 1996.

Parker, D.B. *Fighting Computer Crime: A New Framework for Protecting Information.* New York: John Wiley & Sons, 1998.

Power, R. *Tangled Web: Tales of Digital Crime from the Shadows of Cyberspace.* Indianapolis: Que, 2000.

Shimomura, T., and J. Markoff. *Takedown: The Pursuit and Capture of Kevin Mitnick, America's Most Wanted Computer Outlaw—by the Man Who Did It.* New York: Hyperion, 1996.

Slatalla, M., and J. Quittner. *Masters of Deception: The Gang that Ruled Cyberspace.* New York: HarperCollins, 1995.

Smith, G. *The Virus Creation Labs: A Journey into the Underground.* Tucson, AZ: American Eagle Publications, 1994.

Sterling, B. *The Hacker Crackdown: Law and Disorder on the Electronic Frontier.* New York: Bantam Doubleday Dell, 1992.

Stoll, C. *The Cuckoo's Egg: Tracking a Spy Through the Maze of Computer Espionage.* New York: Pocket Books (Simon & Schuster), 1989.

Winkler, I. *Corporate Espionage: What It Is, Why It Is Happening in Your Company, What You Must Do About It.* Rocklin, CA: Prima Publishing, 1997.

4.9   NOTES

1. Donn B. Parker, *Fighting Computer Crime: A New Framework for Protecting Information* (New York: John Wiley & Sons, 1998).

2. Sarah Gordon, "Inside the Mind of Dark Avenger" (abridged). Originally published in *Virus News International* (January 1993); *www.research.ibm.com/antivirus/SciPapers/Gordon/Avenger.html.*

—— "The Generic Virus Writer I." Paper presented at 4th International Virus Bulletin Conference, 1994; *www.research.ibm.com/antivirus/SciPapers/Gordon/GenericVirusWriter. html.*

—— "Technologically Enabled Crime: Shifting Paradigms for the Year 2000." Originally published in *Computers and Security* (1994); *www.research.ibm.com/antivirus/SciPapers/ Gordon/Crime.html.*

—— "The Anti-Virus Strategy System." Originally published in *Virus Bulletin* (1995); www.research.ibm.com/antivirus/SciPapers/Gordon/Strategy.html.

—— "The Generic Virus Writer II." Paper presented at the 6th International Virus Bulletin Conference, 1996; *www.research.ibm.com/antivirus/SciPapers/Gordon/GVWII.html.*

—— "Virus Writers: The End of Innocence?" Paper presented at the 10th International Virus Bulletin Conference, 2000; *www.research.ibm.com/antivirus/SciPapers/VB2000SG.htm* and *www.research.ibm.com/antivirus/SciPapers/VB2000SG.pdf.*

3. Computer Security Institute, "Financial losses due to Internet intrusions, trade secret theft and other cyber crimes soar." *www.gocsi.com/prelea/000321.html.*

4. ICSA Labs, Computer Virus Prevalence Survey: full report from *www.trusecure.com/ html/tspub/pdf/vps20001.pdf* and an executive summary from *www.trusecure.com/html/ tspub/pdf/vps20002.pdf*

5. CERT-CC, *www.cert.org/current/current_activity.html.*

6. *Wall Street Journal,* June 6, 1996.

7. UPI, October 14, 1996.

8. *Press Association News,* October 29, 1996.

9. See *techweb.cmp.com/iw/602/02mtsec.htm.*

10. Associated Press, November 21, 1996.

11. See *www.fish.com/survey.*

12. *Press Association News,* January 2, 1997.

13. *Press Association News,* February 13, 1997.

14. *Press Association News,* February 20, 1997.

15. *EDUPAGE,* March 9, 1997.

16. Associated Press, June 9, 1997.

17. PR Newswire, June 27, 1997.

18. *Information Systems Update,* June 30, 1997.

19. *Newsbytes,* September 5, 1997.

20. Privacy Guild, November 8, 1997.

21. *Australasian Business Intelligence*; *www.abix.com.au,* January 4, 1998.

22. *Nihon Keizai Shimbun* via COMLINE News Service, January 5, 1998.

23. *EDUPAGE,* February 19, 1998.

24. *Communications Week*, March 24, 1998.

25. *RISKS* 19.81, June 16, 1998, *http://catless.ncl.ac.uk/Risks/19.81.html#subj1.*

26. *St. Petersburg* (Florida) *Times,* June 18, 1998.

27. *RISKS* 19.82, June 20, 1998, *http://catless.ncl.ac.uk/Risks/19.82.html#subj6.*

28. *EDUPAGE,* July 17, 1998.

29. *EDUPAGE,* September 29, 1998.

30. *Advertising Age,* October 26, 1998, *www.adage.com/interactive/articles/19981026/ article6.html.*

31. For details, contact *www.ktgroup.co.uk. Newsbytes,* October 30, 1998.

32. *Business Wire,* November 10, 1998.

33. *Newsbytes,* January 8, 1999.

34. OTC, February 18, 1999.

35. *National Business Review* (New Zealand), February 19, 1999.

36. Reuters, February 22, 1999.

37. *The Australian,* February 23, 1999.

38. *Detroit News,* April 7, 1999, *www.gocsi.com/prelea990301.htm.*

39. OTC, April 19, 1999.

40. *Information Week UK* via CMPWeb, April 20, 1999.

41. OTC press release, April 30, 1999.

42. *USA Today* Online, May 2, 1999.

43. Reuters, May 2, 1999.

44. *Los Angeles Times,* May 3, 1999.

45. *EDUPAGE, Los Angeles Times,* May 13, 1999.

46. Reuters, AP, May 21, 1999.

47. *Computer Reseller News Online,* May 25, 1999.

48. *Courier Mail* (Brisbane, Australia), *Sydney Morning Herald, Australian Financial Review,* June 16, 1999.

49. *Computer Economics,* June 18, 1999.

50. *E-Commerce Times* Online, June 21, 1999.

51. *Information Week,* July 12, 1999, *www.informationweek.com/shared/printArticle? article=infoweek/743/prsecur.htm&pub=iwk.*

52. *www.securityfocus.com/templates/forum_message.html?forum=2&head=32&id=32% 20%20,* August 11, 1999.

53. IDG News Service, September 1, 1999.

54. SANS, *Computerworld Online,* September 16, 1999.

55. *USA Today,* September 22, 1999.

56. Reuters, October 3, 1999.

57. OTC, November 17, 1999.

58. *Guardian Weekly,* November 29, 1999, p. 13.

59. *Corporate Insurance & Risk,* November 30, 1999.

60. *Newsbytes,* December 6, 1999.

61. *ACM TechNews, Newsbytes,* December 29, 1999.

62. See *www.digitalcentury.com/encyclo/update/crime.html.*

63. *Guardian Weekly,* January 29, 2000.

64. *EPIC Alert,* January 27, 2000.

65. Associated Press, February 18, 2000.

66. *NewsScan,* February 22, 2000.

67. *NewsScan,* February 2, 2000; *Washington Post, www.washingtonpost.com/wp-dyn/ business/A56622-2000Mar1.html.*

68. Reuters; CSI, *www.gocsi.com/prelea_000321.htm; NewsScan,* March 22, 2000; *Los Angeles Times.*

69. *NewsScan* (reprinted with permission); *Investor's Business Daily,* May 25, 2000.

70. AP/*Los Angeles Times,* May 25, 2000. *NewsScan, Los Angeles Times,* May 25, 2000.

71. *NewsScan, New York Times,* June 12, 2000, *www.partners.nytimes.com/library/tech/ 00/06/biztech/articles/12mark.html.*

72. *NewsScan,* June 15, 2000, *Wall Street Journal.*

73. *NewsScan,* June 15, 2000.

CHAPTER 5

TOWARD A NEW FRAMEWORK FOR INFORMATION SECURITY

Donn B. Parker

CONTENTS

5.1 PROPOSAL FOR A NEW INFORMATION SECURITY FRAMEWORK. Information security discussions historically have been clouded by the lack of a comprehensive, complete, and analytically sound framework for thinking about the issues. The persistence of the classic triad of "CIA" (confidentiality, integrity, availability) is inadequate to describe what security practitioners think about and implement when doing their jobs. We need a new information security framework to express, in practical language, the means for information owners to protect their information from any adversaries.

The current focus on computer systems security is attributable to the understandable tendency of computer technologists to protect what they know best—the computer and network systems rather than the application of those systems. With a technological hammer in hand, everything looks like a nail. The primary security challenge comes from people misusing or abusing information, and often—but not necessarily—using computers and networks. Yet the individuals who currently dominate the information security folk art are neither criminologists nor computer application analysts.

This chapter presents a comprehensive new information security framework that I believe resolves the problems of the existing models. The chapter demonstrates the need for six security elements—availability, utility, integrity, authenticity, confidentiality, and possession—to replace the CIA foundation in the new security framework. This new framework is used to list potential information losses. I also present the new models in another form, the *Threats, Assets, Vulnerabilities Model,* and include detailed descriptors for each topic in the model. At the end of the chapter, I present the *Clark-Wilson Integrity Model,* which is particularly important for business transaction systems. These models support the new security framework, demonstrating their contribution to advance information security from its current technological stage as a folk art into the basis for an engineering and business art in cyberspace.

The new security framework model incorporates six essential components:

1. *Foundation* elements or characteristics of information to be preserved are:
   - Availability
   - Utility
   - Integrity
   - Authenticity
   - Confidentiality
   - Possession

2. *Sources* of loss of these characteristics are:
   - Intentional acts of abusers and misusers
   - Accidental occurrences
   - Physical forces

3. *Losses* are:
   - Destruction
   - Interference with use
   - Use of false data
   - Modification or replacement
   - Misrepresentations or repudiation
   - Misuse or failure to use
   - Location
   - Disclosure
   - Observation
   - Coping
   - Taking
   - Endangerment

4. *Safeguards and practices* to protect information from the losses are:
   - Avoidance
   - Deterrence
   - Detection
   - Prevention
   - Mitigation
   - Transference
   - Investigation
   - Sanctions and rewards
   - Recovery

    ○ Correction

    ○ Education

5. *Selecting* safeguards and practices by:

    ○ Standards of due care

    ○ Diligence

    ○ Special needs

6. *Objectives* to be achieved by information security are:

    ○ Avoidance of negligence

    ○ Orderly and protected society

    ○ Meeting laws and regulations

    ○ Ethical conduct

    ○ Successful commerce

    ○ Privacy

This model is based on my goal of meeting owners' needs to preserve the desired *security elements* of their information from intentional and accidental *acts* of abusers and misusers (and from physical forces) that would cause *losses*. This is done by applying *safeguards and practices* that are selected by *standards of due care* and from special needs to achieve desired *objectives*.

5.1.1   Six Essential Foundation Elements.   At least six foundation elements in the proposed framework model are essential to information security. If any one of them is omitted, information security is deficient in protecting information owners. I use six scenarios of information losses, all derived from real cases, to demonstrate my contention. Then I show how each scenario violates one, and only one, element of information security. Thus, if we omit the element from information security, we also must remove the scenario from the concerns of information security. I think readers all will agree that these scenarios fall well within the range of the abuse and misuse that we need to protect against.

5.1.1.1   Loss Scenario 1—Availability.   A rejected contract programmer, intent on sabotage, removed the name of a data file from the file directories in a credit union's computer. Users of the computer and the data file no longer had the file available to them because the computer operating system recognizes the existence of information available for users only if it is named in the file directories. The credit union was shut down for two weeks while another programmer was brought in to find and correct the problem so that the file would be available. The perpetrator was eventually convicted of computer crime.

The other elements of information security—utility, integrity, authenticity, confidentiality, and possession—do not address this loss, and their state does not change in the scenario. The owner of the computer (the credit union) retained possession of the data file. Only the availability of the information was lost, but it is a loss that clearly should have been prevented by information security. Thus, the preservation of availability must be accepted as a purpose of information security.

It is true that good security practice might have prevented the disgruntled programmer from having use of the credit union application system, and his work could have been monitored more carefully. The credit union should not have depended on the technical capabilities and knowledge of only one person and should have employed several controls to preserve or restore the availability of data files in the computer, such as by maintaining a backup directory with the names of erased files and pointers to their physical location. The loss might have been prevented, or minimized, through good backup practices, good usage controls for computers and specific data files, use of more than one name to identify and find a file, and the availability of utility programs to search for files by content or to mirror file storage.

The severity of availability loss can vary considerably. A perpetrator may destroy copies of a data file in a manner that eliminates any chance of recovery. In other situations, the data file may be partially usable, with recovery possible for a moderate cost, or the user may have inconvenient or delayed use of the file for some period of time, followed by complete recovery.

5.1.1.2   *Loss Scenario 2—Utility.*

In this case, an employee routinely encrypted the only copy of valuable information stored in his organization's computer, then accidentally erased the encryption key. The usefulness of the information was lost and could be restored only through successful cryptanalysis.

Although this scenario can be described as a loss of availability or authenticity of the encryption key, the loss focuses on the usefulness of the information rather than on the key, since the only purpose of the key was to facilitate encryption. The information in this scenario is available, but in a form that is not useful. Its integrity, authenticity, and possession are unaffected, and its confidentiality is greatly improved.

To preserve utility of information in this case management should require mandatory backup copies of all critical information and control the use of powerful protective mechanisms such as cryptography. Management should require security walk-through tests during application development to limit unresponsive forms of information. It should minimize the adverse effects of security on information use and control the types of activities that enable unauthorized persons to reduce the usefulness of information.

The loss of utility can vary in severity. The worst-case scenario would be the total loss of usefulness of the information with no possibility of recovery. Less severe cases may range from a partially useful state with the potential for full restoration of usefulness at moderate cost.

5.1.1.3   *Loss Scenario 3—Integrity.*

In this scenario, a software distributor purchased a copy (on diskette) of a program for a computer game from an obscure publisher. The distributor made copies of the diskette and removed the name of the publisher from the diskette copies. Then, without informing the publisher or paying any royalties, the distributor sold the diskette copies in a foreign country. Unfortunately, the success of the program sales was not deterred by the lack of an identified publisher on the diskette or in the product promotional materials.

Because the diskette copies of the game did not identify the publisher who created the program, the copies lacked integrity. (*Integrity* means a state of completeness, wholeness, and soundness, or adhering to a code of moral values.) However, the copies did not lack authenticity, since they contained the genuine game program and only lacked the identity of the publisher, which was not necessary for the successful use of the product. Information utility was maintained, and confidentiality and availability were not at issue. Possession also was not at issue, since the distributor bought the original diskette. But copyright protection was violated as a consequence of the loss of integrity and unauthorized copying of the otherwise authentic program.

Several controls can be applied to prevent the loss of information integrity, including using and checking sequence numbers, checksums, and/or hash totals to ensure completeness and wholeness for a series of items. Other controls include performing manual and automatic text checks for required presence of records, subprograms, paragraphs, or titles, and testing to detect violations of specified controls.

The severity of information integrity loss also varies. Significant parts of the information can be missing or misordered (but still available), with no potential for recovery. Or missing or misordered information can be restored, with delay and at moderate cost. In the least severe cases, an owner can recover small amounts of misordered or mislocated information in a timely manner at low cost.

5.1.1.4 *Loss Scenario 4—Authenticity.*

In a slight variation of the preceding scenario, another software distributor obtained the program (on diskette) for a computer game from an obscure publisher. The distributor changed the name of the publisher on the diskette and in title screens to that of a well-known publisher, then made copies of the diskette. Without informing either publisher, the distributor then proceeded to distribute the diskette copies in a foreign country. In this case, the identity of a popular publisher on the diskettes and in the promotional materials significantly added to the success of the product sales.

Because the distributor misrepresented the publisher of the game, the program did not conform to reality: It was not an authentic game from the well-known publisher. Availability and utility are not at issue in this case. The game had integrity because it identified a publisher and was complete and sound. (Certainly the distributor lacked *personal* integrity because his acts did not conform to ethical practice, but that is not the subject of the scenario.) The actual publisher did not lose possession of the game, even though copies were deceptively represented as having come from a different publisher. And, although the distributor undoubtedly tried to keep his actions secret from both publishers, confidentiality of the content of the game was not at issue.

What if someone misrepresents your information by claiming that it is his? Violation of CIA does not include this act. A stockbroker in Florida cheated his investors in a Ponzi (pyramid sales) scheme. He stole $50 million by claiming that he used a super-secret computer program on his giant computer to make profits of 60 percent per day by arbitrage, a stock trading method in which the investor takes advantage of a small difference in prices of the same stock in different markets. He showed investors the mainframe computer at a Wall Street brokerage firm and falsely claimed that it and the information stored therein were his, thereby lending believability to his claims of successful trading.

This stockbroker's scheme was certainly a computer crime, but the CIA foundation does not address it as such because its definition of integrity does not include misrepresentation of information. Integrity means only that information is whole or complete; it does not address the validity of information. Obviously, confidentiality and availability do not cover misrepresentation either. The best way to extend CIA to include misrepresentation is to use the more general term *authenticity*. We can then assign the correct English meaning to the phrase "integrity of information": wholeness, completeness, and good condition. Dr. Peter Neumann at SRI International is correct when he says that information with integrity means that the information is what you expect it to be. This does not, however, necessarily mean that the information is valid. *Authenticity* is the word that means conformance to reality.

A number of controls can be applied to ensure authenticity of information. These include confirming transactions, names, deliveries, and addresses; validating products;

checking for out-of-range or incorrect information; and using digital signatures to authenticate documents.

The severity of authenticity loss can take several forms, including lack of conformance to reality with no recovery possible; moderately false or deceptive information with delayed recovery at moderate cost; or factually correct information with only annoying discrepancies. If the CIA foundation included authenticity, with misrepresentation of information as an associated threat, Kevin Mitnick (the notorious criminal hacker who used deceit as his principal tool for penetrating security barriers) probably would have faced a far more difficult challenge in perpetrating his crimes. Computer vendors might have understood the need to prove computer operating system updates genuine to avoid misrepresentation with fakes before their customers ingested them into their computers.

5.1.1.5   Loss Scenario 5—Confidentiality.
A thief deceptively obtained technical information from a bank's technical maintenance staff. He used a stolen key to open the maintenance door of an automated teller machine (ATM) and secretly inserted a radio transmitter that he purchased from a Radio Shack store. The radio received signals from the touch-screen display in the ATM that customers use to enter their personal identification numbers (PINs) and receive account balance information. The radio device broadcast the information to the thief's radio receiver in his nearby car, which recorded the PINs and account balances on tape in a modified videocassette recorder. The thief used the information to loot the customers' accounts from other ATMs. The police and the Federal Bureau of Investigation caught the thief after elaborate detective and surveillance efforts. He is now serving a 10-year sentence in federal prison.

The thief violated the secrecy of the customers' PINs and account balances, and he violated their privacy. Availability, utility, integrity, and authenticity were unaffected in this violation of confidentiality. The customers' and the bank's exclusive possession of the PINs and account balance information was lost, but not possession per se because they still held and owned the information. Therefore, this was primarily a case of lost confidentiality.

According to most security experts, confidentiality deals with disclosure, but confidentiality also can be lost by observation, whether that observation is voluntary or involuntary, and whether the information is disclosed or not disclosed. For example, if I leave sensitive information displayed on my unattended computer monitor screen, I have disclosed it and it may or may not lose its confidentiality. If I turn the monitor off, leaving a blank screen, I have not disclosed sensitive information, but if someone turns the monitor on and reads its contents without my permission, then I have lost confidentiality by observation. We must prevent both disclosure and observation in order to protect confidentiality.

Controls to maintain confidentiality include using cryptography, training employees to resist deceptive social engineering attacks intended to obtain their technical knowledge, and controlling the use of computers and computer devices. Good security also requires that the cost of resources for protection not exceed the value of what may be lost, especially with low incidence. For example, protecting against radio frequency emanations in ATMs (as in this scenario) is probably not advisable, considering the cost of shielding and the paucity of such high-tech attacks.

The severity of loss of confidentiality can vary. The worst-case scenario loss is when a party with the intent and ability to cause harm observes a victim's sensitive information. In this case, unrecoverable damage may result. But information also may be known to several moderately harmful parties, with a moderate loss effect, or be known to one harmless, unauthorized party with short-term recoverable effect.

5.1.1.6 Loss Scenario 6—Possession.

A gang of burglars aided by a disgruntled, recently fired operations supervisor broke into a computer center and stole tapes and disks containing the company's master files. They also raided the backup facility and stole all backup copies of the files. They then held the materials for ransom in an extortion attempt against the company. The burglary resulted in the company's losing possession of all copies of the master files as well as the media on which they were stored. The company was unable to continue business operations. The police eventually captured the extortionists with help from the company during the ransom payment, and they recovered the stolen materials. The burglars were convicted and served long prison sentences.

Loss of possession occurred in this case. The perpetrators delayed availability, but the company could have retrieved the files at any time by paying the ransom. Alternatively, the company could have re-created the master files from paper documents, but at great cost. Utility, integrity, and authenticity were not issues in this situation. Confidentiality was not violated because the burglars had no reason to read or disclose the files. Loss of ownership and permanent loss of possession would have been accomplished if the perpetrators had never returned the materials or if the company had stopped trying to recover them.

The security model must include protecting the possession of information so as to to prevent theft. Confidentiality, by definition, deals only with what people possess and know, not what they possess without knowing. Our increasing use of computers magnifies this difference; huge amounts of information are possessed for automated use and not necessarily held confidentially for only specified people to know. Computer object programs are perfect examples of information we do not know but possess by selling, buying, bartering, giving, receiving, and trading until we ultimately control, transport, and use them. We have incorrectly defined confidentiality if we include the protective efforts for possession.

We protect the possession of information by preventing people from unauthorized taking, from making copies, and from holding or controlling it—whether or not confidentiality is involved. The loss of possession of information also includes the loss of control of it and may allow the new possessor to violate its confidentiality at will. Thus, loss of confidentiality may accompany loss of possession. But we must treat confidentiality and possession separately to determine what actions criminals might take and what controls we need to apply to prevent their actions. Otherwise, we may overlook a particular threat or an effective control. The failure to anticipate a threat is one of the greatest dangers we face in security.

Controls that can protect the possession of information include using copyright laws, implementing physical and logical usage limitations, preserving and examining computer audit logs for evidence of stealing, inventorying tangible and intangible assets, using distinctive colors and labels on media containers, and assigning ownership to enforce accountability of organizational information assets.

The severity of loss of possession varies with the nature of the offense. In a worst-case scenario, a criminal may take information, as well as all copies of it, and there may be no means of recovery—either from the perpetrator or from other sources such as paper documentation. In a less harmful scenario, a criminal might take information for some period of time but leave some opportunity for recovery at a moderate cost. In the least harmful situation, an owner could possess more than one copy of information, leaving open the possibility of recovery from other sources (e.g., backup files) within a reasonable period of time.

5.1.1.7   Conclusions about the Foundation Elements.

We need to understand some important differences between integrity and authenticity. For one, integrity deals with the intrinsic condition of information, while authenticity deals with the extrinsic value or meaning relative to external sources. Integrity does not deal with the meaning of the information with respect to external sources, that is, whether the information is timely and not obsolete. Authenticity, in contrast, concerns the question of whether information is genuine and not out of date with respect to external sources. A user who enters false information into a computer possibly has violated authenticity, but as long as the information remains unchanged, it has integrity. An information security technologist who designs security into computer operating systems is concerned only with application information integrity because the designer cannot know if any user is entering false information. In this case, the security technologist's job is to ensure that both true and false information remain whole and complete. It is the information owner, with guidance from the information security advisor, who has the responsibility of ensuring that the information conforms to reality—in other words, that it has authenticity.

Some types of loss that information security must address require the use of all six elements of the framework model to determine the appropriate security to apply. Each of the six elements can be violated independently of the others, with one important exception: A violation of confidentiality always results in loss of exclusive possession, at the least. Loss of possession, however—even exclusive possession—does not necessarily result in loss of confidentiality.

Other than that exception, the six elements are unique and independent, and often require different security controls. Maintaining the availability of information does not necessarily maintain its utility; information may be available but useless for its intended purpose, and vice versa. Maintaining the integrity of information does not necessarily mean that the information is valid, only that it remains the same or, at least, whole and complete. Information can be invalid and, therefore, without authenticity, yet it may be present and identical to the original version and, thus, have integrity. Finally, who is allowed to view and know information and who possesses it are often two very different matters.

Unfortunately, the written information security policies of many organizations do not acknowledge the need to address many kinds of information loss. This is because their policies are limited to achieving CIA. To define information security completely, the policies must address all six elements presented. Moreover, to adequately eliminate (or at least reduce) security threats, all six elements need to be considered to ensure that nothing is overlooked in applying appropriate controls. These elements are also useful for identifying and anticipating the types of abusive actions that adversaries may take—before such actions are undertaken.

For simplification and ease of reference, we can pair the six elements into three double elements, which should be used to identify threats and select proper controls, and we can associate them with synonyms so as to facilitate recall and understanding:

availability and utility   → usability and usefulness

integrity and authenticity   → completeness and validity

confidentiality and possession → secrecy and control

Availability and utility fit together as the first double element. Controls common to these elements include secure location, appropriate form for secure use, and usability of backup copies. Integrity and authenticity also fit together; one is concerned with internal structure and the other with conformance to external facts or reality. Controls for both include double entry, reasonableness checks, use of sequence numbers and checksums or hash totals, and comparison testing. Control of change applies to both as well. Finally, confidentiality and possession go together because, as discussed, they are interrelated. Commonly applied controls for both include copyright protection, cryptography, digital signatures, escrow, and secure storage.

The order of the elements here is logical, since availability and utility are necessary for integrity and authenticity to have value, and these first four elements are necessary for confidentiality and possession to have material meaning.

5.1.1.8   *What the Dictionaries Say about the Words We Use.* The following definitions of security and the elements are relevant abstractions from *Webster's Third New International Dictionary* and *Webster's Collegiate Dictionary,* 10th edition.

Security—Freedom from danger, fear, anxiety, care, uncertainty, doubt; basis for confidence; measures taken to ensure against surprise attack, espionage, observation, sabotage; resistance of a cryptogram to cryptanalysis usually measured by the time and effort needed to solve it.

Availability—Present or ready for immediate use.

Utility—Useful, fitness for some purpose.

Integrity—Unimpaired or unmarred condition; soundness; entire correspondence with an original condition; adherence to a code of moral, artistic or other values; the quality or state of being complete or undivided; material wholeness.

Authenticity—Quality of being authoritative, valid, true, real, genuine, worthy of acceptance or belief by reason of conformity to fact and reality.

Confidentiality—Quality or state of being private or secret; known only to a limited few, containing information whose unauthorized disclosure could be prejudicial to the national interest.

Possession—Act or condition of having or taking into one's control or holding at one's disposal; actual physical control of property by one who holds for himself, as distinguished from custody; something owned or controlled.

We lose credibility and confuse information owners if we do not use words precisely and consistently. When defined correctly, the six words are independent (with the exception that information possession is always violated when confidentiality is violated). They are also consistent, comprehensive, and complete. In other words, the six elements themselves possess integrity and authenticity, and therefore they have great utility. This does not mean that we will not find new elements or replace some of them as our insights develop and technology advances. (I first presented this demonstration of the need for the six elements in 1991 at the fourteenth U.S. National Computer Security Conference in Baltimore.)

My definitions of the six elements are considerably shorter and simpler than the dictionary definitions, but appropriate for information security.

Availability—Usability of information for a purpose.

Utility—Usefulness of information for a purpose.

Integrity—Completeness, wholeness, and readability of information and quality being unchanged from a previous state.

Authenticity—Validity, conformance, and genuineness of information.

Confidentiality—Limited observation and disclosure of knowledge.

Possession—Holding, controlling, and having the ability to use information.

5.1.2   Comprehensive List of Information Losses.   The threats that cause losses come from people who engage in unauthorized and harmful acts against information, such as embezzlers, fraudsters, thieves, saboteurs, and hackers. They engage in harmful using, taking, misrepresenting, observing, and every other conceivable form of human misbehavior. Natural physical forces such as air and earth movements, heat and cold, electromagnetic energy, living organisms, gravity and projectiles, and water and gases also are threats to information, as are inadvertent human errors.

Extensive lists of losses often include fraud, theft, sabotage, and espionage along with disclosure, usage, repudiation, and copying. The first four losses in this list are criminal justice terms at a different level of abstraction from the last four and require an understanding of criminal law, which many information owners and security specialists lack. For example, fraud includes theft only if it is performed using deception, and larceny includes burglary and theft from a victim's premises. What constitutes "premises" in an electronic network environment?

Many important types of information loss, such as false data entry, failure to perform, replacement, deception, misrepresentation, prolongation of use, delay of use, and even the obvious taking of information, are frequently omitted from lists of losses. Each of these losses may require different prevention and detection controls, a fact that is easy to overlook if our list of potential losses is incomplete—even though the losses we typically omit are among the most common reported in actual loss experience. The people who cause unusual losses often are aware that information owners have not provided adequate security. It is, therefore, essential to include all types of potential losses in our lists, especially when unique safeguards are applicable. Otherwise, we are in danger of being negligent, and those to whom we are accountable will view information security as incomplete or poorly conceived and implemented when a loss does occur.

The "Complete List of Potential Information Losses" (Section 5.1.2.1) presents a comprehensive, nonlegalistic list of potential losses to information that I compiled from my 30 years in research about computer crime and security. I have simplified it to a single level of abstraction to facilitate understanding by information owners and to enable them to select effective controls. The list makes no distinction among the causes of the losses; as such, it applies equally well to accidental and intentional acts. Cause is largely irrelevant at this level of security analysis, as is the underlying intent or lack thereof. (Identifying cause is important at another level of security analysis. We need to determine the sources and motivation of threats in order to identify appropriate avoidance, deterrence, and recovery controls.) In addition, the list makes no distinction between electronic and physical causes of loss, or among spoken, printed, or electronically recorded information.

The loss pairs (e.g., availability and utility, etc.) correspond to the six elements of information security outlined previously. Some types of loss in one element grouping may have a related effect in another grouping as well. For example, if no other copies of information exist, destroying the information (under *availability*) also may cause loss of possession, and taking (under *possession*) may cause loss of availability. Yet loss of possession and loss of availability are quite different, and may require different controls. I have placed losses in the most obvious categories, the places where a loss prevention analyst is likely to look first.

5.1.2.1   Complete List of Potential Information Losses

- *Availability and Utility Losses*
  - Destruction, damage, or contamination
  - Denial, prolongation, acceleration, or delay in use or acquisition
  - Movement or misplacement
  - Conversion or obscuration
- *Integrity and Authenticity Losses*
  - Insertion, use, or production of false or unacceptable data
  - Modification, replacement, removal, appending, aggregating, separating, or reordering
  - Misrepresentation
  - Repudiation (rejecting as untrue)
  - Misuse or failure to use as required
- *Confidentiality and Possession Losses*
  - Locating
  - Disclosing
  - Observing, monitoring, and acquiring
  - Copying
  - Taking or controlling
  - Claiming ownership or custodianship
  - Inferring
  - Exposing to all of the other losses
  - Endangering by exposing to any of the other losses
  - Failure to engage in or to allow any of the other losses to occur when instructed to do so

Users may be unfamiliar with some of the words in the lists of losses, at least in the context of security. For example "repudiation" is a word that we seldom hear or use outside of the legal or security context. According to dictionaries, it means to refuse to accept acts or information as true, just, or of rightful authority or obligation. Information security technologists became interested in repudiation when the Massachusetts Institute of Technology (MIT) developed a secure network operating system for its internal use. The system was named *Kerberos,* taking the name of the three-headed dog that guarded the underworld in Greek mythology. Kerberos provides a means of forming secure links and paths between users and the computers serving them. Unfortunately, however, in early versions it allowed users to falsely deny using the links. This did not present any particular problems in the academic environment, but it did make Kerberos inadequate for business, even though its other security aspects were attractive. As the use of Kerberos spread into business, repudiation became an issue, and nonrepudiation controls became important.

Repudiation is an important issue in electronic data interchange (EDI) used by many corporations to automate their purchasing functions and Internet commerce, which require digital signatures, time stamps, and other authentication controls. I could, for example, falsely claim that I never ordered merchandise and that the order form or electronically transmitted ordering information that the merchant possesses is false. Repudiation is also a growing problem because of the difficulty of proving authorship or the source of electronic missives. And the inverse of repudiation—claiming that an act that did not happen actually did happen, or claiming that false information is true—is also important to security, although it is often overlooked. Repudiation and its inverse are both types of misrepresentation, but I include both "repudiation" and "misrepresentation" on the list because they often require different types of controls.

Other words in the list of losses may seem somewhat obscure. For example, we seldom think of prolonging or delaying use as a loss of availability or a denial of use, yet they are losses that are often inflicted by computer virus attacks.

I use the word "locate" in this list rather than "access" because access can be confusing with regard to information security. Although it is commonly used in computer terminology, its use frequently causes confusion, as it did in the trial of Robert J. Morris Jr. for releasing the Internet worm of November 2, 1988, and in computer crime laws. For example, access may mean just knocking on a door or opening the door, but not going in. How far "into" a computer must you go to "access" it? A perpetrator can cause a loss simply by locating information, because the owner may not want to divulge possession of such information. In this case, no access is involved. For these reasons, I prefer to use the terms "entry," "intrusion," and "usage"—as well as "locate"—to refer to a computer as the object of the action. I have a similar problem with the use of the word "disclosure." Disclose is a verb that means to divulge, reveal, make known, or report knowledge to others. We can disclose knowledge by:

- Broadcasting
- Speaking
- Displaying
- Showing
- Leaving it in the presence and view of another person
- Leaving it in possible view where another person is likely to be
- Handing or sending it to another person

Disclosure is what an owner or potential victim might do inadvertently or intentionally, not what a perpetrator does, unless it is the second act after stealing, such as selling stolen intellectual property to another person. Disclosure can be an abuse if a person authorized to know information discloses it to an unauthorized person, or if an unauthorized person discloses knowledge to another person without permission. In any case, confidentiality is lost or is potentially lost, and the person disclosing the information may be accused of negligence, violation of privacy, conspiracy, or espionage.

Loss of confidentiality also can occur by observation, whether the victim or owner disclosed knowledge, resisted disclosure, or did nothing either to protect or to disclose it. Observing is an abuse of listening, spying by eavesdropping, shoulder surfing (looking over another person's shoulder or overhearing), looking at or listening to a stolen copy of information, or even by tactile feeling, as in the case of reading Braille. We should think about loss of confidentiality as a loss caused by inadvertent disclosure by the victim and observation by the perpetrator. Disclosure and observation of information that is not knowledge converts it into knowledge if cognition takes place. Disclosure always results in loss of confidentiality by putting information into a state where there is no longer any secrecy, but observation results in loss of confidentiality only if cognition takes place.

Loss of possession of information (including knowledge) is the loss from the unintended or regretful giving or taking of information. At a higher level of crime description, we call it larceny (theft or burglary) or some kind of fraud. Possession seems to be most closely associated with confidentiality. The two are placed together in the list because they share the common losses of taking and copying (loss of exclusive possession). I could have used "ownership" of information, since it is a synonym for possession, but "ownership" is not as broad, because someone may rightly or wrongly possess information that is rightfully owned by another. The concepts of owner or possessor of information, along with user, provider, or custodian of information, are important distinctions in security for assigning asset accountability. This provides another reason for including possession in the list.

The category *endangerment* is quite different from, but applies to, the other losses. It means that a person has been remiss (and possibly negligent) by not applying sufficient protection to information, such as leaving sensitive or valuable documents in an unlocked office or open trash bin. Leaving a computer unnecessarily connected to the Internet is another example. Endangerment of information may lead to charges of negligence or criminal negligence and civil liability suits that may be more costly than direct loss incidents. My baseline security methodology invokes a standard of due care to deal with this exposure.

The last loss in the list—failure to engage in or allow to occur any of the other losses when instructed to do so—may seem odd at first glance. it means that an information owner may require an act resulting in any of the losses to be carried out. Or the owner may wish that a loss be allowed to occur, or information be put into danger of loss. There are occasions when information should be put in harm's way for testing purposes or to accomplish a greater good. For example, computer programmers and auditors often create information files that are purposely invalid for use as input to a computer to make sure that the controls to detect or mitigate a loss are working correctly. A programmer bent on crime might remove an invalidity in a test input file to avoid testing a control that he or she has neutralized or that he or she has avoided implementing for nefarious purposes. The list would surely be incomplete without this type of loss, yet I have never seen it included or discussed in any other information security source.

I describe the losses in the list at the appropriate level for deriving and identifying appropriate security controls. At the next lower level of abstraction (e.g., read, write, and execute), the losses would not be so obvious and would not necessarily suggest important controls. At the level that I choose, there is no attempt to differentiate losses that make no change to information from those that do, since these differences are not important for identifying directly applicable controls or for performing threat analyses. For example, a loss from modification changes the information, while a loss from observation does not, but encryption is likely to be employed as a powerful primary control against both losses.

5.1.2.2   *Examples of Loss and Suggested Controls.*   The following examples illustrate the relationships between losses and controls in threat analysis. Sets of loss types are followed by examples of the losses and applicable controls.

5.1.2.2.1   Destroy, Damage, or Contaminate.   Perpetrators or harmful forces can damage, destroy, or contaminate information by electronically erasing it, writing other data over it, applying high-energy radio waves to damage delicate electronic circuits, or physically damaging the media (e.g., paper or disk) containing it.

Controls include disaster prevention safeguards such as locked facilities, safe storage of backup copies, and write-usage authorization requirements.

5.1.2.2.2   Deny, Prolong, or Delay Use or Acquisition.   Perpetrators can make information unavailable by hiding it or denying its use through encryption and not revealing the means to restore it, or by keeping critical processing units busy with other work, such as in a denial-of-service attack. Such actions would not necessarily destroy the information. Similarly, a perpetrator may prolong information use by making program changes that slow the processing in a computer or by slowing the display of the information on a screen. Such actions might cause unacceptable timing for effective use of the information. Information acquisition may be delayed by requiring too many passwords to retrieve it or by slowing retrieval. These actions can make the information obsolete by the time it becomes available.

Controls include making multiple copies available from different sources, preventing overload of processing by selective allowance of input, or preventing the activation of harmful mechanisms such as computer viruses by using antiviral utilities.

5.1.2.2.3   Enter, Use, or Produce False Data.   Data diddling, my term for false data entry and use, is a common form of computer crime, accounting for much of the financial and inventory fraud. Losses may be either intentional, such as those resulting from the use of Trojan horses (including computer viruses), or unintentional, such as those from input errors.

Most internal controls such as range checks, audit trails, separation of duties, duplicate data entry detection, program proving, and hash totals for data items protect against these threats.

5.1.2.2.4   Modify, Replace, or Reorder.   These losses result from actions that are often intelligent changes rather than damage or destruction. *Reordering,* which is actually a form of modification, is included separately because it may require specific controls that could otherwise be overlooked. Similarly, *replacement* is included because users might not otherwise include the idea of replacing an entire data file when considering modification. Any of these actions can produce a loss inherent in the threats of entering and modifying information, but including all of them covers modifying data both before entry and after entry, since each requires different controls.

Cryptography, digital signatures, usage authorization, and message sequencing are examples of controls to protect against these losses, as are detection controls to identify anomalies.

5.1.2.2.5   Misrepresent.   The claim that information is something different from what it really is or has a different meaning from what was intended arises in counterfeiting, forgery, fraud, impersonation (of authorized users), and many other deceptive activities. Hackers use misrepresentation in social engineering to deceive people into revealing information needed to attack systems. Misrepresenting old data as new information is another threat of this type.

Controls include user and document authentication methods such as passwords, digital signatures, and data validity tests. Making trusted people more resistant to deception by reminders and training is another control.

5.1.2.2.6   Repudiate.   This type of loss, in which perpetrators generally deny having made transactions, occurs in electronic data interchange (EDI) and Internet commerce. Oliver North's denials of the content of his e-mail messages is a notable example of repudiation, but as I mentioned earlier, the inverse of repudiation also represents a potential loss.

Repudiation can be controlled most effectively through the use of digital signatures and public key cryptography. Trusted third parties, such as certificate authorities with secure computer services, provide the independence of notary publics to resist denial of truthful information as long as they can be held liable for their failures.

5.1.2.2.7   Misuse or Fail to Use as Required.   Misuse of information is clearly a part of many information losses. Misuse by failure to perform duties such as updating files or backing up information is not so obvious and needs explicit identification. Implicit misuse by conforming exactly to inadequate or incorrect instructions is a sure way to sabotage systems.

Information usage control and internal application controls that constrain the modification or use of trusted software help to avoid these problems. Keeping secure logs of routine activities can help catch operational vulnerabilities.

5.1.2.2.8   Locate.   Unauthorized use of someone's computer or data network to locate and identify information is a crime under most computer crime statutes—even if there is no overt intention to cause harm. Such usage is a violation of privacy, and trespass to engage in such usage is a crime under other laws.

Log-on and usage controls are a major feature in many operating systems, such as Microsoft Windows NT and some versions of Unix as well as in add-on utilities such as *RACF* and *ACF2* for large IBM computers and *Watchdog* and *DACS* security products for PCs.

5.1.2.2.9   Disclose.   Preventing information from being revealed to people not authorized to know it is the purpose of business, personal, and government secrecy. Disclosure may be verbal, by mail, or by transferring messages of files electronically or on disks or tape. Disclosure can result in loss of privacy and trade secrets.

5.1.2.2.10   Observe or Monitor.   Observation, which requires action on the part of a perpetrator, is the inverse of disclosure, which results from actions of a possessor. Workstation display screens, communications lines, and monitoring devices such as recorders and audit logs are common targets of observation and monitoring. Observation of output from printers is another possible source, as is shoulder surfing—the technique of watching screens of other computer users.

Physical entry protection for input and output devices represents the major control to prevent this type of loss. Preventing wiretapping and eavesdropping is also important.

5.1.2.2.11   Copy.   Copy machines and the software *copy* command are the major sources of unauthorized copying. Copying is used to violate exclusive possession and privacy. Copying can destroy authenticity, as when used to counterfeit money or other business instruments.

Location and use controls are effective against copying, as are unique markings such as those used on U.S. currency and watermarks on paper.

5.1.2.2.12   Take.   Transferring data files in computers or networks constitutes taking. So does taking small computers and diskettes or documents for the value of the information stored in them. Perpetrators can easily take copies of information without depriving the owner of possession or confidentiality.

A wide range of physical and logical location controls applies to these losses; most are based on common sense and a reasonable level of due care.

5.1.2.2.13   Endanger.   Putting information into locations or conditions in which others may cause loss in any of the previously described ways clearly endangers the information, and the perpetrator may be accused of negligence, at the least.

Physical and logical means of preventing information from being placed in danger are important. Training people to be careful, and holding them accountable for protecting information, may be the most effective means of preventing endangerment.

5.1.2.3   Physical Information and Systems Losses.   Information also can suffer from physical losses such as those caused by floods, earthquakes, radiation, and fires. Although these losses may not directly affect the information itself (e.g., knowledge of operating procedures held in the minds of operators), they can damage or destroy the media and the environment that contain representations of the information. Water, for example, can destroy printed pages and damage magnetic disks; physical shaking or radio frequency radiation can short-out electronic circuits, and fires can destroy all types of media. Overall, physical loss may occur in seven natural ways by application of:

1. Extreme temperature
2. Gases
3. Liquids
4. Living organisms
5. Projectiles
6. Movements
7. Energy anomalies

Each way, of course, comes from specific sources of loss (e.g., smoke or water). And the various ways can be broken down further to identify the underlying cause of the source of loss. For example, the liquid that destroys information may be water flowing from a plumbing break above the computer workstation, caused in turn by freezing weather. The next list presents examples of each of the seven major sources of physical loss.

1. *Extreme temperature.* Heat or cold. Examples: sunlight, fire, freezing, hot weather, and the breakdown of air-conditioning equipment.
2. *Gases.* War gases, commercial vapors, humid or dry air, suspended particles. Examples: Sarin nerve gas, PCPs from exploding transformers, release of Freon from air-conditioners, smoke and smog, cleaning fluid, and fuel vapors.
3. *Liquids.* Water, chemicals. Examples: floods, plumbing failures, precipitation, fuel leaks, spilled drinks, acid and base chemicals used for cleaning, computer printer fluids.
4. *Living organisms.* Viruses, bacteria, fungi, plants, animals, and human beings. Examples: biological warfare, sickness of key workers, molds, contamination

from skin oils and hair, contamination and electrical shorting from defecation and release of body fluids, consumption of information media such as paper or of cable insulation, shorting of microcircuits from cobwebs.

5. *Projectiles.* Tangible objects in motion, powered objects. Examples: meteorites, falling objects, cars and trucks, airplanes, bullets and rockets, explosions, explosions, and windborne objects.

6. *Movements.* Collapse, shaking, vibration, liquefaction, flows, waves, separation, slides. Example: dropping or shaking fragile equipment, earthquakes, earth slides, lava flows, sea waves, adhesive failures.

7. *Energy anomalies.* Electric surge or failure, magnetism, static electricity, aging circuitry; radiation: sound, light, radio, microwave, electromagnetic, atomic. Examples: electric utility failures, proximity of magnets and electromagnets, carpet static, electromagnetic pulses (EMP) from nuclear explosions, lasers, loudspeakers, high-energy radio frequency (HERF) guns, radar systems, cosmic radiation, explosions.

Although falling meteorites, for example, clearly pose little danger to computers, it is nonetheless important to include all such unlikely events in a thorough analysis of potential threats. In general, every possible loss should be included in a threat analysis. Then consider it carefully; if it is too unlikely, document the consideration and discard the item. It is better to have thought of a source of loss and to discard it than to have overlooked an important one. Invariably, when one presents a threat analysis to others, someone will try to surprise the developer with another source of loss that has been overlooked.

Insensitive practitioners have ingrained inadequate loss lists in the body of knowledge from the very inception of information security. Proposing a major change at this late date is a bold action that may take significant time to accomplish. However, we must not perpetuate our past inadequacies by using the currently accepted destruction, disclosure, use, and modification (DDUM) as a complete list of losses. We must not underrate or simplify the complexity of our subject at the expense of misleading information owners. Our adversaries are always looking for weaknesses in information security, but our strength lies in anticipating sources of threats and having plans in place to prevent the losses that they may cause.

It is impossible to collect a truly complete list of the causes of information losses that can be caused by the intentional or accidental acts of people. We really have no idea what people may do—now or in the future. We base our lists on experience, but until we can conceive of a loss or until a threat actually surfaces or occurs, we cannot include it on the list. And not knowing the threat means that we cannot devise a plan to protect against it. This is one of the reasons that information security is still a folk art rather than a science.

5.1.2.4 Challenge of Complete Lists.

I believe that my lists of physical sources of loss and information losses are complete, but I am always interested in expanding them to include new sources of loss that I may have overlooked.

While I was lecturing in Australia, for example, a delegate suggested that I had omitted an important category. His computer center had experienced an invasion of field mice with a taste for electrical insulation. The intruders proceeded to chew through the computer cables, ruining them. Consequently, I had to add rodents to my list of sources. I then heard about an incident in San Francisco in which the entire evening shift of computer operations workers ate together in the company cafeteria to celebrate a birthday. Then they all contracted food poisoning, leaving their company without sufficient operations staff for two weeks. I combined the results of these two events into a category "Living Organisms."

5.1.3   Functions of Information Security.   The model for information security that I have proposed includes 11 security functions instead of the three (prevention, detection, and recovery) included in previous models. These functions describe the activities that information security practitioners and information owners engage in to protect information as well as the objectives of the security controls that they use. Every control serves one or more of these functions.

Although some security specialists add other functions to the list, such as quality assurance and reliability, I consider these to be outside the scope of information security; there are other specialized fields that deal with them. Reliability is difficult to relate to security except to say that perpetrators can destroy the reliability of information and systems, which is a violation of security. Thus, security must preserve a state of reliability but need not attempt to improve it. Security must protect the auditability of information and systems while, at the same time, security itself must be reliable and auditable. My colleague Peter Neumann is right about the overlap of security and reliability, but I believe that my security definitions include destruction of the reliability and auditability of information at a different level of abstraction. For example, reliability is reduced when the authenticity of information is put into question by changing it from a correct representation of fact.

Similarly, I do not include such functions as auditing, authentication of users, and verification in my lists, since I consider these to be control objectives to achieve the 11 functions of information security. Auditing as performed by licensed auditors, for example, achieves the detection of deficiencies and anomalies in systems.

There is a definite logic to the order in which I present the 11 functions in my list. A methodical information security practitioner is likely to apply the functions in this order when resolving a security vulnerability.

1. *Avoidance:* The practitioner must determine if a security problem can be avoided altogether.

2. *Deterrence:* If the problem cannot be avoided, the practitioner needs to try to deter potential abusers or forces from misbehaving.

3. *Detection:* If the threat cannot be avoided or deterred, the practitioner attempts to detect its activation.

4. *Prevention:* If detection is not assured, then the practitioner tries to prevent the attack from occurring.

5. *Mitigation:* If prevention fails and an attack occurs, then the practitioner needs to stop it or minimize its harmful effects through mitigation.

6. *Transference:* The practitioner needs to determine if another individual or department might be more effective at resolving the situation resulting from the attack, or if another party (i.e., an insurer) might be held accountable for the cost of the loss.

7. *Investigation:* After a loss occurs, the practitioner needs to search for the individual(s) or force(s) that caused or contributed to the incident as well as for any parties that played a role in it—positively or negatively.

8. *Sanctions and Rewards:* When identified, all parties should be sanctioned or rewarded as appropriate.

9. *Recovery:* After an incident is concluded, the victim needs to recover or assist with recovery.

10. *Correction:* The stakeholders should take corrective actions to prevent the same type of incident from occurring again.

11. *Education:* The stakeholders must learn from the experience in order to advance their knowledge of information security and teach it to others.

5.1.4   Selecting Safeguards Using a Standard of Due Care.   Information security practitioners usually refer to the process of selecting safeguards as risk assessment, risk analysis, or risk management. Selecting safeguards based on risk calculations can be a fruitless and expensive process. While many security experts and associations advocate using risk assessment methods, many organizations ultimately find that using a standard of due care (or diligence) is far superior and more practical. Often one sad experience of using risk assessment is sufficient to convince information security departments and corporate management of their limitations.

The standard of due care approach is simple and obvious; it is the default process that I recommend and that is commonly used today instead of more elaborate "scientific" approaches. The standard of due care approach is recognized and accepted by many legal documents and organizations and is documented in numerous business guides. The 1996 U.S. federal statute on protecting trade secrets (18 USC § 1831), for example, states in (3)(a) that the owner of information must take "reasonable measures to keep such information secret" for it to be defined as a trade secret (see Chapter 45).

5.1.5   Threats, Assets, and Vulnerabilities Model.   Pulling all of the aspects of losses together in one place is a useful way to analyze the threats and vulnerabilities in real crimes and to create effective scenarios to test real information systems and organizations. The model illustrated in Exhibit 5.1 is designed to help readers do this. Users can outline a scenario or analyze a real case by circling and connecting the appropriate descriptors in each column of the model.

In this version of the model, the Controls column lists only the subject headings of control types; a completed model would contain hundreds of controls. If the model is being used to conduct a review, I suggest that the Vulnerabilities section of the model be converted to Recommended Controls. This model is probably incomplete; Dr. Fred Cohen at Sandia Laboratory in Livermore, California (*www.sandia.gov*), is currently attempting to create a more comprehensive version.

5.2   CONCLUSION.   The security foundation and the framework models proposed in this chapter represent an attempt to overcome the dominant technologist view of information security by focusing more broadly on all aspects of security, including the information that we are attempting to protect, the potential sources of loss, the types of loss, the controls that we can apply to avoid loss, the methods for selecting those controls, and our overall objectives in protecting information. This broad focus should have two beneficial effects: advancing information security from a narrow folk art to a broad-based discipline and—most important—helping to reduce many of the losses associated with information—wherever it exists.

Exhibit 5.1 Threats, Assets, and Vulnerabilities Model

Threats				Assets	Vulnerabilities (Missing and deficient controls)		
Offenders Have/Acquire	Abuse/Misuse	Methods	Losses	Assets Lost	Control Objectives	Controls (types)	Control Guides
Skills learning technology people **Knowledge** direct indirect **Resources** computer services transport financial **Authority** employment contract ownership possession custodian right other	Errors Omissions Negligence Recklessness Delinquency Civil Disputes Conspiracy Nature Disruption Destruction Theft Privacy Trespass Burglary Larceny Forgery Counterfeiting Smuggling Fraud Scam Embezzlement Bribery	**External** Heat, cold Gases, air water chemical bacteria viruses people animals insects collision collapse shear shake vibrate liquefy flows waves separate slides electric magnets aging radiate	**Availability and Utility** destroy damage contaminate deny prolong accelerate delay move misplace convert obscure **Integrity and Authenticity** insert use produce modify replace remove append reorder misrepresent	**Information** spoken printed magnetic electronic optical radio biological **Computer** **Commlines** **Networks** **Facilities** **Buildings** **Transport** **People**	Avoidance Deterrence Prevention Detection Mitigation Sanction Transfer Investigate Recovery Correction	Organization Physical Development Automation Operation Voice Network Access Training Motivation Management Applications Printing Audit Disaster Recovery	Cost effective Due care Complete Consistent Performance Sustain Automatic Tolerated Consequences Override Failsafe Default Instrument Auditable Non-repudiate Secrecy Universal Independent Unpredictable Tamperproof Compartment Depth Isolate Least

(continued)

Exhibit 5.1 Threats, Assets, and Vulnerabilities Model (continued)

Threats				Assets	Vulnerabilities (Missing and deficient controls)		
Offenders Have/Acquire	Abuse/Misuse	Methods	Losses	Assets Lost	Control Objectives	Controls (types)	Control Guides
Motives No intent negligence errors and omissions **Intentional** problem solving gain higher ethic **Extreme** **Advocacy** social political religious	Extortion Racketeering Infringement Plagiarism Piracy Espionage Antitrust Contract Securities Employment Kickbacks Laundering Libel Drugs Pornography Harassment Assault Sex attack Kidnapping Murder Suicide	sound light radio atomic **Masquerade** impersonate spoof **Programmed** Trojan Virus Bomb Bypass Trapdoor **Authority** Violation **Active** Deny service False data entry **Passive** Browse Observe **Failure** Omit duty **Indirect** Crime use	repudiate fail to use **Confidential and Possession** locate disclose observe monitor acquire copy take control own infer **Expose** to loss **Endanger** Fail instruction				Accountability Trust Multifunction Deception Positional Transparent

Source: Donn B. Parker, *Fighting Computer Crime* (New York: John Wiley & Sons, 1998).

PART TWO

THREATS AND VULNERABILITIES

CHAPTER 6

THE PSYCHOLOGY OF COMPUTER CRIMINALS

Quinn Campbell and David M. Kennedy

CONTENTS

6.1 INTRODUCTION. We are currently experiencing a technological revolution where many individuals, businesses, and organizations are becoming increasingly reliant on computer networks and the Internet for daily communication. NUA, an Internet consulting firm, indicates that there were an estimated 407 million individuals online in November 2000, with North America alone comprising 167 million users.[1] As societies embrace these new forms of technology, numerous unforeseen consequences will have far-reaching effects on all aspects of our culture. Musicians, legislators, law enforcement, social scientists, and numerous other social groups are struggling to adapt to the cultural changes caused by this technological revolution. In more technologically advanced nations, computer security and personal privacy recently have become key points of concern due to the widespread reliance on technology and the amount of information stored and transferred via computer networks.

6.1.1 Computer Crime Cost and Prevalence. Pricewaterhouse Cooper's Global Security Survey[2] indicated that security breaches had cost global corporations $1.5 trillion in losses in 2000. According to the fifth annual Computer Crime and Security Survey by the Computer Security Institute (CSI), 90 percent of survey respondents detected cyberattacks in 2000 with 273 organizations reporting an estimated $260 million in financial losses. In their 1998 survey, only 64 percent of survey respondents reported breaches in computer security, with 520 organizations reporting $137 million in financial loss due to computer crime.

Several Fortune 100 corporations also have reported financial losses totaling more than $10 million as a result of a single computerized attack.[3] Computer crimes increased 45 percent in the United Kingdom over a three-year time span. U.K. organizations reported experiencing over 500 cyberattacks and a combined loss of £3.9 million.[4] In 1997 the U.S. Department of Defense's (DoD) computer networks were attacked over 250,000 times, with a 60 percent success rate. Only 4 percent of the attacks were actually detected by network administrators, and of those only 27 percent were reported.[5] In an independent investigation by Exopa Terra, an electronic journal dealing with technology and society, in 1997 computer crime cost society $1.2 trillion worldwide.[6] According to Attrition, a Web site that mirrors Web server attacks, there have been over 6,000 confirmed Web site defacements since August 1999.[7] The Computer Emergency Response Team (CERT) reported in its annual review that in 1999 it handled 8,268 computer security incidents and received 419 vulnerability reports which affected over 4 million Internet hosts.[8]

The 2000 Information Security Industry Survey of 1,897 high-tech and info-security professionals, conducted by *Information Security* magazine, revealed that electronic crimes from both external forces and dangerous insiders continue to increase.[9] Some corporations are reporting spending in excess of $1 million per year on information security and increase of 188 percent over two years. The survey also indicated that 80 percent of corporations have experienced destructive virus attacks in the previous year. Of the corporations surveyed, e-commerce sites reported experiencing the most attacks.[9]

Computer crime is an obvious financial and societal problem that shows no signs of slowing. Studies suggest that the number of electronic intrusions and the resultant financial losses from these attacks will continue to increase. Douglas Campbell, president of the Syneca Research Group Inc., states that "the dominant threat to the United States is not thermonuclear war, but the information war."[10]

One solution that has been offered in an effort to slow down this disturbing trend is to examine the underlying motivations of computer criminals from a psychological perspective. Researchers suggest that understanding the psychological motivations behind cybercriminals would aid in both cybercrime prevention and protection.[11–12] According to researchers, a psychological profile of computer criminals would aid in creating preventive initiatives as well as more effective countermeasures in the fight against computer crime.[11–12] Since computer crime is not solely a technological issue but one involving human agents, social psychological theories regarding anonymity, aggression, social learning, and disinhibition may enable us to better understand the behaviors and motivations of the computer criminal.[13] Information security consultant Donn Parker suggests that the creation of an effective malicious hacker profile still remains an elusive goal in the information security field.[11] Therefore, this chapter surveys past and current literature surrounding the psychological motivations of computer criminals. Theories from both social and personality perspectives are presented to attempt to explain some possible motivations behind computer crime. Finally, the chapter reviews classification theories of computer criminals and details the difficulty researchers have had when trying to develop a single all-encompassing theory to account for the behaviors of all computer criminals.

6.1.2   Recent Examples of Computer Crime.   In April 2001, Chinese crackers began a Web page defacement campaign targeting Web sites in the United States.[14] The Chinese crackers claimed to be attacking U.S. Web sites in retaliation for the collision between a Chinese fighter jet and an North American spy plane that resulted in the death of Chinese pilot Wang Wei.[14] In retaliation for the Web defacements, U.S. cracker groups began defacing Chinese Web sites, resulting in a small-scale, but much-hyped, international cyber skirmish.[15]

In March 2001, the National Infrastructure Protection Center (NIPC) issued an advisory indicating that several e-commerce and e-banking sites were being extorted by Eastern European computer criminals.[16] According to the NIPC, the crackers were exploiting unpatched Microsoft NT operating systems and then downloading customer and credit card databases from the victims.[16] The advisory further stated that an estimated 1 million customers' credit cards from more than 40 companies had been compromised as a result of the attacks. The crackers also contacted the compromised companies, threatening to post the stolen data and details of the hack on the Internet unless they were paid off.[16]

In September 2000, Western Union's Internet Web site was compromised by a computer criminal. The intruder cracked into Western Union's customer database and downloaded the private information and credit card numbers of 15,700 patrons of the companies Internet service.[17] Affected customers were notified and advised to cancel their credit cards.

In mid-February 2000, a cracker using a distributed denial of service (DDoS) attack crippled several major Internet companies including Yahoo, ebay, CNN Interactive, and Amazon.com, rendering their Web sites inaccessible. The resulting downtime for the companies cost them an estimated "tens of millions of dollars."[18] A 15-year-old Canadian teenager who went by the Internet moniker "Mafiaboy" eventually was charged in the attacks.[19]

In December 2000, a computer criminal who used the pseudonym "Maxus" cracked into the Internet database of CD Universe, an online music realtor, and claim to have stolen 300,000 customers' credit cards. Maxus then contacted CD Universe and offered to tell them how he compromised their database in exchange for $100,000. When the company refused his blackmail attempt, Maxus began posting portions of the CD Universe customer database on his Internet Web site.[20]

In the summer of 2000, a Philippine student is thought to have released a computer worm, dubbed the "Love Bug," which rapidly spread via e-mail. The worm sent copies of itself to every address listed in an infected user's Microsoft Outlook address book, clogging and slowing down e-mail servers. The worm also attempted to delete multimedia files from the infected users' hard drives. The Love Bug worm caused an estimated $1 billion in financial loss to businesses worldwide.[21]

6.2   SOCIAL PSYCHOLOGICAL ASPECTS OF COMPUTER CRIME.   Many acts of computer crime can be categorized as demonstrations of aggressive behaviors. For example, cracking into a company's Web server and defacing a Web page or launching a denial-of-service (DoS) attack on an organization's computer network, thereby crippling its Internet connection, are common malicious and aggressive acts engaged in by computer criminals. Social psychological theories on hostility and violence suggest that people are more likely to commit acts of aggression when the perpetrator of these acts remains anonymous and the threat of retaliation is low.[22] It is extremely difficult to correctly identify the perpetrators of computer attacks. These cybervandals frequently use nicknames ("nicks" or "handles"), stolen accounts, and spoofed Internet Protocol (IP) addresses when they engage in illegal activities. Computer criminals who deface Web pages are so confident that they are anonymous that they regularly "tag" the hacked Web site by leaving their handles and the handles of their friends, and in some cases even their Internet e-mail addresses.[7] These Web vandals are confident that their crimes cannot and will not be traced back to their true identities.

Social psychological theories suggest that because current Internet technology and practices make it easy to remain anonymous, and because the technical abilities of cybercriminals allow them to further obfuscate their offline identities, the resulting anonymity may be one factor that facilitates aggression on the Internet in the form of Web site defacement, DoS attacks, and other forms of computerized intrusions. For example, it is an extremely difficult and tedious task to identify computer criminals who launch DoS attacks and DDoS attacks against computer networks. The attacker plants DoS programs into "hacked" or compromised shell accounts controlled by a master client. The master client will instruct every "slave" DoS programs to *cooperatively* launch an attack at the victim's host at a configurable time and date. Thus, the DoS attacks are not launched by the criminal's own computer; rather, the attacks come from innocent networks that have been compromised by the cracker. This degree of indirection makes it all the more difficult to trace the original attacker. Much like the Web site vandals, DDoS attackers are also confident that the attacks will not be traced back to their actual identities. Frequently DDoS attackers will even brag on Internet Relay Chat (IRC) channels about how many host nodes they have compromised and against which domain they are planning to launch attacks against.[23]

6.2.1   Anonymity, Aggression, and Computer Crime.   Stanley Milgram's research examining obedience and conformity illustrated how ordinary individuals are capable of committing egregious acts of cruelty and violence. Milgram demonstrated how easily situational factors could be manipulated to make participants engage in these aggressive behaviors.[24] In a series of experiments, participants (teachers) were instructed to administer painful shocks, with increasing severity, to a second participant every time the learner made a mistake on a memory task. The second participant (learner), actually a confederate of Milgram's, was not really receiving the punishments, but deceptively screamed and yelled in fake agony after every shock.[24]

Milgram found that a significant proportion of his participants increased the severity of the shocks to life-threatening levels despite the screams, pleas, and the eventual unconscious state of the victim. Many study participants did complain and attempt to stop administering the shocks, but the researcher calmly told them to continue and most obeyed.[22] Milgram found that participants would deliver higher levels of shock when the victim was in an adjoining room than when the victim and participant were in the same room. The wall or window between the two rooms acted as a buffer for the participant's harmful actions. However, when victims were in the same room as participants, participants could not ignore the victims' pleas and screams and consequently would not administer as high levels of shock. In another scenario where Milgram had the participants pull a lever to instruct a second person to shock the victim, almost all of the participants (95 percent) obeyed until life-threatening levels had been administered.[22] Participant interviews revealed that the attitudes of teachers who administered shocks shifted to accommodate their negative actions. In an attempt to justify their actions, teachers started to dislike and derogate the learners, engaging in victim blame behavior. Milgram's seminal research demonstrated how various situations can influence ordinary people into committing aggressive and cruel acts against innocent victims.[22]

Situational influences on behavior and attitudes work similarly in cyberspace as they do in the real world. Computer criminals who commit aggressive acts against their innocent victims do not see the immediate consequences of their actions. The computer screen and ephemeral nature of the Internet can act an electronic wall between the criminal and the victim. Like Milgram's participants who were separated from their victims by a wall, computer criminals do not see the consequences of their actions. When computer criminals release automated attacks against organizations, they are further removed from the presence of the victims. Like Milgram's participants who pulled a lever to have someone else deliver an electric shock, computer criminals in a sense issue commands to automated "slave" programs that then attack their victims. Milgram's research illustrates how situational factors can influence behavior. Through his research we can see the "banality of evil"[25] and how ordinary people are capable of committing cruel acts. Automated cracking and DoS scripts coupled with a lack of social presence in computer-mediated interaction may be contributing to the behaviors of cybercriminals. It is easier to act aggressively against an entity that is depersonalized as well as emotionally and physically distant.[22] Also like many of Milgram's participants, computer criminals engage in victim blame in an attempt to justify their electronic aggressions. Cybervandals often criticize their victims for not properly securing their computer networks, suggesting that the victims deserved to be attacked.

6.2.2 Social Presence and Computer Crime. Social psychologist Sara Kiesler and colleagues have examined social presence in computer-mediated interactions. In traditional face-to-face interactions, individuals cognitively attend to social context cues and use them to guide their behaviors.[26-27] The researchers suggest that the lack of social-context cues in computer-mediated communication due to reduced social presence may lead to antinormative and disinhibited behavior. Group members communicating via computer-mediated communication are more hostile toward one another, take longer to reach decisions, and rate group members less favorably than comparable face-to-face groups.[26] Kiesler and Lee Sproull suggest that the absence of social-context cues in computer-mediated communication hinders the perception of and adaptation to social roles, structures, and norms.[27] The reduction of social-context cues in computer-mediated communication can lead to deregulated behavior, decreased social inhibitions, and reduced concern with social evaluation. The most common variables examined in these experiments are hostile language in the form of "flaming" (aggressive, rude, and often ad hominem attacks) and post hoc perceptions of group members. The results of one experiment indicated that there were 102 instances of hostile flaming behavior in 24 computer-mediated groups compared to only 12 instances of hostile commentary in the face-to-face groups.[27]

According to some researchers, the lack of social context cues and social presence on the Internet leads to aggressive behaviors.[26-27] Computer criminals may be engaging in hostile behaviors due to this reduction of available context cues. Crackers who harass and victimize system administrators and IRC users may be engaging in these activities due to their disinhibited state and reduced attention and concern with social evaluations, a direct result of social cue reduction. There are numerous anecdotal accounts of computer criminals "taking over" IRC channels, harassing people online, deleting entire computer systems, and even taunting system administrators whose networks they have compromised. Their criminal and aggressive behaviors may be partially attributed to the reduced social context cues in computer-mediated communication and the resulting changes in their psychological states.

6.2.3   Deindividuation and Computer Crime.   Disinhibited behaviors have also been closely linked to the psychological state of deindividuation.[26, 28–29] Deindividuation is described as a loss of self-awareness that results in irrational, aggressive, antinormative, and antisocial behavior. The deindividuated state traditionally was used to describe the mentality of individuals who comprised large riotous and hostile crowds (e.g., European soccer crowds, mob violence). Social psychologist Phillip Zimbardo suggested that a number of antecedent variables, often characteristic of large crowds, lead to the deindividuated state.[28] The psychosocial factors associated with anonymity, arousal, sensory overload, loss of responsibility, and mind-altering substances may lead to a loss of self-awareness, lessening of internal restraints, and a lack of concern for social or self-evaluation.[28]

Many of antecedent variables that could lead to a deindividuated state also are associated with the use of computers and the Internet. Internet users are relatively anonymous and often use handles to further obscure their true identities. Many of the Web sites, software programs, and multimedia files that typify the computing experience are sensory arousing and in some cases overwhelming. The Internet can be viewed as a large global crowd that individuals become submersed in once they go online. It is possible that the physical and psychological characteristics associated with the Internet that make it so appealing may lead individuals to engage in antisocial and antinormative behaviors due to psychological feelings of immersion and deindividuation.

Deindividuation is brought upon by an individual's loss of self-awareness and psychological immersion into a crowd due to certain antecedents.[28] The aggressive, hostile, and antinormative actions of computer criminals may be linked to deindividuation theory. Zimbardo found that when participants were deindividuated, operationalized by anonymity, darkness, and loud music, they would administer higher levels of electric shocks to experimenter confederates and for longer lengths of time than nondeindividuated participants.[28] Like Zimbardo's participants, computer criminals may be engaging in hostile and aggressive behavior due to deindividuation—that is, as a direct result of anonymity, subjective feelings of immersion, and the arousing nature of computer and Internet use.

For a more extended discussion of anonymity and identity in cyberspace, see Chapter 53.

6.2.4   Social Learning Theory of Computer Crime.   Computer criminal researcher Marc Rogers suggests that social learning theory may offer some insight into the behavior of computer criminals.[30] According to psychologist Albert Bandura, individuals learn behaviors by observing the actions of others and their associated consequences. Social learning theory is similar to B. F. Skinner's operant-conditioning model of learning where behaviors are learned or extinguished via direct reinforcement. However, Bandura's theory suggests that social learning occurs when an individual simply observes others behaviors and reinforcements and cognitively associates the two actions. Once the behavior is acquired, the learned actions are subject to external reinforcement, as in operant conditioning or in self-directed reinforcement.[30]

Recently there has been a growing amount of social and media attention focused on information security and computer criminals in particular. National newspapers, magazines, and electronic news sources have reported thousands of incidents, interviews, and commentary related to computer crime. A number of these articles appear to glamorize hacking and computer criminals.[32] The articles compare computer criminals to rock-and-roll superstars, James Bond–like spies, and international freedom fighters. Motion pictures and television shows like *Mission Impossible, Hackers, Swordfish,* and *The X-Files* have all bestowed a superhero-like status on computer criminals. According to social learning theory, individuals acquire behaviors by vicariously observing the consequences of another's actions.[22] With the media's glorification and glamorization of hacking and computer criminals, adolescents and adults learn that it pays to be a computer criminal—at least, from a social psychological point of view. Many crimes involving computer are extremely difficult to investigate and prosecute. The public learns via the media that computer criminals often are afforded fame and notoriety among their peers and the information security field for their illegal activities. There are very few instances of computer criminals' being convicted and serving jail time as a consequence of their actions. Usually the criminals are given a light sentence. Their notoriety garners them media interviews, book and movie deals, even consulting and public speaking jobs.[20] Once an action is learned, social learning theory states that the behavior will be maintained via self-directed and external reinforcement. Computer criminals are rewarded for the illegal activities via the acquisition of knowledge and their elevated status in the hacker community.[33] If the popular media continues to glamorize and focus on the positive consequences associated with computer crime, the cost and prevalence of these illicit actions will continue to grow. Younger generations of computer users also will learn that there are more positive as opposed to negative consequences associated with computer crime, which will serve to encourage their engagement in illegal behaviors. Social learning theorists would suggest modeling appropriate use of computers and the Internet as one solution for computer crime. Instead of focusing on the positive consequences, media outlets should stress the negative repercussions of computer crime for both the victims and the perpetrators. Social learning theory may offer one explanation for the illegal behaviors of computer criminals, especially the marked increase in recent years.[22]

6.2.5   Individual Differences and Computer Criminals.   Although situational factors can account for some of the behaviors of computer criminals, one must not discount the power of the individual. Attitudes and behaviors are often the product of both situational influences and individual personality.[22] Based on published biographies and interviews of computer deviants, information security professor M.E. Kabay suggests that computer criminals demonstrate personality traits consistent with antisocial personality disorder. He suggests that consistent with the *Diagnostic and Statistical Manual of Mental Disorders IV* (DSM-IV) criteria for antisocial personality disorder, computer criminals appear to exhibit insincerity and dishonesty in combination with superficial charm and an enhanced intellect. Also consistent with DSM-IV criteria for the disorder, computer criminals commit their illegal behavior for little or no visible rewards despite the threat of severe punishment. Another central characteristic of antisocial personality disorder is lack of clear insight by perpetrators regarding their behaviors.[35] Researchers have noted that computer criminals do not view their criminal actions as harmful or illegal.[33, 36] The criminals rationalize their behaviors by blaming the network administrators and software designers for not properly securing their computers and programs.

6.2.5.1   *Narcissistic Personalities Personalities and Computer Criminals.*
Computer crime researchers M.E. Kabay, Eric Shaw, Keven Ruby, and Jerrold Post
also have suggested that computer criminals demonstrate personality characteristics
consistent with narcissistic personality disorder.[34, 36] According to the *Diagnostic Statistical Manual* 4th edition (DSM-IV) criteria, narcissistic individuals are attention
seekers with an exaggerated sense of entitlement.[35] Entitlement is described as the
belief that one is in some way privileged and owed special treatment or recognition.
Shaw and associates suggest that entitlement is characteristic of many "dangerous
insiders," or information technology specialists who commit electronic crimes against
their own organizations.[36] When corporate authority does not recognize an individual's inflated sense of entitlement, the criminal insider seeks revenge via electronic
criminal aggressions. Anecdotal evidence suggests that external computer criminals
also may demonstrate an exaggerated sense of entitlement as well as a lack of
empathy for their victims, also characteristic of narcissistic personality disorder. One
self-identified computer criminal states, "we rise above the rest, and then pull
everyone else up to the same new heights . . . We seek to innovate, to invent. We,
quite seriously, seek to boldly go where no one has gone before."[37] Narcissistic individuals also frequently engage in rationalization to justify and defend their behaviors.[35] Toxic Shock again writes, "We are misunderstood by the majority. We are
misunderstood, misinterpreted, misrepresented. All because we simply want to learn.
We simply want to increase the flow of knowledge, so that everyone can learn and
benefit."[37] Although is a mistake to generalize these hypotheses to the entire population without any empirical support, certain subsets of computer criminals may
demonstrate characteristics that are consistent with both narcissistic and antisocial
personality disorders.

6.2.5.2   *Asperger Syndrome and Computer Criminals.*   Recently researchers
have suggested a possible link between computer hackers and a relatively new developmental disorder named Asperger syndrome (AS).[38–39] Asperger syndrome is a disorder that resides at the mild end of the pervasive developmental disorder (PDD)
spectrum with classic autism at the more severe end. PDDs are characterized by primary developmental abnormalities in language and communication, social relations
and skills, and repetitive and intense interests or behaviors.[38, 40] Unlike autism, individuals who are diagnosed with AS have higher cognitive abilities and IQ scores
ranging from normal to superior.[38] Individuals with AS also have normal language
and verbal skills, although there are noticeable deficits in social communication.

Clinicians recently have proposed several criteria that are necessary for a diagnosis
of AS.[35] According to clinical psychologist Kenneth Gergen, individuals must
demonstrate social impairment. They may have a lack of desire or inability to interact
with peers, and may engage in inappropriate or awkward social responses.[41] These
individuals may have extremely limited or focused interests and are prone to engage
in repetitive routines. Although language development is often normal, these individuals may demonstrate unusual speech patterns, rate, volume, and intonation. Individuals with AS also may demonstrate clumsy motor behaviors and body language as
well as inappropriate facial expressions and gazing.[38, 41]

The central feature of Asperger syndrome is the obsessive or extremely focused
area of intellectual interest that the individuals demonstrate.[41] Children with AS often
show an obsessive interest in areas such as math, science, technology, and machinery.
They strive to read, learn, and assimilate all information about their area of specialized interest. Researchers have indicated that their preoccupied interests may last

well into adulthood leading to careers associated with their obsessions. Much of their social communication is egocentric revolving around their obsessive interests, often leading to strained and difficult social interactions. Although children with AS desire normal peer interaction, their egocentric preoccupations, lack of appropriate social behaviors, and inability to empathize with others often leaves them frustrated, misunderstood, teased, and sometimes ostracized.[38]

Researchers have noticed similarities in the characteristics associated with Asperger syndrome and traits stereotypically associated with computer hackers.[39] Based on over 200 personal interviews with computer criminals, cybercrime expert Donn Parker reports finding significant similarities between AS sufferers and criminal hackers.[39] Many of the computer criminals he has interviewed demonstrated the social awkwardness, unusual prosody, and lack of social empathy during interactions that are characteristic of Asperger syndrome.[39] Anecdotal evidence suggests that computer hackers often have an obsessive interest in technology and computers, similar to that seen in individuals with AS, that forms a salient component of both their individual and social identities. Due to their egocentric preoccupations, many computer hackers often feel misunderstood and frustrated in social situations.

To date there has been no empirical evidence to suggest a link between Asperger syndrome and computer criminals. There is no evidence whatsoever to suggest that Asperger syndrome causes computer hacking. In fact, most sufferers of AS have been characterized as being extremely honest and lawful citizens.[39] It would be a mistake to assume that all computer hackers are suffering from Asperger syndrome or that every AS sufferer a computer hacker.[39] The term "hacker" also has been over used and misused in the popular media. Characteristics of Asperger syndrome appear more common in computer hackers, those who explore and tinker with computers and technology, rather than in computer criminals, or "crackers," who break into computers or use them for illegal activities. At present, there is still no one all-encompassing personality profile that applies to all computer criminals. In fact, many feel that it is inappropriate to try to create a single personality profile that applies to all computer criminals.[39]

6.2.5.3   *Computer Addiction and Computer Crime.* Researchers have indicated that a subset of computer criminals appear to demonstrate addiction-like tendencies associated with their use of computers and the Internet.[42-44] Technological addiction is described as having an addiction involving human−computer interaction, characterized by salience, mood modification, tolerance, withdrawal, conflict, and relapse.[45] Information security researchers Kent Anderson and Jerrold Post suggest that computer criminals appear to have obsessive or compulsive-like characteristics surrounding their computing behaviors.[43, 46] Cybercriminals will work for 18 or more hours a day on their computers trying to gain unauthorized access to one single computer system with little or no external reward for doing so. Anderson states that computer attacks sometimes take months of planning along with numerous trial-and-error attempts.[46] Anderson reports that one U.S. judge even attempted to sentence a computer criminal to psychological treatment for his compulsive computer use.[46]

Personality theorists state that for some computer criminals, committing electronic crimes is an experience similar to that of a drug high. Computer criminals commit illegal acts because of the euphoric rush they receive from their actions. Information security researcher August Bequai compares the actions of computer criminals to electronic joyriding.[47] He equates the feeling of unauthorized access and usage of a computer network to that of stealing a sports car and joyriding around the neighborhood.

One computer cracker interviewed by computer-crime researcher, Dorothy Denning described hacking as "the ultimate cerebral buzz."[42] Other crackers have commented that they received a rush from their illegal activities that felt as if their minds were working at accelerated rates. Some computer criminals have suggested that the euphoric high stems from the dangerous and illegal nature of their activities.[42] Computer criminals have compared the feelings they receive from their illegal intrusions and attacks to the rush that is felt when participating in extreme sports such as rock climbing and skydiving.

As in substance abuse or athletic thrill seeking, tolerance also may develop with computer crime. Tolerance occurs when increased amounts of a substance or an activity is needed in order to obtain a "high" or euphoric rush. Tolerance is common in hard drug users who find themselves injecting or smoking increasing amounts of a substance to achieve their original euphoric state. Anecdotal evidence suggests that computer criminals go through a stage of evolution with each step leading to more dangerous and riskier behaviors. Many cybercriminals begin by pirating and cracking the copy protection algorithms of software programs. When the "warez" (pirated software) scene loses its thrill, they migrate to chat room or IRC harassment. The criminals may then begin launching damaging DoS attacks against servers and defacing Web sites in order to obtain that initial rush that originated with simple warez trading. Similar to a drug addiction, the euphoric psychological states and resulting tolerance associated with excessive computer use may explain why computer criminals repeatedly engage in illicit activities even after they have been caught and punished.

6.2.6   Ethics and Computer Crime.   Researchers have suggested that computer criminals may have an underdeveloped sense of ethics or moral maturity.[42–43, 48] Because of this ethical immaturity, computer hackers may think that many of their illegal actions are justified and ethical. Many computer criminals feel that they are ethically entitled to have access to all information. These individuals also feel that it is morally right to use inactive computer processing power and time, regardless of who owns the computer system. Computer criminals do not feel that breaking into a computer network should be viewed in the same fashion as breaking into an individual's house. Often computer criminals rationalize their illegal activities and justify their behaviors by blaming the victims for not securing their computer networks properly. Most computer criminals are adolescents, which may account for the underdeveloped sense of ethics in the community.[42]

Vincent Sacco and Elia Zureik, in their investigation of ethics and computer usage, administered an anonymous survey to university students enrolled in computer courses at a Canadian university.[49] They used a 22-page questionnaire containing questions about computer behaviors, perceptions, and general attitudes. They examined attitudes toward computer crimes and assessed judgments regarding the ethical nature of illegal computing behaviors, beliefs about the prevalence of the illegal behaviors, and beliefs about probability of detection. Questions about self-reported computer misuse dealt with the use of unauthorized passwords, illegal reproduction of software, avoidance of charges while using programs, and looking at discarded paper for interesting programs, passwords, and the like.

The researchers hypothesized that there would be a significant relationship between self-reported computer crime and the measures of attitude regarding the crimes. As they predicted, there was a strong positive correlation. Viewing illicit computing behaviors as ethical increased the reported likelihood that the respondents had engaged in such actions. Computer crime was least reported when the behavior was seen as being more unethical. Their findings were similar to the ethical computing theories proposed by Denning, Winkler, and Post.[42–43, 48]

Journalists Steven Levy and Steve Mizrach suggest that computer hackers may have a separate code of ethics from the general Internet population.[50–51] Hackers feel that access to computers and computing time should be unlimited and free of restrictions. From their point of view, hours of potentially useful computing time are needlessly restricted and therefore wasted in today's computing world. They also believe that all nonsensitive information should be free and easily accessible to any individual, regardless of control or authorship. Information should not be hoarded by anyone in power but rather openly shared so that those who crave it can have access to it. Computer hackers claim to promote decentralization of government and politics. They have an ardent mistrust of authority. Hackers feel that other hackers should be judged not on superficial criteria, such as age, gender, or ethnicity, but by the quality of their computing and hacking skills. They also feel that the proper use of computers can create beauty and art, equivalent to more traditional creative methods such as painting or poetry. Computer hackers believe that computers have the ability to improve the quality of living.[50] They feel that it is ethical to crack into computer systems as long as no data is harmed, stolen, or vandalized in the process.[51]

Information security specialist Ira Winkler further suggests that computer hackers, because of their generally young age, do not fully understand the possible repercussions associated with their actions.[48] They demonstrate an infantile version or complete lack of empathy for their victims.[48] Hackers fail to fully realize the consequences of their electronic intrusion into computer systems. The adolescents do not fully comprehend that their mere presence on a computing network could potentially cost companies thousands of dollars as well as cost systems administrators their jobs within an organization.[13] According to Winkler, many computer hackers learn and develop a sense of computer ethics from their online and offline peers.[48] In other words, unlike most instruction on morality and ethics that stem from a responsible adult, computing ethics are socially learned from other adolescents over the Internet. Computer hackers learn the "dos and don'ts" of hacking and computing from elder statesmen in the hacking community who may be no more than a few years older than themselves. Often, in today's technological society, children know more about computers and the Internet than their parents do. When adolescents have problems or need guidance in ambiguous situations, many times their parents and mature role models are unable to offer them guidance and assistance. Therefore, the youngsters seek out the knowledge from their peers, who may or may not offer them the most ethical or wise advice.

As individuals grow older, they develop a more mature or adult sense of ethics. Adults have legal authority over the lives of their children because adolescents are not yet fully capable of making every decision on their own. Adults need to extend this legal responsibility and authority into cyberspace. Many children are making judgments and performing actions on their own without adult supervision while on the Internet. Adolescents do not have the same ethical maturity that adults have, yet unsupervised on the Internet they are given as much power, authority, and responsibility as ethically mature adults.[52] Neil Patrick, the leader of one particularly malicious group of phone-system hackers known as the 414's, stated that he did not know that his hacking was illegal or unethical. In fact, asked when, if ever, he began to question the ethics of his actions, Patrick stated that ethics never came into his mind until the Federal Bureau of Investigation was knocking on his front door.[52] Patrick and the other young members of the 414's did not see anything wrong with their actions. To them, breaking into proprietary telecommunications networks was not a crime. They saw nothing ethically wrong with their actions.

Psychologist Lawrence Kohlberg developed a three-level theory to explain normal human moral development. The first level deals with avoiding punishments and obtaining rewards, the second level emphasizes social rules, and the third level emphasizes moral principles. Each of his three levels contains two stages that an individual passes through during adolescence on the way to adult moral development.[53] Computer criminals appear to be operating in the lower three stages of Kohlberg's model: the two stages comprising level 1 and the first stage in level 2. The moral judgments of computer criminals appear to be determined by the necessity to satisfy their own needs and to avoid disapproval and rejection by others. These individuals do not appear to be aware of or concerned with the third level of moral development, where moral judgments are motivated by civic respect and one's own moral conscience.[53] Computer criminals may be functioning at the third level of moral development in the physical world, a level appropriate for teens and adults. However, they may be functioning at lower levels of moral development while on the Internet.[52] Their entire cyberspace behavior appears to be aimed at satisfying their own needs. They break into computer networks to satisfy their own curiosity and to gain the approval of their peers. One notorious hacker who was known as the Mentor states, "We explore, you call us criminals. We seek after knowledge and you call us criminals. . . . I am a criminal. My crime is that of curiosity."[54]

According to Shaw and associates, there is a notable lack of ethical regulation and education in organizations, schools, and homes regarding proper computing behavior.[36] Computer criminals who lack ethical maturity fail to realize that their actions are sometimes just as damaging as physical aggression. Cybervandals do not see the immediate repercussions of their actions because of the physical distance and lack of social presence in computer-mediated interactions. This ethical immaturity is a result of the technology gap between young computer users and their parents. In real-world situations, parents and teachers strive to instill responsibility and ethics in adolescents. Therefore, young adults become capable of making informed decisions regarding ethical and unethical behaviors. However, the same adolescent who demonstrates ethical behavior in the physical world may be ethically bereft in cyberspace, partly due to the lack of adult guidance and instruction. Research has indicated that computer criminals are primarily white males in their teenage years.[42, 44] Anecdotal evidence suggests that in today's society, adolescents recreationally use and are more familiar with computers and the Internet than their parents. Many times, these young adults learn the about the Internet-related behaviors and attitudes on their own or via peer-to-peer interaction. Adolescents are socialized on the Internet by other adolescents, which may lead to a *Lord of the Flies* scenario, where children construct social rules and guidelines to govern their behaviors.[55] These socially constructed norms and guidelines may be both morally and ethically different from real-world norms.

Scholastic Incorporated demonstrated in a recent survey that 48 percent of elementary and middle school students did not consider computer hacking to be a crime.[56] Recently the Department of Justice (DoJ) formed a cybercitizen awareness program in an effort to educate parents, teachers, and children about ethical and unethical computing practices. The program seeks to educate individuals through ethics conferences, multimedia presentations, and speaking engagements at schools around the country. This program and others like it may aid to increase moral responsibility and ethical behaviors of adolescents on the Internet.

6.3   CLASSIFICATIONS OF COMPUTER CRIMINALS.   For both ordinary and abnormal behaviors, it is difficult if not impossible to find one theoretical perspective that can account for every behavior in a given a situation. Attitudes and behaviors are the product of the combined influence of an individual's personality and the current social situation. Therefore, it stands to reason that no single theory or theoretical perspective can account for the various types of computerized crimes and the criminals who engage in these activities. The difficulty lies in the fact that there are numerous types of computerized crimes, ranging from trading pirated software, to cloning cellular phones, to sniffing network passwords. Along with the different variations of computerized crime, there are many different types of computer criminals, ranging from the AOL-password thief to the professional spy. Any theory that would account for the behavior of computer criminals would have to consider, first, the type of illegal activity the person was engaged in and, second, the type of cybercriminal category that the individual falls into.[33] Computer criminals are by nature paranoid and secretive agents who exist in a similar community. They use handles to conceal their true identities and, except for annual hacker conventions or local meetings, seldom interact with each other in the real world. Therefore, it is difficult for researchers to identify and categorize the various subgroups that exist. However, recently researchers using interview and survey techniques have attempted to do so.

The term "computer hacker" has been both overused and misused as a way of classifying the entire spectrum of computer criminals.[33] The motivations and actions of one subgroup of computer criminals may be entirely different from those of a second group; therefore, it is imperative that in any psychological analysis of computer criminals, the various subcategories be taken into consideration. Many theories have attempted to account for the motivations and behaviors of computer criminals as a whole when the theorists actually were referring to one specific subgroup in the underground culture.[34, 42, 48] Computer criminals are a heterogeneous culture; therefore, one single theory or perspective cannot explain all their actions. The fact that researchers traditionally have treated computer criminals as a homogeneous entity has limited the validity and generalizibilty of their findings. Even researchers who have taken into account the heterogeneous nature of the computing underground have had difficulty with experimental validity. Experimenters have allowed participants to use their own self-classification schemes or attempted to generalize the results of a single subgroup to the entire underground culture.[33]

6.3.1   Early Classification Theories of Computer Criminals.   Over the past few decades, several researchers have attempted to develop a categorization system for individuals who engage in various forms of computer crime.[33–34, 43, 57–58] A comprehensive review of this research is beyond the scope of this chapter. For an extensive review, see Rogers's analysis and development of a new taxonomy for computer criminals.[33] Bill Landreth, a reformed computer cracker, was one of the earliest theorists to develop a classification scheme for computer criminals.[57] His system divided criminals into five categories based on their experience and illegal activities.

1. The "novice" criminals have the least experience with computers and cause the least amount of electronic disruption from their transgressions. They are considered to be tricksters and mischief-makers.[33, 5] AOL users who annoy chatroom members with text floods and DoS-like punting programs (software used to interfere with other user's connections in chat rooms) would be considered novices.

2. The "students" are electronic voyeurs. They spend their time browsing and exploring unauthorized computer systems.

3. The "tourists," according to Landreth, commit unauthorized intrusions for the emotional rush that results from their actions.[57] This subgroup of computer criminals is similar to Bequai's electronic joyriders.[47] The tourists are thrill-seekers who receive a cerebral buzz from their illegal behaviors.

4. The "crashers" are malicious computer criminals. This subgroup is composed of the darkside criminals that Kabay refers to.[34] The "crashers" will crack into networks and intentionally delete and destroy the computer systems.

5. Landreth's final classification of computer criminal is the "thieves."[57] Criminals who fit into this category commit their illegal actions for monetary gain. These individuals are the equivalent of the dangerous insiders that Post has analyzed.[43] Thieves may work alone, or they may be under contract from both foreign and domestic corporations and governments.

Former Australian Army intelligence analyst Nicolas Chantler conducted one of the few empirical examinations of computer criminals and their culture.[44] This survey-based study attempted to gain a deeper understanding of the underground culture as well as develop a categorization system for cybercriminals. Chantler posted questionnaires to bulletin board systems (BBSs), Usenet newsgroups, and chat rooms owned or frequented by computer criminals. An analysis of the data yielded five primary attributes—criminal activities, hacking prowess, motivations, overall knowledge, and length of time hacking—that Chantler used to create three categories of computer criminals: lamers, neophytes, and elites.[33]

1. "Lamers" have the least technical skill and they have been engaged in their illegal activities for the shortest period of time. This group of criminals is primarily motivated by revenge or theft of services and property.[33, 44]

2. "Neophytes" are more mature than lamers. They are more knowledgeable than the previous category and engage in illegal behaviors in pursuit of increased information.[33, 44]

3. Members of the "elite" group have the highest level of overall knowledge concerning computers and computer crime. They are internally motivated by a desire for knowledge and discovery. They engage in illegal activities for the intellectual challenge and the thrill they receive from their criminal behaviors.[33, 44]

According to Chantler, the largest proportion of computer criminals, 60 percent, fall into the neophyte category. Thirty percent of the computer criminals fall into the elite category while 10 percent are lamers.[44]

As cited by Rogers, Donn Parker developed a seven-level categorization scheme for computer criminals.[33, 58] He formalized his scheme through years of interaction and structured interviews with computer criminals.

1. "Pranksters" are characterized by their mischievous nature.

2. "Hacksters" are motivated by curiosity and a quest for knowledge. Pranksters and hacksters are the least malicious computer criminals.

3. "Malicious hackers" are motivated by a need for disruption and destruction. They receive pleasure from causing harm to computer systems and financial loss to individuals.

4. "Personal problem solvers" commit illegal activities for personal gain. Problem solvers, the most common type of computer criminal according to Parker, resort to crime after failed legitimate attempts to resolve their difficulties.[58]

5. "Career criminals" engage in their illegal cyber behaviors purely for financial gain.

6. "Extreme advocates" have strong ties to religious, political, and/or social movements. Recently these types of cybercriminals have been dubbed "hacktivists," a combination of computer hacking and activism.

7. "Malcontents, addicts, and irrational individuals" comprise the final category in Parker's scheme. Individuals in this category usually are suffering from some form of psychological problem such as addiction or antisocial personality disorder.[58]

6.3.2   Rogers's New Taxonomy of Computer Criminals.   After an extensive review of past categorization theories, Rogers has advanced a new taxonomy for computer criminals.[33] This classification scheme is comprised of seven independent but not mutually exclusive categories.

1. "Newbie/toolkit" (NT) criminals have the least amount of technical knowledge and skill. Members of this category are relatively new to the scene and use prewritten and compiled scripts and tools to commit their computerized crimes.

2. "Cyber punks" (CPs) are the second category in Rogers's taxonomy.[33] Members of this category are slightly more advanced than the newbies. These criminals are novice programmers limited in experience with computer systems and networks. Cyber punks also commit malicious criminal acts, such as mail bombing, Web page hijacking, and credit/calling card theft. Winkler (1994) suggests that the majority of computer criminals fall into either the cyber-punk or newbie categories. He estimates that between 35,000 and 50,000 computer criminals, well over 90 percent of their total estimated number, fall into these categories, whom he dubs "clueless."

3. "Internals" (ITs) consist of disgruntled workers or former workers who hold information technology positions in an organization. Members of this category have an advantage over external attackers due to their job and status within the corporation. Research indicates that internals are responsible for the majority of computer crimes and associated financial loss.[33, 59]

4. Coders (CD) are computer criminals with advanced technical knowledge and skill. These individuals are responsible for writing many of the exploit code and programs (e.g., stack overflows, rootkits, etc.) that are used by the less knowledgeable "newbie/toolkit" and cyber-punk crackers in their cyber attacks.

5. The "old guard" (OG) hackers, according to Rogers, are not criminals in the traditional sense. However, they have a relaxed sense of ethics regarding privacy and intellectual and personal property found in other computer criminals. OG hackers engage in behavior according to the traditional hacker ethic and ideology described by Levy.[50] Their illegal behaviors are motivated by a quest for knowledge and information.

6&7. "Professional criminals" and "Cyber-terrorists" comprise the final two categories. According to Rogers, these two groups present the most danger to individuals and organizations. These criminals are traditionally older and more knowledgeable about technology than the previous categories. Members of these categories are former government and intelligence operatives who are motivated by money or radical ideology. Professional criminals and cyber-terrorists have access to advanced technology and are adept at industrial espionage.

The annual survey by Computer Security Institute consistently indicates that employees (the category similar to Rogers's "internals") are responsible for most acts of computer crime against an organization.[33, 59] According to their 2000 survey, outside attacks cost organizations an average of $172,000, while insiders accounted for more than $1 million in financial loss.[59] Shaw and associates classify computer criminals into two categories: outside intruders and dangerous insiders.[36] The researchers focus on the critical IT insiders who are typically programmers, technical support staff, networking operators, administrators, consultants, and temporary workers in an organization. Malicious insiders are a subgroup of such employees who are motivated by greed, revenge, problem resolution, and ego gratification. According to Shaw and coauthors, these dangerous insiders typically have introverted personalities.[36] They demonstrate a preference for solitary intellectual activities over interpersonal interaction. Members of this subgroup may have had numerous personal and social frustrations that have hindered their interpersonal interactions and contributed to their antiauthoritarian attitudes. Researchers also have suggested that these computer criminals may have developed a dependence on or an addiction to computers.[36]

The malicious subgroup of critical information technologists has been characterized as having a loose or immature sense of ethics regarding computers. The dangerous insiders rationalize their crimes by blaming their company or supervisors for bringing any negative consequences on themselves. They feel that any electronic damage they cause is the fault of the organization for treating them unfairly.[36] The researchers also note that many insiders identify more with their profession than with the company for which they work. This heightened identification with the profession undermines an insider's loyalty to an organization. This reduced loyalty is evidenced by the high turnover rates of jobs in the IT industry. According to Shaw and associates, the unstable bond between insiders and their organizations creates undue tension with regard to security practices and intellectual property rights.[36]

Researchers also have suggested that dangerous insiders are characterized by an increased sense of entitlement and hostility toward organizational authority. Entitlement, one of the characteristics of narcissistic personality disorder, is described as the belief that one is privileged and owed special treatment or recognition.[35] According to Shaw and coauthors, when an unfulfilled sense of entitlement is combined with previous hostility toward authority, malicious acts or revenge against the organization may result.[36]

6.3.3   Virus Creators.   Although the phrase "computer criminal" is synonymous with the term "hacker," there are other types of computer-related crimes than electronic intrusions such as cracking software protection, software pirating, and spreading computer viruses. The motivations and behaviors of virus creators have been examined less than those of traditional computer criminals. However, recently researchers have begun to interview and survey members of the virus-writing culture in an effort to understand their actions and motivations.[59–61]

Using case studies and interviews, researchers Andrew Bissett and Geraldine Shipton examined the factors that influence and motivate virus writers.[61] The researchers suggest that it is difficult to generalize their findings to all virus creators because of the limited published literature and research regarding virus writers as well as the lack of clinical populations and theories. Virus creators appear to demonstrate conscious motivations for their potentially destructive actions that are similar to the motivations of traditional computer criminals. Virus writers create and distribute their code for reasons of nonspecific malice, employee revenge, ideological motives, commercial sabotage, and information warfare.[61] Bissett and Shipton's review of Sarah Gordon's interview with Dark Avenger reveals some of the motivations behind one of the most notorious virus writers.[61] They suggest that Dark Avenger consistently denies responsibility for his creation and, like traditional computer criminals, engages in victim blaming. Dark Avenger states that it is human stupidity, not the computer, that spreads viruses. The virus writer also appears to self-identify with his malicious code. Dark Avenger seems to project his persona onto viruses in a process called projective identification.[60] During the interview Dark Avenger stated that the United States could prevent him from traveling to the country but it is unable to stop his viruses. Dark Avenger also attempted to justify creating destructive viruses by commenting that most personal computers did not store data of any value and therefore his malicious programs were not doing any real harm.[61] The researchers suggest that Dark Avenger creates malicious viruses because he is envious of other's computers and of the work and bond that they form with these systems. In the interview, Dark Avenger commented that he hates it when people have more powerful computers than he does, especially when the individuals do not use the resources for anything that he deems constructive.[61]

Anti-virus expert Sarah Gordon examined the ethical development of several virus writers using interview and survey methodology.[59–60] Her initial four case studies involved an adolescent virus writer, a college-age virus writer, a professionally employed virus writer, and an ex–virus writer. The interviews revealed that all four individuals appeared to demonstrate normal ethical maturity and development consistent with Kohlberg's stage theory. Gordon suggests that there appears to be many different reasons why individuals create and distribute viruses, including boredom, exploration, recognition, peer pressure, and sheer malice.[60]

Gordon suggests that the virus underground is currently populated by a second generation, or "next-generation," of virus writers whose skill and ability at virus construction is comparable to that of the "old school," or original virus writers.[60] On the surface, these second-generation creators maintain a public façade that suggests that they are extremely cruel, obnoxious, and more technologically advanced than previous generations. The next-generation virus writers appear to be more aware of the ethical responsibilities surrounding virus creation and distribution; however, the exact definition of "responsible virus creation and distribution" varies from individual to individual. [60] Many of these next-generation virus writers have considerable technical skill and are motivated by the challenge to defeat the virus countermeasures implemented by antivirus vendors.

According to Gordon, another group of virus creators populating the virus underground is the "new-age" virus writers.[60] These individuals are motivated by current trends, such as political activism, virus exchange, freedom of information, and challenges to write the most destructive or sophisticated virus, as opposed to technical exploration. These virus writers are motivated by boredom, intellectual curiosity, mixed messages surrounding the legality of virus creation, and increased access to ever-more powerful technological resources.[60] Gordon suggests that these "new-age" virus writers may be older and wiser than the second or "next-generation" creators.[60] They are very selective as to who has access to their creations and do not share their findings or accomplishments with members outside their group. Unlike the next-generation creator, new-age virus writers will not stop or "grow out of" writing viruses, as they are most likely already adults. They will continue to write and distribute more sophisticated viruses in part due to the mixed messages concerning the ethical nature of virus creation propagated by the popular media, academia, and the culture of the Internet.[60]

Similar to the popular views surrounding computer hackers, researchers have stated that we must be careful not to view virus creators as a homogeneous group.[60–61] Instead we must monitor the virus-exchange community while pursuing in-depth case histories that may aid in our understanding of virus writers. Education about the ethical nature of virus creation and distribution and the repercussions associated with malicious code may attenuate these potentially destructive activities.

6.4   SUMMARY AND CONCLUSIONS.   According to PricewaterhouseCooper's annual CSI/FBI security survey, computer crimes are becoming increasingly more widespread, diverse, and financially damaging. With the advent of broadband technologies such as DSL (digital subscriber line) and cable modems, computer crimes are no longer simply problems for the corporate realm but are affecting the casual home user as well.

Examining the behaviors of computer criminals from a social psychological perspective, which emphasizes the influence of situational factors on behaviors, may offer possible explanations for the motivations and actions of computer criminals. Research regarding computer-mediated interaction suggests that the characteristics inherent to the electronic environment may contribute to antinormative behaviors. Anonymity, reduced social context cues, and a deindividuated-like state may all contribute to the aggressive and antisocial behaviors of computer criminals.

Social learning theory suggests that computer criminals learn their illegal behaviors from watching the actions and associated consequences of other cyber-deviates. Recently the popular media has been criticized for glorifying computer criminals by presenting them as Robin Hood–like rebels or technological activists. This type of glorification may lead individuals to associate positive consequences with illegal activities, thereby increasing the probability of their occurrence.

Personality theorists suggest that computer criminals demonstrate characteristics associated with antisocial and narcissistic personality disorders, which may contribute to their illegal behaviors. Researchers also have indicated that computer criminals may develop an addiction to computers and Internet resources as well as a druglike rush from their illegal behaviors. In addition, computer criminals have been characterized as having an underdeveloped sense of ethics and ethical maturity, although some virus writers have demonstrated normative ethical development.

The few empirical studies that have examined computer criminals have been primarily descriptive in nature and have attempted to generalize their results to the entire population.[33, 43] In order to develop predictive theories regarding the attitudes and behaviors of computer criminals, researchers need to take into account the categories and personalities of computer criminals. There is no one single profile or typical computer criminal. Researchers have developed numerous classification systems that group hackers according to their skill levels, motivations, and goals into independent categories ranging from neophyte hackers to professional cyberterrorists.

The computer criminals who comprise one category may have vastly different motivations and attitudes from the typical members of another category. Psychological theories that account for the behaviors and attitudes of one category of cybercriminals may fail when applied to another category of criminals. Thinking of computer criminals as a homogeneous entity limits the understanding of their criminal behaviors and attitudes.

Research and attention from popular culture and the media traditionally has focused on computer criminals in the cyber-punk category due to their sheer numbers and the visible nature of their crimes. However, many theories regarding this group of criminals have been inappropriately generalized to the computer criminal population as a whole, resulting in faulty explanations and misattribution of their behaviors. Although there has been ample theoretical speculation regarding computer criminals in general, there has been a paucity of research on criminals in specific subsets or categories.

Social psychological theories offer various explanations that may influence criminal activities on the Internet. These situational influences may interact with various individual personality traits to further contribute to illegal behaviors. The current task for researchers is to untangle these personality and situation influences on electronic behavior. They must determine what situations and characteristics are influencing the various types of computer criminals. There is no simple explanation as to why computer criminals engage in hostile and destructive acts. The answer lies in a complex mixture of factors that depends on the social environment and individual personality factors. There are numerous types of computer criminals ranging from script kids to the professional criminal, each with varying personalities. The interaction of personality variables and environmental factors will determine how a computer criminal reacts in any given situation.

6.5   NOTES

1. NUA, "NUA Internet: How Many Online?" (2000), Available: *www.nua.ie/surveys/how_many_online/index.html.*

2. PriceWaterhouseCoopers, "Global Security Survey" (2000). Available: *www.pwcglobal.com/extweb/ncpressrelease.nsf/DocID/7ABBA8E73B1E901D8525693500548A34.*

3. T. Wilson, "Profits Embolden Hackers," *InternetWeek* (1998). Available: *web.lexis-nexis.com/more/cahners-chicago/11407/3116583/3.*

4. Special report, "Internet Services: Workplace Crime? Police the PCs," *Daily Telegraph,* March 20, 1998. Available: *www.telegraph.co.uk.*

5. Cyberstats, "Net Security" (1997). Available: *www.zdnet.com/icom/cyberstats/1997/12/.*

6. Exopa Terra, "The Cost of High-tech Crime Is Soaring" (1997), Available: *www.exopa-terra.com/special1.htm.*

7. Attrition, "Attrition Defacement Archive" (2000), Available: *www.attrition.org.*

8. CERT, "CERT® Coordination Center 1999 Annual Report (Summary)" (2000), Available: *www.cert.org/annual_rpts/cert_rpt_99.html.*

9. Andrew Briney, "2000 Information Security Industry Survey," *Information Security Magazine* (2000), Available: *www.infosecuritymag.com/2000survey.pdf&e=42.*

10. Douglas Campbell, "A Detailed History of Terrorist and Hostile Intelligence Attacks Against Computer Resources" (1992). Available e-mail: Dcampb@aol.com.

11. Donn Parker, "How to Solve the Hacker Problem," *Journal of the National Computer Security Association,* No. 5 (1994), pp. 4–8.

12. Jerrold Post, "The Dangerous Information Systems Insider: Psychological Perspectives" (1998). Available e-mail: jmpost@erols.com.

13. M.E. Kabay, "Ethics." Available: *www2.norwich.edu/mkabay/ethics/index.htm.*

14. Michelle Delio, "A Chinese Call to Hack U.S.," *Wired* (2001). Available: *www.wired.com/news/politics/0,1283,42982,00.html.*

15. Michelle Delio, "Crackers Expand Private War," *Wired* (2001). Available: *www.wired.com/news/business/0,1367,43134,00.html.*

16. NIPC, "Update to NIPC Advisory 00-060 "E-Commerce Vulnerabilities," *2001 NIPC Advisories* (2001). Available: *www.nipc.gov/warnings/advisories/2001/01-003.htm.*

17. Mark Obmascik, "Hacker Hits Western Union," *Denver Post,* September 2000. Available: *www.denverpost.com/news/news0911a.htm.*

18. Computer Security Institute, "Issues and Trends: 2000 CSI/FBI Computer Crime and Security Survey" (2000). Available: *www.gocsi.com/prelea_000321.htm.*

19. Sascha Segan, "Tracking 'Mafiaboy's' Steps," ABCNews.com (2000). Available: *abcnews.go.com/sections/tech/DailyNews/webattacks000420.html.*

20. Mike Brunker, "Web Site Offering 'Free' Credit Cards Seen as Scheme to Sell Rest of Data," *MSNBC* (2000). Available: *www.msnbc.com/news/355593.asp.*

21. CNN, "Internet Provider in Philippines Homes in on Virus Author," *CNN* (2000). Available: *www.cnn.com/2000/TECH/computing/05/05/iloveyou.01.*

22. David Meyers, *Social Psychology,* 6th ed. (New York: McGraw-Hill, 1999).

23. Bob Sullivan, "DoS attacks: What Really Happened," *MSNBC* (2000). Available: *www.zdnet.com/zdnn/stories/news/0,4586,2553035,00.html.*

24. Stanley Milgram, *Obedience to Authority* (New York: Harper & Row, 1974).

25. Hanna Arendt, *Eichmann in Jerusalem* (New York: Viking Press, 1963).

26. Sara Kiesler, Jane Siegel, and Timothy McGuire, "Social Psychological Aspects of Computer-mediated Communication," *American Psychologist,* No. 39 (1984), pp. 1123–1134.

27. Sara Kiesler and Lee Sproull, "Group Decision Making and Communication Technology," *Organizational Behavior and Human Decision Processes,* No. 52 (1992), pp. 96–123.

28. Phillip Zimbardo, "The Human Choice: Individuation, Reason, and Order Versus Deindividuation, Impulse, and Chaos," *Nebraska Symposium on Motivation,* No. 17 (1969), pp. 237–307.

29. Edward Diener, "Deindividuation, Self-awareness, and Disinhibition," *Journal of Personality and Social Psychology,* No. 37 (1979), pp. 1160–1171.

30. Marc Rogers, "Modern-day Robin Hood or Moral Disengagement?" (1999). Available: *www.escape.ca/~mkr/moral_doc.pdf.*

31. Albert Bandura, "The Social Learning Perspective: Mechanisms of Aggression." In H. Toch (ed.), *Psychology of Crime and Criminal Justice* (New York: Holt, Rinehart & Winston, 1979).

32. Matt Richtel, "The Hacker Myth Crumbles at Convention," *New York Times* (1998), [On-line], Available, *www.nytimes.com/library/tech/98/08/cyber/articles/02hacker.html.*

33. Marc Rogers, "A New Hacker Taxonomy" (2000). Available: *www.escape.ca/~mkr/hacker_doc.pdf.*

34. M.E. Kabay, "Totem and Taboo in Cyberspace," *Journal of the National Computer Security Association* (1996), pp. 4–9. Available: *www2.norwich.edu/mkabay/ethics/totem_taboo_cyber.htm.*

35. American Psychiatric Association, *Diagnostic and Statistical Manual of Mental Disorders,* 4th ed. (Washington, DC: American Psyciatric Association, 1994).

36. Eric Shaw, Keven Ruby, and Jerrold Post, "The Insider Threat to Information Systems," *Security Awareness Bulletin,* No. 2 (1998), pp. 1–10.

37. Toxic Shock, "Another View of Hacking: The Evil That Hackers Do," *Computer Underground Digest,* No. 2 (1990). Available: *ftp.eff.org/CUD.*

38. Stephen Bauer, "Aspgerger Syndrome (2001). Available: *www.asperger.org/asperger/asperger_bauer.htm.*

39. M.J. Zuckerman, "Hacker Reminds Some of Asperger Syndrome," *USA Today,* March 3, 2001. Available: *www.usatoday.com/news/health/2001-03-29-asperger.htm.*

40. Rosalyn Lord, "Asperger Syndrome" (2001). Available: *www.asperger.org/asperger/asperger_as.htm.*

41. S. Ehlers and Christopher Gillberg, "The Epidemiology of Asperger Syndrome: A Total Population Study," *Journal of Child Psychology and Psychiatry and Allied Disciplines,* Vol. 34, No. 8 (1993), pp. 1327–1350.

42. Dorthy Denning, "Concerning Hackers Who Break Into Computer Systems," *CPSR* (1990). Available: *www.cpsr.org/cpsr/privacy/crime/denning.hackers.html.*

43. Jerrold Post, Eric Shaw, and Keven Ruby, "Information Terrorism and the Dangerous Insider," Paper presented at the InfowarCon 98, Washington, D.C.

44. A.N. Chantler, "Risk: The Profile of the Computer Hacker." Ph.D. dissertation, Curtin University of Technology, 1995.

45. Mark Griffiths, "Internet Addiction: Does It Really Exist?" In J. Gackenbach, ed., *Psychology and the Internet: Intrapersonal, Interpersonal and Transpersonal Applications* (New York: Academic Press, 1998), pp. 61–75.

46. K.E. Anderson, "International Intrusion: Motives and Patterns" (1994). Available: *www.aracnet.com/~kea/Papers/paper.shtml.*

47. August Bequai, *Technocrimes* (Lexington, MA: Lexington Books, 1987).

48. Ira Winkler, "Why Hackers Do the Things They Do?" *Journal of the National Computer Security Association,* No. 7 (1996), p. 12.

49. Vincent Sacco and Elia Zureik, "Correlates of Computer Misuse: Data from a Self-Reporting Sample," *Behavior & Information Technology,* No. 9 (1990), pp. 353–369.

50. Steven Levy, *Hackers* (New York: Dell Publishing, 1984).

51. Steve Mizrach, "Is There a Hacker Ethic for '90s Hackers?" (1997). Available: *www.infowar.com/hacker/hackzf.html-ssi.*

52. Brian Harvey, "Computer Hacking and Ethics" (1998). Available: *www.attrition.org.*

53. Lundy Gill and Carolyn Magee, "Lawrence Kohlberg's Stages of Moral Development" (1998). Available: *gsep.pepperdine.edu/gsep/class/ethics/kohlberg.*

54. Mentor, "The Conscience of a Hacker," *Phrack Magazine* (1986). Available: *www.phrack.com.*

55. William Golding, *Lord of the Flies* (London: Faber and Faber, 1954).

56. Peter Smith, "The Cybercitizen Partnership: Teaching Children Cyber Ethics," *Cybercitizen Partnership* (2000). Available: *www.cybercitizenship.org/ethics/whitepaper.html.*

57. Bill Landreth, *Out of the Inner Circle* (Redmond, WA: Microsoft Books, 1985).

58. Donn Parker, *Fighting Computer Crime: A New Framework for Protecting Information* (New York: John Wiley & Sons, 1998).

59. Sarah Gordon, "The Generic Virus Writer," 4th International Virus Bulletin Conference, Jersey, U.K. (September 1994). Available: *www.research.ibm.com/antivirus/SciPapers/Gordon/GenericVirusWriter.html.*

60. Sarah Gordon, "The Generic Virus Writer II," 6th International Virus Bulletin Conference, Brighton, U.K. (September 1996). Available: *www.research.ibm.com/antivirus/SciPapers/Gordon/GVWII.html.*

61. Andrew Bissett and Geraldine Shipton, "Some Human Dimensions of Computer Virus Creation and Infection," *International Journal of Human Computer Studies,* Vol. 52, No. 5 (2000).

CHAPTER 7

INFORMATION WARFARE

Seymour Bosworth

CONTENTS

> *Information warfare is the offensive and defensive use of information and infor-*
> *mation systems to deny, exploit, corrupt, or destroy, an adversary's information,*
> *information-based processes, information systems, and computer-based networks*
> *while protecting one's own. Such actions are designed to achieve advantages over*
> *military or business adversaries.*
>
> —Dr. Ivan Goldberg, Institute for Advanced Study of Information Warfare

7.1   INTRODUCTION.   Until recently, warfare was conducted by armed forces representing adversarial nations or by revolutionary elements opposing their own governments. Today, although such conflicts still exist around the world, the ubiquitous nature of computers and associated technology has created new forces, new threats, new targets, and an accompanying need for new offensive and defensive weapons. Information warfare (IW), also known as e-warfare or cyberwar, is actually or potentially waged by all segments of the U.S. armed forces and by those of other nations as well as by commercial enterprises, activist groups, and even by individuals acting alone.

Conventional wars, whether large or small, are regularly reported by the news media. Information wars, on the other hand, are largely ignored except by those with a professional interest in the field. One reason for this is that conventional warfare is a matter of life or death; photos and eyewitness accounts are dramatic reminders of human cruelty and mortality. In contrast, IW has been conducted bloodlessly, with only economic and political consequences. However, it is becoming increasingly evident that IW may soon be conducted in ways that could equal or exceed the death and destruction associated with conventional weapons.

Conventional wars are fought by known combatants with clearly defined allies and antagonists, but IW often is waged by unknown entities with uncertain allegiances and goals. IW may be conducted on many fronts simultaneously, with wars fought within wars and with both civilian and military targets devastated.

The motives for conventional warfare were almost always territorial, religious, political, or economic. These are still important, but to them must be added the psychological motivations of groups and individuals—groups far more widely distributed and less easily overcome.

This chapter discusses information warfare in terms of the vulnerabilities of targets, participants' objectives, the sources of threats and attacks, the weapons used, and defenses against those weapons.

7.2   VULNERABILITIES.   Until recently, concerns over the security of the technological infrastructure in technologically advanced nations have been viewed with skepticism. However, by the mid-1990s, opinion leaders in government, industry, and the security field were coming to grips with widespread vulnerabilities in the critical infrastructure.

7.2.1   Critical Infrastructure.   In 1998, President Bill Clinton circulated Presidential Decision Directive 63, which outlined his administration's policy on critical infrastructure protection:

> Critical infrastructures are those physical and cyber-based systems essential to the minimum operations of the economy and the government . . . . They include, but are not limited to, telecommunications, energy, banking and finance, transportation, water systems and emergency services, both government and private."[1]

Having defined the very broad, vital areas that require protection, the paper went on to describe succinctly their vulnerability:

> The United States possesses both the world's strongest military and its largest national economy. Those two aspects of our power are mutually reinforcing and dependent. They are also increasingly reliant upon certain critical infrastructures and upon cyber-based information systems . . . .
>
> Because of our military strength, future enemies, whether nations, groups or individuals, may seek to harm us in non-traditional ways including attacks within the United States. Our economy is increasingly reliant upon interdependent and cyber-supported infrastructures and non-traditional attacks on our infrastructure and information systems may be capable of significantly harming both our military power and our economy.

A few examples of specific weaknesses were given by Jack L. Brock, Jr., Director, Governmentwide and Defense Information Systems, United States General Accounting Office:

> In May 1999 we reported that, as part of our tests of the National Aeronautics and Space Administration's (NASA) computer-based controls, we successfully penetrated several mission-critical systems. Having obtained access, we could have disrupted NASA's ongoing command and control operations and stolen, modified, or destroyed systems software and data.
>
> In August 1999, we reported that serious weaknesses in Department of Defense (DOD) information security continue to provide both hackers and hundreds of thousands of authorized users the opportunity to modify, steal, inappropriately disclose, and destroy sensitive DOD data.[2]
>
> Although these "attacks" were carried out one at a time, and without malicious intent, it is apparent that they, and many others, could have been launched simultaneously and with intent to inflict the maximum possible damage to the most sensitive elements of the national infrastructure.

In a memorandum to its chairman, describing a report of the Defense Science Board Task Force on Defensive Information Operations, Larry Wright stated that

> The threats to the DoD infrastructure are very real, non-traditional and highly diversified . . . . The vulnerabilities of these United States are greater than ever before, and we know that over twenty countries already have or are developing computer attack capabilities. Moreover, the Department of Defense should consider existing viruses and "hacker" attacks to be real "Information Operations or Warfare," what early aviation was to Air Power. In other words, we have not seen anything yet![3]

The report concluded that "It is the view of this task force that DoD cannot today defend itself from an Information Operations attack by a sophisticated nation state adversary."

7.2.2   Off-the-Shelf Software.   One characteristic of almost all military and civilian infrastructures is that they share, with more than 100,000,000 computers, a single ubiquitous operating system, and many of the same applications programs such as word processors, spreadsheets, and database software. These commercial off-the-shelf (COTS) products are available around the world, to friend and foe alike, and they appear to be more intensively studied by malefactors than by their security-inadequate producers. Each of these products presents entry points at which one common vulnerability may be exploited to damage or destroy huge portions of the national infrastructure. Until, and unless, this software is rendered significantly more resistant to attack, all of its users remain at risk.

7.2.3   Dissenting Views.   Not every influential observer concurs in these possible scenarios. Dr. Thomas P.M. Barnett, a professor and senior decision researcher at the Decision Support Department, Center for Naval Warfare Studies, U.S. Naval War College, voices a fairly typical disagreement:

> If absence makes the heart grow fonder, network-centric warfare is in for a lot of heart-break, because I doubt we will ever encounter an enemy to match its grand assumptions regarding a revolution in military affairs. The United States currently spends more on its information technology than all but a couple of great powers spend on their entire militaries. In a world where rogue nations typically spend around $5 billion a year on defense, NCW is a path down which only the U.S. military can tread.[4]

7.2.4   Rebuttal.   It may be of some benefit to have spokespersons for this unworried viewpoint, but their opinions must be weighed against those, for example, of Scott Henderson, of the Navy-Marine Corps intranet, who said: "One of our critical capabilities will be how we are to defend our information and our information systems from an adversary's attack."[5] He stated that successful intrusions, or attacks, on Navy computer systems increased from 89 in 2000 to 125 in 2001, an annualized increase of 80 percent. Those figures did not include successful attacks that went undetected or unsuccessful attempts that may have identified a weak point from which to launch future, and probably more successful, attacks.

A highly significant factor in IW that most of the dissenters miss is what has been called its asymmetric nature. The barriers to entry for attackers are very low; their weapons can be inexpensive, easily obtained, highly effective, easily automated, and used with negligible risk of personal harm. In contrast, defensive measures are extremely costly in time, money, and personnel, and they may be ineffective against even unsophisticated attackers using obsolete computers.

Considering the nature and extent of already successful attacks against major elements of U.S. military and civilian infrastructures, there appears to be no justification for discounting the views of those who believe that IW, in both its offensive and defensive roles, must be accorded the attention that surrounds any potentially cataclysmic force. This handbook, especially Chapters 9, 10, 11, and 13, contains many examples of viruses, worms, and other malware that have created massive disruptions in very large networks. The worst-case scenarios presented here should serve to awaken a measured response in those who may have been unaware or unconcerned.

7.3   GOALS AND OBJECTIVES.   Attacking forces, in information warfare, will always have a variety of strategic and tactical motives behind their actions; defensive forces generally have only one tactical goal—to blunt the enemy's attack and, if possible, to counterattack. Only after this is accomplished, and the nature of the attackers has been studied, can strategies for long-range operations be determined and effected.

7.3.1   Infrastructure.   Depending on the target, an attacker's goals may vary widely, but in almost every instance attackers want to damage, subvert, or destroy the infrastructure. In doing so, an attacker would hope to bring government, the economy, and military operations to a standstill—to instill fear, uncertainty, and doubt, and ultimately to induce widespread chaos that could cost many lives.

Although this view is entirely appropriate to wars between nations or to wars fought by terrorists, it is somewhat extreme for commercial warfare, whose main goal is competitive advantage.

7.3.2 Military.   Today, information warfare is a vital concern of area commanders under battlefield conditions. They must obtain complete, accurate, and timely information about their opponents' actions, intentions, weaknesses, and resources, while denying the same to their adversaries. The ultimate objective for all of these activities is to support the military tactics that will maximize the enemy's body count, or at least to render its defenses ineffective, so that surrender becomes the only viable option. The other side of the coin, defensive tactics, are aimed at preventing enemies from accomplishing their objectives. In the United States, the Joint Chiefs of Staff (for Army, Navy, Marine Corps, Coast Guard, and Air Force) have formulated the *Joint Doctrine for Operations Security* to be followed by all commanders of combatant commands in planning, preparation, and execution of joint operations. The publication states:

> Operations Security (OPSEC) is a process of identifying critical information and subsequently analyzing friendly actions attendant to military operations and other activities, to: (a) identify those operations that can be observed by adversary intelligence systems; (b) determine what indicators adversary intelligence systems might obtain that could be interpreted or pieced together to derive critical information in time to be useful to adversaries; and (c) select and execute measures that eliminate or reduce to an acceptable level the vulnerabilities of friendly actions to adversary exploitation.[6]

OPSEC is a process that could be applied to every element of civilian infrastructure as well as to the military, although all sources of information commonly used by the military are not available to the civilian sector. Other military code words for intelligence activities are as follows:

- *HUMINT* (Human Intelligence) is the most widely used source of information, as it has always been for both the civilian and military sectors. HUMINT is often the only source capable of direct access to an opponent's plans and intentions. Some intelligence gathering is quite open, but covert or clandestine operations must be conducted in secrecy, so as to protect the sources of confidential information.

- *SIGINT* (Signals Intelligence) is obtained from communications (COMINT), electronics (ELINT), and foreign instrumentation signals (FISINT).

- *COMINT* (Communications Intelligence) is information intended for others and intercepted without leaving a trace.

- *ELINT* (Electronic Intelligence) derives technical or geographic location data from an opponent's electromagnetic radiations, other than those that arise from communications or from nuclear detonations or radioactive sources. The primary ELINT sources are radars (radio detection and ranging).

- *FISINT* (Foreign Instrumentation Signals Intelligence) is obtained from intercepting and analyzing metered performance parameters electronically transmitted from sources such as a ballistic missile.

- *MASINT* (Measurement and Signal Intelligence) is scientific and technical in nature. Its purpose is to identify distinctive features associated with a source, emitter, or sender so as to facilitate subsequent identification or measurement. These features include wavelength, modulation, time dependencies, and other unique characteristics derived from technical sensors.

- *IMINT* (Imagery Intelligence) is produced by photography, infrared sensors, lasers, radars, and electro-optical equipment. This equipment, operated from land, sea, air, or space platforms, provides strategic, tactical, and operational information.

- *TECHINT* (Technical Information) is derived from the exploitation and analysis of captured or otherwise acquired foreign equipment.
- *OSINT* (Open Source Intelligence) is available to the general public from news media, unclassified government publications, public hearings, contracts, journals, seminars, and conferences. The World Wide Web has become an important tool of OSINT.

The *Joint Doctrine for Operations Security* lists several generic military activities with some of their associated critical information. It must be the objective of all information warfare to acquire this critical information about their opponents while denying such information to them.

- *Diplomatic negotiations* include military capabilities, intelligence verification, and minimum negotiating positions.
- *Political-military crisis management* includes target selection, timing considerations, and logistic capabilities and limitations.
- *Military intervention* requires information about intentions, military capabilities, forces assigned and in reserve, targets, and logistic capabilities and constraints.
- *Counterterrorism* involves forces, targets, timing, strategic locations, tactics, and ingress and egress methods.
- *Open hostilities* information involves force composition and disposition, attrition and reinforcement, targets, timing, logistic constraints, and location of command and control (C^2) nodes.
- *Mobilization* requires information about an intent to mobilize before public announcement, impact on military industrial base, impact on civilian economy, and transportation capabilities and limitations.
- *Intelligence, reconnaissance, and surveillance* information includes purpose and targets of collection, timing, capabilities of collection assets, and processing capabilities.

In addition to the Joint Chiefs' doctrines, the Department of Defense and each individual branch of service has been charged with the responsibility for establishing task forces, advisory groups, training and awareness programs, and virtual information networks to mobilize IW forces and to bring into being a strong defense against enemy attack.

Further evidence of the importance of military information and the vulnerabilities that exist at this time is contained in the 2001 report of the Secretary of Defense to the President and Congress:

> Information superiority is all about getting the right information to the right people at the right time in the right format while denying adversaries the same advantages. The United States enjoys a competitive advantage in many of the technical components of information superiority, but the U.S. also has vulnerabilities stemming from its increasing dependence on high technology. Experiences from Somalia to the Balkans have shown that low technology adversaries also can wage effective information campaigns, especially in urban environments.[7]

In the Information Age, the opportunities and obstacles to achieving national security objectives often are informational in nature. Information superiority is a principal component of the transformation of the Department. The results of research, analyses, and experiments, reinforced by experiences in Kosovo, demonstrate that the availability of information and the ability to share it significantly enhances mission effectiveness and improves efficiencies. Benefits include: increased speed of command, a higher tempo of operations, greater lethality, less fratricide and collateral damage, increased survivability, streamlined combat support, and more effective force synchronization. Kosovo also highlighted the shortage of assets for intelligence, surveillance, and reconnaissance, as well as the need for more secure interoperability and information protection, especially within coalitions.

> To ensure that the above prerequisites are in place, DoD is developing appropriate policy and oversight initiatives, actively pursuing opportunities to improve international cooperation in the areas of Command, Control, Communication, Computers, Intelligence, Surveillance, and Reconnaissance (C4ISR) and space-related activities, partnering with industry, and working to anticipate and understand the implications of emerging information technologies.
>
> The quality of DoD's infostructure will be a pacing item on the journey to the future. The ability to conceive of, experiment with, and implement new ways of doing business to harness the power of Information Age concepts and technologies depends upon what information can be collected, how it can be processed, and the extent to which it can be distributed. The ability to bring this capability to war will depend upon how well it can be secured and its reliability. DoD envisions an infostructure that is seamless with security built-in, one that can support the need for increased combined, joint, and coalition interoperability, leverages commercial technology, and accommodates evolution.

Although not as well publicized as are the U.S. defensive efforts, equal attention, time, and resources are being expended on actual and possible offensive operations. Every objective, every tactic, and every recommendation above, and some too sensitive to discuss, are subjects for study and implementation of offensive strategies and tactics aimed at enemies, present and future.

7.3.3 Government. The objectives of government, at every level, must be to protect the lives and welfare of its constituencies. Any breakdown in an essential government function may produce marked unrest, rioting, vandalism, civil disobedience, and possibly much bloodshed.

Just as in the military, government must be able to defend itself against an information attack waged by any enemy of the established order. Although not every element of government is perceived by all to perform a useful function, there are agencies without which it would be virtually impossible to sustain a developed nation's day-to-day activities.

At the federal level, civil servants' salaries, Social Security payments, tax collections and disbursements, military expenditures, lawmaking, and a myriad of other functions and activities can be carried out only with the active and pervasive use of computers and computer networks. In the past, some of these computer operations have been penetrated by hackers, crackers, and political dissidents, but only one at a time. It does not require a science fiction writer to imagine what the effect would be if simultaneous attacks were successfully launched against major federal government agencies.

At state levels, although the effects would be more constrained geographically, a great deal of damage could be done to emergency response units, to police and judiciary functions, and to health and welfare services. All of these depend on computerized functions that are protected even less than those of federal agencies.

For municipalities and even smaller governments, zoning enforcements and other local functions can be suspended without serious consequences, but police radio and computer networks are easily penetrated, and their ability to maintain law and order compromised.

As demonstrated by many previous incidents, government functions at any level are susceptible to information warfare. Natural events, Murphy's law (what *can* go wrong *will* go wrong), poorly configured systems, flawed operating systems and application programs, together with inadequate security measures underlie the vulnerability of government systems.

7.3.4   Transportation.   Airplanes, trains, trucks, and ships are all likely targets for physical and information warfare. Because all of them are necessary to support the infrastructure by transporting personnel and materials, any disruption can cause severe problems. Because all of these transportation systems increasingly rely on sophisticated telecommunications and computing resources, they are subject to information warfare.

7.3.4.1   Aviation.   The most visible, and potentially the most vulnerable, component of the transportation infrastructure is the aviation industry. Unlike the fly-by-the-seat-of-your-pants technology of aviation's early days, today's airplanes and the systems that dispatch and control them in flight are almost totally dependent on electronic communications and instruments, both analog and digital.

To a great extent, almost every airplane depends on its global positioning system (GPS) to determine its position in space, its course, speed, bearing to an airfield, and other important functions. Airplanes generally are required to fly at certain altitudes, in specific corridors, avoiding restricted areas, bad weather, and other aircraft. These requirements are met by a combination of GPS, ground and airborne radar, internal instruments, and communications from ground controllers. In the original design of these types of equipment, little or no consideration was given to security; as a result, all of them are susceptible to information warfare attacks.

On the other hand, the accuracy and reliability of GPS and airborne radar has led federal aviation authorities to consider implementing a system where ground controllers and published restrictions would no longer determine altitude, speed, clearance distances, and other flight parameters. Instead, pilots would have the option to choose any flight parameter that they believed to be safe. This new system is intended to increase the number of flights that can safely traverse the limited airspace. It is undoubtedly capable of doing so, but at the same time, it will greatly increase the dangers of flight should information warfare be waged against airplanes and the aviation infrastructure.

7.3.4.2   Railroads.   Less so than airplanes, but not to a negligible degree, trains are possible targets of IW. Train movements; switch settings; communications between engineers, trainmen, and control centers—carried on by insecure radio communications and wired lines. Attacks against any or all of these can prevent the railroads from carrying out their important functions, possibly by causing disastrous wrecks.

7.3.4.3   Trucking.   The great majority of domestic goods shipments are carried by tractor-trailer trucks. Foodstuffs, especially, depend on this relatively fast, reliable means of transportation. If even a short disruption were to be caused by IW, untold quantities of foodstuffs would rot in the fields, as would additional stockpiles awaiting distribution from central warehouses. Data for scheduling, routing, locating trucks, setting times and locations of pickup and delivery, and performing maintenance could be prevented from reaching their destinations.

7.3.4.4   Shipping.   Ships are indispensable means for transporting vast quantities of materials over long distances. Navigational data, such as position, speed, course to steer, and estimated time of arrival, are a few of the parameters determined by computers and GPS on virtually every ship afloat. Conventional radar and communications by VHF and high-frequency radio are in common use, with satellite communications becoming more prevalent, despite an early start that met with technical and economic difficulties.

Radar and communications jamming are old established weapons of IW, as is interception of critical information. Little attention has been paid to security in designing or operating this equipment, and that places ships at great risk, as does the threat of physical attacks.

7.3.4.5 Other Transportation Vulnerabilities.   Recognizing the importance of transportation to a nation's infrastructure, IW attackers could create wide-ranging disruptions if they were to intercept and successfully prevent receipt of critical information within the transportation industry. Recently, as a leader in new technology, the Port Authority of New York and New Jersey has begun converting to a wireless infrastructure at its many airports, train stations, bus terminals, tunnels, bridges, and shipping facilities. It requires no stretch of the imagination to predict what a determined attacker might accomplish in damaging or destroying such an infrastructure. The danger is especially great in light of the general lack of security from which wireless transmissions suffer.

Ironically, the last paragraph was written just one week before the World Trade Center (WTC) was destroyed by terrorist action. The Port Authority's offices in the WTC were completely destroyed, and more than 70 of its employees were officially listed as deceased or missing. Although that catastrophe points up the need for greater physical security, it also demonstrates how the Internet can be used in emergency situations. The Port Authority site, *www.panynj.gov*, was used to convey operational messages to the public as well as information for tenants, employees and prospective employees, vendors, suppliers, contractors, and the media.

7.3.5 Commerce.   In 1924 in an address to the American Society of Newspaper Editors, then-President Calvin Coolidge said: "After all, the chief business of the American people is business. They are profoundly concerned with producing, buying, selling, investing, and prospering in the world. I am strongly of the opinion that the great majority of people will always find these are moving impulses of our life."[8]

Now, more than 75 years later, these statements are no less true. Producing, buying, selling, and investing are the commercial means by which U.S. citizens and guest workers can hope to achieve prosperity. Although not recognized earlier, infrastructure is the glue that ties these functions together and permits them to operate efficiently and economically.

If these bonds were to be broken, American business would come to a virtual standstill; it is that reality which makes the commercial infrastructure so inviting a target. Without complete, accurate, and current information, no investors would put their money at risk, and no transactions would take place among producers, buyers, and sellers.

In a populace lacking food, utilities, prescription drugs, money, and other necessities, civil disorder would be widespread. With the breakdown of commerce and the citizenry's unwillingness or inability to perform their customary functions, government at every level might cease to operate. This, in turn, would make military defensive actions highly problematic, and an enemy who combined IW with conventional force attacks would be difficult to resist.

On a less catastrophic level, there have been several cases of deliberate stock manipulation by means of insertion of false information into various news channels; an enemy could cause significant disruption in the stock market by forcing a few key stocks into unwarranted declines. In addition, the widespread use of automated trading tools that respond to significant drops in specific shares or in particular aggregate stock indexes could precipitate major economic problems in the developed world.

7.3.6   Financial Disruptions.   Money is the lifeblood of every developed nation. For an economy to be healthy, its money supply, like the body's blood supply, must be strong, healthy, and free-flowing. For an IW attacker, disruptions in the enemy's money supply and in its free flow are important objectives. Likely targets in the financial infra-structure include payment systems, investment mechanisms, and banking facilities.

7.3.6.1   Payment Systems.   Every government employee, every member of the armed forces, every office worker, factory hand, service worker, engineer, and retired person—in fact, almost every individual in the United States—depends on regular receipt of funds necessary for survival. Paychecks, dividends, welfare and unemployment benefits, commissions, payments for products, and fees for services comprise most of the hundreds of millions of daily checks, direct deposits, and wire transfers without which most people would be unable to purchase their essential needs—assuming that products and services were available to meet those needs.

The great majority of payroll systems are computerized. Many of them, including those of the federal and state governments, depend on a few centralized computer payroll services. Even if those services were not damaged by infrastructure attacks, the banks on which payroll funds are drawn might be. This would halt, or at least impede, the cutting of physical checks, the direct deposits, cash withdrawals, wire transfers, and any other means by which payments are made. Such a situation has never occurred within the United States except in small local areas and for only brief periods of time. No one can predict what the consequences would be for a widespread attack and surely, no one would want to find out.

7.3.6.2   Investment Mechanisms.   Various stock, bond, and commodity exchanges provide the principal means by which individual, institutional, and corporate entities easily and expeditiously can invest in financial instruments and commodity goods.

Each exchange has all of its computers and communications located within a single facility, with connections to tens of thousands of terminals worldwide. Disruption in these systems would not have as disastrous an effect as would a payment system disruption, but it would not be long before a breakdown in investment mechanisms would produce a commercial meltdown.

Because of the vast sums of money involved, exchange systems largely have been hardened against intrusion, and most have remote, redundant facilities, but there have been instances where hardware and software problems as well as physical exploits have brought down an exchange infrastructure.

7.3.6.3   Banking

The banking industry is the foundation of the modern financial system, and by extension both American and foreign capitalist economies. At some point, every important financial transaction is conducted through the banking system. As such it is vital to economic health. With the advent of information warfare, the electronic, interdependent nature of banking—and finance in general—combined with its critical nature, makes the banking system a likely target for a strategic attack against a country. This is a new viewpoint for an industry focused on crime, traditional financial crises, and the more recent phenomenon of low-level hacking. It is critical, however, that we master this viewpoint and adapt our banking industry to it, for the threats information warfare poses are different than traditional bank security threats, and will increase as the age of information warfare develops. Focused correctly, a well prepared attack could cause chaos throughout the international system.[9]

The ubiquitous banking system is as highly automated and as security conscious as any other element of the world's infrastructure. With ATMs, online banking, funds-transfer networks, and check clearing, banks are integral to virtually every commercial transaction.

As an example of the scope of banking operations involving money transfers, FED-WIRE, operated by the Federal Reserve Board, serves 9,000 depository institutions, providing transfers that are immediate, final, and irrevocable. It processed 108 million transactions in the year 2000, with a total value in excess of $379 trillion. The average daily volume was over 429,000 transactions, valued at more than $1.5 trillion.[10]

The Clearing House Interbank Payment System (CHIPS) processes transfers for more than 1000 financial institutions. Each day, CHIPS transfers an average of $1.3 trillion, in 238,000 transactions.[11]

The Society for Worldwide Interbank Funds Transfer (SWIFT) has over 7,000 users in 193 countries. In July 2001 it had processed 860 million messages, year to date.[12] Information about dollar value is not made public, but the amounts are known to be huge.

If any of these systems were to be attacked successfully, the consequences for the financial well-being of many nations would be disastrous. Despite intensive efforts to safeguard the networks, attacks could be launched against the central computers, the computers of each user, and the networks that connect them.

7.3.7 Medical Security. In hospitals, as in group and private practice, the primary functions are carried out in a decentralized mode, making large-scale attacks impracticable. However, ancillary functions, such as sending invoices to the government, to health maintenance organizations, and to individuals, for services provided, and placing orders for drugs and supplies require interconnections with centralized computers.

Although the medical profession is often slow to adopt new infrastructure elements, network-connected computers have been mandated at least for payments, and they are becoming increasingly popular for maintaining patient data, for research, and for other functions. There have been reports that hospital systems have been penetrated, with prescriptions switched and HIV negative patients advised that their test results were positive.

So far, only isolated incidents of sadistic cruelty have been reported, but they indicate that the vulnerabilities may be more than is apparent on the surface. Chapter 49 of this *Handbook* treats medical information security in detail.

7.3.8 Law Enforcement. The objectives of law enforcement are to facilitate the apprehension of criminals and wrongdoers. To accomplish this, facilities in common use include computers in every squad car connected to precinct headquarters, and networks that interconnect local, state, federal, and international databases. In spite of these cooperative efforts, much remains to be done. The laws of different governments are often not in alignment. A typical case, and one of great and tragic consequences, is that of Osama bin Laden. Although he was wanted for heinous crimes against the United States, he has been sheltered and supported by governments unfriendly to the

United States. Politics and religion have become embedded in law enforcement; unless these elements can be eliminated or resolved, enforcement of laws across international boundaries will remain, at least in part, an unachievable goal.

With local law enforcement, it is clear that jamming, or noise interference on emergency channels, or denial of computer services would greatly exacerbate the effects of physical attacks. At worst, a state of panic and chaos might ensue.

7.3.9   International and Corporate Espionage.   Espionage has been a recognized military activity since at least the biblical story of Joshua; however, its application to civilian commerce dates only from the Industrial Revolution. Since then, industries and indeed nations have prospered to the extent that they could devise and retain trade secrets. In the United States, the unauthorized appropriation of military secrets has been legally proscribed since the country's inception, with penalties as severe as death during wartime.

Only recently have economic espionage and the theft of trade secrets become the subjects of law, with severe penalties whether the law is broken within or outside of the United States or even via the Internet.

The "Economic Espionage Act of 1996" was signed into law by President Clinton on October 11, 1996. Section 1832 provides that:

(A)   Whoever, with intent to convert a trade secret, that is related to or included in a product that is produced for or placed in interstate or foreign commerce, to the economic benefit of anyone other than the owner thereof, and intending or knowing that the offense will injure any owner of that trade secret, knowingly—

   (1)   Steals, or without authorization appropriates, takes, carries away, or conceals, or by fraud, artifice, or deception obtains such information;

   (2)   Without authorization copies, duplicates, sketches, draws, photographs, downloads, uploads, alters, destroys, photocopies, replicates, transmits, delivers, sends, mails, communicates, or conveys such information;

   (3)   Receives, buys, or possesses such information, knowing the same to have been stolen or appropriated, obtained, or converted without authorization;

   (4)   Attempts to commit any offense described in any of paragraphs (1) through (3); or

   (5)   Conspires with one or more other persons to commit any offense described in any of paragraphs (1) through (3), and one or more of such persons do any act to effect the object of the conspiracy,

   Shall, except as provided in subsection (b), be fined under this title or imprisoned not more than 10 years, or both.

(B)   Any organization that commits any offense described in subsection (A) shall be fined not more than $5,000,000.[13]

Although the foregoing lists all of the actions that are proscribed, it is not specific as to which assets are to be protected as trade secrets. For this, see the Defense Security Service paper "What Are We Protecting?"[14] There, the five basic categories of People, Activities/Operations, Information, Facilities, and Equipment/Materials are expanded into 42 specific assets, with the admonition that every company official must clearly identify to employees what classified or proprietary information requires protection. Only if the owner has taken reasonable measures to keep such information secret, and the information derives actual or potential economic value from not being generally known to or readily obtainable through proper means, will the courts view it as a trade secret.

For further information on intellectual property, including trade secrets, see Chapter 12.

7.3.10   Communications.

Communications are the means by which all elements of a civilization are tied together. Any significant destruction of communications media would disrupt the most important segments of society. Without adequate communications, transactions and services would come to a complete halt. In the United States, communications have been disrupted frequently, but fortunately, the infrastructure has been so vast and so diverse that the consequences have rarely been more than temporary. Even after the WTC disaster of September 11, 2001, when Verizon's downtown telephone facilities centers were heavily damaged, service was restored within four days to the New York Stock Exchange and to other important users in the area.

Contrary to popular belief, the Internet is so widely used and concentrated in so few backbone points that a coordinated attack actually could destroy its functioning. For many years, backup facilities have included redundant computers and all of their associated peripherals, often in remote locations. Too often, however, alternate communications facilities are not provided. Unless this is rectified, the same disaster that brings down one installation will disable all.

7.3.11   Destabilization of Economic Infrastructure.

A major difference between wealthy, developed nations and poor, undeveloped countries lies in the strength of their economic infrastructures. The existence of strong capital markets, stable banking and lending facilities, and efficient payment processes, all tied together by fast, technically advanced communications capabilities, are essential to healthy, growing economies.

At opposite ends of this spectrum lie Afghanistan and the United States. Although this is being written only three months after the attacks on the Pentagon and the WTC, and the eventual outcome of this event cannot be predicted, one thing appears certain. The perpetrators of the attack, now identified as Osama bin Laden and his Al-Qaeda organization, operating out of Afghanistan, chose as their target the symbols and the operating centers of America's military operations and its economic infrastructure.

It seems certain at this time that the United States and the entire world is being impelled into a serious recession. With hundreds of thousands thrown out of work and with investment capital drying up, the entire economic infrastructure of the world has suffered a great blow. How and when it will recover is a subject of speculation, but of one thing there can be no doubt: Every effort must be bent toward preventing another attack. Security can no longer be the duty of a few technical people; it has become everyone's responsibility.

7.4   SOURCES OF THREATS AND ATTACKS.

The actual and potential originators of information warfare are numerous and powerful. One need not be paranoid to feel that an attack may come from any direction. This section lists sources that have already proven their capabilities for conducting cyberwar.

7.4.1   Nation-States.

U.S. military preparations for cyberwar were described in Section 7.3.2. This section details some of the measures that another great power—China—is effecting toward the same ends. Most of the material is from a paper titled "Like Adding Wings to the Tiger: Chinese Information War Theory and Practice."[15]

7.4.1.1   *China and Information Warfare.*

Although China is a nuclear power, it does not yet have the arsenal necessary to threaten a superpower like the United States.

However, it can do so with its IW forces; adding wings to the tiger makes it more combat worthy. Nor is Chinese IW entirely theoretical. On August 3, 2000, the *Washington Times* reported that hackers suspected of working for a Chinese government institute took large amounts of unclassified, but sensitive information from a Los Alamos computer system. A spokesman stated that "an enormous amount of Chinese activity hitting our green, open sites" occurs continuously.[16]

According to an article in the Chinese Armed Forces newspaper, the *Liberation Army Daily,* their first attack objectives will be the computer networking systems that link a country's political, economic, and military installations, as well as their general society.[17] A further objective will be to control the enemy's decision-making capability in order to hinder coordinated actions.

Expanding on Mao Zedung's theory of a People's War, IW can be "carried out by hundreds of millions of people using open-type modern information system."[18] In this war, combatants can be soldiers or teenagers, or anyone who has a computer as a weapon.[19] Ironically, China, with its long-standing fear of outside information as a possible spur to counterrevolutionary action, now views arming large numbers of intelligent people with computers and access to the Internet as a necessary survival measure. It remains to be seen just how many personal computers will be made available and how China will ensure that they will be used only as the government intends.

7.4.1.2   Strategies.   The People's Liberation Army (PLA) with 1.5 million reserve troops has been carrying out IW exercises on a wide scale. One such, in Xian Province, concentrated on conducting information reconnaissance, changing network data, releasing information bombs, dumping information garbage, disseminating propaganda, applying information deception, releasing clone information, organizing information defense, and establishing spy stations.[20] The antecedents of these tactics can be found in a book of unknown authorship, first mentioned about 1500 years ago, entitled *The Secret Art of War: The 36 Stratagems.*" Strategy 25 advises: "*Replace the Beams with Rotten Timbers.* Disrupt the enemy's formations, interfere with their methods of operations, change the rules in which they are used to following, go contrary to their standard training. In this way you remove the supporting pillar, the common link that makes a group of men an effective fighting force."[21]

The 36 stratagems deserve close study; many of them are obviously in use even today by China and others. For example, strategy 3 says: "*Kill with a Borrowed Sword.* When you do not have the means to attack your enemy directly, then attack using the strength of another."[22] Lacking the weapons to attack the United States directly, the perpetrators of the WTC attack used the airliners belonging to their targets.

Strategy 5 says: "*Loot a Burning House.* When a country is beset by internal conflicts, when disease and famine ravage the population, when corruption and crime are rampant, then it will be unable to deal with an outside threat. This is the time to attack."[23]

At the time of this writing, the anthrax dispersion following the WTC disaster seems to follow this strategy, although the source of the infectious material has not yet been ascertained.

Some of the strategies might well be employed by the United States. For example, strategy 33 advises: "*The Strategy of Sowing Discord.* Undermine your enemy's ability to fight by secretly causing discord between him and his friends, allies, advisors, family, commanders, soldiers, and population. While he is preoccupied settling internal disputes his ability to attack or defend, is compromised."[24] To accomplish this, IW may prove to be an effective weapon.

7.4.1.3 Training. Several high-level academies and universities have been established to conduct IW instruction for the PLA. In addition, training is planned for large numbers of individuals to include:

- Basic theory, including computer basics and application, communications network technology, the information highway, and digitized units
- Electronic countermeasures, radar technology
- IW rules and regulations
- IW strategy and tactics
- Theater and strategic IW
- Information systems, including gathering, handling, disseminating, and using information
- Combat command, monitoring, decision making, and control systems
- Information weapons, including concepts, principles of soft and hard destruction, and how to apply these weapons
- Simulated IW, protection of information systems, computer virus attacks and counterattacks, and jamming and counterjamming of communications networks[25]

It is doubtful that all of these training objectives have been accomplished yet, but there seems to be a major commitment to do so, and sooner rather than later.

China and the United States are only two of the nations that are openly preparing for, and actually engaged in, information warfare. It is obvious that many others are similarly involved and that these measures, combined with conventional weapons or weapons of mass destruction, have the potential to elevate warfare to a destructive level never before possible and hardly conceivable.

7.4.2 Cyberterrorists. " 'Cyberterrorism' means intentional use or threat of use, without legally recognized authority, of violence, disruption, or interference against cybersystems, when it is likely that such use would result in death or injury of a person or persons, substantial damage to physical property, civil disorder, or significant economic harm."[26]

Cyberterrorists, those who engage in cyberterrorism, generally are able to carry out the same sort of cyberwar as nation-states; in fact, they may be state-sponsored. The major difference is that terrorist attacks are usually hit-and-run, where nations are capable of sustained and continuous operations. Although conventional warfare always was carried out in an overt fashion, it is the nature of IW that it can be engaged in without a declaration of war and without any clear indication of who the attacker actually is. In fact, it may not be recognized that a war is being conducted; it may seem only that a series of unfortunate, unconnected natural failures of computers and communications are disrupting an economy.

Terrorists, especially when state-sponsored, would be very likely to conceal their IW activities in this manner, so as to avoid the retribution that would inevitably follow. On the other hand, some terrorists would publicly take credit for their actions, in order to bolster their apparent strength, and to gather added support from like-minded individuals and organizations.

The seriousness of terrorist threats has resulted in the appointment, in October 2001, of Tom Ridge as head of the Office of Homeland Security, responsible for coordinating antiterrorist measures among federal, state, and local agencies. Mr. Ridge is also head of the new Homeland Security Council, consisting of the Attorney General, the Secretary of Defense, the head of the CIA, and the Director of the FBI, as well as the heads of other security-related agencies. Whether this appointment proves effective in reducing or eliminating terrorism within the United States will depend on solving the problems of overlapping authorities, inertia, incompatible databases, turf wars, funding, management, the predictability of terrorist actions, and a host of political and technological issues.

7.4.3   Corporations.   The threats aimed at or directed by corporations are far less deadly than those of the military or of terrorists, but they are no less pervasive. Thefts of data, denial of service, viruses, and natural disasters traditionally have been at the heart of individual corporate security concerns. These concerns have not abated, but to them have been added fears that attacks on large segments of the information infrastructure are more likely to create damage than is an attack against any single enterprise. To guard against this, every installation should operate behind strong firewalls and effective access controls.

In the wake of the September 11 attacks, Richard Clarke, who had been National Coordinator for Security, Infrastructure Protection and Counterterrorism since May 1998, was appointed to a new post. As special advisor to the president for cyberspace security, Mr. Clarke has warned that terrorists are out to hurt our economy and that they can use viruses in massive, coordinated attacks against corporate IT systems. He recommends, at a minimum, that disaster recovery plans include near-online, off-site backup facilities and redundant communications paths.

7.4.4   Activists.   The line between terrorists and activists is often thin and indistinct. Throughout the world, many organizations and individuals feel very strongly about globalization, territorial claims, environmental concerns, abortion, human rights, poverty, and other seemingly intractable issues. These organizations, and like-minded individuals, operate along a spectrum that extends from the completely intellectual and peaceable at one end, to the radical, confrontational, and militant at the other. For example, activists have sabotaged World Wide Web sites to express opposition to the World Trade Organization, support for Kashmiri independence, and distaste for Japanese revisionist history about atrocities in World War II.[27]

Given this wide range of motivations and actions, proactive steps and active responses must be carefully measured so as to be consistent with the nature of specific activist threats. The countermeasures may range anywhere from simple public relations announcements to shuttered and barricaded facilities, with strong cyberwar defenses in place.

7.4.5   Criminals.   While all of the earlier-mentioned sources of threat may have political or ideological motives, there is a large class of security risks whose sole motivation is personal financial gain. Their illegal activities include manipulating stock prices, stealing services, fraudulently transferring funds to their own accounts, and using stolen or invented credit card numbers; they also trade in stolen customer lists, product designs, marketing plans, and other proprietary information, which they offer to sell to competitors or back to their original owners. Although the materials may have been stolen for personal gain, their ultimate use may be as weapons in cyberwar, such as transnational commercial competition.

Chapters 4 and 12 of the *Handbook* describe in detail many criminal threats and the measures that may be taken to thwart them.

7.4.6 Hobbyists. The term "hackers" originally was applied to those individuals with expert programming capabilities, who derived satisfaction from delving into the internal structures and functions of software. The goal was to increase their own level of sophisticated technical knowledge and to share this learning with others; their motives were never malevolent.

To this day, there are many students of computer science and pure hobbyists with these same objectives, who would never intentionally attack a computer or its software. On the other hand, there now appear to be as many, or possibly more, persons whose intent is to damage or destroy computer systems for what appears to be malicious pleasure. Rather than sharing knowledge for academic reasons, these individuals do so in order to acquire bragging rights and a reputation among their peers. When a single hobbyist or a group with malicious intent attack any Internet site, they are engaging in cyberwar.

Most of the original hackers resent the use of this appellation to describe malicious system penetrators; instead, they would like the malefactors to be known as crackers. Especially they resent the fact that many crackers have little or no technical knowledge. Those, known as "script kiddies," can do no more than initiate a program given to them by others, but they are inordinately pleased by the amount of damage they can do.

For a full discussion of hackers, see Chapter 6.

7.5 WEAPONS OF CYBERWAR. The weapons used in information warfare have existed for many years, but newer and more malevolent versions are produced with increasing frequency. For this reason, system security cannot be considered as static, but rather as part of an ongoing process that must be continuously monitored and strengthened. This section briefly describes the most common and most dangerous IW weapons, with references to other chapters where more detailed information is available.

7.5.1 Denial of Service and Distributed Denial of Service. Denial of Service (DoS) and Distributed Denial of Service (DDoS) are means by which computers, network servers, and telecommunications circuits can be partially or completely prevented from performing their designated functions. Any computer element that has been designed for a specific maximum capacity, if flooded by messages or data inputs that greatly exceed that number, can be slowed or even brought to a complete halt.

A DoS attack is carried out by a single computer that has been programmed to overwhelm the target system's capacity, usually by generating, automatically, a very large number of messages. A DDoS attack is implemented by planting a small program on hundreds or thousands of unaware computers. At a signal from the attacker, all of the agents (sometimes called zombies or daemons) send many messages simultaneously, thus flooding the victim's system or preempting all of its bandwidth capacity.

Details of many of these attacks and the recommended defenses are contained in Chapter 11.

7.5.2 Malicious Code. Malicious code includes viruses, worms, and Trojan horses, as described in Chapter 9. Mobile code such as Java, ActiveX, and VBScript were developed to increase the functionality of Web sites, but all three, as described in Chapter 10, also can be used maliciously.

There have been innumerable instances where malicious code has actually been used to damage or deface Web sites, both civilian and military. Apparently, all of these exploits have been perpetrated by single individuals or by very small groups of unaffiliated crackers. However, in the event of actual cyberwar, it seems certain that large groups of coordinated, technically knowledgeable attackers will attempt to wreak havoc on their opponents' infrastructures through the use of malicious code.

Just as U.S. military and governmental agencies, and most of their allies, are engaged in large-scale operations to develop defensive capabilities, it is essential that all commercial enterprises exert major efforts to do the same. Initiatives have begun to form close working relationships between government and the private sector. Also, industry groups have begun advocating relaxation of those laws that prohibit close cooperation of competitors. This will be necessary before information can be shared as required to strengthen the infrastructure. Similarly, groups are requesting that shared information be protected from those who would use the Freedom of Information Act to force disclosure.

Every prudent organization will support these initiatives and will work with appropriate government agencies and industry groups to ensure their own survival and the welfare of the country itself.

7.5.3 Cryptography.   Military operations, since the earliest recorded times, have utilized cryptography to prevent critical information from falling into enemy hands. Today, information is a vastly more important resource than ever before, and the need for cryptography has increased almost beyond measure. Not only the military, but every financial institution, every competitive commercial enterprise, and even many individuals feel impelled to safeguard their own vital information. At the same time, access to the secret information of enemies and opponents would provide inestimable advantages.

Recognizing this, powerful supercomputers, directed by mathematicians, theoretical scientists, and cryptographers, are being applied to improving the processes of encryption and decryption. The most notable achievement in the recent past was the British construction of a computerized device to break the German Enigma code. The information thus obtained has been widely credited with a significant role in the outcome of World War II.

The development of effective mechanisms for spreading computations over millions of personal computers has greatly reduced the time required for brute-force cracking of specific encrypted messages; for example, messages encrypted using the 56-bit Digital Encryption Standard (DES) were decrypted in four months using 10,000 computers in 1997, 56 hours using 1,500 special-purpose processors in 1998, and 22 hours using 100,000 processors in 1999.[28]

A major issue, yet to be resolved, is the strength of cryptographic tools that may be sold domestically or exported overseas. The contending forces include producers of cryptographic tools who believe that if the strength of their product is in any way restricted, they will lose their markets to producers in other countries with more liberal policies. Similarly, proponents of privacy rights believe that unbreakable cryptographic tools should be freely available.

The countervailing view is that virtually unbreakable cryptographic tools shipped overseas will inevitably find their way into the hands of unfriendly governments who may use them in conducting cyberwars against us. Domestically, law enforcement agencies believe that they should have "back-door" entry into all cryptographic algorithms, so that they may prevent crimes as wide-ranging as embezzlement, drug trafficking, and terrorism.

As domestic crimes and terrorist attacks grow in number and intensity, it seems certain that at least a few civil liberties, including privacy rights, may be infringed. The hope is that an optimum balance will be struck between the need for security and the core values of our democracy.

Tutorial 5 on the *Handbook* Internet site at *www.wiley.com/go/security/handbook* and Chapter 5 both contain further discussions of cryptography.

7.5.4   Psychological Operations.

Psychological operations (PSYOP) may be defined as planned psychological activities directed to enemy, friendly, and neutral audiences in order to influence their emotions, motives, attitudes, objective reasoning, and behaviors in ways favorable to the originator. The target audiences include governments, organizations, groups, and individuals, both military and civilian.

One of the most potent weapons in information warfare, PSYOP, attempts to:

- Reduce morale and combat efficiency within the enemy's ranks
- Promote mass dissension within, and defections from, enemy combat units and/or revolutionary cadres
- Support our own and allied forces cover and deception operations
- Promote cooperation, unity, and morale within one's own and allied units, as well as within friendly resistance forces behind enemy lines[29]

The information that accomplishes these ends is conveyed via any media: by printed material such as pamphlets, posters, newspapers, books, and magazines, and by radio, television, personal contact, public address systems, and of increasing importance, through the Internet.

A classic example of successful PSYOP application was the deception practiced prior to the Allied invasion of the European mainland. Through clever "leaks," false information reached Germany that General Patton, America's most celebrated combat commander, was to lead an army group across the English Channel at Pas de Calais. As a consequence, German defensive forces were concentrated in that area. For weeks after the Normandy invasion was mounted, Hitler was convinced that it was just a feint, and he refused to permit the forces at Calais to be redeployed. Had this PSYOP failed, and had more of Germany's defensive forces been concentrated in Normandy, the Allied landing forces might well have been thrown back into the sea.

Although generally considered not to involve a PSYOP action, the September 11 attacks and the subsequent spread of anthrax spores made clear that a physical action can have the greatest and most far-reaching psychological effects. Beyond mourning the death of almost 5,000 innocent civilians, the new sense of vulnerability, and powerlessness caused great psychological trauma throughout the nation and much of the Western world. The full consequences to the travel, entertainment, and hospitality industries, as well as to every segment of the world economy, are likely to be both disastrous and long-lasting.

At the time of this writing, President George Bush and Mayor Rudy Giuliani of New York were attempting to counter the PSYOP defeat, but what is required is a major, integrated, expert PSYOP mission to restore morale and encourage behavior that can reverse a downward spiral.

7.5.5   Physical Attacks.

Prior to September 11, 2001, physical attacks, as a part of cyberwar, were generally considered in the same light as attacks against any military objective, and defensive measures were instituted accordingly. In the civilian sector, starting with student attacks against academic computers in the 1960s and 1970s, there have been occasional reported physical attacks against information processing resources.

Although access controls have been almost universally in place, their enforcement often has been less than strict.

Another indication of the susceptibility of the information infrastructure to physical attack is the prevalence of "backhoe attacks" in which construction crews accidentally slice through high-capacity optic cables used for telecommunications and as part of the Internet backbones.[30] The signs indicating where not to dig can serve as markers for those deliberately targeting single points of failure.

The destruction of the WTC and a portion of the Pentagon have brought the possibility of additional physical attacks very much into the forefront of cyberwar thinking for both the military and civilian infrastructures. Car bombings and packaged bombs had become almost commonplace, especially in the Mideast. Successful attacks had been launched against U.S. embassies and troop barracks, as well as against Israel, England and France. To guard against such actions, perimeter defenses were widened, and in some areas personal searches at strategic points were instituted.

These defenses have proven to be of limited value, and suicide bombers seem to be increasing in numbers, and in the effectiveness of their weapons. The use of commercial aircraft, fully loaded with fuel, as manned, guided missiles was apparently never considered, prior to 11 September. After that date, there has been wide-spread recognition that protective measures must be taken that will prevent a recurrence of those tragic events. Airport security has become a direct federal responsibility, under a new Transportation Security Administration in the Department of Transportation. On November 11, 2001, President Bush signed a bill that requires all airport baggage screeners to be U.S. citizens and to undergo criminal background checks before becoming federal employees. At the same time, five airports were selected at which security will be provided by private contractors to test the relative merits of governmental and private responsibility. While even minimal safeguards against known weapons are being debated, there appears to be little thinking directed toward other types of attacks that might even now be in the planning stage.

7.5.6   Biological and Chemical Weapons and Weapons of Mass Destruction. Although the use of these weapons can affect every element of society, they have a particular potency in destroying the infrastructure of a targeted nation. While the WTC attacks have had long-lasting psychological effects, the results of the anthrax dissemination may be even more deeply traumatic. Already, the presence of anthrax spores has interfered with the functioning of the Congress, the Supreme Court, the U.S. Postal Service, hospitals, and many other institutions. How much more of the infrastructure will be damaged is unknowable at this time. Unless the culprit is apprehended quickly and countermeasures taken against these and future attacks, the infrastructure damage already evident is certain to increase greatly.

7.5.7   Weapons Inadvertently Provided.   There are many widespread vulnerabilities to computer systems that are not created as weapons, but whose presence makes the targets of cyberwar highly vulnerable. Poor software designs and inadequate quality control create opportunities for attackers to damage or destroy information, and the information systems themselves. Chapters 25, 26, and 36 of this *Handbook* are especially useful in identifying and eliminating these sources of security vulnerabilities.

7.6   DEFENSES.   A variety of defenses may be employed both to prevent attacks and to mitigate their effects. Because each of these defenses may have only limited utility, it is evident that new and more effective defenses must be developed.

7.6.1   Legal Defenses.   As a defense against IW attacks or as a framework for apprehending and prosecuting attackers, the international legal system has been generally ineffective. The reasons for this include:

- Information warfare is not prohibited under the United Nations (UN) Charter, unless it directly results in death or property damage.
- Laws that are not recognized and enforced lose their power to compel actions.
- There is little or no police power to enforce those few laws that do exist.
- The issue of sovereignty as it relates to transborder communications is unresolved.
- Neither the United States nor any other major power has pressed for international laws to govern information warfare. This may be attributed to the fact that such laws, while desirable for defense, would impair their own offensive operations.
- Many nations do not recognize cyberwar attacks as criminal actions.
- In many lands, political considerations determine judicial outcomes.
- Few countries support extradition of their citizens even when indicted for terrorist or criminal activities.
- Terrorists, drug cartels, the international mafia, and even individual hackers have every reason to circumvent the law and usually possess the resources that enable them to do so.
- Identifying attackers may be difficult or even impossible.
- New technologies arrive at a rate much faster than appropriate legislation.

Further acting to constrain law as a deterrent, is the fact that there has been no universal acceptance of definitions for IW-relevant terminology—attacks, acts of war, aggression, hostilities, combatants, crimes, criminals—all remain vague concepts. Until such terms, as applied to IW, are clearly defined, there can be no legal strictures against them.

The difference between acceptable and unacceptable targets is obscured by the dual-use, civilian and military, characteristics of infosystems and infrastructures. Similarly, it is difficult to condemn denial of service, when peacetime boycotts and economic sanctions are widely applied to further economic or political ends.

Clearly, legal defenses against cyberwar are inadequate at this time. Whether the United States will pursue effective international legislation remains doubtful until the question of building adequate defenses, without hobbling offensive operations, is resolved.

7.6.2   Forceful Defenses.   If IW attacks are accepted as acts of war, the use of retaliatory military force would be highly likely. The strategic and tactical decisions that would follow are well beyond the scope of this chapter, but six considerations are relevant.

1. The United States has shown considerable reluctance to engage in combat without the sanction of the United Nations and without the concurrence of major allies. If the provocation is limited to an IW attack, it may be difficult to build a coalition or even to avoid UN condemnation.

2. The identity of the attacker may be unclear. Even after the September 11 attacks, the United States had no enemy who admitted culpability. As a consequence, the

United States could not declare war on any nation or state but could only declare a war on "terrorism."

3. The attacker may be misidentified. Through the use of "spoofing," and routing an attack through unaware nations, the anonymous culprit may escape detection, while blame falls on an innocent victim.

4. There may be difficulty in determining whether a particular event is an act of information warfare or simply the result of errors, accidents, or malfunctions.

5. The attackers may not be a foreign government, against whom war can be declared, but a criminal organization, a disaffected group, activists, commercial competitors, or even individuals bent on mischief.

6. The United Nations, and international sentiment in general, require that military force only be used in response to armed attack and, further, that the response be proportional to the attack that provoked it.

In light of these considerations, it seems unlikely that information warfare, unless it results in catastrophic injuries and deaths, will be met by a forceful reaction.

7.6.3 Technical Defenses.   The technical defenses against IW are many and varied. Almost the entire contents of this volume are applicable to safeguarding against cyberwar attacks. In particular, Chapters 8 to 11, 13 to 24, 27 to 29, 34 to 43, 45 to 47, and 50 to 53 will prove helpful in building powerful defenses.

These same measures can prove equally effective in defending against IW, criminals, activists, competitors, and hackers.

7.6.4 In-Kind Counterattacks.   A cyberwar defense that has been used often is an in-kind counterattack, where flaming is met by flaming, DDoS by DDoS, site defacement by site defacement, and propaganda by propaganda. Recent examples include exchanges between Israelis and Arabs, Kashmiris and Indians, Serbs and Albanians, Indians and Pakistanis, Taiwanese and Chinese, and Chinese and Americans.

Although there may be personal satisfaction in originating or responding to such attacks, the net effect is usually a draw, and, therefore, in-kind attacks generally have been short-lived. In the future, such attacks may no longer be the output of only a few individuals but may be mounted by large numbers of similarly minded cyberwarriors, organized into coordinated groups, with sophisticated tools and with covert or overt state sponsorship.

In that event, the asymmetric nature of the adversaries' infrastructures would be telling. Clearly, if the Taliban, for example, were to mount another full-scale cyberterrorist attack against the United States, with the help of their supporters throughout the world, the effects could be devastating. Although the United States might mount a highly sophisticated in-kind response, it probably would have no effect on the Taliban's organization, their economy, their military effectiveness, or their ability to carry out suicide missions, biological warfare, or other physical attacks. A great and powerful nation may lack the ability to destroy a small, primitive, almost nonexistent infrastructure.

7.6.5 Cooperative Efforts.   Although the United States has been moderately successful in building coalitions in support of military operations, it has shown little inclination to build an international consensus dealing with information warfare. This may be so because of the legal difficulties outlined in Section 7.6.1 above or because any prohibitions against offensive cyberwar will limit U.S. options. Nevertheless, whether by treaty, convention, agreement, or UN directive, technical people, diplomats, and statesmen of all well-intentioned countries should work together to define unacceptable and harmful actions and to devise means for detecting, identifying, and punishing those who transgress.

7.7   SUMMARY.   The potential for information warfare to damage or destroy the infrastructure of any nation, any corporation, or in fact, any civilian, governmental, or military entity is unquestionable. Until now, the only incidents have been isolated and sporadic, but the possibility of sustained, coordinated, simultaneous attacks is strong. If these attacks are combined with physical, chemical, or biological warfare, the effects are certain to be devastating.

Although the types of potential attackers, and the probable weapons they will use, are well known, the available defenses do not at this time offer any great assurance that they will be effective. The United States and many of its allies are engaged in great efforts to remedy this situation, but formidable obstacles are yet to be overcome. The military is generally better prepared than the civilian sector, but much of the military's infrastructure is woven into and dependent on transportation, communications, utilities, food production and distribution, and other vital necessities that are owned by private enterprises.

Recent terrorist attacks and the probability of future offensives should serve as an immediate impetus to devote whatever resources are needed to combat the threats to our way of life, and in fact, to our very existence.

7.8   FURTHER READING

Campen, Alan D., and Douglas H. Dearth, eds. *Cyberwar 3.0: Human Factors in Information Operations and Future Conflict.* Fairfax: AFCEA International Press, 2000.

Denning, Dorothy E. *Information Warfare and Security.* Reading, MA: Addison-Wesley, 1998.

Erbschloe, Michael, and John Vacca. *Information Warfare.* New York: McGraw-Hill, 2001.

Gollman, Dieter. *Computer Security.* New York: John Wiley & Sons, 1999.

Greenberg, Lawrence, et al. *Information Warfare and International Law.* National Defense University Press; *www.iwar.org.uk/law/resources/iwlaw/iwilindex.htm.*

Henry, R., and C.E. Peartree, eds. *The Information Revolution and International Security.* Washington, DC: Center for Strategic and International Studies, 1998.

Kahn, David. *The Codebreakers.* New York: Scribner, 1996.

Marsh, R.T., chair. "Critical Foundations: Protecting America's Infrastructures. The Report of the President's Commission on Critical Infrastructure Protection." See *www.pccip.gov/info.html* for details and ordering information.

Parker, Donn. *Fighting Computer Crime: A New Framework for Protecting Information.* New York: John Wiley & Sons, 1998.

Price, Alfred, and Charles A. Horner. *War in the Fourth Dimension: U.S. Electronic Warfare, from the Vietnam War to the Present.* London, England: Greenhill Books/Lionel Leventhal, 2001.

Schwartau, Winn. *Information Warfare: Chaos on the Electronic Superhighway,* 2nd ed. New York: Thunder's Mouth Press, 1996.

Zalmay, Khalilzad, et al., eds. *Strategic Appraisal: The Changing Role of Information in Warfare.* New York: McGraw-Hill, 1999.

7.9   NOTES

1. White Paper, the Clinton Administration's Policy on Critical Information Protection: Presidential Decision Directive 63, May 22, 1998. Available at: *www.fas.org/irp/offdocs/pdd/pdd-63.htm.*

2. Critical Infrastructure Protection, Fundamental Improvements Needed to Assure Security of Federal Operations. Testimony before the Subcommittee on Technology, Terrorism and Government Information, U.S. Senate, October 6, 1999. Available at: *www.senate.gov/~judiciary/10699jlb.htm.*

3. Protecting the Homeland, Report of the Defense Science Board Task Force on Defensive Information Operations, Vol. 2, Office of the Undersecretary of Defense for Acquisition, Technology, and Logistics, March 2001. Available at: *www.cryptome.org/dio/dio.htm.*

4. "The Seven Deadly Sins of Network-Centric Warfare," *Proceedings,* Vol. 125, No. 1 (January 1999): 36–39; adapted from an essay Dr. Barnett wrote for the Center for Naval Analyses, where he served on the research staff. Available at: *www.milnet.com/milnet/infowar/usni-7-sins.htm.*

5. Gerry G. Gilmore, "Navy-Marine Corps Intranet Girds for Cyber-Attacks," Armed Forces Press Service, July 6, 2001.

6. Joint Chiefs of Staff, *Joint Doctrine for Operations Security,* Joint Publication 3-53; available in pdf at: *www.dtic.mil/doctrine/jel/new_ pubs/jp3_13.pdf.*

7. William S. Cohen, Secretary of Defense, Annual Report to the President and the Congress, 2001, Chapter 8: "Information Superiority and Space." Available in HTML at: *www.dtic.mil/execsec/adr2000/chap8.html;* in pdf at: *www.dtic.mil/execsec/adr2001/Chapter08.pdf.*

8. See: *www.calvin-coolidge.org/pages/history/research/quotations/quotesb.html.*

9. Edward J. Browne, "Information and Finance: A Strategic Target," Political Science Department, U.S. Air Force Academy, Colorado, December 1996; available as a MS-Word file at: *www.securityfocus.com/data/library/infowar/papers/FinancialInfowar.doc.*

10. See: *www.federalreserve.gov.htm.*

11. See: *www.nych.org/pay.htm.*

12. See: *www.nacic.gov/pubs/eea_96.htm.*

13. See: *http://law2.house.gov/usc.htm.*

14. See: *www.dss.mil/cithreats/protect.htm.*

15. Timothy L. Thomas, "Like Adding Wings to the Tiger: Chinese Information War Theory and Practice," Foreign Military Studies Office, Fort Leavenworth, Kansas; see: *www.iwar.org.uk/iwar/resources/china/iw/chinaiw.htm.*

16. Bill Gertz, "Hackers Linked to China Stole Documents from Los Alamos," *Washington Times,* August 3, 2000, p. 1.

17. Shen Weiguang, "Checking Information Warfare Epoch Mission of Intellectual Military," *Jiefangjun Bao,* February 2, 1999, p. 6, as translated and downloaded from the Foreign Broadcast Information System (FBIS) Web site on February 17, 1999.

18. Wei Jencheng, "New Form of People's Warfare," *Jiefangjun Bao,* June 11, 1996, p. 6, as translated and reported in FBIS-CHI-96-159, August 16, 1996.

19. Shen Weiguang, "Focus of Contemporary World Military Revolution—Introduction to Research in IW," *Jiefangjun Bao,* November 7, 1995, p. 6, as translated and reported in FBIS-CHI-95-239, December 13, 1995, pp. 22–27.

20. *Qianjin Bao,* December 10, 1999, provided by William Belk via e-mail to Timothy L. Thomas. According to Mr. Thomas, Mr. Belk is the head of a skilled U.S. reservist group that studies China.

21. Quotation from Stefan H. Verstappen, *The Thirty-Six Strategies of Ancient China* (Books and Periodicals, 2000). As described at: *www.chinastrategies.com.*

22. Ibid.

23. Ibid.

24. Ibid.

25. Zhang Zhenzhong and Chang Jianguo, "Train Talented People at Different Levels for Information Warfare," *Jiefangjun Bao,* February 2, 1999, as translated and downloaded from FBIS Web site on February 10, 1999.

26. Article 1.2 of "Proposal for an International Convention on Cyber Crime and Terrorism by the Center for International Security and Cooperation. See: *http://cisac.stanford.edu/docs/sofaergoodman.pdf.*

27. B.I. Koerner, "To Heck with Hactivism: Do Politically Motivated Hackers Really Think They're Promoting Global Change by Defacing Web Sites?"; see: *www.salon.com/tech/feature/2000/07/20/hacktivism.*

28. Curtin, M., and J. Dolske. "A Brute-Force Search of DES Keyspace" (May 1998): *www.interhack.net/pubs/des-key-crack/;* "Frequently Asked Questions (FAQ) About the Electronic Frontier Foundation's DES Cracker Machine": *www.eff.org/Privacy/Crypto_misc/DESCracker/HTML/19980716_eff_desfaq.html;* "RSA Code-Breaking Contest Again Won by Distributed.Net and Electronic Frontier Foundation (EFF): DES Challenge III Broken in Record 22 Hours" *www.eff.org/Privacy/Crypto_misc/DESCracker/HTML/19990119_deschallenge3.html.*

29. See: *www.geocities.com/Pentagon/1012/psyhist.html.*

30. June 27, 1997: In one such inadvertent 'backhoe attack,' a construction crew sliced through a major component of the Internet backbone in Florence, NJ. WorldCom's service to UUNet Technologies and MFS Communications as well as several other ISPs were severely affected. Many users were unable to access the Net and e-mail transfers were erratic throughout the U.S."—M.E. Kabay, "INFOSEC Year in Review 1999": w*ww2.norwich.edu/mkabay/iyir/1999.pdf.*

September 30, 1999: "An Ohio gas company worker accidentally cut a 40 Gbps east-west optic fiber cable at the end of September. Internet traffic was slowed as much as 50 times, as terabits of data were rerouted through alternate connections. Repairs took about a day."

October 16, 1999: "A backhoe accident destroyed a major fiber-optic cable in Massachusetts. AT&T, MCI Worldcomm, and the Mass Turnpike Authority lost channels, resulting in major problems for people on the East Coast of the United States."

November 26, 1999: "In Canada, a railway backhoe operator severed an AT&T Canada optic fiber cable, causing computer crashes, shutdown of phone lines, and communications problems throughout southern Ontario. The Bank of Nova Scotia was without computer services, and Internet services were slow because rerouted connections went through the United States on the Thanksgiving holiday."—M.E. Kabay, "INFOSEC Year in Review 1999": w*ww2. norwich.edu/mkabay/iyir/1999.pdf.*

CHAPTER 8

PENETRATING COMPUTER SYSTEMS AND NETWORKS

Chey Cobb, Stephen Cobb, and M.E. Kabay

CONTENTS

8.1 SECURITY: MORE THAN A TECHNICAL ISSUE. Information systems security has both technical and nontechnical aspects. The primary nontechnical factor is human behavior, which can defeat just about any technical security measure. More than anything else, security depends on human beings to understand and carry out security procedures. Consequently, information systems security must be integral to the corporate culture, which must have a consistent approach to all of its functions. Without this, systems and networks will not be able resist attempts at penetration.

Security often is represented as a structure of concentric circles. Protection of the central, secured element is then dependent on the barriers imposed by each successive ring. These barriers can be physical or figurative, but the goal of information system security is to protect the integrity, confidentiality, and availability of information processed by the system. This goal is reached using identification, authentication, and authorization. *Identification* is a prerequisite, with each user required to proffer an identifier (ID) that is included in the authorization lists of the system to be accessed. *Authentication* consists of proving that the user really is the person to whom the ID has been assigned. *Authorization* consists of defining what a specific user ID, running specified programs, can legally do on the system. The security perimeter can be penetrated by compromising any of these functions.

8.1.1 Organizational Culture. An organization's general attitude toward security is the key to an effective defense against attack. Security is difficult to sell, especially to an organization that has never experienced a significant problem. In fact, the better the defenses, the less evidence there is of their utility. A basic principle of security is that practitioners must act as if they are paranoid, continuously on guard against attacks from any direction. Many organizations view security precautions as an attack on the integrity of employees. Wearing badges, for example, is sometimes viewed as dehumanizing and offensive. This attitude leads to absurdities such as having only visitors wear badges. If only visitors wear badges, then taking off the badge automatically reduces the likelihood that a dishonest intruder will be challenged.

Some individual employees also consider security precautions as personally offensive. For example, locking a terminal or workstation when leaving it for a few minutes may be seen as evidence of distrust of other employees. Refusing to allow piggybacking—that is, permitting several colleagues to enter a restricted area on one access card—may be seen as insufferably rude. Where employees are taught to be open and collegial, securing removable computer media and paperwork at night can seem insulting.

These conflicts occur because years of socialization, starting in infancy, are diametrically opposed to the tenets of information security. Politeness in a social context is a disaster in a secure area; for instance, piggybacking into a computer room impairs the accuracy of audit trails kept by the access-control computers. Lending someone a car is kind and generous, but lending someone a user ID and a personal password is a gross violation of responsibility.

Carrying out effective security policies and procedures must resolve these conflicts between normal standards of politeness and the standards required in a secure environment. Organizations must foster open discussion of the appropriateness of security procedures, so that employees can voluntarily create a corporate culture conducive to protection of corporate information. For more on corporate culture and security, see Chapters 28, 29, and 35.

8.1.2 Chapter Organization. Section 8.2 looks at methods of tricking people into allowing unauthorized access to systems. Section 8.3 examines technical measures for overcoming security barriers and specific techniques (*exploits*) for penetration, while Section 8.4 describes legal and political aspects of system penetration.

8.2 NONTECHNICAL PENETRATION TECHNIQUES

8.2.1 Misrepresentation (Social Engineering). Social engineering relies on falsehood. Lies, bribes, and seduction can trick honest or marginally dishonest employees into facilitating a penetration. An attacker might trick an employee into revealing login and authentication codes or even into granting physical access to an otherwise secure site. System penetration can then be accomplished by numerous means, from walking up to an unsecured workstation, to installing Trojan code or a network packet-sniffing device.

8.2.1.1 Lying. Someone intent on obtaining unauthorized access to a system can obtain valuable information by telling lies. Lies work by playing on the natural human tendency to interpret the world by our internal model of what is most likely. Social psychologists call this model the *schema.* Well-dressed businesspeople who walk briskly and talk assertively are probably what they seem. In a phone conversation, a person who sounds exasperated, impatient, and rude when demanding a new password is probably an exasperated, impatient, and rude employee who has forgotten a password. Unfortunately, criminals know that these interpretations help get them into secured systems.

Noticing details is sometimes called the figure-ground problem. The normal becomes the background, and the objects of our attention become figures standing out from the ground. The schema influences what is noticed; only deviations from expectation spark figure-ground discrimination. Criminal hackers take advantage of this effect by fading into the background while penetrating security perimeters.

8.2.1.1.1 Impersonating Authorized Personnel. Criminal hackers and unscrupulous employees call security personnel, operators, programmers, and administrators to request user IDs, privileges, and even passwords. The telephone is a bad medium for granting security privileges; if staff were trained to refuse requests made over the phone, many attempts to penetrate systems could be thwarted. In sites where employees wear ID badges, intruders have a hard time penetrating physical security by posing as employees. However, physical security in these cases depends on the cooperation of all authorized personnel to challenge everyone who fails to wear a badge. This policy is critically important at entry points. To penetrate such sites physically, criminals can steal or forge badges or work with confederates to obtain real but unauthorized badges.

Sites where physical security includes physical tokens, such as cards for electronic access control, are much harder for criminals to penetrate. They must obtain a real token, perhaps by theft or by collusion with an employee. Perimeter security depends on keeping the access codes up to date so that cards belonging to ex-employees are inactivated. Security staff must immediately inactivate all cards reported lost. In addition, it is essential that employees not permit *piggybacking,* the act of allowing another person, possibly unauthorized, to enter a restricted zone along with an authorized person. Too often, an employee, in an act of politeness, will permit others to enter a normally locked door as he or she exits. Once inside a building, criminals can steal valuable information that will allow later penetration of the computer systems from remote locations.

8.2.1.1.2 Impersonating Third-Party Personnel. Even if employees are willing to challenge visitors in business suits, it may not occur to them to interfere with people who look as if they are employees of an authorized support firm. For example, thieves often have succeeded in entering a secured zone by dressing like third-party computer technicians or building cleaners. Few employees will think of checking the credentials of a weary technician wearing grimy overalls, an authentic-looking company badge, a colorful ID card, and a tool belt. When such a suitable-looking individual claims to have been called to run diagnostics on a workstation, many nontechnical employees will acquiesce at once, seizing the opportunity to grab a cup of coffee or to chat with colleagues. Minutes later, the thief may have copied sensitive files from CDs, floppies, hard disks, or network servers.

8.2.1.2   Subversion.   People make moral choices constantly. There is always a conscious or unconscious balancing of alternatives. Criminal hackers try to reach their goals by changing the rules so that dishonesty becomes more acceptable to the victim than honesty.

8.2.1.2.1   Bribery.   The value of industrial or commercial information sometimes can be measured on the black market. The price of a competitor's engineering plans may be a year's salary for a computer operator responsible for making backups. There is little likelihood that anyone would notice the subverted operator copying a backup at 3:00 A.M. or a secretary taking an extra CD out of the office. Many organizations have failed to install software to prevent a manager sending electronic mail with confidential files to a future employer.

Government espionage is well known, but industrial espionage is likely to increase as competition grows worldwide, especially among multinational corporations. Building a corporate environment in which employees legitimately feel themselves to be part of a community is a bulwark against espionage. When respect and a sense of exchange for mutual benefits inform the corporate culture, employees will rebuff spies or even entrap them, but the disgruntled employee whose needs are not addressed is a potential enemy.

8.2.1.2.2   Seduction.   Sometimes criminal hackers and spies have obtained confidential information, including access codes, by tricking employees into believing that they are loved. This lie works well enough to allow access to personal effects, sometimes after false passion or drugs have driven the victim into insensibility. It is not unknown for prostitutes to seduce men from organizations that they and their confederates are seeking to crack. Rifling through customers' wallets can often uncover telltale slips bearing user IDs and passwords.

No one can prevent all such abuse. People who are enthralled by expert manipulators will rarely suspect that they are being used as a wedge through a security perimeter. Along with a general increase in security consciousness, staff members with sensitive codes must become aware of these techniques so that they may be less vulnerable. Perhaps then they will automatically reject a request for confidential information or access codes.

8.2.1.2.3   Extortion.   Criminals can threaten harm if their demands are not met. Threaten someone's family or hold a weapon to the throat and few will, or should, resist a demand for entry to a secured facility or for a login sequence into a network. Some physical access-control systems include a duress signal that can be used to trigger a silent alarm at the monitoring stations. The duress signal requires a predetermined, deliberate action on the part of the person being coerced into admitting unauthorized personnel. This action may be adding an extra number to the normal pass code, pressing the pound sign (#) twice after entering the code, or entering 4357 (H-E-L-P) into the keypad. The duress signal quietly notifies security that an employee is being forced to do something unwillingly. Security can then take appropriate action.

8.2.1.2.4   Blackmail.   Blackmail is extortion based on the threat of revealing secrets. An employee may be entrapped into revealing confidential data, for example, using techniques just described. Classic blackmail includes seduction followed by pictures *in flagrante delicto,* which the criminals then threaten to reveal. Sometimes a person can be framed by fabricated evidence; a plausible but rigged image of venality can ruin a career as easily as truth. Healthy respect for individuals and social bonds among employees, supervisors, and management can make it difficult for blackmailers to succeed. If employees feel they can inform management when they are victims of a blackmail attempt, without suffering inappropriate negative consequences, the threat may be mitigated to a certain degree. Perhaps the last, best defense against blackmail is honesty. The exceptionally honest person will reject opportunities that lead to black-mail and laugh at fabrications, trusting friends and colleagues to recognize lies when they hear them.

8.2.2 Human Target Range.   Organizations should not underestimate the range of targets at which the above techniques may be directed. While the terms "employees," "authorized personnel," and "third-party personnel" are used in the preceding para-graphs, it is important to understand that the target range includes all manner of ven-dors, suppliers, and contractors as well as all levels of employees: from software and hardware vendors, through contract programmers, to soft drink vendors, and cleaning staff. It may even include clients and customers, some of whom possess detailed knowl-edge of the organization's operations. These days employees at every level are likely to be computer literate, with varying degrees of skill. For example, unlike 10 years ago, it is quite possible that someone working as a janitor today knows how to operate a computer and may even know how to surf hacking sites on the Web and download penetration tools.

In short, anyone who comes into contact with the organization has the potential to provide an attacker with information useful in the preparation and execution of an attack. The human targets of a social engineering attack may not, on an individual basis, possess or divulge critical information, but they may provide clues—pieces of the puzzle, as it were—an aggregation of which can lead to successful penetration and compromise of valuable data and resources. In fact, use of this process is a hall-mark of some of the most successful criminal hackers. The term "incremental infor-mation leveraging" was coined for this use of less valuable data to obtain more valuable data.[1]

8.2.3 Incremental Information Leveraging.   By gathering and intelligently uti-lizing small and seemingly insignificant pieces of information, it is possible to gain access to much more valuable information. This technique of incremental information leveraging is a favorite tool of hackers, criminal and noncriminal. One important ben-efit of the tool that is particularly appreciated by criminal hackers is the low profile it presents to most forms of detection. At the same time, it is very powerful. By accu-mulating seemingly innocuous pieces of information over a period of time, and by making intelligent deductions from them, it is possible to penetrate systems to the highest level.

As a result of a very early exploit, Kevin Mitnick served almost five years behind bars for breaking into computers, stealing data, and abusing electronic communi-cation systems. Illegal acts committed by Mitnick include the 1981 penetration of Computer System for Mainframe Operations (COSMOS), a Pacific Bell facility in downtown Los Angeles. COSMOS was a centralized database used by many U.S. phone companies for controlling basic record-keeping functions. Mitnick and others talked their way past a security guard and located the COSMOS computer room.

They stole not only computer passwords but also operating manuals for the COSMOS system and combinations to the door locks on nine Pacific Bell central offices. Mitnick later employed knowledge of phone systems and phone company operations to penetrate systems at Digital Equipment Corp. (DEC).

Following his release in January of 2000, Mitnick spoke before Congress and at several other public venues on information security. He described social engineering as such a powerful tool that he "rarely had to resort to a technical attack." As to technique, he stated: "I used to do a lot of improvising . . . I would try to learn their internal lingo and tidbits of information that only an employee would know." In other words, by building up a knowledge of the target, using a lot of information that is not protected or proprietary, it is possible to gain access to that which is poorly protected. The power of incremental information leveraging is the equivalent of converting a foot in the door into an invitation to come inside.

Protection against incremental information leveraging, and all other aspects of social engineering, begins with employee awareness. Employees who maintain a healthy skepticism toward any and all requests for information provide a strong line of defense. Another powerful defense mechanism, highlighted by Mitnick, is the use of telephone recording messages, such as "This message may be monitored or recorded for training purposes and quality assurance." An attacker who hears a message like this will think twice about proceeding with attempts to use voice calls to social engineer information from the target.

8.2.4 Data Scavenging.   The term "data scavenging" describes the process that feeds incremental information leveraging in many forms, both digital and analog. Perhaps the most widely known is "dumpster diving," sorting through whatever an organization throws away. The classic example is a discarded internal phone directory, which can provide a social engineer with valuable data to use when making calls to employees. An employee who hesitates to comply with an attacker's bogus request for information over the phone may well be persuaded if the attacker says something like "I understand your hesitation; if you like you can call me back at extension 2645." If 2645 is a legitimate internal extension, the caller gains considerable credence. The properly trained employee will hang up and make the call to 2645 rather than take the easy option and say "I guess that's okay then, here is the information you wanted." See Section 8.3.3.4 for more details of scavenging.

8.3 TECHNICAL PENETRATION TECHNIQUES.   Technical penetration attacks may build on data obtained from social engineering, or they may be executed on a purely technical basis. Techniques used include eavesdropping, either by listening in on conversations or by trapping data during transmissions, and breaches of access controls (e.g., trying all possible passwords for a user ID or guessing at passwords). Weaknesses in the design and implementation of information systems, such as program bugs and lack of input validation, may also be exploited in technical attacks.

8.3.1 Data Leakage: A Fundamental Problem.   Unfortunately for information security (INFOSEC) specialists, it is impossible, even in theory, to prevent the unauthorized flow of information from a secured region into an unsecured region. The imperceptible transfer of data without authorization is known as data leakage. Technical means alone cannot suppress data leakage.

Consider a tightly secured operating system or security monitor that prevents confidential data from being copied into unsecured files. Workstations are diskless, there are no printers, employees do not take diskettes into or out of the secured facility, and there are strict restrictions on taking printouts out of the building. It would appear that these mechanisms should suffice to prevent data leakage.

Not really. It is unlikely that anyone could prevent dishonest employees from writing notes on paper and concealing the notes in their clothing or personal possessions. Unless employees are strip-searched, no guard can stop people with crib sheets full of confidential data from walking out of the building. For that matter, anyone with a penchant for mnemonics or with a photographic memory could simply remember information and write it down after leaving the facility.

Criminals can use steganography—concealing valuable information in large amounts of unexceptional information—for more systematic, large-scale data leakage. For example, a corrupt employee determined to send a confederate information about a chemical formula could encode text as numerical equivalents and print these values as, say, the fourth and fifth digits of a set of engineering figures. No one would notice that these unimportant numbers contained anything special.

The unauthorized transfer of information cannot be absolutely prevented because information can be communicated by anything that can fluctuate. Theoretically, one could transfer data to a confederate by changing the position of a window shade (slow but possible). Or one could send ones and zeros by the direction of oscillation of a tape reel; or one could send coded information by the choice of music. Even if a building were completely sealed, it would still leak heat outward or transfer heat inward—and *that* would be enough to carry information.

In practical terms, system managers can best meet the problem of data leakage by a combination of technical protection and effective management strategies.

8.3.2   Intercepting Communications.   Criminal hackers and dishonest or disgruntled employees can glean access codes by monitoring communications between a peripheral node such as a terminal, workstation, or client system and a mainframe, minicomputer, or server host. Attackers can exploit various vulnerabilities of communications technologies.

8.3.2.1   Wiretapping.   Wiretapping consists of intercepting the data stream on a communications channel.

8.3.2.1.1   Asynchronous Connections.   Point-to-point connections (e.g., using EIA-232D lines) generally are easy to tap. Physical connection at any point on twisted pair or multiwire cables allows a monitor to display and record all information passing between a node and its host. Asynchronous lines in large installations often pass through patch panels, where taps may not be noticed by busy support staff as they manage hundreds of legitimate connections. Such communications usually use phone lines for distances beyond a few hundred meters (or about a thousand feet).

Wiretappers must use modems configured for the correct communications parameters including speed, parity, number of data bits, and number of stop bits, but these parameters are easy to find out by trial and error.

Countermeasures include:

- Physical shielding of cables and patch panels
- Multiplexing data streams on the same wires
- Encryption of data flowing between nodes and hosts

8.3.2.1.2   Synchronous Communications.   Because synchronous modems are more complex than asynchronous models, and because their bandwidths (maximum transmission speeds) are higher, they are less susceptible to attack, but they are not risk-free.

8.3.2.1.3   Dial-up Phone Lines.   Used for both data and voice communications, dial-up lines supplied by local telephone companies and long-distance carriers are vulnerable to wiretapping. Law enforcement authorities and telephone company employees can install taps at central switching. Criminals can tap phone lines within a building at patch panels, within cabling manifolds running in dropped ceilings, below raised floors, or even in drywall. They also can tap at junction boxes where lines join the telephone company's external cables.

The same countermeasures apply to phone lines as to asynchronous or synchronous data communications cables.

8.3.2.1.4   Leased Lines.   Leased lines use the same technology as dial-up (switched) lines, except that the phone company supplies a fixed sequence of connections rather than random switching from one central station to another. There is nothing inherently more secure about a leased line than a switched line; on the contrary, it is easier to tap a leased line at the central switching station because its path is fixed. However, leased lines usually carry high-volume transmissions. The higher the volume of multiplexed data, the more difficult it is for amateur hackers to disentangle the data streams and make sense of them. At the high end of leased line bandwidth (e.g., carriers such as T1, T2, etc.), the cost of multiplexing equipment makes interception prohibitively expensive for all but professional or government wiretappers.

Data encryption provides the best defense against wiretapping on leased lines.

8.3.2.1.5   Long-Distance Transmissions.   Dial-up and leased lines carry both short-haul and long-distance transmissions. The latter introduce additional points of vulnerability. Microwave relay towers carry much of the long-distance voice and data communications within a continent. The towers are spaced about 40 kilometers (25 miles) apart; signals spread out noticeably over such distances. Radio receivers at ground level can intercept the signals relayed through a nearby tower, and because microwaves travel in straight lines, rather than following the curvature of the earth, they eventually end up in space, where satellite receivers can collect them. The difficulty for the eavesdropper is that there may be thousands of such signals, including voice and data, at any tower. Sorting out the interesting ones is the challenge. However, given sufficient computing power, such sorting is possible, as is targeting of specific message streams. Spread-spectrum transmissions, or frequency hopping, is an effective countermeasure.

8.3.2.1.6   Packet Switching Networks.   Packet switching networks, including X.25 carriers such as Telenet, Tymnet, and Datapac, use packet assembler-disassemblers (PADs) to group data into packets addressed from a source to a destination. If data travel over ordinary phone lines to reach the network, interception can occur anywhere along these segments of the communications link. However, once the data have been broken up into packets (whether at the customer side or at the network side), wiretappers have a difficult time making sense of the data stream.

8.3.2.1.7   Internet Connections.   Transmission control protocol/Internet protocol (TCP/IP) connections are no harder to tap than any others. Unless the data stream is encrypted, there are no special impediments to wiretappers.

8.3.2.2   LAN Packet Capture.   Local area networks (LANs) such as Ethernet (IEEE 802.3) or Token-Ring (IEEE 802.5) systems, including all popular network operating systems such as Novell and VINES, are similar to packet-switching networks: Both network protocols send information through cables in discrete packages. Each package has a header containing the address of its sender and of its intended recipient. Packets are transmitted to all nodes on a segment of a LAN. Normally, a node is restricted to interpreting only those packets that are intended for it alone. However, it is possible to place devices in "promiscuous mode," overriding this restriction. This can be done with software that surreptitiously converts a device, such as an end-user workstation, into a listening device, capturing all packets that reach that node. Of course, network administrators can intentionally create a packet-capturing workstation for legitimate purposes, such as diagnosing network bottlenecks. It is also possible to connect specialized hardware called LAN monitors to the network, either with or without permission, for legitimate or illegitimate purposes. Sometimes called network sniffers, these devices and programs range from basic freeware to expensive commercial packages that can cost tens of thousands of dollars for a network with hundreds of nodes. (Note that the term "Sniffer," although in common use, is a registered trademark of Network Associates Technology, Inc.).

The more sophisticated packet sniffing programs allow the user to configure profiles for capture; for example, the operator can select packets passing between a host and a system manager's workstation. Such programs allow an observer to view and record everything seen and done on a workstation, including logins or encryption keys sent to a server.

Packet sniffing poses a serious threat to confidentiality of data transmissions through LANs. Most sniffing programs do not announce their presence on the network. Although it may not be apparent to the casual observer that a workstation is performing sniffing, it is possible, as a countermeasure, to scan the network for sniffing devices. Stealthier packet sniffing technology is constantly improving, and tight physical security may be the best overall deterrence.

LAN users concerned about confidentiality should use LAN protocols that provide end-to-end encryption of the data stream or third-party products to encrypt sensitive files before they are sent through the LAN. Routers that isolate segments of a LAN or WAN (wide area network) also reduce the threat of sniffers.

8.3.2.3   Optical Fiber.   Although optical fibers were once thought to be secure against interception, new developments quickly abolished that hope. An attacker can strip an optical fiber of its outer casing and bend it into a hairpin with a radius of a few millimeters ($\frac{1}{8}$ inch); from the bend, enough light leaks out to duplicate the data stream. Luckily, most optical cables carry hundreds or thousands of fibers, making it almost impossible to locate any specific communications channel. In addition, the equipment for converting optical signals into usable data is costly, preventing its use by casual criminal hackers.

8.3.2.4   Wireless Communications

8.3.2.4.1   Radio and Wireless Phones.   Ordinary citizens' band (CB) radio is by definition public. According to notorious phone phreak John Draper, known as Cap'n Crunch, speaking at the HoHoCon meeting of hackers in Austin, Texas, in December 1993: "In Oakland, hackers with a modem and radio managed to intercept police data links and read the data on their screens. About 10% of U.S. police departments are now encrypting their transmissions."

Wireless phones, also referred to as cordless phones, also broadcast their signals. Older models of wireless phones often allowed crosstalk between neighboring phones; newer models use a range of frequencies and reduce such accidental eavesdropping. However, wireless phones usually have no hook on the base station; access to the phone line is controlled by the handset. This design flaw allows a criminal to "steal dial tone" by using a compatible handset while roaming through a neighborhood or apartment building. Whenever the criminal obtains a dial tone, it becomes possible to make long-distance or toll calls at the victim's expense. The same compatibility allows eavesdropping on communications or on modem transmissions.

Wireless phones should be used for confidential voice or data traffic only when encryption is enabled and activated.

8.3.2.4.2   Cellular Phones and Modems.   Early analog cellular phone systems were equivalent to shouting a message through a megaphone from a rooftop. Calls on such phones are easily intercepted using scanners purchased from local electronics stores. Although recent legislation has banned such sales, the equipment is still available. While encryption is possible on the newer digital cell phones that are now widely used, the encryption is not always turned on, due to the burden it imposes on the cell company switching equipment. Check with the carrier before assuming that cell calls are encrypted. Also bear in mind that, although digital cell phone calls are harder to intercept than analog ones, there is a thriving black market in devices that make such interception possible.

As a rule, confidential information should never be conveyed through cellular phones or modems without encrypting the messages first.

8.3.2.4.3   Packet Radio.   Several vendors, such as Ardis, RadioMail, and SkyPage, are using radio transmissions for packets of data. The equipment for hacking such transmissions was once considered too expensive for amateurs, but the constant downward trend in electronics prices is eroding that assumption.

8.3.2.4.4   Spread-Spectrum Technology.   In the 1980s, the Department of Defense declassified spread-spectrum technology and provided an excellent wireless medium for secure transmissions. Spread-spectrum systems use frequency-agile modems and tuned oscillators to send data through rapidly changing frequencies. The only way to make sense of what sounds like low-intensity radio noise is to pass the signal through a receiver that changes frequency in step with the transmitter. Spread-spectrum transmissions are generally much harder to tap.

8.3.2.5   Van Eck Freaking.   This attack is named for Wim Van Eck, a Dutch electronics researcher, who in 1985 proved to a number of banks that it was possible, using technology, to read information from their CRTs at distances of almost a mile away. This is possible because many types of electronic equipment emit radio-frequency signals. Receivers that capture these signals can be used to reconstruct keystrokes, video displays, and print streams. Using simple, inexpensive wide-band receivers, criminals can detect and use such emissions at distances of tens or hundreds of meters (yards).

Since radio-frequency signals leak easily through single-pane windows, PCs should never be placed in full view of ground-floor windows. Attenuators that "tap" the window at irregular intervals can be installed to defeat such leakage. A special double-pane window with inert gas between the panes also can lessen the strength of radio signals leakage.

Other countermeasures include special cladding of hardware, such as computers and printers, to attenuate broadcast signals. This protection is often referred to by the name of the classified government standard for protection of sensitive military systems, TEMPEST. Although TEMPEST was allegedly a classified code word to begin with, it is now sometimes expanded as "Transient ElectroMagnetic Pulse Emission STandard" or Telecommunications Electronics Material Protected from Emanating Spurious Transmissions.

TEMPEST-certified equipment costs roughly 10 times more than the same equipment without TEMPEST cladding (e.g., $20,000 for a PC that sells for $2,000). A less expensive alternative is to emit electromagnetic noise that masks meaningful signals. Such add-on devices cost about $1,000 for a PC. Yet another approach to protection against this threat is to locate systems within buildings, or rooms within buildings, that have been constructed to TEMPEST standards. There are federal regulations concerning the methods of building "sensitive compartmented information facilities" (SCIFs), and the testing to obtain a TEMPEST rating is quite stringent. These measures include such things as cladding of all walls and ceilings, cladding of all electrical and network cabling, lead-lined doors, and the absence of any external windows.

8.3.2.6 Trapping Login Information.
Criminals can capture identification and authentication codes by inserting Trojan Horse programs into the login process on a server host and by using macro facilities to record keystrokes on a client node.

8.3.2.6.1 Host-based Login Trojans. A Trojan Horse is a program that looks useful but contains unauthorized, undocumented code for unauthorized functions. The name comes from Greek mythology, in which Odysseus (Ulysses in Latin), weary of the never-ending siege of Troy, sailed his ships out of sight as if he and his warriors were giving up but left a giant wooden horse at the gates of Troy. Entranced by this magnificent peace offering, the Trojans dragged the great horse into the city. During wild celebrations that night, the soldiers Odysseus had secreted in the belly of the hollow horse let themselves out and opened the gates to their army. The Greeks slaughtered all the inhabitants of the city and the Trojan War was over.

In February of 1994, the Computer Emergency Response Team Coordination Center (CERT-CC) at Carnegie Mellon University in Pittsburgh issued a warning that criminal hackers had inserted Trojan Horse login programs in hundreds of Unix systems on the Internet. The Trojan captured the first 128 bytes of every login and wrote them to a log file that was later read by the criminals. This trick compromised about 10,000 login IDs.

In another trick, a victim sits at a terminal used by several people (e.g., in a terminal room at a university). The victim enters a user ID and, after a suitable prompt, a password. At that point, the terminal displays a system message such as "Invalid password—try again," and the user does so. This time the login is accepted, and the victim continues working, unaware that the user ID and password have been recorded for later use by a criminal.

The victim has unwittingly been interacting with a "spoof" of the operating system. A trickster loads a program that simulates the normal login procedure, displaying the expected screen and dialog. Once the victim has typed in a password, the spoof program writes the identification and authentication codes to a file and then shows a misleading message. The spoof program then terminates and the regular program is ready for login.

Such a case occurred in April 1993 in a suburb of Hartford, Connecticut. Shoppers noticed a new automatic teller machine (ATM) in their mall. At first, the device seemed to work correctly, disbursing a few hundred dollars to bank card users on demand. It quickly changed to a more sinister mode. Users would insert their bank card and respond as usual to the demand for their personal identification numbers (PIN). At this point, the new ATM would flash a message showing a malfunction and suggesting that the user try an adjacent bank machine. Most people thought nothing of it, but eventually someone realized that the ATM was not posting the usual "Out of Order" indicator after these supposed errors. In addition, banks began receiving complaints of a rash of bank card frauds in the immediate area. Investigators discovered that the ATM had no connection to any known bank—that it had been purchased used, along with equipment for manufacturing bank cards. The ATM was a spoof; it was merely collecting the user ID and PIN of every victim for later pickup by the criminals who had installed it without permission in the mall. The criminals were caught after having stolen about $100,000 over a four-week period using fraudulent bank cards.

8.3.2.6.2 Macro Facilities.   Another threat to identification and authentication codes is the ability to record keystrokes for later playback or editing. MS Windows, for example, includes a simple macro facility. More sophisticated terminate/stay resident (TSR) programs automate quality assurance tests. Such tools lay in wait on a workstation and record everything the user does with the mouse and types with the keyboard. Later, the criminal can harvest the records and pick out the login codes and other valuable information.

Both types of traps depend on repeated use of a user ID and password. The simplest countermeasure is to switch to one-time passwords generated by microprocessors. One-time passwords are discussed Chapter 16.

8.3.3   Breaching Access Controls.   Criminals and spies use two broad categories of technical attacks to deduce access phone numbers, user IDs, and passwords: brute-force attacks and intelligent guesswork. In addition, ways to manipulate people into revealing their access codes; these techniques are discussed in the section on social engineering.

8.3.3.1   Brute Force Attacks.   Brute force attacks consist of using powerful computers to try all possible codes to locate the correct ones. Brute force is applied to locating modem or network numbers, user IDs, and passwords.

8.3.3.1.1 Demon (War) Dialing.   The most common form of external access to a system is via a dial-up phone line using a modem. The telephone number of the modem connected to the host or server is sensitive and should not be posted or broadcast.

Demon dialers are programs that can try every phone number in a numerical range and record whether there is a voice response, a fax line, a modem carrier, or no answer. When phones ring all over an office in numerical order, one at a time, and when there is no one on the line if a phone is picked up, it is undoubtedly the work of someone using a demon dialer.

One criminal hacker at HoHoCon '93 (a hacker convention) reported using a demon dialer to harass a victim who carried a pager. The criminal hacker programmed a demon dialer to call thousands of pager numbers and send the tones representing the victim's phone number. The innocent intermediaries called the victim at all hours of the day and night.

Some youngsters have been reported to "farm" entire telephone exchanges during the night; they sell the fax numbers the next day for a dollar a number to unscrupulous junk-fax services that then retail the fax lines to advertisers.

8.3.3.1.2   Exhaustive Search.   The same approach as demon dialing can find user IDs and passwords after a connection has been made. The attacker uses a program that cycles systematically through all possible user IDs and passwords and records successful attempts. The time required for this attack depends on two factors:

1. The keyspace for the login codes

2. The maximum allowable speed for trying logins

In today's technical environment, any inexpensive computer can generate login codes far faster than hosts permit login attempts. Processor speed is no longer a rate-limiting factor. Note that this type of attempt to "guess" passwords is different from password cracking, described later, which operates on captured or stolen copies of encrypted password files.

8.3.3.1.2.1   Keyspace.   The keyspace for a code is the maximum number of possible strings that meet the rules of the login restrictions. For example, if user passwords consist of exactly six uppercase or lowercase letters or numbers and the passwords are case-sensitive (i.e., uppercase letters are distinguished from lowercase letters), the total number of possible combinations for such passwords is calculated as follows:

- There are 10 digits and 52 upper- or lowercase letters (in the English alphabet) = 62 possible codes for any of six positions.
- If there are no restrictions on repetition, a string of n characters to be taken from a list of r possibilities for each position will generate r^n possible combinations.
- Thus, in our example, there are 62^6 possible sequences of 62 codes taken in groups of six = 56,800,235,584 (more than 56 billion) possible login codes.

If there are restrictions, the keyspace will be reduced accordingly. For example, if the first character of a password of length six must be an uppercase letter instead of being any letter or number, there are only 26 possibilities for that position instead 62, thus reducing the total keyspace to $26 \times 62^5 = 23,819,453,632$ (more than 23 billion) possibilities.

8.3.3.1.2.2   Login Speed.   Generating login codes is not hard. The greatest barrier to brute-force login attacks is interruptions in the login whenever the host detects an error. Most operating systems and security monitors allow the administrator to define two types of login delays following errors:

1. A (usually brief) delay after each failed attempt to enter a correct password

2. A (usually long) delay after several failed login attempts

Suppose each wrong password entered causes a one-tenth-second delay before the next password can be entered; then for our example involving six repeatable uppercase or lowercase letters or numbers, it would take 5,680,023,558 seconds, or 1,577,784 hours, or 180 years, to try every possibility.

Suppose, in addition, that after every fifth failed login attempt, the system were to inactivate the user ID or the modem port for three minutes. Such interference would stretch the theoretical time for a brute-force exhaustive attack to around 650 years.

Should the security manager completely inactivate the ID if it is under attack? If the ID is inactivated until the user calls in for help, user IDs become vulnerable to inactivation by malicious hackers. Attackers need merely provide a bad password several times in a row and the unsuspecting *legitimate* user will be locked out of the system until further notice. A widespread attack on multiple user IDs could make the system unavailable to most users. Such a result would be a denial-of-service attack (see Chapter 11).

Should the port be inactivated? If there are only a few ports, shutting them down will make the system unavailable to legitimate users. This drastic response may be inappropriate—indeed, it may satisfy the intentions of criminal hackers. A short delay, perhaps a few minutes, would likely be sufficient to discourage brute-force attacks.

In all of these examples, the illustrations have been based on exhaustive attacks (i.e., trying every possibility). However, if passwords or other codes are chosen randomly, the valid codes will be uniformly distributed throughout the keyspace. On average, then, according to a principle of statistics called the Central Limit Theorem, brute-force searches will have to search half the keyspace. For large keyspaces, the difference between a very long time and half of a very long time will be negligible in practice (e.g., 325 years is not significantly different from 650 years if everyone interested will be dead before the code is cracked).

8.3.3.1.3   Scavenging Random Access Memory.   Not all attacks come from outside agents. Criminals with physical access to workstations or authorized users who can use privileged utilities to read main memory can scavenge memory areas for confidential information such as login IDs and passwords.

On a workstation using a terminal emulator to work with a host, ending a session does not necessarily unload the emulator. Many emulators have a configurable screen display buffer, sometimes thousands of lines long. After an authorized user logs off and leaves a terminal, a scavenger can read back many pages of activity, sometimes including confidential information or even login codes. Passwords, however, usually are invisible and therefore not at risk.

If a workstation is part of a client/server system, an application program controlling access may leave residues in random access memory (RAM). A RAM editor, easily available as part of utility packages, can capture and decode such areas as file buffers or input/output (I/O) buffers for communications ports. However, rebooting the workstation after communication is over prevents RAM scavenging by reinitializing memory.

8.3.3.2   Intelligent Guesswork.   Users rarely choose random passwords. Much more frequently, passwords are chosen from a subset of all possible strings. Instead of blindly batting at all possible sequences in a keyspace, an attacker can try to reduce the effective keyspace by guessing at more likely selections. Likely selections include canonical passwords, bad passwords, and words selected from a dictionary. Hardware and software often come from the factory, or out of the box, with user IDs and passwords that are the same for all systems and users.

For example, all multiuser computer systems have user IDs for manufacturers' field personnel to do their job of preventive maintenance and repair. Naturally, these user IDs are set up with the same password. (For example, FIELD.SUPPORT on a

Xylol Systems computer might have the password XSONLY.) Such systems always include instructions to change the passwords, but too many administrators and users neglect to do so. Criminals are familiar with factory presets and exploit them to penetrate systems. The simple routine of changing all canonical passwords prevents hackers from gaining easy access to systems and software.

8.3.3.3   *Stealing.* Criminal hackers have few scruples about using other people's property when they enter computer systems; they have none at all concerning using other people's trash.

8.3.3.4   *Dumpster Diving.* Discarded printouts, carbon papers, printer ribbons, and punch cards often end up in trash containers where they are easily accessible to *dumpster divers* after hours. In some areas, if one visits an office or industrial park at night, one can see half a dozen people rummaging about, sometimes headfirst in the dumpsters. Criminal hackers use the information thoughtlessly discarded by naïve office workers as a source of procedures, vocabulary, and proper names that can help them impersonate employees over the phone or even in person.

Some printouts contain confidential information that can lead to extortion or system penetration. For example, a thief who steals a list of patients with HIV infection could torment the victims and extort money. A memory dump from a midrange or mainframe computer may contain terminal buffers, file buffers, and system tables—any of which may contain highly privileged information. Terminal buffers contain login IDs and passwords as well other images of information sent to a screen or typed at a keyboard. File buffers may contain data from a password file or any other kind of file on the system. System tables may contain privilege masks, showing which special capabilities a user ID owns, that can help target powerful IDs for later attack.

Every piece of paper to be discarded should be evaluated for confidentiality. Unless the information is worthless to everyone, employees should shred paper before disposal or arrange to send paper to a bonded service for destruction. It also would be well to analyze the sensitivity of unshredded paper sent to recycling.

8.3.3.5   *Discarded Magnetic Media.* Discarded paper poses a threat; discarded magnetic media are a disaster. Naïve users use the DOS ERASE command to delete files without realizing that all of the data in the files remains accessible until they are overwritten. Any UNERASE or UNDELETE function will find the original file clusters and offer to regenerate any part of the original file that has not yet been overwritten.

Backup tapes may contain valuable information about the system security structure. For example, in the 1970s and 1980s, system backups on one brand of minicomputer contained the entire directory, complete with every user ID and password *in the clear* on the first tape. Using a simple file copy utility, any user could read these data.

To destroy information on magnetic media, users either must overwrite the medium several times with random data or physically destroy the medium. Degaussers are inadequate unless they meet military specifications, but such units typically cost tens of thousands of dollars.

The problem of readable data is especially bad on broken hard disk drives. Users have received disk drives originally from other users as replacements for their own broken units. Sometimes the replacement disks have not even been reformatted; they contain entire directories of correspondence, customer databases, and proprietary software. Because it is by definition impossible to overwrite data on a defective disk drive, military security specialists routinely destroy defective hard disks using oxy-acetylene torches.

8.3.4   Spying.   Some techniques used by criminal hackers seem to have been lifted directly from spy novels.

Hackers surreptitiously steal people's access codes by watching their fingers as they punch in secret sequences. *Shoulder surfers* capture telephone calling-card codes, which they sell to organized crime rings. They surf in public places such as New York's Grand Central Station; as well as peering over shoulders of neighboring callers, they also use binoculars, telescopes, and video cameras to track their victims' flying fingers.

Shoulder surfing can occur within installations as well. For example, most users of punch key locks pay no attention to the visibility of their fingers. Some people even stand aside obligingly as if to show their trust in their visitors by displaying in detail exactly which buttons they push in sequence.

Whenever punching in a code, users should guard against observation by unauthorized people. In public places, users should stand up close to the keypad. In fixed installations, facilities' managers should cover keypads with opaque sleeves allowing unimpeded access but concealing details of the access codes.

8.3.5   Penetration Testing, Toolkits, and Techniques.   Verifying and improving the security of systems by attempting to penetrate them is a relatively new practice among security professionals and system administrators. Although some were practicing this technique earlier, it was not openly discussed prior to 1993. That year, Dan Farmer and Wietse Venema released the pioneering paper entitled "Improving the Security of Your Site by Breaking into It."[2] This paper advanced the notion of assessing system security by examining a system through the eyes of a potential intruder. Farmer and Venema showed that scanning for seemingly benign network services can reveal serious weaknesses in any system. Prior to the publication of this important paper, many system administrators were unaware of the extent of vulnerabilities affecting their systems.

Following the release of their paper, Farmer and Venema released a network testing program called SATAN (Security Analysis Tool for Auditing Networks). The reaction to the program among security professionals and system administrators was both applause and anger. Some system administrators cheered the availability of an "all-in-one" tool that revealed security holes but did not exploit them. On the other hand, some questioned the authors' motives in releasing a free and readily available tool that hackers could use to attack networks. While the debate raged on, system administrators and hackers alike began using SATAN to interrogate networks.

8.3.5.1   *Common Tools.*   Since that time, literally hundreds of penetration toolkits have appeared; they are commonly referred to as scanners. Today one can find innumerable freeware tools or can invest in one of the highly marketed, although expensive, commercial tools. Scanners vary in complexity and reliability. However, a majority of the tools employ the same basic functions to test a network: query ports on the target machines and record the response or lack of response.

Used in the proper manner, these tools are quite effective in discovering and recording vast amounts of data about a network of computer systems and revealing security holes in the network. Many scanner packages also include packet sniffing applications, described earlier. Administrators can use this information to reduce the number of systems that can be compromised.

A wide variety of network tools may be used in any penetration test. These tools may include mundane programs such as PING, FINGER, TRACEROUTE, and NSLOOKUP. However, most serious penetration tools make use of an automated vulnerability analysis tool consisting of a series of port queries and a database of known vulnerabilities. Some tools also attempt to exploit identified vulnerabilities in order to eliminate false positives. Once the vulnerabilities have been found, it is remarkably easy to obtain "exploits" or programs with which to launch an attack against the susceptible machines. All the tools make use of the basic operations of the TCP suite of protocols. While these protocols will operate on different port numbers, they all share a common structure of a three-way handshake. All TCP protocols look for a connection attempt (connect), a synchronization and acknowledgment exchange (SYN/ACK), various conditions (FLAGS), and a close port request (FIN). Therefore, the operation of port scanners is quite similar. They attempt to find open, or listening, ports on a machine, ask for a connection, and then log the results to a file to be compared to the internal database. The scanner will display the results of the scans by listing the open ports and the services that appear to be running. At this point the various programs differ. Some attempt an in-depth analysis of the possible security holes associated with the ports and services along with the appropriate security measures to secure them. The more malicious scanners also include automated scripts for exploitation of the vulnerabilities thus revealed.

The most common commercial tools are Internet Security Scanner (ISS) and Cybercop. ISS is available for the NT platform and Cybercop is available for both NT and Linux. These programs are well established and respected but are quite expensive, especially for use on large networks. The only real difference between the commercially available tools and the freeware tools is that the commercial products will not try to exploit any of the vulnerabilities they find.

Of the freeware tools, Nessus, Netcat, and nmap are probably the best known and most widely used by administrators and hackers. SATAN is still available, as are its spin-offs, SAINT and SARA. A fair amount of skill is required to use these tools as they are fairly sophisticated, and some of the scans can quickly overload a system and cause it to hang or crash.

8.3.5.2   Common Scans.   As previously mentioned, most of the scanners/sniffers available will run through the same basic routines in order to develop a picture of a machine as a whole. The purpose is to determine what is running on the machine and what its role is in the network. The following sections describe most basic scans and their results.

8.3.5.2.1   TCP Connect (TCP).   This is the most basic form of TCP scanning. This system call is provided by the operating system. If the port is listening, the attempt at a connection will proceed. This scan does not require root or supervisor privileges. However, this scan is easily detectable, as many connection and termination requests will be shown in the host's system logs.

8.3.5.2.2   TCP SYN.   This scan does not open a full connection and is sometimes referred to as a "half-open" scan because a full handshake never completes. A SYN scan starts by sending a SYN packet. Any open ports should respond with a SYN|ACK. However, the scanner sends an RST (reset) instead of an ACK, which terminates the connection. Fewer systems log this type of scan. Ports that are closed will respond to the initial SYN with a RST instead of an ACK, which reveals that the port is closed.

8.3.5.2.3   Stealth Scans.   Also referred to as Stealth FIN, Xmas Tree, or Null scans, the stealth scan is used because some firewalls and intrusion detection systems watch for SYNs to restricted ports. The stealth scan attempts to bypass these systems without creating a log of the attempt. The scan is based on the fact that closed ports should respond to a request with an RST and open ports should just drop the packet without logging the attempt.

8.3.5.2.4   UDP Scans.   There are many popular User Datagram Protocol (UDP) holes to exploit, such as an rpcbind hole or a Trojan program, like cDc Back Orifice, which installs itself on a UDP port. The scanner will send a 0-byte UDP packet to each port. If the host returns a "port unreachable" message, that port is considered closed. This method can be time consuming because most Unix hosts limit the rate of Internet Control Message Protocol (ICMP) errors. Some scanners detect the allowable rate on Unix systems and slow the scan down, so as not to flood the target with messages.

8.3.5.2.5   IP Protocol Scans.   This method is used to determine which Internet Protocol (IP) protocols are supported on a host. Raw IP packets without any protocol header are sent to each specified protocol on the target machine. If an ICMP unreachable message is received, then the protocol is not in use. Otherwise it is assumed to be open. Some hosts (AIX, HP-UX, Digital Unix) and firewalls may not send a protocol unreachable message so all protocols appear to be open.

8.3.5.2.6   ACK Scan.   This advanced method usually is used to map out firewall rule-sets. In particular, it can help determine whether a firewall is stateful or just a simple packet filter that blocks incoming SYN packets. This scan type sends an ACK packet with random-looking acknowledgment/sequence numbers to the ports specified. If an RST comes back, the ports is classified as "unfiltered." If nothing comes back, or if an ICMP unreachable is returned, the port is classified as "filtered."

8.3.5.2.7   RPC Scan.   This method takes all the TCP/UDP ports found open and then floods them with SunRPC program NULL commands in an attempt to determine whether they are RPC ports and, if so, what program and version number they return.

8.3.5.2.8   FTP Bounce.   This scan looks like it is an FTP proxy server within the network (or trusted domain). It could eventually connect to an FTP server behind a firewall. Once the FTP server has been found, scanning of ports normally blocked from the outside can be made from the internal FTP server. Of course, reading and writing to directories can be checked from this server as well.

8.3.5.2.9   Ping Sweeps.   This scan uses Ping (ICMP echo request) to find hosts that are up. It can also look for subnet-directed broadcast addresses on the network. These are IP addresses that can be reached externally. Ping sweeps often are used to try to "map" the network as a whole.

8.3.5.2.10   OS Fingerprinting.   As many security holes are dependent on the operating system of the host, this scan attempts to identify which operating system is running, based on a number of suppositions. It uses various techniques to detect subtleties in the underlying OS network stack of the computers being scanned. The data gathered are used to create a "fingerprint" that is compared to the scanner's database of known OS fingerprints. If an unknown fingerprint is found, attackers can check Web sites and newsgroups on which information about fingerprints is freely traded, to discover what a particular OS might be. Once the OS has been identified, it is quite easy to find exploits by simply using a search engine on the Web. OS fingerprinting is unnecessary if the OS can be discovered by reading the banners. For example, if one was to telnet to a machine, the response could be as follows:

badguy~> telnet abcd.efg.com
Trying 163.143.103.12 . . .
Connected to abcd.efg.com
Escape character is '^]'.
HP-UX hpux B.10.01 A 9000/715 (ttyp2)
login:

The banner, which was included in the default configuration, simply indicates that the OS is HP-UX. A good system administrator will turn off the banners on all services that have them.

8.3.5.2.11 Reverse Ident Scanning.   This scan usually is used to see if a Web server on the network is running as root. If the *identd* daemon is running on the target machine, then a TCP Ident request will cause the daemon to return the username that "owns" the process. Therefore, if this request is sent to port 80 (hex), and the return user is root, then that server can be used for an attack on the system. This scan requires a full TCP connection to the port in question before it will return the username.

8.3.5.3   Basic Exploits.   Using the results of a scanning program, the next logical step for hackers would be to try to exploit the apparent weaknesses in the system. Hackers seek to compromise a machine on the network by getting it to let them run programs or processes at will at the root level. Once hackers "own" that machine, the possibilities are endless. Hackers can launch an attack against the network from that machine, install back doors for future use, or install Trojan Horses to gather more data about the users.

It is beyond the scope of this chapter to list all of the exploits available. There are simply too many, with new ones appearing every day. The number of Web sites devoted to hacking is enormous. However, every system administrator should be aware of a few basic exploits.

8.3.5.3.1 Buffer Overflow.   The most common vulnerability in a system has to be the enormous number of buffer overflows that can be used to gain access to a system. Simply put, each protocol has a predetermined number of bytes in which to communicate. If a communication goes over the limit, then the extra data is dumped into an overflow area. The data keeps writing and overwriting in the overflow area until it reaches an end. It is like sending a message that says, "hi hello how are you I heard your mom was sick and you crashed your car the weather here has been crazy and there's flooding all over" instead of simply saying "hello."

The possible effects of buffer overflows are numerous. A buffer may overflow into an adjoining buffer and corrupt it. The overflow condition alone may be enough to crash the process. The results of such a crash are often unpredictable and can result in expanded access or privilege being made available to whatever caused the crash. Buffer overflows occur in applications as well as protocols. Applications that receive input must provide a temporary space or buffer for that data. If more data is supplied than expected and no provision is made to limit input, or respond to excess input in an orderly manner, errors can occur, resulting in crashes, increased access, and the like.

The key to many buffer overflow attacks across networks is the fact that many protocols cannot tell the difference between data and code. Hackers try to get the last bit of data written to the overflow area to be a command or a bit of code that will execute a command. In the end it would be like sending a string that says, "hi hello how are you I heard your mom was sick and you crashed your car the weather here has been crazy and there's flooding all over and oh by the way when you get to the end of this, change to the root directory and give me all privileges."

The first line of defense against buffer overflow attacks is to patch the software whenever an overflow vulnerability is discovered. Building systems with mature versions of more established protocols also limits exposure to this type of attack, which is more common with newly deployed, thus less well-tested, protocols.

8.3.5.3.2   Password Cracking.   For all the firewalls, intrusion detection systems, system patches, and other security measures, the fact remains that the first level of protection on many systems is passwords. Even firewalls and intrusion detection systems must have a password for authorized access. And for all the rules and regulations and training about "good" passwords, attackers can count on at least a few people using "bad" passwords. Their rationale for choosing bad passwords is often that they are sure that they will never be found out. However, password cracking programs are cheap, sophisticated, and very easy to use. Some of the most popular password crackers in use are L0phtCrack, John the Ripper, Crack, and Brutus.

These programs rely on two features of network password systems. First, the encryption used to scramble passwords on a network is easily defeated. Second, the encrypted passwords on a network are relatively easy to obtain. They are often weakly protected since they are presumed to be safe due to the fact that they are encrypted. Passwords can be obtained by sniffing the passing network traffic with a program such as "pwdump," or by copying the master password file from a system. Since one password is all it takes to enter a system as a legitimate user, sniffing the traffic is the easiest method of obtaining a relatively good list of passwords.

Once the list has been obtained, it is saved as a simple text file and the password cracking program begins checking the encrypted words in the file against a dictionary of words that have previously been encrypted with the same algorithm. Whenever a match is found between an encrypted string in the file and a word in the encrypted dictionary, the cracking program displays and records the plain text of the encrypted dictionary word. Thus the password is revealed.

In addition to checking ordinary dictionary words, some password crackers check for both upper-case and lower-case letters, numbers before and after a word, and numbers used in lieu of vowels within a word. The speed at which these programs operate, even on a cheap Pentium III computer, is impressive, and it is entirely possible to obtain cracked passwords within seconds. Indeed, a useful security awareness exercise is to demonstrate such a program—the first passwords to be cracked will be the weakest ones, and that can serve as a warning to users who choose such words.

A good security officer will ensure that passwords on a network are checked regularly with a password cracker or by implementing one of the many "strong" password enforcers. Password enforcers augment the password program by comparing the passwords chosen by the user to the rules set by the enforcer. See Chapter 16 for more details on identification and authentication.

8.3.5.4   Rootkits.   Rootkits are one of the many tools available to hackers to disguise the fact that a machine has been "rooted." A rootkit is not used to crack into a system but rather to ensure that a cracked system remains available to the intruder. Rootkits are comprised of a suite of utilities that are installed on the victim machine. The utilities start by modifying the most basic and commonly used programs so that suspicious activity is cloaked. For example, a rootkit often changes simple commands such as "ls" (list files). A modified "ls" from a rootkit will not display files or directories that the intruder wants to keep hidden.

Rootkits are extremely difficult to discover since the commands and programs appear to work as before. Often a rootkit is found because something did not "feel right" to the system administrator. Since rootkits vary greatly in the programs they change, one cannot tell which programs have been changed and which have not. Without a cryptographically secure signature of every system binary, an administrator cannot be certain to have found the entire rootkit.

Some of the common utilities included in a rootkit are:

- Trojan Horse utilities
- Backdoors that allow the hacker to enter the system at will
- Log-wiping utilities that erase the attacker's access record from system log files
- Packet sniffers that capture network traffic for the attacker.

8.3.5.4.1   Trojan Horse.   A Trojan Horse follows the mythology in that it is something other than it appears to be. In this case, the Trojans are the changed programs in a rootkit that allow an intruder's tracks to be hidden or allow the program to gather more information as it sits silently in the background. Local programs that are Trojaned often include "chfn," "chsh," "login," and "passwd." In each case, if the rootkit password is entered in the appropriate place, a root shell is spawned.

The replacement for "login" is one of the oldest Trojans around. To the user, the normal login screen appears. After the username and password are entered, the login screen appears again. Most users simply assume that they typed something incorrectly and go through the login process once more to gain entry. What has actually happened is that the initial login screen simply captured the keystrokes and saved them to a file. The hacker can then pick up the file at will and have access through additional usernames and passwords.

8.3.5.4.2   Backdoors.   Backdoor utilities often are tied to programs that have been Trojaned. They are used to gain entry to a system when other methods fail. Even if a system administrator has discovered an intrusion and has changed all the usernames and passwords, there is a good chance that he or she does not know that the backdoors exist. To implement the backdoor, the hacker needs only to enter a password or command where one is not usually entered.

For example, "inetd," the network super daemon, is often Trojaned. The daemon will listen on an unusual port (rfe, port 5002 by default in Rootkit IV for Linux). If the correct password is given after connection, a root shell is spawned and bound to the port. The manner in which the shell is bound makes it essential to end all commands with a semicolon (";") in order to execute any command line.

The function "rshd" is similarly Trojaned. A root shell is spawned when the rootkit password is given as the username. The command "rsh [hostname] −l [rootkit password]" will obtain access to the compromised machine.

8.3.6   Penetration via Web Sites.   In 1995, many companies had not even heard of the World Wide Web. By 2001, more than 20 million domain names had been registered with the commercial "dot com" extension (.com). Some 16 million additional domain names had been registered, with .net or .org extensions, or with country-specific extensions such as.uk. Many of these country-specific extensions are also company domains, as in .co.uk or .com.sa. A vast new network territory opened up in the final decade of the twentieth century, devoted to commerce and driven by attempts to make money from a technology that originally had been developed for military and academic purposes. For example, by 2001 Singapore had over 30,000 .com.sg domains. Not surprisingly, this new territory became a playground for hackers, from the merely curious to the seriously criminal.

Despite the dot-com market correction of April 2000 and the subsequent demise of numerous pioneering Internet companies, the Web still presents a "target-rich" environment for people seeking unauthorized access to other people's information systems. There are several reasons for this; chief among them is the fact that many organizations, both commercial and governmental, have external, public Web sites that are connected, in some way, to internal, private networks. This connection provides a system penetration path that can be exploited in many different ways, which are outlined in this section.

8.3.6.1   Web System Architecture.   Standard practice when placing a commercial Web site on the Internet is to screen it from hostile activity, typically using a router with access control lists (ACLs) or a firewall, or both. However, unless the Web site is of the basic, "brochure-ware" kind, which exists only to provide information on a read-only basis, the site has to allow for user input of data. Input is required for something as simple as a guest book entry or an information request form; more complex applications such as online shopping have more complex input requirements.

The most widely used method of processing input is the Common Gateway Interface (CGI). This is a standard way for a Web server to pass user input to an application program and to receive a response, which can then be forwarded to the user. For example, when a user fills out a form on a Web page and submits it, the Web server typically passes the form information to a small application program. This application processes the data and may send back a confirmation message. This method is named CGI, and it forms part of the Hypertext Transfer Protocol (HTTP). Because it is a consistent method, applications written to employ it can be used regardless of the operating system of the server on which it is deployed. Further adding to the popularity of CGI is the fact that it works with a number of different languages including C, C + +, Java, and PERL. The term "CGI" is used generically for Web server code written in any of these languages.

Any system that receives input must provide a path within the system through which that input can flow. This is referred to as an "allowed path." The necessity of allowed paths, combined with the ability to exploit them for penetration attacks, led the system security expert David Brussin (author of Chapter 20 in this book) to coin the term "allowed path vulnerabilities" for this class of vulnerability. The two leading categories of exploit that employ allowed paths are input validation exploits, which often abuse CGIs, and file system exploits, which abuse the Web server operating system and services running on the server.

Of course, there are other ways to abuse Web sites as well. Denial-of-service attacks can be used to inhibit legitimate access and thus compromise availability. (Chapter 11 covers DOS attacks.) Not every attack is aimed at further penetration of systems; the

Web pages themselves may be the target of attack, as in a defacement, an unauthorized change to Web pages. Defacement often is committed to embarrass the Web site owner, publicize a protest message, or enhance the reputation of the criminal hacker who is performing the defacement. But in terms of penetration, the primary goal of attacks on Web sites is to compromise internal networks that might be connected to the Web server. Exploitation of allowed path vulnerabilities is the most common form of such attacks.

8.3.6.2   Input Validation Exploits.   Whenever an allowed path is created to accommodate user input, the possibility exists that it will be abused. Such abuse can lead to unauthorized access to the system. This section describes a range of penetration methods using this approach, all of which somehow employ invalid input, or input that is:

- Not expected by the receiving application on the server
- Not "allowed" according to the rules by which the receiving application is operating.

How is it possible to submit such unallowed or unexpected input to a server? The answer lies in the architecture of the Internet and the paradoxical nature of the client system that is accessing the server. The typical Web client is a client in name only. It is often a powerful machine, capable of being a server in its own right, and very difficult for any other server to control, due to the inherent peer-to-peer nature of the huge network that is the Internet. All nodes of the Internet are considered hosts. And, of course, many of these hosts are outside the physical control of the organizations hosting those machines that are acting as servers. This fact has serious implications for security.

Unless the server can install a tightly controlled application code on the client and restrict user input to that code, it must rely on the code most commonly used to implement Web client-server interaction, HTML and HTTPD. Both are complex and immature. For example, they do not automatically identify the source of the input. Consider an HTML form on a Web page, designed to be presented to a visitor to the Web site who fills in the fields and then clicks a button to submit the form to the Web server. There is nothing on the client side to control the user's input. So instead of entering a first name in the First Name field, a user might enter a long string of random characters. Unless the application processing this data field performs extensive input validation, the effects of such action can be unpredictable, even more so if the user includes control characters. Similarly, if the Web server itself is not designed to validate page requests, a user might cause problems by submitting a bogus URL (Universal Resource Locator). This will be discussed later in the context of the "dot dot" attack.

The problem is even more severe than this. Unless the Web server application is specifically written to defeat the following abuse, it can be used to cause all sorts of problems that potentially lead to successful penetration. Suppose that, instead of simply filling out a form, the user creates a local copy of the page containing the form, then alters the source code of the form, saves the file, and submits it to the Web site, instead of the original page. This does not violate the basic protocols of the Web but clearly provides considerable penetration potential. Many Web sites are still vulnerable to attacks of this type. Space does not permit detailed description of all of the possible exploits of Web servers, but one detailed example is provided since many of the other forms of attack are very similar in terms of scope and technique.

8.3.6.2.1   Hidden Tags: An Input Validation Example.   While conducting penetration tests for corporate clients in 1997, network security specialists at Miora Systems Consulting (MSC) found a number of corporate Web sites susceptible to penetration via a specific weakness in HTML forms. These forms are the primary means of accepting user input on Web pages. The weakness was in a feature or tag known as the hidden form field. Warnings about its security implications had been around for many years, in places as prominent as the World Wide Web Security Frequently Asked Questions (FAQs). But upon further investigation, MSC discovered several undocumented aspects of this vulnerability, including its potential to provide a means of unauthorized access. Research also revealed a large number of high-profile public Web sites susceptible to this avenue of attack. After developing a fix for the problem, MSC decided to publicize it, since existing knowledge of the problem was clearly limited. It became known as the MSC Hidden Form Field vulnerability (MSCHFF or "Mischief" vulnerability). This is a classic example of the input validation problem.

Hidden form fields contain information that is, by default, not displayed by the Web browser. This information is passed along to the input processing programs, along with user input, in order to assist in processing. To find hidden form fields in an HTML document, a user can select the "view source" option in a Web browser and look for fields laid out as follows:

```
<INPUT TYPE="HIDDEN" NAME="abc" VALUE="defghijk">
```

As Web content became more interactive with the advent of forms and user response mechanisms, Web designers were faced with three problems:

1. The protocol on which the Web is based (HTTP) is "stateless," meaning it does not have the ability to recognize or identify the fact that certain requests are part of one user's "session."

2. CGI programs can be expensive to build, so a mechanism permitting their reuse is very attractive.

3. As designers considered moving sensitive information to Web servers, they needed a mechanism for implementing some security requirements.

Web designers have tended to see hidden form fields as a solution to all of these problems. Hidden form fields store session identifiers to preserve state information, provide a variety of different run-time parameters to CGI programs, and preserve security and user authentication information for use in electronic commerce applications. Unfortunately, many Web designers do not realize the serious security implications of their actions. Since the Mischief vulnerability is an allowed path vulnerability, it is not addressed by firewalls, which are primarily designed to block nonallowed traffic.

8.3.6.2.2   Hidden Form Fields and Unexpected Input.   Unexpected input is one of five major aspects to the Mischief vulnerability, impacting critical and diverse segments of Web server, electronic commerce, and Internet architecture operation. All of these aspects can be explained by means of David Brussin's banking analogy, known as the "Teller Window" authentication model. When customers walk up to the teller window at a bank, they are asked for certain pieces of information, based on the type of transaction they want to perform. If, for example, they are making a deposit, they will be asked for a deposit slip with their account number, plus the currency or endorsed checks that they are depositing. If making a withdrawal, however, they might be asked for a withdrawal slip and some form of identification. This Teller Window authentication model works because the bank teller consults specific bank policy regarding the procedure for a given transaction. If the bank teller expected or allowed the customers to dictate procedure for a transaction, the bank would soon find a line of swindlers waiting to make fraudulent transactions.

Consider an example of a broken teller window model: A customer walks up to the counter and tells the clerk that she is making a deposit. However, instead of handing the teller a deposit slip, she presents a withdrawal slip. The teller is thinking "deposit," so does not ask for identification, but instead processes the withdrawal and hands over the cash. This sounds absurd, but only because people are very familiar with the properly functioning teller model, and because human tellers are better equipped to know when a situation "feels" wrong than are their digital counterparts.

Consider an example of CGI program reuse through hidden form fields breaking the Teller Window authentication model. MSC encountered a site designed so that different types of users would utilize different Web pages to log on to the system. One type was "customer," which could perform certain restricted functions; another type was "vendor," which could perform numerous sensitive operations across the entire system. When a user of either type logged on from the designated page, the username and password were checked against a database and then logged in with the appropriate authority and options. Since these login functions were similar, it made sense to the Web designer to reuse the same CGI program and to provide options via hidden form fields. The only distinction between a customer and a vendor was made through a "user type" hidden form field located on the login pages. The field contained "customer" on the customer page and "vendor" on the vendor page, and the CGI program provided authority and options based on that field. Since this hidden form field provided the user with an element of control over the authentication process, it broke the Teller Window model. Not surprisingly, it allowed MSC penetration testers to log in with greater authority than they should have been given.

Consider another example: The login page on a sensitive project management system overtly requested only a username and password. Behind the scenes, however, this login page contained a hidden form field with the destination directory the user should reach upon successful authentication. MSC quickly used this field to gain access to sensitive portions of the system. It is important to realize that any impact the user has on an authentication process, no matter how small that impact appears to be, weakens the security system. That decrease in protection may be sufficient to break the process.

8.3.6.2.3   Hidden Form Fields and Attacks on Applications.   While some Web designers realize that the contents of hidden form fields are not actually hidden, they do not realize that hidden form fields are "user-submitted content," just as any other form field would be. When used to provide run-time options to CGI programs and to perform other tasks, Web designers assume that these fields will be submitted as designed. In fact, an attacker can modify these forms to create unexpected results in CGI programs.

Consider a Web page dedicated to collecting feedback information from users. It might do extensive checks on the size and content of user-submitted fields to prevent buffer overflow attacks (see Section 8.3.5.3.1 for more on buffer overflows). But if this page contains a hidden form field with, for example, an identifier for type of user information being gathered, that form may not be recognized as user-submitted content and may be accepted without any check. An attacker could modify the contents of that hidden field, creating a "buffer overflow" situation within the CGI program on the Web server, thus compromising the system.

There is also a more subtle problem. It is possible to modify the field contents of a hidden form field in such a way that the length is still legal, the characters used are still legal, but the CGI program performs unexpectedly. For example, if an attacker removes the content of a hidden form field, the corresponding CGI program could "crash" or deliver sensitive data.

It is vital to realize that all form fields, hidden or not, are user-submitted content. All of these fields may be modified for content or length by a user or attacker, and must be checked by the CGI program or validated in some other way. Typical checks include length, allowable characters, and allowable content. This final check, allowable content, means that extensive error checking must be performed to protect the CGI program from unexpected results.

8.3.6.2.4   Unexpected User Control of Applications.   When hidden form fields are modified to contain legal information that will pass all safety checks, it is extremely difficult to determine whether or not that legal content will create the intended result or some nefarious one. This problem is more difficult to address than the problem described in the previous section. For example, MSC researchers were able to attack sensitive systems behind a firewall by exploiting the hidden form fields in a page that called a common CGI "e-mail response" program. The CGI program was designed to process user feedback and requests on Web sites and to accept hidden form field input to specify the destination address for the e-mail.

Although several well-known vulnerabilities with such e-mail response programs center on the CGI program's failing to check the contents of a form field, the more subtle vulnerability found here was in the presence of the field itself. MSC Labs' researchers were able to specify arbitrary but legal e-mail recipients, then use "Sendmail" attacks against systems behind the firewall. In this case the hidden form fields provided the attacker with some unneeded element of control over the behavior of a CGI program, something a Web client should never have allowed.

8.3.6.2.5   Hijacking and Replay Attacks.   Hidden form fields often are deployed to maintain state information for Web servers, since those servers typically have no mechanism for handling such information. Hidden form fields can enable compromise of these "state" mechanisms, permitting simple hijacking attacks as well as replay attacks. An electronic commerce server, for example, might use hidden form fields to store a "session number," so that a user could log in to the system once, then perform a series of functions, such as adding items to a "shopping cart." Without some type of state information, the Web server would be forced to reauthenticate the user for every operation. Since hidden form fields are vulnerable to modification, an attacker could log on to the system, modify the session number, and hijack the sessions of other users. On systems such as online banking and electronic commerce, this could mean that an attacker with one account could attack numerous other accounts.

Another common method used to maintain state on Web servers involves storing the username and password, or sometimes an encrypted hash of the password, in a hidden form field. When this is done, attackers can obtain the hidden form field contents from client systems and used them later in a "replay" attack.

8.3.6.2.6   Sensitive Information and Application Details.   In addition to the "active" attacks just discussed, "passive" hidden form field vulnerabilities can disclose sensitive information and facilitate further attacks. These are part of a very large class of attacks that can be characterized as "leaky client" attacks. The vast majority of computers used as clients in Web applications lack adequate access controls or proper system administration. Often they are left unattended, with not so much as a password between any attacker who has physical access to the system and complete access to all of the machine's files, applications, resources, and network connections. In some environments, client machines are shared between users with little or no separation of privileges.

Just like the contents of files left open on an unprotected and unattended machine, or the contents of disk and memory caches, the contents of current and recently used hidden form fields are accessible to a local attacker. They are hidden or even obscured, so most users do not know that an attacker can retrieve even sensitive data from them such as username, password, encrypted authentication data, or other sensitive information stored in these invisible fields. And because users often are unaware of the dangers of leaving their client systems unattended, they can be lulled into a false sense of security by the fact that their sensitive information does not actually appear on the screen.

The use of hidden form fields to provide options and run-time information to CGI programs also gives attackers access to an undesirable level of detail about the operation of those CGI programs, including the options and their format. Using the technique of incremental information leveraging, this information can facilitate more sophisticated attacks.

8.3.6.2.7   Field and Application Overflows.   As described earlier in the context of hidden form fields, it is possible to gain access to Web servers by supplying more input than expected. Such an attack is possible with any field on a user-submitted form, not just a hidden field. The defense is to build extensive error-checking into the application that processes the form.

Overflow attacks, which were described in general terms earlier, also can be directed at applications or services running on the Web server. For example, in June of 2001, CERT announced a remotely exploitable buffer overflow in one of the Internet Server Application Programming Interface (ISAPI) extensions installed with most versions of Microsoft Internet Information Server 4.0 and 5.0, specifically the Internet/Indexing Service Application Programming Interface extension, IDQ.DLL. An intruder exploiting this vulnerability may be able to execute arbitrary code in the local system security context, giving the attacker complete control of the victim system.

8.3.6.3   File System Exploits.   Another category of attack against Web sites exploits problems with the file system of the Web server itself. Ever since Web servers started appearing on the Internet, there has been a constant procession of vulnerability announcements arising from file system issues. The main ones are presented here, but the possibility of others appearing is high due to a lack of what David Brussin has called vulnerability class analysis. A vulnerability class is a type of problem, such as buffer overflow or file system access control. Developers of Web servers, and many other applications, are often adverse to, or resource-constrained from, the elimination of vulnerabilities as a class, being focused instead on the hole-by-hole fixing of specific instances of the vulnerability as they arise. This phenomenon is largely a result of the rapid pace at which the Web has been developed and deployed, driven by powerful commercial forces.

8.3.6.3.1   Dot Dot, Slash, and Other Characters.   Persons responsible for the security of information systems that employ Web servers must be alert for new vulnerabilities. Web server software has proven particularly susceptible to certain categories of vulnerability that tend to recur in new versions. Whenever these vulnerabilities are discovered, attackers quickly exploit them. Typically, software vendors issue patches to solve the problem, but systems remain susceptible until patched and attackers use automated tools to scan the Internet for servers that are still susceptible. For example, in April of 2001 a flaw was discovered in versions of Microsoft Internet Information Server (IIS) in use at that time. This flaw made it possible for remote users to list directory contents, view files, delete files, and execute arbitrary commands.

In other words, if a Web server running IIS was connected to the Internet, anybody using the Internet could potentially copy, move, or delete files on the Web server. With this level of access, it was possible to use the Web server to gain access to connected networks unless strong internetwork access controls were in place. In alerts that were issued to warn users of this software, exploitation of this vulnerability was described as "trivial." Indeed, a large number of sites were penetrated because of it, and many suffered defacement, that is, unauthorized changes to the appearance of their Web sites. In other cases, attackers downloaded sensitive customer data and uploaded and installed backdoor software.

Particularly worrying about this vulnerability was the fact that it was essentially a recurrence of the so-called dot dot directory traversal attack, which was possible on a lot of early Web servers. These servers would, upon request, read ".." directories in URLs, which are unpublished parent directories of the published directory. Thus attackers were able to back out to the Web root directory and then to other parts of the server's directory structure. This technique basically allowed attackers to navigate the file system at will. Many Web servers, including IIS, began to incorporate security measures to prevent the "dot dot" attack, denying all queries to URLs that contain too many leading slashes or ".." characters.

The vulnerability published in April 2001 involved bypassing these restrictions by simply substituting a Unicode translation of a "/" or "\." Attackers found that, by appending the ".." and a Unicode slash or backslash after a virtual directory with execute permissions, it was possible to execute arbitrary commands. Attackers could execute any command via a specially crafted HTTP query.

8.3.6.3.2 Metacharacters.   Dots and slashes used in field system references are closely related to metacharacters, which also can be used to attack Web systems. A metacharacter is a special character in a program or data field that provides information about other characters, for example, how to process the characters that follow the metacharacter. Users of DOS or Unix are probably familiar with the wildcard character, a metacharacter that can represent either any one character or any string of characters. If used inappropriately, for example in user-supplied data, metacharacters can cause errors that result in unintended consequences, including privileged access.

8.3.6.3.3 Server-Side Includes.   Server side includes or SSIs are special commands in HTML that the Web server executes as it parses an HTML file. SSIs were developed originally to make it easier to include a common file, called an include file, inside many different files; examples include files containing a logo or text files consisting of the page, date, author, and so on. This capability was expanded to enable server information, such as the date and time, to be included automatically in a file. Eventually several different types of include commands were provided on Web servers: config, include, echo, fsize, flastmod, exec. The last of these, exec, is quite powerful, but it is also a security risk, as it gives to the user of the Web client permission to execute code. A number of attacks are possible when exec is permitted within an inadequately protected directory.

Analogous to SSIs are ASPs or Active Server Pages and JavaServer Pages, as well as PHP3. All are technologies that facilitate dynamic page building and allow execution of codelike instructions within an HTML page. All should be employed with special attention to security implications.

8.4   POLITICAL AND LEGAL ISSUES.

Thanks to the World Wide Web, the Internet has become a self-documenting phenomenon. One can use the Internet to find out everything one wants to know about the Internet, including how to penetrate information systems that employ Internet technology. However, the penetration information available on the Internet is not restricted to Internet systems, and the Internet is not the only source of penetration information. Furthermore, the very availability of penetration information is fraught with political and legal issues. These are discussed briefly in this final section of the chapter.

8.4.1   Exchange of System Penetration Information.

The sharing of system penetration information—that is, information that could facilitate illegal penetration of an information system—is the subject of a long, heated, and ongoing debate. This debate encompasses both practical and ethical aspects of the issue. While complete coverage is not possible within the confines of this chapter, we do review the question of full disclosure, along with some of the sources for penetration information.

8.4.2   Full Disclosure.

How should we handle known vulnerabilities and dangerous viruses? Should we publish full details, conceal some details, or suppress any publication that would allow exploitation until patches or updates are available from manufacturers?

At the European Institute for Computer Anti-Virus Research (EICAR) conference in Brussels the first week of March 2000, one of the topics discussed by researcher Sarah Gordon of the T. J. Watson Center of IBM was the range of attitudes toward disclosure of vulnerabilities and exploits. Gordon described how the antivirus (AV) world and the information security (INFOSEC) world differ significantly in their disclosure models. In general, the AV world frowns on open disclosure of detailed virus codes; in contrast, the general INFOSEC world has developed venues for full disclosure of system or network vulnerabilities and exploits (e.g., BugTraq). Support for full disclosure of such details, down to the source code or script level, from professional, honest security experts (the Good Guys) is based on subsets of several key beliefs:

- The Bad Guys know about the vulnerabilities anyway.
- If they do not know about it already, they will soon with or without the posted details.
- Knowing the details helps the Good Guys more than the Bad Guys.
- Effective security cannot be based on obscurity.
- Making vulnerabilities public is an important tool in forcing vendors to improve their products.

There is indeed a criminal underground where viruses and exploits are widely exchanged and explored. VX (virus exchange) bulletin boards are widespread; in the criminal hacker underground, there are open discussions on IRC (Internet Relay Chat) channels of new methods for breaking into sites, and there are restricted Web sites for exchange of exploits. Since the criminals usually are aware of these techniques before system administrators and security experts learn of them, it makes sense—so the argument goes—to spread the knowledge where it can do some good. In addition, it is widely accepted that cryptographic techniques ought to be exposed to public scrutiny by experts to detect vulnerabilities and to avoid future failures; so why should other aspects of security not be made public too?

As for putting pressure on manufacturers, one colleague describes an incident that illustrates the frustrations that sometimes underlie full disclosure. He informed an important software supplier of a major security vulnerability. The product manager ignored him for a month. At that point, patience gone, the colleague informed the product manager that he had exactly one more day in which to produce a patch; otherwise, he said, he would publish the hole in full in the appropriate Usenet group. A patch was forthcoming within one hour.

Why would anyone object to full disclosure of detailed viral code and exploits? The arguments are:

- Nobody except researchers needs to know the details of viruses or even of specific exploits.
- Publishing in full gives credibility to ill-intentioned Bad Guys who do the same.
- Full disclosure makes children more susceptible to criminals' propaganda about the acceptability of illegal computer abuse.

How, exactly, does publishing the details of a new virus help system administrators? In one view, such details should be exchanged only among colleagues who have developed trust in each other's integrity and who have the technical competence to provide fixes. The "zoo" kept by ICSA Labs serves this function: All of the members of the Anti-Virus Product Developers' Consortium have complete access to all the viruses that are contributed; the members sign a Code of Ethics that forbids distributing viruses casually to anyone who wants samples. Sarah Gordon states that opponents of this stance see the attitude as arrogant and elitist.

However, should exploits be published where thousands of eight-year-old children can use them for automated attacks on Web sites? Doesn't this give naïve people the impression that it is OK to publish any attack code, regardless of consequences? What is the difference, then, between publishing vulnerabilities or exploits and actually creating attack tools? Was creating and publishing BackOrifice a morally neutral or even useful act? BackOrifice is a tool that is explicitly designed to install itself surreptitiously on systems and then hide in memory, using stealth techniques modeled on what some viruses use. Is this a contribution to security?

Faced with vendor inability or unwillingness to fix security vulnerabilities in a timely manner, some users and experts can be expected to turn to full disclosure of security information, even though many of them may deplore using such tactics.

8.4.3   Sources.   There are many sources for information about how to penetrate systems. The motives behind these sources range from the highly ethical to the downright immoral.

8.4.3.1   Bulletin Board Systems.   There are thousands of bulletin board systems (BBSs) run by individuals or groups throughout the world. Most of these are innocent avenues for the exchange of legitimate information among honest people. However, several hundred cater to people who actively break the law by seeking to gain unauthorized access to systems belonging to other people. These criminal BBSs include information such as

- Modem telephone numbers for private or government computer systems
- Stolen user IDs and passwords
- Information on taking control of phone switches, networks, and computer operating systems
- Security holes in different versions of operating systems
- Password cracking programs and demon dialers
- Collections of computer viruses and virus-writing kits, some of which may be used to create viruses that send confidential information from an infected system to the outside world (see Chapter 9)

Such BBSs allow beginners quickly to absorb the culture of the underground. Many BBS operators close certain sections and require an initiation ritual to be allowed into the inner circle. Initiation most commonly consists of uploading private information stolen from a computer system the beginner has cracked.

8.4.3.2 Usenet Groups. Usenet groups are early Internet equivalents of BBSs, where legitimate sharing of information occurs alongside the exchange of illegal information, pirated code, and so on. Some groups are moderated and so maintain certain ethical standards. Others follow the Internet tradition of anything goes. System administrators and employees should never participate in these groups with company e-mail addresses. In a popular strategy, hackers wait for platform-specific vulnerabilities to be announced, then search newsgroups for messages from people using that platform, look at their e-mail addresses to see where they work, and attack systems at those companies in the hope that patches are not yet installed.

8.4.3.3 Publications. Over the years many publications have specialized in hacking. Often these provided information on how to penetrate systems. Some publications were primarily electronic, such as *Phrack,* while others have been print-based, such as *2600,* which is now widely distributed through conventional magazine channels as well as through paid subscriptions.

8.4.3.4 Hacker Support Groups. Numerous groups of people exist to share hacking information, ranging from relatively stable entities with their own publications (e.g., *2600* and *cDc*) to annual conventions with thousands of participants (e.g., DefCon). Although some members of these groups may have committed criminal acts and some participants at hacker conventions actually have been convicted of such and served time, there is usually a diverse mix of elements with different motivations in these groups and meetings. DefCon, for example, draws not only people who openly advocate unauthorized security testing of other people's systems and networks but also law enforcement personnel and legitimate security experts. Some participants go to DefCon specifically to convince young people not to break laws in trying to learn about security.

Many security professionals would prefer that the line between white-hat hacking and black-hat hacking to be clearer and more sharply enforced; however, some companies overlook past transgressions in order to gain the perceived value of the hackers' technical security expertise. Indeed, in recent years, investors have even cooperated with groups of hackers in founding security consulting companies, complete with some employees who continue to use hacker handles. Some of the best technical training in the field is provided by people who gained their expertise in criminal (or quasi-criminal) hacking but who now help fight such penetrations.

8.4.4   The Future of Penetration.   Several factors suggest that attempts to penetrate information systems will not decrease any time soon. Indeed, the trend at the time of writing is definitely up, and looks set to continue in that direction. Consider these factors:

- The declining cost, and increased access to, penetration technology—from processors used to crack passwords to eavesdropping and interception devices, the trend is lower cost and wider availability.
- The continuing practice of fielding inadequately tested systems, built with immature technology and with insufficient attention to security.
- The increased availability of automated hacking tools with easy-to-use interfaces.
- The continually growing allure, and portrayal in popular culture, of hacking as a "cool" activity, without regard to its legality, or consideration of its morality.

Although some companies are actively pursuing improved responses to these threats, others are not. Through lack of concern, resources, or time to address these trends, many entities are at increasing risk. Too often answers are sought in technological quick fixes. While improvements are possible, such as simplified background encryption and allowed path protections, the root causes of vulnerability, namely human behavior and employee awareness of security issues, are not receiving the attention and resources they deserve.

8.5   SUMMARY

- Penetration of information systems is possible by means of a wide range of methods, some of which are very hard to defend against.
- Those responsible for securing systems have to defend against this wide range of penetration methods.
- Making sure all defenses against all attacks are effective all the time is a lot harder than finding a single point of failure within those defenses.
- While all systems do not need to defend against all types of attack equally, the cost of even the more exotic attack strategies is constantly falling, expanding the range of possible attackers.
- The cheapest and most effective attacks are often nontechnical, exploiting human frailty rather than weaknesses in the technology.
- Experienced criminal hackers tend to favor the nontechnical attack over the technical; and the best defense, employee awareness, is also nontechnical.
- Systems can be attacked at the client, at the server, or at the connection between the two.
- Both wired and wireless systems are highly susceptible to eavesdropping and interception.
- Many systems today are built with immature and insecure technology, making them susceptible to a wide range of attacks.

- New attacks come to light with alarming but predictable regularity.

- Many of these new attacks are old attacks reborn, due to a lack of vulnerability class analysis. As a result of economic pressures, faulty reasoning, and insufficient desire for security, vulnerabilities are fixed one instance at a time rather than one class at a time.

- Allowed path attacks against Web sites are consistently the most effective strategy for system penetration whenever a system is Web-connected or Web-enabled.

- Penetration testing, both by internal staff and objective external experts, always should precede system deployment.

- Given the inevitability of penetration attempts and the high probability of their eventual success, systems should be designed to survive attacks, limiting the scope of compromise from any single point of failure.

- Penetration of systems will continue to fascinate the curious and tempt them to break the law by illegally accessing systems. The potential gains from system penetration, in terms of money, power, competitive advantage, and notoriety, will continue to motivate those to whom laws and morality are not effective deterrents.

- Penetration of systems will become increasingly automated and simplified, further widening the range of possible attackers.

- Human nature, not technology, is the key to defense against penetration attempts. Only by raising society's ethical standards and educating employees to understand the willingness of others to behave unethically can the occurrence of criminal hacking into information systems be significantly reduced.

8.6   FURTHER READING

8.6.1   Web Sites

CERIAS Hotlist: *www.cerias.purdue.edu//hotlist.*
Lessig, L., D. Post, and E. Volokh (1997). *Cyberspace Law for Non-Lawyers.* Published via e-mail: *www.ssrn.com/update/lsn/cyberspace/csl_lessons.html.*
ICSA Labs/TruSecure Corporation's *Hype or Hot* index: *www.trusecure.com/html/tspub/hypeorhot/index.shtml.*
Information Security Resources: *www.security.isu.edu.*
INFOSEC and INFOWAR Portal: *www.infowar.com.*
INFOSYSSEC links, news and search engines: *www.infosyssec.com/infosyssec/index.html.*
SecurityFocus: *www.securityfocus.com.*

8.6.2   Books

Chirillo, J. *Hack Attacks Revealed: A Complete Reference with Custom Security Hacking Toolkit.* New York: John Wiley & Sons, 2001.
Fialka, J. J. *War by Other Means: Economic Espionage in America.* New York: W.W. Norton, 1997.
Goodell, J. *The Cyberthief and the Samurai: The True Story of Kevin Mitnick—and the Man Who Hunted Him Down.* New York: Dell, 1996.
Hatch, B., J.B. Lee, and G. Kurtz. *Hacking Linux Exposed.* New York: McGraw-Hill, 2001.
Power, R. *Tangled Web: Tales of Digital Crime from the Shadows of Cyberspace.* Carmel, IN: Que, 2000.
Scambray, J., S. McClure, and G. Kurtz. *Hacking Exposed,* 2nd ed. New York: McGraw-Hill, 2000.

Scambray, J., and S. McClure. *Hacking Exposed Windows 2000: Network Security Secrets & Solutions.* New York: McGraw-Hill, 2001.

Schwartau, W. *Terminal Compromise.* Seminole, FL: Inter.Pact Press, 1991.

Shimomura, T., and J. Markoff. *Takedown: The Pursuit and Capture of Kevin Mitnick, America's Most Wanted Computer Outlaw—by the Man Who Did It.* New York: Hyperion, 1996.

Slatalla, M., and J. Quittner. *Masters of Deception: The Gang that Ruled Cyberspace.* New York: HarperCollins, 1995.

Sterling, B. *The Hacker Crackdown: Law and Disorder on the Electronic Frontier.* New York: Bantam Doubleday Dell, 1992.

Stoll, C. *The Cuckoo's Egg: Tracking a Spy Through the Maze of Computer Espionage.* New York: Pocket Books/Simon & Schuster, 1989.

Winkler, I. *Corporate Espionage: What It Is, Why It Is Happening in Your Company, What You Must Do about It.* Rocklin, CA: Prima Publishing, 1997.

8.7   NOTES

1. Cobb, S., *The Stephen Cobb Guide to PC & LAN Security* (New York: McGraw-Hill, 1992).

2. Dan Farmer and Wietse Venema, "Improving the Security of Your Site by Breaking into It" Available at *http://nsi.org/Library/Compsec/farmer.txt* or from *www.fish.com/security/admin-guide-to-cracking.html.*

CHAPTER **9**

MALICIOUS CODE

Roger Thompson

CONTENTS

9.1   INTRODUCTION.   This chapter is not intended to provide detailed virus information. Excellent virus descriptions can be found at most antivirus (AV) vendors' Web sites. It is not intended to provide a detailed history of the virus industry. More complete historical anecdotes can be found in earlier books, many of which were written by knowledgeable people close to the sources themselves. Instead, the purpose of this chapter is to trace the important milestones of the virus and AV industries, because there well may be many parallels between the early 2000s and the early 1990s. More than ever, if we ignore the lessons and mistakes of the past, we will be condemned to repeat them in the future. What this chapter tries to show is that, although the IBM PC and disk operating system (DOS) were released in 1981, it took about another six years for the body of information about operating system internals to build up to the point where virus writing was possible, and another four or five years for it to build to the point where sophisticated viruses, using stealth, tunneling, and encryption, were commonly being written.

Then, in 1995, when Microsoft released Windows 95, most of the system internal knowledge became obsolete, along with most of the viruses that existed at that time, and only high-level language viruses, such as macroviruses, could be written. However, the knowledge of how to program at the innermost levels of Windows 95 and higher, and Windows NT 4 and higher, has been building up, and has reached the point where highly sophisticated and successful assembler language viruses will be seen again.

Fred Cohen is generally credited with coining the original definition of a virus in his 1984 thesis: "We define a computer 'virus' as a program that can 'infect' other programs by modifying them to include a possibly evolved copy of itself. With the infection property, a virus can spread throughout a computer system or network using the authorizations of every user using it to infect their programs. Every program that gets infected may also act as a virus and thus the infection grows."[1]

Although the virus industry is about 15 years old, a time span that is arguably four or five generations in the microcomputer industry, that definition still works pretty well today.

For more information on AV techniques, see Chapter 24.

9.2   EARLY HISTORY OF VIRUSES.   Although there was a very early virus written at Texas A&M University around 1981 for the Apple II computer, it eventually died out by itself and was largely forgotten by most of the world until long after the fact. However, the early viruses of greatest significance were the first DOS viruses recorded as infecting the PCs of the general population, as opposed to languishing in a collection somewhere. These DOS viruses started appearing around the world in 1987.

9.2.1   Late 1987.   The earliest viruses included Brain, Lehigh, and the Christmas-Tree worm.

9.2.1.1   *Pakistani or Brain Virus.*   The first virus that received much publicity was the Brain boot sector infector. It was, by later standards, quite big for a boot sector infector, marking three clusters (six sectors) bad, and hiding itself in there, together with the original boot sector. The virus contained text attributing it to two brothers in Lahore, Pakistan. Although it was one of the earliest viruses, it was remarkably advanced in that it used a stealth technique to hide by redirecting attempts to read the boot sector to the stored copy of the boot sector. No versions of it ever infected hard drives, and it is now considered extinct. This virus was the first one that illustrated the concept of *hooking an interrupt*—the process of modifying the operating system so that normal calls to specific system routines could be intercepted and the nature of the system call could be modified to suit the purposes of the virus writers.

9.2.1.2   *The Lehigh Virus.*   The Lehigh virus broke out at Lehigh University in late 1987. It was a program infector, in that it would infect copies of command.com, but it infected *only* command.com. This restriction limited its ability to spread in those prenetwork days, because the only floppies that contained a copy of command.com were those formatted as bootable. Nevertheless, it represented one of the early program-infecting viruses.

9.2.1.3   *Christmas Tree Worm.*   In December 1987, IBM mainframe computers connected to the EARN network began experiencing a mailstorm; that is, they were overloaded by E-mail. It eventually turned out to be a worm, written in an IBM-specific language called REXX. The *worm* (a free-standing program that replicates through a network) generated a rough drawing of a Christmas tree, and while it was displaying this on the screen, it would search for names of people that either sent mail to or received mail from this account, and would propagate itself to them.

   Although this was strictly a mainframe problem, it is worth including here because, in an uncanny parallel of today's events, this was even an interpretive script language.

9.2.2   Early 1988.   Early in 1988, information technology (IT) support personnel at one site thought they might have a virus. They had noticed that one of their PCs would periodically develop a small "hole" on its screen. They had tried all the obvious things, such as changing the video board, and even the mother board, when suddenly several other PCs began developing small, identical holes. As a result, they decided that they had better call a virus expert.

   It turned out that they did indeed have a virus, which came to be known as Jerusalem.1813. It was so named because Jerusalem was about the first place it was ever noticed, and it was about 1,813 bytes in length. Once the victim ran it, it stayed memory resident and infected every .exe and .com file that the user ran thereafter.

   There were many variations, but the most common was one that deleted, rather than infected, programs that were run on any Friday the 13th; this variant also made the hole on the screen 30 minutes after the first virus-infected file was run.

One of the earliest versions was known as the Israeli or the Palestinian virus; it was initially thought to be politically oriented, because the first trigger date for file deletion fell on a day that happened to be the 40th anniversary of the day before the founding of the State of Israel.

Most AV researchers later agreed that this date was just an accident, and that really the virus was just trying to trigger on Black Fridays (i.e., Friday the 13ths).

9.2.3   Stoned/New Zealand/Marijuana Virus.

Between 1989 and 1991, a small (less than 400 bytes) boot sector–infecting virus was easily the most common virus in the world. When a victim was unfortunate enough to attempt to boot from an infected floppy, the Stoned virus would infect the master boot record (MBR) on the hard drive by moving the true MBR from sector 1 to sector 7 of the first side (side 0) of the first cylinder (cylinder 0) of the hard drive; the virus then wrote itself in its place.

There was a one in seven chance that on the initial infection of the hard drive the virus would also display the message "Your PC is now stoned! Legalize marijuana." In those early days, it was probably just as well that it occasionally displayed the message, otherwise most users would never have known that they were infected.

Although the principle of the Stoned virus was copied to the point of mind-numbing tedium from the technical community's point of view, it originally broke much new ground. Until it was released, most people had no clue that hard drives were addressed in terms of side, cylinder, and sector, and that most of side 0, cylinder 0 was empty, and just perfect for hiding viruses and master boot records. Until it was released, most people had no clue that there were actually two boot records on a hard drive: the MBR (at side 0, cylinder 0, sector 1) and the DOS boot record (DBR, at side 1, cylinder 0, sector 1). In fact, some of the most popular disk utilities available at the time didn't seem to know either, and made no provision for examining the MBR. By now, most of this information has probably been forgotten, and may be used again by malefactors.

9.3   VIRUS VARIETIES.

By 1995, many different virus paths had been explored, and it is worth spending some time to understand some of the more important variations. The virus industry has always been a competition between the virus writers, or *vXers,* who find some way to evade detection, and the AV folks, or *Avers* (pronounced "a-v -ers"), who change their software to detect it. As explained in Chapter 24, AV tools started off using recognition of characteristic sequences (virus signatures) of executable code in viruses. Later generations included *heuristic* engines to recognize abnormal, virus-like behavior of programs. By 1993 and 1994, the virus-writing industry was six or seven years old—an established element in the microcomputer world. As one might expect of a mature industry, the early, simple infectors had evolved into a significant number of different types of viruses, some of which were quite clever, complex programs that delved deep into the operating system and used many approaches to eluding AV products.

9.3.1   Virus Factories/Code Generators.

Code generators are not a new idea, and it didn't take long for them to be introduced to the virus-writing world. They made it easy for a relatively untrained and unskilled person to write an assembly language virus, which sometimes worked, but which had two flaws that prevented them from becoming little more than a curiosity.

The first flaw was that serious virus writers have always believed that they had to write their own code. It has never been "cool" simply to modify someone else's work, and that is all they would ever be doing using the virus generators.

The second, and more serious flaw, is that it was soon discovered that there was so much common code in the generated output that AV programmers could find all possible generations using just a few signatures.

The ultimate test of this was in the mid-1990s, when someone generated 15,000 samples using the Phalcon/Skism mass-produced code generator (PSMPC), but all the AV companies were able to detect them within about a week.

There have always been lots of virus code generators, but two of the most interesting from this period were the Virus Creation Laboratory code generator (VCL) and PSMPC.

- **VCL**—This was a pretty piece of code that was written using one of the prominent Borland compilers of the time, either Turbo Pascal or Turbo C, and included state-of-the-art (for that time) Turbo Vision libraries. This gave it a user interface that had pull-down menus, modern (for that time) dialog boxes, and interactive help, and that supported mouse operations. This was around 1993, and was done in DOS-style, text-based displays rather than the graphical Windows interface that is so familiar today. Although the code it generated was easy to detect, it made great presentation fodder for some AV marketing people wishing to impress audiences with the cunning of virus writers.

- **PSMPC**—Rather than being interactive and menu-driven, this was written in a batch-oriented, compiled language. After parameters were set, the program ran and generated code. Like the VCL output, the code it generated was relatively easy to detect.

9.3.2   Program Infector Viruses.   These were viruses that infected executable files, such as those that ended in .exe, .com, or .sys. One of the beliefs of the time, later proven unfounded, was that data files did not have to be scanned, because even if a data file contained a virus, there was no way for it to get into the execution stream of the PC. In other words, it could never start.

Program infectors were categorized in two ways. One set of categories was the means used to evade detection, and included polymorphic, stealth, tunneling, retro, companion, and path-companion. The second set of categories referred to the infection method and location; it included memory-resident, nonresident, prepending, appending, and midfile.

9.3.2.1   Polymorphic Viruses.   Polymorphic viruses arose as the logical zenith of using encryption to evade signature scanners. The first encrypted viruses had a small, simple decryption loop at the start of the code, whose job it was to decrypt the virus before allowing it to run. Because scanner-developing Avers simply took their signatures from the decryption loop instead of the body of the virus, the vXers tried making the decryption loop more complicated and variable, with each version having a different signature.

The biggest problem with this approach was the difficulty of writing in assembly language. The Bulgarian programmer (or perhaps more properly, group of programmers) called the Dark Avenger, solved this problem by creating the first polymorphic virus writing kit (DAME, or Dark Avengers mutation engine). This was a semicompiled program called an object file (.obj) that could be linked to any other virus, and that could then provide professional quality polymorphism with just a couple of well-executed calls. Virus writers could concentrate on the rest of their code and, once it was working as they wanted, simply link the mutation engine into it.

Dark Avenger provided documentation with the kit, and was even said to provide technical support via e-mail. The vXers quickly released several other mutation engines, including the Trident polymorphic engine (TPE) and Dark Slayer's mutation engine (DSME).

The AV industry countered by developing emulators that allowed the scanner to step through the decryption loop until the underlying virus was exposed in memory. At that point, the AV product could use simple signatures to identify the virus.

9.3.2.2   Stealth Viruses.   These viruses were developed to evade check-summing AV programs. Check summers monitored each program on a hard drive, usually at boot time, and if nothing had changed, then probably no virus was active. On the other hand, if several programs were reported to have changed, and if the user had not updated those programs, then probably a virus was on the system.

Once active on a PC, stealth viruses would watch for any attempt to open a program file for reading, as opposed to simply executing. The stealth code would interpret that as either an AV check summer or scanner about to look for it in that file. It would pause the calling program while it removed itself from the victim program. In fact, it would restore the victim program to its original state and would then allow the calling program to complete the scan or check sum. The stealth code would also be watching for the call to close that file, and as soon as it intercepted the call, the virus would reinfect the originally infected file — or any file that was being opened and closed.

The result of this strategy was that the stealth virus would follow the AV program throughout the entire disk, infecting every program on it in just one pass. They were very effective spreaders, and troublesome to remove from a system.

Once a stealth virus was on a PC, the only way to get rid of it was either a complete restore from a backup, or booting the system from a known clean DOS boot floppy, and running the scanner from the floppy. To prevent infections, the only recourse that AV product developers had was either to identify the virus before it could run or to scan the memory of the PC. Fortunately, stealth viruses were hard to write and never widely disseminated.

9.3.2.3   Tunneling Viruses.   These viruses evolved to evade behavior-blocking memory-resident AV programs. These AV programs tried to stop viruses by watching for virus-like behavior, and then intercepting and disallowing that behavior. For example, it was rarely natural for a program to want to write to the boot sector of a hard drive, so a behavior blocker would intercept that call and ask the user for permission to complete the operation.

A tunneling virus overcame this barrier by putting the machine into single-step mode and issuing an innocuous version of some system call. It would then trace the addresses that were returned by the call until it felt that it had derived the true address of the system call in read-only memory (ROM) or in random-access (live) memory (RAM), and would subsequently call that routine directly, instead of making a normal system call that would be blocked.

Fortunately, these too were hard to write, and were not common.

9.3.2.4   Retroviruses.   A retrovirus is a virus that fights back. It deliberately tries to bypass the operation of specific AV programs.

Some virus writers knew that they would be more successful if AV programs could be rendered ineffective, so they added code to detect popular AV programs, and then to neutralize them. For example, memory-resident AV programs commonly have a call available that tells them not to scan anything until further notice. This exists so that an on-demand scanner can open files for scanning without the resident scanner interfering. Another possibility is that sometimes these programs need to remove themselves from memory so they can be updated.

AV people tried hard to hide these implementation details, but vXers spent just as many hours reverse-engineering AV programs looking for those calls. When such a call was found, it was common for the information to be published on the vX underground, and for new viruses using that information to follow shortly thereafter.

9.3.2.5 Memory-Resident Viruses.
Most programs run, do their job, and then terminate. Once they terminate, the memory they used is returned to the pool for other programs. Memory-resident viruses are those that, once run, don't actually terminate. Typically, they detach themselves from a host program, and even when the host terminates, they stay active in memory, looking for files to infect.

9.3.2.6 Nonresident Infectors.
Nonresident infectors run when the host program is run, just the same as their resident cousins, but once they have infected one or more files, they terminate.

9.3.2.7 Prependers, Appenders, Overwriters, and Midfile Infectors.
All viruses, except overwriters, try to maintain the functionality of the original target program by preserving all the original code. They do so by moving one or more instructions from the original code and using JUMP codes to branch from the virus modifications back to the fragment of original code and then on to the rest of the program.

Prependers infect files by placing their viral code at the beginning of the victim file, whereas appenders infect by placing themselves at the end of the victim file. Overwriters, as the name implies, simply overwrite all or part of the victim file. Overwriters damage the functionality of the infected program, and so are usually noticed immediately after they infect their target; as a result, overwriting viruses do not spread easily.

Midfile infectors generally try to move some code from the middle of a program and write themselves into the file in its place. This is obviously a much harder programming task than, say, appending, and as a result, it has not been as popular a method.

It should be noted that modern *metamorphic* viruses are a form of midfile infector combined with polymorphism. So far, the AV scanners have been able to keep up with this, but it seems likely the virus writers will continue to explore this idea.

Another infection plan involved the idea of not touching the victim file at all. The idea of *companion viruses* was that they would position themselves so that they would be found and run first. For example, in the DOS days, .com files were run before .exe files. If a companion virus wanted to infect an .exe file called hello.exe, it would simply write itself into the same directory, calling itself hello.com. Whenever someone tried to execute "hello," the .com version would run first, and then quietly run the .exe version.

In a variant of the scenario above, a *path companion* would find a directory closer to the beginning of the search path, and would write itself into that directory.

9.3.2.8 Multipartite Viruses.
This refers to viruses that infect more than one category of targets. In the DOS days, we had viruses such as NATAS, which would infect both boot records and program files. The idea was that this would give them a better chance of spreading. If users booted from an infected disk, the virus would be in memory, and ready to go; if they ran an infected program, the virus would also be in memory.

9.3.3   Boot Viruses.   Boot viruses infect a system when a user attempts to boot from an infected floppy. For most of the early 1990s, despite the fact that they never accounted for more than two or three percent of the known viruses, they were responsible for 80 or 90 percent of the reported infections.

People who were aware of the problem always claimed that they would never boot their PC from a floppy, but what often happened was that they would unknowingly leave an infected floppy in the drive when they went home. When they powered up the PC next morning, it would actually boot from the floppy, and thus infect the system.

9.4   MICROSOFT SOFTWARE AND RECENT VIRUSES.   The release of Microsoft Windows 95 in 1995 marked the beginning of the rapid decline of boot viruses. Under Windows 95, boot viruses could still infect the hard drive, but they were usually detected immediately because the operating system reported them as an error. Not only that, but under Windows 95 and higher, boot viruses could no longer infect floppies.

As the vXers continue to refine their understanding of Windows internals, the possibility continues to increase that they may again learn how to make boot sectors a viable vector.

9.4.1   August 1995: Windows 95 Released.   The release of Windows 95 in 1995 was a watershed event in the virus world. It was the first commonly adopted operating system that used what was called protected mode. DOS and Windows 3.1 worked in what is known as real mode. Basically, real mode meant that any program could write into the address space of any other program. Programmers were supposed to write well-behaved programs that took care not to overwrite any other programs in memory, but there was no enforcement of that at either the hardware or software level.

Protected mode involves using a combination of hardware and software to prevent any given program, accidentally or intentionally, from writing into the address space of any other program.

Most of the viruses that existed at that time, particularly, the stealthy and tunneling ones that burrowed deep inside the operating system and generally caused the most grief, no longer worked.

More importantly, the huge body of information that had built up about DOS internals, and which had allowed viruses to be written in the first place, became obsolete and irrelevant overnight. In fact, the Windows 95 programming model was so different from the known and well-understood DOS model that many low-level programmers on both sides never climbed the learning curve.

9.4.2   August 1995: MS-Word Macro Viruses Appear.   Although Windows 95 wiped out most of the world's viruses when it was released, it was a case of one hand taking away, but the other hand giving. MS-Office 95, including Word 6.0, released at the same time, included a powerful macro language that was a derivative of Visual BASIC, called Word BASIC.

At almost the same time, a compact disc read-only memory (CD-ROM) was distributed that contained a working example of a macro virus written in Word BASIC. This was immediately named the Concept virus by the AV community, partly because it provided a road map for hundreds of would-be virus authors who could no longer use any of the older virus models, and partly because it contained a routine named, ominously, PayLoad. The PayLoad routine actually had no real code in it, just a remark that said, "And that's enough to prove my point."

To further complicate matters, the executable macro code was actually stored within the document file itself. For the first time, this meant that executable code was stored in, and could activate from, a data file. For years, AV support people had been telling users, "You shouldn't scan data files. Viruses can't execute from a data file." That was now the wrong advice. Not only could viruses reside in what seemed to be a plain data file, but Word documents were fast becoming the most popular vector for new viruses. Suddenly, support people had to start saying "Well, you don't have to scan *most* data files, but you do have to scan some."

The reason for this apparent anomaly was that Word documents were actually structured storage files. This meant that these files were like a file system within a file system. Each single, structured storage file contained one or more directories, known as *storages,* and each storage contained zero or more separate files, now known as *streams.* Word Basic macros were in one storage within the document file, and the words of the document itself in a different storage.

Although it has always been possible to write viruses in high-level languages like BASIC, C, and Pascal, before the advent of Windows 95, "real" virus writers only wrote in assembly language. After 1995, though, not only was it well nigh impossible to write in assembly language, but writing macro viruses emerged as an excellent alternative. As a result of this technology, and because of the widespread popularity of Windows 95 and its Office suite, viruses could be written for all Office platforms.

9.4.3   July 1996: First Excel Virus—XM/Laroux.a.   Almost a year after the Concept virus, the first Excel macro virus was discovered. It was mostly harmless, except that it showed that the bad guys were starting to explore other Office products as potential vectors.

9.4.4   January 1997: Office 97 Released.   Office 97 offered an enhanced macro language, Visual BASIC for Applications (VBA), which was standard across all Office products. This meant that cross-platform macro viruses were now a probability, rather than a possibility.

At the same time, the internal security capability was enhanced. If a document contained macros, Word would now warn the user, and would offer to open the document without allowing the macros to run. This was not a perfect solution, because it relied on the user to make the right decision. An even more critical problem was that the warning dialog also contained a little check box that said something like "Don't ask this question again." Thus users could easily disable the very security that might save them.

9.4.5   February 1997: First E-Mailing Virus—WM/ShareFun.a.   This was a Word macro virus that had the distinction of being the first e-mail aware virus. Every time an infected file was activated, a pseudo-random number generator ensured that there was a one in four chance that the mailing portion of the virus would activate. If MSMAIL (an early e-mail program from Microsoft) was running, the virus would randomly select three addresses from the MSMAIL address list, and would attempt to send e-mail to them, with an infected copy of the document attached.

Interestingly, the chosen subject line was "You have GOT to see this!", which is not all that different from many of the current, successful strategies.

WM/ShareFun.a was originally found in the wild, but was never very successful, mostly because it worked with the relatively unpopular MSMAIL, rather than the ubiquitous Outlook.

9.4.6   March 1998: First Access Virus—A97/AccessiV.a.   This was nothing more than a proof of concept virus, and was never found in the wild. Few viruses have been written in Access since, and none has ever been a problem for normal users.

9.4.7   June 1998: Windows 98 Released.   One of the important features of Windows 98, at least from a virus or AV point of view, was that Windows Scripting Host was installed by default. Previously, it had to be specifically installed, or it came with certain Internet Explorer versions. Once installed by default, and therefore ubiquitous and homogeneous, it became a viable option for the virus writers to explore.

9.4.8   September 1998: First Office Cross-Infector—O97/Shiver.a.   There is little that is important about this virus except that it was the first that could infect both Word documents and Excel spreadsheets. As with WM/ShareFun.a, this was possible because, with the release of Office 97, all Office products began using VBA as a common macro language.

9.4.9   November 1998: First .vbs Virus—VBS/VBSFirst.   This was a trivial, proof of concept that claimed to be written by Lord Natas of CodeBreakers. It did little more than spread itself, but it certainly helped make people aware of the ease of use, and the immense power of Windows Scripting Host.

9.4.10   December 1998: First PowerPoint Virus—PP97/Attach.a.   PP97/Attach.a infected all PPT files in the "C:\My Documents" folder, that contained user forms. Because user forms are uncommon in PowerPoint programs, this, along with other design flaws, made it unlikely that the virus would ever succeed in the wild. It is mentioned here only because it was the first PowerPoint virus, and it rounds out the list of Office infectors.

9.4.11   January 1999: First Modern Worm—Happy99@m.   Happy99 is known as the first modern worm. It was certainly successful, and several of its techniques have been adopted by other worm developers. For example, it was the first, or one of the first, to patch winsock.dll to watch for outgoing e-mail addresses to send itself to. It was easy to detect, and most AV programs could detect it shortly after its initial discovery. Fortunately, for the many home users who either did not have AV programs at all, or did not update their AV programs frequently enough, the virus was fairly harmless. Its only payload was the occasional display of a fireworks graphic, and some users actually liked it. By targeting home users, and not corporations, the author didn't really make anyone mad enough for the authorities to bother with him.

Even though it was considered a slow mailer, rather than a mass mailer, the fact that it was harmless and subtle, together with its targeting of home users, combined to give it a long life span and allowed it to be the most prominent virus in the world for quite a while.

9.4.12   March 1999: First Outlook Mass Mailer—W97/Melissa.a@mm.   W97/Melissa.a@mm arrived as a Word document, called list.doc, which purported to be a list of passwords to adult-content Web sites. Early on the morning of March 26, 1999, users all around the world began receiving an e-mail with a document attached. The accompanying e-mail bore a subject of "Important message from <someone you know>," and the e-mail body said "Here is that document you asked for . . . Don't show anyone else ;-)."

The combination of being from someone known, and therefore probably trusted, together with the intriguing, collaborative message, was enough to trick a large portion of the public into opening the document. When they did so, the worm e-mailed itself to the first 50 addresses in each of their address books.

The author of the worm is reported to have said that he tried to limit the effect of the code by only going for the first 50, but what he didn't take into account was that the first 50 addresses very often included groups of addresses, which massively multiplied the worm's effect.

9.4.13   April 1999: First Virus to Attempt to Flash ROM—CIH Virus.   CIH was a virus written by a Taiwanese college student, who called it his "little virus game." The importance of this virus is that it had quite a damaging payload. On its trigger date, it would overwrite a portion of the victim's hard drive, and, much worse, would attempt to overwrite the flash ROM of the PC. Hard drives can be recovered by users, provided they have a reasonable backup, but an overwritten flash ROM is not trivial to replace. Laptops, in particular, usually have to go back to the factory.

The AV community was quite worried about this virus because it was known to have spread widely. Although it was discovered in about June 1998 and detection had been available since about July 1998, questions kept coming in to AV support people, and it gradually became obvious that the most widespread variant was one that triggered only once per year, on April 26.

When the trigger date finally arrived, most U.S. and European computers turned out to be adequately protected, but Asian computer users paid a heavy penalty.

9.4.14   June 1999: First Worm to Spread by Both Mass Mailing and Network Shares—Zipped Files.   ZippedFile.exe arrived as an e-mail attachment, from someone to whom the victim had just written an e-mail. The e-mail said something similar to "I received your e-mail and I shall send you a reply ASAP. Till then, take a look at the attached zipped docs."

What victims usually failed to realize was that the e-mail was not really from their contacts, but from the worm itself, which would analyze and reply to incoming messages on an infected machine.

As well as spreading by e-mail, this worm would also look for, and infect, shared network drives on the local area network. This gave it a fast method of distribution; combined with its payload of overwriting many data files, this worm was much more painful on a local area network than WM/Melissa.

9.4.15   October 1999: First Self-Mailing Virus Able to Run Without Opening an E-Mail—JS/Kak@m.   Kak is a worm that embeds itself within an e-mail, rather than within an attachment. It does this by replacing Outlook Express's signature file, which then infects every e-mail sent via Outlook Express thereafter.

The significance of Kak is that it executes when the user views the message in the preview pane of Outlook Express, without the user's opening an e-mail or clicking on an attachment.

9.4.16   December 1999: W32/Babylonia.a@mm.   Babylonia was probably not the first self-updating worm, but it was an important precursor to W32/Hybris@mm. When Babylonia ran on a victim's machine, one of its first steps was to try to contact a particular Web site and download plug-in modules to be run on the victim machine.

What this meant was that the worm could change its functionality and potentially become more damaging every time a new plug-in was released and added to the Web site.

Given the timing of this release, this may have been an attempt to cause a Y2K (year 2000) virus problem.

Fortunately, for the world, but unfortunately for the success of this worm, the AV industry was able to put enough pressure on the Web host that the Web site was shut down, effectively blunting Babylonia's power.

9.4.17   May 2000: Fastest Spreader?—VBS/LoveLetter.a@mm.   On May 4, 2000, AV people around the world started asking if anyone had seen a new mass mailing worm that arrived as an attachment named LOVE-LETTER-FOR-YOU.txt.vbs. Not surprisingly, almost everyone was seeing it. It seemed to spread all around the world at the same time, from which it can be inferred that it infected an extremely large address book very early.

9.4.18   October 2000: W32/Hybris@mm.   W32/Hybris@mm was more than a simple virus or worm—it was an environment. It could update itself with plug-in modules downloaded from the news group alt.comp.virus. The virus author had learned from his previous work, Babylonia, that updates from a Web page could easily be shut down by authorities. Therefore, Hybris was updated from the Usenet, which no one controls, making this part of its activity virtually unstoppable.

Hybris itself does little more than infect a PC and spread from there. It spreads by patching a component of Windows, wsock32.dll (winsock), and then watching the data stream for anything resembling an e-mail address. This might be from a genuine e-mail being sent or received, or it might be an e-mail address inside an e-mail message or even in a local document or a Web page.

When it sees an address, Hybris waits for a while, and then sends itself to that address via an anonymous remailer. By using the anonymous remailer, Hybris disguises where it came from, and by waiting a while, it prevents the victim from identifying the earlier clean mailer as the culprit. With Hybris, the vXers have shown considerable social engineering skills (in the sense that they seem to understand how to exploit normal human behavior) as well as programming skills. They've demonstrated that it doesn't matter if a virus can be detected by AV software because enough people will neglect to update their AV software that the virus will still be able to generate many infections.

The vXers have also demonstrated that by targeting home users more than corporate users, they are unlikely to make anyone who has sufficient resources to catch them, *want* to catch them; the ones who do want to catch them don't have the resources. This development is significant because as the Melissa and LoveLetter worms showed, if enough important people are mad enough, they *can* catch the culprit.

Although Hybris itself is fairly harmless, the updatable plug-in architecture makes it possible for the virus author to add a module to do something nasty. By uploading to the newsgroup, a module could update all infected computers, worldwide, in a matter of hours.

9.4.19   February 2001: VBS/VBSWG.J@mm (a.k.a. OnTheFly, Anna Kournikova). The release and subsequent success of the Anna Kournikova worm proved two things. The first was that the vX world had polarized into two camps: assembler programmers in one camp writing sophisticated, successful viruses such as Hybris, and relatively unskilled bottom feeders using kits to generate pretty stupid, successful worms like this one.

It arrived as an e-mail attachment called AnnaKournikova.jpg.vbs. Windows by default hides known file extensions, so all most people saw was an attachment called AnnaKournikova.jpg. The e-mail was, naturally, from someone you knew, saying "Hi: Check this!" and it looked like the file ought to be a picture of the attractive eponymous tennis player.

Evidently that was enough, and large numbers of people all round the world double-clicked the attachment and were shocked to find that their computer sent the file to all of their friends and colleagues. That is, those who understood what had happened were shocked. Among support staff, stories are legion of users who double-clicked it twice, because they didn't see a picture the first time.

The alleged perpetrator admitted that he could not write a program, but had simply made a few menu choices and mouse clicks in a kit known as VBSWG to generate the worm.

Part of the official name of this worm is VBSWG.J, which indicates that it was actually the 10th worm generated by this kit and released to either the public or to virus collections, but none of the first nine actually were propagated. At this writing, AV researchers are locked in a debate over the phenomenon of missing variants of worms. One position is that worm outbreaks happen when one or more of the major AV developers can't detect the worm at release time. The other position is that it doesn't matter whether or not the worm can be *detected* because, in fact, worm outbreaks can't be *prevented,* as long as someone with a big address book and an out-of-date AV program can be counted on to let it loose. This is called "getting lucky."

Adding fuel to this fire was the fact that, just three months later, another worm generated by the same kit also resulted in a large outbreak. This worm was VBS/ VBSWG.X@mm, better known as VBS/Homepage (see Section 9.4.21). Again, this was different enough that some large scanners couldn't detect it without a signature update, which tended to support the argument that the lack of signature updates facilitates outbreaks. The opposition points out, however, that 13 other worms from the same kit had been identified and collected during those three months, some of which had resulted in minor outbreaks, but none of which had resulted in major outbreaks. In other words, they claim this supports their side of the argument, in that the worms just hadn't gotten lucky.

The truth probably lies somewhere in the middle. Massive outbreaks happen when someone with a big address book runs a mass-mailing worm that the installed AV can't detect. This initial mailing gives it a start, but if the reason it couldn't be detected was simply an out-of-date signature file, and the majority of AV programs can detect the worm, then the outbreak quickly dies out. If, however, the worm gets a start because a major AV couldn't detect it without an upgrade to the detection engine itself, then that means that all the clients of that AV will be similarly unprotected, and the outbreak becomes major.

It is also worth noting that the mass-mailing outbreaks, although spectacular, are short lived. Usually, they peak within 24 hours, drop off dramatically within the next 24 hours, and die out completely within a few months. The reason for this pattern is that the AV community receives nearly instantaneous notification of such outbreaks and can count on their high news value to get news of the signature updates out to the public very quickly.

See the note under the Worms section for some good preventative advice.

9.4.20   March 2001: W32/Magistr@mm.   This virus was first isolated in March 2001, and combines both mass-mailing and flash overwriting capability. This makes it possibly the most dangerous virus ever seen. AV developers hope that this combination is not a sign of things to come, but given the propensity for causing damage in the virus-writing community, there may be more of these vicious viruses in the future.

9.4.21   May 2001: VBS/VBSWG.X@mm (a.k.a. Homepage).   VBS/Homepage was different from most kit-generated worms because it was clearly modified significantly by hand. This was necessary because the authors wanted the worm to point to one of four different adult-content Web sites, based on a random number from 1 to 4, but the kit did not offer that option. VBSWG kit-generated code is generally untidy, which is perfectly acceptable to a PC, but very hard for a human being to read and modify. No lines are indented, routine and variable names are just a random jumble of letters, and of course, there are no comments.

A probably unexpected by-product of the tidying process performed by the authors is that they changed the worm sufficiently so that no AV could detect it, thus allowing the worm to get an initially wide distribution.

When it arrived at the victim's desktop, it was, as usual, from someone the victim knew. The e-mail message said simply "You've got to see this!" and the attachment was called HOMEPAGE.html.vbs. Again, because the Windows default is to hide known file extensions, all most people saw was HOMEPAGE.html. Evidently, lots of people thought that .html had to be safe, and double-clicked it. As usual, the worm then e-mailed itself to everyone in each of the exposed address books and the cycle began anew (see the note under the Worms section for some good preventative advice).

9.4.22   July 2001: W32/CodeRed.   This was one of the really significant malicious code events for 2001, and came just one month after the buffer overflow attack that it used was announced to the public.

On June 18, 2001, a security company announced that it had discovered a buffer overflow in Microsoft's Internet Information Server, IIS version 4. At the time, IIS 4 was probably the most widely used Web server in the world. Following the commonly adopted Full Disclosure Model, the company made enough details of the discovery available that responsible network administrators would be able to fashion protection against anyone trying to exploit the vulnerability. Buffer overflows have long been understood to allow a malicious attacker to gain remote control of a computer, but have also long been understood to be quite difficult to implement. It seems likely, though, that the authors of the CodeRed worm already had most of their code prepared and were simply waiting for someone to find an appropriately widespread vulnerability. In any case, around July 13, less than a month after the initial announcement, Network Administrators around the world began noticing large numbers of attacks trying to exploit that vulnerability. It quickly became obvious that a worm now existed that had spread widely.

The worm was named CodeRed, allegedly for no better reason than that the discoverers were drinking lots of that particular soda at the time. More importantly, disassembly revealed that the worm had two main functions. The first was to spread as far as it could. Second, on a particular date, all infected machines were to try to bombard the official White House Web site with massive numbers of requests, thus overwhelming the Web site and denying service to genuine Web visitors. In reality, although the worm infected massive numbers of Web servers, the authors used a hard-coded IP address, and the White House Web site administrators simply "moved" the White House by changing DNS entries to a different IP address, so the actual payload part of the attack missed completely.

A slightly patched version of the worm, CodeRed.B, was soon discovered. The patch generated generate completely random IP target addresses, allowing the worm to spread further.

The worm had two other significant points of interest. While active in a Web server, it would dynamically generate a Web page claiming that the Web site had been "Hacked by Chinese." Because this occurred shortly after an unfortunate collision between a U.S. military plane and a Peoples' Republic of China fighter jet, with a corresponding rise in tensions between the two countries, it seems possible that the worm was in fact written in the Peoples' Republic of China. The second interesting point is that this worm never actually wrote itself to the hard drive of the victim computer. It resided entirely in RAM. This meant that the worm disappeared as soon as a Web server was rebooted, but unless the server was patched before being restarted, it would soon be probed by another infected PC and the whole cycle started again.

9.4.23 August 2001: W32/CodeRed II (a.k.a. CodeRed.C). This was another significant event for 2001, discovered on or about August 2 or 3. Internally, the worm called itself CodeRed II. Although it was a completely different code base from the initial worm, it worked through the same vulnerability, and a large part of the AV industry officially called it CodeRed.C. The main difference between the .A variant and Code-Red II was that the new one also carried a backdoor program with it, which it dropped on any server it infected. Therefore, this presented a bigger problem for infected corporations. Any infected machine was effectively compromised, and corporations were forced to choose between simply removing the backdoor and hoping that nothing new or different had been added while the machine was compromised, or reinstalling all software on the machine and starting again. Reinstalling was obviously the safer alternative, but this was not a pleasant choice for corporations with hundreds or even thousands of infected machines.

Early in August, I had begun wondering exactly what was bouncing off port 80 on my firewall. I thought it was probably a CodeRed, but which one? A, B, C, or something new? Needing some way to know, I wrote a program to listen on port 80, and checksum whatever came in. Known captures were to be reported every hour, and new captures would be reported immediately. I began deploying WormCatcher in mid-August, and almost immediately, caught CodeRed.D, a minor variation of CodeRed II which had been modified to allow it to spread further and faster. Thus it came about that by the end of August, there was a large body of compromised machines, and a small but growing number of WormCatcher nodes.

9.4.24 September 2001: W32/Nimda.a@mm. Exactly one week after the terrible events of September 11, 2001, at 9:05 A.M., one of my WormCatcher nodes went off three times in less than a minute. That proved little, because in order to avoid overwhelming my mailserver in the event of a massive outbreak, WormCatcher had a couple of built-in limiting algorithms, one of which was that only three variants per hour would be immediately reported—more than three would simply be stored locally and reported on the hour. Minutes later, while I was still considering the implications of this event, another WormCatcher, in a different country, began reporting the same sequence of probes. Five minutes later, a third node reported the same probing sequence, and it became obvious to me that a new worm was afoot. Within 30 minutes, in fact, all WormCatcher nodes, all around the world were reporting the same thing.

The timing, exactly one week after September 11, at 9:00 A.M., caused some concern that this was somehow related to those awful events, but in time, it became clear that the author was simply being opportunistic.

We knew we had a worm, but not a sample or a name. That problem was solved by Righard Zwienenberg, a Dutch AV researcher. Righard was also running a Worm-Catcher node, and called me saying, "Am I the only one?" I assured him that all nodes were seeing exactly the same thing, and he said "I have the worm. I've called it Nimda, as a working name until we agree on something better."

An examination of the visible strings inside the worm revealed that the author really wanted his creation called CV (Concept Virus), but most anti-virus researchers choose some name other than what the author wanted, and as Righard searched for a better name, he noticed that the worm came as a file called admin.dll, and admin, spelled backwards is Nimda. As far as he was concerned, it was simply a working name, so it did not matter that it was nearly unpronounceable. For better or for worse, the name stuck, and over the next few weeks was variously referred to as Nidma, Nimad, and Nidam, before it became properly understood as Nimda.

It was more than slightly amusing,when the next version of Nimda was released, to see that the author had, almost plaintively, left the following note visible in the code, "This's CV, no Nimda."

Compared to the slick, elegant code of the CodeReds, Nimda was conventional to the point of being almost pedestrian. It was written in C, as opposed to the much harder Assembly language of the CodeReds. Although the author thought of it as a concept virus, most of its tricks were nothing new. Self-emailing worms are common, and local-share-traveling worms are common. Infecting programs and HTML in Web pages was also common. Even the idea of using security vulnerabilities to launch a worm was not new, and the vulnerabilities it used were nearly twelve months old by the time the author used them. Combining multiple techniques is also not new—"multi-partite" is a term that has long been used to describe exactly this property in viruses.

Nimda's success can be traced to three factors that came together in an ill-timed confluence. The first was the large number of Web servers already compromised by Code-Red II's backdoor. This meant that every one of those Web servers was immediately infected by Nimda. The second was that networks tend to be hard and crunchy on the outside but soft and chewy on the inside. This means that if Nimda got into a network by any means, it spread like wildfire via local network shares, which are mostly unprotected because of the implicit trust in coworkers. The real impact of this, however, was that it infected previously uncompromised Web servers from the *inside*. The third factor was that a vast number of Web surfers were running unpatched browsers, which were entirely vulnerable to a Nimda-infected Web page. A user would surf to a favorite Web page and suddenly become infected, after which the whole cycle started again.

There are three lessons to be drawn from the CodeRed and Nimda events. The first is that the authors of these worms are unknown, and there is no reason to think they are not working on new creations. Two or three such events can be expected each year, for the next few years. The second lesson is that these things spread faster than either AV updates or vulnerability patches can be applied, although both could have been avoided, or at least ameliorated, by configuring systems wisely. The answer then, is not "Patch, patch, patch" but "Configure, configure, configure." The third lesson is that the answer to the typical question: "When can you relax?" is, of course: "Never."

9.5   WORMS.   The commonly accepted definition of a worm is that it is a program that replicates without "infecting" other programs with a copy of itself. Generally, worms spread either as e-mail attachments or by being network-aware, and by using network-specific calls to get from one place to another. For example, worms can spread by using network calls to find shared, writable drives across the network, to which they copy themselves.

9.5.1 Prevention of Worms and Other E-Mail–Carried Malicious Code. Most of the modern, massive worm outbreaks could actually be easily prevented if network administrators simply filtered off the principal file extensions. For example, nearly all worm attacks seen in 2000, and early 2001, used just a few extension types. Those were .vbs, .exe, .scr, and .pif. This list is not exhaustive, but it does cover most attacks, and others can easily be added as they become necessary.

Filtering should be done at the e-mail gateway based on file extensions. Security administrators can easily do this, using almost any AV gateway products, which, at the same time, can scan for known viruses. For example, if a .vbs file must be sent by e-mail, the sender should be made to zip or compress it. This would not be completely bullet proof, but it would require greater effort from a perpetrator.

9.5.2 Morris Worm of 1988. Many volumes have been written about this worm, the first significant worm the Internet had yet seen. The worm was released on November 2, 1988, by Robert T. Morris, Jr. In those early days, many systems had common, easily exploited holes (e.g., buffer overflows in *fingerd* and a debugging option in *sendmail*), and this is what the worm did very well. It replicated itself so quickly, and so widely, that it brought the Internet to its knees for a few days.

9.6 NONREPLICATING THREATS. Not all malicious code actually replicates. Starting in about December 1999, increasingly large numbers of remote access Trojans (RATs) were being posted to the Usenet, as would-be hackers realized that the Internet was a fantastic replicator all by itself. The purpose of these programs is to gain control of other people's computers. Typically, the programs are posted to adult-content newsgroups thinly disguised as an adult-oriented digital movie, for example— "16YearOldHasSexForFirstTime.mpg.exe" or "HardCore.avi.scr." As explained earlier, by default, Windows hides known file extensions, so most users who downloaded either of the two examples above would not see the .exe or the .scr parts of the name, and most were fooled into thinking it to be an .mpg or .avi file—in other words, a movie.

To determine the actual type of a Windows file, the easiest way is to right-click the file in Windows Explorer and look at the Properties page. That will show, among other things, the full file name, including the true extension. Overriding the default that hides file extensions is also useful. This is accomplished by opening a window in Windows Explorer, right-clicking on "View," right-clicking "Folder options," and right-clicking the "View" tab. In the menu, "Hide extensions for known file types" should be unselected, before clicking "OK."

Whenever a file apparently has two extensions, such as .jpg.vbs or .mpg.exe, the file is probably malicious, and should either be deleted or examined by an expert before activation.

If the victim is unwary enough to run a RAT, usually nothing seems to happen, and the victim usually concludes wrongly that the movie was corrupted in the download, and keeps on surfing the newsgroups, or performing any other function. However, what has really happened is that the RAT will have changed its name, copied itself deep into the Windows directories (where few people really know what should be there), and then added itself to the start-up path. After the next start-up, the program will always be running in the background.

From then on, every time the victim connects to the Internet, the RAT "phones home." It contacts the perpetrator, usually by joining a given IRC channel, and waits for commands. Anytime the perpetrator wants, he can then do almost anything on that machine. He can download any file he wants, including password caches or accounting and online banking files. He can upload any file or program he wants, including more sophisticated remote control programs, such as DDoS (distributed denial of service) clients, and then make the PC (or even all the PCs under his control) attack some other victim. Even big, commercial Web sites can be brought to their knees if enough PCs attack them simultaneously.

The number of different RATs keeps growing, but the most popular, and most commonly seen include SubSeven and one that is generally, and loosely called Multidropper.

9.6.1   SubSeven.   SubSeven is written by someone who calls himself MobMan, and who claims that his program is for "Internet Entertainment" only. While that may well have been his intention, it is fairly obvious that some people are bent on using it for other purposes, because 600 to 1,000 copies of it are posted to the Usenet each month, disguised as adult movies.

SubSeven actually comes in three parts: Client, Server, and EditServer. Server is the program that the perpetrator tries to plant on the victim's PC, and Client is the piece that the perpetrator runs to send commands to the Server, hence controlling the victim's PC. The EditServer program is used to configure the Server options. There are actually many options, but a few examples are what ports to use for communication, how to notify when the victim is online, whether to use ICQ or IRC for notification, and which start-up method to use when the PC is rebooted.

For protection against reverse engineering, the binary code is usually compressed by the author using the Ultimate Packer for eXecutables (UPX) compressor/decompressor prior to release. All these parameters are stored inside the Server program itself, in a block at the end of the file, and then the block is encrypted and usually protected with a password to stop prying eyes.

By far the most popular version is 2.1, which itself is broken down into three or four minor variations. Although at this writing version 2.2 has been out for several months, it seems to be unable to gain even a fraction of 2.1's popularity.

9.6.2   Multidropper.   The RAT known mostly as Multidropper is not really a program at all, but an odd little collection made up of two programs and several scripts, all bound together into a single file by a program called a binder. If the file is run, the binder knows how to split the individual files up, and where to put them. It, too, is posted to the Usenet in large numbers each month, disguised as adult movies.

Possibly the most interesting part of this is that, unlike SubSeven, there is no actual RAT involved. Instead, one of the programs within the collection is a copy of the extremely popular shareware program, MIRC. This version of MIRC has been optioned to allow uploading and downloading of files without asking the victim for permission, and without telling the victim that it's happening. The second program in the collection is a shareware or freeware utility that can hide or unhide windows. Naturally, this is used to hide MIRC, so that the user never sees it. The other files in the collection are either .ini files, used to set parameters for MIRC, or scripts, used to drive MIRC to perform certain functions. The point of using a commonly available and popular program rather than a RAT is that an AV program won't report it, because MIRC is a

CHAPTER 10

MOBILE CODE

Robert Gezelter

CONTENTS

10.1 INTRODUCTION. Several definitions, as used by United States military forces but applicable to all, are useful in considering the content of this chapter:[1]

- An *enclave* is an information system environment that is end-to-end under the control of a single authority and has a uniform security policy, including personnel and physical security. Local and remote elements that access resources within an enclave must satisfy the policy of the enclave.

- *Mobile code* is software obtained from remote systems outside the enclave boundary, transferred across a network, and then downloaded and executed on a local system without explicit installation or execution by the recipient.

- *Mobile code* is also a powerful software tool that enhances cross-platform capabilities, sharing of resources, and Web-based solutions. Its use is widespread and increasing in both commercial and government applications . . . . Mobile code, unfortunately, has the potential to severely degrade . . . operations if improperly used or controlled.

- *Malicious mobile code* consists of mobile code software modules designed, employed, distributed, or activated with the intention of compromising the performance or security of information systems and computers, increasing access to those systems, providing the unauthorized disclosure of information, corrupting information, denying service, or stealing resources.

10.1.1   Mobile Code from the World Wide Web.   On the World Wide Web, the phrase "mobile code" generally refers to executable code supplied by a Web server for execution on the client's computer; aside from Hypertext Markup Language (HTML) and related languages (e.g., Extensible Markup Language, XML). The most common development languages for mobile code are ActiveX, Java, and JavaScript (also known as ECMAScript). Mobile code can perform covert functions on a client system, accessing information or altering the operation or persistent state of the system.

Although malicious software such as viruses, worms, and Trojan horse programs written in compiled, interpreted, or scripting languages such as VisualBasic also might be considered mobile code, these pests are not generally labeled as such; this chapter deals only with ActiveX *controls,* Java *applets,* and JavaScript programs. See Chapter 9 for details of other types of malicious software.

The most spectacular problems with mobile code involve system or application crashes, which disrupt user sessions and workflow. However, covert access to or modification of client system data are more serious problems. For example, some Web sites covertly obtain e-mail addresses from users' browsers, resulting later in unwanted commercial e-mail.

Mobile code presents a complex set of issues to information technology (IT) professionals. Allowing mobile code into an operating environment comprises any enclave; however, even commercial off-the-shelf (COTS) programs breach the integrity of an enclave. The differences between mobile code and other forms of code are primarily in the way these external programs are obtained, installed, and documented. In an enterprise computing environment, COTS acquisition normally involves conscious and explicit evaluation of the costs and benefits of installing a particular named and documented program. In contrast, mobile code programs are installed largely without notification of the user and generally without documentation of any kind. Unless client-system firewalls are set to reject mobile code automatically, system administrators cannot be certain exactly which software has been executed on client machines under their nominal control. Even though such control is often illusory, due to user circumvention of restrictions on installation of unauthorized software, the use of mobile code, installed by external Web sites, seriously compromises any remaining control over employee software configurations.

10.1.2   Design and Implementation Errors.   Design and implementation errors take a variety of forms. The simplest cases involve software that malfunctions on a constant predictable basis. More pernicious and more dangerous are those errors that compromise the strict containment of a multiuser environment. Errors in such prophylactic layers, known as brick walls or sandboxes, compromise the integrity of the protection scheme. In the worst cases, they permit unfettered access to system-level resources by unprivileged user programs.

Design and implementation errors can occur within any program or procedure, and mobile code is no exception. *Sandboxes* (nonprivileged, restricted operating it is extremely difficult to see how individual developers can be expected to create their own equivalent of the sandbox for each control. In light of these hazards, the authors of the CERT/CC report wrote that "there is a large number of potential failure points."

10.2.4   Case Studies.   Several security breaches or demonstrations mediated through ActiveX have occurred since the introduction of this technology in the mid-1990s.

10.2.4.1   *Internet Exploder.*   In 1996, Fred McLain wrote Exploder, an ActiveX control designed to illustrate the broad degree of trust conferred on an ActiveX control by virtue of its having been "signed." Exploder, when downloaded for execution by Internet Explorer, will shut down the browser's computer (the equivalent of the *Shut down | Shut down* sequence from the Start menu on a Windows system). This operation is operationally disruptive but not actually corrupting of the system. McLain notes in his frequently asked questions (FAQ) on Exploder that it is easy to build destructive or malicious controls.[5]

Exploder raises an important question: Who and what are the limits on trust when using signed code? In normal commercial matters, there is a large difference between an inauthentic signature, a forgery, and a properly signed but unpayable check. In software, there is a large difference between an inauthentic control and a dangerous one.

10.2.4.2   *Chaos Computer Club Demonstration.*   On January 27, 1997, a German television program showed members of the Chaos Computer Club demonstrating how they could use an ActiveX control to steal money from a bank account. The control, available on the Web, was written to subvert the popular accounting package Quicken. A victim need merely to visit a site and download the ActiveX control in question; it automatically checked to see if Quicken was installed. If so, the control ordered Quicken to issue a transfer order to be saved in its list of pending transfers. The next time the victim connected to the appropriate bank and sent all pending transfer orders to the bank, all the transfers would be executed as a single transaction. The user's personal identification number (PIN) and transaction authorization number (TAN) would apply to all the transfers, including the fraudulent one in the pile of orders. Most victims would be unaware of the theft until they received their next statement—if then.[6]

Dan Wallach of Princeton University, commenting on this case, wrote, "When you accept an ActiveX control, you're allowing completely arbitrary code to rummage around your machine and do anything it pleases. That same code could make extremely expensive phone calls to 900 numbers or over long distances with your modem; it can read, write, and delete any file on your computer; it can install Trojan horses and viruses. All without any of the subterfuge and hackery required to do it with Java. ActiveX hands away the keys to your computer."[7]

Responding to criticisms of the ActiveX security model, Bob Atkinson, architect and primary implementor of Authenticode, wrote a lengthy essay explaining his point of view. Among the key points:

- Microsoft never claimed that it would certify the safety of other people's code.
- Authentication is designed solely to permit identification of the culprits *after* malicious code is detected.
- Explorer-based distribution of software is no more risky than conventional purchases through software retailers.[8]

Subsequent correspondence in the RISKS Forum chastised Mr. Atkinson for omitting several other key points, such as:

- Interactions among ActiveX controls can violate system security even though individual controls are apparently harmless.
- There is no precedent in fact for laying liability at the feet of software developers even when you can find them.
- Under attack, evidence of digital signature is likely to evaporate from the system being damaged.
- Latency of execution of harmful payloads will complicate identification of the source of damage.
- Malice is not as important a threat from code as incompetence.
- Microsoft has a history of including security-threatening options, such as automatic execution of macros in Word, without offering any way of turning off the feature.
- A Web site can invoke an ActiveX control that is located on a different site or that already has been downloaded from another site, and can pass, by means of that control, unexpected arguments that could cause harm.[9]

10.2.4.3   Certificates Obtained by Imposters.   In January 2001, VeriSign issued two *Class 3 Digital Certificates* for signing ActiveX controls and other code to someone impersonating a Microsoft employee. As a result, users receiving code signed using these certificates would receive a request for acceptance or rejection of a certificate apparently signed by Microsoft on January 30 or 31, 2001. As Russ Cooper commented on the NTBUGTRAQ Usenet group when the news came out in March 2001:

> The fact that unless you actually check the date on the Certificate you won't know whether or not its [sic] one you can trust is a Bad Thing‰, as obviously not everyone (read: next to nobody) is going to check every Certificate they get presented with.
> You gotta wonder how VeriSign's issuance mechanism could be so poorly designed and/or implemented to let something like this happen.
> Meanwhile, Microsoft are [sic] working on a patch which will stick its finger in this dam.
> Basically, VeriSign Code-Signing Certificates do not employ a Certificate Revocation List (CRL) feature called CDP, or CRL Distribution Point, which causes the Certificate to be checked for revocation each time its read. Even if you have CRL turned on in IE, VeriSign Code-Signing Certificates aren't checked.
> Microsoft's update is going to shim in some mechanism which causes some/all Code-Signing Certificates to check some local file/registry key for a CRL, which will (at least initially) contain the details of these Certificates. Assuming this works as advertised, any attempt to trust the mis-issued Certificates should fail.[10]

Roger Thompson, technical director of malicious code research for TruSecure (and author of Chapter 9 herein), explained that the imposters' motives would determine how bad the results would be from the fraudulent certificates. "If it was someone with a purpose in mind, then six weeks is a long time to do something," he said. "If the job was to install a sniffer, then there could be a zillion backdoors as a result of it." Published reports indicated that the failure of authentication occurred due to a flaw in the issuing process at VeriSign: The certificates were issued *before* receiving verification by e-mail that the official customer contact authorized the certificates. This case was the first failure of authentication in over 500,000 certificates issued by VeriSign.[11]

10.3   RESTRICTED OPERATING ENVIRONMENTS.   From a Web perspective, the term "sandbox" defines what could otherwise be referred to as a restricted operating environment. Restricted operating environments are not new; they have existed for over 40 years in the form of multiuser operating systems, including MULTICS, OS/360 and its descendants, OpenVMS, UNIX, and others. See Chapter 17 for an overview of operating systems security.

In simple terms, a restricted, or nonprivileged, operating environment prohibits normal users and their programs from executing operations that can compromise the overall system. In such an environment, normal users are prohibited from executing operations such as HALT that directly affect hardware. User programs are prevented from executing instructions that can compromise the operating system memory allocation and processor state and from accessing or modifying files belonging to the operating system or to other users. Implemented and managed carefully, such systems are highly effective at protecting information and data from unauthorized modification and access. The National Computer Security Center (NCSC) *Orange Book* contains criteria for classifying and evaluating trusted systems.[12]

The strengths and weaknesses of protected systems are well understood. Permitting ordinary users unrestricted access to system files can compromise the integrity of the system. Privileged users (i.e., those with legitimate access to system files and physical hardware) must be careful that the programs they run do not compromise the operating system. Last, most protected systems contain a collection of freestanding programs that implement useful system functions requiring some form of privilege to operate. Often these programs have been the source of security vulnerabilities.

10.3.1   Java.   Java is a language developed by Sun Microsystems for platform independent execution of code, typically within the context of a Web browser. The basic Java environment includes a Java Virtual Machine (JVM) and a set of supporting software referred to as the Java Run Time Environment. Applets downloaded via the World Wide Web (intranet or Internet) have strict limitations on their ability to access system resources. In particular, these restrictions prevent the execution of external commands and read or write access to files.

The Java environment does provide for *signed applets* that are permitted wider access to files. Dynamically downloaded applets also are restricted to initiating connections to the system that supplied them, theoretically limiting some types of third-party attacks.

In concept, the Java approach, which also includes other validity tests on the JVM pseudocode, should be adequate to ensure security. However, the collection of trusted applets found locally on the client system and signed downloaded applets represent ways in which the security system can be subverted. Without signature, the Java approach is also vulnerable to attack by domain name system (DNS) spoofing.

Multiuser protection and virtual machine protection schemes also are totally dependent on the integrity of the code that separates the nonprivileged users from privileged, system-compromising, operations. Java has not been an exception to this rule. In 1996, a bug in the Java environment contained in Netscape Navigator Version 2.0 permitted connections to arbitrary URLs.[13] Later, in 2000, errors were discovered in the code that protected various resources.[14]

Additionally, since unsigned code can take advantage of errors in underlying signed code, there is no guarantee that complex combinations of untrusted and trusted code will not lead to security compromises.

10.4   DISCUSSION.   Mobile code security raises important issues about how to handle relationships in an increasingly interconnected computing environment.

10.4.1   Asymmetric, and Transitive or Derivative, Trust.   It is common for cyber-relationships to be *asymmetric* with regard to the size or power of the parties. This fact increases the potential for catastrophic interactions. It also creates opportunities for mass infection across organization boundaries. Large or critical organizations often can unilaterally impose limitations on the ability of partner organizations to defend their information infrastructure from damage.

The combination of a powerful organization and insufficient controls on signing authority, or, alternatively, the obligatory execution of unsigned ActiveX controls, is a recipe for serious problems. The powerful organization is able to obligate its partners to accept a low security level, such as would result, for example, from using unsigned ActiveX controls, while abdicating responsibility for the repercussions.

All organizations should, for security and performance reasons, use the technology that requires the least degree of privilege to accomplish the desired result. JavaScript/ECMAScript can provide many functions, without the need for the functionality provided by Java, much less ActiveX.

Earlier in this chapter, it is noted that Web servers represent an attractive vector for attacks. Signing (authentication) methods are a way to control damage potential, if the mechanisms used for admitting executable code are properly controlled. Failure to control these mechanisms leads to severe side effects.

In Chapter 22, it is noted that protecting Web servers requires that the contents of the servers be managed carefully and that it is appropriate and often necessary to isolate Web servers on separate network segments, separated from both the Internet and the organizational intranet by firewalls. These precautions are even more necessary when servers are responsible for supplying executable code to clients.

Security practitioners should carefully examine the different functions performed by each server. In some cases, such as OpenVMS hosts, where network servers commonly run unprivileged in separate contexts and directory trees, it is feasible to run multiple services on a single server. In other systems, such as UNIX and Windows NT, where it is common for applications services to execute as privileged, with full access to all system files, a logic error in a network service can compromise the security of the entire server, including the collection of downloadable applets.

Much more serious is *transitive* (or derivative) trust: Alpha trusts Beta who trusts Gamma. A security compromise—for example, an unsigned Java applet or a malfunctioning or malevolent ActiveX control supplied by Gamma—compromises Beta. Beta then causes problems with Alpha's systems. This cascade can continue repeatedly, leading to numerous compromised systems far removed geographically and organizationally from the original incident.

10.4.2   Multidimensional Threat.   Mobile code is a multidimensional threat, with several different aspects that must each be treated separately. Signing code, such as Java applets or ActiveX controls, addresses the problem of authenticity and authority to release the code. However, the integrity of the signature mechanism requires that the integrity of the PKI infrastructure be beyond reproach. In a very real sense, the PKI infrastructure is beyond the control of the organization itself. Any compromise or procedural slip on the part of the certificate authority or signer invalidates the presumptions of safety.

Signing, however much it contributes to resolving the question of authenticity, does not address safety or validity. As an example, the Windows Update ActiveX control, distributed by Microsoft as part of the various Windows operating systems, has as its underlying purpose the update of the operating system. A failure of that control would be catastrophic. Fortunately, Microsoft gives users the choice of using the automatic update facility or doing updates manually. Many Web applications are not so accommodating.

The problem is not solely a question of malfunctioning applets. It is possible that a collection of applets involved in a client's overall business activities may collide in some unanticipated fashion, from attempting to use the same Windows registry key in contradictory ways, to stepping on each other's use of a temporary file name. Similar problems often occur with applications that presume they have a monopoly on the use of the system.

These issues are, for the most part, completely unrelated to each other. A solution in one area would neither improve nor worsen the situation with regard to the other issues.

10.4.3   Server Responsibilities.   Earlier in this chapter, it is noted that Web servers represent an attractive vector for attacks. Signing (authentication) methods are a way to control damage potential, provided the mechanisms used for admitting executable code are properly controlled. Failure to control these mechanisms leads to severe side effects.

There is little reason to impose the use of ActiveX for the purposes of changing the color of a banner advertisement. JavaScript/ECMAScript is capable of many powerful, fairly safe display-related operations. Using Java to maintain a shopping cart (price, quantities, and contents) is reasonable and does not require the use of a signed applet, with its attendant greater capabilities and risks. At the other end of the scale, it is plausible that a system update function (e.g., the Windows Update function, which automatically downloads and installs changes to the Windows operating system) requires the unbridled power of a signed ActiveX control.

When the power of signed applets or controls is required, good software engineering practice provides excellent examples of how to limit the potential for damage and mischief, as discussed in Chapter 25.

Good software implementation isolates functions and limits the scope of operations that require privileged access or operations. Payroll applications do not directly manipulate printer ports, video display cards, network adapters, or disk drives. Privileged operating system components, such as device drivers and file systems, are responsible for the actual operation. This separation, together with careful parameter checking by the operating system kernel and the privileged components, ensures safety.

The same techniques can be used with applets and controls. Because they require more access, they should be programmed carefully, using the same defensive measures as are used when implementing privileged additions to operating systems. As an example, there is little reason for an SMTP (Simple Mail Transfer Protocol) server to be privileged. An SMTP server requires privileges for a single function, the delivery of an individual electronic mail message to a recipient's mailbox. This can be accomplished in two ways:

1. Implement the application in a nonprivileged way, by marking users' e-mail files and directories with the necessary access for the mail delivery program to create and modify e-mail files and directories. Such a mechanism is fully in conformance with the NCSC *Orange Book's* C2-level of security.

2. Alternatively, implement a separate subcomponent whose sole responsibility is the actual message delivery of the message. The subcomponent must be written defensively to check all of its parameters, and does not provide an interface for the execution of arbitrary code. This approach is used by Compaq's OpenVMS operating system.

The UNIX *sendmail* program, by contrast, is a large, multifunctional program that executes with privileges. *sendmail* has been the subject of numerous security problems for over a decade and has spawned efforts to produce more secure replacements.[15]

10.5   SUMMARY.   Mobile code provides many flexible and useful capabilities. The different mechanisms for implementing mobile code range from the innocuous (HTML), to fairly safe (JavaScript/ECMAScript), and with increasing degrees of power and risk through Java and ActiveX.

Ensuring security and integrity with the use of mobile code requires cooperation on the part of both the provider and the client. Clients should not accept random signed code and controls. Providers have a positive responsibility to:

- Follow good software engineering practices
- Grant minimum necessary privileges and access
- Use defensive programming
- Limit privileged access, with no open-ended interfaces
- Ensure the integrity of the signing process and the associated private keys

If caution is taken, there is no reason why mobile code cannot be a constructive, powerful part of intranet and Internet applications, both within an organization and in cooperation with its customers and other stakeholders.

10.6   BIBLIOGRAPHY

Carl, Jeremy. "ActiveX Security: Under the Microscope," *Web Week,* Vol. 2, No. 17, November 4, 1996; see: *www.webdeveloper.com/activex/activex_security.html.*

CERT, "Java Implementations can Allow Connection to an Arbitrary Host": *www.cert.org/advisories/CA-1996-05.html.*

CERT, "Netscape Allows Java Applets to Read Protected Resources": *www.cert.org/advisories/CA-2000-15.html.*

CERT, "NIMDA Worm": *www.cert.org/advisories/CA-2001-26.html.*

CERT, "Results of the Security in ActiveX Workshop," Pittsburgh, PA, August 22-23, 2000: *www.cert.org/reports/activeX_report.pdf.*

CERT, "sadmind/IIS Worm," May 8, 2001: *www.cert.org/advisories/CA-2001-11.html.*

CERT, "Unauthentic 'Microsoft Corporation' Certificates," March 22, 2001: *www.cert.org/advisories/CA-2001-04.html.*

Felten, Edward. "Security Tradeoffs: Java vs. ActiveX," last modified April 28, 1997: *www.cs.princeton.edu/sip/faq/java-vs-activex.html.*

Felten, E., and G. McGraw. *Securing Java: Getting Down to Business with Mobile Code.* New York: John Wiley & Sons, 1999. Also free and unlimited Web access from *www.securingjava.com.*

"Frequently Asked Questions—Java Security," revised March 29, 2001: *java.sun.com/sfaq/index.html.*

McGraw, G., and E.W. Felten. *Java Security: Hostile Applets, Holes and Antidotes—What Every Netscape and Internet Explorer User Needs to Know.* New York: John Wiley & Sons, 1997.

McLain, Fred, "The Exploder Control Frequently Asked Questions (FAQ)," last updated February 7, 1997: *www.halcyon.com/mclain/ActiveX/Exploder/FAQ.htm.*

Microsoft, "Introduction to Code Signing" (with appendix), © 2001: *http://msdn.microsoft.com/workshop/security/authcode/intro_authenticode.asp* and *http://msdn.microsoft.com/workshop/security/authcode/appendixes.asp.*

Microsoft, "Microsoft Security Bulletin MS01-017: Erroneous VeriSign-Issued Digital Certificates Pose Spoofing Hazard," March 22, 2001: *www.microsoft.com/TechNet/security/bulletin/MS01-017.asp.*

Verisign, "Verisign Security Alert Fraud Detected in Authenticode Code Signing Certificates," March 22, 2001: *www.verisign.com/developer/notice/authenticode/index.html.*

10.7   NOTES

1. Memorandum, November 7, 2000, from Arthur M. Money, Assistant Secretary of Defense for C3I and CIO, to Secretaries of the Military Departments, Chairman of the Joint Chiefs of Staff, Chief Information Officers of the Defense Agencies, et al. SUBJECT: Policy Guidance for Use of Mobile Code Technologies in Department of Defense (DoD) Information Systems; *www.c3i.osd.mil/org/cio/doc/mobile-code11-7-00.html.*

2. Advanced Software Logic, "What Is Authenticode?"; *www.webcomponentdeployment.com/faq.htm.*

3. CERT/CC, Results of the Security in ActiveX Workshop, Pittsburgh, Pennsylvania, August 22–23, 2000; PDF download available at *www.cert.org/archive/pdf/activeX_report.pdf.*

4. Ibid., pp. 6–9.

5. F. McLain, "The Exploder Control Frequently Asked Questions (FAQ)," last updated February 7, 1997: *www.halcyon.com/mclain/ActiveX/Exploder/FAQ.htm.*

6. D. Weber-Wulff, "Electronic Funds Transfer without Stealing PIN/TAN," *RISKS,* Vol. 18, No. 80 (1997): *catless.ncl.ac.uk/Risks/18.80.html.*

7. D. Wallach, "RE: Electronic Funds Transfer without Stealing PIN/TAN," *RISKS,* Vol. 18, No. 81 (1997): *catless.ncl.ac.uk/Risks/18.8.html.*

8. B. Atkinson, "Comments and Corrections Regarding Authentication," *RISKS,* Vol. 18, No. 85 (1997).

9. *RISKS,* Vol. 18, No. 86 (1997), et seq.

10. R. Cooper, "Alert: Microsoft Security Bulletin MS01-017," NTBUGTRAQ list server, 2001; archive at *http://archives.neohapsis.com/archives/ntbuttraq/2001-q/0046.html.*

11. R. Lemos, "Microsoft Says Beware of Stolen Certificates," *ZDNet News,* March 22, 2001; *http://news.cnet.com/news/0-1003-200-5222484.html.*

12. For full text, see *www.radium.ncsc.mil/tpep/library/rainbow/5200.28-STD.html.*

13. CERT, "Java Implementations Can Allow Connection to an Arbitrary Host": *www.cert.org/advisories/CA-1996-05.html.*

14. CERT, "Netscape Allows Java Applets to Read Protected Resources": *www.cert.org/advisories-CA-2000-15.html.*

15. For example, the ICAT Metabase (*http://icat.nist.gov/icat.cfm*) shows that the Common Vulnerabilities and Exposures (CVE) database includes a total of 29 unique vulnerabilities involving *sendmail,* of which 15 are dated 2000 and 2001.

CHAPTER 11

DENIAL OF SERVICE ATTACKS

Diane E. Levine and Gary C. Kessler

CONTENTS

11.1 INTRODUCTION. This chapter discusses Denial of Service (DoS) and Distributed Denial of Service (DDoS) attacks. These attacks seek to render target systems and networks unusable or inaccessible by saturating resources or causing catastrophic errors that halt processes or entire systems. Furthermore, they are increasingly easy for even *script kiddies* (children who follow explicit attack instructions or execute attack programs) to launch. Successful defense against these attacks will come only when there is widespread cooperation among all Internet service providers (ISPs) and other Internet-connected systems worldwide.

Working in a variety of ways, the DoS attacker selects an intended target system and launches a concentrated attack against it. While initially deemed to be primarily a nuisance, DoS attacks can incapacitate an entire network, especially those with hosts that rely on Transmission Control Protocol/Internet Protocol (TCP/IP). DoS attacks on corporate networks and ISPs have resulted in significant damage to productivity and revenues. DoS attacks can be launched against any hardware or operating system platform because they generally aim at the heart of Internet Protocol (IP) implementations.

Because IP is the typical target, the DoS attack tools that run under one operating system (Linux is a common choice) can be aimed at any operating system running IP. Additionally, because IP implementations are similar for different platforms, one DoS attack may target several operating systems and work on each. Once written for one platform and released, new DoS attacks appear to evolve (via the examination and participation of hackers and crackers) so that in a short period of time (approximately two weeks) mutations of the DoS attack appear that work on virtually all platforms.

Because of the critical impact that DoS attacks can have, they cannot be taken lightly. DoS attacks have been around in one form or another since the 1980s; in 1999, they evolved into Distributed DoS attacks, primarily due to the heavy use of internal networks and the Internet. DDoS tools launch coordinated DoS attacks from many sources against one or more targets simultaneously.

This chapter describes first DoS and then DDoS attacks. This arrangement is primarily due to the fact that DoS attacks historically predate DDoS attacks. In addition, some DDoS attacks make use of DoS techniques. However, the attacks themselves, the terminology, and the defenses are sufficiently different that they warrant separate discussion.

11.2   DENIAL OF SERVICE ATTACKS.   Historically, any act that prevented use of a system could be called a denial of service. For example, in some mainframe and minicomputer systems, typing a malformed command could cause a system failure; pressing the RETURN key on the system console could monopolize the device-recognition process of the operating system and use up all the central processing unit (CPU) cycles, thus preventing any further activity on the system. Typing one or more characters on the system console without pressing the RETURN key could block all further system messages on the console, causing system buffers to fill up with unprinted messages; when the system buffers were exhausted, no system action requiring notification to the console could take place (e.g., logons, logoffs, special-form requests, or tape-mount requests). However, such events were usually the result of bugs in the operating system, inadequate numbers of buffers for critical data, or accident.

11.2.1   History of Denial of Service Attacks.   One of the first major DoS incidents that made headlines and ripples far and wide was probably accidental. It took place in December 1987, when an employee of IBM in Europe sent out a holiday greeting e-mail message. The e-mail message, however, contained a program that drew a nice Christmas tree on the recipient's terminal—and read the recipient's NAMES and NETLOG files listing the user's address book as well as the e-mail addresses of individuals that this user had recently sent mail to or received mail from, respectively (sound familiar, Outlook users?). The Christmas Tree program then triggered the automatic transmission of copies of itself to all e-mail addresses found in NAMES and NETLOG. The result overloaded the IBM corporate network worldwide and brought it crashing down both in Europe and the United States. In addition, messages "escaped" from IBM's corporate network and wreaked havoc on the BITNET/EARN education and research networks in North America and Europe. Although the cause of the outage was originally thought to be a computer virus, and the incident has been referred to as a virus, a worm, and a prank, the result was a true denial of service.

Perhaps the most famous Internet DoS resulted from the Morris Worm, also referred to as the Internet Worm, which occurred in November 1988. Cornell graduate student Robert T. Morris Jr. co-wrote an article about some vulnerabilities in *sendmail* and *fingerd* on Unix systems. Most of the TCP/IP community dismissed the vulnerabilities as theoretical; apparently Morris wanted to demonstrate that the vulnerabilities actually could be practically exploited. To demonstrate the problem, his program had to invade another system, guess some passwords, and then replicate itself. Morris said after the incident that he wanted the program to replicate just a few times to demonstrate that it was real; unfortunately, a programming error led the worm to replicate often and quickly in addition to superinfecting already-infected systems. The worm clogged the Internet with hundreds of thousands of messages and effectively brought the entire network down—most sites that did not actually crash were disconnected from the network by their system administrators to avoid being infected and to allow disinfection. Regardless of intent, the Morris Worm inadvertently caused a DoS.

Moving to more recent times, on Friday, September 6, 1996, PANIX, a public access Internet provider in Manhattan, was struck by a DoS attack that consisted of many messages flooding the server with massive amounts of data. The attacks were made against mail, news, name, and Web servers as well as user shell account machines. The attackers successfully eluded tracking, and the attacks went on for several days. About a week after the attacks began, PANIX went public with the story, and dozens of other online service providers acknowledged that they too were the victims of similar attacks.

In 1997, a disgruntled former employee of Forbes, Inc., used a former colleague's password to remotely access the firm's computer systems. Deliberately tampering with the system, he deleted budgets and salary information and caused five of the eight network servers to crash. When Federal Bureau of Investigation (FBI) agents caught the perpetrator, his home was filled with hacking tools, proprietary information from Forbes, Inc., and other incriminating material.

In February 1998, hackers from Israel and northern California attacked the U.S. Department of Defense (DoD). In a carefully organized attack that exploited buffer overflow, these hackers systematically perpetrated a DoS attack that lasted over a week on 11 DoD sites.

In March 1988, all across the United States, system administrators found their Windows NT servers under apparently automated attack. Systems crashed repeatedly until they were updated to the latest patches from Microsoft. There appeared to be no file damage from the attacks, which lasted more than a day. Sites affected included:

- Carnegie Mellon University (OH)
- Massachusetts Institute of Technology
- NASA Goddard Space Flight Center (MD)
- NASA Dryden Flight Research Center (CA)
- NASA Independent Validation and Verification Facility (WV)
- NASA Jet Propulsion Laboratory (CA)
- NASA Wallops Flight Facility (VA)
- NASA Stennis Space Center (MS)
- NASA White Sands Test Facility (NM)
- NASA Headquarters in Washington (DC)
- NASA Langley Research Center (VA)
- NASA Ames Research Center (CA)
- NASA Marshall Space Flight Center (AL)
- NASA Moffett Federal Airfield (CA)
- NASA Kennedy Space Center (FL)

- NASA Lewis Research Center (OH)
- Northwestern University
- University of California, San Diego
- University of California, Los Angeles
- University of Minnesota
- University of California campuses in Berkeley
- University of California, Irvine
- U.S. Navy (unclassified servers)

Yet another mailstorm erupted in May 1998 when an Australian official set autoreply on his e-mail package while he was away. Unfortunately, he inadvertently set his destination for these largely useless messages to be all 2,000 users on his network—and requested autoconfirmation of delivery of each autoreply, which generated yet another autoreply, and so on ad infinitum and ad nauseam. Within four hours, his endless positive-feedback loop generated 150,000 messages before his autoreply was shut down. The ripples lasted for days, with the perpetrator saddled with 48,000 messages in his in-basket and a stream of 1,500 a day pouring in. This was another case of an inadvertent DoS attack.

In January 1999, someone launched a sustained DoS attack on Ozemail, an important Australian Internet service provider. E-mail service was disrupted for users in Sydney.

In March 1999, the Melissa e-mail-enabled virus/worm swept the world in a few days as it sent copies of itself to the first 50 addresses in victims' e-mail address books. Because of this high replication rate, the virus spread faster than any previous virus in history. On many corporate systems, the rapid rate of internal replication saturated e-mail servers with outbound automated junk e-mail. Initial estimates were in the range of 100,000 downed systems. Antivirus companies rallied immediately, and updates for all the standard products were available within hours of the first notices from the CERT Coordination Center (CERT/CC). The Melissa macro virus was quickly followed by the PAPA MS-Excel macro virus with similar properties but that, in addition, launched DoS attacks on two specific IP addresses.

More recent attacks are discussed in the sections below describing modern DoS tools.

11.2.2 Costs of Denial of Service Attacks. What are the effects of these DoS attacks in terms of productivity and actual financial costs? It is difficult to place an exact monetary figure on DoS attacks. DoS attacks can interrupt critical processes in an organization, and such interruption can be costly. When a company's computer network is inaccessible to legitimate users and they cannot conduct their normal business, productivity is lowered. The negative effect is bound to carry over to the financial aspects of the business. However, putting exact figures to these effects is uncertain at best, and the estimates are widely disputed, even among security and business experts. In addition, many companies do not comment on the exact losses they suffer because they fear that the negative publicity will decrease their market share. This latter point is significant: In an early 1990s study of Wall Street firms, some of the companies suggested that if they were to be without their network for two to three days, they might never reopen their doors.

In the case of the Christmas Tree worm, it took IBM several days to clean up its network and resulted in the loss of millions of dollars, both for cleansing the system and in lost business because of lost connectivity and related productivity. Additionally, there was the embarrassment suffered by IBM, a noted technology company. The individual who launched the worm was identified and denied access to any computer account, while IBM had to write a letter of apology to the European Academic and Research Network (EARN) administrators.

In 1988, at the time of the Morris Worm, the Internet consisted of 5,000 to 10,000 hosts, primarily at research and academic institutions. As a result, although the Morris Worm succeeded in bringing many sites to a halt and gained worldwide notoriety, the financial and productivity impact on the commercial world was minimal. A similar incident today would wreak havoc and cost millions of dollars in losses.

By 1996, however, commercial reliance on the Internet was already becoming a matter of course. Working around the clock, the management at PANIX and at Cisco, the ISP's router vendor, kept the service provider up and running, but the network received 210 fraudulent requests per minute. Although the systems did not crash, thousands of subscribers were unable to receive their e-mail messages. Other sites were attacked in the same time frame as PANIX, including Voters Telecommunication Watch. No one took the blame for these attacks, and it has been widely assumed that they were triggered by articles on SYN DoS attacks (see the description below) that had recently appeared in *2600 Magazine* and *Phrack,* journals that cater to hackers.

According to Forbes, Inc., the losses suffered by the firm because of the DoS attack perpetrated by the disgruntled former employee exceeded $100,000. Could it have been prevented? According to the firm, it is highly unlikely, since Forbes had no reason to suspect the individual was maintaining either the firm's confidential and sensitive material at home or that he was thinking of hacking into the computer system and deliberately doing damage. While the firm had security on its systems, the perpetrator used the password of a legitimate, authorized user.

The DoS attack launched against the DoD computers in 1998 proved that attackers could deny access to vital military information. In this particular instance, the attack was directed at unclassified machines that had only administrative and accounting records, but it proved to be a blow to the confidence of the Defense Department. Tying up the computers for over a week presumably reduced productivity, but the government would not comment on the actual cost from loss of machine time and personnel productivity.

These cases show that a DoS attack on a computer or network can be devastating to an organization. Important equipment and networks and even an entire organization can be disabled by such attacks.

Early DoS incidents often were described as annoying, frustrating, or a nuisance. However, with increasing sophistication and dependency on networking, it has become difficult to keep a sense of humor about such incidents. Especially in corporations, where the mission is to make a profit for the shareholder, company managers find it increasingly difficult to excuse being incapacitated because of a DoS or DDoS attack.

As these forms of attack become more sophisticated, so must the tools and methods for detecting and fighting them. Current products scan equipment and networks for vulnerabilities, trigger alerts when an abnormality is found, and frequently assist in eliminating the discovered problem.

11.2.3 Types of Denial of Service Attacks. DoS attacks, whether accidental or deliberate, result in loss of service; either a host or a server system is rendered inoperable or a network is rendered inaccessible. DoS attacks are launched deliberately by an *intruder* (the preferred term for attacker in this context). Systems and networks that are compromised are referred to as the *victims.* And while DoS attacks can be launched from the intruder's system, they often are launched by an automated process that allows the intruder to start the attack remotely with the push of a few keystrokes. These programs are known as *daemons* and they are often placed on another system that the hacker has already compromised.

There are three basic types or categories of DoS attack:

1. One type of attack seeks to deprive computers and networks of scarce, limited, or nonrenewable resources that are essential in order for the computers or networks to operate. Resources of this type include CPU time, disk space, memory, data structures, network bandwidth, access to other networks and computers, and environmental resources such as cool air and power.

2. Another type of attack destroys or alters configuration information. Because poor or improperly configured computers may fail to operate or operate inadequately, this type of attack can be very severe.

3. The final type of attack physically destroys or alters network components. To guard against this type of attack, it is necessary to have good physical security to safeguard the computers and other network components. This chapter does not deal with physical damage.

11.2.4   Specific Denial of Service Attacks.   The following discussion of some specific DoS attacks covers the main methods extant at the time of writing (December 2001); however, new types of attacks are anticipated.

11.2.4.1   Destructive Devices.   Destructive devices are programs that accomplish either harassment or destruction of data. There are mixed opinions regarding how severe destructive devices are, but if they threaten a computer's or network's ability to function properly and efficiently, then they may be the instruments of DoS attacks. Viruses, e-mail bombs, and denial of service tools all can be considered destructive devices. In fact, viruses and e-mail bombs are known to cause DoS attacks. More about viruses and other malicious software and their actions can be found in Chapter 9 of this *Handbook,* while DDoS tools and E-mail bombs are discussed below.

11.2.4.2   E-mail (and E-mail Subscription) Bombing.   E-mail and e-mail subscription *bombing* were among the first documented DoS attacks. An *e-mail bomb* consists of large numbers of e-mail messages that are used to fill up a victim's electronic mailbox. A huge number of messages can tie up an online connection, slow down mail delivery, and even overload the e-mail server system until the system crashes. Most e-mail bombings are thought to be deliberate attacks by disgruntled people; specific targets may be victims of someone with a particular grudge. For example, a San Francisco stock broker received 25,000 messages on September 23, 1996, consisting of the word "Idiot" from a consultant with whom he had had a disagreement. The flood of messages prevented him from using his computer, so in December the victim sued the perpetrator's employer for $25,000 of damages. On occasions in the past, such as with the Christmas Tree worm and the Internet Worm, the DoS is thought to have been accidental.

E-mail bomb packages automate the process of launching and carrying out an *e-mail bombing* DoS attack. With names like Up Yours, Kaboom, Avalanche, Gatemail, and the Unabomber, these packages can be placed on a network server during a DoS attack and used to attack other systems. Administrators who are aware of these names and others should regularly scan their drives for associated filenames and eliminate them.

To safeguard computers and/or servers, tools such as mail filters and exclusionary schemes can automatically filter and reject mail sent from a source address using e-mail bomb packages. Mail filters are available for Unix, Windows, Macintosh, and Linux systems. Most computer operating systems and most ISPs now offer filtering tools for eliminating unsolicited commercial e-mail and other e-mail. Although perpetrators often disguise their identity and location by using a false address, most filters can be set to screen and eliminate these addresses.

With *e-mail subscription bombing,* also known as *list linking,* a user is subscribed to dozens of mailing lists by the attacker without the knowledge of the user. For example, one of the earliest subscription-bombing incidents was perpetrated by someone calling himself "johnny [x]chaotic." In August 1996, he claimed the blame for a massive mail-bombing run based on fraudulently subscribing dozens of victims to hundreds of mailing lists. In a rambling and incoherent letter posted on the Net, this person made rude remarks about famous and not-so-famous people whose capacity to receive meaningful e-mail was obliterated by up to thousands of unwanted messages a day. Today, filtering packages have point-and-click mechanisms that provide automatic list linking. A user conceivably could start to receive hundreds or thousands of mail messages per day if linked to just 50 to 100 lists. Once linked to the various lists, the victim has to manually unsubscribe from each individual mailing list. If an attack takes place while the victim is away and without access to e-mail, a user could have a backlog of thousands of messages by the time they return.

List server software should never accept subscriptions without sending a request for confirmation to the supposed subscriber; however, even this safety mechanism can generate a wave of many single e-mail messages if a mail bomber abuses the list servers.

Speaking of being away, vacation messages and return receipts are another way in which individuals can inadvertently start an *e-mail storm.* Many users set their e-mail clients to automatically request a return receipt of all messages sent. Then, the users go on vacation and set up an auto-reply vacation message. When a message is received, the client sends back the vacation message and also requests a receipt. The returned receipts, in turn, generate more auto-reply vacation messages.

Another variant on this feedback loop occurs when an employee goes on vacation and forwards all mail to an external ISP that has a local access number in the locale of the vacation. If the employee decides not to check the mail while away (perhaps because of high local access fees or so as not to interfere with the vacation), the ISP mailbox will fill up with forwarded messages. If the mailbox fills up, the ISP will send a bounce message back to the corporate server—which then forwards the bounced message back to the ISP, which generates yet another bounce message. Eventually, even the corporate mail server will fill up with a single individual's bounce messages, causing an e-mail DoS.

11.2.4.3   Buffer Overflow.   *Buffer overflow* attacks can be insidious and damaging. It is possible to send an input string to a target program that contains actual code and is long enough to overflow the memory space or input buffer. Sometimes this surreptitious code is placed on the process stack (the area in a computer's memory where the operating system keeps track of the program's input and related code used for processing the inputs), and the code then is processed. An overflow can occur when the input data overflows its buffer space and flows into the stack, where it overwrites the previous data and return address. If the program is written so that the stack address

points to the malicious code located in the return buffer, the code executes with the original program's privileges. Buffer overflow is the result of poor programming, where the programmer does not check the size of the input compared to the input buffer; the Internet Worm attack was based, in part, on such poor programming. Although buffer overflows have been around for years and should have been eradicated by now, new buffer overflow attacks pop up monthly.

Not all buffer overflows allow the user to insert executable code. DoS attacks such as the Ping of Death merely attach a data block that is larger than allowed by the IP protocol (i.e., greater than the 65,536 bytes). Because the packets are broken into fragments for transmission, they manage to get through the network and, probably, the router and firewall. Once reassembled at the target, however, the packets cause the IP kernel's buffer to overflow and the systems crashes.

Another example is an old flaw in Microsoft's Internet Information Server (IIS) that could be exploited to allow the Web service to be halted. To do this, an attacker would request a document with a very long URL from an IIS-based Web site. Upon receipt of the request, an access violation occurred and the server would halt. Although Microsoft issued a patch for this "security hole," successful attacks continue to take place today. (And how does one identify an IIS site? If a Web site use pages with the .htm or .asp extensions, it is a good guess that the site is running IIS.)

11.2.4.4 Bandwidth Consumption.   *Bandwidth consumption* involves generating a large number of packets directed to the network under attack. Such attacks can take place on a local network or can be perpetrated remotely. If the attacker has, or can access, greater bandwidth than the victim has available, the attacker can flood the victim's network connection. Such saturation can happen to both high-speed and low-speed network connections. Although any type of packet may be used, the most common are Internet Control Message Protocol (ICMP) Echo messages (generated by Pinging). By engaging multiple sites to flood the victim's network connection, attackers can amplify the DoS attack. To do this successfully, the attackers convince the amplifying system to send traffic to the victim's network. Tracing the intruder who perpetrates a bandwidth consumption attack can be difficult since attackers can spoof their source addresses.

The most common bandwidth consumption attack is called a *SMURF* attack. This attack is particularly interesting (and clever) since it uses tools that reside on every IP system and employs a third-party site without actually having to take control of any system anywhere. As Exhibit 11.1 shows, the SMURF attack starts when the intruder (at *attacker.com*) sends a continuous string of very large Ping messages to the IP broadcast address (* in the exhibit) of the unsuspecting third party, *stooge.com.* The intruder spoofs the source IP address of the Ping message so that it appears that these messages come from, say, the router at the target network, *router.victim.com.* If the intruder sends a single 10,000-byte Ping message to the broadcast address of an intermediate site with 50 hosts, for example, the responses will consume 4 megabytes (Mb).[1] Even if *victim.com* has a T1 line (with a bandwidth of 1.544 Mb per second), the attacker can swamp a victim's line merely by sending a single large Ping per second to the right stooge site. The intermediate site is called, for obvious reasons, the amplifying network; note that the attacker does not need to compromise any systems there. The ratio of originally transmitted packets to the number of systems that respond is known as the *amplification ratio.*

A variant of the SMURF attack is called a *Fraggle* attack. In this variant, the attackers send spoofed User Datagram Protocol (UDP) packets instead of Echo messages to the broadcast address of the amplifying network. Each system on the amplifying network

Exhibit 11.1   SMURF DoS Attack

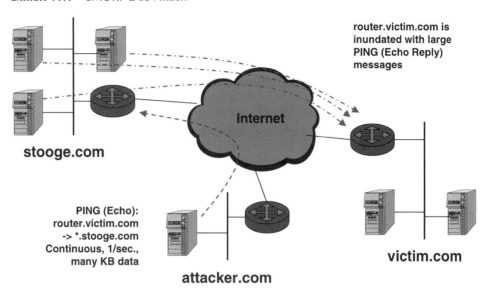

that has the specific broadcast address port enabled will create a large amount of traffic by responding to the victim's host; if the port is not enabled, the system on the amplifying network will generate ICMP Host Unreachable messages to the victim's host. In either case, the victim's bandwidth is consumed.

Kernel panic attacks are not due to programming flaws per se. The Intel Pentium chip that could not correctly divide two particular legal inputs had a programming flaw. An IP kernel that fails when receiving a packet that should never occur in the first place is, indeed, a gap in the program's logic but not the same as failing to handle legal input.

A specific example of kernel panic occurs in Linux kernel v.2.2.0 when a program usually used for printing shared library dependencies is used instead to print some core files. Under certain circumstances, *munmap( )*, a function call used to map and unmap devices into memory, overwrites critical areas of kernel memory and causes the system to panic and reboot.

And there are other examples of these kinds of attacks. A *Land* attack occurs when a spoofed packet is sent to a target host where the TCP Source Port and Destination Port are set to the same value, and the IP Source Address and Destination Address also are set to the same value. Since this is confusing to the host, it results in 100 percent CPU utilization and then a halt. Land attacks have been directed at just about all operating systems.

Teardrop attacks are also the result of behavior when receiving "impossible" packets. If an IP packet is too large for a particular network to handle, the packet will be fragmented into smaller pieces. Information in the IP packet header tells the destination host how to reassemble the packet. In a Teardrop attack, the attacker deliberately crafts IP packets that appear to overlap when reassembled. This, too, can cause the host to crash. Teardrop attacks have been targeted against Microsoft operating systems and all variants of Unix.

11.2.4.5   *Routing and Domain Name System Attacks.* *Routing and Domain Name System (DNS) attacks* are clever attacks that are achieved repeatedly. By tampering with the Domain Name System (DNS), a site's domain name resolves to the IP address of some other site.

In August 1999, Gary D. Hoke, Jr., a disgruntled engineer for PairGain Technologies, provided a direct link to a bogus but authentic-looking Bloomberg News Service page he had created. Hoke, who owned PairGain shares, posted false information about PaiGain's supposed acquisition by an Israeli company, pumping up the price of PairGain stock worldwide and creating havoc in the market through his pagejacking exploits. Although a nontraditional DoS attack, Hoke's antics did deny users access to the site that they desired, with serious consequences. Another example occurred in July 1997 when Eugene Kashpureff filed fraudulent information with InterNIC for its DNS updates in July, forcing domain name servers around the globe to recognize temporary and unauthorized Internet addresses ending in .xxx, .mall, .nic, and .per. A few weeks later, he inserted false information that forced people trying to access the Web site of Network Solutions Inc. to end up at Kashpureff's Alternic site.

In another example of a routing and DNS attack, RSA Security, Inc., after announcing that it had developed a method to combat Web site hackers, found that users were unwittingly being rerouted to a counterfeit RSA Web site. The fraudulent site looked exactly like the original RSA Web site but made fun of the fact that the hacker had managed to achieve his DoS goal.

As far back as 1997, weaknesses were found in and documented about BIND implementations in versions preceding 4.9.5+P1. The earlier versions would cache bogus DNS information when DNS recursion was enabled. The vulnerability enabled attackers to exploit the process of mapping IP addresses to hostnames in what is known as *PTR record spoofing.* This type of spoofing provides the potential for a DNS DoS attack.

11.2.4.6   SYN Flooding.   *SYN flooding* is a DoS attack that fits into the consumption-of-scarce-resource category. This DoS attack exploits the three-way handshake used by TCP hosts to synchronize the logical connection prior to data exchange. In a normal TCP host-to-host connection, the two hosts exchange three TCP segments prior to exchanging data, as shown in Exhibit 11.2:

1. The client sends a segment to the server with its initial sequence number (ISN). The SYN (synchronization) flag is set in this segment.

Exhibit 11.2   Normal TCP 3-Way Handshake

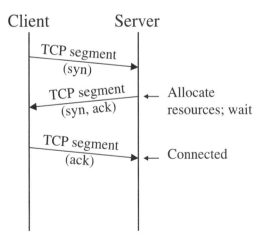

Exhibit 11.3   TCP SYN DoS Attack

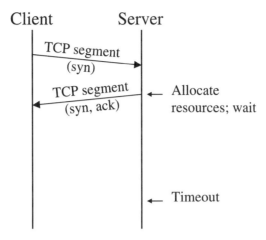

2. The server responds by sending a segment containing its ISN and acknowledges the client's ISN. This segment will have both the SYN and ACK (acknowledgement) flags set. At this point, the server allocates resources for the about-to-be-established connection and waits for the third segment.

3. The client sends a segment acknowledging the server's ISN. This and all subsequent segments until the end of the session will have only the ACK flag set.

A SYN flood takes advantage of the three-way handshake and the fact that a server can only have a finite number of open TCP connections. The attack is launched when an attacker initiates connections for which there will never be a third segment (see Exhibit 11.3). After the server sends the segment in step 2 above, it waits for a response. Under normal circumstances, the client will respond within a few seconds. The server might wait, say, 10 seconds before timing out and releasing the resources. But suppose the attacker sends hundreds of connection messages per second on a sustained basis. When these bogus connection attempts "flood" the target faster than they can time-out, there will not be any resource left in which to establish a legitimate connection. This is the type of attack that was launched against PANIX in 1996.

11.2.4.7   Resource Starvation.   *Resource starvation* is a catch-all category for many other types of DoS attacks that are the result of some scarce resource—be it bandwidth, processing power, disk space—being consumed and exhausted. One example uses a novel UDP DoS attack, where an intruder forges UDP packets and uses them to connect the *echo* service of one machine (UDP port 7) to the character generator (*chargen*) service on another machine (UDP port 19). When this occurs, the two machines consume all available network bandwidth, and all machines on the same networks as the target machines can be affected and starved for resources.

But such attacks can happen locally, as well. Unfortunately, many authorized users carry out *local DoS attacks* that either consume system resources or deny users access. Numerous resource starvation attacks and programming flaws attack specific systems. For instance, by exceeding imposed quotas on disk space, multiuser systems can suffer from a resource starvation attack. Most operating systems limit the amount by which a user can exceed disk quota. Windows 2000 has a twist on this; while individual files can exceed their quota by only a small amount, if *every* file exceeds the quota, a user can consume a lot of extra disk space.

11.2.4.8   Java.   *Java* is another avenue for DoS attacks. One such DoS attack exploits the fact that whenever specific internal elements of the Netscape and HotJava browsers lock, additional host lookups via the browser are prevented. Another DoS occurs by forcing the overutilization of the CPU and random-access memory (RAM), resulting in the browser halting or freezing. During both of these events, the origin of further attacks could be obscured.

It is also possible for the Java browser's proxies to be neutralized or knocked out with the victim's DNS queries being rerouted to an untrusted DNS server. Such an untrusted server would provide misinformation in regard to host names, and this would snowball into a root compromise.

Java also can force a reboot on Windows 9x systems. A demonstration applet that works for Netscape Communicator 4.x can kill a Windows box.

11.2.4.9   Router Attacks.   *Router attacks* have been developed for a wide variety of routers. Because routers are the backbone of the Internet and the gateway through which organizations connect to the Internet, killing a router denies network service for hundreds of machines. Productivity and financial repercussions from a hardware attack can be very severe. Popular targets for these kinds of attacks are routers from Ascend, Cisco, Livingston (now Lucent), and 3Com. Unfortunately, many network managers make the attacks easy by employing Telnet or HTTP for remote access and do not properly secure the network against remote access by anyone over the Internet.

11.2.4.10   Other Denial of Service Attacks.   Even this list of specific DoS attacks is not exhaustive. For example, *Bonk* and *boink* (aka *bonk.c*) are DoS attacks that cause a target Windows 9x/NT system to crash. *Arnudp* (*arnudp100.c*) forges UDP packets to implement a DoS against UDP ports 7 (*echo*), 13 (*daytime*), 19 (*chargen*), and 37 (*time*), services that frequently run on Unix and Windows NT systems. And *cbcb.c* is a *cancelbot* that destroys existing Usenet news postings that fit certain criteria. (Some argue that *cbcb.c* does not actually carry out a DoS attack; however, once activated, the program denies access to postings for targeted Usenet users.)

The CERT/CC (*www.cert.org*) and SANS (*www.sans.org*) have the most comprehensive lists of various DoS attacks.

11.2.5   Preventing and Responding to Denial of Service Attacks.   DoS attacks are best prevented; handling them in real time is very difficult. And the most important way to protect a system is to harden the operating systems: Install them with security in mind, monitor sites to be aware of security vulnerabilities, maintain the latest versions of software where possible, and install all relevant security patches.

But a large measure of the prevention consists of packet filtering at network routers. Because attackers frequently hide the identity of the machines used to carry out the attacks by falsifying the source address of the network connection, techniques known as *egress filtering* and *ingress filtering* are commonly used as protective measures. As discussed later in this chapter, egress and ingress filtering are methods of preventing packets from leaving or entering the network, respectively, with an invalid source address. By blocking addresses that do not fit the criteria for legitimate source addresses and making certain that all packets leaving an organization's site contain legitimate addresses, many DoS attacks can be thwarted.

Other packet filtering methods that will help prevent DoS are to block all broadcast messages and most ICMP messages. There is no reason that a site should accept messages being broadcast to all hosts on the site. Furthermore, there is probably no good reason to allow all hosts to respond to Ping or traceroute messages; in fact, most ICMP messages probably can be blocked.

In some instances, victims have set up response letters triggered to send and resend in large quantities so that they flood the attacker's address. Doing this is generally not a good idea. If these messages are sent to a legitimate address, the attacker may "get the message" and stop. But the attackers generally spoof the source IP address, so responding in kind is not a good defensive posture because it may harm innocent victims. The best defense will involve the ISP.

In instances where the attacker's service provider can be identified and contacted, the victim can request that the service provider intervene. In these instances, it is usual for the ISPs to take appropriate action to stop the attack and find the perpetrator. However, in instances where a DoS appears to be emulate or mimic another form of attack or when it continues for an unusually long period of time, the victim may want to take more aggressive action by contacting CERT/CC, the Federal Bureau of Investigation, and other authorities that have experience with DoS attacks and some jurisdiction if the perpetrators are caught.

Real-time defenses are difficult but possible. Many routers and external intrusion detection systems (IDSs) can detect an attack in real time, such as too many connection requests per unit time from a given IP host or network address. A router might block the connection requests or an IDS might send a pager message to a security administrator.

However, attacks such as SMURFs can suck up all of the bandwidth even before the packets get to the target site. Cooperation by ISPs and end-user sites is required to fully combat DoS attacks. This issue will be addressed further as part of the discussion of responding to DDoS.

11.3   DISTRIBUTED DENIAL OF SERVICE ATTACKS.   DDoS tools use amplification to augment the power of the attacker. By subverting poorly secured systems into sending coordinated waves of fraudulent traffic aimed at specific targets, intruders can overwhelm the bandwidth of any given victim.

In a DDoS attack, the attacking packets come from tens or hundreds of addresses rather than just one, as in a standard DoS attack. Any DoS defense that is based on monitoring the volume of packets coming from a single address or single network will fail since the attacks come from all over. Rather than receiving, for example, 1,000 gigantic Pings per second from an attacking site, the victim might receive one Ping per second from each of 1,000 attacking sites.

One of the other disconcerting things about DDoS attacks is that the handler can choose the location of the agents. So, for example, a handler could target several North Atlantic Treaty Organization (NATO) sites as victims and employ agents that are all in countries known to be hostile to NATO. The human attacker, of course, might be sitting in Canada.

Like DoS attacks, all of the DDoS attacks employ standard TCP/IP messages—but employ them in some nonstandard ways. Common DDoS attacks have such names as Tribe Flood Network (TFN), Trin00, Stacheldraht, and Trinity. The following sections present some details about these attacks.

11.3.1   Short History of Distributed Denial of Service.   Denial of service attacks under a number of guises have been around for decades. Distributed DoS attacks are much newer. In late June and early July of 1999, groups of hackers installed and tested a DDoS tool called Trinoo (see below) to launch medium to large DDoS attacks. Their tests involved over 2,000 compromised systems and targets around the world.

Most of the literature suggests that the first documented large-scale DDoS attack occurred in August 1999, when Trinoo was deployed in at least 227 systems (114 of which were on Internet2) to flood a single University of Minnesota computer; this system was down for more than two days.

On December 28, 1999, CERT/CC issued its Advisory CA-1999-17 (*www.cert. org/advisories/CA-1999-17.html*) reviewing DDoS.

On February 7, 2000, Yahoo was the victim of a DDoS during which its Internet portal was inaccessible for three hours. On February 8, Amazon, Buy.com, CNN, and eBay were all hit by DDoS attacks that caused them to either stop functioning completely or slow down significantly. And, on February 9, E*Trade and ZDNet both suffered DDoS attacks. Analysts estimated that during the three hours Yahoo was down, it suffered a loss of e-commerce and advertising revenue that amounted to about $500,000. According to book seller Amazon.com, its widely publicized attack resulted in a loss of $600,000 during the 10 hours it was down. During their DDoS attacks, Buy.com went from 100 percent availability to 9.4 percent, while CNN.com's users went down to below 5 percent of normal volume and Zdnet.com and E*Trade.com were virtually unreachable. Schwab.com, the online venue of the discount broker Charles Schwab, was also hit but refused to give out exact figures for losses. One can only assume that to a company that does $2 billion weekly in online trades, the downtime loss was huge.

11.3.2   Distributed Denial of Service Terminology and Overview.   To describe and understand DDoS attacks, it is important to understand the terminology that is used to describe the attacks and the tools. While the industry has more or less settled on some common terms, that consensus did not come about until well after many DoS/DDoS attacks had already appeared in the hacker and mainstream literature. Early descriptions of DDoS tools used a jumble of terms to describe the various roles of the systems involved in the attack. At the CERT/CC Distributed System Intruder Tools Workshop held in November 1999, some standard terminology was introduced. Those terms are used in the paragraphs that follow (see *www.cert.org/reports/dsit_workshop-final.html* or *www.cert.org/reports/dsit_workshop.pdf*). To align those terms and the terms used by the hacker literature as well as early descriptions, here are some synonyms:

- Intruder: Also called the *attacker* or *client.*
- Master: Also called the *handler.*
- Daemon: Also called an *agent, bcast (broadcast) program,* or *zombie.*
- Victim: Also called the *target.*

DoS/DDoS attacks actually have two victims, namely the ultimate target as well as the intermediate system(s) that were exploited and loaded with daemon software. In this chapter, the focus is on the end-of-the line DoS/DdoS victim.

DDoS attacks always involve a number of systems. A typical DDoS attack scenario might follow roughly the following three steps:

1. The *intruder* finds one or more systems on the Internet that can be compromised and exploited (see Exhibit 11.4). This is generally accomplished using a stolen account on a system with a large number of users or inattentive administrators, preferably with a high-bandwidth connection to the Internet. (Many such systems can be found on college and university campuses.)

2. The compromised system is loaded with any number of hacking and cracking tools, such as scanners, exploit tools, operating system detectors, rootkits, and

Exhibit 11.4   DDoS Phase 1

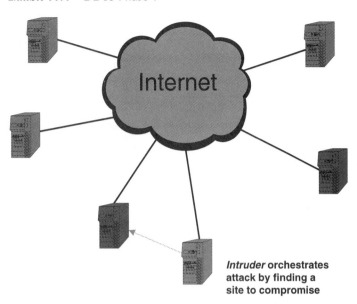

Intruder **orchestrates**
attack by finding a
site to compromise

DoS/DDoS programs. This system becomes the DDoS *master.* The master software allows it to find a number of other systems that can themselves be compromised and exploited. The attacker scans large ranges of IP network address blocks to find systems running services known to have security vulnerabilities. This *initial mass-intrusion phase* employs automated tools to remotely compromise several hundred to several thousand hosts, and installs DDoS agents on those systems. The automated tools to perform this compromise are not part of the DDoS toolkit but are exchanged within groups of criminal hackers. These compromised systems are the initial victims of the DDoS attack. These subsequently exploited systems will be loaded with the DDoS *daemons* that carry out the actual attack (see Exhibit 11.5).

Exhibit 11.5   DDoS Phase 2

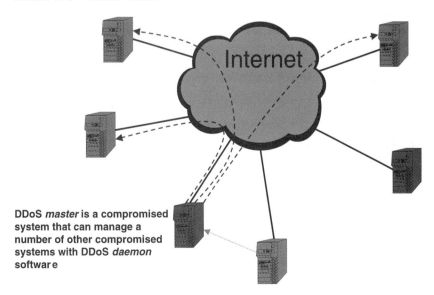

DDoS *master* **is a compromised**
system that can manage a
number of other compromised
systems with DDoS *daemon*
softwar e

Exhibit 11.6   DDoS Phase 3

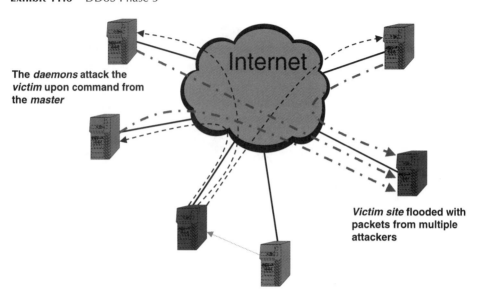

The *daemons* attack the *victim* upon command from the *master*

Victim site flooded with packets from multiple attackers

3. The intruder maintains a list of *owned systems,* the compromised systems with the DDoS daemon. The actual *denial of service attack phase* occurs when the attacker runs a program at the master system that communicates with the DDoS daemons to launch the attack. Here is where the intended DDoS victim comes into the scenario (see Exhibit 11.6).

Communication between the master and daemons can be obscured so that it becomes difficult to locate the master computer. Although some evidence may exist on one or more machines in the DDoS network regarding the location of the master, the daemons normally are automated so that it is not necessary for an ongoing dialogue to take place between the master and the rest of the DDoS network. In fact, typically techniques are employed to deliberately camouflage the identity and location of the master within the DDoS network. These techniques make it difficult to analyze an attack in progress and difficult to block attacking traffic and trace it back to its source.

In most cases, the system administrators of the infected systems do not even know that the daemons have been put in place. Even if they do find and eradicate the DDoS software, they cannot help anyone determine where else the software may have been placed. Popular systems to exploit are a site's Web, e-mail, name, or other servers since these systems are likely to have a large number of open ports, a large amount of traffic, and are unlikely to be quickly pulled off-line even if an attack can be traced to them.

11.3.3   Distributed Denial of Service Tool Descriptions.   This section provides some details about how some of the major DDoS tools work.

11.3.3.1   Trinoo (Trin00).   *Trinoo,* also called *Trin00,* was the first known DDoS tool, appearing in June or July 1999. The typical installation of Trin00 is similar to the scenario painted above where an attacker plants handler software on a system and the handler, in turn, loads the attack software on the agents. Trin00 is a distributed SYN DoS attack.

Trin00 uses a number of TCP and UDP ports:

- Masters listen on TCP port 27665 for attacker-to-master communication.
- Daemons listen on UDP port 27444 for master-to-daemon communication.
- Masters listen on UDP port 31335 for daemon-to-master communication.

These are default port numbers, of course, and future implementations could use other ports. The human attacker can control a Trin00 master (the handler) remotely via a connection to TCP port 27665. After connecting, the attacker gives the expected password, *betaalmostdone*.

The trinoo master program is typically named *master.c* and the daemon is *ns.c*. Communication between the trinoo master (handler) and daemons (agents) is via UDP. Master-to-daemon communications use UDP datagrams on port 27444. All commands contain a password, the default being *l44adsl*. All valid commands contain the substring *l44*.

Communication from the trinoo daemons to the master use UDP datagrams on port 31335. When the daemon starts, it sends a message to the master containing the string **HELLO**. The Trin00 *keep alive* function is accomplished by an exchange between the master and daemon: The master sends a trinoo *mping* command, which sends the string *png* to a daemon; the daemon responds by sending the string *PONG* to the master.

The passwords are here to prevent system administrators from being able to take control of the masters and daemons that form the trinoo network. Other default passwords in the initial attacks were *gOrave* to start the trinoo master server and *killme* to control the master's *mdie* command to kill the trinoo processes. Like the port numbers, the passwords can be changed easily.

Intrusion detection software or system management routine analysis can look for a number of things that might indicate the presence of trinoo:

- A system listening on UDP port 27444 could be a trinoo daemon.
  - Trinoo daemon communication will contain the string *l44*.
  - The SYN flood mechanism picks the destination port using a random number generator function.
  - A trinoo daemon will send the string *PONG* if it receives a *png* command.
- A system listening on TCP port 27665 could be a trinoo master.
- A system listening on UDP port 27444 could be a trinoo master.
  - UDP packets will contain the string *l44adsl*.

A detailed analysis of trinoo by Dave Dittrich can be found at *http://staff.washington. edu/dittrich/misc/trinoo.analysis*. The National Infrastructure Protection Center (NPIC) also has posted an alert and detection tool for trinoo (and other DDoS) tools at *www. nipc.gov/warnings/alerts/1999/trinoo.htm*.

11.3.3.2   *Tribe Flood Network.*   The Tribe Flood Network (TFN) appeared after trinoo. TFN runs primarily on compromised Unix systems exploited using buffer overrun bugs in the RPC services. TFN client and daemon programs implement a DDoS network capable of employing a number of attacks, such as ICMP flood, SYN flood, UDP flood, and SMURF-style attacks.

TFN is noticeably different from trinoo in that all communication between the client (attacker), handlers, and agents use *ICMP ECHO* and *ECHO REPLY* packets.

Communication from the TFN client to daemons is accomplished via *ICMP ECHO REPLY* packets. The absence of TCP and UDP traffic sometimes makes these packets difficult to detect because many protocol monitoring tools are not configured to capture and display the ICMP traffic.

Remote control of the TFN network is accomplished by executing a program on the client system. The program also can be executed at the handler system by the client via some host-to-host connection method, such as connecting to an exploited TCP port or using a UDP- or ICMP-based remote shell. The program must be supplied:

- The IP address list of hosts that are ready to carry out the flood attack
- The type of attack to be launched
- The IP address list of target hosts
- The port number for SYN attack

No password protection is associated with TFN. Each command to the daemons is sent in the Identifier field of the ICMP packet; values *345, 890,* and *901* start the *SYN, UDP,* and *ICMP* flood attacks, respectively. The Sequence Number field in the *ECHO REPLY* message is always set to *0x0000,* which make it look like the response to the initial *ECHO* packet sent out by the *ping* command.

The TFN client program is typically named *tribe.c* and the daemon is *td.c.* A detailed analysis of TFN by Dave Dittrich can be found at *http://staff.washington.edu/dittrich/misc/tfn.analysis.*

11.3.3.3   Stacheldraht.   *Stacheldraht* (German for "barbed wire") is a DDoS tool that appeared in August 1999 and combines features of trinoo and TFN. It also contains some advanced features, such as encrypted attacker-master communication and automated agent updates.

Stacheldraht uses a trinoo-like client/server architecture. The handler listens on TCP port 16660 for client (intruder) commands, and the agents listen on TCP port 65000 for commands from the handler. Agent responses to the handler employ *ICMP ECHO REPLY* messages. The possible attacks are similar to those of TFN; namely, ICMP flood, SYN flood, UDP flood, and SMURF attacks.

Trinoo and TFN exchange commands in plaintext. Trinoo, being TCP-based, is also subject to common TCP attacks such as session hijacking. Stacheldraht addresses these deficiencies by employing an encrypting "telnet alike" client. ("Telnet alike" is a Stacheldraht term.) The client uses secret key cryptography.

The Stacheldraht network comprises a number of programs. The attacker uses an encrypting client called *telnetc/client.c* to control one or more handlers. The handler program is called *mserv.c,* and each handler can control up to 1,000 agents. The agent software, *leaf/td.c,* coordinates the attack against one or more victims upon command from the handler.

Dave Dittrich's analysis of stacheldraht can be found at *http://staff.washington.edu/dittrich/misc/stacheldraht.analysis.*

11.3.3.4   TFN2K.   Tribe Flood Network 2K (TFN2K) was released in December 1999 and targets Unix and Windows NT servers. TFN2K is a complex variant of the original TFN with features designed specifically to:

- Make TFN2K traffic difficult to recognize and filter.
- Remotely execute commands.

- Hide the true source of the attack using IP address spoofing.
- Transport TFN2K traffic over multiple transport protocols including UDP, TCP, and ICMP.
- Confuse attempts to locate other nodes in a TFN2K network by sending "decoy" packets.

TFN2K, like TFN, can consume all of a system's bandwidth by flooding the victim machine with data. But TFN2K, unlike TFN, also includes attacks designed to crash or introduce instabilities in systems by sending malformed or invalid packets, such as those found in the Teardrop and Land attacks.

TFN2K uses a client-server architecture in which a single client issues commands simultaneously to a set of TFN2K agents. The agents then conduct the DoS attacks against the victim(s). The agent software is installed in a machine that already has been compromised by the attacker.

An early description of TFN2K from CERT/CC can be found at *www.cert.org/ advisories/CA-1999-17.html*.

11.3.3.5 Other Types of Distributed Denials of Service. Trinoo, TFN/TFN2K, and Stacheldraht are the best known, and still most widely used, DDoS tools, but more tools are becoming available.

In November 1999, for example, the Shaft DDoS tool became available. A Shaft network looks conceptually similar to a trinoo network with client-managing handler programs ("shaftmaster") that, in turn, manage agent programs ("shaftnode"). Like trinoo, handler-agent communication uses UDP, with the handler(s) listening on port 20433 and the agent(s) listening on port 18753. The client communicates with the handler by telnetting to TCP port 20432. The attack itself is a packet-flooding attack, and the client controls the size of the flooding packets and duration of the attack. One signature of Shaft is that the sequence number for all TCP packets is always 0x28374839. Additional information about Shaft can be found at *www.sans.org/y2k/shaft.htm*.

In August 2000, a DDoS attack against Apache Web servers was first detected. The attack took advantage of a vulnerability whereby a URL sent to an Apache Web server containing thousands of forward slashes ("/") would put the server into a state that would consume enormous CPU time. This particular attack was launched by over 500 compromised Windows computers and would, presumably, succeed against Apache Web servers prior to version 1.2.5.

During the following month, a new DDoS tool called Trinity was reported. Trinity is capable of launching several types of flooding attacks on a victim site, including UDP, fragment, SYN, RST, ACK, and other floods. Trinity agent software must be placed on Linux systems compromised by a buffer overflow vulnerability. The agent binary code typically is found in */usr/lib/idle.so*. Communication from the handler or intruder to the agent, however, is accomplished via Internet Relay Chat (IRC) or America Online's ICQ. Whereas the attacker has to keep track of the IP addresses of compromised systems with Trinoo and TFN, all of the Trinity agents report back to the attacker by appearing in the same chat room. The original reports were that the Trinity agent communicated over an IRC channel called *#b3eblebr0x;* other IRC channels presumably are being used for DDoS, as well. IRC uses TCP ports 6665 to 6669, and Trinity appears to use port 6667. In addition, a binary called */var/spool/uucp/uucico* is a backdoor program that listens on TCP port 33270 for connections; an attacker connecting on that port and providing the password !@# will achieve rootshell on the affected system.

Zombie software is not always distributed by an attacker exploiting a vulnerability of an exposed system. Indeed, very often the user is the culprit. Trojan horses are often the mechanism for distributing the zombie code. The SubSeven Defcon8 software, for example, is a backdoor virus that is rapidly spreading. SubSeven gets on a user's system because it is distributed within programs available via Usenet and other Internet sites, such as some game or pornography programs (e.g., SexxxyMovie.mpeg). Potential attackers frequently scan computer systems today, particularly residential systems connected to the Internet via DSL or cable modem, for the presence of SubSeven, which provides a potential backdoor into users' systems; system administrators also are learning to scan for this dangerous program on their own systems.

11.3.3.6   Denial of Service Using Exploitable Software.   The tools above employ the common DoS approach; an attacker exploits a vulnerability of a potential victim and uses that system to launch attacks on the intended victim. The latest round of DDoS attacks, however, use code that is commonly available and that has known vulnerabilities.

In May 2001, a buffer overflow exploit was discovered in the Microsoft Internet Information Service (IIS) Indexing Service. In mid-June, Microsoft released a security bulletin warning that administrative scripts (.ida files) and Internet data queries (.idq files) did not do proper bounds checking. As it happens, what seems like the vast majority of IIS servers did not get the patch and, in essence, every unpatched IIS server became a DDoS zombie.

In July, eEye Digital Security and several other security organizations around the Internet saw an alarming number of TCP port 80 scans on the Internet. What they eventually discovered was what became known as the Code Red Worm.

Code Red has three distinct phases. The *propagation phase* occur during the first 19 days of the month. During this phase, the attacking system scans target systems on TCP port 80, and sends a specially crafted HTTP GET request that exploits the IIS buffer overflow (even if the Index Service is not running). If the exploit is successful, the worm runs in RAM of the infected server and spawns 99 new threads to attack a quasi-random set of IP addresses. If the exploited server's native language is English, the server's Web page is defaced with a message that says "Welcome to http://www. worm.com! Hacked by Chinese!" This message would stay up for 10 hours and then disappear.

The *flood phase* occurs on days 20–27 of the month. This is when the attack really happens: Every day between 8:00 and 11:59 p.m. UTC, the compromised servers send 100 KB packets to the IP address 198.137.240.91, which formerly was assigned to *www.whitehouse.gov.*

Days 28–31 of the month are the *termination phase,* when the worm becomes dormant. Code Red was relatively innocuous to what it could have been; once asleep, the worm stayed asleep although it could be reawakened. Removing the worm program from RAM only required a reboot and the patch from Microsoft would prevent further infection.

As an aside, although only IIS servers could be exploited, many other devices that listen on port 80 were also affected. Cisco 600 DSL routers and HP JetDirect devices, for example, listen on port 80 and would crash when they received the buffer overflow packet.

Three different variants of Code Red existed on the Internet, all acting as described above. In August, a couple of new variants appeared that have been called Code Red II. Unlike Code Red, Code Red II did not deface Web pages nor did it launch a DDoS attack on any given site. Instead, this worm was destructive, installing backdoors on infected servers, changing many registry settings, installed a Trojan horse version of *explorer.exe* (Windows Explorer), and disabling the System File Checker (SFC) utility. The worm also spread very quickly, employing up to 300 threads at a time looking for other systems to infect.

The next evolution appeared in September 2001, and was called NIMDA. NIMDA, a play on the term *admin,* was truly unique because it exploited multiple vulnerabilities in Microsoft code, namely IIS, Internet Explorer (IE), and the Message Application Program Interface (MAPI). As a result, NIMDA had four distinct propagation vectors:

- *IIS:* When a Web server is found, the attacker attempts to exploit various IIS vulnerabilities, including IIS sadmind, a Code Red II root.exe or other backdoor program, or IIS Directory Traversal. If successful, the attacker uses tftp from cmd.exe to send the worm code (admin.dll) to the victim.

- *Web browser:* The worm on an infected server creates a copy of itself in a file called *readme.eml.* The worm also alters every Web-content file at the infected site with a small JavaScript code that points to this file. When some user browses to the infected Web server, the infected page's JS code is activated, and *readme. eml* is downloaded. Vulnerable versions of Internet Explorer will auto-execute the file while most other browsers won't.

- *E-mail:* NIMDA sends itself to all of the e-mail addresses found in the InBox and Address Book of an infected server in a MIME-encoded, 56KB attached file named *readme.exe.* The file contains an "audio/x-wav" section that contains the worm. E-mail clients using IE 5.1 or earlier to display HTML will automatically execute the attachment if the *message* is opened or previewed.

- *Network shares:* When on an infected system, the worm copies itself to all local directories on victim host and to all open, writeable network shares. The worm also sets up shares on the victim host.

NIMDA also makes the GUEST account a member of Administrator group.

11.3.4   Defenses against Distributed Denials of Service.   As with DoS attacks, a site cannot in isolation defend itself from DDoS attacks. Members of the Internet community must work together to protect every site against becoming the source of attacks or forwarding the attacks. This section discusses some ways to help prevent the spread of DDoS attacks by limiting the distribution of the tools and by limiting the propagation of the offending attack packets.

Although not discussed in detail here, another point needs to be made about DDoS attack responses. As discussed in Chapter 38, victims of such an attack should maintain detailed logs of all actions they take and events they detect. These logs may prove invaluable in understanding the attack, in preventing other attacks at the initial target and others, and in aiding law enforcement efforts to track down the perpetrators.

11.3.4.1   User and System Administrator Actions.   The following seven steps should be taken to minimize the potential that an individual system will be compromised and attacked or used as a stepping-stone to attack others:

1. Keep abreast of the security vulnerabilities for all of the site's hardware, operating systems, and application and other software. This sounds like a Herculean task, but it is essential to safeguarding the network. Apply patches and updates

as soon as possible. Standardize on certain hardware, operating systems, and software where feasible to help manage the problem.

2. Use personal firewall software on workstations to detect an attack.

3. Monitor systems periodically to test for known operating system vulnerabilities. Also periodically check to see what TCP/UDP ports are using the "netstat –a" command; every open port should be associated with a known application. Turn off all unused applications.

4. Regularly monitor system logs and look for suspicious activity.

5. Use available tools to periodically audit systems, particularly servers, to ensure that there have been no unauthorized/unknown changes to the file system, registry, user account database, and so on.

6. Do not download software from unknown, untrusted sites. If possible, know the author of the code. Even better, download source code, review it, and compile it on a trustworthy system rather than downloading binaries or executables.

7. Keep up with and follow recommendations from the CERT/CC, SANS Institute, Internet Engineering Task Force (IETF), Requests for Comments (RFCs), and other best practices.

11.3.4.2 Local Network Actions. Even if users lock down their systems so that no vulnerability has gone unpatched and no exposure unprotected, the local network itself still can be at risk. Local network managers and network administrators can take a number of steps to protect all of their own users as well as the rest of the Internet community:

1. Every network connected to the Internet should perform egress address filtering at the router. *Egress filtering* means that the router should examine the IP Source Address field of every outgoing packet to the Internet to be sure that the NET_ID matches the NET_ID of the network. Historically, users' firewalls have been used to protect users from attacks from the outside world. But those attacks come from somewhere, so sites should also use the firewall to protect the outside world.

2. Networks should block incoming packets addressed to the broadcast address (the all-ones HOST_ID). There is no legitimate reason that an external network device should be sending a broadcast message to every host on a network.

3. To prevent a site from being used as a broadcast amplification point, turn off the Directed Broadcast capability at the router unless it is absolutely essential. If it is essential, reexamine the network to see if there is not a better way. Even where Directed Broadcasts are useful, they are typically needed only *within* the enterprise and are not required for hosts on the outside. RFC 1918 defines three blocks within the IP address space that are reserved for private IP networks; these addresses are not to be routed on the Internet.

IP Address Range	Network ID/Subnet Mask	Number of Equivalent Classful IP Networks
10.0.0.0-10.255.255.255	10/8 prefix	One Class A network
172.16.0.0-172.31.255.255	172.16/12 prefix	Sixteen Class B networks
192.168.0.0-192.168.255.255	192.168/16 prefix	256 Class C networks

In addition, there are a number of reserved IP addresses that are never assigned to "public" networks or hosts, including:

0.0.0.0/32	Historical broadcast address
127.0.0.0/8	Loopback network identifier
169.254.0.0/16	Link-local Networks
192.0.2.0/24	TEST-NET
224.0.0.0/4	Class D Multicast address range
240.0.0.0/5	Class E Experimental address range
248.0.0.0/5	Unallocated
255.255.255.255/32	Broadcast

Attackers commonly use IP address spoofing, generally by using one of the RFC 1918 private addresses or one of the other reserved addresses. Firewalls should immediately discard *any* packet that contains any RFC 1918 or reserved IP address in the IP Source Address or Destination Address field; such packets should never be sent to the Internet.

1. Block all unused application ports at the firewall, particularly such ports as IRC (6665–6669/tcp) and those known to be associated with DDoS tools.

2. Use some form of intrusion detection system to protect the network. For example, one can install personal firewall software on every workstation to help detect an attack on individual systems; this strategy is particularly useful at sites (e.g., ,colleges) that have a large number of systems *in front* of a firewall. It is no coincidence that so many daemons reside on college and university computers that have been taken *owned* (i.e., taken over by hackers).

3. Regularly monitor network activity so that aberrations in traffic flow can be detected quickly .

4. Educate users about things to watch for on their systems and how to report any irregularity that might indicate that someone or something has tampered with their system. Educate the help desk and technical support to assist those users who make such reports. Have an intelligence-gathering system within the organization so that such reports can be coordinated centrally to spot trends and to devise responses.

5. Follow CERT/CC, SANS, and other best practices procedures.

11.3.4.3   Internet Service Provider Actions.   Internet service providers offer the last hope in defeating the spread of a DDoS attack. While the ISP cannot take responsibility for locking down every customers' host systems, ISPs have—and should accept—the responsibility to ensure that their network does not carry packets that contain obviously "bad" packets. Some of the steps that ISPs can take include:

- As mentioned, attackers commonly employ IP address spoofing using an RFC 1918 private address or other reserved address. Amazingly, many ISPs will route these packets. Indeed, there is no entry in their routing table telling them where to send the packets; they merely forward them to a default upstream ISP. *Any* packet that contains any RFC 1918 or reserved IP address in the IP Source Address or Destination Address field should be discarded immediately.

- Perform ingress (and egress) address filtering. *Ingress filtering* means that ISPs should examine every incoming packet to their network from a customer's site and examine the IP Source Address field to be sure that the NET_ID matches the NET_ID assigned to that customer. Doing this will require additional configuration at the router and may even result in slight performance degradation, but the trade-off is certainly well worth the effort. The ISPs also should perform egress filtering to check their outbound packets to upstream and peer ISPs.

- Disable IP directed broadcasts.

- Pay careful attention to high-profile systems (servers) and customers.

- Educate customers about security and work with them to help protect themselves.

Most of the ISP community takes at least some of these steps. Users should insist that their ISPs provide at least these protections and should not do business with those who do not. The ICSA Labs ISP Security (ISPSec) community (*www.icsa.net/html/communities/ispsec/*) is a good source of information for ISPs.

11.3.4.4   Code Red/NIMDA Defensive Actions.   There are a number of defensive steps that can be taken to avoid or mitigate problems due to NIMDA, although several of these are controversial:

- If you are using IIS, consider using alternate Web server software. If you must use IIS, the only way to clean up after NIMDA is to reinstall IIS on a new, clean installation of the underlying operating system. Keep IIS and the operating system up to the latest patch revision. Microsoft's IIS Cumulative Patch does *not* clean a system of Code Red II backdoors or NIMDA.

- If you use the Internet Explorer, consider using alternate browser software. If you must use IE, secure it against MIME auto-execution. IE 5.01 requires a patch whereas IE 5.5 SP2 and IE 6.0 are already immune.

- Disable any and all unused accounts on your system. In particular, enable the Guest account or anonymous access only if necessary.

- Disable JavaScript, Java, and ActiveX on your browser and turn those features on only if they are needed while you are on a safe site.

- Do not execute readme.exe or *any* e-mail attachment unless expected, known, and verified.

- Use most up-to-date anti-virus signature files.

- Unbind file and print sharing from TCP/IP. In some cases, this will require installing NetBEUI for file and print sharing.

11.3.4.5   Other Tools under Development or Consideration.   Responses to DDoS attacks are not limited to the defensive steps just listed. Indeed, proactive responses to the prevention and detection of DDoS attacks is an active area of research.

One method that is being discussed is to examine the network at the ISP level and build a type of intelligent, distributed network traffic monitor; in some sense, this would be like an IDS for the Internet. ISPs, peering points, and/or major host servers would have traffic monitor hardware using IP and the Internet for communications, much like today's routing protocols. Each node would examine packets and their contents, doing a statistical analysis of traffic to learn the normal patterns. These devices would have enough intelligence to be able to detect changes in traffic level and determine whether those changes reflected a normal condition or not. As an example, suppose that such hardware at Amazon.com were to identify a DoS attack launched from an ISP in Gondwanaland; the traffic-monitoring network would shut off traffic to Amazon coming from that ISP as close to the ISP as possible. In this way, the distributed network of monitors could shut traffic off at the source.

The hardware would need to be informed about traffic-level changes due to normal events, such as a new Super Bowl commercial being posted at the Ad Critic Web site or a new fashion show at Victoria Secret's Web site. The hardware also would need to prevent the attacker community from operating under the cover of these normal events.

RSA Laboratories has proposed another potential defense to DDoS attacks against Web servers that employs cryptographic methods. The approach uses a *client puzzle* protocol designed to allow servers to accept connection requests from legitimate clients and block those from attackers. A client puzzle is a cryptographic problem that is generated in such a way as to be dependent on time and information unique to the server and client request.

Under normal conditions, a server accepts any connection request from any client. If an attack is detected, the server selectively accepts connection requests by responding to each request with a puzzle. The server allocates the resources necessary to support a connection only to those clients that respond correctly to the puzzle within some regular TCP time-out period. A bona fide client will experience only a modest delay getting a connection during an attack, while the attacker will require an incredible amount of processing power to sustain the number of requests necessary for a noticeable interruption in service, quickly blocking the attack (in effect, a reverse DoS). This scheme might be effective against a DDoS attack from a relatively small number of hosts each sending a high volume of packets but would appear to have limited effectiveness against a low-volume attack from a large number of systems.

A third tool that is under consideration is that of *IP Traceback*. The problem with DoS/DDoS attacks is that packets come from a large number of sources, and IP address spoofing masks those sources. Traceback, in concept, is a relatively straightforward idea. Every packet on the Internet goes through some number of ISP routers. The processing power, memory, and storage are available for routers to mark packets with partial path information as they arrive. Since DoS/DDoS attacks generally comprise a large number of packets, the traceback mechanism does not need to mark every packet, but only a sample size that statistically is likely to include attack packets (e.g., one packet out of every 20,000). The feature allows the victim to locate the approximate source of the attack without the aid of outside agencies and even after the attack has ended. Another traceback proposal would define an ICMP Traceback message that would be sent to the victim site containing partial route information about the sampled packet. While both of these proposals requires a change to tens of thousands of routers in the Internet, it is a solution that can be implemented gradually, is backward compatible, and results in no negative effects on users.

These three proposals are merely samples of some ways for dealing with DDoS attacks: The first adds new hardware to the Internet; the second requires changing Web server and client software; and the third requires incrementally changing software in all of the Internet's routers. Upgrading Web browsers is probably the most practical strategy even though there are millions of copies in distribution; the vast majority come from two vendors, and users tend to upgrade. And there are even more proposals— such as ICSA's Host Identity Payload (HIP) protocol—under discussion.

11.4   MANAGEMENT ISSUES.   One of the greatest shortcomings in many organizations is that the highest levels of management do not truly understand the critical role that computers, networks, information, and the Internet play in the life of the organization. It is difficult to explain that there is an intruder community that is actively working on new tools all the time, and history has shown that as the tools mature and become more sophisticated, the technical knowledge required of the potential attacker goes down and the number of attacks overall goes up. Too many companies insist that "no one would bother us" without realizing that *any site* can become a target just by being there.

DoS attacks come in a variety of forms and aim at a variety of services, causing increased complexity and difficulty for system defense. DoS attacks should be taken seriously because of the potential threat they present, and attempts should be made to educate operational staff before such attacks occur, to document DoS attacks if they do occur, and to review the documentation and actions taken after the incident is over. Discussion of what steps were taken, what actions went into effect, and what the overall result was will help in determining whether the procedures carried out and techniques utilized were those best suited to the situation. A frank review and discussion will help achieve the best, most rapid, and most effective deployment of resources.

If anything proves the intertwined nature of the Internet, it is the defense against DDoS attacks. DDoS attacks require the subversion and coordination of hundreds or thousands of computers to attack a few victims. Defense against DDoS attacks requires the cooperation of thousands of ISPs and customer networks. Fighting DDoS requires continued diligence in locking down all of the hosts connected to the Internet as well as fundamental changes in the nature of TCP/IP connection protocols. As these changes are not likely to happen quickly, it is equally unlikely that DdoS attacks will disappear immediately.

11.5   SUGGESTED RESOURCES.   Several books and articles describe the early history of DoS attacks.

Brenton, C. *Mastering Network Security.* San Francisco: Sybex, 1999.

Denning, D.E. *Information Warfare and Security.* Reading, MA: Addison Wesley, 1999.

Hutt, A., S. Bosworth, and D. Hoyt. *Computer Security Handbook,* 3rd ed. New York: John Wiley & Sons, 1995.

Maximum Security, 2nd ed. Indianapolis: SAMS, 1998.

Pipkin, D.L. *Information Security.* Upper Saddle River, NJ: Prentice-Hall, 2000.

Scambray, J., S. McClure, and G. Kurtz. *Hacking Exposed, Network Security Secrets & Solutions,* 2nd ed. Berkeley, CA: Osborne/McGraw-Hill, 2000.

Spafford, E.H. "The Internet Worm: An Analysis." *Computer Communication Review,* January 1989.

Most of the best current references, however, are on the Web. Some of the sites that readers should monitor for updated DoS/DDoS information are:

Attrition.org's "Denial of Service (DoS) Database": *www.attrition.org/security/denial.*

CERT/CC's Web site: *www.cert.org.*

Dave Dittrich's Web page: *www.washington.edu/People/dad.*

Denialinfo.com's "Denial of Service (DoS) Attack Resources" page: *www.denialinfo.com.*

PacketStorm's "Distributed Attack Tools" page: *http://packetstorm.securify.com/distributed.*

Rekhter, Y. et al. "Address Allocation for Private Internets." RFC 1918/BCP 5: *www.ietf.org/rfc/rfc1918.txt.*

SANS Global Incident Analysis Center (GIAC) page: *www.sans.org/giac.htm.*

TruSecure's "DDoS Attacks" page: *www.icsa.net/html/communities/ddos/index.shtml.*

11.6   NOTE

1. 10 KB $\times$ 8 b/B $\times$ 50 hosts = 4 Mb.

CHAPTER 12

THE LEGAL FRAMEWORK FOR PROTECTING INTELLECTUAL PROPERTY IN THE FIELD OF COMPUTING AND COMPUTER SOFTWARE

William A. Zucker and Scott J. Nathan

CONTENTS

12.1 THE U.S. APPROACH

12.1.1 Concept of Proprietary Rights. For many years, unless an idea was patentable, the primary protection for internal business data, confidential or proprietary information, and computer code was through the common law doctrine of trade secrets.[1] Generally, a trade secret might be considered any internal, nonpublished manufacturing know-how, drawings, formula, or sales information used in a trade or business that has commercial applicability and that provides a business with some strategic advantage. Such information, so long as it was (1) not published or disseminated to others who were not obligated to maintain its confidentiality[2] and (2) maintained in confidence with the protecting organization, could be protected as a trade secret.

The law of trade secret thus recognized a business's ownership or proprietary interest in such information, data, or processes. There are, however, important practical limitations on the application of trade secret protection. First and foremost, for any product sold in the market, the law does not protect against a competitor seeing the product and then using it to figuring out how to manufacture like or similar items. Competitors are therefore free to "reverse engineer" a product so long as the reverse engineering is done wholly independently.

The second caveat is that an organization has to prove not only that the information qualifies for trade secret protection but also that it protected the secrecy of the information as required by the law of the applicable jurisdiction. This means that ownership will be a matter not of record but of case-by-case proof, making enforcement of trade secret protection time-consuming and expensive later on. Generally, the proof required consists of a showing that there was an active security program in place that was sufficient to protect the information as confidential. Various programs may be deemed adequate, depending on the circumstances, but usually such programs have five things in common:

1. An inventory of trade secret information that is periodically updated.
2. A security program to protect the technology at issue, often on a need-to-know basis with clear marking of information as "confidential, access restricted."
3. A written description of the security program that is provided to all employees.
4. An enforcement officer or oversight procedure.
5. An enforcement program, including litigation, if necessary, to enjoin unauthorized access or distribution.

In the field of computing, these principles often mean that source code or other readable formats should be secured in a locked file and marked "confidential." All representations of the code as stored on magnetic or other medium should be marked "confidential" and secured. Computerized information should be password protected with restrictions on circulation of the password and periodic password changes. A notice of confidentiality should be displayed as soon as access to the program is obtained, with appropriate warnings on limitation of use. Levels of access should be controlled so that privileges to copy, read, and write are appropriately restricted. Surveillance of entries and logon should be conducted routinely to verify that there has been no unauthorized entry. Finally, periodic audits should be conducted to test and substantiate the security procedures.

Security and trade secret law are forever linked together. A trade secret cannot exist without such security. The watchwords "Eternal vigilance is the price of liberty," spoken by Wendell Phillips in 1852, should be restated, in the context of business information protection, as "Eternal vigilance is the price of trade secret protection." It is not as catchy a phrase, but it is the price each business must pay if it relies in whole or in part on trade secret law for protection.

12.1.2   Copyright Law and Software.   Because of anxiety over the true extent of protection afforded software under patent and copyright law, software programs initially were protected as trade secrets. Such protection became increasingly problematic in today's society, where information technology and pressure for the free flow of information makes confidentiality controls more difficult to police. Copyright law has evolved to include computer programs.

Since 1964, the United States Copyright Office has permitted registration of computer programs, although judicial decisions were divided on the applicability of the Copyright Act. In 1976, Congress passed the Copyright Act of 1976, which did little to resolve the ambiguity. Clarification finally was obtained in the Computer Software Copyright Act of 1980, which explicitly extended the protection of the copyright laws to software.[3] Any type of work that can be fixed in any tangible medium is protected, even if the work can be reproduced by machine only.

Copyright protection, however, does not protect "ideas."[4] Rather, it protects the particular expression of the idea. As can be seen by the parallel proliferation of spreadsheet programs, the idea for the spreadsheet program cannot be protected, but the particular code that produces the spreadsheet can be. In order to qualify for copyright protection, the work must be (1) original, (2) fixed in a tangible medium, and (3) not just the embodiment of an idea. Once obtained, copyright protection grants to the copyright owner the exclusive right to reproduce and publish the copyrighted article. In 1990, Congress passed the Computer Software Rental Amendments Act,[5] which added to the list of copyright infringements the distribution of a computer program for commercial advantage. Materials copyrighted after 1978 are protected for the lesser of 75 years from the date of first publication or 100 years from the date of creation.

Copyright law has additional limitations, some of which are discussed in the following sections.

12.1.2.1   Formulas.   Formulas cannot be copyrighted.[6] This means that when formulas are part of a computer program, other modes of defense need to be considered, such as trade secret or possibly patent protection. If one were to disclose the formula through copyright publication, one would lose the ability to protect that information.

12.1.2.2   First Sale.   Copyright protection is limited to a first sale of the item. Once the item is placed in commerce, subsequent transfers cannot be restricted. To avoid what sometimes can be a problem if the program winds up in the hands of a competitor, companies often prefer to license the item instead of selling it outright. However, if the license has all the basic indicia of a sale, it will be treated as one, notwithstanding what it is labeled.

12.1.2.3   Fair Use.   All copyright protection is subject to the doctrine of fair use.[7] Despite its codification in the 1976 Copyright Act, fair use remains a nebulous doctrine—an equitable rule of reason with each case to be decided on its own facts.[8]

12.1.2.3.1   Reverse Engineering.   Within the field of computer software, recent cases have considered whether "dissection" in order to reverse engineer the program is a violation of the copyright. To those involved in protecting software programs, the answer appears to be that reverse engineering does not constitute an infringement, even though the disassembly of the program falls squarely within the category of acts prohibited by the copyright act because of the doctrine of fair use. The Ninth Circuit in *Sega Enterprises Ltd. v. Accolade, Inc.*[9] found as a matter of law that "where disassembly is the only way to gain access to the ideas and functional elements embodied in a copyrighted computer program and where there is a legitimate reason for seeking such access, disassembly is a fair use of the copyrighted work."[10]

The Ninth Circuit is not the only one that has upheld reverse engineering against a copyright claim. The Federal Circuit reached a similar conclusion regarding reverse engineering of object code to discern the "ideas" behind the program in *Atari Games*

Corp. v. Nintendo of America, Inc.[11] The fair use rationale of *Sega* also was adopted by the Eleventh Circuit in *Bateman v. Mnemonics, Inc.*[12] on the grounds that it advanced the sciences. Thus, unless careful thought is given to the application of copyright protection, merely copyrighting the software will not necessarily protect against imitation.

12.1.2.3.2 Interfaces.   The issue as to whether copyright protects the format for interfacing between application and data is an open one. Competitors particularly in the area of gaming look to reverse engineer the interface format to make new modules compatible with existing hardware. Such reverse engineering has been held not to violate the copyright laws, so long as the new product does not display copyrighted images or other copyrightable expressions.[13] Thus, the nonprotectable interface may be protected if such copyrighted images or expressions are embedded in the display.

12.1.2.3.3 Transformative Uses.   One of the factors that the doctrine of fair use considers is the "amount and substantiality of the portion used in relation to the copyrighted work as a whole."[14] In practical terms, this means that courts look at how much was taken and for what purpose. One could take a little but still take the essence of the program. One also could take a little that did not attempt to duplicate but rather used the copyrighted material as a springboard for a new creation. Out of this qualitative and quantitative investigation comes the notion of transformative use, which became the coin of analysis in the Supreme Court's 1994 decision in *Campbell v. Acuff-Rose Music, Inc.*[15] *Campbell* addressed the concept in terms of a claim of copyright infringement involving a rap parody of a popular song. Taking its clues from the opening language of Section 107 codifying fair use, the U.S. Supreme Court asked whether the "new" work "adds something new, with a further purpose or different character, altering the first with new expression, meaning or message; it asks, in other words, whether and to what extent the new work is transformative."[16] The Court then laid down the test to be applied:

> Although such transformative use is not absolutely necessary for a finding of fair use, . . . the goal of copyright, to promote science and the arts, is generally furthered by the creation of transformative works. Such works thus lie at the heart of the fair use doctrine's guarantee of breathing space within the confines of copyright, . . . and the more transformative the new work, the less will be the significance of other factors, like commercialism, that may weigh against a finding of fair use.[17]

Thus, a transformative use may play off of a prior copyright and still not be deemed an infringement so long as the resulting new work is just that—new.

12.1.2.4 Derivative Works.   Under Section 106 (2) of the Copyright Act, the copyright owner has the exclusive right "to prepare derivative works based upon the copyrighted work." The Copyright Act defines a "derivative work" as:

> a work based upon one or more pre-existing works, such as a translation, musical arrangement, dramatization, fictionalization, motion picture version, sound recording, art reproduction, abridgement, condensation, or any other form in which a work may be recast, transformed, or adapted. A work consisting of editorial revisions, annotations, elaborations, or other modifications which, as a whole, represent an original work of authorship, is a "derivative work.

A derivative work thus is defined as an original work that is independently copyrightable. To infringe the exclusive right to prepare a derivative work granted by the Copyright Act to the copyright owner, the infringer need not actually have copied the original work or even have fixed in a tangible medium of expression the allegedly infringing work.[18] The right, therefore, to create the derivative work can be a useful tool in counterbalancing attempts to pirate computer programs and the issue of fair use.

The Copyright Act creates an exemption for a lawful owner of a purchased license for a computer program to adapt the copyrighted program if the actual adaptation "is created as an essential step in the utilization of the computer program in conjunction with a machine and it is used in no other manner."[19] The adaptation cannot be transferred to a third party. The right to adapt is, in essence, the right to modify or, in the language of the Copyright Act, to create a derivative work. Such changes can be made even without the consent of the software owner so long as such modifications are used only internally and are necessary to the continuing use of the software.[20]

12.1.2.5   Copyright and the Issue of "Look and Feel" for Software Products.
Copyright protection ordinarily extends to the physical manifestation of the computer program in the source code and object code. The operation of that code, as it translates to what the human mind perceives, has been described as the "look and feel" of the program. In attempting to quantify the concept of "look and feel," courts have considered whether the organization, structure, and sequence of the program can be protected. In the United States, *Whelan Associates, Inc. v. Jaslow Dental Lab., Inc.*[21] gave the greatest extension to protecting "look and feel." In that case, none of the code had been copied and the program operated on a different platform. Nonetheless, copyright infringement was found because the organization, structure, and sequence of the program had been copied. The court recognized that the structure and logic of the program are the most difficult to create and that the idea could be protected as it was embodied in the program structure since, given the variety that was possible, the structure was not necessarily just an extension of the idea. Since *Whelan,* courts in the United States have retreated from such broad protection. In 1992, *Computer Associates, Inc. v. Altai, Inc.*[22] developed the so-called abstraction-filtration test. The results of that test define as unprotectable: (1) program structures that are dictated by operating efficiency or functional demands of the program and therefore deemed part of the idea and (2) all tools and subroutines that may be deemed included in the public domain. Only what remains is to be compared for possible copyright infringement.

While protection of "look and feel" may vary among the different federal circuits, in general, the courts are swinging away from broader protection. However, this may not necessarily be true internationally; English law appears to grant the broader protections afforded by the *Whelan* decision.

12.1.2.6   Digital Millennium Copyright Act.   In 1998, Congress passed the Digital Millennium Copyright Act (DMCA) to address concerns raised by the Internet and copyright issues in the context of our increasingly technological society. The DMCA creates a civil remedy for its violation as well as criminal penalties starting after October 2000. One of the purposes of the DMCA is to protect the integrity of copyright information. Removal of copyright notice, or distribution knowing that such copyright has been removed, is now actionable.[23] Both civil and criminal remedies also now exist if one circumvents "a technological measure that effectively controls access to a work protected" by the Copyright Act.[24] Thus, efforts to circumvent access limitations on copyrighted software are now punishable under the DMCA. In addition, it is a civil violation and a crime to "manufacture, import, offer to the public, provide or otherwise traffic in any technology, product, service, device, component, or part thereof" that "is primarily designed or produced for the purpose of circumventing

a technological measure that effectively controls access to a work protected" under the Copyright Act.[25]

A technological measure effectively controls access to a work if the measure, "in the ordinary course of its operation, requires the application of information or a process or a treatment, with the authority of the copyright owner, to gain access to the work."[26] One circumvents such technology measure if one uses a means "to descramble a scrambled work, to decrypt an encrypted work, or otherwise to avoid, bypass, remove, deactivate, or impair a technological measure," without the authority of the copyright owner.[27]

The DMCA, however, explicitly carves out all defenses to copyright infringement, including the doctrine of fair use, as being unaffected by the passage of the act. Moreover, while the DMCA prohibits the act of reverse engineering if such an act requires circumvention of a technology measure as defined in the DMCA, the act also creates an important exception that recognizes the right to reverse engineer if (1) the person has lawfully obtained the right to use a copy of a computer program, and (2) the sole purpose of circumventing the technology measure is to identify and analyze "those elements of the program that are necessary to achieve interoperability of an independently created computer program with other programs."[28] The DMCA creates a similar exemption for circumvention for the purpose of "enabling the interoperability of an independently created computer program with other programs, if such means are necessary to achieve such interoperability."[29] The term "interoperability" is defined to encompass the "ability of computer programs to exchange information and of such programs mutually to use the information which has been exchanged."[30] The information acquired through these permitted acts of circumvention also may be provided to third parties so long as it is solely used for the same purposes.[31]

Exempt from the DMCA, as well, are "good faith" acts of circumvention where the purpose is encryption research. A permissible act of encryption research requires that (1) the person lawfully have obtained a copy, (2) the act is necessary to the research, (3) there was a good faith effort to obtain authorization before the circumvention, and (4) such act does not constitute an infringement under a different section of the Copyright Act or under the Computer Fraud and Abuse Act of 1986. With the caveat that it must be an act of good faith encryption research, the technological means for circumvention can be provided to others who are working collaboratively on such research. The issue of good faith encryption research looks to what happened to the information derived from the research. If it was disseminated in a manner that was likely to assist infringement, as opposed to reasonably calculated to advance the development of encryption technology, then the act still falls outside of the exemption. Other factors that go into the determination of "good faith" are whether the person conducting the research is trained, experienced, or engaged in the field of encryption research and whether the researcher provides the copyright owner with a copy of the findings.

The DMCA also has a bias against the collection or dissemination of personally identifying information. Thus, it is not a violation of the DMCA to circumvent a technology measure that essentially protects, collects, or disseminates personally identifying information, provided that the circumvention has no other effect and provided that the program itself does not contain a conspicuous notice warning of the collection of such information and a means to prevent or restrict such collection.[32]

Finally, in so far as relevant to this chapter, the DMCA also excludes from its scope "security testing." The DMCA grants permission to engage in security testing that, but for that permission, would violate the terms of the act. If the security testing, for some reason, violated some other provision of the Copyright Act of the Computer

Fraud and Abuse Act of 1986, then it is still an act of infringement. The DMCA, in part, considers whether a violation occurred by how the information was used. The factors to be considered include if the information was used to promote the security of the owner or operator of the computer network or system, was shared with the developer, and was used in a manner that would not facilitate infringement.[33] For purposes of the DMCA, security testing means accessing either an individual computer or network for the purpose of "good faith testing, investigating, or correcting, a security flaw or vulnerability, with the authorization of the owner or operator."[34]

The criminal penalties for violation of the DMCA can be quite severe. If the violation is willful for commercial gain, the first offense bears a fine of up to $500,000 or five years' imprisonment. Subsequent violations bear fines of up to $1 million or 10 years' imprisonment. Civil remedies include an order to restrain the violation, damages for lost profits, damages for recovery of the infringer's profits, or statutory damages for each violation. Depending on the section of the DMCA at issue, each violation can generate fines of up to $2,500 or $25,000. Since each act of infringement can constitute a violation, the statutory fines can become quite substantial.

12.1.2.7   Semiconductor Chip Protection Act of 1984.   The Semiconductor Chip Protection Act of 1984 (SCPA) protects as part of the Copyright Act "mask works fixed in a semiconductor product."[35] What the SCPA actually protects is not the product itself but the circuit design or blueprint from being copied. Because of reverse engineering, the protections afforded by SCPA are limited in practice.

12.1.2.8   Computer Fraud and Abuse Act of 1986.   In 1984, Congress passed the original version of the Computer Fraud and Abuse Act (CFAA).[36] The general purpose was to protect "Federal interest computers" by criminalizing intentional and unauthorized access to those computers that resulted in damage to the computers or the data stored on them. The statute was substantially amended in 1986[37] and again in 1996[38] and now contains both criminal and private civil enforcement provisions.

The statute proscribes the following activities:

- Knowingly accessing a computer without authority or in excess of authority, thereafter obtaining U.S. government data to which access is restricted and delivering, or attempting to deliver, the data to someone not entitled to receive it.[39]

- Intentionally accessing a computer without authority or in excess of authority and thereby obtaining protected consumer financial data.[40]

- Intentional and unauthorized access of a U.S. government computer that affects the use of the computer by or for the U.S. government.[41]

- Accessing a computer used in interstate commerce knowingly and with the intent to defraud and, as a result of the access, fraudulently obtaining something valued in excess of $5,000.[42]

- Causing damage to computers used in interstate commerce by (1) knowingly transmitting a program, code, and so on that intentionally causes such damage, or (2) intentionally accessing the computer without authority and causing such damage.[43]

- Knowingly, and with the intent to defraud, trafficking in computer passwords for computers used in interstate commerce or by the U.S. government.[44]

- Transmitting threats to cause damage to a protected computer with the intent to extort money or anything of value.[45]

The criminal penalties range from fines to imprisonment for up to 20 years for multiple offenses. As discussed in the "Piracy" section below, the CFAA has become a prominent element of claims by the U.S. government and private parties seeking to protect data that is not always protected by other statutory schemes.

12.1.3   Patent Protection.   Ideas, which are not protected by copyright, can be protected through a patent. In general, the patent laws protect the functionality of a product or process. A patent can be properly obtained if the invention is new, useful, nonobvious, and disclosed. The patent exchanges a grant of an exclusive monopoly for the invention in return for disclosure. Disclosure is the trigger point for patentability. The disclosure supports the claims of patentability—that is, it sets up the claim that the invention is both new and nonobvious—and also the scope of what can be protected. Thus, 35 U.S.C. § 112 provides:

> The specification shall contain a *written description* of the invention, and of the manner and process of making and using it, in such full, clear, concise and exact terms as to *enable any person skilled in the art* to which it pertains, or with which it is most nearly connected, to make and use the same, and shall set forth the *best mode* contemplated by the inventor of carrying out his invention.
> The specification shall conclude with one or more claims particularly pointing out and *distinctly claiming* the subject matter which the applicant regards as his invention (emphasis added).

A patent, therefore, must disclose the best mode for implementing the invention, a clear written description of the invention, sufficient detail so that a practitioner can understand and make use of the description, and distinct claims, in order for a patent to issue. The application gives notice of the technology involved in the patent so as to put the public on fair notice of what would constitute an infringement, by adequate disclosure of the invention. From a public policy perspective, the disclosure enlarges the public knowledge. From the inventor's perspective, the trade-off is disclosure for exclusivity. Depending on how the invention is to be used and the areas in which protection will be necessary, disclosure may not be the best means of protecting the invention. This is particularly true if the inventor is not convinced it will be deemed nonobvious from prior art, in which case it will be subject to challenge, or if, after disclosure, other companies may legally use the disclosed information for competitive advantage. The effects of disclosure should be carefully considered before applying for patent protection.

12.2   APPLICATION INTERNATIONALLY

12.2.1   Brief Overview.   Because the laws of the United States are just the laws of one nation among many, the enforcement of U.S. law and the protection of intellectual property rights in large part depend on international treaty. To the extent that the infringing acts or acts of piracy may be deemed to occur in the United States, or the infringers can be found in the United States, then the United States has sufficient jurisdiction over these acts to enforce its laws. In other words, such actors can be sued directly in the courts of the United States for violation of the laws of the United States.

Apart from direct enforcement, international protection is usually a vehicle of bilateral agreements between the United States and individual countries or a function of international protocols or treaties to which the United States is a signatory. Thus, for example, the Paris Convention for the Protection of Industrial Property[46] establishes a system for recognizing priority of invention, but only among member countries. In addition, there is the Patent Cooperation Treaty (PCT), a multilateral treaty with more than 50 signatories. The PCT permits the filing of an international application that simplifies the filing process when a patent is sought in more than one nation. For copyright protection, there is also a series of international treaties and agreements that include the Berne Convention,[47] the Universal Copyright Convention, and the World Trade Organization (WTO) Agreement.[48] Canada, Mexico, and the United States also signed the North American Free Trade Agreement (NAFTA) in December1992. NAFTA addresses intellectual property and requires that member states afford the same protection to intellectual property as members of GATT (General Agreement on Tariffs and Trade). At a minimum, members of GATT must adopt four international conventions, including the Paris Convention and the Berne Convention.

These agreements, conventions, and treaties in large part do not attempt to reconcile the differences in the national laws of intellectual property. The particular national rules and nuances are simply too complicated and there are too many differences of opinion to expect that these differences could be reconciled internally. Rather, in large measure, these international accords attempt to codify comity between the member nations so that each will recognize the legitimacy of the intellectual property rights in the other.

12.2.2 Agreement on Trade-Related Aspects of Intellectual Property Rights. On December 8, 1994, the Agreement on Trade-Related Aspects of Intellectual Property Rights (TRIPS) was signed into law in the United States. The signing of TRIPS required changes to be made in U.S. statutes and regulations to bring them into conformity with international norms. TRIPS, however, was a product of the United States and other industrial countries pressing for stronger, more uniform standards for treating internationally with intellectual property. The basic structure of TRIPS is to set the minimum standard of protection for intellectual property with each member nation free to adopt more stringent standards. Under the rubric used in the United States, TRIPS applies to copyrights, patents, trademarks, service marks, masks works (integrated circuit designs), and trade secrets. It also covers geographical indications[49] and industrial designs.[50] Not addressed by TRIPS, although part of the international jargon for intellectual property, are breeder's rights[51] and utility models.[52] Thus, TRIPS establishes no standards for these concepts; each nation is left to set the parameters of protection unimpeded by TRIPS.

It is not by accident that TRIPS was negotiated within the context of GATT, which had set the international standards for trade tariffs and had provided remedies of trade retaliation if such standards were not adhered to. The structure of GATT provided the means under which developing countries agreed to reduce their trade tariffs in exchange for the right to export innovative products under an exclusive monopoly conveyed by intellectual property rights. The second benefit to the GATT format was to provide a means for trade retaliation if under the dispute resolution provisions of TRIPS, the WTO has determined that there is noncompliance. In reality, it is obvious that TRIPS benefits industrial nations, which are more likely to be at the forefront of innovation and more concerned with the protection of their citizens' intellectual property.[53] The major concession wrung by the developing countries under TRIPS was obtaining a period of four to 11 years to implement TRIPS and to bring their national laws into conformity.

TRIPS generally reflects the U.S. view that focuses on the economic underpinnings for intellectual property rights as serving the greater societal interests. There is thus a shift from "societal" interests to "enterprise" interests. In particular, TRIPS adopts high minimum standards for patents standards that will require significant legislative changes in developing countries. On the other hand, the copyright section affords less protection than may be afforded by European nations, but it is in line with treatment in the United States. In short, TRIPS responds to the concern of enterprises in the United States that too loose a system of international protection has enabled imitation of U.S. innovations through copying and outright piracy.

12.2.2.1 *Trade-Related Aspects of Intellectual Property Rights and Trade Secrets.*
Under its category for "Protection of Undisclosed Information," TRIPS provides protection for the type of information routinely referred to as trade secrets in the United States. Member nations are required to implement laws that safeguard information, lawfully possessed, from being disclosed to, acquired by, or used by others without consent and contrary to "honest commercial practices" if such information is (1) a secret in that it is not in the public domain, (2) has commercial value because it is a secret, and (3) has been subject to reasonable steps to maintain its secrecy.

Because discussions that led to TRIPS are not institutionally preserved, unlike the U.S. congressional record, there is no negotiating history to be consulted to flesh out the meaning of the spare paragraphs instituting trade secret protection. There do, however, appear to be differences from the total panoply of protections afforded in the United States. The concept of public domain articulated by TRIPS is information that is "not, as a body or in the precise configuration and assembly of its components, generally known among or readily accessible to persons within the circles that normally deal with the kind of information in question." This articulation appears to address technological formulations of information as opposed to general commercial information, such as financial information, that is generally considered proprietary and confidential in the United States. The focus on a technology formulation for protected information is bolstered by TRIPS' requirement that the information have commercial value. Thus, other types of information that are not part of a traded article may be deemed to have no commercial "value" and therefore to fall outside of the scope of protection. Depending on the particular jurisdiction in the United States, there is a distinction between confidential information and trade secrets based on the requirement that a trade secret must have commercial value. This, in turn, has been held to mean that information that is not exploited commercially is unprotectable under the law of trade secret. For example, the results of failed experiments that never resulted in a commercial product lack commercial value, even though such experiments certainly are helpful in the next round of exploration, in that they are signposts of what not to do.

The lesson to be drawn is that one should not assume symmetry of protections just because of the TRIPS provision. Instead, as part of the reasonable steps to maintain secrecy, enterprises need to consider carefully thought out and structured contractual provisions as well as a system of data caching that leaves truly confidential data in the United States, even if access is permitted outside. Improper takings of such data are, arguably, acts that occur in the United States, and such acts are subject to enforcement and punishment under the laws of the United States.

12.2.2.2 *Trade-Related Aspects of Intellectual Property Rights and Copyright.*
TRIPS embraces the United States general model for copyright protection in its opening statement that: "[c]opyright protection shall extend to expressions and not to ideas, procedures, methods of operation or mathematical concepts as such." All member nations agree that, as to the protection of copyrights, the Berne Convention will apply. Under the Berne Convention, the duration of a copyright is the life of the author plus 50

years. If the life of a natural person is not involved, then it is ordinarily 50 years from publication. In addition, computer programs, whether in source or in object code, are to be protected as literary works under the Berne Convention. TRIPS also recognizes that compilations of data can be protected as creative works. Article 10, paragraph 2 explicitly provides:

> Compilations of data or other material, whether in machine readable or other form, which by reason of the *selection* or *arrangement* of their contents constitute *intellectual creations* shall be protected as such. Such protection, which shall not extend to the data or material itself, shall be without prejudice to any copyright subsisting in the data or material itself (emphasis added).

TRIPS, therefore, does establish some minimum standard in the growing debate over what protections will be afforded a database. In the United States, the clear demarcation point for unprotected information is compilations that represent no more than "sweat-of-the-brow" efforts. Such compilations cannot be copyrighted.[54] The classic example of a "sweat-of-the-brow" is the copying and alphabetical organizing of names, addresses, and telephone numbers that are in telephone books. In the United States, the key for copyright protection is the creator's original contribution of selection and arrangement. Thus, arguably, the TRIPS provision mimics the law of the United States.

The European Union (EU) has taken a more protective path. In its 1996 European DataBase Directive, the EU granted databases *sui generis* protection as their own, unique form of intellectual property. Under the EU directive, a database is "a collection of independent works, data or other materials arranged in a systematic or methodical way and individually accessible by electronic or other means." A database may be protected either because it represents a work of "intellectual creation" or because it was compiled through "substantial investment." The EU directive protects such databases from unauthorized extraction or use for a period of 15 years, with the ability to extend the period for an additional 15 years if there was a "substantial new investment" in the database. Such protection extends to databases of EU members and to databases of nationals of other countries that offer protections similar to the EU.

The United States, despite a number of legislative proposals, has not adopted a concomitant rule. The result, at least for multinationals, is that entities which rely on databases should consider "locating" such databases within an EU member country so as to take advantage of the EU's database protections.

12.2.2.3 Trade-Related Aspects of Intellectual Property Rights and Patents.
TRIPS requires that all members recognize the right to patent products or processes in all fields of technology. A patentable invention must be new and inventive and have an industrial application. The patent application must fully and clearly disclose the invention so that a person skilled in the art could carry out the invention. The best mode for carrying out the invention as of the filing date also must be disclosed. Patent rights are to be enforced without discrimination as to place of invention or whether the product is imported or produced locally. The patent of a product conveys the exclusive right to prevent, without consent of the inventor, the making, using, offering for sale, selling, or importing of the product. The patent of a process conveys the exclusive right to prevent all of the above for products that result from the process as well as the use of the process itself. The holder of a patent also has the rights to assign, transfer, or license the patent. The minimum period for a protecting a patent is 20 years from filing.

TRIPS gives each member state the right to carve out from patentability certain subject matters that have as their purpose the protection of human, animal, or plant life, or to avoid serious prejudice to the environment. In addition, TRIPS permits a member state to allow other use without authorization from the patent holder. The section defining when such use is permissible is the most detailed section among the patent provisions of TRIPS. In general, it permits such use only (1) after an effort to obtain a license from the patent holder on reasonable commercial terms and conditions, (2) with adequate remuneration to the patent holder, (3) if such use is limited predominantly to the domestic market of the member nation, and (4) if there is a review of the decision to permit, as well as the compensation, by a "higher authority in that Member."

One of the circumstances envisioned by TRIPS is the granting of a second patent that cannot be exploited without infringing an earlier (first) patent. In such cases, a member nation may grant authority if the invention embodied in the second patent represents an "important technical advance of considerable economic significance" with respect to the first patent's invention, and a cross-license on reasonable terms is granted to the holder of the first patent to use the second patent. For process patents, TRIPS creates a limited burden on the alleged infringer to prove that the identical product was produced using a different process. In particular, a member state can create a presumption that the process patent was violated in circumstances where the product is new, or where the patent holder is unable to demonstrate what process was actually used.

12.2.2.4 *Trade-Related Aspects of Intellectual Property Rights and Anticompetitive Restrictions.*

TRIPS acknowledges that some licensing practices or other conditions with respect to intellectual property rights may restrain competition, adversely effect trade, and impede the transfer and dissemination of technology. Accordingly, TRIPS permits member nations to specify practices that constitute an abuse of intellectual property rights, and to adopt measures to control or limit such practices, so long as the regulation is consistent with TRIPS' other provisions. In the event that a national of a member nation violates another member's laws and regulations regarding anticompetitive activity, TRIPS provides for the right of the involved nations confidentially to exchange information regarding the nationals and their activities.

12.2.2.5 *Remedies and Enforcement Mechanisms.*

Each member nation is expected to provide an enforcement mechanism under its national laws to permit effective action against any act of infringement. Such procedures are to include remedies to prevent acts of infringement as well as to deter future acts. TRIPS imposes the obligation that all such procedures be "fair and equitable" and not be "unnecessarily complicated or costly" or involve "unwarranted delays."[55] In general, these remedies mean access to civil judicial procedures with evidentiary standards that shift the burden of going forward to the claimed infringer, once the rights holder has presented reasonably available evidence to support its claim. Damages may be awarded sufficient to compensate the rights holder for the infringement if the "infringer knew or had reasonable grounds to know that he was engaging in infringing activity." This means that vigilance and notice are essential to have meaningful protection for intellectual property rights, since notice is the best means for setting up a damage claim. TRIPS permits its members to allow the recovery of lost profits or predetermined (statutory) damages even when the infringer did not know that it was engaged in infringing behavior. While injunctive relief is to be provided for, remedies may be limited in circumstances involving patent holders, as discussed above, where adequate compensation is paid and the alleged infringer has otherwise complied with the provisions of its national law permitting such use upon payment of reasonable compensation. In order to deter further infringement, infringing materials may be ordered destroyed or disposed of noncommercially.

In addition to civil remedies, TRIPS requires criminal penalties in cases of "willful trademark counterfeiting or copyright piracy on a commercial scale."[56]

12.3 PIRACY

12.3.1 The Marketplace. For as long as ideas and innovation have been a source of commercial or social value, the terms on which these ideas and innovations have been available for use and exchange by others have been the subject of significant tension. While inventors and creators of commercially viable products and processes want to maximize the return on their investment, marketplace pressure for cost efficiency (and human and corporate greed) fuels a constant drive to remove the inventors' and creators' royalties from the cost of production. And as we have seen repeatedly over the past 15 years in the technology context, many people believe that innovations and creations that make computing easier should be freely available to the marketplace. Consequently, the ancient notion of piracy, the unauthorized boarding of a ship to commit theft and now used to refer to the unauthorized use of another's invention or production,[57] remains alive and well.

The demand for unlicensed access to and use of software and entertainment media increases annually. In its sixth annual survey regarding computer security among corporate and governmental institutions, the Computer Security Institute and the U.S. Federal Bureau of Investigation (FBI) found that 91 percent of all respondents discovered employees who abused Internet privileges by, among other things, downloading pirated software.[58] A study by the Business Software Association and the Software & Industry Information Association estimates that the worldwide revenue loss from the piracy (unlawful copying and distribution) of software exceeded $12 billion in 1999.[59] In a separate study by the Business Software Alliance, the piracy rate in the United States in 2000 was 24 percent; in several Asian countries, it exceeded 90 percent.[60] In countries such as China, piracy is not merely sanctioned; it constitutes an investment by government agencies.[61]

In recent years, in large part due to the saturation of Internet access, there has been a tremendous proliferation of technologies designed to access and distribute (without authorization) protected software applications and entertainment media. This proliferation has posed a tremendous challenge for license holders, legislators, and law enforcement authorities. The results have included attempts to punish both unauthorized access and use of protected material. In the process, the definition of what is protected has been transformed, and some confusion has arisen about the extent of that protection when the Internet is involved.

12.3.2 Authorized Use. The availability of, and access to, data on and through the World Wide Web is raising new questions about the scope of intellectual property protection. From the internal process employed in downloading Web pages to the use of automated tools to search for and extract information from millions of Web sites and databases, new standards are being considered to accommodate advanced technology that retains protected interest in the creator's work. Currently, the discussions focus principally on two areas: authorized use and authorized access. This section briefly addresses the parameters of authorized use. The next section discusses the genesis and current standards governing authorized access. The discussion in each section assumes that there is no express permission to use or access the original work or data.

12.3.2.1   Database Protection.

Databases, the organized compilation of information in an electronic format, are prominent elements of any discussion concerning copyright protection. Compilations of information, data, and works are protectable under the Copyright Act.[62] To secure copyright protection for a compilation, a party must demonstrate that (1) it owned a valid copyright in the compilation; (2) the alleged infringer copied at least a portion of the compilation; and (3) the portion so copied was protected under the Copyright Act. See *Feist Publications, Inc. v. Rural Telephone Service Co., Inc.*[63] In this context, the Copyright Act protects the "original" selection, coordination, or arrangement of the data contained in the compilation.[64]

To the extent that compilations contain purely factual information—for example, existing prices of products and services—there is no protection because the facts themselves lack originality.[65] It does not matter that the author "created" the facts of the prices being charged for the product or service.[66] To sustain a claim of copyright protection for compilations of fact, the author must demonstrate creativity in the arrangement of the data. Standard or routine arrangements are likewise beyond the act's umbrella.[67]

Recently, the United States Supreme Court held that the compilation into a database of original works by contributing authors to newspapers and magazines violates the copyrights of the individual authors when the database does not reproduce the authors' articles as part of the original collective work to which the articles were contributed. In *New York Times Co., Inc. v. Tasini*,[68] authors who contributed articles and other works to the *New York Times, Time* magazine, and *Newsday* sued when they learned that the articles that they sold to the publishers for use in the respective publications were being reproduced and made available online, through LEXIS/NEXIS, an online database, and on CD-ROM. In most instances, the reproductions were of the individual articles outside of the newspaper or magazine context that is, the collection of works separately protected by the Copyright Act. The Supreme Court held that, because the publishers of the new collective works made no original or creative contribution to the individual authors' original works, they could not reproduce and distribute those works outside of the format that each publisher created for the original collections of works, without permission from, or payments to, each author.[69]

12.3.2.2   Applications of Transformative and Fair Use.

The concepts of transformative use and fair use (to the extent that they are separable) discussed earlier in this chapter have played a substantial role in recent decisions involving the authorized use of electronic media and the Internet. The starting point for this application of the doctrine is the U.S. Supreme Court's decision in *Sony Corporation v. Universal City Studios, Inc.*,[70] the famous battle over Betamax initiated by the movie industry. At issue was whether electronic recording machines could record television programs to permit individuals to "time shift" television programs (to record programs for viewing at a time other than the time of airing). In its decision, the Court found in *Sony* that time shifting was a productive use of the television programs for a purpose other than the original commercial broadcast and was not an attempt either to duplicate the original purpose or to impact the commercial market for these programs. The Court emphasized the noncommercial element inherent in time shifting.[71]

12.3.2.3 Internet Hosting and File Distribution. The growth of the breadth and scope of the Internet has been accompanied by increasing questions about the extent to which the distribution of otherwise protected expressions change their form when converted into an electronic format. These questions arise for Internet service providers (ISP), which provide the pathway for distributing protected material, and for end users who post such materials on their Web sites and bulletin boards. For ISPs, the DMCA provides some initial comfort.

Title II of the DMCA, designated the "Online Copyright Infringement Limitation Act,"[72] establishes a safe harbor for any provider of "online services or network access, or the operator of facilities thereof, . . ." including "digital online communications, between or among points specified by user, of material of the user's choosing, without modification to the content of the material as sent or received."[73] Those that qualify are protected from direct copyright infringement claims "by reason of the storage at the direction of a user of material that resides on a system or network controlled or operated by or for the service provider," so long as the service provider can show that (1) it has no actual or constructive knowledge that its system contains infringing materials and, once it learns of such materials in its system, acts expeditiously to remove those materials; (2) receives no financial benefit directly attributable to the infringing activity; *and* (3) upon receipt of a notice of infringing material on its system, responds expeditiously to remove, or disable access to, the material.[74]

Assuming that the safe harbor does not apply (as, e.g., because the ISP failed to act on a notice of infringing activity), many service providers may nonetheless escape liability. In the first, and seminal, case on this topic, *Religious Technology Center v. Netcom On-Line Communication Services, Inc.,* 907 F.Supp. 1361 (N.D. Cal. 1995),[75] an ISP hosted a bulletin board service on which Church of Scientology publications were posted by a former minister. The district court held that the ISP must demonstrate that its use was of public benefit (facilitating dissemination of creative works including, but not limited to, the infringing work); that its financial gain was unrelated to the infringing activity (e.g., subscription fees from providing e-mail systems rather than fees from the display or sale of the infringing work); that its use was unrelated to the use of the owner of the work; that the ISP copied only what was necessary to provide its service; and that its use of the material had no demonstrable effect on the potential market for the work.[76]

For Web site owners and users who post allegedly infringing material, the courts have had much less difficulty discarding the transformative fair use arguments. This has been particularly true in the purely commercial setting, as where the infringing party gains direct financial benefit from the infringing material[77] and where the posted material is an exact copy of the protected work without any transformation to something creative or original.[78] In a case that goes to the heart of the open-access nature of the Internet, one court recently held that a copyright owner who posts work on the Internet for free distribution as shareware may defeat a transformative fair use defense by also posting an express reservation of distribution rights.[79]

12.3.2.4 Web Crawlers and Fair Use. The Internet, premised on open exchange of data and economic efficiency, has spawned a spate of data search and aggregation software tools that scan the Web looking for information requested by the user. The process used by these search engines[80] includes identifying data on the Web that conforms to the search parameters and then downloading that data. Since the copying usually occurs without the express permission of the copyright owner, some have argued that such copying constitutes an infringement. While there is very little precedent concerning the application of transformative fair use to automated data retrieval systems, at least one court has upheld the use of the defense to an infringement claim.[81]

12.3.2.5   File Sharing.   Transformative fair use will not protect the verbatim retransmission of protected work in a different medium when there is a substantial and detrimental impact on the market for the protected work. In *A&M Records, Inc. v. Napster, Inc.,*[82] Napster enabled users to share music files over the Internet by downloading the file-sharing software to their hard drive, using the software to search for MP3 music files stored on other computers, and transferring copies of MP3 files from other computers. The Court of Appeals held that Napster users were merely retransmitting original works in a different medium and that this did not constitute a transformation of the original work. The court also found that sharing of music files over the Internet had, and would have, a significant and detrimental impact on the existing and potential market for CDs and digital downloads of the copyright owners' works. Picking up on the *Sony* decision's emphasis on the distinction between commercial and personal use, the Court of Appeals found that Napster's Web site effectively made the works available for use by the general public and not simply for the personal use of individual users.[83]

12.3.3   Authorized Access.   In addition to the traditional protection afforded the work itself, there has been an increasing effort over the past decade to protect access to the work—in effect, to restrict the keys to the copy machine. Like the developments surrounding authorized use, authorized access has developed in significant part due to the dynamics of the Internet. The legal foundation for the gatekeeping approach includes the Computer Fraud and Abuse Act (CFAA) and the DMCA. The result, at least in the Internet context, has been a tug-of-war between the open-access nature of the Web, the First Amendment, and protection for commercially proprietary information.

12.3.3.1   Computer Fraud and Abuse Act and "Without Authorization."   The linchpin among the relevant decisions concerning access to data under the CFAA is whether the access is "without authority" or "in excess of authority." The factors considered by the courts include the steps taken by the owner of the information to protect against disclosure or use, the extent of the defendants' knowledge regarding their authority to access or use the data, and the use(s) made of the data after gaining access. The legislative history indicates that the statute was intended to "punish those who illegally use computers for commercial advantage."[84]

Broadly speaking, there are two sets of circumstances to consider. In the first instance, is the actual access authorized either expressly or impliedly? In the Internet context, where there is a presumption of open access, the site or data owners must show that they took some steps to protect the contents of their site and to limit access to the data at issue.[85] Once those steps are taken, the protection constitutes a wall through which even automated search retrieval systems may not go without express permission.[86] Without the wall, there must be some evidence of an intent to access for an impermissible purpose, as when Intuit inserted "cookies" into the hard drives of home computers.[87]

Second, has the authorized access been improperly exceeded? Generally speaking, those who use their permitted access for an unauthorized purpose to the detriment of the site or data owner have violated the CFAA. Examples include employees who obtain trade secret information and transmit it via the employer's e-mail system to a competitor for which the employee is about to begin work[88]; using an ISP subscription membership to gain access to and harvest e-mail addresses of other subscribers in order to transmit unsolicited bulk e-mails[89]; and using access to an employer's e-mail system to alter and delete company files.[90]

12.3.3.2   Digital Millennium Copyright Act and Circumvention of Technological Protection.

Article 11 of the World Intellectual Property Organization Copyright Treaty required all signatory countries to provide adequate legal protection and remedies against the circumvention of technical measures intended to secure copyrights. In response, Congress adopted Section 1201 of the DMCA, which generally prohibits the act of circumventing, and trafficking in the technology that enables circumvention of, protection measures designed to control access to copyrighted work.[91] A spate of recent legal action demonstrates that this legislation will be strictly enforced by the courts and that the technologically savvy will be in no better position to gain access to protected technology than will anyone else.

In *RealNetworks, Inc. v. Streambox, Inc.,*[92] Streambox distributed software that enabled users to bypass the authentication process employed by RealNetworks, which distributes audio and video content over the Internet. Thus, Streambox users could get the benefit of the RealNetworks streaming audio and video content without compensating the copyright owners. The U.S. District Court in Washington state found that the Streambox software was a technological measure that was designed to circumvent the access and copy control measures intended to protect the copyright owners.[93]

In a case involving DVD encryption, a U.S. district court in New York found that posting links to sites where visitors may download the decryption program was trafficking in circumvention technology and was a violation of the DMCA.[94] In *Universal City Studios, Inc. v. Reimerdes,* the court rejected an argument that the use of the decryption software constituted free expression protected by the First Amendment of the U.S. Constitution.[95] And in a direct challenge to the constitutionality of the statute, several professors who responded to an open invitation from the Secure Digital Music Initiative Foundation (SDMIF) to find ways to penetrate copyright protection measures, sued for the right to publish the results of their work.[96] Edward Felten, Bede Liu, and others accepted SDMIF's invitation and successfully "cracked" the copyright security measures employed to protect digital music files. When the professors attempted to deliver a paper describing their success, SDMIF and others threatened litigation based on the anticircumvention provisions of the DMCA. The *Felten* lawsuit challenged the constitutionality of the DMCA in these circumstances.[97]

12.4   DAMAGES.

The Copyright Act contains several sections that specifically address the penalties and remedies for infringement. They include injunctive relief (i.e., a court order terminating the infringing conduct),[98] impounding and disposing of infringing articles,[99] damages,[100] litigation costs and attorneys' fees,[101] and criminal penalties.[102] While this chapter cannot address all of the permutations of remedies and penalties available, a few are worth mentioning.

Generically, a copyright owner must choose between its actual losses (i.e., what it actually lost and any profits realized by the infringer) and statutory damages.[103] Actual damages imply economic losses actually suffered as a result of the infringement. The kinds of actual damages that have been awarded include development costs of the software,[104] the economic consequences of lost customers,[105] lost future sales,[106] the value of the infringer's licensing fees where the licensor is precluded from market sales,[107] lost market value of the material infringed,[108] and lost royalty payments.[109] An award of actual damages is not automatic; the license holder has the burden of proving that the infringing activity and the economic loss are causally connected, at which point the infringing party must show that the license holder would have incurred the loss anyway.[110]

A copyright owner may elect to receive statutory damages rather than actual damages and the infringer's profits.[111] Making the election is mandatory, and it must be done before final judgment is entered. Once the election is made, it is final. The statutory damages generally range from $750 to $30,000 "for all infringements involved in the action, with respect to any one work, for which any two or more infringers are liable jointly and severally, ... For purposes of this section, all the parts of a compilation or derivative work constitute one work."[112] This amount may be increased to $150,000 if the court finds that the infringement was willful and reduced to $200 if the court finds that the infringer "was not aware and had no reason to believe" that their act was an infringement.[113]

Statutory damages are theoretically[114] intended to approximate the actual damages suffered and were crafted as an alternative compensation scheme for copyright owners, when actual damages are difficult to calculate. In determining whether to elect actual or statutory damages, a copyright owner ought to perform a careful analysis to determine how many separate infringements occurred that justify, under the statute, separate awards. While posting different copyrighted computer software programs on a bulletin board for downloading constitutes multiple infringements,[115] making multiple copies of the same cartoon character in different poses constitutes a single infringement because only one work was copied.[116]

As mentioned, this is one of the statutory schemes that discourages frivolous litigation by imposing the cost of litigating on the losing party. The statute permits the substantially prevailing party to recover its reasonable attorneys' fees and costs from the losing party. Who is the substantially prevailing party and what constitutes reasonable attorneys' fees are separate and distinct issues that will be decided by the courts.

There are criminal penalties for the willful and unauthorized copying of copyrighted material for commercial advantage or private financial gain. The acts punishable as a crime include willful circumvention of copyright protection systems[117] and the "reproduction or distribution, including by electronic means," of copyrighted works having a value greater than $1,000.[118] The criminal penalties include up to five years' imprisonment for a first offense and 10 years' imprisonment for subsequent offenses.[119]

12.5   CONCLUSION.   Both in the United States and elsewhere, the issue of intellectual property has assumed an importance almost equal to that of physical property. Throughout the world, as manufacturing becomes more and more commodified and suitable mainly for lowest-cost producers, the value placed on intellectual property increases in inverse proportion. Especially in developed nations, future economic advances appear more likely to come from intellectual property than from any other source.

As with other types of assets, the competition to acquire and retain intellectual property legally is invariably met by unethical and illegal efforts to deprive legitimate owners of their rights. It is necessary, therefore, to be fully aware of the mechanisms and procedures required to protect these rights.

This chapter has attempted to delineate the most important aspects of the problem. However, many facets of the legal questions remain unanswered or have been answered generally rather than in the context of a particular problem. Prudent guardians of intellectual property should continuously monitor the relevant judicial determinations and be certain to integrate them into a planned approach to protect these most valuable assets.

12.6   NOTES

1. See *Kewanee Oil Co. v. Bicron Corp.,* 416 U.S. 470, 473, 94 S. Ct. 1879, 40 L.Ed.2d 315 (1974).

2. The need to protect the information from general dissemination is what, in part, has given rise to the practice of nondisclosure agreements.

3. The 1980 Computer Software Copyright Act carved out for owners of computer programs a right to adapt, and for that purpose to copy, the program so that it functions on the actual computer in which it is installed. See discussion under the subheading "Derivative Works."

4. Ideas, if protectable at all, are protected by patent.

5. The Copyright Act, 17 U.S.C. § 109(b).

6. The Copyright Act, 17 U.S.C. § 102(b).

7. The Copyright Act itself in sections 108 through 121 provides detailed limitations on the copyright owner's exclusive rights. These limitations are simply a matter of statutory construction. In addition, courts developed the doctrine of fair use in an effort to balance the rights of copyright owner and the public interest. That doctrine is now codified as part of the copyright statute in 17 U.S.C. § 107.

8. See the House Report No. 94-1476, 94th cong., 2d Sess. 62 (1976) on the 1976 Act.

9. 977 F.2d 1510 (9th Cir. 1992), amended, *Sega Enterprises Ltd. v. Accolade, Inc.,* 1993 U.S. App. Lexis 78.

10. 977 F.2d at 1527-28.

11. 975 F.2d 832 (Fed. Cir. 1992), *petition for rehearing denied,* 1992 U.S. App. Lexis 30957 (1992).

12. 79 F.3d 1532 (11th Cir. 1996).

13. Compare *Micro Star v. Formgen Inc.,* 154 F.3d 1107 (9th Cir. 1998) (infringement found because copyrighted images displayed) with *Lewis Galoob Toys, Inc. v. Nintendo of America, Inc.,* 964 F.2d 965 (9th Cir. 1992) (no infringement although product compatible with Nintendo product).

14. 17 U.S.C. § 107.

15. 510 U.S. 569 (1994).

16. Id. at 577.

17. Id. at 580.

18. See the House Report No. 94-1476, 94th Cong., 2d Sess. 62 (1976) on the 1976 Copyright Act.

19. 17 U.S.C. § 117,

20. *Aymes v. Bonelli,* 47 F.3d 23 (2d Cir. 1995).

21. 797 F.2d. 1222 (3rd Cir. 1986)

22. 982 F.2d .693 (2d Cir. 1992).

23. 17 U.S.C. § 1202(b).

24. 17 U.S.C. § 1201(a).

25. 17 U.S.C. § 1201(a)(2).

26. 17 U.S.C. § 1201(a)(3).

27. Ibid.

28. 17 U.S.C. § 1201(f)(1).

29. 17 U.S.C. § 1201(f)(2).

30. 17 U.S.C. § 1201(f)(4).

31. 17 U.S.C. § 1201(f)(3).

32. 17 U.S.C. § 1201(i)(1).

33. 17 U.S.C. § 1201(j)(3).

34. 17 U.S.C. § 1201(j)(1).

35. 17 U.S.C. § 901(a)

36. Pub. L.98-474, codified at 18 U.S.C. § 1030.

37. Pub. L.99-474.

38. National Information Infrastructure Protection Act of 1996, Pub. L.104-294.

39. 18 U.S.C. § 1030(a)(1).

40. 18 U.S.C. § 1030(a)(2).

41. 18 U.S.C. § 1030(a)(3).

42. 18 U.S.C. § 1030(a)(4).

43. 18 U.S.C. § 1030(a)(5). *See Hotmail Corporation v. Van Money Pie, Inc.,* 1998 WL 388389, 47 U.S.P.Q.2d 1020 (N.D. Cal. 1998).

44. 18 U.S.C. § 1030(a)(6).

45. 18 U.S.C. § 1030(a)(7).

46. The Paris Convention was initially concluded in 1883 and updated in 1967. It is administered by the World Intellectual Property Organization, an agency of the United Nations. The Paris Convention has provisions that apply to patents, trademarks, service marks, industrial designs (similar to design patents), and unfair competition. Approximately 100 nations are now signatories to the Paris Convention.

47. Until the adoption of TRIPS, the Berne Convention was the other major international agreement. Like the Paris Convention, it is administered by the World Intellectual Property Organization. The Berne Convention, first adopted in 1886, has undergone a series of revisions. The convention includes "every production in the literary, scientific and artistic domain whatever may be the mode or form of its expression." Berne Convention, Art. 2, ¶1. Essentially, it assures that a work protected within a member state will also be protected outside of the member state without being subject to discriminating formalities. The number of signatories to the Berne Convention presently exceeded 80 nations.

48. The WTO effectively began operating on July 1, 1995, as a result of the 1994 Uruguay Round Agreements. The WTO replaces GATT (General Agreement on Tariffs and Trade), which had been operable since 1950. Congress ratified the Uruguay Round Agreements in December 1994. The WTO acts similarly to other international economic organizations in the area of international trade.

49. Geographical indications are marks or other expressions that state the country, region, or place in which a product or service originates.

50. Industrial designs protect the aesthetic look of the product and is similar but not identical to the U.S. notion of trade dress. Products may be afforded protection based on novelty or originality of design, depending on national law.

51. Breeder's rights confer protection on new and different plant varieties.

52. Utility models protect the manner in which a product works or functions and as such are different from industrial design, which protects only the aesthetics of the product. Generally, utility models address mechanical functioning, which in the United States is not protectable unless patentable. Thus, the innovation in the United States must be significant to warrant protection.

53. Until 1989, the developing countries largely refused to negotiate standards. Threats by the United States of trade sanctions under the United States Trade Act played a significant role in altering the positions of economically weaker developing countries. In particular, China, India, Taiwan, and Thailand were all investigated.

54. *Feist Publications v. Rural Telephone System,* 499 U.S. 340 (1991).

55. TRIPS, Article 41.

56. TRIPS, Article 61.

57. *Webster's Seventh New Collegiate Dictionary* (1967 ed.), p. 644.

58. *Computer Security Issues and Trends,* Vol. VII, "2001 CSI/FBI Computer Crime and Security Survey" (hereafter the CSI/FBI Survey) p. 4.

59. *SIIA's Report on Global Software Piracy 2000,* p. 2.

60. Business Software Alliance, *Sixth Annual BSA Global Software Piracy Study,* pp. 5-6. In its report, the BSA notes that software piracy was in decline for several years prior to 2000 but increased slightly in that year over 1999. Notwithstanding this increase, the dollar value of the losses sustained as a result of piracy decreased in 2000 over 1999 by 3.5 percent. The

BSA membership includes Adobe, Microsoft, Compaq, Dell, IBM, Intel, Apple Computers and Symantec.

61. See Lamb and Rosen, *Global Piracy and Financial Valuation of Intellectual Property,* pp. 11.1–11.3.

62. "The subject matter of copyright . . . includes compilations." 17. U.S.C. § 103.

63. 499 U.S. 340, 361 (1991).

64. Id. at 350–351. *See* 17 U.S.C. §§ 101–103.

65. Id. at 344, 348–9. *See Ticketmaster Corp. v. Tickets.com, Inc.,* 2000 U.S. Dist. LEXIS 12987 (C.D. Cal. Aug. 10, 2000), *aff'd* 2001 U.S. App. LEXIS 1454 (9th Cir. Jan. 22, 2001).

66. *Feist Pub., Inc. v. Rural Tel., supra,* at 352–354, where the Court rejected the so-called "sweat-of-the-brow" doctrine.

67. *Matthew Bender & Co., Inc. v. West Publishing Co.,* 158 F.3d 674, 682 (2d Cir. 1998) ("[t]he creative spark is missing where: (i) industry conventions or other external factors so dictate the selection that any person composing a compilation of the type at issue would necessarily select the same categories of information, or (ii) the author made obvious, garden-variety, or routine selections").

68. 121 S.Ct. 2381; 150 L.Ed. 2d 500; 2001 U.S. LEXIS 4667; 69 U.S.L.W. 4567 (2001).

69. The Court found interesting the publishers' decision not to assert a claim of transformative fair use. Id. at 2390. See Section 12.1.2.3.3 (transformative use section), *supra.*

70. 464 U.S. 417 (1984).

71. Transformative fair use was recently applied to the use of Rio devices, which permit individual users to download purchased MP3 music files to a hard drive and then play them either on the PC or a CD. These devices were analogized to the Betamax time shifting discussed in *Sony* and were upheld primarily on that basis. *See Recording Industry Association of America v. Diamond Multimedia Systems, Inc.,* 180 F.3d 1072 (9th Cir. 1999).

72. DMCA, § 201, Pub. L. 105-304, 112 Stat. 2877 (1998) (codified at 17 U.S.C. § 101 note).

73. 17 U.S.C. § 512(k).

74. 17 U.S.C. § 512(c)(1). See *ALS Scan, Inc. v. RemarQ Communities, Inc.,* 239 F.3d 619 (4th Cir. 2001), where the Court of Appeals determined what notice was sufficient to remove the safe harbor protection.

75. The *Netcom* decision predated the DMCA and provided part of the rationale and reasoning used by Congress in drafting and passing Title II of the DMCA. *See* House Rep. 105-551(I), at 11.

76. The church raised a question of fact about the impact of the ISP's activity on its potential market by asserting that the posting of the church's materials on the bulletin board discouraged active participation by existing and potential congregants. Therefore, the court could not find for the ISP as a matter of law.

77. See e.g., *Playboy Enterprises, Inc. v. Frena,* 839 F. Supp. 1552 (M.D. Fla. 1993). The *Frena* decision, insofar as it holds the bulletin board service provider liable for infringement, has been expressly overruled by Title II of the DMCA. See House Rep. 105-551(I), at 11.

78. *Los Angeles Times v. Free Republic,* 2000 U.S. Dist. LEXIS 5669 (C.D. Cal. April 5, 2000). In the *Free Republic* decision, the court recognized the public benefit of posting articles for commentary and criticism but found that the initial postings contained little or no commentary that might transform the article into a new original work.

79. *Storm Impact, Inc. v. Software of the Month Club,* 13 F. Supp. 2d 782 (N.D. Ill. 1998).

80. There are various names for the components of the software programs that actually travel through the Web looking for data, including bots, crawlers, spiders, scrapers, and automated data retrieval systems.

81. *Kelly v. Arriba Soft,* 77 F. Supp. 2d 1116 (C.D. Cal. 1999).

82. 239 F.3d 1004 (9th Cir. 2001), *amended,* 2001 WL 314734 (9th Cir. April 3, 2001)

83. *See also UMG Recordings, Inc. v. MP3.com, Inc.,* 92 F. Supp. 2d 349 (S.D. N.Y. 2000), where the district court held that storing recordings from purchased CDs on MP3.com's servers for retransmission to other users was infringement and not transformative fair use.

84. Senate Rep. 104-357, pp. 7–8.

85. *Register.com, Inc. v. Verio, Inc.*, 126 F. Supp. 2d 238 (S.D. N.Y. 2000).

86. Id.

87. *In Re Intuit Privacy Litigation*, 138 F. Supp. 2d 1272 (2001). But see *U.S. v. Czubinski*, 106 F.3d 1069 (1st Cir. 1997), where the Court of Appeals found that an IRS employee who accessed private tax information in violation of IRS rules but did not disclose the accessed information could not be prosecuted under 18 U.S.C. § 1030(a)(4) because he lacked an intent to deprive the affected taxpayers of their right to privacy.

88. *Shurgard Storage Centers, Inc. v. Safeguard Self Storage, Inc.*, 119 F. Supp. 2d 1121 (W.D. Wash 2000).

89. *America Online, Inc. v. LCGM, Inc.*, 46 F. Supp. 2d 444 (E.D. Va. 1998).

90. *U.S. v. Middleton*, No. 99-10518 (9th Cir. November 16, 2000).

91. *Universal City Studios, Inc. v. Reimerdes*, 111 F. Supp. 2d 294, 316 (S.D.N.Y. 2000).

92. 2000 U.S. Dist. LEXIS 1889 (W.D. Wash. 2000).

93. Id. at pp. 19–21.

94. *Universal City Studios, Inc. v. Reimerdes, supra.*

95. Although defendant Shawn Remeirdes settled with the plaintiffs after the injunction was issued, his co-defendant, Eric Corley, appealed the District Court's decision to the Second Circuit Court of Appeals. On November 28, 2001, the Second Circuit upheld the injunction entered by the District Court. In its decision, the Court of Appeals provided a lengthy discussion about the protection afforded digital communications by the free speech clause of the First Amendment. *See Universal City Studios, Inc. v. Corley,* Second Circuit Court of Appeals Docket No. 00-9185 (November 28, 2001).

96. *Edward Felten, et al v. Recording Industry Association of America, Inc., et al,* U.S.D.C. Civil Action No. CV-01-2660 (D. N.J.) (First Amended Complaint filed June 26, 2001).

97. The suit filed by Felten was dismissed by the District Court shortly during the final editing of this article. As of that time, the deadline for filing an appeal had not expired.

98. 17 U.S.C. § 502

99. 17 U.S.C. § 503

100. 17 U.S.C. § 504

101. 17 U.S.C. § 505

102. 17 U.S.C. § 506.

103. 17 U.S.C. § 504(a).

104. *See Harris Market Research v. Marshall Marketing and Communications, Inc.,* 948 F.2d 1518 (10th Cir. 1991).

105. *See Regents of the University of Minnesota v. Applied Innovations, Inc.,* 685 F. Supp. 698, *aff'd* 876 F.2d 626 (8th Cir. 1987)

106. Id.

107. *See Cream Records, Inc. v. Jos. Schlitz Brewing Co.,* 754 F.2d 826 (9th Cir. 1985).

108. *See Eales v. Environmental Lifestyles, Inc.,* 958 F.2d 876 (9th Cir. 1992), *cert. den.* 113 S.Ct. 605.

109. *See Softel, Inc. v. Dragon Medical and Scientific Communications Ltd.,* 891 F. Supp. 935 (S.D.N.Y. 1995). Interestingly, in this case, the court also held that any increase in the infringer's profit may be considered when calculating the profit that must be disgorged to the license holder.

110. *See Harper & Row Publishers, Inc. v. Nation Enterprises,* 471 U.S. 539, 105 S.Ct. 2218 (1985); *Data General Corp. v. Grumman Systems Support Corp.,* 36 F.3d 1147 (1st Cir. 1994).

111. 17 U.S.C. § 504(c)(1).

112. Id.

113. 17 U.S.C. § 504(c)(2).

114. The theoretical nature of the relationship between actual and statutory damages is dramatically illustrated when the copyright owner demonstrates that the infringement was willful. *See Peer International Corp. v. Luna Records, Inc.,* 887 F. Supp. 560 (S.D. N.Y. 1995),

where the music publisher's president willfully infringed licensed and unlicensed works and was assessed $10,000 for the licensed works, $15,000 for the unlicensed works, and $25,000 that the president used in derivative format without permission even though actual damages were $4,107. Presumably this resulted from the court's attempt to find a way to punish the infringer since the statute makes no provision for punitive damages.

115. *See Central Point Software, Inc. v. Nugent,* 903 F. Supp. 1057 (E.D. Tex. 1995).

116. *See Walt Disney Co. v. Powell,* 897 F.2d 565 (D.C. Cir. 1990).

117. 17 U.S.C. §§ 1201, 1204(a).

118. 17 U.S.C. § 506(a)(2). For an interesting discussion of the applicability of this section, and the No Electronic Theft Act of 1997, P.L. 105-80, to the kind of file sharing offered by and through Napster, see Joseph D. Schleimer and Kenneth D. Freundlich, "Criminal Prosecution of Online File Sharing," *Journal of Internet Law,* Vol. 5, No. 2 (August 2001):14.

119. 18 U.S.C. § 2319.

CHAPTER 13

E-COMMERCE VULNERABILITIES

Anup K. Ghosh

CONTENTS

13.1 INTRODUCTION. This chapter provides a systematic look at the primary software components that make up e-commerce applications and provides an overview of the risks to each of these components.[1] The goal of this chapter is to point out that every system will have risks to its security and privacy that need to be systematically analyzed and ultimately addressed.

13.2 BREAKING E-COMMERCE SYSTEMS. To make a system more secure, it may be advisable to break it. Finding the vulnerabilities in a system is necessary in order to strengthen it, but breaking an e-commerce system requires a different mindset from that of the programmers who developed it. Instead of thinking about developing within a specification, a criminal or cracker looks outside the specifications.

Crackers believe that rules exist only to be broken, and they will always use a system in unexpected ways. In doing so, they usually will follow the path of least resistance. Those areas perceived to provide the strongest security, or most resistance to cracking, will likely be ignored. For example, if a system uses Secure Sockets Layer (SSL) to encrypt Web sessions between Web clients and the Web server, a cracker will not try to break the encryption stream but instead will look for an easier way to get at the data after they are decrypted and stored in the clear.

Crackers go where the money is—sometimes literally, sometimes not. They typically try to crack into a site only if there is some reward for their effort. Sometimes crackers are motivated by money, but as often by the lure of fame and notoriety. The level of protection should be commensurate with the value of the resource being protected. For instance, a Web site that publishes the menus for local restaurants may not run the risk of a full-scale denial of service or any other attack. It simply is not as attractive a target as a bank's online Web site. Similarly, most people do not bother encrypting e-mail messages because most potential snoopers are not interested in ordinary e-mail. On the other hand, sensitive e-mail from a high-profile organization should be encrypted.

It is important to remember that the e-commerce system is a chain that is only as strong as its weakest link.[2] Crackers naturally attempt to attack the weakest link. This explains why a site may deliberately set up a sacrificial machine (a "honey pot") with appealingly vulnerable services in order to track and monitor potential crackers. In e-commerce systems, because cryptography often is perceived to provide the strongest links, crackers generally attack host-side services and client-side content.

Maintaining strong host security, both inside and outside of firewalls, is critically important. One unfortunate side effect of corporate firewalls is that system administrators tend to relax host security. The result is that once crackers make it through or around the firewall, they can leverage the trust relationships inside so as to compromise many machines. The prudent administrator will exercise equal concern both at the entry to systems and within those systems.

13.3 CASE STUDY OF BREAKING AN E-BUSINESS. Consider an online investing e-business application and how a cracker might go about disassembling its security for malicious gain. Online investing has become very popular for several reasons. Rather than waiting for quarterly statements in the mail or dealing with a phone menu, customers can quickly view the status, balances, and current value of investment holdings by visiting the Web pages of their portfolio managers. If they wish to buy and sell equity shares on demand, they can establish online Web-enabled brokerage accounts. Exhibit 13.1 shows a simplified workflow diagram of an online investing application that enables users with established accounts to view portfolio holdings and cash balances, to update the stocks tracked, and to conduct online trades.

To see how this application can be broken, it is helpful to look at a sample network architecture that implements the online application. Exhibit 13.2 shows the network architecture of the system that implements the online investing application, along with example exploits. The system consists of the end users' client machines, the Internet, routers, firewall, front-end Web and e-mail servers, application servers, databases, and workstations.

There are many ways a cracker could break this online application. Exhibit 13.2 shows one possible scenario. In step 1 of the attack, the cracker uses the Internet and a Web browser to misuse one of the CGI (computer graphics information) scripts that implement the application on a server. The CGI script could be a development CGI script inadvertently left on the server before going into production, a default CGI script from an application server distribution, or a script that implements flawed logic in the online investment application. Exploiting CGI scripts is a common

Exhibit 13.1   Online Investing Application

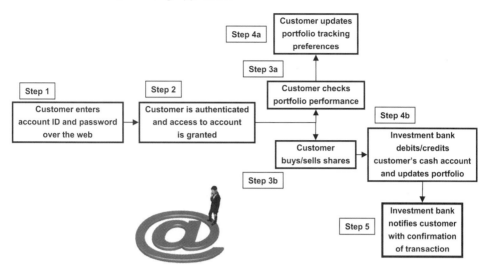

method that crackers use to gain shell access to Web servers. CGI script vulnerabilities are discussed later in this chapter.

The vulnerability need not be in a CGI script. Application servers can be implemented in Java, C, C++, Perl, or Python in various application server frameworks. The difficulty lies not in which language the business application logic is developed; more important are the vulnerabilities introduced by the complex logic at this middleware layer. One of the key problems in the development of application middleware is

Exhibit 13.2   Breaking an E-Business

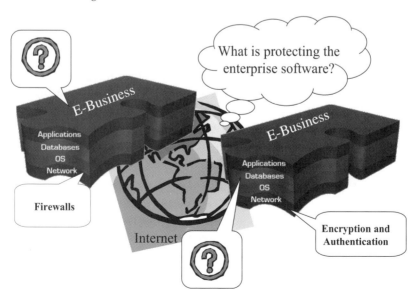

poor input sanity-checking; that is, the developers fail to impose limits on acceptable input. The cracker can exploit the lack of input sanity-checking to feed the application server unexpected input used in system commands. This technique can gain shell privileges on the machine.

Although application server misuse is a common way of breaking into systems, there are many other ways to gain the initial access in step 1 of the attack. For instance, the Web and mail servers may be running any of several network services, such as *FTP* and *BIND/DNS,* that may be misconfigured. The Web and mail server software themselves may be vulnerable to attack. Most of the popular commercial Web and mail servers always been vulnerable to buffer overrun attacks that often permit full system root privileges on the host.[3] Once attackers gain system privileges on an internal host, they can exploit the Web of trust often woven among machines on a local network to gain access to other machines on the network. This strategy is precisely what the attacker follows in step 2 of the attack illustrated in Exhibit 13.2.

Once attackers have access to the various file systems on the application server, they can view the source code of CGI scripts or other application middleware to discover customer account numbers, passwords, and even database administrator passwords for accessing the back-end databases. From there, they can download important and confidential client information stored in the database. In step 3 of the attack, the attacker leverages the internal privileges gained to plant backdoors into the system unnoticed. A suite of software, commonly known as a "rootkit" and available to crackers, allows them not only to get into a system unnoticed but also to erase their tracks in audit logs. In the example shown, the cracker installs a rogue remote administration program known as Back Orifice, which provides the ability to remotely administer the network with the same privileges and power as the authentic system administrator.

At this point in the attack, the cracker has assumed total control of the e-business, with many options including:

1. Blackmailing the business with threats of discrediting it
2. Defacing the Web pages
3. Working in a stealthy manner to uncover proprietary business information and confidential client information
4. Subverting the application for personal gain

Step 4 of the attack illustrates the last case, where the attacker credits a personal cash account. The cracker must move quickly enough to withdraw these funds before traditional back-end auditing discovers the discrepancy. There have been many defaced Web pages of government agencies, and other important sites, and many reported instances of the other cases. Of course, financial institutions are understandably reluctant to publicize such events that might lessen customer confidence.

Unfortunately, it takes only a single flaw or overlooked vulnerability for a cracker to compromise a system. Although *defense-in-depth* (using multiple forms of security, such as firewalls on the perimeter and intrusion detection inside the network) is a popular strategy, often multiple layers of defense fall like a house of cards when a single hole is exploited. For example, an attacker who gains *root* capability can disable all other security measures. The problem is known as an *asymmetric* attack because it is much more difficult and costly to defend against such an attack than to launch one.

The number of flaws that can be exploited is staggering, considering all the different platforms and devices that make up current information technology (IT) infrastructures.

Compounding the problem is the fact that a cracker can work in relative anonymity using a $500 computer and modem to launch attacks. Even worse, crackers can work from any number of Internet kiosks available in airports, malls, cafés, and even laundromats. As crackers get more sophisticated, and as more easily utilized scripts become available, attacks will be launched from mobile devices that can roam in and out of different geographic zones and then be discarded—making tracking of the attacker next to impossible.

13.4   E-COMMERCE SYSTEM SECURITY.   In spite of the fairly bleak picture painted here, businesses can effectively manage their risk from crackers. As in many other security domains, the security posture or stance assumed by the business is critical for deterring and thwarting crackers. To use a physical-world analogy, consider burglars who intend to break into homes in a nice neighborhood. As the burglars scope out potential targets, they will notice some houses with burglar alarms—complete with conspicuous signs of the alarm systems—and some without. In all likelihood, the burglars will bypass the houses with the burglar alarms and move on to the other, less well-protected targets. Thus, the security stance assumed by the owner plays an important role.

Every business must first determine its desired security stance as documented in its security policy. System administrators use the security policy to configure the systems, routers, firewalls, and remote access solutions. Without an explicit security policy, there is no way to determine what the security stance of the business is, how to configure its systems, or even if a nonobvious security breach has occurred. Once the security policy is developed, the actual security implementation must be assessed. That is, the system must be tested and evaluated to determine how well it meets its security policy. Usually there is a difference between the desired stance and the actual stance. This difference is the security gap between where the organization would like to be (secure against particular threats) and where it actually is in practice.

The process of developing a security policy and evaluating the business systems against that policy will identify not only the gaps between the actual security stance and the desired posture but also weaknesses in the security policy itself. It is important to have an independent party, preferably an outside party, evaluate the security stance of the organization. A third party can fairly assess whether the organization's system upholds the security policy. If the group that develops the security policy or the system configuration is also responsible for evaluating it, the evaluation may be biased, and potential vulnerabilities may be overlooked. This may occur not through ill will or dishonesty but rather because of the difficulty of being objective about one's own work.

13.5   PROTECTING E-COMMERCE APPLICATIONS.   E-commerce systems security can be understood from different views. First, consider the view of e-businesses in Exhibit 13.3. The diagram shows two e-businesses communicating over the Internet, perhaps performing business-to-business types of transactions.

In this view, the lowest layer of the e-business is the *networking layer.* At the networking layer, there are concerns about the reliability, integrity, and confidentiality of the data that runs over the communications channel. This layer is of particular concern because the Internet is a public switched network, meaning that any number of third parties may have access to the data that traverses the nodes of the Internet on the way from the data source to its destination. Also, the Internet Protocol (IP) is a connectionless protocol, which means there is no dedicated circuit between source and

Exhibit 13.3   Layered View of E-Businesses

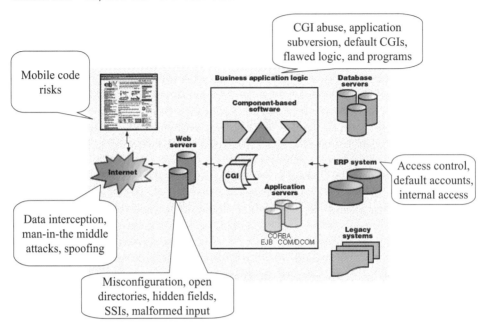

destination. As a result, packets sent during a given session may take different routes to their destination, depending on traffic congestion and routing algorithms. Because the IP is an unreliable datagram protocol (i.e., IP uses independent packets forwarded from node to node, but there is no guarantee of successful transmission), the networking layer includes a connection-oriented reliable transmission layer such as TCP (transmission control protocol) that ensures that dropped or lost packets are retransmitted and that bit flips that may have occurred during transmission (e.g., over wireless networks) are corrected.

Although TCP/IP provides for more reliable delivery of Internet packets, TCP/IP does not provide *secure* connection services. Typically, this means that there is no *guarantee* of confidentiality, identification, or even delivery of packets sent from one Internet host to another. Because Internet packets often traverse several Internet nodes from source to destination, packet contents can be intercepted by third parties, copied, substituted, or even destroyed. This is the risk that most people citing Internet risks of e-commerce have decried; they have overlooked the more substantive risks of e-commerce dealing with server- and client-side security and privacy. Fortunately, we have good solutions to the data confidentiality problem. Cryptography techniques can provide strong guarantees for data confidentiality, authentication of parties, and integrity of data sent during the transmission. Furthermore, digital signatures can be used to sign received mail in a "return receipt" application that provides guarantees of delivery of e-mail. Thus, as shown in Exhibit 13.3, we can use encryption services to protect data transmitted over the network.

The operating system (OS), or *platform,* that hosts the e-business applications lives on the networking layer. In a layered model, the services of one layer use the services of the lower layer and provide services to upper layers. The network layer often is thought of as a core portion of the operating system; however, from a layered services point of view, the OS software runs on top of the network layer.

Operating systems are notoriously rife with software flaws that affect system security. Operating systems are vulnerable because commercial OSs today are immensely complex; for instance, the Windows 2000 operating system is purported to have more than 50 million lines of source code. It is impossible to catch all software design and programming errors that may have security consequences in a platform this complex. Even though Unix operating systems have been in use for the better part of 30 years, new flaws in OS utilities are found on a weekly basis across all the different Unix platform variants.[4]

Security holes in the platform are critical by nature. That is, if the OS itself is vulnerable to exploitation, security provided by the application can be compromised by holes in the platform. The OS is always the foundation on which applications are built, so that cracks in the foundation make for weak security at the application layer. As Exhibit 13.1 suggests, firewalls provide protection against some operating system flaws. One of the key roles of firewalls is their ability to shut down services offered to *logical domain addresses.*

Using Internet domain addresses, the firewall administrator can partition Internet addresses into *trusted* and *untrusted* domain ranges. For instance, any Internet address outside the company's domain can be considered untrusted. As a result, all OS services, such as remote logins, can be shut down to everyone outside of the company's domain. Even within a company, the domains can be partitioned so that certain *subdomains* are trusted for access to certain machines, but others are not. The key benefit then of firewalls is their ability to restrict access to the platform through *offered services* (i.e., specific functions that pass data through the firewall). As a result, firewalls can make it easy to hide OS flaws from untrusted entities.

Even so, firewalls are vulnerable to data- or code-driven attacks through offered services. For instance, an attack through *SMTP* (mail) or *HTTP* (Web) will not be stopped by a firewall if the firewall is configured to let e-mail and Web services through, as is necessary for e-commerce. Firewalls also will not stop OS exploits from insiders or from the trusted entities who are granted access to the platform. For the purpose of this discussion, however, it is important to realize that firewalls, if properly configured, can close down exposure to a significant number of platform vulnerabilities simply by denying untrusted outsiders access to platform utilities and services. Exhibit 13.3 illustrates reasonable protection from network- and platform-based attacks but not from application and database attacks. The database layer is shown separately in the diagram because of the importance of its role in e-commerce; however, database attacks usually can be considered as a type of application attack.

Application-based attacks represent a critical issue that has yet to be addressed adequately by the industry. One reason is that there is no simple solution. Another reason is the sense of security provided by a firewall, an SSL-enabled Web site, and encryption, together with digital certificates and signatures. These measures are necessary but not sufficient. Applications, above all, *are* the online business.

The front-end Web servers, back-end databases, and OS platforms are fairly standard and uniform from business to business. The online applications, though, are what make each business unique. Since Web pages are merely packaging that captures each enterprise's unique application logic, the software must be custom-developed in-house or outsourced to an e-business development group.

Furthermore, because online applications are increasingly sophisticated, the software that implements the application logic has become highly complex, requiring component-based and object-oriented paradigms such as Enterprise Java Beans, CORBA, and DCOM/COM services. Collectively, these are known as *application servers.* The key point, however, is that because the application logic is custom and complex, it is often rife with errors in implementation or logic that can be and often are exploited by crackers.

Application security must not be confused with marketing claims. A secure online application is one that is resistant to attacks. It is not simply one that authenticates end users, encrypts transaction data, provides nonrepudiation of transactions, and guarantees service. These are all matters of importance that address characteristics of the transaction, not properties of the software. The remainder of this chapter addresses the software problem in some detail. the next section provides a different view of e-commerce systems from the layered view discussed previously. It identifies vulnerabilities in the different software components and strategies for managing the risks.

13.6   COMPONENTS AND VULNERABILITIES IN E-COMMERCE SYSTEMS.

Exhibit 13.4 shows a generic *n*-tier architecture of an e-business, together with a summary of the types of vulnerabilities and risks to each of the major components. Using the Internet, Web clients (running on PCs or hand-held devices) interface with a front-end Web server, a middleware layer of business application logic, back-end databases, an Enterprise Resource Planning (ERP) system, supply-chain management software, and even some legacy systems that are now brought to the Internet.

13.6.1   Client-Side Risks.

Most e-commerce is performed using standard Web browsers and mail clients. Increasingly, e-commerce is being performed on hand-held mobile devices such as personal digital assistants (PDAs) and mobile phones. The security risks particular to wireless devices are covered elsewhere in this volume.

Exhibit 13.4   Client/Server *N*-Tier Architecture of an E-Business

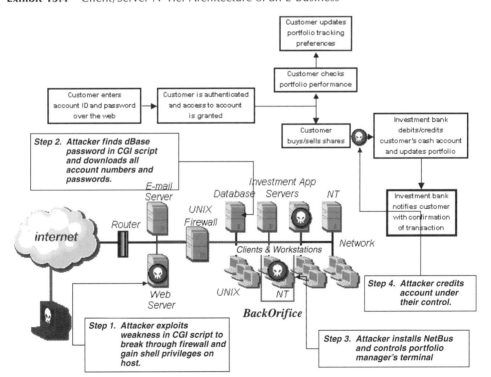

Client-side security risks are mainly from malicious mobile code such as Web scripts, ActiveX controls, and hostile Java applets.[5] Another major risk in client-side software is loss of privacy.[6] Each computer and its related software receives and transmits a great deal of personal identifying information (PII). For instance, browsers may convey information about the computers (name, IP address, browser type, version, company name) and sometimes about the users themselves, particularly if automatic form-filling features have been enabled. Browsers also are used to track movements through the Web. For instance, every Web site the browser visits typically gets a record of the previous site from which the user entered. Banner ads in Web pages also track which sites have been visited in order to create a profile of Web usage.

A class of more insidious programs, known as *spyware,* can send information about computer usage out to specific sites, often without the user's knowledge or approval. One of the key risks with client-side software is that users simply do not know what the programs are revealing about themselves, or to whom. A simple principle is that a program should not be sending out any data that the user does not know about. An audit of the programs on any given machine probably would reveal that quite a few are in violation of that principle. While most spyware programs are written to provide marketing data for software vendors, so as to profile and target their customers more effectively, some are specifically written to spy on usage activity. For example, SpectorSoft markets a spyware tool known as eBlaster to people who suspect their spouses are engaging in illicit online affairs. This type of spyware program spies on user activity, from keystrokes to screen shots, and sends a log of the activity out over the network. Spyware can be identified using diagnostic programs such as *optout* from Gibson Research Corporation (*http://grc.com*).

A final client-side risk that businesses need to be especially concerned about is the risk of malicious executables that run on their user workstations. The desktop machine is like a petri dish for software: It is constantly changing and growing with new software executables—some of an unsavory nature. Malicious software, or *malware* as it is now known, finds many ways of infecting machines. For instance, one common way of disseminating malicious software is via e-mail attachments. Another is by masquerading as legitimate software on a Web page available for download. Users often upload and download software to and from internal network file shares. In addition, even the old-fashioned floppy disk is still a viable way of transmitting malicious software. The Back Orifice 2000 (BO2K) "remote administration kit" is one example of malicious software that will allow anyone—including a hacker—to administer and control one's machine remotely. Some malware products, running on an internal machine, may compromise the entire network by losing and stealing data. It is essential, therefore, that corporations closely monitor the applications software that is downloaded and run on their machines.

13.6.2   Network Protocol Risks.   Network risks primarily arise from sending confidential data over the Internet—a public, packet-switching network. Many good protocols address the risks of sending confidential data over the Internet.[7] In fact, a few years ago, the list included the following:

- SET
- SSL
- S/HTTP
- S/MIME
- CyberCash

Although some of these protocols are still around in one form or another, the industry has generally accepted SSL as the protocol of choice for secure Web browser transactions. The objective of most secure network protocols is to layer security properties on top of the TCP/IP network layers. While TCP/IP provides reliable and robust delivery of datagrams over the Internet, it does not provide confidentiality, authentication, or strong message-integrity services. These are the properties that secure protocols provide. Some go even further. For instance, SET-compliant protocols leave the credit card number encrypted even at the merchant site. Since the merchant does not need to know the consumer's credit card number, by hiding the number from the merchant, a significant portion of credit card fraud can be eliminated. Rather than decrypting the credit card number at the merchant site, it is passed in encrypted form from the merchant to the credit-issuing bank. There it is decrypted, and the merchant's account is credited the amount of the purchase. The protocol details of SET, SSL, and other e-commerce protocols are described in Chapter 3 in *E-Commerce Security: Weak Links, Best Defenses* as well as in other books.[8]

Depending on the needs of an online business application, there is a requirement for more or less of the security properties afforded by secure protocols. For most Web browsing, a secure protocol is unnecessary; the standard Web protocol, HTTP, suffices. However, when customers send confidential or personal information to a site, a secure protocol that encrypts the data is preferable. The de facto secure protocol standard is Secure Sockets Layer, now implemented in every standard Web browser. SSL will not only negotiate a secret session key between the Web site and a client to encrypt the data, but it also will authenticate the Web site. The Web site must have a valid certificate endorsed by a Certificate Authority, which the users implicitly trust. Using a list of trusted Certificate Authorities maintained within the client browser, access can be prevented to other, untrusted sites. Once the connection is established, the user can verify that the Web site is, in fact, the one intended by examining the site certificate. Users rarely do this in practice, but the certificate is available and should be more widely utilized.

These secure properties—that is, encrypted sessions and host site authentication—serve the purpose for most online commerce applications. Some applications, though, may demand even stronger security services. For instance, banking and investment applications often transmit highly confidential information, with the possibility of huge financial losses through inadvertent error or intentional fraud. These types of transactions require not only confidentiality of the data but also authentication of the client. A financial institution must never give access to account information and permit transactions without authenticating the user.

Common identification schemes on the Internet include simple user name and password authentication. A much more secure solution is to require strong client authentication using client certificates. SSL supports client certificates, although sites rarely use this capability because it involves requiring customers to obtain a certificate from a Certification Authority.

In the future, e-commerce protocols will need to be increasingly sophisticated if they are to meet the stringent security and privacy requirements of new Internet applications. For example, as criminal, medical, patent, and other important databases migrate to the Internet, the protocols developed for accessing them need to consider the security and privacy needs of the database owners and maintainers as well as those of the client or requester. Today, the progress in genomics is producing much information about the likelihood of developing deadly disease based on a genetic DNA sequence. While this knowledge raises moral and ethical questions as to how much information about potential diseases should be revealed to doctors and patients, it also raises the specter of such information getting into the wrong hands once it is accessible on the Internet.

Consider the case of a doctor querying an online genetic disease database with a patient's DNA sequence. The online application attempts to match the DNA sequence with diseases that might develop in the future. If the database were maintained by a commercial entity such as an insurance provider, the patient almost certainly would not want the company to know of any disease that might be returned as the result of a query, because that information could be used to deny both insurance and employment.

Likewise, the database maintainer probably would not want to know of the query or of its result, as such knowledge might put it at risk for lawsuits, should the information be leaked. Furthermore, the database maintainer would want the rest of the database to remain inaccessible except for specific results returned to an approved inquiry. Preventing access to any other information in the database would help to protect the commercial interests of the company, because then the database could not be duplicated easily. Nor could queries be made without a cost-tracking mechanism. To support this dual model of secure and private information access, e-commerce protocols need to be developed and commercialized that not only encrypt data in transmission but also consider the total security and privacy needs of both parties to the transaction.

Another e-commerce application area that will require better security and privacy protocols involves applications that accept e-cash or digital coin payments. Currently, most online payment schemes use either credit or debit cards, with payments made from the buyer's checking account at a bank. Payments are made either with online verification of funds or with offline batch payments at the end of the day. A number of applications, particularly those involving payments of a few dollars or even pennies, are being created that cannot support the costs of a bank-based transaction.

Many commercial services and products, such as vending machines and parking meters, are coin-activated and do not require customers to have an account or a line of credit. Although efforts are being made to convert such services to computerized devices, with micropayment capabilities, it will be many years before this is actually accomplished. In any case, there will always be customers who want to pay with cash or its electronic equivalent so that the transaction cannot be tracked by a third party, such as a bank or a creditor.

Newer online applications for micropayments may include collecting fees for downloading music, data, weather reports, stock quotations, articles from magazines, and pages from books. While many of these applications are provided today without charge and supported by banner advertising, a concern for profits is motivating most Web sites to seek additional sources of income. Whatever the application, there is a need for cash-based alternatives to the current account-based system for making payments. The key security and privacy concerns are with ensuring that e-cash is properly spent and accounted for and that anonymity is preserved throughout. Although several protocols have been developed with these goals in mind, none has reached commercial success or adoption by the vendor community. As mobile e-commerce begins to drive more traditionally cash-based transactions (i.e., parking meters, vending machines, and ticket booths), wireless vendors may adopt these new digital cash-based protocols.

Regardless of the network protocol used in an e-commerce application, the key concern is for those attackers who will attempt to breach the easiest obstacle in their quest to obtain system privileges and unauthorized access to data. If the security provided by the network protocol is perceived to be strong, attackers will look for alternatives that bypass the network security. For instance, the following types of standard attacks from the cracker's toolkit will bypass the security provided by most e-commerce protocols:

- Man-in-the-middle attacks: capturing transmissions in transit for eavesdropping or forgery.
- DNS attacks: altering records in the worldwide Domain Name System to misdirect connections to the wrong addresses.
- War dialing: automated testing of every phone number in a block of numbers to find modems.
- Exploiting software vulnerabilities in network services such as FTP, Bind, SMTP, and HTTP servers.
- Internal access: improper use of authorized access by an insider (employee, contractor).
- Leveraging trusted hosts: attacking from another system that has a privileged relationship with the target system.
- Brute-force crypto attacks: automated testing of all possible decryption keys to decipher a ciphertext.

In summary, it is important not only to select the appropriate network protocol for each online application but also to avoid a false sense of security that might arise from use of a "secure" network protocol. Good security engineering will consider vulnerabilities in other components of the system that are more attractive targets to determined crackers.

13.6.3   Business Application Logic.   The business application logic pictured in Exhibit 13.4 represents one of the key areas of vulnerability in e-commerce systems. The program logic encodes what the online business is offering in terms of products and services. It also defines the look and feel of the Web site and provides all of the interactive features, such as dynamic Web pages, personalized Web pages, and online transaction capabilities. Because each application is unique, the software that implements the logic must be custom-developed for each particular site.

In contrast, most of the other software components of a Web site are commercial off-the-shelf (COTS) software. For instance, the Web server, back-end databases, and supply-chain logistics software are often purchased off the shelf from software vendors. With COTS software, the end user has no control over the code and therefore is not responsible for coding bug fixes. When software bugs in COTS software are discovered, the software vendor usually issues a patch or incorporates a bug fix in the next release version. Although software vendors can fix discovered bugs, they depend on customer sites to actually apply the patches or upgrades to the software. In practice, this occurs less often than desired and is a significant reason why many Internet-based systems are vulnerable.[9] The most important task in securing COTS software systems is to make sure that: (1) they are properly configured for a secure installation according to the site's security policy and (2) the software is properly updated to the current version and patch level.

Because business applications are custom-developed, either by an in-house staff or, more frequently, by outsourcing to an e-business developer, the program represents a key risk for several reasons. The dynamic, interactive nature of e-businesses, coupled with increasingly sophisticated online services, requires a significant amount of development to code the logic. As a result, the application programs tend to be very complex pieces of software, likely to contain flaws, and susceptible to the kinds of attacks launched against Web sites. In practice, errors in design and implementation of business application logic often compromise the security of an e-business.

Traditionally, the middle tier of software is implemented on Web servers using the Common Gateway Interface or (CGI). CGI scripts are programs that run on the Web server machine as separate processes from the Web server software. These general-purpose programs are invoked by the Web server in response to user requests. The CGI script's main function is to process user input and to perform some service such as retrieving data or dynamically creating a Web page for the end user. Because CGI scripts process untrusted user input, the security risks associated with the CGI, and other forms of middle-tier software, are extremely high. Many attacks against Web-based systems are implemented by exploited CGI scripts. Although CGI scripts can be written in any general-purpose programming language, they are written most often in Perl, C, Tcl, and Python.

More recently, component-based software (CBS) is making inroads in e-commerce applications. The purpose of CBS is to develop, purchase, and reuse proven software in order to implement application logic quickly, easily, and with high quality. Two of the more popular component frameworks for e-commerce applications are Enterprise JavaBeans (EJB) and Java 2 Enterprise Edition (J2EE), which support component-based Java. Other component models include the Object Management Group's (OMG) Common Object Request Broker Architecture (CORBA) and Microsoft's Common Object Model (COM) and Distributed COM (DCOM). These component frameworks are the glue that enables software components to use standard infrastructure services while hiding the details of the implementation by using well-defined interfaces.

Business application logic, when coded in CBS systems, usually runs on application servers with particular component models, such as EJB, CORBA, COM, and DCOM. CBS also provides an interface to back-end services such as database management, enterprise resource planning (ERP), and legacy software systems.

In addition to supporting traditional CGI functions, component-based software is expected to enable distributed, business-to-business applications over the Internet. The component-based software paradigm also supports good software engineering, as described later. The Unified Modeling Language (UML) facilitates object-oriented analysis and design for component-based frameworks. In addition, as the market for component-based software expands, many standard business application components will be available for purchase off the shelf.

Although the benefits of component-based software are numerous, they pose security hazards similar to those of CGI scripts. Component-based software enables development in general-purpose programming languages such as Java, C, and C++, which can execute with all the rights and privileges of server processes. Like CGI, they process untrusted user input, and because component-based software can be used to build sophisticated, large-scale applications, the likelihood for errors may be even greater than for simple CGI scripts. Regardless of the implementation—CGI or application servers—the security risks of server-side software are great, and therefore server-side software must be designed and implemented carefully.

The key risks in the middleware layer of e-commerce sites are these:

- Misconfiguration of the CGI
- Default and development CGI scripts being left on the production server

- CGI misuse
- Application subversion
- Flawed logic
- Programming errors

13.6.4   CGI Script Vulnerabilities.   CGI scripts are frequent targets of attackers because they are often misconfigured and vulnerable to misuse.[10] When designing CGI scripts, it is prudent to expect the unexpected, particularly the malicious attack. Although the Web designer has control over the content of CGI scripts, there is no control over what end users are going to send to them. Also, often overlooked are vulnerabilities of CGI scripts that exist on the server as part of the distribution but that are not actually used in the application. Some CGI scripts included as part of the Web server distribution have well-known flaws that can be exploited to obtain unauthorized access to the server. Even if the default CGI scripts are not used as part of the Web server pages, anyone can access them by simply knowing the script names.

One of the most common—yet easily preventable—security hazards is misconfiguration of software, especially CGI scripts. One feature supported by many Web servers is the ability of individuals throughout an organization to write CGI scripts and have them execute from their own directories. While useful for prettying up personal Web pages, this feature also can introduce system security hazards. In e-commerce applications, the Web server should be configured to prevent CGI scripts from executing anywhere but in a single CGI directory under control of the system administrator.

The script-aliased CGI mode for Web servers ensures that CGI scripts will execute only from an explicitly named directory in the server configuration file. In addition, the CGI script path is not named in the URL to the CGI. Rather, the server "aliases" the explicit path to the CGI script to a chosen name, such as *cgi-bin*. Thus, running the server in script-aliased CGI mode prevents rogue CGI scripts from executing while it also hides the explicit path to the CGI scripts.

The CGI script directories also should be properly configured using OS access controls. For instance, if CGI scripts are written in a compiled language such as C, the script sources should be excluded from the document root of the Web server so that they cannot be accessed via the Web. They should be accessible to the system administrator or Web content development group only and inaccessible to everyone else in the organization. If the script sources fall into the hands of malicious perpetrators, the source code can be inspected for flaws, making the perpetrator's job even easier. Access to the CGI executables directory, frequently called the cgi-bin, should be properly controlled as well. Only the Web server and administrator need access to this directory. Liberal access permissions to the CGI executables directory give malicious insiders the opportunity to place their own scripts on the e-business site.

Most CGI scripts are written in scripting languages such as Perl, JavaScript, and Python. While scripting languages are useful for rapidly prototyping systems, they also let the developer write dangerous code very easily. For instance, it is easy to construct system commands with user input, a potentially dangerous situation. Writing the same system functionality requires several lines of C code and knowledge of system libraries. The easy accessibility of scripting languages makes them appealing but also threatening to security-critical applications. It is also important to prohibit access to interpreters from the Web server. For instance, system administrators may be tempted to include the Perl interpreter in CGI script directories; however, doing so provides direct Web access to interactively execute Perl commands—an extremely dangerous configuration.

Finally, administrators should account for every CGI program on the server in terms of its purpose, origin, and modifications. Remove CGI scripts that do not serve a business function. View with suspicion and carefully screen CGI scripts that are distributed with Web servers, downloaded from the Internet, or purchased commercially. These steps will eliminate most of the potentially dangerous CGI scripts. Once a stable set of CGI programs is established, make a digital hash of the program executables (e.g., using MD5) to enable future integrity checks.

13.6.5   Application Subversion.   Application subversion attacks are not discussed often in relation to e-businesses, but they represent a significant threat to most online applications. Application subversion is a form of program misuse. Unlike buffer overrun attacks, application subversion attacks exploit the program logic without violating program integrity, in order to elevate user privileges and gain unauthorized access to data. It is the very complexity of the target program that gives the attacker the means to gain unauthorized access. Application subversion attacks use programs in ways that the program's designers and developers did not anticipate. Typically, these attacks are not scripted but rather developed from online interactive use and subsequent abuse.

Referring to Exhibit 13.1, an application subversion attack will attempt to discover ways of short-circuiting paths in the workflow. For instance, there may be a hidden path that lets the user gain access to account information without being authenticated to that account. Many such attacks work on the premise that access to confidential information is not properly authenticated.

Another common attack sends malformed input to a program. Many Web pages use forms extensively to drive the application, while the data input on the form is checked using client-side JavaScript. An attacker can take advantage of the fact that many online application developers assume that the client is going to use the form properly and that the JavaScript will check all input sent to the site. The attacker can examine the data stream sent by the form and then, rather than using the form, send a modified data stream. An attacker may be able to obtain access to the application by placing system commands in the input stream. If the input stream is subsequently used in a *system()* call by the online application, the end user may force the execution of system commands on the attacker's behalf.

Some application developers rely heavily on hidden fields in the HTML document. Hidden fields allow the Web developer to include information on the page that is not displayed, although the end user can see the hidden field data simply by viewing the HTML source. The mistake application developers make is in first believing that the end user cannot see the hidden fields and, second, in relying on the integrity of the hidden field data for making online decisions. Some online merchants have made the mistake of including pricing information for items in the hidden fields and using those prices to determine the cost of the online transaction. The end user can simply change the pricing in the hidden fields and send lower prices back to the merchants for a discounted purchase.

Another misuse of hidden fields is to redirect application output. For instance, some Web sites include file system path information in hidden fields on their Web pages. This information is used by a server-side script to determine where to read or write transaction information. Attackers, by simply changing the hidden field, can overwrite files or read files to which they should not have access. In some cases, it may be possible to store a program entered in a form field to be used later as a means of running a shell on the remote system.

In summary, rigorous software quality assurance is necessary through the design and development of e-business applications, including front-end Web pages, application middleware, and operating systems. Once the software is believed to be immune to application misuse and subversion attacks, the system administrator must perform other activities to ensure the security of the e-business middleware:

- All unnecessary scripts or application server programs must be eliminated from the production server.

- Source code of application middleware must be carefully guarded against download or unauthorized access.

- Proper configuration of the CGI and application middleware is necessary to ensure executable access only to the correct application middleware, with the lowest practical privilege level. Sanity-checking of inputs to application middleware must be done to ensure that only well-formed input is accepted.

13.6.6   Web Server Exploits.   Web server security has been written about and covered in detail, including in Chapter 4 of *E-Commerce Security: Weak Links, Best Defenses* and *The Web Security Source Book,* among other titles.[11] Here we highlight some of the common exploits of Web servers used against many e-businesses.

13.6.6.1   *Configuration.*   The key to Web server security is its configuration. Like other complex pieces of software, Web servers are highly configurable to meet the needs of any given site. By default, most software vendors configure the software application for maximum functionality but minimum security. Thus, by default, when the server is first started, it is likely to be more permissive than any given company's security policy would like. The principal premise for configurability is in the variations that exist among sites.

A correctly configured Web server is the result of a policy that defines what access is allowed to which individuals for each resource. This policy, in turn, is used to configure routers, firewalls, and all public servers, such as the Web server. Configuring the Web server, while necessary, is by no means sufficient to secure the system. The discussion of application server exploits in Section 13.6.5 demonstrates this principle.

13.6.6.2   *HTML Coding and Server Side Includes.*   Once the Web server is configured as securely as possible, it is important to ensure that the Web pages themselves do not open holes in the security. Many Web page developers fall into some common pitfalls that may compromise the site's security. The preceding section mentioned the problem of relying on hidden fields in HTML for security or business-critical data. Users can abuse the hidden field data to subvert an application.

HTML offers other potential vulnerabilities. One that is most often criticized is *Server Side Includes* (SSI). The SSI configuration option, if enabled, allows directives to be embedded in HTML that the server will execute. For instance, if the following statement were embedded in an HTML document, it would direct the server to display the contents of the system password file:

<CF> <!--#exec /bin/cat /etc/passwd -->

Certainly Web pages should not be written with SSIs without a compelling reason. Although access to the HTML code is normally under control of the site, there are many ways an attacker might get an SSI into an HTML page. First, the attacker may have found another way into the system (e.g., by a CGI script exploit) but may want to provide either an easier back door or a redundant back door in case the CGI script vulnerability is found and closed. Once the CGI script is exploited, the attacker may implant an SSI directive within one of the site's HTML pages. Another way for an attacker to gain access is to have the server generate a Web page with the SSI of choice embedded in the HTML. How can an attacker do this? One approach exploits a server that generates dynamic HTML depending on the end user's data, preferences, or history. If the Web server ends up using some of the attacker's data to generate the HTML page, the attacker may be able to insert an SSI directive in the HTML. In summary, a better solution than continuously monitoring the HTML pages is simply to disable the SSI. In that event, even if SSIs were embedded, the server would not execute them. This is a configuration option, and like all system configuration files, the Web server configuration file should be protected by both file permission protection and file integrity checks to ensure that it cannot be tampered with.

Although SSIs are often highlighted, a more common risk results from keeping documents or files in a publicly accessible portion of the Web server. The accessible portion of the Web server is called the *document root*. This root specifies the portion of the file system that the Web server can read and display to a Web client if requested. The document root can be a superset of the Web pages that are actually displayed when the user clicks through a Web site. There may be other documents in the document root that are not linked to or from Web pages. This does not mean they are not accessible, however. Simply giving the correct address for any document will result in either displaying or downloading the document to any Web client. Therein lies the problem.

13.6.6.3   *Private Documents in Public Directories.*   Private documents inadvertently placed in a public directory can result in a compromise of confidential information and loss of privacy. For example, if a database file of credit card numbers (say, *cardnumbers.mdb*) were stored in the document root of the Web server for a fictitious company, *mycompany.com,* the following URL address typed in a Web browser could download the file: *www.mycompany.com/cardnumbers.mdb.*

This risk is even greater if *directory browsing,* another configurable feature, is enabled. Directory browsing allows an end user to view the contents of the file system at a given directory level if a Web page does not exist with the same name. Directory browsing is really a way to explore the file system of another site using a Web browser. Users may view this feature if they go back one level from a given Web page by deleting the right-hand section of a page's URL and viewing its higher-level directory (e.g., in *http://a.b.com/d/e.htm,* one would remove the "e.htm" thus attempting to browse *http://a.b.com/d/*). Attackers can learn a lot of valuable information from viewing the contents of a directory containing private files. Furthermore, the browser itself provides for clicking on a file name in the directory structure, which causes the file to be downloaded. Again, directory browsing, if enabled, is an open vulnerability and an unfortunately easy way to download private or confidential information.

13.6.6.4   *Cookies.*   Finally, another potential vulnerability for an e-business is the use of *cookies.* Because HTTP is a *stateless protocol,* each new Web page that is visited has no memory of the last Web page that was visited by that user. Cookies are used to "keep state" between different Web pages visited in a given session. Cookies can make an e-business transaction appear to be seamless, sequential, and coordinated.

Most people, when discussing the risks of cookies, focus on the client-side privacy risks. While these certainly exist, cookies also pose risks to the businesses that employ them. If the information contained in cookies is trusted, much the same way that the content in hidden fields is trusted, then the e-business may be vulnerable to cookie exploits called *cookie poisoning*. Some Web sites use cookies to carry authentication information for a given user who traverses its pages. Once users have authenticated themselves, their token of authentication may be carried with them via cookies from one Web page to all subsequent pages at that site. Using cookies is a fairly weak form of authentication. The cookie can be stolen easily by someone snooping a user's local area network or the Internet and then, with the information gained, to access the user's personal pages on the Web site. Secure protocols such as SSL should be employed to mitigate this risk.

Cookies also are used for other purposes that can introduce new vulnerabilities into critical transactions. Because cookies are under the control of end users, they can be changed in whatever manner a user chooses. If cookies are designed to instruct a Web server where to write a customer-specific file, by changing the cookie data, an end user might overwrite other customer files or even replace critical system files. Similarly, if cookies are used for carrying order information, as is common in electronic shopping carts, then changing the contents of the cookies would corrupt the transaction. This could result in an unauthorized, deep discount to the customer.

Regardless of the technology used, it is important to examine the features and functions of Web servers from a security-critical viewpoint. Dependence on a specific technology for critical transactions demands that the technology be trustworthy, so that it does not provide vulnerable points of attack.

13.6.7   Database Security.   Databases traditionally have represented an important intellectual property of information-based companies. As a result, they have almost always been company proprietary and unavailable to public access. In the new model of business, however, many of these proprietary databases are made available on the Internet, often without careful consideration of the risks involved. The Web browser becomes the database query interface, often to unknown and untrusted entities.

Although there has been much research in database security over the last two decades, the commercial sector has adopted only two key tenets: authenticating and authorizing principals to certain objects. Access to databases thus is controlled by properly authenticating the credentials of the requesting principal and then verifying which objects the authenticated principal is authorized to access. Any online database application must perform these two functions rigorously so as to protect the most valuable assets of an e-business as well as customer privacy.

Although many vendors claim secure channel access from the Web server to the database, there are many pitfalls. To start with, the fundamental reason why databases are vulnerable is that Web interfaces are commonly appended to what once may have been a closed and proprietary interface, without concern for overall security. Second, unsecured middleware programs such as CGI scripts or application servers usually mediate access from the Web server to the database. Web servers can provide client authentication from simple user name and password entry to strong certificated authentication. The needs of the business and the size of the accessing community will dictate which solution is feasible.

Despite obvious security advantages, most users do not store encrypted information in their databases, primarily for performance reasons. Encrypting and decrypting information on the fly during search, retrieve, and store operations can be too slow for real-time transactions. Also, even encrypting the data in a storage unit would not provide complete protection, as the online application must be able to read from and write to the database in clear text. Application-based attacks would still be able to get at the data while it was in plain, unencrypted text format.

Another key vulnerability of online databases also arises from application-based attacks. As described earlier, attacks that exploit vulnerabilities in the business-application logic often can provide unrestricted access to a database.

Attacks that exploit a buffer overflow vulnerability in an application server program usually will be able to get command shell access on the remote server. From there, the attacker usually is able to find source code for the application server programs, such as Perl scripts or even C code, that are used to access the database. Because these programs *need* access to the database, they also must know the passwords used to access the various data partitions. If the programmers have foolishly *hard-coded* the passwords, then simply reviewing the source code may be enough to discover these passwords. With passwords in hand, the attacker can use the application server program via the Web interface to gain unauthorized access to the database. More directly, with a password it is possible to query a database from the command shell, using SQL commands or commands from the database language of choice.

Finally, like the other complex programs that run e-businesses, databases must be securely configured. Basic steps that the database administrator (DBA) needs to take include:

- Enforcing Web client authentication to the database.
- Enforcing Web client authorization for access to database records.
- Eliminating default database and database platform accounts.
- Ensuring that passwords are read from encrypted files, not stored in program code.
- Changing easily guessed passwords.
- Configuring and maintaining internal access controls.
- Auditing log files for suspicious activity.

Account maintenance can be a key vulnerability in database management. Often the database software vendor will create a DBA account with an easily guessed password. Worse, DBAs may use the default account and password distributed with the database installation. This permits an attacker who has knowledge of the default passwords to gain access to all portions of the database by assuming the identity of the database administrator.

13.6.8   Platform Security.   One area alluded to earlier in this chapter concerns the platforms that host components of an e-business. The platform, or operating system, represents the foundation of the e-business, but it is a potentially weak link in security. If there are cracks in the foundation, there is very little that even strong application software can do to keep the business secure. Therefore, it is imperative that system administrators properly patch platform vulnerabilities and maintain the security of the platform itself. As mentioned earlier, firewalls can go a long way toward blocking access to platform vulnerabilities by unauthorized outsiders. However, authorized but unprivileged users within the firewall can exploit known platform vulnerabilities to yield root privileges on a business-critical machine. Outsiders able to gain user privileges on the platform through any means also may be able to penetrate platform holes into severe security breaches.

Some key steps necessary to maintain platform security include:

- Eliminating default accounts generally installed with the operating system.
- Prohibiting easily guessed passwords.
- Enforcing password expiration.
- Deactivating any unnecessary services that may be running by default.
- Regularly applying security patches to the operating system.
- Updating the operating system to its most recent release.
- Ensuring that file access permissions are properly enforced, so as to prevent unnecessary access to critical files.
- Enabling audit logging with intrusion monitoring.
- Running system file integrity checks regularly.

Some administrators believe that deploying a firewall is an acceptable substitute for configuring their platforms securely. Furthermore, with the plethora of different platforms running their enterprises, many system administrators give up on installing the latest OS patches and on securely configuring their platforms. They mistakenly assume that firewalls will protect them from all threats, even without maintenance. Unfortunately, relaxing host security can make the job of crackers easy. By hopping from machine to machine they usually can find the valuable information they are looking for, or if that is their goal, they can wreak maximum damage.

13.7   SUMMARY.   This chapter has provided an overview of the weakest links in e-commerce systems, including Web clients, network protocols, front-end Web servers, back-end databases, application servers, and the platforms on which they run. Secure network protocols are necessary but certainly not sufficient for securing e-commerce. The vulnerabilities described here are largely based on software flaws that exist in the application layer of e-commerce transactions.

Perhaps the most common vulnerability in e-commerce systems is misconfiguration of software. Because the responsibility for software configuration lies with the user, a security policy must be implemented and enforced. Once a system is configured, it is important to subject it to third-party validation and testing. A third-party audit can ensure that the configured system, including routers, firewalls, servers, and databases, meets the specifications of the security policy. The system also should be tested periodically against well-known, common attacks as well as against newer threats as they arise .

Like any software system, commercial off-the-shelf software has flaws, many of which are security-critical. It is imperative that system administrators stay current with vendor Web sites, with hacker sites, with newsgroups, and with wherever threats and patches to their software are released. Both the security and hacker communities are constantly at work finding flaws in COTS that software vendors and security firms generally correct quickly. Software consumers—those who buy and use the software— must do their part by applying all relevant patches to their vulnerable software.

For custom-developed software, which includes front-end Web pages, application servers, CGI scripts, and mobile content such as ActiveX or Java, developers must do everything possible to ensure that their software is not vulnerable to attack and that it does not infringe on users' privacy.

13.8   FURTHER READING

Anderson, R. *Security Engineering: A Guide to Building Dependable Distributed Systems.* New York: John Wiley & Sons, 2001.

McGraw, G., and E. Felten. *Securing Java.* New York: John Wiley & Sons, 2000.

Rubin, A. *White Hat Security Arsenal: Tackling the Threats.* Reading, MA: Addison-Wesley, 2001.

Rubin, A., D. Geer, and M. Ranum. *The Web Security Sourcebook.* New York: John Wiley & Sons, 1997.

Viega, J., and G. McGraw. *Building Secure Software: How to Avoid Security Problems the Right Way.* Reading, MA: Addison-Wesley, 2001.

13.9   NOTES

1. This chapter is adapted from Chapter 4 of Anup K. Ghosh, *Security and Privacy for E-Business* (New York: John Wiley & Sons, 2001); adapted by permission.

2. Anup K. Ghosh, *E-Commerce Security: Weak Links, Best Defenses* (New York: John Wiley & Sons, 1998).

3. C. Cowan, P. Wagle, C. Pu, S. Beattie, and J. Walpole, "Buffer Overflows: Attacks and Defenses for the Vulnerability of the Decade," *Proceedings of the DARPA Information Survivability Conference and Exposition* (DISCEX 2000), January 25–27, 2000, Hilton Head, S.C. Published by IEEE Computer Society Press, Los Alamitos, CA.

4. Ibid.

5. G. McGraw and G. Morrisett, "Attacking Malicious Code: A Report to the Infosec Research Council," *IEEE Software,* Vol. 17, No. 5 (September/October 2000), pp. 33–41.

6. Ghosh, *Security and Privacy for E-Business,* chap. 7.

7. B. Schneier, *Applied Cryptography: Protocols, Algorithms, and Source Code in C,* 2nd ed. (New York: John Wiley & Sons, 1995).

8. Ghosh, *E-Commerce Security.*

9. W.A. Arbaugh, W.L. Fithen, and J. McHugh, "Windows of Vulnerability: A Case Study," *IEEE Computer,* Vol. 33, No. 12 (December 2000), pp. 52–59.

10. L. Stein, *Web Security: A Step-by-Step Reference Guide* (Reading, MA: Addison-Wesley, 1998).

11. A. Rubin, D. Geer, and M. Ranum. *The Web Security Sourcebook* (New York: John Wiley & Sons, 1997).

CHAPTER 14

PHYSICAL THREATS TO THE INFORMATION INFRASTRUCTURE

Franklin N. Platt

CONTENTS

14.1   INTRODUCTION.   This chapter describes physical threats that can affect an information system (IS). The infrastructure affected can be any component of a computer system or communications network, any of the cables or wiring that transport data, or any of the support services or utilities needed to sustain full IS performance. The speed and accuracy of any system is dependent on a long chain of physical components as well as on the performance and productivity of all the people who use and maintain each component. Anything less than full system performance can become very costly.

A physical threat is any situation that can disrupt the performance of an information system; the list of potential disruptions of the information infrastructure is long and varied. Disruptions can result directly from accidents, misuse, improper installation or maintenance, equipment failure, natural or man-made hazards, spying, and, increasingly, deliberate attack.

Remote incidents that occur elsewhere—often at considerable distance—also can threaten IS performance. Whether direct or indirect, physical threats often compound themselves and trigger additional situations that cascade through the systems and quickly become disruptive and costly.

Although some threats will certainly happen, costly disruptions need not occur, and protection need not be costly. On the contrary, good security is a process that can add value. This process begins by identifying all potential threats. Then the process can, if possible, assess the likelihood (or even the approximate likelihood) of each threat and evaluate the possible impact in terms of disruption, costs, embarrassment, and loss of business. Once the potential threats are quantified, they can be prioritized, and effective protection can be implemented as part of a strategic risk management process that maximizes value, enhances morale and productivity, and best serves customers. Absent a thorough planning process, security becomes a flawed selection of vendors or solutions, which can only add cost.

The events of September 11, 2001 sounded a shattering wake-up call that threats can actually happen and that even the best security products, practices, and services are of little value without proper planning, implementation, and support. This chapter suggests a comprehensive security planning process that can add value and help avert disaster. Chapter 15 then goes on to suggest implementation that can optimize morale, productivity, and profitability.

14.2   BACKGROUND AND PERSPECTIVE.   History and statistics are of little value in predicting future threats. The past is no longer prologue because many new risks are emerging, and incidents are increasingly widespread, complex, damaging, and costly. Proliferating and increasingly dispersed system and network components are often fragile and hard to protect. Hybrid configurations of new and legacy systems vastly complicate protection.

As discussed in Chapter 4, there are few reliable threat statistics. Many security incidents are never detected. Even when incidents are detected, the majority are not reported for fear of embarrassment, liability, or loss of business. Many security incidents are covered up as quality-control problems for the same reasons, or are misdiagnosed because no one had time to determine the true cause(s). Lacking reliable precedents, predicting future threats is especially difficult—yet increasingly necessary.

Most incidents happen suddenly, without warning, and often where least expected. Many threats once thought to be unlikely now occur widely and strike with surprising intensity and devastation. Inexperience and complacency are very likely to turn threats into costly incidents. Businesses that are well prepared will survive, while many others will not.

14.2.1 Today's Risks Are Greater.   Today's risks are increasingly sophisticated, unpredictable, potentially serious, and commonplace. Disruptive events can result from mistakes, accidents, hacking, snoopers, vandalism, disgruntled or disruptive persons, labor disputes, demonstrations, or civil unrest, extremists of many stripes, and, increasingly, domestic and international terrorism. Although violent crime statistics have decreased in recent years, these data are misleading because they rarely include workplace-related events. Violence in the workplace is becoming increasingly common and often occurs without warning. Incidents can include harassment, bomb scare, robbery, hostage situation, shooting, or arson. The use of weapons of mass destruction is increasingly possible. These include biological and chemical agents that are far more dangerous than conventional weapons,.

Today's would-be perpetrators tend to be dedicated, well trained and equipped, persistent, and patient. Almost anyone can cause trouble: full-time employees, temporary or contract workers, service personnel, maintenance or construction crews, repair persons, inspectors, meter readers, building personnel, visitors, vendors, consultants, or anyone posing in any of these roles.

Physical threats can extend beyond direct attacks. Many scares do not result in actual violence, and disruptive incidents can occur outside of or well removed from the workplace. However, and wherever, they happen, violence-related incidents are increasingly commonplace, disruptive, and costly.

What was once the stuff of melodrama is now thought to be commonplace and proliferating. All too many people with access to the workplace have backgrounds, allegiances, and emotional drives that are entirely unknown. Even previously trustworthy people may be forced into espionage, sabotage, or other criminal activities. Some are ideologically motivated, while others are simply duped. Still others are drawn by opportunities for personal gain. And there is very little risk of detection or apprehension for most would-be perpetrators. Government officials can substantiate some of the incidents, but much of this information is not public. Only the most egregious cases are publicized.

Informed opinion suggests that such crimes are already widespread and rapidly increasing. Yet few incidents are detected and fewer still ever reported. Worse yet, there are scant data on the extent of crimes against information systems, theft of data, espionage, or similar activities that can clearly cause huge business losses.

Those who threaten the IS infrastructure must at least gain access to it, but often this can be done inconspicuously, by deception, or simply by forced entry. A physical attack may be the best way to compromise an information system. Often many vital system components are vulnerable, exposed, or easily accessible. These components include wiring and cable runs, connection and junction points, system and network equipment, and the utilities that support them. Attacks or spying by physical means are often easy, fast, safe, and sure.

14.2.2   Likely Targets.   Businesses and organizations are increasingly likely to be targets of hackers, disgruntled employees, competitors, disturbed persons, demonstrators, hate groups, extremists, and even terrorists. Motives may include a conspicuous, tempting, or challenging target; rage or revenge, opportunity for adverse publicity, or a political statement; extortion, blackmail, or personal profit (which can be very substantial). Often there are no discernable motives. And beyond being likely targets, most businesses are convenient, easy, and safe targets as well, because most are unaware and unprepared for today's threats. Government facilities remain preferred targets, but many are now better protected than most businesses.

Another likely threat arises from the need of extremists and terrorists to finance their activities. Many groups and all independent, self-directed cells are dependent on crime to fund a long and expensive list of their necessities. Robberies, equipment theft, extortion, blackmail, spying, and pirating software are all credible threats to business. In addition, many foreign governments, businesses, and criminal organizations are actively engaged in spying. Although these are mainly corporate security and logical security problems, they are also potential physical threats that must be deterred.

14.2.3   Productivity Issues.   Good security is strongly correlated with high productivity, customer satisfaction, and goodwill. Good security can strategically enhance each of these factors to add both value and profit. Anything less than good security only invites wasted time and money.

People who do not feel safe will not be productive. This applies to employees, visitors, vendors, and others on premises as well as to customers, stockholders, and other stakeholders at remote locations. Everyone must be comfortable that information systems are uninterruptible, that privacy is assured, and that everyone using these systems is physically safe. Therefore, everyone concerned must be involved in implementing good security.

Whenever a security incident occurs, morale and productivity are likely to plummet and can remain low for weeks or months. Whether or not the infrastructure is actually affected, significant disruption of operations is likely. Even when there is no injury or damage, the perception of such an event can be costly; it can disrupt productivity, lose business and customers, and jeopardize goodwill. Even an unrelated incident, accident, nearby event, or a medical emergency can cause significant and prolonged disruption before productivity eventually climbs back to normal. The costs of recovering from any such event can be enormous.

Some examples of incidents observed by the author:

- An outside accountant died from a heart attack during a meeting with several managers.
- A construction worker collapsed with a heart attack in front of many employees and died just as an ambulance crew arrived.
- A senior officer in his early 40s choked at a company reception and died in front of over 100 employees.

All three people died in the workplace, but all three could have been saved had there been proper medical equipment and trained people. In each case, morale and productivity plummeted and remained so for weeks. The business costs were enormous.

In another incident, an executive was robbed at gunpoint in a men's rest room that was publicly accessible. While he managed to flee without injury, the entire office was traumatized and little work was done for weeks. To make matters worse, there were rumors of similar robberies within the building complex. Here again, morale plummeted and took even longer to restore. Little work was done. Customers who were initially sympathetic soon took their business elsewhere. Again, the cost was high.

None of these incidents related directly to information systems. Yet each incident caused significant and prolonged disruptions that good infrastructure security might have prevented. Prior to those events, senior management had discussed the risks but had decided that no special protection was needed. Their premises security people viewed these threats as minimal, based on assurances from the landlords that the buildings were amply protected. Each of the threat assessment processes was therefore flawed.

No one knows how often productivity-related events occur. Businesses do not report them, and neither do the media. But they do happen, and most can be prevented or at least substantially mitigated at far less cost than the consequences.

14.2.4   Terrorism and Violence Are Now Serious Threats.   Acts of terrorism and violence are now a reality that can occur anywhere in the world. September 11, 2001 and the events that followed have brought home the stark reality that violence can happen anywhere and can cause massive damage and disruption. Information systems far removed from the actual incidents can be disrupted.

Workplace violence is also happening with increasing frequency and often at facilities thought to be safe. Bomb and biological or chemical scares, personal threats, harassment, hostage situations, and shootings all happen with increasing regularity. Whether or not actual violence occurs, these are all productivity-related events that can seriously disrupt the performance of information systems for a long time. Therefore, these become infrastructure security issues that require special protection and should not be left to premises security personnel to prevent.

There are other serious threats from domestic groups generally unknown to the public. Some of these are explained well in the Project Megiddo report published by the Federal Bureau of Investigation (FBI) in 1999 in anticipation of the Millennium. The report provides "an FBI strategic assessment of the potential for domestic terrorism in the United States undertaken in anticipation of or response to the arrival of the new millennium."[1] The risks cited remain unchanged.

Attempted violence is now a serious threat to all IS infrastructures. However, thorough security planning can do much to avoid trouble and needless expenses.

14.2.5   Costs of a Threat Happening.   Direct costs of system downtime can exceed many thousands of dollars per hour. The losses include inactivity of people who cannot use the systems, support and maintenance people diverted to restoring operations, recovery expenses, overtime, and often lodging and food. Usually, many outside resources are needed for response and recovery. Everything becomes very expensive, very quickly.

Indirect costs can be significant also. Reestablishing and keeping good public relations can be expensive. Often many public announcements, new releases and briefings to the news and financial media and to stockholders are needed to neutralize public embarrassment and control rumors. Key customers must be contacted and reassured and pending orders rescheduled. Still more costs include lost business or market share and dropping stock prices. Competitors often will take as much advantage as they can, which necessitates further costs defending brands and reputation.

These costs can be fatal for the enterprise unless strong security measures are deployed effectively and quickly. Any infrastructure outage of more than a few hours is usually devastating. Many victims never recover.

Before any threat assessment can be meaningful, a list of possible costs for response and recovery is needed. These should include all foreseeable direct and indirect costs and expenses and a large contingency amount for unforeseen costs that will likely occur.

14.2.6   Who Must Be Involved?   Many threats to information systems also involve corporate or premises security whose role is to protect people and property within and surrounding the workplace. But the computer infrastructure requires additional protection. It must be strong, fast-acting, focused on specific targets, and closely monitored. Effective early-warning systems are necessary in order to prevent threats from becoming events. In reality, each security function will have its own needs and priorities and use its own resources. But during a serious incident, security for the premises, the information systems, and the infrastructure must coordinate efficiently and effectively. They must also work smoothly with local fire and police and other emergency responders and with the many resources they can provide.

Who, then, should manage the process of determining the threats to the IS infrastructure? And who are the stakeholders who should be involved in this process?

The best person to manage the physical security of information systems is one who knows a great deal about possible threats and the infrastructure. The office manager, facilities manager, or corporate security director is usually ill equipped to determine or manage IS security. Often, too, the chief information officer (CIO) and IS security officers deal with protecting data and data processing and are not the best persons to understand physical security, especially in a large installation. Therefore, the best person is a trusted individual with the right knowledge and experience and enough time to manage the process well.

Another consideration is that no one person should know all the secrets, a point that becomes especially important in dealing with the IS infrastructure. When trouble comes, many experts must mobilize very quickly and effectively. To do this, the responders must be familiar with all the information systems and have fast access to the infrastructure. But they do not need to know much about the facility's defenses or the logical defenses. Neither do the corporate and premises security personnel need to know the logical (i.e., data-related) or infrastructure security. It is wise to divide the secrets so that no one group knows or has access to them all. Having done this, multiple persons can then share each portion of the secrets, so that no one person is indispensable.

Only the defense implementations should be secrets. The process of determining the underlying threats should be common knowledge among all the stakeholders involved.

14.2.7   A Standard Process.   Most businesses use "disaster response," "crisis management," "damage control," or similar terms. These processes are usually proprietary and do not share common language or standardized procedures that can be understood by everyone involved. Many regulated industries must develop emergency response plans using terms and formats dictated by the regulating agency, which makes these terms and formats proprietary as well. Examples are industries that use hazardous or nuclear materials or operate dams.

Many organizations that are involved in emergency response—such as hospitals and emergency medical services, schools, volunteer agencies, National Guard and military units—use still other terms and models.

During an emergency that involves a large area, these many and disparate approaches present major communications barriers and cause unnecessary misunderstandings, delays, and wasted resources.

Everyone experiences essentially the same threats, is likely to be overwhelmed in a major emergency, and can benefit enormously from outside resources. Yet each venue tends to use dissimilar models, terms, and procedures that are often unintelligible to the others. In many cases, their models become file-and-forget plans and procedures that no one understands or accepts. A standard process and language are needed.

Governments use the term "emergency management" and are beginning to adopt a comprehensive model developed by the Federal Emergency Management Agency (FEMA), which encompasses all hazards, coordinates all resources efficiently, and is clear, concise, understood, and accepted by everyone involved.[2]

Fortunately a new standard is emerging, one developed and supported by every organization involved: U.S. and foreign government agencies, business and industry, associations, insurers, and academic institutions where emergency management is taught. The new standard contains several components, all of which can be helpful in determining and controlling threats.

The National Fire Protection Association (NFPA) has published Standard 1600, *Recommended Practices for Disaster Management.* This standard "establishes a common set of criteria for disaster and emergency management programs in both the public and private sectors." A fire marshal or a large fire department may have a copy of this standard and can provide briefing. It is also obtainable directly from NFPA.[3]

NFPA Standard 1600 evolved from FEMA's SLG-101, *State & Local Guide for All-Hazard Emergency Operations Planning,* and subsequent formats and toolkits adapted by many states. Local emergency managers should have SLG-101 and state-specific formats and toolkits. If not, contact the regional or state office of emergency management.

FEMA's CAR (Capability Assessment for Readiness) reporting procedure to assess emergency preparedness also will be helpful as an emerging standard procedure. CAR was developed as an annual reporting procedure to evaluate emergency preparedness and highlight shortcomings. The format is a comprehensive checklist that can be adapted easily to any security need. Contact local or state emergency officials for more information.

Another useful model to standardize the security planning process is the *Incident Command System* (ICS) of emergency response command, control, and coordination. While there are some state-specific variances, the ICS model is used by most fire, police, medical, and emergency responders, and is embedded in many state and local emergency operations plans. Information and guidelines are available from the National Interagency Incident Management System (NIIMS). Local and state emergency officials can provide information as to regional versions.

Security preparedness based on one or more of these standards may become mandatory for many organizations and essential for others that want to avoid liability, obtain insurance, or use capital markets to mitigate risk. Knowing these standards will help the threat assessment process and, later, can provide better protection.

14.2.8 Liability Issues.   Aside from the need for efficient emergency response, another issue is becoming increasingly important, potentially costly, and often overlooked. This is the issue of liability. Any organization has a legal and fiduciary responsibility to protect people and property within and surrounding its premises. If any injury or damage occurs for almost any reason, accusations of negligence are likely to follow. The resultant legal costs, bad publicity, fines, and awards can be devastating.

If negligence is alleged, the question is whether the organization was properly prepared for any emergency. The question arises: Did management perform its duty to protect the organization? An affirmative answer would require at least:

- Evidence of a thorough threat assessment process
- Good security policies that have been well implemented
- Proper training and current security awareness
- Periodic drills, exercises, security reviews, and feedback from known events
- Periodic updates to assure that security remains effective

If it can be demonstrated that these measures were not taken, or that there were deviations from generally accepted standards, the result could be punitive as well as compensatory damage awards. If gross negligence is alleged, insurance may not defend the accused organizations or individuals, who would then be personally liable. Even with insurance in effect, it may not be sufficient to cover the very large penalties that juries commonly award.

Hence, emphasis must be placed on carefully determining the threats, so that protection can be based on a threat assessment and not on the availability of commercial products or solutions.

14.2.9   Definitions and Terms.   Information system security is simply a means of performance assurance—another element of quality control. Good security precludes any IS infrastructure disruption that might cause a slowdown or loss of productivity, a loss of data, breach of privacy, or a disruption of the systems, networks, and utilities that support any IS. Good security assures that all information systems remain fully operational, robust, and accurate and that all data remain private and cannot be compromised.

There are three elements of IS security. Each element must be specifically designed to protect against different threats of varying scope and intensity. The three elements include

1. *Logical security,* which is also known as information systems security, protects only the integrity of data and of information processing. Data are not physical because they consist only of electronic, magnetic, or optical bits.
2. *Physical security,* which is also called infrastructure security, protects the rest of the information systems and all of the people who use, operate, and maintain the systems. Physical security also must prevent any type of physical access or intrusion that can compromise logical security.
3. *Premises security,* which is also known as corporate or facilities security, protects the people and property within an entire area, facility, or building(s), and is usually required by laws, regulations, and fiduciary obligations. Premises security protects broad areas. It often provides perimeter security, access control, smoke and fire detection, fire suppression, some environmental protection, and usually surveillance systems, alarms, watchmen, and guards. Premises security is often an extension of law enforcement.

14.3   THREAT ASSESSMENT PROCESS.   Effective security planning begins with a threat assessment. This process begins by establishing an organization, staffing, and budget approval, and then forming a steering committee that includes all the stakeholders (see also Chapters 42, 46, and 47). The first tasks are to identify all potential threats, to determine their likelihood and to estimate the direct and indirect costs of each threat, to evaluate and prioritize each threat, and to prepare and present a final report that each committee member signs. This report becomes evidence of due diligence to avoid liability and becomes the basis for protecting the infrastructure, which is described in Chapter 15.

14.3.1   Set Up a Steering Committee.   The security planning process is not effective unless everyone involved participates (see also Chapter 35). The best way to do this is to establish a steering committee that will help identify and assess potential threats and later help develop a comprehensive protection plan.

The committee should represent all stakeholders and include as much experience, knowledge, and perspective as possible. It should include users, administrators, management, key partners, customers, and vendors. Legal, financial, and human resources representatives should participate, as should objective outside experts, facilitators, and a project manager. The best committee chair is often an outside facilitator who is immune from political or cultural bias, loyalties, or product preferences.

This can be a virtual committee and need never meet in full session. Communications can be electronic or by phone. Staff can interview members and gather data. Confidentiality need not be an issue, either. The committee's purpose is advisory and to assist in planning. No member need have knowledge of the resulting security systems and procedures. Each member, however, must sign off on the committee's final report.

Once its initial mission is completed, it is well for this committee to convene at least annually to review new and changing threats and to assess how well the security systems have performed. This committee not only represents all involved stakeholders but can provide assurance that management does not neglect to exercise, review, and update the security plan. In effect, the committee provides due diligence that management has fulfilled its fiduciary responsibilities.

14.3.2   Sources of Information and Assistance.   Historical information is the starting point. This includes data from the weather bureau, fire and police departments, utility companies, newspapers, and local knowledge of relevant events that have occurred in the region. Power and communications utility companies can provide outage reports, but their terms must be clearly defined. Their terms used can be very misleading. For example, an "outage" may include only interruptions of more than a specified duration. Regional and state regulatory authorities, public utility commissions, industry and professional organizations, and business development groups may provide similar material.

Most emergency managers in the local government have a hazard mitigation plan that lists all hazards that have occurred throughout the state and provides dates, descriptions, and map locations that often go back for a century. Often these documents reveal that certain threats are far more prevalent than one might imagine. Emergency managers and a state's Office of Emergency Management may be of considerable assistance about similar data for man-made and technical hazards.

Another useful source is FEMA CPG I-35, *Capability and Hazard Identification Program* (CHIP), published in 1985 and no longer available at FEMA's Web site as of this writing. However, many states have issued a newer, broader version. Many state and local officials have implemented a CHIP program, including a hazard assessment workbook, hazard identification, and vulnerability assessments. Exact titles may vary among states.

Finally, expert advice on technical and man-made threats may be available from vendors, suppliers, neighboring businesses, service and maintenance personnel, consultants, and academics.

14.3.3   Identify All Possible Threats.   The first step is to identify all possible threats that might affect the IS infrastructure. This can be a very long list. It should include threats that are direct as well as indirect and threats that could affect the general area while also disrupting IS operations. It is best to list all threats, including ones that are very unlikely to occur, as a precaution against inadvertently omitting some that might have more importance than is apparent at first glance. A CHIP document can be used as a checklist to assure that all threats have been listed.

Do not rely on force majeure—for example, the threat of a major earthquake—as an excuse that a particular threat may be unavoidable. Force majeure does not limit liability. Even though such an event is an act of God and therefore cannot be prevented, the threat is still real and likely can be mitigated. Nor may acts of war hold up as an excuse.

14.3.4   Determine the Likelihood of Each Threat.   The steering committee should estimate the likelihood that each risk may happen. Usually, likelihood is expressed as an annual probability and using a relative scale from zero (none) to five (very likely) is suggested. If, for example, the community's floodplain maps show that a site is within an area where major flooding has occurred only once in the past century, the committee might rate the likelihood as 1, provided that it is reasonably certain that such a flood will not actually occur every five or every 10 years because of the world's changing weather patterns. It is often wise to include risks deemed totally unlikely, although with a 0 rating, to indicate that the committee has not overlooked those risks.

14.3.5   Approximate the Direct Costs.   Once all the possible risks are determined and the likelihood of each one is estimated, the next step is to assess the potential losses and costs associated with each risk. A relative scale of one (very low) to five (very high) is suggested. Ideally, the group can settle on approximate order-of-magnitude estimates corresponding to each of these values, thus reducing the extent of variation in the responses. Threat assessment usually uses a worst-case scenario, because this tends to be the most realistic. There will be many line items to consider, with frequent disagreement as to the appropriate dollar value of each one. It is important to be sure that all possible line items are included and to obtain some consensus as to a possible range of direct costs.

Direct costs include estimated costs, both direct and consequential, to locate the trouble(s), stabilize the infrastructure, repair and install replacements, reboot, restore databases, and thoroughly test the systems. Temporary facilities and outside services may be needed. There may be costs to repair property damage and restore premises as well as costs of premium time, special services, and food and lodging.

Directly attributable threat costs can include loss of productivity of system users, overtime needed to regain production schedules, contracted services, and interim facilities—any of which can far exceed expectations. Loss of business, customers, and market share, falling stock price, and the cost of public relations efforts to offset rumors and adverse news reports are some of the indirect costs that may result from each risk.

The direct costs will continue to accumulate during the response phase, throughout the recovery period, and possibly long after. There will certainly be discussions of the possible dollar amounts. Precise figures are impossible, so simply agree on representative amounts. The relative ratings, from one to five (but perhaps carried to one decimal place), are the important numbers because they serve primarily to direct discussion to what the group generally accepts as important.

14.3.6 Consider Cascading Costs.

Some threats can trigger consequential threats. These become secondary threats—often called cascading threats—that add still more impact costs. For example, during a serious fire there will likely be loss of electrical power, cooling, ventilation, communications, and water damage. Each of these conditions is a separate risk in itself. In reality, few hazards occur in isolation, and many of the cascading events can be unexpected and unpredictable, and can trigger still more consequential events and collateral costs.

Nonetheless, it is well to add another calculation to indicate which secondary events might be associated with each primary threat. The first step is to list the potential cascading threats. The next step is to add their cost factors to show a composite cascading cost factor. Use the same scale for each cost factor.

Applying secondary impact costs realistically poses problems. Some economies of scale occur during a disaster, so the total cost of a disaster can be less than the sum of the individual threats. Here is where the experience and perspective of the steering committee becomes valuable. It can develop consensus cost factors for the cost/value analysis described in Chapter 15.

14.3.7 Prioritize the Threats.

Deciding which risks are the most important tends to be subjective and controversial, and often is based on past estimates rather than on actual experience. The steering committee must present a proactive, comprehensive analysis, even though individual opinions will likely differ. Once the committee settles on all the possible risks and the relative likelihood and impact costs of each risk, the evaluation process begins.

First, prioritize the threats. By rating likelihood on a scale from zero to five and impact costs on a scale from one to five, the product of these two factors calculates the relative importance of each individual risk. The suggested formula is:

$$\text{Importance} = \text{Likelihood} \times [\text{Direct Cost} + \text{Secondary Cost(s)}]$$

The resultant values indicate the relative importance of each threat. The higher the value, the greater the importance. And by including very unlikely threats with a scale value of zero, they become of zero importance but remain on the preliminary versions of the list to show that these threats were not forgotten.

The list should then be sorted in order of importance; at this point, those items considered unimportant can be deleted. The list that is generally circulated to all interested parties—usually members of the management team—will name the threats listed in order of importance, but it is generally unwise to include any evaluation data. In some situations, the whole list may be considered confidential.

14.3.8 Completing the Threat Assessment Report.

Once the threat list is prioritized, the committee should prepare a report for general circulation, which will stand as the reference source data for the planning process that follows. Be very careful that this report does not suggest vulnerabilities to would-be troublemakers. Indeed, the report might best be classified. Each member should sign his or her concurrence, then the report must be presented to and discussed with senior management for their approval. The work of the steering committee is done at this point.

Chapter 15 describes a planning process that relates to specific threats and how to manage these risks. The remainder of this chapter deals with the many and varied risks that can impact the infrastructure of information systems.

14.4   GENERAL THREATS.   Many potential threats can disrupt the information system infrastructure. These threats are separated for discussion into natural, technical, and man-made events. But these categories are not important. In actuality, some threats can fall into any or all of these categories.

Accidents, misuse, curiosity, and blunders are likely to cause the most problems. But other threats, such as spying, can happen frequently, are often undetected, and can be very costly. Vandalism and other physical attacks are increasingly likely and can cause significant damage if unforeseen. The most costly and disruptive physical threats come from violence and possibly terrorism, which must be deterred or mitigated to avoid devastating costs.

Most of these risks pertain to premises security but are included here because premises or logical security alone generally does not protect the IS infrastructure. Whereas premises security needs to provide reasonable protection when an event occurs, good IS security requires deterrence, early warning, fast response, and contingency plans to keep vital information systems performing. Threats to the infrastructure present special needs that are different from logical threats.

14.4.1   Natural Events.   Natural events are becoming ever more frequent and widespread as weather patterns seem to be changing. Severe flooding, lightning, strong winds and tornadoes, snow and ice conditions, wildfires, earthquakes, drought, disease, and contamination are increasingly likely to impact IS performance. Natural events can disrupt business in any number of direct and consequential ways—many unexpected—depending on the locations of information systems, networks, terminals, data storage, cables, and utilities. While natural events cannot be prevented, their impact can be mitigated. Natural threats can include the following:

14.4.1.1   Blight.   A blight or infestation caused by disease, weather, or insects can disrupt operations, support systems, and utilities.

14.4.1.2   Building or Bridge Collapse.   Even indirectly, this can require evacuation, disrupt productivity, and isolate workers.

14.4.1.3   Dam Failure.   Any obstacle downstream or below a dam can be destroyed if it breaches. Most dams are well maintained and protected from natural hazards but are still at risk to technical and man-made threats. Few people imagine this could ever happen. But, if it does, even far away, damage and disruption will be significant.

14.4.1.4   Drought.   A prolonged period without rain increases the dangers of fire, smoke damage, shortages of potable or cooling water, and transportation disruptions. People cannot work and equipment cannot function in dust or smoke, and most facilities cannot be sealed. Evacuation may be necessary. Hydroelectric power may be rationed.

14.4.1.5   Earthquake and Volcanic Eruption.   Many areas of the United States are at moderate risk and likely to experience only moderate and infrequent earthquake activity. But authorities believe that some major metropolitan areas that have no history of earthquake activity are at high risk of a major earthquake. Even moderate earthquakes can disrupt utilities, keep people from work, or topple equipment cabinets and wall racks. In addition, sections of the West and Northwest are considered prone to severe volcanic activity.

14.4.1.6 *Epidemic.*   A widespread outbreak of disease can severely impact business operations.

14.4.1.7 *Landslide.*   A landslide, mudslide, or avalanche can disrupt transportation and utilities, damage property, and isolate workers. Coastal erosion during a severe storm can cause the same problems.

14.4.1.8 *Flood.*   Heavy rain, snowmelt, or ice-jams cause flooding that can damage buildings and utilities, disrupt transportation, and isolate people. Urban flooding (in developed areas) can be caused by the same events and by broken water mains, overflowing storm sewers, and fires. Any of these events can disrupt IS operations. Ironically, floods often create a shortage of potable and cooling water that businesses need to operate.

14.4.1.9 *Hurricane or Tornado.*   Severe storms can disrupt a wide area, damage buildings, interrupt utilities, disrupt transportation, and require evacuation. Repairs and restoration can take weeks.

14.4.2 Technical Events.   Many possible threats can disrupt the IS infrastructure directly or indirectly. Worse yet, threats often cascade to trigger other threats that can further disrupt the infrastructure.

14.4.2.1 *Utility Disruptions.*   Blackouts, brownouts, outages, and lightning all affect electrical power and will necessitate uninterruptible power supplies (UPS), surge suppressors, and emergency backup generators to continue operations and avoid damaging equipment.

14.4.2.2 *Physical Attacks.*   Electronic (logical) hacking from within the organization, over its networks, or from anywhere in the world via the Internet, dial-up, wireless channels, or dedicated communications lines are the most common ways to penetrate information systems. Although electronic attacks can be thwarted, physical attacks are more difficult to deter or detect; they require carefully guarded assets and an effective early-warning system, to prevent the serious damage that can result very quickly.

14.4.2.3 *Coordinated Attacks.*   Just as electronic attacks often occur simultaneously and in great numbers, multiple physical attacks are increasingly likely as determined groups target information systems. Some attacks may be diversions in order to plant a surveillance device, malicious software, or a back door that hackers can use to enter the system electronically. Other coordinated attacks may intend significant damage and disruption that will be long and hard to repair. Therefore, even the remote possibility of a coordinated attack requires very strong, fast, and well-implemented security.

14.4.2.4   Hazardous Material (HAZMAT) Incidents.   Uncontrolled release of a hazardous material during storage, processing, or transportation can be a major threat that requires considerable outside assistance. A HAZMAT incident can injure or kill people, severely damage property, disrupt transportation and utilities, and may require immediate evacuation of a large area. HAZMAT accidents within the facility, nearby, or in the region usually occur without warning and can be particularly serious. Chemical weapons of mass destruction that might be used by terrorists are another HAZMAT risk.

14.4.2.5   Radiological Incidents.   Uncontrolled release of radioactive material could pose a serious threat to any persons in the vicinity and those downwind of the site, with consequent disruption of business operations. Many medical service providers, laboratories, and industries commonly use radioactive materials, and many of these are delivered as needed and taken away soon after. Normally, radioactive materials are transported and handled safely so there is no danger, even in the event of a moderate transportation accident. However, trouble does happen occasionally, caused by rogue shippers, a severe fire or explosion, carelessness, criminal activity, and perhaps terrorism.

Generally, except for fallout from a nuclear event, the actual threat during a radiological incident is small, but hysteria and disruption can be widespread. Often, evacuations are ordered. During the Cold War, every U.S. community had one or more civil defense radiation kits with portable equipment to measure actual radioactivity levels and dosimeters to be worn by those who responded to measure accumulated radiation. Many communities still have instruments that are accurately calibrated and people trained to use them. Most of this equipment can be obtained very cheaply through government surplus and calibrated inexpensively. It would be useful to have on hand if any radiological event ever develops. The Federal Emergency Management Agency offers a free home study course on using this equipment.

14.4.2.6   Biological Hazards.   Much the same issues arise when considering biohazards as in other HAZMATs and radioactive substances in particular. At the time of this writing, deadly anthrax spores were being detected in widely-dispersed area. With several deaths, and about two dozen victims already identified, the eventual outcome is completely unknown.

Adding to the actual damages, there is the very real threat of psychological and emotional harm that can be done, even by false rumors of additional biological attacks. Like radiological hazards, biological threats are particularly suited to hoaxes because of the small amount of material required to pose a credible threat; for instance, in one case packages of paste were mailed to office workers with labels indicating that the material contained anthrax. Hoaxes are easily perpetrated by anyone using information readily available from the news media. Actual attacks require materials and skills that many terrorists already possess. Both hoaxes and actual threats can be dispersed throughout widely separated areas.

Biologicals differ from chemical agents, which usually act quickly, and from radiological materials that are readily detectable. Biological agents take longer to detect and identify and can cause considerable disruption.

14.4.3   Fire and Smoke.   Urban and wildfires can wreak havoc on business operations, even when the actual fire is miles away. Utilities and communications can be disrupted, people may be unable to get to or from work, or evacuations may be required.

Smoke is toxic, very hard on electronic equipment, and easily sucked into ventilating systems. Nearby building fires can be a significant threat for the same reasons. Even though the actual fire is well away from the information systems, flooding, smoke conditions, and utility disruptions are likely if the fire is not quickly contained.

A smoke condition or fire inside an equipment room is potentially disastrous. Heated wiring, circuit boards, and plastic components can emit large amounts of toxic chemicals similar to mustard gas. Even though the smoke does not appear thick, a few breaths can be fatal. Smoke also contains carbon monoxide, which is particularly dangerous because people do not realize they are breathing it. Heat buildup inside an equipment room can destroy hardware, components, and wiring rapidly. If not quickly exhausted, smoke condenses on circuit boards and connectors, which begin to corrode. Soon their circuits will be disrupted. Worse yet, small amounts of heat or smoke can significantly hasten component failures, while the cause may not be apparent. This is the principal reason why smoking inside an equipment room must be prohibited and the ban enforced by smoke detectors.

The first priority in any smoke condition is to get people away to a safe area and not let anybody breathe smoke. No one should enter a smoke condition, even briefly. The only safe fire procedure is to evacuate immediately.

14.4.4   Water Leaks and Flooding.   Water or other stored liquids can disrupt information systems in many ways, some of which are unexpected. A burst or frozen pipe many floors above can quickly spread laterally and downward. Roofs and setbacks often cause floods due to ice, clogged drains, or heavy rains. Windows can break, be left open, or leak sufficiently to damage areas below. Unless absolutely unavoidable, there should be no pipes or liquid storage inside, near, or within two floors above any equipment or wiring. This includes heat and water risers, soil lines, roof and setback drains, and, especially, air-conditioning pipes—any of which can corrode and eventually leak or burst.

Sprinkler systems are another major cause of water damage. Usually, sprinklers are activated by temperature sensors, but all too often they are subject to burst pipes or to false temperature sensing. Water can come from any part of the building and can drain laterally and downward to any other part. Some building codes require sprinklers inside equipment rooms, which is often the best and cheapest means of fire suppression, provided the rooms are designed to handle this.

No matter how unlikely a leak or water damage may seem, temperature and flood alarms in all information system areas are wise insurance. Unless it is cost prohibitive, all systems equipment and wiring should be inside enclosed, waterproof cabinets. Desktop units should use water-repellent dust covers during off hours. Sufficient spares should be safely stored in a remote location and brought in to replace any damaged units.

14.4.5   Environmental Problems.   Lack of environmental controls where information system equipment is located can cause major troubles. Dirty air, humidity that is too high or too low, or lack of temperature control will eventually disrupt operations. These are threats often overlooked. Eventually they cause system failures that are usually attributed to faulty equipment and not recognized as environmental problems.

14.4.5.1   *Dust.* Dust is a threat because it blocks ventilation, reduces radiation cooling, and limits convection cooling, any of which conditions can overheat components and greatly shorten their lives. Air within an equipment room should be dust free. It should also be free of exterior contaminants and pollutants. Equipment rooms should utilize separate process-cooling systems which are better suited for, and less expensive than, air-conditioning systems (see Chapter 15).

14.4.5.2   Humidity.   Humidity that is too low or too high threatens the performance of electronic equipment. Relative humidity below 40 percent causes static electricity buildup as people move about. Anyone who is statically charged can destroy electronic equipment by a sparking that may not even be felt. For example, someone statically charged who touches a keyboard can easily destroy chips within the keyboard or the computer, or destroy a hard-disk sector. Relative humidity routinely goes well below 40 percent in cold weather. The higher the humidity, the less static electricity buildup will occur. The only effective protections are humidity control systems. Nonstatic floors or carpeting can help. Floor coatings or sprays are only temporary.

Relative humidity above 60 percent is a threat also. It causes one of two chemical reactions that eventually will damage connectors and disrupt circuits. Either electrolysis or galvanic action will occur, depending on the presence of external direct current. Usually, the reaction is galvanic action that requires no external current. The result in either case is electroplating, whereby metal from one connector slowly migrates to the mating connector. In turn, this bonds the connector so it cannot be opened and eventually changes electrical impedance enough to disrupt the circuits. Examples are circuit boards that become stuck in their sockets and connectors stuck together. The damage is not reversible. The components must be replaced. The only prevention is to keep relative humidity below 60 percent.

14.4.5.3   Temperature.   Temperature of equipment is not as important. Usually, it is enough to keep the room comfortable for people. A room temperature of $72° \pm 3°F$ (about 22° C) is usually comfortable for both people and equipment, although component temperatures inside a unit can be 20°F (11°C) or more higher than the room temperature. Any equipment that uses very much electrical current also generates heat and may need extra cooling. Equipment and wiring should be kept in enclosed cabinets, where temperature can be monitored and well controlled.

14.4.5.4   High-Intensity Radio Frequency Flux.   High-intensity radio frequency flux has been documented in several data centers as a cause of disruption. Nearby commercial radio stations and microwave relay antennas, for example, can emit enough electromagnetic radiation to disrupt control systems in adjacent buildings. Even relatively weak emitters can disrupt computer equipment at close range; cellular phones, for example, are routinely excluded from intensive-care units in hospitals because of documented effects on some medical electronics. Cellular phones have been implicated in specific cases of processor and disk-controller crashes as well as in avionics disruption in commercial aircraft. Many data centers now require cellular phones to be powered off, much as airlines do.

14.4.6   Utility Problems.   Utility problems are similar to environmental problems. They include electrical power that is "dirty," voltage surges and spikes, undervoltage and brownout events as well as blackouts and power outages. Any of these can cause significant disruption and damage, and all are occurring with increasing frequency as power demands accelerate.

Problems can be caused by power coming into the building, by problems within the building, or by interference within the premises. Exterior problems can include feeders, transmission lines, substations, transformers, insufficient power available, loss of generation, and weather-related events, such as ice, wind, and rain. Many problems are due to improper premises wiring or use of power outlets. Power problems also can result from fires and other natural hazards and from technical and man-made events.

To determine the threats, it is necessary to measure and analyze the power into key systems using a recording device that logs all unusual events for a period of at least several days. A competent electrical expert is necessary to interpret the recordings and to consider the likelihood of any power event occurring, whether or not it has already happened in the past.

Threats can be determined only by measuring the protections already in place. Protections include some combination of surge suppressors, power filters, battery backup systems, and emergency generators. These must sustain not only vital information systems but also the people and critical functions necessary to operate and maintain these systems. Many large organizations were caught short in prior blackouts when their generators failed to start, especially in winter or stormy weather. Generators were damaged when the power cycled on and off before the actual outage—as it often does—and the generators would not start. There were no provisions for emergency power to ventilate and cool equipment, power vital workstations and task lighting, gain access to sites in high-rise buildings, or carry more fuel to the generators. And many similar failures occurred that could only be termed shortsighted.

Communications utilities present very similar problems. Unless data lines are fiber optic, voltage surges, spikes, and interference induced onto copper wiring can cause major problems. Lines outside the building can be broken, flooded, damaged by rodents, short-circuited by power lines, severed by an accident, or deliberately cut. There are many potential threats to consider. The only protection is redundancy using other paths and media.

Copper communications cables, terminations, and patch panels also can be tapped for surveillance, which is a significant threat that is rarely detected. Because fiber optic cables and connections must be interrupted to apply a workable tap, they are relatively safe, at least for the moment. See "Wiretaps" below.

14.5 MAN-MADE THREATS. While the general threats tend to be generic and somewhat predictable in their impact, man-made threats tend to be unexpected and to occur suddenly, without warning. They often focus on specific targets but can escalate and cascade rapidly. Because man-made threats are increasingly complex, varied, and potentially serious, these risks must be considered carefully.

14.5.1 Accidents. Most security problems are the result of accidents, lack of quality control, bad design, improper installation, failure to update, or poor maintenance. Disruption often occurs during maintenance. Snooping, blunders, pranks, vandalism, deliberate attacks, and spying are all increasingly prevalent and sophisticated but are still overshadowed by accidents and blunders.

Moving furniture or equipment, especially by outsiders, can damage wiring, connectors, and other equipment sufficiently to crash systems. And while it rarely happens, substantial "accidental" damage can occur during a labor dispute, especially when an outside trade union is brought on site.

Construction work, alterations, repairs, and wiring changes often damage information systems. Crews often drape dropcloths over workstations and equipment to keep off dust and debris. But no one thinks to shut down the equipment first, so it becomes overheated and will probably fail either immediately or soon after. Crews also plug in power tools, floor waxing machines, or vacuum cleaners in whatever outlets are handy. If these happen to be dedicated outlets for systems equipment, damage may well result. In like manner, workstation users often plug time stamps, electric staplers, refrigerators, fans, and immersion heaters into outlets intended for information systems. Such mistakes can cause random problems that are difficult to locate.

Determining accident vulnerabilities involves careful premises inspection, continuing user training and supervision, and enforcement of good rules, policies, and procedures.

14.5.2 Civil or Political Disorder. Certain types of facilities and businesses may become targets for demonstrations, protests, strikes, picketing, or attempted blockades. Incidents can include harassment and intimidation, physical threats and injuries, and armed conflict. Disorder also can result from an economic emergency, such as business closures, an energy shortage or high prices. Public services, such as transit or sanitation, may be disrupted or utilities affected. Violence within or near the workplace is increasingly possible, such as a bomb scare, a violent public disturbance or riot, sabotage, a shooting incident, a knife attack, a hostage incident, or, worse, a threat of weapons of mass destruction. Other potential threats include a deranged person, a work stoppage or lockout, intentional obstruction, or sabotage. Still other threats now increasingly possible include contaminated facilities, air, ground, food, or drinking water. The threat of disruption is very real.

Disruption can easily spill over from trouble happening elsewhere. If violence or severe crimes occur elsewhere, morale and productivity will plummet unless workers receive extra protection and continuous reassurance. During a regional emergency, workers may need to be sheltered and fed inside the facility to maintain operations.

Most of these threats will never occur. But if any do, the impact can be devastating. It is prudent therefore to carefully assess which threats are possible and what can be done to deter or at least mitigate them.

14.5.3 Wiring Runs and Exposed Wire. Wiring and cabling are already vulnerable in many ways—and are becoming increasingly more so. The number and length of IS cables are proliferating and the data they carry is increasingly vital and must not be disrupted. Cables are becoming increasingly fragile and easily damaged by accident, mistake, vandalism, or deliberate attack.

Fiber optic cables are especially fragile. Any unusual pressure or a sharp bend can alter transmission characteristics and may cause failure. Fiber is fast replacing copper wiring as increased capacity is needed for horizontal connections and vertical and backbone runs for local, wide-area, and remote networks. Communications utilities and other information systems are rapidly adding and upgrading their fiber optic capacity.

Copper data cables are generally not much tougher than fiber cables. Crimps or tight bend radii can disrupt them also. In addition, copper wiring is vulnerable to many added risks, including electrical and magnetic interference from light fixtures, motors, and transformers. Lightning is attracted to, and electrical power surges may be induced onto, copper data cables.

Wiring and cables are often damaged during construction or alterations—damage that may not become apparent until the wiring is utilized to full capacity. Generally, but not always, installers are experienced. Other construction workers generally do not understand signal wiring and may not even know they are working near it. Moves, additions, or changes to the systems often disrupt and damage existing wiring, especially nearby cables that are used by other systems.

Cables, patch cords, and connectors are often exposed to accidental damage during routine premises maintenance and cleaning. Vacuum cleaners and shampooing and waxing machines can easily damage both signal and power wiring. Carpet shampooing can soak connections and flood underfloor wiring. Chair and equipment casters and moving or shifting of furniture often damage cables and connectors.

Power cables to critical systems can be threatened also. Generally, compliance with local electrical codes provides strong physical protection but no early warning that trouble may be approaching. Unrestricted access to electrical closets or power distribution panels poses the threat of critical circuits being damaged by accident or deliberately. Cable runs are even more vulnerable, whether the cables are exposed, within partitions, or above ceilings.

A thorough threat assessment requires careful inspection and consideration of everything that might be vulnerable.

14.5.4 Intrusion.   There are many ways to gain access to the infrastructure of information systems. And once an intrusion does occur, disruptions may follow due to accidents, mistakes, snooping, hacking, spying, vandalism, extortion, or deliberate attack. Intrusion threats are not the same as premises access control. The infrastructure's vulnerabilities are different, and early warning is necessary to prevent possible trouble before it happens.

Intrusions via wiring and cabling are covered in the prior section. Here the emphasis is on preventing access to hardware, distribution and termination panels, patch panels, or any of the utilities that support them. Assessing the possible threats first involves inspecting the existing defenses. It is also necessary to determine what physical threats are not covered by premises and logical security.

Unauthorized persons should not be allowed access to any type of equipment room, rack, or closet. Everyone granted access, including visitors, should be logged in and out. And as a second layer of protection, a gatekeeper should always be at hand to observe everyone who enters and leaves, authenticate each person's identity, and know why they need access. Gatekeepers may include guards, receptionists, supervisors, or managers. This function can be performed remotely, using closed-circuit television. In addition, critical hardware should utilize a third layer of protection with surveillance cameras and motion detectors.

Workstations located outside of equipment rooms are generally protected logically—using login procedures, tokens such as smart cards, and biometric devices—depending on the sensitivity of the data they handle. Guards and surveillance equipment may be used also as a part of premises security.

Theft of equipment or components is possible, especially during nonbusiness hours. These are issues best addressed by premises security, except that no sensitive data should be stored in components that could be copied or stolen. The best defense is to keep all removable media and easily transported laptops under lock and key. In the event of theft, media backups and a supply of spare parts and equipment should be available from safe storage.

Thieves often cut the cables between the wall outlets and workstations, rather than take extra time to disconnect them. More frequently, these cables fail due to accidental damage. The only defense is a good supply of spare cables.

Theft and intrusion prevention devices can include case locks and various mechanisms that clamp or tether equipment to walls or furniture. These devices can be intrusive, may hinder maintenance and repair, and are often ineffective against heavy-duty wire cutters or a pry bar. More effective are equipment alarms triggered whenever a case or cabinet is opened or a data cable disconnected. Some equipment manufacturers include these capabilities, which generally work well, provided the equipment is operating and not shut down.

Cabinet locks are generally an effective deterrent, provided that both the locks and the cabinets are sturdy and the cabinets themselves are not easily removed.

14.5.5   Wiretaps.   Fiber optics circuits are difficult and expensive to tap. For the moment at least, a fiber connection must be interrupted to apply a workable tap. And opening a connection should trigger an immediate alarm. Copper circuits, however, are much easier to tap. Wiretaps are very hard to detect—if not impossible—except by close visual inspection, which in itself is cumbersome, difficult, and must be repeated periodically. Most wiretaps are at best inconspicuous. And most taps can be placed quickly and inconspicuously even in occupied spaces.

In general terms, and using information that is commonly known, wiretaps into copper wires are done in several ways. Small, inconspicuous induction coils placed next to a wire can easily pick up the signals without penetrating the insulation. Sometimes the taps are done with tiny probes that reach around the circumference of a wire. Induction taps are generally undetectable, except visually. Wiretaps also are made by bridging circuits with a physical connection at a terminal strip, patch-wiring, test panel, or connector. Bridged wiretaps can be inserted anywhere along a wire by penetrating the insulation with a needle or cutting away a tiny piece of insulation in order to splice a tap wire. Taps are easily connected to an accessible junction box or termination strip. Bridged taps are usually high impedance, so they do not alter the circuit; therefore, like induction taps, they are undetectable, except visually.

Many logical security breaches are set up by "back door" entrances into the systems that are hacked electronically via LANs, the Internet, or a dial-up connection. However, back-door intrusions also can be done physically and these are often much harder to detect or locate. Physical access also can be safer and easier for the intruder. And wiretaps can be far more effective than logical hacking.

Taps are used for spying, changing or erasing data, stealing software, theft of service, planting worms or viruses, or planting decoys to trick responders into thinking they have found the true cause of an incident. Any physical access to the interconnect points, cable runs, servers, clients, or network equipment is a major vulnerability. An experienced person can place a tap within a couple of minutes, unobtrusively, even when under escort and closely watched.

Once a wiretap is in place, it leads to a transmitter, to a storage device with a dial-up modem, or to a monitoring point in a safe place where no one is likely to notice the equipment or people coming or going. The better taps use system power, not batteries. Monitoring can occur within the building or outside, from a vehicle or via a pay telephone anywhere in the world.

At one time, phone taps in the United States were sent on leased telephone lines to another country (usually Mexico) where wiretapping was actually legal. The leased line was a huge expense and, once detected, could easily be traced. This illustrates how profitable wiretaps used to be, even though they could monitor only telephone conversations. Today, all this is completely unnecessary. Powerful wiretaps are now easily installed, effective, inexpensive, harder to trace even if detected, and can yield much more useful data.

There are actually two different wiretap threat situations. One is an experienced professional who can place a tap undetected. The other threat is someone inexperienced who blunders and disrupts the systems.

14.5.6 High-Energy Radio Frequency Weapons. A controversial area of research is high-energy radio frequency (HERF) weapons, which some experts claim pose a serious threat of remote-control damage and disruption to processors. Demonstrations of prototypes at security conferences have shown that bulky apparatus constructed from easily obtained components can cause personal computers to malfunction; however, at this time there is no evidence that available portable equipment exists to project beams of radio frequency emissions at sufficient power to harm computers more than dozens of meters away from the source. In any case, the defense against all HERF weapons is the Faraday cage, which surrounds vulnerable equipment, or even entire rooms or facilities, in copper mesh as part of the casings or walls. However, many skeptics hotly deny the existence of portable, useful HERF weapons.

14.5.7 Workplace Violence and Terrorism. The use of force, harassment, or physical violence is an increasing reality within the workplace. Workplace drug- and alcohol-related incidents are on the upswing, as are workplace crimes necessary to support and conceal such habits. Adding to the threats is the increasing prevalence of rage within or upon the workplace. Any of these incidents can cause widespread trauma and disrupt business operations for months.

Any violence situation—whether threatened, imagined, actual, or peripheral—can seriously disrupt information systems. The infrastructure may be directly affected. More likely, productivity and morale will plummet for a long time following any perceived or actual threat. A safe working environment, security training, and awareness are essential throughout the premises as a whole and specifically for the IS infrastructures.

While most violence and drug-related precautions are beyond the scope of this book, good IS infrastructure security is obviously necessary.

The probable tools of choice for inflicting workplace violence will soon be cheap and easily made weapons of mass destruction (WMD) rather than guns, bombs, or arson. WMDs are far more dangerous, yet small and easily carried in a pocket, package, or briefcase. They are generally inconspicuous, even when placed and activated, and usually very hard to detect, even by those with expert training and expensive equipment.

A small, common-looking object containing biological toxins and powered by a flashlight battery can kill every person inside the largest of office buildings. A vial no larger than one's finger but carrying virulent hemolytic viruses can kill every person within a 20- to 50-mile radius, if it is dispersed correctly. As few WMD compounds have much odor or color, occupants, visitors, bystanders, and responders are all likely victims until the true cause is determined. Illness can begin within minutes, hours, or days. Ordinary personal protective gear and breathing apparatus provide little or no protection.

WMDs can be enormously destructive. A national FEMA, Department of Justice training exercise conducted in May 2000, simulating a biological attack on Denver, Colorado, resulted in an estimated 57,000 fatalities.

WMDs include chemical, biological, incendiary, radiological, and explosive devices. The first two are the most dangerous and difficult to deal with. The explosive elements are likely low power and used to disburse chemical or biological agents. Explosive devices also may be used to disperse radioactive materials to cause greater panic. Because these threats can devastate IS personnel and operations, strong security is needed to prevent their use near information systems or the utilities needed to support them.

Most details on WMD and extremist or terrorist threats are classified, but state and federal authorities can explain the threats, the degree of potential risk, and the possible targets.

14.6   OTHER THREATS.   Additional potential threats can disrupt the information system infrastructure. Some may be direct threats, but many are incidents that can lead to physical disruptions later if they are not precluded or at least well monitored. Examples include opportunities for troublemakers to "case" a facility, observe its systems, and note the defenses. Others are a variety of preventable incidents that will likely lead to accidents later. While most of these situations are premises security issues, they can readily disrupt the IS infrastructure.

Assessment of each of these other threats must include examination of existing premises and protections.

14.6.1   Off-Hour Visitors.   Cleaning and maintenance personnel usually work off hours, hired by a landlord who rarely provides much, if any, supervision or training. Very few of the personnel are aware of security precautions, and most know very little about the systems their equipment can damage. Many are poorly paid, forced to rush their work, and may understand little English.

Waxing floors and shampooing carpets are often outside services. Moving furniture and changing workstations are often done after hours, as are repairs, alterations in occupied office space, and major maintenance. Almost always, these people are unescorted and many are not even logged into or out of the premises or identified in any way. Worse yet, many of these people prop open doors so they can work faster and sometimes so they can take advantage of air-conditioning in adjacent spaces. People often come and go from the premises without proper authorization.

A floor waxing machine grinds everything it touches and will destroy unprotected wiring or connectors, whether or not they are visible to the machine operator. Carpet shampoo uses a lot of liquids and can flood floor-level outlet boxes and drain into underfloor conduits. Threat assessment must first determine whether premises design invites damage, even though cleaning and maintenance personnel work carefully.

Users often compound these threats. Workstations are left unsecured. Systems are often left running continually and not shut down and covered, as they should be before major cleaning or construction. Chairs and wastebaskets that must be moved for cleaning often hide wiring and receptacles. Electrical plugs, receptacles, and unauthorized extension cords for critical equipment are often unlabeled; the well-meaning cleaning staff can unknowingly unplug servers to power their cleaning equipment.

Messengers and deliveries are another source of trouble, especially during off hours. While the majority of messengers and delivery personnel are legitimate and honest, some are not. The best policy is to admit no outsider into any workplace. Everyone should be stopped at the reception or delivery desk, with no access into the workplace. This has the added security feature that the deliverer cannot see where money, wallets, or handbags are kept. A night bell or intercom outside a locked door should be used to prevent entry to a sensitive facility.

14.6.2   Storage Rooms.   Rooms used to store computer supplies, paper, or forms are especially dangerous if a fire occurs. For example, cartons of multipart computer forms and reams of paper expand when they burn. Then the carton bursts and the paper explodes into a conflagration that spreads quickly and burns at a very high temperature. Such a fire occurred in a high-rise office building in Manhattan. Even though the fire was quickly contained, building columns were so weakened that the building nearly toppled. The cause of this fire was determined to be a cigarette butt that fell between several closely stacked cartons.

Any room containing flammable materials must have smoke detectors, sprinklers, and sufficient fire extinguishers nearby. Storage rooms should be kept locked and access should be limited to trusted persons, if only to protect the value of the contents.

Backup tapes, diskettes, and optical storage media should be kept securely in locked rooms or in fireproof storage cabinets. Duplicate backups also should be stored in a safe place off site. These rooms should have access control, open-door alarms, and smoke detectors.

14.6.3   Medical Emergencies.   Most medical emergencies will cause information system disruptions. Some emergencies will be minor, but others can disrupt operations seriously and for a prolonged period. Offices with many or high-level visitors especially need emergency medical capability. Vendors also must be protected while on or near the premises Few managers realize how much trouble can ensue or for how long operations may suffer following a medical emergency. Therefore, it is prudent to consider these threats and how information systems can be protected.

Increasingly, places where people work, visit, or congregate have first aid equipment, supplies, and personnel on hand who have been trained to use them. Increasingly, such equipment includes oxygen and a defibrillator. Many personnel in such places should be currently certified in cardiopulmonary resuscitation and first aid.

14.6.4   Using an Illicit Terminal.   A convenient method to set up a logical intrusion or attack is to unplug a desktop terminal or workstation that has limited functionality and substitute a full-featured machine. Anyone with a full-featured notebook computer and physical access to the network may be able to substitute it for such a terminal easily.

The illicit user may then be able to log onto the network (possibly as a trusted user with his or her own password), search for restricted information, and use the full-featured machine to copy the information. Or the illicit user simply connects a modem to a nearby telephone receptacle to export data conveniently.

The illicit user may use hacking programs to gain supervisory status to access more sensitive information, crack passwords, steal software, infect the network with malicious software, or install a back-door entrance into the network that an accomplice can use to spy, monitor network traffic, modify or destroy data, and, very likely, obliterate evidence of any intrusion.

Such an intrusion can be done quickly, the full-function computer removed, and the original workstation reconnected. A service technician, vendor, or consultant could breach the network during business hours in the guise of checking the client's machine or LAN connection. Maintenance personnel working off-hours also could substitute a terminal inconspicuously.

Security awareness is the best prevention. No one should be swapping equipment or connections unless a manager, supervisor, or nearby workers know the person's identity and what he or she is doing. If in doubt, the activity should be reported. The second best prevention is good network security, with alarms when any desktop systems are opened, disconnected, or shut down.

14.7   CONFIDENTIAL INFORMATION ABOUT THREATS.   Many other threats should not be mentioned publicly: they are easily accomplished and likely to be used by anyone with a grievance. Many can easily incite copycat incidents. Other such threats use tools or devices that are easily obtained, are inconspicuous while in use, and can be safely hidden after the crime. Avoiding such threats is difficult, and apprehension is unlikely. Nonetheless, mitigation is possible, and sometimes even deterrence, once these threats are known and understood.

Most vendors, installers, and consultants have long lists of possible ways to disrupt, snoop, or destroy specific types of information systems. No threat assessment can be complete without asking all persons involved for whatever attack methods they can suggest as well as for methods of preventing or mitigating each threat.

There are also useful sources of information and guidance that are not generally public. Some material is derived from classified information, but briefings and even limited copies may be made available to those who need it. More general information may be available from local, state, and federal agencies, regulatory bodies, peer groups, business associations, volunteer organizations, vendors, and consultants involved in emergency response.

14.8 SUMMARY. Many threats can damage the infrastructure of information systems and disrupt operations. These are increasingly frequent, widespread, severe, and potentially costly. Although perception and acceptance of most potential threats remains low, the risks to the IS infrastructure are steadily increasing.

Maintaining full IS performance is increasingly vital, and any threat to the infrastructure can quickly disrupt operations and prove extremely costly. The only realistic protection is to carefully consider all the potential threats that can occur, assess the likelihood that each may happen, and evaluate the probable impact if it does. Impact costs must include all of the costs of response and recovery, such as time and expenses and loss of business, customers, or reputation as well as the costs of reestablishing brand recognition. Impact costs also must include the potentially huge value of data lost to others, destroyed, or otherwise unavailable for full IS performance.

Once the likelihood and potential impact of each threat is known, potential threats can be prioritized and effective protections developed. Good security is therefore a process, not a product or packaged solution. When planned, implemented, and maintained carefully, security adds value. Anything less can only waste time and money.

14.9 FURTHER READING

Brownlee, N., and E. Guttman. *Expectations for Computer Security Incident Response.* RFC 2350, 1998; *www.cis.ohio-state.edu/htbin/rfc/rfc2350.html.*

BSI. *IT Baseline Protection Manual: Recommended Measures to Meet Medium-Level Protection Requirements.* 1997. Prepared by the Bundesamt für Sicherheit in der Informationstechnik of the German Federal Government. English version at *<www.bsi.bund.de/gshb/english/menue.htm.>*

Campen, A. D., D. H. Dearth, and R. T. Goodden, eds. *Cyberwar: Security, Strategy, and Conflict in the Information Age.* Fairfax, VA: AFCEA International Press, 1996.

Critical Infrastructure Assurance Office: *www.ciao.gov.*

Department of Commerce Critical Infrastructure Protection Program: *www.doc.gov/cio/oipr/CIP.html.*

Federation of American Scientists. *White Paper—The Clinton Administration's Policy on Critical Infrastructure Protection: Presidential Directive 63: www.fas.org/irp/offdocs/paper598.htm.*

InfraGard Program: *www.infragard.net.*

National Infrastructure Protection Center (NIPC): *www.nipc.gov.*

Office of Critical Infrastructure Protection (OCIP): *ocip.anl.gov.*

President's Commission on Critical Infrastructure Protection: *www.info-sec.com/pccip/web.*

Rotenberg, M. "Critical Infrastructure Protection and the Endangerment of Civil Liberties."
EPIC (Electronic Privacy Information Center), 1998: *www.epic.org/security/infowar/epiccip.
html.*

14.10   NOTES

1. *www.cesnur.org/testi/FBI_004.htm.* Every U.S. police department received a copy of
the Project Megiddo report and may provide access.

2. *www.fema.gov.*

3. National Fire Protection Association, 1 Batterymarch Park, Quincy, MA 02269. *www.
nfpa.org.*

PROTECTING THE INFORMATION INFRASTRUCTURE

Franklin N. Platt

CONTENTS

15.1   INTRODUCTION.   The information infrastructure must be well protected from any number of potential physical threats in order to assure the full performance of all its component systems. The vulnerable infrastructure can be any component of a computer or communication system, network, any of the cables or wiring that transport data, or any of the support services or utilities needed to sustain full information system (IS) performance. While protecting the infrastructure is important in itself, assuring uninterrupted system performance is critical and this requires proactive planning and response. Many physical threats can disrupt the infrastructure and thereby degrade system performance. Therefore, the protection must be effective and warn of impending accidents, system failures, intrusions and physical hacking, attacks, violence, and many types of remote threats. While the threats are numerous, effective protection is possible, and there are many ways to avoid risks.

First, the protection must be threat-specific. This requires an understanding of all the threats that might affect the infrastructure. Chapter 14 describes potential threats and a threat assessment process to prioritize potential threats according to their likelihood and resultant costs. The comprehensive planning process described in this chapter utilizes the information from Chapter 14 to develop infrastructure protection that can be effective, nonintrusive, and cost-efficient.

Once trouble starts, the costs and disruptions can be enormous. And trouble often escalates and spreads to a much wider area, so that full recovery can take days, even weeks. Therefore, security protection must be proactive. Protection must deter or significantly mitigate most potential threat situations, and there must be sufficient early warning to ensure that few problems actually occur.

Infrastructure protection is often inappropriate or obsolete as new threats emerge. And infrastructures are becoming increasingly vulnerable, as the hardware rapidly expands and especially when old and new systems are intermixed. In spite of these facts, risk perception generally remains low and the threats continue to escalate.

Protecting the information infrastructure is not simply an extension of premises security. The requirements, threats, vulnerabilities, and strategies are much different. Premises security protects people and property within and around a facility. It often relies on compliance with building codes, security guards, and apprehending troublemakers after damage has occurred. In contrast, infrastructure security must trigger an effective response *before* trouble happens.

Good protection starts in the boardroom and must involve management and everyone else with access to the information systems. All of the stakeholders should be represented in the planning process, including all IS users, key customers, suppliers and vendors, stockholders, and local government officials. Everyone involved must understand and support good security. Every group can assist during an emergency and help speed recovery. And because hardware, threats, security needs, and business opportunities can change rapidly, the plans and procedures must be reviewed and updated frequently.

Effective security is a planning process, not a product. Simply choosing products, vendors, or standard solutions is not enough and can easily be ineffective, risky, and wasteful. Protection by comparison shopping among vendors and consultants is neither planning nor strategic. Therefore, the planning process is the key to good protection.

15.2   A STRATEGIC PLANNING PROCESS.   Good infrastructure protection begins with a thorough planning process. The resultant plan must protect the entire infrastructure and all of its data, ancillary systems, and supporting utilities. Protection also must be threat-specific and not generic. The plan must address every possible threat (see Chapter 14) and be kept current. Preparation only for what has happened in the past is almost certain to be ineffective and costly. The plan also must protect all users from any type of physical threat that would disrupt productivity.

The planning process must optimize the defenses strategically, to add value and contribute to profits, while recognizing that good security cannot be intrusive or reduce morale or productivity.

The planning process must be comprehensive as well. Response and recovery must utilize all possible resources efficiently. Often, outside assistance is needed and there are many resources that can be incorporated into an effective plan. But without good planning and preparation, resources can easily be overwhelmed, while unnecessary and costly disruptions can readily occur. The consequences can be fatal.

Good security is expensive, but the cheapest approach is to stop trouble before it happens. Too much protection is costly and often counterproductive, too little risks potentially huge recovery costs. The process of protecting the information infrastructure is necessarily a cost-value analysis—a strategic planning process designed to sustain IS performance, productivity, and morale—and to optimize profit.

The first step is a plan that covers all possible threats, prioritized in order of importance as determined by their likelihood and impact costs. The next step is to consider the possible defense strategies. Finally, the planning process develops a comprehensive infrastructure security plan that can be optimized to add value, best serve customers, and enhance future profitability. Senior management and all stakeholders must be involved, so that the protection plan becomes part of a strategic risk management plan. Absent a comprehensive strategic planning process, protection is likely to be weak, unreliable, and very costly.

15.2.1   Attractive Targets.   Many types of physical threats are increasingly likely to target information systems. The infrastructure is attractive because it's widely disbursed, often easily accessible, and perpetrators are less likely to be caught. Often a physical attack is easier to inflict and much more costly than a logical attack. Vandalism and sabotage are becoming increasingly prevalent in the workplace, as is the threat of injury or violence, which disrupts IS performance for extended periods. Systems old and new are becoming increasingly vulnerable to accidents, misuse, snooping, and equipment failures. Utilities and support systems can be undependable, while many types of accidents, situations, and threats can occur elsewhere and disrupt the infrastructure. All these events require effective defenses.

Much of this chapter deals with what amounts to physical hacking. Like its electronic counterpart, attacks cannot be predetermined as to when or where or how they will occur. Electronic hacking from within the organization, over its networks, or from anywhere in the world via the Internet is still the best way to break into most information systems. However, physical intrusion can be harder to detect and locate and often is more damaging and costly.

The information systems must remain fully operational. In order to ensure this, threats must be deterred, significantly mitigated, and detected before they occur.

15.2.2   Defensive Strategies.   There are many effective defensive strategies to consider. The planning process must evaluate each approach and how best to combine them strategically to maximize protection and minimize costs. The following defensive strategies are common.

- *Deterrence* so that specific threats are not likely to occur.
- *Mitigation* to reduce each threat to tolerable levels.
- *Redundancies* so there are no critical links in the infrastructure. There are many methods of redundancy, such as multiple data paths; data loops that are bidirectional; parallel or distributed processing; alternative support systems and utilities; and many more.
- *Early warning* to detect impending trouble and delay onset so that fast response can prevent or minimize any disruption.
- *Layers of Security,* which are like the concentric layers of an onion, so that several layers of security must be penetrated before a target can be reached. This adds reliability, because a failure or breach of one layer does not compromise the other concentric layers.
- *Insurance* that can reimburse some of the recovery costs but usually few of the response costs. Insurance coverage often excludes many threats and can be costly. Terrorist and act-of-war coverage may be unavailable.
- *Capital markets,* which are less costly than insurance and better able to lay off larger and broader risks.
- *Self-insurance* to establish retentions (which are funds accumulated for the purpose) in the hope nothing serious ever happens.
- *Contract services* that are performed inhouse, which basically transfer risks but do not necessarily mitigate threats.
- *Outsourcing,* another option that introduces still other threats and vulnerabilities.

15.2.3   Who Is Responsible?   Effective security begins in the boardroom. A senior executive must oversee IS security. Top management must actively sponsor it and insist that everyone involved understands, supports, and respects the security plan and procedures. Accountability and oversight are essential, as is insistence on periodic security exercises, review, and updating.

Often the role of protecting the infrastructure is sloughed off to someone with little authority, experience, training, or knowledge of the threats. Many times this person is burdened with many other unrelated responsibilities. Given today's potential for catastrophic losses, the IS security manager must be well trained, highly experienced, and well motivated to create and maintain strong system security. There must also be a clear chain of command laid out in the plan: Who is in charge? And who in the organization has what responsibilities?

If possible, the infrastructure security manager should not also be in charge of IS or corporate or premises security. While managers of these areas face similar threats and their groups must work closely together, their priorities and levels of response to any incident are much different. It is best therefore that two or more specialized security groups report to one senior executive officer. Even if the role cannot be full time, an infrastructure security manager is a wise investment.

15.2.4   One Process, One Language.   There are now all too many proprietary systems, solutions, and procedures for risk management. Most are applied with varying approaches, interpretations, procedures, languages, and acronyms. Crisis management or response, disaster recovery, damage control, emergency management, and some other terms describe basically the same process. But each process tends to use its own planning and operating procedures and terminology. Regulated businesses often must comply with far different procedures, and insurers may impose still more terms and conditions. However, all these procedures share the same objectives: managing threats. The many approaches and languages only serve to confuse and hinder people who otherwise might be of considerable assistance in an emergency.

Inconsistency is yet another problem. Some processes are better than others, some are extensions of outdated, obsolete, and often inefficient procedures, and some are product oriented. Many security plans are not risk-specific or comprehensive, and they do not utilize all possible resources effectively. The protection-planning process should be very simple: What are the potential risks? What is the likely impact should each risk happen? What are the options to deter or mitigate? What security implementations will add the most strategic value? Is the security plan comprehensive? Does it cover all potential risks and include and coordinate all possible assets and resources? Is the plan clear, concise, understood, and accepted by everyone concerned? Do all the external resources that can help in an emergency understand the plan? Is there provision to periodically exercise and test, review, and update the plan?

15.2.5   Guidelines of the Federal Emergency Management Agency.   The following guidelines are recommendations only, but they are becoming commonly accepted standard practices that executives can ill afford to ignore. The guidelines are accepted in court, whereas proprietary practices will be expensive to defend whenever negligence is claimed, which is likely to be increasingly often. Nonstandard practices also invite allegations of gross negligence against officials personally and that can result in huge awards. It is well to consider the many advantages of adopting the guidelines of the Federal Emergency Management Agency (FEMA) as standard procedures, not the least of which is that FEMA has far more experience than any other organization in the world and has no commercial bias.[1]

The FEMA plans and procedures are the product of long years of experience and countless major disasters. They clearly define the best practices for emergency preparedness, response, and recovery. The FEMA model has been developed by representatives from all government agencies, business organizations, national standards groups, the insurance industry, medical service providers, and the many volunteer agencies that can assist during and after a disaster. Therefore, FEMA's guidelines, standards, and procedures can benefit any organization. And FEMA offers a wide range of free material and independent-study courses to understand and help implement its model.

FEMA makes the distinction between an emergency—which is a situation that an organization can handle with its own resources—and a disaster, which is when internal resources are likely to be overwhelmed. It recommends preparation for worst-case situations, that is, disasters. Many threats can become disasters to a business, even when outside resources respond quickly. For example, the consequences of an equipment room fire can be disastrous when the local fire department responds with axes and water hoses and cuts off all electrical power to the building. Even a major incident outside a business, where building power is cut off and everyone ordered to evacuate, can be very serious. Many similar scenarios demonstrate the need for a good, comprehensive, well-implemented infrastructure protection plan to avoid disastrous consequences.

Emergency planning is beginning to coalesce into one comprehensive standard that is common to both government and private organizations. The evolving standards are in three parts. FEMA SLG-101 covers emergency operations planning. National Fire Protection Association (NFPA) Standard 1600 augments this with a common set of criteria for emergency, disaster, or crises management.[2] FEMA's Capability Assessment for Readiness (CAR) reporting process determines compliance.

The FEMA bible for emergency planning is publication SLG-101, *Guide for All-Hazard Emergency Operations Planning.* This is comprehensive and rather lengthy, and is currently available online, in PDF format, on FEMA's Web site. Toolkits, checklists, and model plans from local and state emergency management agencies also will be helpful.

Some of FEMA's CAR evaluation reporting is also available on its Web site. All state emergency management offices must report annually and may be better able to provide a model.

NFPA Standard 1600, *Recommended Practices for Disaster Management,* is available from the National Fire Protection Association. It sets forth a unified standard to integrate and coordinate public, private, and support sectors. The report uses terminology and procedures that are clear, concise, and consistent, so that everyone involved understands and accepts them. A fire marshal or library may have a copy.

Many resources can assist. Every community, most regions, and all states have an emergency management agency, although the exact title can vary. These agencies have access to these documents and can explain them. Most of these agencies have Web sites.

A word of caution, however. As of this writing, many state and local communities are not familiar with all three standards. Many still use boilerplate plans that are not comprehensive, clear, and concise, or lack important elements, or are fraught with legal pitfalls that require careful customization and editing. Nonetheless, the new guidelines are publicly available, and many people are well trained in these procedures and able to advise and assist.

Being comprehensive, these documents are also lengthy. Developing a plan involves choosing the relevant material, then customizing and editing carefully to avoid unnecessary liabilities. If needed, less relevant parts of these documents can be incorporated by reference to the source. Procedures for promulgation and concurrence, which are sometimes required by law, are important to avoid liability. Assistance from an independent expert can save time and money.

Avoiding needless liability is a major issue. Whenever trouble comes—even minor, unimportant events—someone may claim damage or injury, and allegations of negligence will surely follow. Asserting such claims has become a major and very profitable industry. Defense is at best very expensive and disruptive even when it is successful.

Three simple yes/no questions will likely determine whether a claim is quickly dropped or a lawsuit is filed.

1. Was the organization adequately prepared?
2. Was there a good emergency plan that was well implemented?
3. Did everyone follow proper procedures?

Anything less than a clear "yes" to any of the questions can readily result in major damage awards. Using the FEMA model is clear evidence of due diligence and likely to dissuade most plaintiffs from filing suit. Any "yes" answer qualified by use of a proprietary model is likely to incur a very costly defense. Any "no" answers can trigger allegations of gross negligence, exposing both officers and organizations to large awards that liability insurance may not defend or cover.

15.2.6 Segmented Secrets.   To maintain good security, no one person should know all the details or inner workings of the security systems and procedures. If total understanding of the security systems is segmented into several parts, there is much less likelihood of misuse, fraud, error, or loss of a key person.

On the other hand, the more people with knowledge of the security systems and procedures, the more these systems become vulnerable. The list of those who know may include managers, administrators, maintenance personnel, users, partners, suppliers, customers, vendors, and consultants. Although many individuals must know at least some of the details, no one needs to know everything.

Secrets can be segmented among individuals, so that no one individual knows the entire security system, yet everyone shares the details needed to perform efficiently. Usually, a manager knows which subordinates understand which segments of the entire system. The subordinates do not know each other's secrets or who may share the same segments. And the managers need to know only enough information to be sure the subordinates are well trained and are following proper procedures and practices.

There are significant benefits to segmenting secrets. No one person is indispensable. Segmented knowledge can be redundant, so one person who is unavailable or leaving the organization cannot compromise the whole security system. No individual can be tempted or extorted into spying, because the knowledge possessed is too fragmented. There is an intimidation factor also, if the protection is well designed. Everyone believes that strong security exists, even though each person only understands a small part of it, so that no one is likely to snoop or experiment. Finally, mounting a successful attack requires collaboration.

Beyond segmenting, there is another precaution needed for good protection. If members of the same group must share sensitive knowledge, a "two-person" rule should apply. This is especially important when anyone is able to modify the security system or event logs. The two-person rule says that any modification to the security system requires two authorized persons working together and an audit trail of who did what and when. This procedure also is used when two or more groups share responsibility for parts of the security system.

15.2.7 Confidential Design Details.   It is often easy for people to identify and locate critical infrastructure components. Various documents often clearly label IS rooms and infrastructure and readily show the locations of equipment, wiring, utilities, and cable runs. Good protection requires that all such information remain confidential. Documents likely to reveal sensitive information include building floor and office layout plans and furniture, wiring, and equipment location plans. Alteration and construction plans, electrical schematics, architectural drawings, and engineering documents customarily show sensitive information, as do shop drawings, installation plans, maintenance diagrams, and documents filed with regulatory agencies. A wide range of people can access these sources easily. Interested contractors, bidders, vendors, and suppliers often receive copies. Building managers, landlords, and real estate offices may have copies. Many are publicly available or easily obtainable by court order.

Wide distribution of these documents is necessary and unavoidable. Therefore, none must reveal anything confidential. There should be no sensitive information on any plan, detail, drawing, specification, or other document that cannot be controlled and safeguarded.

Here are but a few examples of sensitive information and how to hide it. All room and area designations should always be alphanumerical. Do not use descriptive or functional names. This caveat pertains to the entire premises, public areas of the building, and all building mechanical and core areas. Functional designations or terms such as "treasurer," "marketing director," "security desk," "computer room," "network closet," or "telephone room" should never appear. Nor should the names of occupants, groups, or tenants; only alphanumeric designations should be used. And no documents that cannot be controlled and safeguarded should reveal any information about the locations of IS equipment, infrastructure, cable runs, or any of their support systems and utilities. Never include floor plans, titles, or area numbers in a phone book, directory, or anything available to the public.

Lists that correlate room numbers, functions, and descriptive names should be kept in a locked file, as should equipment room details and wiring plans. All these must be readily available to system administrators in the event of a system failure or a need to modify or upgrade, but never to the public or anyone else without a need to know. Any documents that show locations of security devices or wiring should be classified and available only on a need-to-know basis. Ideally, system administrators and management do not have access to this information, except when accompanied by security personnel.

Even within the organization, there should be no sensitive information on any documents generally available—either as printed material or Web accessible. All sensitive information should appear only on documents that can be controlled, stored securely, and issued only to those who need to know. Only security personnel who know what information is sensitive can review internal and public documents before they are issued. Security should be able to sign-off that the information does not violate security policies.

15.2.8   Difficulties in Protecting the Infrastructure.   In the past, most computers were housed inside one computer room, and most of the terminals and peripheral equipment were located in nearby rooms. Access controls, alarms, and surveillance easily covered the critical areas. Cable runs were short and generally also within secure areas. Although there was not as much infrastructure in those days, and there were far fewer threats, in many cases protection was poorly planned. Many organizations were lucky in the past, but a few incidents did occur and often at great cost.

Today, information systems are much larger and more widely distributed, interconnected, and interdependent, and the risks are many times greater. So too are the potential costs of any IS disruption. Data processing, transmission, and storage now occur throughout the premises and far beyond. Many and diverse intra- and interoffice transmission media exist, and still more that may connect a vast number of remote sites. The infrastructure has become much harder to protect.

The IS infrastructure now includes equipment and network rooms, telephone and utility closets, and diverse desktop, peripheral, and remote nodes. Interconnections now include direct and switched wiring, wireless topologies, infrared coupling, and usually many dial-up connections. Many widely scattered interconnect points must be protected, as must many more and longer cables runs. Once, one or two vendors, the landlord, and in-house staff could protect everything. Now the infrastructure involves many vendors and is increasingly widespread, diverse, and fragile. The infrastructure is now far more vulnerable while continuous performance is now more critical; everything must be well protected, and any potential trouble must be detected well before it happens.

15.3   ELEMENTS OF GOOD PROTECTION.   Protecting the infrastructure generally requires different and stronger defenses than premises security or IS logical security can provide. The protection must be efficient, reliable, and cost effective. Yet, it must also be user and visitor friendly and nonintrusive. Too much protection is unnecessarily costly, counterproductive, and inconvenient. Too little can be even more costly and impede productivity, morale, and goodwill.

The appearance of an armed fortress, which usually intimidates visitors and staff more than it protects them, must be avoided. Also, guards and receptionists should not be stationed behind glass, unless this is deemed absolutely necessary. Such barriers tend to enrage someone who may be already upset, can provoke attacks, and do not function very well either. Even if the glass is bulletproof, the pass-through windows usually are not. Glass partitions can be breached and the occupants injured. Some years ago, banks rushed to put their tellers behind thick glass panels but soon discovered that the glass provoked trouble rather than deterring it. The banks quickly removed the glass, which many businesses then bought and installed, with similar results. Proper violence protection is achieved with good facilities design, good security systems and access controls, and good training in security awareness and violence prevention.

Finally, security personnel should review all proposed construction plans, alterations, moves, or changes before they are issued. These documents include invitations to bid, specifications, changes, and every other similar document produced throughout the project. Internal security should review all these as a matter of policy. If they do not have sufficient time or experience to do this effectively, outside independent experts can be valuable. When properly chosen, these experts can provide experience, broader perspective, and evidence of due diligence, so that management cannot later be accused of negligence in protecting people and property.

Proper labeling and tagging of the infrastructure, within protected boundaries, is important to good security. Signal and power cables should be consistently and clearly labeled, using generally accepted cable management procedures, in order to speed up changes, maintenance, and troubleshooting. It is especially important that all authorized personnel understand the labeling system. Many vendors, installers, contract personnel, and in-house staff tend to use their own labeling and tagging systems, some of which are adequate but others are not. Many changes are not documented, especially when wires are abandoned and not removed, or even retagged. The status of in-house personnel, installers, and maintainers is likely to change frequently, creating all the more misinformation and confusion. The inevitable result is poor protection and slow response to a security incident.

Even more important is keeping the correlation documents confidential. These documents relate the alphanumerical codes to the current functional names. If labeling is done right, few will ever need access to the correlation documents and good security can be maintained.

The Telecommunications Industry Association/Electronic Industry Alliance (TIA/EIA) publishes the generally accepted authority, TIA/EIA Standard 606, *Administration Standard for the Telecommunications Infrastructure of Commercial Buildings,* that describes labeling of cables and equipment.[3] It also requires labeling firestops, grounding, and banding connectors. Also, the *National Electric Code,* published by the National Fire Protection Association, includes standards for labels. Local codes may require conformance to one or both of these standards. Any physical changes or additions may require that the entire physical plant be brought up to the current standards, which may be a wise investment in good infrastructure security.

15.3.1   Reliability and Redundancy.   The first requisite of reliable system performance is the use of high-quality equipment, systems, and infrastructure. Inexpensive or unproven components pose a major reliability risk. Beyond reliability, however, is the need for redundancy to ensure fail-safe systems performance. Servers should be redundant and have redundant power supplies, fans, and hard drives that can be diagnosed quickly and hot-swapped easily. Storage systems should be Redundant Array of Independent Disks (RAID) compliant with any critical data fully mirrored.

Multiple parallel servers with load balancing are a wise investment, so that one server will automatically take over another's load if it falters or must go offline. Network components and cable runs should be reliable and redundant also, and so should backup systems so critical data are stored safely both on- and off-site.

There are many avenues to redundancy. Supporting equipment can be located on any node of a local or wide area network (LAN or WAN) or outsourced, even though extra bandwidth and dedicated lines may be needed. Data paths should be redundant also, as well as physically distant from each other, so a failure of one path cannot become a failure of many. If this is not practical, automatic fail-over paths should be provided.

Good manageability is another vital requirement. This includes hardware that can detect trouble before it happens and, if possible, pinpoint the exact location. It also includes good management software with warning and alert capabilities and good logging systems. Remote management must be secure and private. Any changes or disabling of alarm parameters should require two authorized persons to be physically present inside the equipment room and simultaneously logged on. Manageability adds some cost but is a wise investment in security and accountability.

15.3.2   Proper Installation and Maintenance.   Good protection requires that all information systems, equipment, and wiring be installed properly, according to the manufacturer's instructions. All the wiring must conform to, or exceed, local code requirements. Data wiring should be independently tested and certified that it meets specifications as well as current and anticipated future needs.

Out-of-the-box equipment hookups and installations are common, and the cause of many system failures. Most security features are disabled when components and software are shipped. Proper installation requires careful setup, customization, and performance testing, for which adequate time and resources must be allocated. Administrators, users, and maintenance personnel must be properly trained. And once installed, the information systems and infrastructure must be periodically reviewed, tested, and kept up-to-date.

Promptly installing the latest modifications, service packs, updates, and security patches is also vital to maintaining strong protection. Days, weeks, and even months often intervene.

Given the limited staff, time, and budget available, there is often more lip service than actual performance in infrastructure protection. Management should be forewarned, however, that proper installation, upkeep, and maintenance together constitute cheap and effective assurance that IS performance is never compromised.

15.3.3 Threats from Smoke and Fire. Smoke and fire must be prevented within any equipment room. Otherwise, considerable damage and disruption will occur very quickly. No matter how small the incident, its effects are cumulative, and systems eventually will fail. Obviously, smoking must be prohibited—but it often occurs because an equipment room may seem to be a safe place to smoke unobserved.

The first level of prevention is to keep everything combustible outside of equipment rooms. Paper and supplies not in actual use should be stored outside, never within an equipment room. Any reference materials or documents that must be kept within the room should be stored inside fire-resistant files or cabinets when not in actual use. There should be no trash receptacles within an equipment room, and shredders should be outside, under strict control. There should be a clear and firm policy that nothing combustible can remain inside an equipment room, and frequent inspections should be held to verify compliance.

There should be no unnecessary furniture within equipment rooms, especially desks that can become cluttered and that are not rated as fire resistant. A metal table with one small drawer and one or two metal chairs with fire-resistant upholstery are usually sufficient. Because plastic accessories, furniture, and upholstery may burn readily and generate large amounts of toxic smoke, they must be excluded from most areas and especially from equipment rooms.

Equipment rooms must be designed to protect equipment and not to accommodate personnel. These are not to be "occupied spaces." Regardless of the actual furniture or its intended use, any space that accommodates a workstation, or where people can congregate, is considered to be occupied space. Any area labeled as a computer room or data center is also usually considered to be occupied space.

This designation is of extreme importance because building and occupancy codes, the Occupational Safety and Health Administration (OSHA), and other regulatory agencies require proper heating, ventilation, and air conditioning (HVAC), lighting, and easy means of egress for all occupied spaces. Requirements are many and varied. For example, the room air must be ventilated continuously so that occupants can breathe fresh air. HVAC systems are designed to accommodate people and not to protect equipment well. They are generally unreliable in continuous use, inefficient, and very costly in an equipment room, but necessary by code within occupied space.

On the other hand, process-cooling systems are designed specifically to cool equipment, not people. As a result, process cooling is reliable, efficient, and much less costly to operate (see Section 15.6.7). Smoke already within the room can be contained within the room, and exterior smoke can be sealed out, often without having to stop cooling the room.

Smoke and fire originating inside or outside an equipment room can be equally damaging. It is well to coordinate protection among fire-safety and premises security personnel and to solicit advice from local fire departments. Good operating policies and frequent facilities inspections can substantially reduce the likelihood of trouble.

Inadequate firestops are a major threat that is often overlooked. A firestop prevents smoke from penetrating an opening in a partition, floor, or ceiling. It also stops the spread of flame. Many firestops are needed throughout the premises, including the building core and the mechanical, utility and equipment areas—even within a one-story building. Firestops are rigorously required by many codes, but compliance is often inadequate, with the devices often breached by subsequent alterations or wiring changes.

Partitions, floors, and ceilings must all be fire-rated in accordance with local building codes and many other regulations. Proper construction usually is specified by an architect or engineer and inspected or certified as soon as the construction is complete. This inspection often occurs before the mechanical and wiring installations are finished. Subsequently, if any penetration or opening is made through a wall, floor, or ceiling, its fire rating is invalidated and should be recertified.

An approved firestop with a fire rating equal to or better than the surface penetrated must then be installed and certified. Underwriters Laboratory (UL) or similar recognized authorities rate and approve commercial firestops. Each manufacturer then specifies the proper application, installation, and maintenance procedures necessary for compliance. It is therefore wise to utilize specialized vendors with extensive training and experience installing and inspecting firestops and to have them conduct periodic premises inspections.

Inadequate firestops are particularly common in the core areas of older buildings or where tenants occupy multiple floors. While proper firestops may have been provided during construction, installation of piping, cables, conduit, and subsequent wiring changes often breach them. The firestops must be restored and inspected whenever changes occur. Many installers do not understand this or assume others will take care of it.

There can be substantial liabilities if people are harmed or equipment is damaged because of improper firestops. A routine inspection by a fire inspector will quickly discover building violations such as inadequate firestops that can be very costly.

15.3.4 Equipment Cabinets. Most IS equipment is now open-rack mounted, as an economy measure and for easier access. Although enclosed equipment cabinets cost more than racks, they offer much better protection, usually with little loss of floor space. Equipment mounted within an enclosed cabinet may escape damage from smoke or water and even from a quickly extinguished fire inside the cabinet. Cabinets with inside fans can better monitor and maintain ventilation and cooling, so that more equipment can be mounted in less space. In all, cabinets can provide an additional layer of protection against accidental or deliberate damage to the infrastructure.

A fire suppression system is usually required within any equipment room—and is certainly desirable for good infrastructure protection. With equipment inside closed cabinets, a water system with mist sprinkler heads is an excellent, inexpensive fire suppression system. Eliminating the high costs of chemical systems will more than pay for the best equipment cabinets.

15.3.5 Good Housekeeping Practices. All food and drink must be kept out of equipment rooms, since they can cause considerable damage if spilled on a keyboard, connectors, or equipment. Space for food and drink should be provided outside the equipment room, where routine maintenance personnel can keep the area clean.

Loose papers, books, supplies, newspapers, and trash are fire hazards and also must be banned from every equipment room.

15.3.6   Overt, Covert, and Deceptive Protections.   Effective protection of the IS infrastructure requires many hidden elements, such as concealed wires, as well as some clearly visible components. It is important to consider which items are best hidden for reliable protection and which should be visible as deterrents.

Overt devices are ones that are evident to workers and visitors, or whose presence is implied by other visible objects, such as warning notices. These visible devices, which suggest that some sort of security exists, are intended to deter troublemakers, so that all but the most determined attackers will go elsewhere. Examples are surveillance cameras, access controls, and visible alarm warnings and sensors. While most overt devices are active and record data, some may be inexpensive dummy devices that only look real. Covert protection, on the other hand, must not be noticeable to either visitors or insiders. There must be no indication that these protections exist, how they might function, or where they are located. Most effective security systems operate covertly; examples include stealth and silent alarms, concealed early-warning systems, perimeter and proximity sensors, access controls and surveillance devices that are not readily seen.

It is important also to conceal the wiring that interconnects all protective systems and the utilities that support them. Whether or not any part of a system is visible, the wiring that connects it should not be.

Another approach to protection involves deception. Many simple, inexpensive, and effective deceptive techniques should not be mentioned publicly (see Section 15.8 below), but here are some of the possibilities that can be described.

Dummy surveillance cameras, access control devices, and alarm sensors can be placed to attract troublemakers, who may think they can physically damage or disable the system. These visible devices are intended to divert potential troublemakers away from vulnerable areas. Some devices are deceptive in that they are not what they appear to be, but are actually alarm sensors to measure motion, proximity, sound, or anything that disturbs the device. Whether or not a person is diverted, real surveillance devices are placed to monitor the event, issue alarms, and collect evidence of possible wrongdoing. These devices may be well concealed or just not readily apparent, such as distant cameras with zoom lenses.

Deceptive devices often are used to divert troublemakers away from vulnerable people and infrastructure, by offering them a "honey pot": an attractive target, but one equipped with an alarm device, surveillance cameras, or other means of identifying a perpetrator and gathering evidence. While such devices are clearly deceptive, anyone caught probably intended to commit a crime.

There is a gray area between what management can legitimately do to protect its information systems and what may be unethical or illegal actions. Management has a legal and fiduciary responsibility to protect people and property, and those who support deception say that it is increasingly necessary to protect an organization. Others insist that this amounts to entrapment or violates privacy rights. State and local regulations and interpretations vary widely and are continually changing. It is necessary to check carefully with local officials, legal advisors, and insurers to determine what is acceptable and how to manage such risks. Management must then decide to what extent these techniques are necessary, and whether they should be used.

Whether protection is overt, covert, or deceptive, the systems themselves must not be obvious. No one seeing or knowing about parts of a security system should be able to deduce the details of the system, the functionality, or where and how it is monitored. While an observer may notice a particular device or product or the appearance of a vendor's standard solution, the particulars of the protection systems must remain obscure, and all the wiring that supports them must be hidden or disguised as well.

Everyone involved must be aware of the security policies. Conspicuous signs should advise anyone within the premises that they may be monitored. Employees and other on-site personnel should receive periodic security-awareness briefings. All of the overt protections systems, procedures, and policies must be understood and accepted by everyone involved.

Finally, protection must not be intrusive. Security cannot limit office productivity or IS performance in any way. Instead, the protection must contribute to a feeling of safety and security within the workplace and thereby enhance productivity.

15.4   ACCESS CONTROL.   Access control systems are only one layer of infrastructure protection. They are usually used in conjunction with surveillance and perimeter control systems in order to provide sufficient early warning to head off trouble before it happens. Effective access control requires three tiers of support. The strength of each tier and its integration with other security layers determines the level of protection.

- *Privileges*—This determines whether a person seeking entry is authorized. One or more people may possess the same requisite means of access. Examples are a key, a common password, or an entry-lock combination. Unfortunately, the privileges also can extend to include duplicated, lost, or stolen keys, passwords, and combinations disclosed to others, and lock-picking tools that can open a lock almost as quickly as a valid key. This first tier can only assume that the privileges are being invoked by an authorized person.

- *Authentication*—It is usually necessary to identify a person seeking entry with some degree of certainty. To do this, the person must possess or know something unique that others cannot readily duplicate. Examples include personal identification numbers (PINs), electronic keys, entry cards, and biometric devices. PINs and passwords may be used, provided they are strong and well implemented.

- *Audit Trail*—A log is required of each entry attempt, the date and time, identification of the person, and action taken by the access control system. Access-denied and unable-to-identify events should trigger immediate alarms. Logs must be analyzed in a timely manner for improper events or patterns. Where better access control is needed, each person's exit also must be authenticated and logged.

For more details about identification and authentication access controls, see Chapter 16.

15.4.1   Locks and Hardware.   Strong protection begins with high-quality locks, door hardware, and access control systems that are nonintrusive yet able to prevent most unauthorized entry. Locks should be hard to pick and should use keys that are hard to duplicate. Examples are Medico® locks and keys with dimpled sides. Ace® locks with circular keyways require special tools to pick but also tend to signal that there is something important beyond the door. Keys can be made from lock numbers, so keep these numbers locked away safely. No lock is completely safe. Someone with equipment, experience, and time can open any lock, often very quickly and without causing attention. Additional layers of protection are, therefore, needed.

Interior areas accessed only by a few people usually can be secured with a strong push-button, combination lock. Key locks are not appropriate, because the keying cannot be changed periodically or quickly when a key is lost or someone leaves. And lost keys may not be reported for days or weeks. However, key locks may be the best alternative for outside areas or for doors that remain open during business hours. Wherever keys access critical areas, there should be spare lock cylinders and new keys stored on site that can be utilized quickly when a change is needed. Once a lock cylinder is changed, the old cylinder should be rekeyed and a new set of keys produced.

Locks that use an electronic key are particularly effective. Electronically activated cylinders can replace existing mechanical cylinders, so the cost of upgrading is minimal. These systems do not require any wiring. Electronic keys are not much larger than a standard key. Most have a small cylindrical tip that is touched to the lock for access. Both the lock and the key can log each event, identify the specific key used, the date and time, and whether access was granted.

Another inexpensive upgrade is the card-access locks similar to the ones used by hotels. Some of these systems do not require any wiring but are battery operated and can be programmed and quickly changed by an administrator. However, unless centrally wired, most offer limited security and cannot trigger an alarm or log events.

Simple and inexpensive access control can be accomplished with two independent locks. The first lock is a push-button, combination lock. The second lock is a "buzz lock" using an electric door strike, with an intercom or telephone to someone who identifies the person seeking entry, logs the event, and releases the buzz lock. To enter, someone must first know the lock combination and then be identified by voice. Everyone with access rights knows the combination, which is easily changed. A bypass key opens both locks in an emergency. This system is inexpensive and usually sufficient for doors that are rarely used. But for higher traffic and better security, other systems are stronger, less intrusive, and often cost very little more.

Absent a vault-type door and hardware, a determined attacker with pistol and silencer can gain access readily. A newer device that can breach a standard metal door with one shot and less noise is a small water cannon that is transported in what looks like a toolbox. Effective security obviously requires multiple layers of protection.

15.4.2   Card Entry Systems.   The best means of access control is a card entry system, especially the newer systems that are increasingly capable and less expensive than older systems. A card entry system often controls the entire premises: all entrances, exits, and interior doors. Access cards can be similar in size to a business card and carried concealed or worn as identification badges.

The means of encoding data on the cards include bar code, magnetic stripe, smart cards, and cards with embedded bits of metal. Simple bar code is not secure; it can be photocopied to gain access. Although the newer, two-dimensional bar codes are nearly tamper-proof, they cannot store much information. Magnetic-striped cards also have many drawbacks; they cannot store much data, and they are easily erased (often by accident), altered, or copied onto another card. In time, the data decays and must be reprogrammed. Magnetic card readers are not practical outdoors, because of weather and vandalism. And, heavily used magnetic card readers and the cards themselves wear out quickly.

Cards with embedded metal bits are effective. The encoding cannot be seen except by X-ray, and it is durable and permanent. The cards must be held against, or inserted into, a reader. They hold very limited data, the coding is factory installed and cannot be changed, and spare cards must be inventoried. Smart cards with embedded logic chips are now a better solution. These hold much more data, which can be read from and written into the card's memory. Some include miniature batteries to store more data and avoid having to come in contact with the card reader.

Many states and Canadian provinces now issue driver's licenses with a photo ID and a magnetic stripe, or a two-dimensional bar code. While used mostly to identify retail customers and verify age, businesses can use drivers' licenses in a card reader very effectively for authentication. The cards are hard to copy or fake because each state guards the algorithms used to generate the identity code.

Methods of using entry cards include proximity, touch, insertion into a slot, or swiping the card through a narrow channel or in and out of a slot. Swiping is fast, but the card must be hand held. And wear, weather, or vandalism can damage the card reader. Inserting a card has the same shortcoming as swiping and is often slower. Proximity and touch cards and devices are described next.

15.4.3   Proximity and Touch Cards.   The best of the new card access systems use proximity or touch cards. These cards communicate with readers using infrared or microwave transmissions. The reading device powers some types of cards, while others contain miniature batteries. Physically, the cards and card readers are weatherproof and vandal-resistant and do not wear out. Proximity card readers can be surface mounted, recessed flush into a wall, or entirely concealed within a partition so that they do not call attention to a security door. Proximity systems are convenient and safe because the cards can remain concealed inside a wallet, handbag, or pocket.

Touch cards are functionally similar to proximity cards, but they must be held briefly against a visible sensor. Touch cards cost a little less than proximity cards and are good only for entrances with little traffic. The touch-card system is slower and the cards more easily lost, stolen, or forcefully taken.

The new systems provide many useful functions. The cards or badges usually are imprinted with a color photograph, name, title, and department of the bearer. They are usually laminated and sealed to prevent wear, damage, or alteration. Individual cards are quickly prepared, activated, and canceled—all on site. The system can restrict entry to specific places, days, and times, and holiday restrictions also can be programmed. Any card can be locked out immediately if lost or stolen or when the owner leaves.

The newer 13.56 MHz proximity cards function up to three feet away from the card reader; older cards were limited to a range of about four inches. The newer cards are also faster, hold more data, and offer more functionality. Many of the card readers also can write data to the card. There is a trade-off, however, between useful operating range and the amount of data stored. The farther the range, the less the data stored. But most proximity systems are adjustable. For example, on outer perimeter doors, where quick, convenient access is more important than tight security, the systems are set for maximum range. Inner doors that need higher security are adjusted to store more information and to function at a shorter distance, which is still far greater than the older systems allowed.

There are also self-expiring visitor badges that noticeably change color or prominently display the word "expired" after an elapsed period. Self-expiring badges are reusable and come with a fixed expiration time that is usually from two to 24 hours after each activation. Badges that are not returned or that are lost cannot be reactivated, except with very sophisticated equipment.

Cards are not the only proximity or touch devices. Keys or patches also are used. The keys can be small, rugged, and easily attached to a key ring or to a small handheld wand that a security guard might use. The patches work in place of touch cards, or with separate access control systems, to upgrade existing legacy systems. The patches are about the size and thickness of a quarter and are easily attached to anything a person normally carries, such as an ID card or badge, a pager or cell phone, or the inside of a wallet.

Card access often is used for all equipment rooms containing servers, network components, and telephone gear; for off-hour access to information systems by users, technicians, and administrators; and for any areas where high-value items are stored. Card systems usually are integrated with premises security to control access to the building, elevators, service areas, parking, and rest rooms; they also can provide efficient access to any parts of the infrastructure.

Each entry into a controlled area should be logged in a way that cannot be compromised. Logs should provide an accurate audit trail of everyone who sought entry, when, and whether access was denied. Where stronger security is needed, each egress should be logged in the same way. The logging system is best monitored by software that can review all system data in real time, flag trouble quickly, issue periodic summary reports, and quickly search and summarize unusual events. Reviewing logs manually is a cumbersome, time-consuming task. If only manual auditing is possible, there must be a firm policy to do this every few days.

Plan ahead and consider where additional access control points may someday be needed. Piecemeal additions at a later date can be costly.

Card entry systems by themselves do not provide strong protection. Therefore, some degree of authentication is required.

15.4.4 Authentication.   Anyone can use a card that may be borrowed, lost, stolen, or taken by force. Another layer of security, authentication, is needed to establish with some degree of certainty the identity of the person seeking entry. Authentication devices commonly include a numeric keypad, visual or voice identification by a computer or by another person, or a biometric scanner. All come in varying strengths of security, and any can be used in combination.

When an access card is read, the system must verify that the card has the requisite privileges for that place, date, and time. If it does, it then becomes necessary to authenticate the person holding the card. For this purpose, a numeric keypad is the most common device. The card user enters a personal identification number via the keypad. If the system validates the PIN, it activates an electric door strike to momentarily unlock the door. PINs are like individual passwords; every one is different and each must be kept private. However, keypads are not very secure and can be slow and cumbersome, while PINs can be forgotten, lost, or discovered by others.

Visual or voice identification by another person is a better approach. The other person can be a guard or receptionist who can see the entrance or monitor it via a surveillance camera or a video intercom. Emergency-type video intercoms work well because they provide the remote authenticator with a visual image and can monitor sound continuously, so that the authenticator can speak with and challenge whoever approaches the door. When authentication is complete, the other person activates the electric door strike to unlock the door. This system offers stronger security and is faster than a keypad. It also facilitates logging all entrances and exits, especially during off hours, and can visually record events as well.

Biometric scanners offer the best security at this time. They are faster and do away with the need to remember a PIN. Biometric scanners can read any of the following personal attributes, in order of current popularity: fingerprint patterns, facial characteristics, voiceprint, handprint, signature, retinal details, or height and weight.

Most biometric systems can be adjusted to be highly sensitive (which is slower and may require repeated entry attempts, but is very hard to breach) or less sensitive (which is still fast but may result in some false authentications). Before choosing a biometric system, it is necessary to determine that the users understand and will accept it. Many people balk at having to use a retina scanner. Others may feel that biometric devices are invasions of privacy. Most biometric systems cannot be used to investigate a person's background, to identify a person to another agency, or to steal an identity. For these reasons, biometric systems are not generally considered to be invasions of privacy.

Some biometric scanners store their data on an access card or badge as a one-to-one verification that the person seeking entry is the same as the card owner. Others store data centrally and use a one-to-many comparison to identify an individual from a database of registered users. In either case, the data must be encrypted within the scanning device or the system may be defeated easily.

Fingerprint scanners are the most common and are becoming increasingly powerful. Initially, these utilized optical scanning, which could be fooled by photographs, wax impressions, or breached by a severed digit. The newer capacitive scanners use electronics rather than optics and can provide nearly certain identification. Usually, three of the user's fingers are "enrolled" in case some fingers are bandaged or dirty, and single-use passwords can be used to bypass the system.

Most fingerprint scanners cannot identify an individual by name, but only that a person seeking entry matches the person whose biometric identity has been enrolled. Most scanners do not conform to the automatic fingerprint identification standards of police departments. Instead, they scan a small area of the finger and apply proprietary algorithms and encryption. A template from one system is usually meaningless to another.

Accuracy of fingerprint scanning is affected by the angle and position of the finger and by the pressure applied. Most systems allow sensitivity adjustment to optimize enrollment and verification times and success rates as well as to minimize delays and false negatives that require repeated access attempts. While well suited to most applications, fingerprint scanners may not be appropriate where the user could have dirty or thickly callused hands or wear gloves.

Facial recognition is another popular scanning system. It uses graphics technologies and any camera to measure the size and relationship of parts of the face. Most systems are proprietary and cannot be used to identify an individual by name, but some are compatible with law enforcement standards. Sensitivity is dependent on the position and angle of the head as well as on the background lighting. Cameras at all entry points must be positioned to photograph the subject at the same angle. Not all facial recognition systems offer strong protection that is nonintrusive. Some can be fooled by a face mask. Others are best left at their highest sensitivity to avoid spoofing, which may require multiple attempts at entry.

Voice-print scanning can be used, but mostly for access to a terminal or workstation. The better systems display random words on the monitor so a tape-recorded voice cannot be used. Most use the PC's microphone. Voice scanners can be affected by hoarseness, so there should be a password access provision. These systems can be useful for remote login, although the low bandwidth of typical telephone circuits may lessen the system's sensitivity.

Retina or iris scanners are considered the best security, but authentication can take five to 10 seconds. For access control, the user must generally look closely into an eyepiece, which is traumatic to some people. But for access to a terminal or workstation, the camera is generally placed on top of the monitor, 17 to 19 inches from the eye. The user's head must be shifted to align a white dot within a colored circle. The user must hold still, without blinking, while the scan proceeds automatically. Some systems also function as standard video cameras.

15.4.5   Integrated Card Access Systems.

Biometric scanners are used increasingly by other applications, and most can readily coordinate with an access control system. Applications include network user authorization and access to terminals and workstations and to software and data. Keyboards and mice, and readers for access cards, badges and smart cards, are beginning to incorporate biometrics — usually fingerprint scanners. Once open standards emerge, fingerprint scanners may be common on notebooks, handhelds, and other portable devices as well. Scanners that are mostly proprietary are currently integrated with encryption systems (e.g. virtual public networks, public key infrastructure, and smart cards) to authenticate transactions including credit cards, financial, banking, and automatic teller machines. Biometrics are increasingly used to authenticate hospital patients, welfare recipients, people who frequently enter the United States, and similar applications that involve the public.

Infrastructure protection can be independent or integrated into a comprehensive premises security system. Either cards or badges can provide many other functions beyond basic access control. Applications include: off-hour access to the building, elevators, and premises; control of private building entrances, rest rooms, and parking areas (especially at night); purchases at a cafeteria, company store, or concierge; or for charging stationery or materials picked up from a supply room.

A proximity card may be used for access control while it is concealed inside a pocket, handbag, or wallet. Or a proximity badge that everyone in the workplace wears at all times can access both doors and workstations without being touched. Temporary badges customarily are issued to all visitors, even when escorted, and can be used for access control and to monitor areas entered. Temporary badges are quickly activated with specific privileges and can be revoked automatically and immediately when necessary. Longer-term temporary badges can be issued to vendors, contractors, and external employees, although it is best that security personnel store visitor and vendor badges safely while the person is outside the premises.

For greater protection and efficiency, an integrated enterprise-wide, Web-based system can control access to premises, locked doors, infrastructure components, networks, workstations, applications, secure data, and Web connections. This arrangement offers comprehensive security by logging every event. Centralized logs can yield much more meaningful security information, because an integrated system provides better early warnings to head off trouble before it happens.

15.4.6   Bypass Key.

Whatever the systems used, there should be one bypass key that can open every door that uses electronic or electrical controls. The bypass key is for emergency use only. It is a unique key that is not on any mastering system and available only to a few highly trusted people. The cylinders should be heavy duty and very hard to defeat, with the keys nearly impossible to copy. Careful control and protection of each key is essential. The loss of a key may not be discovered quickly, and the time and costs of rekeying every lock will be substantial. Meanwhile, every door on the access control system is vulnerable.

Bypass passwords for individual users also may be needed. These passwords should trigger a silent alarm whenever used, so that security can respond to the site or verify identity by telephone, surveillance, or intercom. One-time passwords provide the best security.

15.4.7   Intrusion Alarms.

Intrusion alarms are necessary to provide early-warning and perimeter alarms and are usually needed as extra layers of security. There are several methods of intrusion detection. Digital surveillance cameras with motion detection are best because they can monitor visually what is happening inside the area and record what they see. Other methods include proximity and pressure sensors mounted within the perimeter walls or floors or inconspicuously within the room. While most of these sensors can detect intrusion and forced entry and can pinpoint the location of trouble, they provide no details, monitoring, or evidence-recording capabilities. Proximity and pressure sensors can protect long perimeter distances, cable runs, and utilities inexpensively. Concentric layers of such devices are necessary for sufficient early warning to prevent trouble from happening.

The best motion detectors use digital closed circuit television (CCTV) surveillance cameras that can sense movement while observing and recording the event. Miniature cameras that are inconspicuous or concealed are particularly effective and increasingly inexpensive. Several cameras can record pictures from many angles and often can identify an intruder positively. In a larger area, cameras often use swivel-tilt mounts and zoom lenses, which can be controlled automatically and remotely as well. Color cameras are preferable, as are cameras that automatically adjust to light conditions, including near darkness.

Some CCTV cameras include a military-type night-scope mode, which works well in total darkness. These cameras also work well in normal light and can switch automatically to night-scope mode when necessary to see clearly and to record evidence.

Other intrusion detectors that do not use CCTV are independent of ambient lighting. Some monitor infrared light beams generated by the detection system. Others use radar or changes in capacitance or inductance to sense intrusion. Most sound an alarm as soon as they are disabled or lose power. Detectors may be wall- or ceiling-mounted devices as an overt means of deterrence, but they are vulnerable to spray paint, wire cutters, or a club. Therefore, these types of intrusion detection sensors are usually concealed, or at least inconspicuous. Perimeter alarms are especially important in building core areas or public areas inside and outside a building to provide ample early warning of an intrusion that might impact a secure area. Digital CCTV cameras are best for this but may be impractical or too expensive for all applications. Therefore, many proximity devices are used to monitor intrusion. Most utilize long sensor wires that are surface-mounted inconspicuously or hidden within partitions, ceilings, and sometimes conduit. These systems detect the presence of a standing adult or a large animal that may come within a few feet of the sensor wire. Each sensor is often very long, so zoning is often necessary to pinpoint an incident at least within a general area of the facility.

A better and cheaper alternative can be the newly available fiber optic perimeter alarms. Developed for the military and national security installations, the fiber optic systems are very sensitive and can monitor, evaluate, and record events. The sensor wires can be embedded inside drywall or masonry partitions, ceilings, floors, or conduit and will detect both pressure changes and sound. Because they do not measure proximity and can monitor and evaluate events, false alarms are less likely. They can warn of an impending accident or efforts at forced entry, and may soon be able to locate the event as well. These systems use software that can discriminate between recognized events, ones an operator ought to evaluate, and situations that are clearly dangerous. All the events are recorded and can be replayed and analyzed by a remote operator at any time (see Section 15.8 below).

In addition to intrusion alarms, environmental alarms should be provided to measure temperature, humidity, and smoke, fire and flood situations within all critical rooms and equipment cabinets as well, as described below.

15.4.8   Other Important Alarms.   A duress alarm system is recommended within most critical areas. This is usually a large red button or an emergency intercom conspicuously mounted near the exit. It is used if someone is injured or ill, when trouble occurs that other alarms will not immediately sense, or if violence is threatened. The emergency intercom types are best. Those with a CCTV camera are described below, but many inexpensive intercoms that provide audio only can be useful. They constantly monitor all sounds within a secure area, and anyone inside can readily talk with security personnel.

Beyond access control and authentication, it is also important to know whenever a locked door is not fully closed. There should be a sensor that warns whenever a controlled door is open or ajar. The sensor is normally built into the door buck (frame) to provide a silent alarm. A door-ajar alarm system allows a few seconds for one authorized person to enter or exit normally. This prevents propping a door open during off hours for cleaning, maintenance, or removing equipment. Locked doors tend to be propped open during off hours for the convenience of persons going in and out and so that equipment room cooling reaches into areas where the air conditioning has been shut down. An alarm should trigger whenever a door is open for too long or when anyone enters or exits improperly.

A door-ajar alarm also deters "piggybacking" whereby two or more people enter together. And this alarm can prevent "double-dipping" so the same person cannot request multiple entries in order to admit unauthorized persons. The door-ajar sensors should be concealed at all times so users are unaware of their existence. Otherwise, they may be taped or jammed so the door appears closed.

15.5   SURVEILLANCE SYSTEMS.   Today, surveillance systems are laid out and designed to fully document every event, to facilitate positive identification, and to provide evidence acceptable to a court. Older analog CCTV cameras and film cameras generally cannot do this, no matter how good the components. The best surveillance systems are now entirely digital and utilize high-speed broadband connections, over fiber optic cable and the Internet, to continuous recording devices. The newer systems are much less expensive than older ones, and costs are still falling. Existing older systems are fast becoming a liability, except for some ancillary applications.

If the protection is designed well, cameras can provide an undisputable, accurate historical record that is available instantly. Cameras never sleep and are not distracted by repetitive tasks or boredom. More important, they can provide early warning, document events, and gather evidence concurrently and synchronously. Cameras increasingly incorporate microphones and interface with emergency audio intercoms to better assess a situation, assist people on the scene, or challenge suspicious persons. The very presence of visible but inaccessible cameras usually deters most attacks. Protecting the infrastructure requires both early warning and identifying the nature of trouble before it can happen. The new CCTV systems can do this effectively. They can be integrated with other alarms and with premises security systems for seamless and very strong protection.

15.5.1   Surveillance Cameras.   Surveillance cameras are far more effective and much less expensive than guards or watchmen. Equipment rooms once relied on motion detectors for security, but now digital cameras with motion detection work better. Digital cameras function well indoors and under most light conditions, from sunlight shining into the camera to near, if not total, darkness. When used outdoors, digital cameras are immune to all but very severe weather conditions. They are, however, affected by heavy smoke, snow, ice, or rain. Wind-blown objects and sometimes birds or animals can distract their motion-detection systems.

Film cameras provide poor protection at best. These cameras are large, easily disabled, expensive, and offer very limited functionality. There is no early warning. Pictures cannot be viewed for hours, or even days, after the film is removed and processed. Worse yet, film cameras are generally not motion-picture cameras but only expose the film in lapse time, providing a limited number of exposures. Film can easily miss an event in progress because of the interval between exposures or because the camera was triggered too soon and ran out of film. Resolution is poor compared to digital CCTV capabilities, and few film cameras record date and time of each exposure to enable synchronization. The exact sequence of events is often unascertainable and the perpetrators may be unidentifiable.

Today's digital CCTV systems are far more reliable and functional than either film- or analog-based systems. Cameras were once the weak link because details were not clear. Now cameras are much smaller, less expensive, and yield far better pictures. Most systems use color to provide better evidence and easier identification. Color digital cameras work well even in near darkness, and some incorporate an inexpensive, monochrome, night-scope mode that works well in total darkness. Digital cameras automatically correct electronically and mechanically for varying ambient light conditions. Most can correct for background lighting conditions that would otherwise cause subjects to be underexposed, for sunlight glaring directly into the lens, and for unusual brightness that would otherwise wash out a useful image. Most automatic corrections can be overridden remotely. Images can be viewed in real time, searched at any time, edited, and saved—even while the events continue to record.

All but the smallest CCTV cameras now include a microphone so that both video and audio are recorded. Some installations interface with an emergency intercom so background sound is continuously monitored and dialog recorded. Emergency intercoms are particularly good deterrents because security personnel can confront possible troublemakers and advise them that they are being recorded. Most will back off or flee before trouble occurs.

Although many camera control systems provide electronic zoom, the primary zoom function should be mechanical. Although electronic zoom systems are inexpensive, they lose resolution and images can quickly become unidentifiable. The better systems also provide a mechanically adjusted aperture to maintain a clear image. While the camera images are recorded unedited, monitoring equipment should provide electronic zoom, brightness, contrast, and other electronic enhancing functions.

Miniature CCTV cameras can be particularly useful and save money as well. The new one-quarter-inch-diameter lenses provide sharp detail, and many of these cameras are smaller than a pack of cigarettes, even with a zoom lens. Very small, stealthy mounts with tilt-swivel capabilities make miniature cameras very effective.

Opinions vary as to the ethics of using concealed cameras, and some state laws limit their use as invasions of privacy. Generally, the rules of good surveillance practice are the same as monitoring telephone conversations, e-mail, or Internet use. Signs must be posted so that workers and the public can easily see that all persons entering the premises may be monitored for safety and security purposes. Company policies that explain this, and why surveillance is necessary, should be formulated and widely distributed.

15.5.2   Camera Locations and Mounts.   To serve as a deterrent, some cameras must be readily visible, but this may present some problems. Overt cameras placed too high are not good for identification, while cameras placed too low can be spray-painted, covered, or smashed. Any visible camera can be shot out. Older cameras are good for overt use because they are large and may provide backup surveillance. Another option is dummy cameras, some of which have visible indicator lights or automatically pan to attract attention. Some dummy cameras are in fact alarms that will trigger if the unit is disturbed or if its wires are cut.

Surveillance systems must be able to identify troublemakers and gather evidence that can be admissible in court if needed. Otherwise, except for their deterrent effect, it is hard to justify the cost of surveillance. The areas monitored, the camera angles, and the lenses selected are all important. It is said that more than 1 billion facial images are stored in government databases worldwide, so a good surveillance system may indeed be useful. But the police standard face-recognition technology requires a frontal full-face view, which is possible only when the camera position is not much higher than the person's head. Surveillance of a wider area requires an elevated camera that can see greater distances, zoom in on details (especially faces and vehicle license plates), and closely follow an event. Wide-area views are also necessary to spot multiple troublemakers. Several camera angles will likely be needed to gather good evidence.

Large outdoor cameras are protected inside weatherproof enclosures attached to a swivel, tilt mount. Generally, there is no attempt at concealment because the cameras are too high to reach. The direction that the lens is pointed is clearly visible, but not the area covered or the amount of zoom. Large outdoor cameras provide good deterrence as well as protection.

Interior cameras, on the other hand, are often mounted inside small, spherical domes. Swivel-tilt-zoom miniature cameras can be mounted in an object as small as a tennis ball, but generally domes are about the size of a bowling ball. The mount protects the camera and should conceal its wiring as well. Most domes are inconspicuous rather than concealed. Most domes use hardened glass or plastic that can resist most impacts and are sufficiently opaque that an onlooker may not notice the camera or see where it is pointed. Surface-mounted domes can be wall or ceiling mounted, or domes can be suspended on pendants hung from the ceiling for better viewing angles. Cameras recessed in a partition or ceiling offer better concealment and protection. Only a small opaque window is outwardly visible, but the viewing angles are far more restricted than dome mounts.

The smallest of the miniature cameras usually include their own mounts for surface, recessed, or covert installation. With a fixed lens, these units can be tiny and concealed in an object as small as a tie clip.

15.5.3   Recording Systems.   Many special VCR units can record the continuous output of multiple cameras, with resolution similar to a motion picture, and can afterward revert to variable lapse-time images when there are no events in progress. Many use standard VHS tape cartridges because of their low cost. Ideally, 31 tapes are used— one for each day of the month—to provide a month's historical record after which each tape is inspected and reused. Using less than 31 tapes is unwise. If an event does occur or is suspected, a review of the past month's surveillance can be valuable.

Other recording systems use costly, high-capacity tape cartridges or, increasingly, dedicated hard drives. Magnetic tape is a fragile medium; data on magnetic tape can be destroyed by heat or a strong magnetic field, and the tape will decay in time and become unreadable. Although hard drives are also magnetic, the media can be better protected, are easily backed up off premise for redundancy, and can be burned onto CD-ROM for cheap, permanent storage. A hard drive can store two to four weeks of continuous output from two to three cameras or the same data in time-lapse format for nearly a year. Data on a hard drive can be viewed in real time, searched, and manipulated for clarity—all while the system continues to record without interruption.

15.5.4   Camera Control Systems.   Camera control systems commonly adjust swivel (pan), tilt, mechanical zoom, aperture, and background lighting. Not all cameras will need all these functions initially, but control units with all these features are not a major cost. Most also include electronic enlargement and reduction, which is not as powerful and far less clear than a mechanical zoom lens. Some control systems can pan cameras automatically back and forth across large viewing areas. Motion detection is usually done by the control system, so panning does not diminish the motion sensitivity. Some systems can follow automatically and zoom in on an event until an operator manually intervenes. This is a valuable feature that must be covert and carefully applied so the system is not distracted by spurious events or deliberate diversions.

A major advantage of a digital system is that each camera provides continuous images, usually at about 30 frames per second, which fiber optic and other broadband connections bring to the recording system in real time. The recording system and operator are able to decide whether to record every image or to use lapse-time storage, which can be adjusted to any desired interval. This provides far better surveillance and flexibility to meet present and future needs at very little added cost.

The newer digital recording systems offer many functions available at one or more system consoles. An operator can routinely observe six, eight, or more cameras as small images on one screen, or the system can routinely sequence among groups of cameras displayed on one screen. When a suspicious event occurs, one or more remote operators can quickly and independently review the multiple images, monitor selected split-screen views, expand any camera to full screen in real time, or scroll to and enhance any image—all while the digital system records all incoming data continuously. Playback functions usually include search, scrolling, freeze frame viewing, video zoom, cropping, and color, brightness, and contrast correction. Any operator also can print, file, or export images or a video sequence via a LAN, the Internet, telephone, fax, diskette, or a CD-ROM. Yet another advantage is a precise time and date stamp recorded with each image.

With an audio signal received from each camera, ambient sounds and any dialog between an operator and the scene can be recorded, and any part of the audio can be played back in any manner, enhanced and forwarded, either separately or along with the video.

15.5.5   Broadband Connections.   The advantage of broadband camera connections is that continuous data are available immediately and more camera control functions are possible. Fiber optic cabling does this best but should be dedicated and well protected. Remote locations can be controlled via a broadband LAN or Internet connection, if done carefully so that other traffic is not impeded.

Multiplexing is another advantage of broadband connections, and an economy as well. Broadband once necessitated fewer frames transmitted per second, even though each camera provided continuous images. Now digital multiplexing allows all data from all cameras to be transmitted continuously. Multiplexing is accomplished remotely as signals from several cameras are combined at a remote location into a single broadband connection to the control system. Connections among control systems are also multiplexed to minimize line charges. The signal interfaces between each camera and the multiplexer can be fiber optic, microwave, a network, or the Internet. This way, hundreds of cameras can be networked economically.

Coaxial cable and Category 5 or higher communications cables are rarely used in new installations because other media can move more data, faster, and cheaper.

15.6   OTHER DESIGN CONSIDERATIONS.   Good protection begins with good facility design that will ensure the safety of the information infrastructure and the people who use it. Protective systems become expensive and inefficient when the premises themselves do not accommodate good security. Proper interior design, facilities layout, engineering, and construction will minimize security costs, enhance productivity and morale, and generally contribute to profits. The starting point is an inspection of all sites and review of all construction documents.

Premises inspection and review of construction documents are best assisted by outside, objective experience. Comprehensive and objective architectural, engineering, and security experience are needed and may not be available internally or from vendors. The inspection and review process always must be threat-specific. This requires a careful threat assessment, a prioritized list of all possible threats, and the approximate response and recovery costs for each threat. (See Chapter 14.) With all this data, a comprehensive cost/value analysis can minimize costs.

The special purpose of infrastructure protection is to prevent trouble from happening. To do this, there must be effective deterrence or ample early warning. Facilities design, premises security, and infrastructure protection must all support this special purpose and work together seamlessly. To the extent that security cannot foresee all threats and prevent all incidents, protection must significantly mitigate trouble and delay its onset.

Good facilities design can be efficient, nonintrusive, cost-effective, and inexpensive — even within existing facilities. Here are some guidelines and suggestions.

15.6.1   Choosing Safe Sites.   Sites for equipment rooms and utility closets should be easily protected from potential threats. Infrastructure sites should be located far away from all piping, tanks, or equipment that uses any liquid that could possibly leak or spill. Most plumbing tends to leak unexpectedly at some time, so it is well to assume that any pipe, connection, container, or pump will eventually burst or leak. Placing sensitive sites at a distance from such threats is safer and cheaper than any other form of protection. The zone of danger must include ample horizontal area, at least one floor below, and a widening inverted pyramid that extends upward for several floors. Most buildings require fire-suppression sprinklers, and their activation by accident, vandalism, or a fire must be considered. So, too, must infrastructure sites be located away from windows, exterior walls, roofs, skylights, building setbacks, and storm drains, since all are potential threats. Treated water used in heating, air conditioning, and solar systems is another problem; it can quickly destroy electronic equipment, connectors, and wiring.

If all of the infrastructure cannot be located at a safe distance from all liquids, there must be special protections and alarms. Protections include sealed, waterproof construction and drains to divert liquids. Environmental alarm sensors must be placed near the plumbing and where liquids may approach protected areas. Floor drains must protect the equipment areas, especially those that use sprinklers.

Infrastructure sites should not be visible or accessible from public areas. And infrastructure wiring or cables should not run through the building core, public, or mechanical areas, within rest rooms or stairwells, or in any other area where an unauthorized person might loiter. All equipment room entrances should be clearly visible from workplaces where employees can readily observe all comings and goings. Choosing inherently safe sites and entrances greatly reduces both risk and costs because less security is needed.

There should only be one access point to each critical area, for both entry and exit. However, if local fire or building codes require a secondary means of egress, a delayed-access panic bar with a surveillance camera is usually acceptable. Such a system delays releasing the exit lock for a few seconds, while an alarm sounds and the camera is triggered.

Locked doors should look as alike as possible from the outside and be identified only by a room number that looks similar to that of any other premises door. No functional name, person's name or title, or any other means to identify what is inside a locked area should be apparent. No signage or directory should include a functional, personal, or departmental name, but only area or room numbers and directional arrows if needed. Only floor, room, or suite numbers should appear on premises signs or floor or building directories.

15.6.2   Physical Access.   Physical access to all parts of the information infrastructure should be restricted. All information system and network equipment must be inside equipment rooms that are always locked and accessible only to those who need to be there. All utility and wiring closets, power distribution panels, patch panels, wiring blocks, and terminations should be located inside equipment rooms that are always locked. If possible, do not allow unrelated systems, equipment, or utilities inside a locked area, so that a technician working on one system cannot access other systems. If this cannot be avoided, IS personnel always should escort others entering these areas. People entering tightly secured areas also should be escorted. Guards and premises security personnel are not good escorts if they do not know the infrastructure. All visitors must be positively identified and each visit logged.

It is wise to put critical electrical distribution panels inside an equipment room, so they are quickly accessible and secure. This is a safety issue as well; anyone working on a power circuit can readily see that the circuit breaker is off. Other electrical distribution panels should always be locked, unmarked from the outside other than by a coded location number. Whenever an electrical panel controls anything critical, access to the area should be restricted and the room alarmed. These precautions reduce any possible loss of power to critical systems by accident or intentionally.

A mantrap can best control access to critical equipment rooms. This is a two-door arrangement with an inner door, outer door, and a short corridor in between. Both doors are interlocked; one must be closed before the other can open. The corridor usually is constructed with a sturdy, full-height glass partition on one or both sides for surveillance. Both the doors are usually windowless, and each door must have a strong access control system. Usually one or more CCTV cameras are positioned to identify anyone entering or leaving the mantrap.

Emergency intercoms within the mantrap corridor and at the entrance and exit points are strongly suggested. Conspicuous duress/assistance buttons should activate silently, so security personnel can monitor the area and speak with or challenge anyone who cannot pass through properly. The intercoms also can include miniature CCTV cameras to save money. This arrangement can avoid many problems if someone is ill or somehow becomes trapped.

Mantraps serve many purposes. They make "piggybacking"—one person closely following a person who has been authorized to enter—very difficult. Whether or not the second person is authorized, access must be logged. Mantraps not only preclude propped-open doors but also make removal of objects from the room difficult and risky. The access control log and surveillance recordings can identify troublemakers and provide strong evidence to convict those who might otherwise be suspects or persons unknown.

Mantraps are usually covert, in that only the outer door is visible to anyone entering. This can provide a strong deterrence or an effective deception, depending on how the mantraps are designed. In either case, a well-designed mantrap can be valuable for all but heavily traveled entrances.

15.6.3   Protective Construction.   Equipment rooms require sturdy building walls and interior partitions for many reasons. The walls must structurally support the extra weight of wiring and equipment, which can be a considerable weight that most walls are not designed to accommodate. Moreover, the walls must remain safe and stable during any seismic activity, such as heavy road traffic or a sonic boom, explosion, or earth tremor. Sturdy walls and partitions also deter forced entry.

Security doors should be sturdy also. They should be metal, fire rated, and relatively heavy duty and use heavy-duty hardware. Try not to call attention to controlled doors by any distinctive appearance. If many occupied areas use wood doors, the security doors should not stand out. Use wood-faced metal doors and hardware that looks similar to all other doors. Sometimes secure-looking dummy doors that lead to nothing important are used for deception or as a honey pot to draw troublemakers away from secure areas.

Well-constructed partitions and ceilings will seal out smoke and contain it in the event of an interior fire. Weather stripping around the perimeter of each door is recommended to keep out dust, airborne contaminants, and possibly smoke.

If possible, any wiring inside a door should be routed within the hinges so that no wiring is visible at any time. Exposed wires can be damaged by accident, cut, or compromised in many ways. The major hinge manufacturers can supply special hinges to conceal most wiring and match the appearance of other premises hardware.

Masonry partitions are usually unnecessary unless there are special structural or very high security requirements. Drywall partitions with metal studs are usually sufficient but should be extra sturdy. Type-X fire-rated drywall panels at least three-quarters of an inch thick are recommended. Better yet, use double half-inch- to three-quarter-inch-thick panels. Existing drywall partitions can easily be double-paneled for added strength. Masonry partitions are usually faced with fire-rated plywood for attaching equipment supports and wiring.

Do not use a suspended ceiling in any equipment room. Suspended ceilings just add cost, inconvenience, and diminish the size of the room. The plenum space above the suspended ceiling is a fire hazard, and everything inside it must be fire rated, including any exposed cables, which adds unnecessary costs. Most building codes require separate fire detection zones and suppression heads within every part of each plenum, which represent substantial and unnecessary costs. And a suspended ceiling diminishes the useful space within the room, takes away space better utilized for cable trays, and makes maintenance and changes unnecessarily difficult.

Avoid raised floors for the same reasons. Most raised floors are now more cosmetic than functionally necessary, and they are very costly. Like suspended ceilings, raised floors create a plenum space that needs separate fire detection zone and suppression heads. Raised floors usually restrict the ceiling height because the slabs were not designed for this, so the room must be enlarged to accommodate everything, and often with little provision for the future. Raised floors soon become dust traps and, in time, usually a clutter of new, old, and abandoned cables that no one can figure out. Many equipment failures have been caused by overheating due to airflow restricted by too shallow a raised floor or by too many obstructing cables. A raised floor plenum is rarely needed for cooling air supply or return. Surface-mounted ducts and registers usually can do the job better and cheaper, and are easily cleaned and modified. All of the wiring usually can be routed efficiently above and between the equipment or by using inexpensive cable troughs mounted on walls and ceilings. If needed, floor outlets can access trench ducts in the floor, which often already exist. Or use conduit through the floor and along the ceiling below for special needs.

It is important that all wiring outside of equipment rooms is protected inside of metal conduit. This conduit should not be thin-wall or plastic, but rugged, heavy-duty metal. Metal conduit is stronger, hard to damage, harder to breach, and provides good magnetic and electronic shielding. Metal conduits can easily be and should be well grounded. Obtain expert advice on where and how to connect the grounds. Metal conduit also may serve as a proximity sensor to warn when something gets too close.

The federal government has standards for very secure installations needed for national security. A "red" standard covers very secure installations, while a "black" standard covers important installations that are less critical. These installations require metal conduit, extra electrical insulation, grounding, and separation distances from other wiring. While equipment compliance can be monstrously expensive, the cabling requirements and room design is similar to what is suggested in this chapter.

All conduits should look alike whether they carry power or data or control security systems. While the diameter of the conduit must vary, keep the general appearance the same. Do not label or mark the outside of any conduit except with an alphanumeric code. Cables and wires inside of a conduit should not be marked either. The wiring inside of conduit should be labeled only where it emerges inside of a locked closet, equipment room, or junction box.

Cabling and wires, whether copper or fiber optic, are fragile. Any undue pressure, bending, stretching, vibration, or crimping can alter transmissions and may cause failure. Fiber optic cables are especially fragile. Metal conduit is usually the best and least expensive protection. Special cable sheathings are cumbersome and costly.

Any cable or wire can be installed or terminated improperly, whether or not it is inside conduit. While substandard wiring or installations may function well initially or temporarily, future failure is likely and will be expensive. Therefore, it is important that all cables be acceptance-tested and certified by an independent expert before the installer is fully paid.

Critical cable runs should be alarmed from end to end, whether the conduit carries power, data, or security. There are several ways to alarm a cable run. Outdoor conduits often are pressurized with nitrogen to keep out humidity, or with a special gel to keep out oxygen and humidity and to stabilize the wires inside. Interior conduits can be alarmed in the same way. Whatever the fill, the pressure is monitored to detect a leak or an intrusion; any loss triggers an alarm. The system is effective and provides early warning, but breaches cannot be pinpointed, and any future wiring changes may be difficult.

Proximity and pressure-sensitive sensors also can alarm the entire length of critical cables. A monitored conduit can be very long and may lead through many areas that are difficult to protect and yet may offer concealment to a troublemaker. While surveillance and intrusion detectors can protect vital areas, there often are many other areas that can be protected only with long sensor wires along the conduit. Mechanical pressure sensors will detect unusual vibration, while proximity sensors indicate a change in the magnetic or electronic environment surrounding the cable or conduit. While the conduit itself may become the sensor, good sensitivity often requires the sensor wires outside of the conduit. But neither approach may provide enough early warning to locate and stop trouble.

However, a better system is evolving, using technology recently developed for the military. The new systems are far more sensitive, discerning, and cheaper than older methods, and the sensor wires can be concealed inside the conduit (see Section 15.8).

15.6.4   Using Existing Premises Alarms.   Various codes require workplaces to have visible and audible fire alarms. And most workplaces have voice paging, emergency intercom, surveillance, and premises security systems as well. All of this equipment can be utilized effectively to augment and support the information infrastructure.

Audible alarms are used when those at the scene must take immediate action, such as an evacuation. Conversely, silent alarms provide early warning and allow security to monitor the scene discreetly and to respond and assist if needed. All these alarms can be integrated into infrastructure protection systems to provide better early warning and extra layers of protection.

All alarms and alerts should be transmitted to a central security desk or guard station. The purpose is to document and manage incident response, summon resources quickly, monitor the scene, gather evidence, and support those at the scene. Central management is especially necessary when multiple incidents occur, as they often do. Security managers, IS managers, the infrastructure security manager, and key department heads also should be notified immediately. Some of these people may be off site or at remote locations but will need to communicate effectively with at least the response control center. Notifications and the subsequent communications should be quick, private, and secure. Each message receipt should be acknowledged in a similar way. Communications may utilize any combination of a network, wireless pager, cell phone, or fax with direct or dial-up connections. If everyone involved is activated quickly, disruption may be averted.

An effective method of premises-wide alert uses voice codes broadcast over a paging system. These are usually scripted and often prerecorded so that alerts can be initiated automatically, remotely or manually. Hospitals do this effectively with what are equivalent to silent alerts that do not seem unusual to the public. For example, types of threats can be coded as the names of colors, common objects, or fictitious persons in a large organization. Alphanumeric codes can identify the general location of an incident. As in a hospital, it is well to add similar codes for other routine purposes, so the public will generally tune out all the paging. This system is particularly useful when violence is threatened or has occurred.

Everyone inside the premises needs to know when an emergency threatens. Indeed, everyone has a legal right to know and to promptly receive safety instructions. Anything short of this will result in considerable liability. Effective procedures, clear simple instructions, good preparation, and periodic training can protect everyone.

15.6.5   Clean Electrical Power.   Protecting electronic equipment requires a source of electrical power that is consistently "clean." While blackouts, power outages, and interruptions (discussed in the next section) are some obvious problems, good protection begins with a power distribution system that can eliminate all disturbances.

Many terms are used to describe power problems. In addition to blackouts and power outages, there are brownouts, dips and sags, spikes, transients, magnetic and radio frequency interference, and more. Understanding each term is not as important as knowing that a wide variety of problems commonly occur randomly and without warning.

Even when some of the specific problems are known, mitigation can be expensive, complicated, and sometimes uncertain. The problems are dynamic and likely to change. Therefore, ensuring sufficiently clean electrical power is a process where independent outside expertise can be valuable.

Brownouts are particularly harmful. These are voltage reductions by the electric utility that will cause equipment to overheat. The effect is not linear; as the heat increases as the square of the current. For example, a modest 25 percent brownout may cause more than a doubling of heat buildup, which is likely to overwhelm most cooling and ventilation systems.

Few power disturbances will destroy circuits or crash systems immediately, but all can cause cumulative damage. Each incident can weaken electronic circuits that will eventually fail for no apparent reason. Poor equipment quality usually is blamed, because no one thought to investigate the true cause. Worse, replacement equipment will fail also.

All power disturbances can be measured to determine whether or not a particular circuit is clean. Usually, a recording device is left in place for at least a week to measure and log the details of every event that occurs. Avoid any test instrument that logs only an unnamed event but provides no details. An independent engineer who is not a vendor may best provide testing that is comprehensive and objective.

First, thoroughly test every phase into the main service panel to determine that the power coming into it is clean. The tester should test each phase separately as measured between both the ground and the neutral buses, then test between these two buses, and then test between every pair of phases. Once the main service looks okay, check each receptacle or utility box that powers vital information system infrastructure. Some circuits are likely to show intermittent disturbances caused by something nearby within the building and sometimes by improper wiring. Knowing the power problems coming in through the main service helps to isolate where other disturbances may originate. There may indeed be multiple causes of power disturbances, and all of them may be intermittent,which is why seven-day tests are recommended.

Another major electrical problem is improper or inadequate grounding that can damage IS equipment and cables. While electricians must comply with national and local electrical codes that protect people, they do not necessarily understand or provide the special grounding necessary for reliable IS performance. The power connection to each component of the IS infrastructure should provide an isolated ground connection with a dedicated wire all the way back to the central building ground. Isolated ground wires serve only one connection and are not shared. Although recommended by many equipment manufacturers, isolated grounds are usually not required by code. Some manufacturers do not provide installation specifications unless asked, and some vendors disregard them to remain price competitive.

Opinions vary as to the best building ground configuration for information systems, and as local conditions can vary significantly, no one approach is best. It is wise to consult an independent engineer to recommend, inspect a proper grounding system, and certify local code compliance.

It is also important to provide separate circuits for all IS equipment, so that one circuit breaker controls no more than one receptacle or hard-wired utility box. Separate circuits also are required for all equipment that can draw high current, especially if the load can cycle on and off. This is required by code for large motors, such as pumps, air conditioning and elevators, which can create large power disturbances along other circuits. But copiers and large laser printers (especially older ones) can create electrical disturbances when starting and when the fuser-heaters cycle. All types of lights, except a few incandescents, can cause a dip or a surge when the fixtures are switched on or off. (Fluorescent light fixtures with electronic ballasts conserve power and cause much less trouble.) A separate circuit somewhat isolates the hot and neutral connections from other circuits, but trouble may be spread through standard grounding wires that often are daisy chained with other circuits.

Do not share a dedicated circuit with any of the following equipment, which can readily disrupt and damage electronic equipment: time stamps, electric staplers, coffeepots, refrigerators, heaters, fans, or any other device with a motor or solenoid. Even if inaccessible, a dedicated outlet should be a single receptacle, not a duplex. It is all too easy for vacuum cleaners, power tools, or maintenance equipment to use the other half of the duplex outlet. This will cause a severe disturbance and may open the circuit breaker. There must be plenty of convenience outlets that are readily accessible for all noncritical needs.

Yet another cause of power problems is excessive solar activity. These events can be measured only when they occur, which is randomly during an unpredictable interval of several years that peaks about every 11 years. Power disruptions occur mainly during daylight hours. (But data disruptions caused by solar activity can occur at any hour.) High solar activity occurred in 1988, causing major power outages and disruptions in Montreal, Canada. Activity has been high since mid-2000 but with no known damage yet. Daily activity reports, forecasts, pictures, and historical records are available on the Web, at *www.dxlc.com/solar,* for example.

There are three remedial options when power disturbances are encountered or believed possible:

1. Eliminate the problem at the power distribution panel. Better grounding, more separate circuits, suppressors, filters, and isolation transformers may help. But this type of remediation can be difficult, costly, or unreliable.

2. Use a surge suppressor near the equipment it protects. This is inexpensive but useless against brownouts, outages, and severe disruptions.

3. Employ an uninterruptible power supply (UPS) for each piece of critical infrastructure equipment. One type of UPS is switched on only when the incoming power fails, although its battery is always being charged. Another type is always online acting to filter the incoming power, suppress most surges, compensate for minor brownouts, and maintain full system power for five to 10 minutes following an outage, to allow an orderly system shutdown. A third (and best) type always powers its load from batteries, thus isolating the load and providing clean power. When the UPS battery is not in use, it is continuously maintained in a state of full charge.

UPS units should power the computer, monitor, and sometimes fax machines. They may power inkjet printers or other peripherals that draw very little current. On the other hand, laser and dot matrix printers do not need UPS protection. Most UPS units provide unswitched, unfiltered outlets for the printers, transformer "bricks," and peripherals that do not need to be kept running. Small printers and peripherals can be expendable and quickly replaced by spare units, so they do not need clean power.

Individual UPS units placed near the equipment they protect cost less and can be shut off by the operator to better protect equipment that may be vulnerable, even when shut off. Larger UPS units are used in equipment rooms where they also can monitor and log all power events and trigger alarms. Most good UPS units can shut the equipment down automatically when the UPS batteries are low, unless the user intervenes.

Many UPS units also provide telephone line suppression; this should be utilized if possible. Disruptions transmitted over communications wires can readily damage telephone instruments and modems. Power line and telephone spikes can occur almost simultaneously and devastate equipment that one disturbance alone would not damage. A good UPS unit with telephone line suppression is best able to stop both spikes.

15.6.6   Emergency Power.   Most of the critical systems and infrastructure must remain fully operational during any electrical power problem. Filtration and suppressors cannot compensate for power outages and most brownouts. Uninterruptible power supplies can deal with these conditions, but only briefly. Therefore, a backup emergency generator is the only way to continue operations during a sustained power outage.

While backup generators are often the only alternative, they are not a panacea. Generators are expensive and complex to install, require monthly "exercise," and are not entirely reliable. Their voltage regulation is marginal; when the load changes, the output voltage and frequency may change as well. As the load increases, the current flowing through the load, wiring, and generator increases in a linear proportion, but the amount of electrical heat generated increases as the square of the current. If the source cannot supply the required current, then its voltage will drop. Generators, therefore, must have ample reserve capacity beyond the anticipated equipment loads.

Because backup generators are expensive and complex, planning is often shortsighted and many installations are not adequately tested. The inevitable result is that many generators do not do what is expected. Here are a few examples of what can be overlooked.

After considerable discussion at a major money-center bank in Manhattan about what seemed to be the excessive cost of a backup generator, the project was begrudgingly approved. The generator was to power two identical computer systems running in parallel to support a securities trading operation. Two identical computers were necessary to maximize reliability. Because the generator would cost more than the two computers, cost was an issue until the bank realized that the generator would pay for itself within one day of use. Soon after completion, a citywide blackout erupted and a three-day outage ensued. Despite much inconvenience carrying fuel from the elevator up a flight of stairs to the rooftop generator, the generator performed flawlessly—one of the few systems in Manhattan that did.

Many other generators did not start or cut over properly, despite warm, clear weather conditions, and others did not support the necessary infrastructure. One problem was that some other generators did not supply power for their computers' air coolers, which had to be shut down quickly. Other necessary support functions not on some emergency power systems included communications systems, lighting for users, an elevator for key people and to carry fuel to the generator, security and access control systems, and at least basic provisions for food and rest for those keeping the vital systems running. Few businesses thought to include the necessary support functions on their generator systems.

This incident happened some years ago when power outages were considered very unlikely. Today, blackouts are far more likely. They can happen anywhere and may last for days while transmission systems are repaired. In the future, as in the past, many organizations will inevitably suffer the devastation resulting from poor planning.

A related example of shortsightedness occurred recently in a large suburban luxury hotel operated by a prestigious hotel chain. Following a severe thunderstorm, the power utility advised the hotel that power would be shut down for several hours to repair a substation. Given ample notice, the hotel set out hundreds of candles in the dining, lounge, reception, and pool areas and started the emergency generator, which cut over automatically as soon as the blackout occurred. Emergency exit signs and emergency lights in the corridors and stairs all worked properly, although many were battery powered and soon darkened. The generator powered one elevator, the computer and telephone systems, the access control system, and all the room locks. The generator seemed to work as expected, but the emergency response procedures did not.

Even with ample warning, no one thought to shut down the other elevators or to post signs to use the stairs. Two very frightened people were trapped in the dark, between floors, proving that a generator can be a liability and not a benefit unless operating procedures are carefully planned, well implemented, and periodically reviewed.

Another recent example involved a state's civil defense command center, designed to remain fully operational no matter what events might occur. The generator powered all the critical systems. Everything had been tested many times and had worked smoothly as expected. When an actual power failure occurred during a thunderstorm, the power flickered several times and then returned to normal. The generator tried to start, and then damage occurred that prohibited starting the engine. As it turned out, the generator was not needed at that time, but it was actually disabled until parts could be replaced. Another, far more tragic event occurred when New York City's Emergency Management Center in the World Trade Center was entirely demolished on 11 September. Fortunately, a secondary site was quickly established that was able to coordinate the rescue efforts without delay.

Most power failures begin with flickering, which can incapacitate a generator system that is not set up properly. Most mission-critical generators are set up to start the engine automatically, and many transfer power automatically as soon as the generator comes up to speed. Manual start-up and transfer are more reliable and cheaper, if trained personnel are always available.

The best way to sequence automatic operation is as follows:

1. After only one start-up pulse, the start-up sequence is locked on until the engine starts or a failed-start timeout occurs, or the engine is shut down manually.

2. Power does not transfer until the generator is fully up to speed and operating temperature, and the utility power is unusable. Both conditions must occur before transfer, and there should be a manual override as well.

3. All generator shutdowns should be manual.

There are countless examples of critical backup generators failing to work as expected. Here are six suggestions to determine whether a generator is necessary for protecting information systems and how to implement a generator efficiently and economically:

1. Investigate the outage history of the utility feeders that serve the premises. The electric utility can usually provide this data; if not, the state's Public Utilities Commission usually can. Be sure to ask how the terms are defined, because an outage may only include interruptions that continue for more than two minutes.

Also ask whether more reliable feeders are possible. Loop feeders that are powered from both ends are more reliable and often serve critical buildings. Ask which distribution transformers isolate and filter out power disturbances and which can regulate voltage.

2. Find other customers who use the same feeders, discuss their experiences, and determine if they use heavy machinery. While some improvements are possible and may be at little or no cost to the utility customer, past history is not always a reliable guide to the future. Today, the threat of extended power problems is far greater than in the past and is increasing rapidly. Motor generators are a necessity in mission-critical applications.

3. Determine which systems need emergency power. Most critical information systems, equipment, networks, and infrastructure must remain fully operational. And so must all the facilities, systems, utilities, and personnel needed to operate and support them. Outages can drag on for days or weeks with key people isolated and living inside the facility to keep it running. The generator must power these needs also.

4. Consider the following support systems that may require emergency power:
   ○ All the IS protections, monitoring, access controls, alarm systems, security stations, and consoles.
   ○ Heating, ventilation, air conditioning, and process-cooling systems, including all the controls, fans, pumps, and valves needed to operate the critical and support systems. In addition to equipment cooling, it is best to provide room comfort for users, operators, and administrators. Area air conditioning may not be possible, but heating in winter and adequate ventilation will be needed.
   ○ Sufficient lighting for key personnel, equipment rooms, utility closets, corridors, restrooms, and food service. Local light switches can conserve power, provided the lights are off when the generator starts. Battery-powered lights are suitable only for immediate emergency egress and cannot provide area lighting.
   ○ Enough convenience outlets for test equipment, work lights, and any accessories that must be used. Live receptacles may be needed for portable fans.
   ○ Sufficient food service equipment and refrigeration, running water and sanitary facilities, and a sleeping area for 24/7 operations that may have to continue for several days.
   ○ An elevator for access to the site, for delivery of food and supplies and to carry fuel for the generator.

5. Compile a list of all the items a generator must power. Then copy the rated power of each item to determine the size of the generator and the number of circuits needed. Power ratings usually are shown on a nameplate near the power connection and listed in the instructions. Ratings may be given in watts, amperes, or volt-amps. Generally, watts and volt-amps are considered equivalent; the latter value is the product of multiplying the rated voltage (e.g., 120 volts) by the rated amperes, while the former multiplies that number by the equipment's power factor. Large generators are rated in kilowatts (1,000 watts) of continuous power. However, low-cost generators are intended to run for only a few hours. An experienced engineer should review this process.

6. Consider the costs per hour of lost productivity, business, and goodwill if any information systems are unreliable.

Electric codes may require, and good practice dictates, that the generator be sized to handle the sum of the individual rated loads. This may seem wasteful because not all loads operate at once and average operating power will be somewhat less. It is nonetheless a wise practice to provide for the maximum rated load, with additional spare capacity for improved reliability and future additions. There are several reasons for oversizing. When power is first transferred to the generator, the initial surge can exceed by far the rated-power loads. All of the UPS units and other battery-operated devices may need to recharge, and all equipment motors may concurrently draw their maximum surge currents. Extra generator capacity ensures a smoother startup, better voltage regulation, and enhances the system's reliability.

Most generators produce three-phase power. Each of the three output phases should be balanced so that each "leg" draws about the same current. To do this, heavy motors, multiple light fixtures controlled by one switch, and other surge-producing equipment may have to be divided among the three legs. Existing wiring at the distribution panels probably will need changing to balance the legs. It is desirable, but not always possible, to reserve one leg for clean power to critical single-phase electronic systems.

As many electronic systems as possible that are powered by generators should be protected by UPS as well. There will be large voltage surges, dips, sags, and overvoltage conditions as the generator loads change. Power disturbances will be much greater because electrically noisy equipment cannot be isolated. Without plenty of extra protection from UPS units, electronic equipment will be stressed and may soon fail.

Locating the generator is the next challenge. The choices are on a roof or setback, inside the premises, or outdoors. Each site has advantages and obstacles. Outdoor generators can be the easiest and cheapest to install but also more expensive to operate. Outdoor generators are noisy, often unsightly, subject to vandalism, and local ordinances may prohibit them. Weatherproof housings protect the engine, generator, and fuel tank. Most engines used outdoors need to be kept heated, which can become a high overhead cost. Noise is another problem, and persons nearby may object. It is important to use good mufflers and to get written permission from nearby property owners and other tenants. Outdoor units should be fenced with plenty of room for maintenance and fueling. A generator shed is best, if possible, but does not reduce the need for heating or a good muffler. The whole installation should be well locked and alarmed with motion-detecting surveillance cameras. Floodlights may deter vandalism and will assist refueling.

Generators on roofs or building setbacks present other problems and these installations, too, may be limited by local codes. The first problem is weight. Structural reinforcement probably will be needed. The next problem is getting the unit in place, which may require a crane or a licensed rigger. Very few building elevators come up to a roof level. All the generator components may have to be hauled up stairs that are usually narrow. Installations on top of building setbacks will need a special access door, and moving heavy equipment across a finished floor requires heavy planks and floor protection (e.g., sheets of Masonite or plywood) under the casters to avoid considerable damage. There must be sufficient space on the roof or setback to safely fuel and service the generator. Noise will usually be a problem, and vibration as well.

Indoor installations offer both advantages and challenges. An indoor location that is sometimes possible is a heated garage-type ground-floor room with a standard garage door to open when the generator operates. This arrangement is good because it is inconspicuous, fireproof, easily protected, and convenient for fueling and maintenance. Should a generator fail, a trailer-mounted unit can be hooked up easily.

Inside generators may be prohibited by building or fire codes. Large rooms are needed to facilitate fueling and maintenance, and large ventilation systems to dissipate the considerable engine heat. The engine exhaust can be well muffled and piped outside, while engine-intake air is ducted in from outside. Heating and ventilating the room must be designed correctly, for both hot and cold weather. The room must be fireproof and soundproof, with fire alarms and a suppression system that uses chemicals or dry-head sprinklers that cannot freeze. The floor may need reinforcement and vibration isolators. And a floor drain is advisable and must be environmentally approved.

There are advantages to indoor installations. The generator and its fuel can be kept warm easily. Starting is easier and more reliable. Fueling is easier without having to brave the elements. There is less chance of water in the fuel, which can be fatal to diesel engines. Last, maintenance is easier.

Problems with indoor installations include building codes that allow only small day tanks for fuel. Every few hours, a lot of fuel must be carried in to keep the generator running. Fuel cannot be stored inside most buildings, and an elevator may not be running or available to help carry in fuel cans.

There are many possible fuels for emergency generators. Larger units usually use diesel engines, which are hard to start, especially in cold weather, and cannot be hand-cranked. Diesel engines, however, can operate continuously under full load. They use less fuel but pollute more, and diesel fuel tanks should be drained periodically to keep the fuel fresh. Sometimes, fuel from a heating oil tank powers a diesel generator, but this requires extra fuel filters and careful design. The advantage of using oil from the heating system is that the fuel does not age in a tank that is little used.

If liquid fuel is used, the fuel tank should be full at all times to avoid condensation. Fuel additives can prevent gumming and assist starting. Make sure all diesel fuel is treated for use in a cold climate. Refiners normally do not use this process except in winter, but untreated diesel fuel turns to jelly near freezing and will not flow. Never let a dealer "cut" diesel fuel with kerosene, which is corrosive. Diesel fuel also requires additives to avoid bacteria buildup that will clog fuel lines.

Natural gas or propane is the most convenient fuel. Either one eliminates the day tank and refueling. These engines are the least polluting and they start much easier, require no preheating, and can be hand cranked, but they may not sustain full output power for extended periods. Gasoline engines are rarely used except in portable generators. Gasoline is far more dangerous to handle and store, and gasoline engines do not hold up well under heavy loads.

Continually monitor the engine oil level. Most generators automatically shut down when the oil level is low. Some also shut down when overheated. An unexpected generator shutdown will be catastrophic, so monitor closely for early warning signs of trouble.

Once the desired size and type of generator is decided, here are some other considerations:

- Automatic engine controls and load transfer switches can be unreliable and may cause damage. Avoid these if possible. However, generators can be controlled remotely as well as on-site.

- Automatic starting can be unreliable. If the engine does not start quickly, the battery will discharge. If at all possible, someone should be present during the starting process, using a checklist to verify proper operations, and then transferring the load manually when the generator is ready. Switches that automatically transfer the load are expensive and sometimes fail. Always transfer back to utility power manually, and do this only after sensitive systems are put into a standby mode. Automatic transfer can cause major damage if the utility power flickers and goes out again, or if the voltage fluctuates, as it often does. Do not shut off the engine automatically. This is best done manually, and not until utility power is flowing smoothly.

- An emergency generator must be exercised regularly. The manufacturer will specify when and how the units should be exercised. Usually, this must be done monthly and at medium to heavy load. Good practice, when critical systems are involved, is to exercise the generator weekly. There should be a written, initialed log entry for each exercise, including inspection, maintenance, oil checks, and refueling. Always log operating hours.

Despite the cost and complexity, there is a great feeling of contentment in having a good emergency generator system that performs smoothly, while other organizations may be floundering. Once the generator runs well during a real emergency, even skeptics realize the value added.

15.6.7   Climate Control.   Even though today's information systems do not need as much cooling or the precise climate controls that legacy systems once demanded, good control of temperature and humidity, good ventilation, and clean air are still important. Information systems can function reliably only when proper environments are maintained in both equipment rooms and user workplaces. But each area requires a different approach.

Air conditioning is basically intended to cool people. On the other hand, equipment should be cooled by an entirely different system, which is best called process cooling. The systems should not be intermixed, nor should either one substitute for the other. Building codes require heating, ventilation, and air conditioning within all occupied spaces, that is, where people may congregate or where there are workstations. Building codes set minimum ventilation requirements for occupied space. And the codes require a minimum percentage of makeup (outside) air continually brought into occupied spaces so the inside air does not become stale. Most codes do not mention the needs of electronic equipment.

Equipment has many special needs, and many are incompatible with the code-required people comforts. Most equipment operates continually, whereas air conditioning operates only during business hours. Air-conditioning equipment can be shut down for maintenance, during off hours, or in cool weather.

By contrast, process cooling must operate at all times, so parallel and redundant systems are often used. The same air should be well filtered and recirculated with no makeup air added. Better humidity control will be needed. But less cooling capacity is needed in equipment rooms than in occupied spaces, so process-cooling systems can be smaller. Process cooling systems are easier and faster to maintain and quickly cleaned. Often components are redundant and hot-swappable. Increasingly, the cooling unit is on the floor or ceiling of the equipment room, so that no ducts, dampers, or registers are needed.

All IS processing, storage, and network equipment should be inside dedicated equipment rooms, which also should be unoccupied spaces to avoid the code-imposed air-conditioning requirements. Avoid using terms such as "computer room" or "data center," which are usually construed to be occupied spaces.

Both process cooling in equipment rooms and air conditioning in IS areas must provide humidity control. It is important that relative humidity be controlled between 40 and 60 percent at all times, regardless of the climate or season.

When the relative humidity falls below 40 percent, which can easily happen in cold weather, static electricity is generated as people move about. Electrical charges can quickly accumulate many thousands of volts, and a spark will jump to any object a person touches that is differently charged. Even though a spark may not be felt, several thousand volts can destroy electronic circuits. For example, a static charge jumping to a keyboard can cause serious damage to storage media and circuits. Much of the damage may not be readily apparent. Actual failure may be delayed, so the cause is not identified. Grounded strips can be installed on workstations and service personnel can wear grounded wrist straps, but these do not completely stop the problem. The best solution is always to keep the relatively humidity above 40 percent.

Relative humidity above 60 percent also causes problems that will eventually destroy equipment and wiring. Above 60 percent, condensation and mold will begin to damage some components. Above roughly 80 percent, galvanic action occurs and quickly becomes serious. This is often called silver migration because most electronic connections are silver-plated. The process is similar to electrolysis (electroplating), but the two metals are immersed in high humidity rather than a liquid. Molecules of one conductor begin to physically move toward and attach themselves to another less-active metal. Even though both metals may be silver or copper, it is likely that they differ in composition, and therefore galvanic action will occur whenever the humidity is too high. Connector pins and sockets can disintegrate, fuse together, or fail electrically due to pitting. Printed circuits can also fail. While this happens slowly, it accumulates and is irreversible.

The only protection is to control humidity in both equipment rooms and work areas. Process cooling and air conditioning systems commonly do this by several methods. Both systems dehumidify naturally when cooling and can use a reheat coil to warm output air if the temperature is too low. Humidification is added with a water spray, atomizer, or a water screen through which supply air is pumped.

There are additional protections, which are wise to install and maintain. In a cold climate, all areas and workplaces with electronic equipment should have low-static floor surfaces. This can be low-static carpeting or floor tile made for this purpose. Do not rely on sprays to control static electricity; they soon dissipate. Be sure that equipment room walls and doors are well sealed so that humidity, dust, and contaminants cannot migrate. Be sure the walls are well sealed from slab to slab and that slabs themselves are impervious to dust and humidity. (See also the information on firestops in Section 15.3.3.)

15.6.8 Smoke and Fire Protection.   Smoke can be far more dangerous than flame, and all smoke is toxic. It contains high levels of carbon monoxide, which is invisible, odorless, and quickly fatal. Smoke is a product of the combustion of many materials, and most of these are dangerous to breathe, if not very quickly fatal. Even a little smoke can do much harm to humans and considerable harm to electronic equipment. Smoke is deceptive even when there does not seem to be very much smoke or heat, and visibility looks good, people within or passing through the area quickly become disabled and may soon die.

The first priority is the safety of people. Get everyone away immediately from any smoke, and keep everyone away. Only trained responders with proper clothing, equipment, and breathing apparatus should enter any smoky area. There must be no heroics; crawling through smoke on the floor or breathing through a wet rag is a desperate measure that should be attempted only by people who are already trapped. Otherwise, everyone must wait until firefighters arrive and then follow their instructions.

The best way to prevent an equipment room fire is to keep anything combustible outside the room. Documents, manuals, and supplies should be stored outside the room in closed metal cabinets. Inside furniture should be limited to a metal table and a chair or two. All waste receptacles should be outside.

Once combustible materials are eliminated, the only smoke that develops will be from electrical overheating. Electrical fires rarely occur in an equipment room, and those that do occur are likely to be very small, brief, and cease as soon as the electrical power is removed. While often acrid and still potentially toxic, there is usually little smoke. Nonetheless, sensitive fire and smoke detectors and an effective means of fire suppression are needed and required by most building and fire codes. Good detectors can provide enough early warning to ward off trouble.

Enough heat to cause damage requires a high electrical current. Very few items within an equipment room are able to draw enough current to cause much, if indeed any, smoke. Circuit breakers and fuses usually will open before there is enough heat to cause more than a puff of smoke. Perhaps the greatest risk is smoke from ballasts in low-quality light fixtures.

The 110- and 220-volt power circuits and wiring can short and generate considerable heat and some smoke until a circuit breaker opens. But if power circuits are designed and installed properly, high voltage circuits rarely cause trouble. The majority of electronic circuits use very low voltages and draw very little power, so they present almost no risk of smoke or personal injury.

There are, however, many external fire and smoke threats. Smoke and flame may spread from fires elsewhere. These and possibly an explosion may be the result of arson or may be a diversion preceding a crime or terrorism attack. Therefore, strong and comprehensive protection is necessary.

In every equipment room, there should be smoke detectors that are connected to a central alarm system. There should be enough detectors to cover the entire volume of each room. Each detector should include an electric eye to detect visible smoke, ionization sensors that can detect smoke well before it is noticed by humans, and a rapid-rise-in-temperature detector in case there is enough heat to cause damage. Even though detected, nothing will stop smoke generated by overheated wiring or components until the electrical power is cut off.

There must be a fire suppression system in every equipment room. This is best done with sprinkler heads that spray water mist, although computers and other equipment may be damaged if the water is not immediately effective. Waterproof covers are often kept near equipment, but no one should waste time trying to apply them if there is smoke in the room.

Wiring, connections, and most components will dry themselves, even when soaked. Or the process may be hastened with a lint-free towel and careful use of a hair dryer. Keyboards, monitors, UPS units, power supplies, some disk or tape drives, and especially printers may be damaged and should be replaced until they can be inspected. Hard drives are usually hermetically sealed. A few other components could be damaged by excessive heat. Plenty of replacement items should be safely stored. Handling damaged low-voltage components (such as most circuit boards) presents little risk to people provided there is not too much water and the people involved know what they are doing and how to avoid damaging the components. If in doubt, shut down the equipment temporarily.

Enclosed equipment cabinets offer the best protection regardless of the fire suppressant. And enclosed cabinets can monitor temperature and humidity, detect and contain smoke, sound alarms, and often suppress a fire before damage occurs.

Halon 1301 fire suppressant was once widely used in critical areas. But Halon is a fluorocarbon whose manufacture has been banned for many years. Today's chemical systems are designed differently; one example uses the FM200 Suppression Agent made by Siemens. The claimed advantage of the chemical suppressants is that humans can breathe the agent. Another fire suppression system uses carbon dioxide, which is effective and less expensive, but can kill people as well as extinguish fires. The problem with all chemical agents including carbon dioxide is that they quickly mix with smoke and become very toxic. The agent may be safe to breathe, but the smoke mixed with it is not. These systems are also very expensive.

Regardless of the suppression system, there should be controls and a shutoff near the room's exit, but not accessible to a perpetrator. Generally, an audible, continuous alarm indicates that the suppression system is about to activate. There should be postpone buttons on the control panel, and perhaps remotely as well, that will delay activation for about two minutes while someone intervenes. The postpone-mode generally pulses the audible alarm. A silent alarm indication should remain activated whenever a fire suppression system is disabled or the alarms are silenced.

The next level of protection is several fire extinguishers. These are the most useful protections because a suppressant can be aimed where it is needed and not throughout the room. Carbon dioxide is best because it does not leave a residue. Chemical, powder, and foam extinguishers also work well but are hard to clean up. ABC-type extinguishers are best because they are effective with combustible materials, flammable liquids, and electrical fires, respectively. Several handheld extinguishers are better than a few large, heavy units. All fire extinguishers should be conspicuously wall-mounted or placed immediately inside and outside of entrances. An OSHA-approved red patch placed on the wall nearest to every extinguisher is immediately obvious. Also, check other OSHA, local code, and insurance requirements that may apply.

Supply air from the process cooling equipment should be shut down quickly and automatically to contain smoke. The IS equipment may have to be shut down soon thereafter before it overheats. It is best to shut down everything promptly in an orderly sequence—cooling, IS equipment, electrical power, and lighting—and then evacuate. Shut down the lighting, in case it is part of the problem. Shut-down should occur automatically with manual intervention from controls inside the room or remotely. Battery-powered emergency lights are advisable so responders do not need flashlights.

A so-called crash cart is a good investment. This is used during a smoke condition, a water leak, and, it is hoped, before a fire suppression system activates. A crash cart is kept outside or near major equipment rooms and rolled to where it is needed. The cart usually contains covers to keep smoke and water out of racks and off equipment, large fire extinguishers, and sometimes respirators or self-contained breathing apparatus. The crash cart should include quick-reference procedures, a checklist for protecting and shutting down the room, and safety and notification procedures—usually printed on plastic. The crash cart should be inspected and the procedures reviewed monthly, and there should be periodic training and exercises to practice using the equipment. Before the smoke and water covers are used, be sure the equipment is first powered off. Crash carts were important for yesterday's computer rooms but are increasingly unnecessary in a well-designed equipment room. Finally, be sure to utilize something to purge the room of smoke quickly. Most fire departments have portable purge fans with long fabric and wire hoses to reach outside. Do not allow anyone to use a respirator or breathing apparatus without training and experience. Respirators and breathing apparati are dangerous because, if they do not fit properly, people can be injured or killed before they realize they are in trouble.

15.7   MITIGATING SPECIFIC THREATS.   Several other threats must considered before good protection is possible. Some are not very likely to happen. But if they ever do, the costs can be enormous.

15.7.1   Preventing Wiretaps.   Most wiretaps are placed at wiring junction points. Vulnerable spots are within equipment rooms, wiring closets, junction boxes, wiring blocks, or data receptacles. With copper wiring, physical bridge connections or inductive couplers are easy and quick to install, and very hard to identify among a plethora of look-alike wiring. Bridges may tap onto wires or terminals that are already exposed, or connect where insulation has been scraped away. Couplers need only press against the wiring, but often the cable jacket must be split open and wires shifted so the coupler can touch the desired wire. Because of their high impedance, bridges are usually undetectable, except visually. Inductive couplers do not affect the signal lines in any way and are therefore undetectable, except visually (see also Section 14.5.5).

Fiber optic wiring is much more difficult to tap. Currently, the only way to place a tap is to insert a splitter or possibly an inline repeater or converter that can output to a copper tap wire. None of these devices can be inserted without interrupting the circuit, which should trigger an alarm. Fiber wiretapping requires a diversion or distraction to make the interruption look like a normal event.

The tap wire is likely to be a small cable that is hardly noticeable, running to an inconspicuous place. Or the tap can utilize an unused pair of wires within a legitimate cable that leads to an inconspicuous place. Once removed to a safe place, the data can be extracted by phone, radio, Internet, or recording. Tapped data may even be encrypted and stored on the victim's own network.

Unless all voice, date, and image data is encrypted, wiretap protection must be strong because detection is difficult at best. First, determine which cables are critical and where the entire run is located. All cables should be inside of metal conduit. Data and power conduits should look similar and with no markings or labels except alphanumeric codes. Keep critical conduits as inconspicuous as possible and away from places the public might access. There must be strong access controls, intrusion alarms, motion detectors, or surveillance where terminations, connectors, or wires can be accessed. Critical cable runs must be protected over their entire length (see Section 15.4.7).

In addition to possible wiretaps, data cables between the desktop and wall or floor outlets are hard to protect and easily damaged by accident, prolonged usage, rage, or vandalism. Cables, harnesses, and connectors inside office furniture are vulnerable also. Reasonably good protection is possible with design and devices that harden the data cabling against the possibility of a wiretap and that may detect tampering with any data wires. It is wise to consider provisions to patch into temporary cables, standby circuits, or unused outlets in case receptacles or wiring in the wall or floor are damaged. Store a variety of spare components for this use also.

Wiring trouble can occur at any time and without warning. Disruption, however, can be minimal. The best protection is preparation. Store spare cables and components safely. Extra spares may be needed following a major office move or a fire, flood, earthquake, or vandalism spree.

The recommendations in this chapter can protect the information infrastructure quite well for all but the most stringent requirements.

15.7.2   Remote Spying Devices.   Special radio receivers exist that can monitor information system data through walls or from outside the building without the use of a wiretap. These devices can simply listen to the data from afar. Such equipment is not available publicly and is well beyond the means of all but the best-financed intelligence agencies. However, there are many such systems in use today, and many more will be available as prices drop. Any organization whose data are very valuable is a potential target. Unfortunately, most victims will never discover the theft, which can continue undetected at the will of the spy organization.

15.7.3   Bombs, Threats, Violence, and Attacks.   Violent events are unpredictable and potentially devastating. These are not accidents but deliberate attacks intended to disrupt, cause damage, and spread fear. The tragic attacks of September 11, and their aftermath, have proven the vulnerability of people and of their infrastructures.

Protection against violence must be threat-specific, and all possible threats must be addressed. (See Chapter 14.) Effective deterrence and mitigation then becomes a matter of strengthening the defenses described throughout this chapter, which need not be very costly. Premises or corporate security must deal with most threats of violence, but the infrastructure needs special protections to avoid disruption and to mitigate the downtime and cost consequences of any such event.

Lesser bomb threats now happen frequently. Many threats are hoaxes; some deploy harmless but frightening devices; some weapons fail; and a few do not. There is usually no advance warning of serious events. Bomb threat risks are too great to be ignored. Protections and preparation will at least reduce the otherwise huge liabilities when any event occurs. The Federal Bureau of Investigation (FBI) offers considerable information on dealing with bomb threats, including a standard checklist for anyone receiving a warning phone call. Use of the checklist can help deter threats and apprehend perpetrators.

Some well-known bomb devices made with materials that are readily available from local stores include pipe bombs made with metal or plastic plumbing and inserted into sports balls, books, dolls, or teddy bears. An explosion can be set off by a fuse, timer, radio, motion sensor, pressure- or sound-activated trigger, or a mechanism to injure anyone attempting to defuse the bomb. A new device now showing up in schools is a tennis ball that will explode with considerable force when it is thrown.

Reasonably good protection can be simple and inexpensive but does require special knowledge. Details cannot be described publicly, but state and regional bomb squads or explosives units can advise and assist in many ways, including current briefings. Weapons of mass destruction (WMDs), other than nuclear weapons, are fast becoming a real threat, especially because many are small and easily concealed. WMDs include chemical and biological agents, incendiary devices, and even small amounts of radioactive materials disbursed by an explosive, or through the mails; all can spread panic. The government considers these devices very serious threats, with businesses and their infrastructures as likely targets.

A few cups of a chemical agent can kill hundreds of people. Victims are usually stricken within minutes or hours, and for no apparent reason. Chemical agents are not contagious. Biological agents are even harder to detect quickly. A small vial the size of a lipstick can kill every person within a large metropolitan area. Biological victims usually do not react for several hours or days, and they may be highly contagious. With either agent, death is likely unless the right procedures and antidotes are administered quickly.

Should any suspected WMD event occur, call for government help and stay well away from the scene (at least 600 feet upwind, uphill, and upstream) until properly trained and equipped specialists arrive. Advise state and regional emergency officials that mass decontamination may be required before victims can be transported or enter hospitals. Decontamination requires copious amounts of water (fire hoses set on a gentle spray), plenty of detergent, and, possibly, diluted household bleach. Provisions should be made to keep victims comfortable and to protect their modesty.

FBI, fire, police, and emergency management officials, trained in WMD and terrorism, should be consulted to better understand the possible threats and how best to deal with them.

15.7.4   Medical Emergencies.   Although medical emergencies are primarily premises security problems, preventing them is vital to avoid disrupting the performance of information systems.

Medical emergencies include heart attack, choking, smoke inhalation, asthma or allergic attacks, falls, and many other accidents, illnesses, or injuries that can occur in and around the workplace. As devices to test for biological and chemical hazards become available, these, too, will become necessary components of good security. Even minor cuts, bruises, and sprains should be treated promptly, especially if they are business-related. Employees, visitors, vendors, maintenance and delivery personnel, and messengers are all vulnerable. Senior executives may be especially vulnerable.

A serious medical emergency is very likely to happen eventually. Any such event can devastate morale and productivity and severely affect IS performance for an extended period. The event can be excessively costly if not promptly treated.

Mitigating medical emergencies requires a first aid room on the premises, first aid and some medical supplies, oxygen, a defibrillator, a nurse if possible, and many workers trained in first aid and cardiopulmonary resuscitation (CPR). All security personnel and guards should be certified in first aid and CPR.

Cardiac arrest occurs in the workplace and can hit anyone, visitors, vendors, or staff. Fast response, adequate equipment, and proper training are essential—minutes count. Waiting for a 911 response usually results in death or permanent impairment, even if emergency medical technicians arrive quickly. An automated external defibrillator (AED) on site will save lives and can be operated by anybody in an emergency. A portable AED currently costs about $1,000, and the suggested training is inexpensive. An AED is required in all federally managed buildings. Many shopping malls, places of public assembly, and commercial aircraft are now equipped with one or more units.

Oxygen is often necessary to save lives and prevent permanent impairment. Most sites equipped with an AED also have oxygen units. Good portable units cost about $1,000 and can be operated by almost anyone, without training.

15.8   INFORMATION NOT PUBLICLY AVAILABLE.   Many special threats cannot be mentioned publicly because the tools are easily obtained, concealed, and disposed of after the crime. It is not possible to describe these threats without explaining how anyone can perpetrate them. Apprehension is difficult, sometimes impossible, so the only protection is deterrence and detection before trouble happens. Chapter 14 excludes these threats.and it is equally inappropriate to discuss their specific mitigation in this chapter.

Generally, however, here are effective ways to mitigate these special threats as well as more common ones. It is best to compile a comprehensive list of possible threats and how to mitigate them by talking with a wide array of experienced consultants, contractors, installers, maintenance personnel, and vendors who are not product-oriented. Most vendors, installers, and consultants have long lists of ways to disrupt, snoop, or attack information infrastructures, along with recommended countermeasures. No protection can be comprehensive until these resources have been asked for suggestions. Once the potential threats and protective strategies are understood, effective deterrence or mitigation can be relatively inexpensive.

Just like some threats, there are effective security products that cannot be mentioned. These are not marketed publicly and therefore are unknown to dealers, resellers, or distributors. The costs can be reasonable because they are only sold direct. Developers may supply classified systems for military or government use and offer declassified versions to selected users. In this way, vendors restrict knowledge of their products to as few people as possible, so that others cannot discover how to recognize or circumvent them.

One example is a perimeter detection system developed for the military that is now available, but not yet publicly. This system offers major improvements and economies. It can be used effectively to protect cable runs of any length, equipment rooms, interior spaces, and outside facilities. The system is sensitive, reliable, and can record suspicious events.

Many consultants who have worked with financial, regulated, or very large clients know some of these specialty vendors. Usually, a consultant will approach the vendor and discuss what is needed; the vendor may then contact the customer directly.

15.9 COMPLETING THE SECURITY PLANNING PROCESS

15.9.1 A Cost-Value Approach. The threat assessment procedures described in Chapter 14 can generate a prioritized list of all potential threats as well as the probability that each threat may occur and the approximate response and recovery costs that may result. This chapter suggests what protections are needed, alternatives for reducing the risk, and some optional solutions. The next step is a cost-value analysis to determine the best alternative.

A cost-value analysis is at best an approximation. Nonetheless, valid conclusions are possible and potentially valuable. Consider the following premises:

1. A specific threat might occur every 10 years.

2. Whenever it does happen, the resultant costs will be (say) $25,000.

3. The initial cost of strong protection is $10,000 and the ongoing cost is $500 per year.

Each of these premises is a best-guess approximation. The question is how to reduce this threat profitably.

Simple cost-value conclusions suggest that self-insuring will average $2,500 every year ($25,000 divided by 10 years), while strong protection can pay for itself in five years. A $10,000 capital expense amortized over five years equals $2,000 per year, plus maintenance of $500 per year totals $2,500 per year for the first five years. Thereafter, the strong protection costs only $500 annually. Compared to self-insurance, strong protection represents a saving of $2,000 per year, a $10,00 total savings. The same approach can be used to evaluate the approximate value of lease-purchase, outsourcing, insurance, or a surety bond. The best combination of each alternative should provide adequate protection against each specific threat.

There are other factors to consider as well: cost of funds, tax implications, the useful life of the alternatives, and whether the threat will diminish or increase in the future. It is necessary to develop an analytical model that is comprehensive and best suits the circumstances. Although educated guesses must be used, the process still can yield valid results.

This example covers only one hypothetical threat, whereas a threat assessment will provide a list of many actual threats. While protection is ineffective unless it is threat-specific, there are many common defenses. Unfortunately, there are also cascading situations where one threat can cause others to occur and the ultimate costs may be far greater than expected. (Cascading is described in Chapter 14.) For example, in addition to the repair costs following a fire, there will likely be water damage, equipment damage, and data lost as a result of loss of power.

The cost-value process is not easy and cannot be abbreviated. All the stakeholders should be involved, should agree on the objectives, and should concur on the final strategy. It also may be prudent to seek outside assistance and advice, but the process should not be placed entirely in outsiders' hands.

15.9.2   Plan Ahead.   Information systems and their infrastructure are constantly changing, and at an ever-increasing pace. So, too, are the requirements for protection. It is wise to develop contingency plans for changes, relocations, expansions, and even downsizing that could occur in the future. Before any new systems are installed, and before any modifications are made to existing systems, future needs should be evaluated and incorporated into the designs, if feasible. Once a protective system is installed, changes can be expensive, but contingency provisions for the future often can be implemented inexpensively. Preparedness can save time and money.

15.9.3   Keep Well Informed.   To know what is happening in security, it is necessary to be aware of threats as they occur in similar information systems. Reading relevant literature, attending security seminars and conferences, keeping current with security patches and advisories, and participating in discussions with peers to share experience are minimum requirements. Relationships should be maintained with local emergency management, police, fire, and other officials who can provide advice and assistance. Senior management must be well briefed as to security risks, opportunities for improvement, and ways to add value.

Continuing awareness of improved security tools and new approaches as they emerge will permit better protection, generally at lower costs than catch-up changes.

15.10   SUMMARY.   No silver bullets or out-of-the-box solutions provide adequate protection. Security needs and risks vary considerably and keep changing. Today's threats are numerous, escalating rapidly, often complex, and increasingly dangerous. Serious terrorist attacks, accidents, mistakes, vandalism, hacker exploits, and spying are ever more frequent. Threats must be avoided because the consequences are potentially devastating. Businesses are increasingly likely targets for risks that are escalating, as information infrastructures become increasingly complex and fragile and, therefore, more vulnerable.

The infrastructure must be well protected so that IS performance cannot be compromised. Any lapse or shortcoming of the defenses will inevitably result in enormous costs, disruptions, loss of business, and embarrassment. Therefore, strong protection is necessary, and it must be implemented and maintained in a cost-effective manner.

The information infrastructure requires special protection beyond what premises or corporate security can provide. Ample early warning is essential so that trouble is discovered before any disruption can occur. Covert protective systems, components, wiring, and procedures are needed and must be inconspicuous, so that employees and visitors cannot determine what exists, how it functions, or where it is located. Effective deterrence that requires some exposed devices is also needed so that trouble will be directed elsewhere. In addition, deceptive devices may be needed to divert potential troublemakers from sensitive areas or to entrap them.

Good planning, design, and management are all essential to strong protection; everyone involved must understand the infrastructure's security needs. Many stakeholders must be involved in planning and must support good security. Effective protection also must be threat-specific, comprehensive, and utilize all resources efficiently. The result can be added value and enhanced productivity, goodwill, and morale. Good protection that is well implemented and maintained is a good investment. Anything less is a waste of time and money.

15.11   NOTES

1. FEMA's Web site is *www.fema.gov*. Local and state emergency management officials can assist, as can regional FEMA offices.

2. The National Fire Protection Association is located at 1 Batterymarch Park, Quincy, MA 02269; tel (617) 770-3000; *www.nfpa.org*.

3. The Telecommunications Industry Association/Electronic Industry Alliance can be reached at 2500 Wilson Boulevard, Arlington, VA 22201; tel. (703) 907-7700; *www.tiaon-line.org*.

CHAPTER 16

IDENTIFICATION AND AUTHENTICATION

Ravi Sandhu

CONTENTS

16.1 INTRODUCTION. *Authorization* is the allocation of permissions for specific types of access to restricted information. In the real world, authorization is conferred on real human beings; in contrast, information technology normally confers authorization on *user identifiers* (IDs). Computer systems need to link specific IDs to particular authorized users of those IDs. Even inanimate components, such as network interface cards, firewalls, and printers, need IDs. *Identification* is the process of ascribing an ID to a human being or to another computer or network component. *Authentication* is the process of *binding* an ID to a specific entity. For example, authentication of a user's identity generally involves narrowing the range of possible entities claiming to have authorized use of a specific ID down to a single person.

The focus of this chapter is on person-to-computer authentication. In practice, we also need computer-to-person authentication to prevent spoofing of services on a network. This type of authentication is increasingly important, especially on open networks such as the Internet, where users may be misled about the identity of the Web sites they visit. For example, some criminals send unsolicited e-mail messages in Hypertext Markup Language (HTML) to victims; the messages include links that are labeled to suggest an inoffensive or well-respected Web site, but the underlying HTML actually links to a fraudulent site designed to trick people into revealing personal information such as credit card numbers or details to support theft of identity. More generally, computer-to-computer authentication, typically in both directions (i.e., mutual authentication), is essential to safeguard critical transactions such as those of interbank transfers and business-to-business electronic commerce.

In the early decades of computer usage, most computers authenticated users who accessed mainframes from within a single enterprise. User IDs therefore could be assigned in a centralized and controlled manner. Even so, identifiers have never necessarily been unique, for there is no obligatory one-to-one relationship between a user ID and a human being's real-world identity. For example, an account such as inventory_clerk could be shared by several people without interference from the computer; at most, the operating system might be configured to prevent simultaneous sharing of an ID by limiting to one the number of sessions initiated with a specific ID.

Conversely, a single user often has many user IDs. For example, there may be unique identifiers for each of dozens of Web sites for music clubs, book clubs, enterprise e-mail, and so on. Even on the same computer, a given user might have several accounts defined for different purposes; jane_doe and jdoe might be identifiers for two different application packages on a system. These multiple identifiers cause problems for administrators if they do not know that the same user is associated with the different IDs; they also cause practical problems for users who have to use different authentication methods for a range of IDs. One of the critical goals of today's identification and authentication (I&A) research and development is to develop reliable and economical methods for *single signon,* whereby users would not have to reidentify and reauthenticate themselves when accessing different computer systems linked into an internet. For details of I&A in facilities security, see Chapter 15.

16.2   FOUR PRINCIPLES OF AUTHENTICATION.   Authentication of a claimed identity can be established in four ways:

1. What you know (passwords and passphrases).
2. What you have (tokens: physical keys, smart cards).
3. What you are (static biometrics: fingerprint, face, retina, and iris recognition).
4. What you do (dynamic biometrics: voice, handwriting, and typing recognition).

These methods can be combined; for example, passwords often are combined with tokens or biometrics to provide stronger authentication than is possible with either one alone. A familiar example of this *two-factor authentication* occurs with automatic teller machine (ATM) cards. Possession of the card (the token) and knowledge of the personal identification number (the PIN, corresponding to a password) are required to access a user's bank account.

This chapter introduces each of these four authentication methods and provides additional details for each.

16.2.1   What You Know.   Password- or passphrase-based authentication on the basis of a password or passphrase that only the user should know is so widely used that any person who has had any contact with computers and networks probably has had several passwords. Although password technology is often poorly administered and insecure and frustrating for users and administrators, passwords can be deployed much more securely and conveniently than they usually are. Although many security professionals have felt and hoped for years that passwords eventually would be phased out to be replaced by tokens or biometrics, today the consensus is that passwords are not likely to disappear soon and that they will continue to be the dominant authentication technique for years to come.

Demonstrating knowledge of a password does not directly authenticate a human being. All it does is authenticate knowledge of the password. Unauthorized knowledge of, or guessing at, a password can lead to impersonation of one user by another, called *spoofing.* The theft of a password can be difficult to detect since it is not a tangible asset. Passwords are also very easy to share. It is common for senior executives to give their passwords to their secretaries to facilitate their work, even though assigning proxy privileges would be as effective and more secure.

16.2.2   What You Have.   Authentication based on possession of a token is used where higher assurance of identity is desired than is possible by passwords alone. As with passwords, possession of a token does not directly authenticate a human being; rather it authenticates possession of the token and ability to use it. Sometimes a password or PIN is required to use the token, thus establishing two-factor authentication; the theory is that the requirement to have both elements decreases the likelihood of successful spoofing.

Tokens can take on a variety of forms. The oldest token is the physical key for a physical lock, but these are not much used for securing computer systems. *Soft tokens* are carried on transportable media or even accessed over a network from a server. Soft tokens contain only data; they typically require a password to access the contents. Modern tokens usually are implemented in self-contained hardware with computing capability; examples include:

- Credit card–size devices with a liquid crystal display (LCD) that display pseudo-random numbers or other codes
- LCD devices in the shape of a key fob using the same algorithms as the credit card–shape devices
- Hardware devices called *dongles* that plug into input-output ports on computers. Examples include dongles for serial ports, parallel ports, Universal Serial Bus (USB) ports, and PC-card interfaces

All tokens used for computer authentication require software to process information residing in or produced by the token. The most significant distinction is whether the tokens require electronic contact with the authentication system. *Contactless* tokens are easier to deploy because they do not require specialized readers. For example, the credit card and key fob pseudorandom number generators simply require the user to enter the visible code in response to a prompt from the authentication software. On the other hand, contactless tokens are more limited in function than *contact tokens.* For instance, a contact token can be used to create digital signatures whereas a contactless token cannot do so practically.

In cyberspace, a token does not authenticate by means of physical characteristics. Rather the token has some secret, either exclusive to itself or possibly shared with a server on the network. Authentication of the token is really authentication of knowledge of the secret stored on the token. As such, authentication based on possession of a token is tantamount to authentication based on what the token knows. However, this secret can be longer and more random than a secret that a user has to retain in human memory as a password. Unfortunately, building cost-effective and secure tokens from which the secret cannot be extracted by tampering or by brute-force guesswork has proven much more difficult than initially anticipated. In the early 1990s, many security professionals believed that tokens would replace passwords; in fact, however, although tokens continue to be an attractive authentication technology, they probably will not become pervasive soon.

16.2.3   What You Are.   Biometrics take authentication directly to the human being. As humans, we recognize each other by a number of characteristics. Biometric authentication seeks to achieve a similar result in cyberspace. A *static biometric* is a characteristic of a person such as fingerprints, a hand geometry, or an iris pattern; more dramatically, it could be the DNA of an individual. The likelihood of two individuals having identical fingerprints, iris patterns, or DNA is minuscule (with exceptions for genetically identical siblings). Biometrics require specialized and expensive readers to capture the biometric data, making widespread deployment difficult.

Biometrics also suffer from the problems of replay and tampering. Thus, the biometric reader must itself be trusted and tamper-proof to reduce the likelihood of an attacker's capturing the data input and replaying it at a later time or creating false biometric profiles to trick the system into accepting an imposter. Moreover, the biometric data themselves must be captured in proximity to the user to reduce the likelihood of substitution, such as stolen blood used to fool a DNA-based biometric system. If the data are transmitted to a distant server for authentication, the transmission requires a secure protocol, with extensive provisions for time-stamping and rapid expiration of the data.

16.2.4   What You Do.   *Dynamic biometrics* capture a dynamic process rather than a static characteristic of a person. A well-known example is that of signature dynamics. Signature dynamics involves recording the speed and acceleration of a person's hand as a signature is written on a special tablet. Rather than merely the shape of the signature, it is the dynamic characteristics of motion while writing the signature that authenticates the person—motions that are extremely hard to simulate. Another possibility is to recognize characteristics of a person's voice as he or she is asked to read aloud some specified text. Keystroke dynamics of a person's typing behavior is another alternative.

As in all other forms of authentication, dynamic biometrics depends on exclusion of capture and playback attacks, in which, for example, a recording of someone's voice might be used to fool a voice-recognition system. Similarly, a signature-dynamics system might be fooled by playback of the data recorded from an authentic signature. Encryption techniques help to make such attacks more difficult.

Security experts agree that biometrics offer a stronger guarantee of authentication than passwords, but deployment on a large scale remains to be demonstrated. Whether this technology becomes pervasive may ultimately be determined by its social and political acceptability as much as by improved technology.

16.3 PASSWORD-BASED AUTHENTICATION. Passwords are the pervasive technology for authentication in cyberspace today. At a conservative estimate, there are close to a billion password-based authentications per day. Examples include the vast number of Internet users and the number of passwords each one uses every day. However, the current deployment of password technology needs to be improved in many ways. Today users must remember too many identities and corresponding passwords. Also, the deployed technology is more fragile than it needs to be; for example, many users choose passwords that can be guessed easily. Passwords are never going to be as secure as the strongest biometric systems, so one would not use them as the sole basis for, say, launching nuclear missiles. However, their use can be made strong enough for many less critical transactions.

The following sections review the major risks of password use and their mitigation by technical, social, and procedural means.

16.3.1 Access to User Passwords by System Administrators. One of the most dangerous practices in use today is the storage of unencrypted user passwords accessible to system administrators. In some sites, new users receive passwords that are assigned and written down by system administrators. If these passwords are used only once, for the initial logon, the user can be forced to choose or create a truly secret password that no one else knows. However, in many such sites, administrators keep control of a paper or electronic record, usually for quick access when users forget their own passwords. Such access completely destroys an important element of I&A: *nonrepudiation.* If someone else has access to a password, then authorized users can reasonably *repudiate* transactions by claiming that their identities were spoofed. It is difficult to counter such a repudiation, especially in a court of law considering an accusation of malfeasance by the authorized user of that password. In general, passwords that will be used repeatedly should not be written down, and they should not be accessible to system administrators. Critical passwords can be written down, stored in tamper-proof containers, and locked away where at least two signatures will be required for retrieval in case of emergency.

16.3.2 Risk of Undetected Theft. Perhaps the biggest intrinsic risk with passwords is that they can be stolen without knowledge of the user. Observation of somebody typing in a password is sufficient to leak it. This can happen surreptitiously without the victim's explicit knowledge. A related risk is disclosure of a password to an attacker who persuades the legitimate user to reveal it by posing as a systems administrator who needs the password to do something beneficial for the user. Loss of a physical token eventually may be discovered since it is missing, although the possibility of cloning these devices remains. Loss of a password, on the other hand, can be discovered only by detecting its misuse or by finding it in the possession of an unauthorized user (e.g., in a list of passwords cracked by using a dictionary-based *password-cracking* program, as described in section 16.3.5).

There are several mitigations of this risk. First, user education and awareness are critically important. People need to treat important secrets with the care they deserve. Typing a password in an unsafe environment should be done discreetly. Efforts to be discreet should be positively reinforced while negligence in exposing passwords during entry should be considered akin to bad social behavior.

User education and awareness, although extremely important, can never be the whole solution. People will inevitably slip up and make mistakes. Some of us are more negligent than others. Others will be surreptitiously observed. In some cases passwords will be revealed to computers with Trojan horses (see Chapter 9) that capture them. Technologists must pursue technical and human solutions to mitigate these risks.

Since some losses of control over passwords are inevitable, it logically follows that password-based authentication should be used only in situations where misuse detection is not only feasible but actually convenient to do in real time. To make this possible, the system architecture should centralize the information needed for misuse detection in one place. If the required information is dispersed across many servers, it will be difficult to coordinate the different audit trails. Traditionally, users of password systems have not considered the need for misuse detection. However, modern security is firmly based on a mix of prevention and detection techniques. Security professionals should apply similar thinking to authentication systems. Ease of misuse detection should be an important criterion in the design of any authentication system. For password-based systems, misuse detection capability should be considered an essential requirement. (For information on intrusion-detection systems, see Chapter 37.)

What else can system designers do to mitigate this risk? It should be made easy for users to change their passwords themselves. Having a system administrator change a password that will be used more than once is illogical.

If a user feels that a password may have been compromised, changing it should be a simple matter. In particular, the system should never prevent a user's attempt to change a password. Some deployed systems will deny change of a password if the password was changed recently, say in the past 24 hours. Although there are reasons for this kind of restriction, it may create a bigger risk than the one it purports to prevent.

Users should be encouraged to change their passwords fairly often; a typical allowable lifetime for a password is between 30 and 90 days. Without occasional changes, a compromised password could be held until the malicious attacker finds opportunity to use it. Frequent changes to passwords reduce the window of opportunity for such attackers.

16.3.3   Risk of Undetected Sharing.

Another major risk of passwords is the ease with which they can be shared. There are many examples of sharing between executives and their secretaries, between physicians and office staff or nurses, between professors and their secretaries or students, and among coworkers in any activity. User education and strict policies against password and account sharing are obvious first steps to deter this possibility. Strict policies can be effective within an organization, but their deterrent effect may not carry over to large consumer populations. Misuse detection also can be employed to enforce a strict policy.

The root cause of password sharing within an organization is the lack of effective delegation mechanisms whereby selected privileges of one user can be delegated to another. Better authorization mechanisms could eliminate much of the perceived need for password sharing. It should be possible for secretaries to read their boss's e-mail under their own identity and password. In fact, the bosses should be able to segregate the e-mail that the secretaries can read while denying access to more sensitive e-mail. Moreover, reading the boss's e-mail should be possible without allowing the secretary to send e-mail under the boss's identity; a proxy privilege could allow secretaries to answer their boss's e-mail while signing the replies with their own names. In the nonelectronic world, secretaries routinely answer mail for other people without impersonating them, and this should be the practice with computers as well.

Sharing of passwords among consumers is likely to occur when the cost to the consumers is minimal. While consumers are unlikely to share passwords for an online bank or brokerage account with others, they may be willing to share passwords for an online subscription service, possibly with many friends. An enterprising consumer may even make a business of reselling the service. One way to deter such consumer piracy would be to tie exposure of the password to exposure of a sensitive secret of the consumer, such as a credit card number.

16.3.4   Risk of Weakest Link.   One of the frustrations of passwords is that users have to remember too many. Thus, users tend to repeat selection of the same password at multiple sites. This is a very insidious risk. Exposure of a user password at a poorly maintained site can lead to penetration of the user's account at numerous other sites. It is not easy to deploy technical measures to protect directly against this risk. A particular site can force a user to pick a complex password or can even choose the password for the user. However, it cannot prevent use of the same password elsewhere. This is one area where user education, awareness, and self-interest are paramount. Malicious attackers can set up rogue Web sites easily, to entice users to register for attractive services, whereupon the user's password for other sites may be revealed.

A technical solution to mitigate this problem is to avoid the requirement that a user has to register at multiple sites with user IDs and passwords. Instead, the user should register at a few trusted sites, but the user ID should be usable at multiple sites by secured sharing of assurances that the user has in fact been identified and authenticated sufficiently for business to continue. This is essentially what public key infrastructure (PKI) seeks to do. With authentication based on client certificates, it is not necessary to expose a user's password to multiple sites. An effective marriage of passwords and PKI would reduce the exposure to the weakest link. For more details of PKI, see Chapter 23.

A similar approach stores sensitive information in one place and then directs businesses to that place for payment information. For example, today a number of systems (e.g., the Microsoft *Passport*) allow a user to register credit card information once with a trusted service and then refer online retailers (e-tailers) to that service for payment.

16.3.5   Risk of Online Guessing.   Authentication systems are susceptible to guessing attacks. In *online guessing,* an attacker tries to authenticate using a valid user ID and a guessed password. If the password has been poorly selected, the attacker may get lucky. The attacker also may be able to exploit personal knowledge of the victim to select likely passwords. This approach exploits the documented tendency of naïve users to select passwords from lists of obvious words, family, friends, pets, sports, commercial brands, and other easily obtained information. For example, studies of password files consistently show that the most frequently selected password in the world is "password"; the second most frequent is the user ID itself or the user ID backward. An account with the same password as the user ID is often called a *Joe account,* as in User ID: joe; Password: joe.

Another kind of password vulnerable to guessing is a password assigned by default; for example, many software installations create accounts with the same password on all systems. Documentation usually warns users to change those *canonical passwords,* but many people ignore the warning. Canonical passwords are particularly dangerous when they grant access to powerful accounts such as root accounts or to support functions.

The first line of defense against online attacks is to enforce password complexity rules, in addition to user education and awareness. Many systems today require a minimum of eight-character passwords with a mix of upper- and lower-case letters, numerals, and possibly special characters. Nonetheless, online guessing attacks are still possible, and system logging (see Chapter 38) or application logging (see Chapter 39) can be helpful in identifying successful impersonation. For example, log files may show that a particular user has never logged on to a particular account outside working hours, yet someone has logged on as that user in the middle of the night.

Some systems react to online attacks by a simple rule that locks the account after a certain number of failed attempts. This rule may have been borrowed from a similar rule with ATM cards. The rule actually makes sense in the context of ATMs with two-factor authentication based on possession of the card and knowledge of the PIN. However, in a password-only scheme, the "three strikes and out" rule can lead to denial of service to legitimate users. An attacker can easily lock up many accounts by entering three wrong passwords repeatedly. A more graceful rule would slow down the rate at which password guessing can be attempted so that a legitimate user may be perceptibly slowed down in authentication but not denied. For example, locking an account for a couple of minutes after three bad passwords suffices to make brute-force guesswork impractical. See Chapter 8, section 8.3.3.1 for examples of brute-force attack speeds.

In addition, intrusion-detection systems can be configured to alert system administrators immediately upon repeated entry of bad passwords. Human beings then can intervene to determine the cause of the bad passwords—user error or malfeasance.

16.3.6   Risk of Offline Dictionary Attacks.   The paramount technical attack on password-based authentication systems is the *dictionary attack*. Such attacks start with copying the password file for a target system and placing it on a computer under the attacker's control. The password file normally uses *one-way encryption* that allows the system to encrypt an entered password and compare it to the encrypted form of the legitimate password. If the two encrypted strings match, the entered password is presumably correct and so the system authenticates the user ID.

The dictionary attack is described as offline because the attacker obtains the necessary information to carry out the attack and then performs the computations offline to discover the password from this information. It is a guessing attack because the attacker tries different likely passwords from an extensive list of possible passwords (the *dictionary*). The list of likely passwords is called a dictionary because it includes words from one or more natural languages such as English and Spanish; specialized versions used with *password-cracking* programs may sort words by frequency of use rather than alphabetically to speed up successful guesses.

The initial response to dictionary attacks was to stop users from selecting passwords that could be cracked via a dictionary attack. In essence, the system would try a dictionary attack; if it succeeded, it would prohibit the user from selecting this password. This is not a productive approach because attackers' dictionaries are often ahead of the system's dictionaries. The productive approach is to prevent the attacker from collecting the information necessary to carry out the dictionary attack.

Designers of password-based authentication systems were slow to recognize the risk of dictionary attacks. It has long been understood that passwords should not be stored on a server in cleartext because this becomes a single point of catastrophic failure. Time-sharing systems of the early 1970s stored passwords in a "hashed" form.

Knowledge of the hashed form of a password did not reveal the actual password. Authentication of passwords was achieved by computing the hash from the presented password and comparing with the stored hash. The Unix system actually made the hashed form of user passwords easily readable, since reversing the hash was correctly considered computationally infeasible. However, knowledge of the hashed form of a password is sufficient for dictionary attacks. The attacker guesses a password from a list, or dictionary, of likely passwords, computes its hash, and compares with the stored hash. If they match, the attacker's guess is verified; otherwise the attacker tries another guess. Since the late 1980s Unix systems have stopped making the file of hashed passwords easy to read, so this vulnerability has been reduced.

Unix also introduced the concept of a *salt* to make dictionary attacks more difficult. The user password and a random number called the salt are hashed together and stored on the server. The salt is also stored on the server. To authenticate a user, the presented password and the stored salt are hashed and compared with the stored hash value. Use of a salt means that a separate dictionary attack is required for every user since each password guess must be hashed along with the salt.

16.3.7 Risk of Password Replay. If a password is transmitted in cleartext from client to server, it is susceptible to being picked up on the network by an intruder. This is called *password sniffing*. Many systems require the password to be sent to the server in cleartext. Others require transmission of a hash of the password (usually without a salt). Transmitting the hash of a password is risky for two reasons:

1. The hash is sufficient for a dictionary attack unless a salt is used and kept secret.

2. The attacker does not even need to recover the password. Instead, the attacker can replay the hash of the password when needed.

Many existing systems are susceptible to sniffing of passwords on the network in cleartext or hashed form. Fortunately, technical solutions to this problem do exist.

One approach to the replay threat is to use the server's public key to encrypt any transmission of password-related information to the server: Thus, only the server can decrypt the information by using its private key. This is essentially what server-side SSH (Secure Shell) and server-side SSL (Secure Sockets Layer) do. The server-side mode of both SSL and SSH require the server to have a public key certificate. The client-side mode of these protocols requires that the client also have a public key certificate. This approach can be effective but has its own risks.

An alternate approach is to avoid transmitting the password but instead to employ a protocol that requires knowledge of the password to run successfully. One of the earliest and best-known systems to take this approach is Kerberos. In this system, a user's password is converted to a secret key on the client machine and also stored on the Kerberos server. When the user requests authentication, the Kerberos server sends the user's machine a secret session key encrypted using the shared secret key derived from the user's password. The ability to decrypt this message correctly demonstrates knowledge of the password without actually transmitting it, in cleartext, hashed, or encrypted form. Unfortunately, the Kerberos protocol is susceptible to dictionary attacks: Any client machine can pretend to be any user and can obtain the necessary information required for a dictionary attack.

Kerberos also does not use a salt, so the same dictionary attack can be applied to multiple users. Kerberos Version 5 provides for a preauthentication option, which makes it somewhat harder to gather the information for a dictionary attack. The data are no longer available by simply asking the Kerberos server for them; instead they must be sniffed on a network. Recent experiments have shown that dictionary attacks on Kerberos are very practical, so this is a serious vulnerability of a widely deployed password-based authentication system.

Since the early 1990s, many password-based authentication protocols have been published that do not suffer from the dictionary attacks to which Kerberos is so vulnerable. In particular, *zero-knowledge password proofs* are based on the idea that two parties (computers, people) can demonstrate that they know a secret password without revealing the password. These methods depend on the ability to establish that the two parties both independently selected the same number—but without knowing what the specific number is. One popular conceptual model of this process is the business-card zero-knowledge password proof, which runs as follows:

1. Two people want to test whether they share a secret number (in this thought experiment, a single digit between 1 and 10). In this example, the shared number is 3.
2. The two people have a deck of 10 blank cards.
3. The first person counts down to the third card and makes a mark on the right edge of that card.
4. The deck of business cards is arranged so that the second person can mark the left edge of the cards but cannot see the right edge.
5. The second person also counts down to the third card (in this example) and marks the right edge.
6. The card deck is shuffled so that the sequence order is lost and then displayed to both parties.
7. If a single card has a mark on both the right edge and the left edge, then the two parties share the secret number but neither had to reveal exactly which number it was.

Today we understand how to construct such protocols. Products built on these safer protocols are commercially available. No longer do customers of password-based authentication products need to be exposed to dictionary attacks. This is a truly important development because it closes the most significant technical vulnerability of passwords.

16.3.8   Risk of Server Spoofing.   As mentioned earlier, one widely used approach to preventing password exposure in transit on a network is to send passwords from client to server encrypted using the server's public key. The server, which has the corresponding private key, can decrypt the password to recover it. Knowledge of the public key is not sufficient for a spoofer to determine the private key. Naïve protocols for protecting the private key can be susceptible to replay attacks. However, there are two well-designed protocols in widespread use today.

Server-side SSL is the protocol that has been used by most Web surfers. In this protocol, the server's public key is used to secure transmission of the user's password from client to server. Like all public key–based schemes, the Achilles' heel of this protocol lies in authentic knowledge of the server's public key. The technology of public key certificates seeks to provide public keys with good assurance of the identity of the server to which they belong. A full discussion of issues with Public Key Infrastructure technology appears in Chapter 23, but it suffices to observe that there are pitfalls with the use of certificates for authentication of servers. A server can collect a user's password by pretending to be something other than what it is. Relying on the look and feel of a Web page for server authentication is hardly sufficient, since it is easy to copy an entire Web page for use as a decoy and to establish confidence before capturing confidential information. Authenticity of the server's certificate can be spoofed in many ways that are hard for the user to detect, and manipulation of the trusted root certificates that are configured in the user's Web browser is possible. Moreover, while trust ultimately chains up to a root certificate, the owner of a single certificate below a trusted root is capable of considerable mischief. Server-side Secure Shell is a similar protocol, typically used to provide secure remote access to Unix servers. SSL and SSH share the same fundamental vulnerabilities: Server-side SSL and server-side SSH can be spoofed by certificate manipulation. The use of server-side SSL to protect transmission of passwords from client to server is prevalent on the Internet today, but it is important for customers of authentication products to understand the risks inherent in this approach.

On the other hand, in the client-side mode of these protocols, there is no need for a password to be transmitted from client to server, since client-to-server authentication is based on the client's use of the private key to generate a digital signature. Hence client-side protocols are not vulnerable to password capture by server spoofing.

16.3.9   Risk of Password Reuse.   The need to change passwords with some reasonable frequency is well recognized, but what is reasonable frequency? And how draconian should the enforcement be? It seems that security administrators have pushed too far on these questions. Forcing users to change passwords every month and enforcing such rules ruthlessly actually could lead to less security rather than more. There is a real risk here, created by well-meaning security administrators who have made the problem worse than it inherently is.

Systems that choose a password for the user have their own set of problems and are generally too user-unfriendly to be viable in the Internet age. This discussion focuses on systems that allow users to select their own passwords.

How does exposure of a password increase with time? Even the strongest password-based system, with immunity to offline dictionary attacks and password capture by server spoofing, faces increased exposure as time passes. Over a long period of time, a slow, ongoing, online guessing attack could be successful. Also, the likelihood of inadvertent disclosure by surreptitious observation or exposure on a Trojan horse–infected computer increases with time. Nevertheless, a good password, carefully chosen by the user to be safe from dictionary attacks and well memorized by the user, should not be changed casually. A change every six months may be appropriate for well-chosen, brute-force–resistant passwords.

Enforcing password changes is a complicated business, and one where the security community has not really done a good job. It is not difficult to keep track of the age of a password and to force a change when an appropriate time has passed. The difficulty is in forcing the new password to be independent of the old one. In fact, the likelihood is that the new password will be a slight variation of the old one. For example, appending the numeral designating a month to a fixed string enables users to have almost the same password, even if they are forced to change it every month. Some systems will keep a history of recently used passwords to prevent their reuse. A system that keeps a history of, say, five passwords can be fooled by rapidly changing the password six times. To prevent this, there are systems that will not allow a user to change a password more than once a day. This has the unfortunate effect of actually increasing risk of password exposure, since a user who realizes that the current password may have been inadvertently exposed cannot change it, exactly when the need to do so is greatest.

16.4   TOKEN-BASED AUTHENTICATION.   Token-based authentication relies on something that the user possesses. This authentication can be achieved in many ways, including:

- One-time password generators
- Smart cards and dongles
- Soft tokens

16.4.1   One-Time Password Generators.   A popular form of token, such as the SecurID from RSA Data Security Inc., displays a *one-time password,* typically a six- or eight-digit numeral, which changes every one to three minutes. The password is generated using a proprietary algorithm and uses both a unique token identifier stored on the token and a time signal generated by an onboard clock. The user authenticates by entering the user ID and current value displayed by the token.

The password is called *one-time* because it expires at the end of its allowable period for use. The token is contactless in that it does not need electrical contact with the computer where the user is presenting authentication data. The user transfers the necessary information from the token via a keyboard or other input device. To make this a two-factor authentication, a fixed user password is also required in addition to the changing one-time password displayed by the token. These tokens are based on shared secret keys, so both the token and the server have a shared secret. The server and the token need to be initialized and then kept synchronized for this scheme to work. If the time discrepancy between a specific token and the authenticating system exceeds a specified limit, the authenticating software adjusts a value in an internal table to compensate for the time slippage.

Password generators and smart cards must be protected against physical tampering. These devices typically include several measures to cause destruction of the electronic circuits if the outer case is opened; for example, in addition to epoxy-resin glue, tokens may include light-sensitive components that are destroyed immediately by exposure to light, rendering the unit unusable. Some password generators and smart cards cannot even be opened to replace batteries, so the entire card must be replaced on a pre-dictable schedule. Tokens of this kind are available that are guaranteed to last one year, two years, or three years without having the batteries wear out.

16.4.2   Smart Cards and Dongles.   Another form of token is a smart card. These cards can go into a PC-card reader, or they can be read by a specialized reader. *Dongles* are smart cards that fit into input-output ports such as USB. A smart card has its own processing capability and typically stores a private key associated with the user. Often a password or PIN is required to access the card, thereby achieving two-factor authentication. The smart card enables user authentication by signing some challenge presented to it with the user's private key. The signature is verified by means of the user's public key. A complete discussion of such smart cards involves consideration of public key cryptography, public key certificates or so-called digital certificates, and supporting infrastructure or PKI (Public Key Infrastructure). Suffice it to say that smart cards have long been considered essential for widespread use of public key technology but so far have not been widely deployed.

Hardware tokens offer the potential for stronger authentication than passwords but have only seen limited use due to their costs and their infrastructure requirements. Whether they can be deployed in a scale of millions of users remains to be seen. Authentication by tokens is really authentication by something that the token knows. Since tokens can be programmed to remember and use secrets much more effectively than humans can, they offer the potential of strong cryptographic authentication, but tamperproof tokens are not easy to produce. In recent years, attacks based on differential power analysis have proven effective in determining the secret keys and PINs stored on smart cards. These attacks require physical access to a card whose loss probably would be known, so, although they may not always be feasible, they certainly call into question the presumed tamper-proof nature of smart cards. As smart cards are more widely deployed, other ingenious attacks are likely to be pursued. Smart cards are more susceptible to secret extraction than tokens because their computations leak such information in the form of electromagnetic radiation.

In comparing tokens with passwords one can argue that undetected theft is easier with passwords. The token is a physical object whose absence is noticeable. On the other hand, tokens create their own problems. They can be lost, misplaced, malfunction, or break, thereby denying access to the user. So some fallback to password-based authentication may still be needed. The potential for undetected sharing is definitely reduced since a token can be used by only one person at a time.

16.4.3   Soft Tokens.   The notion of *soft tokens* has been proposed as a low-cost alternative to hardware tokens. Early soft tokens consisted of a user's private key encrypted with a password and stored on some transportable medium, such as a floppy disk. Such a scheme is extremely vulnerable to dictionary attacks because a guessed password can be verified easily (by testing a putative private key to see if it decrypts a message encrypted using the user's known public key). Moreover, the physical transport of floppy disks and the possible lack of floppy disk drives have led people to store these soft tokens on network servers so they are accessible as needed. Unfortunately, this location also makes them easily accessible to attackers. Protecting access to soft tokens on a network server by means of a password simply returns to the problems of password-based authentication.

It has been suggested that a user's public key could be kept secret and known only to trusted servers to avoid dictionary attacks on the encrypted private key. This approach comes at the severe cost of a closed PKI rather than an open PKI. Schemes for retrieving the private key by means of a secure password-based protocol have been published and are being implemented by some vendors. These schemes ultimately revert to password-based authentication as their foundation. Schemes based on splitting the private key into two parts have been developed. One part of the private key is computed from the password; the other part is stored on an online server, which functions as a network-based virtual smart card. Both parts of the private key are needed for user authentication but are never brought together in one place.

An alternative scheme would be to store the user's entire private key on an online server and make its use contingent on a secure password-based protocol. This approach allows the server to impersonate any user at will and may not be suitable in all environments.

16.5   BIOMETRIC AUTHENTICATION.   Biometric authentication looks like an excellent solution to the problem of authentication in cyberspace. However, there are several challenges in implementing biometrics.

16.5.1   Binding Biometrics to a Known Identity.   The analogy of a picture ID should make it clear that biometrics alone is not sufficient. A driver's license or passport serves as an effective authentication precisely because it is a paper document issued by a trusted authority. The fundamental problem remains: binding a token to a specific identity. For example, passports and driver's licenses can be obtained by deceit, and they do get forged and misused. Passports often are stolen for exactly this purpose. The photograph on a stolen passport is skillfully replaced by one belonging to another person. It is not the biometric that is stolen and compromised but rather an infrastructure document.

When public key cryptography was first invented, many cryptographers felt that knowledge of a private key, proven by means of signing a challenge, would suffice for authentication. Today we understand much better the complexity and cost of the infrastructure, or PKI, necessary to make this dream a reality. To be useful on a large scale, biometric authentication will have to take place in the context of some secure authentication infrastructure. Biometrics alone is not going to make this infrastructure secure.

16.5.2   Input of Biometric Data.   Another problem with biometrics is the need for specialized readers. The cost of these devices has been dropping in recent years; for example, at the time of writing in August 2001, stand-alone USB fingerprint readers were being sold for around $150, but new computer systems are increasingly supplied with such devices integrated into a mouse, keyboard, or touchpad.

16.5.3   Power of Discrimination.   It is widely believed that biometric authentication systems are relatively poor at discriminating between authorized and unauthorized users. This problem is usually referred to as high rates of false positives (incorrectly identifying an unauthorized user as authorized) and of false negatives (incorrectly identifying an authorized user as unauthorized). Static biometrics, such as fingerprints or iris scans, are less prone to such failure than, say, voiceprints or signature dynamics. However, despite the general prejudice against biometrics, current error rates for fingerprint recognition are as low as 1 in 10,000.

16.5.4   Loss of Biometric Identifier.   In theory, one problem particular to biometrics is that the biometric characteristic can be destroyed. For example, one might have a hand or a specific finger amputated, thus impeding hand geometry or fingerprint recognition; similarly, an eye might be damaged in an accident or changed through a disease process, making iris or retinal pattern recognition impossible. In practice, however, the availability of other members (fingers, the other hand, the other eye) may allow reenrollment in the I&A system. In any case, I&A difficulties are not likely to be ranked as the primary disadvantage of such accidents or diseases.

16.5.5   Security of Templates.   An intrinsic characteristic of biometrics is that the user needs to be compared with respect to a reference template. A fingerprint has to be compared against a stored fingerprint, and so on. Where is the reference template stored and compared? The biometric reader itself can store the template and do the comparison, but this limits portability. How is a distant ATM going to store biometric templates? The reference templates can be stored on an online server, but then the system requires protocols to authenticate this server. Moreover, the server must be trusted not to impersonate the user to other servers on the network. Alternatively, the biometric template could be carried by the user on a smart card. This approach requires another reader for the smart card.

16.5.6   Privacy Concerns.   Many concerns have been voiced by privacy activists about the dangers of biometric authentication systems. In particular, some less technically aware people believe that biometric authentication data could be used as the equivalent of the dreaded universal identifier; that is, if fingerprint data are widely used to authenticate the user ID on computer systems, then government bodies could abuse those data to track specific individuals, and all of their activities.

However, security experts expect all biometric authentication systems to store one-way encrypted data. A user can be authenticated by comparing the encrypted input to the encrypted template, but it does not follow that such template data would be identical in different systems. Unless the same format and algorithms were used to encrypt the template data, biometric authentication will be no worse a threat to privacy than any other technology for I&A.

There is also concern about a related technology: facial recognition. In addition to allowing for biometric authentication, facial recognition systems are deployed in applications such as gaming casinos, where they are used to identify customers viewed as undesirable and to prevent them from gambling. Facial recognition systems also are used in conjunction with surveillance cameras in public places, where they have successfully identified criminal suspects or escaped prisoners. For more discussion of privacy issues, see Chapter 52.

16.6   CONCLUDING REMARKS.   Identification and authentication are the foundations for almost all other security objectives in cyberspace. In the past, these problems often were viewed as simple ones whose solution was assumed before the real security issues came into play. Important standards for computer security were published and practiced without much attention to identification and authentication. In cyberspace, the problems associated with I&A are severe, and they have barely begun to be solved effectively. A robust, scalable identification and authentication infrastructure is vital to achieving security. Technologies such as tokens and biometrics hold out considerable promise, but their deployment requires infrastructure costs dominated by the cost of hardware for readers and the like. Meanwhile, passwords continue to be strengthened, as we better understand the real risks in using them and as we develop technical means to mitigate those risks. The fact that modern operating systems continue to provide simple password-based authentication, vulnerable to dictionary attacks, reflects poorly on the pace at which security technology is adopted in the marketplace. Looking to the future, one can predict that we will see a mix of passwords, biometrics, and tokens in use, perhaps in two- or three-factor configurations. Biometrics and tokens are likely to dominate the high-assurance end, while passwords will dominate the lower end.

The U.S. National Institute of Standards and Technology has organized a Biometric Consortium to serve as a focal point for research and standards in this arena.

16.7   SUMMARY.   Passwords are widely used in practice and will continue to be a dominant form of user authentication. There are many risks in deploying passwords, and a number of widely used password systems have serious vulnerabilities. Nonetheless, technical measures can mitigate the inherent vulnerabilities of passwords. While it takes great skill and care, with our current understanding it is technically possible to build and deploy strong password-based authentication systems, using commercial products. The truly inherent risks of undetected theft and undetected sharing can be largely mitigated by new technologies, such as intrusion detection systems. Undetected sharing may be deterred further by a system that couples high-value secret data, such as credit card account numbers, with passwords. Tokens are available to generate one-time passwords or to communicate directly with authentication systems. Although costs have been dropping, tokens are still not as widely deployed as early predictions suggested they would be.

Biometric authentication methods are improving in power and accessibility, but they are currently met with considerable skepticism, engendered by fairly high costs and by problems associated with privacy concerns. Although biometrics have been implemented only infrequently and on a small scale, they offer great potential, especially for high-security applications.

As we reflect on the events of September 11, 2001, the need for strong identification and authentication in the physical space of airline travel has become painfully evident to the general public at large. Many technologies discussed in this chapter are relevant to the airline travel situation, but the inherent difficulties of this task are becoming evident to the lay public and to political and corporate leaders. When we deal with large populations, it is very difficult, perhaps even impossible, to guarantee foolproof identification and authentication in free societies. As cyberspace technologists we realize that absolute guarantees can not be achieved in cyberspace. Too many security professionals seek absolute goals and too many security technologies are marketed as being stronger than they really are. Our profession will benefit greatly if we address practical problems with practical cost-effective techniques, and develop a sound security discipline that contains, bounds and mitigates the inevitable residual risk that we must face in any large-scale human situation.

16.8   FURTHER READING

Anderson, J., and R. Vaughn. *A Guide to Understanding Identification and Authentication in Trusted Systems,* 1991. "Light Blue Book" in the Rainbow Series, NCSC-TG-017, *www.fas.org/irp/nsa/rainbow/tg017.htm.*

Biometric Consortium: *www.biometrics.org.*

Counterpane Internet Security Biometrics Links: *www.counterpane.com/biometrics.html.*

Gupta, M. "Biometric Technologies Overview," 2001: *www.sans.org/infosecFAQ/authentic/biometric2.htm.*

Integrity Sciences: "Bizcard ZKPP: A Zero-Knowledge Password Proof with Pencil and Paper," 2001: *www.integritysciences.com/zkppcard.html.*

Jablon, D., et al. "Publications on Strong Password Authentication," 2001: *www.integritysciences.com/links.html.*

Jain, L.C., et al. , eds. *Intelligent Biometric Techniques in Fingerprint and Face Recognition.* Boca Raton, FL: CRC Press International Series on Computational Intelligence, 1999.

Kabay, M.E. "Identification, Authentication and Authorization on the World Wide Web," 1998: *www.trusecure.com/html/tspub/whitepapers/iaw.pdf.*

National Biometrics Test Center of San José University: *www.engr.sjsu.edu/biometrics.*

Schneier, B. "Biometrics: Truths and Fictions," 1998: *www.counterpane.com/crypto-gram-9808.html#biometrics.*

Schneier, B. "Biometrics: Uses and Abuses," 1999: *www.counterpane.com/insiderisks1.html.*

Smith, R.E. *Authentication: From Passwords to Public Keys.* Reading, MA: Addison-Wesley, 2001.

Tung, B. *Kerberos: A Network Authentication System.* Reading, MA: Addison-Wesley, 1999.

Wayman, J.L. "The Functions of Biometric Identification Devices," 1998: *www.engr.sjsu.edu/biometrics/publications_tech.html.*

Wayman, J.L. "Biometric Technology: Testing, Evaluation, Results," 1999: *www.engr.sjsu.edu/biometrics/publications_technology.html.*

Wu, T. "A Real-World Analysis of Kerberos Password Security." Proceedings of the 1999 Network and Distributed System Security Symposium, *www.isoc.org/ndss99/proceedings/papers/wu.pdf.*

CHAPTER 17

OPERATING SYSTEM SECURITY

William Stallings

CONTENTS

17.1 INFORMATION PROTECTION AND SECURITY. This chapter reviews the principles of security in operating systems. Some general-purpose tools can be built into computers and operating systems (OSs) that support a variety of protection and security mechanisms. In general, the concern is with the problem of controlling access to computer systems and the information stored in them. Four types of overall protection policies, of increasing order of difficulty, have been identified:

1. *No sharing:* In this case, processes are completely isolated from each other, and each process has exclusive control over the resources statically or dynamically assigned to it. With this policy, processes often "share" a program or data file by making a copy of it and transferring the copy into their own virtual memory.

2. *Sharing originals of program or data files:* With the use of reentrant code, a single physical realization of a program can appear in multiple virtual address spaces, as can read-only data files. Special locking mechanisms are required for the sharing of writable data files, to prevent simultaneous users from interfering with each other.

3. *Confined, or memoryless, subsystems:* In this case, processes are grouped into subsystems to enforce a particular protection policy. For example, a "client" process calls a "server" process to perform some task on data. The server is to be protected against the client discovering the algorithm by which it performs the task, while the client is to be protected against the server's retaining any information about the task being performed.

4. *Controlled information dissemination:* In some systems, security classes are defined to enforce a particular dissemination policy. Users and applications are given security clearances of a certain level, while data and other resources (e.g., input/output [I/O] devices) are given security classifications. The security policy enforces restrictions concerning which users have access to which classifications. This model is useful not only in the military context but in commercial applications as well.[1]

Much of the work in security and protection as it relates to OSs can be roughly grouped into three categories.

1. *Access control:* concerned with regulating user access to the total system, subsystems, and data, and regulating process access to various resources and objects within the system.

2. *Information flow control:* regulates the flow of data within the system and its delivery to users.

3. *Certification:* relates to proving that access and flow control mechanisms perform according to their specifications and that they enforce desired protection and security policies.

This chapter looks at some of the key mechanisms for providing OS security and then examinesWindows 2000 as a case study.

17.2   REQUIREMENTS FOR OPERATING SYSTEM SECURITY

17.2.1   Requirements.   An understanding the types of threats to OS security that exist requires a definition of security requirements. OS security addresses four requirements:

1. *Confidentiality:* requires that the information in a computer system be accessible only for reading by authorized parties. This type of access includes printing, displaying, and other forms of disclosure, including simply revealing the existence of an object.

2. *Integrity:* requires that computer system assets can be modified only by authorized parties. Modification includes writing, changing, changing status, deleting, and creating.

3. *Availability:* requires that computer system assets are available to authorized parties.

4. *Authenticity:* requires that a computer system be able to verify the identity of a user.

17.2.2   Computer System Assets.   The assets of a computer system can be categorized as hardware, software, and data. Let us consider each of these in turn.

17.2.2.1   Hardware.   The main threat to computer system hardware is in the area of availability. Hardware is the most vulnerable to attack and the least amenable to automated controls. Threats include accidental and deliberate damage to equipment as well as theft. The proliferation of personal computers and workstations and the increasing use of local area networks (LANs) increase the potential for losses in this area. Physical and administrative security measures are needed to deal with these threats.

17.2.2.2   Software.   The OS, utilities, and application programs are what make computer system hardware useful to businesses and individuals. Several distinct threats need to be considered.

A key threat to software is an attack on availability. Software, especially application software, is surprisingly easy to delete. Software also can be altered or damaged to render it useless. Careful software configuration management, which includes making backups of the most recent version of software, can maintain high availability. A more difficult problem to deal with is software modification that results in a program that still functions but that behaves differently than before. A final problem is software secrecy. Although certain countermeasures are available, by and large the problem of unauthorized copying of software has not been solved.

17.2.2.3   Data.   Hardware and software security are typically concerns of computing center professionals or individual concerns of personal computer users. A much more widespread problem is data security, which involves files and other forms of data controlled by individuals, groups, and business organizations.

Security concerns with respect to data are broad, encompassing availability, secrecy, and integrity. In the case of availability, the concern is with the destruction of data files, which can occur either accidentally or maliciously.

The obvious concern with secrecy, of course, is the unauthorized reading of data files or databases, and this area has been the subject of perhaps more research and effort than any other area of computer security. A less obvious secrecy threat involves the analysis of data and manifests itself in the use of so-called statistical databases, which provide summary or aggregate information. Presumably, the existence of aggregate information does not threaten the privacy of the individuals involved. However, as the use of statistical databases grows, there is an increasing potential for disclosure of personal information. In essence, characteristics of constituent individuals may be identified through careful analysis. To take a simple example, if one table records the aggregate of the incomes of respondents A, B, C, and D and another records the aggregate of the incomes of A, B, C, D, and E, the difference between the two aggregates would be the income of E. This problem is exacerbated by the increasing desire to combine data sets. In many cases, matching several sets of data for consistency at levels of aggregation appropriate to the problem requires a retreat to elemental units in the process of constructing the necessary aggregates. Thus, the elemental units, which are the subject of privacy concerns, are available at various stages in the processing of data sets.

Finally, data integrity is a major concern in most installations. Modifications to data files can have consequences ranging from minor to disastrous.

17.2.3   Design Principles.   Saltzer identifies a number of principles for the design of security measures for the various threats to computer systems. These include:

- *Least privilege:* Every program and every user of the system should operate using the least set of privileges necessary to complete the job. Access rights should be acquired by explicit permission only; the default should be "no access."

- *Economy of mechanisms:* Security mechanisms should be as small and simple as possible, aiding in their verification. This usually means that they must be an integral part of the design rather than add-on mechanisms to existing designs.

- *Acceptability:* Security mechanisms should not interfere unduly with the work of users, while at the same time should meet the needs of those who authorize access. If the mechanisms are not easy to use, they are likely to be unused or incorrectly used.

- *Complete mediation:* Every access must be checked against the access-control information, including those accesses occurring outside normal operation, as in recovery or maintenance.

- *Open design:* The security of the system should not depend on keeping the design of its mechanisms secret. Thus, the mechanisms can be reviewed by many experts, and users can have high confidence in them.[2]

17.3   PROTECTION MECHANISMS.   The introduction of multiprogramming brought about the ability to share resources among users. This sharing involves not just the processor but also the following:

- Memory
- I/O devices, such as disks and printers
- Programs
- Data

The ability to share these resources introduced the need for protection. Pfleeger points out that an OS may offer protection along the following spectrum:

- *No protection:* This is appropriate when sensitive procedures are being run at separate times.

- *Isolation:* This approach implies that each process operates separately from other processes, with no sharing or communication. Each process has its own address space, files, and other objects.

- *Share all or share nothing:* The owner of an object (e.g., a file or memory segment) declares it to be public or private. In the former case, any process may access the object; in the latter, only the owner's processes may access the object.

- *Share via access limitation:* The OS checks the permissibility of each access by a specific user to a specific object. The OS therefore acts as a guard, or gatekeeper, between users and objects, ensuring that only authorized accesses occur.

- *Share via dynamic capabilities:* This extends the concept of access control to allow dynamic creation of sharing rights for objects.

- *Limit use of an object:* This form of protection limits not just access to an object but the use to which that object may be put. For example, a user may be allowed to view a sensitive document but not print it. Another example is that a user may be allowed access to a database to derive statistical summaries but not to determine specific data values.[3]

The preceding items are listed roughly in increasing order of difficulty to implement, but also in increasing order of fineness of protection that they provide. A given OS may provide different degrees of protection for different objects, users, or applications.

The OS needs to balance the need to allow sharing, which enhances the utility of the computer system, with the need to protect the resources of individual users. This section considers some of the mechanisms by which OSs have enforced protection for these objects.

17.3.1   Protection of Memory.   In a multiprogramming environment, protection of main memory is essential. The concern here is not just security but the correct functioning of the various processes that are active. If one process can inadvertently write into the memory space of another process, then the latter process may not execute properly.

The separation of the memory space of various processes is easily accomplished with a virtual-memory scheme. Either segmentation or paging, or the two in combination, provides an effective means of managing main memory. If complete isolation is sought, then the OS must simply ensure that each segment or page is accessible only by the process to which it is assigned. This is easily accomplished by requiring that there be no duplicate entries in page and/or segment tables.

If sharing is to be allowed, then the same segment or page may appear in more than one table. This type of sharing is accomplished most easily in a system that supports segmentation or a combination of segmentation and paging. In this case, the segment structure is visible to the application, and the application can declare individual segments to be sharable or nonsharable. In a pure paging environment, it becomes more difficult to discriminate between the two types of memory, because the memory structure is transparent to the application.

Segmentation especially lends itself to the implementation of protection and sharing policies. Because each segment table entry includes a length as well as a base address, a program cannot inadvertently access a main memory location beyond the limits of a segment. To achieve sharing, it is possible for a segment to be referenced in the segment tables of more than one process. The same mechanisms are, of course, available in a paging system. However, in this case the page structure of programs and data is not visible to the programmer, making the specification of protection and sharing requirements more awkward. Exhibit 17.1 illustrates the types of protection relationships that can be enforced in such a system.

An example of the hardware support that can be provided for memory protection is that of the IBM System/370 family of machines, on which OS/390 runs. Associated with each page frame in main memory is a 7-bit storage control key, which may be set by the OS. Two of the bits indicate whether the page occupying this frame has been referenced and changed; these bits are used by the page replacement algorithm. The remaining bits are used by the protection mechanism: a 4-bit access control key and a fetch-protection bit. Direct memory accesses (DMA) and Input/Output (I/O) memory references must use a matching key to gain permission to access that page. The fetch-protection bit indicates whether the access control key applies to writes or to both reads

Exhibit 17.1   Protection Relationships Between Segments

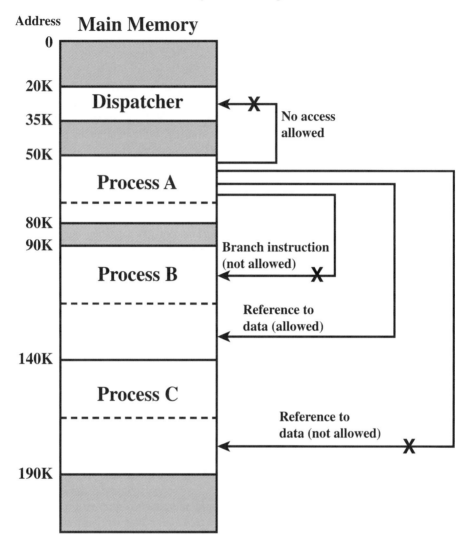

and writes. In the processor, there is a program status word (PSW), which contains control information relating to the process that is currently executing. Included in this word is a 4-bit PSW key. When a process attempts to access a page or to initiate a DMA operation on a page, the current PSW key is compared to the access code. A write operation is permitted only if the codes match. If the fetch bit is set, then the PSW key must match the access code for read operations.

17.3.2   User-Oriented Access Control.   The measures taken to control access in a data processing system fall into two categories: those associated with the user and those associated with the data.

User control of access is sometimes referred to as authentication. Because this term is now widely used in the sense of message authentication, it is not applied here. The reader is advised, however, that this usage may be encountered in the literature.

The most common technique for user access control on a shared system or server is the user logon, which requires both a user identifier (ID) and a password. The system will allow a user to log on only if that user's ID is known to the system and if the user knows the password associated by the system with that ID. This ID/password system is a notoriously unreliable method of user access control. Users can forget their passwords and accidentally or intentionally reveal their password. Hackers have become very skillful at guessing IDs for special users, such as system control and system management personnel. Finally, the ID/password file is subject to penetration attempts.

User access control in a distributed environment can be either centralized or decentralized. In a centralized approach, the network provides a logon service, determining who is allowed to use the network and to whom the user is allowed to connect.

Decentralized user access control treats the network as a transparent communication link, and the destination host carries out the usual logon procedure. Of course, the security concerns for transmitting passwords over the network still must be addressed.

In many networks, two levels of access control may be used. Individual hosts may be provided with a logon facility to protect host-specific resources and application. In addition, the network as a whole may provide protection to restrict network access to authorized users. This two-level facility is desirable for the common case, currently, in which the network connects disparate hosts and simply provides a convenient means of terminal-host access. In a more uniform network of hosts, some centralized access policy could be enforced in a network control center.

17.3.3   Data-Oriented Access Control.   Following successful logon, the user has been granted access to one or a set of hosts and applications. This is generally not sufficient for a system that includes sensitive data in its database. Through the user access control procedure, a user can be identified to the system. Associated with each user, there can be a profile that specifies permissible operations and file accesses. The OS can then enforce rules based on the user profile. The database management system, however, must control access to specific records or even portions of records. For example, it may be permissible for anyone in administration to obtain a list of company personnel, but only selected individuals may have access to salary information. The issue is more than just one of level of detail. Whereas the OS may grant a user permission to access a file or use an application, following which there are no further security checks, the database management system must make a decision on each individual access attempt. That decision will depend not only on the user's identity but also on the specific parts of the data being accessed and even on the information already divulged to the user.

A general model of access control as exercised by a file or database management system is that of an *access matrix* (see Exhibit 17.2a), based on a figure in Sandhu, 1994. The basic elements of the model are:

- *Subject:* An entity capable of accessing objects. Generally, the concept of subject equates with that of process. Any user or application actually gains access to an object by means of a process that represents that user or application.
- *Object:* Anything to which access is controlled. Examples include files, portions of files, programs, and segments of memory.
- *Access right:* The way in which an object is accessed by a subject. Examples are read, write, and execute.

One dimension of the matrix consists of identified subjects that may attempt data access. Typically, this list will consist of individual users or user groups, although access

Exhibit 17.2   Example of Access Control Structures

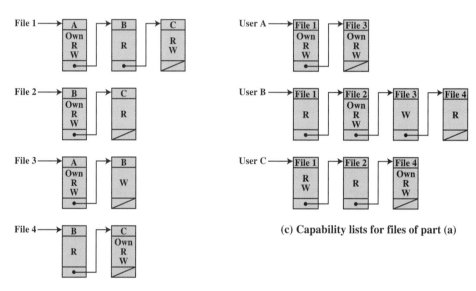

(a) Access matrix

(c) Capability lists for files of part (a)

(b) Access control lists for files of part (a)

Source: Based on a figure in Sandhu (1996).

could be controlled for terminals, hosts, or applications instead of or in addition to users. The other dimension lists the objects that may be accessed. At the greatest level of detail, objects may be individual data fields. More aggregate groupings, such as records, files, or even the entire database, also may be objects in the matrix. Each entry in the matrix indicates the access rights of that subject for that object.

In practice, an access matrix usually is sparse and is implemented by decomposition in one of two ways. The matrix may be decomposed by columns, yielding *access control lists* (see Exhibit 17.2b). Thus for each object, an access control list details users and their permitted access rights. The access control list may contain a default, or public, entry. This allows users who are not explicitly listed as having special rights to have a default set of rights. Elements of the list may include individual users as well as groups of users.

Decomposition by rows yields *capability tickets* (see Exhibit 17.2c). A capability ticket specifies authorized objects and operations for a user. Each user has a number of tickets and may be authorized to lend or give them to others. Because tickets may be dispersed around the system, they present a greater security problem than access control lists. In particular, the ticket must be unforgeable. One way to accomplish this is to have the OS hold all tickets on behalf of users. These tickets would have to be held in a region of memory inaccessible to users.

Network considerations for data-oriented access control parallel those for user-oriented access control. If only certain users are permitted to access certain items of data, then encryption may be needed to protect those items during transmission to authorized users. Typically, data access control is decentralized, that is, controlled by host-based database management systems. If a network database server exists on a network, then data access control becomes a network function.

17.3.4 Protection Based on an Operating System Mode. One technique used in all OSs to provide protection is based on the mode of processor execution. Most processors support at least two modes of execution: the mode normally associated with the OS and that normally associated with user programs. Certain instructions can be executed only in the more privileged OS mode. These would include reading or altering a control register, such as the program status word; primitive I/O instructions; and instructions that relate to memory management. In addition, certain regions of memory can be accessed only in the more privileged mode.

The less privileged mode often is referred to as the *user* mode, because user programs typically would execute in this mode. The more privileged mode is referred to as the *system mode, control mode,* or *kernel mode.* This last term refers to the kernel of the OS, which is that portion of the OS that encompasses the important system functions. Exhibit 17.3 lists the functions typically found in the kernel of an OS.

Exhibit 17.3 Typical Kernel Mode Operating System Functions

Process Management

- Process creation and termination
- Process scheduling and dispatching
- Process switching
- Process synchronization and support for interprocess communication
- Management of process control blocks

Memory Management

- Allocation of address space to processes
- Swapping
- Page and segment management

I/O Management

- Buffer management
- Allocation of I/O channels and devices to processes

Support Functions

- Interrupt handling
- Accounting
- Monitoring

The reason for using two modes should be clear. It is necessary to protect the OS and key OS tables, such as process control blocks, from interference by user programs. In the kernel mode, the software has complete control of the processor and all its instructions, registers, and memory. This level of control is not necessary and for safety is not desirable for user programs.

Two questions arise: How does the processor know in which mode it is to be executing, and how is the mode changed? Regarding the first question, typically there is a bit in the program status word that indicates the mode of execution. This bit is changed in response to certain events. For example, when a user makes a call to an OS service, the mode is set to the kernel mode. Typically, this is done by executing an instruction that changes the mode. When the user makes a system service call or when an interrupt transfers control to a system routine, the routine executes the change-mode instruction to enter a more privileged mode and executes it again to enter a less privileged mode before returning control to the user process. If a user program attempts to execute a change-mode instruction, it will simply result in a call to the OS, which will return an error unless the mode change is to be allowed.

More sophisticated mechanisms also can be provided. A common scheme is to use a ring-protection structure. In this scheme, lower-numbered, or inner, rings enjoy greater privilege than higher-numbered, or outer, rings. Typically, ring 0 is reserved for kernel functions of the OS, with applications at a higher level. Some utilities or OS services may occupy an intermediate ring. Basic principles of the ring system are:

- A program may access only those data that reside on the same ring or a less privileged ring.
- A program may call services residing on the same or a more privileged ring.

An example of the ring protection approach is found on the VAX VMS OS, which uses four modes:

1. *Kernel:* executes the kernel of the VMS OS, which includes memory management, interrupt handling, and I/O operations.
2. *Executive:* executes many of the OS service calls, including file and record (disk and tape) management routines.
3. *Supervisor:* executes other OS services, such as responses to user commands.
4. *User:* executes user programs, plus utilities such as compilers, editors, linkers, and debuggers.

A process executing in a less privileged mode often needs to call a procedure that executes in a more privileged mode; for example, a user program requires an OS service. This call is achieved by using a change-mode (CHM) instruction, which causes an interrupt that transfers control to a routine at the new access mode. A return is made by executing the REI (return from exception or interrupt) instruction.

17.4   FILE SHARING.   Multiuser systems almost always require that files can be shared among a number of users. Two issues arise: access rights and the management of simultaneous access.

17.4.1   Access Rights.   The file system should provide a flexible tool for allowing extensive file sharing among users. The file system should provide a number of options so that the way in which a particular file is accessed can be controlled. Typically, users or groups of users are granted certain access rights to a file. A wide range of access rights have been used. The following list indicates access rights that can be assigned to a particular user for a particular file:

- *None:* The user may not even learn of the existence of the file, much less access it. To enforce this restriction, the user would not be allowed to read the user directory that includes this file.
- *Knowledge:* The user can determine that the file exists and who its owner is. The user is then able to petition the owner for additional access rights.
- *Execution:* The user can load and execute a program but cannot copy it. Proprietary programs often are made accessible with this restriction.
- *Reading:* The user can read the file for any purpose, including copying and execution. Some systems are able to enforce a distinction between viewing and copying. In the former case, the contents of the file can be displayed to the user, but the user has no means for making a copy.
- *Appending:* The user can add data to the file, often only at the end, but cannot modify or delete any of the file's contents. This right is useful in collecting data from a number of sources.
- *Updating:* The user can modify, delete, and add to the file's data. This normally includes writing the file initially, rewriting it completely or in part, and removing all or a portion of the data. Some systems distinguish among different degrees of updating.
- *Changing protection:* The user can change the access rights granted to other users. Typically, only the owner of the file holds this right. In some systems, the owner can extend this right to others. To prevent abuse of this mechanism, the file owner typically is able to specify which rights can be changed by their holder.
- *Deletion:* The user can delete the file from the file system.

These rights can be considered to constitute a hierarchy, with each right implying those that precede it. Thus, if a particular user is granted the updating right for a particular file, then that user also is granted the following rights: knowledge, execution, reading, and appending.

One user is designated as owner of a given file, usually the person who initially created a file. The owner has all of the access rights listed previously and may grant rights to others. Access can be provided to different classes of users:

- *Specific user:* Individual users who are designated by user ID.
- *User groups:* A set of users who are not individually defined. The system must have some way of keeping track of the membership of user groups.
- *All:* All users who have access to this system. These are public files.

17.4.2   Simultaneous Access.   When access is granted to more than one user to append or update a file, the OS or file management system must enforce discipline. A brute-force approach is to allow a user to lock the entire file when it is to be updated. A finer-grained control locks individual records during update. Issues of mutual exclusion and deadlock must be addressed in designing the shared access capability.

17.5   TRUSTED SYSTEMS.   Much of what has been discussed so far has been concerned with protecting a given message or item from passive or active attack by a given user. A somewhat different but widely applicable requirement is to protect data or resources on the basis of levels of security. This is commonly found in the military, where information is categorized as unclassified (U), confidential (C), secret (S), top secret (TS), or beyond. This concept is equally applicable in other areas, where information can be organized into gross categories and users can be granted clearances to access certain categories of data. For example, the highest level of security might be for strategic corporate planning documents and data, accessible by only corporate officers and their staff; next might come sensitive financial and personnel data, accessible only by administration personnel, corporate officers, and so on.

When multiple categories or levels of data are defined, the requirement is referred to as *multilevel security.* The general statement of the requirement for multilevel security is that a subject at a high level may not convey information to a subject at a lower or noncomparable level unless that flow accurately reflects the will of an authorized user. For implementation purposes, this requirement is in two parts and is simply stated. A multilevel secure system must enforce:

1. *No read up:* A subject can only read an object of less or equal security level. This is referred to in the literature as the *simple security property.*

2. *No write down:* A subject can only write into an object of greater or equal security level. This is referred to in the literature as the **-property* [4] (pronounced *star property*).

These two rules, if properly enforced, provide multilevel security. For a data processing system, the approach that has been taken, and has been the object of much research and development, is based on the *reference monitor* concept. This approach is depicted in Exhibit 17.4. The reference monitor is a controlling element in the hardware and OS of a computer that regulates the access of subjects to objects on the basis

Exhibit 17.4   Reference Monitor Concept

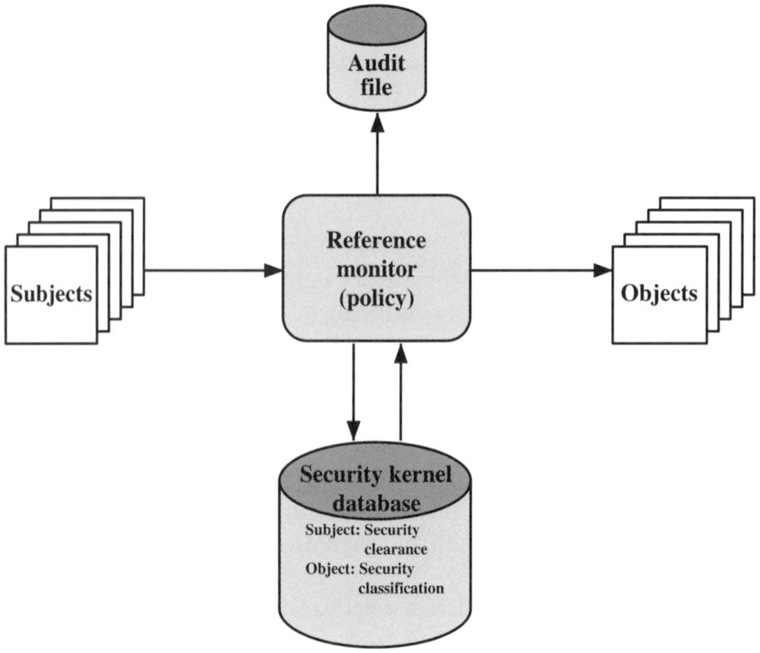

of security parameters of the subject and object. The reference monitor has access to a file, known as the *security kernel database,* that lists the access privileges (security clearance) of each subject and the protection attributes (classification level) of each object. The reference monitor enforces the security rules (no read up, no write down) and has the following properties:

- *Complete mediation:* The security rules are enforced on every access, not just, for example, when a file is opened.
- *Isolation:* The reference monitor and database are protected from unauthorized modification.
- *Verifiability:* The reference monitor's correctness must be provable. That is, it must be possible to demonstrate mathematically that the reference monitor enforces the security rules and provides complete mediation and isolation.

These are stiff requirements. The requirement for complete mediation means that every access to data within main memory and on disk and tape must be mediated. Pure software implementations impose too high a performance penalty to be practical; the solution must be at least partly in hardware. The requirement for isolation means that it must not be possible for an attacker, no matter how clever, to change the logic of the reference monitor or the contents of the security kernel database. Finally, the requirement for mathematical proof is formidable for something as complex as a general-purpose computer. A system that can provide such verification is referred to as a *trusted system.*

A final element illustrated in Exhibit 17.4 is an audit file. Important security events, such as detected security violations and authorized changes to the security kernel database, are stored in the audit file.

In an effort to meet its own needs and as a service to the public, the U.S. Department of Defense in 1981 established the Computer Security Center within the National Security Agency (NSA) with the goal of encouraging the widespread availability of trusted computer systems. This goal is realized through the center's Commercial Product Evaluation Program. In essence, the center attempts to evaluate commercially available products as meeting the security requirements just outlined. The center classifies evaluated products according to the range of security features that they provide. These evaluations are needed for Department of Defense procurements but are published and freely available. Hence, they can serve as guidance to commercial customers for the purchase of commercially available, off-the-shelf equipment.

17.6   TROJAN HORSE DEFENSE.   One way to secure against Trojan horse attacks is the use of a secure, trusted OS. Exhibit 17.5 illustrates an example. In this case, a Trojan horse is used to get around the standard security mechanism used by most file management and OSs: the access control list. In this example, a user named Bob interacts through a program with a data file containing the critically sensitive character string "CPE170KS." User Bob has created the file with read/write permission provided only to programs executing on his own behalf: that is, only processes that are owned by Bob may access the file.

The Trojan horse attack begins when a hostile user named Alice gains legitimate access to the system and installs both a Trojan horse program and a private file to be used in the attack as a "back pocket." Alice gives read/write permission to herself for this file and gives Bob write-only permission (see Exhibit 17.5a).Alice now induces Bob to invoke the Trojan horse program, perhaps by advertising it as a useful utility. When the program detects that it is being executed by Bob, it reads the sensitive character

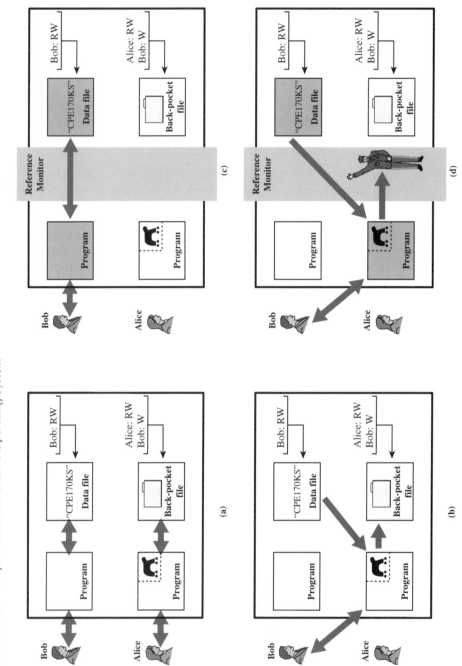

Exhibit 17.5   Trojan Horse and Secure Operating System

string from Bob's file and copies it into Alice's back-pocket file (see Exhibit 17.5b). Both the read and write operations satisfy the constraints imposed by access control lists. Alice then has only to access Bob's file at a later time to learn the value of the string.

Now consider the use of a secure OS in this scenario (see Exhibit 17.5c). Security levels are assigned to subjects at logon on the basis of criteria such as the terminal from which the computer is being accessed and the user involved, as identified by password/ID. In this example, there are two security levels, sensitive (gray) and public (white), ordered so that sensitive is higher than public. Processes owned by Bob and Bob's data file are assigned the security level sensitive. Alice's file and processes are restricted to public. If Bob invokes the Trojan horse program (see Exhibit 17.5d), that program acquires Bob's security level. It is therefore able, under the simple security property, to observe the sensitive character string. When the program attempts to store the string in a public file (the back-pocket file), however, the *-property is violated and the attempt is disallowed by the reference monitor. Thus, the attempt to write into the back-pocket file is denied even though the access control list permits it: The security policy takes precedence over the access control list mechanism.

17.7 WINDOWS 2000 SECURITY. A good example of the access control concepts discussed in this chapter is the Windows 2000 (W2K) access control facility, which exploits object-oriented concepts to provide a powerful and flexible access control capability.

W2K provides a uniform access control facility that applies to processes, threads, files, semaphores, windows, and other objects. Access control is governed by two entities: an access token associated with each process and a security descriptor associated with each object for which interprocess access is possible.

17.7.1 Access Control Scheme. When a user logs on to a W2K system, W2K uses a name/password scheme to authenticate the user. If the logon is accepted, a process is created for the user and an access token is associated with that process object. The access token, whose details are described later, includes a security ID (SID), which is the identifier by which this user is known to the system for purposes of security. When the initial user process spawns any additional processes, the new process object inherits the same access token.

The access token serves two purposes:

1. It keeps all necessary security information together to speed access validation. When any process associated with a user attempts access, the security subsystem can make use of the token associated with that process to determine the user's access privileges.

2. It allows each process to modify its security characteristics in limited ways without affecting other processes running on behalf of the user.

The chief significance of the second point has to do with privileges that may be associated with a user. The access token indicates which privileges a user may have. Generally, the token is initialized with each of these privileges in a disabled state. Subsequently, if one of the user's processes needs to perform a privileged operation, the process may enable the appropriate privilege and attempt access. It would be undesirable to keep all of the security information for a user in one systemwide place, because in that case enabling a privilege for one process enables it for all of them.

A security descriptor is associated with each object for which interprocess access is possible. The chief component of the security descriptor is an access control list that specifies access rights for various users and user groups for this object. When a process attempts to access this object, the SID of the process is matched against the access control list of the object to determine if access will be allowed.

When an application opens a reference to a securable object, W2K verifies that the object's security descriptor grants the application's user access. If the check succeeds, W2K caches the resulting granted access rights.

An important aspect of W2K security is the concept of impersonation, which simplifies the use of security in a client/server environment. If client and server talk through a Remote Procedure Call (RPC) connection, the server can temporarily assume the identity of the client so that it can evaluate a request for access relative to that client's rights. After the access, the server reverts to its own identity.

17.7.2   Access Token.   Exhibit 17.6a shows the general structure of an access token, which includes the following parameters:

- *Security ID:* Identifies a user uniquely across all of the machines on the network. This generally corresponds to a user's logon name.

- *Group SIDs:* A list of the groups to which this user belongs. A group is simply a set of user IDs that are identified as a group for purposes of access control. Each group has a unique group SID. Access to an object can be defined on the basis of group SIDs, individual SIDs, or a combination.

- *Privileges:* A list of security-sensitive system services that this user may call. An example is create token. Another example is the set backup privilege; users with this privilege are allowed to use a backup tool to back up files that they normally would not be able to read. Most users will have no privileges.

Exhibit 17.6   Windows 2000 Security Structures

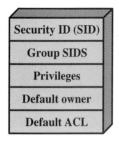

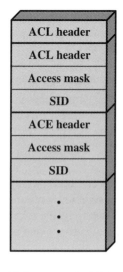

    (a) Access token   **(b) Security descriptor**   **(c) Access control list**

- *Default owner:* If this process creates another object, this field specifies who is the owner of the new object. Generally, the owner of the new process is the same as the owner of the spawning process. However, a user may specify that the default owner of any processes spawned by this process is a group SID to which this user belongs.

- *Default ACL:* This is an initial list of protections applied to the objects that the user creates. The user may subsequently alter the Access Control List (ACL) for any object that it owns or that one of its groups owns.

17.7.3   Security Descriptors.   Exhibit 17.6b shows the general structure of a security descriptor, which includes the following parameters:

- *Flags:* Defines the type and contents of a security descriptor. The flags indicate whether or not the System Access Control List (SACL) and Discretionary Access Control List (DACL) are present, whether or not they were placed on the object by a defaulting mechanism, and whether the pointers in the descriptor use absolute or relative addressing. Relative descriptors are required for objects that are transmitted over a network, such as information transmitted in a RPC.

- *Owner:* The owner of the object generally can perform any action on the security descriptor. The owner can be an individual or a group SID. The owner has the authority to change the contents of the DACL.

- *System Access Control List (SACL):* Specifies what kinds of operations on the object should generate audit messages. An application must have the corresponding privilege in its access token to read or write the SACL of any object. This is to prevent unauthorized applications from reading SACLs (thereby learning what not to do to avoid generating audits) or writing them (to generate many audits to cause an illicit operation to go unnoticed).

- *Discretionary Access Control List (DACL):* Determines which users and groups can access this object for which operations. It consists of a list of access control entries (ACEs).

When an object is created, the creating process can assign as owner its own SID or any group SID in its access token. The creating process cannot assign an owner that is not in the current access token. Subsequently, any process that has been granted the right to change the owner of an object may do so, but again with the same restriction. The reason for the restriction is to prevent users from covering their tracks after attempting some unauthorized action.

Access control lists are at the heart of the W2K access control facility (see Exhibit 17.6c). Each list consists of an overall header and a variable number of access control entries. Each entry specifies an individual or group SID and an access mask that defines the rights to be granted to this SID. When a process attempts to access an object, the object manager in the W2K executive reads the SID and group SIDs from the access token and then scans down the object's DACL. If a match is found, that is, if an ACE is found with a SID that matches one of the SIDs from the access token, then the process has the access rights specified by the access mask in that ACE.

Exhibit 17.7 shows the contents of the access mask. The least significant 16 bits specify access rights that apply to a particular type of object. For example, bit 0 for a file object is File_Read_Data access, and bit 0 for an event object is Event_Query_Status access.

Exhibit 17.7   Windows 2000 Access Mask

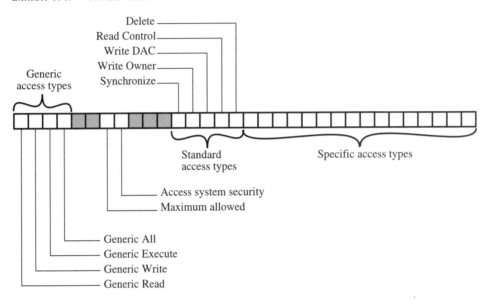

The most significant 16 bits of the mask contain bits that apply to all types of objects. Five of these are referred to as standard access types:

1. *Synchronize:* Gives permission to synchronize execution with some event associated with this object. In particular, this object can be used in a wait function.

2. *Write_owner:* Allows a program to modify the owner of the object. This is useful because the owner of an object always can change the protection on the object. (The owner may not be denied Write DAC access.)

3. *Write_DAC:* Allows the application to modify the DACL and hence the protection on this object.

4. *Read_control:* Allows the application to query the owner and DACL fields of the security descriptor of this object.

5. *Delete:* Allows the application to delete this object.

The high-order half of the access mask also contains the four generic access types. These bits provide a convenient way to set specific access types in a number of different object types. For example, suppose an application wishes to create several types of objects and ensure that users have read access to the objects, even though read has a somewhat different meaning for each object type. To protect each object of each type without the generic access bits, the application would have to construct a different ACE for each type of object and be careful to pass the correct ACE when creating each object. It is more convenient to create a single ACE that expresses the generic concept allow read, simply apply this ACE to each object that is created, and have the right thing happen. That is the purpose of the generic access bits, which are:

- *Generic_all:* Allow all access
- *Generic_execute:* Allow execution if executable
- *Generic_write:* Allow write access
- *Generic_read:* Allow read only access

The generic bits also affect the standard access types. For example, for a file object, the Generic_Read bit maps to the standard bits Read_Control and Synchronize and to the object-specific bits File_Read_Data, File_Read_Attributes, and File_Read_EA. Placing an ACE on a file object that grants some SID Generic_Read grants those five access rights as if they had been specified individually in the access mask.

The remaining two bits in the access mask have special meanings. The Access_System_Security bit allows modifying audit and alarm control for this object. However, not only must this bit be set in the ACE for a SID, but the access token for the process with that SID must have the corresponding privilege enabled.

Finally, the Maximum_Allowed bit is not really an access bit but a bit that modifies W2K's algorithm for scanning the DACL for this SID. Normally, W2K will scan through the DACL until it reaches an ACE that specifically grants (bit set) or denies (bit not set) the access requested by the requesting process or until it reaches the end of the DACL, in which latter case access is denied. The Maximum_Allowed bit allows the object's owner to define a set of access rights that is the maximum that will be allowed to a given user. With this in mind, suppose that an application does not know all of the operations that it is going to be asked to perform on an object during a session. There are three options for requesting access:

1. Attempt to open the object for all possible accesses. The disadvantage of this approach is that the access may be denied even though the application may have all of the access rights actually required for this session.

2. Only open the object when a specific access is requested, and open a new handle to the object for each different type of request. This is generally the preferred method because it will not unnecessarily deny access, nor will it allow more access than necessary. However, it imposes additional overhead.

3. Attempt to open the object for as much access as the object will allow this SID. The advantage is that the user will not be artificially denied access, but the application may have more access than it needs. This latter situation may mask bugs in the application.

An important feature of W2K security is that applications can make use of the W2K security framework for user-defined objects. For example, a database server might create its own security descriptors and attach them to portions of a database. In addition to normal read/write access constraints, the server could secure database-specific operations, such as scrolling within a result set or performing a join. It would be the server's responsibility to define the meaning of special rights and perform access checks. But the checks would occur in a standard context, using systemwide user/group accounts and audit logs. The extensible security model should prove useful to implementers of foreign files systems.

17.8   FURTHER READING.

Two books with extensive coverage of OS security issues are Gollman (1999) and Pfleeger (1997). Singhal (1994), Sinha (1997), and Stallings (1998) also contain considerable coverage of these topics. Gasser (1988) provides a comprehensive study of trusted computer systems. Viega (2000) is a good comparison of Windows and Unix security approaches.

17.9   REFERENCES

Boebert, W., R. Kain, and W. Young. "Secure Computing: the Secure Ada Target Approach." *Scientific Honeyweller* (July 1985). Reprinted in M. Abrams and H. Podell, *Computer and Network Security.* Los Alamitos, CA: IEEE Computer Society Press, 1987.

Bransted, D., ed. *Computer Security and the Data Encryption Standard.* National Bureau of Standards, Special Publication No. 500-27, February 1978.

Gasser, M. *Building a Secure Computer System.* New York: Van Nostrand Reinhold, 1988.

Gollmann, D. *Computer Security.* New York: John Wiley & Sons, 1999.

Denning, P., and R. Brown. "Operating Systems." *Scientific American* (September 1984).

Pfleeger, C. *Security in Computing.* Upper Saddle River, NJ: Prentice-Hall PTR, 1997.

Saltzer, J., and M. Schroeder. "The Protection of Information in Computer Systems." *Proceedings of the IEEE,* September 1975.

Sandhu, R., and P. Samarati. "Access Control: Principles and Practice." *IEEE Communications* (September 1994).

Singhal, M., and N. Shivaratri. *Advanced Concepts in Operating Systems.* New York: McGraw-Hill, 1994.

Sinha, P. *Distributed Operating Systems.* Piscataway, NJ: IEEE Press, 1997.

Stallings, W. *Cryptography and Network Security: Principles and Practice,* 2nd ed. Upper Saddle River, NJ: Prentice-Hall, 1998.

Viega, J., and J. Voas. "The Pros and Cons of Unix and Windows Security Policies. *IT Pro* (September/October 2000).

17.10   NOTES

1. P. Denning and R. Brown, "Operating Systems." *Scientific American,* September 1984.

2. J. Saltzer and M. Schroeder, "The Protection of Information in Computer Systems." *Proceedings of the IEEE,* September 1975.

3. C. Pfleeger, *Security in Computing* (Upper Saddle River, NJ: Prentice-Hall PTR, 1997).

4. The "*" does not stand for anything. No one could think of an appropriate name for the property when the first report on the model was being written. The asterisk was a dummy character entered in the draft so that a text editor could rapidly find and replace all instances of its use once the property was named. No name was ever devised, and so the report was published with the "*" intact.

CHAPTER 18

LOCAL AREA NETWORKS

Gary C. Kessler and N. Todd Pritsky

CONTENTS

18.1 INTRODUCTION. This chapter discusses generic issues surrounding local area network (LAN) security. Securing the LAN is essential to securing the Internet because LANs are where most of the attackers, victims, clients, servers, firewalls, routers, and other devices reside. The systems on the Internet that are exploited open other systems on that local network to attack as well as systems on the Internet as a whole. Many of the general issues mentioned herein are described in more specific terms in other chapters, while Tutorial 3 of this book covers LAN terms, standards, protocols, and equipment.

18.2 POLICY AND PROCEDURE ISSUES. Twenty years ago, all users had accounts on a shared mainframe or minicomputer. A single system manager was responsible for security, backup, disaster recovery, account management, policies, and all other related issues. Today all users are system managers, and, in many cases, individuals have responsibility for several systems. Since the vulnerability of a single computer can compromise the entire LAN, it is imperative that there be rules in place so that everyone can work together for mutual efficiency and defense. But where polices and procedures can be centralized, they should be because most users do not take the security procedures seriously enough.

The following list, modified from Fraser RFC 2196[1], is a rough outline of LAN-related security policies and procedures that should at least be considered:[2]

I. Administrative Policies Framework
    A. Information Security Issues
        1. Password management procedures
            a. Are passwords assigned or chosen by user?
            b. Are password auditing procedures in place?
            c. Are password policies enforced (e.g., minimum length, allowed and required characters, expiration, blacklisting)?
            d. How many passwords are required to access all systems?
        2. Virus protection
            a. Are servers protected?
            b. Is there an e-mail "viruswall"?
            c. Is virus protection a centrally managed activity or up to each user?
            d. How do users maintain the current virus signature database?
        3. Encryption and certificates
        4. Security event handling
    B. Network Connectivity Issues
        1. Dial-up access
        2. Hubs versus switches
        3. Identification and authentication
            a. Passwords and management
            b. Authentication systems
            c. Two-factor authentication?
            d. Single sign-on?
            e. Biometrics
    C. Physical site security and disaster recovery
        1. Physical security of systems
        2. Dial-up access lines and modems
        3. Scheduling backups
        4. Access to servers
        5. Storing and limiting access to backup media
        6. Disaster recovery and contingency plans
    D. Operating system and LAN security
        1. Operating system-specific issues
            a. Monitoring operating system security vulnerabilities
            b. Apply security patches
            c. Securing OS during installation
            d. Auditing the systems
        2. Is DHCP employed?

    3. Log analysis software and procedures
    4. Vulnerability testing
    5. Intrusion detection tools

II. User Policies Framework

  A. Written, published network security policy

  B. Network/Internet Appropriate Use Policy (AUP)

  C. User training and education

    1. Security (general issues)

    2. Importance of protecting customer data, client information, and other data subject private information such as medical claim records and patient information

    3. Policies and AUPs

    4. Suggestions for how to be safe

  D. Virus protection

    1. Using antivirus software

    2. Maintaining current virus signature database

  E. Choosing good passwords

  F. Best practices

    1. E-mail (netiquette and handling attachments)

    2. Browser (shut off Java, JavaScript, ActiveX, and other auto-execution)

    3. Microsoft Office Suite

      a. Use of macros

      b. Implications for document management

    4. Protecting files on the server and your own system

      a. Use of Windows "shares" and Unix NFS

      b. Use of NetWare, NTFS, and Unix access control

        i. Spotting a possible compromise (methods for identifying intrusions or other unauthorized activity)

        ii. What to do and whom to contact if a compromise is suspected

  G. When trouble strikes (computer emergency response procedures)

Most of these topics are discussed in other parts of this *Handbook,* although they all apply in one way or another to the LAN. Not every issue will apply to all networks, but each LAN is an ever-evolving entity and the policies guiding its operation also must evolve.

18.3   PHYSICAL SITE SECURITY.   The physical protection of the site is very important but too often overlooked. One reason that site security is often lacking is that some of the policies and procedures can be perceived as sending a message to employees that they are not trusted. Nevertheless, physical site security includes many aspects of protecting network servers, communications facilities, individual user's systems, and information. Some of the precautions to consider include:

- Installing an uninterruptible power supply (UPS) for hubs/switches, routers, servers, and other critical systems.

- Protecting all other power connections against surges and spikes.

- Securing hubs, switches, routers, servers, and other critical systems in a locked room or closet.

- Training maintenance and janitorial staff never to unplug any computer equipment, never to connect any maintenance equipment into a socket not expressly marked for that purpose, and always to give switches and controls a wide berth.

- Removing signs on server room doors that advertise the contents or function of the room.

As the terrifying events of September 11, 2001, have shown us, no matter what steps we take there are many things beyond our control. People and companies are moving on after the tragedy, and it has become very clear that it is extremely important to develop a business continuation plan to deal with catastrophe. This plan should include policies specifying how often information is backed up and how often backups are rotated off-site. It should also identify people who will take the lead when disaster strikes.

A lesson learned by many companies is that having good backups of data is only half the story. Many companies lost all of their computer equipment in the World Trade Center, so while their data was indeed safe, they had no machines to restore the data. Given that access to corporate information is often considered mission-critical, consideration should be given to overall redundancy—for example, mirroring facilities in geographically diverse locations.

Even anthrax and other toxic substances must now be a part of our physical security equation. As of this writing, authorities still know very little about exactly how contagions like anthrax spores can be distributed. There is the distinct possibility that spores could make their way through ventilation systems, for example. Thus, many companies are hardening not only their mail facilities in response to the mail-based threat already seen, but actually shoring up defenses in computer and other facilities as well. Nobody wants to be alarmist, but in the absence of understanding, everybody should probably err on the side of caution.

For more information on facilities security, see Chapters 14 and 15 of this *Handbook*.

18.4   PHYSICAL LAYER ISSUES.   The LAN itself has a number of additional vulnerabilities because the systems and media are so widely dispersed. This section discusses securing the LAN infrastructure.

18.4.1   Sniffers and Broadcast LANs.   Traditional LAN medium access control (MAC) schemes operate assuming a logical, if not physical, broadcast topology. In a broadcast network, every station hears every transmission. When operating in *promiscuous mode,* a LAN station will read every frame that goes by regardless of whether the frame is addressed to the station or not.

When protocol analysis, or *sniffer,* software became available in the 1980s, every station on the LAN became a potential network analysis and management tool—or a surreptitious eavesdropper. Since so many of the network's applications—particularly TCP/IP-based applications—transmit passwords and files in plaintext, this type of software is potentially dangerous.

A number of sources offer commercial packet sniffing software that is powerful and flexible, such as Network Associates' SnifferPro and Novell's LANalyzer. These packages usually have additional capabilities such as network monitoring, performance monitoring, and traffic analysis. Prior to 1990, network protocol analysis required a special piece of hardware with a connection to the network. Today, a large number of software packages that do TCP/IP packet sniffing can help an intruder because they can be installed directly on an individual's laptop or desktop computer. Some of these packages include:

- BUTTsniffer (Windows NT)
- Ethereal (Windows, Unix)
- Network Monitor (free with, and for, Windows NT)
- Sniffit (Linux, SunOS, Solaris, FreeBSD, Irix)
- snort (Unix)
- Solsniff (Solaris)
- tcpdump (Unix)
- WinDump (Windows 9x/NT)

Relatively few countermeasures can be taken against these kinds of tools. Fortunately, they are effective only on a broadcast network such as a hubbed LAN. If an Ethernet hub, for example, is replaced with a switch, the only traffic broadcast to all hosts on the network are those frames actually addressed to the LAN's broadcast address. In this case, a station can sniff only that traffic that is going to or coming from the station with the sniffer software. Replacing all hubs with switches may be unreasonable in many environments, but placing all servers on a switch instead of a hub will improve both performance and security.

Other network-based tools that can detect a host with a network interface card (NIC) in promiscuous mode, such as AntiSniff (Windows) and sentinel (Unix). These tools work by performing a number of tests to detect the promiscuous host; they check the network hosts' operating systems, domain name system (DNS) activity, and network and machine latency. An excellent overview of antisniffer tools can be found at *www.securitysoftwaretech.com/antisniff/tech-paper.html*.

Sniffers can be defeated using cryptography. Use of secure IP (IPsec) and secure shell (SSH) for TCP/IP applications can provide privacy and integrity to all communication and applications. IPsec is available from any of the IPsec Developers Forum members (*www.ip-sec.com*), and SSH is available from SSH Communications Security (*www.ssh.com*).

18.4.2   Attacks on the Physical Plant.   The most common medium employed today on LANs is copper-based, unshielded twisted pair (UTP) cable. All copper media, including UTP and coaxial cable, emanate a magnetic field because of the changing current on the wire. Van Eck monitoring devices can pick up these emanations remotely and reproduce the frames on the wire or keystrokes at a machine. As far-fetched as this might sound, the vulnerability is very real. The U.S. government and military have a set of standards to reduce and limit electromagnetic radiation (EMR) called TEMPEST, and the National Security Agency (NSA) even has a list of products that are TEMPEST-compliant. Indeed, this vulnerability may not be a major problem in most organizational networks, but there is some set of networks where this is a concern. An excellent source of TEMPEST information can be found at *www.eskimo.com/~joelm/tempest.htm*.

An alternative to encasing workstations in Faraday cages (i.e., copper mesh layers surrounding all components) is to generate random electronic noise that masks meaningful radiated data transmissions.[3]

One way to reduce or eliminate EMR is to reduce or eliminate the amount of copper media on the network. Optical fiber, for example, has no EMR because there is no electricity on the line. It does not eliminate the EMR at the desktop itself, but it does prevent its entry into all interconnecting fiber cables.

Users also can be the source of some types of denial-of-service (DoS) attacks, either purposely or accidentally. Consider coaxial cable Ethernet networks (10BASE-5 or 10BASE-2) where nodes are attached to a common LAN medium. In both cases, the coaxial cable has a terminating resistor at the end of the wire to eliminate reflection of the signal. If the resistor is removed, it allows extra noise on the wire that can block all traffic on the network. End-of-cable resistors should be beyond the reach of users if at all possible.

Similar DoS attacks may occur whenever users modify the wiring scheme of the network. Removal of terminating resistors is only one action that can cause problems. Hubs in common areas might be unplugged or have network connectors removed. A token ring hub-to-hub connection can be detached, breaking the integrity of the ring and thus preventing LAN hosts from communicating with other hosts and denying service to users.

The bottom line is that the physical network should be secured to the extent possible. LAN managers should educate users to avoid the accidental problems that might occur and even how to recognize nefarious attacks.

18.4.3 Modems, Dial-up Servers, and Telephone Lines.   Modems anywhere on the LAN are a potential danger, particularly those that are connected directly to a user's system, with or without official sanction. Modems can provide a back door into the LAN, possibly bypassing the firewall, strong authentication, proxy server, and any other network security.

In general, all modems should be concentrated at the network's dial-up server. Individual user systems should, in most cases, be banned from having modems on the network. This is a difficult rule to enforce, however, because laptops and an increasing number of desktop systems usually include preinstalled modems, and a user can always connect an external modem to the serial port of any system. This is an example of why security managers have to integrate policies into the culture of an organization. Otherwise, users will find a way around what they perceive to be prohibitive and onerous policies, and modems are one way to circumvent the corporate firewall.

Modems in auto-answer mode are particularly dangerous. Although most companies do not advertise their dial-in telephone numbers, these numbers do not remain secret for very long from someone who wants to find them. Anyone with a telephone directory can easily start mapping an organization's block of corporate telephone numbers. For example, if the main number is 802-555-3700, attackers have a place to start. When attackers call the main number and ask the receptionist for the organization's fax number, they obtain even more information. Using war-dialer software, attackers can scan an entire block of telephone numbers (e.g., 555-3700 through 555-3799) and obtain a list of which numbers are active, which respond with a tone, and what the tone represents (e.g., fax, modem, etc.). If a user has an auto-answer modem on a computer, attackers may gain access to the user's system without so much as a password. Security managers should work with their local telephone companies to obtain telephone numbers for modem lines that are not in the organization's telephone block.

The dial-up server, then, is the place to concentrate the modems and the authentication of dial-up users. There are several strategies for authentication at the dial-up server, the strongest being some form of two-factor authentication, such as a combination of passwords and a token. Another strong protection mechanism is to implement a dial-back mechanism so that once a bona fide user logs in, the system hangs up and calls back to a preconfigured telephone number. This is an effective scheme that works well with fixed-location telecommuters, but not with roaming employees. In addition, attackers have been known to tamper with the central switch of a telephone company to call-forward from an assigned number to the attacker's own modem.

When a user requires two separate logons, one to the dial-up server and then one to a domain server, security restrictions should control what the caller is allowed to do after passing the first test. One of the authors of this chapter worked with a company that had a shared secret (an oxymoron) telephone number for its modem bank and then a single shared username and password for all the users to authenticate to the dial-up server. To access files and shared network resources, the user then had to authenticate to the domain controller. But after passing the identification and authentication for the first server, an attacker was on the organization's LAN and had complete, unfettered access to the Internet and an identity that implicated the company in any possible malfeasance.

Configure all software and modems so that a user logout forces the modem to disconnect. Some guidelines for securing dial-up servers include:

- Maintain and monitor telephone logs.
- A modem disconnect forces a user logout.
- Configure the modems so that they return to their default configuration after every connection.
- Implement a dial-back mechanism, where possible.
- Use two-factor authentication for roaming users.
- Periodically scan internal telephone numbers for unauthorized modems.
- Prevent the display of any banner message when the user connects to the modem, and certainly do not display any sort of *welcome* message.
- Train the organization help desk in social engineering techniques and prohibiting them from giving out modem telephone numbers, user names, or other sensitive information that could help attackers.

18.4.4   Wireless LAN Issues.   Wireless LANs (WLANs) have vulnerabilities their wired counterparts do not. The most obvious difference between wired and wireless networks is the medium itself. Although copper-based LANs emit a small amount of radiation that can be intercepted, the entire basis of wireless LANs is transmitting data using radiation in some form.

There are WLANs based on infrared signals that cannot penetrate building walls and so achieve some degree of security due to the limited propagation of those signals. Such LANs are typically found in networks requiring high levels of security. However, most WLANs today use radio transmission techniques. In these networks, anyone on a nearby street can use a listening device to intercept data and even capture the network identifiers required to connect to the LAN. The practical range of interception is governed by the inverse-square law for the signal strength (it declines as the square of the distance from the source) and by the sensitivity and signal-to-noise characteristics of the receivers.

Fortunately there is a certain measure of security within the physical layer itself. IEEE 802.11-based LANs employ either Direct-Sequence Spread Spectrum (DSSS) or Frequency-Hopping Spread Spectrum (FHSS) techniques. As always, depending on range and noise levels, it is possible to eavesdrop. However, interpreting the signals is made more difficult by how DSSS and FHSS work.

To make sense of the transmissions, the receiver must know either the *chipping code* used in a DSSS network or the *frequency-hopping pattern* in an FHSS implementation. Without such information, the signal will appear to be nothing more than background noise to the illicit receiver. It is not an insurmountable problem for the would-be eavesdropper, but the work factor is definitely increased when compared to narrowband radio techniques. The spread spectrum approach also offers more reliability in the face of interference from denial of service (i.e., intentional jamming), as the signal is spread over a broad range of frequencies. Some vendor equipment also comes with software components that allow for tuning around interference.

For greater privacy than that provided by the physical layer alone, the 802.11 standard includes an optional encryption method called Wired Equivalent Privacy (WEP). This technique is truly optional so not all vendors support the standard. WEP uses a 40-bit form of the RC4 algorithm by default, although some products support stronger, 128-bit versions. It is a good idea to choose a product that offers more than just the 40-bit version, as a 40-bit keyspace does not provide great security given today's computing power.

Because WEP does not offer strong encryption and does not describe a standard key-exchange mechanism, many vendors have implemented layer 3 tunneling methods, such as those found in virtual private networks (VPNs), to provide greater privacy. These VPN-based approaches generally employ other encryption processes (e.g., Microsoft Point-to-Point Encryption as used in the Point-to-Point Tunneling Protocol (PPTP) that use longer keys than WEP and often support Public Key Infrastructure (PKI) or other key-exchange mechanisms. Some implementations also provide authentication through standards such as Remote Access Dial-In User Service (RADIUS) for more flexible client management. The major problem is that these approaches are not all interoperable and are not necessarily multiprotocol-capable.

WEP also can be used for authentication to prevent unauthorized access to the WLAN itself. Such authentication adds another layer of protection to the username and password combination employed by typical server software. Before gaining access to information resources on the server, a client must first gain access to the physical medium. Using the shared key scheme, a wireless device must possess the same encryption key as the LAN's access point, the device enabling wireless connectivity to the wired portion of the LAN. Any data transmitted must be encrypted with the key or the frame will be ignored. Many wireless access products also have the capability to create access control lists based on MAC addresses to filter LAN connections.

In summary, network managers should consider the following security items when evaluating wireless network components:

- Physical layer schemes
  - *Infrared*—cannot penetrate walls and is good for high-security applications
  - *Frequency-Hopping Spread Spectrum*—signal hopping provides good level of security, but complexity of technique limits bandwidth
  - *Direct-Sequence Spread Spectrum*—low "spreading ratio" can increase available bandwidth but also the possibility of interception and jamming

- Encryption options
  - *Wired Equivalent Privacy*—optional default is low-grade encryption, 40 bit, strength
  - *Alternative Encryption Methods*—often more secure than WEP but not always interoperable
- Authentication methods
  - *Wired Equivalent Privacy*—requires clients to have the same encryption key as the LAN Access Point, which introduces key management issues
  - *Access Control List*—allows only certain clients to gain physical access to the LAN, based on the MAC address; this adds complexity to client management
  - *Server-Based Authentication*—flexible user authentication with RADIUS for an additional layer of protection from illicit connections

18.5   NETWORK OPERATING SYSTEM ISSUES.   In the early 1990s, it was common to find desktop systems running the Windows operating system *and* the Novell NetWare network operating system (NOS). Desktop applications ran over Windows, and NetWare was used only to move files to and from the shared file space, or to print documents.

Today, the distinction among the desktop operating system, server operating system, and NOS is disappearing. Operating systems such as Linux, Mac OS, Unix, and Windows all provide desktop application suites with networking capabilities, including communications protocols such as TCP/IP. There are some general security considerations for all LANs regardless of the specific operating system:

- Use whatever capabilities are provided by the operating system to employ strong passwords.
- Create password policies that force strong passwords. Change passwords periodically and do not allow reuse. Periodically audit passwords using password-cracking tools such as L0phtCrack (Windows NT) or crack (Unix). Ensure that the administrator and root accounts are given passwords that are not widely distributed or guessed.
- Disable (or uninstall) any services that are not being used.
- Keep the operating system and application software up to date, and with the latest security patches installed.
- Carefully manage access control lists for files and other system/network resources.
- Strictly define users, groups, and network/domain trusts.
- Tightly secure any running applications.
- Log on as administrator or root only when necessary; otherwise log on as a regular user.
- Allow operators and administrators to log on only locally at server systems.
- Limit use of guest, demo, or anonymous accounts.
- Where feasible, put boot and system files as well as application files and data on different partitions, hard drives, or I/O controllers.
- Regularly audit server systems.

- Monitor log files.

- Remove the floppy and CD drives from servers after the system has a stable configuration.

- Implement best industry practices when securing the operating system.

- Use vulnerability assessment tools on a regular basis to scan servers.

- Use intrusion detection tools to monitor potential attacks on the LAN that are launched from the internal network.

- If using the Simple Network Management Protocol (SNMP) for network administration, carefully choose community names and block external access to the SNMP service. Make Management Information Bases (MIBs) read-only, where possible.

- Avoid use of the Domain Name System (DNS) HINFO (host info) resource record to identify the (central) processing unit type and the installed operating system.

Specific operating system vulnerabilities are beyond the scope of this chapter; entire books and Web sites are devoted to securing some of these individual operating systems. At a minimum, network managers must monitor their operating system vendor's Web site and all other sites that cover the NOS's security. The following paragraphs provide some general observations and comments about the various network operating systems.

18.5.1   Windows 9x.   All of the Windows operating systems (including NT and 2000) support peer-to-peer resource sharing and are vulnerable to exploitation of Net-BIOS file and print sharing. In particular, when file and print sharing is enabled, the service is, by default, bound to TCP/IP. While this does not cause an additional exposure to systems on the local network (since shares can be seen by other nodes on the LAN anyway), it does provide a potential vulnerability for hosts connected to the Internet. File and print sharing can be unbound from TCP/IP using Start, Control Panel, Network.

Windows 9x (including Windows 95, Windows 98, and Windows ME) systems also have a vulnerability in the way authentication is performed when a user wishes to access a remote share. Windows uses the challenge-handshake authentication protocol (CHAP) for all passwords that need to be sent over the network, so passwords never appear in plaintext on the LAN. However, Windows 9x uses the *same* challenge during a given 15-minute period so that an intruder with a physical access to the LAN and to a sniffer could effect a replay attack by resending a duplicate authentication request and remapping a share on the Windows 9x system. This example illustrates the critical role of physical security in preventing compromise of LANs.

One of the best-known Trojan horse programs for Windows 9x is Back Orifice (BO). Advertised as a remote Win9x administrator tool, it can be used by a nefarious user to take total control of someone else's system, including the capability to modify the Registry, reboot the system, transfer files, view cached passwords, spawn processes, and create shares. NetBus is another tool that can be used to take control of a remote Windows system. Some commercial virus scanners can detect these programs on individual systems, and several workstation firewalls exclude communications characteristic of these Trojans.

Windows 9x has no particular logon security mechanism. Although every user might be forced to log on to a system, any user can log in with any username and any password to get at least basic access. Several password-cracking programs are available through the Internet to break Windows' .PWL password files, which are accessible once a user has access to the network. If a password-protected screen saver is preventing an attacker from logging in, there is an easy way around this as well: Simply reboot the computer. However, third-party security programs include non-breakable secure logins and screen savers; many include bootlock functions that prevent any access whatever unless a valid password is entered. Current examples of such software can easily be located using buyers' guides such as the annual listing from the Computer Security Institute (see *http://gocsi.com*).

18.5.2   Windows NT/2000.   From a security perspective, Windows 2000 Millennium Edition (ME) is not significantly stronger than Windows 9x. Network administrators should periodically scan the network's public shares to ensure that they are appropriate. Windows NT Server, NT Workstation, and 2000 Server editions are built for security and network services and have the software architecture to support these services. However, a security vulnerability announcement related to these operating systems seems to come out almost weekly. Many of the hacking tools available for Win9x also are available for Windows NT and 2000; Back Orifice 2000 (BO2K), for example, is an NT/2000 version of BO and NetBus also can take control of an NT/2000 host.

Scripting holes in Internet Explorer (IE) and Office 2000 make all Windows systems susceptible to a variety of new virus and worm attacks. Although the early viruses such as Melissa and I LOVE YOU required users to open e-mail attachments, that is no longer so. Microsoft Outlook and Outlook Express will execute HTML and script code in the body of an e-mail by default. Several ActiveX components also will execute from an e-mail containing HTML and script code; examples of such controls include Scriplet.typlib (ships with IE 4.x and 5.x) and the UA control (Office 2000). The best protection against these types of vulnerabilities are to define Outlook and Outlook Express to read e-mail in the "Restricted Sites Zone" and disable all Active Scripting and ActiveX related settings in that zone. This vulnerability affects all Windows systems with Office 2000 or Internet Explorer 4.x/5.x installed, even if IE is not used.

Securing Windows NT/2000 systems is well beyond the scope of this chapter, but some of the precautions, in addition to the list above, are as follows:

- Format the drive using NTFS rather than FAT.
- Use long file names and disable the DOS 8.3 naming format.
- Disable the Everyone group.
- Rename the Administrator account.
- Turn auditing on. (It is off by default.)

All NT-based systems have been given the C2 security rating by the National Computer Security Center. At the time of this writing, Windows NT 3.5 and 4.0 and Windows 2000 SQL Server version 8.0 have completed the evaluation process. Windows 2000 Server has been submitted by Microsoft and is expected to be given the C2-level rating. This means that when Windows is installed correctly, it meets evaluation criteria set forth in the NCSC's "Orange Book" of security specifications. C2 certification is not applied to the operating system itself; rather, it is applied to a particular installation. Microsoft provides tools to audit a site so administrator(s) can deploy the correct hardware and software configurations to achieve this level of security in a network.

Windows 2000 introduced a new feature that administrators might want to employ. Windows NT introduced the ability to compress and decompress files on the fly. Windows 2000 introduces the capability to encrypt and decrypt files on the fly. The Encrypting File System (EFS) uses public key cryptography and the Data Encryption Standard (DES) to encrypt files on the hard drive. EFS includes an optional capability for a recovery mechanism in case of key loss. Organizations using EFS on critical systems should consider employing this mechanism to protect against loss or destruction of the private key.

Microsoft's newest OS, Windows XP, was released just prior to the completion of this chapter, so its security details are still not fully known. Microsoft claims users of XP will enjoy vastly increased security, but the major improvement appears to be the inclusion of a firewall capability in both the Home Edition and Professional versions. Professional goes a couple steps further by offering EFS file encryption, Kerberos[4] and smart card support, and a new software restriction feature allowing administrators to mitigate the impact of viruses and Trojan horses. XP also supports raw sockets, which in itself is not unusual—UNIX and Linux do as well. This feature is intended to increase the functionality of Internet services, but in Microsoft's implementation it is available to any user, no matter what privilege level. Thus hackers can possibly gain control of a computer running XP, and use it to initiate DoS attacks by commanding the OS to generate a flood of traffic.

One of the most important capabilities for the network security manager is to audit the Windows server systems to protect their integrity. The following tools are part of the base operating system or the Windows NT Resource Kit:

- Netstat examines open ports.
- Event Viewer examines application, security, and system logs.
- Net start, net user, net group, net local group display running services, users, groups, and local groups.
- Dumpel converts Event Viewer logs to ASCII files.
- NetMon displays network traffic.
- Netsvc displays local and remote running services and drivers.
- Addusers displays users and groups.
- Findgrp displays local and domain groups for a user.
- Local and global show all members of specific local or global groups.
- Dommon displays trusted domains.
- Xcacls examines the file Access Control Lists (ACL).
- Perms examines the ACLs associated with a user.
- Sysdiff displays changes in the Registry and file system.
- Regdmp creates an ASCII version of the Registry.
- Ralist lists a domain's Remote Access Servers (RAS).
- Rasusers lists users authorized for dial-in access.

18.5.3   Novell NetWare.   Novell's NetWare NOS is fundamentally different from Windows and Unix, which support client/server access to services as well as peer-to-peer networking. In the NetWare environment, client systems (workstations) can communicate only with a server, while servers can communicate with workstations or other servers. NetWare has a generally well-deserved reputation for being a secure operating system. Passwords are protected on the network, the NetWare Directory Service (NDS) efficiently and effectively scales to large organizations and networks, and it includes several powerful logging and auditing tools. NetWare 4.11 also has a C2 level "Red Book" evaluation, which includes additional networking and file sharing criteria and is thus more stringent than the "Orange Book" specifications.

However, NetWare is not impervious to attack. In most installations, it is rather easy for any user, including those not logged on to any NetWare server, to discover network servers, trees, groups, printers, and usernames; the easiest way to do this is to use Windows' Network Neighborhood. An attacker also can use Novell's On-Site Admin product to learn the status of all network servers and browse the complete NetWare tree without logging on. Since the "attacker" cannot gain access to these resources without authenticating, these features may not be fatal flaws. However, an attacker can learn a lot about a potential victim with little or no work. It is best to disable the default (public) browse capability.

To launch effective attacks against NetWare systems, the attacker generally has to be more sophisticated than a Windows attacker, although automated tools will make this easier over time. One potential vulnerability of NetWare is *connection hijacking,* where an intruder sends information to a server and spoofs being a currently logged-in administrator. NetWare's solution to this is a scheme called *packet signatures,* where the server and workstation digitally sign every frame using a shared, secret key. There is a possible attack on packet signatures, but the attack does not break the encryption. It attempts to convince the workstation and server not to use the signatures scheme.

NetWare also includes a script called SECURE.NCF that can improve the security of the network. When run during server startup, SECURE.NCF can disable support for unencrypted passwords, disable access to system auditing information by nonadministrators, enable automatic repair of bad volumes during start-up, and reject bad NetWare Core Protocol (NCP, which is the NetWare equivalent to the Presentation Layer supporting NDS) packets.

The SecureConsole command provides security features to protect the server system from an attack launched by someone at the server console. The Secure Console command is run from the server console, allowing only the server to load software located in the system directory. It also disables the console debugging utility and prevents the date or time from being changed by any user other than the console operator. Once invoked, these features can be disabled only by rebooting the server.

These are important tools to protect the server because the goal of most serious attacks on a NetWare network is to become the Admin user. *Nwpcrack* is one of several tools that can be used to crack NetWare 4.x passwords. The best defense against any password-guessing attack is to enable NetWare's intruder detection and password-blacklisting features; the former sends the network administrator an alert if it detects too many events that have predefined attack signatures, and the latter automatically locks an account if there are more than a predetermined number of consecutive failed logins on an account.

Network administrators also can test their network for security vulnerabilities using additional tools; unfortunately, attackers can use these same tools to identify security weaknesses. Tools such as AuditWare for NDS (*www.cheyenne.com*), Kane

Security Analyst for Novell NetWare (*www.intrusion.com*), and LT Auditor+ (*www. bluelance.com*) will perform these tasks, but it is noteworthy that most of these tools require physical access to the console—which again shows the importance of physically securing LAN servers.

18.5.4   Unix.   Unix is the oldest operating system still in widespread, growing use today. Originally developed in 1969 at AT&T Bell Laboratories, Unix became the first operating system to integrate network communications when TCP/IP was bundled into Berkeley Software Development (BSD) 4.2 Unix in 1984. Unix had traditionally been reserved for server systems and hardcore computer users. With the development of the X-Windows interface for Unix and the wide deployment of Linux since the mid-1990s, Unix and its variants represent the only significant competition to Windows in the desktop and server environment.

Like TCP/IP and the Internet itself, Unix was developed for functionality and use within a trusted user community. As such, while Unix has many powerful tools, it does not have a cohesive security architecture, nor is it an inherently secure operating system.

Unix has most of the basic operating system protections: passwords, access control lists, groups, user privilege levels, and so on. But Unix also comes with a large variety of services (daemons) enabled by default, including *FTP, Telnet, finger, echo, chargen, daytime, RPC, BIND,* and more. In addition, nearly every Unix daemon has had some sort of security vulnerability reported at one time or another, with buffer overflows being quite prevalent.

The SANS Institute (*www.sans.org*) has a list of 20 (recently expanded from the original 10) most critical Internet security threats. Given Unix's longevity, it is interesting that six of these threats specifically affect Unix or its variants:

1. The *Berkeley Internet Name Daemon* (*BIND*) service has several weaknesses that can allow an attacker root access to Unix systems. Because of *BIND's* ubiquity in the Internet, a single flaw has significant ramifications.

2. Weaknesses in the *Remote Procedure Call* (*RPC*) capability of several applications can lead to a root compromise. RPC allows programs on one computer to execute programs on a remote computer and is widely used to access network services such as shared files in Sun's *NFS.*

3. *Sendmail* and Multipurpose Internet Message Extensions (MIME) buffer overflows as well as pipe attacks might allow immediate root compromise. *Sendmail* is the software responsible for sending, receiving, and forwarding e-mail while MIME defines multimedia file types for e-mail (and other applications). Buffer overflows can exploit the *sendmail* application (as per the Internet Worm in November 1988), and a MIME-encoded program can cause *sendmail* to execute a set of instructions placed by an attacker.

4. Buffer overflows in *sadmind* (an application that provides a graphical interface to remote administration functions for Solaris systems), and *mountd* (software that controls access to NFS mounts) can be exploited to allow an attacker to gain root access to a system.

5. Improperly configured NFS exports on TCP port 2049 can expose system files or give full file system access to an attacker.

6. Buffer overflow vulnerabilities and/or incorrect configuration in e-mail client programs using the Post Office Protocol (POP) and Internet Message Access

Protocol (IMAP) expose systems to attacks. Firewalls usually have holes in them for these services to allow external e-mail access, and attackers frequently gain root access via this path.

There are many things that an administrator should consider when securing a Unix/Linux system. In addition to the general steps just listed, the security manager might also:

- Disable (or remove) any unused services, particularly *finger,* the BIND name daemon (*named*), RPC, *sendmail,* Trivial FTP (tftp), POP/IMAP, *sadmind, mountd,* and NFS.
- Install the latest version and security patch of all installed software.
- Take great care when configuring access control lists and other sharing.
- Do not run *Sendmail* in daemon mode (turn off the -bd switch) on machines that are neither mail servers nor mail relays.
- Limit use of the "r" remote access protocols.
- Use shadow password files.
- Implement TCP Wrappers to control access to services.
- Consider using encrypted communication protocols, such as Secure Shell (SSH) or Secure Sockets Layer (SSL), for remote access. Prevent transmission of cleartext passwords over the Internet.

One of the most important capabilities for the network/security manager is to audit the Windows server systems to protect their integrity. The following tools are part of the base operating system or the Windows NT Resource Kit:

- Netstat examines open ports.
- Lsof displays hidden file space and network connections.
- Tcpdump displays network traffic.
- Who displays users that are logged on and the *utmp* log file.
- Last displays login history, and the *wtmp* log file.
- Lastb display a history of bad logins (and the *btmp* log file).
- Syslogd is a central server facility for managing and logging system messages.
- TCPWrapper monitors and manages incoming service requests.

18.5.5   Mac OS.   Although the Macintosh operating systems have mostly given way to Windows and Unix, at least for server systems, they are still worth mentioning. The Macintosh was the first desktop operating system that included networking and resource sharing as integral elements. But like Unix and TCP/IP before it, the Mac OS is designed for convenience and usability but not for security.

Because of its peer-to-peer nature, Mac OS has a number of potential exposures. Although Windows and Unix also can operate in a peer-to-peer mode, a novice user generally will not know how to share resources and thereby inadvertently open holes. On the Mac, however, every user is a system administrator and can accidentally open holes to the system. Consider, for example, that a user can share individual files, folders, or disk volumes. Unlike Windows, where a directory is marked as not shared, read, or full, Mac file sharing is more complex and allows the user to establish a set of trusts that require a fair amount of cooperation and knowledge by the users.

Network communication is via the proprietary AppleTalk protocol, but this sharing capability is also available over TCP/IP in Mac OS.

A nefarious Mac network user can quickly see what servers and shares are available on the network by using the *Chooser* accessory. Network administrators are advised periodically to scan the network in order to ensure that no users have accidentally enabled more "Guest" access than they intended. However, such guest access is a potentially gaping hole if using TCP/IP. Personal file sharing should be disabled, but if file sharing is required, administrators should establish a central file server, with security provisions.

In desktop use, Macs have relatively little security. Password protection is provided by default only with some laptop systems, and not even a password-protected screen saver comes standard with the system. In short, there is very little standing between a determined attacker and a Mac computer. Third-party software is required to provide password protection against access to the system and files or for data protection with disk encryption.

Mac-based viruses and worms are much less prevalent than their Windows counterparts, but Macs are not totally immune. First, those viruses that depend on Microsoft Office Suite software will work because the Mac versions of Word and Excel employ macros. Second, Internet-based attacks aimed at TCP/IP—such as the Ping-of-Death, Teardrop, and SMURF—can still affect a Mac server. There are a few third-party antivirus packages specific for the Mac, for example, Norton Antivirus.

Increased security can, indeed, be added to individual Mac systems, using such tools as:

- DiskLocker software that write-protects the hard drive, and FileLock that allows write-protecting individual files
- Empower, which adds strong access control to applications and files
- MacPassword and Sesame that provide complete password protection for a Mac system, including multiple password levels as for administrators and users

Any system that can employ passwords will also have password crackers, and the Mac is no exception. Password crackers abound for the Mac but they do not target the Mac OS itself, since the operating system does not have passwords. Instead, the crackers attack passwords associated with certain Mac OS applications, such as:

- FirstClass Thrash! and PassFinder, which attack FirstClass passwords, an application often used to transform a Mac into an Internet mail and news server
- FMProPeeker, FMP Password Viewer, and MasterKey, which crack FileMaker passwords
- Password Killer, which circumvents PowerBook security
- Remove Passwords and RemoveIt both break passwords associated with StuffIt archives

It is just as important to keep the version of Mac OS up-to-date as the other operating systems. Macs running System 7.1 and 7.8, for example, are known to crash if they are subject to a large volume of port scans. Many schools and businesses use FoolProof to limit user access to files and other resources; it also appears to store passwords in memory in plain text so that any user with a memory editor can access password lists. And the installation of System 8.0 on top of earlier versions of Mac OS (on a PowerBook) can disable the Password Control Panel and any password protection. These examples demonstrate the need to stay abreast of security warnings and patches.

A number of Mac administrative tools can be used to improve security. Among these are:

- InterMapper, an SNMP-based network management tool for both AppleTalk and IP
- MacRadius, a Mac version of RADIUS to protect dial-in servers and services
- NetLock, a powerful data security application that employs encryption to protect network sessions, passwords, logins, and other information
- Network Security Guard, software that scans Mac OS systems for security vulnerabilities

There are fewer Mac OS security incidents reported because the greater popularity of Windows NT and Unix servers make it easier to learn about them, because there are more potential targets, and because one single attack can affect more systems. Put another way, there are fewer attacks on Macs because the hacker community is not as familiar with them, and there are fewer attractive targets.

18.6   CONCLUSION.   A good administrator can secure almost any NOS, although no NOS is secure initially. The network administrator needs continuous vigilance and monitoring, while recognizing that the operating system is only a part of the overall security plan for the LAN and network services. Most network administrators, due to the nature of their job and training, focus exclusively on the computers attached to the LAN and to the LAN's operating system and software. Unfortunately, this approach is too narrow in its scope. Personal firewall software also might be employed to protect individual systems against attack, but almost all of these products are oriented toward IP-based attacks and miss attacks that employ the NOS's native operating system.

Routers, network firewalls, and proxy servers are essential for protecting LAN systems from attack by an external source. The network administrator also must provide tools to protect servers and workstations from other users on the LAN.

18.7   REFERENCES AND FURTHER READING.   This section lists some books, articles, and Web sites that cover the issues addressed in this chapter. Administrators should monitor vendor, operating system, and security Web sites that will have up-to-date, timely additional information.

Brenton, C. *Mastering Network Security*. San Francisco: SYBEX, 1999.

Edwards, M.J. *Internet Security with Windows NT*. Loveland, CO: Duke Press, 1998.

Fraser, B., ed. "Site Security Handbook." RFC 2196/FYI 8, September 1997, *ftp://ftp.isi.edu/in-notes/rfc2196.txt* (November 24, 2000).

Garfinkel, S., and G. Spafford. *Practical Unix and Internet Security*. Sebastopol, CA: O'Reilly & Associates, 1996.

IEEE Working Group for WLAN Standards, *http://grouper.ieee.org/groups/802/11/*.

Landau, T. *Sad Macs, Bombs, and Other Disasters,* 4th ed. Berkeley, CA: Peachpit Press, 2000.

L0pht. "Overview of AntiSniff," *www.securitysoftwaretech.com/antisniff/tech-paper.html* (November 24, 2000).

Mann, S., and E.L. Mitchell. *Linux System Security: The Administrator's Guide to Open Source Security Tools*. Englewood Cliffs, NJ: Prentice-Hall, 2000.

Maximum Security, 2nd ed. Indianapolis: SAMS, 1998.

McNamara, J. "The Complete, Unofficial TEMPEST Information Page" (October 2, 2000), *www.eskimo.com/~joelm/tempest.html* (November 21, 2000).

National Computer Security Center. "Commercial Product Evaluations." *www.radium.ncsc. mil/tpep* (August 16, 2001).

Payne, W.H., T. Sheldon, and B. Payne. *The Complete Reference to Netware 5.* New York: McGraw-Hill, 1999.

Rizzo, J., and K.D. Clark. *How Macs Work,* Millennium ed. Indianapolis: Que, 2001.

SANS Institute. "How to Eliminate the Ten Most Critical Internet Security Threats: The Experts' Consensus" (V1.32, January 18, 2001). *www.sans.org/topten.htm* (March 6, 2001).

Sans Institute. "Securing Linux Step-by-Step Guide" (V1.0). *www.sansstore.org* (November 23, 2000).

Sans Institute. "Securing Windows NT Step-by-Step Guide" (V2.15, July 30, 1999). *www. sansstore.org* (November 23, 2000).

Scambray, J., S. McClure, and G. Kurtz. *Hacking Exposed,* 2nd ed. Berkeley, CA: Osborne/ McGraw-Hill, 2001.

Schmidt, J., T. Hadden, T. Davis, D. Bixler, and A. Kachur. *Microsoft Windows 2000 Security Handbook.* Indianapolis: Que, 2001.

Steen, W., ed. *Netware Security.* Indianapolis: New Riders Publishing, 1996.

University of Toronto. "Local Area Network Security Guidelines." *www.utoronto.ca/security/ LAN.htm* (November 21, 2000).

Wireless Ethernet Compatibility Alliance, *www.wirelessethernet.org.*

Wireless LAN Association, *www.wlana.com.*

18.8   NOTES

1. Fraser, ed. RFC2196, 1997. *Site Security Handbook,* RFC 2196, SEI/CMU, September 1997.

2. See *www.ietf.org/rfc/rfc2196.txt.*

3. For details of software-based TEMPEST, see the work of Kuhn and Anderson (1998; *www.cl.cam.ac.uk/~mgk25/ih98-tempest.pdf*) for details of software-based TEMPEST). "Soft Tempest: Hidden Data Transmission Using Electromagnetic Emanations," appeared in David Aucsmith, ed., *Information Hiding,* Second International Workshop, IH'98, Portland, OR, April 15–17, 1998; see also *Proceedings,* LNCS 1525, pp. 124–142, Springer-Verlag.

4. Microsoft came under fire for its original implementation of Kerberos in Windows 2000. Microsoft's version used a piece of proprietary data in the authentication process, making it impossible for third party Kerberos servers to work with Windows. The company has since released interoperability information.

CHAPTER 19

E-COMMERCE SAFEGUARDS

Jeffrey B. Ritter and Michael Money

CONTENTS

19.1 INTRODUCTION. Electronic commerce (e-commerce) is, fundamentally, the electronic execution of business transactions. But that simple concept disguises significantly greater complexities. E-commerce requires replacing a global marketplace's tradition of signed writings as the ultimate best evidence of the information upon which a transaction is based with electronic, intangible records. Under most commercial law—whether the transaction is a purchase, a lease, a payment, a license, a sale of real estate, a grant of a security interest, or a transfer of securities—the paper record has been given superior validity. Recently, the law has responded to the explosive use of e-commerce, permitting more and more electronic records to be given legal equivalent value. However, the law rarely establishes standards for when an electronic record will be considered conclusive proof—the value of an electronic record often depends on the effectiveness of the security controls that have been instituted to protect the authenticity and integrity of the record.

This chapter has two objectives:

1. Describe the legal framework that has been adopted for the use of electronic commercial practices—e-commerce—and the role of the contract as an essential tool for implementing e-commerce solutions.

2. Describe the various security services, together with a basic methodology, by which the integrity and trustworthiness of the electronic records can be achieved and preserved as an effective substitution for the paper record.

Those managing security for e-commerce applications must understand the legal framework as well as the security services that are available. Without integrating both into the applications and solutions that are developed, significant risks arise that the resulting business records will not be acceptable as evidence of the transaction that was intended or performed.

19.2   THE LEGAL FRAMEWORK.   One of the most difficult aspects of doing business through electronic communications is that jurisdictional differences can complicate planning, execution, and risk management whenever cross-boundary traffic is involved. This section examines commercial law in the United States and under international agreements; in addition, we review salient features of contract law that affect e-commerce.

19.2.1   State of Uniformity in Commercial Law.   Historically, commercial laws were extremely focused on local market requirements. However, through the twentieth century, the United States progressively worked to harmonize and establish uniformity in its commercial laws, a trend that was replicated in international laws during the past decade. In many respects, the requirements for e-commerce provoked the international harmonization efforts. This section will review the uniformity that exists. To the extent that uniformity in the applicable laws does not exist, those managing security must be careful to take into account the nonuniform components and design their systems and operations to meet the variations in law.

19.2.1.1   The United States.   In the United States, both state and federal laws provide a source of uniformity. Generally, state laws are uniform through voluntary efforts among the states to harmonize their laws toward certain uniform standards. Federal law works to establish a single standard applicable to all of commerce.

19.2.1.1.1   The Uniform Commercial Code.   Electronic commercial practices challenge a basic architecture of existing commercial law. Until the final years of the twentieth century, modern commercial law was remarkably local in its focus and its applicability. The communications infrastructure had not yet stimulated significant reform in the legal architecture. Faced with transactions that crossed borders of states, provinces, and nations, the parties to commercial agreements would routinely include in their contracts choices of the law that would govern the transactions, and the jurisdiction in which their disputes, if any, would be resolved.

In the 1960s, the United States witnessed a remarkable revolution as the state governments collaborated in the formulation of a uniform commercial code (UCC). The UCC governs the core transactions of commerce—notably sales, checks, negotiable instruments, warehouse receipts, bills of lading, securities, and security agreements. The UCC served to simplify, clarify, and modernize the law governing commercial transactions and, in doing so, sought to achieve uniformity in the law among the various states.[1]

The 50 states proceeded to adopt the UCC on a voluntary basis and, although numerous variations existed, substantial uniformity was accomplished. During the past three decades of the twentieth century, significant revisions were made to certain essential articles of the UCC, and new articles were added to govern leases and fund transfers. These revisions and additions included, to a significant degree, provisions that would allow for the transactions governed by the UCC to be negotiated and concluded by electronic means.

In many respects, the UCC continues to be a viable and valued body of law for commercial transactions. Although the states were often slow to modernize their laws to the initial version of the UCC, later revisions—particularly those affecting electronic commercial practices—have been adopted by the states more quickly and with fewer nonuniform variations. The UCC articles governing letters of credit, funds transfers, and secured transactions—each of which is strongly focused on electronic commercial practices—are now mainly uniform among the states.

In marked contrast to the ongoing reforms of the UCC, however, the fundamental article (Article 2–Sales) has remained largely unchanged since its creation in the early 1960s. Among its provisions is § 2-201, the "Statute of Frauds." This section sets forth the prevailing law in the United States: "a contract for the sale of goods for the price of $500 or more is not enforceable . . . unless there is *some writing* sufficient to indicate that a contract for sale has been made between the parties and *signed* by the party against whom enforcement is sought" (emphasis added). As a result, absent special agreement among the parties to do business electronically, many normal electronic purchasing practices could be challenged as unenforceable.

Efforts to modernize Article 2–Sales of the UCC have been in progress for nearly 10 years. Those efforts have not succeeded, in part because of the struggles among vested interests to retain certain provisions of the Article unchanged, including the Statute of Frauds. But the failure to achieve reform of Article 2–Sales has not suppressed the use of electronic commercial practices for sales transactions. Instead, commercial parties have relied on an important provision of the UCC that permits parties, with few exceptions, to mutually agree to variations in the applicability of the UCC.[2]

As a result, commercial parties have routinely negotiated and executed commercial agreements under which they mutually agree to accept electronic messages as the signed writings otherwise required by the UCC. These contracts, often referred to as interchange agreements or trading partner agreements, take many forms—they can be bilateral agreements, incorporated into Web site terms and conditions, established as the rules of a trade association, or stated as part of a buyer (or supplier) master agreement.[3]

Indeed, the use of commercial agreements to overcome legal obstacles to e-commerce is an important factor to those managing computer security. The commercial agreement can serve as an effective venue in which to obtain the commitment of trading partners to the implementation of mutually beneficial security controls, together with rules regarding the certainty to be given to particular communications. This requires collaboration among the legal, technical, and business units of a company, but the resulting electronic records have significantly greater value to all concerned. As discussed in later sections of this chapter, the emerging legal infrastructure for e-commerce continues to emphasize the importance of the commercial agreement as a supplement to the statutory rules.

19.2.1.1.2 Electronic Signatures: State Law.   Concurrently with the revisions of the UCC during the 1990s, state legislatures enacted laws to eliminate the inhibiting effect of other laws that mandated the use of tangible writings or manual signatures on a large variety of commercial and other legal documents. These states struggled to enact laws that facilitated commerce under immense lobbying pressure from vendors of particular technologies, specific industries that actually wished to retain paper documents, and consumer protection groups afraid that the adoption of electronic commercial practices would endanger the protections provided by required written disclosures and would isolate large segments of the public with limited or no access to computers.

Electronic signature laws in the various states take many forms. There is no uniformity in their provisions, although a few general structures predominate:

- *Technology neutral laws*—these laws enable electronic signatures without specifying a particular technology to be used.

- *Digital signature laws*—these laws specifically favor and validate the use of public key infrastructure (PKI)-based digital certificates as the required element for any electronic signature to be given legal effect.

- *Hybrid laws*—these laws endorse the use of electronic signatures on a neutral basis, but provide favorable presumptions when digital signature technologies are used.

These laws also addressed related legal issues regarding electronic records: What constitutes an "original"? What types of records cannot be produced in electronic form (based on public policy considerations, e.g., wills and trusts)? What types of notices or agreements must be accomplished to give legal effect to the electronic signatures or records? However, taken as a whole, the electronic signature laws did not achieve uniformity; to the contrary, the enacted legislation was quite nonuniform. For businesses within the United States, as well as international trading partners, the resulting mix handicapped companies wishing to adopt standardized business practices, and often deterred companies from proceeding with technologically feasible solutions.

19.2.1.1.3   Uniform Electronic Transactions Act.   The nonuniform nature of the electronic signature laws of the states motivated one of the sponsors of the UCC—the National Conference of Commissioners on Uniform State Laws (NCCUSL)—to prepare the Uniform Electronic Transactions Act (UETA). The text of the UETA was finalized in 1999. The UETA serves to establish the functional equivalency between records and signatures that are either in electronic or paper form:

- Between parties that agree to conduct transactions by electronic means, records and signatures cannot be denied legal effect or validity solely on the ground that they are in electronic form.

- If a law requires a record to be in writing or requires a signature, that requirement is satisfied by an electronic record or electronic signature.

For the purposes of the UETA, "agreement" may be determined from the surrounding circumstances, including the parties' conduct. No formal consent, contract, or explicit agreement is required; however, it is helpful to have such an agreement in place.[4] The UETA has broad applicability—it applies to both consumer and commercial transactions, as well as transactions with governments, to the extent of an agreement to conduct electronic transactions. Accordingly, if a transaction is governed by the law of a state that has enacted the UETA, generally the parties can have confidence that the transaction can be documented by electronic means, provided the necessary agreement is in place.

As of July 2001, 37 states in the United States had enacted the UETA. Generally, its enactment has been uniform, but some states have adopted exceptions or limitations to its applicability. The existence of these exceptions provokes a sense of nonuniformity that is comparable with that arising in connection with the electronic signature laws. Indeed, one of the biggest sources of confusion is determining the manner in which the UETA, if enacted, reconciles with earlier electronic signature laws in those states that had enacted them.

The UETA is important to those implementing electronic commerce solutions because of the implications of the UETA as it relates to several corollary legal principles, many of which are influenced by the manner in which security controls are introduced into the transaction processes.

Legal rules requiring that certain writings be provided, sent, or delivered to a person can be satisfied by an electronic record if the record is "capable of retention by the recipient at the time of receipt." Thus, a recipient must be able to store or print the electronic record.

Any technology that a sender uses to inhibit the ability of a recipient to store or print the transmitted electronic record disqualifies the ability of the sender to enforce the electronic record against the recipient.

An electronic record is sent only when:

- It is addressed or otherwise properly directed to a system the recipient has designated or used for receiving electronic records and from which the recipient can retrieve the electronic record;
- The record is in a form capable of being processed by the receiving system; and
- The record enters a system outside the control of the sender.[5]

An electronic record is received only when it meets corollary rules for receipt. When the law requires a record be retained, that law is satisfied by an electronic record that:

- Accurately reflects the information set forth in the record after it was generated in its final form as an electronic record or otherwise; and
- remains accessible for later reference. Ancillary information, such as computer codes, headers and communication data, need not be retained.[6]

As the preceding rules indicate, the precise methods by which electronic signatures are implemented, and how the electronic records are transmitted and stored, are vital to assuring the legal adequacy of the resulting records. E-commerce solutions that are installed and do not reflect coordination of the legal, business, and technology efforts are at substantial risk for producing legally insufficient electronic records.

The UETA is also distinguished by the exclusions that are made from the scope of its provisions. As drafted, the Act is limited to apply only to those provisions of the UCC within Article 2–Sales and Article 2A–Leases; all other articles are excluded from the effects of the UETA. This has the result of overcoming the Statute of Frauds; however, the scope language is optional, and many states have elected not to extend the UETA to apply to any provisions of the UCC. As a result, state-by-state determinations are required to verify whether the UETA has any impact upon the UCC.

19.2.1.1.4 E-Sign: Federal Intervention.   Commercial pressure to achieve legal uniformity in the rules governing electronic records and electronic signatures was also focused at the federal level. Several industries with national operations were frustrated in their ability to implement automated processes on a consistent basis across widely varying state laws. In October 2000, the Electronic Signatures in Global and National Commerce Act became effective (commonly referred to as "E-Sign"). If a state has *not* enacted the UETA in the official form, as it was approved by the NCCUSL, then generally E-Sign pre-empts any state law that conflicts with its provisions. States have a limited ability to modify, limit, or supersede E-Sign's effect upon state laws.

E-Sign is comparable with the UETA in many respects. For commercial transactions, the federal and uniform state laws function similarly. Indeed, E-Sign also excludes the UCC from its scope to the same extent as the UETA. Under each law, the use of electronic signatures and records must be voluntary; however, E-Sign does not contain any explicit requirement for an agreement to be in place to do so. E-Sign introduces some important additional requirements with regard to the use of electronic signatures with consumers: an informed, affirmative consent must be obtained from consumers before electronic records can be used.[7]

Like the UETA, E-Sign is technology neutral. However, E-Sign acknowledges that state and federal regulators must make some selections in order to implement valid electronic records—agencies could not possibly support all possible technologies. Accordingly, agencies may establish their own standards and formats for electronic filings, including performance standards, provided appropriate findings are made of "important governmental objectives" that are advanced by such specifications.

19.2.1.2   *International Environment.* The need for uniformity in legal standards for e-commerce solutions is a global requirement. For multinational businesses, or those conducting transactions across multiple jurisdictions, as well as the vendors providing the solutions, uniform legal rules facilitate achieving maximum efficiency and cost-benefit results. As a result, the international legal community also has sponsored the development of uniform statutory solutions.

19.2.1.2.1   United Nations Model Law on Electronic Commerce.   In 1996, the United Nations Commission on International Trade Law (UNCITRAL) finalized the text of the Model Law on Electronic Commerce.[8] The Model Law was approved by the UN General Assembly prior to the final version of the UETA or the enactment of E-Sign; however, experts have strong differences of opinion as to the degree to which the U.S. legal solutions emulated the legal principles set forth in the UN Model Law. For other nations, the UN Model Law has been an indispensable resource; however, its success in producing uniform statutory enactments has been inconsistent. Many nations have proceeded to enact laws that vary from the language of the UN Model. As a result, those implementing e-commerce solutions must proceed carefully to assure that the solution will produce electronic records and electronic signatures that will be given legal validity in the nations in which the transactions are occurring.

The UN Model Law is highlighted by the following rules and characteristics, which are analogous in many respects to the principles of the UETA and E-Sign:

- The Model Law applies to a wide range of electronic "data messages" and specifically includes electronic mail, electronic data interchange (EDI), telex, and telecopies (facsimiles).

- Information in a data message is not to be denied legal validity or enforceability solely because it is in the form of a data message.

Legal requirements for signatures can be satisfied in relation to a data message where:

- A method is used to identify the sender and to indicate that person's approval of the information contained in the data message; and
- That method is as reliable as was appropriate for the purpose for which the data message was generated or communicated, in light of all the circumstances, including any relevant agreement.

Where the law requires information to be presented or retained in its original form, that requirement is met by a data message if:

- There exists a reliable assurance as to the integrity of the information from the time when it was first generated in its final form, as a data message or otherwise; and
- Where it is required that information be presented, that information is capable of being displayed to the person to whom it is to be presented.

The Model Law distinguishes itself from the U.S. laws because of the degree to which the legal rules are made conditional on the surrounding circumstances. The concepts of "as reliable as was appropriate for the purpose" and "a reliable assurance" introduce the opportunity for security methods used in a particular application to be second guessed and possibly invalidated if a judicial review determines that insufficient care was taken with the implementation.

The Model Law also addresses another dimension of e-commerce solutions: When will a record be attributed to the sender? Here, the security protocols used become particularly important, because the Model Law allows receivers to rely on certain messages even if, in fact, they were not sent by the identified sender. Under the Model Law, a data message is attributed to the sender if:

- The sender sent the data message itself.
- The originator had the authority to send the data message on behalf of the sender.
- An information system programmed by, or on behalf of, the sender transmitted the message.

In addition, a receiving party can rely upon a data message attributed to the sender if:

- The receiving party properly used a procedure previously agreed to by the sender for ascertaining the originator of the data message; and
- The receiving party had no reason to doubt the source of the data message and had not otherwise been advised by the sender that a message was not authentic.

Similarly, the Model Law defines the legal effect of electronic acknowledgments. Many e-commerce solutions use technology in order for the parties to assure efficiently that the content of transmitted messages has not been altered during transit. Acknowledgments can either verify the type of message received or can more precisely confirm the accuracy of the data received. Under the Model Law, if the parties have agreed on a process for acknowledgment, transmitted messages cannot be relied on unless the required acknowledgment has been sent.[9]

The Model Law also establishes rules for ascertaining the time at which data messages are determined to be sent and received. Data messages are sent at the time they enter an information system outside the control of the originator; however, when they are received depends on the agreement of the parties as to the applicable procedures. If an information system has been designated by the receiver, then the data message is deemed to be received at the time the message enters that system; if the message is sent to a different system, then the message is deemed received at the time the receiver retrieves the message (if at all). If no system is designated, receipt occurs when the message enters any system of the addressee.[10]

In 2001, UNCITRAL also finalized a Model Law on Electronic Signatures.[11] The Model Signature Law goes beyond the scope of the Model Law and establishes legal principles for determining the reliability of electronic signatures. The Model Signature Law provides that a signature requirement is met when an electronic signature is used that is "as reliable as appropriate for the purpose for which the data communication was generated or communicated, in the light of all of the circumstances, including any relevant agreement." Of course, in the absence of an explicit agreement, parties are left uncertain under this test whether any particular solution will be appropriate. Accordingly, the Model Signature Law establishes a statutory presumption that an electronic signature will be deemed to be reliable if it meets the following criteria:

- The signature creation data are, within the context in which they are used, linked to the signatory and no other person;
- The signature creation data were, at the time of signing, under the control of the signatory and no other person;
- Any alteration to the electronic signature, made after the time of signing, is detectable; and
- Where the integrity of the content is legally important, any alteration to that content after the time of signing is detectable.

The Model Signature Law, by providing this statutory presumption, endorses the use of digital certificate-based electronic signatures. Because the Model Signature Law follows the adoption of the European Directive (see subsection 19.2.1.2.2), it is apparent that the Model Signature Law was adopted in a manner that gives support to the European approach (as opposed to the technology-neutral approach of the UETA and E-Sign).

19.2.1.2.2 European Directive.   In 1999, the Parliament of the European Communities adopted Directive 1999/93/EC establishing a legal framework for electronic signatures within the European Communities.[12] The Directive is distinguished from the Model Law and E-Sign by its adoption of a hybrid regulation that validates electronic signatures but also enables, and gives certain preferences to, "advanced electronic signatures" and the certification providers that are required for such purposes. This result, which requires the enactment of enabling national legislation by each of the member states who belong to the European Commission, is in stark contrast to the U.S. solutions.

Advanced electronic signatures are those electronic signatures with the following features:

- Uniquely linked to the signatory;
- Capable of identifying the signatory;
- Created using means that the signatory can maintain under its sole control; and
- Linked to the data to which it relates in such a manner that any subsequent change of the data is detectable.

That definition is, on its face, technology neutral; however, under the Directive, legal advantage is only given to "advanced electronic signatures which are based on a qualified certificate and created using a secure-signature-creation device" (i.e., a PKI solution). Member states must ensure, for those types of signatures, that:

- The signatures satisfy the legal requirements in relation to electronic data in the same manner that a manual signature satisfies applicable requirements for paper-based data; and

- The signatures are admissible as evidence in legal proceedings.

Much of the remainder of the Directive provides the legal architecture in which certificate providers can conduct business in support of commercial demand for those certificates.

The Directive's departure from the technology-neutral approach adopted by the UETA and E-Sign challenges commercial businesses wishing to implement electronic signatures. Clearly, the Directive provides superior legal certainty for "advanced electronic signatures"; however, those familiar with solutions more affordable than digital certificates believe that the same legal certainty can be achieved by combining the technology functionality with the legal agreement of the parties set forth in appropriate commercial agreements.

The Directive does not address several other legally significant topics considered by E-Sign, the UETA, and the UN Model Law—rules for "original" status, time of sending and receipt, and contract formation are not included. Nor does the European Directive make any conspicuous distinction with regard to consumer-based transactions.

19.2.1.2.3   Other Initiatives.   The legal facilitation of electronic commercial practices continues to be a priority of governments. Many nations, motivated by the initial rapid pace at which U.S. state governments enacted electronic signature laws, enacted legislation that also reflected different structural approaches. The Model Law has been a useful resource to many nations,[13] whereas others have proceeded to develop independent statutes that tend to align toward either the European Directive or E-Sign. Many experts believe that the battle for certain technologies to emerge as the "standard" for signatures will continue for some time, influenced by commercial demand and often advanced—or hindered—by legislative preferences. The challenge for those implementing related technologies is to achieve the confidence that the solution produces the intended results—legally valid and effective electronic records and signatures. The solution requires the management of suitable and appropriate commercial contracts and agreements, as well as the installation and use of technologies appropriate to the business needs.

19.2.2   Contract Infrastructure of E-Commerce.   This section discusses the use of contracts as part of the portfolio of tools with which those managing computer security achieve their control objectives. It reviews the significance of contracts and the architecture of agreements that are part of doing business through e-commerce, and summarizes the substantive provisions that are often included from a computer security management perspective in the applicable agreements.

19.2.2.1   Significance of Contracts.   As indicated by the statutes adopted to facilitate e-commerce, the contract or agreement between commercial parties implementing electronic commercial practices can be a vital tool for assuring that electronic records are produced that are legally valid and enforceable. Indeed, despite all the automation that is part of e-commerce, the many different commercial actors involved in the development and operation of electronic services require a significant number of varied commercial agreements. For businesses that operate on the Internet, for example, Exhibit 19.1 presents a typical architecture of the contracts required to establish and operate an online marketplace that services multiple commercial parties.

Achieving suitable electronic records, therefore, hinges significantly on the mutual agreements reached among the commercial parties regarding the structure, format, communication methods, security protocols, and record retention practices to be used by the various parties. Based on the methods used, key legal aspects of the electronic records can be assured. That objective is important; if the processes used leave the records vulnerable to legal challenge, the intended cost-benefit results are significantly put at risk.

Strategic planning of these various requirements across the different kinds of contracts used for e-commerce is necessary. For each agreement, parties must evaluate the variables on which there must be accord between them in order for the messages to be effectively communicated. In many instances, the requirements are mutual; in other instances, parties must require certain conduct that falls solely on one party or another in order to produce the expected results. The goal is to produce trusted communications that are also legally adequate when measured against the applicable law.

Section 3 of this chapter presents a methodology for developing information security for e-commerce solutions and selecting the appropriate security services that are

Exhibit 19.1   E-Commerce Retail System Contract Infrastructure Timeline

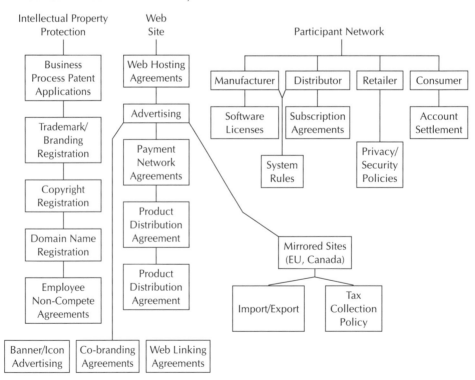

© 1999 Kirkpatrick & Lockhart LLP

needed. The remainder of section 2 outlines the various aspects of those security services that are incorporated into the requirements of the various related commercial agreements. It is not possible to outline which of these requirements are to be addressed in which agreement. The objective is to assure that each commercial party that creates or has custody of relevant records adopts the necessary security procedures that allow the record to have its intended legal effect. The contract becomes the most effective tool for achieving that objective.

19.2.2.2 Common Safeguards.

To facilitate trusted, legally effective electronic transactions, commercial agreements often require the parties to agree to various safeguards and security procedures that serve as the building blocks toward trustworthy communications. The following is a representative list of the topics that can be addressed. In many cases, the agreements reference more complete technical specifications that are presented in a separate document; however, the result is the same. The parties commit to conduct their electronic communications pursuant to the defined standards.

19.2.2.2.1 Data Standards. Based on the method of communication, the standards around which the data will be structured are defined. These standards may include both the message structures (e.g., EDI formats, such as ANSI x.12, or UN/EDIFACT, or more contemporary standards such as BXML) and the methods of communication to be used (e.g., value-added networks, Internet, or business-to-business exchanges).

19.2.2.2.2 Information Certainty. As contemplated by the various e-commerce laws, the parties may establish by agreement when their electronic communications are to be given effect. Indeed, various commercial laws often depend on whether messages have been sent or received, and consequences can hinge on the time at which these events occur. Accordingly, contracts can define:

- The information systems used by the parties to send and receive communications
- The rules for determining whether a message has been sent (e.g., the transmission logs of a value-added network)
- The rules for determining whether a message has been received
- The rules for measuring the time at which certain messages are sent or received

19.2.2.2.3 Security. The detail with which commercial agreements define security requirements among commercial parties varies significantly. One factor to consider, of course, is whether the contracts should discuss topics on which confidentiality is vital to preserve. As a result, many contracts will commit parties to use security procedures that are separately defined and exchanged in a manner that maximizes their confidentiality.

As enterprises become more interdependent on their trading partners, the justification increases for requiring greater detail and more specific compliance with security procedures. The security requirements can be defined for virtually every layer of the information architecture, and can address:

- Physical facility security
- System access
- Authentication and identification

- Network security and controls
- Record retention and access control

As illustrated by the review of applicable e-commerce laws, the use of electronic signatures, particularly those involving digital certificates, involves mandating particular security procedures and processes. The rules for the use of digital certificates for electronic signatures can become quite complex. The rules are often set forth in certification practice statements and similar materials. These materials are often referenced in the commercial agreements and can be substantially negotiated in order to achieve a suitable balance between their requirements and the allocations of risk associated with noncompliance.

Security should be included as a provision in the contract. One common approach is to make the contract stipulate that security controls are required to be at least compliant or exceed the *customer's* policies and processes. If the vendor's security policies and processes are superior to the client's, then little action is required. However, when the reverse is true, where the client's policies and processes are superior to the vendor's, action is required by the vendor to improve its security practices. Banks and other financial institutions are required to assure compliance via periodic reviews. This is especially true when the vendor has access to or processes customer information, and according to the provisions of the Gramm-Leach-Bliley Act (GLB) for nonpublic customer information. For more information about the GLB, see Chapter 52.

If the contracting company does not have policies or documented procedures, the process becomes more complicated. The contract should specify information security practices that the vendor company must heed. The suggested "best practices" that should be considered in the contract include the following:

- Effective access management—user IDs and passwords for all, with periodic password changes, no sharing, and acceptable configuration (including numbers and symbols and avoiding common words or names).
- Track users and purge those that no longer require access.
- The information technology department acts to resolve known vulnerabilities, including viruses; controls are in place to detect and prevent their introduction and distribution.
- Effective architecture—the perimeter is secured by including firewalls, intrusion detection, back-up, and segmented networks, while connected to the contractor's site.
- Roles and responsibilities for information security are defined, documented, and communicated, with responsible individuals identified. People are generally aware of good information protection practices, including security event recognition, escalation, and resolution.
- Management supports the information security department with adequate staffing, budgets, and training. The information security department participates in infrastructure, application, and technology decisions.
- Hardened servers—deny services that are not required, and maintain security patches as suggested by manufacturers.
- Log and monitor—log user access, and periodically monitor for anomalies and retain for accountability.

The impact of nonperformance needs to be discussed in the contract. Required security practices need to be stipulated as being implemented and verified prior to the agreement being finalized. This will optimize the leverage created by the agreement. Once the contract is signed, it will be difficult to monitor compliance and (in a worst-case scenario) to switch vendors.

19.2.2.2.4   Audit and Access.   The efficiency of e-commerce requires commercial parties to be able to assure that their respective records are in alignment—the interdependent nature of many commercial transactions faces immediate disruption if the message content is not accurate. Accordingly, commercial contracts often require the parties to cooperate in providing to each other the opportunity to access their information systems and periodically audit the compliance with the security controls and other procedures used.

The requirement for such audits has become particularly conspicuous when the data records relate to personal information that is otherwise subject to privacy laws. Under those laws, the transfers of personal information routinely must occur pursuant to commercial agreements that permit verification procedures to be used for assuring the integrity of the record and the efficacy of security controls used to protect the related personal information from alteration, loss, or improper disclosure.[14]

19.2.2.2.5   Recourse.   Establishing requirements has little value unless the agreements also specify the remedies that may be available when a party fails to comply with those requirements. The nature of the recourse can include:

- Economic credits, particularly if the breach results in measurable losses,
- Reimbursement of legal expenses or other costs paid to third parties,
- Sanctions against further misconduct, and
- Termination of the relationship

Regardless of the recourse selected, the agreement should define the manner in which the recourse is to be pursued and resolved. Many e-commerce agreements have rejected reliance on judicial venues; instead, alternative dispute resolution techniques are adopted. These techniques can involve mediation, arbitration, or other nonjudicial approaches, which tend to invite faster resolution of the situation and promote the continued commercial relationship of the parties.

19.2.2.3   Legal Management of Risks.   The commercial agreement also makes available certain tools that can be used for allocating the risks associated with e-commerce. Notwithstanding the good faith efforts of businesses, various factors can result in losses attributed to the inadequacy of the electronic records. Records can be altered, lost, inadequately preserved, or otherwise compromised in a manner that produces loss. What legal tools are available to allocate the losses that relate to such risks?

19.2.2.3.1   Service Level Standards.   Commercial agreements can establish service level standards associated with the various technical requirements. By establishing these standards, performance can be measured against defined criteria and, if performance falls below the applicable standards, economic charges can be assessed accurately and precisely. This approach is particularly useful for third parties that serve as intermediaries in e-commerce; their efficiency is essential to achieving trustworthy e-commerce, and service level standards, if tied to objective measurements of their services, can be particularly effective in motivating acceptable performance.

19.2.2.3.2 Exception Management.   Errors or miscommunications will occur. When they do, the precision with which the parties have defined the next steps to be taken can be vital to mitigating potential losses and restoring the confidence of the parties in the e-commerce solutions used. Many companies overlook this important feature that legal agreements can provide. Specifically, parties should be encouraged to develop, and agree to implement, procedures for addressing exceptional situations. E-commerce is not intended to be a trap for the unwary; if the selected standards and procedures do experience an interruption, parties should be mutually committed to appropriate correction processes. These may include:

- Mutual notices of errors or miscommunications.
- Notices to intermediaries and other dependent third parties.
- Retransmittal of suspect messages or data.
- Escalation procedures for persistent problems.

19.2.2.3.3 Force Majeure.   Many commercial agreements contain force majeure ("acts of God") clauses. These provisions relieve parties of their duties in circumstances in which events outside their control interfere with their abilities to perform. Historically, these clauses have been overlooked; however, for e-commerce, careful attention to their provisions is appropriate. Those attentive to security concerns will focus on whether storms, floods, or similar circumstances for which disaster recovery arrangements are in place should excuse substandard performance (i.e., lower than specified in the contract). In addition, many clauses will indicate that nonperformance by suppliers or telecommunication carriers provides a basis for excusing performance by the primary party. However, often the selection of such related service providers is part of the package upon which parties rely; standard legal terms should be carefully reviewed to determine whether the risks associated with poor choices should be excused.

19.3 TECHNICAL DEFENSES

19.3.1 E-Commerce Security Services: A Basic Methodology.   In the complex world of e-commerce security, best practices are constantly evolving and new protocols and products are announced regularly. Before the Internet explosion, most companies rarely shared their data and their proprietary applications with any external entities, and information security was not a priority with many business and development staffs. Now, companies taking advantage of e-commerce need sound application security architectures. Effective information security has become a business issue. This chapter provides a flexible framework for building secure e-commerce applications, and it provides assistance in identifying the appropriate and required security services. The theoretical examples shown are included to facilitate the reader's understanding of the framework in a business-to-customer (B-to-C) and business-to-business (B-to-B) environment.

The best place to start when discussing e-commerce security is to develop a framework that:

- Defines information security concerns specific to the application

- Defines the security services needed to address the security concerns
- Selects security services based on a cost-benefit analysis, and risk versus reward issues

This three-step approach is recommended to define the security services selection and decision-making processes.

19.3.1.1 Step 1: Define Information Security Concerns Specific to the Application.
The first step is to define or develop the application architecture and the data classification involved in each transaction. This step considers how the application will function. As a general rule, if security issues are defined in terms of the impact on the business, it will be easier to discuss with management and easier to define security requirements.

The recommended approach is to develop a transactional follow-the-flow diagram that tracks transactions and data types through the various servers and networks. This should be a functional and logical view of how the application is going to work—that is, how transactions will occur, what systems will participate in the transaction management, and where these systems will support the business objectives and the organization's product value chain. Data sources and data interfaces need to be identified, and the information processed needs to be classified. In this way a complete transactional flow can be represented. Common tiered architecture points will include:

Clients—These may be PCs, thin clients (devices that use shared applications from a server and have small amounts of memory), personal digital assistants (PDAs), and wireless application protocol (WAP) protocol telephones.

Servers—These may include World Wide Web, application, database, and middleware processors, as well as back-end servers and legacy systems.

Network devices—Switches, routers, firewalls, modems, and Internet service providers.

Network spaces—Network demilitarized zones (DMZs), intranets, extranets, and external hosting sites.

It is important at this step of the process to identify the criticality of the application to the business and the overriding security concerns: transactional confidentiality, transactional integrity, or transactional availability. Defining these security issues will help justify the security services selected to protect the system. The more completely the architecture can be described, the more thoroughly the information can be protected via security services.

19.3.1.2 Step 2: Develop Security Service Options.
The third step considers the security services alternatives for each architecture component and the data involved in each transaction. Each architectural component and data point should be analyzed and possible security services defined for each. Cost and feasibility should not be considered to any great degree at this stage. The objective is to form a complete list of security service options with all alternatives considered. The process should be comparable with, or use the same techniques as, brainstorming. All ideas, even if impractical or far-fetched, should be included. Decisions should not be made during this step; that process is reserved for Step 3.

Information security is an organization that provides services to an enterprise. The services provided by information security organizations vary from company to company. Several factors will determine the required services, but the most significant considerations include:

- Industry factors
- The company's risk appetite
- Maturity of the security function
- Organizational approach (centralized or decentralized)
- Impact of past security incidents
- Internal organizational factors
- Political factors
- Regulatory factors
- Perceived strategic value of information security

Several factors contribute to the services that information security organizations provide. Security services are defined as safeguards and control measures to protect the confidentiality, integrity, and accountability of information and computing resources. Security services that are required to secure e-commerce transactions need to be based on the business requirements, and on the willingness to assume or reduce the risk of the information being processed. Information security professionals can be subject-matter experts but are rarely equipped to make the business decisions required to select the necessary services. Twelve security services that are critical for successful e-commerce security have been identified:

1. *Policy and procedures* are a security service that defines the amount of information security that the organization requires, and how it will be implemented. Effective policy and procedures will dovetail with system strategy, development, implementation, and operation. Each organization will have different policies and procedures; best practice dictates that organizations have policies and procedures at some level based on the risk the organization is willing to take with its information. At a minimum, organizations should have a high-level policy that dictates the proper use of information assets and the ramifications of misuse. Chapters 28, 31, 33, and 35 provide details of security policy development, content, and implementation.

2. *Confidentiality and encryption* are a security service that secures data while they are stored or in transit from one machine to another. A number of encryption schemes and products exist; each organization needs to identify those products that best integrate with the application being deployed.

3. *Authentication and identification* are a security service that differentiates users and verifies that they are who they claim to be. Typically, passwords are used, but stronger methods include tokens, smart cards, and biometrics. These stronger methods verify what you have (e.g., token) or who you are (e.g., biometrics), not just what you know (password). Two-factor authentication combines two of these three methods and is referred to as strong authentication. Chapter 16 reviews these issues.

4. *Authorization* determines what access privileges a user requires within the system. Access includes data, operating system, transactional functions and processes. Access should be approved by management who own or understand the system before access is granted. For example, authorized users can access only the information they require for their jobs.

5. *Authenticity* is a security service that validates a transaction and binds the transaction to a single accountable person or entity. Also called nonrepudiation, authenticity ensures that a person cannot dispute the initiation of a transaction. This is especially useful for contract and legal purposes.

6. *Monitoring and audit* provide an electronic trail for a historical record of the transaction. Audit logs consist of operating system logs, application transaction logs, database logs, and network traffic logs. Monitoring these logs for unauthorized events is considered a best practice. Chapters 38 and 39 review logging in detail.

7. *Access controls and intrusion detection* are technical, physical, and administrative services that prevent unauthorized access to hardware, software, or information. Data are protected from alteration, theft, or destruction. Access controls are preventative—stopping unauthorized access from occurring. Intrusion detection catches unauthorized access after it has occurred, so that damage can be minimized and access cut off. These controls are especially necessary when confidential or critical information is being processed. Chapters 17 and 37 examine these topics in detail.

8. *Trusted communication* is a security service that assures that communication is secure. In most instances involving the Internet, this means that the communication will be encrypted. In the past, communication was trusted because it was contained within an organization's perimeter. Communication is currently ubiquitous and can come from almost anywhere, including extranets and the Internet.

9. *Anti-virus* is a security service that prevents, detects, and cleans viruses, Trojan horse programs, and other malware. Chapters 9, 10, and 24 examine these issues.

10. *System integrity controls* are security services that help to assure that the system has not been altered or tampered with by unauthorized access.

11. *Data retention and disposal* is a security service that keeps required information archived or deletes data when they are no longer required. Availability of retained data is critical when an emergency exists such as a systems outage especially in light of the terrorist activities from September 11, 2001. Chapter 41 reviews backup policies.

12. *Data classification* is a security service that identifies sensitivity and confidentiality of information, guides for information labeling, and protection during the information's life.

Once an e-commerce application has been identified, the team must identify the security issues with that specific application and identify the necessary security services. Not all of the services will be relevant, but using a complete list and excluding those that are not required is an excellent starting point that will assure a comprehensive assessment of requirements and security built into the system's development. In fact, management can reconcile the services accepted with their expectations of risk acceptance.

19.3.1.3 *Step 3: Select Security Service Options Based on Requirements.* The third step uses classical cost-benefit and risk management analysis techniques to make a final selection of security service options. However, we recommend that all options identified in step 3 be distributed along a continuum, such as shown in Exhibit 19.2, so that they can be viewed together and compared.

Exhibit 19.2   Format for Listing Security Services Options

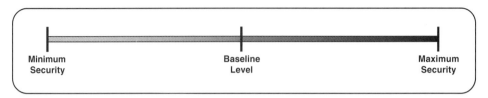

Gauging and comparing the level of security for each security service and the data within the transaction will facilitate the decision process. Feasible alternatives can then be identified and the "best" solution selected based on the requirements. The most significant element to consider is the relative reduction in risk of each option compared with the other alternatives. The cost-benefit analysis is based on the risk versus reward issues. The effectiveness information is very useful in a cost-benefit model.

Four additional concepts drive the security service option selection:

- Implementation risk or feasibility
- Cost to implement and support
- Effectiveness in increasing control, thereby reducing risk
- Data classification

Implementation risk considers the feasibility of implementing the security service option. Some security systems are difficult to implement due to factors such as product maturity, scalability, complexity, and supportability. Other factors to consider include skills available, legal issues, integration required, capabilities, prior experience, and limitations of the technology.

Cost to implement and support measures hardware and software implementation, support, and administration costs. Consideration of administration issues is especially critical because support of the security service is vital to its success.

Effectiveness measures the reduction of risk proposed by a security service option once it is in production. Risk can be defined as the impact and likelihood of a negative event occurring after mitigating strategies have been implemented. An example of a negative event is the theft of credit card numbers from a business's database. Such event causes not only possible losses to consumers, but also negative public relations that may impact future business. Effective security service options reduce the risk for a negative event occurring.

Data classification measures the sensitivity and confidentiality of the information being processed. Data require being classified and protected, regardless of storage format, throughout their life (creation through destruction) from misuse, disclosure, theft, or destruction. Usually the originator of the information is considered to be the owner of the information and is responsible for classification, identification, and labeling. The more sensitive and confidential the information, the more information security measures will be required to safeguard and protect it.

19.3.2   Using the Security Services Framework.   The next two sections are examples to demonstrate the power of the security services methodology. The first example is a B-to-C model. The business could be any direct-selling application. The second example is a B-to-B model. Both businesses are taking advantage of the Internet to improve their product value chain. The examples are a short demonstration of the security services methodology, and neither are complete nor representative of any particular application or business.

19.3.2.1   Business-to-Customer Security Services.   The first example is a B-to-C case. The company desires to contact customers directly through the Internet and allow them to enter their information into the application. The following assumptions are made to prepare this B-to-C system example:

1. Internet-facing business
2. Major transactions supported
3. External customer-based system, specifically excluding support, administration, and operations
4. Business critical application
5. Data classification is highly sensitive
6. Three-tiered architecture
7. Untrusted clients, because anyone on the Internet can be a customer

Exhibit 19.3 shows a high-level architecture of this example. There are five layers that need to be secured:

1. The *presentation layer* is the customer interface and is what the client sees or hears using the Web device. The client is the customer's untrusted PC. The security requirements at this level are minimal because the company will normally not dictate the security of the customer.

2. The *network layer* is the communication connection between the business and customer. The client, or customer, uses an Internet connection to access the B-to-C Web applications. The security requirements are minimal but sensitive, and confidential traffic will need to be encrypted.

3. The *middle layer* is the Web server that connects to the client's browser and can forward and receive information. The Web server supports the application by being an intermediary between the business and the customer. The Web server needs to be very secure. Theft, tampering, and fraudulent use of information need to be prevented. Denial of service and Web site defacement are also common risks that need to be prevented in the middle layer.

4. The *application layer* is where the information is processed. The application serves as an intermediary between the customer requests and the fulfillment systems internal to the business. In Exhibit 19.2, the application server and database server are the same server because both the application and database reside on the same server. This could reside with the Web server, but is shown separately for this example.

5. The *internal layer* is the business's legacy systems or databases that support customer servicing. Back-end servers house the supporting application, including order processing, accounts receivable, inventory, distribution, and other systems.

For each of these five levels, Exhibit 19.3 shows four security services:

1. Trusted communications
2. Authentication/identification

Exhibit 19.3   Trust Levels for B-to-C Security Services

Client

Presentation Layer

Trusted Communication	Authentication/ Identification	Audit	Access Control
• HTTP • HTTPS • Certificates • SSL Encryption • WAP • TLS	• None Required	• None Required	• None Required

Firewall

Firewall

Network Layer

Trusted Communication	Authentication/ Identification	Audit	Access Control
VPN	None Required	None Required	None Required

Web Server

Middle Layer

Trusted Communication	Authentication/ Identification	Audit	Access Control
• HTTP • HTTPS • SSL • SET • IOTP	• Application Password • PKI	• Transaction Logs • OS Logs	• OS • Application (RBAM)

Firewall *

Application Server

Application Layer

Trusted Communication	Authentication/ Identification	Audit	Access Control
• TCP/IP • IPSec	• App • OS • DB	• OS • APP • Database	• OS • DB Database (App Password)

Firewall *

Back-End Server

Internal Layer

Trusted Communication	Authentication/ Identification	Audit	Access Control
• TCP/IP • IPSec	• OS • Database	• OS • Database	• OS • Database

*Firewall should be between the web layer/application layer or the application/back-end layers depending on the company's architecture.

3. Audit

4. Access controls

19.3.2.1.1   Step 1: Define Information Security Concerns Specific to the Application.
Defining security issues will be particular to the system being implemented. To understand the risk of the system, the best starting place is with the business risk; then define risk at each element of the architecture.

Business Risk:

- The application needs high availability because customer will demand product at off-hours and on weekends.

- The Web pages need to be secure from tampering and cyber-vandalism because the business is concerned about customer confidence as a result of negative publicity.

- Customers must be satisfied with the level of service.

- The system will process customer credit card information and will be subject to the privacy regulations of the GLB.

Technology Concerns. Exhibit 19.4 shows the five architectural layers in this example that need to be secured:

- The *presentation layer* will not be secured or trusted. The communication between the client and the Web server will be encrypted.

- The *network layer* will need to filter traffic that is not required, prevent denial of service (DoS) attacks, and monitor for possible intrusions.

- The *middle layer* will need to prevent unauthorized access, be tamper proof, contain effective monitoring, and support efficient and effective processing.

- The *application layer* will need to prevent unauthorized access, support timely processing of transactions, provide effective audit trails, and process confidential information.

- The *internal layer* will need to prevent unauthorized access, especially through Internet connections, and to protect confidential information during transmission, processing, and storage.

19.3.2.1.2   Step 2: Develop Security Services Options.   The four security services reviewed in this example are the most critical in an e-commerce environment. Other services such as nonrepudiation and data classification are important but not included in order to simplify the example. Services elected are:

- Trusted communication

- Authentication and identification

- Monitoring and auditing

- Access control

Many security services options are available for the B-to-C case, with more products and protocols on the horizon. Exhibit 19.4 shows the B-to-C architecture on the left and candidate security services options on the right in five architectural layers for each of the services defined in step 1.

- *Presentation layer.* Several different options can be selected for trusted communication. Hypertext transfer protocol (HTTP) is the most common, with secure socket layer (SSL) certificates in a PKI, or digital signatures, being even less common, and WAP for wireless communications and transport security layer protocol (TLS) for encrypted Internet communications being the most rare. Because the client is untrusted, the client's authentication, audit, or access control methods cannot be relied upon.

- *Network layer.* Virtual private networks (VPNs) are considered best practice for secure network layer communication. Firewalls are effective devices for securing

Exhibit 19.4   B-to-C Security Architecture and Security Service Options

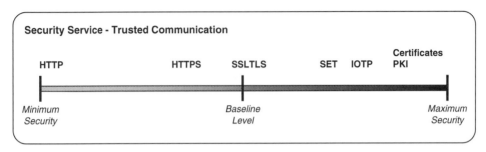

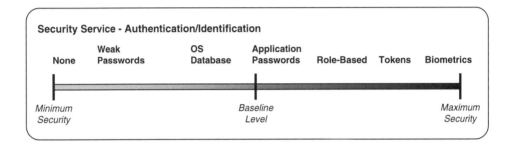

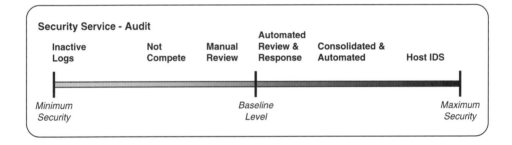

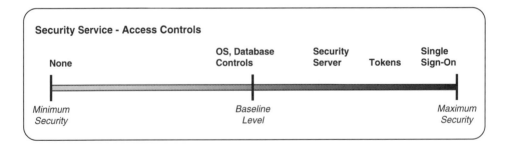

network communication. The client may have a personal firewall. If the client is in a large corporation, there is a significant likelihood that a firewall will intervene in communications. If the client is using a home or laptop computer, then a personal firewall may protect traffic. There will be a firewall on the B-to-C company side of the Internet. Chapter 20 reviews firewalls in detail.

- *Middle layer.* The Web server and the application server security requirements are significant. Unauthorized access to the Web server can result in Web site defacement by hackers who change the Web data. More importantly, access to the Web or application server can lead to theft, manipulation, or deletion of customer or proprietary data. Communication between the Web server and the client needs to be secure in e-commerce transactions. HTTP is the most common form of browser communication. Although Web transactions using HTTP are unsecured, over 33% of credit card transactions use HTTP.[15] SSL and HTTPS are the next most common secure protocols, but the encryption key length is critical: the larger the key, the more secure the transaction is from deciphering. Digital certificates in a PKI, and digital signatures, are not as common, but they are more effective forms of security. Another protocol that has achieved some acceptance in the banking industry is secure electronic transactions (SET). The SET protocol can be used to deliver secure, authenticated electronic payments, especially in the area of credit card processing. The Internet open trading protocol (IOTP) is gaining acceptance as a multipurpose trading/exchange engine. Chapters 21 and 22 provide details of protection for Internet-connected systems in general and Web sites in particular.

- *Application layer.* The application server provides the main processing for the Web server. This layer may include transaction processing and database applications. This layer needs to be secured to prevent erroneous or fraudulent processing. Depending on the sensitivity of the information processed, the data may need to be encrypted. Interception and the unauthorized manipulation of data are the greatest risks in the application layer.
- *Internal layer.* In Exhibit 19.4, the example shows how the internal layer is secured by a firewall protecting the external-facing system. This firewall helps the B-to-C company protect itself from Internet intrusions. Database and operating system passwords and access control measures are required.

The format of Exhibit 19.4 is a presentation tool that shows the spectrum of options for each security service. Management can decide which security capability is required and at what level. This format can be repeated to discuss security services at all levels and all systems, not just e-commerce–related systems.

19.3.2.1.3 Step 3: Select Security Service Options Based on Requirements. In step 3 the B-to-C company can analyze and select the security services that best meet its legal, business, and information security requirements. As described in Section 19.3.1.3, there are four stages required for this analysis:

- Implementation risk or feasibility
- Cost to implement and support
- Effectiveness in increasing control, thereby reducing risk
- Data classification

Implementation risk is a function of the organization's ability to effectively roll out the technology. In this example, we assume that implementation risk is low and resources are readily available to implement the technology.

Costs to implement and support are paramount to the decision-making process. Both costs need to be considered together. Unfortunately, the cost to support is difficult to quantify and easily overlooked. In this example, resources are available to both implement and support the technology.

Effectiveness in increasing control is an integral part of the benefit and risk management decisions. Each component needs to be considered in order to determine cross-benefits where controls overlap and supplement other controls. In this case, the control increase is understood and supported by management.

Data classification is the foundation for requirements and will help drive the cost-benefit discussions because it captures the value of the information to the underlying business. In this example, the data are considered significant enough to warrant additional security measures to safeguard the data against misuse, theft, and loss.

Exhibit 19.4 shows some of the technology decisions required to secure the example environment. Management can use this chart to plot the security levels required by the system. For example, for "system audit services," in order of minimal service to maximum:

- The minimal level of security is to have systems with a limited number of system events logged. For example, the default level of logging from the manufacture is used but does not contain all of the required information. The logs are not reviewed but are available in the event of a security incident for forensics.

- A higher level of security is afforded with a log that records more activities based upon requirements and not, for example, the manufacturer's default level. As in the minimal level of security, the activities are logged and available to support forensics but not reviewed. In this case, the type of information recorded in the system logged is more adequate but may not contain all that is required. Sufficient log is kept on each server and is manually monitored for anomalies and potential security events. Log is automatically reviewed by software on each server.

  System logs are consolidated on to a centralized security server. Data from the system logs is transmitted to the centralized security server and software is then used to scan the logs for specific events that require attention. Events such as attempts to gain escalate privileges to root or administrative access can be flagged for manual review.

- The maximum service level is host-based intrusion detection system (IDS). This is used to scan the system logs for anomalies and possible security events. Once these are detected, action needs to be taken to resolve the intrusion. The procedure should include processes such as notification, escalation, and automated defensive response.

19.3.2.2   *Business-to-Business Security Services.* The second case study uses the security services framework in a B-to-B example. The following discussion is a theoretical discussion of how the framework can be applied to discuss B-to-B e-commerce security. The following assumptions may be made in this B-to-B system example:

1. It is Internet-facing.
2. It supports major transactions.
3. Descriptions will be external and customer-based (excluding support, administration, and operations security services).
4. Trusted communication is required.
5. It has three-tier architecture.
6. It has an untrusted client.
7. The business application is critical.
8. Data are classified as highly sensitive.

Exhibit 19.5 shows a high level architecture of this example. There are five layers in this example that need to be secured:

1. The *presentation layer* is the customer interface and is what the client sees or hears using the Web device. The client is the customer's untrusted PC, but more security constraints can be applied because the business can dictate enhanced security.

Exhibit 19.5   B-to-B E-Commerce Security Services

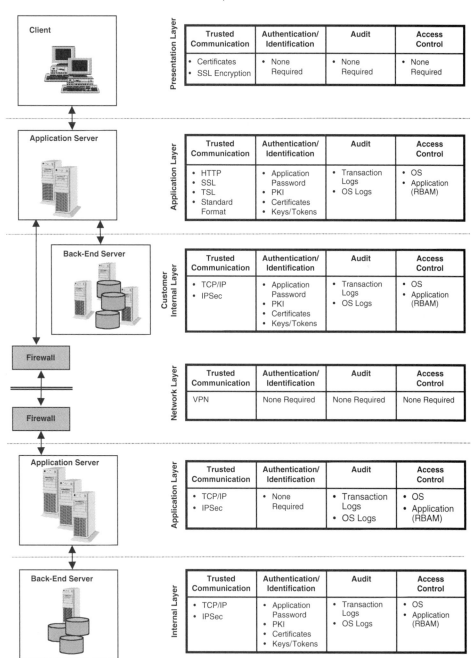

2. The *application layer* is where the information is processed. The application serves as an intermediary between the business customer's requests and the fulfillment systems internal to the business (the back-end server). The application server is the supporting server and database.

3. The *customer internal layer* is the interface between the application server supporting the system at the customer's business location, and the customer's own internal legacy applications and systems.

4. The *network layer* is the communication connection between the business and another business. The Internet is used to connect the two businesses. Sensitive and confidential traffic will need to be encrypted. Best practice is to have the traffic further secured using a firewall.

5. The *internal layer* is the business's legacy systems that support customer servicing. The back-end server houses the supporting systems, including order processing, accounts receivable, inventory, distribution, and other systems.

For each of these five levels, Exhibit 19.5 shows four security services. In order to simplify this example, only two firewalls are shown. Additional firewalls can be added as required. The four security services are:

1. Trusted communications

2. Authentication/identification

3. Audit

4. Access controls

19.3.2.2.1   Step 1: Define Information Security Concerns Specific to the Application. Defining security issues will be particular to the system being implemented. To understand the risk of the system, the best starting place is with the business risk; then define risk at each element of the architecture. For example, for business risks:

- Communication between application servers needs to be very secure. Data cannot be tampered with, stolen, or misrouted.

- Availability is critical during normal business hours.

- Cost savings from switching from electronic data interchange (EDI) to the Internet is substantial and will more than cover the costs of the system.

Technology Concerns. Exhibit 19.5 shows the six architectural layers in this example that need to be secured:

1. The *presentation layer* will not be secured or trusted. The communication between the client and the customer application is trusted because it uses the customer's private network.

2. The *application server* will need to be secure. Traffic between the two application servers will need to be encrypted. The application server is inside the customer's network and demonstrates a high degree of trust between the two companies.

3. The *customer's internal layer* will be secured by the customer.

4. The *network layer* needs to filter traffic that is not required, prevent DoS attacks, and monitor for possible intrusions. Two firewalls are shown: one to protect the client and the other to protect the B-to-B company.

5. The *application layer* will need to prevent unauthorized access, support timely processing of transactions, provide effective audit trails, and process confidential information.

6. The *internal layer* will need to prevent unauthorized access (especially through Internet connections) and protect confidential information during transmission, processing, and storage.

19.3.2.2.2   Step 2: Develop Security Services Options.   There are four security services reviewed in this example. Others could have been included, such as authenticity, with nonrepudiation and confidentiality, but they have been excluded to simplify this example. Elected security services include:

- Trusted communication
- Authentication/identification
- Audit
- Access control

Many security services options are available for B-to-B environments. This is where an architectural picture such as Exhibit 19.5 is helpful because it clearly describes each element. The architecture is on the left and security services on the right.

- *Presentation layer.* Several different options can be selected for trusted communication. HTTP is the most common. The communications between the client and the application server, in this example, are internal to the customer's trusted internal network and will be secured by the customer.
- *Application layer.* Communication between the two application servers needs to be secure. The easiest and most secure method of peer-to-peer communication is via a VPN.
- *Customer internal.* Communications between the customer's application server and the customer back-end server are internal to the customer's trusted internal network and will be secured by the customer.
- *Network layer.* It is common in a B-to-B environment that a trusted network is created via a VPN. The firewalls will probably participate in these communications, but hardware solutions are also possible.
- *Application layer.* The application server is at both the customer and B-to-B company sites. VPN is the most secure communication method. The application server also needs to communicate with the internal layer, and this traffic should be encrypted as well.
- *Internal layer.* The internal layer may be secured with another firewall from the external-facing system. This firewall helps the B-to-B company to protect itself from intrusions and unauthorized access. In this example, a firewall is not shown so the external firewall and DMZ need to be very secure.

The selections made are noted in Exhibit 19.5. The format of that Exhibit captures the architecture and security services choices in a concise format. Intrusion detection, log reading, and other devices not shown can easily be added and discussed with management. This format can be repeated to discuss security services at all levels and all systems, not just e-commerce–related systems.

19.3.2.2.3   Step 3: Develop Security Service Options.   In step 3 the B-to-B company can analyze and select the security services that best meet its legal, business, and information security requirements. The biggest difference between B-to-C and B-to-B systems is that the B-to-C system assumes no level of trust. The B-to-B system assumes trust, but additional coordination and interface with the B-to-B customer or partner is required. This coordination and interoperability must not be underestimated, because they may prove difficult and expensive to resolve. There are four stages required for this analysis:

1. Implementation risk or feasibility

2. Cost to implement and support

3. Effectiveness in increasing control, thereby reducing risk

4. Data classification

Implementation risk is a function of the organization's ability to effectively roll out the technology. In this example, we assume that implementation risk is low and resources are readily available to implement the technology.

Cost to implement and support are paramount to the decision-making process. Both businesses' costs need to be considered. Unfortunately, the cost to support is difficult to quantify and easily overlooked. In this example, resources are available both to implement and to support the technology.

Effectiveness in increasing control is an integral part of the benefit and risk management analysis. Each security component needs to be considered in order to determine cross-benefits where controls overlap and supplement others. In this example, increased levels of control are understood and supported by management.

Data classification is the foundation for requirements and will help drive the cost-benefit discussions because it captures the value of the information to the underlying business. In this example, the data are considered significant enough to warrant additional security measures to safeguard the data against misuse, theft, and loss.

Exhibit 19.6 is an example of B-to-B security services presented in a continuum. Each security service can be defined along this continuum, with implementation risk, cost, and data classification all considered. Management can use this chart to plot the security levels required by the system. This example outlines the effectiveness of security services options relative to other protocols or products. Each organization should develop its own continuums and provide guidance to Web developers and application programmers as to the correct uses and standard settings of the security services. For example, for "authentication/identification" services, in order of minimal service to maximum:

- The minimal level of security is to have no passwords.

- Weak passwords (e.g., easy to guess, shared, poor construction) are better than no passwords but still minimal levels of security.

- Operating or database level passwords usually allow too much access to the system but can be effectively managed.

- Application passwords are difficult to manage but can be used to restrict data access to a greater degree.

- Role-based access distinguishes users by their need to know to support their job function. Roles are established and users are grouped by their required function.

Exhibit 19.6   B-to-B Security Services

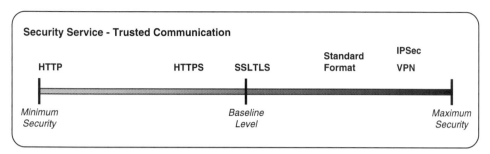

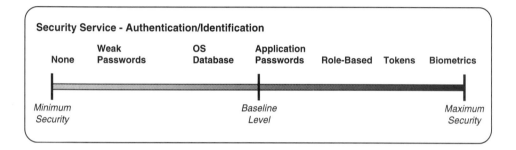

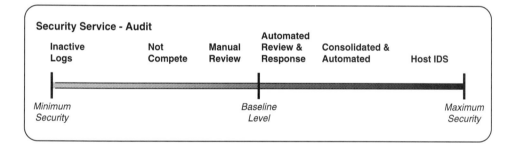

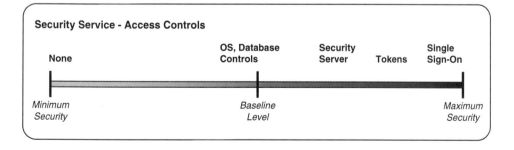

- Tokens are given to users and provide for two-part authentication. Passwords and tokens are combined for strong authentication.
- Biometrics are means to validate the person claiming to be the user via finger-prints, retina scans, or other unique body function.

19.4 CONCLUSION.   Internet e-commerce has changed the way corporations conduct business with their customers, vendors, suppliers, and business units. The B-to-B and B-to-C sectors will likely continue to grow. Despite security concerns, the acceleration toward increased use of the Internet as a sales and marketing channel continues. The challenge for information security professional is to keep pace with this change from a security perspective but not to impede progress. Another equal challenge is that the products that secure the Internet are new and not fully functional or mature. The products will improve, but meanwhile, existing products must be implemented, and later retrofitted, with improved and more secure security services. This changing environment, including the introduction of ever more serious and sophisticated threats, will remain difficult to secure.

The process described in this chapter will allow the security practitioner to provide business units with a powerful tool to communicate, select, and implement information security services. Three steps were described and demonstrated with two examples. The process supports decision making. Decisions can be made and readily documented to demonstrate the cost-effectiveness of the security selections. The risk of specific decisions can be discussed and accepted by management. The trade-offs between cost and benefit can be calculated and discussed. Therefore, it becomes critical that alternatives be reviewed and good decisions be made. The processes supporting these decisions need to be efficient and quickly applied. The information security services approach will allow companies to implement security at a practical pace. Services not selected are easily seen. The risk of not selecting specific security services needs to be accepted by management.

19.5 FURTHER READING

Bernstein, T., A.B. Bhimani, E. Schultz, and C.A. Siegel. *Internet Security for Business.* New York: John Wiley & Sons, 1996.

Ford, W. and M.S. Baum. *Secure Electronic Commerce: Building the Infrastructure for Digital Signatures and Encryption.* Upper Saddle River, NJ: Prentice Hall, 1997.

Garfinkel, S. and G. Spafford. *Web Security and Commerce.* Sebastopol, CA: O'Reilly & Associates, 1997.

Ghosh, A.K. *E-Commerce Security: Weak Links, Best Defenses.* New York: John Wiley & Sons, 1998.

Khare, R., ed. *Web Security: A Matter of Trust.* Sebastopol,CA: O'Reilly & Associates, 1998. *World Wide Web Journal* 2(3).

Wright, B. *The Law of Electronic Commerce: EDI, E-mail and Internet—Technology, Proof and Liability.* 2d ed. Boston: Little, Brown, 1996.

19.6 NOTES

1. UCC § 1-102 (2).

2. UCC § 1-102 (3) provides: "The effect of provisions of this Act may be varied by agreement, except as otherwise provided in this Act and except that the obligations of good faith, diligence, reasonableness and care prescribed by this Act may not be disclaimed by agreement."

3. The substantive provisions of these types of agreements are reviewed in Section 19.2.2.2.

4. UETA § 5(b). The official text of the UETA may be found at *www.nccusl.org.*

5. UETA § 15(a).

6. UETA § 12.

7. E-Sign, § 101(c).

8. The complete text of the Model Law and accompanying report may be found at *www.uncitral.org/english/texts/electcom/ml-ec.htm.*

9. See, generally, Model Law, Article 14.

10. See, generally, Model Law, Article 15.

11. The complete text may be found at *www.uncitral.org.*

12. See the complete text at *http://europa.eu.int/comm/internal_market/en/media/sign/Dir99-93-ecEN.pdf.*

13. Nations that have relied on the Model Law in enacting statutes include Australia, Bermuda, Colombia, France, Hong Kong, Ireland, Philippines, Republic of Korea, Japan, Singapore, and Slovenia. Canada's law was reported to be influenced by the Model Law. See *www.uncitral.org,* status of texts/Model Law on Electronic Commerce.

14. See, generally, Chapter 52, Privacy.

15. See Eric Murray's article "Survey on Information Security," in *Information Security Magazine,* October 2000.

CHAPTER **20**

FIREWALLS AND PROXY SERVERS

David Brussin

CONTENTS

20.1 INTRODUCTION. The firewall has come to represent both the concept and the realization of network and Internet security protections. Through its rapid acceptance and evolution, the firewall has become the most visible of security technology throughout the enterprise chain of command. In distinct contrast to virtually any other single piece of technology, there is not likely to be a chief executive officer in this country who cannot say a word or two about how firewalls are used to protect enterprise systems and data.

Firewalls and proxy servers as network security mechanisms have provided protection necessary for unprecedented enterprise connectivity to external networks, most visibly the public Internet. These devices have very specific roles, however, and do not provide the types of protection often ascribed to them. However, they do excel at certain tasks and are certainly a necessary component in any secure architecture.

20.1.1   History and Background.   Changing computing paradigms, changing models for business interaction, and the global change introduced by the emergence of Internet-centric computing have dramatically altered the responsibilities and capabilities of traditional security components.

For more details about the history of computing and security, see Chapter 1.

20.1.1.1   Changing Network Models.   As connections between systems have changed the way computers are used, security issues have shifted to accommodate the new approach. The progression from mainframe-centric information processing to increasingly broad networks of systems has changed the idea of the security perimeter. Additionally, as a result of the new connections, the requirements for application security have grown to include new concerns about network and host security.

The mainframe-based information processing approach had established security technology and procedures. The transition to client/server computing left these behind to a significant extent, and the continued shift to network-centric computing made clear the need for a new approach.

20.1.1.1.1   Mainframe-Centric Computing.   Early information processing systems centered on a "glass house" approach to networking. Mainframe systems were often solitary, and when multiple systems were present, their connections typically were limited to a single data center. Wide area networks (WANs) were limited to direct leased-line connections between data centers.

Network and physical perimeters were typically the same, with client access provided primarily by "green screen" terminal services. The need for application security was limited by this single, available and allowed path. Network security in this environment was the responsibility of the mainframe services connected to network interfaces. For example, these services had security features that controlled access and frequently were located in separate mainframe regions.

Mainframe operating systems predicted the evolution of networks and firewalls to some extent. These operating systems typically ran as instances on a lightweight virtual machine, as in the case of IBM MVS/VM, or were otherwise divided into partitions or regions. The interactions between these virtual systems could be regulated, even to the level of implementing Mandatory Access Control (MAC).

20.1.1.1.2   Enterprise Client/Server Computing.   As mainframe resources were augmented with midrange servers, running operating systems such as Unix, NetWare, OS/2, and Windows NT, the number and type of network connections increased rapidly. Also, terminal-based clients were replaced in large part by personal computer (PC)–class client systems with network connections.

This shift represents the initial change in the traditional security perimeter. Network connections reached outside of the data center to the individual desktop, and WANS expanded to connect these systems across the enterprise and beyond. Among the advantages of the midrange server approach was the broad suitability of their operating systems to office productivity, back-end computing, transaction processing, database service, and other tasks. Along with these capabilities came complexity, including default configurations designed to enable maximum functionality out of the box.

As data centers, and even wiring closets, became populated with servers, the network connections and associated available network services became increasingly complex. The security perimeter no longer had any distinct boundaries within the enterprise, as clients and server were connected in increasingly complex ways. Application security was redefined, as application functionality spread across mainframe, server, and PC-class client platforms. The interactions between these platforms within a single application created multiple allowed paths, and the many available network services on a given platform created opportunities to circumvent the intended application flow.

20.1.1.1.3   Network-Centric Computing.   As the Internet has emerged as an important commercial platform, it has influenced enterprise technology both directly and indirectly. Directly, Internet connections and HTTP and other Web services have driven enterprise networks toward the TCP/IP standard. Also, as infrastructure vendors standardized on Internet protocols and technologies, the available components for internal enterprise use settled on TCP/IP as well.

Enterprise applications have migrated from PC-class client applications tied to back-end midrange servers, to multitier applications with lightweight Web browser-based client interfaces linked to HTTP servers backed by transaction and database midrange servers.

The result of these changes is a broad, homogenous network environment that uses TCP/IP to provide connectivity ranging from customer access, to marketing materials, to intermainframe and interserver back-end transactions. Additionally, the connected environment has further degraded security perimeters, requiring TCP/IP connections outside the enterprise via such paths as leased lines, frame relay, and the Internet.

20.1.2   Progression of Network Security Mechanisms.   The changing problem of perimeter security has produced a succession of network security mechanisms designed to restrict allowed paths and inspect network traffic.

20.1.2.1   Router Access Control Lists.   Routers are the heart of TCP/IP networks, directing traffic from segment to segment. Router vendors recognized the need for security controls at the boundaries between different segments and networks, and implemented simple controls that could be activated with negligible performance impact. Using explicit "allow" and "deny" statements, router access control lists (ACLs) restrict IP traffic based on source and destination addresses and ports. In addition, these controls can limit traffic based on other parameters, such as whether or not a packet is in response to an established connection. Routers inspect each packet in a vacuum, without any context of previous traffic.

20.1.2.2   Dedicated Host-based Firewall Applications.   While routers did an effective job of implementing access control rules, it was clear that they were not suited for more complex requirements. Dedicated server-based firewalls were created to provide for additional capabilities, including protocol traffic inspection, contextual traffic inspection, comprehensive logging and alerting, and air-gap application gateways, which completely rebuild network packets to protect systems on internal networks.

These firewall applications typically are built on top of an existing operating system (OS). Various Unix variants and Windows NT are commonly used, often with special hardening or system monitoring components added to the OS. In some cases, hardening is implemented to the extent that components of the network stack within the underlying OS are completely replaced.

The full OS permits firewalls with significantly greater functionality than available on routers. Also, development scope and effort can be reduced by using commercial off-the-shelf (COTS) components and scripting languages and building on real-time process scheduling, network input/output (I/O), and file system functionality. Unfortunately, these benefits come at a price: added complexity, unpredictable configurations, third-party component interactions, and uncontrolled changes.

20.1.2.3   Purpose-Built Firewall Appliances.   An extension of the host-based firewall concept, the firewall appliance is an effort to realize the benefits of a full operating system upon which to build functionality while providing the controlled operating and maintenance characteristics of routers and network appliances. In taking control of the entire host, vendors can closely control software versions and configuration and prevent undesired system changes. In order to do so, vendors must increase their expertise to include appliance hardware and operating systems and will have to bear additional challenges as a hardware vendor as well as possible licensing fees for included software components.

20.1.2.4   Personal Firewalls.   In recognition of the new role of client workstation as network server, personal firewalls have emerged as a client software solution designed to insulate vulnerable desktop OS from attacks.

Such products are of particular value in a corporate environment when the remote client workstation is viewed as an extension of the network perimeter, such as in the case of Virtual Private Network (VPN) connectivity for remote users.

The growth of residential and small-business broadband Internet access also has increased the need for personal firewalls. The spread of various Distributed Denial of Service (DDoS) attacks, which work by compromising a large number of unsuspecting workstations, has helped to bring the issue of workstation protection to the forefront. See Chapter 11 for more information about DDoS.

20.2   ROLE OF NETWORK SECURITY MECHANISMS.   Recognition of the value of network security mechanisms has changed the way systems are built and managed from the largest government network to the individual personal workstation. While information technology (IT) managers have increased their expertise and recognized the need for these mechanisms, they often have unrealistic expectations about their capabilities. Network security mechanisms are far from the easy answer to Internet security concerns that some believe them to be. An understanding of the capabilities and roles of these components permits the most effective realization of their benefit, both direct and otherwise, without the undesired consequence of insufficient protection in other areas.

20.2.1   Perimeter Protection.   As the de facto network perimeter expanded and lost definition during the transition from mainframe-centric computing, through client/server, to the current network-centric approach, the requirement for reinforcement of that boundary line emerged. In their various forms, firewalls and proxy servers control aspects of network traffic, such as parties to the communication, traffic types, direction and flow, and even content.

Most important, these devices draw a line between external and internal so that inherent weaknesses, misconfigurations, and other vulnerabilities in various components are hidden behind the controlled interface of the perimeter device. This represents a dramatic change from the unprotected network environment where every system was in fact external and a part of the perimeter.

In order properly to fit this role and to facilitate the allowed path controls that follow, perimeter controls must follow the principle of least privilege. To be a useful definition of perimeter, these devices must implicitly block all traffic that is not explicitly permitted. One area of concern regarding the measure of perimeter protection afforded by these devices is the extension of perimeter via allowed traffic. Clearly a firewall or proxy server that forwards traffic from one network to another in accordance with defined rules is exposing internal systems to external traffic. Care must be taken to ensure that the systems within the internal network are capable of acting as part of the logical network perimeter. Essentially, perimeter protection from firewalls and proxy servers allows network administrators to focus security efforts on a fixed group of systems.

For more information about perimeter-focused security, see Chapters 8, 21, and 22.

20.2.1.1 *Control of Allowed Paths.* While network security devices such as firewalls and proxy servers create a distinct physical perimeter between different networks, they also create a logical perimeter that extends to systems within protected networks. Just as the teller windows in a bank branch office restrict customers' interactions with bank personnel to those that are intended, the allowed path protections afforded by a firewall ensure that outside traffic is able to flow only in expected and intended ways.

The perimeter protection and allowed path control roles of the network security mechanism combine to form a "least privilege gateway" that comprises the original "firewall" function. Network security professionals quickly learned that the dangers of external traffic could easily extend to the defined "allowed paths." Significant security responsibility still rested with the destination host within the protected network. The many generations of network security mechanisms that followed focused on abstracting more of this responsibility back to the firewall or proxy server itself.

20.2.1.2 *Intrusion Detection.* The final primary role of the network security mechanism is that of intrusion detection: sounding an alarm when all is not well with the network perimeter. Depending on how these mechanisms are deployed, alerts may provide extremely valuable information about real problems or a torrent of information about attempted attacks rather than actual intrusions. Tactics for addressing these issues will be discussed in detail later in this chapter.

When network security mechanisms are working properly, intrusion detection information is really "threat level" information, useful in maintaining knowledge of the background levels of hostile activity directed at the protected network. Tests have shown that new Internet hosts are probed and attacked within hours of being placed online and are probed almost continuously thereafter.

Some firewalls incorporate pattern-matching features, such as those found in dedicated intrusion detection systems, in order to detect hostile traffic along allowed paths. Similar in some ways to virus scanning via pattern matching, this method can detect certain "known" attacks on specific protocols.

Since multiple firewalls and proxy servers often are used in a given architecture, intrusion detection data also can report actual security failures. When a network security mechanism observes and rejects traffic that architecturally should never have been present, security failure of an upstream device is possible.

For more details of intrusion detection, see Chapter 37.

20.2.2   Additional Roles of the Firewall and Proxy Server.   Network security mechanisms, for a combination of security and practical reasons, have been assigned various responsibilities beyond those just discussed. Actual or perceived security impact of various functions has resulted in these devices adding capabilities. Additionally, the practical location of these components on the network between, in many cases, the Internet and internal networks has resulted in the addition of nonsecurity network-related functionality.

20.2.2.1   Intrusion Response.   Network administrators, responsible for reacting to the alerts from firewall intrusion detection components, knew that there had to be a more efficient way to deal with these critical events. Firewall vendors began to integrate various types and levels of intrusion response capability into their products, producing automated responses to intrusion detection alerts.

20.2.2.1.1   Connection Termination.   The simplest of intrusion response capabilities, connection termination involves the firewall terminating a specific allowed path connection from a specific address and port when intrusion detection components detect traffic on that allowed path that matches known attack patterns. Typically implemented in TCP via an "RST," or connection reset command, this functionality also can be implemented on connectionless UDP (User Datagram Protocol) allowed paths through packet dropping.

This intrusion response capability is effective at blocking known attacks on allowed paths but suffers from several drawbacks. Unfortunately, skilled attackers can use this capability to create a denial of service against legitimate clients on specific ports. In many cases the clients rebuild their connections, but a successful attack might deny service completely for some period of time. Also, this technique is not useful for preventing attackers from attempting additional, perhaps unknown, attacks following connection termination of initial attacks.

20.2.2.1.2   Dynamic Rule Modification.   The dynamic rule modification technique takes connection termination to the next level, ensuring that attackers are prevented from attempting further attacks from the same address. By dynamically modifying the network security mechanism rule base to block traffic from the offending address, further potential attacks are blocked.

While this technique addresses one of the failings of connection termination, namely the exposure to unknown attacks that might follow known attacks, it is even more exposed to the denial of service issues just discussed. Since dynamic rule modification creates a semipermanent barrier for traffic from a given address, attackers can deny service to broad groups of users for an extended period. Since many enterprises and Internet service providers (ISPs) use only a few proxy server source addresses for all traffic, an attack could quickly deny service for a very large group, such as all AOL users.

20.2.2.1.3   "Hack-Back" Reactive Intrusion Response.   A large step beyond the functionality of dynamic rule modification is the "hack-back" reactive response method. This technique, which typically uses denial of service and other attacks, attempts to attack and disable the source of hostile traffic.

For ethical, legal, and practical reasons, this technique has never been widely adopted, although a few products have offered it. Not only could networks be subject to denial of service, but an attacker also could easily use "hack-back" functionality to target innocent third parties. The ethical and liability issues associated with this type of intrusion response are staggering. For further discussion of this topic, see Chapter 30, Ethical Decision Making.

20.2.2.1.4 System-Level Action. Most network security mechanisms perform internal monitoring of component processes and the underlying operating system. In the event of internal problems or evidence of compromise, or certain external intrusion detection events, system-level action can be initiated.

Actions taken can range from firewall interface deactivation to firewall system shutdown. It is important to test firewall shutdown behavior carefully before using this response, as several firewall products have in the past, upon shutdown, permitted open routing of traffic via the underlying operating system.

20.2.2.2 Encryption. Security and practical concerns have prompted the inclusion of encryption technology in network security mechanisms. Valid concerns over centralization of responsibility for security decisions, components and perimeter protection, as well as cost and complexity savings have resulted in a variety of hardware and software encryption solutions as part of firewalls and proxy servers.

20.2.2.2.1 Virtual Private Networks. Virtual private networks (VPNs), which extend the security perimeter of a network to include remote systems as if they were on an internal network, have increased in popularity as a mechanism for allowing remote enterprise access without extensive hardware infrastructure. VPNs over the public Internet are most commonly used in this role.

Savvy network administrators realize that remote VPN clients are very different from true internal hosts and seek a way to mitigate the risk that comes along with them. Utilizing the perimeter protection and allowed path control capabilities of the firewall, it is possible to create a special rule base specifically for VPN clients.

The "P" in VPN, which stands for private, is implemented through encryption technology. When the firewall is responsible for allowed path control on traffic from remote VPN clients, it must be able to deal with unencrypted traffic. Rather than place additional servers or appliances outside the firewall, where they might be vulnerable to Internet attacks, vendors chose to integrate the encryption technology directly into the firewall.

20.2.2.2.2 SSL Acceleration. SSL, or Secure Sockets Layer, is the standard encryption protocol for protecting Web-related network traffic. In order to centralize acceleration hardware, enable intrusion detection and allowed path inspection, reduce Web server load, and simplify secure Web implementations, vendors have integrated support for SSL, frequently using hardware acceleration, into the network security mechanisms.

20.2.2.3 Content Inspection. The inspection of content along various allowed paths is most easily performed at a choke point, where all of the traffic flows through one set of components, resulting in the integration of content inspection functionality in network security mechanisms.

20.2.2.3.1 Content Filtering. Content filtering is not strictly a security capability. In most cases, this technology permits policy enforcement with respect to the actions of internal rather than external users. Business policy regarding the use of enterprise resources, for example, is often enforced through HTTP content inspection and filtering. HTTP (Hypertext Transfer Protocol) and SMTP (Simple Mail Transfer Protocol) filtering are used to isolate users from undesired materials, such as those they might consider offensive.

This technology, which is far from perfect, uses a variety of approaches to filter content. Address-based filtering, which uses IP (Internet Protocol) addresses of destination Web sites, for example, is efficient and easy to implement. This technique requires constant updates to a "blocked address" list, however, and can easily block sites unintentionally due to virtual hosts sharing IP addresses. Name-based filtering is a slight improvement, using actual domain and resource names, but still suffers from the list management problem.

In an attempt to address the list management issues, a resource-intensive technique based on real-time content scanning was developed. This technique, which can incorporate anything from keyword scanning to image analysis, also results in significant erroneous filtering.

See Chapter 51 of this *Handbook* for more details on content filtering.

20.2.2.3.2   Virus Scanning.   Virus scanning within network security mechanisms takes various forms, from SMTP message and attachment scanning to HTTP traffic inspection. Typically based on existing pattern recognition virus scanning systems, this integration sometimes loops traffic through dedicated scanning systems rather than performing the work on the firewall or proxy server itself. See Chapters 9 and 24 for more about viruses, worms, and other malware.

20.2.2.3.3   Active Code Scanning and Filtering.   Active code, such as ActiveX, VBScript, and JavaScript, can pose a security threat to internal systems. Many network security mechanisms have been enhanced to support filtering and/or scanning of these components on certain allowed paths.

On HTTP connections, for example, active code filtering might simply prevent the transfer of certain types of active code. More sophisticated scanning technology can be used to identify hostile code through pattern recognition and/or sandbox execution.

SMTP connections have seen significant new attention in this area due to active code weaknesses in popular mail clients. The scanning and filtering of active code in SMTP traffic is now being used to address a new breed of e-mail viruses.

20.2.2.4   Caching.   Proxy server vendors quickly realized that their devices could dramatically reduce Internet bandwidth consumption and improve internal performance by caching frequently requested items on various protocols. HTTP, FTP (File Transfer Protocol), and streaming media caches are common on enterprise networks.

20.3   TECHNICAL DETAIL: FIREWALLS.   Firewalls implement the primary and secondary roles discussed above, with constant attention to several basic security requirements. Each successive generation of firewall products has introduced new techniques for serving its basic roles. These advances have focused heavily on the area of allowed path control, adding various levels of allowed path traffic inspection.

20.3.1   Security Tasks.   In implementing perimeter protections and control of allowed paths, firewalls must satisfy several basic security requirements. It is useful to refer to the primary role of the firewall and to its satisfaction of these requirements when considering the security impact of secondary roles for such a device.

20.3.1.1   Authorization.   The authorization of access is the most basic function of the network gatekeeper, or firewall. This authorization can be based on parameters such as the source and destination address and port information or can incorporate elements like user identity and credentials.

Most firewalls support at least these levels of authorization, frequently enabling complex user-based authorization through secondary firewall roles. For example, user-based authorization might permit HTTP traffic for a particular user, but user-based content inspection functionality might block the active code components of the desired Web resource.

20.3.1.2   Availability.   It is often said that no enterprise would ever install security software for its own sake. Similarly, an enterprise must carefully manage risk when connecting to outside networks such as the Internet and when controlling those connections with firewalls. In many business contexts, the role of the firewall is to enable connectivity and provide protections, rather than the other way around. Intrusion response plans must take into account these requirements, particularly when developing automated intrusion response configurations for firewall systems.

20.3.1.3   Accounting and Audit.   In addition to security issues such as forensic records and intrusion detection, business needs can also drive accounting and audit requirements. Secondary roles such as content inspection and filtering have driven business requirements related to enforcement of acceptable use policies.

20.3.2   Firewall Architectures.   As network security mechanisms have evolved from functionality added to existing routing devices, to dedicated systems and appliances, the techniques used to implement firewall functionality have evolved as well. Always balancing security requirements against performance and network throughput, vendors have introduced a variety of approaches.

20.3.2.1   Rule Processing on Routing Devices.   The first firewalls were in fact routers, both dedicated routing appliances and Unix-based "bastion hosts." Of such devices, routing appliances with ACLs (access control lists) are still widely used as network security mechanisms. Some routing appliances use the stateful inspection architecture discussed later in this section.

Routers using ACLs make authorization decisions for allowed path control based strictly on the packet currently being processed by the router. This decision, without context of previous traffic, is based on such packet data as source and target addresses, and port and packet flags such as the synchronizing field (SYN) present in packets attempting to initiate connections.

This focused view of individual packets has resulted in several vulnerabilities. One such vulnerability exploited combinations of the poorly compliant IP implementation in Windows NT and the strictly compliant implementation in the routers. Attackers crafted fragmented IP packets such that the initial SYN packet contained headers conforming to an ACL on the router. The following packet, however, had a fragment offset that placed new header data into the packet upon reassembly in the Windows NT host behind the firewall. Since this second fragment did not contain a SYN flag, it was not blocked at the router. Windows NT patches and router changes that prevented fragments with offsets within the packet header have addressed this vulnerability. The practice of reassembling fragmented packets at the router also became common as a preventive measure against this type of attack.

The deployment section later in this chapter shows how existing routing infrastructure, in combination with dedicated network security mechanisms, can be used to enhance security architectures.

20.3.2.2   Packet-Filtering Firewalls.

Packet-filtering firewalls are appliance, or host-based, firewalls that use the ACL method described above for allowed path authorization but add additional firewall capabilities. These systems typically do formal logging, are capable of user-based authorization, and have intrusion detection and alerting capabilities.

Unfortunately, these firewalls also have suffered from weaknesses due to lack of context information, as described above. Additionally, host-based packet-filtering firewalls have suffered from various weaknesses in the network stacks of the underlying operating systems.

Very few firewall vendors currently offer traditional packet-filtering firewalls, but many nonsecurity products now have packet-filtering capabilities. For example, various load balancers, Web caches, and switch products now offer packet-filtering firewall capabilities.

Packet-filtering firewalls are ideally suited to load-balanced and highly available environments, as they can load-balance connections among devices, between each packet, with no additional overhead and can similarly fail-over between devices in the middle of an established connection.

20.3.2.3   Stateful Inspection Firewalls.

In recognition of the problems with authorizing allowed path traffic based on the information in a single packet, vendors developed several new technologies. The basic design behind application gateways, discussed below, was considered by some to be too computationally expensive for real-time processing on firewall devices. A competing technology, stateful inspection, was developed to provide connection context information for allowed-path authorization and still provide for good performance, scalability, load balancing, and fail-over capabilities.

This technique calls for a table of connection information, providing context, to be maintained in memory on the firewall. In order to improve throughput, the information in this table is stored in the form of binary representations of IP packet header information. This information then can be compared to the binary header of an incoming IP packet very efficiently, in many cases using only a few native CPU instructions.

This technique, as it inspects only certain portions of the incoming packet, is effective only against known or predicted classes of IP attack. Attacks that use ignored portions of the packet to attack weak IP implementations on back-end hosts still succeed. As a result, this type of firewall, while it may be configured with a least-privilege rule base, is partially comparable to the packet filter in that it does not do least-privilege data inspection.

Some stateful inspection systems have focused so heavily on performance that they offer a "fast mode" that reduces inspection dramatically once a connection has been opened successfully. This mode, while very efficient, is strongly discouraged by network security experts as sacrificing too much security.

Stateful inspection technology lends itself well to load balancing and highly available solutions, albeit with significant overhead traffic. In order to support load balancing and fail-over between packets and within established connections, the state tables between clustered or paired devices must be synchronized. This operation typically is conducted via in-band network traffic or out-of-band interdevice connectivity, such as through RS-232, a standard that specifies physical connectors, signal voltage characteristics, and an information exchange protocol.

20.3.2.4   *Application Gateway Firewalls.* A second approach to adding context information to the allowed path access decision came in the form of application gateway firewalls. These firewalls utilize protocol-specific proxies on each allowed path port to make access decisions, extract required protocol information, and build "internal" packets for distribution to the back-end host. Since these firewalls are performing far more complex operations than stateful inspection systems, they have some significant performance challenges to overcome.

The benefit of the "air gap" approach to the packet inspection, access decision, data extraction, and packet assembly workflow is that it is effective at protecting against not only known or predicted classes of attack but also against unknown attacks. Since unused packet elements are discarded, they present no danger to internal systems.

Application gateways do not lend themselves easily to load balancing and highly available solutions. Load balancing typically is accomplished through affinities, where connections will be balanced at their initiation and not change devices thereafter. Failover can be accomplished through operating system–level synchronization and failover mechanisms, but typically not without disrupting connections in progress.

20.3.2.5   *Hybrid Firewalls.* Hybrid firewalls have emerged as a compromise between the speed and efficiency of the stateful inspection approach and the increased security of the application gateway approach. In fact, most commercial firewalls available today can be classified as hybrids.

Hybrid firewalls, evolved from stateful inspection systems, typically perform their normal inspection for all but a few protocols. These protocols, such as HTTP, are subject to additional application gateway-style inspection and/or proxy.

Application gateways in the hybrid category have always used the proxy approach for known protocols. These systems now implement stateful inspection for unknown or encrypted protocols and offer a "fast mode" that performs stateful inspection rather than application gateway functionality on established connections.

20.3.3   Technical Detail: Proxy Servers. Proxy servers address the primary and secondary roles of network security mechanisms in a manner related to, but quite different from, that of the firewall. These devices serve as part of the network perimeter, but largely in that they keep internal systems from becoming exposed to attack through access to external resources. These components protect internal systems from the hazards of network connections, from protocol-specific attacks, and from undesired content.

In addition to the security requirements for network security mechanisms discussed above, proxy servers have some technical characteristics unique to their category. Proxy servers can be implemented using a number of techniques. Some fall into the category of transparent proxy, which use network intercepts to implement proxy functionality. Others are visible, and require standardized or proprietary client-side support, such as SOCKS (Socket Secure) or HTTP.

Both categories of proxy server typically support user-based authorization; they collect credentials in the form of HTTP "get" or "post" data, cookies, and even notoriously weak source IP address information.

20.4   AVAILABLE AND EMERGING TECHNOLOGIES. A number of newly available and forthcoming technologies have the potential to change the way network administrators utilize and interact with network security mechanisms. Among the challenges of current network security mechanism implementations is the consistent configuration, monitoring and alerting, and management of disparate devices. New movement toward consolidated interfaces, unified protocols, and application program interfaces (APIs) may help improve the situation.

20.4.1   Consolidated Management Consoles.   Network security mechanisms, and the various network infrastructure devices around them that also accept security responsibility, have until recently been administered through a variety of different interfaces. Many devices, even of the same vendor and model, had to be maintained independently.

Several products are available from firewall vendors and third-party integrators that attempt to address this problem by providing a single interface to all network security components, from ACLs on routers to firewall configurations and rule bases. The cross-vendor nature of these offerings is a major shift from the vendor-specific management consoles traditionally provided.

These products can be of particular value when configuring screened subnets and multilayer firewall architectures, where rules must match up exactly across disparate components and platforms.

20.4.2   Unified Intrusion Detection.   Unified intrusion detection infrastructure, while not available yet, is emerging based on new Intrusion Detection System (IDS) APIs and proposed interaction standards. Unified intrusion detection infrastructure will provide significant new data on threat profile and actual intrusions. With various products from different vendors all contributing data to real-time and trend analysis, much more meaningful information will become available. In particular, the ability to coordinate ACL failure logs from external routers with routers on other network perimeters and allowed path firewall logs will provide significant value.

20.4.3   Unified Alerting and Reporting.   Available to a limited extent today, often through custom integration, unified alerting also is being developed based on emerging standards. Consolidated logging and alerting of security, IDS, and operational events is of importance to successful maintenance and incident response functions. Particularly in the face of larger and more complex implementations, this capability will provide data in an efficient manner to security and operational teams.

20.4.4   Content Vectoring.   Introduced under various names by firewall vendors, content vectoring is emerging as the next evolutionary step beyond hybrid firewall technology. This approach simply vectors specific types of traffic to ancillary internal or external handlers for additional inspection or other processing. This technology provides an opportunity for vital allowed-path data inspection between DMZ networks, which are partially protected from outside attack yet not trusted by internal networks, and internal systems. These interactions typically are implemented via transaction and data access protocols, and inspection is necessary to safeguard internal systems from hostile user-supplied data.

20.4.5   Multifunction Devices.   Integration of multiple security products into existing platforms already has provided several new offerings. Emerging technologies point to commercial IDS components integrated with firewall products, full-featured commercial firewalls integrated with router platforms, and proxy servers integrated with Web caching and acceleration products.

20.4.6   Automated Allowed-Path Inspection.   Perhaps most significant among the newly available technologies is the automated allowed-path inspection afforded by new products designed to protect HTTP servers and applications. These go far beyond the traditional HTTP inspection, and attack-pattern recognition, built into application gateways and hybrid firewalls, providing actual inspection and sanity checking of user-supplied data.

Inspections and tests seek to satisfy three basic requirements:

1. Continued authentication of Web users across sessions

2. Authorization to invoke Web functionality

3. Conformance of request and data submitted

These products represent a new opportunity to establish properly the logical network perimeter and to control better the actual content of allowed paths. When such products are available for protocols other than HTTP, so that the transactional and data access interactions across the more significant perimeter between DMZ systems and internal networks can be protected, this technology will become even more valuable.

20.5   SUCCESSFUL DEPLOYMENT OF NETWORK SECURITY MECHANISMS

20.5.1   Screened Subnet Firewall Architectures.   The external router is an architecture's first line of defense against attacks from the outside world. The ACLs on this router should mirror the allowed-path configuration of the external firewall interface, in order to provide the front half of a screened subnet on which the firewall can operate. This screened subnet provides several important benefits.

The firewall is able to operate at maximum efficiency, since traffic that would be rejected based on packet-filtering rules normally would never reach the firewall. This permits the firewall to focus, in terms of load, on protocol inspection.

The firewall is able to respond immediately to unexpected conditions. If, for example, the firewall inspects a packet that should never have passed the external router's ACLs, the firewall can assume that the router is not behaving normally. The firewall is then free to respond appropriately, with such actions as a firewall shutdown, to a single inappropriate packet.

Finally, the screened subnet provides redundancy in the form of a hardened infrastructure. This redundancy protects the internal network even in the case of individual component failures. In this case, the firewall would detect a failure by the external router as soon as inappropriate traffic appeared. A failure by the firewall, on the other hand, would not result in any immediate compromise of DMZ or internal systems, since the external router still would be enforcing the allowed paths.

20.5.2   Management and Monitoring Strategies.   It is important to define the security requirements for management and monitoring of network security components. The following requirements will be discussed for the functionality of a monitoring solution:

- Monitoring (health and availability)
- Alert facility (enerate alerts based on thresholds applied to monitoring data)

- Maintenance (any control of any aspect of a component system)
- Logging (collection of detail logs from components)

In general, the most secure method for accomplishing any of these requirements is by using a direct console via native hardware console ports, for monitoring and management purposes, with no in-band management or monitoring whatsoever. (*In-band* control signals are transmitted using the same channel or frequencies as the data signals.) Functionality is understandably limited in this approach, but all of the above requirements can be accomplished in a nonautomated manner. A lower, but acceptable, level of security can be achieved using automated out-of-band management and monitoring techniques. This level, which utilizes connections such as RS-232 console connections clustered on terminal servers, can provide most functionality in a primarily automated manner. (*Out-of-band* signals are transmitted using a separate channel for communications; for example, sending a pager or telephone message when an alert is received is an *out-of-band* transmission.) A lower, acceptable level of security is achieved by using carefully isolated in-band network connectivity with one-way, read-only reporting by component systems. The monitoring, alert, and logging functions are implemented easily in a very automated manner using this approach, but maintenance must be implemented carefully. A final approach, though highest in risk, is the most straightforward to implement. Given acceptable risk tolerance, network security mechanisms can be monitored and maintained using entirely in-band techniques. Such systems typically depend on encryption technology for strong authentication, authorization, and data confidentiality and integrity.

20.5.2.1   Direct Console Method.   The direct console method depends on the existing physical and operational security and introduces no new connectivity.

20.5.2.2   Out-of-Band Method.   The out-of-band method establishes new connectivity over a limited, point-to-point path. Connectivity should be directly to management stations, which should have no unencrypted network connectivity. Access should be protected using dual-factor (e.g., a token plus a personal identification number or password) or other restrictive authentication methods, especially for access outside to a secured data center. (See Chapters 14 and 15 for a discussion of physical and facilities security.)

20.5.2.3   Isolated In-Band Management.   Isolated in-band management establishes new connectivity over a limited, point-to-point path. Connectivity should be directly to a management station, using individual Network Interface Cards (NICs) with any protocol-forwarding or routing features disabled. Management station should have no additional in-band network connectivity. Out-of-band connectivity to an isolated (and secured) terminal or graphical user interface (GUI) workstation is acceptable. A management station should have local access only, in a secured data center facility.

All access by management and monitoring protocols should be passive and read-only. This manner of Simple Network Management Protocol (SNMP) (or other management protocol) access may be implemented in two ways: (1) unidirectional at the network transport level or (2) unidirectional at the protocol level. If the solution design calls for information "pulled" (requested) from component systems, rather than "pushed" (sent without request) to the management station, the protocol level must be used to allow the management station to make requests of the component systems. The ability to respond to such requests must be severely limited at each component system, with appropriate ACLs implemented. If information can be pushed to the management station at regular intervals without a requirement for specific requests in the other direction, transport-level ACLs can be implemented in appropriate routers and firewalls as an additional measure.

Connectivity to the management paths should be established from firewall systems only, not from routers or other component systems. Management traffic should flow in the external direction from all component systems and should never pass through a firewall, except onto an isolated management path. Thus, all firewalls requiring management path connectivity, and all firewalls more external than components requiring management path connectivity, should be connected directly to the management paths. The most internal firewall systems along any production path are special cases. Such systems may be managed internally or through a connection to the described management path. Component systems more internal than these special-case firewalls must be managed internally.

Component systems more external than the most external firewall along any production path should not be managed through this method. The isolated management band should permit only the appropriate management protocol, such as SNMP or Remote Monitor (RMON) and the transport protocol (IP) required for the management protocol.

20.5.2.4   Full In-Band Management.   Full in-band management uses the production application paths for monitoring and management data. The key to successful implementation of this technique is the use of appropriate strong credentials for authentication, such as two-factor hardware token-based authentication. Appropriate link-layer encryption is essential to protect the confidentiality and integrity of monitoring and management traffic, as well as to protect sessions in progress from hijacking. Careful restriction of unencrypted traditional monitoring and management traffic along in-band paths, such as SNMP and RMON, is essential to ensure that the mitigation effected by the authentication mechanisms and encryption is maintained.

20.5.3   Firewall and Proxy Server Configuration and Management

20.5.3.1   Rule Creation.   The creation of rules, which define and control access to allowed paths, is central to the configuration of any network security component. It is vital that every rule base begin as a "deny all," where all traffic not explicitly permitted is denied.

20.5.3.1.1   Identify Allowed Paths.   Allowed paths, specific protocols used to implement communication, must be identified. In a typical Internet environment, business services require allowed paths such as HTTP, SSL (HTTP/S), SMTP, and Domain. These requirements will vary, but for an environment each allowed path should be directly related to a required external service.

Starting from an implicit or explicit (depending on the platform) "deny all" rule, allowed paths will be added as "allow" rules, such as PERMIT HTTP, with specifics determined by the following sections.

20.5.3.1.2   Identify Endpoints.   The systems or groups of systems that will be permitted to send and receive traffic along a specific allowed path are the endpoints of that communication. While network addressing does not provide effective authentication of systems or users, restrictive endpoints can make it much more difficult for an attacker to exploit an otherwise straightforward vulnerability. It is also important to identify carefully the internal endpoints, particularly in cases where these endpoints might reside in internal rather than DMZ networks. An example of such a rule is:

PERMIT HTTP SOURCE-ADDRESS DESTINATION ADDRESS

20.5.3.1.3   Identify Direction of Traffic.   The direction of traffic, indicated by the source of connection initiations, is useful for the rule definitions for several reasons. First, rules can be written so that only responses to internally originated allowed paths are allowed in from the external network, rather than permitting the protocol bidirectionally. Also, firewalls process rules at different times based on design or configuration, as discussed below. It is valuable to understand the direction of traffic flow so that rules can be implemented, and firewalls configured, so that they are consistently enforced. Such a rule might be:

PERMIT HTTP SOURCE-ADDRESS DESTINATION ADDRESS ESTABLISHED

20.5.3.1.4   Behavior and Configuration of Rule Engine.   Various firewalls implement rule enforcement by interface, in a configurable number of directions. For example, firewalls can be configured to inspect traffic as it enters the system, as it exits the system, or both. Since firewall systems now are frequently configured with many interfaces to support environments such as DMZ networks, multiple external and internal networks, and administrative networks, many new variables have been introduced.

Understanding the structure and behavior of the rule enforcement engine within a firewall is vital to successful configuration as well as to effective rule creation. Firewalls implement various protocols using methods and shortcuts that can have an impact on security. Passive (PASV) FTP access (the form of FTP in which a client sends the PASV command to request a port number for a data connection; defined in RFC 959), for example, is implemented on some stateful inspection firewalls in such a way that attackers have been able to use it to create a path for their hostile traffic from the external network.

20.5.3.2   Implicit Rules and Default Configurations.   Certain firewalls, most notably CheckPoint FW-1, use implicit rules to implement certain default behaviors and functionality. Since these rules are not visible to the administrator without specific request, their impact on overall rulebases can be easily overlooked.

FW-1 typifies commercial firewalls in another aspect: The default configuration is not designed to be the most conservative or secure. In the case of certain versions of FW-1, SNMP access, Internet Control Message Protocol (ICMP) traffic, and Domain traffic (TCP port 53) are all permitted by default from external interfaces. Also, the default SNMP "read" string is set to the default "public," exposing internal configuration and operational data. Finally, the remote administration ports are enabled externally by default. These, almost typical, flaws point up the necessity of examining all implicit rules and defaults in out-of-the-box software to eliminate security vulnerabilities.

20.5.4   A Constantly Changing Security Landscape.   Since much of the technology used in information systems is complex and often immature, particularly in an Internet-connected infrastructure, changes in the security landscape can have a dramatic impact on risk levels. Emerging technical vulnerabilities can result in immediate, significant risk to internal systems and data. While the impact is often negligible in the immediate term for robust infrastructures built with a resistance to successive compromise, action still must be taken quickly so that all levels of protection are in place. The process flow looks like this:

Exhibit 20.1   Vulnerability and Patch Process Flow

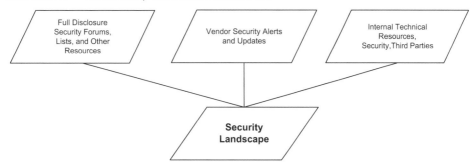

20.5.4.1   *Full Disclosure Security Forums and Resources.* Such full disclosure security forums as Bugtraq and NTBugtraq as well as various security research Web sites often provide timely information on newly discovered or publicized technical vulnerabilities. Often such information is available prior to the release of vendor fixes. Use of such fixes can reduce the period of exposure.

20.5.4.2   *Vendor Security Alerts and Updates.* Vendor security alerts typically are provided once a fix is available, unless public discussion has forced an informational alert prior to the availability of a fix. Frequently these alerts provide little data or ability to take appropriate action. Correlation between vendor and public data may yield enough information for mitigating action.

Vendors frequently include security fixes in bundled updates and do not necessarily disclose their presence. Strong vendor relationships can improve this situation, but in some cases bundled updates may have to be treated implicitly as if they address security issues.

20.5.4.3   *Internal Technical Resources.* Internal evaluation of network security mechanisms occasionally will uncover security issues. These issues should be directed through a well-defined channel to an established incident response function for review. Additionally, internal evaluation and testing of bundled updates from vendors can uncover security-related items through detection of updated files and subsystems.

20.6   FURTHER READING

Amoroso, E., and R. Sharp. *PCWEEK Intranet and Internet Firewall Strategies: Identify Your Security Requirements and Develop a Plan to Protect Your Information.* Emeryville, CA: Ziff-Davis Press, 1996.

Chapman, D.B., and E.D. Zwicky. *Building Internet Firewalls.* Sebastopol, CA: O'Reilly & Associates, 1995.

Cheswick, W., and S. Bellovin. *Firewalls and Internet Security: Repelling the Wily Hacker.* Reading, MA: Addison Wesley, 1994.

Curtin, M., and M.J. Ranum. *Internet Firewalls: Frequently Asked Questions, Revision 10.0,* 2000; available online at *www.interhack.net/pubs/fwfaq/,* 2000.

Garfinkel, S., and G. Spafford. *Practical UNIX and Internet Security,* 2nd ed. Sebastopol, CA: O'Reilly & Associates, 1996.

Garfinkel, S., and G. Spafford. *Web Security and Commerce.* Sebastopol, CA: O'Reilly & Associates, 1997.

Gonçalves, M. *Firewalls Complete.* New York, NY: McGraw-Hill, 1998.

Shinder, T.W., D.L. Shinder, and M. Grasdal. *Configuring ISA Server 2000.* Rockland, MA: Syngress Media, 2001.

Ziegler, R. *Linux Firewalls.* Indianapolis, IN: New Riders Publishing, 2001.

Zwicky, E.D., S. Cooper, D.B. Chapman, and D. Russell. *Building Internet Firewalls,* 2nd ed. Sebastopol, CA: O'Reilly & Associates, 2000.

CHAPTER 21

PROTECTING INTERNET-VISIBLE SYSTEMS

Robert Gezelter

CONTENTS

21.1 INTRODUCTION. Throughout the enterprise, people and information are physically safeguarded. Even the smallest organizations have a locked door and a receptionist to keep outsiders from entering the premises. The larger the organization, the more elaborate the precautions. Small businesses have simple locked doors; larger enterprises often have many levels of security, including electronic locks, security guards, and additional levels of receptionists. Companies also jealously guard the privacy of their executive conversations and research projects. It is inconceivable that any organization would consider it reasonable to broadcast all meetings and conversations over the public address loudspeakers in the parking lot for all the public, and competitors, to hear.

Despite these norms, it is not unusual to find that information security practices are weaker than physical security measures. Connection to the Internet (and within the company, to the intranet) worsens the problem by greatly increasing the risk and decreasing the difficulty of attacks.

This chapter examines techniques, policies, strategies, and tactics for protecting *Internet-visible systems.* Internet-visible systems are those with any connection to the worldwide Internet. Chapter 22 covers additional issues relating specifically to World Wide Web (WWW) servers and applications.

21.1.1   Not Solely a Technical Issue.   It is tempting to consider protecting Internet-visible systems as a purely technical issue. However, technical and business issues are inseparable in today's risk management. For example, the degree to which systems should be exposed to the Internet is fundamentally a business risk-management issue. Protection technologies and the policies behind the protection can be discussed only after the business risk questions have been considered and decided, setting the context for the technical discussions. In turn, business risk-management evaluation (see Chapters 47 and 54) must include a full awareness of all of the technical risks. Ironically, nontechnical business managers can accurately assess the degree of business risk only after the technical risks have been fully exposed.

Additional business and technical risks result from outsourcing. Today, many enterprises include equipment owned, maintained, and managed by third parties. Some of this equipment resides on the organization's own premises, and other equipment resides offsite; for example, at application service provider facilities.

21.1.2   Ubiquitous Internet Protocol (IP) Networking.   Business has been dealing with the security of internets (i.e., interconnected networks) since the advent of internetworking in the late 1960s. However, the growing use of transmission control protocol/internet protocol (TCP/IP)[1] networks and of the public Internet has exposed much more equipment to attack than in the days of closed corporate networks. In addition, a much wider range of equipment, such as voice telephones based on voice-over IP (VoIP), fax machines, copiers, and even soft drink dispensers, are now network accessible.

IP connectivity has been a great boon to productivity and ease of use, but it has not been without a darker side. Network accessibility also has created unprecedented opportunities for improper unauthorized access to networked resources and other mischief. It is not uncommon to experience probes and break-in attempts within hours or even minutes of unannounced connection to the global Internet.

Protecting Internet-visible assets is inherently a conflict between ease-of-access and security. The safest systems are those unconnected to the outside world. Similarly, the easiest to use systems are those that have no perceivable restrictions on use. Adjusting the limits on user activities and access must balance conflicting requirements.

21.1.3   Internal Partitions.   Complex corporate environments can often be secured effectively by dividing the organization into a variety of interrelated and nested security domains, each with its own legal, technical, and cultural requirements. For example, there are specific legal requirements for medical records (see Chapter 49) and for privacy protection (see Chapter 52). Partners and suppliers, as well as consultants, contractors, and customers, often need two-way access to corporate data and facilities. These diverse requirements mean that a single corporate firewall is often insufficient.

Different domains within the organization will often require their own firewalls and security policies. Keeping track of the multitude of data types, protection and access requirements, and different legal jurisdictions and regulations makes for previously unheard of degrees of complexity.

21.1.4 Critical Availability. Networks are often critical for second-to-second operations; as a result, the side effects of ill-considered countermeasures may be worse than the damage from the actual attack. For example, shutting down the network, or even part of it, for maintenance or repair can wreak more havoc than penetration by a malicious hacker.

21.1.5 Accessibility. Users must be involved in the evolution of rules and procedures. Today, it is still not unheard of for a university faculty to take the position that any degree of security will undermine the very nature of their community, compromising their ability to perform research and inquiries. This extreme position persists despite the attention of the mass media, the justified beliefs of the technical community, and documented evidence that lack of protection of any Internet-connected system undermines the safety of the entire connected community.

Connecting a previously isolated computer system or network to the global Internet creates a communications pathway to every corner of the world. Customers, partners, and employees can obtain information, send messages, place orders, and otherwise interact 24 hours a day, seven days a week, 365 days a year, from literally anywhere on or near Earth. Even the Space Shuttle and the International Space Station have Internet access. Under these circumstances, the possibilities for attack or inadvertent misuse are limitless.

Despite the vast increase in connectivity, some businesses and individuals do not need extensive access to the global Internet for their day-to-day activities, although they may resent being excluded. The case for universal digital dial-tone is therefore a question of business policy and political considerations.

21.1.6 Appropriate Responses to Attacks. Long before the advent of the computer, before the development of instant communications, international law recognized that firing upon a naval vessel was an act of war. Captains of naval vessels were given standing orders summarized as "fire if fired upon." In areas without readily accessible police protection, the right of citizens to defend themselves is generally recognized by most legal authorities. Within the body of international law, such formal standards of conduct for military forces are known as "rules of engagement," a concept with global utility.

In cyberspace, it is tempting to jettison the standards of the real world. It is easy to imagine oneself master of one's own piece of cyberspace, without connection to real-world laws and limitations on behavior. However, information technology (IT) personnel do not have the standing of ships' captains with no communications to the outside world. Some argue that *fire if fired upon* is an acceptable standard for online behavior. Others maintain that such an approach does not take into account the legal and ethical issues surrounding response strategies and tactics.

Any particular security incident has a range of potential responses. Which response is appropriate depends on the enterprise and its political, legal, and business environment. Acceptability of response is also a management issue, as well as potentially a political issue. Determining what responses are acceptable in different situations requires input from management on policy, from legal counsel on legality, and from technical staff on technical feasibility. Depending on the organization, it also may be necessary to involve unions and other parties in the negotiation of what constitutes appropriate responses.

What is acceptable or appropriate in one area is not necessarily acceptable or appropriate in another. Often the national security arena has lower standards of proof than would be acceptable in normal business litigation. In U.S. civil courts, cases are decided upon a preponderance of evidence. Standards of proof acceptable in civil litigation are not conclusive when a criminal case is being tried, where guilt must be established beyond a reasonable doubt.

Gambits or responses that are perfectly legal in a national security environment may be completely illegal and recklessly irresponsible in the private sector, exposing the organization to significant legal liability.

Rules of etiquette and behavior are similarly complex. The rights of prison inmates in the United States remain significant, even though they are subject to rules and regulations substantially more restrictive than for the general population. Security measures, as well, must be appropriate for the persons and situations to which they are applied.

21.1.7   Counter-Battery.   Some suggest that the correct response to a perceived attack is to implement the cyberspace equivalent of *counter-battery,* that is, targeting the artillery that has just fired upon you. However, counter-battery tactics, when used as a defensive measure against Internet attacks, will be perceived, technically and legally, as an attack like any other.

Counter-battery tactics may be emotionally satisfying, but are prone to both error and collateral damage. Counter-battery can only be effective when the malefactor is correctly identified and the effects of the reciprocal attack are limited to the malefactor. If third parties are harmed in any way, then the retaliatory action becomes an attack in and of itself. One of the more celebrated counter-battery attacks gone awry was the 1994 case when two lawyers from Phoenix, Arizona, spammed over 5,000 Usenet newsgroups to give unsolicited information on a U.S. Immigration and Naturalization Service lottery for 55,000 green cards (immigration permits). The resulting retaliation—waves of e-mail protests—against the malefactors flooded their internet service provider (ISP) and caused at least one server to crash, resulting in a denial of service to all the other, innocent, customers of the ISP.[2]

21.1.8   Protecting Employees.   It is critical that Internet policies adopt a *hold harmless* position. That is, if employees act in good faith, in accordance with their responsibilities, and within documented procedures, management should never punish them for such action. If the procedures are wrong, managers should improve the rules and procedures, and not blame the employees. Disciplinary actions are inappropriate in such circumstances.

21.2   TECHNICAL ISSUES.   There are many technical issues involved in protecting Internet-accessible resources. The technologies used to protect network assets include routers, firewalls, proxy servers, redundancy, and dispersion. When properly designed and implemented, security measures produce a positive feedback loop, where improvements in network security and robustness are self-reinforcing. Each improvement makes other improvements possible and more effective.

21.2.1   Inside/Outside.   Some visions of the future include a utopian world where everything is directly accessible from anywhere without effort, and with only beneficial results. The original Internet operated on this basis, until a number of incidents (including the 1988 Morris worm) caused people to rethink the perceived inherent peacefulness of the networked world.

The architecture and design of protective measures for a network depend on differentiating *inside* trustable systems from *outside* untrustworthy systems. This is equally true for intranets, the Internet, or an *extranet,* so called to distinguish private interconnections of networks from the public Internet. Unfortunately, trust is not a black and white issue. A system may be trustworthy from one perspective and untrustworthy from another, thus complicating the security design. In addition, the vast majority of inappropriate computer use is thought to be done by those with legitimate access to some aspect of the system and its data.

Basic connectivity configuration is one of those few areas that are purely technical, without a business risk element. One of the most obvious elements involves the tables implemented in routers connecting the enterprise to the public carrier-supplied IP connection. The table rules must prevent *IP spoofing,* which is the misrepresentation of IP packet origins.

There are three basic rules for preventing IP spoofing applicable to all properly configured networks:

1. Packets entering the network from the outside should never have *originator* addresses within the target network.

2. Packets leaving a network and going to the public network must have *originator* addresses within the originating network.

3. Packets leaving a network and going to the public network must not have *destination* addresses within the originating network.

A corollary to these rules is that packets with originator or destination addresses in the intranet addresses range (RFC1597, superseded by RFC1918)[3] or dynamic IP addresses,[4] should never be permitted to enter or leave an internal network.

21.2.2 Hidden Subnets. Firewalls funnel network traffic through one or more choke points, concentrating the security task for a small number of systems. The reasoning behind such concentration is that the likelihood of a security breach of the entire network rises rapidly with the number of independent access points.

Firewalls and proxy servers (see Chapter 20) are effective only in topologies where the firewall filters all traffic between the protected systems and the less-trusted world outside its perimeter. If the protected systems can in any way be accessed without going through the firewall, then the firewall itself has been rendered irrelevant. Security audits often uncover systems that violate this policy; relying on administrative sanctions to preclude such holes in the security perimeter generally does not work.

The simplest solution to this problem is the use of RFC 1918 (formerly RFC 1597)[5] addresses within protected networks. RFC1918 provides a range of IPv4 addresses guaranteed by the Internet Assigned Numbers Authority (IANA) never to occur in the normal, public Internet. The address ranges used for dynamic IP address assignment[6] have similar properties. These address ranges are listed in Exhibit 21.1.

Filtering these addresses on both inbound and outbound data streams is straightforward and highly effective at stopping a wide range of attacks.[7] Requiring the use of such addresses, and prohibiting the internal use of externally valid addresses, goes a long way toward preventing the use of unauthorized protocols and connections.

Exhibit 21.1   Private IPv4 Addresses[1]

Ranges TEST-NET (RFC1878)
   192.0.2.0–192.0.2.255 (192.0.2.0/24)

RFC1918 Address Allocation for Private Networks (formerly RFC 1597)
   192.168.0.1–192.168.255.255 (192.168.0.0/16)
   172.16.0.0–172.131.255.255 (172.16.0.0/12)
   10.0.0.0–10.255.255.255 (10.0.0.0/8)

Non-DHCP Server Autoconfiguration (Dynamic IP Address Assignment)[2]
   169.254.0.0–169.254.255.255 (169.254.0.0/16)

---

[1] CIDR representation form parenthesized. See T. Pummill and B. Manning, "RFC 1878—Variable Length Subset Table for IPv4," December 1995.
[2] See Stuart Cheshire and Bernard Aboba, "Dynamic Configuration of IPv4 Link-Local Addresses" (Draft RFC), March 1, 2001.

21.2.3   What Need Be Exposed?   A security implementation starts with an analysis of the enterprise's mission, needs, and requirements. All designs and implementations are a compromise between absolute security, achieved only in a powered down or disconnected system, and total openness, in which a system is completely open to any and all access from the outside.

Although in most cases communications must be enabled between the enterprise and the outside world for normal business functions, total disconnection, known as an *air gap,* is sometimes both needed and appropriate between specific components. Industrial real-time control systems, life-critical systems, and systems with high requirements for confidentiality are appropriate candidates for total air gaps.

Often, systems that do not need to receive information from outside sources must publish statistical or other information to less secure systems. This requirement can often be satisfied through the use of limited functionality links such as media exchange, or through tightly controlled one-way transfers. These mechanisms can be implemented with IP-related technologies, or with more limited technologies including KERMIT,[8] UUCP, or vendor-specific solutions.

In other cases, restrictions reflect policies for permitted use and access rather than for protection against outside attack. For example, it is reasonable and appropriate for a public library to limit access to HTTP and related protocols, while prohibiting access to such facilities as FTP and TELNET. In these cases, firewalls are a reasonable solution, so long as their limitations are recognized. For example, firewalls do not prevent mobile code such as Active-X and JAVA from working around prohibited functions.

21.2.4   Multiple Security Domains.   Many networks implement security solely at the point of entry, where the organization's network connects to the public Internet. Such a *monolithic firewall* is a less than effective choice for all but the most simple of small organizations. As a starting point, systems available to the general population should be outside of the internal security domain (Exhibit 21.2) in a "no man's land" between the public Internet and the private internal net; such a barrier is referred to as a *demilitarized zone* (DMZ). These systems should be afforded a degree of protection by sandwiching them between an outer firewall (protecting the DMZ from the public network) and an inner firewall (protecting the internal network from the public network

Exhibit 21.2   Servers between Inner and Outer Firewalls

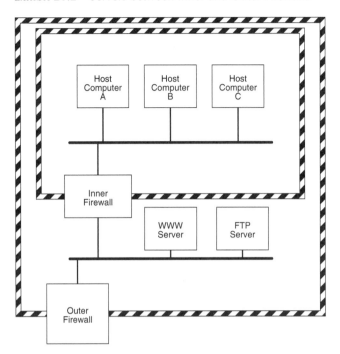

and controlling the communications between the publicly accessible servers located in the DMZ to the internal network). Such a topology permits implementation of the differing security restrictions applicable to the two networks. Systems located within the DMZ should also be suspect, as they are targets for compromise.

Although the industry as a whole agrees on the need for DMZ configurations, it is less appreciated that such restrictions also have a place within organizations. Different groups, departments, and functions within an organization have different security and access requirements. For example, in a financial services firm, the security requirements differ dramatically among departments (Exhibit 21.3). Three obvious examples of departments with different requirements are Personnel, Mergers and Acquisitions, and Research and Development.

Exhibit 21.3   Sibling and Nested Security Domains

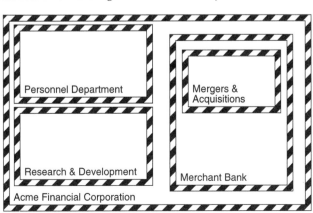

The Personnel Department is the custodian of a wide range of sensitive information about the firm, its employees, and often outsiders who are either regularly on company premises or work regularly with the company on projects. Some of this information, such as residence addresses, pay levels, and license plates, is sensitive for personal or cultural reasons. Other information subjects the organization to legal or regulatory sanctions if it is improperly disclosed or used. In the United States, examples of sensitive data include social security numbers, age, sexual orientation, and human immunodeficiency virus (HIV) or other medical status.

The Mergers and Acquisitions Department handles sensitive information of a different sort. Information about business negotiations or future plans is subject to strict confidentiality requirements. Furthermore, the disclosure of such information is subject to a variety of regulations on governmental and securities industry levels. Within the Mergers and Acquisitions Department, access to information often must be on a need-to-know basis, both to protect the deal and to protect the firm from exposure to civil and criminal liability.

Some information in the Research and Development Department is completely open to the public, whereas other information is restricted to differing degrees.

A full implementation of an adequate security environment will require protections that are not only logically different on a departmental basis, but also require that different departments be protected from each other. It is difficult, therefore, if not impossible, for a single firewall, located at the connection to the outside world, to implement the required security measures.

Securing systems in isolated logical areas is not an example of distrust, but merely a matter of ensuring that the interactions between the third party systems and the outside world are as allowed. As an example, consider the straightforward situation at Hypothetical Brokerage. Hypothetical Brokerage uses two trading networks, Omega and Gamma. At first glance, it would seem that that it would be acceptable to place Omega's and Gamma's network gateways on the usual DMZ, together with Hypothetical's WWW servers (Exhibit 21.4).

However, this grants a high degree of trust to Omega and Gamma, and all of their staff, suppliers, and contractors. The most important operative question is whether there is a credible hazard.

Exhibit 21.4   Omega and Gamma Servers on
Hypothetical's DMZ

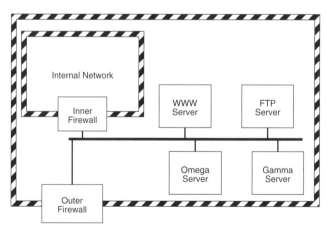

Either of the two gateways is well situated to:

- Monitor the communications traffic to and from Hypothetical's WWW servers
- Monitor the traffic between Hypothetical and the other, competing network
- Attack the other gateway
- Disrupt communications to and from the other gateway
- Attack Hypothetical's network

Network providers also represent an attractive attack option. A single break-in to a network provider–supplied system component has the effect of compromising large numbers of end-user sites. There is ample history of private (PBX) and public (carrier-owned) switches being preferred targets.[9]

The solution is to isolate the third-party systems in separate DMZs, with the traffic between each of the DMZs and the rest of the network scrupulously checked as to transmission control protocol and user datagram protocol (TCP/UDP), port number, and source and destination addresses, to ensure that all traffic is authorized. One method is to use a single firewall, with multiple local area network (LAN) ports, each with different filtering rules, to recast Hypothetical's original single DMZ into disjoint, protected, DMZs (Exhibit 21.5)

21.2.5 Compartmentalization. Breaking the network into separate security compartments reduces the potential for total network meltdown. Limiting the potential damage of an incident is an important step in resolving the problems.

The same rule applies to the DMZs. For example, in a financial trading or manufacturing enterprise, it is not uncommon to have gateways representing access points to trading and partner networks (Exhibit 21.4). Where one places these "friendly" systems

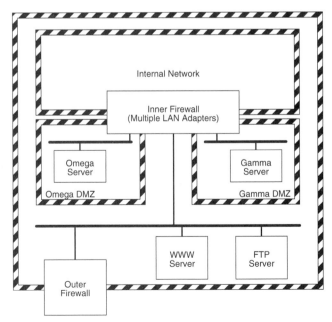

Exhibit 21.5   Omega and Gamma Servers in Separate DMZs from Hypothetical's Server

is problematic. Many organizations have chosen to place these systems within their regular DMZ.

Sites have belatedly discovered that such gateways have, on occasion, been found to have acted as routers, taking over that function from the intended routers. In other cases, the gateways have experienced malfunctions and impaired the functioning of the rest of the network (or DMZ). As always, the only solutions certain to work are shutdown or isolation.

Compartmentalization also prevents accidents from cascading. A failure in a single gateway is not likely to propagate throughout the network, because the unexpected traffic will be stopped by the firewall isolating the gateway from the network. Such an event can be made to trigger a firewall's attack alarms.

The network problem is not limited to externally provided nodes. An errant system operating in a noncompartmented network, located as it is within the outer security perimeter, can wreak havoc throughout the entire corporation. Constructing the network as a series of nested and peer-related security domains, each protected by appropriate firewalls, localizes the impact of the inevitable incidents. The larger the network, the more expensive an incident is. It is quite conceivable that the entire budget for compartmentalizing a corporate network will be less expensive than the single hour of downtime resulting from the first errant system.

21.2.6   Need to Access.   Sometimes it is easy to determine who requires access to which resources and information. However, the question of access control often involves painful choices with many nuances and subtleties. Legal and contractual responsibilities further complicate the question. For example, lack of access may be a benefit to persons alleged to have misused information.

Physical and logical access controls (see Chapters 14, 15, and 16) need to be implemented for Internet-accessible systems as for any other sensitive and critical system. Controls for such systems must be enforced, and respected by all members of the organization. It is important that personnel with restricted access to the network and security infrastructure understand and comprehend the reasons for the security rules, and that they not take measures that circumvent those rules. The integrity of an organization's firewalls and network infrastructure is only as good as the physical and logical security of the personnel, equipment, infrastructure, and systems comprising the firewall and network. Regular auditing of both physical and logical access to infrastructure assets is critical and necessary.

The need to maintain information security on communications within the organization argues for the extensive use of security technologies, even when the data packets are never expected to leave the premises. It is not far-fetched to propose that, even within the enterprise, any application with privacy or confidentiality requirements should make use of privacy infrastructure such as the secure sockets layer (SSL) for WWW-based applications, or tunneling such as layer 2 tunneling protocol (L2TP)[10] and point-to-point tunneling protocol (PPTP).[11]

21.2.7   Accountability.   People often talk about impenetrable systems. However, despite the castle-and-moat analogies used in many discussions of security, no perimeter is likely to be perfect. Given the likelihood of successful attacks, security personnel must use both technical and managerial measures for effective response.

When securing infrastructure, priority should be given to protective measures that ensure accountability for actions. Just as it is desirable to prevent inappropriate activity, it is even more important to ensure that activities can be accounted for.

For example, there are many ways to carry out denial-of-service attacks. The most troublesome are completely legal. Although some of these attacks, such as distributed denial of service, are belligerent or politically and ideologically motivated, involving remote-control *zombie* programs as described in Chapter 11, many accidental denials of service can occur without malice in the course of software development. For example, two of the most famous worms that inadvertently led to denial of service, the Morris worm and the WANK worm, were detected due to implementation errors in their replication mechanisms. Errors in the replication mechanisms caused both worms to proliferate at extremely fast rates, effectively producing denial-of-service attacks and subsequent detection.

It is important to analyze security breaches to distinguish among attacks, accidents, and experiments. It is better for weaknesses to be uncovered, even accidentally, within an organization, than it is to deal with a truly belligerent security breach. Policies and practices should therefore encourage employees to report accidents rather than try to hide them. As for false alarms caused by overenthusiastic security neophytes, management should avoid punishing those who report illusory breaches. Accountability provides the raw material to determine what actually happened. The resulting information is the critical underpinning for analysis and education, thus enabling the enterprise to evolve to higher levels of security and integrity.

21.2.8   Read-Only File Security.   Many sites allow downloads, usually via FTP, of large numbers of files. These files may include copies of forms, manuals, instructions, maps, and service guides. If such file serving is provided, then it is critical to ensure that:

- The servers supporting the ftp service are secure.
- The contents of the publicly accessible file store are read-only and subject to change control.
- The entire contents of the public file store can be restored quickly in the event of a possible compromise.
- There is a designated party who is responsible for maintaining and protecting the public file service.

21.2.9   Exposures.   There are as many different types of exposure on the Internet as there are connections and users. In that context, every connected site is a potential target for some form of attack. Containing the risk is the critical requirement.

The potential exposures are business risk management issues as well as technical issues. Although technical issues are important, the business risks such as liability and damage to reputation are more significant than the purely technical exposures.

Downtime and corruption, while technically tedious to correct, are more damaging in the context of an enterprise's financial well being.

21.2.10   Going Offline.   The responsiveness required to a problem with an Internet-connected system is directly related to the out-of-service costs. In some organizations, this may be the cost of lost business; in other organizations, the cost may be that of lost professional time, of damaged public relations, and of lowered morale. In any event, the larger the proportion of the organization (or its customers) affected by the problem, the higher the cost, and the greater the urgency to effect repairs.

Today's interconnected world makes Internet disconnection a truly painful option for a network or security manager. Although the cost of disconnection can run into hundreds of thousands of dollars in lost business and productivity, disconnection in certain situations is both necessary and appropriate. At times, disconnection presents the lowest cost, most effective way to protect users, systems, and the public. For example, on May 4, 2000, during the epidemic spread of the Microsoft Outlook-exploiting "I Love You" virus attack, network managers at Ford Motor Company[12] disconnected Ford's network from the outside world to limit the entry of contaminated e-mail into Ford's systems, and to prevent Ford's systems from spreading the contagion. The response achieved its goals. It was not painless, but the alternatives were more painful.

The primary issue surrounding disconnection is what can be disconnected, on whose authority. According to well-known corollaries of Murphy's Law, such important incidents require short response times, always on occasions when senior managers are not available. The best way to provide for this contingency is to furnish the personnel who are present with guidelines, and with the authority to act within those guidelines without fear of reprisal, in order to defend the systems. If an organization chooses, as some do, not to authorize such actions, they also forswear the benefits.

21.2.11   Auditing.   In any organization, facilities usage should be monitored and analyzed, including network activity. Because people interested in attacking or subverting the enterprise's networks will attack when they wish, such monitoring and analysis must be part of a continuing process. Ongoing observation and review should include:

- Physical communications infrastructure
- Firewalls, router tables, and filtering rules
- Host security
- File security
- Traffic patterns on backbones, DMZ, and other network segments
- Physical security of systems and communications infrastructure

These areas are both synergistic and independent. They are synergistic in that the combination of all of them is mutually reinforcing in promoting a secure computing environment. They are independent because any one of them may represent a weak point in an otherwise secure environment. See Chapter 36 for audit guidelines.

21.2.12   Planning.   It is generally conceded that all plans are inherently imperfect, particularly when addressing technical issues that come in an almost infinite variety. However, plans do serve an important function: they crystallize the decision-making process and determine what options are available.

Planning for Internet-related security and availability issues should emphasize the ranges of permissible response options and how each potential response will affect the enterprise. Decision makers need to visit each of the issues before a crisis occurs, so that when the time comes to make decisions with critical impact, the complexities will have been explored in advance. See Chapter 40 for a discussion of emergency response.

Planning should be a wide-ranging exploratory process, rather than a narrow effort to develop specific reaction plans. Although specific scenarios and required responses will certainly be developed; the thinking and analysis of the processes are more important than the actual contents of the resulting checklists and procedures.

21.2.13   Site Hardening.   Site hardening, that is, maximizing the survivability of resources in the case of an outside event (e.g., power failure) is often a reflexive action when building potentially critical resources. Data centers have been hardened for years, including via auxiliary generators, isolated compartments, and other measures. Although reasonable hardening remains a useful strategy, hardening must be viewed in the context of what Internet-accessible resources are used for: accessing the outside world.

The original ARPAnet packet-switched network was an experiment in building a network that could survive the obliteration of individual nodes comprising the network. Although military conflict was the original motivation; the concept and the lessons learned have more global utility. In particular, extreme site-hardening measures are less effective, in terms of Internet connectivity, than a redundant, dispersed network with multiple, diverse connectivity.

That is not to say that reasonable business continuity precautions (Chapter 42) are not appropriate, merely that they must be viewed in context. See Chapters 14 and 15 for details of infrastructure protection.

21.2.14   Site Dispersion.   Security-related penetrations, worms, viruses, and other harmful attacks can damage an organization's entire Internet-accessible systems, regardless of their physical location.

However, many "Internet" failures are actually failures of physical infrastructure, of outside communications providers, of specific physical problems such as leaking roofs and fires, or of environmental factors such as floods, tornadoes, and hurricanes. Defending against these problems is most cost effectively addressed by dispersing the Internet access points, by providing a network with multiple routes, and by alternate backup facilities. The best defense against floods, tornadoes, hurricanes, and major infrastructure problems is locating alternate sites in different geographic and weather areas.

21.2.15   Benefits and Drawbacks of Hardening and Dispersion.   Neither hardening nor dispersing a site is a cure-all. In a sense, hardening and dispersion represent end points of a continuum of potential configuration and location options, with the scale of the facility and infrastructure having a major impact on costs and feasibility.

Small to medium organizations can organize alternate facilities at modest cost, often more inexpensively than any potential site-hardening option. More extensive sites will incur greater costs.

The key to effective decisions involving hardening or dispersion is a careful analysis of the costs and benefits. Organizations will almost always benefit from a combination of the two approaches. For any critical element of network infrastructure, some form of protected power, such as an uninterruptible power supply is an absolute necessity, although creating a secondary facility may be a better option than installing an expensive long-term power-generating facility.

In other situations, such as health-care facilities, where a distant computer facility is unfeasible, a secondary facility could be located on the same campus, but in a different building, to prevent a problem with the primary physical facility from completely shutting down access.

21.3   APPLICATION SERVICE PROVIDERS.   In recent years, it has become increasingly common to outsource entire applications services. External organizations providing such services are known as *applications service providers,* more commonly referred to as ASPs.

The security and integrity issues surrounding the use of ASPs are the same as those surrounding the use of an internal corporate service. Questions of privacy, integrity, and reliability remain relevant, but as with any form of outsourcing, there are additional questions. For example, are databases for different clients comingled? What data security measures are taken? What network security measures are enforced? What business continuity measures are in place? What are the hiring and vetting practices of the ASP?

The bottom line is that although outsourcing promises speedy implementation, lower personnel costs, and economies of scale, the customer organization will suffer considerable harm if there is a problem with the ASP.

21.4   SUMMARY.   Internet access and Internet-accessed resources are a critical part of the modern information infrastructure, which warrants the same degree of care and concern present in the rest of the enterprise. The overall issues involved in protecting Internet-visible systems are first and foremost business risk issues—with both a technical overlay in terms of feasibility and hazards—and a degree of technological due diligence.

One of the underappreciated keys to developing effective and reasonable policies for protecting Internet-visible assets is an understanding of what types of access are necessary and appropriate for each part of the enterprise to accomplish its tasks. The best functioning security and protective measures are those that prevent misuse while having a minimal impact on legitimate use. Policies that become an everyday obstruction to effective work will be the source of later problems. Appropriate precautions and preventative measures are feasible, both to assure continuing use and to protect the integrity and operation of the enterprise.

Reactions to attacks (and natural disasters) must be responsible. Counter-battery and other reactive responses, while emotionally satisfying, are counterproductive. More critical is the delegated management authority to take necessary defensive actions, including disconnection, without fear of disciplinary retaliation.

Organizations can be effectively viewed as a collection of smaller organizations, each with its own requirements and obligations. Following the same rules within the organization as without reduces risk substantially. Some systems need to be absolutely protected from the outside, and these systems should be air-gapped.

Redundant facilities and network connectivity are a critical component to ensuring 24/7/365 availability. Hardening is useful, but connectivity or regional problems are more probable than specific casualties. Planning for specific failure syndromes is futile; plan to shift to redundant facilities to maintain capability. Do the post-mortem analysis later.

21.5   BIBLIOGRAPHY

Alderman, Ellen, and Caroline Kennedy. *The Right to Privacy.* New York: Alfred A. Knopf, 1995.

Bernstein, David. "We've Been Hacked." *Inc Technology,* No. 3, 2000.

Bradsher, Keith. "With its E-mail Infected, Ford Scrambled and Caught Up." *The New York Times,* May 8, 2000.

Cheshire, Stuart, and Bernard Aboba. "Dynamic Configuration of IPv4 Link-Local Addresses." March 2001 (RFC number awaiting assignment at time of press).

da Cruz, Frank, and Christine M.Gianone. *Using C-KERMIT,* nd. Boston, MA: Digital Press 1997.

deGroot, G., D. Karrenberg, V. Moskowitz, and Lear E. Rekhter. "RFC1597—Address Allocation for Private Internets." March 1994. Available at *www.ietf.org/rfc.html.*

deGroot, G., D. Karrenberg, V. Moskowitz, and Lear E. Rekhter. "RFC1918—Address Allocation for Private Internets." February 1996.

Derfler, Frank J., and Jay Munro. "Home Appliances Hit the Net." *PC Magazine,* January 2, 2001.

Electronic Communications Privacy Act of 1986; 18 USC § 2510 et seq.

Gezelter, Robert. "Internet Security." *The Computer Security Handbook,* 3rd ed. New York: John Wiley & Sons, 1995.

Gezelter, Robert. "Internet Security." *The Computer Security Handbook,* 3rd ed, Supplement. New York: John Wiley & Sons, 1997.

Gezelter, Robert. "Security Prosecution: Records and Evidence." *DECUS Magazine,* Spring 1996.

Gezelter, Robert. "Stopping Spoofed Addresses Can Cut Down on DDoS Attacks." *Network World Fusion,* August 14, 2000.

Gezelter, Robert. "System Security—The Forgotten Issues." Conference Session, US DECUS Symposium, Las Vegas, Nevada, Fall 1990 (available from *www.rlgsc.com/presentations.html*).

Hamzeh, K., G. Pall, W. Verthein, J. Taarud, W. Little, and G. Zorn. "RFC 2637—Point-to-Point Tunneling Protocol." July 1999.

Janofsky, Michael. "Police Seek Record of Bookstore Patrons in Bid for Drug Charge," *The New York Times,* November 24, 2000.

Kahn, David. *Codebreakers.* New York: MacMillan, 1970.

Kahn, David. *Seizing the Enigma.* Boston: Houghton Mifflin, 1991.

Klensin, J., ed. "RFC 2821—Simple Mail Transfer Protocol" (obsoletes RFC 821, RFC 974, and RFC 1869), May 2001. Available at *www.ietf.org/rfc.html.*

Layton, Edwin. *And I Was There: Pearl Harbor and Midway–Breaking the Secrets.* William Morrow, 1985.

Littman, Jonathan. *The Fugitive Game: Online with Kevin Mitnick.* Boston: Little, Brown, 1996.

Neumann, Peter G. "The Green Card Flap." *RISKS Forum Digest* 15.76, April 18, 1994 and ff.

Postel, J, and J.K. Reynolds. "RFC 854—Telnet Protocol Specification." May 1983.

Postel, J., and J.K. Reynolds. "RFC 959—File Transfer Protocol." October 1985.

Pummill, T., and B. Manning. "RFC 1878—Variable Length Subnet Table for IPv4." December 1995.

Schwartau, Winn. *Information Warfare—Chaos on the Information Superhighway,* 2nd ed. New York: Thunder's Mouth Press, 1996.

Shimormura, Tsutomo, and John Markoff. *Takedown.* New York: Hyperion, 1996.

Slatalla, Michelle, and Joshua Quittner. *Masters of Deception.* New York: HarperCollins, 1995.

Stoll, Clifford. *The Cuckoo's Egg.* New York: Bantam Doubleday, 1989.

Timms, Kevin. Telephone interview, Summer 2001.

Townsley, W., A. Valencia, A. Rubens, G. Pall, G. Zorn, and B. Palter. "RFC 2661–Layer Two Tunneling Protocol 'L2TP'." August 1999.

Weizenbaum, Joseph. *Computer Power and Human Reason.* San Francisco: WH Freeman, 1976.

21.6 FURTHER READING

www.ietf.org Internet Standards.

www.cert.org Security related information.

Alderman, Ellen, and Caroline Kennedy. *The Right to Privacy.* New York: Alfred A. Knopf, 1995. Well-written work concerning legal issues relating to privacy, particularly in the United States.

Kahn, David. *Codebreakers.* New York: MacMillan, 1970. Well-regarded work on the history of cryptography.

Kahn, David. *Seizing the Enigma.* Boston: Houghton Mifflin, 1991. Well-written account of the electronic intelligence effort against Germany during World War II, and instructive to those interested in electronic security.

Layton, Edwin. *And I Was There: Pearl Harbor and Midway–Breaking the Secrets.* William Morrow, 1985. Memoirs of electronic intelligence gathering in the Pacific Theatre, World War II.

Stoll, Clifford. *The Cuckoo's Egg.* New York: Bantam Doubleday, 1989. Well-written account of a series of Internet-cracking incidents.

21.7 NOTES

1. The third main fundamental protocol of the protocol suite is the User Datagram Protocol (UDP). UDP and TCP are peer protocols at the same level in the protocol stack. Referring to the protocol suite as "TCP/IP" is somewhat incorrect but has become common usage.

2. Peter G. Neumann, "The Green Card Flap," *RISKS Forum Digest* 15.76, April 18, 1994.

3. G. deGroot, D. Karrenberg, V. Moskowitz, and Lear E. Rekhter, "RFC1597—Address Allocation for Private Internets," March 1994; and G. deGroot, D. Karrenberg, V. Moskowitz, and Lear E. Rekhter, "RFC1918—Address Allocation for Private Internets," February 1996.

4. Stuart Cheshire and Bernard Aboba, "Dynamic Configuration of IPv4 Link-Local Addresses," March 2001 (RFC number awaiting assignment at time of press).

5. deGroot et al. "RFC1597"; deGroot et al. "RFC1918."

6. Cheshire and Aboda, "Dynamic Configuration."

7. Robert Gezelter, "Stopping Spoofed Addresses Can Cut Down on DDoS Attacks," *Network World Fusion,* August 14, 2000.

8. Frank da Cruz and Christine M.Gianone, *Using C-KERMIT* (Boston, MA: Digital Press 1997).

9. Michelle Slatalla and Joshua Quittner, *Masters of Deception* (New York: HarperCollins, 1995).

10. W. Townsley, A. Valencia, A. Rubens, G. Pall, G. Zorn, and B. Palter, "RFC 2661–Layer Two Tunneling Protocol 'L2TP'," August 1999.

11. K. Hamzeh, G. Pall, W. Verthein, J. Taarud, W. Little, and G. Zorn, "RFC 2637—Point-to-Point Tunneling Protocol," July 1999.

12. Kevin Timms, Telephone interview, Summer 2001; Keith Bradsher, "With its E-mail Infected, Ford Scrambled and Caught Up," *The New York Times,* May 8, 2000.

CHAPTER 22

PROTECTING WEB SITES

Robert Gezelter

CONTENTS

22.1   INTRODUCTION.   Protecting a World Wide Web (WWW or Web) site means ensuring that the site and its functions are available 24 hours a day, seven days a week, 365 days a year. It also means ensuring that the information exchanged with the site is accurate and secure.

The preceding chapter focused on protecting Internet-visible systems, predominantly those systems used within the company to interact with the outside world. This chapter focuses on issues specific to Web interactions with customers, as well as to supply and distribution chains. Practically speaking, the Web site is an important, if not the most important component of an organization's interface with the outside world.

Web site protection lies at the intersection of technology, strategy, operations, customer relations, and business management. Web site availability and integrity directly affect the main streams of cash flow and commerce: an organization's customers, production chains, and supply chains. This is in contrast to the general Internet-related security issues examined in the preceding chapter, which primarily affect those inside the organization.

Availability is the cornerstone of all Web-related strategies. Idle times have become progressively rarer. Depending on the business and its markets, there may be some periods of lower activity. In the financial trading community, there remain only a few small windows during a 24-hour period when updates and maintenance can be performed. As global business becomes the norm, customers, suppliers, and distributors increasingly expect information when requested at any time of the day or night, even from modest size enterprises.

Causation is unrelated to impact. The overwhelming majority of Web outages are caused by unglamorous problems. High-profile, deliberate attacks are much less frequent than equipment and personnel failures. The effect on the business organization is indistinguishable. Having a low profile is not a guard against a random scanning attack.

External events, and their repercussions can also wreak havoc, both directly and indirectly. The September 11, 2001 terrorist attacks which destroyed New York City's World Trade Center complex had worldwide impact, not only on systems and firms located in the destroyed complex. Telecommunications infrastructure was damaged or destroyed, severing Internet links for many organizations.

Parts supply and all travel was disrupted when North American airspace was shutdown. New York City was sealed to exits and entries, while within the city itself, and throughout much of the world, normal operations were suspended. The September 11 attacks were extraordinarily disruptive, but security precautions similar to those described throughout this *Handbook* served to ameliorate damage to Web operations and other infrastructure elements of those companies that had implemented them.

Best practices and scale are important. Some practices, issues, and concerns at first glance appear relevant only to very large organizations, such as Fortune 500 companies. In fact, this is not so. Considering issues in a large organization permits them to appear magnified, and in full detail. Smaller organizations are subject to the same issues and concerns, but may be able to implement less formal solutions. Formality does not necessarily imply written procedures. It may mean that certain computer-related practices, such as modifying production facilities in place, are inherently poor ideas and should be avoided. Very large enterprises might address the problems by having a separate group, with separate equipment, responsible for operating the development environment.

22.2   RISK ANALYSIS.   Protecting an organization's Web sites depends on an accurate, rational assessment of the risks. Developing effective strategies and tactics to ensure site availability and integrity requires that all potential risks be examined in turn.

Unrestricted commercial activity has been permitted on the Internet since 1991. Since then, enterprises large and small have increasingly integrated Web access into their second-to-second operations. The risks inherent in a particular configuration and strategy are dependent on many factors, including the scale of the enterprise and the relative importance of the Web-based entity within the enterprise. Virtually all high-visibility Web sites (e.g., Yahoo, America Online, cnn.com, Amazon.com, and eBay) have experienced significant outages at various times.

The more significant the organization's Web component, the more critical is availability and integrity. Large, traditional firms with relatively small Web components can tolerate major interruptions with little damage. Firms large or small that rely on the Web for much of their business must pay greater attention to their Web presences, because a serious outage can quickly escalate into financial catastrophe.

22.2.1   Business Loss.   Business losses fall into several categories, any of which can occur in conjunction with an organization's Web presence. In the context of this chapter, customers are both outsiders accessing the Internet presence, and insiders accessing intranet applications. In practice, insiders using intranet-hosted applications pose the same challenges as the outside users.

22.2.1.1   PR Image.   The Web site is the organization's public face 24/7/365. This ongoing presence is a benefit, making the firm visible at all times, but the site's high public profile also makes it a prime target.

Government sites in the United States and abroad have often been the targets of attacks. In January 2000, "Thomas," the Web site of the U.S. Congress, was defaced. Earlier, in 1996, the Web site of the U.S. Department of Justice was vandalized. Sites belonging to the Japanese, U.K., and Mexican governments also have been vandalized.

In the corporate world, company Web sites have been the target of attacks intended to defame the corporation for real or imagined slights. Some such episodes have been reported in the news media, whereas others have not been the subjects of extensive reporting. The scale and newsworthiness of the episode is unimportant; the damage done to the targeted organization is the true measure. An unreported incident that is the initiating event in a business failure is more damaging to the affected parties than a seemingly more significant outage with less severe consequences.

Other cybervandalism episodes (e.g., sadmind/IIS) have used address scanners to target randomly selected machines. Obscurity is not a defense against address-scanner attacks.

22.2.1.2   Loss of Customers/Business.   Internet customers are highly mobile. Web site problems quickly translate into permanently lost customers. The reason for the outage is immaterial; the fact that there is a problem is often sufficient to provoke erosion of customer loyalty.

In most areas, there is competitive overlap. Using the overnight shipping business as an example, in most U.S. metropolitan areas there is (in alphabetical order) Airborne Express, Federal Express, United Parcel Service, and the United States Postal Service. All of the firms offer Web-based shipment tracking, a highly popular service. Problems or difficulties with shipment tracking will quickly lead to a loss of business in favor of a different company with easier tracking.

22.2.2   Interruptions.   Increasingly, modern enterprises are being constructed around ubiquitous 24/7/365 information systems, most often with Web sites playing a major role. In this environment, interruptions of any kind are catastrophic.

22.2.2.1   *Production.*   The past 20 years have seen a streamlining of production processes in all areas of endeavor. Twenty years ago, it was common for facilities to have multiple day supplies of components on-hand in inventory. Today, "zero latency" environments are common, forcing large facilities to have no inventory. Fiscally, zero latency environments are very efficient; operationally, they may be very fragile, subject to disruption by any number of hazards.

22.2.2.2   *Supply Chain.*   Increasingly, it is common for Web-based sites to be in the supply chain. Firms may encourage their vendors to use a Web-based portal to gain access to the vendor side of the purchasing system. XML-based[1] gateways, together with other Web technologies, are used to arrange for and manage the flow of raw materials and components required to support production processes.

22.2.2.3   *Delivery Chain.*   Web-based sites, both internal and external, also have become the vehicle of choice for tracking the status of orders and shipments, and increasingly as the backbone of many enterprises' delivery chain management and inquiry systems.

22.2.2.4   *Information Delivery.*   Banks, brokerages, utilities, and municipalities are increasingly turning to the Web as a convenient, low-cost method for managing their relationships with consumers.

Firms are also supporting downloading records of transactions and other relationship information in formats required by personal database programs and organizers. These outputs, in turn, are often used as inputs to other processes, which then generate other transactions. Not surprisingly, as time passes, more and more people and businesses depend on the availability of information on demand. Today's Web-based customers presume that information is accessible wherever they can use a personal computer, or even a Web-enabled cellular telephone. This is reminiscent of usage patterns of automatic teller machines in an earlier decade, which allowed people to base their plans on access to teller machines, often making multiple $20 withdrawals instead of cashing a $200 check weekly.

22.2.3   Proactive versus Reactive Threats.   Some threats and hazards can be addressed proactively, whereas others are inherently reactive. When strategies and tactics are developed to protect a Web presence, the strategies and tactics themselves can induce availability problems.

As an example, consider the common strategy of having multiple name servers responsible for providing the translation of domain names to internet protocol (IP) addresses. It is required before a domain name (properly referred to as a domain name service (DNS) zone) can be entered into the root level name servers, that at least two name servers be identified to process name resolution requests.

Updating DNS zones requires care. If an update is performed improperly, then the resources referenced via the symbolic DNS names will become unresolvable, regardless of the actual state of the Web server and related infrastructure. The risk calculus involving DNS names is further complicated by the common, efficient, and appropriate practice of designating internet service provider (ISP) name servers as the primary mechanism for the resolution of domain names. In short, name translation provides a good example of the possible risks that can affect a Web presence.

22.3   THREAT AND HAZARD ASSESSMENT.   Some threats are universal, whereas others are specific to an individual environment. The most devastating and severe threats are those that simultaneously affect large areas or populations, where efforts to repair damage and correct the problem are hampered by the scale of the problem.

22.3.1   What Are Threats and Hazards?   On a basic level, threats can be divided into several categories. The first is between deliberate acts and accidents. Deliberate acts comprise actions done with the intent to damage the Web site or its infrastructure. Accidents include natural phenomena (Acts of God) and clumsiness, carelessness, and unconsidered consequences ("Acts of Clod").

22.3.2   Hostile and Deliberate Acts, in Order of General Probability.   Broadly put, a deliberate act is one whose goal is to impair the system. Deliberate acts come in a broad spectrum of skill and intent. For the purpose of risk analysis and planning, deliberate acts against infrastructure providers can often appear to be acts of God. For example, an employee attack against a telephone carrier simply appears to an organization running a Web site to be a service interruption of unknown origin.

No enterprise or agency should consider itself anything but a likely target. Recent high-profile incidents have targeted the FBI (May 26 and 27, 1999), major political parties, and interest groups in the United States. On the consumer level, numerous digital subscriber line (DSL)-connected home systems have been targeted for subversion as preparation for the launching of DDoS attacks.

22.3.2.1   Employee Misbehavior (Deliberate or Accidental).   Employee (or former employee) misbehavior is among the most common deliberate acts, usually by insiders who have an intimate knowledge of procedures, plans, and vulnerabilities. Revenge is not an uncommon motive for attacks by former employees. Preventing them is a challenge, requiring good personnel and access control policies (see Chapters 14, 15, 21, 31, and 32).

Active employees represent a different type of challenge. With active personnel, attacks are likely to be more subtle than overt. Embezzlement and other white-collar crimes are more likely than out-and-out destructive attacks. With active personnel, the major deterrents, and the best defensive measures, are generally based on access control and accountability. In that sense, the files, servers, and infrastructure supporting a Web site are no different from any other type of IT resource.

22.3.2.2   Crackers.   Crackers often describe themselves as individuals who wish to explore systems for the pure technical challenge. As a hobby, such technical curiosity is not offensive, when permission has been given for the activities. Responsible individuals set up their own laboratory systems to experiment upon; less responsible individuals attempt to exploit systems belonging to other people and organizations without their permission. Unauthorized activity is what the general media refer to as *cracking* or *hacking.*

Many crackers incorrectly believe that their efforts are harmless. Data disclosure and accidental damage are two distinct types of damage associated with crackers. However, "because the systems are there" is perhaps the most dangerous motivation for the activity. Most other deliberate acts are intended to cause harm. Cracking often causes harm as a side effect. What is worse is that many of the people involved in cracking are doing it for pure fun, which means that no time limitations are involved. (For further information on hackers, see Chapter 6.)

22.3.2.3 Angry Customers.

Dissatisfied customers are not often the source of major Web security problems. However, e-mail flooding attacks are merely an electronic form of traditional letter-writing campaigns, magnified in their potential impact by the leverage afforded by the technology.

It is also plausible that an individual or group with the skills and inclination to attack systems could be motivated to attack a specific target because of an earlier unsatisfactory transaction.

22.3.2.4 Political Activism.

Although it is not common, Web sites, particularly those belonging to high-profile groups, are attractive targets for political extremists. In the United States, sites belonging to a variety of political and interest groups, and government entities have been attacked for political reasons.

Outside the United States, governments including Japan, the United Kingdom, and Mexico, and multinational organizations such as the WTO (World Trade Organization) and OPEC (Organization of Petroleum Exporting Countries), have been attacked and vandalized. Many of these incidents are specifically targeted by individuals and groups with political agendas.

22.3.2.5 Terrorism.

Terrorist actions can have a severe impact on information infrastructure, including Web sites. The severity of the impact can be illustrated by the destruction of New York City's World Trade Center complex by a terrorist attack on September 11, 2001. The same complex had been previously damaged in an attack with a truck bomb on February 29, 1993.

The "Twin Towers," the two 110-story office buildings in the World Trade Center complex, were known throughout the world as a prominent signature of Manhattan's skyline. More than 2,893 people were killed[2] in the attack, and numerous others injured. The Twin Towers were estimated to contain hundreds of businesses, more than 300 mainframes, and 15 trading floors.[3] The other buildings in the World Trade Center complex were destroyed or fatally damaged by the collapse of the twin towers, and buildings adjacent to the World Trade Center complex (including the World Financial Center) were heavily damaged. In all, nearly 20 percent of the high-quality office space in downtown Manhattan was either damaged or destroyed, with severe damage to computer and communications infrastructure.[4]

The utility substation responsible for a substantial section of southern Manhattan was destroyed. The telephone Central Office supporting the Financial district was damaged. Cellular and pager infrastructure was damaged. Long-haul leased lines and Internet connections were disrupted.

In the earlier 1993 attack, terrorists had detonated a truck bomb underneath the World Trade Center. The explosion caused major damage to utility levels of the building and forced the shutdown and evacuation of numerous firms, each of which attempted to implement its disaster plan. Unfortunately, there were fewer hot-site facilities available than firms declaring emergencies. Thus, many firms experienced significant problems with their operations.

The 1993 attack occurred before Web operations had become widespread. The 2001 attack had an extensive and extended impact on information technology related infrastructure, which continued for months after the attack. The impact on many firms' Web applications was significant, but other firms' disaster plans dealt adequately with the operational problems.

22.3.2.6   Criminals.   White-collar crimes such as embezzlement by employees have occurred on the Web many times, and criminal activity by third parties also has become part of the environment. Criminal threats on the Internet have included:

- Kidnapping domain names for ransom (web.net, bali.com).
- Downloading information and threatening disclosure (e.g., CD Universe with 300,000 credit card account numbers and their expiration dates, and CreditCards.com with 55,000 credit card numbers and their expiration dates).
- Threatening to disable production systems unless a payoff is made.

In a production environment, these threats and the hazards they represent must be taken seriously. See Chapter 32 for details of operations security.

22.3.3   Competitors.   The Web operates on a global basis, but business ethics, mores, and laws are not uniform throughout the world. The majority of publicized security penetrations involve crackers, only a few of whom are acknowledged to have been well paid to steal competitive intelligence. With monetary motivation supplanting the desire for notoriety amongst their peers, it is not surprising that such activities have not been publicly identified. It is a safe assumption that such "cracking for compensation" occurs, and is likely to be undetected, or at least unadmitted, in the majority of incidents.

From a different perspective, the majority of reported extortion episodes seem to imply that the underlying security penetration was not detected until the extortion demand was received. If this is correct, it is not unreasonable to presume that were the financial desires of the perpetrators met through other means, the penetrations would not have been detected.

22.3.4   Damage by Nonhostile Acts.   Deliberate hostile intent is not required to produce severe damage. Significant incidents occur on a daily basis. The overwhelming majority are neither widespread nor public enough to be deemed newsworthy; those that are represent only a small sampling of episodes in the past 20 years. Numerous similar incidents occur daily, ranging from backhoes breaking cables, to storms, floods, and earthquakes.

Newsworthiness is immaterial. Local telephone line outages are an example. It is not unusual for cable-splicing crews to stand by while road crews repave roads. The presence of the splicing crew is reassuring until one realizes that the crew would not be there were trouble not expected. It is not unusual in such situations to experience a cable break every few days. Such cable break incidents are rarely newsworthy, but the service interruptions are certainly important to those enterprises whose voice and data services are interrupted.

22.3.5   Acts of God.   Insurance professionals refer to fires, storms, earthquakes, and floods as "Acts of God," which are viewed as inevitable. Despite the impressive achievements of the modern IT environment, "Acts of God" remain hazards to the operations of Web sites and other online systems.

22.3.5.1   Weather.   Severe weather storms, tornadoes, floods, lightning, and icing occur frequently throughout the year, with major impacts on information infrastructure availability.

During December 2000, a series of severe ice storms shut down large parts of the southeast United States, including much of Texas and Arkansas. In Texas, the Dallas–Fort Worth airport, one of the busiest in the United States, was shut down for days. In Arkansas, ice storms shut roads and damaged utility infrastructures, with over 400,000 homes and businesses without power at one point.[5] The impact on Web presences in the affected areas was catastrophic.

22.3.5.2   Earthquake.   Many major metropolitan areas are vulnerable to earthquakes. San Francisco, Los Angeles, Mexico City, Tokyo, and other international business centers are located in earthquake zones.

As an example, on October 17, 1989, a 7.2 magnitude earthquake occurred in Loma Prieta, approximately 100 km south of San Francisco, California. The earthquake caused extensive damage to the San Francisco area, including disrupting electricity, gas, and telephone utilities. It destroyed the double-level Nimitz freeway in nearby Oakland, and caused the collapse of one 30-foot segment of the Oakland Bay Bridge. While some of the interruptions were quickly repaired, other problems remained for weeks or months.

22.3.5.3   Fire.   Modern buildings are generally low fire risks. However, fires within a computer facility are almost always catastrophic. The damage is not solely caused by the flames themselves, but also by the secondary effects of smoke and water infiltration into the equipment. In addition to equipment, power and communications cabling and other infrastructure elements are often severely damaged.

The most well-publicized incidents involving fire damage to telecommunications facilities were the May 9, 1988, fire in the AT&T Long Lines switching facility in Hinsdale, Illinois, and the February 27, 1975, fire in a New York Telephone Central Office in New York City. In May 5, 1996, a data center in Paris, France, belonging to Credit Lyonnais was destroyed by fire, although operations continued uninterrupted at a sibling facility located remotely.

In each case the damage was severe, with the repercussions lasting weeks if not months. The most serious damage in such an incident is neither the lost equipment nor the structure. The worst damage is the destruction of cabling connected to and within the facility. Splicing large numbers of cables is a tedious, manpower-intensive task. Completely rebuilding a major central office takes many man-years of effort.

22.3.5.4   Bridge and Tunnel Failure.   Bridges and tunnels often carry utility cables and pipelines in addition to vehicular and rail traffic. Derailments, major vehicular accidents, floods, and earthquakes can damage bridges and tunnels. A single accident can disrupt several routings believed to be redundant, but which are, in actuality, traveling in the same or adjacent conduits in or on the same structure.

In 1970, a cargo vessel collided with the Chesapeake Bay Bridge-Tunnel, destroying a 375-foot section of one of the bridges. In October 1989, the Oakland Bay

Bridge suffered severe damage in an earthquake. Other bridge and tunnel accidents happen on a regular basis.

22.3.5.5   *Hardware Failure.*
Computing hardware is perhaps the most reliable equipment in human history. In the past 50 years, mean time between failures (MTBF) has dropped from a matter of minutes or hours to years. Without this dramatic increase in reliability, today's Internet applications would be totally infeasible. However, the complexity of the systems and the number of interconnected elements has increased even more dramatically than the MTBF.

There are sufficient elements in most Web applications to virtually assure that at least one component related to the environment will be out of service at any one time. Because most of the equipment is sufficiently reliable that preventive maintenance is now considered a danger, rather than a benefit, most failures are not detected until they prevent the equipment from performing its intended task. In many environments, the most common failure is equipment overheating due to fan failure or accumulated dust clogging the unit.

22.3.5.6   *Vehicle Accidents.*
In many areas, utility poles are immediately adjacent to roads, making them vulnerable to vehicular accidents. A single truck or car striking a pole can shut down power or communications to an entire industrial park for hours, a catastrophe for Web sites in the affected area.

22.3.6   Acts of Clod.
Deliberate acts and acts of God are not the only problems that can impair a Web site's operations. Often, the reasons for an outage are simply lack of care, or just plain clumsiness.

22.3.6.1   *Death by Backhoe or Pile Driver.*
On April 13, 1992, a work crew was driving protective pilings around a bridge over the Chicago River in Chicago, Illinois. In the process, one of the pilings punctured and flooded tunnels under The Loop, Chicago's central business district. The tunnels, formerly used for a variety of purposes, had been pressed into service for routing numerous utility cables. Water flowed through the tunnels and the utility areas of many buildings, forcing evacuations, cutting off power and communications, and causing massive water-related damage.

Less spectacularly, throughout the fall of 2000, work on the extension of the Bay Area Rapid Transit (BART) from South San Francisco to San Francisco International Airport regularly interrupted power and communications services in San Bruno as construction crews repeatedly damaged underground cables. A pile driver incident also occurred on September 8, 1998, at Newark International Airport (outside of New York City). In that episode, a pile being driven to support a new parking garage destroyed the majority of the power feeder cables supplying power to the airport. Power was only restored several hours later.

22.3.6.2   *Operator Error.*
Operator errors inevitably happen. Most go publicly unreported. One of the more spectacular publicly reported errors began innocently enough, on September 17, 1991, when operators at an AT&T facility in New York routinely switched to internal power from utility supplied power. At the time of the changeover, a failure occurred that shifted power sources to emergency batteries. The batteries lasted for the designed period, at which point the entire switching complex shut down for lack of electrical power, disrupting the AT&T network in Metropolitan New York. This incident occurred only months after AT&T maintenance personnel

accidentally cut the fiber optic cable linking New York to the rest of the network (January 4, 1991).

A similar accident befell the Internet's domain name system on July 17, 1996, when an incorrect database update was applied to the root name servers, causing a major disruption for several hours until the problem was corrected.

22.3.6.3   Poorly Executed Updates or Maintenance of Hardware or Software.
Upgrade failures are not uncommon when upgrading software and hardware. Part of the planning for upgrades of hardware and software supporting Web sites should be measures to ensure that the site is operational while the upgrade is in progress. The plan also should include a provision in the event that the upgrade does not install correctly.

On August 7, 1996, America Online was offline for 19 hours due to a failed router update. The unavailability of America Online, in particular its e-mail receiving nodes, caused many problems to percolate throughout the Internet, even affecting systems and users unrelated to America Online.

Such incidents happen daily, but they are rarely admitted, and are even more rarely considered newsworthy.

22.3.6.4   Failures of Planning.
The physical risks described in the preceding sections are compounded by plans that fail to take the risks into account. Planning should start with presumptions that virtually anything can happen. Presumptions about personnel and equipment should be challenged and checked at every opportunity.

22.3.6.5   Accidental Worms.
Worms and other attacks are generally examples of malicious behavior. However, the combination of Web-based applications and scripted e-mail can easily lead to spontaneous creations with many, if not all, of the aspects of worms. This is a challenge for reaction plans to ensure that decision makers do not prematurely label an incident as a deliberate act when it could have been caused by an unforeseen combination of otherwise innocuous software components.

22.4   RULES OF ENGAGEMENT.
The Web is a rapidly evolving, complex environment. Dealing with customers electronically is a challenge. Web-related security matters raise many sensitive security issues. Attacks against a Web site always need to be taken seriously. As an example, the Victoria's Secret online lingerie show, in February 1998, exceeded even the most optimistic expectations of its creators, and the volume of visitors caused severe problems. Obviously, the thousands of people were not attacking the site; they were merely a "virtual mob" attempting to access the same site at the same time. Similar episodes have occurred when sites were described as "interesting" on Usenet newsgroups.

Repeated, multiple attempts to connect to a server could be ominous, or they could represent a customer with a technical problem. Depending on the source, large numbers of failed connects or aborted operations coming from gateway nodes belonging to an organization could represent a problem somewhere in the network, an attack against the server, or anything in between.

There is a difference between protecting Internet-visible assets (Chapter 21) and protecting Web sites. For the most part, Internet-visible assets are not intended for public use. Thus, it is easier to account for traffic patterns. With Web sites, activity is subject to the vagaries of the worldwide public. A dramatic surge in traffic could be an attack, or it could be an unexpected display of the site's URL in a television program. Differentiating between belligerence and popularity is difficult.

Self-protective measures that do not impact customers are always permissible. However, care must be exercised to ensure that the measures are truly impact free. As an example, some sites, particularly public FTP servers, often require that the IP address of the requesting computer have an entry in the inverse domain name system, which maps IP addresses to host names (e.g., node 192.168.0.1 has a PTR, or pointer record, of 1.0.168.192.in-addr.arpa)[6] as opposed to the more widely known domain name system database, which maps host names into IP addresses. It is true that many machines do have such entries, and many sites, including company networks, do not provide inverse DNS information. Whether this entire population should be excluded from the site is a policy and management decision, not a purely technical decision.

Logging interactions between customers and the Web site is also a serious issue. A Web site's privacy policy is again a managerial, legal, and customer relations issue with serious overtones. Technical staff needs to be conscious that policies, laws, and other issues may dictate what information may be logged, where it can be stored, and how it may be used. For example, the 1998 Children's Online Privacy Protection Act (COPPA)[7] makes it illegal to obtain name and address information from children under the age of 13 in the United States. Many firms are party to agreements with third-party organizations such as TRUSTe[8], governing the use and disclosure of personal information.

Dealing with legal authorities is similarly complicated. Attempts at fraudulent purchases and other similar issues can be addressed using virtually the same procedures that are used with conventional attempts at mail or phone order fraud. Dealing with attacks and similar misuses is more complicated and depends on the organization's policies and procedures, and the legal environment. The status of the Web site is also a significant issue. If the server is located at a hosting facility, or is owned and operated by a third party, the situation becomes even more legally complicated. Involving law enforcement in a situation will likely require that investigators have access to the Web servers and supporting network, which may be difficult. Last, there is a question of what information is logged, and under what circumstances.

In summary, when protecting Web sites and customers, defensive actions are almost always permissible, and offensive actions of any kind are almost always impermissible. Defensive actions that are transparent to the customer are best of all.

22.5 TECHNICAL ISSUES. Protecting a Web site begins with the initial selection and configuration of the equipment and its supporting elements, and continues throughout its life. In general, care and proactive consideration of the availability and security aspects of the site from the beginning will reduce costs and operational problems. Although virtually impossible to achieve, the goal is to design and implement an automatic system, with a configuration whose architecture and implementation operates even in the face of problems, without customer impact.

That is not to say that a Web site can operate without supervision. Ongoing, proactive monitoring is critical to ensuring the secure operation of the site. Redundancy is only a means to bypass a problem; it does not eliminate the underlying cause. The initial failure must be detected, isolated, and corrected as soon as possible. Otherwise, the system will operate in its redundancy mode until it also fails, at which time the system will fail completely.

22.5.1 Applications Design. Protecting a Web site begins with the most basic steps. First, a site processing confidential information should always support the hypertext transfer protocol secure (HTTPS) protocol, typically using transmission control protocol (TCP) port 443. Properly supporting HTTPS requires the presence of an appropriate digital certificate (see Chapter 23).

When the security requirements are uncertain, the site design should err on the side of using HTTPS for communications. Although the available literature on the details of internet eavesdropping are sparse, the Communications Intelligence and Signals Intelligence (COMINT/SIGINT) historical literature from World War II makes it abundantly clear that encryption of all potentially sensitive traffic is the only way of protecting information. See Chapter 7 for details of information warfare.

Encryption also should be used within an organization, possibly with a different Digital Certificate, for sensitive internal communications and transactions. The preceding chapter noted that organizations are not monolithic security domains. This is nowhere more true than when dealing with human resources, employee evaluation, compensation, benefits, and other sensitive employee information. There are positive requirements that this information be safeguarded, and few organizations have truly secured their internal networks against internal monitoring. It is far safer to route all such communications through securely encrypted channels. Such measures also demonstrate a "good faith" effort to ensure the privacy and confidentiality of sensitive information.

It is also important to avoid providing all of the authentication information on a single page, or for that matter, in a sequence of pages. As an example, when parts of information are suppressed, for example, portions of a credit card or account number, the division between suppressed and displayed portions should be maintained. Displaying all of the information, even if it is on different screens, is an invitation to a security breach.

22.5.2   Provisioning.   Although today's hardware has unprecedented reliability, any failure of hardware between the customer and the data center will impair an enterprise's Web presence. For a highly available, frontline Web site, the effective requirement is a minimum of two diversely located facilities, each with a minimum of two servers. This is not necessarily an expensive proposition. Fairly powerful Web servers can be purchased for less than $5,000, so the total hardware expenditure for four servers is reasonable, substantially less than the annual cost of a single technician. In most cases, the cost of the extra hardware is more than offset by the business cost of downtime, which can sometimes exceed the total cost of the duplicative hardware by as much as a factor of 100 on an hourly basis in a single episode.[9]

Duplicative hardware and geographic diversity ensure constant customer access to some degree of functionality. The degree of functionality that must be maintained depends on the market and the customers. Financial firms supporting online stock trading have different requirements than supermarkets. The key is matching the support level to the activities. Some degree of planned degradation is generally acceptable. Total unavailability is not an option.

22.5.3   Restrictions.   All Web servers should be located behind a firewall in a "demilitarized zone" (DMZ; see Chapter 21). Incoming and outgoing services should be restricted using protocols such as HTTP, HTTPS, and internet control message protocol (ICMP). For troubleshooting purposes, it is desirable to implement ICMP, which is used by PING, an echo requester, as a way to check connectivity. All unused ports should be disabled. The disabled ports should furthermore be blocked by the firewalls separating the DMZ from the outside world.

Customer information should, to the extent possible, be stored on systems separate from the systems actually providing Web serving. Many security episodes appear to exploit file protection errors on the Web server, in order to access the database directly. Segregating customer data on separate machines, and ensuring that the only way to access customer data is through the documented pathways, is likely to severely impede attempts to improperly access the data.

These safeguards are especially important for high-security information such as credit card numbers. The number of incidents in which malefactors have downloaded credit card numbers directly from Web site is an indication of the importance of such precautions. The systems actually storing the sensitive information should never be accessible from the public Internet.

22.5.4   Multiple Security Domains.   The front-line Web servers, and the database servers supporting their activities, comprise two different security domains.

The Web servers, as noted previously, need to be globally accessible via HTTP, HTTPS, and ICMP. In turn, they need to access the database servers, and *only* the database servers. In a production system, it is preferable that database servers interact with the Web servers using a dedicated, restricted-use protocol. Properly implemented, such a restriction prevents a hijacked Web server from exploiting its access to the database.

The database servers should be in a security domain separated by restrictive firewalls from the externally accessible Web servers. This seems like a significant expenditure, but it is often less expensive and lower risk than a single significant incident.

22.5.5   What Needs to Be Exposed?   Publicly accessible Web sites need publicly accessible Web servers to perform their functions. Providing the desired services to the public, without simultaneously providing levers that can be used in unauthorized ways to subvert the site, is the challenge. A penetration incident leads to significant financial losses, embarrassment, and potential financial and (in some cases) criminal liability.

No system on the Web site should be directly connected to the public Internet. All connections to the public network should be made through a firewall system, with the firewall configured to only pass Web-related traffic to those hosts.

Many sites will opt to place externally visible Web servers in a security compartment of their own, on a separate port of the firewall (if not a totally separate firewall), using a separate DMZ from other publicly accessible resources. These precautions may seem excessive, but having improperly secured systems can lead to security breaches that are extremely difficult to correct, and can lead to extended downtime while the problems are analyzed and remedied. In this case, an ounce of prevention is worth substantially more than a pound of cure.

22.5.6   Exposed Systems.   Exposed systems are inherently a security hazard. Systems that are not accessible from the public network are not compromisable from the public network. Only systems that absolutely need to be publicly accessible should be so configured. Minimizing the number of exposed systems is generally desirable. However, this is best considered in terms of machine roles, rather than actual counts of systems. Increasing the load on each publicly accessible server by increasing the size of the server, thus increasing the amount of capacity impacted by a single system outage, is not a benefit.

22.5.7   Hidden Subnets.   The servers directly supporting the Web site need to be accessed by the outside world, and thus must generally have normal Internet addresses. However, all of the other systems supporting the Web servers have no legitimate need for access from or to the public network.

The safest address assignments for supporting, non-outside visible systems are the IPv4 addresses allocated for use in "Private Internets."[10] Needless to say, these systems should be in a separate security compartment than the publicly accessible Web servers, and that compartment should be isolated from the publicly accessible compartment with a very restrictive firewall.

22.5.8   Access Controls.   Publicly accessible systems are both the focus of an organization's security efforts and the primary target of attempts to compromise that security. The number of individuals authorized to make changes to the systems and the ways in which changes may be made need to carefully controlled, reported, and monitored. The cleared individuals should use individual accounts, and the accounts should be immediately invalidated if the individual's access is no longer authorized.

22.5.9   Site Maintenance.   Maintaining and updating the Web site requires great care. The immediate nature of the Web makes it possible for a single-character error in a major enterprise level application to cause hundreds of thousands of dollars of damage within moments. Web servers need to be treated with respect; the entire enterprise is riding on the electronic image projected by the server. Cybervandalism, which most commonly consists of defacing the home page of a well-known site, requires unauthorized updating of the files comprising the site. In 2000 alone, well-known public and private entities including the FBI, OPEC, World Trade Organization, and NASA, as well as educational institutions including the University of Limerick, have been harmed in this way.

The Web is inherently a highly leveraged environment. Small changes in the content of a single page percolate throughout the Web in a matter of minutes. Information disseminates easily and quickly at low cost. Leverage helps tremendously when things go right; when things go badly, leverage compounds the damage.

The normal process for updating applications software in small shops involves little fear of severe damage to large numbers of people. As the size of the customer base expands, the need for testing and careful concern increases dramatically. When things get to the scale of mission-critical enterprise software, where millions of dollars, and many lives, can be at risk if an error slips through, the procedures for making changes to programs must be formulated with utmost precision, completely tested with extreme precision, and put into production only when the possibilities of error have been reduced to the vanishing point.

All development and testing work on a Web site should be done first in a test mode on a system not publicly available, preferably on an isolated network. If there are problems, they should happen there, not in a way that will impact a wide user community. Live updates must be done with a high degree of caution. Once testing is completed, the tested site, as a complete entity, should be archived, using a utility such as ZIP, GNUZIP, PKZIP, tar, or OpenVMS BACKUP, to create an archive. The archive can then be used for:

- The initial propagation of the Web site to the production systems
- Comparison with the production system in the event of an integrity question
- Restoration of the production system in the event of a fatal hardware problem

Managing the Web site as a single entity, or as a modest number of smaller ones, rather than as a large number of individual files, is an important safety precaution. It is very easy to accidentally fail to include one or more files among a very large number in a partial update, and extremely difficult to track down the error. Some useful precautions are:

- Always be prepared to regress. Despite all of the testing that will have been performed, it is likely that some problems will slip through. Be prepared to switch back to the old operative condition if the revised system shows problems. It is better to fall back and regroup than to try to fix large amounts of damage or to endure a long service disruption.

- Place the new files in a separate directory tree. Do not overlay new files on top of existing files, so that if there were a problem with the new files, it would be a simple matter to revert to the original ones rather than to perform extensive file manipulations.

- Make every possible effort to maintain the validity of links stored on the site, both from present pages and from hyperlinks that users may have bookmarked. It is particularly important to keep current links valid because users will become frustrated if links in presently available pages suddenly change. If a site is sufficiently stable, there is a way to prevent alterations. The Web server can be set up to serve files directly from a CD-ROM. Because CD-ROMs are not easily removed, copied, modified, and reinserted without setting off alarms, the danger of unauthorized modification to the site is greatly reduced. CD-ROM–based server software, together with a tightly run, secure operating system, where the server software has no elevated privileges, offers a very high degree of security.

It is certainly possible for a small or moderate size site to run without rigid controls. However, the more formalism introduced into the update process, the less chance for error. Manually maintaining a site with a hit rate of hundreds of pages a day does not need the degree of care that must be exercised when maintaining a site with hundreds of thousands, or even millions of hits per day. The simple act of keeping the test site separate from the production site—and propagating entire copies of the site from the development to production environments—is a rather simple procedure, with significant benefits and reductions in risk.

22.5.10   Maintaining Site Integrity.   Every Web site and its servers is a target. Antagonists can be students, activists, terrorists, disgruntled former employees, or unhappy customers. Because Web sites are an enterprise's most public face, they represent extremely desirable targets.

Maintaining integrity requires that updates and changes to the site be done in a disciplined manner. Write access to the site must be restricted, and those authorized must use secure methods to access the Web servers. The majority of reported incidents appear to be the result of weak security in the update process. For example, unsecured FTP access from the general Internet is a poor practice. Safer mechanisms include:

- Secure FTP
- FTP from a specific node within the inner firewall
- KERMIT on a directly wired port
- Logins via SSH
- Physical media transfers

Most of the technologies do not inherently require that a physically on-site individual perform server updates, which would preclude remote maintenance. It does mean that in order to get to a machine from which an update can be performed, it is necessary to come through a virtual private network with point-to-point tunneling protocol or Layer2 tunneling protocol (VPN PPTP/L2TP) authenticated by at least one of the secure gateways.

22.6 ACCEPTING LOSSES. No security scheme is foolproof. Incidents will happen. Some reassurance can be taken from the fact that the most common reasons for system compromises in 2001 appear to remain the same as when Clifford Stoll wrote *The Cuckoo's Egg* in 1989.[11] Then and now, poorly secured systems have:

- Obvious passwords into management accounts
- Unprotected system files
- Unpatched known security holes

However, eliminating the simplest and most common ways in which outsiders can compromise Web sites does not resolve all problems. The increasing complexity of site content, and of the applications code supporting the dynamic site, means that there is an ongoing design, implementation, testing, and quality assurance challenge. Security hazards will slip into Web sites, despite the best efforts of developers and testers. The acceptance of this reality is an important part of the planning necessary to deal with the inevitable incident. When it is suspected that a Web site, or an individual component, has been compromised, the reaction plans should be activated. The plans required are much the same as those discussed in Chapter 21. The difference is that the reaction plan for a Web site has to take into consideration that the group primarily impacted by the plan will be the firm's customers. The primary goal of the reaction plan is to contain the damage.

Severe reactions may create as much, if not more, damage than the actual attack. The reaction plan must identify the decision-making authority and the guidelines to allow effective decisions to be made. This is particularly true of major sites, where attacks are likely to occur on a regular basis. Methods to determine the point at which the Web site must be taken offline to prevent further damage need to be determined in advance.

22.7 ETHICAL ISSUES. Managing a Web site poses a variety of ethical issues, mostly surrounding the information that the site accumulates from processing transactions, from performance tracking, problem identification, and auditing. Policies need to be promulgated to ensure that information is not used for unauthorized purposes, and the staff running such systems needs to be aware of, and conform to, the policies. Many of these ethical issues have civil and criminal considerations as well. The topic of information privacy is more completely addressed in Chapter 52.

22.7.1 Monitoring

27.7.1.1 Employee Monitoring. It is important to differentiate between monitoring employees engaged in non-critical internet usage and monitoring those involved in running mission-critical servers, although the monitoring specific to an important Web site is not categorically different from that required for any other mission critical system.

The ethics and issues involved in monitoring employees are covered in Chapter 51.

22.7.1.2   Carnivore Issues.   In late 1999, the FBI obtained an order instructing EarthLink, an ISP with a facility in Pasadena, California, to permit the installation of a device, referred to as Carnivore, to its backbone network. Carnivore, according to testimony before Congress, is a modified version of a commercially available LAN analysis package, which extracts e-mail and other electronic communications between a suspect's computer and other computers. Questions arose as to whether use of Carnivore was proper without the execution of a specific search warrant in each case. Earth-Link subsequently filed an action to constrain the installation of Carnivore on the EarthLink network, but the Court of Appeals ruled against them, and the FBI installed the device on the backbone network. An agreement was subsequently negotiated between the FBI and EarthLink to accommodate the investigation while protecting the integrity of the EarthLink network.

In the course of these proceedings, many objections were voiced in the press, on television, and in sessions of Congress decrying Carnivore as the government's ultimate invasion of privacy. In one response, on August 7, 2000, the FBI's John E. Collingwood, Assistant Director of the Office of Public and Congressional Affaires, wrote to the *Los Angeles Times* as follows:

> Contrary to what has been asserted we are not recruiting Internet Service Providers to "spy on U.S. citizens." We cannot ask them to do that and they cannot lawfully do so for us. Only after a court concludes that there is probable cause to believe that a serious crime has or is being committed, the e-mails to or from a specific person are about that crime and the interception is necessary to obtain evidence about the crime can an order be obtained to intercept the content of any e-mails. The orders by statute are very limiting and specific. Carnivore ensures the intercept matches the court orders, nothing more, and provides an audit trail to double ensure that is what happened.

Assistant Director Collingwood is absolutely correct. However, Carnivore and similar technologies are powerful tools; which can easily be misused. Many believe that improper or unauthorized use of Carnivore to monitor innocent individuals is a serious hazard. Such data-monitoring technologies are always controversial. A typical backbone network contains traffic from a multitude of customers, and a Carnivore-type device or any other network analysis tool is capable of capturing the data of criminal suspect and innocent user alike. Further complicating the problem is the fact that crude but effective network capture devices are implementable by moderately skilled programmers at the cost of only a few hundred dollars.

Monitoring devices are another argument in favor of isolating Web servers within their own DMZ. These devices further necessitate that any connection between the servers and their supporting database systems be via a second DMZ. This permits the traffic coming from the public network into one or more Web servers to be captured, without exposing other traffic to malfunctions or misprogramming of the monitoring device. The privacy risk of such monitoring argues in favor of encrypted communications for all customer information.

22.7.1.3   Liabilities.   The liability environment surrounding Web servers is too new for litigation to have run its course. However, there is no reason to believe that the myriad laws governing the disclosure of personal information will not be fully enforced in the context of Web sites.

Web sites increasingly handle sensitive information. Financial industry sites routinely handle bank and securities transactions; e-mail services handle large volumes of consumer traffic, and more and more insurance companies, employee benefits departments, and others are using Web sites to deal with extremely sensitive information covered by a variety of regulations.

Part of the rationale for recommending careful attention to the control of Web servers and their supporting systems is the need to create an environment of due diligence, where an organization can show that it took reasonable steps to ensure the integrity, safety, and confidentiality of information.

22.7.2 Customer Monitoring, Privacy, and Disclosure. Customer monitoring is inherently a sensitive subject. The ability to accumulate detailed information about spending patterns, for example, is subject to abuse. A valid use of this information helps to pinpoint sales offerings that a customer would find relevant, while eliminating contacts that would be of no interest. Used unethically, or even illegally, such information could be used to assemble a dossier that could be the subject of embarrassing disclosure, of insurance refusal, and even of job termination. The overall problem predates the Web. In fact, more than 15 years ago, a major network news segment reconstructed someone's life using nothing more than the information contained in the person's canceled checks, supplemented with publicly available information. The resulting analysis was surprisingly detailed. A similar experiment was reported in 1999, using the Web.[12]

Organizations sometimes violate the most basic security practices for protecting online information, when all of the information required to access an account improperly is contained on the single page of a billing statement. There have been repeated incidents (e.g., CDUniverse, CreditCard.com) where extremely sensitive information has been stored unencrypted on Web-accessible systems. These incidents recur with regularity, and are almost always the result of storing large amounts of sensitive client information on systems that are Internet accessible. There is little question that it is inappropriate to store customer credit card, and similarly sensitive data, on exposed systems.

The security and integrity of systems holding customer order information is critical. The disclosure of customer ordering information is a significant privacy hazard. Failure to protect customer banking information (e.g., credit card numbers and expiration dates) can be extremely costly, both in economic terms and in damaged customer relations. Credit card merchant agreements also may subject the enterprise to additional liabilities and obligations.

A Web site, by its monitoring of customer activity, will accumulate a collection of sensitive material. It may be presumed that the information is only useful for the site, and is inherently valid, but there are a variety of hazards here, most of which are not obvious:

- Information appearing to originate from a single source may indeed be a compilation of data from multiple sources. Shared computers, firewalls, and proxy servers can give rise to this phenomenon.

- Casual correlations may arise between otherwise unrelated items. For example, it is not an uncommon acceptable business practice for one member of a business group to pay for all expenses of a group of traveling colleagues. Failure to correctly interpret such an event could be misconstrued as proof of illicit or inappropriate behavior.

The problem with casual associations is the damage they can cause. In the national security area, the use of casual associations to gather intelligence is a useful tool, albeit one that is recognized to have serious limitations. In other situations, it is an extremely dangerous tool, with significant potential to damage individuals and businesses. An example:

> A Texas-based married businessman flies to New York City. When he arrives, he checks into a major hotel. A short time later, he makes a telephone call, and shortly, a young woman goes up to his room and is greeted warmly. This appears to be a compromising situation. The businessman is old enough to be the woman's father. In fact, he is her father. That single fact changes apparently inappropriate behavior into a harmless family get-together. Peter Lewis of *The New York Times* correctly notes that this single fact, easily overlooked, dramatically changes the import of the information.

The danger with correlations and customer monitoring is that there is often no control on the expansive use of the conclusions generated. The information often has some degree of validity, but it is both easy to overstep the bounds of validity, and difficult to correct the damage, once damage has been done.

22.8 LITIGATION.   The increasing pervasiveness of the Web has led to increasing volumes of related litigation. In this chapter, the emphasis is on litigation or regulatory investigation involving commercial or consumer transactions, and the issues surrounding criminal prosecution for criminal activities involving a Web site. More detailed information on this subject appears in Chapter 2 of this *Handbook*.

22.8.1 Civil.   Web site logs and records can become involved in litigation in many ways. In an increasing number of cases, neither the site owner nor operator is a party to the action; the records merely document transactions involved in a dispute. The dispute may be a general commercial matter, a personnel matter, or even a domestic relations matter involving divorce.

It is important that records handling and retention policies be developed in concert with counsel. The firm's management and counsel also must determine what the policy is to be with regard to subpoenas and related requests. The counsel also will determine what materials are subject to which procedures and regulations. For example, in a case of an e-mail provider (e.g., Hotmail.com), material may be subject to the Electronic Communications Privacy Act of 1986.[13] Other material may be subject to different legal or contractual obligations.

22.8.2 Regulatory.   A wide range of rules are enforced (and often promulgated) by various regulatory agencies. In the United States, such agencies exist at the federal, state, regional, and local level (outside the United States, many nations have agencies at least at the national and provincial levels). Many of these agencies have the authority to request records and conduct various types of investigations. For many organizations, such investigations are significantly more likely than civil or criminal investigations. Regulatory agencies also may impose record keeping and retention requirements on companies within their jurisdiction.

22.8.3 Criminal.   Criminal prosecutions receive more attention than the preceding two categories of investigation, yet are also much less frequent. Criminal matters are expensive to investigate and prosecute, and must pass a higher standard of proof than regulatory or civil prosecutions. Relatively few computer-related incidents reach the stage of a criminal prosecution, although because of its seriousness, the process is the most visible.

22.8.4   Logs, Evidence, and Recording What Happened.   The key to dealing effectively with any legal proceeding relating to a Web site is the maintenance of accurate, complete records in a secure manner. This is a complex topic, some details of which are covered in Chapters 34 and 38.

In the context of protecting a Web site, records and logs of activity should be offloaded to external media, and preserved for possible later use, as determined by the site's policy and its legal obligations. Once offloaded, these records should be stored using the strict procedures suitable for evidence in a criminal matter. The advent of inexpensive CD-ROM and DVD writers greatly simplifies the physical issues of securely storing such media.

Archival records not intended for evidentiary use also should be stored offline, either physically, or at least on systems that are not accessible from the public Internet.

The media should be stored in signed, sealed containers in an inventoried, secure storage facility with controlled access. For this reason, the copies archived for records purposes should not be the copies normally used for system recovery. In the event of an investigation or other problem, these records will be carefully examined for possible modification or misuse.

22.9   TECHNOLOGY

22.9.1   Protecting Customers.   Some of the information on every Web server is inherently public. The name of the company, the company's address, telephone number, and e-mail address of the Webmaster are not generally confidential, and no hazard exists from disclosing them. However, once a Web site goes beyond storing public information, disclosure hazards arise.

Unquestionably, Web sites are highly desirable means for customers to access information about their past, present, and future dealings with a firm. Making information available to customers is generally a win-win situation; it benefits customer relations and satisfaction, and simultaneously reduces costs to the supplier. A customer service telephone inquiry typically costs the organization several dollars. The equivalent Web-based inquiry typically costs significantly less than a dollar, often just a few pennies, even including amortized development and infrastructure costs.

The anonymity of Web accessors makes inappropriate access a serious privacy hazard. Hazards such as "snooping" must be considered in light of the information that can be gained. Much of the attention on privacy has focused on the interception of unencrypted network communications. Less effort has focused on extremely weak security mechanisms. In some cases, mere knowledge of an account number can get access to a wealth of private information. In other cases, a single copy of the account statement contains all that is needed to access the account. It is true that such inquiry systems often do not permit theft, but they do permit disclosure, which can be even more damaging than an actual theft. The killing of actress Rebecca Schaeffer was directly linked to disclosure of motor vehicle records.[14] This and similar incidents led to the passage in 1994 of the Driver's Privacy Protection Act.[15]

Conventional security systems are fundamentally based on "something you have" or "something you know" (see Chapter 16). The same rules should apply to customer private information available through the Web.

Many systems do not use secure sockets layers (SSL) for sessions displaying customer information. While tapping the backbone of the public network is difficult, and generally not feasible, monitoring near either end point of the connection is generally low in cost and effort, and high in yield. This is especially true of internal corporate systems, where a variety of confidentiality obligations may exist by law and contract.

Most if not all browsers and Web servers support SSL and HTTPS. There are overwhelming reasons for using secure connections for all communications involving customer or employee information.

22.9.2   Protecting Staff.   Intranet applications require the same precautions as Internet applications. All personnel require the same precautions and safeguards when accessing internal systems (e.g., payroll and benefits) as do external customers.

Proper procedures for the storage, processing, and transmission of customer information also protect staff from temptation and accusations. As an example, if all customer traffic uses encryption between the customer's browser and the Web server, there is no potential for an employee to breach security by monitoring the network.

22.9.3   Protecting Partners.   When there is any possibility that information being transmitted between a Web site and a partner is private, only secure, encrypted communications such as SSL, HTTPS, or VPN should be used. Distributed, but unjustified, trust is a pernicious problem in an interconnected world. Taking extra precautions is far safer and less costly than later discovering that there has been a security breach.

22.9.4   Protecting a Site with Damage Control.   Regardless of the security and robustness measures taken in designing, implementing, and provisioning a Web site, there will be security events. The inevitable incident may be the result of a deliberate act by a cracker, an act of God, such as an earthquake, or an act of clod with an errant backhoe. The actual impact on operations will be determined by the effectiveness of a damage control plan.

Attempts to address the problem by exhaustively enumerating the possibilities can never be entirely successful. There will always be unforeseen problems. In this effort, the IT world has much to learn from naval architecture.

Long ago, naval architects stopped attempting to enumerate all of the ways in which things could go awry. Instead, they assumed that damage would occur, and they described means for containing that damage. Naval officers use the same term, *damage control,* for dealing with battle damage as they do for dealing with naturally inflicted damage, or catastrophic equipment failure. How the damage occurred is irrelevant, what is important is preventing the damage from incapacitating or sinking the ship.

The analogy is clear. For a Web site, total unavailability to customers is the equivalent of incapacitation or a sinking. The reason for an outage is relatively unimportant, but the speed and effectiveness of the response is of greatest consequence. On the Web, where availability is a vital element, customers only care that they cannot do business. They do not care if the outage was caused by a coding error, an ISP unplugging a component, or a backhoe causing a cable break.

The most important aspect of a damage control plan is the degree of containment and recovery covered by the plan, not what possible failures it enumerates. The highest degree can usually be attained by providing a complete second site for Web support, operating in real-time, and in parallel with the basic site. The cost can be quite modest, even for fairly small enterprises. The cost of configuring two dedicated Web servers, located at two different widely disbursed geographic locations, is modest. The cost of downtime is quite high, often a factor of 1,000 more than the cost of the backup systems on an amortized basis.[16] The loss of customer goodwill is even more damaging.

22.9.4.1   File Security.   The files comprising the Web site must, at a minimum, be able to be replaced completely from an approved master copy. It may be that the only way to ensure that the files comprising a Web site have not been tampered with is to run the site directly from a CD-ROM. This may sound extreme, but the idea is not without merit.

The integrity of the server system is critical. It does not matter if the host is internal, co-located at a hosting facility, or a shared resource provided and managed by an ISP. Access from the servers to individual user accounts should be strictly limited, using the principle of minimum privileges, granted only where required. Otherwise, poor host security in the future, as in the past, will continue to be the means of entry for the overwhelming majority of break-ins.

Regardless of how a site's server is operated, appropriate security measures should be followed at all times. As a matter of course, all files comprising the Web site's content and scripts should be protected so that they cannot be altered. If possible, the Web server software should be running from a non-privileged account, one with only read/execute permissions to the Web site files.

22.9.4.2   Going Offline.   A previous section discussed a damage control plan. One of the most critical pieces of policy in such a plan is under what conditions the duty supervisor has the authority to totally shut down part or all of the Web site.

Every high-availability resource has an emergency shutdown plan. Airports, sports stadiums, power plants, and conference centers all have emergency evacuation procedures and a list of personnel who are authorized to declare and execute emergency shutdowns.

Web resources are no different. Despite all of the precautions using firewalls, proxy servers, routers, DMZs, and other measures, at some point an incident will occur. Any damage control plan must contain a set of guidelines and rules as to the situations under which components of the site, or indeed the entire site, can be taken offline. These procedures must be in writing, and they must be completely understood and strictly enforced. If a supervisor determines that the conditions have been met, then shutdown is necessary, and no criticism should ever be leveled. If the action later seems inappropriate, the guidelines and rules should be changed for the future. Otherwise, fear of retaliation will prevent necessary shutdowns.

22.9.4.3   Monitoring.   Monitoring a Web site is somewhat like being a night watchman—a routine yet vital job with high potential for boredom. Part of the job is waiting for the alarms to ring, or for e-mail messages relating problems to arrive, and part should be proactive: checking the site to ensure that nothing untoward is happening.

On a production system for a moderate-sized enterprise, the Web server should be separate from the server processing e-mail. The e-mail should go through a separate path, to prevent messages relating to a security incident from being compromised by the same incident. The files comprising the Web site should be compared regularly with the files in the base site distribution. Although it is certainly useful to run periodic checksums of the files using cryptographic checksums, such as MD5, there is no substitute for periodically checking the actual contents of the files on a bit-for-bit basis.

Monitoring does not stop at checking the contents of the files. On a regular basis, staff not associated with the development team should browse the site, to ensure that the interface presented to the outside world does indeed conform to requirements.

Site content should be treated in the same manner as program source codes; namely, subject to an ongoing quality control and monitoring effort. Problems should be tracked so that they are not repeated. Regression tests for all modifications should be performed; not only should the new elements be tested, but all tests previously run should be repeated, to ensure that the new changes have not improperly affected the existing system.

22.9.4.4 Planning. In the constantly changing Web context, elaborate reaction plans are sometimes out of date before the plans have been widely distributed. The Web's 24/7/365 environment requires a fast reaction time, often faster than the appropriate part of the plan can be identified and implemented. However, the analyses behind the plans are crucial.

Military planners know that battle plans rarely survive initial contact, and contingency plans in the online world are little better. Plans must be outlines of desired actions rather than scripts to be slavishly executed. The underlying analyses and requirements, options and restrictions, permissions and authorities do, however, need to be discussed and agreed to in advance, and tested in simulation.

In Chapter 21, it was mentioned that network operations and security personnel must have clear, unambiguous guidelines as to what actions are permitted, and what actions are prohibited. That chapter focused on internal access to the Internet. This chapter focuses on the enterprise's primary presence in its Web site. If, in an emergency, people have to start digging through elaborate binders of material to determine what to do, the battle has probably already been lost.

Planning, however, does need to be done. The concentration must be on the important issues:

- Who has authority for what action?
- Under what circumstances can the site or any of its components be taken offline?
- Who has to be notified of a situation?
- Who has permission to involve external agencies and authorities?
- Who is responsible for preserving evidence?
- Who can switch primary operations away from the primary site?

While each of the preceding questions has tactical elements, they are not inherently tactical issues, but rather, policy and strategic issues, with impact on corporate operations. The need is to get line departments and senior management into formulating the policies and strategies, not just to review and rubber stamp the results. The Legal, Public Relations, Customer Service, and Operations Departments all need to be involved in the planning, as well as in the implementation of the plans.

22.9.4.5 Compartmentalization. Although planning for damage prevention is necessary, the overriding goal is damage containment and limitation. The first line of defense in such a situation is the content itself. If using the various dynamic Web technologies, whether on the client side (e.g., JAVA and JAVASCRIPT) or on the server side (e.g., application service providers (ASPs), PERL, etc.), the code must be carefully checked and continually tested, both by the developers and by the auditors to ensure that it correctly handles errors, ranging from servers becoming unreachable to databases not working correctly. Checklists and reviews are excellent; regression collections of past failures are invaluable. It is easier, cheaper, and less disruptive to check code against a set of known past problems than it is to deal with thousands of disrupted customers. As a good lawyer once said, "I measure success by how rarely I end up in court." It is infinitely safer to make decisions in the comfort of a conference room or cubicle rather than under the gun of an actual security incident.

Servers and resources should be examined with an eye toward determining which resources are critical to which functions. Some functions are more important than others, and should have a priority on resources. If functions are not interrelated, they should not arbitrarily be coupled. It is acceptable for different functions to share resources, for example ISP lines, but the firm must be clear on the relative priorities of the various functions. When a problem occurs, for example a security breach or line outage, the people responsible for dealing with the problem need to have a clear understanding of which applications are most time critical. "All of them" is not an acceptable answer. Compartmentalization aids in damage control by limiting the potential of a problem to cascade into other enterprise activities. It is beneficial to share resources under normal circumstances, as long as operations knows which adjustments need be made to isolate the different elements when an emergency occurs. Certain applications may be so critical that they should operate normally in an isolated mode, and only use shared resources in the event of an emergency. If this is the case, it must be ensured that the security of the critical applications and services is not compromised by the act of connecting the critical application to the shared resource.

In other instances, the critical operation shares facilities with other, less important, applications. In an emergency it must be possible to isolate the critical function so that it may be restored in the shortest time possible, without concern for secondary applications.

22.10 PHYSICAL DEPLOYMENT. Site hardening and other point defenses are ineffective protection against certain types of incidents. Only strategic or area defenses, such as dividing the Web server facilities geographically, can ensure that no single physical problem, be it an act of God, or an act of clod, catastrophically incapacitates the organization's Web presence. The September 11 attacks in New York City and Washington, D.C., only underscore the reality of this hazard. See Chapters 14 and 15 for details of site security.

22.10.1 Site Hardening. Many site planners routinely presume that site hardening is a solution to external problems. Sites install large collections of ancillary equipment, including satellite dishes, auxiliary turbine generators, uninterruptible power supplies (UPS), pumps, and other devices to deal with power outages, water-main breaks, and other problems. These measures, if economically feasible, should be taken in any event. However, relying solely upon these enumerated threats and solutions is a serious operational hazard.

Although enumeration is useful to a point, its effectiveness is limited by the ability to construct all possible failure scenarios. In short, the fact that a particular scenario is beyond an individual's imagination does not prevent the scenario from occurring.

Handling obvious failure possibilities is an important task, and certainly a critical site should have backup communications, power, and other utilities.

Enterprises that have experienced floods, hurricanes, or earthquakes are well aware that in the event of a natural disaster, the data center will not be at the top of the priority list for assistance from utilities or other agencies. Service will be restored, but the timescale will be days or weeks, not seconds or minutes.

In 2000 and 2001, California suffered a severe electricity shortage, with major industries suffering power reductions and blackouts. Auxiliary generators are usually designed for hours of operations, not days and weeks, and their fuel supplies are often correspondingly limited.

If only one enterprise is affected by an easily corrected problem, the odds are high that the problem will be fixed quickly. Where there are thousands of victims and the problem is extensive in scope, the infrastructure may be out of service for an extended time.

When an incident happens, it is too late to take defensive measures. Availability strategies must be implemented before incidents occur; otherwise, timely recovery is not possible.

22.10.2 Site Dispersion.   If hardening the site does not solve all availability problems, what approach can? Dispersion, a strategic defense placing redundant systems in geographically separated facilities, permits the Web presence to operate without interruption, even in the face of a major casualty at a single site.

The problem behind the research that evolved into the original ARPAnet was to develop a network that could survive a nuclear attack. The solution was to disperse the network's intelligence, throughout many interconnected networks, and to permit automatic rerouting of data packets. The individual nodes were not extensively hardened. A similar strategic approach is suitable for Web sites.

Dispersing a critical Web site and its auxiliary equipment over multiple, widely separated servers is highly desirable. The servers should not be sited in the same river basin, power grid, or weather region. Ideally, all servers would be active all of the time, with the load divided between them.

On some levels, site dispersion is easily accomplished. If the Web presence is static and informational, then deploying the same content to two different sites requires care, but is not technically challenging. Adding the DNS entries to point to the different sites simultaneously is also not a particular problem.

If the site is more interactive, then the problems become more challenging. There are a variety of shadowing and data distribution technologies that enable databases to be duplicated at several separate sites. Even if single point dependencies cannot be totally eliminated, it is possible to significantly reduce the primary site workload. For example, limiting the primary site to database activity only, instead of transaction processing as well, often reduces its workload by a significant factor. In that event, the power and communications demands to support the site are correspondingly reduced, making emergency resources last longer.

Chapter 21 discussed how geographical dispersion was desirable for Internet-accessible resources. In terms of the Web, geographic dispersion is even more critical. When Internet-accessible assets were discussed, the focus was on assets and activities within the enterprise. When discussing the Web presence, the focus is on interactions with entities outside of the enterprise. Impeding internal operations is dispiriting and costly, but interrupting customer interactions is far more costly and damaging to the enterprise.

Implementing dispersion is not necessarily expensive. Satellite facilities can be located at out-of-area hosting facilities. Organizations with offices in other parts of the country also can serve as their own hot-site providers, reducing the cost of implementing dispersion to the minimal cost of a hundred square feet of office space, together with the cost of some electrical, communications, and air-conditioning work. Geographic dispersion is cheaper than site hardening, and it is substantially more robust; protecting Web capability against a wide spectrum of hazards.

Because the Web operates continuously, there is no idle time, and no safe time where systems can be taken down for maintenance or upgrade. All such operations must be performed with no apparent interruptions to users. Replicating individual items of equipment, and even full sites, is the key to creating an environment that keeps information available all of the time.

Often, provisioning raises the question of guarantees. ISPs are asked for guarantees of service and bandwidth; Web hosting facilities are asked about power, environment, and spare parts for servers; individuals are asked to wear their beepers or cell phones at all times. In the 24/7/365 world of the Web, such guarantees are not much more rewarding than a money-back guarantee on a parachute. Although an incident may result in a refund from a service provider, its value is almost minuscule in proportion to the losses incurred.

Most IT continuity plans rightly emphasize preventing damage from happening, but the most effective strategies include damage control procedures. They all start with the assumption that damage has already happened, and then describe measures to isolate the injury and to control its impact. The first general rule is that damage control is easier with multiple small systems than with fewer large ones. For example, an application might require two $100,000 computers, or forty valued at $5,000 each. With the larger system, a single problem would cause a reduction in capacity of at least 50 percent, which would almost certainly be visible to users. Because the small-system approach permits dispersion, either within a single facility or at remote locations, a single incident, even one affecting eight of the small servers, would only affect 20 percent of serving capacity, which is likely to pass unnoticed. Maintaining overall functionality without serious impairment is the key to achieving effective operations, even in the midst of a security incident.

Geographic dispersion is an important facet of the same concept. Having multiple widely dispersed sites, no two in the same weather region or power grid, connected via different ISPs, means that operations will continue automatically, even in the face of a catastrophic disruption to a single site. The overriding concept is to have on-site personnel able and authorized to deal with problems immediately, using the damage control manual. If people have to be paged before actions can be taken, their responses will be too late to prevent customer effects. Inspections, analysis, and determination of future responses can take place after an event has been resolved.

22.10.3   Application Service Providers.   Conceptually, ASPs are not new. Many organizations have historically outsourced payroll processing and other applications. Theoretically, the ASP is responsible for the entire application. Often, paying a package price for the application seems attractive: no maintenance charges, no depreciation costs, lower personnel costs, latest technology, and moderately priced upgrades. However, just as a ship's captain retains responsibility for the safety of his ship, despite the presence of a harbor pilot, an enterprise must not forget that if something goes wrong, the enterprise, not the ASP, will likely bear the full consequences. In short, the ASP must be required to answer the same questions, and held to the same standards, as an inside IT organization regarding privacy, security, and integrity issues.

If using an ASP, what precautions are there to ensure the availability and safety of operations and information? Is stored information commingled with that of other firms, perhaps competitors? Is information stored encrypted? What backup provisions exist? Is there offsite storage of backups? What connectivity does the ASP have? Where are the ASP's servers, and are they dispersed? What are the personnel practices of the ASP? Does the ASP itself own and operate its facilities, or does it in turn contract out to other providers?

None of the items cited may be reason to justify a negative finding on ASPs as a group. They should, however, serve as reminders that each of the issues related to keeping a Web presence secure, available, and effective apply no less to an ASP than they do to an in-house IT organization.

22.11   REACTION PLANS.   It is not possible to successfully deal with all possible problems and situations through planning. Every plan or technology, no matter how sophisticated or well thought out, will have gaps. Inevitably, every Web site experiences an incident.

The damage control plan for a site determines the severity of the repercussions. The most important elements of any reaction plan include:

- Who has the authority to initiate the plan?
- Who has the authority to make decisions when the plan has been activated?
- What actions are permissible?
- Who has the authority to involve outside organizations?
- What are the escalation steps?

The difference between the reaction plan for a Web site and a conventional reaction plan is that the plan for a Web site is likely to have far more interaction with outside suppliers, customers, and related parties.

22.11.1   Computer Emergency Response Teams (CERTs).   The CERT response for a Web site is, of necessity, more extensive than a CERT response for a computer-related problem limited to systems internal to the company. Because the Web site is the organization's interface with suppliers, customers, and others, responses must be measured, and must not cause more damage than the actual incident.

In many cases, measures, which might be appropriate and timely on a purely technical basis, will have to be deferred to prevent excessive collateral damage to the enterprise. See Chapter 40 for a discussion of CERTs.

22.11.2   CERT Auxiliaries.   All response teams need to include representatives from non-IT departments. In a conventional CERT, for example, a representative from the corporation counsel is desirable, in the event that a problem will require legal input before action is taken. The CERT responsible for a Web site has an even greater need for such non-IT expertise.

At the outset, it was noted that protecting the Web site is a multidisciplinary corporate exercise, not a purely technical exercise. The Web site is a firm's portal to its customers and suppliers; a shutdown may have severe side effects. Operations, Legal, and other non-IT departments must provide the collateral capabilities to support an emergency response. In some cases, the collateral may be nothing more complicated than a telephone list. In other cases, the response may need to include provisions for alerting call centers to increase operator staffing needed to deal with a suddenly greater volume of voice inquiries.

Decisions affecting the entire enterprise may require that senior managers be the final arbiter of any limitation or shutdown. In terms of personnel, it is important that the plan include a protocol for preparatory alert messages, and escalation protocols to ensure that when decisions need to be made, the people who are in a position to make the decisions are either physically present, or can be reached via telephone. See Chapters 42 and 43 for more details of business continuity planning and disaster recovery.

22.12   SUMMARY.   Availability is the cornerstone of all Web-related strategies. In both this chapter and Chapter 21, it was noted that redundant hosting and routing were necessary to ensure 24/7/365 availability. It was also noted that although some providers of services offer various guarantees, these guarantees almost never provide adequate compensation for the consequential damage done to the enterprise. In the end, an enterprise's only protection is to take adequate measures to ensure their own security and integrity.

Operating guidelines and authority are also critical to ensuring the availability of Web resources on a 24/7/365 basis. Systems must be architected and implemented to enhance availability, on an overall level. Operating personnel must have the freedom and authority to take necessary actions, without fear of reprisal if the procedures do not produce the desired outcome.

Privacy and integrity of information exchanged with the Web site is also important. The implementation and operation of the site and its components must be in compliance with the appropriate laws, regulations, and obligations of the site owner, in addition to being in conformance with the expectations of the user community.

22.13   BIBLIOGRAPHY

Albitz, Paul, and Liu Cricket. *DNS and BIND.* Sebastopol, CA: O'Reilly & Associates, 1994.

Alderman, Ellen, and Caroline Kennedy. *The Right to Privacy.* New York: Alfred A. Knopf, 1995.

Barnes, Steve. "In Ice-Coated Arkansas and Oklahoma, Chaos Rules." *The New York Times,* December 28, 2000.

Bernstein, David. "We've Been Hacked." *Inc Technology,* No. 3 (2000).

CERT. "sadmind/IIS Worm." May 8, 2001: *www.cert.org/advisories/CA-2001-11.html.*

Children's Online Privacy Protection Act of 1998. 15 U.S.C. § 6501 et seq.

da Cruz, Frank, and Christine M. Gianone. *Using C-KERMIT,* 2nd ed. Boston, MA: Digital Press, 1997.

deGroot, G., D. Karrenberg, V. Moskowitz, and Lear E. Rekhter. "RFC1597—Address Allocation for Private Internets." March 1994. Available at *www.ietf.org/rfc.html.*

deGroot, G., D. Karrenberg, V. Moskowitz, and Lear E. Rekhter. "RFC1918—Address Allocation for Private Internets." February 1996.

Derfler, Frank J., and Jay Munro."Home Appliances Hit the Net." *PC Magazine,* January 2, 2001.

Electronic Communications Privacy Act of 1986; 18 U.S.C.A. § 2510 et seq.

Fraser, B. "RFC2196—Site Security Handbook." September 1997.

Gezelter, Robert. "Internet Security." *The Computer Security Handbook,* 3rd ed. New York: John Wiley & Sons, 1995.

Gezelter, Robert."Internet Security." *The Computer Security Handbook,* 3rd ed. Supplement. New York: John Wiley & Sons, 1997.

Gezelter, Robert. (1996). "Plain Talk Management Needs to Hear from Its Technical Support Staff." Speech presented at *Commerce in Cyberspace: Expanding Your Enterprise via the Internet* Symposium, The Conference Board, February 1996; available from *www.rlgsc.com/tcb/plaintalk.html.*

Gezelter, Robert (1996). "Security Prosecution: Records and Evidence." *DECUS Magazine,* Spring 1996.

Gezelter, Robert. "Stopping Spoofed Addresses Can Cut Down on DDoS Attacks." *Network World Fusion,* August 14, 2000.

Gezelter, Robert. "System Security—The Forgotten Issues." Speech presented at Conference Session, US DECUS Symposium, Las Vegas, NV, Fall 1990; available from *www.rlgsc.com/publications.html.*

Glater, Jonathan."Hemming in the World Wide Web." *The New York Times,* January 7, 2001.

Guernsey, Lisa. "Keeping the Life Lines Open." *The New York Times,* September 20, 2001, p. G1.

Hamzeh, K., G. Pall, W. Verthein, J. Taarud, W. Little, and G. Zorn. "RFC2637—Point-to-Point Tunneling Protocol." July 1999.

Janofsky, Michael. "Police Seek Record of Bookstore Patrons in Bid for Drug Charge." *The New York Times,* November 24, 2000.

Kahn, David. *Codebreakers.* New York: MacMillan, 1970.

Kahn, David. *Seizing the Enigma.* Boston, MA: Houghton Mifflin, 1991.

Kelley, Tina. "An Expert in Computer Security Finds His Life Is a Wide Open Book." *The New York Times,* December 31, 1999.

Klensin, J., ed. "RFC2821—Simple Mail Transfer Protocol" (obsoletes RFC821, RFC974, and RFC1869). May 2001.

Layton, Edwin. *And I Was There: Pearl Harbor and Midway—Breaking the Secrets.* New York: William Morrow, 1985.

Littman, Jonathan. *The Fugitive Game: Online with Kevin Mitnick.* Boston, MA: Little, Brown, 1996.

Llosa, Mario Vargas. "Crossing the Moral Boundary" (OpEd). *The New York Times,* January 7, 2001.

Mockapetris, P.V. "RFC 1034—Domain Names: Concepts and Facilities." November 1, 1987.

Mockapetris, P.V. "RFC 1035—Domain Names: Implementation and Specification." November 1, 1987.

Neumann, Peter G. "The Green Card Flap." *RISKS Forum Digest* 15.76, April 18, 1994, and ff.

The New York Times. "Employees in the Twin Towers," September 16, 2001, pp 10.

Overbye, Dennis. "Engineers Tackle Havoc Underground." *The New York Times,* September 18, 2001, pp. F1.

Postel, J., and J.K. Reynolds. "RFC854—Telnet Protocol Specification." May 1983.

Postel, J., and J.K. Reynolds. "RFC959—File Transfer Protocol." October 1985.

Schwartau, Winn. *Information Warfare—Chaos on the Information Superhighway.* New York: Avalon, 1994.

Shimormura, Tsutomo, and John Markoff. *Takedown.* New York: Hyperion, 1996.

Simmons, Matty. *The Credit Card Catastrophe.* Fort Lee, NJ: Barricade Books, 1995.

Slatalla, Michelle, and Joshua Quittner. *Masters of Deception.* New York: HarperCollins, 1995.

Stoll, Clifford. *The Cuckoo's Egg.* New York: Bantam Doubleday, 1989.

Talbot, Margaret. "The Devil in the Nursery." *New York Times Magazine,* January 7, 2001.

TechWise Research, Inc. "Quantifying the Value of Availability." June 2000.

Townsley, W., A. Valencia, A. Rubens, G. Pall, G. Zorn, G., and B. Palter. "RFC 2661–Layer Two Tunneling Protocol 'L2TP'." August 1999.

Weinberg, Gerald. *The Psychology of Computer Programming.* New York: Van Nostrand Reinhold, 1971.

Weizenbaum, Joseph. *Computer Power and Human Reason.* San Francisco, CA: W.H. Freeman, 1976.

Westin, Alan, et al. "Databanks in a Free Society." *NYT Quadrangle,* 1972.

Wright, Peter. *Spycatcher.* Viking Penguin, 1987.

Zoellick, Bill. "Wide Use of Electronic Signatures Awaits Market Decisions about their Risks and Benefits." *New York State Bar Association Journal,* November/December 2000.

22.14   FURTHER READING

www.cert.org
www.eff.org
www.ietf.org

The historical literature on ELINT/COMINT/SIGINT has many books that detail the degree to which collected information can be exploited (see Kahn 1970, Layton 1985, Wright 1987, all listed in the Bibliography). The events in these books relate to World War WII and the following era and were classified for many years. Although not computer related, the techniques for collecting and exploiting information are very relevant. More recent books of interest are listed below.

Alderman, Ellen, and Caroline Kennedy, *The Right to Privacy* (New York: Alfred A. Knopf, 1995) is a well-written book on general privacy issues, with some chapters directly relating to electronic privacy.

Weizenbaum, Joseph, *Computer Power and Human Reason* (San Francisco: W.H. Freeman, 1976) discusses many topics related to reasoning with computer systems, including a significant amount of material relating to ELIZA, a simple script-based psychology program. He brings out the point that people often believe what the computer says, regardless of its actual accuracy or obvious limitations.

Westin, Alan, et al. *Databanks in a Free Society* (New York: NYT Quadrangle, 1972). Although dated, this is one of many books that discuss the political implications of large-scale databases in a free society.

22.15   NOTES

1. Extensible Markup Language: A universal standard for structured documents and data on the world wide web sponsored by the World Wide Web Consortium (W3C): www.w3c.org.

2. As of the time of publication, the casualty count was still considered preliminary by New York City authorities. The number cited is as reported in *The New York Times* of January 13, 2002.

3. *Newsweek,* September 24, 2001, pp 46-47.

4. Ibid.

5. Steve Barnes, "In Ice-Coated Arkansas and Oklahoma, Chaos Rules," *The New York Times,* December 28, 2000.

6. P.V. Mockapetris, "RFC 1034—Domain Names: Concepts and Facilities," November 1, 1987, and "RFC 1035—Domain Names: Implementation and Specification." November 1, 1987.

7. 15 U.S.C. § 6501, et seq.

8. *www.truste.org.*

9. TechWise Research, Inc., "Quantifying the Value of Availability," June 2000.

10. G. deGroot et al., "RFC1918."

11. Clifford Stoll, *The Cuckoo's Egg* (New York: Bantam Doubleday, 1989).

12. Tina Kelley, "An Expert in Computer Security Finds His Life Is a Wide Open Book," *The New York Times,* December 31, 1999.

13. 18 U.S.C.A. § 2510 et seq.

14. Ellen Alderman and Caroline Kennedy, *The Right to Privacy.* New York: Alfred A. Knopf, 1995.

15. 18 U.S.C.S. § 2721 et seq.

16. TechWise, "Quantifying the Value."

CHAPTER 23

PUBLIC KEY INFRASTRUCTURES AND CERTIFICATE AUTHORITIES

Santosh Chokhani

CONTENTS

23.1 INTRODUCTION. In today's computing and networking environment (see Exhibit 23.1), security must cover physical resources, operating systems, and even applications software, as well as the data that they store and process. In addition, network

Exhibit 23.1   Today's Computing and Communication Environment

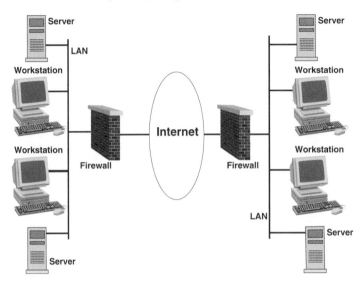

access controls, firewalls, and other filtering technologies are necessary to protect the enterprise perimeter.

Outside the perimeter, unprotected data sent and received by the organization over networks are vulnerable to disclosure, modification, insertion, deletion, and replay attacks. To protect the data being transported over untrusted networks, the only practical and cost-effective technology is cryptography. Cryptography is at the heart of both virtual private networks (VPNs) and public key infrastructures. For further information on encryption, see Chapter 50, and for a tutorial on cryptography, see the *Computer Security Handbook's* Internet site at *www.wiley.com/go/securityhandbook.*

23.1.1   Secret Key Cryptography Not Practical for Network Security.   Secret key symmetrical cryptography uses the same key to encrypt cleartext into ciphertext and to decrypt ciphertext back into cleartext.

In order for n parties to communicate with each other securely, a secret key cryptosystem will require $n*(n-1)/2$ keys (see Exhibit 23.2), although any one party needs to know only n keys. For a community of six users, this means merely 15 keys. But for a community of 1,000 users, managing and securely exchanging almost half a million secret keys is impractical.

Exhibit 23.2   Symmetric Keys

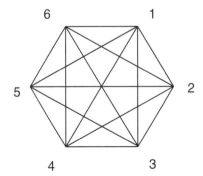

23.1.2 Public Key Cryptosystem. In contrast to secret key cryptosystems, public key cryptosystems (PKCs) use pairs of related keys that are generated together. The ciphertext produced by one key can be decrypted only with the other member of the same key pair. One of these keys is kept secret (the *private* key) and the other is published for all to use (the *public* key).

To conceal a message in transit so that only the desired recipient may read it, the cleartext is encrypted using the recipient's public key. Only the recipient's secret key can decrypt the transmitted ciphertext.

Similarly, to verify message integrity and authenticity, it is possible to encrypt information with a sender's private key. This allows anyone with access to that sender's public key to validate the message by decrypting the ciphertext successfully.

23.1.3 Advantages of Public Key Cryptosystem over Secret Key Cryptosystem. For securing data transmissions, public key cryptosystems are preferred over secret key cryptosystems for the following reasons:

- Public key cryptosystems require fewer keys to manage: each party (n) has a key pair, so the total number of keys is $2n$, instead of being proportional to n^2 as for secret key cryptosystems.

- Because private keys need not be distributed or otherwise managed, public key cryptosystems require only demonstrated integrity and authenticity of the public keys themselves. Users (the *relying parties*) must have assurance that their public keys truly belong to the publishers.

- Because no secret keys are transmitted over any network, PKCs are not susceptible to compromise even when public keys have to be changed. PKCs can be used to encrypt temporary keys (*session keys*) that can be used one time for secret key cryptography to obviate the heavier computational load of the PKC.

- To encrypt a message so that multiple PKC users can receive and decipher the ciphertext securely, PKC software can create a session key. This secret key is then encrypted with each recipient's public key and sent with the ciphertext to all recipients without compromising confidentiality.

- PKC-based digital signatures can provide the basis for nonrepudiation in the event of a dispute. Only the possessor of a private key could have sent a message decrypted by its public key. In contrast, because of the use of shared secrets, symmetric secret key cryptosystems alone cannot reasonably support nonrepudiation.

23.2 NEED FOR PKI. The PKC depends on the integrity of each public key and of that public key's binding to a specific entity, such as a person, an institution, or a network component. Without mechanisms for ensuring integrity and authenticity, a relying party is vulnerable to masquerading attacks through public key substitution.

To illustrate, suppose that ABC Company wants to send a confidential message to XYZ Corp. that no one else can read. ABC could use XYZ's public key to encrypt the message, although, for the sake of efficiency, ABC probably would use a symmetric algorithm to encrypt the message and the public key algorithm to encrypt the symmetric key. However, if ABC can be tricked into using Perp's public key as if it were XYZ's public key, then Perp would be able to decrypt the message. This technique is known as public key *spoofing.*

Such public key spoofing by Perp would, however, make it impossible for XYZ to read the message from ABC, as was originally intended. Therefore, such an attack probably would continue with Perp reencrypting ABC's message, using XYZ's real public key, and sending it on to XYZ. Such interception and reencryption is an example of a *man-in-the-middle* attack.

Another example of breaching the connection between a public key and its owner involves digital signature verification. Suppose ABC wants to verify XYZ's signature. If Perp could trick ABC into using Perp's public key as if it were XYZ's public key, then Perp would be able to sign messages masquerading as XYZ using Perp's private key. ABC would unknowingly use the replaced public key and be spoofed into thinking that the message actually was signed by XYZ.

In summary, both for digital signature and encryption services, the relying party must use the public key of the correct party in order to maintain security. There are various manual, electronic, and hybrid mechanisms for the distribution of public keys in a trusted manner, so that the relying party can be sure to have the correct public keys of the subscribers. These mechanisms for distribution and binding of public keys are known as a public key infrastructure (PKI).

23.3   PUBLIC KEY CERTIFICATE.   The technique that is most scalable uses a public key certificate issued by a trusted party called the *certification authority* (CA). A CA issues public key certificates to the various subscribers by putting together subscriber information and signing the information using the CA's private key. The generally accepted standard for public key certificates is the X.509 version 3.[1] Each CA's certificate contains the following key information:

- Version number of certificate standard
- Certificate serial number (unique for every certificate issued by the CA)
- Algorithm and associated parameters used by CA to sign the certificate
- CA name
- Validity period for the certificate
- Subscriber name
- Subscriber public key, public key algorithm, and associated parameters
- CA unique identifier (optional)
- Subscriber unique identifier (optional)
- Extensions (optional)
- CA's digital signature

The relying parties require the CA's public key so that they can verify the digital signatures on the certificates issued by the CA. The relying party must trust the CA's public key. As described below, this public key most likely is obtained during the registration process. Once the signatures are verified, relying parties can use the subscriber name and subscriber public key in the certificate with as much confidence in the accuracy of the information as they have in the trustability of the CA.

In some situations, a CA may need to revoke the binding between a subscriber and that subscriber's public key. For example, the subscriber private key may be compromised (i.e., there may be reason to believe that the secret key has fallen into the hands of someone else). Since a public key certificate is an electronic object and can reside in several places at the same time, it is neither practical nor possible to recall, delete, or erase all the copies of the subscriber certificate in a distributed environment. Thus, to invalidate a public key certificate by severing the binding between the subscriber and the subscriber public key, the CA creates a list of invalid certificates. This list is called a *certificate revocation list* (CRL). The relying parties must check that a certificate is not on the CRL prior to using the public key in the certificate. If the certificate is on the CRL, the relying party must not use it. The CA signs the CRL to allow the relying parties to verify the CRL's integrity and authenticity. The key information in the X.509 version 2 CRL is as follows:

- Version number of CRL standard
- Algorithm and associated parameters used by CA to sign the certificate
- CA name
- This CRL issuance time
- Next CRL issuance time (optional)
- List of revoked certificates (for each certificate the following is contained)
  - Certificate serial number
  - Time CA was notified of revocation
  - Extensions related to the revoked certificate (optional)
- Extensions related to CRL (optional)
- A's digital signature

23.4   ENTERPRISE PKI.   Each group of users covered by a CA is called a *domain.* Subscribers in a domain are issued public key certificates by the appropriate CA. Exhibit 23.3 illustrates the components of the PKI for a domain. The CA is responsible for generation of subscriber certificates and for CRL generation. The CA posts these signed objects to the repository where the relying parties can obtain them. The CA also archives the certificates and CRLs in case they are required in the future to resolve disputes among the subscribers and the relying parties.

The *registration authority* (RA) is the trusted representative of the CA and is responsible for authenticating the subscriber identity. The RA typically performs the following functions:

- Authenticates the subscriber's claimed identity. For example, the RA could require the subscriber to provide a valid photo ID, such as a driver's license or a passport.
- Obtains the subscriber public key from the subscriber.

Exhibit 23.3   Enterprise Public Key Infrastructure Components

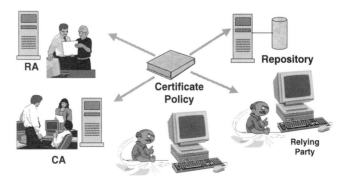

- Provides the CA public key to the subscriber. A *trust anchor* is a CA's public key that the relying party trusts. This trust generally is established by obtaining the public key from a trusted source using trusted means such as physical hand-off or via Secure Sockets Layer (SSL) from a trusted or known Web site. The CA public key becomes a subscriber trust anchor.

- Sends the certificate creation request to the CA. Typically, the RA creates an electronic mail message containing the subscriber name and the subscriber public key, digitally signs the message, and sends the message to the CA. Other transport means, such as manual or on the Web, also are appropriate as long as there is assurance that the subscriber identity and the public key are not changed. X.509 standard does not specify a protocol for certificate generation requests. The PKIX working group of the Internet Engineering Task Force (IETF) has developed Internet standards in this area.[2]

23.5 CERTIFICATE POLICY.   To ensure the security of the PKI, the PKI components need to operate with a high degree of security. For example:

- Private keys must be kept confidential.
- Private keys must be used only by the owners of the keys.
- Trust anchors' public key integrity must be assured.
- Initial authentication of the subscriber (private key holder and the subject of the public key certificate) must be strong so that identity theft does not occur at the point of certificate creation.
- CA and RA computer systems and applications must be protected from tampering.

In addition to the security requirements, in order to facilitate electronic commerce, the PKI must address obligations of all parties and liabilities in case of dispute. These issues of security, liability, and obligations are articulated in a *certificate policy* (CP).

According to the American National Standards Institute (ANSI) standard X.509, a CP is "a named set of rules that indicates the applicability of a certificate to a particular community and/or class of application with common security requirements." A certificate user may use a certificate policy to decide whether a certificate, and the binding implied between the certificate and its owner, is sufficiently trustworthy for a particular application. The CP addresses security and obligations of all PKI components, not just the CA; this includes the CA, RA, repository, subscriber, and relying party.

A more detailed description of the practices followed by a CA in issuing and managing certificates is contained in a *certification practice statement* (CPS) published by or referenced by the CA. According to the American Bar Association's *Digital Signature Guidelines* (hereinafter referred to as "ABA Guidelines"), "a CPS is a statement of the practices which a certification authority employs in issuing certificates."[3]

Although a CP and a CPS both address the same topics, the CP defines the security requirements and obligations for an enterprise PKI and the CPS describes how these requirements are satisfied by the enterprise PKI.

The CP and CPS also are used differently. The CP forms the basis for cross-certification across enterprise boundaries to facilitate secure, interenterprise electronic commerce. An *object identifier* (OID) representing the CP used to create a certificate can be put into the "certificate policies" extension of X.509 certificates. The OID thus enables relying parties to learn the care taken during the generation of certificates, recommended usage, and obligations of the various parties.

The CPS enables PKI personnel to use and administer the PKI components. The CPS also forms the basis for compliance audits in order to ensure that the PKI components are operating in accordance with the stipulations of the CPS. Exhibit 23.4 illustrates the components of CP and CPS. Components are divided further into subcomponents, which in turn are divided into elements. Components may be appropriate for various PKI entities but may be applied in the same way or differently. For example, technical security controls may apply to CA, RA, subscribers and relying parties. These controls may be different for each of these entities, being most stringent for the CA, then the RA, and then the subscribers and relying parties. In the exhibit, the line labeled "Repository" represents the five dimensions to consider in managing PKI.[4]

23.6   GLOBAL PKI.   The principles of an enterprise PKI with a single CA can be extended to support global, secure electronic commerce by relying on multiple CAs and/or CAs to certify other CAs and each other. How the CAs certify each other is also called *trust model, trust graph,* or *PKI architecture.* For one person to communicate securely with another, there must be a trust path from the trust anchor(s) of the relying party to the subscriber whose signature needs to be verified or to whom an encrypted message is to be sent.

23.6.1   Trusted Paths.   The trust model can be viewed as an arrow, with its tail a certificate-issuing CA and its head the subscriber (i.e., the subject of the certificate). The subscriber can be another CA or an end entity. To ascertain the trustworthiness of a certificate, it is necessary to start with the relying party trust anchor and to follow in the direction of the arrow until the subscriber (of interest to the relying party) is reached. Global secure communications require that there be a trust path from every subscriber to every other subscriber.

The relying party can start with its trust anchor and verify the certificates issued by the trust anchor. Once that happens, the public keys can be trusted and used to verify the certificates issued by these CAs. This can be done recursively by the relying party until the public key certificate of the subscriber of interest is verified. Then the subscriber public key can be used to verify digital signatures and to perform encryption.

Exhibit 23.4   Certificate Policy and Certification Practices Statement Framework

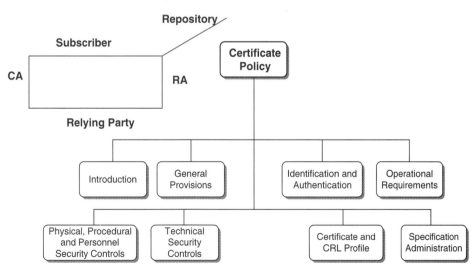

Exhibit 23.5   Certification Path

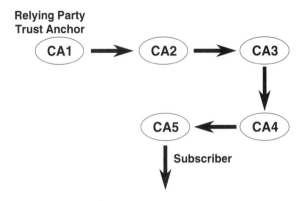

Exhibit 23.5 illustrates this pathway. The arrows represent certificates, and the chain of arrows is also called a *certification path* or a *certificate chain.*

23.6.2   Trust Models.   The following are examples of trust models in PKI:

- Strict hierarchy
- Hierarchy
- Bridge
- Multiple trust anchors
- Mesh (anarchy)
- Combination

23.6.2.1   Strict Hierarchy.   Exhibit 23.6 illustrates a strict hierarchy. It is a tree structure with a single root. In a strict hierarchy, for two parties to communicate with each other securely, they require the public key of their common ancestor as the trust anchor. Verifiable certificate chains require that the parties have a common ancestor.

Exhibit 23.6   PKI Trust Model: Strict Hierarchy of
Certificate Authorities and End Entities

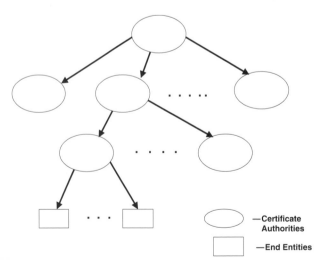

For all parties to communicate securely with each other, they require the root as the trust anchor, since it is the only common trust anchor.

23.6.2.2   Hierarchy.   In a (nonstrict) hierarchy, the subordinate CAs certify their parents. Exhibit 23.7 below illustrates this model. Since the directed graph is bidirectional, any CA can be trust anchor for the relying parties. But, from practical, operational, and performance (i.e., certificate path length) viewpoints, the local CA should be the trust anchor. The local CA is the CA that issued a certificate to the relying party.

23.6.2.3   Bridge.   Another trust model is the bridge. Under this model, one CA cross-certifies with each CA from various domains. The domains can be organizations or vertical segments, such as banking or healthcare. Exhibit 23.8 illustrates the bridge

Exhibit 23.7   PKI Trust Model: Hierarchy

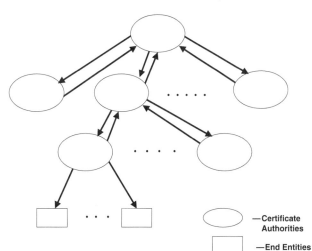

Exhibit 23.8   PKI Trust Model: Bridge

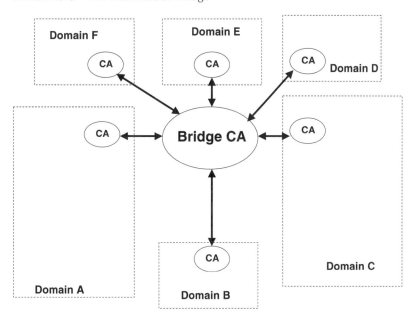

CA. The bridge CA is not the trust anchor for any relying party. A CA in the domain of the relying party is the trust anchor.

Within a domain, there are no constraints on the trust model. The domain PKI itself could be organized as any of the trusted models, including bridge, leading to possible layers of bridge CAs.

23.6.2.4   Multiple Trust Anchors.   Another alternative is for the relying party to obtain the public keys of the various CAs in a trusted manner and then use those public keys as trust anchors. This approach is attractive when the CAs cannot, or are not willing to, cross-certify, and the relying party needs to communicate securely with the subscribers in the domains of the originating CAs. This approach is called *multiple trust anchors.* Each trust anchor representing a domain could be a single CA or a PKI with a collection of CAs in a trust model.

23.6.2.5   Anarchy.   The final example of trust model is an anarchy. Anarchy describes any directed graph representing trust among the CAs without any particular rules or patterns. This model sometimes is known as a web of trust and is particularly associated with the original design of pretty good privacy (PGP), one of the early popular systems implementing a PKC.

23.6.3   Choosing a PKI Architecture.   Whether a domain (enterprise) chooses a single CA or multiple CAs for its intradomain operation should be determined from a variety of factors, including:

- Management culture
- Organization politics
- Certification path size
- Subscriber population size
- Subscriber population distribution
- Revocation information

In many situations, the politics or management structure may dictate that there be multiple CAs within the domain. In other words, organizations at business-unit level, regional office level, corporate level, or national level may want to create a CA in order to provide them with certain degree of control, independence, autonomy, and prestige. How these CAs are organized (bilateral cross certification, hierarchy, etc.) also will depend on the management and political landscape of the domain. The trust model should be such that it keeps the certification path size manageable; otherwise, end users will see unacceptable performance degradation in obtaining certificates and CRLs and in verifying digital signatures on the certificates and the CRLs.

Similarly, large subscriber populations may require more than a single CA in order to ensure that the CA can manage the subscribers and to keep the CRL size small. If CA products that issue partitioned CRLs are selected, the CRL sizes can be kept manageable even for a very large subscriber population. For further discussion of the CRL issue, see Section 23.7 on revocation alternatives.

When considering interdomain cross-certification, similar issues should be considered.

23.6.4   Cross-Certification.   In the simplest form, cross-certification consists of two CAs that certify each other by issuing each other a certificate. The certificates can be stored in specific attributes of the directory entry in a certificate; examples include the "cross-certificate attribute pair" or the "CA certificate."

There are two practical problems with cross-certification. One deals with the commercial products. If the two domains use different products, their CAs may not be able to exchange information to cross-certify, and their directories may not be able to chain to permit the relying parties to retrieve certificates.

The other problem is operational. Before certifying another CA, the certificate-issuing CA needs to make sure that the subject CA is operating in accordance with the acceptable controls, articulated in a CP. The issuing CA asserts the appropriate CP in the "certificate policies" extension of the X.509 version 3 certificate of the subject CA.

In practice, the two CAs cross-certify each other after reviewing each other's CP and after ensuring that the CPs can be claimed to be equivalent. This does not mean that all the security controls and obligations are identical, but they need to offer roughly similar amounts of trust and of obligations, and similar liability and financial relief.

When two CAs cross-certify each other, the trust generally is for a limited set of policies, through assertions in "certificate policies" extensions, and trust is only bilateral. In other words, trust will not commute; it will remain between the two CAs. The CAs ensure this by inhibiting policy mapping through the "policy constraints" extension. Policy constraint extensions permit differing policy mapping inhibitions down the certificate chain. In most direct cross-certifications, policy mapping should be inhibited immediately. In the case of cross-certification using the bridge CA model, in order to take advantage of the policy mapping services of the bridge CA, the policy mapping inhibition should be different for one certificate (namely, the bridge CA certificate).

In addition, the two CAs should use the "name constraints" extension in the X.509 version 3 certificates to ensure that they trust the other domain for the names over which the other has control. The use of this extension also minimizes the chances of name collision.

Exhibits 23.9 and 23.10 illustrate cross-certification examples. These examples are for illustrative purposes only and do not represent real-world entities.

In the case of bilateral cross-certification, policy mapping should be inhibited immediately by using a value of "0" in the "inhibit policy mapping" field of the "policy constraints" extension in X.509 certificates. When bridge CA is used for interdomain interoperability, a value of "1" should be used in this field. This will permit the issuing CA domain to map its policies to the bridge CA policies and then permit the bridge CA to map its policies to the subject CA domain, in effect mapping from the issuing CA domain to the subject CA domain.

As long as the issuing CA uses its control on inhibit policy mapping, the bridge CA need not use inhibit policy mapping to control the mapping inhibition.

23.6.5   PKI Interoperability.   The complexity of the technology, standards, and products makes the PKI technology difficult to interoperate from one domain to another, and from one product to another. Yet, without interdomain interoperability, there can be no global trust.

The following factors play a critical role in ensuring PKI interoperability:

- Trust path
- Cryptographic algorithms
- Certificate and CRL formats
- Certificate and CRL dissemination

- Certificate policies
- Names

Exhibit 23.9   Bilateral Cross-Certification

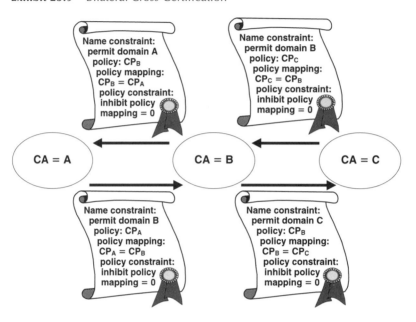

Exhibit 23.10   Cross-Certification via Bridge CA

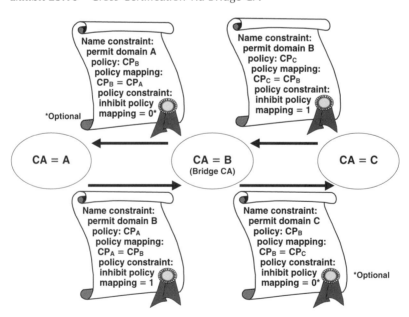

23.6.5.1   Trust Path.   The communicating parties must be able to form trust paths from their trust anchors to their subscribers. This can be achieved through multiple trust anchors, cross-certification, and other trust models described earlier.

23.6.5.2 Cryptographic Algorithms. The communicating parties must implement the cryptographic algorithms, such as hashing, digital signatures, key encryption, and data encryption, used by each other.

In addition, the parties should be able to communicate to each other the algorithms they use. In X.509 certificates and CRL, this information may be contained in the objects themselves, as in the *algorithm* field. In X.509 certificates, for the information being communicated, algorithms such as the digital signature and key encryption algorithm may be carried in the end-entity certificate. The hashing algorithm and the data encryption algorithm can be part of the implicit agreement between the parties or can be carried with the information being communicated. The information also can be obtained from the *supported algorithms* attribute of the X.500 directory entry of the user, although this option is not widely used.

In all these situations, the algorithm is identified using the object identifiers. Different organizations may register the same algorithm under their OID arc. Thus, it is important that either the two domains use the same OID for the algorithms or that their software interpret the multiple OIDs as the same algorithm. For this reason, OID proliferation for algorithms in not recommended.

Variants of the same base algorithm further exacerbate the problems of algorithm interoperability. For example, there are subtle padding and other differences between the RSA algorithm as defined in the Public Key Cryptography Standards (PKCS) and in the ANSI X9 committee. Similarly, the Diffie Helleman algorithm has various modes and various ways to reduce the calculated secret to symmetric key size (i.e., ways to make session keys smaller). Any of these differences in algorithms must be documented through different OIDs so that the OID invokes the appropriate implementation.

23.6.5.3 Certificate and Certificate Revocation List Format. The communicating parties must share, or must be able to understand, each other's certificate and CRL formats. The most common way to achieve this is to use a common standard, such as X.509. Many times this has not been sufficient due to the ambiguity in the standard and associated encoding schemes, although, over time, those bugs have been worked out. The primary reason today why certificates and CRLs issued by one product may not be understood by another is that either one or both are not compliant with the standard, or one product does not implement all the features of the standard used by the other product.

23.6.5.4 Certificate and Certificate Revocation List Dissemination. The communicating parties must obtain the certificates and CRLs issued by the various CAs in each other's domain. These certificates and CRLs may be obtained from a repository such as an X.500 and Lightweight Directory Access Protocol (LDAP) server. Alternatively, the certificates and CRLs can be carried as part of the communication protocol between the parties for example, as defined in S/MIME (Secure/Multipurpose Internet Mail Extension) version 3.

The X.500 and LDAP repositories are based on hierarchical databases. Each node in the hierarchical tree structure belongs to an object class. The node's object class determines the attributes that are stored for that node. Examples of attributes are job title, phone number, fax number, and the like. Certificates and CRLs are also attributes.[5]

X.500 and LDAP have defined a standard schema for PKI certificates and CRLs. For certificates, these attributes are *userCertificate, cACertificate,* and *crossCertificatePair.* The end-entity certificates should be stored in *userCertificate* attribute. All CA certificates should be stored in the forward element of the *crossCertificatePair* attribute of the subject CA. In addition, all certificates issued to the CAs in the same domain should be stored in the *cACertificate* attribute of the subject CA.

Various revocation lists should be stored in the *cRL, aRL,* and *deltaCRL* attributes of the issuing CA as applicable.

If the certificates and CRLs are not stored in these standardized attributes, the relying-party software may not be able to obtain these objects. Furthermore, X.500 directory products still may not always interoperate due to additional complexity of the X.500 standard and to product differences. When implementing X.500 directories and connecting X.500 directory products from different vendors, implementers should allow time to make the products and directories interoperate.

23.6.5.5   *Certificate Policies.* In order to trust each other and cross-certify, the CAs in two domains need to operate under similar policies. Users in the two domains should be able to accept or reject certificates of each other's domains based on the security requirements of the application and the policy under which the certificates were issued.

In order to determine the similarity, or equivalency, of the policies of the two domains, the CP should be written using the IETF standard RFC-2527 framework. The CP is represented using an OID in the certificate. To ensure that the user software accepts and rejects certificates based on the application requirements and on the CP, PKI products should be selected and configured so that the CA asserts the certificate policies, policy mapping, and policy constraints extensions appropriately. The user's PKI-enabling software must process these extensions appropriately and fully in compliance with the requirements of X.509 certificate-path validation rules.

23.6.5.6   *Names.* The communicating domains must not assign the same name to two different entities. X.500 *distinguished names* (DN) are steps in that direction, but not sufficient to achieve this.

To illustrate the point, consider, for example, CygnaCom. CygnaCom is a company incorporated in the Commonwealth of Virginia. While it is highly unlikely that there is another CygnaCom in Virginia, there is no assurance that there is no CygnaCom incorporated in other U.S. states. Thus, it would be possible that c = US, O = CygnaCom could be asserted by the CAs for several different domains.

In order to avoid this name collision and ambiguity, the *name constraints* extension in X.509 should be used. The CA for one domain can prevent any other entity from using a name registered in that domain. The issuing CA (CA "Y" in this example) uses the *name constraints* extension to assert priority and control over the specified identifier. For example, the first CA that certifies a company called CygnaCom in its domain should set the *name constraint* attribute in its certificate for its CygnaCom stating that only its CygnaCom is allowed to issue certificates under the name space c = US, O = CygnaCom. If another CygnaCom were to come along, CA "Y" would ask the second CygnaCom to choose another name in order to avoid name collision. Although this example focuses on the DN, the *name constraint* can be used for any hierarchical name forms, including DN, RFC 822-compliant names, and others.

PKI products should be selected and configured so that the CA asserts the *name constraints* extension appropriately. The user's PKI-enabling software must process this extension appropriately and fully in compliance with the requirements of X.509 certificate-path validation rules.

23.7   FORMS OF REVOCATION. As discussed earlier, a PKI includes mechanisms for key revocation.

The first form of revocation designed was the CRL. It seems the most appropriate form of revocation given the distributed authentication framework of PKI. The CRL mechanism allows the CA to generate the objects and the relying parties to process them securely without worrying about the security of the servers or system that supply the CRL and without concerns about the network(s) over which the CRL has traveled.

23.7.1   Types of Revocation-Notification Mechanisms.   However, there have been several concerns about the CRL, and these concerns have led to several other forms of revocation-notification mechanisms. Many of these mechanisms are variations on the CRL in the sense that these are revocation lists, but they are not complete. The second category of revocation mechanisms defers the processing of revocation information by a server. A third category of mechanisms lets the users check the status of a single certificate from the directory and allows the CA to update the status of that certificate in the directory. A final category lets a CA or another trusted server organize the revocation information in a hash tree.

Which mechanism(s) to choose depends on a variety of factors, such as the following:

- The communication model (i.e., which class of users is communicating with which other class). For example, if a user communicates with several users who are subscribers to the same CA, a single CRL from that CA will provide relevant information about all those targeted users. On the other hand, if a user is communicating with users who belong to different CAs, each CRL provides information about only one user.
- The directory architecture: where they are located and what portions of the directory information is replicated or shadowed?
- The communication bandwidth available.
- The bind time (i.e., the time to set a connection with the repository in order to perform retrievals and updates) to access the repository.
- The size of the revocation response from the repository (e.g., the CRL size).
- The processing load on the repository, especially for digital-signature generation on the revocation information.
- The processing load on the user workstation, especially for digital signature verification on the revocation information.

23.7.2   Certificate Revocation Lists and Their Variants.   The first set of mechanisms, CRL and its various forms, is the most versatile, effective, and recommended approach for revocation notification. There are several basic types of CRL, and they should be carefully considered, based on the user communication model and anticipated revocation rate:

- Full and complete CRL
- Authority revocation list (ARL)
- Distribution-point CRL
- Delta CRL

23.7.2.1   *Full and Complete CRL.*   The full and complete CRL is a CRL that contains the revocation information for all certificates issued by a CA.

23.7.2.2   *Authority Revocation List.*   The ARL is a CRL that contains the revocation information for all the CA certificates issued by a CA. That is, the ARL is subset of CRL for certificates issued to the CAs only. The ARL is a very desirable mechanism for the following reasons:

- It is likely to be short: A CA is likely to certify fewer CAs than other types of subscribers. Also, given that CAs are expected to operate with a great deal of vigilance, and given that CAs are not going to be revoked for reasons such as name change or organizational affiliation change, CAs will be revoked far less often than the end entities. These factors will contribute to making the ARL very small.

- For all of the certificates except one, only the ARL needs to be checked, since in a certificate path all but the last certificate is issued to a CA.

Due to a security flaw in X.509 version 1, a CA should never issue ARLs defined using that version. In X.509 version 1, there is no difference between the CRL format and the ARL format. Since both CRLs and ARLs are signed by the same CA, if an adversary (directory or network adversary) were to supply an ARL to the relying party in lieu of a full CRL, the relying party would have no way of knowing that it had received an ARL instead of the requested CRL. The ARL would not have end-entity revocation information and therefore could mislead the relying party into using the revoked certificate of an end entity.

The X.509 version 2 ARL fixes this security flaw using an *issuing distribution point* extension. An ARL must use this extension and assert a field that states that the list contains only CA certificates. The presence of this field in the signed ARL tells the relying party that it is not a full CRL. Now, if an adversary were to supply an ARL in lieu of a CRL, the relying party would detect this substitution by using the *issuing distribution point* field.

This is one of the several security reasons that PKI-enabling software must be able to process the various extensions properly in accordance with the requirements stated in X.509 standard.

23.7.2.3   Distribution-Point CRL.   Distribution-point CRL is a mechanism that has several useful functions. It can be used

- To replicate a CRL,
- To consolidate revocation information from the various CAs so that the relying parties only need to obtain one CRL, or
- To partition the revocation information for the subscribers of a CA into multiple smaller pieces.

This latter function, partition, is achieved by asserting the *CRL Distribution Point* extension in the certificate that points to the name entry under which revocation information for the certificate will appear. The partitioned CRL will assert the same name in the *Distribution Point* field of the *issuing distribution point* extension in the CRL.

Since all the partitioned (distribution point) CRLs are signed by the same CA, it is not sufficient for the relying party simply to validate the CA's signature on the Distribution Point CRL. The relying party must match the Distribution Point name in the *issuing distribution point* extension of the CRL with the Distribution Point name in the *distribution point* extension in the certificate.

23.7.2.4   Delta Certificate Revocation List.   Yet another way to reduce the size of the CRL is to publish changes to the revocation information since the last CRL. The

CRL that contains changes only is called the delta CRL, and the CRL to which changes are published is called the base CRL. The delta CRL can be applied to any of these CRLs: CRL, ARL, and Distribution Point CRL. In order to construct current revocation information, the latest delta CRL and its base must be used.

23.7.3   Server-Based Revocation Protocols.   Server-based revocation uses protocols, such as On-Line Certificate Status Protocol (OCSP) and Simple Certificate Validation Protocol (SCVP). In general, these protocols suffer from several flaws, including the following:

- Since the revocation information is produced at the server, the communication channel between the relying party and the server must be secured, most likely by using digital signatures.
- Signed operations will limit server scalability since digital signature generation is computationally intensive.
- Since the revocation information is produced at the server, the scheme requires a trusted server as opposed to an untrusted repository.
- Revocation of a server public key requires a method for checking the server public key status. This method is likely to use the server public key as an additional trust anchor or to rely on a CRL mechanism.
- There needs to be a nonsuppressible mechanism for the CA to provide revocation information to the trusted server; that is, the CA should know whether the revocation information has or has not reached the trusted server. Although a CA itself can act as a trusted server, this is not recommended for security reasons; in addition, we do not want to impose the high performance requirement on the CA architecture. The trusted server must be a high-performance system.
- There are no standards in the area of CA to provide nonsuppressible mechanisms for transmitting the revocation information to the trusted server.

These mechanisms may be desirable under one of the following situations:

- Need to have thinnest possible PKI client.
- Need to generate revenue for CA services
- Need to check changing credentials, such as available credit
- Need to update dynamic credentials, such as the remaining credit line

The last two situations permit the trusted server to provide the revocation information and to check or change the credentials of the subscriber.

Delta CRLs and server-based revocation protocols are not being standard-compliant, are covered by patents, and provide information relevant only to a single certificate or to a few. These factors will cause smaller total information transfer but will require many more accesses to the repository.

23.7.4   Summary of Recommendations for Revocation Notification

- The most scalable and versatile revocation-notification mechanism can be achieved by using a combination of the following:
  - CRLs
  - Replication of the CA directory entry, at locations determined by the enterprise network topology, for fast access to CRL
  - Use of ARLs

- Consolidation of ARLs for all CAs in a domain through the use of distribution points. Consolidation is achieved by placing the name of a CA who can revoke a certificate in the certificate's CRL *Distribution Point* extension.

- Consolidation of all the reason-codes of key compromise for all certificates in a domain through the use of the *Distribution Point* extension. This CRL can be issued very frequently to meet the freshness requirements of the domain. This mechanism makes the CRL mechanism as current as the Online Certificate Status Protocol (OCSP).

- Partitioning routine revocation information using Distribution Point CRLs if CRLs become too large.

Several other techniques can help improve CRL retrieval efficiency:

- Repositories may store both enciphered CRLs to send to the relying parties and also deciphered (plaintext) CRLs to perform fast searches. Storing both forms reduces the overhead that would result from using encryption or decryption at the time of each request.

- If the repository does not store any private information, bind operations for retrieval can be configured to require no authentication, thus eliminating another potential performance bottleneck.

- CRL size can be reduced by having a short validity period for the certificates, by using a coarse domain name so that reorganization does not invalidate a name, and by allowing some changes (e.g., name change or transfer) without forcing revocation.

23.8   REKEY.   The public key certificates for the subscribers have a defined validity period. Once the validity period expires, subscribers require new public key certificates. There are two primary reasons why public key certificates have a limited life. One relates to the life of a private key based on the potential cryptanalysis threat. Another reason is to help control CRL size since no certificate gets off a CRL until it expires.

No public key should be used longer than the estimated time for brute-force cryptanalysis using current technology (its *cryptanalysis threat period*). At that point, the certificate should be assigned a new public key (i.e., it should be *rekeyed*). However, before the cryptanalysis threat period expires, the same key can be renewed or *recertified*. Certificates can be renewed easily by having subscribers send a digitally signed request to the CA, or by having the CA perform automatic renewal. During renewal, any information (other than the subscriber public key) may be changed.

Certificates can be rekeyed easily also by the having the subscriber send a digitally signed *rekey request message* that also contains the new public key. The message is signed using the current private key so that it can be verified using the current public key. If the subscriber being rekeyed is a CA, the following requirements also come into play:

- The relying parties should be able to verify certificates chains after the CA is rekeyed.

- The relying parties should be able to verify CRLs issued by the CA.

- The rekey should not have a ripple effect on the PKI. Just because one CA rekeys, other CAs or end entities should not have to rekey.

- The length of certificate paths should be minimized.
- The operational impact on the PKI entities should be minimal.

A good way to meet these requirements is for the CA to do the following:

- Issue all current valid certificates when it rekeys, without changing the validity periods in the subscriber certificates.
- Continue to sign CRL with all current valid private keys. This will result in multiple CRLs, all with the same information. A CA private key is considered valid until all certificates signed using that key have expired.

If the CA is a trust anchor, it can use one of two approaches to rekey itself in-band, over the untrusted network:

1. The CA can send out a rekey message that contains its new public key and is signed using the current key. The CA needs to ensure that all the subscribers receive and process the rekey message prior to expiration of the current key.
2. The CA can provide the hash of the next public key and parameters (if the cryptographic algorithm has parameters; RSA does not have parameters, but DSS does) with the current key. When it is time to publish the new public key, the CA can publish a new self-signed public key certificate that contains the new public key and parameters as well as the hash of the next public key and parameters.

23.9   KEY RECOVERY.   Subscriber public keys can be used to encrypt data-encryption keys (for symmetric-key encryption). Such data-encryption keys are used to encrypt data quickly with the lower overhead of symmetric-key encryption. Subscribers require their private keys to decrypt the data-encryption keys and thus allow decryption of the data.

It is critically important to distinguish between *signing* keys and *data-encryption* keys. The former may *never* be subjected to key recovery; the latter *may* be protected using key-recovery techniques.

Sometimes a subscriber's private-key token (e.g., a diskette, hard drive, smart card, etc.) may be corrupted or the subscriber may forget the password associated with the token. Similarly, sometimes a subscriber may not be available yet the subscriber's employer may need to decrypt corporate information encrypted by the missing subscriber. Key-recovery techniques are designed to meet these emergency needs for access to encrypted information. Inherently, they provide a form of back door to the keys, but they also impose additional overhead costs. Thus, the need to provide key recovery should be balanced carefully against potential costs and complexity.

The two most popular forms of key-recovery mechanisms are:

1. *Key escrow:* Under this form, the subscriber's long-term private decryption key is provided to a trusted third party called a *key recovery agent* (KRA)
2. *Key encapsulation:* Under this form, the subscriber encrypts the data-encrypting key using the public key of the KRA so that the KRA can decrypt the data.

Of these two schemes, key escrow is becoming more widely available in the PKI products because:

- It is simpler to implement at the infrastructure level.

Exhibit 23.11   Key Recovery System Components

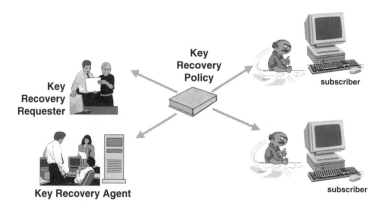

- It is independent of organization boundaries between the sender and receiver of encrypted communications. If a party's private date-encryption key is escrowed, then communications to the party can be decrypted.

Exhibit 23.11 illustrates the components of a key-recovery system.

Subscribers may always recover their own data-encryption key from the key-recovery system. Authorized third parties, such as a subscriber's employer, also may request keys. Such an authorized party is called a *key recovery requester* (KRR). All of the components are governed by a *key recovery policy* (KRP) and associated *key recovery practices statement* (KRPS). The KRP and KRPS are akin to the *Certificate Policy* (CP) and *Certification Practice Statement* (CPS), but have some differences. One of the main differences is in the technical security-controls sections. There are several requirements to check the communication protocols among the components to ensure confidentiality, integrity, and authorization. Exhibit 23.12 illustrates the components of a good KRP and KRPS.

A general criticism of key recovery is that it provides secrets to a single party, namely a KRA. One way to mitigate that concern is to share the secret among multiple

Exhibit 23.12   KRP and KRPS Framework

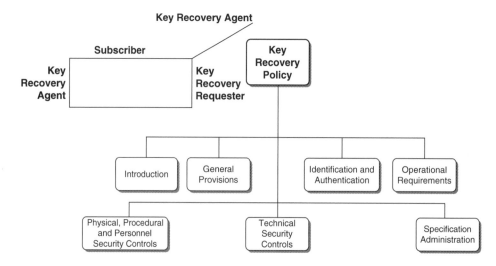

recipients in a way that requires cooperation (if it is authorized) or collusion (if it is not) among two or more holders of the escrowed secret. For example, superencryption (encryption of ciphertext) can make unauthorized discovery of a key more difficult. The secret key S is encrypted with one recipient's public key (say, K_1), producing a ciphertext, represented as $E(S,K_1)$, and then that ciphertext is superencrypted using a second recipient's public key, K_2, to produce the ciphertext $E(E(S,K_1),K_2)$. Unlike encryption of the same message for two recipients, where each recipient can decrypt the ciphertext independently, superencryption requires decryption by each recipient in the reverse order of priority. Thus if a user encrypts a secret key using A's public key and then superencrypts the ciphertext using B's public key, key recovery requires decryption by B using the corresponding private key and then decryption of the resulting ciphertext by A with that user's private key.

To use superencryption so that fewer than all recipients may decrypt the key, the sender encrypts to a first group of recipients and then superencrypts to a second group of recipients. Thus, any one of the members of the first group and any member of the second group of recipients can cooperate to decrypt the secret key.

This technique allows key escrow even in the absence of a formal PKI, such as in informal webs of trust using "Pretty Good Privacy" (PGP).

Another solution to making collusion more difficult in key escrow is to split the key using Shamir's *n out of m rule*.[6] In a properly implemented key-splitting scheme, parts of a secret key are distributed to m destinations and at least n recipients are required to reconstitute the secret key. Thus, $n-1$ or fewer persons colluding together cannot determine even a single bit of the escrowed key. Successful collusion requires at least n individuals. The split-key approach can be applied to key escrow, in which case the private key can be split and different splits can be provided to different KRAs. Alternatively, the split-key key approach may be applied to encapsulation, where the session key can be split and different splits can be encrypted using public keys of different KRAs.

This strategy also theoretically allows full reconstitution of the secret key to be performed by the authorized recipient of the partial keys instead of by any of the escrow agents.

23.10   PRIVILEGE MANAGEMENT.   The primary purpose of PKI is to provide entity authentication in a global, distributed environment. In most systems and applications, authentication becomes the basis for access control. There are three fundamental ways to implement access control:

1. The systems and applications can perform access control on their own. The PKI continues to provide the authentication framework.

2. The privileges, attributes, roles, rights, and authorizations, can be carried in a public key certificate in the *subject directory attribute* extension.

3. The privileges, attributes, roles, rights, and authorizations can be carried in an *attribute certificate.* The X.509 Standard is being revised to include the concept of attribute certificates. The attribute certificates carry privileges and authorizations instead of the public key, and thus provide a distributed authorization framework.

Exhibit 23.13 summarizes the pros and cons of each of the three approaches.

These factors should be considered while architecting an access infrastructure. Although the attribute certificate seem to be the latest fad in the PKI world, users should

Exhibit 23.13   Privilege Management Alternatives

Alternative	Pros	Cons
Application Based Access Control	Easy to implement Does not require additional infrastructure, so saves cost	Need to manage privileges on an application-by-application basis Synchronization of privileges may be hard as applications increase and as they are distributed Security may be compromised if privileges are not removed from all applications Higher operational costs
Public Key Certificate	Easy to add to PKI Privileges can be managed easily by revoking certificate	Changes in privileges require revocation of identity certificate. In some situations this is a small price to pay for savings that result from not having to deploy and operate a separate privilege management infrastructure (PMI) Parties issuing identity certificate may not have authority to bestow privileges
Attribute Certificate	Privileges can be managed easier by revoking attribute certificates Change in privilege does not require revocation of public key certificate	Cost of privilege management infrastructure (PMI)

carefully study putting privileges in public key certificates to save the cost of implementing a privilege management infrastructure (PMI) over and above the cost of PKI.

23.11   TRUSTED ARCHIVAL SERVICES AND TRUSTED TIME STAMPS.   PKI technology supports global electronic commerce through the use of digital signature technology. Digital signature technology is a detection or passive mechanism. In other words, the technology does not *prevent* someone from modifying data in storage or in transit, nor from impersonating someone else. The technology merely detects that an attempt had been made to modify the data, or that someone had tried to impersonate someone else.

In a court of law, digital signatures may be disputed long after they were applied if, for example, the cryptanalysis threat period for the keys has expired. In those circumstances, producing a document with a verified digital signature may not prevent repudiation. A party could claim that the cryptanalysis threat period has passed and the private key might have been discovered or broken by an adversary.

To mitigate both of these threats—data corruption and expiry of the cryptanalysis threat period—trusted archival services are required for transactions with a potential for this kind of dispute. Such an archival service also would be able to safeguard associated certificates and CRLs. Trusted archival services should depend on controls such as physical security, stable media (e.g., write-once read-many WORM devices), and appropriate techniques to maintain readability despite changing technologies. Such services should be capable of error-free transcription of data on older media and of translating outdated encoding into more modern media and current encoding schemes. For example, EBCDIC-encoded data on nine-track magnetic tapes could be copied onto optical disks using ASCII encoding.

A related technology is the trusted time stamp, where a trusted third party attaches the current valid time to a document and signs it to prove the existence of the document at a given time. If the document owner does not want to reveal the contents of the document to the time stamp server, then a hash of the document may be stamped and signed instead.

In most applications, a trusted archival service may obviate the need for trusted time stamp service because, for the long term, the trusted archival service can attest to the time of the transaction. For the short term, both parties can date and digitally sign the transaction when it is consummated, rendering it valid as a contract. If the date is not acceptable to any party—it is either too far in the future or in the past—that party can either reject the transaction or invoke some dispute-resolution procedure immediately.

23.12 COST OF PKI. One of the misconceptions about PKI technology is that it is too costly, but these costs should be compared to the alternatives.

Short of taking a major risk, there is no practical technology other than cryptography to protect data in transit over untrusted network. The only choice, then, is between symmetric key cryptography and public key cryptography (PKC). Aside from the difficulties of distributing and supporting symmetric, secret keys, such cryptosystems require approximately n^2 keys for a group of n individuals who must communicate with each other.

While a secret key cryptosystem requires n^2 keys to be kept confidential, with their integrity maintained, PKI requires managing only n keys. Clearly, it should be cheaper to maintain integrity of n keys than to manage n^2 keys and their confidentiality and integrity. We need PKI to manage the public keys.

PKI costs seem large when they must provide global trust and interoperability, something not asked of most systems or infrastructures. Currently no other technology works as well or is as cost-effective as PKI to achieve global secure, trusted communication and electronic commerce. The alternative is to assume the risk without PKI or to continue with the last century's approach of paper-based trust.

23.13 FURTHER READING

Adams, C., S. Lloyd, and S. Kent. *Understanding the Public-Key Infrastructure.* Indianapolis, IN: New Riders Publishing, 1999.

Adams, Carlisle, and Steve Lloyd. *Understanding Public Key Infrastructure.* New York: Macmillan, 1999.

American Bar Association, *Digital Signature Guidelines: Legal Infrastructure for Certification Authorities and Electronic Commerce,* Draft 1995.

Austin, T. *PKI: A Wiley Technical Brief.* New York: John Wiley & Sons, 2000.

Australian Government Public Key Infrastructure: *www.govonline.gov.au/projects/publickey/index.asp.*

Baltimore Technologies Learning Center. *Introduction to PKI: www.baltimore.com/library/pki.*

Chokhani, S., and W. Ford. "RFC 2527—Certificate Policy and Certification Practices Framework," April 1998.

Ford, Warwick, and Michael S. Baum. *Secure Electronic Commerce: Building the Infrastructure for Digital Signatures and Encryption.* Upper Saddle River, NJ: Prentice-Hall, 1997.

Housley, Russ, and Tim Polk. *Planning for PK: Best Practices Guide for Deploying Public Key Infrastructure.* New York: John Wiley & Sons, 2001.

Howes, Tim, et al. *Understanding and Deploying LDAP Directory Services.* New York: Macmillan, 2002.

IETF Public-Key Infrastructure (X.509) charter: *www.ietf.org/html.charters/pkix-charter.html.*

Menezes, Alfred, Paul van Oorschot, and Scott Vanstone. *Handbook of Applied Cryptography.* Boca Raton, FL: CRC Press, 1996.

Schneier, B. *Applied Cryptography: Protocols, Algorithms, and Source Code in C,* 2nd ed. New York: John Wiley & Sons, 1995.

Shamir, Adi. "How to Share a Secret." *Communications of ACM,* Vol. 22, No. 11 (1979): 612–613.

Vacca, J.R. *Public Key Infrastructure.* Boca Raton, FL: CRC Press, 2001.

23.14   NOTES

1. Additional details on X.509 certificates can be obtained from X.509 standard ISO/IEC 9594-8.

2. These standards can be obtained from *www.ietf.org.*

3. American Bar Association, *Digital Signatures Guidelines: Legal Infrastructure for Certification Authorities and Electronic Commerce.* Draft, 1995.

4. Further details on CP and CPS format and contents can be found in S. Chokhani and W. Ford, "RFC 2527—Certificate Policy and Certification Practices Framework," April 1998.

5. For further discussion on repositories, see Tim Howes et al., *Understanding and Deploying LDAP Directory Services.* New York: Macmillan, 2002.

6. Adi Shamir, "How to Share a Secret," *Communications of ACM,* Vol. 22, No. 11 (1979): 612–613.

CHAPTER 24

ANTIVIRUS TECHNOLOGY

Chey Cobb

CONTENTS

24.1 INTRODUCTION. For over two decades, computer viruses have been a persistent, annoying, and costly threat to the security of computer systems. There is no shortage of vendors offering to provide a cure for the virus problem, but the mere existence of viruses is understandably vexing to those charged with system security. In some ways, the high cost of virus-related losses is ironic because many viruses were not designed to cause harm, and those that contain malicious code seldom work as planned. However, because viruses are designed to subvert legitimate program operations and to spread across a large number of systems, they are far more likely than legitimate software to cause unexpected problems. These problems often result in damaged data and system downtime, even if the virus code was not actually designed to cause intentional damage. In addition, all execution of unauthorized code on a computing platform destroys the basis for trust in the results from that system; this problem is known as *destroying the trusted computing base.* Finally, the cleanup required to recover from even a "benign" virus infection can be very expensive in terms of lost productivity and unbudgeted labor costs.

Although this threat remains and has grown even larger in recent years, the technology deployed to defend computers against viruses is one of the least understood aspects of security architecture; as a result, antivirus defenses are often set up improperly. This chapter describes available antivirus technologies and how they work. Their effective application within a comprehensive program of computer security is outlined. For details of viruses and other malicious software, see Chapters 9 and 10.

24.1.1 Antivirus (AV) Terminology. The acronym *AV* is widely used to describe the industry, the products, and the programs that have been developed to defeat computer viruses. Early AV programs used simple scans to search for a specific text string hidden within a specific file. This is the origin of the term *AV scanner,* which is now widely used as a generic term for all AV programs. That is how the term is used in this chapter, although it should be pointed out that many of today's AV scanners do much more than merely scan.

When exploring AV product literature, it is common to see statements about the number of viruses that exist. It is not unusual to see five-digit estimates of the number of viruses, and three-digit estimates of the number of new viruses created every month. However, it is important to bear in mind that not all virus numbers are created equal. For a start, there is a difference between viruses that exist only in a research setting (in the zoo) and those that are actively infecting users' computers (in the wild). The term *in the wild* is applied to viruses that are active, as tracked by virus researchers, notably Joe Wells, who pioneered the WildList (www.wildlist.org). Starting in the early 1990s, Wells developed a coordinated reporting procedure that synchronizes the work of responsible AV researchers around the world, resulting in a reliable and consistent monthly accounting of virus activity. It often comes as a surprise to people when they find out there are only a few hundred viruses in the wild (e.g., 225 in March 2001 versus over 50,000 in the zoo).

The viruses in the zoo have been catalogued, but most are not currently being detected in the wild. A less stringent parameter requiring only a single sighting is also reported each month by the WildList organization (there were 427 on that list in March 2001). Viruses enter the zoo by various channels. Samples are sometimes sent directly to virus researchers by virus writers. A virus also may appear in the wild, be sampled and catalogued, and then die out.

24.1.2 Antivirus Issues. Many early viruses rarely worked for more than a couple of infections before they died on their own. This made the job of finding viruses and cleaning the systems a lot easier than it is today. However, as viruses have become more complex and harder to find, the number of infections has increased tremendously. Viruses are no longer easy to find and eradicate. AV scanners have become sophisticated logic machines. This new level of complexity of both the problem and the solution has made it even more confusing for users.

Few people understand how scanners detect and eliminate viruses from their systems, due in part to the sophistication of AV scanners and the lack of easy-to-understand documentation. Therefore, AV scanners are often misconfigured (improperly set up) and out of date; these deficiencies are probably why reports of the Love Bug virus were still appearing a year after its first release. Improper configuration of AV scanners means they can do little or nothing to protect the systems on which they were installed, and can threaten the security of downstream connections. Again, the Love Bug virus highlighted this problem when the virus crossed over from the public Internet to classified government systems.

Many system administrators do not regularly update their virus signature files but wait until reports of a virus outbreak reach a fever pitch. This despite the fact that viruses are often detected and reported several months before end-users are aware of their existence, and the AV vendors generally offer updates well ahead of a mass infection. Unfortunately, because people are not keeping their scanners updated, a virus can take hold and quickly reach epidemic proportions despite the ready availability of countermeasures. As a result, there is a mass scramble to the vendors' Web sites by users trying to find and download the update. Sometimes these inquires overwhelm the Web servers, further delaying the distribution of updated protection mechanisms.

Some virus epidemics have occurred because the virus exhibited completely new code, and behaviors that the scanners did not anticipate. AV scanners are largely based on what has happened before. They attempt to anticipate new viruses, but that is not their strong point.

Antivirus scanners also have suffered from a lack of support from upper management. They are often viewed as a high-cost/low-return item and are given a low priority in the security budget. The information technology (IT) team of an organization needs resources for the constant upgrading of AV packages. Considering the plethora of AV products from which to choose, and the large number of patches introduced each day, many system administrators despair. They will install just what they have time for, and call it good enough.

24.2   A HISTORY OF VIRAL CHANGES.   Shortly after the first viruses began appearing on PCs, AV scanners made their debut. The first scanners only detected the presence of a virus and did nothing to disinfect the system. At that time, there were a limited number of viruses, and most were distributed via floppy disks, because personal computer networks and the Internet were not widely used at that time. Changes in the computing environment are responsible for both the type of viruses and the rate at which they infect. For example, until 1992 the number of boot sector viruses and file-infecting viruses were roughly equivalent. In 1992, the number of file-infecting viruses began to decrease and boot sector viruses began to increase. This trend continued through 1995, when the change from DOS-based computing to Windows-based computing tipped the scales in favor of boot-sector viruses for a while. Most PCs were still diskette based, and boot disks were standard equipment. Users frequently swapped information between computers via floppies on the "sneaker net" because interconnected computers were rare. Infected floppies that were left in the drive during the boot process allowed the virus to take up residence in the computer's memory and would subsequently infect every disk used on that machine. Because boot sector viruses did not cause Windows to crash, many users did not realize that they had been infected until they, themselves, had infected a number of disks.

Another factor tending to favor boot sector viruses for a time was the complexity of Windows 3.1 relative to earlier operating systems (OS). When Windows was new to the market, virus writers did not have much experience in writing viruses that worked well with Windows. Because most file-infecting viruses of that period caused Windows to crash, and because Windows 3.1 was itself notoriously unstable, users frequently reformatted hard drives and reinstalled the OS as a matter of course. As a result, whether or not the users were aware of the fact that a virus was resident, the file-infecting viruses were quickly eliminated.

The introduction of Windows 95 again changed the course of viruses. Once more, the virus writers had a new OS with which to contend, and they quickly discovered that Windows 95 included an enhancement that warned users when changes were made to the boot sectors. These warnings would alert users that a virus might be present. Boot sector viruses stalled at this point, and the rate of file infectors slowed until the virus writers caught up with the new technology. Eventually it was the new OS's ability to allow multiple programs to share the same information that led to the next stage in virus evolution and the subsequent rampant plagues—the macro virus.

Microsoft's dominance of the office suite market through its MSOffice products (Word, Excel, PowerPoint, and Access) provided a uniform platform for the spread of macro viruses based on its proprietary Visual BASIC programming language. Because macros are easy to develop and can be quickly exchanged among users, it is natural that macro viruses quickly became the most prevalent type of virus. These facts, combined with increased connectivity between systems and networks, made macro viruses able to spread faster than the traditional boot sector or file-infecting viruses. Additionally, the Microsoft macro language is the key that allowed viruses to cross platforms. Prior to this, a Windows-based virus could never infect a Macintosh. With the advent of macro viruses, an MSWord virus could infect beyond the traditional boundaries of similar platforms, as long as users depended on MSOffice.

Early viruses also required the interaction of a human being to assist it in spreading. The user had to execute the infected program, copy it from a hard disk to a floppy, and physically move it to another machine. However, as these tasks have become more automated, viruses no longer require human interaction to execute. The data files used by most common applications today can harbor code, which makes execution and transfer of data imperceptible to the user. These include ActiveX, Visual Basic, and Java (see Chapter 10). Many recipients of infected e-mail messages do not realize that by simply opening a message, they have automatically executed a program that contained a virus because the virus was written with one of these applications. For more details of viruses and other malicious software, see Chapters 9 and 10.

24.3   ANTIVIRUS BASICS.   AV scanners are a bit like police officers walking the beat. They try to watch everything that's going on around them, look out for suspicious behavior, and attempt to intercede when they think something bad is happening, or about to happen. Both police and AV scanners look for certain patterns and behaviors, and they leap into action when a suspect crosses a predetermined threshold of acceptability. Like the police, however, AV scanners sometimes reach the wrong conclusions. This is usually caused by insufficient data or new behavioral patterns. Virus detection is an inexact science, and it is impossible to create an AV scanner with a 100% success rate. It is simply not possible to know the intent of every bit of code that enters a computer, and it is not feasible to test every bit of code before it executes. To do so would demand so much of the processing power of the CPU that valid programs would not be able to execute. The best an AV scanner can do is to look for clues of a virus based on a database of what has been seen before. Additionally, it is not always possible for a user to be able to tell when a virus has infected a system. Viral behaviors are subject to broad variations, and there are no longer hard and fast rules that a user can apply to determine if a system harbors a virus.

24.3.1 Early Days of AV Scanners. When viruses first started appearing with regularity, their detection and eradication was relatively straightforward. This was because the viruses were quite simple, and normally did not spread very quickly. The AV community could research them, determine what made them work, and publish an effective fix in short order. At that time, the fixes tended to be written for a specific virus and were only effective in finding that particular type. Users who suspected that their systems harbored a virus first had to identify which virus (or type of virus) they thought they had, then go in search of a program that would fix it. Because Internet connectivity was not as prevalent as it is now, users frequently spent much time calling friends and associates in the hope that they had a copy of the AV program that could be sent to them. Additionally, there were no naming conventions for viruses, and it was difficult to determine with any conviction that the fix obtained would actually work.

Viruses of that period generally inserted their code in predictable sections of a program. The early scanners ran a search for a specific string of characters. If they found it, they would delete that string and attempt to restore the host program to its original form. Failing that, the scanner would usually advise the user that disinfection was incomplete and that they should delete the program and reinstall it.

As the number of viruses began to climb, software companies that had ventured into the AV market began to realize that the job of creating and distributing individual fixes was no longer feasible. Instead, they began to develop more comprehensive scanners that could look for more viruses, both old and new. The new generation of scanners were comprised of two components: the scanning engine and the signature files. Each component was entirely dependent on the other to work. The engine consisted of the user interface and the program that scanned the files for viruses. The signature files were a database of the fingerprints of known viruses. Although many of these early scanners did a good job, others did not. None of them were able to catch all known viruses. With the number of viruses on the increase and a very competitive AV market, there was even some suspicion that, in an attempt to boost sales, AV vendors had released new viruses that only their scanners would catch.

24.3.2 Validity of Scanners. The vendors of software scanners in the late 1980s and early 1990s faced a number of obstacles. It seemed there was a new AV vendor appearing every month and the market became highly competitive as user awareness of the virus problem grew. Given this competitive state, there was vast dissension among the AV community as to how viruses for research should be stored and tested. Many AV vendors kept a library of viruses for their own use, and this fact was used in their marketing. Claims that one program worked better than another because it checked for more viruses were misleading. No one knew how many viruses existed, and there was no method of commercial or independent testing to check the validity of these claims. Additionally, there was a problem of naming the viruses. Each vendor created its own names for viruses, and it was not uncommon for one virus to be known by several names.

The AV vendors also disagreed on how AV scanners should operate in principle. Some vendors felt that AV scanners should only look for new viruses, and others felt that a good product should search both old and new viruses. While this argument raged, viruses looked as though they would eventually gain the upper hand, especially as virus writers began to use underground bulletin boards, and later the Internet, to share and distribute virus code.

With no standards for the AV products, the public had little to go by other than the vendors' marketing copy and the advice of other users. However, if a recommendation was made by a friend for Brand X Antivirus because no viruses were found on the friend's system, it could have been possible that no viruses had ever been introduced, and that Brand X could not find old viruses, new viruses, or any viruses at all.

Two things happened that revolutionized the AV scanner market. In 1993, Joe Wells, a research editor with a business magazine, began collecting viruses and virus reports from experts around the world, and began assembling a library of these viruses. As was noted earlier, he named this library of viruses the "WildList" and made it available to legitimate AV researchers. His list divided viruses into those known to have infected systems (in the wild) and those that had been written but were not actively infecting (in the zoo). A naming convention of viruses also began to emerge in order to maintain an efficient and searchable database. The other notable event was the development of commercial AV testing and certification by a company known as the National Computer Security Association (NCSA), which later became ICSA.net, then TruSecure Corporation. The NCSA started a consortium of AV vendors who, for a fee, submitted their products to be tested. NCSA and Joe Wells began a collaboration for the use of his WildList, and Dr. Richard Ford, a noted virus expert, created a virus testing laboratory for NCSA. Dr. Ford fashioned an environment in which AV scanners were put through their paces to see if they could detect all of the viruses in the WildList. AV vendors submitted their products every time a new version of their product was about to be released. Although the original test results were dismal (many scanners could not detect more than 80% of the viruses in the list), an environment had been created in which measurable improvements in the effectiveness of AV technology could be achieved. Naturally, the public and the press began to look for AV products that had been certified by NCSA. Other commercial and independent test laboratories independently developed their own certification schemes to help users find reliable AV products. For a detailed analysis of security standards, see Chapter 27.

24.3.3   Scanner Internals.   PCs and Macintosh computers run simplified operating environments (Windows 9x, and Mac OS, respectively) that lack segregation between system routines and user routines. In contrast, operating systems such as Windows NT, Windows 2000, UNIX variants and mainframe operating systems make it very difficult for viruses and other malicious code to execute at the OS level because they include a *security kernel* as part of the operating system that grants access to processes running on the computer system. Macro viruses are another matter, because they operate within the environment provided by MSOffice. For more information on security features of operating systems, see Chapter 17.

Determining whether a program on a computer running the Windows 9x or Mac OS is a legitimate program or a virus is nearly impossible. If AV scanners could be developed with 100% accuracy, the code could be written into the operating systems and there would be no need for individual AV products. However, operating systems are constantly executing programs, changing files, swapping memory, making system calls, and moving data. To expect that an OS lacking a security kernel could also monitor every program to determine if it has hostile or unauthorized intentions is unrealistic. In this sense, AV products are compensating for a fundamental flaw in popular operating environments.

As was noted earlier, an AV scanner cannot simply put each program aside in memory and test it for viruses before it is allowed to execute. To do that would require all the resources of the CPU, and users would be stuck with a system that barely operated. Therefore, AV scanners can only operate within the confines of the OS. To the OS, the AV scanner is just another program to be managed.

In order to operate efficiently and in harmony with the other programs on a computer, AV scanners have had to resort to numerous tricks to prevent virus infections, find infections, disinfect programs, and still operate at speed without bringing the entire system to a halt. They use four basic methods of operation:

- Detection—looking for infections by known viruses.
- Prevention—monitoring changes, or attempted changes to files.
- Heuristics—scanning for previously unknown viruses using a rule-based scan.
- Immune systems—monitoring the health of all systems that are connected to a centrally based reporting system.

24.3.4 Antivirus Engines and Antivirus Databases. The AV engine and its database work in concert to prevent and detect viruses entering a system. The engine generally serves as the user interface and provides a library of commonly used functions. It consists of dozens of complex searching algorithms, CPU emulators, and various forms of programming logic. The engine determines which files to scan, which functions to run, and how to react when a suspected virus is found. However, the engine knows absolutely nothing about the viruses themselves and is almost useless without the signature database.

The *signature database* (also known as the *dat* file by some vendors) contains the fingerprints of thousands of viruses. As new viruses appear at an accelerating rate, it is imperative that the signature database be updated often. In 1995 the experts advised updating the database files at least once a month, but with so many viruses appearing daily, users today are advised to update at least weekly. Some AV manufacturers now provide products that check for updates automatically and download changes whenever a user is connected to the Internet.

In the early days of the AV industry, signature database files were unencrypted, resulting in floods of false positives as soon as a user installed more than one AV product on the same system. Vendors quickly began encrypting their signature databases to preclude such false-positive results.

The database also contains the rule sets used in the heuristic scans. These types of scans tend to be slower and more intrusive than simple signature scans, and their design and implementation varies greatly between products. Most products now give users configurable options to lessen or increase heuristics as desired. Although signature scans can be considered a heuristic in themselves, the term is more commonly used to identify the more complex AV functions that attempt to locate viruses even when their signatures are not within the database.

Because the distinction between a scanning engine and a signature database is not obvious to many system administrators, many religiously update the database but are unaware that the engine also may need updating. This is a poor strategy that can result in many viruses slipping by the scanner undetected, or by a sudden increase in false-positive detections.

24.4 SCANNING METHODOLOGIES. Scanning is not necessarily automatic. The AV product is configurable by the user or the system administrator, and it can be set to scan upon startup, constantly, or on demand. To be at its most effective, a scanner should be set to a continuous scan, but many users running older, slower AV programs will find that this degrades the system performance. Many scanners need to use much of the system's memory on continuous scans in order to be able to test sections of code, which may make the applications slow to nearly a complete halt. Therefore, a happy medium must be found—the AV scanner must be able to protect the system, and the user must be able to have full use of the system.

There is no one scanning method that is superior to the others. All of the scanning methods have their advantages and disadvantages, but none are able to detect viruses with unfailing accuracy. A scan is looking for code and behaviors that have been noticed in other viruses, and if a new virus exhibits new, previously unknown behaviors, it can pass by undetected. Therefore, most AV scanners do not rely upon only one scanning method to detect viruses, but have several included in their design.

24.4.1   Detection.   As a virus copies itself from one executable file to another, it leaves bits of its code in the infected file, or host body. The sequence of code that is specific to the virus is referred to as the fingerprint, or signature of that virus. To detect the presence of a virus, the scanner looks for the signature, removes its code from the host file, and attempts to restore the infected program to its original state. In early viruses, it was discovered that the signatures were usually found within specific bytes of a program, so the scanners set out to inspect only those bytes rather than scanning an entire program from top to bottom. This saved vast amounts of time and processing power. However, not all virus signatures appear in the same area of a program.

Every vendor's AV product has a different implementation of scanner and database, although the signature scanning technique is the most common. Signature scans can identify whether or not a program contains one of the many signatures contained in the database, but it cannot say for certain whether or not the program has actually been infected by a virus (e.g., the virus may be present but has not executed). Users can only trust the guess of the AV scanner, because the odds are in the scanner's favor. It is possible, however, that a program that is suspected of being infected actually contains random data that only coincidentally looks like a virus signature. The legitimate program could contain instructions that by sheer chance matched the search string in the virus database. However, when there is a possibility that the code is actually from a virus, the scanner reports it as a positive hit.

False-positive reports are the main drawback to signature scanners. If users notice that their scanner falsely reports the presence of viruses too often, they view this as an annoyance, and will likely seek to disable the software or find ways of circumventing the scans.

24.4.2   Prevention.   As more complex viruses appear, the job of scanning programs solely for signatures has become less effective at finding viruses. Some new viruses have been found to have very short signatures or none at all. There are viruses that attempt to hide in different areas of a program than have been seen before, or they store themselves in directories that are not normally scanned for viruses, such as the CAB files. Viruses use encryption, change their form, and mutate in the hopes that the AV scanner will not find them. Today's operating systems and legitimate programs have bloated to millions of lines of code, so that finding a virus signature is resource intensive. Because many viruses are malicious, it is not a good strategy to let them infect and then attempt to clean up the mess. This may be suitable for a single system that is not used often, but on interconnected networks, this would spell disaster. A better strategy is to try to find the viruses before they infect, and prevent them from doing harm.

The use of a cyclical redundancy check, or checksums, was added to AV scanners to aid in the prevention of viral execution. This method of detection is also found in many firewalls because it tracks changes made to programs and files. A virus, or a hacker, entering a program changes the size of that program. To track those changes, a fingerprint of each executable program is computed and stored in a database when the AV product is first installed. These fingerprints are quite small; usually consisting of less than 100 bytes of information—this is the "sum" or checksum of the program. Because viruses must change files or boot records in order to infect them, the checksums of the fingerprints are compared with any newer version of the programs, looking for these changes. If the checksums vary, then the AV scanner runs other routines to investigate further. If the change in the size of the program cannot be attributed to a known virus in the signature files, or to a legitimate operation, then a generic disinfection routine is run to see if it can restore the program to its original state.

Other prevention methods, such as brute force decryption and emulation, are also used in AV scanners. An encrypted virus's code begins with a decryption algorithm and continues with scrambled or encrypted code for the remainder of the virus. Each time it infects, it automatically encodes itself differently, so its code is never the same. However, if the encryption algorithm can be decrypted in the laboratory, then the scanner includes this information in the signature files.

Other viruses that morph or change form require a different tactic—that of attempting to emulate what the program will do without affecting the entire system. Because many polymorphic viruses interrupt a program at a specific point that is quite different from normal programs, a routine was included in AV scanners to determine if that interrupt exists. If it does not, then the program is probably not virus infected and precious computing cycles are not required.

24.4.3 Heuristics.   By adding heuristics to their AV scanners, the vendors looked to increase the efficacy of their products. The scanners could now look for viruses that were new and unknown and not contained within the signature database.

The word *heuristic* comes from a Greek word meaning "to discover." The term is used today in computer science to describe algorithms that are effective in solving complex questions quickly. A heuristic algorithm makes certain assumptions about the problem it is trying to solve. In the case of an AV scanner, it analyzes a program's structure, its attributes, and its behavior to see if these meet the rules that have been established for identifying a virus, even without its signature on file. The drawback to heuristic scanning is that it makes intelligent assumptions, but is nevertheless bound to make mistakes. Another problem with heuristic scanning is that, on slower systems, it may take a long time to run and may require user interaction. For example, at least one AV scanner has options that are set by the user. The user is offered no explanation as to what this feature is or what it does. When it is turned on, the user must answer questions in persistent dialog boxes as to what to do with "possible" viruses. Most users consider this intrusive and annoying and quickly turn off the feature. By combining both signature scanning and heuristic scanning in their products, AV vendors have increased their effectiveness and speed.

Heuristic scanners use a rule-based system to verify the existence of a virus. It applies all the rules to a given program and gives the program an overall score. If the score is high, there is a good likelihood that a virus is present. Generally, the scanner looks for the most likely location for a virus to attach itself to a program. This is a crucial step because program files can be tens of megabytes in size. A well-designed heuristic scanner will limit the regions of the program to be examined in order to scan the highest number of suspects in the shortest possible time. The scanner then examines the logic of the suspected program to determine if it might be a virus. This is considered to be a *static* scan. The static method applies the rules and gives a pass/fail score to the program—whether or not the program has actually executed.

The other type of heuristic scanning is called the *dynamic method.* This method applies basically the same rules as the static method, and if the score is high, it attempts to emulate the program. Rather than examining the logic of the suspected code, the dynamic scanner runs a simulation of the virus in a virtual environment. This technique has come to be known as *sandbox* emulation, and is effective for attempting to identify new viruses that do not appear in the signature database.

Neither of these heuristic scanning methods is necessarily better than the other, but in concert they give fairly good results. Although a static heuristic scan may miss some viruses because they have not yet executed and started an infection, the dynamic heuristic scan can catch previously unknown viruses before they execute. When the Melissa virus was released in April 1999, at least one AV scanner actually caught the virus even though it was new and not in any of the signature databases.

24.5   IMMUNE SYSTEMS.   For more than 10 years AV vendors have been struggling to develop a way of making a computer heal itself without interaction with, or intervention from, a human user. Researchers have considered how a body's immune system deals with viruses, and they have tried to model a similar system for networked computers. The computer immune system that the researchers are attempting to create can monitor the state of its health, try to heal itself when it is sick with a virus, or call for help when it cannot cure itself. There are currently only a few AV vendors who have implemented immune systems of this type, and their sales have largely been limited to corporate users. Because the technology has only been newly implemented, there are few data on the effectiveness of such a system, but it holds considerable promise for the future of AV technology.

24.5.1   How Does the Immune System Work?   An isolated computer, that is, one unconnected to any other, would have no method of healing itself after attack by an unknown virus because it would lack resources. In contrast, a computer linked to a network can share resources to help fight the virus infection.

In prototypes of the computer immune system, at least one central server provides support for fighting new viruses. The central server can be located on a user's property or at the AV vendor's laboratory. All of the individual computers and workstations on the network are loaded with a monitoring system that uses a variety of heuristics to constantly monitor the state of health of the individual machines. The heuristics look at system behaviors, suspicious changes to programs, and signatures that may contain viral code. If the AV program suspects that an individual computer is infected by a new virus it cannot handle with its current knowledge base, the AV program makes a copy of the suspect program or document files and sends it to the central server for analysis.

Upon receipt of the suspect files, the central server sends copies to another system that provides a controlled environment where the virus may execute safely. The test system is segregated on its own subnet with controls to keep it from communicating with any systems on the network other than the central server. The central server communicates with the test systems only when predetermined conditions are met.

The test system begins a series of steps to get the suspect virus to replicate. It runs programs, copies and moves files, and starts and stops various services. At the end of the test, the program is analyzed by other components on the test machine to see if, indeed, a virus is present. The hoped-for end result is that the analysis extracts the virus signature, and produces a scan to verify and remove the virus. The resultant signature and scan are sent back to the central server where they are permanently stored in its database with appropriate cures.

The central server then sends the new scan back to the computer that initially reported the suspect virus. It also contacts all the other computers on the network and installs the new scan to immunize the entire system.

All of this happens with no human intervention, ideally while unnoticed by the user. Human intervention should be required only when the testing and analysis systems are unable to create an AV on their own. In that case, the virus sample is forwarded to researchers who are also connected to the larger system.

24.5.2 Will It Work? Many questions are still to be answered with respect to the efficacy of an immune system for networks. Just as there were no standards for AV scanners when they first appeared, there are no standards for an immune system. Whether or not standards would be necessary is also unclear. It is understood that an immune system certainly would require a strong security posture to prevent contamination by any viruses that are detected and then tested, and also to prevent tampering with, or abuse of, the immune system.

There is also the question of testing and verifying that such systems actually work. Under whose control would immune systems operate and who, if anyone, is liable when they do not work? Some vendors hope to be able to deploy an Internet-wide immune system. For this to be effective, all connected systems would be required to install that vendor's immune system monitoring software, and they would have to be completely interoperable with all other AV vendors' immune systems. Because immune systems require a robust architecture to be able to sustain their operations, they may prove to be too expensive for widespread use.

24.6 CONTENT FILTERING. Until fairly recently, computer security experts often allayed the fears of computer users by telling them that they could never catch a computer virus from e-mail. This assurance was based on the fact that e-mail was almost exclusively composed of ASCII text documents, with no ability to execute program code. At the same time, other experts were saying, "never say never." The skeptics won. First there were several waves of macro virus–infected documents sent as file attachments to e-mail. This led to the modified assurance that one could never catch a computer virus from an e-mail message attachment if it was not opened. Then virus writers started experimenting with embedded commands that use the HTML and scripting capability of newer e-mail programs. This led to the further modified assurance that a computer virus could not be caught from unopened e-mail. This assurance in turn proved unwarranted, because e-mail preview capabilities were exploited to trigger malicious code even without user intervention. At one point, merely highlighting a message subject in MSOutlook was enough to execute an attachment, although this default was later changed.

Virus writers also began to exploit the user's e-mail facility by forwarding copies of the virus to entries in the user's e-mail address book. The Melissa virus was the first virus that really leveraged e-mail to spread rapidly. Since the Melissa virus, advice to users has been changed to suspect just about any unsolicited e-mail. Virus writers are constantly looking for new delivery methods and they were richly rewarded when e-mail programs began to allow executable code within the e-mail. Although users enjoy the point-and-click convenience of this feature, it is allowing new viruses to proliferate at a rate not seen before.

The Web also has seen an explosion in malicious code distribution. Although ActiveX and Java have not been used to release a virus via the Web, some experts have warned of this possibility for years. Web-based e-mail is a popular application, and because the browser is able to execute desktop applications, it too must be protected from virus infections passing through.

Content filtering is an effective way of controlling both e-mail and Web-based threats. It consists of a server-based application that interrogates all incoming and outgoing traffic, according to its configuration and rule sets. Early versions were cumbersome to configure due to a text-based interface that required all rules to be composed in a laborious text editor. Misconfigurations were commonplace because administrators were not often sure which of the text files was causing a failure.

The new generation of content filters has increased user-friendliness using interactive graphic user interfaces to set and adjust policies. Administrators are able to fine-tune policies so that they meet the specific needs of their organizations. For example, all e-mail containing executable attachments may be blocked, quarantined, or simply deleted. This may be established as a rule for some users or all users. The policy also may be set to strip macros out of all incoming e-mail, thus preventing any micro viruses from entering the system via this route.

Content filters have been used effectively in preventing recent infections of e-mail–borne viruses, even before the AV was even released. For example, when the security officer of one government office heard of the Love Bug virus on the morning news, that person set the content filters to block all e-mail attachments containing the extension ".vbs," thus averting infection of a large network. No user interaction was required, and most users were not aware that the block had been placed. The costs and downtime of a virus attack were prevented.

24.6.1   How Content Filters Work.   These applications work in the same general manner that AV scanners do. They scan all incoming data on specific ports on the server and compare the traffic to rules and strings in the database. One of the main differences between an AV scanner and a content filter is that the filter is not limited to scanning just executables. Because content filters are capable of blocking more than one type of file or program, they have the ability to scan text files, graphics, zipped files, self-extractors, encryption formats, and various executables. Although most content filters do not contain AV scanners in the program, they are able to interoperate with multiple AV scanning products. Thus, if an e-mail does contain a virus, it can be intercepted and disinfected before it is sent to the recipient.

The standards for e-mail have long been in place and detail the type of information in every byte. It is quite easy for a program to look for particular information within these bytes to determine what is included in the message. Content filters first begin by disassembling a message to look at its various parts before scanning the message for the items to be allowed or denied into the system. Before sending the message onward, it is reassembled and checked for the conditions specified in the configurations. For example, a condition may state that any attachments be stripped and deleted, that the message body be sent to the recipient, and that an outward e-mail be sent to the sender stating that attachments are not allowed in e-mail.

In terms of computer security, a content filter adds several elements that are beyond the traditional AV scanner. For example, message and attachment content can be scanned for inappropriate material. This might be proprietary company information that employees should not be sending out via e-mail, or it could be offensive material such as pornography, that should not be coming into the company's e-mail system. Content filtering also can stop the spread of common forms of spam mail, such as chain letters and get rich quick schemes.

24.6.2 Efficiency and Efficacy. Of course, speed of operations is a concern with content filtering mechanisms, given the large volume of e-mail traffic in some organizations. However, because the operations are all contained within the server, the users will not notice any change in performance of their desktop systems. When examining large attachments, waiting mail will queue up, and delivery of mail may suffer for a period. Putting a limit on the size of attachments is one method of reducing these lags.

Content filters are also subject to the same failures as traditional AV scanners. New viruses can be missed if the data are not present in the scanning database. Additionally, the configuration of the product and the application of patches and updates are crucial to its successful operation. False positives are also a problem, where a legitimate message inadvertently includes content that triggers a block. It is possible to quarantine questionable messages and have a system administrator follow up with the sender; this can lead to refinement of the filters, or to the detection of serious offenses. Before a content filtering system is deployed, it is important to put in place the response mechanisms, so that abuses of e-mail policy can be addressed appropriately. This may well involve several departments besides security, including legal and human resources.

24.7 ANTIVIRUS DEPLOYMENT. AV scanners can be installed on the desktop or on the servers. Each strategy has its advantages and disadvantages. For example, if the system is server based, viruses on floppy disks and CDs on the desktop will not be scanned. The consensus of most experts, however, is to use both. With the advances in AV products and network management systems, it is entirely possible to install scanners on both the desktop and on servers, while still maintaining an acceptable level of control and performance.

24.7.1 Desktops Alone. If an organization's computer security policy allows unrestricted use of floppies and CDs, then it is imperative that AV scanners be deployed to the desktop. It is not uncommon to hear that a network has been infected and reinfected many times by one floppy disk that contained a macro virus. Unless these devices are locked or disabled, there is no way, other than scanning, to prevent users from accidentally introducing viruses. The preferences of a desktop AV scanner can be set to automatically scan external media. However, most users will complain of the intrusive nature of these scans and often try to disable the feature. Additionally, large files can take a long time to scan and will test the user's patience. An easy solution to prevent the spread of boot sector viruses, but not other types of floppy-borne malicious software, is to configure the basic input-output system of a PC to boot only from its hard disk instead of from a floppy disk; all subsequent boot operations will ignore any floppy. If necessary, this switch can be reversed in an emergency to permit booting from a recovery diskette.

Updates to desktop AV scanners can now be distributed via a central server. This is particularly effective when new signature files are needed to prevent the infection by a newly discovered virus. The updates can be pushed to the desktop and the users need not be present at the workstation, although the desktop system must be on and connected to the network at the time. If the updates are scheduled after working hours, it is important to verify that desktop systems were not shut down by the users as they went home. Desktops that were offline at the time of the update will need to be updated individually by the system administrator, a tedious and time-consuming task.

In order to prevent unauthorized changes, it is possible to prevent the users from changing the configuration of their desktop AV scanners, but that is not the default installation. Once such a restriction is imposed, the individual users must not be granted administrative privileges on their machines.

24.7.2   Server-Based Antivirus.   Many companies have sought to reduce the number of user complaints about AV scanners by limiting their installation to the server. Depending on the size of the network and its architecture, AV scanners can be installed on all servers, which would require different products or versions for different operating systems, or they could be installed on servers used for specific tasks or processes.

A common-sense approach is to install AV scanners on the servers where downloads are frequently stored and traffic is high. This is particularly important for e-mail servers because the majority of recent viruses use this path for infection.

A server-based AV scanner can be configured to send alerts to administrators when a suspected virus is detected. Like the desktop-based scanners, the response to a virus detection can be predetermined. Many system administrators set the program to erase all infected files, rather than to send them to quarantine. This strategy works to lessen the possibility that a quarantined virus can be "released" by mistake.

One of the major drawbacks of a server-based AV strategy is the need to use different scanners for the different operating systems. There are far fewer AV scanners for UNIX systems than Windows systems because there are fewer UNIX viruses. However, it is entirely possible for a Windows virus to traverse a UNIX system, leaving that system unscathed, and eventually find its way into a Windows system and begin infecting. A UNIX-based AV scanner should have the ability to scan for Windows viruses.

24.8   POLICIES AND STRATEGIES.   In the battle against viruses, the promulgation of appropriate policies and the implementation of realistic plans of action are far more likely to succeed than the simple installation of an AV scanner. The policies should not only spell out in detail what actions are allowed or denied, but it should also be very specific about the users' responsibilities. The policies and responsibilities should be updated whenever major changes occur in the organization, or in the pattern of virus infections.

End-user AV awareness training should be high on the list of priorities in every organization. Users are more likely to cooperate in preventing and quarantining infections if they are aware of the types of viruses that may infect the system and the damage they can cause. A simple virus bulletin board in a central location is an easy and effective way to communicate with users. E-mail is probably not an effective method of distributing virus awareness because users become confused between the education effort, actual and legitimate virus alerts, and bogus virus alerts.

The roles and responsibilities of each person within an organization should be clearly defined and communicated to the general populace. For example, the responsibilities of an average user will be different from those of a system administrator, and the responsibilities should be reflected in their roles. An individual user's role may describe the actions required of the user if a virus is detected on a workstation, while the system administrator's role may describe how to handle the report from the user and prepare for disinfection.

Many large virus infections have occurred after normal working hours. Some viruses have included trigger dates of national holidays, thus ensuring that the infection would start when no one was around to stop it. Problems and catastrophes will always occur when they are least expected, so every organization should have an emergency response plan in its policies. The emergency plan should detail the list of persons to be called in an emergency and the priority order in which they should be called. There are a number of resources available on the Internet for the establishment of virus response teams, and these can be adapted for internal use.

For every virus infection event within an organization, care must be taken that a "lessons learned" session be undertaken as soon after the event as possible. No matter how well written a policy may be, it cannot be proven effective until it is put into use. An actual infection will highlight the failures of a policy in action, which should be rectified before the next attack. Recent macro virus infections have shown that these viruses are highly likely to morph and reinfect a system.

Management's support for such policies is vital. Support is required not only to approve the AV budget and the policies, but also to abide by the policies themselves. It is highly unlikely that users will follow a policy that upper management routinely flouts.

24.9   CONCLUSION.   AV technology has progressed rapidly over the past decade and largely remains in step with virus technology. This fact is often overlooked when people read about the major outbreaks of the past few years, some of which have caused billions of dollars worth of damage. In fact, the "success" of the viruses in these cases is largely due to the failure of people, not AV technology. However good the AV technology gets, it will not make a serious dent in the virus problem unless it is appropriately implemented by organizations, and properly employed by users who act responsibly. Hopefully, as AV technology improves, and becomes better understood, it will be used more widely and more wisely.

24.10   FURTHER READING

Antiviral Software Evaluation: *www.claws-and-paws.com/virus/faqs/avrevfaq.shtml.*
The AntiVirus CookBook: *www.bocklabs.wisc.edu/~janda/av_cookbook.html.*
The Anti-Virus FAQ: *www.claws-and-paws.com/virus/faqs/vlfaq200.shtml.*
IBM Research—Antivirus Research Papers: *www.research.ibm.com/antivirus/SciPapers.htm.*
Polk, W. Timothy, et al. *Anti-Virus Tools and Techniques for Computer Systems* (Advanced Computing and Telecommunications Series). New Jersey: Noyes Publications, 1995.
Virus Bulletin: *www.virusbtn.com/.*
The WildList Organization: *www.wildlist.org/.*

CHAPTER 25

SOFTWARE DEVELOPMENT AND QUALITY ASSURANCE

Diane E. Levine

CONTENTS

25.1   INTRODUCTION.   Software development can affect all of the six fundamental principles of information security as described in Chapter 5, but the most frequent problems caused by poor software involve integrity, availability, and utility.

Despite the ready availability of packaged software on the open market, such software frequently has to be customized to meet its users' particular needs. Where this is not possible, programs must be developed from scratch. Unfortunately, during any software development project, despite careful planning, unforeseen problems inevitably arise. Custom software and customized packages frequently are delivered late, are faulty, and do not meet specifications. Generally, software project managers tend to underestimate the impact of technical as well as nontechnical difficulties. Because of this experience, the field of software engineering has developed; its purpose is to find reasonable answers to questions that occur during software development projects.

25.2   GOALS OF SOFTWARE QUALITY ASSURANCE.   In the IEEE *Glossary of Software Engineering Terminology* quality is defined as "the degree to which a system, component, or process meets customer or user needs or expectations." In accordance with this definition, software should be measured primarily by the degree to which user needs are met. Because software frequently needs to be adapted to changing requirements, it should be adaptable at reasonable cost. Therefore, in addition to being concerned with correctness, reliability, and usability, the customer also is concerned with testability, maintainability, portability and compliance with the established standards and procedures for the software and development process. Software Quality Assurance (SQA) is an element of software engineering that tries to ensure that software meets acceptable standards of completeness and quality. SQA acts as a watchdog overseeing all quality-related activities involved in software development.

The principle goals of SQA are as follows:

- Uncover all of a program's problems
- Reduce the likelihood that defective programs will enter production
- Safeguard the interests of users
- Safeguard the interests of the software producer

25.2.1   Uncover All of a Program's Problems.   Quality must be built into a product. Testing can only reveal the presence of defects in the product. To ensure quality, SQA monitors both the development process and the behavior of software. The goal is *not* to pass or certify the software; the goal is to identify all the inadequacies and problems in the software so that they can be corrected.

25.2.2   Reduce the Likelihood that Defective Programs Will Enter Production.   All software development must comply with the standards and policies established within the organization to identify and eliminate errors before defective programs enter production.

25.2.3   Safeguard the Interests of Users.   The ultimate goal is to achieve software that meets the users' requirements and provides them with needed functionality. To meet these goals, SQA must review and audit the software development process and provide the results of those reviews and audits to management. SQA, as a functioning department, can be successful only if it has the support of management and if it reports to management at the same level as software development.

25.2.4   Safeguard the Interests of Software Producers.   By ensuring that software meets requirements, SQA can help prevent legal conflicts that may arise if purchased software fails to meet contractual obligations. When software is developed inhouse, SQA can prevent the finger-pointing that otherwise would damage relations between software developers and corporate users.

25.3   SOFTWARE DEVELOPMENT LIFE CYCLE.   Good software, whether developed inhouse or bought from an external vendor, needs to be constructed using sound principles. Because software development projects often are large and have many people working on them for long periods of time, the development process needs to be monitored and controlled.

While progress of such projects is difficult to measure, using a phased approach can control the projects. In a phased approach, a number of clearly identifiable milestones are established between the start and the finish of the project. A common analogy that is used is that of constructing a house, where the foundation is laid initially and each phase of construction is achieved in an orderly and controlled manner. Frequently, with both house construction and software development, payments for phases are coupled with reaching the designated milestones.

When developing systems, we refer to the phased process as the System Development Life Cycle (SDLC). The SDLC is the process of developing information systems through investigation, analysis, design, coding and debugging, testing, implementation, and maintenance. These seven phases are common, although different models and techniques may contain more or fewer phases.

Generally milestones identified in the SDLC correspond to the points in time when specified documents become available. Frequently the documents explain and reinforce the actions taken during the just-completed phase of the SDLC. We therefore say that traditional models for the phased development are "document driven" to a large extent.

There are problems and drawbacks inherent in the document-driven process. The method of viewing the development process via the SDLC is not totally realistic to the actual projects. In reality, errors are found in earlier phases, are noted, and "fixes" are developed, prototyping is introduced, and solutions are implemented. This, in effect, is more than what is assumed will be necessary in the debugging and maintenance phases. Also, often the problems are solved before those phases are reached. Because of the recognition that much of what in traditional models is referred to as maintenance is really evolution, other models of the SDLC, known as evolutionary models, have been developed.

In traditional models, the initial development of a system is kept strictly separate from the maintenance phase. The major goal of the SDLC is to deliver a first version of the software system to the user. It is not unusual for this approach to result in excessive maintenance costs to make the functioning or final system fit the needs of the real user. There are other models available, and it is necessary, for each project, to choose a specific systems development life cycle model. To do this, it is necessary to identify the need for a new system and to follow this by identifying the individual steps and phases, possible interaction of the phases, the necessary deliverables, and all related materials.

There are four major system development techniques:

1. Traditional systems development life cycle (SDLC)
2. Waterfall model (a variant of the traditional SDLC)
3. Rapid application development (RAD)
4. Joint application development (JAD)

Although these four development techniques frequently are seen as mutually exclusive, in truth they represent solutions that place different emphasis on common elements of systems design. Defined at different times, each methodology's strengths demonstrate the technology, economics, and organizational issues that were current at the time the methodology was first defined.

Software generally is constructed in phases, and tests should be conducted at the end of each phase before development continues in the next phase. Four major phases that are always present in software construction are:

1. The analysis phase, where software requirements are defined
2. The design phase, based on the previously described requirements
3. The construction, programming or coding phase
4. The implementation phase, where software is actually installed on production hardware, and finally tested before release to production

The programming phase always includes unit testing of individual modules and system testing of overall functions. Sometimes, in addition to testing during programming and implementation, a fifth phase, solely devoted to functional testing, is established. Review and modification generally follow all phases, where weaknesses and inadequacies are corrected.

25.3.1   Phases of the Traditional Software Development Life Cycle.   The seven phases discussed here comprise the most common traditional SDLC:

1. Investigation
2. Analysis
3. Design
4. Decoding and debugging
5. Testing
6. Implementation
7. Maintenance

From this traditional model, other models with fewer or more phases have been developed.

25.3.1.1   Investigation.   This phase involves the determination of the need for the system. It involves determining whether a business problem or opportunity exists and conducting a feasibility study to determine the cost effectiveness of the proposed solution.

25.3.1.2   *Analysis.*   Requirements analysis is the process of analyzing the end users' information needs, the environment of the organization and the current system, and developing functional requirements for a system to meet users' needs. This phase includes recording all of the requirements. The documentation must be referred to continually during the remainder of the system development process.

25.3.1.3   *Design.*   The architectural design phase lists and describes all of the necessary specifications for the hardware, software, people and data resources, and information products that will satisfy the proposed system's functional requirements. The design can best be described as a blueprint for the system. It is a crucial tool in detecting and eliminating problems and errors before they are built into the system.

25.3.1.4   *Decoding and Debugging.*   This phase involves the actual creation of the system. It is done by information technology professionals, sometimes on staff within a company and sometimes from an external company that specializes in this type of work. The system is coded and attempts are made to catch and eliminate all coding errors before the system is implemented.

25.2.1.5   *Testing.*   Once the system is created, testing is absolutely essential. Testing proves the functionality and reliability of the system and acts as another milestone for finding problems and errors before implementation. This phase is instrumental in determining whether the system will meet users' needs.

25.3.1.6   *Implementation.*   Once the previous five phases have been completed and accepted, with substantiating documentation, the system is implemented and users are permitted to use it.

25.3.1.7   *Maintenance.*   This phase is ongoing and takes place after the system is implemented. Because systems are subject to variances, flaws, and breakdowns as well as difficulties when integrating with other systems and hardware, maintenance continues for as long as the system is in use.

25.3.2   Classic Waterfall Model.   Although phased approaches to software development appeared in the 1960s, the waterfall model, attributed to Roy Royce, appeared in the 1970s. The waterfall model demands a sequential approach to software development and contains only five phases:

1. Requirements analysis phase
2. Design
3. Implementation
4. Testing
5. Maintenance

25.3.2.1   *Analysis or Requirements Analysis.*   The waterfall model emphasizes analysis as part of the requirements analysis phase. Since software is always part of a larger system, requirements are first established for all system elements, and then some subset of these requirements is allocated to software. Identified requirements, for both the system and the software, are then documented in the requirements specification. A series of validation tests is required to ensure that, as the system is developed, it continues to meet these specifications.

The waterfall model includes validation and verification in each of its five phases. This means that in each phase of the software development process, it is necessary to compare the obtained results against the required results. Testing is done within every phase to answer this question and does not occur strictly in the testing phase that follows the implementation phase.

25.3.2.2   Design.   The design phase is actually a multistep process focusing on data structure, software architecture, procedural detail, and interface characterization. During the design phase, requirements are translated into a representation of the software that then can be assessed for quality before actual coding begins. Once again, documentation plays an important role because the documented design becomes a part of the software configuration. Coding is incorporated into the design phase instead of being a separate phase. During coding, the design is translated into machine-readable form.

25.3.2.3   Implementation.   During the implementation phase, the system is given to the user. Many developers feel that a large problem with this model is that the system is implemented before it actually is ready to be given to the user. However, waterfall model advocates claim that the consistent testing throughout the development process permits the system to be ready by the time this phase is reached. Note that in the waterfall model, the implementation phase precedes the testing phase.

25.3.2.4   Testing.   Although testing has been going on during the entire development process, the testing phase begins after code has been generated and the implementation phase has occurred. This phase focuses on both the logical internals of the software and the functional externals.

25.3.2.5   Maintenance.   The maintenance phase reapplies each of the preceding life cycle steps to existing programs. Maintenance is necessary because of errors that are detected, necessary adaptation to the external environment, and functional and performance enhancements required and requested by the customer.

The waterfall model is considered to be unreliable partly due to failure to obey the strict sequence of phases advocated by the traditional model. In addition, the waterfall model often fails because it delivers products whose usefulness is limited when requirements have changed during the development process.

25.3.3   Rapid Application Development and Joint Application Design.   Rapid application development (RAD) supports the iteration and flexibility necessary for building robust business process support. RAD emphasizes user involvement and small development teams, prototyping of software, software reuse, and automated tools. Activities must be carried out within a specified time frame known as a time box. This approach differs from other development models where the requirements are fixed first and the time frame is decided later. RAD, in an effort to keep within the time box and its immovable deadline, may sacrifice some functionality.

RAD has four phases within its cycle:

1. Requirements planning
2. User design

3. Construction

4. Cutover

The main techniques used in RAD are joint requirements planning (JRP) and joint application design (JAD). The word joint refers to developers and users working together through the heavy use of workshops. JAD enables the identification, definition, and implementation of information infrastructures. The JAD technique is discussed with RAD because it enhances RAD.

25.3.4   Importance of Integrating Security at Every Phase.   Security should never be something added to software at the end of a project. Security must be considered continuously during an entire project in order to safeguard both the software and the entire system within which it functions. Regardless of which software development model is used, it is essential to integrate security within each phase of development and to include security in the testing at each phase. Rough estimates indicate that the cost of correcting an error rises tenfold with every additional phase. For example, catching an error at the analysis phase might require only several minutes—time for a user to correct the analyst—and therefore cost only a few dollars. Catching the same error once it has been incorporated into the specifications document might cost 10 times more; after implementation, 1,000 times more.

25.4   TYPES OF SOFTWARE ERRORS

25.4.1   Internal Design or Implementation Errors.   A general definition of a software error is a mismatch between a program and its specifications; a more specific definition is "the failure of a program to do what the end user reasonably expects." There are many types of software errors. Some of the most important include:

- Initialization
- Logic flow
- Calculation
- Boundary condition violations
- Parameter passing
- Race condition
- Load condition
- Resource exhaustion
- Other errors

25.4.1.1   Initialization.   Initialization errors are insidious and difficult to find. The most insidious programs save initialization information to disk and fail only the first time they are used—that is, before they create the initialization file. The bugs appear only on fresh copies of the program, which might not affect an individual user directly but which could easily affect every employee and customer who uses a fresh copy. Other programs might show odd calculations or other flaws the first time they are used or initialized, and these errors, which are initialization errors, will continue to reappear each time the program is used.

25.4.1.2 Logic Flow.   Modules pass control to each other or to other programs. If execution passes to the wrong module, a logic-flow error has occurred. Examples include calling the wrong function or branching to a subroutine that lacks a RETURN instruction so that execution falls through the logical end of a module and begins executing some other code module.

25.4.1.3 Calculation.   When a program misinterprets complicated formulas and loses precision as it calculates, it is likely that a calculation error has occurred; for example, an intermediate value may be stored in an array with 16 bits of precision when it needs 32 bits. This category of errors also includes computational errors due to incorrect algorithms.

25.4.1.4 Boundary Condition Violations.   Boundaries refer to the largest and smallest values with which a program can cope; for example, an array may be dimensioned with 365 values to account for days of the year and then fail in a leap year when the program increments the day-counter to 366 and thereby attempts to store a value in an illegal address. Programs that set variable ranges and memory allocation may work within the boundaries but, if incorrectly designed, may crash at or outside the boundaries. The first use of a program also can be considered a boundary condition.

25.4.1.5 Parameter Passing.   Sometimes there are errors in passing data back and forth among modules. For instance, a call to a function accidentally might pass the wrong variable name so that the function acts on the wrong values. When these parameter-passing errors occur, data may be corrupted and the execution path may be affected because of incorrect results of calculations or comparisons. As a result, the latest changes to the data might be lost or execution might fall into error-handling routines even though the intended data were correct.

25.4.1.6 Race Condition.   When a race occurs between event A and event B, a specific sequence of events is required for correct operation but this sequence is not ensured by the program. For example, if process A locks resource 1 and waits for resource 2 to be unlocked while process B locks resource 2 and waits for resource 1 to be unlocked, there will be a deadly embrace that freezes the operations.

Race conditions can be expected in multiprocessing systems and interactive systems, but they can be difficult to replicate; for example, the deadly embrace just described might happen only once in 1,000 transactions if the average transaction time is very short. Consequently, race conditions are among the least tested.

25.4.1.7 Load Condition.   All programs and systems have limits to storage capacity, numbers of users, transactions, and throughput. Load errors can occur due to high volume, which includes a great deal of work over a long period of time, or high stress, which includes the maximum load all at one time.

25.4.1.8 Resource Exhaustion.   The program's running out of high-speed memory (RAM), mass storage (disk), central processing unit (CPU) cycles, operating system table entries, semaphores, or other resources can cause failure of the program. For example, inadequate main memory may cause swapping of data to disk, typically causing drastic reductions in throughput.

25.4.1.9   Other Sources of Error.   It is not unusual for errors to occur where programs send bad data to devices, ignore error codes coming back, and even try to use devices that are busy or missing. The hardware might well be broken, but the software also is considered to be in error when it does not recover from such hardware conditions.

Additional errors can occur through improper builds of the executable; for example, if an old version of a module is linked to the latest version of the rest of the program, the wrong sign-on screens may pop up, the wrong copyright messages may be displayed, the wrong version numbers may appear, and various other inaccuracies may occur.

25.4.2   User Interface.   Generally speaking, the term "user interface" denotes all aspects of a system that are relevant to a user. It can be broadly described as the user virtual machine (UVM). This would include all screens, the mouse and keyboard, printed outputs, and all other elements with which the user interacts. A major problem arises when system designers cannot put themselves in the user's place and cannot foresee the problems that technologically challenged users will have with an interface designed by a technologically knowledgeable person.

Documentation is a crucial part of every system. Each phase of development—requirements, analysis, development, coding, testing, errors, error solutions and modifications, implementation and maintenance—needs to be documented. All documents and their various versions need to be retained for both future reference and auditing purposes. Additionally, it is important to document the correct use of the system and provide adequate instructional and reference materials to the user. Security policies and related enforcement and penalties also need to be documented. Ideally, the documentation should enable any technically qualified person to repair or modify any element, as long as the system remains operational.

25.4.2.1   Functionality.   A program has a functionality error if performance that can reasonably be expected is confusing, awkward, difficult, or impossible. Functionality errors often involve key features or functions that have never been implemented. Additional functionality errors exist when:

- Features are not documented
- Required information is missing
- A program fails to acknowledge legitimate input
- There are factual errors conflicting names for features
- There is information overload
- The material is written to an inappropriate reading level
- The cursor disappears or is in the wrong place
- Screen displays are wrong
- Instructions are obscured
- Identical functions require different operations in different screens
- Improperly formatted input screens exist

25.4.2.2   Control (Command) Structure.   Control structure errors can cause serious problems because they can result in:

- Users getting lost in a program

- Users wasting time because they must deal with confusing commands
- Loss of data or the unwanted exposure of data
- Work delay
- Financial cost

Some common errors include:

- Inability to move between menus
- Confusing and repetitive menus
- Failure to allow adequate command-line entries
- Requiring command-line entries that are neither intuitive nor clearly defined on screen
- Failure of the application program to follow the operating system's conventions
- Failure to distinguish between source and parameter files resulting in the wrong values being made available to the user through the interface and/or failure to identify the source of the error
- Inappropriate use of the keyboard when new programs do not meet the standard of a keyboard that has labeled function keys tied to standard meanings
- Missing commands from the code and screens resulting in the user being unable to access information or, utilize programs, failure of the system to be backed up and recoverable, and a host of other commands that leave the system in a state of less-than-optimum operability
- Inadequate privacy or security that can result in confidential information being divulged, the complete change or loss of data without recoverability, poor reporting, and even the undesired access by outside parties to a system

25.4.2.3   *Performance.* Speed is important in interactive software. If a user feels that the program is working slowly, that is an immediate problem. At another level, performance suffers when program designs make it difficult to change their functionality in response to changing requirements. Performance errors include slow response, unannounced case sensitivity, uncontrollable and excessively frequent automatic saves, and limited scrolling speed.

25.4.2.4   *Output Format.* Output format errors can be frustrating and time-consuming. An error is considered to have occurred when the user cannot change fonts, underlining, boldface, and spacing that influence the final look of the output. Errors occur when the user cannot control the content, scaling, and look of tables, figures, and graphs. Additionally, there are output errors that involve expression of the data to an inappropriate level of precision.

25.5   DESIGNING SOFTWARE TEST CASES

25.5.1   Good Tests. No software program can ever be tested completely. Even if all valid inputs are defined and tested, there is no way to test all invalid inputs and all the variations on input timing. It is also difficult, if not impossible, to test every path the program might take, find every design error, and prove programs to be logically correct. Nevertheless, a good test procedure will find most of the problems that would occur, allowing the designers and developers to correct those problems and ensure that the software works properly.

Whenever you expect the same results from two tests, you consider the tests equivalent. A group of tests forms an equivalence class if the tester believes that the tests all test the same thing and if one test catches or does not catch a bug, the others probably will do the same. While classical boundary tests check a program's response to input and output data, equivalence tests teach a way of thinking about analyzing programs that enhances and strengthens test planning.

Finding equivalence classes is a subjective process. Different people analyzing the same program will come up with different lists of equivalence classes because of what the programs appear to achieve. Test cases often are lumped into the same equivalence class when they involve the same input variables, result in similar operations, affect the same output variables, or all handle errors in the same manner.

Equivalence classes can be groups of tests dealing with ranges or multiple ranges of numbers, members of a group, and even time-determined. Equivalence classes are generally the most extreme values such as the biggest, smallest, fastest, slowest. When testing, it is important to test each edge of an equivalence class, on all sides of each edge. Testers should use only one or two test cases from each equivalence class because a program that passes the tests generally will pass any test drawn from that class. Invalid input equivalence classes often allow program bugs to be overlooked during debugging.

25.5.2 Emphasize Boundary Conditions.   Boundaries are crucial for checking each program's response to input and output data. Equivalence class boundaries are the most extreme values of the class; for example, boundary conditions may consist of the biggest and smallest, soonest and latest, shortest and longest, or slowest and fastest members of an equivalence class.

Tests should include values below, at, and above boundary values. When programs fail with nonboundary values, they generally fail at the boundaries too. Programs passing these tests probably also will pass any other test drawn from that class.

Today, the most prevalent security breaches involve buffer overflows in active code (ActiveX and Java), in which inadequate bounds checking on input strings allows overflowing text to be interpreted as code that then can carry out improper operations. Restrictions on input length and type would prevent these exploits.

Tests should also be able to generate the largest and smallest legitimate output values, remembering that input-boundary values may not generate output-boundary values.

25.5.3 Check All State Transitions.   All interactive programs move from one state to another. A program's state is changed whenever something causes the program to alter output (e.g., to display something different on the screen) or to change the range of available choices (e.g., displaying a new menu of user options).

To test state transitions, the test designer should lay out a transition probability matrix to show all the paths people are likely to follow. State transitions can be very complex and often depend not on the simple choices provided but on the numbers the user enters. Testers often find it useful to construct menu maps that show exactly where to go from each choice available.

Menu maps also can show when and where users go when menu or keyboard commands take them to different states or dialogs. Maps are particularly handy when working with spaghetti code (code that has been poorly designed or badly maintained so that logical relationships are difficult to see); maps allow the designer or user to reach a dialog box in several ways and then proceed from the dialog box to several places.

For spaghetti code, the menu maps afford a simpler method of spotting relationships between states than trying to work exclusively from the program itself because the map shows transition between states on paper or on screen. After mapping the relationships, the designer or user can check the program against the map for correctness.

Full testing theoretically requires that all possible paths are tested. However, in practice, complete testing may be unattainable for complex programs. Therefore, it makes sense to test the most frequently used paths first.

25.5.3.1   *Test Every Limit.* It is necessary to test every limit on a program's behavior that is specified by any of the program's documents. Limits include the size of files, the number of terminals, the memory size the program can manage, the maximum size it requires, and the number of printers the program can drive. It is important to check on the ability of the program to handle large numbers of open files on an immediate basis and on a long-term, continuing basis as well. Load testing is actually boundary condition testing and should include running tests the program ought to pass and tests the program should not pass.

25.5.3.2   *Test for Race Conditions.* After testing the system under "normal" load, it should be tested for race conditions. A "race condition" is usually defined as anomalous behavior due to unexpected critical dependence on the relative timing of events. Race conditions generally involve one or more processes accessing a shared resource such as a file or variable, where this multiple access has not been properly controlled. Systems that are vulnerable to races, especially multiuser systems with concurrent access to resources, should undergo a full cycle of testing under load. Race conditions sometimes can be identified through testing under heavy load, light load, fast speed, slow speed, multiprocessors running concurrent programs, enhanced and more numerous input/output devices, frequent interrupts, less memory, slower memory, and related variables.

25.5.4   Use Test-Coverage Monitors. For complex programs, path testing cannot possibly test every path throughout a program. A more practical glass box approach (i.e., with knowledge of the internal design of a program) is to use the source code listing to force the program down every branch visible in the code. When programmers add special debugging code during development, a unique message will print out or be added to a log file whenever the program reaches a specified point. Typically such messages can be generated by calling a print routine with a unique parameter for each block of code. When source code is compiled, many languages permit a switch to be set to allow conditional compilation, so that a test version of the code contains active debugging statements whereas a production version does not. For interpreted code such as most fourth-generation languages, similar switches allow for inclusion or activation of debugging instructions.

Since distinct messages are planted, it is possible to know exactly what point in the program the test has reached. Programmers specifically insert these messages at significant parts of the program. Once these messages have been added, anyone can run the program and conclude whether the different parts actually have run and been tested.

Special devices or tools also can be used to add these messages to the code automatically. Once you feed source code to such a coverage monitor, it analyzes the control structures in the code and adds probes for each branch of the program. Adding these probes or lines of code is called instrumenting the program. It is possible to tell that the program has been pushed down every branch when all the probes have been printed. Besides instrumenting code, a good coverage monitor can capture probe outputs, perform analyses, and summarize them. Some coverage monitors also log the time used for each routine, thus supporting performance analysis and optimization.

A coverage monitor is designed for glass box testing, but knowledge of the internals of the program under test is not needed in order to use the monitor. The coverage monitor counts the number of probe messages, reports on the number of probes triggered, and even reports on the thoroughness of the testing. Because it is possible for the coverage monitor to report on untriggered branches, the monitor can find and identify code that does not belong, such as routines included by default but never used or deliberately inserted undocumented code (a Trojan horse). Some commercially available coverage monitors are, unfortunately, themselves full of bugs. It is important to obtain a full list of the known bugs and patches from the developer. In addition, such tools should themselves be tested with programs that contain known errors, in the process known as seeding, to verify their correctness.

25.5.5   Seeding.   Quality assurance procedures themselves benefit from testing. One productive method, known as seeding, is to add known bugs to a program and measure how many of them are discovered through normal testing procedures. The success rate in identifying such known bugs can help estimate the proportion of unknown bugs left in a program. Such seeding is particularly important when establishing automated testing procedures and test-coverage monitors.

25.5.6   Building Test Data Sets.   One of the most serious errors in quality assurance is to allow programmers to use production data sets for testing. Production data may include confidential information that should not be accessible to programming staff, so access should be forbidden not only to production data but even to copies of production data, or even to copies of subsets or samples from production data. However, *anonymizing* processes applied to copies of production data (e.g., scrambling names and addresses of patients in a medical records database) may produce test data sets suitable for use in quality assurance.

25.6   BEFORE GOING INTO PRODUCTION

25.6.1   Regression Testing.   Regression testing is fundamental work done by glass box and black box testers. The term is used in two different ways. The first definition involves those tests where an error is found and fixed and the test that exposed the problem is performed again. The second definition involves finding and fixing an error and then performing a standard series of tests to make certain the changes or fix made did not disturb anything else.

The first type of regression testing tests that a fix does what it is supposed to do. The second type tests the fix and also tests the overall integrity of the program.

It is not unusual for people who mention regression testing to be referring to both definitions, since both involve fixing and then retesting. It is recommended that both types of testing be done whenever errors are fixed.

25.6.2   Automated Testing.   In some enterprises, every time bug is fixed, every time a program is modified, every time a new version is produced, a tester runs a regression test. All of this testing takes a considerable amount of time and consumes both personnel and machine resources. In addition, repetitive work can become mind-numbing, so testers accidentally omit test cases or overlook erroneous results.

To cut down on the time consumption of personnel and the repetitive nature of the task, it is possible to program the computer to run acceptance and regression tests. This type of automation results in execution of the tests, collection of the results, comparison of the results with known good results, and a report of the results to the tester.

Early test automation consisted essentially of keyboard macros or scripts, with limited capacity for responding to errors; typically, an error would produce invalid results that would be fed into the next step of processing and lead to long chains of meaningless results. Slightly more advanced test harnesses would halt the test process at each error and require human intervention to resume. Both methods were of only modest help to the test team. However, today's test-automation software can include test databases that allow orderly configuration of tests, specific instructions for restarting test sequences after errors, and full documentation of inputs and results. For realistic load testing, some systems can be configured to simulate users on workstations, with scripts that define a range of randomly generated values, specific parameter limits, and even variable response times. Large-scale load testing can connect computers together through networks to simulate thousands of concurrent users and thus speed identification of resource exhaustion or race conditions.

Test automation can be well worth the expenditures required. Automated testing is usually more precise, more complete, faster, and less expensive than the tests done by human personnel. Typically, automated tests can accomplish tenfold or hundredfold increases in the number of tests achievable through manual methods. In addition to freeing personnel to do more rewarding work, such methods greatly reduce overall maintenance costs due to detection of errors before systems reach production.

25.6.3   Tracking Bugs from Discovery to Removal.   Finding a bug is not enough. Even eliminating a bug is insufficient. A system also must allow the causes of each bug to be identified and rectified. For these reasons, it is important to track all problems from the time of their discovery to their removal, to be certain that the problems have been resolved and will not affect the system.

Problem-tracking systems must be used to report bugs, track solutions, and write summary reports about them. An organized system is essential to ensure accountability and communication regarding the bugs. Typical reports include where bugs originate (e.g., which programmers and which teams are responsible for the greatest number of bugs); types of problems encountered (e.g., typographical errors, logic errors, boundary violations); and time to repair. However, problem-tracking systems can raise political issues, such as project accountability, personal monitoring, and control issues regarding the data in the database and who owns them.

Once a tracking system is established, a bug report is entered into the database system and a copy goes to the project manager, who either prioritizes it and passes it along or responds to it personally. Eventually the programmers will be brought into the loop, will fix the problem, and will mark the problem as fixed. The fixed problem then is tested and a status report is issued. If a fix proves not to work, that becomes a new problem that needs to be addressed.

25.7   MANAGING CHANGE.   Many people may be involved in creating and managing systems; whenever changes are made to the system, those changes need to be managed and monitored in an organized fashion to avoid chaos.

25.7.1   Change Request.   The change request is an important document that requests either a fix or some other change to a program or system. Information contained on the change request form generally includes who is requesting the change, the date the request is being made, the program and area affected, the date by which the change is needed, and authorization to go ahead and make the change.

Most companies have paper forms that are retained for monitoring and auditing purposes. As the popularity of digital signatures grows and society continues to move toward a paperless office, it seems logical that some of these change requests eventually will become totally automated.

25.7.2   Tracking System.   The tracking system may be manual, automated, or a combination of methods. Regardless of how it is kept, the original change form generally is logged into a system, either manually filed or entered into an automated database, by some identifying aspect, such as date, type of change, or requesting department.

The system is used to track what happens to the change. When an action is taken, information must be entered into the system to show who worked on the request, what was done, when action was taken, what the result of the action was, who was notified of the actions taken, whether the change was accepted, and related information.

25.7.3   Regression Testing.   When a change or fix has been made, regression testing verifies that the change has indeed been made and that the program now works in the fashion desired, including all other functions.

25.7.4   Documentation.   Documentation is crucial when considering and implementing changes. If information is retained strictly in an individual's head, what happens when the individual goes on vacation, is out sick, or leaves the enterprise permanently? What if the individual simply does not remember what changes were made, or when; how does an organization know who was involved, what actually was done, and who signed off that the changes were made and accepted?

Lack of documentation can mean that unauthorized changes were made. Undocumented changes can result in system crashes, data theft or corruption, embezzlement, and other serious crimes. Lack of documentation is often a violation of corporate policy and is often cited in audits. Since constructing adequate documentation after the fact is almost impossible, documentation must proceed in step with every phase of a system's development and operation. Thereafter, it must be retained according to company policy and legal requirements.

25.8   SOURCES OF BUGS AND PROBLEMS.   Locating and fixing bugs is an important task, but it is also essential to try to determine where and why the bugs and related problems originated. By finding and studying the source, often it is possible to prevent a recurrence of the same or similar type of problem.

25.8.1   Design Flaws.   Design flaws often occur because of poor communication between users and designers. Users are not always clear about what they want and need, while designers do not understand, misinterpret, or simply ignore what the users relate to them. Within the design process, even when users' feelings and requirements are known and understood, design flaws can occur. Often flaws result from attempts to comply with unrealistic delivery schedules. Managers should support their staff in resisting the pressure to rush through any of the design, development, and implementation stages.

28.8.2   Implementation Flaws.   Whenever a program is developed and implemented, there are time limits and deliverable dates. Most problems during development cause delay, so developers and testers often are rushed to get the job done. Sometimes they sacrifice the documentation, the review portion of the project, or even cut short testing, leaving unrecognized design and implementation flaws in place. Managers should emphasize the value of thorough review and testing and allocate enough time to avoid such blunders.

25.8.3   Unauthorized Changes to Production Code.   If problems are traced to unauthorized changes, project managers should examine their policies. If the policies are clear, perhaps employee training and awareness programs need improvement. Managers also should examine their own behavior to ensure that they are not putting such pressure on their staff that cutting corners is perceived to be acceptable.

25.8.4   Incompetent Programmers.   A programmer can make or break a program and a project. Programmers play essential roles in software development. Therefore, it is important that all programmers on a project be capable and reliable. Project programmers should be carefully screened before being placed on a software development project to ensure that their skills meet project requirements. Sometimes holes in programmers' skills can be filled with appropriate training and coaching. However, if problems appear to be consistent, management may want to check a programmer's background to verify that he or she did not falsify information when applying for the job. Truly incompetent programmers need to be removed from the project.

25.8.5   Data Corruption.   Data corruption can occur because of poor programming, invalid data entry, inadequate locking during concurrent data access and modification, illegal access by one process to another process data stack, and hardware failures. Data corruption can occur even when a program is automatically tested or run without human intervention. In any event, when searching for the sources of bugs and other problems, it is important to do a careful review of the data after each round of testing, in order to identify deviations from the correct end-state.

25.8.6   Hacking.   When bugs and problems do occur, hacking—both internal and external—should be considered a possibility and searched for by reviewing the logs of who worked on the software and when that work was done. Managers should be able to spot the use of legitimate IDs when the individuals involved were on vacation, out sick, or not available to log on for other reasons.

Unauthorized changes to code and data sometimes can be identified even if the perpetrator deletes or modifies log files. One method is to create checksums for production or other official versions of software and to protect the checksums against unauthorized access and modification using encryption and digital signatures. Similarly, unauthorized data modifications sometimes can be made more difficult by creating checksums for records and linking the checksums to time and data stamps and to the checksums for authorized programs. Under those conditions, unauthorized personnel and intruders find it difficult to create valid checksums for modified records.

25.9   CONCLUSION.   This chapter has presented a comprehensive look at the software development and quality assurance processes that must be utilized when developing, implementing, and modifying software. Software development involves more than simply selecting and utilizing an approach such as the traditional, waterfall, or RAD methodology. It means working as a team to develop, review, refine, and implement a viable working product. Many good techniques and products can be applied to both the SDLC and the quality assurance portions of producing software; some of the key elements are good documentation, allowing sufficient time for testing in the development and maintenance processes, building good tests, establishing test data, automating testing, and keeping track of change requests.

25.10   BIBLIOGRAPHY AND FURTHER READING

Campanella, J., ed. *Principles of Quality Costs: Implementation and Use,* 2nd ed. Milwaukee, WI: ASQC, Quality Press, 1990.

Horton, W.K. *Designing and Writing Online Documentation: Help Files to Hypertext.* New York: John Wiley & Sons, 1990.

IEEE. *IEEE Standard for Software Quality Assurance Plans.* ANSI/IEEE Std. 730-1981 [The IEEE references are no longer first on the page, since by expanding the reference they now fall consistently in the alphabetical arrangement under "I" instead of "A".] The Institute of Electrical and Electronics Engineers, 1981.

IEEE. *An American National Standard: IEEE Standard for Software Test Documentation.* ANSI/IEEE Std. 829-1983. The Institute of Electrical and Electronics Engineers, 1983.

King, David. *Current Practices in Software Development.* New York: Yourdon, Inc., 1984.

Ould, M.A. *Strategies for Software Engineering: The Management of Risk and Quality.* New York: John Wiley & Sons, 1990.

"Software Quality Assurance": *http://satc.gsfc.nasa.gov/assure/agbsec3.txt.*

"Some Words about Software Engineering": *www.ircam.fr/anasyn/schwarz/da/specenv/ 8_1Some_Words_about_Softwar.html.*

Whitten, N. *Managing Software Development Project.* New York: John Wiley & Sons, 1990.

CHAPTER 26

PIRACY AND ANTIPIRACY TECHNIQUES

Diane E. Levine

CONTENTS

26.1 INTRODUCTION. Piracy is big business. According to Peter Beruk of the SIIA (Software & Information Industry Association), writing in May 2000, "Results of the fifth annual benchmark survey on global software piracy . . . [highlighted] the serious impact of copyright infringement to the software industry. Piracy losses exceeded $12 billion worldwide in 1999 and topped $59 billion during the past five years."[1] The 1999 software piracy estimates indicated that more than one in every three business software applications in use during 1999 was pirated. Piracy losses for the United States and Canada led every other region of the world at $3.6 billion, or 26 percent of the total. The continuing problem means lost jobs, wages, tax revenues, and a potential barrier to success for software start-ups around the globe.

Once thought of as a mere copyright infringement of printed matter or production of a counterfeit audio tape, piracy has grown with technology in the world and has expanded to encompass intellectual property, digital data, DVDs, CD-ROMs, VHS, analog and high-definition TV, and streaming media.

The International Intellectual Property Alliance (IIPA) (*www.iipa.com*) says that in 1996, the major U.S. copyright industries claimed they lost approximately $18 billion to $20 billion in revenue due to piracy outside of the United States. Domestically the losses were in excess of $2.8 billion. Losses increased in the succeeding years leading to the present.

The Software & Information Industry Association (*www.siia.net*) released Year 2000 findings that 91 percent of software being auctioned on Internet auction sites like Yahoo!, eBay, Excite, and Zdnet is pirated. SIIA initiated action against a total of 1,016 companies during that year. Additional action against data pirates was taken in 2001.

To understand why and how piracy occurs and the enormous impact on society worldwide, we need to have a clear understanding of what we mean by the word "piracy." Whenever information is created and published in print, on the Internet, or incorporated into software, that information may be protected by copyright, patent, or trademark law. This principle applies to a broad spectrum of material that includes, for example, the Wright Brothers' specifications for their "Flying Machine;" Microsoft Windows software; the icon Mickey Mouse and all related materials; television shows, plays, and movies; and music created and performed live and on recordings. Making unauthorized copies of such material is referred to as piracy.

26.1.1 Patent, Copyright, and Trademark Laws.   There are differences among the applicable laws and the materials they protect.

Patents give owners exclusive rights to use and license their ideas and materials; patents generally protect nonobvious inventions that can be embodied in computer software and hardware.

Copyrights give owners the exclusive rights to create derivative works, to reproduce original works, and to display, distribute, and conduct their works. Copyrights apply to original works of authorship including paintings, photographs, drawings, writings, music, videos, computer software, and any other works that are fixed in a tangible medium. Copyrights, their infringement, and remedies are described in the Copyright Act of 1976.

Trademarks give owners the right to restrict the use of distinctive marks in certain contexts and apply to words, sounds, distinctive colors, symbols, and designs.

The number of patent infringement lawsuits in the United States doubled between 1982 and 1997. During that same period copyright infringement suits increased by 31 percent and trademark infringement suits increased by 36 percent.[2] See Chapter 12 for a more detailed summary of these issues.

26.1.2 Types of Piracy.   There are several types of piracy. End-user piracy occurs when end users use a single copy of software to run on several different systems, or when they distribute copies of software to others without permission of the software manufacturer. Reseller piracy occurs when unscrupulous resellers distribute multiple copies of a single software package to multiple customers, preload the same software on multiple systems, or knowingly sell counterfeit software to customers.

Internet and bulletin board (BBS) piracy occurs when users download and upload copyrighted materials and use it or make it available for use by others without proper license.

26.2   TERMINOLOGY.   A better understanding of the piracy situation and antipiracy can be obtained by understanding the terminology involved. Some of the most commonly used terms and organizations are listed in this glossary.

ACATS—Advisory Committee on Advanced Television Service.

Anti-Bootleg Statute (Section 2319A)—a U.S. federal statute that criminalizes the unauthorized manufacture, distribution, or trafficking in sound recordings and music videos of "live" musical performances.

ATSC—Advanced Television Systems Committee.

ATV—Advanced Television.

Bootleg recordings—The unauthorized recording of a musical broadcast on radio or television or at a live concert or performance. These recordings are also known as underground recordings.

BSA—Business Software Alliance. A consortium of major software developers including IBM, Microsoft, Novell, Apple, Dell, and Sun Microsystems that is attempting to stem lost revenues from pirated computer software. BSA educates computer users on software copyrights and fights software piracy. Individual members like Microsoft and Adobe have their own antipiracy programs in addition to belonging to the BSA.

CEA—Consumer Electronics Association.

CEMA—Consumer Electronics Manufacturers Association.

CSS—Content Scrambling System. A form of data encryption used to discourage reading media files directly from the disc, without a decryption key. To descramble the video and audio requires a 5-byte, 40-bit key.

DeCSS—Descrambling Content Scrambling System. A utility developed by Norwegian programmers via reverse engineering and posted on the Web. This utility decrypts CSS and allows individuals to make illegal copies of DVD movies. MPAA and DVD CCA sued to have the utility removed from *2600, The Hacker Quarterly* Web site.

DFAST—Dynamic Feedback Arrangement Scrambling Technique.

DMAT—Digital Music Access Technology.

DMCA—The Digital Millennium Copyright Act signed into law October 28, 1998. Designed to implement World Intellectual Property Organization (WIPO) treaties (signed in Geneva in December 1996), DMCA strengthens the protection of copyrighted materials in digital formats.

DVD CCA—DVD Copy Control Association. A not-for-profit corporation that owns and licenses CSS. DVD CCA has filed numerous lawsuits against companies and individuals that make pirated copies of films.

EFF—The Electronic Frontier Foundation. A nonprofit organization working in the public interest to protect fundamental civil liberties, including privacy where computers and the Internet are concerned. The organization frequently disagrees with the steps that other organizations and corporations want to take to protect copyrighted materials.

FAST—The Federation Against Software Theft. A group headquartered in Great Britain represents software manufacturers and works with law enforcement agencies in finding and stopping software pirates in Europe.

FCC—Federal Communications Commission.

grpff—A seven-line, 526-character program of Perl code developed by two students at the Massachusetts Institute of Technology. More compact than DeCSS, the program descrambles DVDs but does not contain a decryption key. The code is readily available on the MIT campus via hats, T-shirts, business cards, and bumper stickers.

HDTV—High definition television. Digital television transmissions that are expected to be the standard for television in the future.

HRRC—Home Recording Rights Coalition represents consumers, retailers, and manufacturers of audio and audiovisual recording products and media. The HRRC dedicates itself to keeping products free of government-imposed charges or restraints on the products' distribution or operation.

IIPA—International Intellectual Property Alliance. A private sector coalition formed in 1984. The organization represents the U.S. copyright-based industries in efforts to improve international protection of copyrighted materials.

MP3—A technology for downloading music files using the MPEG format via the Internet.

MPAA—Motion Picture Association of America. Composed of member companies that produce and distribute legitimate films and videos. This organization serves as the official voice and advocate of the American motion picture industry. MPAA also assists law enforcement in raids and seizure of pirated videocassettes and DVDs.

MPEG—Moving Pictures Experts Group. A generic means of compactly representing digital video and audio signals for consumer distribution. MPEG video syntax provides an efficient way to represent image sequences in the form of more compact coded data.

NMPA—National Music Publishers Association. A trade association that represents 700 U.S. businesses that own, protect, and administer copyrights in musical works.

NTSC—National Television System Committee.

Pirated recordings—Unauthorized duplicates of the sounds of one or more legitimate recordings.

RIAA—Recording Industry Association of America. The group has an antipiracy unit that handles initial examination of product on behalf of the recording industry. Pirates can be turned in by calling RIAA at 1-800-BAD-BEAT.

SAG—Screen Actors Guild. The union for screen actors. Members do not get residuals from pirated films, as they do from authorized copies.

SDMI—Secure Digital Music Initiative. A forum of 175 companies from the electronics, music, telecommunications, and information technology industries, and the RIAA. The mission of this forum is to develop a secure framework for the digital distribution of music.

SIIA—Software & Information Industry Association. A trade organization of the software and information content industries representing over 1,000 high-tech companies that develop and market software and electronic content. The organization provides policies and procedures for dealing with software and Internet use within businesses. SIIA also provides guidelines for telling if software is pirated or counterfeited. The SIIA Anti-Piracy Hotline is 800-388-7478.

SPA—Software Publishers Association, a division of SIIA. This association assists in enforcement in dealing with software piracy and also provides education about software piracy. SPAudit Software is one of the first software audit and inventory tools made available for use by companies (in the 1980s). Improved versions of the software are now available.

Trademark Counterfeiting (Title 18 U.S.C. Section 2320)—A federal statute that deals with sound recordings that contain the counterfeit trademark of the legitimate manufacturer or artists.

Trafficking in Counterfeit Labels (Title 18 U.S.C., Section 2318)—A federal statute that covers counterfeit labels intended to be affixed to a sound recording.

U.S. Copyright Law (Title 17 U.S.C.)—a federal law that protects copyright owners from the unauthorized reproduction or distribution of their work.

WGA—Writers Guild of America. The union for writers of television, video and film scripts.

26.3 HARDWARE-BASED ANTIPIRACY TECHNIQUES. Attempts to regulate the execution of specific software or to use particular equipment have involved accessory devices called *dongles* and also specialized readers.

26.3.1 Dongles. Dongles are hardware lock devices or modules that connect to a computer and communicate with software running on the computer. Without a dongle in place, the controlled external device or regulated software does not work fully or at all.

Initially, dongles were dedicated to printers. Once a dongle was installed on the computer, it provided protection against anyone printing data from the computer without authorization. However, our changing society has created a necessity for protecting all types of devices. Now dongles are used to protect scanners; external drives (e.g., ZIP drives); CD-ROMs and rewritable CD-ROMs; DVD and DVD-R; VHS recorders; Playstation, Nintendo, and Sega video gaming systems; and even Personal Digital Assistants (PDAs).

The most common type of dongle provides a pass-through port to connect a device cable. Generally a dongle incorporates some type of algorithmic encryption in its onboard microelectronic circuitry. The extent of sophistication of the encryption varies depending on the manufacturer and the device. Many dongles provide additional onboard nonvolatile memory for the software to access. Some models even have real-time checks that keep track of date and time information, including when an application's license (temporary or leased) is set to expire.

Dongles provide some definite advantages:

- Because a dongle is an external device, it is fairly simple to install and uninstall on a serial or parallel port. In most cases, since manufacturers support their devices, an ordinary user can install and use a dongle without the need for help from an IT department.

- Dongles also must be registered. Registration provides adequate control over the use of the dongle and thus provides legitimacy to both the device and the users. Registration (dependent on the contract in place) may provide for support for both the software and the hardware.

- Dongles that support encryption provide an extra layer of protection by making transmitted data indecipherable until it reaches its destination, unless the hardware is in place.

There are also disadvantages to using dongles:

- Consumers resist the requirement for installation, maintenance, and additional cost. Most large corporations do not use dongles for their products.

- Dongles can be lost or stolen, and they also may fail.

- Problems can interfere with using the attached device. For example, a dongle used to control software and attached to a printer port may accidentally cause problems for a standard printer.

- Sometimes a dongle will work well with a slow computer but cause errors when installed on a faster computer.

- Since not every manufacturer automatically replaces lost or stolen dongles without charge, there may be additional costs involved in getting a replacement.

- Dongles can present a serious risk-management problem for critical applications where delays in obtaining replacements or registering them may be unacceptable.

- As with any device, there can be a serious problem if the dongle manufacturer ceases to support the model of dongle a company has installed, or if the dongle manufacturer goes out of business entirely.

- Laws regarding encryption usage differ in various countries. Specialized dongles that may be legal to use in the United States may be illegal in another country.

26.3.2   Specialized Readers.   One of the impediments to illegal copying used to be the difficulty and cost of obtaining specialized hardware and software for reading and copying proprietary materials with fidelity. However, today such copying equipment is inexpensive and easy to find. In addition, the media for distributing illegal copies are less expensive than ever.

**26.3.2.1   *Audio.*   According to the Recording Industry Association of America (*www.riaa.org*), the global audio industry loses in excess of $5 billion every year to piracy worldwide. RIAA says that $1 million a day, in just physical product, is lost in the United States alone. The loss of ancillary revenues drives the figures higher. But according to RIAA, these figures are low since they estimate that in some countries up to 98 percent of the music in use are illegal copies.

As part of an industry-wide, organized approach to highlighting and reducing the music piracy problem, the RIAA has become increasingly more active in recent years. It has formed proactive alliances with legal and law enforcement agencies globally and gone after the culprits. In 1998, for example, the RIAA confiscated 23,858 illegal CDs in the first half of the year. Operation Copycat—a joint investigation by RIAA, the MPAA, and the New York Police Department—saw the arrest of 43 CD pirates and the shutdown of 15 illegal manufacturing locations.

Those who finance piracy in the United States and Canada are often overseas. Much of the international piracy trade appears to be headquartered in Asia. The sequence of events has been documented as follows. Organized crime operations in Asia make millions of dollars from drugs and prostitution. The money is sent to the United States, where it is used to purchase hardware, software, and paper goods necessary to produce pirated CDs. Pirated music is then distributed at colleges, on Internet auction sites, or shipped abroad. Proceeds from the sale of the counterfeit CDs are then invested in real estate or wired back to Asia. Despite the vigorous efforts of all the organizations and manufacturers attempting to stop this type of piracy, the problem appears too large to control.

An even greater music piracy problem has grown because of the availability of music files on the Internet. Using free software, anyone can download music tracks and burn their own CDs. One of the original RAM-based music players, the RIO from Diamond Multimedia, is a hand-held device that can download and play back MP3 files. The MP3 file format makes it easy to create, distribute, and share compact music discs. RIAA has instituted several lawsuits claiming that the device is a recording device and the downloads are illegal. However, much of the success of the RIO was due to Web sites offering downloadable programming for free from musicians and independent record labels that adopted the MP3 format to promote their records. These musicians and recording studios claim that they are happy with the content being downloaded and are at odds with RIAA. Naturally, this raises the ongoing question of whether there can ever be one standard that applies to all recorded media.

Some major lawsuits have achieved significant press coverage and have been instrumental in enforcing or changing existing laws, or in causing new laws to be written. For instance, deliberate copyright violations resulted in an award of $50 million in statutory damages and $3.4 million in legal fees to Universal Studios in a suit against the My.MP3.com music service. MyMP3 created a database of over 80,000 albums, which when combined with the MyMP3 software let users access and store music digitally without paying a fee.

Perhaps the most recognizable name in the music field in regard to piracy as this chapter was written was Napster (*www.napster.com*), a site that enabled individuals to share tracks of music via the Internet. The site provided free downloadable software for MP3 and directions on using the software to download tracks of music. Essentially, Napster software turned a user's PC into part of a distributed server network that published available music files. It did not take long for the site to acquire a user group of millions of people who after "sampling" the music might then go to a store and buy the entire CD.

However, since the Napster site did not limit the length of the download, many users simply downloaded the entire track. Most never bought the commercial version of the music. Adding to successful piracy attempts was the development and ready availability of rewritable CD-ROM machines. More and more Napster users decided to download the music tracks they wanted and burn their own CDs without ever purchasing the CDs made by the recording artists and music companies.

Creating a stir in the industry and ultimately a landmark judicial case, Napster was forced to radically alter operations in March 2000 after protracted court proceedings. Upon the verdict, Jack Valenti, president and chief executive officer of MPAA, commented that the consumer would benefit most from the court's decision because "You cannot take for free what belongs to someone else."[3] But the subject of Napster and audio piracy remained highly controversial While some people argued that little-known artists received exposure that they may never have gotten without the free file-sharing service, others, especially large music companies and recording artists, argue that they are being denied the royalties they deserve.

As of this writing, Napster was actively attempting to continue in business by forming relationships with various recording industry giants that would allow downloading only for a paid fee. Napster also was urging its users to notify Congress of their opposition to the ruling; the company encouraged users to join the "Napster Action Line." In addition, Napster was in the process of partnering with Gracenote (*www.gracenote.com*), a vendor with a database of names and authors of copyrighted musical works. Under this scheme, if a Napster user wanted to share songs, Gracenote would compare the identifying information with its own database, the database operated by RIAA, and the databases of other music clearinghouses. Songs protected by copyrights would be blocked. If copyrighted music was desired, there would be a charge. In January 2002, Napster began a six-week trial of a subscription model for legal music swapping.

Because of the combined efforts of industry groups, unions, and law enforcement agencies, new efforts are being made to monitor, control, and charge for access and use of various types of data found on the Web.

These efforts are only a beginning; the problem is widespread, and new technologies emerge frequently to undermine such efforts. Napster, although perhaps the most notorious of the music-sharing Web sites, is only one of many that exist. Some music- and software-sharing systems, such as the software called *Gnutella,* do not use servers at all, linking participants in a spontaneous peer-to-peer network with no central control at all. Without such central control, there is no entity against whom legal action can be instituted. It remains to be seen what will happen to other services after the massive crackdown on Napster.

26.3.2.2   Video.   On the video side, Scour, Inc., provided free downloads of digital movies for DVD and VHS media from its site at *www.scour.com.* The company was started by teenagers but was financially backed by private investors including some well-known Hollywood personalities. Without the need for special software, providing an easy-to-use interface and quick response time, Scour.com seemed too good to be true, but according to dissenters and the courts, it was totally illegal.

Controversy arose because the free downloading circumvented the current copyright and distribution laws by making use of new technology—the Internet. Scour provided full-length video content, including bootleg feature films, on its Internet site. The service had two parts. The first part, Scour Exchange, provided peer-to-peer service like Napster and acted as a link from a user's drive to drives elsewhere. The second service was the basic Web site that worked in a manner similar to Yahoo with searches defined only for media files. The Scour spider read the content on the Web page as well as the codes that label the images, videos, and music files. By delving into the "guts" of a site, it was able to pull up specific types of media files.

In July 2000, MPAA, RIAA, and NMPA sued Scour and accused it of large-scale theft of copyrighted material and trafficking of stolen works. By September 2000, the company was shutting down.

This case did not stop the counterfeiting of video media. Despite increasingly steep fines, judicial rulings, and even raids by various law enforcement agencies, counterfeit video is readily available. For example, within one's own home it is possible to copy one VHS tape from an original to another, using either two machines or a dual-tape machine. In these instances where copying is successful, either the tape does not contain any restrictive mechanism or the copying device is capable of circumventing the mechanism. Although successive copying of analog recordings produces degradation of content, unprotected digital content can be copied repeatedly without suffering degradation in quality.

Along Fifth Avenue in New York City, for $5 to $10 anyone can buy the latest films and DVDs; in markets in Hong Kong, Southeast Asia, and India, the copies are even cheaper. It is true that some of the copies available may have "fallen off a truck," but it is more than likely that the counterfeit or bootleg copies were made illegally from a master copy that was either borrowed or stolen.

26.3.2.3 Television—Analog. Over 50 years ago, some people predicted that television was doomed to failure. Not only were these predictions grossly exaggerated, but even pirated TV transmissions have become big business. On January 20, 2000, a complaint against iCraveTV was filed by major television and entertainment companies. The National Football League and the National Basketball Association filed another complaint the same day against the same company.

According to both complaints, iCraveTV, a Canadian firm, was illegally using television signals without authorization or payment and streaming the signals to the iCrave Internet site where viewers could receive them free of charge. In February 2000, a preliminary injunction was issued against iCraveTV and the individuals behind the Internet site. The injunction claimed that the unauthorized transmissions of broadcast signals into the United States via the Internet were a direct violation of U.S. copyright law, and iCraveTV was ordered to stop. After iCraveTV agreed to an out-of-court settlement, the Internet site was shut down.

Hacking cable decoders is another technique for obtaining services without paying for them. Although it is not illegal to buy, install, or modify equipment for converting encoded cable TV signals from pay-per-view or other commercial suppliers, using such set-top decoders to obtain services without paying for them *is* illegal.

26.3.2.4 Television—HDTV. The first television image was created in 1884 when Paul Nipkow created a mechanical scanning disk. With only 18 lines of resolution, the picture was poor. Current NTSC standard TV transmissions are done with bandwidth that does not exceed 6MHz. The current analog system broadcasts 30 frames per second and 525 lines per frame.

High definition television (HDTV) is a digital television system that offers twice the horizontal and vertical resolution of the current TV system. HDTV has the ability to deliver a video composed of approximately 1,125 lines per frames and 60 frames per second. Viewers then see a picture quality close to that of 35mm film. Obviously, transmitting images containing that large amount of audio and video information requires wide bandwidth, actually about 18MHz. Such bandwidth would permit the transmission of 1,050 lines of 600 pixels per line. However, the Federal Communications Commission (FCC) decided to limit HDTV to a 6MHz maximum bandwidth. In order to meet that requirement, MPEG compression would be used.

MPEG compression applies algorithms to pixel groups and records information that changes within a frame rather than all of the information in the frame. Audio is synchronized to the video. Using MPEG saves storage space and transmission requirements while retaining high image and sound quality. According to the Advanced Television Committee Standard (ASTC), the FCC will require that audio and video compression as well as the transmission of HDTV terrestrial signals follow this standard.

As with all other transmissions and media, there are serious concerns about piracy of HDTV transmissions and programs. At the present time, even though many TV transmissions are scrambled in order to thwart reception, it is fairly simple, although illegal, to purchase a descrambler and unscramble the transmissions. It is also legal for home users to record programming for their own personal use.

The cable television industry is moving forward with a plan to implement a copy protection program that will allow movie studios and cable providers to control what viewers are able to record off future digital TV networks. Cable Television Laboratories filed the patented Dynamic Feedback Arrangement Scrambling Technique (DFAST) with the FCC in a 42-page licensing agreement. DFAST-compliant devices would refuse to record digital TV broadcasts that are electronically marked "copy never" or would make one archive copy of a program marked "copy once." The Consumer Electronics Association (CEA) insists that Hollywood wants to increase its profit by charging for copies. Adoption of DFAST would require that makers of televisions, video recorders, and interactive set-top boxes also adopt DFAST if they want their equipment to be compatible with the new digital cable system. Consumers also undoubtedly would have to invest in new DFAST-compliant hardware.

Meanwhile, in March 2001, television producers notified the U.S. Congress that they might protect themselves and their content by using the Content Scrambling Systems (CSS) and provide content only to channels using CSS. CSS is a form of data encryption that discourages reading media files from the DVD disc without a 40-bit decryption key. Encrypting terrestrial broadcast television programming would secure the transmission but, according to the Home Recording Rights Coalition (HRRC), such encryption will threaten established home recording rights. The HRRC contends that Section 1202(k) of the Digital Millennium Copyright Act provides a carefully balanced approach to analog home recording rights and that mandated technology may not be applied to interfere with consumer recording of free, over-the-air terrestrial broadcasts.

Additionally, CSS is not foolproof. In 2000, a 16-year-old Norwegian programmer cracked CSS and wrote a program called DeCSS that lets anyone bypass CSS. According to the hacker, his success was the result of one of the CSS licensees neglecting to encrypt the decryption key. DeCSS is a small (60KB) utility that copies the encrypted DVD video file and saves it to the hard disk without encryption. A U.S. federal judge ruled in August 2000 that DeCSS was created in violation of the DMCA and ordered the program removed from the Web site of *2600, The Hacker Quarterly.* Norwegian prosecutors indicted the teenager in January 2002. Furthermore, the HRRC contends that encrypting the free television broadcast content will create very little incentive for consumers to switch from regular analog to digital television. Instead of thwarting digital pirates, the HRRC contends that strong encryption will impose unfair and even illegal restrictions on consumers.

HDTV is not currently very popular with consumers. However, in the United States it has been mandated that a certain percentage of programs will have to conform to HDTV standards by 2006. It is possible that, by 2006, HDTV may be mandatory for all television transmissions. This may be delayed because HDTV sets are very expensive, and most viewers feel it is not necessary to spend the money when regular TV provides the same entertainment.

26.3.2.5 Specialized Readers Rejected by Consumers.   When widespread use of the personal computer (PC) evolved, anticopying restrictions failed. Bootlegged copies abounded both in educational environments and commercial corporations. In fact, it was bootlegged copies of programs that resulted in the Pakistani Brain virus being imported into the United States. When the Software Publishing Association

(SPA) was first formed, the group, together with law enforcement agencies, raided the physical premises of companies believed to be using pirated software. As a result of finding quantities of the pirated software, SPA won many legal actions and related settlements.

Some people see encryption as a challenge, and work at breaking the algorithms so they can pirate the data—digital, video, or audio. In addition, the lack of standardization of laws throughout industries and countries has led to controversy and ongoing piracy.

Although average consumers do not think of themselves as intellectual-property pirates, many otherwise honest citizens do get and use illegal programs, applications, games, audio tracks, CDs, DVDs, and VHS and television signals. This situation might be attributed to a lack of ethical education, but many people like to save money and simply do not believe they will be caught and punished for such pilfering. A study by the Pew Internet & American Life Project based on phone interviews with 4,205 adults 18 and over, some 2,299 of whom were Internet users, suggested that around 30 million U.S. residents had downloaded music from the Internet.[4] In a smaller survey published in September 2000, findings suggested that 40 percent of the general population in the United States did not see anything wrong with downloading music from the Internet regardless of copyright; among Internet users, the number of scofflaws rose to over 50 percent; among those who regularly used pirated music, almost 80 percent did not believe that sharing music files was wrong. The study also found that only about 20 percent of its respondents claimed to have bought music that they had "sampled" from the Internet.[5]

26.3.3   Evanescent Media.   There are many interpretations of the term "evanescent media." The broad interpretation includes digital imaging, optics, multimedia and other electronic art, and data that are short-lived or transitory. When such media are original, creative works, society has an interest in protecting them against piracy.

Since most evanescent media involve some visual aspects as well as text, antipiracy techniques now being used or considered for other types of data may be applicable. Such techniques include previously discussed dongles, software keys, watermarks, encryption, and digital rights management.

Part of the problem in electing and implementing a solution is the lack of existing standards that specifically deal with this new area of art and science.

26.4   SOFTWARE KEYS.   Software keys of various kinds are used to secure data and equipment. A software key is generally a string of numbers that is used for identification purposes, either to allow access to the use of equipment or to permit authorized printing, processing, or copying of data.

26.4.1   Examples.   As described earlier in the discussion of dongles, most anticopying hardware devices are accompanied by software that works in tandem with the hardware. A software key activates or deactivates the hardware lock. When the software is working perfectly, there are generally no difficulties. However, all software can malfunction, and when that happens there can be serious problems in getting equipment to work. Additional problems occur when the computer containing the software key malfunctions, and the software key cannot be made to work on a replacement machine.

26.4.1.1   *Video Cassettes versus Copy Machines.*   Watermarking is one of the techniques being seriously considered for protecting videocassettes and DVDs. In 1995, the ASTC formed a Copyright Protection Technical Working Group, which spun off a special Watermarking and Embedded Data Encoding subgroup. The group has broad representation including representatives from the PC market, the Macintosh market, the MPAA, the CEMA and related manufacturers, technicians, and users. Their task is to look for technologies and services that might use hidden visual data clues as a means of inhibiting or barring digital piracy. Using a hidden watermark that can be embedded in the content would then trigger machines either to not make copies or to alert the operator that the videocassette is marked and unauthorized copies would be considered pirated.

26.4.1.2   DVD Area Encoding.   Digital video requires very large storage space — too large for a single CD to hold. However, by applying compression techniques, the digital video can be compressed to fit into the digital video disc's maximum capacity of 17 gigabytes. Two different types of compression are used for encoding audio and video content for DVD: Constant Bit Rate (CBR) and Variable Bit Rate (VBR) compression.

In order to prevent piracy of the content of the DVD, many companies are turning to encryption. The compressed data are encapsulated through a mathematical algorithm that can be decrypted only through the use of a decryption key.

26.4.2   Implementation.   For shorter programs, CBR is ideal. Based on MPEG-2 encoding, CBR compresses each frame of audio and video by a user-selected amount. This degree of compression is then applied to the entire program. Using VBR it is possible to create a database of video content based on the amount of change in each frame or scene. This is particularly useful in programs with a long format. To construct the database, the encoding software does several analytical passes of the master footage and then makes a final digitizing pass. From the created database the computer can encode the video with a variable data rate allowing a higher bit rate for scenes with pans, zooms, and fast motion and giving scenes with little or no motion low data rates. By compressing the areas of lower detail more, areas of higher details can be allocated more space and use less compression.

26.4.3   Watermarks.   Watermarking involves embedding one set of data inside a larger set of data. The embedded set of data identifies the origins or ownership of a specific work, just as a watermark does on paper.

Using digital watermarks can help copyright owners track the use of anything digital, including music, movies, photographs, and clip art. However, there is the question of whether it is possible to mark media without offending the viewer. There is also the question of reliability of detection; for instance, how many false positives and false negatives will occur? Additionally, there is the question of survivability of the mark itself as it is run through various transformations.

As an example of watermarking, a Danish technology firm, CD-Cops, uses the glass-master fingerprinting technique, which imprints the master and every disc made from it with an ID and access code. A replicator must license the technology in order to make legal copies through use of the access code.

Watermark research is still in process. Although at the moment antipiracy techniques appear to be moving in other directions, watermarking may prove to be a viable and economic method of preventing video and audio piracy. The Secure Digital Media Initiative (SDMI) has about 10 proposals for digital watermarking from companies specializing in file compression and signal processing. SDMI has even challenged hackers to attempt to crack the code and remove the watermark from an SDMI-compliant song offered online. The Electronic Frontier Foundation has asked the Internet community to boycott the contest. According to the EFF, the DMAT (Digital Music Access Technology) is designed to put an encryption-based shell around digital audio content and prevent it from being played on any player that does not honor the DMAT. This would mean that manufacturers and users would be forced to adopt the DMAT format in equipment and would create additional expenditures for manufacturers and consumers. Producers of television content have raised the same issue.

In October 2000, a team of computer scientists at Princeton and Rice universities and the Xerox Palo Alto Research Center (PARC) was able to remove the invisible "watermarks" used by the 200-company SDMI to protect digital music files from pirates. SDMI had offered a prize to anyone who could defeat its various security measures, four of six of which made use of watermarks. SDMI's Tala Shamoon said, "I expected some would have fallen. This is part of an empirical process to get the best technology."[6] Professor Ed Felten and colleagues at Princeton University defeated all four of the schemes under test.

26.4.4   Resistance to Reverse Engineering.   Reverse engineering allows a programmer to work backward from the finished program or product. By reverse engineering playback software, encryption keys can be extracted. Reverse engineering can circumvent most antipiracy solutions. As a result, manufacturers of antipiracy software and hardware are strongly opposed to permitting reverse engineering.

DMCA does allow reverse engineering. But the provisions of DMCA were not intended to enable the circumvention of technical protection measures (TMPs) in order to gain unauthorized access to or to make unauthorized copies of copyrighted works.

26.4.5   Published Attacks.   The most notable attack on a software key took place when a licensee of CSS neglected to encrypt a decryption key. Obtaining a key by reverse engineering the XingDVD from Xing Technologies, the hackers were then able to guess many other keys. This left the hackers with a collection of decryption keys; even if the XingDVD key was removed, they could still copy DVDs by using the other keys.

26.5   SOFTWARE USAGE COUNTERS.   Software metering has been popular for several years. Special software monitors system usage and inventories the software on the system or network. This type of software also can be used to block or limit the use of specific software such as browsers and games. In addition to fighting piracy, it can reduce the load on IT personnel by reducing complications due to use of unauthorized software.

26.5.1   Controlling Concurrent Installations.   Software metering products can monitor concurrent installations even on networks used by people in different geographic areas who have different requirements and different software installed. The metering software permits an administrator to maintain a live and updated inventory of the software installed at different locations on the network. The logs show where installation has taken place, when the licenses expire, and when updates are necessary. Alerts can be set to notify system administrators when a license is about to expire or an update has been accomplished.

26.5.2   Controlling Concurrent Usage.   Software metering allows network administrators to identify and resolve cases of illegal installation of unauthorized copies of authorized software and also to catch people who install unauthorized software on the organization's computers. Metering software also allows a company to report and analyze logon and logout times, track software usage, and meter software licenses to keep those in the company legal. In addition to avoiding legal entanglements, monitoring can reduce the demand on system resources, network bandwidth, and technical support staff.

26.5.3   Examples.   Microsoft has announced that to combat piracy, new releases of the Office 2000 program will insert a counting feature that makes the programs malfunction if the owner has not registered the software after launching it 50 times. Microsoft is just one of several companies that is actively participating in antipiracy programs. Prior to this announcement, Microsoft published antipiracy literature and provided a great deal of consumer education regarding the effects of software piracy on society as well as a piracy hotline (1-800-RU-LEGIT). Novell (1-800-PIRATES), Adobe, and Xerox are other companies that have vigorous antipiracy programs in place, but they have not yet announced that they are building metering into their products.

26.5.4   Implementation.   Metering software requires a bona fide license in order for it to be implemented. Typically, companies establish CD-ROM keys that are printed on legitimate copies of their product installation discs or jewel cases. The keys include checksums or message authentication codes that can be checked by the installation routines. The algorithms for the checksums are supposed to cause difficulty for people trying to create counterfeit keys. The security of such measures depends on the cryptographic strength of the validation keys.

Software counters for controlling concurrent usage need to store information securely so that each load operation increments a counter and each program unload operation decrements it. However, the security problem is to store such information in such a way that it cannot be modified easily by dishonest people. Encrypting the data in a complex sequence of operations can stop most people from abusing the system by making the effort required for circumventing the mechanisms more costly than buying a license.

26.6   DIGITAL RIGHTS MANAGEMENT.   Recognizing that piracy is a huge moral and financial problem, software developers have adopted and modified another type of system that can be applied to print, audio, video, and streaming media. Called Digital Rights Management (DRM), the system was originally devised to protect proprietary information and military information. The idea behind the system is to protect all types of intellectual digital content from anyone who would take it without the consent of the developer(s) and/or owners. Major companies like Microsoft, Adobe, and IBM are developing and marketing DRM systems, and dozens of smaller companies are springing up.

26.6.1   Purpose.   The purpose of DRM is to protect all digital content that originators or owners want protected. DRM permits distributors of electronic content to control viewing access to that content. The content can be text, print, music, or images. Basically, DRM systems use a form of customized encryption. When an end user purchases viewing, listening, or printing rights, an individual "key" is provided. The system works on rules, meaning that although a key is provided, it generally comes with limitations regarding the copying, printing, and redistribution.

Unfortunately, there is no agreement on a DRM solution. Lack of standards is hampering businesses from moving forward with online business initiatives. Because there are so many companies promoting their own incompatible forms of DRM, customers will have to download megabytes of code for each version. Maintaining, upgrading, and managing all of those different versions are a major headache for the customers. There does not appear to be a simple solution; rather than being a technology issue, it is really a matter of business and politics.

26.6.2 Application. Typically, when users become prospective owners of digital rights, they download a content file. The DRM software does an identity check of the users, contacts a financial clearinghouse to arrange for the payment to be made, and then decrypts the requested file and assigns the user a key. The key is used for future access to the content.

Because the system works on rules, it is possible to impose restrictions. One user might pay just to view material, while another user might want to have printing privileges. A third user might want to download the content to his or her own machine, and finally, a fourth user might want to have viewing privileges for a specified time. The same content would thus be used by four different authorized users, each of whom would pay according to a rate scale established by the content distributor. And throughout all of the transactions, each user would need a mechanism that allows secure transmissions and identifies that user and his or her level of access privileges.

Although this approach to publishing may sound fairly simple, it is really quite complex. In addition to arranging for different users to access material according to the set rules and to pay according to a rate schedule, it is also necessary for content distributors to handle the back end of the application. Everyone involved in the creation, production, and distribution of the content has to be paid fairly for the use of the content.

Payment is especially important as more and more content providers digitize materials so that they can show or print on demand. Many users will read books online, but some physical printing on paper will continue. However, publishers will be able to print precisely those volumes that are requested. This approach will provide customized printing (e.g., large-print editions) as well as saving paper and physical warehouse storage space.

26.6.3 Examples. Several different types of DRM systems exist. Experts agree that the best DRM systems combine both hardware and software access mechanisms. With the advent of the eBook, the digital pad, PDA modems, Internet access devices, and increasingly smaller laptop computers, tying access rights directly to storage media gives publishers and distributors control of where the content is being used as well as by whom.

With the passage of the Electronic Signatures in Global and National Commerce Act, referred to as the E-Sign Bill and the increasing use of digital signatures, original documents (e.g., legal, medical, or financial) will be stored digitally. President Clinton signed the E-Sign Bill on June 30, 2000, in Philadelphia's Congress Hall, using a ceremonial pen and a digital smart card. The bill went into effect on October 1, 2000. The E-Sign Bill gives an online signature ("John Hancock") the same legal status as a signature etched on paper and makes the digital document the original. Any printout will be considered a copy so the ability to view documents and videos (e.g., living wills) digitally will actually give the viewer access to the original. Eventually records for medical treatment and documents for trials may be totally digital and require submission and viewing digitally. When this becomes the norm rather than the exception, strict adherence to DRM in order to maintain privacy, as well as to provide restitution, will be paramount. In addition, such content-protection schemes will prevent unauthorized modifications of the digital data that would otherwise contribute to fraud.

For example, IBM (*www.ibm.com*) has released antipiracy technology called the Electronic Media Management System that allows for downloading of music tracks but puts controls on how many copies can be made or allows for a copy length limitation to be inserted. Thus, a minute of music could be downloaded to give a listener a taste but not a chance to pirate the entire music track. To obtain the entire track, the user would be required to pay a fee.

Microsoft (*www.microsoft.com*) distributes free software that embeds metatags in each audio file. The metatags refer back to a central server in which the business rules are stored. This approach requires that material be tagged as it is created; otherwise, once it is released without the embedded tags, it can be illegally copied.

While major companies like Xerox, Microsoft, IBM, and Adobe have gotten heavily involved in producing and using this software, a multitude of smaller firms, such as InterTrust (*www.intertrust.com*), Reciprocal (*www.reciprocal.com*), and Sealed Media (*www.sealedmedia.com*) have opened shop.

Some companies, such as Sealed Media, ContentGuard (*www.contentguard.com*), Pay2See (*www.pay2see.com*), and Publish.com (*www.publish.com*), concentrate on protecting the rights of print or text material. Other companies, such as MediaDNA.com (*www.mediadna.com*) and Vypu.com (*www.vyou.com*) apply their technology to all types of data including video, streaming media, audio, print, and Web sites.

While DRM may seem to be the panacea for the piracy problem, on the other side of the coin are dissenters who feel that DRM gives producers and distributors too much control. There are also legal issues that have not been addressed and settled as law yet, so there is very little precedent upon which to base cases that arise. Due to the lack of precedent, many individuals and companies may feel wary about becoming involved in DRM.

26.7   FUNDAMENTAL PROBLEMS.   A number of experts have pointed out that there are fundamental flaws to all the methods for preventing illegal copying of digital materials as described in this chapter. Bruce Schneier, a respected cryptographer, has repeatedly explained that all digital information must be converted to a cleartext (unencrypted) form before it is displayed or otherwise used. Because the cleartext version has to reside somewhere in volatile or nonvolatile memory for at least some period of time to be usable, it is theoretically possible to obtain a copy of the cleartext version regardless of the complexity of the methods that originally concealed or otherwise limited access to the data. For example, if a DVD movie using complex regional encoding is to be seen on a monitor, at some point the hardware and software that decoded the DVD have to send that datastream to a monitor driver. The decoded datastream is vulnerable to interception. By modifying the low-level routines in the monitor driver, it is possible to divert a copy of the raw data stream to a storage device for unauthorized replay or reconstruction. Similarly, a system may be devised to prevent more than one copy of a document from being printed directly on a printer; however, unless the system prevents screen snapshots, a user can circumvent the restrictions by copying the screen as a bit image and storing that image for later, unauthorized use. Although hardware devices such as dedicated DVD or CD players may successfully interfere with piracy for some time, the problem is exacerbated under the current popular operating systems that have no security kernel and thus allow any processes to access any region of memory without regard to security levels.

26.8   SUMMARY.   Piracy is a rapidly growing societal "crime" that is on the rise. Piracy comes in different forms and affects a multitude of people and industries. Although producers may suffer the greatest financial losses, there is a substantial impact on consumers. Pirated copies are generally inferior in quality and are sometimes defective. If anything goes wrong, pirated copies, being illegal, are unsupported. Additionally, producers' financial losses due to pirated copies may push the cost of legitimate copies up.

Retailers and distributors also suffer due to the loss of sales to pirates. Illegal copies generally are sold more inexpensively than legitimate copies, so retailers and distributors cannot compete on price.

Creative talent, whether software developers, writers, musicians, artists, or performers, plus all the people who helped create the book, magazine, record, performance, painting, concert, or other media are cheated out of their royalties by pirates. Frequently, because of the amount of time and effort needed to create the end product, the creators depend on the royalties for their livelihood. In addition, poor quality or stolen concepts can irreparably damage the reputation of the creative talent.

Publishers, record companies, art dealers, and other individuals and companies that invest artistic and technical skill along with money and effort to create an original work also lose revenues when that work is pirated. Because of the expenses already laid out to create the original product, companies frequently have to recoup their losses by raising prices for the consumer.

Due to the sophistication of systems and the increased use of the Internet, piracy has become more widespread and has an even greater financial impact worldwide. Many different types of antipiracy systems and techniques have been developed and implemented in an effort to cut down on the ever-increasing instances of piracy. One drawback to all of the systems is the lack of standards applied to software, audio, video, and other media. One of the most promising antipiracy systems is digital rights management (DRM). However, even DRM systems are not yet standardized, thus creating even more confusion regarding which is best and what to use.

Although DRM has gained a following because of the MP3 and online music piracy incidents, its real significance is in the future when books, newspapers, medical and business documents, music tracks, videos, streaming media, and film will all be online. Traditional publishers are still reluctant to digitize everything. And, as extraordinary as it may seem to the "techies" in society, not everyone has Internet access.

Consumers have not yet passed judgment on what the accepted medium for reading online documents will be. While eBooks may well become an important medium, other devices may prove even more popular. Developers are working on newer and more convenient devices, and they are rapidly appearing in everyday life.

Meanwhile, piracy has become such a great problem worldwide that it cannot be ignored. Piracy has become a big business, and as a result, antipiracy methods and techniques are growing in economic importance.

26.9   REFERENCES

Denning, Dorothy E. *Information Warfare and Security.* Reading, MA: Addison Wesley, 1999.

Hutt, Arthur, Seymour Bosworth, and Douglas Hoyt. *Computer Security Handbook,* 3d ed. New York: John Wiley & Sons, 1995.

Panettieri, Joseph C. "The Software Mobsters." *Smart Reseller,* September 6, 1999, pp. 38–42.

The Copyright Act of 1976 (Public Law 94-553); Title 17 U.S.C. Sections 101–120.

2000 Global Software Piracy Report. BSA/SPA Global Piracy Study, 2001, *www.spa.org/piracy/releases.*

26.10   NOTES

1. Peter Beruk, May 2000. See "Five Years: $59.2 Billion Lost, Software Industry Suffers From Cumulative Impact of Global Software Piracy," *www.siia.net/archive.asp.*

2. Cited in "Insuring Intellectual Property Remains a Niche, Despite Rapidly Growing Need," *Business Wire* (August 4, 1997).

3. Jack Valenti, Napster Statement, February 12, 2001, *www.mpaa.org/Press/Napster_2-12-2001.htm.*

4. Pew Internet and American Life Project (*www.pewinternet.org*), April 2000. See "The Music Downloading Deluge," which states that 37 million American adults and youths have retrieved music files on the Internet, *www.pewinternet.org/reports/toc.asp?Report=33.*

5. "Downloading Free Music: Internet Music Lovers Don't Think It's Stealing," *www.pewinternet.org/reports/toc.asp?Report=23.* The study found that 78 percent of Internet users who downloaded music did not think it was stealing and supported the downloader's right to get music online for free. Of the downloaders, 63 percent said they did not care if the music was copyrighted. While 15 percent of the downloaders bought the music online, 21 percent bought the music on a CD or cassette most of the time, 29 percent bought a CD or cassette some of the time, 19 percent bought a CD or cassette a few times, and 26 percent claimed they never bought a CD or cassette of the music they downloaded. A total of 12,751 people were interviewed between March and August 2000.

6. *www.msnbc.com/news/480521.asp.*

PART FOUR

PREVENTION: HUMAN FACTORS

CHAPTER 27

STANDARDS FOR SECURITY PRODUCTS

Paul Brusil and Noel Zakin

CONTENTS

27.1   INTRODUCTION.   Information technology (IT), with its security concerns, has revolutionized business operations. Security associated with information technology is key to every country's national priorities such as economic competitiveness, government operations, national security, and healthcare. E-business, e-commerce, and e-government business models are transforming nearly all enterprises and industries. Security is no longer a supporting player; it is a major element of information technology.

In this multidisciplinary, multitechnology, multiparty environment, different types of security standards are essential.

Some standards provide consistent ways to stipulate security needs and requirements. Other standards exist to specify security-related software interfaces, naming conventions, and data structures, and to specify the security functionality appearing in products. Standards are also necessary for fostering interoperability of separately built security implementations as well as for consistent security, end-to-end, across different business domains and computing environments. Interoperability testing can assure secure interoperation between autonomous business partners. Still other standards exist to specify how to examine conformance of implementations to functional standards and how to assure the interoperability of implementations that must meet the same functional standard. Conformance testing demonstrates whether an implementation includes the functionality stipulated in a functional standard. However, conformance of different products does not necessarily ensure that these products will interoperate. Conformance means that interoperability is possible, but interoperability needs to be verified by pair-wise testing.

Interoperating, conformant security products cannot necessarily be trusted to provide sound security or to mitigate the risks of greatest concern. Key to developing trust is to build confidence that products mitigate the risks of concern, that products are properly built and behave according to specification, and that products do no more or no less than advertised. Fortunately, standards exist for establishing and testing the degree to which risks and vulnerabilities are mitigated to some specified level of confidence and that the quality of security provided by parties with which businesses interact are comparable.

Customers find standards helpful when specifying the level of security functionality and the degree of assurance they require. Standards also help customers to assess the security functionality and the assurances that product builders claim to provide.

A major goal of standardization efforts is to evolve toward an information technology–driven economy where secure products approach plug-and-play status and where they can be comparably trusted, purchased from multiple competing vendors, and mixed, matched, and integrated to provide requisite secure, trusted IT infrastructures that reduce the risks of greatest concern.

Although several different categories of security-relevant standards should be considered, standards associated with developing product trust are especially important in the emerging, electronically interwoven world. This chapter focuses on such standards, first summarizing various approaches that have existed for about two decades. Then the chapter describes the new, internationally recognized paradigm that provides a standard way for stipulating (1) the risks of concern, (2) the security functional requirements that must be met in order to mitigate stated risks, and (3) the security assurance requirements that must be met to provide confidence that products are built with desired quality. According to this paradigm, risks and requirements are stipulated in a way so that security solutions can be tested in a standard way to verify compliance with the stipulations. This so-called Common Criteria paradigm is presented later herein.

27.2   SECURITY ASSESSMENT STANDARDS ASSOCIATED WITH SECURITY IMPLEMENTATIONS.

Standards of various types, various breadths of acceptance, and various levels of formality exist in the general area of assessing the security associated with implementations of technology. For example, there are informal, standard ways of assessing security-oriented products or the standards-specified security technology within a product. Other standards exist to assess the overall quality and soundness of the builder of a product. Security assessment approaches based on these standards can yield generalized conclusions that "good" vendors build "good" security products. Still other types of standards exist to assess both the quality of a product builder and the quality of specific classes of security products that they build.

27.2.1   Security Technology and Product Assessment Standards.

Many informal, typically consortium-directed, approaches exist to demonstrate conformance of a product to stated security features or to specific security technology standards. In the Internet world, the notion of implementation bake-offs among trial (preproduct) implementations of emerging Internet Engineering Task Force (IETF) standards has been a mainstay in the community for quite some time. Less competitive approaches are also being tried in the security world. The SPOCK program is an example of a recognized approach for demonstrating product conformance to security features and performance claimed by the product builder. The VPN Consortium has developed an approach for demonstrating conformance of a product to a specific security standard.

27.2.1.1   *Security Proof of Concept Keystone.*

The *Security Proof of Concept Keystone* (SPOCK) is a joint government-industry consortium (*coact.com/spock.html*) sponsored by the National Security Agency (NSA). It develops and conducts product-specific tests to demonstrate a vendor's or system integrator's stated claims about implemented security features and performance associated with commercial and government products or systems. Such demonstrations of Commercial-off-the-Shelf (COTS) or prototype COTS products are conducted in government-sponsored test beds and provide a loose conformance and performance verification capability. Reports on products that have undergone SPOCK testing can be obtained via the SPOCK NSA program manager.

27.2.1.2   *VPN Consortium.*

The *VPN Consortium IP Security Testing Program* is providing specific types of conformance testing of virtual private network (VPN) products implementing the IETF's IP security standard. Predefined tasks must be successfully performed with reference test gateways. Due to the nonexhaustive set of tests, passing the VPN Consortium test provides indications that tested products conform in limited part to standards and that interoperability is possible with other products that pass the same tests under the same environmental situations. Details on products that have passed the VPN Consortium's testing can be obtained at *www.vpnc.org.*

27.2.2   Standards for Assessing Security Implementers.

Some standards apply specifically to developers of security products.

27.2.2.1 Capability Maturity Model.   Standards exist to measure the software and security competency of any type of organization including, for example, vendors that build security-oriented products.

A standard for assessing the competency of software developers is the *Capability Maturity Model* (CMM).[1] The "Capability Maturity Model for Software" is a family of Software, Systems Engineering, and Product Development Capability Maturity Models[SM] (CMMs[®]).

The *Systems Security Engineering Capability Maturity Model* (SSE-CMM) approach uses such standards. It can be used as a way to assess the soundness of a security product builder's engineering practices during the many stages of product development, such as during

- Product requirements capture and analysis
- Product concept definition including accurate translation of security requirements into product requirements
- Product architecting
- Product design
- Product implementation

A security product developer can demonstrate competence in building products by means of recognized, so-called capability maturity assessments of the developer's software and security engineering processes. Security-enhanced products built by organizations with demonstrated expertise and maturity can be viewed to merit greater trust than products built by organizations that do not demonstrate mature, competent software design and security engineering capabilities.

The SSE-CMM establishes a framework of generally accepted security engineering principles and a standardized way of measuring (and improving) the effectiveness of an organization's security engineering practices. The SSE-CMM describes the essential characteristics of, and provides tools for assessing, an organization's security engineering process that must exist to ensure good security engineering. These characteristics are graded by a set of security metrics that assess specific attributes about a vendor's processes and the security effectiveness of the results of vendor's processes.

When the level of the SSE-CMM security metrics associated with a specific builder of security-oriented products shows the builder to have mature security engineering capabilities and effective security engineering practices, then confidence is increased that the builder can build sound security products.

Trust in, and assurance about, a product can be established to some degree for measurably competent vendors, rather than by relying on other approaches based on post-implementation testing and evaluation of a product. The quantitative comparability of assurance developed via the SSE-SMM approach to the assurance developed via other approaches such as the Common Criteria paradigm is currently unknown and is the subject of investigation.

Further information about how the System Security Engineering-Capability Maturity Model (SSE-CMM) approach can be used is available at the International Systems Security Engineering Association Web site (*www.sse-cmm.org*).

27.2.2.2 Quality (ISO 9000).   ISO 9000, from the International Standards Organization, is used as a guide to conduct a broad, high-level, horizontal assessment of the quality of systems and of the competence of an organization across all its facets.[2]

Although not specific to organizations that build security products, it does provide some amount of basic information about the potential for quality and repeatability in an organization's ability to meet its mission. In fact, derivative approaches such as the Common Criteria, in part inspired by ISO 9000, are used as standards to accredit the quality associated with security testing laboratories.

27.2.3 Combined Product and Product Builder Assessment Standards. Some standards evaluate both developers and their products. The following sections review the history of national standards and the evolution of international standards.

27.2.3.1 *Competing National Criteria Standards.* To introduce consistency in describing the security features and levels of trust of a limited set of security-enhanced products, and to facilitate comprehensive testing and evaluation of such products, the U.S. Department of Defense (DoD) developed the *Trusted Computer System Evaluation Criteria* (TCSEC) in the early 1980s.[3] The TCSEC—or, more colloquially, the "Orange Book"—defined a small set of six classes of increasing security functionality and increasing assurance (from a "C1 class" to an "A1 class") that applied to operating systems. The TCSEC was extended to networking devices[4] and database management systems.[5] The colors of the covers for these TCSEC related books were distinctive, leading to the term "the Rainbow Series." Government in-house evaluations were offered first, followed by comparable, government-sponsored commercial evaluation services. Use of TCSEC concepts expanded beyond the DoD to other U.S. government sectors as well as to foreign governments.

Partly in reaction to early experiences with the "Rainbow Series" that revealed significantly larger security testing delays and costs than were expected, other countries and world regions started developing other criteria that built on the concepts of the TCSEC. Importantly, these other criteria were more flexible and adaptable to the fact that information technology was beginning to evolve very rapidly. Four European countries banded together to develop the *Information Technology Security Evaluation Criteria* (ITSEC), which arose from the combined inputs of earlier German criteria, French criteria, and U.K. confidence levels.[6] Subsequently, in 1993, the *Canadian Trusted Computer Product Evaluation Criteria* (CTCPEC) were developed as a combination of the TCSEC and ITSEC approaches. The U.S. Federal Criteria development then attempted to combine the CTCPEC and ITSEC with the TCSEC.

With the growing realization that an international market for trusted IT products was building and that competing criteria had the potential to fracture the market and derail its growth, efforts began to harmonize the various criteria into a common criteria that would be internationally accepted and standards-based. It was the set of resources applied to the U.S. Federal Criteria that eventually led to the development of a single, wide-ranging, widely accepted common criteria for providing a fully flexible, highly tailorable approach to the standardization of security functionality and evaluation assurance. Indeed, in the United States, national government policy has been established to use these common criteria instead of the former " Orange Book," TCSEC approach.[7]

27.2.3.2 *Common Consolidated Criteria Standard.* Out of the old cumbersome and costly "Orange Book" approach and the experiences, lessons, and analyses of the other national criteria, a new, commercially driven strategy has emerged for testing products and demonstrating confidence that their security features behave properly. This best-of-all-previous-breeds strategy is based on a new, international standard—

referred to as the Common Criteria (CC). The CC strategy resolves differences among the earlier competing national criteria and accompanying certification and accreditation strategies, and integrates the best aspects of its predecessors. The CC strategy offers a single, internationally recognized approach for specification and evaluation of IT security that is widely useful within the entire international community. The CC benefitted greatly from the combined knowledge and involvement of all the parties that originally created the individual national and regional criteria. Version 1.0 of the CC was published in 1996. Subsequent field-testing of Version 1 established the knowledge base and lessons to develop Version 2 in 1998. This was subsequently standardized, with minor editorial and technical changes, by the ISO in 1999 as International Standard 15408.[8] More about the CC appears later.

27.3   ESTABLISHING TRUST IN PRODUCTS AND SYSTEMS AND MANAGING RISKS

27.3.1   Why Trust and Risk Management Are Important.   Businesses are learning that trust in their electronic processing and electronic storage as well as trust in their electronic interactions among customers, business partners, suppliers, and service organizations is the essential ingredient underpinning electronic business models. The need for trust will only increase as new logarithmically growing, paradigm-shifting technologies proliferate, mutating business models and IT operations and management models further, while introducing new risks and vulnerabilities. All players in the emerging electronic business models need confidence in security products in order for high tech to become the prominent and lasting driving force behind businesses and for it to become the engine of economic prosperity.

Key to a vibrant economy and efficient government is trust that the country's market-sector–specific IT infrastructures will not be compromised by cyberterrorists to the point of curtailing or destroying the availability of IT-powered critical national services and industries like healthcare, telecommunications, transportation, and energy provision. Trust must be established that hostile governments, criminal cartels, or guerrilla groups that may now be conducting clandestine cyberreconnaissance on critical computer infrastructures do not destroy public confidence in the IT systems that support the electronic economy.

The need to protect such IT infrastructures and build trust in their viability was dramatically brought to the national consciousness by Presidential Decision Directive 63.[9] Through this directive, the U.S. White House stipulated that critical national IT-based infrastructures need to be protected. More recently, IT protection plans have begun to be developed under the aegis of the U.S. Critical Information Assurance Office and in partnership with industry to implement the directive.[10] Also, the U.S. Secretaries of Defense and Commerce have been instructed to ensure that critical national IT-based infrastructures like the telecom infrastructure be secured and that they can be trusted to support national security and emergency preparedness.

Another key notion besides trust is the notion of risk management. When electronic relationships are established between parties, there are quantifiable risks associated with such relationships.

Risks are quantifiable in many ways. For example, they can be quantified in terms of assessing the types of possible adverse events. They can be quantified in terms of the likelihood of different types of adverse events and the value of what is to be protected by IT security solutions during an adverse event. They can be quantified in terms of the consequences of adverse events, such as the liability that may be exposed via compromises or the entities that may be hurt by compromises.

Risks then can be mitigated in a number of possible ways. For example, risks can be mitigated by using security solutions that reduce the occurrence or impacts of the adverse events of most concern. When assets of increasing value need to be protected, risks can be reduced by using security solutions that have increased assurance. Risks also can be mitigated by using security solutions that decrease the specific, deleterious liabilities and undesired consequences of greatest concern. Being able to specify the risks of concern and security solutions that mitigate those risks is a powerful strategy.

Linking notions of trust together with notions of risk reduction make for an even more powerful strategy. By establishing trust among e-business players with security solutions of appropriate quality—comparable to the face-to-face handshakes in the old business model—revenues generated can increase via the increased volume of business transactions made possible by electronic trust. By mitigating risks, business losses and costs can be reduced. When trust enhancement is coupled with risk management, the resulting increased revenues combined with decreased losses and lower costs make for significant profit multiplication.

The Common Criteria paradigm provides just such a strategy both for establishing appropriate levels of trust and for specifying and mitigating risks of most concern. Indeed, the Common Criteria paradigm appears to be the only strategy available today for simultaneously establishing trust and managing risk.

27.3.2 Alternative Methods of Establishing Trust. Various ways have been developed and used over the years to build confidence about the quality of security implementations. The focus of such efforts includes establishing trust that (1) a product performs its claimed security functionality completely and correctly and (2) the product builder's processes, from design, to development, to delivery, to maintenance are sound. Not all approaches to establishing trust necessarily address both its aspects: namely trust in implemented security functionality and assurance of the soundness of the builder's abilities and processes.

Typically trust is established by testing the implementation or by analytically evaluating the product and its implementer. Many of the testing and evaluation approaches are not based on standards. Lack of reliance on standards makes for difficulty in comparing testing and evaluation results among products, among testing and evaluation approaches, and even among testing facilities. At this time, few testing and evaluation approaches are based on the use of internationally recognized standards. The Common Criteria is based on such standards.

27.3.2.1 Nonstandard Trust Development Alternatives. A variety of current approaches to security testing and evaluation are not dependent on standard, internationally recognized approaches. They include vendor self-declarations, customer in-house assessments, and third-party approaches including, for example, commercial assessments and assessments by magazines and trade press publications.

27.3.2.1.1 Vendor Self-Declarations. One of the initial, and still widely prevalent, approaches to purportedly providing trust was based on the notion of vendor self-declarations. A vendor can unilaterally claim that a specific product meets the security needs of a class of customers and that the appropriate amount of customer-desired confidence can be placed in the product's implemented security features. In part, the confidence associated with this approach is implicitly tied to the past reputation of a vendor or to the customer's past experience in dealing with the vendor. If the vendor's reputation or customer's experiences are good, there is some sense that the vendor has done an adequate job of implementing security. This approach was typical throughout the early days of IT within the United States, when no independent testing and evaluation houses existed. It is still somewhat prevalent in some regions of the world, such as the Far East. The problem with this approach is that it lacks measurable ways of quantifying the degree of trust that can be associated with a product. It also lacks measurable ways of comparing the relative degrees of trust that can be associated with different products.

Nowadays with the typical torrent of upgrades and revisions to products, this approach may have some merit in establishing some degree of confidence in products that have been changed since the version of the product that may have undergone rigorous security testing and evaluation. If a vendor is known to have good security engineering capabilities—such as can be assessed, in part, by standard Capability Maturity Model approaches—and if the vendor can provide reasonable evidence as to the nature of the upgrade or revision since the product that had undergone rigorous assessment, then there can be some qualitative (albeit, quantitatively unknown) degree of confidence about the upgraded or revised product. Under these conditions, trusting customers can believe that the quality of the changed product is similar to the quality of the version of the product that was tested.

27.3.2.1.2   Proprietary In-House Assessments.   Product consumers can develop the requisite substantial technical expertise in-house to test and evaluate specific security-enhanced products directly. Alternatively, consumers can contract a private evaluator, such as one of the big consulting houses or systems integrators, to do such testing and evaluation. Often these approaches are unique and proprietary.

Some of the large international financial institutions have used this approach. Financial institutions as a whole are very careful to make sure that products they use are trustworthy. The security, integrity, and soundness of all products and systems supporting financial institutions must be consistent and verifiable. These institutions fear that any breech of IT security anywhere within their systems will result in a loss of confidence in the entire institution, not just in the specific, subverted IT product.

Most financial institutions developed their own internal security specifications and evaluation processes as well as evaluation methodology to quantify, compare, approve, and certify general security aspects of competing products. One of the consequences of this approach was that it required substantial, costly duplication of testing infrastructure as well as the costly duplication of testing effort for those products that were candidates for purchase by multiple customers.

Furthermore, as the volume of financial devices such as credit card platforms, operating systems, and thousands of applications continues to increase dramatically, in-house resources are finding it difficult to keep up. They have found this kind of do-it-yourself approach to be a tremendous undertaking in terms of development, implementation, legitimacy demonstration, maintenance, and rejustification. They have found it to be expensive, time-consuming, resource-intensive, hard to maintain, always open to interpretation and debate, and always in need of being justified to regulators and principals in new markets being entered.

While this approach has been effective on thousands of financial products, components, and systems, many of the world's foremost financial players (American Express, EuroPay, Master Card, Mondex, VISA International, etc.) are banding together in alliances such as the Smart Card Security Users Group (*http://csrc.nist.gov/cc/sc/sclist.htm*). Such an alliance has many benefits:

- The users can replace their internal approaches.

- They can pool their resources to address common security testing and evaluation needs by using contemporary, standards-based, Common Criteria, security specification and testing schemes recognized across major financial players.

- It allows them to develop profiles of security requirements for the various common elements of smart cards (e.g., chips, operating systems, applications, crypto engines).

- It allows them to develop common test suites to unify the current hodge-podge of fragmented customer- and vendor-specific testing of smart cards.

- It allows them to outsource security testing and evaluation to competent, accredited testing laboratories whose expertise can be used by all financial institutions.

The experience of these financial institutions is that the Common Criteria paradigm is superior to their old, proprietary evaluation schemes. Increasingly, smart cards and smart card components must be evaluated according to the Common Criteria as a necessary precursor to purchase by the financial institution.

27.3.2.1.3   Hacking.   De facto assurance of the underlying security in a product can arise from aggressive students as well as from professional technicians and users who actively probe new products for security flaws. Such probing may arise from internally sanctioned security probing or from unsanctioned, unexpected probing by individuals of ill will. Hacking approaches do not necessarily follow a consistent or comprehensive approach to evaluating the quality of the security functions and services that are implemented. Hence, the assurance achieved is to some uncertain, unmeasurable, and typically very modest level of trust.

27.3.2.1.4   Open Source Approach.   One of the new trends in software development is so-called Open Source development. According to this approach, as espoused, for example, in the Linux community, software is made publicly available for inspection, for modification of flaws and inefficiencies, and for potential upgrading of capabilities and features. In theory, the public review will improve the quality of the software over time, by the collective, uncoordinated, seemingly semirandom and continuous efforts of potentially thousands of autonomous software developers and testers. The downside of this approach is that the degree of trustworthiness achieved by the process is unmeasurable, and it is unclear how long the public scrutiny process should continue. Furthermore, the trustworthiness of a product is more than just improved code. Product trustworthiness also depends on vendor processes such as the quality of design, the protection provided to security features during the delivery of a product from the vendor to the consumer, vendor strategies for maintaining or upgrading security in the face of new threats, and so on. The part of assurance that deals with such types of vendor processes needs study in the Open Source assurance development model.

27.3.2.1.5   Trade Press.   Many trade press publications and magazines conduct reviews of products that pertain to security. Products are seemingly tested in ad hoc environments and against ad hoc criteria that vary from product to product and magazine to magazine. Such magazines may rely on consultants, staff, or private labs to review products. Some reviews may focus on examining quantitative product details other than security, such as performance or throughput of a product. Tests performed often fall short of assessing the real security aspects of a product. Some reviews rate qualitative parameters, such as product "innovativeness." Because of the potential lack of quantified testing rigor and potential dissimilarity of evaluation metrics, comparisons of trade press reviews from different sources are difficult. Perhaps most important, no evaluations are made of the confidence (assurance) that can be associated with the soundness of the security implementation.

Examples of publications that provide reviews of security products include *Information Security Magazine* (*www.infosecuritymag.com*), *Secure Computing Magazine* (*www.westcoast.com/cgi-bin/redirect.pl*), and IDG's *InfoWorld* (*www.infoworld.com*). Online knowledge centers such as ISP Planet (*www.isp-planet.com*) are other sources of ad hoc product reviews.

27.3.2.1.6   Initial Commercial Approaches.   Initial commercial approaches arose to provide relatively low-confidence, surface-level testing whose results could generate a brand mark for vendors' product brochures and advertisements. Such commercial activities began at a time when there needed to be a lower-cost—albeit lower confidence—alternative to expensive, lengthy, economically inappropriate government evaluations whose technical merits were also coming under question as competing government initiatives were proliferating. Commercial activities also were available to support trade press surveys and magazine reviews of products.

These approaches are still prevalent. They are often based on simple, one-size-fits-all testing that usually provides minimal, cursory checks of some of the implemented security functions. Some of these tests focus on product details other than security, such as performance or throughput. No evaluation is made of the confidence (assurance) that can be associated with the soundness of the security implementation.

An example of a private testing service is provided by West Coast Labs via its Check Mark program (*www.check-mark.com/cgi-bin/redirect.pl*). The Check Mark program establishes private criteria for certain types of computer security products, such as antivirus products, firewall products, and VPN products. The criteria are designed to achieve a very basic level of protection against a number of common hostile attacks. West Coast Labs tests products against the applicable Check Mark criteria and, if successfully tested, produces a certificate which shows that specific releases of products meet specific Check Mark criteria.

Another well-known commercial service is the product-certification program conducted by ICSA Labs (*www.icsalabs.com*). Similar to the West Coast Labs approach, private criteria created outside the recognized standards-development communities are developed via invited participation. Criteria for a number of classes of products have been developed. ICSA Labs test products against appropriate criteria to examine whether products can resist the specific types of common threats and risks predefined by ICSA criteria. Products that pass are entitled to display the ICSA brand mark. Products that fail are reported to their vendors with detailed analysis of the criteria they failed. Once awarded an ICSA certificate, vendors take on the obligation to self-check and self-declare continued certification of evolutions of the specific version product that passed ICSA testing. Spot checks by ICSA are used to verify that currently shipping products still can pass the ICSA tests. The ICSA testing is typically a checklist–oriented approach geared for nonexpert testers. ICSA testing is not based on fundamental design or engineering principles or on assessment of underlying technology. Rather, it is a "black box" testing approach.

Many vendors undergo these types of commercial testing because of the pressures from their competitors' products being so certified. While testing costs are reasonable, such testing provides no inputs (i.e., evaluation reports) that can be analyzed to differentiate products. More comprehensive products are not examined for any of their differentiating capabilities. Instead, such check-mark testing programs merely provide a common denominator floor for products. In fact, typical vendor reaction to these types of "branding" programs is that the check marks are often not very good.[11] Instead, they represent a nuisance and noise that distracts vendors; and, unlike more rigorous testing paradigms such as those based on the Common Criteria, check-mark branding programs do not have processes to help improve the quality of the product under test. Unlike Common Criteria testing labs, many vendors do not see check-mark testing labs as strategic partners looking to improve the product under test.

27.3.2.2 Standard-Based Trust Development Alternatives.

In contrast to the preceding, ad hoc, nonstandard approaches to establishing trust in products, the Common Criteria paradigm presents a fundamentally new strategy that overcomes shortcomings of the above approaches. It provides a recognized, reliable, internationally maintained mechanism to develop trust that (1) security requirements are specified correctly, (2) vendors do not misunderstand the requirements, and (3) vendors design and manufacture products that address the requirements and provide risk integrity.

The Common Criteria provides an unprecedented, fully flexible process for setting and testing common security functional requirements for any and all classes and specific instances of existing or future IT products. Unlike all the other approaches, it provides a way to specify assurance requirements and evaluate how well they are met. Assurance requirements are extremely important and are often not considered. They are the essential ingredients to establishing confidence in implementations of security and in providing the level of trust necessary for economies to rely on new electronic business models.

The Common Criteria also establishes a shared-cost method to develop common tests and evaluation methods and to use them to verify the security aspects of products in competent, accredited laboratories. Assessments of security products are composed of both analysis and testing of the product. Use of standard evaluation criteria and standard evaluation methodology leads to repeatable, objective test and evaluation results. Furthermore, independent review and validation of Common Criteria–based testing and evaluation is available to boost consumers' confidence even further. Well-respected consulting houses have concluded that Common Criteria evaluation provides a substantial improvement over the testing practices used by many vendors today that result in seriously undertested software.[12] The Common Criteria specification and testing approach is equally applicable to any and all types of products, such as products that implement security technologies (e.g., crypto boxes, firewalls, or audit tools) as well as products that are either security-enabled (e.g., messaging or Web e-commerce packages) or security-relevant (e.g., operating systems or network management systems).

The Common Criteria provides the foundation for today's unified choice for developing trust in products and systems. It provides an extra level of due diligence that will result in facilitated insurability, reduced legal liabilities with regard to security breaches, and reduced legal and insurance costs as well as increased security and improved safety. It improves and differentiates products and allows buyers to compare products objectively. It is accepted by mutual agreement in most of the world's largest IT-building and IT-buying countries without question or justification. While some countries still use their own country-specific security testing and evaluation standards, the clear trend is to move away from country-specific standard approaches to the single, internationally standard Common Criteria.

27.4   COMMON CRITERIA PARADIGM.   The Common Criteria paradigm is a scheme based on formal international standards. It is a scheme for:

- Stipulating security requirements
- Specifying security solutions in products and systems
- Testing products according to product-tailored—but standard—criteria and testing methodologies using accredited commercial testing laboratories[13]
- Independently validating test results
- Providing certificates to tested and validated products that obviate any need for further product retesting in all countries that mutually recognize each other's commercial testing capabilities and testing results
- Identifying products that are in the pool of candidate products mandated for purchase for certain government uses and recommended for purchase by all other U.S. government agencies and departments

The benefits of the Common Criteria paradigm are many. It forces consumers to thoroughly analyze and understand: their security requirements; the threats and vulnerabilities that products need to handle; the security policies—both organizational as well as legal and/or regulatory; the environment in which products are to work; and assumptions about the environment that are pertinent to the security offered or needed by a product. It forces vendors and consumers to thoroughly understand the products they build or buy and how they address the security requirements and mitigate the stipulated threats and vulnerabilities.

The Common Criteria paradigm is based on formal international standards that provide for a thorough, step-by-step discipline to define the security requirements of consumers and to define the security capabilities of products. Informal international and national standards define processes, procedures, rules, and infrastructure for testing products and validating test results.

According to the Common Criteria paradigm, the path to trustworthy products begins by consumers using a standard methodology, standard language, and catalog of standard security requirements to develop security profiles tailored to the types of products they want. These standards are stipulated within the Common Criteria standard. The profiles developed in accordance with the Common Criteria standard stipulate the security functional needs. The profiles also stipulate the confidence or assurance desired in products as well as in product builders' processes from product design through maintenance.

Next, product builders use the same standard methodology, language, and catalog of the Common Criteria standard to define their products' security specifications. They define product security specifications both in terms of security functionality as well as security assurance about the product and the builders' processes. The builders' specifications show how their products meet stated consumer security functionality and assurance needs and also may go beyond the consumers' stated needs. That is, the builders' specifications may show how their products meet any additional builder-claimed security features. Then an international agreement on how such products should be tested comes into play. This so-called Mutual Recognition Arrangement

(MRA) outlines in broad terms the scheme of processes and procedures that individual countries should follow in order to have Common Criteria–based testing performed once in any country and accepted internationally. In the United States, the Common Criteria Evaluation and Validation Scheme (CCEVS) is just such a national scheme developed in accordance with the MRA.

The CCEVS defines the processes and procedures for conducting MRA-recognized security testing within the United States. In fact, the CCEVS is the only way available in the United States that is recognized across national borders to demonstrate security requirements conformance of security-capable IT products evaluated in this country. The CCEVS also defines the organizational entities and the processes and procedures for establishing, operating, and maintaining a government-overseen, commercial security testing industry that conducts security evaluations of products and security profiles. What is unique about the CCEVS-fostered security testing industry is that it can test products in a way that allows the testing results to be recognized in accordance with the MRA and hence by all the major IT building and buying countries in the world.

According to the CCEVS, in the United States, CC-specified products and security profiles are tested and evaluated by independent, accredited, commercial security-testing laboratories called Common Criteria Testing Labs. These labs use appropriate, common test methods standard across all Common Criteria Test Labs; and these methods are further tailored to security profiles or to the builders' security claims about a product. These common test methods are used to verify in a standard way that a product under test complies with the builders' claims (1) about the product and (2) about the processes associated with the development and life cycle of the product. Also according to the CCEVS, in the United States a government oversight body can be used to independently validate the testing results generated by the Common Criteria Testing Labs, thereby establishing even greater confidence and trust in the product under test. Last, according to the CCEVS, the CCEVS Validation Body will provide validation certificates that stimulate international sales, especially to all other countries that have agreed to recognize any and all products and security profiles that have earned Common Criteria validation certificates.

27.4.1 Standards that Shape the Common Criteria Paradigm.   Several formal and informal standards shape the Common Criteria paradigm.

The "Common Criteria for Information Technology Security Evaluation" is the ISO standard geared toward the part of the paradigm pertaining to security requirements and product specifications.[14]

The Common Evaluation Methodology is an informal international standard maintained by a board of experts that pertains to product testing methods and evaluation actions.[15]

The Mutual Recognition of the Common Criteria Certifications in the Field of Information Technology Security document, colloquially called the Mutual Recognition Arrangement (MRA), is an informal international agreement among a growing number of national bodies for the purpose of recognizing and accepting testing performed in other signatory nations.[16]

The Common Criteria Evaluation and Validation Scheme is an informal standard developed by the U.S. MRA signatories.[17] These signatories are the National Security Agency (NSA) and the National Institute of Standards and Technology (NIST) operating together in a joint program called the National Information Assurance Partnership (NIAP). The CCEVS document summarizes a set of underlying standards that define the processes and procedures used within the United States to independently test, to independently validate, and to certify products recognized under the terms of the MRA.[18] Other such national schemes for using the Common Criteria exist in other countries.

In addition to the above standards, the Common Criteria Evaluation and Validation Scheme uses other international and national standards that pertain to accrediting prospective security testing laboratories. For example, for the purpose of accrediting testing laboratories, the "General Requirements for the Competence of Calibration and Testing Laboratories" is used as the formal international standard for stipulating testing laboratory competency.[19] Another standard further refines these general requirements for IT testing laboratories.[20] Countries also define technology-specific refinements and extensions to the general, technology-neutral lab competency requirements. For example, the "Information Technology Security Testing—Common Criteria" handbook is the formal U.S. government standard developed by NIAP that stipulates more specific laboratory competency requirements pertaining to security assessment procedures and CC security proficiency of lab staff.[21]

27.4.2   Details about the Common Criteria Standard.   The ISO 15408 standard, commonly referred to simply as the Common Criteria (or just the CC), is a multipart standard. One part of the CC standard identifies the models for two types of security profiles, the methodology for developing such profiles, as well as the structures for each of these types of profiles. The other two parts of the CC standard provide catalogs of security requirements of known validity that can be used, mixed, and matched to express the security requirements of virtually any type of IT product or system.

27.4.2.1   Models for Security Profiles.   The CC standard defines the language and structures for two types of security profiles and the methodology to create such profiles.

One type of security profile is called a Protection Profile (PP). A PP is used to stipulate the generic, product-neutral profile of security requirements for some class of IT product—such as a firewall or a telecommunications switch. Two types of security requirements can be stipulated: functional requirements and assurance requirements. Functional requirements define desired security behavior. Assurance requirements provide the basis for establishing trust. Trust is established by gaining confidence that the security functionalities claimed to be implemented to address specific security functional requirements (1) are effective in satisfying specified security objectives and (2) are implemented correctly and completely. It is also established by ensuring that product developers have sound processes and take specified actions accompanying the life cycle of the product they build, test, deliver, and maintain. PPs are typically developed by prospective consumers or by consortia of IT buyers and their product developers in a specific marketplace. They are developed to create standardized sets of security requirements that meet the needs of prospective buyers. Information on how to develop PPs appears elsewhere in this chapter.

The second type of profile structure defined in the CC is called a Security Target (ST). A ST is a product-specific stipulation of the security requirements addressed by a specific product along with information as to how the implemented product meets the stated security requirements. As stipulated in its accompanying ST, a specific product may claim conformance to one or more generic Protection Profiles. For example, a turnkey healthcare information system product can claim it conforms to a DBMS PP, an operating system PP, a PKI PP, and a firewall PP. Alternatively, a specific product may claim conformance to product-specific security requirements enumerated solely within the ST. Or a specific product can claim conformance to both a PP (or several PPs) as well as to additional product-specific security requirements enumerated within the ST. Information on how to develop STs appears elsewhere in this chapter.

It should be noted that the purpose of subsequent testing and evaluation of the product is to confirm that it meets the product-specific evaluation criteria contained in the ST that describes the product's security aspects.

27.4.2.2   Security Functional Requirements Catalog.   The CC standard contains a catalog of security functional requirements organized into a taxonomy of 11 classes of different types of security functional requirements, such as the Audit class, the Identification and Authentication class, and the Security Management class.

The 11 security functional requirements classes are as follows:

1. Audit (Class FAU)
2. Communications (Class FCO)
3. Cryptographic Support (Class FCS)
4. User Data Protection (Class FDP)
5. Identification and Authentication (Class FIA)
6. Security Management (Class FMT)
7. Privacy (Class FPR)
8. Protection of Security Functions (Class FPT)
9. Resource Utilization (Class FRU)
10. Access (Class FTA)
11. Trusted Path/Channels (Class FTP)

Each class has several families of functional security requirements, each family of which differs in emphasis or rigor in the way the security objectives of the parent class are considered. For example, the Audit class of security functional requirements includes families of requirements that pertain to different aspects of auditing, such as audit data generation and audit event storage. Each family of security functional requirements typically contains several, individual, more specialized security functionality requirements components. These components are the specific security functional requirements that can be stipulated within a PP and an ST as a desired security functionality. For example, the Audit Data Generation family of security functional requirements contains a component that pertains to audit record generation and another component that pertains to the linkage between a user and an auditable event.

To foster versatility and evolution, the CC also permits any new security requirements that do not appear in the taxonomies of standard requirements to be created using the CC's standard language. If additional requirements become popular, future versions of the CC standard may incorporate such additional requirements directly into the CC catalogs.

27.4.2.3   Security Assurance Requirements Catalog.   The CC standard also contains a catalog of assurance requirements organized within a taxonomy of 10 assurance classes, such as classes pertaining to assurance requirements associated with configuration management of the product, delivery and operation of the product, and maintaining assurance.

The 10 evaluation assurance classes are organized into:

- Two classes containing the assurance requirements applicable to the evaluation of profiles

  1. Protection Profile Evaluation (Class APE)
  2. Security Target Evaluation (Class ASE)

- Seven classes containing the assurance requirements applicable to the evaluation of CC-specified implementations

  1. Configuration Management (Class ACM)
  2. Delivery and Operation (Class ADO)
  3. Development (Class ADV)
  4. Guidance Documents (Class AGD)
  5. Life Cycle Support (Class ALC)
  6. Tests (class ATE)
  7. Vulnerability Assessment (Class AVA)

- One class dealing with assurance maintenance requirements:

  1. Maintenance of Assurance (Class AMA)

The taxonomy of assurance requirements is refined in terms of a number of families of such requirements within each assurance requirements class. Furthermore, a number of hierarchical assurance requirements components are contained within each family of assurance requirements.

Seven predefined levels of assurance are defined using successively more rigorous packages of balanced component assurance requirements from with the assurance catalog. These seven levels of so-called Evaluation Assurance Levels (EALs) can be used as a rising scale of objective measures of risk reduction.

The names associated with the seven labels of evaluation assurance levels are as follows:

- EAL1: Functionally Tested
- EAL2: Structurally Tested
- EAL3: Methodically Tested and Checked
- EAL4: Methodically Designed, Tested, and Reviewed
- EAL5: Semi-Formally Designed and Tested
- EAL6: Semi-Formally Verified Design and Tested
- EAL7 Formally Verified Design and Tested

EALs provide a monotonically increasing scale which balances the increasing levels of confidence that can be obtained with the increasing cost and decreasing feasibility of conducting the testing and evaluation necessary to develop a specific, higher level of confidence. EALs range upward from the entry-level EAL1 to a stringent EAL7.

For example, at the low end, EAL1 is used to support the contention that baseline due care has been exercised with regard to protection of personal information and to establish some confidence in correct operation of a product in an environment where the threats to security are not considered very serious. In the middle range, EAL4 specifies more rigorous assurance requirements, such as automated configuration management and development controls that are supported by a life-cycle model. At the highest extreme, EAL7 requires a formally verified design and extensive formal analysis. EAL7 may be applicable to certain highly specific, perhaps one-of-a-kind products, targeted for extremely high-risk situations or where the high value of the assets being protected justifies the extraordinary costs of an evaluation to this level of confidence. Typical commercial products can be expected to fall in the range from EAL1 to EAL4.

Specific EAL levels were designed with the idea of trying to preserve the assurance concepts of the earlier national criteria. For example, an EAL2 level is roughly equivalent to the TCSEC C1 and the ITSEC E1.

Typically, one of these seven EALs is stipulated within a PP or an ST. Alternatively, a PP or ST developer may choose, instead, to stipulate either individual component assurance requirements from the assurance requirements catalog or a specific Evaluation Assurance Level plus additional specific assurance requirements from the assurance requirements catalog.

27.4.2.4   Comprehensiveness of Requirements Catalogs.   The taxonomies of both types of security requirements—functional and assurance—are broad, and both catalogs of security requirements are deep: Hundreds of individual, selectable security requirements are defined. Furthermore, the CC was designed to accommodate evolution of its security requirements catalogs as technologies and security needs evolve. New security requirements that are specified according to the CC language, but that are outside the current CC catalogs, can become potential candidates for new, internationally agreed-on security requirements to be incorporated into later versions of the standard CC catalogs.

Given the breadth, depth, and changeability of possible security requirements that can be stipulated within PPs or STs, the Common Criteria provides the ability to stipulate the requirements and products of virtually an unlimited number of existing and yet-to-be-conceived security product needs (PPs) and security product solutions (STs).

27.4.3   Using the Common Criteria Standard to Define Security Requirements and Security Solutions.   The Common Criteria provides a standard way to stipulate the risks of concern and the security functional requirements that must be met in order to mitigate stated risks. The CC also fosters the stipulation of the security assurance requirements that must be met to provide the confidence desired that products are built with desired quality. Consumers develop Protection Profiles as a way to specify their needs to their suppliers, such as product vendors or system integrators. Product developers create a Security Target to specify how implemented security functions and how assurance measures that are followed meet consumers' needs.

The Common Criteria defines the structures for PPs and STs. Via PPs and STs, the CC articulates a methodology for expressing security objectives, for selecting and defining IT security requirements, and for writing high-level specifications of products or systems. These structures and methodologies are summarized below.

27.4.3.1   Profiles and their Construction.   The purpose of a PP is to provide the set of security functional and assurance requirements that an organization considers appropriate and valuable for a specific type of product in a specific threat environment. The PP states the security problem that a compliant product is intended to solve and stipulates the security requirements that are known to be useful and effective in meeting specific security objectives.

The main contents of a PP include statements about the security environment within which a product is to reside, the security objectives to be met by a product, the security requirements to be addressed by a product, and the rationale that is provided to justify all decisions and choices made in developing the content within a PP.

The following sequence of activities is a useful strategy for developing and creating a PP.

In developing the contents of a PP, the PP must identify the expected threats and vulnerabilities against which a prospective product must be protected. As needed, threat and vulnerability analyses should be conducted. Tools like the Common Vulnerability & Exposures (CVE) dictionary (*http://cve.mitre.org*) may prove useful. The CVE dictionary seeks to identify with standard names all the vulnerabilities on which attackers prey. Over 300 vulnerabilities are included to date. The CVE helps standardize a computer security vulnerability vocabulary so that users can be certain that security tools are finding the same holes and so that systems can be built more securely. Such a standardized vocabulary leads to better understanding of common vulnerabilities that could help the development of PPs. The intended operational environment within which a product is to reside must be described in terms of both its IT and non-IT aspects. Assumptions about the product's usage, administration, and management should be enumerated. All policies to which the product must comply within the intended environment should be enumerated. Such policies include all applicable laws and regulations as well as any organizational policies or rules with which the product must comply.

All natural-language expressions of the environment, threats, policies, and assumptions must be codified via CC terminology and put into the PP. PP development automation tools like the CC Toolbox and the CC Knowledge Base should be considered to help speed and to help check the development of the PP.

Next, realistic and achievable security objectives must be established for both the product and the environment within which the product is to reside. The security objectives should indicate which threats are to be countered by the product and which are to be countered by the IT and non-IT environments in which the product is to operate and in which it is to be administered and managed. The security objectives should indicate with which of the organizational policies the product will comply and which organizational policies the environment will address. All stipulated security objectives should be traceable back to the underlying stipulations of threats, policies, and assumptions.

Then security requirements from the CC catalogs should be selected and refined. Security requirements should be selected to meet the stipulated security objectives and to thwart specified threats. The security functional requirements also should be selected to support the stipulated security policies under the stipulated assumptions pertaining to the operational and administrative environment. The security functional requirements should specify functionality that will meet each security objective stipulated for the product as well as functionality that will meet each security objective that applies to the IT part of the environment in which the product is to reside.

Next, security assurance requirements should be selected from the catalog of assurance requirements. Specific security assurance requirements components or a specific evaluation assurance level package should be selected to provide the desired level of assurance that the security objectives within the PP have been met. The desired level of assurance can be estimated by taking into consideration any of several possible factors, such as (1) the value of the resources to be protected, (2) the risk and extent of possible losses, (3) the level of confidence desired, and (4) any reasonably expected cost and delay factors that may accompany the development and any subsequent testing, evaluation, and validation of a product at a specific level of assurance.

CC requirements components may be used exactly as defined in the CC or, when appropriate, they may be tailored through the use of permitted, standard operations in order to meet a specific security policy or to counter a specific threat. Through such operations, (1) options within the standard, CC-stipulated requirements may be selected; (2) quantifications within specific CC security requirements may be assigned; and (3) any refinements to CC requirements may be made. Any such requirements assignment, selections, or refinement operations that are not completed within a PP may be completed within an ST that claims conformance to the PP.

PP development automation tools may be useful again in terms of selecting a compatible set of standard requirements and, if necessary, to specify requirements in more detail than the standard, generalized requirements in the CC catalogs.

Last, rationale should be provided for all decisions and choices made in developing all of the PP content. Rationale should justify how selected security functional and assurance requirements components are suitable to counter the enumerated threats. Rationale should justify how selected requirements components comply with the enumerated policies or handle the enumerated assumptions stipulated for the environment. The rationale should provide a mapping between stipulated requirements and stated security objectives and then back to the original, underlying, driving needs as stated in terms of threats, policies, assumptions, and the environment in which a product is to reside.

In some instances, it may not be necessary to develop a PP "from scratch." Instead, it may be possible to reuse an existing PP and modify or refine it to meet the new situation. These modifications could, for example, change the intended environment or the threats, policies, and assumptions of the original PP. Such alterations could lead to adding or deleting specific functional and assurance requirements or to modifying values previously assigned to specific requirements, so that the resulting requirements are better tailored to the new needs articulated in the new PP. Guidance for developing PPs is available.[22]

27.4.3.1.1   Example of a PP.   The Protection Profile for a Private Branch Exchange (PBX) style of telecommunication switch provides a simple example of a PP (*www. niap.nist.gov/secrequire.html#TelecomPP*). The PBX PP stipulates threats and vulnerabilities that need to be addressed by a product that claims to comply with this PP. Such threats and vulnerabilities include:

- Theft of telecommunications services.
- Hijacking of resources within the PBX to commit cybercrime or cyberespionage.
- Unauthorized use and modification (or destruction) of processes, system software, applications, and databases embedded within the product that claims compliance to this PP.

Other aspects of the environment are described, such as the types of PBX users and administrators, the types of PBX interfaces, and the types of interconnectivity expected with other telecommunications gear.

Security requirements are provided to thwart specific threats and to support specific policies under specific assumptions. Fifty security functional requirements components were selected from seven classes of security functional requirements. For example, for security auditing, the PP stipulates what the PBX must audit; what information must be logged; what are the rules for monitoring, operating, and protecting logs; who can access logs; and so on. Functional requirements for the PBX PP also were selected from other functional requirements classes, such as:

- Security management
- Authentication handling
- Crypto support
- Protection of security functions within a product claiming conformance to this PP.

Also, over 100 assurance requirements components were selected from seven assurance requirements class. The assurance requirements components are chosen to demonstrate:

- How good are product design and configuration.
- That adequate protection is provided during the design and implementation of the product claiming conformance to this PP.
- That vendor testing on the product is of a specified depth and breadth.
- That security functionality is not compromised during product delivery.
- That there is a specified quality and appropriateness in the product manuals that pertain to product installation, maintenance, and use.

The PBX PP was carefully put together to be realistic in its ability to be met by a variety of specific products with a variety of specific security mechanisms and security functions (that are to be specified in a specific product's Security Target). Care was taken to make sure that the PBX PP is achievable and can be met by products that rely on currently available, commercial technology.

27.4.3.1.2   Benefits of a PP.   For potential consumers of security-relevant products, PPs provide a standard and flexible way to help organize requirements capture and analysis. PPs also provide a standard and flexible way to transform security requirements and policies into unambiguous, widely recognized, exactly tailored security requirements for the desired security functional behavior and assurance levels for any class of desired IT product.

PPs provide a standards-based mechanism to clearly articulate the security needs of a specific market sector. Other market sectors or specific organizations may adopt a PP and its common, product-neutral security requirements, thereby creating a bigger marketplace demand that could be expected to stimulate more suppliers to develop competing, readily procurable, commercial off-the-shelf security-relevant products.

PPs provide a standards-based mechanism to clearly convey an organization's security needs to suppliers, vendors, and business partners. PPs provide the bases for standard, requirements-based testing and evaluation. They allow such entities to specify via assurance requirements the depth and breadth of testing and evaluation they would like to have for the products they would like to buy.

27.4.3.1.3   PPs under Development.   PPs have been created and are being created for many classes of products.

PPs that stipulate security needs for general-purpose technology include:

- The Role Based Access Control PP

- Firewall PPs for packet-filtering firewalls and application-filtering firewalls[23]
- DBMS PPs
- PKI PPs
- C2 and B1 operating system PPs
- The Windows 2000 operating system PP currently under development

Also, PPs exist or are being developed to support specific needs of specific industries. For example, the PBX PP, the telecom switch PP, and the Voice over IP firewall PP apply to the telecommunication industry's needs. PPs for smart cards and smart card components (chips, operating systems, applications, cryptoengine, etc.) and for Certificate Issuing and Management Systems apply to the financial industry. Applicable to the healthcare industry are PPs for medical systems such as a patient admission, discharge, and transfer system and PPs for mobile medical platforms. Also pertinent to the healthcare industry are PP-like security requirements packages that capture the security needs of laws such as the Healthcare Insurance Portability and Accountability Act (HIPAA) (see Chapter 49 in this book) and those that capture the security needs of government regulations, such as the Health Care Finance Administration's use of the Internet.

While no single registry of completed PPs or PPs under development currently exists, a system of linked national registries currently lists many PPs. For example, in the United States, several PPs are listed at either or both *http://csrc.nist.gov/cc/ pp/pplist/htm* and *www.radium.ncsc.mil/tpep/library/protection_profiles/index.html;* in the United Kingdom, several PPs are listed at *www.cesg.gov.uk/cchtml/ippr/*. However, since PP development is decentralized by its very nature of being customer- or industry-specific, information about the existence of a new PP or of ongoing efforts to develop a new PP still tends to arise in a haphazard fashion.

27.4.3.2 Security Targets.
Developers create security targets (STs) to document detailed information about the security aspects of each product they build. An ST is required when a specific product is submitted for CC-based testing; the product-specific ST provides the basis and evaluation criteria against which the testing and evaluation of a product is performed. STs also may be used as a document for conveying detailed information to consumers about the security functionality of a specific product and the configuration in which a product has been formally tested.

STs contain a description of the environment within which the product described via an ST is intended to operate. That is, an ST enumerates the threats to the product; the policies, laws, and regulations with which the product is claimed to conform; and the assumptions about the security aspects of the IT and non-IT environment within which the product is intended to be used. STs delineate the security objectives that the builder of a specific product claims are addressed by that product. STs also enumerate the security requirements that the product builder claims are addressed by the product as well as those requirements to be addressed by the environment within which the product is intended to operate. As such, part of an ST is very much like a PP.

However, the ST goes further than a PP because it also specifies the security functions offered by the product to meet each of the stated security requirements in the ST. It also specifies the assurance measures taken by the product builder to meet all the stated assurance requirements in the ST.

Furthermore, a product builder may claim in the ST that the specific product conforms to one or more PPs. If so, the ST can claim that the product it describes addresses the security functional and assurance requirements stipulated in each of the PPs to which the product is claimed to be conformant. As appropriate, the ST may refine PP-stipulated security requirements that are generic or product-neutral in the PP. The ST can thus specifically tailor to the product any general requirements that may appear in a PP. The ST also may add security requirements over and above any PPs to which the product claims to be conformant.

Last, rationale should be provided for all decisions and choices made in developing the ST content. Rationale should justify how selected security functional and assurance components

- Are suitable to counter the enumerated threats
- Comply with the enumerated policies
- Handle the enumerated assumptions stipulated for the environment.

Rationale should justify how implemented security functions meet stated security functional requirements and how the assurance measures used meet the stated security assurance requirements. Rationale should justify all claims made in an ST about the PPs with which the product conforms. In essence, the rationale provided should demonstrate that the ST contains an effective and suitable set of countermeasures and that this set of countermeasures is consistent, complete, and cohesive.

Guidance for developing STs is available,[24] and ST development automation tools also may be useful.

27.4.3.2.1   Benefits of STs.   Consumers benefit by being able to examine an ST to verify completely and unambiguously whether the claimed security functionality of a product and the claimed assurance associated with the product are consistent with their requirements. Comparing product-specific STs with PPs of interest fosters a common buyer/seller understanding of security needs and security capabilities and confidence in products. By comparing the STs of products, consumers are better able to compare the security features of competing products. Consumers are able to understand what types of tests and evaluations that a specific product underwent. They also are able to determine from an ST whether the configuration in which a product was tested is consistent with the environment into which they intend to use the product. Through these types of benefits, consumers can shorten their acquisition cycles for security-relevant products.

Vendors and suppliers benefit by being able to use a product's ST to improve marketing by showing how a specific product matches customer security requirements.

Evaluators in CC testing laboratories benefit by being able to understand the scope of the product-specific evaluation that needs to be performed on a specific product. That is, claims made within the ST are subject to be evaluated by a testing laboratory.

27.4.3.2.2   What STs Have Been Developed.   STs exist for at least all products that have undergone CC-based testing. Tested products that have further undergone testing validation by a CC Validation Body are listed on the Web sites of the several national bodies and national schemes associated with the CC paradigm. Thus, at least the products listed, for example, on the NIAP Validated Products List (*http://niap. nist.gov/cc-scheme/ValidatedProducts.html*), have associated STs. Many other products also have associated STs. But it is difficult to develop centralized listings of all such products since not all products that have undergone CC-based testing have necessarily been tested at accredited CC testing laboratories; and products that have been tested by such testing labs have not necessarily had their testing validated and listed by a CC national Validation Body.

27.4.3.3   PP/ST Development Tools.

NIAP has developed two automation tools to help security profile developers speed the proper construction of useful Protection Profiles and Security Targets compliant with the CC. One of these tools is called the CC Toolbox™ (*http://niap.nist.gov/tools/cctool.html*). It is a knowledge-base–driven program that guides profile developers through a process of defining the IT security requirements either for their consumer constituency's needs or for their product. It creates a nearly complete PP in the former instance or a nearly complete ST in the latter instance. The toolbox provides structured interviews to aid PP and ST developers in identifying pertinent security requirements and in managing the complexity of the requirements definition process.

The CC Profiling Knowledge Base™ is the database that contains information about commonly occurring security threats, security policies, and security objectives that can be used in drafting PPs and STs. The knowledge base is an intelligent, adaptable module for the CC ToolBox™ and, if desired, can be customized by different communities of interest.

The CC toolbox and knowledge base in tandem provide candidate statements about:

- Commonly occurring policies
- Commonly occurring threats
- Common assumptions
- Security objectives
- Recommendations for accompanying CC security requirements components
- Justifying rationale for all choices made with regard to policies, threats, assumptions, objectives, and requirements

Both tools are available as freeware on the NIAP Web site at *http://niap.nist.gov/niap/projects/tooldev-proj.html.*

27.4.4   Defining Common Text Methodology.

According to the Common Criteria paradigm, security testing and evaluation is conducted as structured and formal processes during which time evaluators carry out a series of standard activities derived from the CC. These activities are designed to determine either if products comply with CC security profiles (in the case of a product being tested) or if CC-based security profiles are sound (in the case of a profile being evaluated). The Common Evaluation Methodology is the informal international standard that defines such standardized testing and evaluation activities. More specifically, it specifies the security assurance requirements that lead to the notion of security evaluation. The Common Evaluation Methodology (CEM) describes to evaluators how to conduct evaluations and what actions to take during evaluations.

27.4.4.1   Common Evaluation Methodology.

The CEM is a two-part standard. One part describes the general model of the methodology, the evaluation process, and the roles of the different stakeholders in the evaluation process. The other part contains complete methodology information on general evaluation tasks. It describes specific methodology, evaluation tasks and evaluator actions for evaluating profiles (both PPs and STs) and products. The CEM stipulates the detailed work required for tests and evaluation to be conducted in association with security profiles or with products claiming assurance levels in the range of EAL1 to EAL4. It is expected that subsequent versions of the CEM may address all other EALs as well as each individual assurance requirement component, such as assurance maintenance, that are not included in the standard EAL assurance packages.

The CEM defines a set of standard assessment procedures, assessment methodologies, and evaluator actions for testing compliance to each requirement within the CC requirements catalogs. For each class of CC requirements there is a class of CEM-defined activities, and for each family of CC requirements, the CEM defines a family of subactivities. For each elementary security requirement and evaluator action stipulated in the CC, the CEM defines one or more work units of testing and evaluation activity. Work units are intended to organize the work that evaluators have to do in evaluating products and security profiles. To conduct a standard evaluation of a product, evaluators select the CEM work units that are associated with the specific CC assurance requirements components and the specific EAL stipulated for the product to be evaluated. To conduct an evaluation of a security profile, evaluators select the CEM work units associated with either a PP evaluation or an ST evaluation. Evaluators then carry out all the selected CEM-defined activities and their associated work units.

27.4.4.2 Benefits of the Common Evaluation Methodology. Use of the CEM provides a common base for independent, autonomous bodies to assess in the same ways whether security-oriented products work as claimed. Such common, well-recognized testing and evaluation approaches reduce needs for customer-unique or country-unique approaches. Vendors' testing costs decrease when they need to prepare for just one test campaign rather than a battery of different test campaigns against different criteria.

Buyers of IT products that each claim to address identical CC-stipulated security requirements and that have each passed security tests and evaluations conducted in accordance with the CEM can be confident that such products were identically examined in their ability to meet such security requirements. Testing and evaluation according to the CEM thus provides a common floor of operational confidence in all products that have been shown to comply with the same PP or set of PPs.

27.4.5   Mutual Recognition of Testing and National Testing Schemes. The goal of the CC paradigm is (1) to get products or security profiles tested, validated, and certified in a competent, consistent, credible way, and (2) to have testing done in a way such that the testing results will be recognized by all countries. In particular, the goal is to test products once, anywhere in world, so that suppliers can sell products everywhere, without further retesting, revalidation, and recertification by different countries or enterprises. As such, it is expected that the number of evaluated security products and Protection Profiles defining product needs will increase.

27.4.5.1 Mutual Recognition Arrangement. The Common Criteria Arrangement on the Mutual Recognition of the Common Criteria Certifications in the Field of Information Technology Security is a multicountry agreement that affirms that countries will recognize each other's security tests and evaluations. This agreement, often called simply the Mutual Recognition Arrangement (MRA), was originally signed by government bodies within Canada, France, Germany, the United Kingdom, and the United States. Since then, 14 countries have signed on to the MRA; and the list of countries still wishing to join is large and growing.

27.4.5.1.1 What Is the Mutual Recognition Arrangement? The MRA identifies the several conditions necessary for mutual recognition of testing, validation, and certification among countries. It also defines the process for expanding to include any number of new countries.

According to the MRA, the conditions for mutual recognition are rooted in the use of the CC and CEM as the basis for evaluation criteria and evaluation methods. The MRA stipulates that national schemes for testing/evaluating, validating, and certifying products need to be established by countries adhering to the MRA. It also stipulates that each country that abides by the MRA must have a Validation Body.

The MRA requires that each country's Validation Body either be accredited by a recognized Accreditation Body in accordance with the governing ISO standard[25] or be established under laws, statutory instruments, or other official administrative procedures valid in the country to meet the requirements established within the above ISO standard.

The purpose of the Validation Body is to establish the country's national scheme for testing, evaluating, validating, and certifying CC-specified products and to monitor all security evaluations that occur in accordance with their country-specific national scheme. The MRA requires the use of accredited laboratories to assure consistent quality and competence across countries and across the pools of private, commercial security testing laboratories performing CC-based evaluations within each country.

Common missions of all national Validation Bodies are established by the MRA. Each country's Validation Body is responsible for defining and maintaining the national scheme for testing/evaluating, validating, and certifying products. As such, each country's Validation Body is responsible for achieving correct, consistent, credible, and competent application of the CC and CEM within their country. Each country's Validation Body must establish processes, procedures, and rules pertinent to itself as well as to the approved CC testing labs within the country. These processes, procedures, and rules are for the purpose of ensuring that:

- The CC and CEM are properly applied
- Tests, valuations, validations, and certifications are impartially performed
- The confidentiality of all proprietary or sensitive information that becomes available during testing, evaluation, validation, and certification is properly protected

The MRA specifies the technical scope of testing that can occur in accordance with the MRA. That is, the MRA pertains to products and profiles that claim conformance to:

- Any of the security functional components defined in the CC (or to any suitably extended CC functional component)
- CC-defined assurance levels in the range of EAL1 to EAL4 (or to any uniquely defined assurance level that only uses assurance components that appear in the standard EAL1 to EAL4 assurance packages)

The MRA does not cover any extended CC assurance components or any assurance maintenance schemes. As such, the MRA benefits product developers by limiting the number of different criteria to which their implementations need to conform.

The MRA also stipulates the minimum requirements that must be met by Certification/Validation Reports that must be generated in association with security testing performed under the jurisdiction of a country's Validation Body. The MRA stipulates that a Common Criteria certificate with a distinctive CC logo be awarded to products that are successfully tested and validated. Such products are entitled to use the distinctive CC mark. As such, the MRA benefits consumers by identifying a wide range of internationally produced and assessed security products, thereby expanding the set of competing products that consumers may wish to purchase.

The MRA also provides a vehicle for countries' Validation Bodies to collaborate in continuously improving the efficiency and cost-effectiveness of security testing and evaluation as well as the validation and certification processes for products and Protection Profiles.

27.4.5.2   *National Schemes.* At the time of this writing, the countries that have agreed to the MRA include Australia, Canada, Finland, France, Germany, Greece, Israel, Italy, The Netherlands, New Zealand, Norway, Spain, the United Kingdom, and the United States. Sweden and Japan are preparing to do so, and several other countries are interested.

Each country has a Validation Body. Each Validation Body is also the evaluation authority for its respective national government and has committed itself to replacing any national evaluation criteria with the Common Criteria. The Validation Body in the United States is the National Information Assurance Partnership (NIAP), a joint NSA and NIST organization established under the administrative procedures of the NIST and the NSA to meet the requirements of ISO/IEC Guide 65.

Each country either has a national scheme or is in the process of developing its national scheme. In the United States, the scheme is called the *Common Criteria Evaluation and Validation Scheme* (CCEVS), and it is implemented and operated by the U.S. Validation Body. The CCEVS Validation Body operates under the requirements of the MRA-stipulated international requirements as well as additional national requirements.

As the CCEVS and the U.S. Validation Body often serve as premier models of national schemes and Validation Bodies for other countries, details about them appear as examples below. Furthermore, exploring the CCEVS as an example provides the opportunity to become familiar with a scheme that establishes some of the highest-quality standards of all countries.

27.4.6   Common Criteria Evaluation and Validation Scheme of the United States. In the United States, the CCEVS defines the MRA-recognized, third-party testing and evaluation scheme. This scheme depends on the availability of accredited, commercial security testing laboratories and on government oversight of those laboratories' security assessment activities.

The purpose of the CCEVS is twofold:

1. It is to establish and to maintain the quality of a CC-based security testing, validation, and certification infrastructure in the United States. The CCEVS makes sure that this infrastructure is available to verify that CC-based security profiles comply with the CC and to verify that CC-specified products comply with the Common Criteria as well as their CC-based specifications.

2. The CCEVS defines the policies, procedures, and processes for performing CC-based, MRA-recognized security testing/evaluation, validation, and certification activities in the United States. The CCEVS also designates those validated and certified products and profiles that are to be internationally recognized according to the MRA.

The CCEVS is designed to meet the terms and intent of the MRA. It also supports the goal of the U.S. government to foster trust in the IT products that become part of critical national infrastructures serving either or both government programs/goals and private industries.

Regarding its first purpose, the CCEVS has developed standard guidance for enumerating, establishing, operating, overseeing, and maintaining all entities that are part of the U.S. CCEVS. In particular, these entities include: (1) accredited security testing laboratories, (2) the NIAP Validation Body, and (3) the NIST and NSA certificate issuing authorities. The roles and responsibilities of these entities are defined. Additionally, the CCEVS supports the accreditation of testing laboratories in the United States. Information about the process of accrediting laboratories and validating the results of a security test and evaluation conducted by an accredited lab appears elsewhere in this chapter. As these topics are not necessarily intended for general audiences, the scope of details provided is high level.

Regarding its second purpose, the CCEVS defines the overall process and sequence of events for testing, evaluating, validating, and certifying products and profiles. In particular, Protection Profiles must be developed in accordance with the CC, and Security Target profiles should be developed in accordance with the CC to describe the claimed security features and assurance claims of specific products. These security profiles or IT products with accompanying Security Targets must be analyzed and tested by CC-savvy, accredited security testing laboratories. Last, the accredited laboratory's testing and evaluation results are to be validated by an independent government oversight body. Products and profiles that have been successfully tested and evaluated and have had their results validated will be issued certificates and added to a Validated Products List. Details about testing and evaluation and about validation and certification are given elsewhere in this chapter.

The CCEVS defines the policies, procedures, and processes for performing CC-based, MRA-recognized security testing/evaluation, validation and certification activities in the United States.

The NIAP Validation Body is responsible for operating and maintaining the scheme according to CCEVS policies and procedures and, as necessary, to interpret or amend such policies and procedures and to interpret any technical ambiguities that may arise regarding the CEM or CC. The NIAP Validation Body is responsible for resolving any disputes concerning the CCEVS.

The NIAP Validation Body is responsible for interfacing with other nations and national schemes to alert other national schemes of newly validated products and to ensure international consistency of any technical interpretations it may make. The full set of requirements for, and responsibilities of, the NIAP Validation Body are specified. These requirements and responsibilities are derived from the international standard guiding all MRA-recognized Validation Bodies. The procedures to be followed by the NIAP Validation Body are also specified. More about the CCEVS is available at *http://niap.nist.gov/cc-scheme.*

27.4.7   Accredited Testing.   According to the CCEVS, accredited, commercial security testing and evaluation services are available to assess security profiles and products.

Laboratory accreditation fosters commonality of testing across all accredited labs. For products, the security testing evaluation results are applicable only to that particular version and release of the product in its evaluated configuration. Users are responsible for determining the security impact of installing or operating an evaluated IT product in a configuration other than the configuration in which it was evaluated.

27.4.7.1   Testing Products and Profiles.   IT security testing and evaluation is conducted by commercial testing laboratories that are accredited by the U.S. Department of Commerce's National Voluntary Laboratory Accreditation Program (NVLAP) and are subsequently approved as "NVLAP-accredited" by the NIAP Validation Body.

27.4.7.1.1   Benefits of Accredited Testing and Evaluation.   CCEVS-based testing by accredited security testing laboratories benefits both manufacturers and their customers.

27.4.7.1.1.1   Helping Manufacturers.   CCEVS-based accredited testing directly helps product manufacturers, and thereby also indirectly benefits product consumers, in a number of ways.

Reliance on standards broadens potential markets. It is important that security evaluations of IT products be carried out in accordance with recognized standards and procedures. The use of standard IT security evaluation criteria and IT security evaluation methodology contributes to the repeatability and objectivity of the results. The use of standards tends to increase the product appeal by various, nonrelated customer constituencies.

CCEVS-based accredited testing helps manufacturers penetrate global markets. It provides access to the MRA, and, as such, products and profiles so tested and validated can be recognized internationally within all countries, without needing to undergo any additional testing.

It helps manufacturers penetrate specific domestic markets. In the United States, for example, national government policy has been established regarding the procurement and use of products that have been tested and evaluated by accredited labs in accordance with the CCEVS.[26] According to this policy, U.S. DoD and 20 other U.S. government agencies must purchase only products tested by accredited testing labs (and subsequently validated and certified in accordance with the CCEVS) whenever products are needed for environments pertaining to matters of national security. The civil sector government agencies also are encouraged to purchase such products for all other applications. Many other countries will likely follow suit.

CCEVS-based accredited testing helps manufacturers lower costs. First, accredited laboratories provide manufacturers with a pool of private security testing labs that have consistent testing quality and competence. The fact that accredited labs are commercial fosters competition. Even when selecting the least expensive testing lab, manufacturers do not have to worry about sacrificing the quality of the testing services they receive. Second, by avoiding any further testing or retesting beyond that performed by the selected testing lab, manufacturers are spared enormous and costly country-specific or customer-specific testing campaigns. Lower testing costs can increase product profit margins or lower product prices or both.

27.4.7.1.1.2   Helping Customers.   CC-based testing by a CCEVS-approved, accredited lab directly benefits product consumers in a number of ways.

It provides consumers an impartial, high-quality assessment of a security profile or a security-focused IT product since it is an assessment that is conducted by an independent entity. The fact that testing by accredited testing labs is done according to standards gives consumers a strong sense that testing is objective and not slanted to benefit the product that was tested.

CCEVS-based accredited testing is a first step to helping consumers understand what features are offered by products, whether products comply with certain stated security requirements, and how trustworthy such products should be considered.

Because CCEVS-based accredited testing is part of the CC paradigm and because the CC paradigm has overcome many of the limitations of other approaches to developing trust in products, products tested by accredited testing labs are, arguably, among the most trustworthy products available. With products that can be trusted, customers will be able to reduce their product acquisition costs by eliminating acceptance testing that duplicates testing already performed on a product by an accredited testing lab.

Through the federal government IT procurement policy mentioned earlier, it is expected that U.S. government agency customers will benefit by procuring tested products and systems that will reduce the risks of cyberattack, cyberterrorism, and cyberwarfare on critical national infrastructures as outlined in Presidential Decision Directive PDD-63.

27.4.7.1.2 Preparing for Testing.   The sponsor of a product or profile to be assessed by an accredited lab must gather and make available a number of items of information for a security assessment. Security-relevant information and documentation produced during the product or profile development should be supplied to the testing laboratory conducting the security assessment. The complete set of specific sponsor obligations to be met before and during testing as well as the required sponsor and product or profile information required in order to begin testing are stipulated.

A sponsor is responsible for selecting a specific accredited security testing lab. The laboratory selection decision is solely the decision of the sponsor and typically is based on factors important to the sponsor. Such factors may include, for example, the cost of the evaluation, the amount of time before a lab can begin an evaluation, the expected length of time to complete an evaluation, the proximity of the testing lab to the sponsor, familiarity of the sponsor with the testing lab and its expertise, the previous experience of the testing lab with the relevant technology, and so on.

The sponsor of a product security assessment and the sponsor-selected testing lab will usually establish a private contract to conduct a security assessment using NIAP-approved test methods, carried out according to CCEVS-specified policies and procedures. The lab also may be used to examine the readiness of the product developer for evaluation and the completeness of a developer's documentation required as inputs to the evaluation. Such documentation includes an ST, any appropriate manuals needed as part of the evaluation such as design and usage manuals, and any other documents needed for the evaluation.

All required items of hardware, firmware, software, and technical documentation associated with a product to be tested are delivered to the testing lab.

27.4.7.1.3 Conducting Testing.   The sponsor-selected lab evaluates the specific profile under evaluation or the specific product under test. The activities associated with conducting these security assessments are standardized.

A profile evaluation determines whether the profile is complete, consistent, and technically sound. For a PP, the evaluation determines whether the evaluated PP is suitable as a statement of requirements for a class of products that can be evaluated. If the profile is an ST, the ST evaluation determines whether the ST is an appropriate description of the features and claims of a specific product.

A product evaluation determines if, and how well, the product under test complies with the security functional and assurance requirements, specifications, and claims within its associated Security Target, and how well it conforms to all parts of any stipulated PPs as may be claimed in the ST. Prior to the product evaluation, the accompanying ST is first evaluated according to requirements stipulated in the CC and CEM.

If the ST claims conformance to a specific PP, then the ST must be evaluated against that PP to substantiate that claim. This evaluation of the ST is conducted in addition to, and in conjunction with, the evaluation of the actual product against its ST.

The evaluation process is a structured and formal process during which evaluators employed by the testing lab carry out a specific set of activities derived from the CC. The work to be performed is as documented in the applicable work units defined in the CEM. The test methods used are common across all accredited security testing laboratories. These test methods are derived from CC assurance requirements as well as from the common evaluation methods stipulated in the CEM. Problems or deficiencies encountered during the evaluation are documented in problem reports provided to the evaluation sponsor.

The results of a security test/evaluation conducted within the CCEVS are described in evaluation technical reports produced by the testing lab. If successfully validated, these security testing and evaluation results also will be summarized in an associated validation report as well as on the associated Common Criteria certificate.

27.4.7.1.4   Testing Oversight.   In the CCEVS, oversight by the NIAP Validation Body is used to ensure that testing, evaluation, and validation activities are performed in accordance with the MRA and CCEVS and that each accredited lab is completely and correctly applying the CC and CEM for the specific product or profile evaluation and assurance level sought. The complexity of such testing or evaluation, and the need for consistency across all testing labs to ensure fairness for any individual lab, make essential the technical oversight and monitoring of each evaluation by the NIAP Validation Body.

The concepts and requirements governing testing oversight are standardized along with the associated activities of the NIAP Validation Body and the interactions between the NIAP Validation Body and the testing lab. Varying levels of oversight are provided, depending, for example, on the strength of assurance required and the complexity of the profile or product under test.

The NIAP Validation Body provides initial oversight before testing efforts commence. In accordance with defined CCEVS procedures, it reviews all documentation provided by the sponsor and reviews testing work plans and schedules developed by the testing lab to ensure all parties are adequately prepared to undertake the proposed security assessment and that work plans and schedules are reasonable and consistent.

Through oversight, the NIAP Validation Body also ensures:

- The provision of competent IT security assessment services by accredited testing labs
- That a testing laboratory uses the highest standards of quality, impartiality, integrity, lack of conflicts-of-interest, and commercial confidentiality
- The consistency of security assessments conducted by all accredited testing labs

The Validation Body establishes an approach to the technical oversight of testing labs, including such factors as the qualifications of a lab's evaluators, what lab activities are to be monitored, and how lab outputs should be reviewed. Validators assigned to specific commercial evaluations would not normally review all documentation and evidence provided by the vendor of the product undergoing evaluation. As the aim of the CCEVS is to build confidence, not certainty, the typical scenario would be for validators to do spot checks of vendor-provided evidence.

As necessary, the NIAP Validation Body also provides technical advice, guidance, training, and support to accredited testing labs. Accredited testing labs may consult with the NIAP Validation Body to discuss technical matters, anomalies that may arise, or any other issues relevant to the security assessment being conducted by the testing lab.

The NIAP Validation Body is also responsible for monitoring the long-term performance of accredited testing labs across many different security assessments, focusing especially on assessing a lab's application and interpretation of, and adherence to, the CC and CEM. If necessary, the NIAP Validation Body may remove specific labs from the NIAP Approved Laboratories List.

27.4.7.2   *Accrediting Security Testing Laboratories.* The next sections describe the procedures for becoming an accredited security testing lab and the benefits of accreditation.

27.4.7.2.1   What Is Accreditation?   In the CCEVS, the procedures for becoming an accredited security testing lab are defined. Accreditation ensures that commercial security testing laboratories have the requisite capability and expertise to conduct CC/CEM-based quality tests and evaluations of CC-specified products and profiles in a consistent manner.

To become accredited to perform CC-based, MRA-recognized security testing and evaluation in the United States, testing labs must go through an accreditation process operated by the U.S. Department of Commerce's National Voluntary Laboratory Accreditation Program. The purpose of NVLAP accreditation is to ensure that prospective testing labs meet the international requirements of ISO/IEC Guide 25 as interpreted for security testing labs by ISO/IEC Technical Report 13233 as well as additional security-specific and Common Criteria-specific national requirements established by the CCEVS. ISO/IEC Guide 25, in part, complements and partly overlaps ISO 9000 by focusing in depth on defining requirements pertinent to developing, implementing, and maintaining both quality and consistency in testing laboratories and on providing a vertical assessment strategy for the quality system and competence of testing laboratories.

Prospective security testing labs need to demonstrate that they have a quality system and a quality maintenance system in place. They need to demonstrate their competence to NVLAP during an NVLAP on-site inspection and evaluation. In particular, they need to demonstrate their competence in performing specific tests, measurements, and services in the field of CC/CEM-based IT security testing, using specific test methods. Prospective labs also must demonstrate personnel proficiency in the fundamentals of CC, CEM, computer science, computer security, information technologies, and applied evaluation skills. The specific proficiency tests required are tailored to the laboratory's proposed scope of accreditation. For example, proficiency need exist only in the CEM test methodologies that a lab intends to use and that are included within the proposed scope of the laboratory's accreditation. Prospective labs only need to show proficiency in applying the CC and CEM to security products and profiles that fall within the proposed scope of accreditation. Trial tests conducted during the accreditation activity allow NVLAP to observe the laboratory in operation in performing an evaluation on a reference implementation. Using a single reference implementation to demonstrate a lab's quality and competence in conducting a mock evaluation provides a measure of standardization in the proficiency tests administered to prospective labs. It also serves to promote consistency of testing skills across all labs that become accredited.

NVLAP accredits labs to a particular scope of accreditation. The scope of accreditation is defined by the lab seeking accreditation. The scope specifies the particular test methods that the laboratory will be able to use in conducting IT security evaluations in the range between EAL1 and EAL4. A testing laboratory will choose the test methods for which it will be accredited to be proficient from an NIAP Approved Test Methods List developed by the NIAP Validation Body. There are currently six different test methods, namely EAL1 through EAL4 evaluations, PP evaluations, and ST evaluations. The minimal accreditation scope is for PP, ST, and EAL1 evaluations.

The CCEVS directs the NIAP Validation Body to maintain the list of NIAP Approved Testing Laboratories. Once NVLAP accredits a lab and the lab demonstrates that it meets other CCEVS-specific requirements, the NIAP Validation Body approves NVLAP's accreditation of the prospective lab. It therefore approves participation of the accredited security testing laboratory in the CCEVS, in accordance with its established policies and procedures. Biannual, on-site visits by NVLAP with laboratory management and evaluators are used to check the continuing proficiency, quality, and competence of accredited testing labs.

Approved, accredited laboratories will be placed on the NIAP Approved Laboratories List (*http://niap.nist.gov/cc-scheme/TestingLabs.html*). At the time of this writing, five testing labs were accredited and approved for testing within the CCEVS. More laboratories were in the processes of becoming accredited; and even more labs were accredited by other countries for participation in their national programs.

27.4.7.2.2   Benefits of Accreditation.   Once NVLAP accreditation is received and any additional scheme-specific requirements are met, the NVLAP-accredited, CCEVS-approved testing laboratory will be publicly recognized and placed on the NIAP Approved Laboratories List. An accredited lab is thus known to be a competent, knowledgeable, proficient, security testing laboratory that exercises known high quality.

Sponsors looking for testing labs can be confident that comparable, consistent, and high-quality security testing skills exist in the processes of all accredited labs. Sponsors looking for CC-based testing and evaluation know for sure that accredited labs are competent to conduct such efforts.

Only products or profiles evaluated by accredited labs can be considered for listing on the NIAP Validated Products List; therefore, only products or profiles evaluated by accredited labs can be considered for mutual recognition and global marketplace acceptance by several countries under the terms of the MRA.

A sponsor looking to engage a lab to perform even non–CC-related security testing tasks can have a greater level of confidence that an accredited lab is competent at performing security-relevant testing and evaluation activities. Furthermore, accreditation by NVLAP has some degree of international recognition; and approval by the NIAP Validation Body further promotes the acceptance of CC-based test results from accredited labs by other countries, even those countries not yet in the MRA.

Consumers of evaluated products can be confident that the testing results performed by different accredited labs are directly comparable.

27.4.8   Testing Validation.   In the United States, the CCEVS defines a process of government oversight to independently validate the testing results of the accredited security testing labs. Such review of the commercial testing and evaluation results by an independent, unbiased third party further elevates the level of trust that consumers can place in a tested product.

27.4.8.1   *Validating Test Results.*   Using defined validation policies and proce-dures, the NIAP Validation Body assesses the results of a security evaluation con-ducted by an accredited testing lab within the CCEVS. The validation review provides independent confirmation that (1) a security assessment has been made in accordance with the CCEVS, (2) the conclusions made by the accredited testing laboratory are consistent with the facts revealed and the evidence assessed, and (3) the CC and CEM have been correctly applied. For tested/evaluated IT products, the validation review determines the extent to which a product meets its ST. For evaluated PPs, the valida-tion review determines the extent to which a PP is complete, consistent, and techni-cally sound.

In conducting this review, the NIAP Validation Body may monitor the product evaluation or the profile evaluation and conduct certain validation activities during an evaluation. It also may seek additional information for clarification of any evaluation-related matters and review specific items of evidence and test results to verify any conclusions drawn in the evaluation report.

The review does not attempt to discern if the product under test is completely free of any exploitable vulnerabilities that were not addressed within the ST. Nor, in the case of a profile under evaluation, does it attempt to pass judgment as to whether the security requirements stipulated in a PP are good, bad, appropriate, or inappropriate for the particular situation.

The Validation Body develops and issues an accompanying validation report. The validation report provides a statement of how well a product conforms to its ST or how well a PP abides by the CC. It confirms that the conclusions in the evaluation report developed by the accredited test lab are correct and that there are no factors which would invalidate the evaluation report.

The validation report is a publicly available document that can be of significant interest to prospective customers. It provides detailed, practical security information about the product and the results of its evaluation. For example, the report identifies the validated product and contains information about the assumptions concerning the evaluation and the scope of the evaluation. It lists product documentation that was part of the evaluation. It provides architectural information and describes the testing approach, the evaluated configuration, and the results of the evaluation. Evaluator comments and recommendations are included. It also may include the product's ST.

If appropriate, the Validation Body authorizes the tested, evaluated, and validated product or profile to be issued a Common Criteria certificate.

27.4.8.2   *Operating and Maintaining the Validation Service.*   One of the prin-cipal objectives of the NIAP Validation Body is to ensure the provision of competent validation services to accompany security assessments performed by accredited testing labs. Additionally, validation processes are used to ensure that consistent technical decisions are made by all accredited labs in their efforts to apply the CC and CEM to product and profile evaluations.

In the CCEVS, the requirements, policies, and procedures are defined for validating the product or profile test and the evaluation report produced by an accredited secu-rity testing lab and for interfacing with other countries to harmonize any new testing methodologies or interpretations. The NIAP Validation Body conducts validation activ-ities, develops a Validation Report, and bestows the Validated Product status to prod-ucts or profiles successfully validated in accordance with these established policies and procedures.

One of the main objectives of independent validation of the testing and evaluation results of various different accredited testing laboratories by a single body—namely, the NIAP Validation Body—is to foster the consistency of security assessment across the pool of accredited testing labs. Validation promotes the comparability of all testing and evaluation results across all accredited testing labs.

27.4.9   Recognizing Validated Products and Profiles.   According to the CCEVS, Common Criteria certificates are awarded to products and profiles whose testing has been validated by the NIAP Validation Body. Validated products with certificates are publicly acknowledged.

27.4.9.1   *Issuing Common Criteria Certificates.*   A CC certificate plus the associated validation report confirm that a specific product or security profile has been evaluated at an accredited testing laboratory using the CEM and CC. They confirm that the security assessment of the product or profiles has been conducted in accordance with the CCEVS. They also confirm that the conclusions of the testing lab are consistent with the evidence presented during the security assessment and that the product or profile is suitable to be recognized worldwide under the MRA. The certificate applies only to the specific version and release of the product in its evaluated configuration.

NIST and NSA (both as MRA signatories) are authorized by the NIAP Validation Body to be the CC certificate issuing authorities for the CCEVS. Issued CC certificates contain information such as the product name and version, a summary of the evaluation, the hardware and software platform on which the evaluated product was operating, any successfully evaluated PP claims, the assurance level associated with the validated product, and the date of the validation.

In other countries, the different national schemes define procedures—sometimes similar, sometimes different—for how Common Criteria certificates are awarded to successfully tested products within their national schemes.

27.4.9.2   *Posting Validations.*   Profiles successfully validated under the CCEVS are placed on a national registry of PPs. Products successfully validated under the CCEVS are placed on a Validated Products List. Validated PPs also can be listed in a special section of the Validated Products List. An evaluated product will remain on the Validated Products List for three years, after which time it will be moved and indefinitely listed on a historical evaluated products list.

The Validated Products List contains a high-level description of the product and the scope (e.g., EAL) of its evaluation. The NIAP Validation Body maintains the NIAP Validated Products List. The Validated Products List also includes or references those products and profiles evaluated, validated, and certified by any of the other MRA-recognized national schemes. Such other products and profiles are listed on the validated products lists maintained by these other national bodies (e.g., the UK Certification Body publishes UKSP06, the UK Certified Products List).

27.4.10   Summary—Common Criteria Paradigm.   The experience gathered from recent security requirements profiling and security product testing efforts has shown the Common Criteria paradigm to be a powerful, flexible, standards-based mechanism. It is a mechanism that facilitates defining IT security and confidence requirements tailored to users' specific needs. It also facilitates stipulating IT product security specifications that are compliant to requirements. Further, it facilitates testing and test verification of products to show they are correct, complete, well built, and compliant to their security specifications. It is a mechanism that facilitates worldwide recognition of tested, CC-specified IT products and systems.

The CC paradigm has been shown to provide cost-effective value. It improves product quality by forcing a meticulous and clear focus on security, by forcing a meticulous security design and development discipline, and by forcing a testing campaign that is appropriate to the normal operation of the product or system so as to verify that the implemented security is correct, complete, and compliant under normal operations.

The CC paradigm helps users understand what risks and vulnerabilities are important (via PPs) and what risks and vulnerabilities are addressed by products (via STs). It helps users understand what level of protection and confidence they want (via PPs) and what level of protection and confidence are provided by products (via STs). It also may help shorten users' product acquisition cycles since PPs can be used as procurement specifications and since users can minimize their own acceptance testing efforts.

The CC paradigm can provide due diligence evidence for users seeking to minimize security-relevant litigation. Such evidence, together with increased trust, can lower insurance liability premiums. Furthermore, by providing a way for demonstrating the traceability of the security aspects of a product or system back to user requirements, as well as to applicable policies, laws, and regulations, the CC paradigm can minimize users' exposure to potential penalties for noncompliance to security-relevant laws or regulations.

The CC paradigm has been shown to provide cost-effective value in terms of helping vendors. It helps vendors describe and demonstrate what level of security they designed and built into their products. It helps vendors show that they understand and meet consumer requirements and that they have nothing to hide. Consumers know exactly what they get in CC-specified and CCEVS-validated products.

The high and consistent testing and verification standards that the CC paradigm provides worldwide allow vendors to outsource the security testing, validation, and certification of their products anywhere around the world. The standards allow testing costs to be capped because it limits the number of necessary security (re)evaluations to only one. The standards allow builders to implement security products anywhere in the world and to test security products anywhere else in the world; and, correspondingly, the use of these standards allow users to buy products with confidence from anywhere around the world.

The CC paradigm improves product quality and therefore helps to differentiate products in terms of verified quality. It facilitates expansion of a stable set of quality products from which to build integrated systems. It raises the level of confidence, credibility, and trust in products as well as in vendors and their product design, development, testing, and maintenance processes.

Most important, the CC paradigm assures that better-engineered, more acceptable products are available from vendors who prepare for and undergo rigorous, independent, CC-based evaluations.

27.5 NOTES

1. "Capability Maturity Model for Software," Carnegie Mellon University Software Engineering Institute, CMU/SEI-91-TR-24, 1991; and Carnegie Mellon University Software Engineering Institute (Mark C. Paulk, Charles V. Weber, Bill Curtis, and Mary Beth Chrissis), *The Capability Maturity Model: Guidelines for Improving the Software Process* (Reading, MA: Addison-Wesley, 1995). The model is described at *www.sei.cmu.edu/cmm/cmms/cmms. html*. See also *www2.umassd.edu/SWPI/processframework/cmm/cmm.html* and *www.secat.com*.

2. "International Standards for Quality Management," 2nd ed., ISO 9000, 1992.

3. "Trusted Computer System Evaluation Criteria" (TCSEC), DOD5200.28-STD, U.S. Department of Defense, December 1985.

4. "Trusted Network Interpretation of the Trusted Computer System Evaluation Criteria" (TNI), National Computer Security Center, National Security Agency, 9800 Savage Rd., Ft. Meade, MD 20755, July 31, 1987.

5. "Trusted Database Management System Interpretation of the Trusted Computer System Evaluation Criteria," NCSC-TG-021, National Computer Security Center, National Security Agency, 9800 Savage Rd., Ft. Meade, MD 20755, April 1991.

6. "Information Technology Security Evaluation Criteria" (ITSEC), Office for Official Publications of the European Communities, Luxembourg, 1991.

7. "Advisory Memorandum on the Transition from the Trust Computer System Evaluation Criteria to the International Common Criteria for Information Technology Security Evaluation," NSTISSAM Compusec/1-99, National Security Telecommunications and Information Systems Security Committee (NSTISSC), *www.nstissc.gov,* NSTISSC Secretariat, National Security Agency, 9800 Savage Rd., Ste. 6716, Ft. Meade, MD 20755-6716, *nstissc@radium. ncsc.mil,* March 11, 1999.

8. "Common Criteria for Information Technology Security Evaluation," Version 2, ISO/IEC International Standard (IS) 15408-1 through 15408-3, ISO/IEC JTC1 SC27 WG3, 1999.

9. "Critical Infrastructure Protection," Presidential Decision Directive/NSC-63, PDD-63, Bill Clinton, The White House, Washington, DC, May 22, 1998.

10. "Defending America's Cyberspace—National Plan for Information Systems Protection," Version 1.0, The White House, 2000.

11. Personal communications from several keynote speakers at the First International Common Criteria Conference, National Information Assurance Partnership, *www.niap. nist.gov,* Baltimore, MD, May 2000.

12. "ISO 15408 for Security and Privacy in Healthcare," W. Rishel, Research Note, Technology, T-10-5507, GartnerGroup, March 2, 2000.

13. The terms "testing" and "evaluation" are a source of ambiguity and confusion. In Europe, there are security "evaluation" laboratories, while in Canada and the United States, there are security "testing" laboratories. However, both types of laboratories perform the same work relative to security products and profiles. Even the CC standard is inconsistent in its use of the terms "testing" and "evaluation." Sometimes it is said that security "testing" laboratories perform security "evaluations." This chapter does not attempt to resolve the discrepancies, and the terms "testing, "evaluation," and "testing and evaluation" are used interchangeably.

14. "Common Criteria for Information Technology Security Evaluation," Version 2.

15. "Common Evaluation Methodology for Information Technology Security," Version 1.0, Common Evaluation Methodology Editorial Board, 1999; *http://csrc.nist.gov/cc/cem/ cemlist.htm.*

16. "Mutual Recognition of the Common Criteria Certifications in the Field of Information Technology Security," initially signed October 5, 1998, and as updated periodically with new signatory countries; *http://niap.nist.gov/cc-scheme/DownloadCCMRA.html.*

17. "Common Criteria Evaluation and Validation Scheme for Information Technology Security—Organization, Management and Concept of Operations," Scheme Publication #1, Version 2, NIAP (a joint NIST NSA initiative), *http://niap.nist.gov,* Department of Commerce, National Institute of Standards and Technology, Computer Security Division, Room 426, NN, 100 Bureau Drive, Mail Stop 8930, Gaithersburg, MD 20899-8930, May 1999 (or succeeding versions), *http://niap.nist.gov/schemeCC.html.*

18. "NIAP Common Criteria Evaluation and Validation Scheme for Information Technology Security—Guidance to Common Criteria Testing Laboratories," Scheme Publication #4; "NIAP Common Criteria Evaluation and Validation Scheme for Information Technology Security—Guidance to Sponsors of IT Security Evaluations," Scheme Publication #5, Version 1.0, August 2000 or succeeding versions; "NIAP Common Criteria Evaluation and Validation Scheme for Information Technology Security—Technical Oversight and Validation

Procedures," Scheme Publication #3; "NIAP Common Criteria Evaluation and Validation Scheme for Information Technology Security—Validation Body Standard Operating Procedures," Scheme Publication #2, Version 1.5, May 2000 or succeeding versions; all from Department of Commerce, National Institute of Standards and Technology, Computer Security Division, Room 426, NN, 100 Bureau Drive, Mail Stop 8930, Gaithersburg, MD 20899-8930; *niap.nist.gov/cc-scheme/GuidanceDocs.html.*

19. "General Requirements for the Competence of Calibration and Testing Laboratories," ISO/IEC Guide 25, 1990.

20. "Information Technology Interpretation of Accreditation Requirements in Guide 25 Accreditation of Information Technology and Telecommunications Testing Laboratories for Software and Protocol Testing Services," ISO/IEC Technical Report 13233.

21. "Information Technology Security Testing—Common Criteria," NIST Handbook 150-20, a technology-specific extension to "National Voluntary Laboratory Accreditation Program—Procedures and General Requirements," J.L. Cigler and V.R. White, eds., NIST Handbook 150, U.S. Department of Commerce, Technology Administration, National Institute of Standards and Technology, U.S. Government Printing Office, Washington, DC 20402-9325, March 1994. (Both NIST 150 and 150-20 can be found at *niap.nist.gov/cc-scheme/ GuidanceDocs.html.*)

22. "Guide for Production of Protection Profiles and Security Targets," Version 0.6, ISO/IEC, JTC1, SC27, WG3, N2172, Draft v0.7, December 1998; *csrc.nist.gov/cc/pp/ pplist.htm#PPGUIDE.*

23. "U.S. Government Traffic Filtering Firewall Protection Profile for Low-Risk Environments," Jack Walsh (NSA) and Wayne Jansen, Department of Commerce, National Institute of Standards and Technology, Computer Security Division, Room 426, NN, 100 Bureau Drive, Mail Stop 8930, Gaithersburg, MD 20899-8930, September 1998 (or succeeding versions); available at *http://csrc.nist.gov/cc/pp/pplist.htm#FIREWALL-REV.*

24. "Guide for Production of Protection Profiles and Security Targets," Version 0.6, ISO/IEC, JTC1, SC27, WG3, N2172, Draft v0.7, Dec 1998; available at *http://csrc.nist.gov/ cc/pp/pplist.htm#PPGUIDE.*

25. "General Requirements for Bodies Operating Product Certification Systems," ISO/IEC Guide 65.

26. "National Policy Governing the Acquisition of Information Assurance (IA) and IA-Enabled Information Technology (IT) Products," *www.nstissc.gov/Assets/pdf/nstissp11.pdf;* National Security Telecommunications and Information Systems Security Policy (NSTISSP) No. 11, National Security Telecommunications and Information Systems Security Committee (NSTISSC), *www.nstissc.gov,* NSTISSC Secretariat, National Security Agency, 9800 Savage Road STE 6716, Ft. Meade MD 20755-6716, *nstissc@radium.ncsc.mil,* January 2000. "Advisory Memorandum for the Strategy for using the National Information Assurance Partnership (NIAP) for the Evaluation of Commercial off-the-shelf (COTS) Security Enabled Information Technology Products," NSTISSAM Inforsec/2-00, National Security Telecommunications and Information Systems Security Committee (NSTISSC), *www.nstissc.gov,* NSTISSC Secretariat, National Security Agency, 9800 Savage Road STE 6716, Ft. Meade MD 20755-6716, *nstissc@radium.ncsc.mil,* February 8, 2000.

CHAPTER 28

SECURITY POLICY GUIDELINES

M.E. Kabay

CONTENTS

28.1 INTRODUCTION. This chapter reviews principles, topics, and resources for creating effective security policy guidelines. It does not propose specific guidelines except as examples. Many of the chapters in this *Handbook* discuss policy; a few examples are listed below:

- Chapter 15 provides an extensive overview of physical security policies.
- Chapter 18 discusses local area network security issues and policies.
- Chapter 25 reviews software development policies and quality assurance policies.
- Chapter 29 looks at methods for enhancing security awareness.
- Chapter 31 provides guidance on employment policies from a security standpoint.

- Chapter 32 makes explicit recommendations about operations management policies.
- Chapter 33 reviews specific recommendations for e-mail and Internet usage.
- Chapter 38 discusses the policies that apply to application design.
- Chapter 46 discusses methods for developing security policies.

28.2   TERMINOLOGY.   One of the pre-eminent leaders in security policy development, Charles Cresson Wood,[1] has emphasized that when developing policy, it helps to segregate information that has different purposes. Specifically, one should create different documents for policy, standards, controls, and procedures.

28.2.1   Policy.   Policy is defined as the rules and regulations set by the organization. Policies are laid down by management in compliance with applicable law, industry regulations, and the decisions of enterprise leaders. Policies are mandatory; they are expressed in definite language and require compliance. Failure to conform to policy can result in disciplinary action, termination of employment, and even legal action. Familiar examples of policy include requirements for background checks when hiring employees, the obligation to follow laws governing the duplication of proprietary software, and restrictions on the use of corporate vehicles for private purposes.

Security policy governs how an organization's information is to be protected against breaches of security (see Chapters 28, 31, and 46); examples include policies on identification and authentication, authorization for specific kinds of access to specific data, responsibilities for data protection, limitations on the use of corporate resources for e-mail and Internet access (see Chapter 33), and restrictions on installation of programs on corporate systems. Policies are the basis for security awareness, training, and education; they are a necessary underpinning for security audits (see Chapter 36). Without policies, it is impossible to demonstrate due diligence in the protection of corporate assets (see Chapter 45).

Policies are focused on the desired results, not on the means for achieving those results. The methods for achieving policies are defined in the following sections on controls, standards, and procedures.

28.2.2   Controls.   When developing a framework for implementing security policies, controls are the measures used to protect systems against specific threats. For example, a policy might stipulate that all production systems (see Chapter 32) must be protected against unauthorized modification of data by programmers; a specific control that could be named in the policy might be that test data extracted by programmers from the production databases must be anonymized to protect confidential data.

28.2.3   Standards.   A standard in computing can be an accepted specification for hardware, software, or human actions. An example of a technical standard is the transmission control protocol/internet protocol (TCP/IP) that governs how systems can be interconnected into the Internet.

Standards can be *de facto* when they are so widely used that new applications routinely respect their conventions; an example is the Hewlett-Packard interface bus (HP-IB), which became so popular that it was eventually turned into a *de jure* standard when the Institute of Electrical and Electronics Engineers (IEEE) based its formal IEEE-488 standard on the HP-IB. In contrast, the Centronix parallel interface, although equally popular and universally used, remains proprietary.

In a corporate environment, a standard refers to specific technical choices for implementing particular policies. For example, a corporate policy might stipulate that strong identification and authentication selected by the technical staff must be used when gaining access to restricted data; the corresponding standard might specify that a particular brand and model of a microprocessor-equipped smart card should be used in satisfying access control restrictions. Typically, the standards are of concern to those who must implement policies; not all standards need be made known to all personnel. Standards also must change in response to a changing technical environment; typically standards change much more rapidly than policies.

28.2.4   Procedures.   Procedures prescribe how people are to behave in implementing policies. For example, a policy might stipulate that all confidential communications from employees traveling outside the enterprise must be encrypted; the corresponding standard might define the proprietary virtual private network (VPN) software and hardware needed to implement that policy; and the corresponding procedure would explain in detail each step required to initiate a secure connection using that particular VPN.

28.3   RESOURCES FOR POLICY WRITERS.   If one is setting out to create policy *de novo* (i.e., without a preexisting policy document), it is critically important to use an existing policy template. Creating policies without guidance from experienced policy writers is a time-consuming, frustrating job that can consume thousands of hours of time, cause dissension within the enterprise, and leave everyone so disgusted that the policies end up turning into *shelfware:* stored, but never used. There are several well-recognized resources for helping policy writers structure their work, avoid pitfalls, and save enormous amounts of time. In the following review, readers will find information about the following resources:

- ISO 17799
- CoBiT
- CERT-CC documentation
- NSA Security Guidelines
- U.S. Federal Best Security Practices
- RFC2196
- IT Baseline Protection Manual
- Commercial policy guides

28.3.1   ISO 17799.   An increasingly popular standard for writing and implementing security policies, especially in Europe, is ISO 17799, which is based on BS7799.

28.3.1.1   *Overview of BS7799 and ISO 17799.*   The British Standard 7799 (BS7799) originated in the U.K. Department of Trade and Industry as a code of practice; it was formally renamed the BS7799 in February 1995. According to *The ISO 17799 Service & Software Directory* (*www.iso17799software.com*), BS7799 was not quickly adopted in Great Britain because it was not flexible enough, it used a simplistic security model, and there were more pressing issues such as the imminent arrival of the Y2K problem. In addition, BS7799 was originally a proprietary standard for which users had to pay the equivalent of several hundred dollars before accessing the full documentation.

Version 2 of BS7799 was published in May 1999, and that year also saw the establishment of formal certification and accreditation methods. At that point, the International Organization for Standardization (*www.iso.ch/iso/en/ISOOnline.frontpage*) began the process of defining BS7799 as an international standard; ISO 17799 was published in 1999.

With the increasing interest in security, ISO 17799 certification has been established as a goal for many organizations throughout the world. Major consultancies have trained their auditing staff for compliance with ISO 17799; e-commerce is also a driving force behind the push for certification. One possible motivation is the experience of the ISO 9000 (quality) certification process in the 1980s; certification soon became a competitive edge and then a competitive requirement to maintain and develop market share.

In the context of policy development, ISO 17799 offers a convenient framework to help policy writers structure their project in accordance with an international standard.

The original BS7799 was organized into ten major sections, each covering a different topic or area (see *www.riskserver.co.uk/bs7799/whatisit.htm* for details):

1. Business continuity planning
2. System access control
3. System development and maintenance
4. Physical and environmental security
5. Compliance
6. Personnel security
7. Security organization
8. Computer and network management
9. Asset classification and control
10. Security policy

Within each section are the detailed statements making up the standard.

28.3.1.2   ISO 17799 Resources.   The full text of ISO 17799 is available in electronic format or on paper from the ISO at *www.iso.ch/iso/en/CatalogueDetail Page.CatalogueDetail?CSNUMBER=33441* for 164 Swiss Francs (approximately U.S. $94). In addition, a variety of guides are available to help organizations develop ISO 17799–compliant policies with minimal rewriting. Examples that provide free versions for evaluation are listed as follows:

Information Security Policies from Security Policy World—
   www.iso17799software.com/policies.exe

SOS Interactive Online Security Policies and Support—
   www.iso17799software.com/sos.exe

Security Professional's Guide—*www.iso17799software.com/iso.exe*

28.3.2   CobiT.   The *Control Objectives for Information and related Technology* (CobiT®) provide a business-oriented set of standards for guiding management in the sound use of information technology. CobiT was developed by volunteers working under the aegis of the IT Governance Institute® (*www.itgovernance.org/index2.htm*), which was itself founded by the Information Systems Audit and Control Association (ISACA).

According to the Frequently Asked Questions (FAQ) file from ISACA (*www.isaca.org/faq_r.htm*):

> COBIT, first released in 1996, is an IT governance tool that has changed how IT professionals work. Linking information technology and control practices, COBIT consolidates and harmonizes standards from prominent global sources into a critical resource for management, control professionals, and auditors. As such, COBIT represents an authoritative, up-to-date control framework, a set of generally accepted control objectives, and a complementary product that enables the easy application of the Framework and Control Objectives called the *Audit Guidelines.* COBIT applies to enterprise-wide information systems, including personal computers, mini-computers, mainframes and distributed environments. It is based on the philosophy that IT resources need to be managed by a set of naturally grouped processes in order to provide the pertinent and reliable information an organization needs to achieve its objectives. With the addition of the Management Guidelines, COBIT now supports self-assessment of strategic organizational status, identification of actions to improve IT processes, and monitoring of the performance of these IT processes. Since the 1st edition of COBIT was released in 1996 it has been sold and implemented in over 100 countries throughout the world.

Most of the COBIT standards documents are available through download as PDF files in English or in Spanish at no cost (*www.isaca.org/ct_dwnld.htm*) by filling out a simple questionnaire. The full set of documents, including the restricted *Audit Guidelines,* is available for purchase on CD and paper.

28.3.2.1 Overview of COBIT. The essential components of COBIT are listed as follows in the FAQ:

- An *executive summary,* consisting of an executive overview background and framework, designed to provide senior management with a succinct description of COBIT's key concepts
- The *framework,* which illustrates and identifies IT business requirements for information through the introduction of high-level control objectives
- *Control objectives,* which contain statements of desired results or purposes to be achieved by implementing the 318 specific, detailed control objectives
- *Audit guidelines,* which provide guidance for preparing audit plans and are linked to the control objectives
- An *implementation tool set,* which describes practical approaches used by those organizations that quickly and successfully applied COBIT in their work environments
- COBIT *Folio* infobase on CD-ROM, which provides detailed indexing and key word searches
- *Management guidelines,* which provide guidance in assessing the status of the organization, identifying critical activities leading to success and measuring performance in reaching enterprise goals

28.3.2.2 COBIT Framework. The *framework* defines IT governance as "a structure of relationships and processes to direct and control the enterprise's goals by adding value while balancing risk versus return over IT and its processes." IT objectives are to

- Align its functions with the organization's overall mission

- Use technology resources responsibly
- Manage risks appropriately

The objectives require a *control function,* which is defined as "the policies, procedures, practices and organizational structures designed to provide reasonable assurance that business objectives will be achieved and that undesired events will be prevented or detected and corrected."

The control function directs IT activities in four dimensions:

1. Planning and organization (planning what will be done)—strategy, tactics, management structures
2. Acquisition and implementation (doing what needs to be done)—technology life cycle, including identification of needs, development or purchase, integration, and maintenance
3. Delivery and support (checking quality constantly)—operations management, data processing, application controls
4. Monitoring (determining what needs to be fixed)—assessment, evaluation, oversight, internal and external audit

The *business requirements for information* include quality, fiduciary, and security requirements, which although distinct nonetheless include some overlap:

- Effectiveness—relevance, pertinence, timeliness, consistency, usability of information
- Efficiency—optimal use of resources, productivity, economy
- Confidentiality—protection against unauthorized disclosure
- Integrity—accuracy, completeness, validity
- Availability—timely access
- Compliance—conformity to laws, regulations, and contractual obligations
- Reliability—appropriateness of information for management to exercise its responsibilities

28.3.2.3   *Control Objectives.* IT control objectives are defined as statements "of the desired result or purpose to be achieved by implementing control procedures in a particular IT activity." The authors state, "The control of IT processes which satisfy business requirements is enabled by control statements considering control practices." This structure is expanded for each of the high-level control objectives; for example, the first such high-level control objective, planning and organization (PO1), is represented as follows, where the boldface terms are common to all such definitions, and the body text serves to demarcate each component of the definition:

Control over the IT process of defining a strategic IT plan **that satisfies the business requirement** to strike an optimum balance of information technology opportunities, and IT business requirements, as well as ensuring its further accomplishment. The plan **is enabled by** a strategic planning process undertaken at regular intervals, giving rise to long-term plans; the long-term plans should periodically be translated into operational plans, setting clear and concrete short-term goals. **The plan should take into consideration:**

- the enterprise business strategy
- a definition of how IT supports the business objectives

- an inventory of technological solutions and current infrastructure
- monitoring the technology markets
- timely feasibility studies and reality checks
- existing systems assessments
- enterprise positions on risk, time-to-market, and quality
- the need for senior management buy-in, support, and critical review.

The CoBiT framework defines 34 IT processes in the four domains:

- Planning and organization (PO)
- Acquisition and implementation (AI)
- Delivery and support (DS)
- Monitoring (M)

Each of these domains is broken down into more detail in the sections below, and a few examples are provided to illustrate the kind of policy statement that users can find for guidance in developing their own policy statements.

28.3.2.3.1   Planning and Organization.   The high-level processes are as follows:

- PO1—Define a strategic IT plan
- PO2—Define the information architecture
- PO3—Determine the technologic direction
- PO4—Define the IT organization and relationships
- PO5—Manage the IT investment
- PO6—Communicate management aims and direction
- PO7—Manage human resources
- PO8—Ensure compliance with external requirements
- PO9—Assess risks
- PO10—Manage projects
- PO11—Manage quality

In turn, process PO1, "Define a strategic IT plan" is itself broken down into the following control objectives:

1.1—IT as part of the organization's long- and short-range plan

1.2—IT long-range plan

1.3—IT long-range planning—approach and structure

1.4—IT long-range plan changes

1.5—Short-range planning for the IT function

1.6—Communication of IT plans

1.7—Monitoring and evaluating of IT plans

1.8—Assessment of existing systems

Control objective 1.1, "IT as part of the organization's long- and short-range plan," is then described as follows:

> Senior management is responsible for developing and implementing long- and short-range plans that fulfill the organization's mission and goals. In this respect, senior management should ensure that IT issues as well as opportunities are adequately assessed and reflected in the organization's long- and short-range plans. IT long- and short-range plans should be developed to help ensure that the use of IT is aligned with the mission and business strategies of the organization.

28.3.2.3.2   Acquisition and Implementation.   The high-level processes are to:

- AI1—Identify automated solutions
- AI2—Acquire and maintain application software
- AI3—Acquire and maintain technology infrastructure
- AI4—Develop and maintain procedures
- AI5—Install and accredit systems
- AI6—Manage changes

28.3.2.3.3   Delivery and Support.   The high-level processes are to:

- DS1—Define and manage service levels
- DS2—Manage third-party services
- DS3—Manage performance and capacity
- DS4—Ensure continuous service
- DS5—Ensure systems security
- DS6—Identify and allocate costs
- DS7—Educate and train users
- DS8—Assist and advise customers
- DS9—Manage the configuration
- DS10—Manage problems and incidents
- DS11—Manage data
- DS12—Manage facilities
- DS13—Manage operations

28.3.2.3.4   Monitoring.   The high-level processes are to:

- M1—Monitor the processes
- M2—Assess internal control adequacy
- M3—Obtain independent assurance
- M4—Provide for independent audit

28.3.2.4   Audit Guidelines.   The proprietary COBIT audit guidelines provide detailed instructions for effective audit of the IT function.

28.3.2.5   Implementation Tool Set.   The introduction to the implementation tool set document summarizes the history and content of this work as follows:

> Immediately after COBIT was released, the COBIT Steering Committee started evaluating how the "global best practices" were being implemented. This *Implementation Tool Set* is the result of their findings. It takes the lessons learned from those organizations that quickly and successfully applied COBIT and places them in a Tool Set for others to use. The newly developed *Management Guidelines* introduce new concepts and tools that will open new perspectives and options for introducing COBIT to the enterprise and their use will evolve, as they are adapted to the specific needs of each organization.
>
> Those lessons included advice to: involve senior management, early on, in discussions; be prepared to explain the framework (both at an overview level and at a detailed level); and cite success stories from other organizations. The COBIT Steering Committee was also asked to improve their explanations of key points and give a step-by-step overview, with examples, of an ideal implementation process. Thus, this *Implementation Tool Set* contains:
>
> - Executive Overview
> - Guide to Implementation, including sample memos and presentations
> - Management Awareness Diagnostics and IT Control Diagnostics
> - Case Studies describing COBIT implementation
> - Frequently Asked Questions and Answers
> - Slide presentations for implementing/selling COBIT.

28.3.2.6   Management Guidelines.   The Executive Summary of the management guidelines document describes the content as follows:

> *Management Guidelines* for COBIT . . . consist of Maturity Models, Critical Success Factors (CSFs), Key Goal Indicators (KGIs) and Key Performance Indicators (KPIs). This delivers a significantly improved framework responding to management's need for control and measurability of IT by providing management with tools to assess and measure their organization's IT environment against the 34 IT processes COBIT identifies.

28.3.2.7   Summary of COBIT.   COBIT is so well developed that it provides not only a practical basis for defining security requirements, but also for implementing them and verifying compliance.

28.3.3   Informal Security Standards.   In addition to the formal standards discussed above, several sets of guidelines have garnered a degree of acceptance as the basis for exercising due diligence in the protection of information systems. These informal standards include:

- CERT-CC security improvement modules
- Security guidelines handbook from the U.S. National Security Agency (NSA)
- RFC2196 from the Internet Engineering Task Force
- IT baseline protection manual from the German Information Security Department

28.3.3.1   CERT-CC Documentation.   The Computer Emergency Response Team Coordination Center (CERT-CC) has compiled a series of security improvement modules (*www.cert.org/security-improvement/*) on the following topics:

- Security for information technology
- Service contracts

- Securing desktop workstations
- Responding to intrusions
- Securing network servers
- Deploying firewalls
- Securing public Web servers
- Detecting signs of intrusion

These modules have been assembled into a text, *The CERT Guide to System and Network Security Practices,* edited by Julia Allen (Addison Wesley, 2000).

28.3.3.2   NSA Security Guidelines.   The National Security Agency (NSA) of the United States has published a freely available *Security Guidelines Handbook* on the Web at *www.tscm.com/NSAsecmanual1.html.* This set of employee policies is tailored to the needs of the high-security NSA, but it provides useful information from which all organizations can adapt some materials to their own requirements. The table of contents lists the following topics:

- Initial Security Responsibilities
  - Anonymity
  - Answering Questions about Your Employment
  - Answering Questions about Your Agency Training
  - Verifying Your Employment
  - The Agency and Public News Media
- General Responsibilities
  - Espionage and Terrorism
  - Classification
  - Need-to-Know
  - For Official Use Only
  - Prepublication Review
  - Personnel Security Responsibilities
  - Association with Foreign Nationals
  - Correspondence with Foreign Nationals
  - Embassy Visits
  - Amateur Radio Activities
  - Unofficial Foreign Travel
  - Membership in Organizations
  - Changes in Marital Status/Cohabitation/Names
  - Use and Abuse of Drugs
  - Physical Security Policies
  - The NSA Badge
  - Area Control
  - Items Treated as Classified
  - Prohibited Items

- ○ Exit Inspection
- ○ Removal of Material from NSA Spaces
- ○ External Protection of Classified Information
- ○ Reporting Loss or Disclosure of Classified Information
- ○ Use of Secure and Non-Secure Telephones
- Helpful Information
  - ○ Security Resources

28.3.3.3   U.S. Federal Best Security Practices.   The Federal Best Security Practices (BSPs) are currently being collected by the Chief Information Officers (CIO) Council of the U.S. government. The Web site *http://bsp.cio.gov/* provides a list of the policies that have been contributed; by the time of this writing (January 2002), there were 20. The site includes some descriptive information about the project and forms for submitting proposals for new BSPs.

In the definitions and framework page (*http://bsp.cio.gov/BSPDefined.cfm*), the CIO Council defines a BSP as "an existing method, proven effective and validated by actual experience, that people use to perform a security-related task." Their contrast between what a BSP is, and is not, is instructive for anyone thinking about security policies.

A BSP:

- is a "human practice; that is, a repeated or customary method used by people to perform some action."
- is not "an IT security mechanism, which is implemented by hardware, software, or firmware although such tools are often essential components of a BSP."
- is "security-related; that is, plays a part in protecting an organization's information, resources, or business operations."
- is not "a business practice, though it supports the organization's business operations."
- is "proven-effective in achieving a security objective as the result of actual operational experience."
- is not "a best possible practice but a best existing practice; not the result of armchair theorizing.
- among the most effective of existing practices used to perform a particular security process."
- is not "necessarily the single best existing practice of a particular sort."

The definitions and security frameworks page includes useful links to a number of federal government security frameworks:

- Security process framework (*http://bsp.cio.gov/spfdescription.cfm*) and tree (*http://bsp.cio.gov/SPFTree.cfm*) from the BSP Program Office
- Security of federal automated information resources (Appendix III to OMB Circular No. A-130) (*www.whitehouse.gov/OMB/circulars/a130/a130.html*) from the Office of Management and Budget
- Federal information technology security assessment framework (*www.cio.gov/docs/federal_it_security_assessment_framework.htm*) from the CIO Council

- Generally accepted principles and practices for security of information technology systems (Special Publications 800-14) (*http://csrc.nist.gov/publications/nistpubs/ index.html*) from the National Institute of Standards and Technology
- Federal information system control audit manual (AIMD-12.19.6) (*www.gao. gov/special.pubs/12_19_6.pdf*) from the General Accounting Office
- System security engineering capability maturity model (*www.sse-cmm.org/*) from the NSA

The list of the current Federal BSPs (*http://bsp.cio.gov/list.cfm*) provides visitors with 20 documents. A few of these interesting and valuable papers are listed as follows:

- Securing POP mail on Windows clients (*http://bsp.cio.gov/getfile.cfm?messageid =00020*) comes from NASA and discusses practical methods for securing common e-mail software.
- Integrating security into the systems development lifecycle (*http://bsp.cio.gov/ getfile.cfm?messageid=00013*) is from the Social Security Administration.
- How to deploy firewalls (*http://bsp.cio.gov/getfile.cfm?messageid=00009*) is from the Software Engineering Institute at Carnegie Mellon University.
- Continuity of operations (*http://bsp.cio.gov/getfile.cfm?messageid=00008*) is from the Department of the Treasury.

28.3.3.4   RFC2196 (Site Security Handbook).   The Internet Engineering Task Force (IETF) has an extensive list of informational documents called requests for comments (RFCs) governing all aspects of the Internet (*www.ietf.org/rfc.html*). One document of particular value to any organization thinking about improving its security practices is the *Site Security Handbook,* RFC2196, edited by B. Fraser of the Software Engineering Institute at Carnegie Mellon University, the same body that hosts the CERT-CC. The work is available at no cost from *www.ietf.org/rfc/rfc2196.txt?number=2196* and from *www.cis.ohio-state.edu/cgi-bin/rfc/rfc2196.html.* The *Handbook* has the following structure:

- Introduction
  - Purpose of this Work
  - Audience
  - Definitions
  - Related Work
  - Basic Approach
  - Risk Assessment
- Security Policies
  - What is a Security Policy and Why Have One?
  - What Makes a Good Security Policy?
  - Keeping the Policy Flexible
- Architecture
  - Objectives
  - Network and Service Configuration
  - Firewalls

- Security Services and Procedures
  - Authentication
  - Confidentiality
  - Integrity
  - Access
  - Auditing
  - Securing Backups
- Security Incident Handling
  - Preparing and Planning for Incident Handling
  - Notification and Points of Contact
  - Identifying an Incident
  - Handling an Incident
  - Aftermath of an Incident
  - Responsibilities
- Ongoing Activities
- Tools and Locations
- Mailing Lists and Other Resources
- References

28.3.3.5 IT Baseline Protection Manual. The German government's computer security arm, the Bundesamt für Sicherheit in der Informationstechnik, has published a useful set of guidelines since 1997, the *IT-Grundschutzhandbuch*. The most recent version was published in October 2000 and is available free in English as the *Baseline IT Protection Manual* from *www.bsi.bund.de/gshb/english/menue.htm*. The work is available in PDF and in HyperText Markup Language (HTML) and has five main sections and numerous subsections:

- Stand-alone systems
  - DOS
  - Unix
  - Laptop PCs
  - DOS PCs
  - Windows NT PCs
  - Windows 95 PCs
  - Stand-alone IT systems
  - Telecommuting
- Networked systems
  - Unix servers
  - Windows NT network
  - Novell Netware 3.x
  - Novell Netware 4.x
  - Peer-to-peer networks

- ○ Server-supported networks
- ○ Heterogeneous networks
- ○ Network and system management
- Communications
  - ○ PBX
  - ○ Firewall
  - ○ Fax server
  - ○ Fax machine
  - ○ Answering machine
  - ○ Modem
  - ○ Mobile telephone
  - ○ Remote access
  - ○ LAN integration using ISDN
  - ○ E-mail
  - ○ WWW server
- Infrastructure
  - ○ Buildings
  - ○ Cabling
  - ○ Office
  - ○ Server room
  - ○ Data media archive
  - ○ Technical infrastructure room
  - ○ Protective cabinet
  - ○ Working place at home
- Methodologies
  - ○ Using the *IT Baseline Protection Manual*
  - ○ IT security management
  - ○ Handling of security incidents
  - ○ Contingency planning
  - ○ Standard software
  - ○ Exchange of data media
  - ○ Databases
  - ○ Computer virus protection
  - ○ Cryptography
  - ○ Data backup policy

In general, each module presents concepts, threats and vulnerabilities, and counter-measures. This work is easy to understand and provides a sound basis for effective information security protection.

28.3.4   Commercially Available Policy Guides.   There are several commercially available policy templates that save time when developing new policies or improving existing policies. Three of particular value are discussed below.

28.3.4.1   *ISPME (Charles Cresson Wood).*   The most widely used commercially available collection of security standards is the work by Charles Cresson Wood, *Information Security Policies Made Easy: A Comprehensive Set of Information Security Policies* (Version 8. Houston, TX: Pentasafe Security Technologies, 2001). See *www.baselinesoft.com* for details. The book includes a CD-ROM for easy access to the text so that users can avoid tedious retyping of existing materials.

Wood integrates the perspectives of both management and technical staff when making recommendations. He was one of the original promoters of information security as a way to achieve a competitive advantage, and a coauthor of the first computer crime investigation manual. He was one of the first to advocate and document integration of information resource management concepts with information security activities, use of head-count ratio analysis to determine appropriate levels of information security staffing, an information security document life cycle for planning and budgeting purposes, and network management tools to achieve consistent and centralized systems security. He also has developed and successfully marketed two unique software packages that automate information security administration activities. He additionally evaluated and recommended U.S. Government policies on open versus classified cryptographic research for Frank Press, President Carter's technology advisor.

One of the outstanding features of this work is that Wood explains every policy and sometimes provides opposing policies for use in different environments. His text is not only a set of templates, it is actually an excellent basis for teaching security principles by looking at the practice of security.

28.3.4.2   *Tom Peltier's Practitioner's Reference.*   Tom Peltier is the *Year 2000 Hall of Fame Award Recipient* from the Information Systems Security Association (*www.issa.org*). The citation (*www.issa.org/tompeltier.htm*) provides the background that explains why Peltier is so highly regarded in the field of security:

> Tom Peltier is in his third decade of computer technology experience as an operator, an applications programmer and systems programmer, systems analyst and information systems security officer. . . . He is the past chairman of the Computer Security Institute (CSI) advisory council, the chairman of the 18th Annual CSI Conference, founder and past-president of the Southeast Michigan Computer Security Special Interest Group and a former member of the board of directors for (ISC)2 the security professional certification organization. He was the 1993 "Lifetime Award" recipient at the 20th Annual CSI conference, the 1999 Information Systems Security Association's (ISSA) Individual Contribution to the Profession Award and the CSI Lifetime Emeritus Membership Award. In 2001, Tom was inducted into the ISSA Hall of Fame. . . ."

Peltier's policy text is *Information Security Policies, Procedures, and Standards: Guidelines for Effective Information Security Management* (Auerbach, October 2001). The book is divided into three sections: Writing Policies, Writing Procedures, and Writing Standards. According to the publisher's description, "the book contains checklists, sample policies, procedures, standards, guidelines, and a synopsis of British Standard 7799 and ISO 17799. Peltier provides the tools needed to develop policies, procedures, and standards. He demonstrates the importance of a clear, concise, and well-written security program. His examination of recommended industry best practices illustrates how they can be customized to fit any organization's needs."

28.3.4.3 SANS Resources. The System Administration and Network Security (SANS) Institute is well known for the excellent security resources it makes available to members and the general public.

28.3.4.3.1 Security Essentials Courses. The SANS Security Essentials Courses (*www.sans.org/giactc/agendas.htm*) provide a solid foundation for understanding the issues underlying security policies. Unit 5, *Basic Security Policies,* lists the following objectives:

- Clearly identify the importance of policy and how it relates to your security infrastructure.
- Present step-by-step, practical guidance for identifying, updating, and implementing policy in your organization, from high-level corporate policy to individual policy.
- Provide specific examples of policies relating to common security issues such as passwords, antivirus software, and incident handling.

    Students who complete this course will be able to:
- Explain why policies actually matter.
- Identify the elements of good policy and explain the differences between good policy and bad policy.
- Identify official and unofficial policies in effect at various levels in an organization.
- Evaluate policy and work effectively with colleagues and management to implement change.
- Understand the relationship between policy and the procedures used to implement and uphold policy.
- Understand the importance of a personal policy and write an effective policy for yourself.
- Write several types of essential policies.

28.3.4.3.2 Step-by-Step Guides. The SANS Institute publishes several useful books and online publications for particular platforms, or for establishing policies covering security needs. For details, see the Web site at *www.sans.org/newlook/ publications/.* Topics include:

- 14 Steps to Avoiding Disaster with your Web site
- Computer Security Incident Handling: Step-by-Step
- Intrusion Detection, Shadow Style: Step-by-Step
- Securing Linux: Step-by-Step
- Solaris Security: Step-by-Step
- Windows NT Security: Step-by-Step Guide

28.4 WRITING THE POLICIES. How should one write security policies? Should they be suggestions? Orders? Positive? Negative? This section affirms that policies should be definite, unambiguous, and directive. In addition, all policies should have explanations for the reasons behind them.

28.4.1 Orientation: Prescriptive and Proscriptive. Security policies should be written with clear indications that all employees are expected to conform to them. Language should be definite and unambiguous; e.g., "All employees must . . ." or "No employees shall. . . ." Some policies require people to do something—these are *prescriptive;* e.g., "Employees must follow the password procedures defined by the Information Protection Group at all times." Other policies prohibit certain actions—these are *proscriptive;* e.g., "No employee shall make or order illegal copies of proprietary software under any circumstances."

28.4.2   Writing Style.   Each policy should be short. Simple declarative sentences are best; writers should avoid long compound sentences with multiple clauses. Details of implementation are appropriate for standards and procedures, not for policies. Policies can refer users to the appropriate documents for implementation details; for example, "Passwords shall be changed on a schedule defined in the *Security Procedures* from the Information Protection Group."

For more details on developing policy, see Chapter 46.

28.4.3   Reasons.   Few people like to be ordered about with arbitrary rules. Trying to impose what appear to be senseless injunctions can generate a tide of rebellion among employees. It is far better to provide explanations of why policies make sense for the particular enterprise; however, such explanations can make the policies tedious to read for more experienced users. A solution is to provide optional explanations. One approach is to summarize policies in one part of the document and then to provide an extensive expansion of all the policies in a separate section or a separate document. Another approach is to use hypertext, as explained in section 28.6.3 below.

28.5   ORGANIZING THE POLICIES.   Policies are distinct from the sequence in which they are presented. It is useful to have two distinct presentation sequences for policies: topical and organizational.

28.5.1   Topical Organization.   Security involves a multitude of details; how one organizes these details depends on the purpose of the policy document. The most common format puts policies in a sequence that corresponds to some reasonable model of how people perceive security. For example, employees can look at security as a series of rings with a rough correspondence to the physical world. Under this model, one might have a policy document with a table of contents that looks like this:

- Principles
- Organizational Reporting Structure
- Physical Security
  - Servers
  - Workstations
  - Portable computers
- Hiring, Management, and Firing
- Data Protection
  - Classifying information
  - Data access controls
  - Encryption
  - Countering industrial espionage
- Communications Security
  - Perimeter controls
  - Web usage and content filtering
  - E-mail usage and privacy

- ○ Telephone and fax usage
- Software
  - ○ Authorized products only
  - ○ Proprietary (purchased) software
  - ○ Development standards
  - ○ Quality assurance and testing
- Operating Systems
  - ○ Access controls
  - ○ Logging
- Technical Support
  - ○ Service-level agreements
  - ○ Help desk functions

28.5.2   Organizational.   The complete set of policies may be comprehensive, concise, and well written, but they will still likely be a daunting document, especially for nontechnical staff. To avoid distressing employees with huge tomes of incomprehensible materials, it makes sense to create special-purpose documents aimed at particular groups. For example, one could have guides such as these:

- *General Guide for Protecting Corporate Information Assets*
- *Guide for Users of Portable Computers*
- *A Manager's Guide to Security Policies*
- *Human Resources and Security*
- *Network Administration Security Policies*
- *Programmer's Guide to Security and Quality Assurance*
- *The Operator's Security Responsibilities*
- *Security and the Help Desk*

Each of these volumes or files can present just enough information to be useful and interesting to the readers without overwhelming them with detail. Each can make reference to the full policy document.

28.6   PRESENTING THE POLICIES.   What options do policy makers have for publishing their policies? This section discusses printing them on paper versus publishing them electronically.

28.6.1   Printed Text.   Policies are not inherently interesting. Large volumes full of policies quickly become shelfware. On the other hand, short paper documents are familiar to people; they can be carried around or placed at hand for easy reference anywhere. Reference cards, summary sheets, stickers, and posters are some of the printed media that can be useful in security awareness, training, and education programs. Printed text, like its electronic versions, provides the opportunity for typeface and color to be used in clarifying and emphasizing specific ideas. However, printed copies of policies share a universal disadvantage: they are difficult to update.

Updating dozens, hundreds, or thousands of individual copies of policy documents can be such a headache that organizations simply reprint the entire document rather than struggle with updates. Updates on individual sheets require the cooperation of every user to insert the new sheets and remove the old ones; experience teaches that many people simply defer such a task, sometimes indefinitely, and that others have an apparently limited understanding of the sequential nature of page numbers. Badly updated policy guides may be worse than none at all, especially from a legal standpoint. If an employee violates a new policy but available manuals fail to reflect that new policy, it may be difficult to justify dismissal for wrongdoing.

28.6.2   Electronic One-Dimensional Text.   Despite the familiarity and ubiquity of paper, in today's world of near-universal access to computers in the work environment, there is a place for electronic documentation of policies. Such publication has enormous advantages from an administrative standpoint: all access to the policies can be controlled centrally, at least in theory. Making the current version of the policies (and subsets of the policies, as explained in section 28.5.2) available for reference on a server obviates the problem of updating countless independent copies. However, it is true that employees determined to defy authority can make their own copies of such files on most systems, leading to the electronic parallel to the normal situation when using paper: chaotic differences among copies of different age.

One solution to this problem of enforcing a single version is to send every user a copy of the appropriate documents by e-mail with a request to replace their copies of lower version number. Although this solution is not perfect, it does help to keep most people up to date. A more active approach, using a centralized computer, would scan all systems whenever they are connected to the corporate network, and actively delete and replace outdated policies by the correct current versions.

28.6.3   Hypertext.   Perhaps the most valuable contribution from electronic publication of policies is the availability of hypertext. Hypertext allows a reader to jump to a different section of text and then come back to the original place easily. On paper, forward and backward references are cumbersome, and most readers do not follow such links unless they are particularly keen on the extra information promised in the reference. In electronic files, however, additional information may be as easy to obtain as placing the cursor over a link and clicking.

The most important function of hypertext for policy documents is to provide definitions of technical terms and explanations of the reasons for specific policies.

Some users are more comfortable with printed policies. Hypertext, like other formats of text, generally permits users to print out their own copies of all or part of their policy documentation. Many of the tools also allow annotations by users on their own copy of a file.

28.6.3.1   HTML and XML.   The most widely used hypertext format today is HTML. Its variant, XML, provides additional functionality for programmers, but from the user perspective the hyperlinks are the same. A simple click of the mouse in a Web browser (e.g., Microsoft Internet Explorer, Netscape Communicator, or Opera) branches to a different page. More sophisticated programming allows the use of frames and, with JAVA or ActiveX, pop-up windows. Navigation buttons allow the user to move backward to a previous page or forward to another page. Links also can be used to open new windows so that several pages are visible at once. All of these techniques allow the user to move freely through a text with full control over the degree of detail they wish to pursue.

28.6.3.2   Rich Text Format and Proprietary Word Processor Files. Some people prefer to use word processor files for hypertext. As long as everyone uses the same word-processing software, this approach can work acceptably. For example, it is usually possible to insert a hyperlink to a section of a single document, to a location in a different file on disk, or to a page on the Web. Some word processors, such as Microsoft Word and Corel WordPerfect, allow one to insert pop-up comments; floating the cursor over highlighted text brings up a text box that can provide definitions and commentary.

In addition to explicit links, modern word-processing programs can display a table of headings that allows instant movement to any section of the document.

Rich text format (RTF) is a general format for interchanging documents among word processors, but the results are not always comparable. For example, a comment created using Microsoft Word shows up as a pop-up box with a word or phrase highlighted in the text; the same comment and marker read from an RTF file by Corel WordPerfect shows up as a balloon symbol in the left margin of the document.

28.6.3.3   Portable Document Format. Adobe Acrobat's portable document format (PDF) provides all the hyperlinking that HTML offers, but it does so in a form that is universally readable, and that can be controlled more easily. The free Acrobat reader is available for multiple operating systems from *www.adobe.com.* PDF documents can easily be locked, for example, so that no unauthorized changes can be made. In addition, unlike HTML and word-processor documents, PDF files can be constructed to provide near-perfect reproduction of their original appearance even if not all the fonts used by the author are present on the target computer system. To create PDF files, one uses the Acrobat product; the installation adds two printers to the printer list. The Acrobat PDFWriter program produces relatively crude output that does not always look identical on all systems, but the Acrobat Distiller program produces highly controllable output with uniform properties. Adobe Acrobat also allows one to create a detailed table of contents for documents.

28.6.3.4   Help Files. Help files also provide hypertext capability. In the Windows environment, one can create help files using utilities such as Help & Manual from *www.ec-software.com* or AnetHelpTool from *www.online-promotion.net/anet/ anethelptool.html.* Entering the search string "create help files" into a search engine such as Google (*www.google.com*) brings up many pages of such tools. Windows Help files can be distributed easily to any Windows user because they are relatively small, and they are loaded almost instantly by the Help subsystem. In addition, users are permitted to add their own notes to such documents and can easily print out sections if they wish.

28.7   MAINTAINING POLICIES. There can be no fixed policy document that covers all eventualities. The information security field changes constantly, and so must policies. Information security is a process much like total quality management: for success, both require a thorough-going integration into corporate culture.

Above all, some named individuals must see maintaining security policies as an explicit part of their job descriptions. Hoping that someone will spontaneously maintain security policies is like hoping that someone will spontaneously maintain financial records. However, as explained in Chapter 46, security policies should represent the best efforts of people from throughout the organization, not the arbitrary dictates of just one person.

28.7.1 Review Process. An information protection working group can meet regularly—quarterly is a good frequency to try—to review all or part of the policies. Employees can be encouraged to suggest improvements in policies or to propose new policies. The working group can identify key areas of greatest change and work on those first, leaving minor policy changes to subcommittees. Members of the working group should discuss ideas with their colleagues from throughout the enterprise, not just with each other. Every effort should contribute to increasing the legitimate sense of involvement in security policy by all employees, including managers and executives.

28.7.2 Announcing Changes. Drafts of the new versions can be circulated to the people principally affected by changes so that their responses can improve the new edition. Truly respectful enquiry will result in a greater sense of ownership of the policies by employees, although few of them will rejoice in the new policies. Some employees will see new security policies merely as a mild irritant, while others may view them as a tremendous obstacle to productivity, and a general nuisance.

Ideally, major changes in policy should be described and explained in several ways. For example, a letter or e-mail (digitally signed, one hopes) from the President, Chair of the Board of Directors, Chief Officers (CEO, CIO, CFO), or the Chief Information Security Officer can announce important changes in policy and the reasons for the changes. A brief article in the organization's internal newsletter, or a spot on the intranet, can also provide channels for communicating the policy decisions to everyone involved.

Finally, the updated policies can be made available or distributed to all employees using some of the channels discussed in section 27.6.

28.8 SUMMARY. The following ten recommendations will help anyone preparing to create and implement security policies:

1. Distinguish among policies, controls, standards and procedures.
2. Use all suitable policy resources from government, industry bodies, and commercial organizations in preparing to create policies.
3. Use unambiguous prose when defining policies: tell people what to *do* and what *not* to do.
4. Use short sentences.
5. Give reasons for policies.
6. Provide different views of policies—topical and organizational.
7. Provide several ways of reading the policies, including printed text, electronic text, and hypertext.
8. Review and improve or adapt policies regularly.
9. Circulate drafts showing changes in policies to interested participants before publishing them.
10. Announce major changes using high-level authorities within the enterprise.

28.9 FURTHER READING

Boran, S. (2000). *IT Security Cookbook. www.boran.com/security/index.html.*

Clarke, R. (1993). *Best Practice Guidelines: Controls over the Security of Personal Information. www.anu.edu.au/people/Roger.Clarke/DV/PDSecy.html.*

INFOSYSSEC list of security standards, laws and guidelines. *www.infosyssec.org/infosyssec/secstan1.htm.*

JCAHO (2001). Accreditation information (healthcare organizations). *www.jcaho.org/trkhco_frm.html.*

NASA (1999). Procedures and guidelines. *http://nodis3.gsfc.nasa.gov/library/displayDir.cfm?Internal_ID=N_PG_2810_0001_&page_name=main.*

Overly, M.E. (1998). *E-Policy: How to Develop Computer, E-Policy and Internet Guidelines to Protect Your Company and Its Assets.* AMACOM.

Security Policy World Download Page, *www.securityauditor.net/security-policy-world/download.htm.*

TruSecure White Papers, *www.trusecure.com/html/tspub/whitepaper_index.shtml.*

28.10   NOTE

1. Wood, Charles Cresson. *Information Security Policies Made Easy,* Version 8. Houston, TX: Baseline Software, 2000.

CHAPTER 29

SECURITY AWARENESS

K Rudolph, Gale Warshawsky, and Louis Numkin

CONTENTS

29.1   AWARENESS AS A SURVIVAL TECHNIQUE.   An organization's staff is the most cost-effective countermeasure against security violations. They are generally the first to be impacted by security incidents, and their compliance with security policy can make or break a security program. A staff that is aware of security concerns can prevent incidents and mitigate damage when incidents do occur. Given the importance of the staff as a security control, awareness is therefore the most important part of an organization's security program. Experts recommend that 40 percent of an organization's security budget be spent on awareness measures.[1] In the animal kingdom, awareness—being alert to danger signals and responding quickly—can be the difference between surviving and not. This is also true for organizations. Bats and dolphins use sonar to detect and avoid dangers, and cats use whiskers and keen senses of hearing, smell, and night vision to probe their environments. Personnel who have developed an awareness of danger signals can function as an organization's sensitive detection instruments. Recognition of events that could indicate a security incident should be a reflex. Awareness activities can build this reflexive behavior.

This chapter provides information on security awareness programs. It addresses:

- Critical success factors
- An approach for developing an awareness program
- Principles of awareness
- Content
- Techniques
- Tools
- Measurement and evaluation
- Resources

29.2   CRITICAL SUCCESS FACTORS.   An organization's security awareness program needs a successful launch for maximum impact. An awareness program pre-flight checklist can help ensure a successful launch. The checklist makes sure that the critical program elements listed below are not overlooked:

- Information security policy
- Senior level management support and buy-in
- Awareness program focus that security, at its core, is a people problem
- Goals (short-term, intermediate, and long-range)
- Audience profiles
- Incorporation of motivational techniques

29.2.1   In Place Information Security Policy.   Security is important and should be addressed by policies that clarify and document management's intention. Policies are an organization's "laws." They set employee expectations and guide behaviors. An effective information security policy includes statements of goals and responsibilities and clearly details what activities are allowed, what activities are not allowed, and what penalties may be imposed for failure to comply.

Information security policies indicate that management wishes to focus attention on security. In addition to saying, "This is important, pay attention," well-defined security policies make it easier to take disciplinary action and prosecute those who compromise security. Established policies are also useful in dealing with personality types who will not do something until "management tells me to."

An information security awareness policy gives the information security program credibility and visibility. It shows that management believes that security is important and everyone will be held accountable for their actions.

An awareness policy should establish three things:

1. That participation in an awareness program is required for everyone, including contractors or other outsiders who have access to information systems. The policy should address new arrivals and existing employees. For example, new arrivals might be required to receive an information security awareness briefing within a specific time frame (e.g., 60 days after hire[2]) or before being allowed system access. Existing employees might be required to attend an awareness activity or take a course within 3 months of program initiation and periodically thereafter (e.g., quarterly or annually). Existing employees also might be required to refresh their security awareness when the organization's information technology environment changes significantly or when the employee enters a new position that deals with sensitive data.

2. That everyone will be given sufficient time to participate in awareness activities. In many organizations, policy also states that employees will be asked to sign a statement indicating that they understand the material presented and will comply with security policies.

3. Who is responsible for conducting awareness program activities. The program might be created and implemented by one or a combination of the training department; the security staff; or an outside organization, consultant, or security awareness specialist.

29.2.2   Senior Level Management Support.   Senior management must be committed to information security. It must visibly demonstrate that commitment by setting an example of security awareness, by providing an adequate budget, and by supporting the security staff.

29.2.2.1   Budget.   Demonstrated, documented top management support prevents middle managers from denying requests to fund information security. Managers often do not allocate employee time for security awareness activities because they do not see a direct connection between them and the "bottom line" for which they are held accountable.

29.2.2.2   Example.   Senior management must lead by example. If senior managers do not take security seriously, the program will lack credibility. For example, if the security policy prohibits employees from bringing software from home for use on the organization's PCs, and senior executives are seen using such software to evaluate their portfolios, employees will perceive the policy as inconsistent, unfair, and not universally applicable.

29.2.2.3   Security Staff Backing.   Senior managers should be prepared to stand behind the organization's policies and the security staff charged with enforcing compliance. This is especially important in areas where security and convenience conflict, such as enforcing a control that removes system access for users whose records do not show that they have completed an awareness refresher during the previous year.

29.2.3   Information Security Is a People Problem.   As early as 1952, UNIVAC, the first commercial computer, was used to predict the outcome of the U.S. presidential election. The human operators refused to believe its prediction, a landslide for Eisenhower, so they reprogrammed it to come up with a different solution. The actual result was, in fact, a landslide for Eisenhower. This caused some to declare that, "The trouble with machines is people."

Many technical people view computer security as a technology problem. They use sophisticated hardware and software solutions to control access and prevent fraud. The reality is that computer security is a people problem. Connecting computers into networks significantly increases risk, and network security depends heavily on the cooperation of each and every user. Security is only as strong as the weakest link, and authorization and identification controls are useless if even one user does not recognize the value of the information assets that are to be protected, and allows the system to be compromised.

29.2.4   Goals.   "Sighted sub. Sank same."—*David Francis Miller, U.S. Navy Pilot, Radio Message, February 26, 1942*

Ideally, the goals of an awareness program should be similar to the one reported on by Pilot Miller: specific, realistic, and measurable. Measuring awareness can be challenging and is covered in greater detail in Section 29.8. An effective awareness program reinforces desired behaviors and gradually changes undesired behaviors.

Employees usually know much of what an awareness program conveys, but the program serves to reinforce this knowledge and to produce security behaviors that are automatic. One goal of an information security awareness program, therefore, could be to make "thinking security" a natural reflex for everyone in the organization. Just as martial artists practice many hours to reinforce techniques until they become automatic responses, awareness programs use repetition to reinforce desired behaviors and attitudes about security.

Another might be to set the stage for training by impressing upon users the importance of information security, and the adverse consequences of its failure. Training involves teaching knowledge and skills to individuals so that they can perform more effectively. Training is more comprehensive and detailed than awareness activities.

29.2.5   Audience Profiles.   A U.S. Critical Infrastructure Assurance Office publication states: "The level of security awareness required of a summer intern program assistant is the same as that needed by the Director, Chief, or Administrator of the agency."[3] This may be true, but the methods for effectively reaching those people with the awareness message may need to be different. It is easier to hit the bull's-eye when one can focus on a specific target.

Several different audiences exist within most organizations, with characteristics based on their needs, roles, and interests:

- *Needs.* Audiences with similar needs will have similar levels of computer knowledge and experience. End users with minimal computer experience may be intimidated by and will not respond well to jargon. Analogies and examples are more appropriate for audiences with little in-depth computer expertise.
- *Roles and interests.* End users are usually interested in getting their job done with as little obstruction as possible. They are usually interested in knowing about the effect of security on their workload, delays, and job performance evaluations. Managers are usually interested in the bottom line and measurable results. They want to know, "How much will this security control cost?" and "What kind of return on the investment will it bring?" Technical staff should receive materials with correct technical terms. Otherwise, they may conclude that the information is beneath them or that it has been prepared by people without technical knowledge.

To create an awareness program, identify the audiences and conduct research to find out what the audiences know and what questions about security they ask most often. Surveys and questionnaires can be used to reveal the starting level of awareness of security issues. This will be useful for measuring progress after the awareness program is implemented.

Historical information also can provide clues as to what the audience knows and does not know. Asking, "What security-related problems has the organization experienced?" may reveal information that can be used to tailor the awareness program.

29.2.6   The Art of Motivation.   An awareness program may seek to change attitudes and behaviors that are ingrained habits or that have emotional significance that makes them hard to change. To overcome this resistance, an awareness program must appeal to other attitudes or preferences. For example, a person who believes that it is acceptable to share another individual's personal data with a coworker, or a password with a new hire who has not been approved for system access, must be shown that people are respected and recognized in the organization for protecting confidential data rather than sharing it.

As long as people associate hackers with being "cool," an awareness program is not likely to impress them with anti-hacker messages. Instead, the message should emphasize something that will appeal to the audience, for example, the damage done when a person's identity or personal data are stolen and that person cannot get a loan or health insurance five years later. An awareness program should deglamorize hackers by focusing on the victims and the harmful results of their activities. People need to be made aware that hackers hurt people, whether they intend to or not.

Messages that call for controls that result in inconvenience, or that require a sacrifice by the audience may not be perceived well. A hostile environment for security can result from people having to comply with cumbersome controls while management is demanding greater productivity.

Another factor in motivation is, "How sensitive are the audience members to the opinions of others?" If the audience is mostly new hires and young people, the message can capitalize on the idea that young people often want to belong. People pass chain letters on because they are superstitious or want the acceptance of being part of the group that has seen the latest Internet humor. If someone receives an e-mail attachment with an interesting subject, there is pressure to open it and respond. The awareness program needs to establish a value in belonging to a group that shuns such harmful activity.

The right message will have a positive spin. Instead of glamorizing the independence of the hackers, the message should emphasize the courage and independence it takes to resist appeals from friends and co-workers to share copyrighted software. Withstanding peer pressure to make unethical or risky choices can be shown in a positive light, so that the people who follow the rules are seen as praiseworthy and not as wimps.

Fear can be an effective motivator, but the primary value of scare tactics is to get the user community to start thinking about security in a new way. Fear-based messages are most effective for motivation when the message includes information on how to avoid or protect oneself from danger.

Potential pitfalls of awareness programs that are not carefully designed include the dangers of:

- Losing the audience's attention
- Alienating the audience
- Overdoing it

An awareness program is like an exercise program. If the audience is bombarded with everything in the awareness arsenal at once, they may become overwhelmed and will not stick with the program. It is important that management understand that effective awareness programs are long-term activities that bring gradual improvement.

29.3   APPROACH

29.3.1   Media Campaign.   Raising awareness is similar to commercial advertising or social marketing, such as the campaigns to reduce smoking or decrease the use of alcohol on college campuses. In the security awareness campaign, the message is the need for security, the product to be sold is the practice of security, and the market is all employees. Communication is the essential tool, and the information disseminated becomes the foundation on which behavioral change is built.

Research and planning are essential and should result in a clear strategy that includes the following:

- Definition of program objectives
- Identification of primary and secondary audiences
- Definition of information to be communicated
- Description of benefits as perceived by the audience

Research can be conducted by observation, surveys, tests, and interviews. Help desk statistics and trends should be reviewed for indications of actual and potential security incidents. A large number of calls for password resets might indicate that password procedures need review or that users need additional training. Ask the staff how they would break into the system—the people closest to the system ought to know its vulnerabilities. Ask the staff to consider questions such as, "Are security breaches predictable?"

Another similarity between commercial advertising and awareness programs is the importance of pretesting materials before distributing them. This can be done with focus group interviews, with in-depth individual interviews, and with interviews where multiple choice or closed-ended questions are used to allow quick responses.

29.3.2   Is a Plan Necessary?   Abraham Lincoln has been quoted as saying that if he had six hours to chop down a tree, he would spend the first five sharpening the ax. Planning is like sharpening an ax, so that awareness materials can be carefully designed to get specific, positive responses.

The security awareness plan can be as short as three to five pages, and should identify:

- The status of the organization's current efforts
- Program goals and objectives, and how progress will be measured
- Actions (with associated dates) that will be taken and by whom

Plans allow for faster reaction and enable organizations to take advantage of current events in the news. Planning also allows coordination around a theme.

29.4   AWARENESS PRINCIPLES

29.4.1   Attention Getting.   Attention is a prerequisite to learning. Awareness activities and materials should be designed to get attention in a positive way. Clever slogans and eye-catching images contribute to the program's success.

29.4.2   Appeal to Target Audience.   Awareness programs that appeal to the existing values and motivations of the target audience will be more successful than ones that try to change them.

29.4.3   Basic: Keep It Simple and Memorable.   Awareness efforts should be simple. Awareness sets the stage for training, but is not intended to be complex. An objective of an awareness program might be to take away the fear and ignorance that has traditionally surrounded information security. Awareness is intended to make people recognize that there is a problem and that they are part of the solution.

29.4.4   Buy-In Is Better than Coercion.   People who have contributed to the awareness program with suggestions, contest entries, or focus group testing are more likely to accept and follow security controls. This assumes that there is feedback for every suggestion submitted. No feedback implies "no management interest."

29.4.5   Current.   Awareness material must be fresh and not stale. Chef Oscar Gizelt of Delmonico's Restaurant in New York said, "Fish should smell like the tide. Once they smell like fish, it's too late." If awareness material is not changed frequently, it, too, begins to smell old and becomes boring.

29.4.6   Credible.   Credibility is crucial for an awareness program to be effective. The message should be clear, relevant, and appropriate to the real world. If the audience is required to use 15 different passwords as a part of day-to-day functions, prohibiting them from writing their passwords may not be as realistic as providing strategies for protecting the written list.

29.4.7   Continuing.   Security awareness programs are long-term efforts and require persistence. Repetition is important and so is variety of the method by which the message is delivered.

29.5   CONTENT.   What should an awareness program address? Below are some suggestions for the minimum topics.

29.5.1   Risks.   All organization members need to be able to answer the question, "What does a threat look like?" Awareness material should address how unauthorized activity might appear on local systems. For example, system users might be taught to recognize that a repeated busy signal on an 800 line could be caused by busy circuits or it could be a cracker trying to break in.

Specific items that apply to most awareness programs include:

- "Malware" (e.g., malicious mobile code, viruses, and worms) and how it can damage an information system
- The principle of shared risk in networked systems, where a risk assumed by one is imposed on the entire network
- The impact of distributed attacks and distributed denial of service attacks
- Privacy issues (including vulnerability of payroll, medical, and personnel records)
- The scope of embedded software and hardware vulnerabilities and how the organization corrects them

The material should be tailored to the needs of the audience. For example, if employees use home computers or laptops to connect to the organization's networks, then the material should address the risks associated with remote access.

29.5.2   Basic Countermeasures.   The next step after getting employees to recognize a security problem is making them aware of how they should react to an incident. This would include:

- Procedures for using information technology systems in a secure manner.
- Personal practices to ensure compliance with applicable policy, for example, password creation and management, handling e-mail attachments, and file transfers and downloads.
- Procedures for reporting potential or actual security events, specifically "who to" and "how to" report unauthorized or suspicious activity. For example, in some situations the telephone is more appropriate than e-mail. This would be indicated if a user suspects that a system is under attack and the attacker may be monitoring e-mail.

29.5.3   Responsibilities.   The awareness program should emphasize that security is everyone's responsibility, that management has made it a priority, and that it applies to everyone in the organization equally. System- or organization-specific rules or codes of behavior should be promulgated so that all employees know exactly what to do and what is expected of them.

29.5.4   Contact Information.   Another key component of material to be presented is contact information for incident reporting, for asking nonemergency security questions, and for making suggestions. People must be made aware of who, how, what, and when:

- *Who*—Contact information, such as telephone and pager numbers, e-mail, and Web site URLs (addresses) should be provided for security staff, the incident response team, and help desk personnel.
- *What*—The types of information that will be needed to report a suspected problem, for example:
  - ○ Affected systems or sites
  - ○ Hardware and operating system
  - ○ Symptoms
  - ○ Date, time, and duration of incident
  - ○ Connections with other systems that were active
  - ○ Actions taken
  - ○ Damage
  - ○ Assistance needed
- *How*—Instructions for reporting suspected problems by telephone or by e-mail using a system that is not suspected of being under attack.
- *When*—Users need to know in what sorts of situations time is of the essence. If immediate reporting can prevent further damage, users should know not to delay.

29.6   TECHNIQUES.   Presentation of awareness materials is crucial. If the employee's reaction is "I knew that," the program is not effective. Desired reactions include:

- "I never thought of it that way."
- "That surprises me!"
- "That's a great idea!"
- "I'd almost forgotten about that."
- "I can use this."

29.6.1   Start with a Bang.   Experienced, in-demand speakers do not start a presentation with a long, dry, boring introduction that lists every law, regulation, policy, standard, guideline, or other requirement that relates to information security. If there were such a thing as a deadly sin in an awareness program, it would be to bore the audience. To get an awareness message across, the audience must identify with the idea, concept, or vision.

29.6.2   Use Logos, Themes, and Images.   Well-designed security logos and mascots can be a source of pride and a showpiece for the organization. Images have greater impact than words. Color and design, as well as the uniqueness of the image, add to the image's effectiveness. Careful use of animated images in presentations, computer- and Web-based courses, and screen savers can enhance the message. A Web-based course used by many U.S. Government organizations opens with the words, "What would happen if someone changed your data?" The words are an animated image that changes a few characters at a time until the message becomes completely unreadable: "Wyad ciunx safper ef stmxune khopgel joor deko?" This image makes a dramatic point about data integrity and availability.

Themes can be used to unite several concepts into a related message. The theme of "Prevention Is Better than Cure" would be appropriate for organizations that process medical data. Give-away items, such as first-aid kits with security slogans and contact information imprinted on them, could tie into a medical theme, as could the concepts of virus checking software and backups being similar to health insurance cards in that they must be current to be of value.

The U.S. Nuclear Regulatory Commission (NRC) celebrates International Computer Security Day each year with a different theme. Recent themes included "Keep It Clean" where an NRC Computer Security Officer (CSO) dressed as Mr. Clean (complete with a bald head and gold hoop earring) passed out antivirus software to employees who attended the event. A large, signed color photograph of the official Mr. Clean was on display. Another year, the theme introduced the agency's new security mascot, Cyber Tyger. Cyber Tyger was featured on posters, on the cover of the antivirus software CD, and on buttons. Again, one of NRC's CSOs arrived in costume and delighted the visitors. Other years the themes have included "It's a Bug's Life" and "PC Doctor," where a "sick" PC was wheeled into the lobby on a gurney while the CSO, dressed in surgical scrubs and mask, explained the symptoms of a virus infection to visitors.

Awareness posters can be built around a common theme, with common design elements, or a phrase or logo. A staged campaign of posters might include a series with numbers on them, for example, "85" on one and "3 million" on another. No explanation of the numbers would be given and a mystery would develop. Later, new posters could explain that 85 is the number of incidents reported at the organization in the past year and that 3 million is the number of dollars of lost business from a distributed denial of service attack.

29.6.3   Use Stories and Examples.   Stories about real people and real consequences (people being praised, disciplined, or fired) are useful in presentations and courses. Sources of stories include individuals who have been with the organization for a long time and have a "corporate memory," news events, Internet special interest bulletin boards, and security personnel who attend special interest group meetings and conferences.

The stories should relate to situations and decisions the audience will be facing. Stories about hackers accessing medical records would be useful to organizations that process medical data, whereas stories about fraud or identity theft would be of interest to personnel involved in the financial industry or the accounting function of an organization.

29.6.4   Use Failure.   Expectation of failure is one of the most important learning accelerators there is. Many people do not pay attention to information that is what they are expecting to hear or see. When an employee takes a computer-based awareness quiz and gets an answer wrong, the employee will pay more attention. Failure should be safe and private. For this reason, computer-based awareness questions and quizzes should provide immediate feedback, but should not record answers. At the awareness level, it is more important to give staff something to think about than to allow them to get every answer correct. To remove anxiety, staff members should be informed that their answers are not recorded.

An example of a quiz question designed to engender thought would be:

The building is on fire. As you exit the building in a safe and orderly manner, you are able to take either the data backups or the backup of your custom-built application. Which do you take?

Ⓐ The data

Ⓑ The backup

Either answer the user chooses is considered correct. The answer screens for each answer tell the user that it does not matter which they picked. The important thing is that they have thought about the possibility of a fire in the building and about making backups. Some users may complain about there not being a single, correct answer; however, more will appreciate the idea behind the question and have a favorable response. In reality, there are times when a person will have to make a difficult choice and often there is not a single right answer.

29.6.5   Ask Questions and Involve the Audience.   Awareness activities that are active and involve the audience are more memorable than passive ones. Whether in person, by poster, or by a Web-based awareness course, involving the audience with questions such as "Did you know . . . ?" and "What would you do if . . ." is an effective awareness technique.

Trivia questions and unexpected or counterintuitive facts are good attention getters. For example, asking:

In the United States, which of the following activities is illegal?

A. Creating a virus that spreads through e-mail

B. Disrupting Internet communications

C. Failing to make daily backups of data

usually results in people choosing the first answer. The question is designed to be tricky, because creating a virus is not actually illegal. Releasing a virus is, but that is not one of the answers. The correct answer is "Disrupting Internet communications." The question is designed to get people to think about security in new ways.

29.6.6   Be Surprising.   Well-crafted awareness material is like a piñata; when the audience breaks it open, it should be full of surprises. An activity that often results in wonderful surprises and learning is role playing. Role play (live, or by means of computer- or Web-based simulations) is an excellent way to show the target audience what is expected of them. At a recent security educators' conference, two educators did an impromptu role play of a worker dealing with a boss who wanted to tail gate, that is to follow the employee through a secure door that had been opened with the employee's cardkey. The audience was entertained and learned by example how to handle such a situation and how to teach others to do the same. Audience members will remember the role play long after they have forgotten the material presented on slides.

29.6.7   User Acknowledgment and Sign-Off.   Another technique for getting people to pay attention is to hold them personally responsible for their actions and choices. Many organizations have established policies requiring that an individual's system access be removed if documented awareness orientations or refreshers are not recorded for those individuals by the end of each fiscal year.

"Noisy prosecutions" are an excellent way to discourage security breaches. Organizations may be reluctant to report security incidents out of concerns for losing public confidence. Reporting incidents, however, allows trends to be tracked and may result in faster identification and response to problems.

29.6.8   Use Analogies.   Analogies, metaphors, and similes help learners to associate new concepts with their previous knowledge or experience. These figures of speech create pictures that connect the teacher and learner to the same idea. Famous U.S. trial lawyer Gerry Spence says, "Words that do not create images should be discarded." Saying that an organization that has a firewall but does not prevent users from installing modems in their desktop PCs is "like putting a steel door on a straw house" allows readers to visualize the concept.

Analogies can be used to make complex topics simpler to understand. Use analogies to form a bridge between what the learner already knows and the new concept or idea that the learner is expected to understand. For example, a common analogy used to explain password protection techniques is that passwords are like toothbrushes (change them often; never share). Another analogy is that passwords are like bubble gum (strongest when fresh; should be used by an individual, not a group; and if left laying around, will create a sticky mess). A memorable analogy, especially if accompanied by an illustration, would be that passwords are like long underwear, and should be long and mysterious; should protect the owner; should be used by one person, not a group; and should be changed periodically. The more creative or unusual the analogy, the more likely it is to be remembered.

Another analogy is that sensitive data are like prescription medicines: they should be used only by those who need them and who are authorized to have them; they should not be transferred, sold, or given to those for whom they are not authorized; and they can cause damage if they are given to people who do not have a legitimate need for them. Cars, medieval castles, and American Indian and European folklore, among other topics, have been used successfully to present information security concepts.

29.6.9   Humor.   Humor is an effective attention getter, and it can be used to motivate people and influence an organization's culture. It also helps people relax, which facilitates learning. Two rules for using humor in awareness presentations, courses, and materials are:

1. The humor must be relevant and should complement or augment the message. Humor must be used for a purpose; otherwise it is a distraction and will cause a loss of credibility.
2. Do not use humor that will offend your audience. Avoid sexist, ethnic, religious, political, and bathroom humor. Do not make fun of something that cannot be changed, such as a physical or social characteristic (e.g., baldness or stuttering).

It is often more acceptable to use humor involving oneself or those in positions of power, such as management and auditors. For example, a presenter might say, "The auditor is the one who arrives after the battle and bayonets the wounded" to an audience of managers. Of course, the possibility of backfiring should be carefully considered. A consultant for disaster recovery sites might explain about having a one-page disaster plan: "The plan is simple. It has only two steps: First, I always keep a copy of my resume up to date; and second, I store a backup copy in a secure, off-site location."

Sources of humor include:

- Cartoons. For example, "Dilbert," drawn by Scott Adams, often deals with organizational and technology humor.
- Humorous definitions. For example, "the Arnold Schwarzenegger virus—it'll be back."
- Security-related poems or lyrics written to the tunes of popular songs or in a specific style, such as an information security rap.
- Here is an example of a security haiku, a 17-syllable poem composed in three lines of five, seven, and five syllables:

  > Computer virus,
  >
  > destroyer of files, survives
  >
  > through lack of scanning.

- David Letterman style "top 10" lists, such as the top 10 excuses for not making a backup.

29.6.10 Address Personality and Learning Styles.   Trainers often mention three primary learning styles: auditory, visual, and kinesthetic. An auditory learner picks up information from hearing it and is effectively reached by lectures and written material. A predominantly visual learner wants to see what is being taught and prefers diagrams, charts, and pictures. A predominantly kinesthetic learner responds well to tactile input and will want to walk through the steps or learn by physically doing the task.

Personality styles are arguably more important than learning styles. Some people will not follow a procedure until they understand the reason for it. To reach these people, present the whys. If an exercise is included as part of an awareness course, once a question is answered, give learners the choice of trying again or receiving the answer. Some personalities learn best and have better retention when they figure out something for themselves. Others just want to see the result and move on to the next topic or exercise.

29.6.11 Take Advantage of Circumstances.   Sometimes it takes an outsider, a security breach, or a disaster to focus attention on security. A disaster, such as a fire, can have an invigorating effect and clear the landscape for new growth. Current events can be an excellent source for material and can add credibility to an awareness program. Several Internet security and technology sites offer subscriptions to electronic security alerts and news clippings. Some organizations have established a "news hawk" program, where rewards are given to the first employee to bring a new, relevant story that can be used as part of the awareness program. This is also a good technique to gain buy-in from the end user community.

29.7 TOOLS.   When choosing tools to convey an awareness message, three questions should be addressed:

1. What tools are most appropriate for the message?
2. What methods are most likely to be credible to and accessible by the target audience?
3. Which methods (and how many methods) are feasible, considering the budget and the time frame?

Using as many methods and tools as possible continually reinforces the message and increases the likelihood that the audience will be exposed to the message often enough or long enough to absorb it.

29.7.1   Intranet and/or Internet.   Browser-based tools include Web sites on the Internet, on the organization's intranet, and Web-based courses. E-mail can be used to send alerts or electronic newsletters (E-zines). Web sites (public or private) can be used:

- As a research tool for gathering information
- To present policies and other documents
- To post alerts
- To collect data on forms, such as for security awareness surveys or incident reporting
- For self-assessments to identify at-risk security practices
- For anonymous reporting of security concerns
- For Web casts of security conferences or presentations

Web-based awareness courses are useful when the organization has many people who are in several locations and who need to take the refresher or course at a time that is convenient for them. Web-based courses are especially well suited for use by individuals who have diverse backgrounds and experience with technology. Online courses offer the following advantages over traditional place-based and instructor-led training:

- Feedback is immediate, so learners do not build on early misunderstandings. Well-designed Web-based training takes cultural and personality differences into account and reassures timid trainees while allowing more confident ones to progress at a faster pace. "Why" buttons or links, "How" buttons, "Show me an example" buttons, and "Give me an alternative" buttons can be set up to let learners with different needs and personalities use the course to learn in ways that are comfortable for them.
- It's convenient for the trainees because a Web-based awareness course can take place at any time the learner wants. It does not have to be scheduled, so those with variable or hectic schedules can arrange to take the course at a time that is good for them.
- Web-based courses allow users to make mistakes and learn from them in a safe, nonthreatening environment.
- Web-based courses are flexible and can be customized to accommodate learners with different levels of experience and different interests. By placing detailed information in subordinate, linked pages, users are able to choose between the "need to know" main pages, and the "nice to know" hyperlinked pages.
- Web-based courses can reduce costs and training time. Updates to courses on the Web eliminate the work involved with distributing the current version and materials to many locations. This can be more efficient and consistent because the content has been reviewed, edited, and tested to make it clear and concise.

Exciting and effective Web-based courses should:

- Start with a bang—a story, an image, a headline, or something that immediately engages the learner's attention. Courses should never start with a dull, "why you need this training" introduction. Writer Paul O'Neil offers some excellent advice to writers that applies to creators of awareness programs: "Always grab the reader by the throat in the first paragraph, sink your thumbs into his wind-pipe in the second, and hold him against the wall until the tag line."

- Be goal based, allowing learners to choose how and when they will meet the course requirements.

- Be active and involve learning by doing.

- Address multiple learning styles and personalities. Appealing to multiple senses increases retention. Appealing to different personality styles ensures that the message will reach a wider audience.

- Challenge the learner's beliefs and expectations and allow learners to fail in interesting and safe ways.

- Use examples and analogies—people learn best from reality and situations where they can relate the learning to prior knowledge.

- Provide feedback, such as immediate answers to questions—feedback is essential to motivation and performance.

- Be memorable. People tend to remember things that are unusual, unexpected, or that carry a visceral impact. Repetition also contributes to how memorable an idea is.

- Include stories. Stories grab people's attention. Organizations should collect stories about security incidents, security heroes, mistakes made, and lessons learned.

- Be accessible. Guidelines for creating Web pages that are accessible to people with vision or hearing impairments are published by the World Wide Web Consortium (W3C).[4] To be accessible, the Web pages should not rely on vision or sound alone to impart meaning. For example, all graphics should be labeled with text that explains what the graphic is, and the contrast between the text and the background should be maximized. An alternative would be to create and maintain two versions of an on-line course.

Well-designed Web-based courses meet the above criteria. A potential problem to be alert for is that some developers have a tendency to get carried away by the technology. Just because an awareness course could have three dozen animated, singing computers decorating the pages does not mean that it should. The technology must be used appropriately; bigger buildings do not make better scholars, and more impressive technology does not necessarily result in a better learning experience. A Web-based course that is overloaded with animations and graphics that do not relate to course content, or that has a poorly-designed user interface, will set the awareness program back.

29.7.2   Screen Savers.   Screen savers are a graphic form of communication and, like posters, they should be eye-catching. Involving a professional artist will help get the message across effectively. Screen savers should contain contact information for the organization's security and incident handling functions. Animations or trivia and questions and answers may make the screen saver more interesting. Screen savers should be updated periodically to keep the message fresh. Commercially produced security screen savers are available with enterprise-wide licensing for entire organizations.

29.7.3   Sign-On Screen Messages.   With some systems, it is possible to add a text message to the log-on or sign-on screen. As with other awareness messages, these should be short, to the point, and frequently changed.

29.7.4   Posters.   A poster series with themes or related designs can be used to highlight specific security issues. Posters should be colorful and should present a single message or idea. Using a professional artist (in-house or external) to design the posters will increase the poster's impact. Posters should be larger than standard letter size to stand out and gain attention. Posters should be changed or rotated regularly and placed at eye level in many locations. Posters can be printed on both sides of the paper, saving paper and shipping costs for organizations with multiple locations.

29.7.5   Videos.   Videos can be formatted for VHS tapes and digitally on CD-ROMs. Videos can be used at orientation briefings and "brown bag" lunches for staff. Popcorn can be provided in bags preprinted with security messages. Videos are useful as starting points for discussions and for briefings. Most security awareness videos are less than 20 minutes long. Advantages of videos include that they provide a consistent message throughout the organization and can be provided to staff at distributed locations, saving instructor travel time and costs. Security awareness videos are available commercially from several vendors, and many videos have been produced by the U.S. Government and are available at no charge. Videos can be expensive to produce, with costs averaging $3,000 per finished minute. Also, as rapidly as technology and threats change, videos can become out of date rather quickly. An option is to produce an awareness video in digital format that is designed in segments to allow for updates to portions as the environment or organizational needs change.

29.7.6   Trinkets and Giveaways.   Various giveaway items can be imprinted with a security slogan and contact information, such as security staff phone numbers or the organization's security Web site address. Examples of giveaway items are:

- Pencils, pens, and highlighters—"Report security breaches—It's the 'write' thing to do."
- Erasers—"Wipe out password sharing."
- Notepads—"Note who should be in your area and challenge strangers."
- Frisbees—"Our information security program is taking off."
- Mouse pads and inserts—The mouse pads have a clear cover over an area into which removable paper inserts are placed; making the cost to change the message far less than the cost of printing new mouse pads.
- Key chains—"You are the key to information security."
- Flashlights—"Keep the spotlight on security."
- Cups or mugs—"Awareness: The best part of SecuriTEA" (where the campaign has explained that TEA stands for training, education, and awareness).
- Magnets, buttons, and stickers—"Stick with security."
- First-aid kits—"Be prepared for security."
- Rulers and calculators—"Security counts."
- Coasters, toys, hand exercisers, informational cards, and other items, including posters, virus scanning software, and screen savers.

Larger, more expensive items such as T-shirts, tote bags, and gift certificates can be used as prizes for raffles at security events. The more useful, beautiful, or cleverly designed the item, the greater the likelihood that it will be kept.

29.7.7   Publications.   Publications, such as newsletters and magazines, in paper or electronically formatted e-zines, may be devoted to security or may contain articles on security-related events or items of interest. Memos and alerts concerning security issues can be distributed to staff. To get attention, consider stapling a facial tissue to stressful memos, such as ones that may be perceived as adding inconvenience or an additional burden on users. Brochures, pamphlets, and comic books can be targeted to specific audiences.

29.7.8   Surveys, Suggestion Programs, and Contests with Prizes and Awards. Surveys, suggestion programs, and contests help to achieve buy-in. Contests to suggest or name a security mascot, to provide poster ideas, or even suggestions for improving security can boost morale and contribute to team spirit. At presentations, speakers can tape prizes or awards under seats in the front row to encourage people to come early and sit up front.

29.7.9   Inspections and Audits.   Inspections and audits raise awareness among the staff being reviewed, at least for the duration of the inspection. Another technique, called SBWA (security by wandering around), involves catching staff members doing something right. If no audits are scheduled, a security staff member can tour the work area at the end of the day and leave certificates of congratulations, thank you notes, or trinkets on the desks of people who have locked all sensitive information in cabinets before leaving to provide motivation. Randomness in such activities is more effective than regularly scheduled inspections. Another possibility would be to have the security personnel periodically demonstrate social engineering by attempting to smooth talk users into giving out their passwords. Users who refuse would be rewarded and users who fall for the scheme would be instructed that they have failed a random security test and will be tested again sometime within the next six months.

29.7.10   Events, Conferences, Briefings, and Presentations.   Participation in events such as International Computer Security Day, on November 30 each year, or in any of the various information security conferences raises awareness. Other events that can contribute to awareness include:

- A "Grill Your Security Officer Cook-Out" where food is served and staff are encouraged to bring any questions about security to the security officer.

- Lectures by dynamic speakers. A boring speaker will hurt the program's credibility, but a talented professional speaker can be eye opening. Sometimes, personnel are more accepting of information presented by an independent subject matter expert. Some organizations sponsor a monthly lecture series or lunch presentation on relevant topics.

- Security awareness briefings. Briefings are typically given to senior executives who have little time to spare and to new arrivals who need an overview of the organization's information security awareness policy prior to being granted system access.

29.8   MEASUREMENT AND EVALUATION.   The price security personnel pay for management support includes measurement. Measurement should include the number of people who received awareness orientations and refreshers. This can be determined through attendance sheets, course registrations or completion notifications for on-line courses, and signed user "acceptance of responsibilities" statements.

As with training, an awareness program that does not reach the intended audience is expensive, even if the per capita cost is low. To assess the effects of an awareness program, several measurements and methods may be used. Empirical evidence such as feedback from presenters, audiences, and supervisors is one of the most useful sources of measurement information. Aspects of the awareness program that can be measured include:

- Audience satisfaction
- Learning or teaching effectiveness
- Skill transfer

29.8.1   Audience Satisfaction.   Audience satisfaction can be measured after the fact with course or presentation evaluations or surveys about the awareness program. "Smiley face" evaluations, where the audience is asked to rate the program or activity on a scale, measure how well the audience liked the course, activity, or materials. User feedback may be requested on the presentation's relevance and effectiveness. Asking for suggestions is also a good approach.

29.8.2   Learning or Teaching Effectiveness.   Pre- and post-tests are useful in determining what the audience remembered, and therefore in tailoring more effective future programs. Unless a preprogram test or preliminary survey is conducted, measuring improvement is virtually impossible.

29.8.3   Skill Transfer or Audience Performance.   This type of evaluation goes beyond the learner to gather input from an outside evaluator, such as a supervisor, security practitioner, incident response team, or help desk personnel. Follow-up interviews, walk-through testing, help desk and incident reporting statistics, and audit findings can be used to measure improvements in awareness and job performance. For example, prior to an awareness campaign on password construction and management, a password-cracking program could be run to identify passwords that are subject to guessing or compromise. The same program could be run after the awareness activities, and the results compared. Or, an evaluator could walk though the work areas at lunch time, testing for terminals that are unattended but not logged off. The same inspection could be performed at various times after the awareness program is initiated. Similarly, a survey of attitudes and specific knowledge could be taken prior to awareness efforts. Staff might be asked to whom they should report an incident or if they may take older versions of upgraded software home for use once newer versions have been licensed by the organization. Similar questions would be asked at intervals after the awareness program is implemented and the results compared. Another measure is to monitor the number and type of incidents, realizing that an initial increase in reported incidents may be a sign that the awareness program is working and should not be considered negative.

Regardless of the specific measurement taken, a baseline is needed and data for the baseline should be gathered before the awareness program is implemented.

As with any awareness campaign, a security awareness effort will require repetition from year to year to achieve and maintain the desired impact on or changes in behavior.

29.9   RESOURCES.   The Federal Information System Security Educators' Association (FISSEA) produces a newsletter, manages a member e-mail list, and presents an annual conference. FISSEA is a part of the National Institute of Standards and Technology (NIST); see *http://csrs.nist.gov/organizations/fissea.html* for more information. Among other documents, NIST is responsible for NIST Special Publication 800-16, "Information Technology Security Training Requirements: A Role- and Performance-Based Model." This document contains a chapter focused on evaluating training effectiveness; see *http://csrc.nist.gov/training/800-16.pdf* for the document.

The Computer Security Institute produces a *Buyer's Guide* that lists products and vendors. The *Buyer's Guide* has a category for awareness materials; see *www.gocsi.com* for more information.

Educational Information Security Materials specifically for children are available from:

> The Computer Learning Foundation, *www.computerlearning.org/*
>
> The Atterbury Foundation, *www.atterbury.org*

Information Security Videos are available from the following vendors:

Commonwealth Films, Inc.
info@commonwealthfilms.com
www.commonwealthfilms.com
(617) 262-5634

Software & Information Industry Association (formerly the Software Publishers Association)
www.siia.net

29.10   NOTES

1. See Patrick McBride's article, "How To Spend a Dollar on Security" in *Computer World,* November 9, 2000.

2. Within 60 days is the requirement for U.S. federal employees according to the Office of Personnel Management (OPM) regulation: 5 CFR Part 930, RIN 3205-AD43.

3. "Practices for Securing Critical Information Assets," January 2000, by the Critical Infrastructure Assurance Office (Chapter 1, page 5).

4. See *www.w3.org/wai.*

CHAPTER 30

ETHICAL DECISION MAKING AND HIGH TECHNOLOGY

James Landon Linderman

CONTENTS

30.1 INTRODUCTION: THE ABCS OF COMPUTER ETHICS

30.1.1 Why an Ethics Chapter in a Computer Security Handbook? In an information age, there are many potential misuses and abuses of information that create privacy and security problems. In addition to possible legal issues, ethical issues affect many groups and individuals—stakeholders such as employees and customers—who have enough at stake in the matter to confront and even destroy an organization over ethical lapses. As is so often the case, consciousness raising is at the heart of maintaining control.

In this chapter, *ethics* refers to a system of moral principles that relate to the benefits and harms of particular actions, and to the rightness and wrongness of motives and ends of these actions. The major sections cover principles of ethics, tests to help recognize ethical and unethical behavior, and approaches to help ensure good ethical conduct.

30.1.2   How Much Time Do You Have for this Chapter?   Every reader of this *Handbook* is invited to spend at least one minute with this chapter, since Section 30.2 really can be read in one minute. Ethics matters, and here are the ABCs:

- Section 30.2 **A**wareness (a one-minute primer)
- Section 30.3 **B**asics (a 10-minute summary)
- Section 30.4 **C**onsiderations (a 100-minute study)
- Section 30.5 **D**etails (a lifetime of ongoing commitment)

30.2   AWARENESS.   The following four sections distill some of the most important issues.

30.2.1   Principle 1: Ethics Counts.   Increasingly, society is holding individuals and organizations to higher ethical standards than in the past; for example, in recent years, many countries have passed privacy legislation, conflict-of-interest restrictions for public officials, and full-disclosure laws for candidates in a variety of public offices. People, individually and collectively, really want to trust others. Two corollaries to the principle that ethics counts are as follows:

1. Good ethical standards are usually good for business.
2. Violations of ethics are almost always bad for business.

In other words, good ethical behavior is usually appreciated by society, and bad ethical behavior is almost always frowned upon and punished—sooner or later.

30.2.2   Principle 2: Ethics Is Everybody's Business.   A second important principle is that good ethics flourishes best when everyone works at it, both in practicing good ethics and in holding others to do so. The reverse of this is also true: those who practice bad ethics or choose to ignore the bad ethics of others are truly part of the problem. Ethics is inescapably everybody's business.

30.2.3   A Test: Put Yourself in Another's Shoes.   One of the best evaluators of whether certain behavior is ethical or not invites you to put yourself in the other person's shoes and ask the role-reversal question, "What if I were on the receiving end of the behavior in question?" This variant of the time-honored golden rule translates to, "If I wouldn't like it done to me I probably shouldn't do it to others."

30.2.4   An Approach: Disclose!   One of the best guidelines to help ensure good ethical behavior is to let your stakeholders in on what you are doing or are about to do. Good ethics flourish in the light of day; bad ethics ultimately rely on concealment. Disclosure buys you two forms of peace of mind: first, you're being openly honest; second, if others do not like it, you have at least given them the opportunity to express their concerns.

For example, consider organizational policy about managers reading employee e-mail. Almost any policy (anywhere from aggressive intervention to complete hands off) is likely to be ethical if and only if employees are made aware of it.

30.3 BASICS. The following expansion of Section 30.2 elaborates on the basic principles enunciated there.

30.3.1 Principle 3: Stakeholders Dictate Ethics. Stakeholders are defined as any individuals or groups with something at stake in the outcome of a decision. In the world of business, stockholders are almost always stakeholders; employees, customers, suppliers, and even competitors are often stakeholders, too. How a decision harms or benefits stakeholders is a major ethical consideration. Effects on stakeholders are so important that the best place to start looking at the ethics of a decision is to identify stakeholders and just what it is they have at stake. Decisions will invariably affect individuals and groups, often in opposite ways: some may stand to gain, others to lose or suffer. The effects and tradeoffs raise the principal ethics concerns.

30.3.2 Principle 4: Traditional Principles Still Apply. Recent generations are not the first to raise questions and develop ideas about ethics, although the concept of business ethics has been mocked as an oxymoron and only recently promoted in academia as a valuable area of study. High technology has complicated some issues, but the following fundamental principles still apply:

- The golden rule ("Do unto others as you would have them do unto you") and its variants have already been mentioned in Section 30.2.3. These principles remain timeless and fundamental.

- Consideration of the interplay of duties, rights, and responsibilities remains important. When making ethical decisions, we normally examine the legal, professional, and customary constraints on behavior that apply to our situation.

- Traditional reasons for good ethical behavior, such as religious principles, egoism, utilitarianism, and altruism, still provide us with a useful taxonomy for discussions about ethics.

The point is that even though modern technology has created new opportunities for unethical behavior and new motivations for good ethical behavior, it has not been necessary to develop new principles to deal with ethics. For example, many of the principles (including politeness) governing the behavior of door-to-door sales still apply to Internet push technology.

30.3.3 More Tests. In Section 30.2.3, we suggested the "other's shoes test" as a really good evaluator of whether certain behavior is ethical or not. Here, we introduce three other tests. The first two are negative in the sense of suggesting behavior is inappropriate; the third is positive and suggests the behavior in question is ethical.

- The "mom test" asks how your mom (spouse, children, best friend, etc.) would react if aware of your actions. If you would be embarrassed having someone close to you knowing what is going on, the odds are pretty good it is unethical.

- The "eye-team test" takes this a step further and considers the results of exposing your actions to the whole world as part of an investigative team broadcast. Again, the more embarrassment, the more likely the unethical nature of the actions.

- The "market test" asks you to think about openly publicizing your actions as a competitive customer relations strategy. Never mind whether or not such a marketing strategy is actually feasible; if such exposure could impress others favorably, chances are you are on solid ethical ground.

30.3.4   A Guideline Approach: Ask!   Section 30.2.4 endorsed disclosure as one of the best guidelines to help ensure good ethical behavior. This simply means letting your stakeholders in on what you are doing or about to do. Having done so, it then becomes an appropriate guideline to explicitly ask those stakeholders for their permission (or acquiescence, or at least acknowledgment) for you to proceed. This can be in the form of allowing stakeholders to "opt out"of certain policies (e.g., disclosure of information to third parties). Many stakeholders prefer an "opt-in" approach rather than a default assumption of acceptability, particularly if that assumption is nonintuitive or otherwise obscure.

30.3.5   Another Guideline Approach: An Ethics Officer.   Designating an individual to serve as a full- or part-time ethics officer in an enterprise is a powerful proactive way to help ensure good ethical behavior. Many large organizations now consider this a position on the top-management team. But even small organizations can formally delegate such responsibilities on a part-time basis that need not require much time and energy of the individual involved. In all cases, the common objectives include:

- Clear management commitment to good business ethics, including adequate resources to support this position.

- Organizational recognition that this individual has appropriate authority and responsibility, and is a conduit of information into and within the organization.

- Hassle-free avenues of access to this person.

30.4   CONSIDERATIONS

30.4.1   Principle 5: Ethics Need Not and Should Not Be a Hassle.   The last thing one wants with business ethics is hassle. An organization's ethics policies should not be obscure, complicated, onerous, or an obstacle to getting things done. The keys to avoiding hassle include:

- Clear and straightforward articulation of ethics policies.
- Consciousness raising as a prime objective of ethics policies.
- Clear, comfortable, and safe access to interpretation (e.g., by an ethics officer).
- Consistency in promulgation, education, application, and enforcement.

Employees should not have to guess what constitutes acceptable behavior, nor should they be encumbered by anxiety, guilt, or fear. Individuals should be able to gain clarification on matters before, during, or after events without delay and without creating the appearance of being a nuisance. Questions about ethics issues deserve unbiased answers, without the presumption that there has been a breach of ethical conduct, or that ulterior motives are involved.

Whenever an individual is uncomfortable with a situation or a potential situation, whether or not the individual is directly involved, and particularly if "whistle blowing" implicates others or even organizational policy, that discomfort needs to be addressed. Even if the individual is wrong and should not be concerned, the discomfort should be dispelled. If the individual is right and there is a legitimate concern, the organization should resolve the issue in a way that does not put the whistle blower on the spot but rather indicates support for such disclosure.

30.4.2   Principle 6: Ethics Policies Deserve Formality.   Like other important policies, an organization's ethics policies deserve formality:

- Clear documentation
- Clear motivation
- Clear sanctions
- Clear management support at every level, including the top

Anything less than the foregoing suggests confusion at best and lip service at worst. Formality should not mean bureaucracy or piles of manuals. Consistent with the fifth principle of avoiding hassles, documentation should be brief and clear, and directed at simplifying matters rather than complicating them. The preparation and presentation of policies should reflect a process of thoughtful and high priority consideration.

A corollary of this principle is peer participation. Policies that ultimately rely on organizational support are best developed and disseminated with peer involvement.

30.4.3   Principle 7: Ethics Policies Deserve Review.   Perhaps the only thing as dangerous as ignorance when it comes to policy is complacency. This is as true of ethics policies as it is of any other organizational policy. In particular, to assume everyone in an organization is on board with policy is naive at best. Review offers a type of preventive maintenance whereby policies and their promulgation are reconsidered with an eye to improvement.

Any organizational policy requires subscription on the part of the members of the organization. Understanding of, and compliance with, any policy suffers a dangerous tendency to lapse when simply gathering dust. Even an occasional mention and discussion of ethical issues or principles during meetings can breathe new life into old policy.

Just as a corollary of Principle 6 was peer participation in the formalization of policy, so is peer involvement a corollary of policy review. Not only does such peer review facilitate fresh insights into policy, but the process itself represents a powerful educational opportunity.

30.4.4   Principle 8: Anticipate.   Few people relish the prospect of a serious breach of organizational ethics, particularly if matters reach the point of embarrassing publicity or even legal action. It is better to contemplate the worst scenarios in advance than to deal with them without preparation and after the fact. In other words, do not let wishful thinking deter the organization from including appropriate issues in formal policy.

It is better to address tough issues head on, than to take anything for granted. The two best ways of doing so are to:

- Have comprehensive policies that cover any foreseeable eventuality.
- Have a full- or part-time ethics officer in place to stay on top of things.

30.4.5   The Smell Test.   Sometimes the other tests discussed above (other's shoes, mom, eye-team, market) can result in fuzzy or ambiguous analysis. It may be hard to put yourself in someone else's shoes, especially if different individuals would have widely different reactions to your behavior. And sometimes your family and friends, the general public, or your customers could be neutral or divided in their reactions. The so-called "smell test" does not require quantitative or even qualitative estimations; it simply relies on your intuition as to whether the behavior in question "smells fishy." In other words, if you catch yourself seeking justifications or a bit uncomfortable even thinking about the implications, the ethics may be as bad or poor as they "smell."

30.4.6   An Approach: Stock Taking.   Where can an organization start with all this if it had not already done so? Things usually start with a concerned individual (you?) doing some stock taking and consciousness raising. The following are questions for you and others in your organization to consider. If you like the answers, then your organization is ethically aware. If you do not like the answers, then your organization must deal with the issues you have uncovered.

- If you felt that a fellow employee was misusing company resources or harassing someone, is it obvious what you should do? Is there someone in the organization you could comfortably talk with?
- Do you have the sense that top management in your organization is aware of ethics issues? Do you have the sense that they care?
- Do you know if your organization monitors employee e-mail or computer usage? How much personal business, such as e-mail and net surfing, is permissible on company time?
- How important is quality to your company's products and services? Are marketing claims consistent with quality?
- What, if any, information does your company capture about customers, suppliers, or employees without their permission? Without even their knowledge? What, if any, information does your company provide to entities outside the organization about customers, suppliers, or employees without their permission? Without even their knowledge?
- Does your organization fully comply with license arrangements and payments for software and hardware?
- Are customers, suppliers, and employees always treated with dignity and respect? How would a stakeholder (e.g., a new employee) become aware of organizational ethics policies?

For each of the above questions, the issue of how one knows must be raised. Ambiguous, confusing, or unreliable knowledge of what is or is not going on should raise red flags of concern. Discomfort with such knowledge may be symptomatic of underlying problems with ethics.

This section was allocated 100 minutes of study because you may need at least that much time not only for the stock taking suggested above but also to translate your work into action steps for your organization. Here are a few suggested actions to get you started.

- Ask some of your peers to consider the same stock-taking questions, and compare their thoughts with yours.

- Itemize and prioritize any concerns.

- Make an appointment with someone fairly high up in management to discuss those concerns. If you are "someone fairly high up in management," make an appointment with two or three peers, and with subordinates who represent the staff.

- Examine the feasibility of appointing a full- or part-time ethics officer, while considering the downside of not having one.

- Ask your internal or external auditors to consider an audit of your ethics policies the next time they do a financial or operational audit.

30.5 DETAILS

30.5.1 How to Keep Up. One of the best ways for individuals and organizations to keep up with matters of good ethics is to spread the job around. Do not try to shoulder the effort alone; it will likely overwhelm any one individual, and collective thinking is valuable in these matters. Without abrogating individual responsibilities, charging the right person with the job of ethics officer will certainly help to keep the enterprise on an appropriate ethical course. A growing number of periodicals, both professional and of general interest, include articles involving ethics. Reading them, and then discussing them with your peers can be invaluable. Additionally, there has been an increase in the number of Web sites addressing ethical issues (see the section "For Further Study" at the end of this chapter.)

30.5.2 Why to Keep Up. Keeping on top of organizational ethics is important because it's the right thing to do. Contemporary business practice embraces the idea of an extended value chain where entities such as customers and suppliers, traditionally seen as outside organizational boundaries, are now viewed as partners. Strategic alliances are being formed with these entities, and keeping business partners satisfied and confident is now a strategic necessity. Souring the relationship by a breach of ethics is completely inconsistent with sound business practices. Even if customers and suppliers are not formally viewed as business partners, they are still essential to doing business and are not to be taken for granted. At the very least, given the range of alternate choices available today, unfair exploitation and other forms of unethical practice expose an organization to outright abandonment.

Finally, in the spirit of total quality management (TQM), whereby everyone in the enterprise is seen to contribute to its success or failure, your enterprise can be said to be counting on you. The converse may also be true: your job and your future career may well depend on the success of your enterprise. The good ethics of your organization reflect favorably on you and your colleagues, but bad ethics will have an opposite effect.

30.6 FURTHER STUDY. The following is a short list of a few books and Web sites that will be helpful to readers seeking further discussion of ethical decision making in general and ethics in business and high technology.

Academic Dialogue on Applied Ethics: *http://caae.phil.cmu.edu/cavalier/forum/ethics.html.*

Anonymous. Internet Usage Policy Guide. Burlington, MA: Elron, 2000; *www.elronsoftware. com/enterprise/iupguide.pdf.*

Australian Institute of Computer Ethics: *www.aice.swin.edu.au/.*

Barger, R.N. "In Search of a Common Rationale for Computer Ethics." 1994. *www.nd.edu/ ~rbarger/common-rat.html.*

Brookings Institution Computer Ethics Institute: *www.brook.edu/its/cei/cei_hp.htm.*

Cavazos, E., and G. Morin. *Cyberspace and the Law: Your Rights and Duties in the On-Line World.* Cambridge, MA: MIT Press, 1996.

Clearinghouse for Engineering and Computer Ethics, North Carolina State University: *www4. ncsu.edu/~jherkert/ethicind.html.*

Computer & Information Ethics Resources on WWW. Center for Applied Ethics, University of British Columbia: *www.ethics.ubc.ca/resources/computer/.*

Computer Ethics. Cyberethics: *http://cyberethics.cbi.msstate.edu/.*

Computer Ethics. ThinkQuest: *http://library.thinkquest.org/26658/?tqskip=1.*

Cyber Citizen Partnership. ITAA & DoJ: *www.cybercitizenpartners.org/.*

Cyberangels: *www.cyberangels.org/.*

Cyberspace Law Institute: *www.cli.org/default.html.*

Cyberspacers (kids' site): *www.cyberspacers.com/home.html.*

Ethics and Information Technology (journal):*www.wkap.nl/journals/ethics_it.*

Floridi, L. *Information Ethics: On the Philosophical Foundations of Computer Ethics,* 2nd ed., Version 2,.0, 1998: *www.wolfson.ox.ac.uk/~floridi/ie.htm.*

Forester, T., and P. Morrison. *Computer Ethics: Cautionary Tales and Ethical Dilemmas in Computing.* Cambridge, MA: MIT Press,

Institute for Global Ethics: *www.globalethics.org/.*

Johnson, D.O. *Computer Ethics,* 3rd ed. New York: Prentice Hall, 2000.

Kallman, E.A., and J.P. Grillo. *Ethical Decision Making and Information Technology: An Introduction with Cases,* 2nd ed. New York: McGraw-Hill, 1996.

Lessig, L., D. Post, and E. Volokh. Cyberspace Law for Non-Lawyers. Published via e-mail, 1997: *www.ssrn.com/update/lsn/cyberspace/csl_lessons.html.*

Online Ethics Center for Engineering and Science: *http://onlineethics.org/.*

Project NEThics at the University of Maryland: *www.inform.umd.edu/CompRes/NEThics/ethics.*

Spinello, R. *Case Studies in Information and Computer Ethics.* New York: Prentice Hall, 1996.

Tavani Bibliography of Computing, Ethics, and Social Responsibility, Mississippi State University: *cyberethics.cbi.msstate.edu/biblio.*

University of British Columbia Centre for Applied Ethics: *www.ethics.ubc.ca.*

Web Wise Kids: *www.webwisekids.com/.*

CHAPTER 31

EMPLOYMENT PRACTICES AND POLICIES

M.E. Kabay

CONTENTS

31.1 INTRODUCTION. Crime is a human issue, not merely a technological one. True, technology can reduce the incidence of computer crimes, but the fundamental problem is that people can be tempted to take advantage of flaws in our information systems. The most spectacular biometric access control in the world won't stop someone from getting into the computer room if the janitor believes it's "just to pick up a listing."

People are the key to effective information security, and disaffected employees and angry ex-employees are important threats, according to many current studies. For example, the annual computer crime survey published by the Computer Security Institute in March 2001 (see *www.gocsi.com/prelea_000321.htm*) consistently suggests that computer crime threats to large corporations and government agencies come from both outside and inside their electronic perimeters.

This chapter presents principles for integrating human resources (HR) management and information security into corporate culture. For guidance on setting policies, see Chapter 28; for details of e-mail and Internet usage policies, see Chapter 33.

31.2 HIRING. The quality of employees is the foundation of success for all enterprises; it is also the basis for effective information security.

31.2.1 Checking Candidate Background. Hiring new employees poses a particular problem; growing evidence suggests that many people inflate their résumés with unfounded claims. A research project run by the Port Authority of New York and New Jersey used an advertisement asking for electricians who were expert at using "Sontag Connectors." They received 170 responses claiming such expertise, even though there was no such device (Peter Levine, quoted in *www.virtualhrscreening.com/ background/whybackground.htm*).

Reviewers should be especially careful of vague words such as "monitored," and "initiated." During interviews or background checking, HR staff should find out what the candidate did in specific detail, if possible. All references should be followed up at least to verify that the candidates really worked where the résumé claims they did.

Unfortunately, there is a civil liberties problem when considering someone's criminal record. Once people have suffered the legally mandated punishment for a crime, whether fines, community service, or imprisonment, discriminating against them in hiring may be a violation of their civil rights. Can one exclude convicted felons from any job openings? From job openings similar to areas in which they abused their former employers' trust? Are employers permitted in law to require that prospective employees approve background checks? Can one legally require polygraph tests? Drug tests?

In some jurisdictions, "negligent hiring" that results in harm to third parties is being punished in civil litigation. Imagine, for example, that a firm were to hire an active criminal hacker as a system administrator without adequate background checking and interviews; if the hacker were then to use his position and corporate resources to break into or sabotage another organization's systems, it is reasonable to suppose that the victim could claim damages from the criminal's employer on the basis of negligent hiring.

Employers should consult their corporate legal staff to ensure that they know and exercise their rights and obligations in the specific legal context of their work.

Even checking references from previous employers is fraught with uncertainty. Employers may hesitate to give bad references for incompetent or unethical employees for fear of lawsuits if their comments become known or if the employee fails to get a new job. Today, one cannot rely on getting an answer to the simple question, "Would you rehire this employee?"

Ex-employers must also be careful not to inflate their evaluation of an ex-employee. Sterling praise for a scoundrel could lead to a lawsuit from the disgruntled new employer.

For these reasons, a growing number of employers have corporate policies that forbid discussing a former employee's performance in any way, positive or negative. All one gets from a contact in such cases is, "Your candidate did work as an Engineer Class 3 from 1991 to 1992. I am forbidden to provide any further information."

It is known in the security field that some people who have successfully committed crimes have been rewarded by a "golden handshake" (a special payment in return for leaving) and sometimes even with positive references. The criminals can then move on to victimize a new employer. However, no one knows how often this takes place.

To work around such distortions, interviewers should question candidates closely about details of their education and work experience. The answers can then be checked for internal consistency and compared with the candidate's written submissions. Liars hate details: it is so much harder to remember which lie to repeat, to which person, than it is to tell the truth.

There are commercial services specializing in background checking (e.g., *www. virtualhrscreening.com*). They provide the necessary forms to allow employers to query credit records and other background information (see *www.virtualhrscreening. com/background/howtoBG.htm*).

Experienced employees should interview the candidate and compare notes in meetings to spot inconsistencies. As director of technical support at a large computer service bureau, I questioned a new employee who claimed to have worked on a particular platform for several years—but didn't know how to log on. Had he chatted with any of the programmers on staff before being hired, his deception would have been discovered quickly enough. Ironically, had he told the truth, he might have been hired anyway.

31.2.2   Employment Agreements.   Before allowing new employees to start work, they should sign an employment agreement which stipulates that they will not disclose confidential information or trade secrets from their previous employer. Another clause must state that they understand that the new employer is explicitly *not* requesting access to information misappropriated from their previous employer or stolen from any other source. The Uniform Trade Secrets Act, which is enforced in many jurisdictions in the United States, provides penalties that are up to triple the demonstrated financial damages caused by the data leakage plus attorney's fees (see Tutorial 5 in this *Handbook's* online Tutorials for more details about employment agreements).

31.3   MANAGEMENT.   Security is the result of corporate culture; therefore, management practices are critically important for successful information protection. External attacks through Internet connections and damage from malicious software are certainly important threats; nonetheless, insider damage due to errors and omissions, as well as through dishonesty or a desire for revenge, are still considered major problems for information security (see Chapter 4 for more details on computer crime statistics).

31.3.1   Identify Opportunities for Abuse.   Security managers do not have to be paranoid, they just have to act as if they are paranoid.

Managers must treat people with scrupulously fair attention to written policies and procedures. Selective or capricious enforcement of procedures may constitute harassment. If some individuals are permitted to be alone in the printer room as salary checks are printed, while other employees of equivalent rank are forced to be accompanied, the latter can justifiably interpret the inconsistency as an implicit indication of distrust. Such treatment may move certain employees to initiate grievances and civil lawsuits, to lay complaints under criminal statutes for discrimination, or even to commit vengeful acts.

31.3.2   Access Is Neither a Privilege Nor a Right.   When management removes access rights to the network server room from a system analyst who has no reason to enter that area, the response may be resentment, sulking, and abuse. People sometimes treat access controls as status symbols; why else would a CEO who has no technical training demand that his access code include the tape library and the wiring closet? Managers can overcome these psychological barriers to better security by introducing a different way of looking at vulnerabilities and access. After identifying an opportunity for a particular employee to use the system in unauthorized ways, one should turn the discussion into a question of protecting the person who has unnecessary access against undue suspicion. For example, if an employee has more access to secured files than required for her job, having such capabilities puts her at risk. If anything ever did go wrong with the secured files, she'd be a suspect. There's no need to frame the problem in terms of suspicion and distrust.

With these principles in mind, managers should be alert to such dangers as permitting an employee to remain alone in a sensitive area, allowing unsupervised access to unencrypted backups, or having only one programmer who knows anything about the internals of the accounting package.

As for language, it would be better to stop referring to access *privileges*. The very word connotes superiority and status—the last things management should imply. Access is a function and a responsibility, not a privilege or a right. Perhaps we can start referring simply to *access functions* or *access authorizations*.

31.3.3   The Indispensable Employee.   For most areas of information processing, redundancy is generally viewed as either a bad thing or an unavoidable but regrettable cost paid for specific advantages. For example, in a database, indexing may require identical fields (items, columns) to be placed in separate files (datasets, tables) for links (views, joins) to be established. However, in managing personnel for better security, redundancy is a requirement. Without shared knowledge, our organization is at constant risk of a breach of availability.

Redundancy in this context means having more than one person who can accomplish a given task. Another way of looking at it is that no knowledge should belong to only one person in an organization.

Unique resources always put our systems at risk; that's why companies such as Tandem, Stratus, and others have so successfully provided redundant and fault-tolerant computer systems for critical task functions such as stock exchanges and banking networks. Such computer systems and networks have twin processors, channels, memory arrays, disk drives, and controllers. Similarly, a fault-tolerant organization will invest in cross-training of all its personnel. Every task should have at least one other person who knows how to do it—even if less well than the primary resource. This principle does not imply that managers have to create clones of all their employees; it is in fact preferable to have several people who can accomplish various parts of any one person's job. Spreading knowledge throughout the organization makes it possible to reduce the damage caused by absence or unavailability of key people.

It is dangerous to allow a single employee to be the only person who knows about a critical function in the enterprise. Operations will suffer if the key person is away, and the enterprise will certainly suffer if this unique resource person decides to behave in unauthorized and harmful ways. Managers should ask themselves if there is anyone in their department whose absence they dread? Are there any critical yet undocumented procedures for which everyone has to ask a particular person?

A client in a data center operations management class volunteered the following story. There was a programming wizard responsible for maintaining a key production program; unfortunately, he had poor communication skills and preferred to solve problems himself rather than to train and involve his colleagues. "It will be faster for me to do it myself," he used to say. During one of his rare vacations, something went wrong with "his" production program, shutting down the company's operations. The wizard was in the north woods, out of reach of all communications; the disaster lasted until he returned.

Not only does the organization suffer, but the indispensable persons suffer from the imbalance of knowledge and skill when no one else knows what they know. Some indispensable employees are dedicated to the welfare of their employer and of their colleagues. They may hesitate to take holidays. If their skills are needed from hour to hour, it becomes more difficult for them to participate in committee meetings. These are the people who wear beepers and cannot sit undisturbed even in a two-hour class. If the indispensable employees' skills affect day-to-day operations, they may find it hard to go to offsite training courses, conferences, and conventions. Despite their suitability for promotion, indispensable people may be delayed in their career change because the organization finds it difficult or expensive to train their replacements. In extreme cases, newly promoted managers may find themselves continuing to perform specialized duties that ought to be done by their staff. Sometimes, even a VP of Operations is the only person who can make changes to a production system that should be performed by a programmer three or four levels down.

A particular kind of indispensability occurs when an employee becomes the *de facto* technical support resource for a particular software package or system. Without authorization from their managers, these employees can find themselves in difficulty. They may be fired by their boss because their productivity drops too low according to their job descriptions, which do not include providing undocumented technical support to other people. They may burn out and quit because of overwork and criticism. Or they may cause resentment among their colleagues and neighbors by declining to help them, or by complaining about overwork and causing a ruckus. Alternatively, they may enjoy the situation, and manage to meet all the demands on their time quite successfully, until others in the information technology department begin to feel threatened, and someone either complains to the higher-ups or begins spreading nasty comments about these unauthorized support technicians.

Looking at this situation from a management point of view, there are problems for the recipients of all this free aid. The longer they can persist in getting apparently free help from their unofficial benefactor, the longer they can avoid letting upper management know they need help with their office automation tools. Then when the bubble bursts and the expert becomes unavailable, managers are confronted with a sudden demand for unplanned resources. In some organizations, unexpected staffing requirements are difficult to satisfy. Managers have a hard time explaining how it is that they were unable to predict the need and budget for it.

Sometimes persons continue to be indispensable because of fear that their value to their employer resides in their private knowledge. Such employees resent training others. The best way to change their counter-productive attitude is to set a good example: managers should share knowledge with them and with others in their group. Education should be a normal part of the way everyone in the enterprise works. Managers can encourage cross-training by allocating time for it. Cross-training can be a factor in employee evaluations. Support discussions of current topics from the trade press and academic journals, for example, in a journal club where people take turns presenting the findings from recent research in areas of interest.

Reluctance to explain their jobs to someone else may also mask unauthorized or illegal activity. Lloyd Benjamin Lewis, assistant operations officer at a large bank, arranged with a confederate outside the bank to cash fraudulent checks for up to $250,000 each on selected legitimate accounts at Lewis's branch. Using a secret code stolen from another branch, Lewis would scrupulously encode a credit for the exact amount of the theft, thus giving the illusion of correcting a transaction error. Lewis stole $21.3 million from his employer between September 1978 and January 1981, when he was caught by accident. For unknown reasons, a computer program flagged one of his fraudulent transactions so that another employee was notified of an irregularity. It did not take long to discover the fraud, and Lewis was convicted of embezzlement. He was sentenced to five years in a federal prison.

Because Lewis was obliged to be physically present to trap the fraudulent checks as they came through the system, he could not afford to have anyone with him watching what he did. Lewis would have been less than enthusiastic about having to train a backup to do his job. If anyone had been cross-trained, the embezzlement would probably not have continued so long, or become so serious.

31.3.4   Vacation Time.

In the example presented above, Lloyd Benjamin Lewis took his unauthorized duties (stealing money from his bank) so seriously that during the entire period of his embezzlement, about 850 days, he was never late, never absent, and never took a single vacation day in over two years. Any data center manager should have been quite alarmed at having an employee who had failed to be absent or late a single day in more than two years. The usual rule in companies is that unused vacation days can be carried over for only a limited time, and then they expire. This is intended to be an incentive to take vacation time; for normal, honest employees it probably works fine. For dishonest employees who have to be present to control a scam, losing vacation days is insignificant.

Every employee should be required to take scheduled vacations within a definite— and short—time limit. No exceptions should be permitted. Excessive resistance to taking vacations should be investigated to find out why the employee insists on being at work all the time.

Unfortunately, this suspicious attitude toward perfect attendance causes problems for the devoted, dedicated, and honest employee. An innocent person can get caught up in a web of suspicion precisely because of exceptional commitment. One may be able to avoid difficulties of this kind by: (1) making the reasons for the policy well known to all employees so no one feels singled out; (2) relying on the judgment, discretion, and good will of the investigating manager to avoid hurt feelings in their most loyal employees; and (3) switching such an employee's functions temporarily to see if anything breaks.

31.3.5   Responding to Changes in Behavior.

Any kind of unusual behavior can pique the curiosity of a manager. Even more important from a security management standpoint, any consistent change in behavior should stimulate interest. Is a normally punctual person suddenly late—day after day? Did an employee start showing up regularly in hand-tailored suits? Why is a usually charming person snarling obscenities at her staff these days? What accounts for someone's suddenly working overtime every day, in the absence of any known special project? Is a competent person now producing obvious errors in simple reports? How is it that a formerly complaisant staffer is now a demanding and bitter complainer?

Any radical change in personality should elicit concern. If the normally relaxed head accountant now has beads of sweat on her forehead whenever you discuss the audit trails, perhaps it's time to look into her work more closely. Why does a good family man begin returning from long lunches with whiskey on his breath? A formerly grim manager now waltzes through the office with a perpetual smile on his face. What happened? Or what is happening?

All of these changes should alert managers to the possibility of changes in the lives of their employees. Although these changes do indeed affect the security of an organization, they also concern managers as human beings who can help other human beings. Mood swings, irritability, depression, euphoria—these can be signs of psychological stress. Is an employee becoming alcoholic? A drug addict? Abused at home? Going through financial difficulties? Having trouble with teenagers? Falling in love with a colleague? Of course managers cannot help everyone, and in some cases help should involve qualified mental health professionals; but at least everyone can express concern and support in a sensitive and gentle way. Such discussions should take place in private and without alarming the subject or exciting other employees. At any time, a manager should feel free to involve the HR or personnel department. They will either have a psychologist or trained counselor on staff or be able to provide appropriate help in some other way, such as an employee crisis line.

There are sad cases in which employees have shown signs of stress but have been ignored, with disastrous consequences: suicides, murders, theft, and sabotage. Be alert to the indicators and take action quickly.

With so much of the enterprise's financial affairs controlled by information systems, it is not surprising that sudden wealth may be a clue that someone is committing a computer crime. A participant in the Information Systems Security Course reported that an accounting clerk at a U.S. government agency in Washington, D.C., was arrested for massive embezzlement. The tip-off? He arrived at work one day in a Porsche sports car and boasted of the expensive real estate he was buying in a wealthy area of the Capital region—all completely beyond any reasonable estimate of his income.

Not all thieves are that stupid. A healthy curiosity is perfectly justified if you see an employee sporting unusually expensive clothes, driving a sleek car after years with a rust-bucket, and chatting pleasantly about the latest trip to Acapulco when that person's salary doesn't appear to explain such expenditures. On the other hand, unsolicited inquiries into people's private lives will usually win no friends. There is a delicate line to walk, but ignoring the issue doesn't make it disappear.

The other kind of change—towards the negative—also may indicate trouble. Why is the system manager looking both dejected and threadbare these days? Is he in the throes of a personal debt crisis? In the grip of a blackmailer? Beset with a family medical emergency? A compulsive gambler on a losing streak? Again, on humane grounds alone one would want to know what's up in order to help; however, a manager concerned with security would have to investigate. In these days of explosive rage and ready access to weapons, ignoring employees with a dark cloud hovering over their heads may be irresponsible and dangerous.

The manager's job in probing behavioral changes is difficult: one must walk the thin and possibly invisible line between laissez-faire uninvolvement, risking lifelong regrets or even prosecution for dereliction of duty, and overt interference in the private affairs of the staff, risking embarrassment and possible prosecution for harassment.

Written policies will help; so will a strong and ongoing working relationship with the HR staff. Making it clear to all employees that managers are available for support, but are also expected to investigate unusual behavior, will also help avoid misunderstandings.

31.3.6   Separation of Duties.   The same principles that apply to the control of money should apply to control of data. Tellers at a bank, when someone deposits a large check, will always go to a supervisor and have that person look the check over and initial the transaction. When bank tellers empty the automatic teller machines at night and fill the cash hoppers, there are always two people present. In most organizations, the person who creates a check is not the person who signs it.

In well-run information systems departments, with good operations security (see Chapter 32), data entry is distinct from validation and verification. For example, a data entry supervisor can check on the accuracy of data entry but cannot enter a new transaction without having a direct supervisor check the work. There is no excuse for allowing the supervisor to enter a transaction and then, effectively, authorize it. What if the entry were in error—or fraudulent? Where would the control be?

In quality assurance for program development (see Chapter 25), the principles of separation of duty are well established. For example, the person who designs or codes a program must not be the only one to test the design or the code. Test systems are separate from production systems; programmers must not have access to confidential and critical data that are controlled by the production staff. Programmers must not enter the computer room if they have no authorized business there; operators must not modify production programs and batch jobs without authorization.

Managers should consider giving up access to functions that have been delegated to two or more subordinates. Maintaining such access could cause more problems than it solves, but in an emergency, access and control could easily be restored. This attitude exemplifies the concept of separation of duties.

In early 1995, the financial world was rocked by the collapse of the Barings PLC investment banking firm. The Singapore office chief, Nicholas Leeson, was accused of having played the futures market with disastrous consequences. The significant point is that he managed to carry out all the orders without independent overview. Had there been effective separation of duties, the collapse would not have occurred.

A related approach is called dual control. As an example of dual control, consider the perennial problem of having secret passwords not known to managers who sometimes need emergency access to those passwords. This problem does not generally apply to ordinary users' passwords, which can normally be reset by a security administrator without having to know the old password. This temporary password should be changed to a truly secret string by the user after a single logon. However, to guard against the absence of the only person who has the root password for a system, possibly because the others are on vacation, it is advisable to store a written copy of the root password in a truly opaque envelope, seal it, sign the seal, tape over the seal with non-removable tape, and then store the envelope in a corporate safe. The principle of dual control dictates that such a copy of the root password should be accessible only if two officers of the organization simultaneously sign for it when taking it out of the corporate safe.

In conclusion, managers should think about the structure of control over information as they design security policies so that separation of duties or dual controls are present throughout all systems.

31.3.7   No Unauthorized Security Probes.   In general, managers—not just security officers—should always be looking for vulnerabilities and opportunities for improving security. However, no one should ever *test* systems for vulnerabilities without the full cooperation of the corporate information protection group and authorization of the right executives. Written approval for explicit tests of security are informally known as "get-out-of-jail cards" because without them, employees can go to jail for unauthorized probes of system security. The case of Randal Schwartz, a consultant to Intel Corporation in Beaverton, Oregon, is a salutary example of the dangers of unauthorized security probes. Mr Schwartz was convicted of three felony counts in July 1995 and was fined $68,000 in restitution as well as being put under five years of probation and having to perform 480 hours of community service (for more information about this case, see *www.lightlink.com/spacenka/fors*).

31.4 TERMINATION OF EMPLOYMENT. Taking our security mandate in the widest sense, we have to protect our employer and ourselves against potential damage from unethical, disgruntled, or incompetent employees and against the legal consequences of improper firing procedures. Common sense and common decency argue for humane and sensitive treatment of people being fired, and those who are resigning.

Firing people is a stressful time for everyone concerned, and it usually leads to increased security risks. Managers should do everything in their power to ensure a courteous, respectful, and supportive experience when terminating employment.

31.4.1 Resignations. Potentially the most dangerous form of employment termination is a resignation. The problem is summed up in the caption of a cartoon. A savage attack is in progress against a medieval town that is in flames; a clan war chieftain confronts a singed and dirty warrior. "No, no, Thor! Pillage, THEN burn!" Like the war chieftain, employees rarely resign without planning. An employee may have an indefinite period during which the action is imminent, while the employer may remain unaware of the situation. If the employee has bad feelings toward, or evil designs on, the current employer, there is a period of vulnerability unknown to management. Dishonest or unbalanced employees could steal information or equipment, cause immediate or delayed damage using programmatic techniques, or introduce faulty data into the system.

The policies discussed in previous sections of this chapter should reduce the risks associated with resignations. The manager's goal should be to make resignations rare and reasonable. By staying in touch with employees' feelings, moods, and morale, managers can identify sources of strain and perhaps resolve problems before they lead to resignations and their associated security risks.

31.4.2 Firings. Firings appear to give the advantage to employers, but there may be complications.

31.4.2.1 Timing. One advantage is that the time of notification to a fired employee can be controlled to minimize effects on the organization and its business. For example, employers might find it best to fire an incompetent, or no longer acceptable, employee before beginning an important new project, or after a particular project has finished.

Some people argue that to reduce the psychological impact on other employees, they should fire people at the end of the day, perhaps even before a long weekend. The theory is that the practice gives everyone a cooling-off period outside working hours. These managers say they don't want the buzz of conversation and speculation that often follow a firing to intrude on the work day. This policy fails to regard the psychological stress to employees who have a ruined weekend, and no way of responding constructively to their potentially catastrophic loss of a regular income.

A better approach to this stressful task is to fire people early on Monday morning in order to provide an unrushed exit interview and, if appropriate, job counseling to help the employee prepare for job hunting. In this scenario, the regrettable necessity (from the manager's point of view) of terminating employment is buffered by professionals in the HR department who can give the departing employee a sense of hope and some practical as well as emotional support in their difficult time. This humane attitude is particularly important during downsizing, or when plants are closed, and many people are being fired—one of the worst experiences possible for both employees and managers and an event that has serious security implications.

In one large company, the personnel department asked their information security staff to suspend the access codes for more than 100 people who were to be fired at 18:00 on Tuesday. On Wednesday at 08:00, the security staff began receiving phone calls asking why the callers' logon IDs no longer worked. It turned out that the personnel staff had failed to inform the terminated employees on time. The psychological trauma to both the employees who were fired and to the security staff was severe. Several security staff members were sent home in tears to recuperate from their unfortunate experience. The harm done to the fired employees was even more serious, and the effect on morale of the remaining employees was a disaster. There could well have been violence in that situation.

31.4.2.2   *Procedures upon Termination.*   In both resignations and firings, security consultants unanimously advise instant action. Not for them the leisurely grace period during which employees wind down their projects, or hand them off to other staff members. Security officers are a hard lot, and they usually advise the following scenario: in a formal exit interview, and in the presence of at least two managers, an officer of the employer informs the employee politely that his or her employment is at an end. During the exit interview, the officer explains the reasons for termination of employment. The officer gives the employee a check for the period of notification required by law or by contract plus any severance pay due. Under supervision, preferably in the presence of at least one security guard, the employee is escorted to the accustomed work area and invited to remove all personal belongings and place them in a container provided by the employer. The employee returns all company badges, IDs, business cards, credit cards, and keys, and is then ushered politely outside the building.

At the same time all this is happening, all security arrangements must be changed to exclude the ex-employee from access to the building and to all information systems. Such restrictions can include:

- Striking the person's name from all security post lists of authorized access
- Explicitly informing guards that the ex-employee may not be allowed into the building, whether unaccompanied or accompanied by an employee, without special authorization by named authorities
- Changing the combinations, reprogramming access card systems, and replacing physical keys if necessary for all secure areas to which the individual used to have authorized access
- Removing or changing all personal access codes known to have been used by the ex-employee on all secured computer systems, including microcomputers, networks, and mainframes
- Informing all outside agencies (e.g., tape storage facilities and outsourced functions) that the ex-employee is no longer authorized to access any of the employer's information or to initiate security or disaster recovery procedures
- Requesting cooperation from outside agencies in informing the employer if ex-employees attempt to exercise unauthorized functions on behalf of their former employer

The task is made more difficult by seniority, or if the ex-employee played an important role in disaster recovery or security. The employer should be assiduous in searching out all possible avenues of entry resulting from the person's position of responsibility and familiarity with security procedures.

In one story circulating in the security community, an employee was fired without the safeguards suggested above. He returned to the workplace the next Saturday with his station wagon and greeted the security guard with the usual friendliness and confidence. The guard, who had known him for years, was unaware that the man had been fired. The ex-employee still had access codes and copies of keys to secure areas. He entered the unattended computer room, destroyed all the files on the system, and then opened the tape vault. He engaged the guard's help in loading all the company's backup tapes into his station wagon. The thief even complained about how he had to work on weekends. This criminal then tried to extort money from the company by threatening to destroy the backup tapes, but he was found by police and arrested in time to prevent a disaster for his ex-employer.

This story emphasizes the importance of promptly reaching *everyone* who needs to know that an employee no longer works for the enterprise.

31.4.2.3 Support in Involuntary Terminations.

Security does sometimes prevent a farewell party, one obvious sign of friendliness. The problem with a farewell party is that there may be litigation if employees leaving under a cloud feel humiliated when other people get a party but they don't. Generally it makes sense to treat all departing employees the same, even if the termination is involuntary.

However, nothing stops a humane and sensitive employer from encouraging employees to arrange an after-hours party even for people who have been fired. On the other hand, if a resignation is on good terms, the employer may even arrange a celebration, possibly during working hours and maybe even at company cost.

A firing or a resignation on poor terms has two psychological dangers: effects on the individual concerned of embarrassment, shame, and anger, and effects on the remaining staff of rumors, resentment, and fear. Both kinds of problems can be minimized by publishing termination procedures in organization documents provided to all employees; requiring all employees to sign a statement confirming that they have read and agreed to the termination procedures; and consistent application of the termination procedures.

The personal shock of being fired can be reduced by politeness and consideration consistent with the nature of the reasons for being fired, although even nasty people should not be subject to verbal or physical abuse no matter how bad their behavior. Their treatment should be consistent with that meted out to other fired employees, and there should be generous severance arrangements, if possible.

Organizational turmoil can be reduced by convening organization-wide or departmental meetings to brief remaining employees on the details of significant termination. Open discussions, including how people feel about the rupture of relationships, can be helpful. The remaining employees may have to suffer grief, as a process, not a state. Grief is a normal and healthy response to disruption of relationships (e.g., death of a loved one, divorce, and even the loss of a co-worker). Some people value social relationships more than other aspects of their work and may be especially affected by firings. Grief involves stages of denial, anger, mourning, and recovery. Trying to forestall such responses by denying that people legitimately have feelings is foolish and counter-productive. It is far better to encourage those who are upset to voice their feelings, and to engage in constructive discussion, than to clamp down pointlessly in a futile attempt to suppress discussion.

31.4.2.4 Style of Termination.

The way an organization handles job termination affects more than internal relations. It also influences its image in the outside world. Prospective employees will think twice about accepting job offers from an organization that maltreats departing employees. Clients may form a negative impression of a company's stability if it abuses its own people. Investors also may look askance at a firm that gets a reputation for shoddy treatment of employees. Bad employee management relations are a warning sign of long-term difficulties.

31.4.2.5   Legal Issues.   There is another dimension to employment termination that depends on local laws and the litigation environment. The United States, for example, is said to be one of the most litigious nations on the planet, perhaps because of the high number of lawyers compared with the total population.

The following is not legal advice; for legal advice, consult an attorney. However, simple experience does teach some principles, even without going to law school. Here are some pragmatic guidelines for preventing legal problems related to firings for cause:

- Build a solid, documented case for firing someone before acting. Keep good records, be objective, and get the opinions of several trustworthy people on record.
- Offer the delinquent employee all reasonable chances to correct his or her behavior.
- Give the employee clear feedback long before considering firing.

Timing is important in employee relations, as it is in almost everything else we do. In particular, if an employee is found to be behaving improperly or illegally, there must be no marked delay in dealing with the problem. Such persons could sue the employer and individual managers. They could argue in court that the very fact that there was a delay in firing them was proof that the firing was due to other factors such as personality conflicts, racism, or sexism. A well-defined procedure for progressing through the decision will minimize such problems.

The critical legal issue is consistency. If rules such as those described above for the day of the firing are applied haphazardly, there could easily be grounds for complaining of unfairness. Those to whom the rules were strictly applied would justifiably feel implicitly criticized. How would we feel if we were singled out by having guards check what we took home from our desk—if others got a party and two weeks' notice? Such inconsistency would be grounds for legal proceedings for defamation of character. The company might lose and it might win, but what nonlawyer wants to spend time in court?

Another issue that arises in connection with firings and resignations is nondisclosure agreements. All such agreements must be included in a contract signed before the prospective employee begins work; it is almost impossible to force an existing employee to sign such an agreement.

Managers, the legal department, and the personnel department should study the necessity and feasibility of instituting a legally binding contractual obligation to protect their company's confidential information for a specified period of time after leaving. One cannot impose indefinite gags on people, but one year seems to be normal. For this measure to be meaningful, the initial employment contract should stipulate that departing employees must reveal their new employer, if there is one at that time.

Noncompetition agreements require the employee to refrain from working for direct competitors for perhaps a year after termination of employment. The key to a successful clause here is that there be a strict, operational definition of "direct competitors." Because this limitation can be an onerous impediment to earning a living, many jurisdictions will forbid such clauses.

31.5 SUMMARY. In summary, information security depends on coordination with HR personnel to ensure consistent policies for hiring, ongoing management, and termination of employment.

Some of the key recommendations from this chapter are as follows:

Hiring

- Investigate the accuracy of every likely job candidate's résumé.
- Perform background investigations when hiring for sensitive positions.
- Arrange for experienced staff members to interview candidates and discuss inconsistencies.
- Require signing of a legally appropriate employment contract.

Ongoing Management

- Identify and resolve opportunities for abuse.
- Assign access functions on the basis of need, not social status.
- Identify indispensable employees and arrange for cross-training of other staff.
- Require employees to take their vacations, or rotate their job functions periodically, as a test of smooth operations.
- Note and respond to sudden changes in behavior and mood; involve human resources as appropriate.
- Enforce separation of duties and dual control for sensitive functions.
- Do not engage in or tolerate unauthorized probes of system security by employees.

Termination of Employment

- Provide an opportunity for fired employees to receive counseling and support.
- Ensure that the HR department collaborates with the information technology group to take all appropriate security measures when anyone leaves the employment of the enterprise.
- Ensure that firings do not cause long-term morale problems.
- Follow the guidance of corporate counsel to avoid wrongful dismissal suits.
- Use legally appropriate nondisclosure and noncompetition clauses in employment contracts.

31.6 FURTHER READING

Bologna, J. *Handbook on Corporate Fraud: Prevention, Detection, Investigation.* Boston: Butterworth-Heinemann, 1993.

BSI. *IT Baseline Protection Manual: Recommended Measures to Meet Medium-Level Protection Requirements.* Prepared by the Bundesamt für Sicherheit in der Informationstechnik of the German Federal Government, 1997. English version available at *www.bsi.bund.de/ gshb/english/menue.htm.* Section 3.2: Personnel, *www.bsi.bund.de/gshb/english/b/32.htm.*

Mathis, R.L. and J.H. Jackson. *Human Resources Management.* 9th ed. Cincinnati: South-Western Publishing, 1999.

McNamara, C. Human Resources Management links, 1999. *www.mapnp.org/library/hr_mgmnt/ hr_mgmnt.htm.*

National Academy of Public Administration: Center for Human Resources Management, *www.hrm.napawash.org/.*

Nottingham Business School. Organisation and Management Theory links from the Department of Human Resource Management, *www.nbs.ntu.ac.uk/depts/hrm/list/hromt.htm.*

Society for Human Resource Management (SHRM). White Papers, *www.shrm.org/whitepapers/default.asp?page=wplist.htm.*

CHAPTER **32**

OPERATIONS SECURITY AND PRODUCTION CONTROLS

Myles E. Walsh and M.E. Kabay

CONTENTS

32.1 INTRODUCTION. Despite the enormous increase in individual computing on personal computers and workstations in the years since the first edition of this *Handbook* was published in 1975, many mainframe computers and their networks are still used for enterprise computing in applications devoted to the core business of the enterprise. This chapter focuses on how to run vital computers and networks safely and effectively.

32.1.1   What Are Production Systems?   A *production system* is one upon which an enterprise depends for critically important functions. Examples include systems for handling accounts receivable, accounts payable, payroll, inventory, manufacturing systems, real-time process control, data entry systems, Web-based client interfaces for e-commerce, clinical information systems, and management information systems.

32.1.2   What Are Operations?   *Operations* consist of the requirements for control, maintenance, and support of production systems. Operations staff are responsible for such functions as:

- Integrating new software systems into an existing configuration
- Running programs and batch jobs to update databases and create reports
- Installing new versions of production programs
- Maintaining production databases for maximal efficiency
- Managing backups (creation, labeling, storage, and disposal)
- Responding to emergencies and recovering functionality
- Mounting storage volumes of tapes, cartridges, or disks in response to user or program requests
- Handling special forms for particular printouts (e.g., check blanks)
- Managing all aspects of production networks, such as configuring routers, bridges, gateways, and firewalls

32.1.3   What Are Computer Programs?   A computer program is a set of instructions that tells a computer what to do to perform a task. Computer programs may be acquired, or they may be internally developed. Internally developed programs are stored in computer systems in two basic forms. Source programs are in the form in which they were written (coded) by computer programmers. The statements in source programs are in languages such as COBOL, Visual BASIC, C++, or Java. Source language programs are kept in files and stored in disk storage folders called source libraries or program libraries. Executable programs have been converted from source code, by compilation, into a program that the computer can execute. Executable programs may be maintained in two separate forms: object and load. An object program is a partially executable module that must be linked to other executable modules, such as input/output modules, to become a load module. As load modules, the programs are said to be in executable form. Executable programs are kept in production libraries, from which they are called when needed. Acquired programs are generally in object and load form. The source code is proprietary to the organization that developed it and is rarely given to the acquiring enterprise.

When internally developed programs have to be changed, programmers work with copies of the source programs. The copies are stored in another type of library, referred to as programmer libraries. The programmers make changes to the copy of the source programs and go through a process of recompiling and testing until the modified program is working properly. When acquired programs require changes, often a contract to make the modifications is issued to the organization from which the programs were acquired. In some situations, internal programmers generate new programs and interfaces to the original acquired programs. The same libraries are used: source libraries for source code, production libraries for executable modules, and programmer libraries for work in progress. These libraries need to be protected. Loss or damage can entail huge costs and considerable inconvenience; recovering them can require a long time, and great expense.

32.1.4 What Are Procedures?

Procedures are sets of statements that tell a computer what to do in certain situations. They are unlike programs in that they are not compiled. Stored in files or databases, they are invoked as needed. Procedural statements are made up of operational commands and parameters. The operational commands tell the computer what to do, and the parameters tell the computer which entity to act upon. Job Control Language (JCL) is an example of a procedural language. Procedural language statements often are used in database management systems and in security software products.

32.1.5 What Are Data Files?

Everything stored and maintained in a computer system takes the form of a file. Programs, procedures, information, all are stored in files, using the concept of a file in its broadest sense; that is, a collection of related items. This has become most apparent with the ubiquitous personal computer (PC). Data files, as distinguished from program files and other types, are those that store information. In a PC environment, data files may be called documents. Documents are created by word processors, spreadsheet programs, graphics generators, and other application programs. In mainframe and midsize computer environments, data files are those created and maintained by applications such as payroll, accounting, inventory, order entry, and sales.

Some data files are transient; that is, they are created, used, and deleted within a short period of time. If lost or damaged, they can be reconstructed quickly, with little difficulty. There is usually no need to protect transient files. Other files, such as master files or organizational databases (groups of files that are linked to one another), contain information that is vital, confidential, or virtually irreplaceable. These files, generated by PCs, mainframe, and midsize computer systems, must be protected by security software and backup procedures, to ensure against loss, destruction, theft, and unauthorized disclosure.

32.2 OPERATIONS MANAGEMENT

32.2.1 Separation of Duties.

Separation of duties is a key control that should be applied to development and modification of programs. In enterprises where there are systems and programming departments that create and maintain custom programs, each individual programmer is assigned a user ID and a password. In these enterprises, where programs are developed and maintained internally, changes are constantly made to programs in order to meet changing business requirements. Modified executable programs, after recompilation and testing by programmers, are moved from their libraries into production libraries. Modified source programs are moved into source libraries. The programmers are responsible for keeping the source libraries current, while computer operations, or some other functional group separated from programming, may be responsible for maintaining the production libraries. When an updated executable program is transferred from the programmer's library to the production library, a transmittal is included, signed off by a manager in the programming department.

A particular consequence of the separation of duties is that a member of the operations staff should always be involved in the functional analysis and requirements definition phases for changes to production programs. The operations perspective is not always clear to programmers, and such issues as logging, backout, and recovery, as discussed later in this chapter, need to be brought to their attention early in the development and maintenance cycles.

32.2.2   Security Officer or Security Administrator.   Contemporary enterprises typically include a mix of mainframes, midsize computers, and local area networks (LANs) comprised of hundreds or thousands of workstations, PCs, terminals, and other devices, all interconnected with one another and with the same mix in other enterprises throughout the world via the Internet. A department or an individual in smaller enterprises has the responsibility for providing and maintaining the security of files, databases and programs. The title that is often associated with this function is security officer. This individual or department has the mandate to carry out the security policy as set down by the senior management of the enterprise. The security officer is empowered to allow or to disallow access to files, databases, and programs. In the language of the security officer, procedures are set up and maintained that establish relationships among individuals, programs, and files. Users, programmers, and technicians are granted privileges for full access, update only, or even read only. The security officer has the power to change or to revoke privileges.

32.2.3   Limit Access to Operations Center.   Physical access to the operations center grants a person enormous power to disrupt production systems. Such access must be tightly controlled.

32.2.3.1   Need, Not Status, Determines Access.   A fundamental principle for effective security is that access to restricted areas is granted on the basis of roles. Employees whose roles do not justify access should be excluded from autonomous access to production systems. In particular, high-placed executives such as the president, chief executive officer, chief financial officer, chief operating officer, chief technical officer, and all vice-presidents should examine their own roles and determine if they should be able to enter the operations center unaccompanied; in most cases, such access is unjustified. Limiting their own access sets an important model for other aspects of security policy and demonstrates that need, not social status or position within the corporate hierarchy, determines access to restricted areas. Chapter 35 explains this issue in more detail.

32.2.3.2   Basic Methods of Access Control.   As explained in Chapter 16, access control depends on identification and authentication (I&A). I&A can be based on:

- What one has (tokens such as physical keys or smart cards)
- What one knows (user IDs and passwords or passphrases)
- What one is (static biometric attributes such as fingerprints, iris patterns, retinal patterns, and facial features)
- What one does (dynamic biometrics such as voice patterns, typing patterns, and signature dynamics)

For more information on physical security issues, see Chapters 14 and 15.

A typical arrangement for secure access to an operations center may involve keypads for entry of a particular code or card readers programmed to admit the holders of specific magnetic-stripe or smart card. If the operations center is a 24-hour operation with full-time staffing, the presence of operators provides an additional layer of security to preclude unauthorized access. Remote monitoring of sensitive areas increases security by discouraging unauthorized access or unauthorized behavior and speeds up the response to possible sabotage

32.2.3.3   Log In and Badge Visitors.

Visitors to a facility that houses sensitive systems should be logged in at a controlled entrance and provided with a visitor badge. In high-security applications, an additional log-in may be required when entering the operations center itself. To encourage return of visitor badges, some security policies require the visitor to deposit a valuable document, such as a driver's license, with the security guards at the main entrance. The effectiveness of visitor badges depends entirely on the use of badges by all personnel at all times; if *not* wearing a badge is acceptable and common, a malicious visitor could simply hide a visitor badge to pass as an authorized employee.

The time of login and of logout can be valuable forensic evidence if malfeasance is detected. However, such records can be shown to be reliable only if the guards responsible for keeping the logs consistently verify the completeness and correctness of all information written into the logs.

32.2.3.4   Accompany Visitors.

No unaccompanied visitors should be permitted to circulate in the operations center or in the facility housing such a center. In high-security facilities, someone must even accompany the visitor to the washroom and wait for the visitor outside the door.

If a consultant or temporary employee is to work on a project for longer than a day, it may be acceptable to grant that person a restricted pass for low-security areas; however, high-security areas, such as the operations center, would still require such a person to be accompanied.

32.2.4   Change-Control Procedures from the Operations Perspective.

When programmers have made changes to production programs and all documentation and testing procedures are complete, the new versions are formally turned over to the operations staff for integration into production.

32.2.4.1   Moving New Versions of Software into Production.

Operations staff must keep in mind the following requirements when moving new versions of software into production:

- *Identification*—tracking which software is in use
- *Authorization*—controlling changes
- *Scheduling*—minimizing disruptions to production
- *Backups*—ensuring that all requisite information is available to restore a prior state
- *Logging*—keeping track of data input for recovery and of errors for diagnosis of problems
- *Backout*—returning to a prior production version in case of catastrophic errors

32.2.4.1.1   Identification.   Knowing precisely which versions of all production software are in use is the basis of production controls. Every module must have a unique identification that allows immediate tracking between executable code and source code; all changes to a particular module must be fully documented by the programming group. Unique identifiers allow the quality assurance process to ensure that the only modules that go into production are those that have been properly tested.

Most production shops use a three-level numbering scheme to track versions. Typically, version *a.b.c* (e.g., 7.13.201) is defined as follows:

c changes every time anything at all—even a spelling mistake—is changed.

b changes when program managers decide to group a number of fixes to errors into a new version for release to production.

a changes when significant new functions are added; often the source code is completely renumbered if the changes are great enough.

The version number of object code must match the number of its source code. All object code should include internal documentation of its version number so that the version can be ascertained instantly, without having to consult possibly inaccurate external documentation.

32.2.4.1.2 Authorization.   Strict procedures must be in place to preclude rogue programmers from introducing modified code into the production suite. In addition to the dangers of introducing untested or undocumented changes, allowing any individual to modify production processes without verification and authorization by an appropriate chain of responsibility can allow hostile code, such as Trojan horses and back doors, to be introduced into the systems. Chapter 25 reviews software development security in detail.

32.2.4.1.3 Scheduling.   Implementing any new version of a production system requires careful planning and scheduling. Operations staff must prepare for changes in all aspects of production that depend on the system in question; for example, there may be requirements for new printer forms, additional magnetic tapes, and other supplies that must be ordered in advance. New requests for operator intervention, or changes in status and error messages during production, necessitate appropriate documentation and training. Effects on other programs may require special preparations that must take into account the scheduling requirements of the other systems that are affected. In addition, new versions of software often are implemented immediately after major production jobs, such as end-of-year or quarterly processing, to maintain consistency within an accounting period. For all these reasons, scheduling is critically important for trouble-free operations.

32.2.4.1.4 Backups.   When modifying production systems, operations staff usually make one or more complete backups of the software and data to be modified. This procedure is essential to allow complete restoration of the previous working environment should there be catastrophic failure of the new software and data structures. Chapter 41 discusses backup methodology.

32.2.4.1.5 Logging.   To allow recovery or backout without losing the new data and changes to existing data that may have been carried out using new software and data structures, all production programs should include a logging facility. Logging keeps a journal of all information required to track changes in data and to regenerate a valid version of the data by applying all changes to an initial starting condition.

Logging requires synchronization with backups to avoid data loss or data corruption. Special requirements may exist when a new version of the production system involves changes to data structures; in such cases, applying the information about changes to the older data structures may require special-purpose application programs. Since programmers sometimes forget about such possibilities, operations staff should be prepared to remind the programming staff about such requirements during the design phases for all changes. Chapters 38 and 39 discuss logging in detail.

32.2.4.1.6   Backout and Recovery.   Sometimes a new version of production software is unacceptable and must be removed from the production environment. This decision may be made immediately, or it may occur after a significant amount of data entry and data manipulation has taken place. In either case, operations should be able to return to the previous version of a production system without data loss. This process involves restoring the earlier complete operating environment, with software and data in synchrony, and then using log files to repeat the data input and data modifications to the extent possible.

Not all of the changes that were made using a new version will necessarily be applicable to the previous data; for example, if new fields were added to a database, the data stored in those fields would not be usable for an older, simpler data structure. Similarly, if fields were removed in the newer database, recovery will involve providing values for those fields in the older database. All of these functions must be available in the recovery programs that should accompany any version change in production systems.

32.2.4.2   Using Digital Signatures to Validate Production Programs.   If an unauthorized intruder or a disgruntled employee were discovered to have gained access to the production libraries, it would be necessary to determine if there had been unauthorized modifications to the production programs.

Date and time stamps on programs can record the timing of changes, but many operating environments allow such information to be modified using system utilities that read and write directly to disk without passing through normal system calls and thereby not creating a time stamp or log entry.

One approach that has been used successfully is to apply checksums to all production components. Checksum software applies computations to programs as if the codes were simply data; the results can be sensitive to changes as small as in a single bit. However, if the checksums are computed the same way for all programs, access to the checksum utility could allow a malefactor to change a module and then run the checksum utility to create the appropriate new checksum, thus concealing the evidence of change. To make such subterfuge harder, the checksums can be stored in a database. Naturally, this database of checksums itself must be protected against unauthorized changes. Storing checksums may make unauthorized changes more difficult to disguise, but it also extends the chain of vulnerabilities.

A better way of determining whether object code or source code has been modified is to use digital signatures. Digital signatures are similar to checksums, but they require input of a *private key* that can, and must, be protected against disclosure. Verifying the digital signature may be done using a corresponding *public key* that can be made available without compromising the secrecy of the private key.

When digital signatures are used to authenticate code, it may be possible to validate production systems routinely, provided that the process is not too arduous to be accomplished as part of the normal production process. For example, it should be possible to validate all digital signatures in a few minutes before allowing the daily production cycle to start.

32.2.5   Using Externally Supplied Software.   Production often uses software from outside the organization; such software may be commercial off-the-shelf (COTS) programs or it may consist of programs modified for, or written especially for, the organization by a software supplier. In any case, external software poses special problems of trust for the production team. There have been documented cases in which production versions of software from reputable software houses have contained viruses or Easter eggs (undocumented features, such as the well-known Flight Simulator in MS-Excel versions, which pops up a graphic landscape that includes a monitor showing the names of the Excel development team). In addition, some consultants have publicly admitted that they deliberately include Trojan horse code (undocumented malicious programming) that allows them to damage data or inactivate the programs they have installed at client sites if their fees are not paid.

In large data centers, it may be possible to run quality assurance procedures on externally supplied code. Such tests should include coverage monitoring, in which a test suite exercises all the compiled code corresponding to every line of source code. However, it is rare that an operations group has the resources necessary for such testing.

The trustworthiness of proprietary external software written or adapted especially for a client ultimately may depend on the legal contracts between supplier and user. Such legal constraints may not prevent a disgruntled or dishonest employee in the supplier organization from including harmful code, but at least it may offer a basis for compensation should there be trouble.

32.2.5.1   Verify Digital Signatures on Source Code if Possible.   If externally supplied code is provided with its source library as well as with compiled modules, operations should try to have the supplier provide digital signatures for all such programs. Digital signatures will permit authentication of the code's origins and may make it harder for malefactors to supply modified code to the user. In addition, the digital signatures can support nonrepudiation of the code (i.e., the supplier will be unable credibly to claim that it did not supply the code) and therefore be useful in legal action if necessary.

32.2.5.2   Compile from Source when Possible.   Wherever possible, it is highly desirable to be able to compile executables from source code on the target machine. Compiling from source allows quality assurance processes to check the source for undocumented features that might be security violations and to couple the executables tightly to the verified source. In addition, compiling on the local system ensures that all system routines that must be linked into executables originate in the current version of the operating system.

Operations staff should express this preference for source code clearly to the person or group controlling acquisition of external software.

32.2.6   Quality Control versus Quality Assurance.   Throughout this chapter, quality assurance has been mentioned as an essential underpinning for operations security. *Quality assurance* refers to the processes designed to ensure and to verify the validity of production programs. However, another aspect of quality concerns the operations group: the quality of output. The process of verifying and ensuring the quality of output is known as *quality control.*

32.2.6.1   Service-Level Agreements.   Unlike mathematical truth, there is no absolute standard of quality for computing operations. Every organization must define the level of quality that is suitable for a particular application. A commonly quoted principle in programming and operations is that there is a complex relationship among quality, cost, and development time: increasing quality increases both cost and development time; shortening development time increases cost, if quality is to be maintained. It follows that every system should include a definition of acceptable performance; such definitions are known as *service-level agreements* (SLAs).

SLAs typically include minimum and maximum limits for performance, resource utilization, and output quality. The limits should be expressed in statistical terms; for example, "The response time measured as the time between pressing ENTER and seeing the completed response appear on screen shall be less than three seconds in 95 percent of all transactions and shall not exceed four seconds at any time." SLAs may define different standards for different types of transactions if the business needs of the users so dictate.

32.2.6.2   Monitoring Performance.   Computer-system performance depends on four elements:

1. Access time and speed of the central processing unit(s) (CPU)
2. Access time and speed of mass storage (disks)
3. Access time and speed of fast memory (RAM)
4. Application design

In addition, network performance depends on communications-channel bandwidth and traffic.

Operations groups should monitor performance to ensure that the requirements of the SLAs are met. There are two approaches to such monitoring: (1) analysis of log files and (2) real-time data capture and analysis.

Log files that are designed with performance analysis in mind can capture the precise times of any events of interest; for example, one might have a record in the log file to show when a particular user initiated a read request for specific data and another record to show when the data were displayed on the user's screen. Such level of detail is invaluable for performance analysis because the data permit analysts to look at any kind of transaction and compute statistics about the distribution of response times. In turn, these data may be used for trend analysis that sometimes can highlight problems in program or data structure, design, or maintenance. For example, an excessively long lookup time in a data table may indicate that the system is using serial data access because it had been designed without an appropriate index that would permit rapid random access to the needed records.

Another approach to performance monitoring and analysis is to use real-time monitors that can alert operations staff to abnormal performance. For example, an application program may be designed to calculate response times on the fly; the results may be displayed numerically or graphically on a *dashboard,* for the operations staff. Values falling below a specified parameter may signal an abnormal condition, using color or sound to alert the operators to the drop in performance. Such *integrated performance metrics* allow the fastest possible response to performance problems.

Even if the application programs lack integrated performance metrics, it is sometimes possible to use system-level online performance tools to analyze system activity. In one instance, for example, a software supplier had promised a response time of 10 seconds or less for all transactions, but one particular operation was taking 43 minutes. Using the online performance tool, it quickly became obvious that the transaction in question was generating an enormous amount of disk I/O (read and write operations). Investigation revealed that the program design was forcing 80,000 random reads in a particular dataset to locate a few target records. Installing and using an appropriate index and compacting the dataset to provide rapid access to blocks of related records reduced response time to six seconds.

32.2.6.3   *Monitoring Resources.* Consistent monitoring of resource utilization is one of the most valuable roles of the operations staff. Data center operations should include regular analysis of system log files to track changes in the number of files, amount of disk free space available, number of CPU cycles consumed, number of virtual-memory swap operations, and less esoteric resource demands such as numbers of lines or pages printed, number of tape mounts requested, number of backup tapes in use, and so on. These data should be graphed and subjected to trend analysis to project when particular resources will be saturated if the trend continues. Operations can then reduce demand either by improving aspects of production (e.g., optimizing programs to require fewer resources) or by increasing available resources (e.g., installing a memory upgrade).

Another level of analysis focuses on specific users and groups of users. Each functional group using the production systems should be analyzed separately to see if there are discontinuities in their trends of resource utilization. For example, a specific department might show a relatively slow and stable rise in CPU cycles consumed per month—until the rate of increase suddenly increases tenfold. If such a rate of increase were to continue, it could surpass all the rest of the system demands combined; operations therefore would investigate the situation before it caused problems. The cause of the discontinuity might be a programming error; for example, there might be a logical loop in one of the programs or a repeated computation that ought to have its result stored for reuse. On the other hand, the change in slope in CPU utilization might be due to introduction of new programs with a rapidly growing database; in such cases, operations would have to act to meet heavy new demands.

Disk space is often a key resource that can cause problems. If users fail to clean up unwanted files, disk space can disappear at an astounding rate. This problem is exacerbated by poor programming practices that allow temporary work files to remain permanently in place. Systems have been designed with tens of thousands of sequentially numbered "temporary" work files that had no function whatsoever after a production run was completed but that were accumulated over several years.

One of the methods widely used to reduce resource waste is *chargeback*. Using system and application log files, system administration charges the users of particular systems a fee based on their use of various resources. Although sometimes these chargebacks are viewed as "funny money" because they are an accounting fiction, requiring managers to budget carefully for computing resources can greatly improve attention to mundane housekeeping matters such as cleaning up useless files; if the chargeback system extends to aspects of program performance such as number of disk I/Os, it can even influence programmers to optimize their design and their code.

32.2.6.4   *Monitoring Output Quality.* The final component of quality control is the meticulous monitoring of everything that is produced in the data center and sent to users or clients. Although much printing is now performed on local printers controlled by users, in many situations the operations group is responsible for documents such as invoices and account status reports. Every operations group must explicitly assign responsibility for verifying the quality of such output before it leaves the data center. Operators should keep careful logs that record various types of error (e.g., torn paper, misaligned forms, or poor print quality) so that management can identify areas requiring explicit attention to improve quality.

32.3 PROVIDING A TRUSTED OPERATING SYSTEM. The operating system (OS) is usually the single biggest and most important example of externally supplied software in a data center. Because the OS affects everything that is done in production, it is essential to know that the software is trustworthy. To this effect, operations staff use procedures to ensure that *known-good* software is always available to reinstall on the system.

32.3.1 Creating Known-Good Boot Medium. The simple principle that underlies known-good operating software is that there shall be an unbroken chain of copies of the OS that have never run any other software. That is, operations will create a boot medium (tape, cartridge, CD-ROM) immediately after installing known-good software.

For example, if boot-medium V1B0 is defined as version 1 of the OS as it is delivered from the manufacturer, its installation would require specific settings and parameters for the particular configuration of the system. Immediately after installing V1B0, but before running any other software, operations would create medium V1B1 and set it aside for later use if V1B0 had to be replaced.

32.3.2 Installing a New Version of the Operating System. Continuing this example of how to maintain known-good operating software, it might become necessary to install a new version of the operating system—say, version 2 on medium V2B0. Before using V2B0, operations would reinstall the current known-good OS, say from V1B1. Only then would V2B0 be installed, and the new boot medium V2B1 would be created immediately.

32.3.3 Patching the Operating System. Often, when it is necessary to modify a small part of the OS, rather than installing a whole new version, manufacturers ask users to *patch* the OS. The patch programs modify the compiled code in place. If checksums or digital signatures are in use to maintain OS integrity, these codes will have to be regenerated after the patch is applied. However, to maintain a known-good status, applying a patch should follow a rigid sequence:

1. Load the current known-good software from the appropriate medium (e.g., V2B1).
2. Install the patch.
3. Immediately create a known-good boot medium before running any other software (in our example, this medium would be V2B2).

32.4 PROTECTION OF DATA

32.4.1 Access to Production Programs and Control Data. Just as the operations center needs restricted access, so do production programs and data. From a functional point of view, there are three categories of people who might be allowed access to programs and data on which the enterprise depends: users, programmers, and operations staff.

32.4.1.1   Users.   The only people who should have read and write access to production *data* are those users assigned to the particular systems who have been granted specific access privileges. For example, normally only the human resources staff would have access to personnel records; only the finance department staff would have full access to all accounts payable and accounts receivable records. Managers and other executive users would have access to particular subsets of data, such as productivity records or budget figures. Of course, *no* user should ever have write access to production *programs*.

32.4.1.2   Programming Staff.   Programmers create and maintain production programs; they naturally have to be able to access the versions of those programs on which they currently are working. However, programmers must not be able to modify the programs currently used in *production*. All changes to production programs must be documented, tested, and integrated into the production environment with the supervision of quality assurance, operations, and security personnel.

Programmers need to be able to use realistic data in their development, maintenance, and testing functions; however, programmers should *not* have privileged access to restricted data. For example, programmers should not be allowed to read confidential files from personnel records or to modify production data in the accounts payable system. Programmers can use extracts from the production databases, but sometimes particular fields may have to be randomized to prevent breaches of confidentiality. Programmers generally resent such constraints, but usually an effective process of education can convince them that such barriers between production systems and systems under development are a wise policy.

32.4.1.3   Operations Staff.   Much as the programmers are responsible for developing and maintaining systems, so the operations staff are responsible for using and controlling these systems. Operations staff perform tasks such as scheduling, error handling, quality control, backups, recovery, and version management. However, operations staff should not be able to modify production programs or to access sensitive data in production databases.

32.4.2   Separating Production, Development, and Test Data.   For obvious reasons, testing with production data and production programs is an unacceptable practice, except in emergency situations. Therefore, programmers who develop new programs or modify existing programs must perform tests using their own libraries. These are frequently referred to as test libraries. Experienced programmers keep copies of the source programs for which they are responsible as well as copies of some of the files that are used by the programs and subsets of others in their own test libraries. To avoid security violations, such copies and subsets should be anonymized to the degree necessary to protect confidentiality. For example, a system using personnel data might substitute random numbers and strings for the employee identifiers, names, and addresses.

It is important to include time stamps on all files and programs, including both production and test versions. This practice serves to resolve problems that arise about program malfunctions. If all programs and files have time stamps, it can be helpful in determining whether the most current version of the load program is in the production library and whether test files and production files have been synchronized.

Final testing prior to production release may entail more formal review by an independent quality assurance section or department; the quality assurance group also may control transfers of programs to the production library.

32.4.3 Controlling User Access to Files and Databases.   Access to files has to be controlled for two reasons:

1. There is information in files that is confidential and is not to be made accessible to everyone.

2. There are other files that are considered auditable.

The information audit may be confidential, but that may not be the reason for controlling access to the files. The information in audit files must be controlled because changing it may be illegal. An example would be an enterprise's general ledger file once the books have been closed. Changing the information in these files gave birth to the pejorative phrase "cooking the books." The original copies of these files are developed on the computer that handles the day-to-day transactions of an enterprise. Some time after the month-end closing of the books, copies of these files are archived. In this form they are the recorded history of the enterprise and cannot be changed. Storing this chiseled-in-stone historical information, combining details and summaries in database format, so as to be accessible for the purpose of analysis is known as data warehousing.

In most large enterprises these files are created on mainframe and midsize computers, although as the speed and storage capacity of microcomputers continue to increase, these files are beginning to appear on microcomputer database servers in LANs. In any event, controlling user access to files is performed in several ways depending on what types of access are allowed. Remote access to online to production databases and files is often done over leased lines—dedicated communication facilities paid for on a monthly basis as opposed to dial-up or switched lines paid for on a when-used basis. Access control may be readily accomplished through the use of front-end security software modules, which in turn feed into database and file handling software and finally into the application software. For example, in an environment using a software product for handling queries and updates of online databases and files, a number of different security software products could be installed. Such products use what are called rules or schemas to validate user IDs and passwords, to authorize types of transactions, and to allow access to files and databases.

Many information system installations allow dial-up communications for many kinds of transactions. Various individuals, including sales representatives entering order information and traveling executives wishing to access current information from databases or files, use dial-up communications. This type of access increases the potential for security breaches. There are security products that limit this potential vulnerability. These products, after validating an individual's ID and password, include a feature that "calls back" to a prearranged or authorized phone number—but this technique is less useful for travelers than for teleworkers. Criminals can tamper with the callback technique by manipulating settings at the central phone switch and thus auto-forwarding calls from the desired destination to their own phone lines.

In both dedicated and switched line arrangements, where there are computers at both ends of the communications hook-up, encryption and tokens may be used to prevent unauthorized individuals from "tapping" and intercepting information from communications lines. (See Chapters 19, 23, and Tutorial 4.)

32.5 DATA VALIDATION.   Just as it is essential to have trusted operating systems and application software for production, the operations group must be able to demonstrate that data used for production are valid.

Validation controls normally are carried out dynamically throughout data entry and other processing tasks. Some validity checks are carried out automatically by database software; for example, inconsistencies between header records and details may be reported as errors by the database subsystems. Bad pointers are usually flagged immediately as errors by the database software; examples include:

- Pointers from a particular master record to a detail record with the wrong key value or to a nonexistent location

- Forward or backward pointers from a detail record to records that have the wrong key value for the chain or that do not exist at all

However, many errors cannot be caught by database subsystems because they involve specific constraints particular to the application, rather than errors in the database itself. For example, it may be improper to allow two chemical substances to be mixed in a processing vat, yet there is nothing in the data themselves that the database software would recognize as precluding those two values to be recorded in the input variables. The programmers must include such restrictions in edit checks; often these relations among variables can be coded in a data dictionary. If the programming environment does not allow such dependencies, the programmers must incorporate the restrictions in lookup tables or in initialization of variables.

From a production point of view, operations staff must run appropriate validation programs created by the database suppliers and by the application programmers to assure the quality of all production data. The following sections review in more detail what is involved in such validation programs.

32.5.1 Edit Checks. Operations should have access to diagnostic programs that scan entire databases looking for violations of edit criteria. For example, if a field is designated as requiring only alphanumeric characters but not special characters such as "#" and "@" then part of the diagnostic sweep should be checking every occurrence of the field for compliance with those rules. Similarly, range checks (greater than, less than, greater than or equal, equal, less than or equal, between) are a normal part of such scans. Lookup tables provide further sophistication for more complex relations and restrictions. In any case, the role of operations staff is to run the diagnostics and identify errors; correction of the errors should fall to authorized personnel, such as the database administrators.

Diagnostic programs should provide detailed information about every error located in the production files. Such details include:

- Configurable view of the record or records constituting an error, showing some or all of the fields

- Unique identification of such records by file name or number, record number, and optionally by physical location (cylinder, sector) on disk

- Error code and optional full-text descriptions of the error, including exactly which constraints have been violated

A diagnostic program should, ideally, also allow for repair of the error. Such repair could be automatic, as, for example, insertion of the correct total in an order-header, or manual, by providing for the database administrator to correct a detail record known to be wrong.

32.5.2   Check Digits and Log Files.   Another form of verification relies on check digits. Programs can add the numerical or alphanumeric results of data manipulations to each record or to groups of records when transactions are completed properly. Finding records with the wrong check digits will signal inconsistencies and potential errors in the processing. Check digits are particularly useful to identify changes in production databases and other files that have been accomplished through utilities that bypass the constraints of application programs. For example, most databases come with a relatively simple ad hoc query tool that permits lookups, serial searches, views, and simple reporting. However, such tools often include the power to modify records in compliance with database subsystem constraints but completely free of application program constraints. An even more powerful type of utility bypasses the file system entirely and works by issuing commands directly to the low-level drivers or to the firmware responsible for memory and disk I/O. In the hands of the wrong people, both database and system utilities can damage data integrity. However, it is usually difficult for the users of these utilities to compute the correct checksums to hide evidence of their modifications. A diagnostic routine that recomputes checksums and compares the new values with the stored values can spot such unauthorized data manipulations immediately.

A similar technique for validating and repairing data uses database and application log files to record information about transactions such as before and after images of modified records. Such log files also can include special marker records to flag different steps in complex transactions; these flags can allow diagnostic programs to identify precisely when transactions have been interrupted or subjected to other forms of failure. Using these log files, it is often possible to identify which defective transactions need to be removed, repeated, or completed.

Commercial data-integrity software is available for a wide range of platforms and databases. Searching on "data integrity software" in the Google search engine (*www.google.com*) locates many references to such products; the site *http://dmoz.org/Computers/Software/Databases/Data_Warehousing/Data_Integrity_and_Cleansing_Tools* listed 16 such tools at the time of writing (July 2001).

32.5.3   Handling External Data.   Before using data provided by external organizations, operations should routinely check for data purity. Diagnostic routines from the programming group should be available to check on all data before they are used in batch processing to update a production database. The same principles of data validation used in checking production databases should apply to all data received from clients, suppliers, governments, and any other organization. Special validation programs can and should be written or obtained to test the data received on any medium, including tapes, cartridges, removable discs, CD-ROMs, and data communications channels.

32.6   SUMMARY.   Up until the mid-1980s, the worlds of mainframe and midsized or minicomputers differed from that of PCs. However, from the mid-1980s into the millennium, these worlds have merged. LANs have proliferated, the Internet has changed the way business is conducted, and bridges, routers, and gateways make it possible for information to move among computer platforms, regardless of type. Security requirements are now universal in scope. There are numerous layers of software and hardware that separate the user and the technician from the information to which they require access. These layers themselves contribute somewhat to system security because it requires some technical skill to get at the information. However, computer literacy is increasing rapidly among all elements of society, so the security provided by the technology is not as significant as it once was.

Security is also an economic issue. If an individual with the requisite skill is determined to gain access to online files or databases, it is extremely expensive to prevent such access. Even with high expenditure, success in achieving complete security is in no way guaranteed. Nevertheless, if the value of the information and its confidentiality justifies additional expense, there are software products available that employ complex schemes to support security. When necessary, information security can be extended down to the field level in records of online files and databases.

Other related security measures, such as physical protection, communication security, encryption of data, auditing techniques, system application controls are covered in other chapters of the text. No one measure can stand alone or provide the ultimate protection for security, but with a proper balance of measures, the exposures can be contained and managed.

CHAPTER 33

E-MAIL AND INTERNET USE POLICIES

M.E. Kabay

CONTENTS

33.1 INTRODUCTION.   The Internet offers every enterprise exciting opportunities to find timely information and to reach potential clients. This very power brings with it risks of damaging corporate and professional reputations. Nontechnical problems in cyberspace include bad information, fraud, loss of productivity, and violations of civil and criminal law as well as violations of the conventions of proper behavior established by custom in cyberspace.

In addition, widespread abuse of Internet access while at work is forcing recognition that clear policies are essential to guide employees in appropriate use of these corporate resources.

Finally, some of the information in this chapter may help security administrators involve their users in a more active role by giving them take-home messages that can help them protect their own families and friends. Getting employees to care about security for their families is a good step to involving them in corporate security.

33.1.1 Topics.   Here is a list of some of the dangers users can encounter on the Internet:

- Damaging the reputation of their enterprise
- Incorrect information
- Hoaxes
- Viruses and other malicious code
- Junk e-mail
- Chain letters and Ponzi schemes
- Get-rich-quick schemes

- Mail storms
- Stolen software
- Stolen music and video
- Plagiarism
- Criminal hackers and hacktivists
- Online auctions
- Online gambling
- Buying on the Web
- Games
- Spyware
- Addiction
- Online dating and cybersex
- Hate groups
- Pornography
- Pedophiles

Each section in this chapter ends with a list of practical guidelines for discussion and action and a list of resources for further study.

33.1.2   General Resources

- Better Business Bureau online publications list: *www.bbb.org/library/searchBy-Subject.asp.*
- Children's Partnership Online: *www.childrenspartnership.org.*
- Children's Protection and Advocacy Coalition: *www.thecpac.com/index3.html.*
- "Cybersafety Guidelines," by the Plainsboro, NJ, police: *www.plainsboropolice.com/cybersafety.htm.*
- *Coping with Dangers on the Internet: A Teen's Guide to Staying Safe Online,* by Kevin F. Rothman. New York: Rosen Publishing Group, 2000.
- *Cybersafety: Surfing Safely Online,* by Joan Vos MacDonald. Berkeley Heights, NJ: Enslow Publishers, 2001.
- GetNetWise: *www.getnetwise.org.*
- *Internet & Computer Ethics for Kids (and Parents & Teachers Who Haven't Got a Clue),* by Winn Schwartau. Tampa, FL: Inter-Pact, 2001.
- "Kids & Youth Educational Page," from the FBI: *www.fbi.gov/kids/6th12th.htm.*
- "Kids Page—Kindergarten to 5th Grade," from the FBI: *www.fbi.gov/kids/k5th/kidsk5th.htm.*
- "A Parent's Guide to Internet Safety" (English and Spanish versions available): *www.fbi.gov/publications/pguide/pguide.htm.*
- "Sociology of Internet/Cyberspace." For a scholarly and thorough set of readings, see the course materials for a 1999 course by Professor Carl Kuneo of McMaster University: *http://socserv.mcmaster.ca/soc/courses/soc4jj3_99/sociology4jj3.htm#IPurpose.*

33.2 DAMAGING THE REPUTATION OF THE ENTERPRISE. When we post information to the Net, we normally indicate who we are in our message headers. In particular, all employees using a corporate e-mail account identify their employer in every posting. It follows that when an employee—for example, joe@acme.com—misbehaves on the Net, it is likely that everyone seeing the misbehavior will associate it with the employer, regardless of futile attempts to dissociate the employee from the employer by statements such as "The opinions above are not necessarily those of my employer."

33.2.1 Violating Netiquette. In brief, employees can embarrass their employers by:

- Flaming: launching rude verbal attacks on others.
- Spamming: sending copies of a message to multiple, often unrelated, USENET groups and mailing lists.
- Sending "junk" e-mail, unsolicited advertising and sales promotions, to people's e-mail addresses without their permission. Often called "spam"—much to the dismay of Hormel, the owners of the Spam™ trademark.
- Mail-bombing: sending many e-mail messages to a single e-mail address to annoy its user.

33.2.2 Netiquette Resources

- Dear Emily Postnews: *www.templetons.com/brad/emily.html*
- Netiquette: *www.pbs.org/uti/guide/netiquette.html*
- Netiquette: *www.primenet.com/~vez/neti.html*
- The Net: User Guidelines and Netiquette: *www.fau.edu/netiquette/net/netiquette.html*
- RFC 1855 Netiquette Guidelines: *http://marketing.tenagra.com/rfc1855.html*

33.2.3 Violating Laws. Employees may engage in illegal activities that can seriously compromise their employer; examples include:

- Industrial espionage
- Stock manipulation
- Criminal hacking, unauthorized penetration of other systems
- Sabotage, denial of service attacks
- Vandalism, defacement of Web sites
- Creating, transmitting, or storing child pornography
- Sending threats (e.g., of harm to the President of the United States)
- Credit card fraud, using stolen or fraudulently generated credit card numbers for purchases made using corporate resources

All such actions should be explicitly forbidden by corporate Internet usage policies.

33.2.4 Ill-Advised E-Mail. There have been too many cases of foolish use of e-mail in recent years. Employees have caused a hostile working environment by sending internal e-mail with lewd or hateful jokes and images; staff members have insulted their bosses or their employees in e-mail that later became public; people have made libelous accusations about other workers or about competing companies. All of these uses are wholly inappropriate for a medium that takes control of distribution away from the originators and that produces records that can be backed up and archived for indefinite periods of possible retrieval.

Common sense dictates that anything sent via e-mail should not be illegal, or even embarrassing if it were published in a newspaper.

On a related topic, it would be wise to explain to users that it is also a poor idea to insult people using e-mail. Sending *flames* that belittle, ridicule, and demean other people is likely to generate more of the same in response, and flaming is an ugly practice that distorts standards for public and private discourse. Even if you decide to respond to rudeness, you do not have to be rude yourself. Tell your employees, and your children, to maintain the moral high ground by refraining from obscenity, profanity, and vulgarity in written as well as in oral discourse. Not only is this a good habit in general, but it avoids the possibility of enraging total strangers who may be physically or electronically dangerous. Criminal hackers have been known to damage credit ratings, participate in identity theft to rack up large bills in the victims' names, and even to tamper with phone company accounts. In one notorious prank, hackers forwarded all incoming phone calls for the famous security expert Donn Parker, who is quite bald, to a hair restoration business.

Anonymizers are services that strip identifying information from e-mail and then forward the text to the indicated targets. However, even anonymizers respond to subpoenas demanding the identity of people involved in libel or threats. The service called *annoy.com* is designed to allow people to send annoying messages to others without reaping the consequences; even that service has a particularly clear message on its refusal to tolerate abuse:

> **WARNING**
>
> It has come to our attention that certain people have been using annoy.com to deliver what some might consider to be threats of physical violence or harm to others.
>
> Do not mistake our commitment to freedom of speech for a license to abuse our service in this manner.
>
> We plan to cooperate fully with law enforcement agencies in whatever efforts they make to find you and punish you—even if it's some renegade authoritarian dictatorship . . . Free speech and annoy.com are not about harassment and definitely not about harm or violence. If you think for a second we will allow cowardly idiots to spoil our free speech party you are making a mistake. A huge mistake.

You might also want to point out that on the USENET, in particular, a message is forever: There are archives of USENET messages stretching back for a decade. Being an abusive foulmouth online may not permanently damage a person's reputation, but it is not likely to *improve* anyone's prospects for getting or keeping a good job, especially if the sender's e-mail address shows a corporate affiliation.

33.2.5   Inappropriate Use of Corporate Identifiers.   Considerable controversy exists as to whether corporate policy should forbid corporate IDs for any personal use on the Internet. There is little reason for posting messages to news groups in the .alt hierarchy, and especially not to groups catering to or sympathetic to criminal activity. If employees of an organization want to participate in vigorous political discussion, conversations about sexual activity, and any other topic unrelated to their work, they are free to do so using their own Internet identities. Employers pay for corporate e-mail identities; people who want to post opinions about, say, basket weaving techniques should pay for their own access and leave their employer out of the postings.

The risks of damaging an organization's reputation by violating netiquette are high. Some abusers have themselves been abused by angry and unscrupulous Internauts. In one notorious early case, back in 1994, a naive executive spammed the Net—he posted messages in a couple of dozen newsgroups. In retaliation, his company's 800-number was posted to phone-sex discussion groups in the .alt hierarchy, resulting in thousands of irate and expensive phone calls by seekers of aural sex. Regular customers were unable to get through, and some staff resigned because of the offensive calls. The executive nearly lost his job.

An additional risk is that employees will inadvertently post company-confidential information to what they erroneously perceive as closed, private groups. Competitors or troublemakers can then exploit the information for competitive advantage or publicize it to harm the enterprise. Even if a discussion group or mailing really is closed, nothing prevents a participant from using or disseminating confidential information without permission. By the time the breach of security is discovered, it can be too late for remediation.

33.3   DISSEMINATING AND USING INCORRECT INFORMATION.   The Internet and in particular the World Wide Web are in some ways as great a change in information distribution as the invention of writing 6,000 years ago and the invention of movable type 600 years ago. In all these cases, the inventions involved *disintermediation:* the elimination of intermediaries in the transmission of knowledge. Writing eliminated the oral historians; one could read information from far away and long ago without having to speak to a person who had personally memorized that knowledge. Print allowed a far greater distribution of knowledge than handwritten books and scrolls, eliminating an entire class of scribes who controlled access to the precious and rare records. The Net and the Web have continued this trend, with a radical increase in the number of people capable of being publishers. Where publishing once required printing presses, capital, and extensive administrative infrastructure, or at least relatively expensive mimeographs (1950s), photocopiers (1960s), and printers (1970s), today publishing to a potential audience of millions can be essentially free. Many Internet Service Providers (ISPs) offer free Web-hosting services and places for people to join electronic communities of every imaginable type.

33.3.1   Disintermediation and Quality.   Web pages can lead to visibility unheard of even a decade ago. For example, one young exhibitionist named Jennifer Kaye Ringley put up a Web site to display images of her home taken through Web-enabled cameras (Web cams); this "jennycam.org" site has received up to *half a million hits per day* since it was established. Another young woman decided to put up a Web site devoted to one of her favorite literary characters, Nero Wolfe. Within a few years, her site was so well respected that she was hired by a Hollywood filmmaker as a technical consultant on a series of Nero Wolfe movies. The fees she was paid, despite offering to help for free, helped her get through her studies for her Ph.D. in social psychology. It would have been virtually impossible for her to achieve this recognition by trying to publish her own hard-copy fan magazine; the paper might have reached a few hundred people, but the Web site reached many thousands.

Unfortunately, all of this disintermediation has negative implications as well as positive ones. Freedom from publishers has liberated the independent thinker from corporate influence, editorial limitations, and standards for house style. However, this freedom also has liberated many people from responsible reporting, adequate research, and even rudimentary principles of spelling and grammar. The dictum "Don't believe everything you read" is even more important when reading Web-based information. Individuals may publish incorrect versions of technical information (e.g., health sites that claim that massaging parts of the ear lobe can cure many known diseases), unsubstantiated theories about historical and natural events (e.g., the Tungska Impact of 1908 was caused by an antimatter meteorite), and off-the-wall revisionist history (e.g., slavery was good for black folks and Hitler never killed Jews).

33.3.2 Libel. Some people have taken advantage of the freedom to publish whatever they want by crossing the boundaries of libel. For example, the self-styled "reporter" Matt Drudge went too far in postings on his electronic scandal sheet in 1997 when he made unsubstantiated accusations about White House advisor Sidney Blumenthal's marriage. Professional journalists pounced on him for shoddy journalism. Blumenthal and his wife filed a $30 million libel suit against Drudge even after he apologized for failing to verify the gossip he disseminated. Drudge then claimed that public White House support for Blumenthal amounted to a threat against free speech.

In another notorious case, Walter Cronkite, whom polls revealed to be the most respected man in the United States in the 1980s, was appalled to discover a page of lies about him on the Web in 1997. A 28-year-old programmer, Tim Hughes, invented and posted a scurrilous story about Cronkite's becoming enraged at the author, shrieking imprecations at Hughes and his wife, boasting about his own infidelity, and spitting in their spice cake at a Florida restaurant. In addition, the anti-Cronkite Web page included falsified photographs purporting to show Cronkite at a Ku Klux Klan meeting. Cronkite threatened to sue for libel; Hughes took the page down and weakly protested that it was all a joke.

The effect of this kind of misinformation on children or immature employees, untrained in critical thinking and lacking in skepticism about information on the Internet, can be damaging.

33.3.3 Practical Guidelines. Here are some practical guidelines to help instruct others in using Internet-based information wisely:

- Explain how to estimate the reliability of sites, realizing that none of the following clues is an absolute guarantee; however, meeting most of these criteria can give more confidence in a site's value than finding few of them:
  - Presence of the author's name, title, institutional affiliation, and academic credentials
  - Date of publication and history of revision
  - References to independent sources of validation
  - Reputation for reliability of the organizations publishing the information (e.g., Amnesty International rather than a dictatorship protesting against the latest human-rights report)
  - Lack of obvious benefit for distortion of information (e.g., Amnesty International rather than that dictatorship protecting its innocence)
  - The degree to which other trustworthy sites concur in the information on a particular site
  - Consistency—lack of self-contradictions
  - The number of reliable Web sites linked to the site under evaluation and the number of reliable search engines that list it

- Show learners some off-the-wall sites that contradict what they already know. Then go to more reputable sites and demonstrate how to cross-check information by using authoritative sources.

- Point out stylistic clues that a site may be less than trustworthy:
  - Anonymous sources
  - Incompetent spelling and grammar
  - Obscenities, vulgarity, and foul language
  - Presence of false information
  - Inclusion of long-outdated information
  - Use of lots of exclamation signs
  - Excessive use of capitalization
  - Statements expressed in absolute terms ("All ___ are ___." or "No ___ can be ___.")
  - Intolerance of ambiguity ("There can be no doubt that _____.")
  - Overblown claims of importance ("ACME wart remover: The most important development in medical history!")
  - Claims that violate common sense ("Using rat poison is better for your teeth than using toothpaste.")
  - Intemperate and *ad hominem* remarks ("Only an idiot would believe that _____" or "Only an idiot would disagree with the statement that _____.")

- Show learners examples of more reliable sources of information: scientific and professional publications, public-interest research groups, industry associations, government Web sites, and reputable news sources.

Another source of information is the USENET—that collection of thousands of discussion groups on every conceivable topic. These discussion groups fall into two major classes: moderated and unmoderated. In a moderated group, messages are either passed through a *moderator* who decides to post them for participants or to delete offensive or otherwise inappropriate messages. Not all moderated groups are reliable, and not all unmoderated groups are unreliable. However, many unmoderated groups distribute unsubstantiated information from people who appear to derive their major pleasure in life by insulting other participants and by making outrageous statements about any topic that comes up. Everyone should be trained to recognize emotional and inflammatory language, and should be encouraged to apply skeptical analysis to all statements, especially to those published in rants.

33.3.4 Credibility Resources

- "An Educators' Guide to Credibility and Web Evaluation," by Toni Greer, Donna Holinga, Christy Kindel, and Melissa Netznik. University of Illinois/Urbana-Champaign, 1999: *http://rs.ed.uiuc.edu/wp/credibility*

- "Evaluating Internet Research Sources," by Robert Harris, 1997: *www.virtualsalt. com/evalu8it.htm*

- *WebQuester: A Guidebook to the Web,* by Robert Harris. Guilford, CT: Dushkin McGraw-Hill, 2000.

33.4   HOAXES.   Pranksters have been using e-mail to fool gullible people for years using a particular sort of incorrect information: deliberate *hoaxes*. A hoax is a mischievous trick, especially one based on a made-up story. There are two major kinds of hoaxes circulating on the Internet: urban myths and false information about viruses. The archives in the Urban Myths Web site are full of hilarious hoaxes, some of which have been circulating for years. Why don't they die out?

The problem is the nature of the Internet. Information is not distributed solely from a centrally controlled site; on the contrary, anyone can broadcast, or rebroadcast, any kind of data at any time. There are neither reliable creation dates nor obligatory expiry dates on files, so those receiving a five-year-old document may have no obvious way of recognizing its age, and they almost certainly have no instant way of knowing that its information is obsolete or flatly wrong. All they see is that the document has been sent to them recently, often by someone they know personally.

33.4.1   Urban Myths.   Here are some notorious examples of the bizarre and sometimes disturbing urban myths that are thoroughly debunked on the www.urbanmyths. com Web site:

- *Expensive cookies:* Someone claims that a Nieman-Marcus employee charged $250 to a credit card for the recipe to some good chocolate chip cookies. This story has been traced to a false claim dating back to 1948 in which a store was accused of charging $25 for the recipe to a fudge cake.

- *Do not flash your car lights:* In a gang-initiation ritual, hoodlums drive down a highway with their car lights off. Flash your lights at them and die!

- *Watch out for poisoned needles:* Insane, vengeful druggies leave needles tipped with HIV+ blood in movie theater seats, gas pump handles, and telephone change-return slots.

- *Lose your kidneys:* Visit a foreign city, go drinking with strangers, and wake up in the morning in a bathtub of ice with two neat incisions through which both your kidneys have been removed.

- *Poor little guy wants postcards:* Craig Shergold is just one of the many real or imaginary children about whom well-meaning people circulate chain letters asking for postcards, business cards, prayers, and even money. Shergold was born in 1980; when he was nine, he was diagnosed with brain cancer and friends started a project to cheer him up—they circulated messages asking people to send him postcards so he could be listed in the *Guinness Book of World Records.* By 1991, he had received 30 million cards and an American philanthropist arranged for brain surgery, which worked: Shergold went into remission. The postcard deluge did not. By 1997, the local post office had received over *250 million* postcards for him, and he was long since sick of the whole project.

- *Wish you would stop Making a Wish:* Around the mid-1990s, some prankster inserted false information about the Make-a-Wish Foundation into the outdated chain letters concerning Shergold. The unfortunate organization was promptly inundated with e-mail and postal mail, none of which was in any way useful or relevant to its work.

33.4.2   Virus Myths.   One category of hoaxes has become a perennial nuisance on the Net: virus myths. There is something wonderful about the willingness of gullible, well-meaning people to pass on ridiculous news about nonexistent viruses with impossible effects. One of the most famous is the Good Times "virus," which appeared around 1994. It and its variants have been circulating uninterruptedly for years. Every few years, there is a new outburst as some newcomers to the Internet encounter an old copy of the warnings and send it to everyone they know.

The original very short warning was as follows, including the incorrect punctuation:

> Here is some important information. Beware of a file called Goodtimes.

> Happy Chanukah everyone, and be careful out there.There is a virus on America Online being sent by E-Mail. If you get anything called "Good Times," DON'T read it or download it. It is a virus that will erase your hard drive. Forward this to all your friends. It may help them a lot.

The Good Times virus claimed that downloading a document or reading a document could cause harm; at that time, such a claim was impossible. Ironically, within a couple of years, it did in fact become possible to cause harm via documents because of the macrolanguage capabilities of MS Word and other programs enabled for scripting languages. Over the rest of the 1990s, foolish people modified the name of the imaginary virus and added more details, sometimes claiming impossible effects such as destruction of computer hardware.

Unaware people circulate virus hoaxes because they receive the hoax from someone they know. Unfortunately, the friendliness of a sender has nothing to do with the accuracy of a message. Transmitting technical information about viruses without verifying that information's legitimacy and accuracy is a disservice to your friends. It makes it harder for experts to reach the public with warnings of real dangers, while it clutters up recipients' e-mail in-baskets with alarming information of no use whatever.

33.4.3   Practical Guidelines

Key indicators that a message is a hoax:

- Use of exclamation marks. No official warning uses them.
- Use of lots of uppercase text, typical of youngsters.
- Misspellings and bad grammar.
- No date of origination or expiration.
- Inclusion of words like "yesterday" when there is no date on the message.
- References to official-sounding sources (such as Microsoft, Computer Incident Advisory Capability (CIAC), Computer Emergency Response Team Coordination Center CERT/CC) but no specific document URLs for details. URLs for a site's home page do not count.
- No valid digital signature from a known security organization.
- Requests to circulate widely. No such request is ever made in official documents.
- Claims that someone is counting the number of e-mail messages containing copies of the hoax.
- Threats about dire consequences if someone "breaks the chain" by refusing to forward the message.
- Claims of monetary rewards that make no sense. For example, the Disney organization will send you $5,000 — for forwarding an e-mail message.

- Use of complicated technical language such as "n-th dimensional infinite complexity control loops" that do not make sense.
- Claims of damage to computer hardware from viruses or other computer software.

Before alerting anyone to apprehended threats, check the antihoax pages on the Web, as suggested in the next section.

33.4.4   Hoax Identification Resources

Virus hoaxes:

- Computer Virus Myths: *www.vmyths.com*
- Datafellows Hoax Warnings: *www.datafellows.com/news/hoax.htm*
- Good Times Virus FAQ, by Les Jones (1995): *www.urbanlegends.com/misc/good_times_virus_faq.html*
- ICSA Labs Hoax List: *www.icsalabs.com/html/communities/antivirus/hoaxes.shtml*
- Trend Micro Hoax Encyclopedia:_*www.antivirus.com/vinfo/hoaxes/hoax.asp*

Other hoaxes:

- Alt.folklore.urban and Urban Legends Archive: *www.urbanlegends.com*
- CIAC Hoaxbusters: *http://hoaxbusters.ciac.org/HoaxBustersHome.html*
- Gullibility on the Net: *www.cwrl.utexas.edu/~roberts/gullibility.html*
- Hoax FAQ: *http://chekware.com/hoax*
- Urban Legends and Folklore: *http://urbanlegends.about.com/science/urbanlegends*
- Urban Myths: *www.urbanmyths.com*

For a scholarly, and fascinating, analysis of why hoaxes spread, see the paper by Sarah Gordon titled "Hoaxes & Hypes" at *www.av.ibm.com/InsideTheLab/Bookshelf/ScientificPapers/Gordon/HH.html* and also her excellent overview entitled "Received . . . and Deceived" at *www.infosecuritymag.com/sept/cover.htm*.

33.5   THREATS.   One particular class of hoaxes deserves a special mention: threats.

33.5.1   Receiving Threats.   If you, your employees, or your children receive threats through e-mail, you have a right, and possibly a duty, to inform your local law enforcement officials. In today's climate of fear and violence, any threat warrants attention. In addition to the distress such messages can generate, they may be warning signs of serious trouble. In particular, threats about violence at work, at school, or against any definable group may be the early warning that allows authorities to step in to defuse an explosive situation.

The other side of the coin is that everyone must understand that sending threatening e-mail is not an acceptable joke or a minor prank, especially if the threat involves violence. Some people, believing that they can mask their real identity, have foolishly sent death threats to the White House; because the Secret Service is obligated by law to investigate *all* threats to the President and the First Family, agents show up within a few hours to interrogate the miscreants. For example, youngsters in grade 10 at Profile High School in Bethlehem, New Hampshire, sent death threats to the White House Web site from their school computers. The messages were traced within minutes by the Secret Service and the children were suspended from school and lost their Internet privileges for the next two years.

33.5.2   Practical Guidelines.   Because most adults understand the issues, the following guidelines focus on parents, teachers, and children.

- Parents and teachers should instruct children never to utter threats of violence or other harm, not even in e-mail messages or chat rooms.
- Encourage your children to report all threats directed at them or at others to parents, teachers, or librarians immediately.
- Search the USENET archive at *groups.google.com* using a variety of mildly offensive terms (e.g., "jerk") to illustrate the foolishness of people who spew abuse at each other.

33.5.3   Threat Policy Resources

- Annoy.com policy on threats: *www.annoy.com/scripts/censure/index.asp*
- "Sample Handbook Language re: Threats of Violence," from the School Administrators of Iowa: *www.sai-iowa.org/threats.html*
- "Special Report: When E-mail Threats Become Real," by Jay Lyman, 2001: *www.newsfactor.com/perl/story/8252.html*
- "Maryland Man Arrested after Santana High E-mail Threat," 2001: *www.cnn.com/2001/US/03/10/school.shooting.01*

33.6   VIRUSES AND OTHER MALICIOUS CODE.   As this chapter is being written, there are over 55,000 distinct forms of malicious program code circulating in cyberspace. Most of these harmful programs are limited to antivirus laboratories and to the computers of virus hobbyists—people who derive pleasure from playing with dangerous toys. For more information about viruses, see Chapters 9, 10, and 24.

Employers should have policies clearly forbidding the creation, exchange, and storage of malicious software on corporate systems.

33.6.1   Practical Guidelines for Everyone

- Keep your virus strings up to date, with at least twice-monthly updates.
- Do not download or use software that purports to help you break the law or cheat people and businesses.
- Do not download or use software that has been copied without permission or in violation of license restrictions. That is software piracy, copyright infringement, or plain theft.
- Do not execute software that anyone sends you through e-mail even if you know and like the person who sent it to you. Just because the person is nice does not mean he or she is qualified to inspect programs for safety.
- Before sending someone an attachment such as a picture or any other kind of file by e-mail, let your recipient know what to expect via a preliminary message; if you do not know the person personally, send an e-mail requesting permission to send the attachment.
- Never open attachments you have received without advance notice, regardless of who sent them or what the subject line or text says. Be especially suspicious of

generic subjects such as "FYI" without details or "You'll like this." If you are really curious about the attachment, phone or e-mail the supposed sender to find out whether it is legitimate. However, remember that you should not run programs you receive as attachments, regardless of what the sender thinks.

- Do not forward programs, even reliable programs, to anyone; instead, tell your friends where to download useful programs from a trustworthy source, such as a legitimate Web site.

- Before sending anyone an MS Word document as an attachment, save the document as an RTF file instead of as the usual DOC file. RTF files do not include document macros and therefore cannot carry macro-viruses.

- Disable automatic execution of macros in MS-Word using the TOOLS | MACROS | SECURITY menu and select the HIGH option, which restricts macro execution to digitally signed macros from trusted sources. If the default value is not changed, there is no security against macros.

- Use the patches offered by Microsoft to shut off automatic execution of attachments in Outlook and Outlook Express.

- Do not circulate virus warnings unless you have personally checked their validity on any of a number of virus-information and hoax sites on the Web.

33.6.2   Virus Resources

- Computer Virus FAQ for New Users, 1999: *www.cs.ruu.nl/wais/html/na-dir/computer-virus/new-users.html*
- F-Secure Virus Database search: *www.f-secure.com/v-descs*
- IBM Antivirus Research: *www.research.ibm.com/antivirus/SciPapers.htm*
- ICSA Labs Virus Alerts: *www.icsalabs.com/html/communities/antivirus/alerts.shtml*
- Online VGrep Search: *www.virusbtn.com/VGrep/search.html*
- Top Ten Viruses (Trend Micro): *www.antivirus.com/vinfo/default.asp*
- Virus Bulletin: *www.virusbtn.com*
- Virus Primer (Trend Micro): *www.antivirus.com/vinfo/vprimer.htm*
- "What Makes Johnny (and Janey) Write Viruses?" by Kim Zetter, 2001: *www.itworld.com/Net/3271/PCW01051534405/pfindex.html*
- WildList Organization: *www.wildlist.org*
- Word Macro Virus FAQ from the Michigan State University: *www.ahdl.msu.edu/ahdl/macrofaq.htm*

33.7   JUNK E-MAIL.   Unsolicited commercial e-mail (UCE) is derisively known as "junk" e-mail but also as "spam." Junk e-mail is spawned by foolish or unscrupulous people who send out thousands, or even millions, of identical messages, almost entirely to unwilling recipients. Junk e-mail clogs victims' in-baskets and wastes their time as they open these unwanted messages and take a few seconds to realize that they are junk. Junk e-mail advertising pornography may be highly offensive to the recipients or to their parents. Junk may even push people's e-mail systems over their server limits if they are not picking up their messages regularly; in such cases, wanted e-mail may bounce because the mailbox is full.

Most junk e-mail uses forged headers; that is, the senders know they are doing something wrong and they deliberately put misleading information in the FROM and REPLY fields to avoid receiving angry responses from the victims of their rudeness. Forging e-mail headers is illegal in the states of Massachusetts, Virginia, and Washington, and, if the perpetrators are identified, can lead to court cases and financial penalties for each message involved in the fraud.

In one famous case, a college student sent out a few thousand junk e-mail messages and followed the instructions in his spam kit by putting a made-up REPLY address using "@flowers.com" without checking to see if there really was such a domain. Indeed there was, and the owner of this reputable floral delivery service, Tracy LaQuey Parker, was none too pleased when her system was flooded with over 5,000 bounce messages and angry letters from customers saying that they would never do business with her again. She sued the student for damages and was awarded over $18,000 by a judge who said he wished he could have been even more punitive.

33.7.1 Practical Guidelines

- Do not buy products or services from anyone who has sent you junk e-mail. If the company is unprofessional or inconsiderate enough to use such methods of advertising, it does not deserve either your business or your trust.

- Do not assume that the FROM address is correct, because often it is either nonexistent or, worse, fraudulently misrepresents the origin by pointing to a legitimate business that is completely innocent of wrongdoing. Never bombard the owner of a FROM address with multiple copies, or even one copy, of abusive e-mail. Such messages, known as *mail-bombs,* will probably reach the wrong target, some innocent addressee.

- Never respond to the address listed for removal from a junk e-mail list unless you know the organization that sent you the message. Since bounces (returned e-mail due to bad addresses) never reach them and there is no incremental cost for sending out addresses to unwilling people, these operators really do not care how you feel about the junk they send. Therefore, the unethical people who send junk e-mail use the REMOVE function primarily to harvest correct e-mail addresses so they can sell them to someone else.

- Do not visit the URLs listed in junk e-mail messages. Some of them are deliberately mislabeled and may bring you to offensive Web sites.

- If a toll-free number is listed in the junk message, you may use it at the sender's cost to let the person know how you feel about being on a junk e-mail list. However, never be rude to the people answering the phone; in general, they are poorly paid employees who have no responsibility for, or knowledge of, the methods being used to reach the public. Just ask to speak to a manager so that the perpetrators' cost of doing business can be increased.

- If you *really* feel angry about a particular e-mail, and you have the time and technical know-how, it is possible to locate the Internet Service Provider or Web-hosting service that carries an offending Web site. Sometimes, a well-documented report can result in cancellation of the perpetrators' Internet access and perhaps even their domain registrations.

- Of course, you should not send junk e-mail yourself, nor allow your employees or your children to do so.

- On a similar note, if you are involved in an e-mail discussion group, especially an unmoderated group, about a specific topic, do not post e-mail to members of the list on a subject that is outside the topic area. A typical class of inappropriate posting is an appeal for support of a worthy cause that has no or only a tenuous relation to the subject area; appealing for support to save whales in a discussion group about gardening is not acceptable. The reasoning is "Likes plants; probably environmentally sensitive; likely to be interested in conservation; therefore will be glad to hear about whales." The problem is that such reasoning could be extended to practically any topic at all, disrupting the focus of the group. This often causes angry retorts, which may be sent to the entire list, instead of only to the sender of the inappropriate mail. Then the angry retorts cause further angry responses, and pretty soon the gardening group is mired in dissension and wasted effort, generating bad feeling and distrust. It leaves a bad taste in everyone's mouth and provides grounds for departure and is much to be regretted.

- As suggested in the preceding paragraph, if you do see inappropriate messages on an e-mail list you care about, do not reply to the entire list; reply only to the sender, with possibly a copy to the moderator, if there is one. The reply should be temperate and polite.

33.7.2   Resources on Junk E-Mail

- ChooseYourMail: *www.chooseyourmail.com*
- Coalition Against Unsolicited Commercial Email: *www.cauce.org*
- "Fight Spam on the Internet": *http://spam.abuse.net*
- JunkEmail.org: *www.junkemail.org*
- JunkBusters: *www.junkbusters.com*
- "Tips For Consumers: What You Should Do About Unsolicited Commercial E-mail," from the Better Business Bureau (1998): *www.bbb.org/library/email.asp*

33.8   CHAIN LETTERS AND PONZI SCHEMES.   A particularly annoying form of junk e-mail is the chain letter. Some chain letters include ridiculous stories about terrible diseases and accidents that have befallen people who refused to forward the message. Others focus on getting victims to send money to someone at the top of a list of names, while adding their names to the bottom of the list, before sending it on to a specified number of recipients. Depending on the length of the list, and the amount to be sent to the person on top, the theoretical return could be in the hundreds of thousands of dollars. In practice, only the originators of the scheme profit. After a while, all possible participants have been solicited with disappointing results, and the chains are broken in many places.

Another type of pyramid is known as a "Ponzi scheme," which is an investment swindle in which high profits are promised, and early investors are paid off with funds raised from later ones. The scam is named after Charles Ponzi (1882?–1949), a speculator who organized such a scheme in 1919 and 1920. The Ponzi scheme tricked thousands of people in Boston when Ponzi guaranteed a 50 percent profit on contributions in 45 days and a doubling of value in 90 days. The con man claimed he was redeeming 1-cent Spanish postal certificates for 6-cent U.S. stamps—a claim ridiculed by financial analysts at the time. Nonetheless, Ponzi took in around $15 million in 1920 dollars and stole around $8 million, paying out the rest to the early participants in order to develop credibility. Six banks collapsed because they invested their depositors' funds in the scheme. Ponzi eventually served over three years in jail but escaped in 1925.[1]

The modern-day e-mail Ponzi scheme typically includes passionate assurances from vaguely identified people about how skeptical they were about the scheme but how they succumbed to curiosity, participated in the scheme, and earned vast amounts of money (e.g., $50,000) within a couple of weeks. The letters often include assurances that everything is legal and point to nonexistent postal information phone lines or claim "As Seen on TV" at various points in the letter.

These letters instruct you to send $1 or $2 or $5 to each of a short list of about four people to receive their "reports." Then add your name and address to the list, while removing the first one, before sending a copy of the new letter to as many people as possible. Some letters go through computations involving such assumptions as "Imagine you send out a hundred, a thousand, or ten thousand messages and get a mere 1%, 2%, or 10% response" and then promise enormous returns.

In fact, the "reports" are nothing but one-page, meaningless blurbs about chain letters. The scammers are trying to get around regulations such as the U.S. Post Office's bar against fraudulent uses of the mail.

Here is the exact text of a letter sent to me on December 1, 2000, by V.J. Bellinger of the Operations Support Group of the United States Postal Inspection Service in Newark, New Jersey. It has some interesting information that will be helpful to readers attempting to convince employees (or family and friends) that such chain e-mail involving postal addresses is illegal:

> A chain letter or a multi-level marketing program is actionable under the Postal Lottery, False Representation, and/or Mail Fraud Statutes if it contains three elements: prize, consideration and chance. *Prize* is usually in the form of money, commissions, or something else of value that the solicitation claims you will receive. *Consideration* is the required payment to the sponsor in order to obtain the prize. *Chance* is determined by the activities of participants over whom the mailer has no control. These types of schemes constitute lotteries and are barred from the mails because they violate the following statutes: Title 18, United States Code, Sections 1302 and 1341 and Title 39, United States Code, Section 3005.
>
> In attempts to appear legal, many chain letter or multi-level marketing mailings offer, for a fee, a product or "report." However, since the success of the program is dependent on the number of people willing to participate, all three elements that constitute a violation continue to be present.
>
> The promoter of this scheme has been advised of the potential violations involved and has been requested to discontinue this type of mailing activity.

A superficially similar phenomenon is known as multilevel marketing. In this nonfraudulent, legitimate system of selling products and services, people are encouraged to recruit distributors from among their friends and acquaintances, but the emphasis is on the value of the products. No one claims that anyone is going to become wealthy without work, and there is no demand for investments. The products have an established market, and the company makes money through sales, not through recruitment.

33.8.1 Practical Guidelines

- Do not participate in any scheme that relies on forwarding large numbers of letters or e-mail messages to everyone you know or to strangers.

- Differentiate between pyramid frauds and legitimate multilevel marketing systems: The former emphasize enrolling participants, whereas the latter emphasize the value of products and services.

- Do not participate in alleged multilevel marketing systems if they require substantial investments.
- If you are interested in a multilevel marketing operation,
  - Check out the owners and officers
  - Talk to people who have bought the products to see if they are happy with their purchases
  - Contact your local Better Business Bureau to see if there have been any complaints
- Do not send money to addresses listed in pyramid frauds.
- Work with your employees and children to demonstrate how a pyramid fraud takes money from a growing number of later victims and shifts it to people who participate earlier in the fraud.

33.8.2   Resources on Chain Letters and Ponzi Schemes

- "Gifting Clubs: A New Twist to the Age-Old Pyramid Scheme," from the Better Business Bureau: *www.bbb.org/library/giftingclub032000.asp*
- "Multi-Level Marketing (How to Tell a Legitimate Opportunity from a Pyramid Scheme)," from the Better Business Bureau: *www.bbb.org/library/tippyra.asp*
- "Pit Stop, Dinner Party, and Other Schemes Target Washington and Idaho Regions," from the Better Business Bureau: *www.bbb.org/alerts/pyramid0802.asp*

33.9   GET-RICH-QUICK SCHEMES.   Other get-rich-quick schemes on the Net play on the victims' wishful thinking, their lack of skepticism, and usually on a lack of common sense. There have been claims that you can earn a quarter of a million dollars a year—grooming poodles in your home. Become a millionaire—working four hours a week—sending out promotional literature for products you do not even have to sell. Some such schemes are promulgated by dangerous people; for example, some extremist militia groups have been charging people hundreds of dollars to learn how to defraud the government by claiming liens on government property and then pledging the nonsensical liens as collateral for loans. Other criminals circulate programs for generating fraudulent credit card numbers and using them to steal goods. In other cases, criminals charge money to teach victims how to falsify their bad credit records so they can obtain yet more fraudulent credit, all the while claiming that their criminal methods are 100 percent legal.

From a corporate standpoint, such chain letters and schemes waste bandwidth and pose a potential for serious embarrassment when enterprise resources are used to spread the nonsense. However, corporate security can win favor with users by helping them avoid the pitfalls of such fraud, even when using their own computer systems. The benefits are particularly strong when helping employees to teach their own children how to avoid this kind of trouble.

To illustrate the trouble kids can get into using these techniques, consider the case of Drew Henry Madden. In 1996, this 16-year-old Australian boy from Brisbane started defrauding businesses using stolen and forged credit card numbers just after leaving school. He stole $18,000 of goods and in February 1997 pled guilty to 104 counts of fraud and was sentenced to a year in jail. However, further frauds were discovered, and it turned out that he had stolen an additional $100,000 in goods and services. In October 1997, he pleaded guilty to an additional 294 counts of fraud. He was given an additional suspended sentence. His defense attorney blamed poor security for the losses: "Madden started with very minor credit card fraud, but it escalated alarmingly, because the safeguards were so inadequate." Despite the youngster's unusual revenue stream, his mother appeared to have accepted his globetrotting ways and massive purchases of lottery tickets without comment. At one point, she told reporters, "If we were a wealthy family he'd be at a private school, where his talents could be directed properly."

A relatively new kind of fraud on the Internet is the diploma mill. These organizations pretend to be educational institutions; actually, they are one or more fraudulent individuals who sell bogus diplomas purporting to represent recognized degrees, but that fool no one but the purchaser.

33.9.1   Practical Guidelines

- Remind everyone to use common sense: Earning lots of money with little or no effort usually marks something impossible or illegal.

- Teach users the mantra of the skeptic: "If it sounds too good to be true, it usually is."

- Explain how dangerous it is to get involved with criminal schemes like using stolen or falsified credit cards. Talk about the victims of such fraud: everyone who pays higher interest rates on unpaid credit card bills and innocent shopkeepers who lose merchandise to e-commerce crooks.

- Especially when talking to children, discuss Internet-mediated theft in the same terms as you discuss shoplifting. Explain how commerce works; point out that everyone suffers from all kinds of theft, including electronic shoplifting.

33.9.2   Resources on Online Scams

- "Is the Internet Becoming a Haven for Diploma Mills?" from the Better Business Bureau: *www.bbb.org/library/diplomamills.asp*

- Tips for Consumers: Internet-Related Business Opportunities—Don't Let Them Fool You!: *www.bbb.org/library/internetbus.asp*

33.10   MAIL STORMS.   A peculiar kind of junk e-mail is sent by accident. These flurries of unwanted messages are called *mail storms.*

Most of us belong to mailing lists; many of us have more than one e-mail address; some of us use autoforwarding to shift e-mail from one address to another automatically; and a few of us use automated responses on our e-mail accounts to let correspondents know when we are out of the office or unable to respond quickly.

All of these factors can contribute to mail storms.

33.10.1   Full Mailboxes.   A mail storm occurs when computers begin sending mail to each other without human intervention. Sometimes mail storms can become a denial of service by saturating communications channels and other resources. The e-mail-enabled worms such as Melissa, the I-love-you message, and others, are examples of malicious software programs whose authors deliberately wrote them to create mail storms.

In a simple situation, a person goes on vacation and decides to receive company e-mail using an ISP with a global presence, such as CompuServe or AOL. By setting an autoforward command on the company account, all incoming mail is sent to a mobile

CompuServe e-mail account. Unfortunately, on the remote tropical island where the vacationer is spending two weeks, it is impossible to access the worldwide ISP without paying a surcharge of $6 a minute for long-distance service to the mainland. This proves too expensive, and no e-mails are received or sent.

Meanwhile the company account dutifully forwards every message it receives to the proper CompuServe account, with its storage limit of 250 messages. That limit is reached within the first week of vacation. At that point, every inbound message generates a bounce informing the sender that the recipient's CompuServe mailbox is full.

The very first bounce message CompuServe sends to the company account is autoforwarded to the vacationer's personal mailbox. That message generates yet another mailbox-full message, which then gets bounced back to the company account and so on without let up. Eventually, even the company mailbox fills up and then the two e-mail systems continue chattering at each other indefinitely. The number of e-mail messages that can be generated by this kind of infinite loop is a function of the latency of the positive feedback system that the user has accidentally created. For example, if it takes exactly one minute for a bounce message to be returned to the originating site, then each message causing an initial error can create 60 additional messages per hour. With new messages arriving at the originating mailbox all the time, new sets of bounced messages in infinite loops are constantly added. It is not uncommon to see tens of thousands of messages accumulating in the recipient mailbox if nobody notices the loops.

33.10.2   Autoforwarding and Out-of-Office Messages.   Several other mechanisms inadvertently create mail storms. For example, people can accidentally autoforward e-mail between two of their own accounts, or if two employees both have full mailboxes, and one sends an e-mail to the other, a mail storm will result.

As another possibility: One person has posted an automatic "out-of-office" response on an e-mail address. Another person sends a message to that address and immediately enables a second out-of-office autoresponder before a response to the first message arrives. That first autoresponder message spawns an equivalent response from the second, and a mail storm begins.

33.10.3   Poorly Configured List Servers.   The user of an autoresponder may belong to a list where the FROM address is actually the broadcast address that sends a response to the entire list. The very first automated out-of-office response to the list will generate a message to everyone on that list, producing an infinite sequence of to-and-from messages. This situation is very embarrassing for the list administrator and intensely annoying for everyone else.

33.10.4   Human Error.   Something analogous to a mail storm results from thoughtless behavior when using a public list. A typical instance occurs when a list member posts to an entire list comments relevant only to one individual. For example, a member asks for a reprint of an article and another answers on the list, "I'll send you a reprint tomorrow." Several thousand unwilling readers now know about this projected e-mail message. One of these irritated people posts a message saying "Did you really have to post that message to the entire list?" This second message is so irritating that at least one other person posts a third message to the entire list criticizing the originator of the second letter for criticizing the writer of the first. This useless tempest of e-mail continues via the public list, creating thousands of copies of useless information.

Another form of inconsiderate behavior is to quote entire messages when responding to e-mail. Only the fragments of text that have elicited a response should be copied to the new message. This principle is particularly important on public lists, where messages have been observed containing the entire text, including Internet headers, for up to seven levels of previous messages. Often the amount of new information contained in messages posted to USENET groups is extremely small; the rest was quotations of quotations of quotations.

33.10.5 Practical Guidelines

Here are some simple suggestions for reducing the likelihood of mail storms:

- Minimize the use of automated responses on your e-mail accounts.
- If you do autoforward your e-mail, do not let your target mailbox fill up.
- If you are receiving autoforwarded e-mail from your primary mailbox, do not autoforward back to the original mailbox.
- E-mail system administrators should receive exception reports identifying accounts with excessive numbers of e-mail messages or excessive traffic, so that they can investigate for mail storms.
- Firewalls that inspect the content of e-mail messages should be able to react to an excessive number of bounce messages from a single originating address by deleting the traffic or informing the system administrator of a likely mail storm.
- Managers of unmoderated lists should configure a FROM address different from the address that participants use to post messages to the list.

Users of list servers who want to send personal messages should reply to the sender, not to the entire list.

33.11 STOLEN SOFTWARE, MUSIC, AND VIDEOS. People have been making unauthorized copies of software since personal computers became common. Families where the parents would be shocked at their kids stealing a dollar candy bar from the local supermarket seem unconcerned about those same kids' theft of software packages costing hundreds of dollars. Unfortunately, some of these parents are guilty of stealing software themselves: Many of the "customers" at software "lending libraries" are adults who know that what they are doing is illegal but just do not care. These people need to understand that software theft is a serious problem with possibly serious consequences.

For example, in May 2000, the FBI arrested 17 people, five of them former or current employees of Intel, on charges of involvement with Internet sites devoted to pirated software. The five were described as having held low-level engineering jobs, and an Intel spokesman said four out of the five were no longer with the company. All 17 suspects were members of a loosely organized group called Pirates with Attitudes, which operated one of the Internet's oldest "warez" sites — a term describing a hacker variation of software sold in stores by merchants. Most warez sites are run as hobbies, and their users are often teenage boys who view downloading a pirated software program to be a rite of passage. The indictments did not allege that the perpetrators were attempting to make money through their activities, but the potential penalties include a $250,000 fine and five years in prison. "This is the most significant investigation of copyright infringement involving the use of the Internet conducted to date by the FBI," said a spokeswoman for the Bureau's Chicago office. "It demonstrates the FBI's ability to successfully investigate very sophisticated online criminal activity."[2]

Even some teachers have fallen into the trap of believing that they are entitled to copy proprietary software without permission. They are quite wrong. For example, in

1998, the Business Software Alliance audited the Los Angeles Unified School District and found 1,400 illegal copies of proprietary software in a single school. Total costs of replacing illegal software throughout the district reached about $5 million. Imagine trying to explain fines and costs at such a level to the voters when the next budget came up, or to the board of directors of a corporation when an even higher amount might be involved.

The plague of intellectual-property theft has recently been extended to music compact discs (CDs) and DVD movies. Napster, Gnutella, Wrapster—do you know if your children are using these *peer-to-peer* packages and others like them? Such software allows people to share digital music and video files through the Internet, even though most of the material is restricted by copyright. Napster lost its court cases in the year 2000 and was forced to begin cooperating with the recording industry to screen out copyright-infringing material from its exchange networks. Individuals received legal notice from infuriated bands such as the heavy-metal group Metallica warning them to destroy their pirated copies of stolen music tracks.

In summary, stealing other people's intellectual property is illegal, unethical, and rude. Although there may never be an instance of an individual prosecuted in court, the entire issue can be discussed with employees and children in terms of the ethical and moral principles involved.

The following sections present, and then argue against, the most common excuses offered to justify theft of intellectual property.

33.11.1   Everyone Is Doing It.   That is simply not true: Not everyone breaches copyright. Furthermore, the fact that some people are violating laws and norms of civility is irrelevant to whether others ought to be doing so. What should a concerned parent say in response to the excuse that everyone is staying out late, using drugs, driving without a license, shoplifting, or plagiarizing? Obviously, there would be strict admonitions not to violate the law or to ignore a family standard of integrity. The number of people who use other people's work without recompense does not make this action right or legal. Ethical behavior is not conditional on the actions of others.

33.11.2   We Will Not Get Caught.   Not getting caught is irrelevant to whether they ought to be doing it. Being caught has no bearing on whether an act is moral or legal. A hit-and-run crime is certainly no less criminal simply because the driver was not caught. Doing bad things gets to be a habit regardless of whether or not anyone finds out about it. Companies that tolerate any kind of illegality by their employees while on company time, or on company systems, are opening themselves up to blackmail, denunciation, and lawsuits. In addition, companies or individuals who countenance unethical or illegal attacks on others are almost certain to find those same acts perpetrated against themselves.

33.11.3   It Is the Music and Software Industries' Fault.   Four responses are appropriate here.

1. Even shareware authors who charge only a few dollars are cheated by people who use their software without paying for it.

2. The owner of the software or of the music copyright has no obligation to meet anyone else's view of appropriate pricing.

3. No one has a right or entitlement to use intellectual property without an agreement with its owner. If the price is unacceptable, there may be a more cost-effective alternative within the law.

4. It is just plain rude to disregard the express wishes of software designers or musicians by using their creative output without their permission. Would you do this if you were face to face with these people? If not, examine your motivations and justifications.

33.11.4 It Is the Producers' Fault. Attempts to blame the victim instead of a criminal attacker are misguided. If someone had entered an office or a home by breaking down the door, and then had removed some valuable property, would any jury excuse the crime because the defense claimed that the property owner was at fault for not having a stronger door? Actually, criminal hackers go to great lengths to violate security measures on the systems they compromise; every attempt to defend against intrusion is met with vigorous activity to find ways around the defenses.

33.11.5 It Does Not Hurt Anyone. But it does. Software vendors, for example, including individual entrepreneurs and employees, suffer from having an estimated one-half to seven-eighths of their potential sales eliminated through theft. In addition to the loss of revenue, there is a loss of incentive, for which everyone suffers. No one knows what great software or musical creations have been lost because of this disincentive.

33.11.6 It Only Hurts a Company, Not an Individual. A company is not a machine, it is a group of people who agree to work together, for the good of the company and to their own benefit. Steal from the company and you steal from employees, owners, and other stakeholders. You may even hurt honest users by contributing to higher prices. Some hackers say that they would steal from a business office but not the property of an employee there. Where is the line they are drawing? Would they steal from a corner store owned by Mom and Pop? What if the business were a sole proprietorship, or had only a few employees? If this were really a political and ideological issue, perhaps the hackers should use the tactics of civil disobedience and present themselves for legal action instead of violating copyright in secret.

33.11.7 The Music Industry Is Violating Musicians' Rights, So Breaching Copyright Is Okay. Many people feel that musicians are being violated by the big music distributors' stranglehold on copyrights and distribution.[3] If there is real concern for musicians' income, unlawful copying of their records could hardly improve the situation. Taking a musician's work without recompensing anyone at all hardly seems like a principled stand against greed—rather the reverse.

33.11.8 Theft Is Helping to Increase Software and Music Sales. The software and music industries carefully develop their marketing strategies, and they have rejected this model. Attempting to force a marketing strategy on such unwilling participants is neither feasible nor acceptable. This is somewhat analogous to stealing the merchandise of a store and giving it away without permission, because "the give-away is a great loss-leader, and the losses will be recouped by increased visibility and sales."

33.11.9 No Software, Music, or Art Should Ever Be Copyrighted—It Should Always Be Free. Many of those who make this argument earn a salary, or at least

they plan to; they do not donate their time. They also buy their computers, drive purchased automobiles, and own VCRs, obviously not in favor of communal property
and voluntary labor for themselves. These people certainly lack the right to determine
that other people's labor should be free. They are at liberty to give away music or software that they themselves create, but their claims to rights over the property of others
is certainly specious. They should not claim to be following a principle that they would
not apply to their own property or labor.

33.11.10   I Need It But Cannot or Do Not Want to Pay for It.   Even if you
could define need so flexibly as to include the wish to use someone else's tools or art
without paying for them, that cannot normally justify theft. Use of the Internet and
special software ought not negate our normal attitudes toward fair dealing with other
people. Cyberspace is not a place, it is just a word for a method of communications;
normal obligations and constraints that govern civil society must not be ignored simply
because modems and T1 lines are in use.

33.11.11   Resources on Software, Music, and Video Theft

- Business Software Association (BSA): *www.bsa.org*
- Copyright and Fair Use Site at Stanford University: *http://fairuse.stanford.edu*
- Recording Industry Association of America (RIAA): *www.riaa.org*
- Software Information Industry Association (SIIA): *www.spa.org*
- Zeropaid: The File Sharing Portal: *www.zeropaid.com*

33.12   PLAGIARISM.   A different kind of fraud involving intellectual property
occurs when people misrepresent someone else's work as their own. Older students
know intellectually that this is supposed to be bad, but for young children, the issue is
completely abstract. The problem today is that plagiarism is easier than ever and harder
for teachers to detect.

Academic guidelines try to make it clear to students that copying other people's
work without attribution is called *plagiarism* and is severely frowned on. Plagiarism
includes not only direct quotation without indications of origin but also paraphrasing
that merely shuffles the ideas around a little or substitutes synonyms for the original
words. In many institutions, plagiarism is grounds for suspension or expulsion. In all
cases, plagiarism defeats the purpose of writing assignments by eliminating the opportunity for critical thinking and creative expression. Few plagiarists remember what they
have copied from others after they hand their material in.

Assuredly, students have traded term papers and other assignments for centuries.
However, the availability of electronic documents and of the World Wide Web has enormously increased both the fund of material that can be plagiarized and the ease of
copying. Worse still, some people are profiting from easy accessibility by selling papers
specifically for plagiarism and even writing papers to order. In one study by Peggy Bates
and Margaret Fain of the Kimbel Library at Coastal Carolina University, the authors
easily located over 100 sites on the Web selling or donating papers to students for plagiarism.[4] To combat this problem, science has come to the aid of beleaguered instructors by providing automated similarity analysis of any paper submitted electronically.
The system uses a bank of more than 100,000 term papers and essays as well as documents located on the Web; analysis uses pattern recognition to measure similarities

among different documents and to estimate the probability of plagiarism. According to the turnitin.org documentation:

> Our system is now being used in the majority of universities in the United States and the U.K., as well as a large number of schools around the world. Many of these institutions, among them UC Berkeley and the fifty-eight member schools of the Consortium of Liberal Arts Colleges, an association of the most respected liberal arts schools in the US, have chosen to ensure the academic integrity of all their students by selecting institution-wide subscriptions to our service. Other universities, such as Harvard and Cornell, have elected to make use of our system on a departmental or single-instructor basis.

Plagiarism is also a risk to the enterprise; having employees misuse other people's or other organization's materials without attribution can lead to lawsuits, embarrassing publicity, and serious financial penalties.

33.12.1 Practical Guidelines

- Discuss plagiarism clearly at home and at school.
- Use examples to illustrate the difference between plagiarism and a legitimate use of other people's work.
- Encourage children to practice summarizing information in their own words.
- Practice writing references to quoted material.
- Have a student submit a sample term paper to the turnitin.org analysis program for an automatic *Originality Report.*
- Discuss how antiplagiarism sites analyze documents to measure similarities and help teachers identify plagiarism.

33.12.2 Resources on Plagiarism

- "Cheating 101: Paper Mills and You," by Margaret Fain and Peggy Bates (revised 2001): *www.coastal.edu/library/papermil.htm*
- Overview of Turnitin.org: *www.turnitin.org/new.html*
- "Plagiarism: What It Is and How to Recognize and Avoid It," from the Indiana University student manual: *www.indiana.edu/~wts/wts/plagiarism.html#plagiarized*
- "Plagiarism and the Web," by Bruce Leland of Western Illinois University: *www.wiu.edu/users/mfbhl/wiu/plagiarism.htm*
- Plagiarism.org: *www.plagiarism.org*

33.13 CRIMINAL HACKING AND HACKTIVISM. As discussed in Chapter 31, it is important that all employees understand and agree that using corporate systems for unauthorized access to computers and networks is grounds for dismissal and possibly criminal prosecution. In particular, no employee should ever imagine that testing for security weaknesses in the enterprise's systems without authorization is a contribution to security.

The motivation for illegal actions does not mitigate the seriousness of computer trespass. Employees should be informed explicitly that regardless of the excuse, no violations of law will be tolerated. For example, hacking into systems in another country to support a war effort is not excusable; nor is destroying child pornography sites a good idea. Cybervigilantes can destroy evidence needed for prosecution.

33.13.1   Practical Guidelines

- Contact your local FBI office and find out if they can send a speaker to your company or to a local meeting of a professional security association for a discussion of computer crime.

- If you or specific authorized staff (e.g., from the security group) do visit Web sites that support criminal hacking, be sure to use a personal firewall and set the parameters to deny access to personal information and to refuse cookies and active code (ActiveX, Java) from such sites.

33.13.2   Resources on Criminal Hacking and Hacktivism

- Campen, A.D., D.H. Dearth, and R.T. Goodden, eds. *Cyberwar: Security, Strategy, and Conflict in the Information Age.* Fairfax, VA: AFCEA International Press 1996.

- Fialka, J.J. *War by Other Means: Economic Espionage in America.* New York: W.W. Norton, 1997.

- Forester, T., and P. Morrison. *Computer Ethics: Cautionary Tales and Ethical Dilemmas in Computing.* Cambridge, MA: MIT Press, 1990.

- Freedman, D.H., and C.C. Mann. *@ Large: The Strange Case of the World's Biggest Internet Invasion.* New York: Simon & Schuster, 1997.

- Garfinkel, S. *Database Nation: The Death of Privacy in the 21st Century.* Sebastopol, CA: O'Reilly, 2000.

- Goodell, J. *The Cyberthief and the Samurai: The True Story of Kevin Mitnick— and the Man Who Hunted Him Down.* New York: Dell, 1996.

- Gordon, S. "Inside the Mind of Dark Avenger (abridged)." Originally published in *Virus News International* (January 1993); *www.research.ibm.com/antivirus/ SciPapers/Gordon/Avenger.html*

- Gordon, S. "Technologically Enabled Crime: Shifting Paradigms for the Year 2000." Originally published in *Computers and Security* (1994); *www.research. ibm.com/antivirus/SciPapers/Gordon/Crime.html*

- Gordon, S. "Virus Writers: The End of Innocence?" Presented at the 10th International Virus Bulletin Conference, 2000: *www.research.ibm.com/antivirus/ SciPapers/VB2000SG.htm* or *www.research.ibm.com/antivirus/SciPapers/ VB2000SG.pdf*

- Hafner, K., and J. Markoff. *Cyberpunk: Outlaws and Hackers on the Computer Frontier.* New York: Touchstone Books, Simon & Schuster, 1991.

- Kabay, M.E. "Making Ethical Decisions: A Guide for Kids (and Parents and Teachers Too) (2000): *www2.norwich.edu/mkabay/ethics/making_ethical_decisions. htm* or *www2.norwich.edu/mkabay/ethics/making_ethical_decisions.pdf*

- Littman, J. *The Fugitive Game: Online with Kevin Mitnick—The Inside Story of the Great Cyberchase.* Boston: Little, Brown and Company, 1996.

- Power, R. *Tangled Web: Tales of Digital Crime from the Shadows of Cyberspace.* Indianapolis, IN: Que, 2000.

- Schwartau, W. *Terminal Compromise.* Seminole, FL: Inter. Pact Press 1991.

- Shimomura, T., and J. Markoff . *Takedown: The Pursuit and Capture of Kevin Mitnick, America's Most Wanted Computer Outlaw—by the Man Who Did It.* New York: Hyperion, 1996.

- Slatalla, M., and J. Quittner. *Masters of Deception: The Gang that Ruled Cyberspace.* New York: HarperCollins, 1995.

- Smith, G. *The Virus Creation Labs: A Journey into the Underground.* Tucson, AZ: American Eagle Publications, 1994.

- Sterling, B. *The Hacker Crackdown: Law and Disorder on the Electronic Frontier.* New York: Bantam Doubleday Dell, 1992.

- Stoll, C. *The Cuckoo's Egg: Tracking a Spy Through the Maze of Computer Espionage.* New York: Pocket Books, Simon & Schuster, 1989.

- Winkler, I. *Corporate Espionage:What It Is, Why It Is Happening in Your Company, What You Must Do about It.* Rocklin, CA: Prima Publishing, 1997.

33.14 ONLINE AUCTIONS.   The theory behind an auction is that the competition for an object or service helps participants determine a fair price. This process can be corrupted in a real-world, physical auction if the seller conspires with confederates to bid up the price artificially. Unfortunately, this is even easier online, where anyone can have as many identities as he or she wants. The ease with which browsers and e-mail systems allow forged headers and forged identifiers means that sellers can inflate the price of their own offerings.

The Federal Trade Commission of the United States reports that online auctions cause the largest number of complaints they receive annually about fraud.

This theoretical discussion does not even begin to address such questions as whether the auctioned items really exist, are as described, or will ever be delivered. A case of such fraud occurred on eBay, where Robert Guest of Los Angeles admitted in court in July 1999 that he defrauded victims of around $37,000 by offering goods for auction via eBay but failing to deliver anything. The customers of Mr. Guest certainly found out the hard way that they were being cheated, but it appears that they could not have known in advance that he was untrustworthy. Although eBay maintains a system whereby potential bidders can see reviews and comments posted by earlier customers of each seller, new sellers such as Mr Guest have no record, and anyone with a bad record can assume a new identity.

eBay has further responded to these concerns by suggesting the use of escrow services and by warning its users that it does not guarantee the legitimacy of the transactions it facilitates.

There are also concerns about the legality of some of the items put up for auction. Someone offered items made from endangered species, in violation of the Convention on International Traffic in Endangered Species. The products included dried feet of elephants and gorillas caught in snares and allowed to die excruciating deaths before being hacked into pieces. In the United States, buying, selling, and possessing such contraband can lead to arrest, prosecution, fines, or imprisonment.

More ludicrously, someone put up a human kidney for sale through eBay in September 1999 and received bids of up to $5.8 million. The auction service canceled the sale because selling human organs is a federal felony with up to $250,000 in fines and at least five years in jail. A week later, eBay had to shut down an auction for an unborn human baby. Prices for the supposed baby had risen into the $100,000 range before eBay shut down that auction. Finally, a fool or a prankster—it is unclear which—

tried to sell 500 pounds of fresh marijuana online. The auction was shut down after 21 hours, during which prices offered had reached $10 million. In August of 2001, a couple offered to name their baby in accordance with the wishes of a high bidder. That auction, too, was ended prematurely.

Most of the bids probably were not legitimate. It is unlikely that everyone who bid for kidneys, pot, and babies really expected to pay for what they were bidding on. They may have been treating the auction like a video game, with no element of reality. Situations such as these invite other abuses, and ordinary users are often at a loss as to how to proceed.

Even if the items being offered for sale online are ordinary things such as software or physical products, they may have been obtained illegally. Online auctions are a frequently used channel for fencing stolen goods.

Corporate users should probably not be using Internet auctions to buy or sell products, except in those closely guarded, industry-specific sites that have proven their worth. Certainly, employees should not be using corporate Internet access to engage in such activities for their private purposes.

33.14.1   Practical Guidelines to Help Your Employees

- Before becoming involved with online auctions, research the value of goods you are interested in buying. Check bricks-and-mortar stores, online retail outlets, and comparative shopping sites that provide you with specific prices.

- Examine the policies and costs on shipping, warrantees, and refunds.

- Set your upper limit before you get involved in an auction. Do not be influenced by the value other people appear to place on a particular product or service, and certainly do not be caught up in a bidding frenzy.

- Do not treat online auctions as a competition you have to win.

- Look for auction services that provide a guarantee of support if you are cheated in a transaction. For example, check for language in the terms of service that covers losses up to a suitable limit. Check for insurance policies, costs, terms, and limits. Use search engines to evaluate the trustworthiness of the service you are thinking of using.

- If possible, use a service that provides an escrow function so that you pay money to the service and then release it only when the product is received in good condition.

- Use the browser functions to print documents, and save Web pages to disk at every stage of each transaction.

33.14.2   Resources on Online Auctions

- "Buying at Online Auctions": *http://gcorner0.tripod.com/other/onlineauction.html*

- "eBay.com Rules & Safety Overview": *http://pages.ebay.com/help/community/index.html*

- "Fraud Grows among Online Auctions," by Jim Carlton and Pui-Wing Tam: *www.zdnet.com/zdnn/stories/news/0,4586,2569405,00.html*

- "How to Survive Online Auctions: Avoiding the Swindlers of Cyberspace," by David Noack, 1999: *www.apbnews.com/safetycenter/specialreport/onlineauctions.html*

- "Online Auctions: Deal or Steal," by Audri and Jim Lanford in *Internet Scam-Busters #43* (2001): *www.scambusters.org*
- "The Scoop on Online Auctions," by Robin Boyd: *www3.lifeserv.com/essentials/fun/article.asp?ArticleID=2438*
- "Tips for Consumers: Online Auctions," from the Better Business Bureau, 1998: *www.bbb.org/library/auctions.asp*

33.15   ONLINE GAMBLING.   It is hard to imagine that any enterprise would authorize employees to gamble online using corporate resources, but providing employees with the following guidance may be a valuable service.

33.15.1   Fraud and Error.   In 1998, the Arizona lottery discovered that no winning number in its Pick 3 game had ever included even one numeral 9.[5] It turned out that the pseudo–random number generator algorithm had an elementary programming error that generated only the digits 0 through 8. All those who had used a 9 in their lottery numbers felt justifiable anger—especially when they were told they could have a refund, but only if they had kept their old losing tickets.

The Arizona lottery used a simulated random process to provide the illusion to gamblers that they were betting on a physical process such as balls mixing together in a barrel and falling out of a tube. One of the problems with the Arizona simulation is similar to a genuine vulnerability in proprietary (i.e., secret) cryptographic algorithms. As cryptographers have stressed over many decades, the security of an encryption scheme should not depend on the secrecy of its algorithm. Had the lottery algorithm been exposed to public scrutiny, its flaws would have been detected sooner. For example, in the 1980s there was much excitement over a new encryption scheme called the knapsack algorithm; after extensive examination by cryptographers, it proved to be flawed. It is conceivable that someone detecting the flaw in the Arizona lottery might have made bets with a higher probability of winning than those of uninformed people, but exposing the algorithm and its implementation to scrutiny before it went into production would have made that less likely.

These examples demonstrate that electronic gambling, as in older, conventional types, is subject to more than the rules of chance. Lack of conformity to good security practices lays both the gambler and the "house" open to abuse, and to inadvertent errors.

33.15.2   Lack of Control.   Physical gaming devices are located in real-world establishments under the nominal control of regulatory and law enforcement officials. Even so, they are always adjusted for a certain predetermined payout. Gambling based on the results of actual sports events or contests is validated by external news reports, although the contests themselves can be rigged. But there is no basis for a gambler to trust the results of computer-generated pseudo–random numbers displayed on a browser screen.

Most individual gamblers will never know if a long-range analysis of the pseudo–random numbers would support their hopes for fairness in the odds. No one is keeping track of these data except the people making money from the participants, and they are not distributing the results.

The disclaimer at one Internet gambling portal, *findinternetcasino.com,* is not very encouraging:

> Although every attempt has been made to ensure fairness and security toward the player at
> each of the links that can be found in the directories, FindInternetCASINO® cannot be held

responsible if discrepancies occur between an Online Gambling operation and you, the player, after following a link from this WWW site. Consult your local authorities prior to registering with any online wagering service. U.S. Citizens: The information at this site is for entertainment and news purposes only. Use of this information in violation of any federal, state or local laws is prohibited.

33.15.3   Legal Issues.   In some jurisdictions, betting online is illegal. In the United States, for example, it is already illegal to use interstate telecommunications to place bets; in addition, there are several initiatives to ban Internet betting even if the host is outside the United States. On February 28, 2000, Jay Cohen was convicted in Manhattan federal court after a two-week trial of operating a sports betting business that illegally accepted bets and wagers on sporting events from Americans over the Internet and telephones. Cohen was convicted of conspiracy to violate the Wire Wager Act and seven substantive violations of the Wire Wager Act in connection with his operation of World Sports Exchange (WSE). On August 6, 2001, his conviction was upheld in federal appeals court.

If your employees insist on gambling, they may want to check the ratings for a specific operation on the Fair Bet site, *www.fairbet.com*. There they can find purportedly objective ratings of any Internet casino.

33.15.4   Practical Guidelines

- Do not gamble with money you cannot afford to lose.
- Do not gamble online, except at well-known sites.
- If you do gamble online, do not gamble with money at sites hosted outside your own country.
- Do not give your credit card number to online gambling centers that are outside your own country.
- Before you gamble online, do some research to find out if there have been complaints about that casino. Contact your Better Business Bureau, or equivalent, and see if you can find friends or acquaintances who have played on the site you are considering.

33.15.5   Resources on Online Gambling

- "Borderless Betting: The Emergence of Online Gambling," by Elliot Almond, 1999: *http://seattletimes.nwsource.com/news/sports/html98/gamb_012499. html*
- Interview with founder of Fair Bet describing fraudulent casino: *http://fairbet. org/cgi-bin/display.pl?page=pop_up*
- Fair Bet: *http://fairbet.org/cgi-bin/display.pl*
- "Hill Stymied by Online Gambling," by Patrick Ross, 2001: *http://news.cnet. com/news/0-1005-200-5192243.html*
- "Jay Cohen Convicted of Operating an Off-shore Sports Betting Business that Accepted Bets from Americans over the Internet," U.S. Department of Justice press release, 2000: *www.usdoj.gov/criminal/cybercrime/cohen.htm*
- "Log on, Double Down," by Michael Bradley, 1997: *www.shorecast.com/html/ Features/ScFeatures/FeatOnlineGam2.html*

- "Online Gambling: Sleazy or Safe?" by Herman Manson: *www.mediatoolbox. co.za/new/aspen_viewartaspen.dll?Aid=1071&temp=12*
- "Wanna Bet? Look Offshore," by Michael Bradley (1997): *www.shorecast.com/ html/Features/ScFeatures/FeatOnlineGam.html*

33.16   BUYING ON THE WEB.   Buying from known merchants through the Web can be as satisfying as buying in their stores. If you know the organizations selling goods and services, there is no more reason to be worried about buying from them through a Web connection than buying from them over the phone or in person at a store. Web sites belonging to recognized merchants or organizations, such as non-profit charities, are trustworthy, especially if they show any of several symbols representing compliance with various standards of security for customer data. Some of the safety seals in common use include:

- TrustWatch from GeoTrust:

  Potential buyers won't spend time on a site unless they know from whom they're getting information or who's really selling the goods and services. . . . Big stores and long-recognized brands are recognized in the physical world, but what about online? In the anonymous world of the Web, consumers want to be certain about the site they're visiting, to know the business behind the site is real. Identity is the foundation for trust.... Without identity, legitimacy will always be suspect. TrustWatch is an identity solution for business Web sites. Site association with a business is checked, and site owners are provided with an active digital icon for their Web site. Consumers, seeking to know and trust the Web domains they visit, will know from the icon if the Web site owner is a TrustWatch member. And, if the site belongs to a TrustWatch member, consumers will have access to business information about that enterprise. It's a way to show legitimate sites and make eCommerce safer.[6]

- TRUSTe:

  TRUSTe is an independent, non-profit privacy initiative dedicated to building users' trust and confidence on the Internet and accelerating growth of the Internet industry. We've developed a third-party oversight "seal" program that alleviates users' concerns about online privacy, while meeting the specific business needs of each of our licensed Web sites.[7]

- WebTrust:

  WebTrust is a service jointly developed by the Canadian Institute of Chartered Accountants (CICA) and the American Institute of Certified Public Accountants (AICPA) and adopted globally by the accounting profession. WebTrust enables consumers and businesses to purchase goods and services over the Internet with confidence that vendors' Web sites meet high standards of privacy protection, business ethics and security.[8]

33.16.1   Dynamic Pricing.   One controversial technique that some firms have been studying is *dynamic pricing*. Dynamic pricing presents a different price to different customers. By building a profile of a specific customer's buying habits, vendors can inflate prices for people who appear to be more willing to buy higher-priced goods and lower prices for those who are cost-conscious. Many bricks-and-mortar stores do the same, in that stores in some parts of town may cater to richer people than in other areas; similarly, some chains of stores have been documented as charging higher prices to poor people in ghettos than in suburbs in part because there is less competition in poor neighborhoods and the cost of doing business may be higher there. A different kind of dynamic pricing occurs in the airline industry, where seats on planes vary in price according to when they are booked and how many seats are expected to be sold. However, unlike these examples, dynamic pricing on the Web resembles traditional automobile sales, where research confirms that women and racial minorities are consistently offered higher prices than the deals for white males. In both automobile sales and dynamic pricing on the Web, the fundamental difference from the normal free-market model is that the prices are varied secretly so that only the victim of the predatory pricing sees the offered price. Without mechanisms for sharing information among purchasers, this model of pricing seems to put the buyers at an immense disadvantage with respect to the seller. It will be interesting to see how this model develops over time.

33.16.2   Privacy.   Another key area of concern when buying products on the Web is privacy. Many consumers prefer their buying habits to remain their own business. Receiving unwanted paper mail or e-mail, because of past purchases, seems intrusive and irritating to them; they classify all such promotions as junk mail. Other consumers appreciate the convenience of receiving targeted information about new products and special sale prices for items they have previously bought. In either case, it is important to pay attention to the privacy policies offered by online vendors. Marketers must decide whether to set up their systems on an opt-in or opt-out basis. If marketers choose the former, then all individuals actually must *agree* to have information about themselves included on lists that may be used within the organization or sold to or traded with third parties. If the system is set up for opt-out, then everyone's information may be freely disclosed, except for those who specifically state that they do not want the list keepers to do so. These are broad general outlines; the privacy policy of each organization must be spelled out in detail. Some sites such as online bookstores and music services may keep detailed records of what each person buys from them, and even what items are simply looked at. These Web sites can then tailor their sales presentations to products that are appropriate to each customer's interests. Amazon.com, for example, tries to be helpful to visitors by suggesting books that may interest the returning visitor based on previous behavior. However, one of the unexpected consequences of customer profiling is that the practice may reveal more than users would wish; if you watch one of your employees enter such a Web site and discover that the predominant theme is, say, weapons and techniques of terrorism, you might want to have some serious discussions with your human resources staff. A less positive application of profiling caused a flurry of interest when information about the purchasing habits of employees of specific companies was accidentally made available to those companies' competitors.

Another issue often raised in discussions of privacy is cookies. Cookies are small text files that a site stores on a visitor's hard disk to store information that can be used the next time the user visits the site. Properly defined cookies can be used only by the site that deposited them. The information stored can include the sequence of Web pages the visitor saw or personal identifiers that allow the Web software to recognize the visitor so that the Web site can build up a preference profile for each visitor or client, and to enable those cheery greetings like "Welcome back, Bob! We have a special deal for you on the newest title in *The Real Man's Guide to Heavy Artillery* series!" Cookies also may be used to accumulate items in a shopping cart; without cookies, each purchase would have to be concluded separately.

In general, cookies are harmless. If you do not like the idea of having identifiers stored on your system, you can block cookies in your browser settings, block them globally or on a site-by-site basis using a personal firewall, or install cookie-sweepers that get rid of all cookies whenever you activate them.

33.16.3   Practical Guidelines

- Before spending a considerable amount of money on a new online merchant's site, do some basic research into the site's reliability. Check the company's reputation; see if it belongs to the Better Business Bureau, and contact the appropriate chapter of the BBB to see if there have been complaints about the vendor.

- Do a Web search using a good search engine, such as Google, to see if there are any up-to-date reports about customer experience on the site you are interested in.

- Pretend that you already have a problem and look for the customer service pages. Are there clear instructions on how to communicate problems? Would you have the choice of e-mail, letters, and phone communications? If you have the time, you may even want to try calling customer service and find out just how they handle calls. If you hit a company that hangs up on you when its lines are busy ("We are sorry, but all our agents are busy; please call back later"), you might want to give serious thought as to whether it is safe doing business with them.

- Read the company's return policy; how does it handle breakage in transit or defective goods? Does it offer guarantees on delivery time? What happens if the company is out of stock on a specific item—does it ship partial shipments or wait for everything to be ready? If it splits your shipment, does it charge extra for delivery of the later parts?

- Read the site's privacy policy. If the text is practically invisible 6-point yellow on white, be suspicious. Look for weasel-words in the clauses that say, for instance, that their policies can be changed at any time without notice. You must check the site regularly to see if the policy has changed, but this is unrealistic. Instead, look for firm, clear assurances that your personal information will not be sold, traded, or given away without your permission. Usually, Web site owners state that they may have to divulge information to partnering organizations that handle such normal functions as billing and order fulfillment. There can be little objection to this provided the partners are bound by acceptable security policies.

- Keep a detailed record of your transactions. Use the browser functions to save copies of, or print out, the relevant Web pages with descriptions of the products, prices, a summary of your order, the order number, promised delivery date, and method of shipment.

33.16.4   Resources on Buying on the Web

- "Be an Educated Consumer: Know the Danger Signals of Scams," from the Better Business Bureau: *www.bbb.org/library/educatedcons.asp*

- "Buying Computers by Mail," from the Better Business Bureau: *www.bbb.org/library/compmail.asp*

- "Check Out a Company," from the Better Business Bureau: *www.bbb.org/reports/bizreports.asp*

- "Cybershopping—What You Need to Know," from the Better Business Bureau: *www.bbb.org/library/cybershop.asp*

- GeoTrust: *www.geotrust.com* and *www.geotrust.com/building_trust/safe_market/trustwatch.asp*

- "Learn to Identify Deceptive Ads," from the Better Business Bureau: *www.bbb.org/library/deceptads.asp*

- TRUSTe home page: *www.truste.org*
- "WebTrust Certification: Your Essential e-commerce Web Site Enhancement": *webtrust.net*

33.17   GAMES.   Some enterprises allow their employees to play games at various times during the day—usually low-usage times such as lunch, or before and after the normal workday. However, some Internet-enabled multiuser games can consume enormous bandwidth; the shoot-'em-up game called Quake is notorious for saturating all available connectivity.

When helping employees understand how to negotiate the perils of the Internet, you might recommend that parents read reviews of video games before allowing their young children to play them. Some games have astonishing levels of graphic violence ("Brilliant Bleeding! Detailed Decapitations!!") and unusual values ("Win points by burning as many residents to death as possible!"). This latter example is based on a notorious case in which a video-game vendor was apparently surprised by the public wave of revulsion over a game that glorified arson. Some military and police shoot-'em-up games explicitly take points off for hitting innocent bystanders; others do not. Some games use graphic nudity; others are more modest. The main point is that relying on the judgment of eight-year-olds to choose their own entertainment may be unwise.

33.17.1   Practical Guidelines

- Learn to play some of the games your kids are enthusiastic about. Take the time to immerse yourself in the imaginary worlds they play in, and study the underlying values that are being communicated by the game creators.
- Use published reviews from online or other media that reflect your own family's values before allowing games into your home.
- Accompany your children to the stores when buying video games. Check for parental warning labels. Talk to the salespeople if you think they are reliable.
- Know the characteristics of your hardware and software before buying recently released games. Do not buy a new game only to discover that it does not run on your obsolescent system. A disappointed child can apply intense pressure to spend money on a new system. Some games are computationally intensive and require expensive, advanced computer hardware and modern sound systems, complete with a high-powered amplifier driving woofers and subwoofers.
- Try making game playing an opportunity for family fun or parent-child bonding instead of the isolating experience games can sometimes be. See if you can all have fun with puzzle- and exploration-oriented games such as *Myst* and *Riven,* neither of which involves violence, and both of which are visually beautiful.

33.17.2   Resources on Games

- "Content Rating and Filtering": *www.efa.org.au/Issues/Censor/cens2.html*
- "Guide to Parental Controls/Internet Safety Products": *www.microweb.com/pep-site/Software/filters.html*
- Platform for Internet Content Selection (PICS): *www.w3.org/PICS*

33.18   SPYWARE.   In December 1999, computer scientist, cybercrime investigator, and writer Richard Smith became curious about a program called *zBubbles* that he had installed on his system to improve online shopping. Created by Alexa, a sub-sidiary of e-tailer Amazon.com, the program provided competitive information about alternative and possibly cheaper sources for particular products. However, Smith dis-covered that there was more going on than met the eye.

Smith monitored his own Internet traffic while he was using zBubbles by using a packet sniffer, a tool that displays details of every piece of information being trans-mitted through a network connection. He found that zBubbles was sending a steady stream of information about him and his surfing habits to Alexa, including his home address, the titles of DVDs he had browsed on Buy.com, and the details of an airline ticket he had verified online. In addition, the program even continued to send infor-mation regularly to Alexa's servers even when Smith was not using his browser. It turned out that zBubbles was not the only program sending information back to its makers.

33.18.1 Surveillance. Many programs are available that, once installed, report on the Web sites you visit, which banner advertisements you click, what products you search for, and any other information the programmers have been instructed to acquire. Even widely used downloading software, such as NetZip, has been shown to report to its providers on the names of every file downloaded by each user.

Sometimes these programs are informally known as "E.T." applications, in a refer-ence to Steven Spielberg's movie of that name, in which an extraterrestrial strives to "phone home"—exactly what the spyware programs are doing.

The term "spyware" is applied to any technology that transmits information without the knowledge of its user. Several programs distributed without charge through the Internet secretly collect information about the user, monitor user behavior, and then send those data to advertisers. The more general class of monitoring software that col-lects information for use by advertisers is known as *advertising-supported software* or *adware*. These programs allow freeware to make money for its creators by gener-ating revenue based on how many users transmit information to the advertisers about their habits.

Although defenders of the advertising-supported programs claim that they are harm-less, privacy advocates argue that the issue is control: Do users know what these pro-grams are doing, or are they collecting and transmitting information covertly? Some adware comes with complicated contracts that use complex legal language to bury the fact that they will monitor and report user behavior. Worse yet, many such contracts explicitly authorize the software supplier to alter the privacy conditions without noti-fication and, preposterously, instruct the user to check the contracts on the Web fre-quently. No one has the time to monitor countless suppliers to see if privacy conditions have been altered, especially if there is no attempt to highlight changes.

Another issue is that some spyware modules have used *stealth* technology charac-teristic of viruses, Trojan horses, and other malicious software. For example, some adware (e.g., TSADBOT) installs itself as a system process and is not listed in the Win-dows task list. Therefore, it cannot easily by aborted by a user. TSADBOT also resists removal; even if the carrier product is uninstalled, TSADBOT persists. If a user's fire-wall blocks outbound transmission by the TSADBOT process, the spyware initiates attempts to reach its target at a rate of 10 per second, potentially leading to central pro-cessing unit (CPU) and network resource overload.

Spyware, like any software, can contain errors that cause system problems. In par-ticular, components of the Aureate/Radiate spyware have been shown to cause system instability and crashes.

One of the most egregious cases of spyware erupted in 1999, when it was discovered that CometCursor, a supplier of cute cartoon-character cursors aimed at children, was sending information back to its servers about what the children were browsing on the Net. According to some attorneys, this kind of covert data gathering about children may be a violation of the U.S. federal Child Online Privacy Protection Act.

Several free software programs have been written to help users identify and remove spyware. In addition, personal firewalls can identify and block unauthorized outbound communications. There is also a specialized program available that runs in the background to monitor and thwart attempts to install spyware.

33.18.2   Practical Guidelines

- Before installing freeware or adware, read the terms and conditions carefully to see if they currently include language permitting automatic transfer of information to the supplier or to third parties. Be aware that these contracts often include language authorizing the supplier to change the terms and conditions at any time and without notifying you.

- Install and use a spyware scanner and removal program, such as the free *Adaware* program from Lavasoft.

- If you are particularly irritated by spyware, install a real-time spyware monitor and blocker such as the inexpensive program *Adaware Plus,* which is also available from Lavasoft.

- Support legislative attempts to force software manufacturers to disclose their use of spyware.

33.18.3   Resources on Spyware

- Information on TSADBOT: *http://cexx.org/tsadbot.htm*
- Lavasoft: *www.lavasoft.de/aaw/aaware.html*
- Radiate/Aureate spyware information: *http://grc.com/oo/aureatemail.htm*
- Spyware Control Act: *http://grc.com/spywarelegislation.htm*

33.19   INTERNET ADDICTION.   Any activity can become the basis of compulsive exaggeration. A small proportion, around 5 percent, of the Internet-using population may qualify as addicted to any of the following computer-mediated activities:

- An uncontrollable desire to find and organize more and more information about an enormous range of topics
- Excessive involvement in games, gambling, and buying things on the Internet
- Excessive concentration on relationships mediated through e-mail and chat rooms to the detriment of real-life relationships
- Involvement in long sessions of viewing pornography or being sexually stimulated via e-mail, chat rooms, pornographic sites, or sexual-fantasy games

None of these activities is a suitable use of corporate computing resources, and employees should be alerted to the policies precluding such activities at work. In addition, everyone should be aware of the dangers of Internet addiction.

33.19.1   Signs of Addiction.   The issue here is what constitutes *excessive* involvement in these activities. Professional psychologists such as Dr. Kimberly Young have identified some of the diagnostic criteria for these disorders, including the following based on her *Internet Addiction Test:*

- Regularly staying online longer than intended
- Often neglecting obligations to spend more time online
- Consistently preferring to spend time online instead of with one's partner
- Frequent complaints by friends and family about excessive Internet use
- Suffering consequences at school or at work because of time spent online
- Giving e-mail a higher priority than other important issues
- Concealing the extent of Internet usage
- Turning to the Internet as a substitute for dealing with disturbing issues
- Feeling that life without the Internet would be devoid of meaning and pleasure
- Getting angry when disturbed during Internet usage
- Losing sleep due to late-night Internet activity
- Yearning to be back online

Those who feel uncomfortable about their level of involvement with the Internet would do well to take this test offered by Dr Young, and, if several of their answers are positive, to seek counseling to prevent possibly tragic consequences of untreated addiction.

33.19.2   Practical Guidelines

- Know the warning signs of Internet addiction and self-monitor.
- Discuss Internet addiction and its warning signs with your employees and your children.
- Encourage open discussion of feelings about the Net, so that children feel free to turn to you for help if they become uncomfortable or unhappy about their own experiences on the Net.

33.19.3   Resources on Internet Addiction

- *Caught in the Net: How to Recognize the Signs of Internet Addiction—and a Winning Strategy for Recovery,* by Kimberly S. Young. New York: John Wiley & Sons, 1998.
- Center for On-Line Addiction: *www.netaddiction.com*
- Computer Addiction Services: *www.computeraddiction.com*
- *Virtual Addiction: Help for Netheads, Cyberfreaks, and Those Who Love Them,* by David N. Greenfield. Oakland, CA: New Harbinger, 1999.

33.20   ONLINE DATING AND CYBERSEX.   As in other topics in this chapter, it is unlikely that corporate policy would allow users to engage in online dating and cybersex. Nonetheless, in line with the overall orientation of this chapter, the following sections will help employees understand the issues in these online activities.

33.20.1   Dating Online.   Thousands of sites on the Web specialize in helping people meet each other. In a sense, chat rooms and bulletin board systems are ways for people with similar interests to communicate about their hobbies and lifestyles. There are also sites that specialize in helping people find others who match particular profiles. Some of these sites are free; others charge fees for participation. Dating service sites usually explicitly restrict participation to people over 18 years old, but most of them depend on possession of a credit card as their sole mechanism for authenticating age. It is very difficult to exclude teenagers, or even younger children, from such sites if they have access to credit card numbers.

Parents, teachers, and employers who want to get a sense of what is going on can type "online dating" in the search field of a search engine such as Google (*www.google.com*) and then visit a few of the sites. If children post information about themselves in such a cyberspace locale, even with false information claiming that they are adults, there is a real risk of attracting unsavory characters or perhaps ordinary people who can become angry at being tricked into exposing their feelings to an imposter.

33.20.2   Sex Talk Online.   In addition to matchmaking, users of the Internet also can get involved in *cybersex*. People chatting online can describe themselves or each other in sexual interactions that are inappropriate for youngsters. Such online chat also has been implicated in a number of divorces, since many spouses find it wholly inappropriate that their beloved is getting sexually excited with a stranger via the Internet.

In August 2001, a 15-year-old girl from Massachusetts was alleged to have been kept captive for at least a week during which she was repeatedly sexually abused by the couple who had brought her to Long Island. According to the criminal complaint, she was also "loaned out" for two days to another man and further abused. The couple had met the teenager in an Internet chat room, where their conversation was explicitly sexual.

Employers should ensure that no one in their employ, none of their colleagues or employees, and none of their children could engage in these activities, whether using corporate resources or home computers.

33.20.3   Practical Guidelines for Parents and Teachers.   The National Center for Missing and Exploited Children (*www.missingkids.org*) suggests that you:

- Do not build online profiles or give out addresses, phone numbers, or school names.
- Do share e-mail accounts with your children, and oversee their messages.
- Keep the computer in a family room where children's activities can be monitored.
- Remember that people may lie when describing themselves online.
- Do not allow children to meet online users without permission, and make all meetings in public places with adult supervision.
- Forward copies of suggestive or obscene messages to your Internet service provider.
- Find ways to block objectionable material.

In addition, you might:

- Discuss online dating with kids so they understand what is involved.
- Ensure that kids understand why it is inappropriate and even dangerous for them to masquerade as adults in online dating services.

33.20.4 Practical Guidelines for Cyberdaters of All Ages

- Do not rush into face-to-face contact; you need to be sure that you are meeting someone who is on the level, not an imposter who has ulterior motives.

- You may want to take advantage of anonymizing services offered by some dating sites to avoid handing out your real e-mail address to complete strangers.

- Be suspicious of anyone who tries to pressure you in any way, including demanding money or insisting on a meeting before you feel confident of the person's good intentions.

- As you are getting to know someone online, ask questions about lots of things you are interested in—for example, hobbies, politics, religion, education, birthdate, family background, and marital history and status.

- Keep the answers you receive and beware of people who provide inconsistent or contradictory information as they are communicating with you—any lie is a danger signal.

- Be suspicious of anyone who seems to be too good to be true; if someone matches you on every single preference or interest you mention, try mentioning the very opposite of what you said earlier in the communications and see if the person agrees with *that* too. Trying too hard to please by lying may mark a manipulative and potentially dangerous personality.

- Be honest about yourself; state your own interests and characteristics fairly, including things you think might be less attractive than stereotypes and cultural norms dictate. A mature, good person will not necessarily be turned off if you do not look like a movie star or if you do not play four musical instruments perfectly, or if you lisp.

- If you get to the point of exchanging pictures, be sure that you see the person in a wide variety of situations and with other people; some online daters send false pictures to misrepresent themselves.

- Talk to the person you are getting interested in over the phone; be suspicious if the person resists such a request for a long time or always has excuses for not being available when you have agreed to talk.

- Listen carefully to how the person sounds on the phone, and be suspicious if you now receive information that contradicts something the person wrote to you about. Any lie should alert you to potential problems.

- Before you agree to meet, get your date's full name, address, and telephone number. Be suspicious if the person refuses to give you a home number: Could he or she have a spouse or a current live-in friend that he or she is trying to deceive? Call the home number a couple of times to see if someone else answers.

- Give the person's information, and the exact details of where and when you are going to meet, to friends and family. Do not ever accept a date with someone who wants to keep the location and time a secret. Be sure the meeting place is well lighted and in a public place such as a coffee shop.

- Do not allow a stranger to pick you up at your house, and be sure you can get home by yourself.

- Before considering further involvement, for safety's sake think about having a background check done on the person you like, using a professional service such as *whoishe.com* or *whoisshe.com*.

33.20.5   Resources on Online Dating and Cybersex

- "Cyberdating Tips from Dateable.com: 7 Things Everyone Should Know about Online Personals": *www.links2love.com/dating_sites_links.htm*
- "Cybersex and Online Relationships": *http://chatting.about.com/internet/chatting/cs/cybersex*
- "Cyborgasms: Cybersex amongst Multiple-Selves and Cyborgs in the Narrow-Bandwidth Space of America Online Chat Rooms." M.A. Dissertation, 1996: *www.socio.demon.co.uk/Cyborgasms.html*
- "Internet Safety Tips for Parents": *www.missingkids.org*
- "Online Dating Advice from the Experts: Information on How to Play It Safe": *www.joylight.com/dating.html*
- "Safety Tips for Cyber-dating": *http://whoishe.com/safety.html*
- "Teen Advice Online: Dating": *www.teenadvice.org/dating*
- 10 Tips for Online Dating Safely": *www.spankoz.com/online_dating_safety.htm*

33.21   HATE GROUPS.   Another source of concern for employers and parents is the easy accessibility of hate literature on the Web. Hatemongers have taken full advantage of the largely unregulated nature of the Net to spread their pernicious messages. One can find Web sites devoted to hatred of every imaginable identifiable group. Race, ethnicity, religion, gender, sexual orientation, immigration status, political ideology—anything can spark hatred in susceptible personalities. Unfortunately, some of the hate groups have been quite successful in recruiting young people through the Web; they publish propaganda such as pro-Nazi revisionist history that may fool uncritical people into believing their rants. Neo-Nazi and racist skinhead groups have formed hate-rock groups that take advantage of kids' enthusiasm for very loud music with aggressive lyrics.

Employers cannot tolerate the slightest involvement of their employees in such activities using corporate resources. Aside from their possible personal revulsion at such hate-mongering, managers also should be aware that toleration of intolerance can lead to a hostile work environment in which targets of hate or contempt can legitimately appeal to the courts for compensatory and punitive damages. Employees must understand and agree that using any corporate resources for participation in hate groups is a serious infraction of Internet usage policy.

33.21.1   Prevalence of Hate Sites.

According to the Simon Wiesenthal Center, there are over 2,300 Web sites advocating hatred, of which over 500 are extremist sites hosted on American servers but authored by Europeans; most European countries have strict antihate laws. Using more stringent criteria, the HateWatch group estimates more than 500 extremist hate sites on the Web; it distinguishes between hate propaganda and those pages that consist largely of racial epithets, dismissed as mere grafitti.

The Southern Poverty Law Center monitors 500 active hate organizations in the United States. It has regularly reported on the growing number and stridency of such sites. In his comments to Keith Perine of *Network World*, spokesperson Mark Potok said, "A few years ago, a Klansman needed substantial effort and money to produce and distribute a shoddy pamphlet that might reach a few hundred people. Today, with a $500 computer and negligible costs, that same Klansman can put up a slickly produced Web site with a potential audience in the millions."[9]

A fundamental reality is that human beings are gregarious. They find it very easy to affiliate with others to form *in-groups,* groups to which they feel entitled to belong. Unfortunately, defining in-groups naturally means it is equally easy to define *out-groups:* groups to which we *do not* want to belong. Grade school and high school cliques are examples of in- and out-groups. A wealth of study in social psychology confirms the validity of the universal impression that we tend to inflate our esteem for in-groups and to reduce our respect and liking for out-groups. However, research also shows that social norms against discrimination can reduce hostility toward out-groups; thus it seems likely that parental and teacher articulation of norms of tolerance can significantly reduce children's susceptibility to the blandishments of hate groups.

33.21.2 Practical Guidelines

- To protect your children against the wiles of these hateful people, the most important step is to discuss the issue of hate speech and hate groups with them openly. You may even want to visit some of the sites listed below *with your kids* to give them a sense of the problem and possible countermeasures.

- Discuss your children's feelings about out-groups in their own lives; for example, encourage them to speak freely, without fear of punishment or reprimand, about whatever groups they do not like. Then pursue the discussion with explanations of such issues as cultural differences, history, or whatever else you feel will help your children gain perspective on their own feelings and behavior. Of course, this positive attitude cannot be applied to hate groups or similar outlaws.

- Provide positive social role models for children with respect to hate groups. Speak out firmly in opposition to intolerance rather than sitting silently by when bigots display their hatred for other groups.

33.21.3 Resources on Hate Groups

- Center for the Study of Hate and Extremism: *www.hatemonitor.org*
- Media Awareness Network: *www.media-awareness.ca/eng*
  - Challenging Online Hate: *www.media-awareness.ca/eng/issues/internet/hintro.htm*
- Partners Against Hate: *www.partnersagainsthate.org*
- Simon Wiesenthal Center: *www.wiesenthal.com*
  - Museum of Tolerance: *www.wiesenthal.com/mot/index.cfm*
- Southern Poverty Law Center: *www.splcenter.org*
  - Intelligence Project: *www.splcenter.org/intelligenceproject/ip-index.html*
  - Teaching Tolerance: *www.splcenter.org/teachingtolerance/tt-index.html*
- Tolerance.org: *www.tolerance.org/index_flash.html*

33.22 PORNOGRAPHY.   Pornography—even with the most restrictive definitions —is widespread on the Internet. Observers of Net culture have commented that the sure-fire way of telling if new technology is going to be a success on the Internet is to see how quickly pornographers can apply it. For example, the appearance in July 2000 of the first WAP (wireless application protocol) pornography sites signaled the adoption of WAP technology into the mainstream. Although the sites offered only tiny grainy images of naked Japanese models, sociologists said that the same expected sequence of rapid technological advances occurred with photography and video cameras.

33.22.1   Prevalence of Porn.   Some studies of Internet traffic have claimed that more than half of the total bandwidth is used for transfer of pornography or solicitations for purchase of pornography.

33.22.2   Trickery.   Pornographers use various tricks to get people onto their Web sites:

- Using a different domain, like "whitehouse.com" to take advantage of interest in "whitehouse.gov."
- Misspellings, such as the now-inactive "micosoft.com," which traded on the likelihood of mistyping "Microsoft.com."
- Junk e-mail invitations with innocent-looking labels for URLs that do not match the actual link, but instead take the viewer to a pornography site.
- Padding porn-site metatags (normally invisible text used to describe a Web site) with inoffensive keywords that place the site high on search engine lists where they can appeal to children.
- Disabling normal features of a browser to trap victims in the porn site. One perpetrator who was shut down by the Federal Trade Commission (FTC) actually ran Java applets that disabled the "back" arrow and defeated the ability to close the browsers. People trapped in porno-hell had to reboot their computers to get out.

Porn sites are notorious for using deceit to defraud their victims. One widely used scam is to demand a credit card number from a visitor as "proof" of their age (it is nothing of the sort), then to charge the card even though the site clearly states that there is a period of free use.

In 1996, viewers of pornographic pictures on the sexygirls.com site were in for a surprise when they got their next phone bills. Victims who downloaded a "special viewer" were actually installing a Trojan Horse program that silently disconnected their connection to their normal ISP and reconnected them (with the modem speaker turned off) to a number in Moldova in central Europe. The long distance charges then ratcheted up until the user disconnected the session—sometimes hours later, even when the victims switched to other, perhaps less prurient, sites. Some victims who stayed online for a long time paid more than $1,000 in long-distance charges. In February 1997 in New York City, a federal judge ordered the scam shut down. An interesting note is that AT&T staff spotted the scam because of unusually high volume of traffic to Moldova, not usually a destination for many U.S. phone calls. In November 1997, the FTC won $2.74 million from the Moldovan telephone company to refund to the cheated customers.

Both of these scams described relied in part on the reluctance of porn-seeking victims to admit to their socially disapproved interest. Few victims were willing to pursue the matter until the damages mounted into the thousands of dollars.

33.22.3   Filtering.   An entire industry has grown up to try to shield (or block) children from seeing pornography or other materials deemed offensive by their parents or by the makers of the blocking software. The popular blocking systems are reviled by many free-speech advocates and often ridiculed for what are described as clumsy, keyword-oriented algorithms. The classic examples of ludicrous blocking include trapping access to any site that uses the word "breast"—including even possibly this very page if you are reading it on the Web. Other simple-minded traps have blocked users from accessing information pages for geographical locations ending in the old British suffix "-sex" such as Wessex, Sussex, Middlesex, and so on. The village of Scunthorpe in England was blocked by software used by a major Internet service provider because its internal filters prevented anyone from using "vulgar" words in their mailing address.

Some of the blocking software products use hidden assumptions about the unsuitability of a wide range of topics, including abortion rights, civil rights, political ideology, and gay liberation. Any parent is entitled to express opinions about any topic; however, parents will want to check on whether a particular program is imposing its makers' political agenda by stealth. In the workplace, employers who use broad-spectrum blocking software may interfere with legitimate research by their employees.

33.22.4   Monitoring.   A different approach to interfering with the nefarious deeds of pornographers is to install monitoring software on the computers that employees use at work or that children will use at home. These products keep a log or audit trail that allows employers and parents to see exactly what users have been doing with their computers.

In the family context, most important, however, is the principle that machines and programs cannot by themselves teach values. Instead of relying only on passive barriers or on snoopware, parents would do well to make surfing the Internet a family activity rather than a private hobby. And when kids express interest in pornography—because our popular culture is full of sexual innuendo that children read, hear, and see—it makes sense to discuss the issues rather than try to pretend that they do not exist. One approach for reducing the power of the forbidden fruit offered by pornographers is to explain to children in a supportive and nonpunitive way why sexual exploitation and degradation are bad for people. Children who stumble on porn sites by accident or at their friends' houses may be better prepared to cope with the sometimes disturbing images and words if their parents have prepared them for this aspect of today's world.

33.22.5   Practical Guidelines for Parents

- Place young children's Internet-access computers in a family area of the home rather than in their bedrooms.

- Interact with your children while they are using the Internet; treat the Web browser like a window on the world and be present to help your children interpret that world in a way consistent with your values.

- Talk with your children about the existence and nature of pornography; as they reach puberty, assure them that there is nothing wrong with being interested in sex, but that pornography is not a healthy way of learning about wholesome, loving relations.

- Warn your children about some of the tricks used by pornographers to get traffic on their Web sites, such as telling them to download special readers. Tell them about the Moldovan porn scam.

- Discuss the issue of junk e-mail that advertises porn sites. Warn children that no one should ever click on a URL from any kind of junk e-mail because it can easily be a trick to get them into dangerous territory.

- Teach your children to keep an eye on the actual URL that appears in the browser window; any discrepancy between the visible URL shown on a page and the actual URL should alert them to the possibility of fraud.

- Explain that pornographers sometimes charge for access to their sites without permission; be sure your children understand how dangerous it would be to give your credit card number to these people for any reason.

33.22.6 Resources on Pornography

- America Links Up!: *www.getnetwise.org/americalinksup*
- Christians Against Internet Pornography: *http://members.tripod.com/~Joseph_Provencial/caip_homepage.htm*
- Feminists' Perspectives on Pornography—Academic Dialogue on Applied Ethics: *http://caae.phil.cmu.edu/cavalier/forum/pornography/porn.html*
- "Marketing Pornography on the Information Superhighway: A Survey of 917,410 Images, Descriptions, Short Stories, and Animations Downloaded 8.5 Million Times by Consumers in Over 2000 Cities in Forty Countries, Provinces, and Territories" by Marty Rimm, 1995: *http://trfn.pgh.pa.us/guest/mrtext.html*
- Yahooligans Parents' Guide: www.yahooligans.com/parents

33.23 PEDOPHILES.   The following section applies primarily to training users for protection of their children.

33.23.1 Pedophiles Online.   Pedophilia is defined as sexual arousal in response to contact with or images of prepubescent children. Some pedophiles misrepresent themselves as youngsters in chat rooms or via e-mail and trick children into forming friendships with what they believe are peers. In one notorious case, Paul Brown Jr., a 47-year-old man, misrepresented himself as a 15-year-old boy in e-mail to a 12-year-old girl in New Jersey. The victim's mother stumbled onto the long-range relationship when she found a package from her daughter to a man she did not know sitting on her own doorstep; the child had put the wrong postage on it and the post office had sent it back. Opening the package, she found a videotape that showed her daughter cavorting naked in front of the family video camera. The distraught mother searched her daughter's room and discovered a pair of size 44 men's underpants in one of the child's bureau drawers.

Brown was arrested in February 1997. Police found correspondence with at least 10 other teenage girls across the country through which Brown convinced his young victims, some as young as 12, to perform various sexual acts in front of cameras and to send him the pictures and videotapes. He pleaded guilty in June to enticing a minor into making pornography. In August of 1997, at his sentencing hearing, one of his many victims told the court that she had suffered ridicule and humiliation as a result of her entrapment and had left her school to escape the trauma. She accused Brown of emotional rape. Displaying an astonishing interpretation of his own behavior, Brown said at his sentencing hearing, "It was just bad judgment on my part." Using good judgment, the court sentenced him to five years incarceration.

In March 2000, Patrick Naughton, a former executive of the INFOSEEK online company, pled guilty to having crossed state lines to commit statutory rape of a child. In August, FBI officials said that Naughton had been providing help in law enforcement investigations of pedophilia on the Net. In return for his cooperation, prosecutors asked the court for five years of probation (instead of a possible 15 years in prison), counseling, a $20,000 fine (instead of the maximum $250,000), and an agreement not to have "unapproved" contact with children and to stay out of sex chat rooms online.

The problem of Internet-mediated pedophile stalking has reached international dimensions. In January 1999, police forces around the world cooperated to track and close down a worldwide ring of pedophiles trafficking in child pornography through the Net.

In June 2000, child safety experts warned the U.S. congressional committee on child online protection that with the average age of online users declining (children between the ages of two and seven are among the fastest-growing user cohorts on the Internet), children increasingly are put at risk by their careless or ignorant online activities. Parry Aftab, a children's advocate, told committee members that 3,000 children were kidnapped in the United States last year after responding to online messages posted by their abductors. A recent survey of teenage girls found 12 percent had agreed to meet strangers who had contacted them online.

33.23.2   Practical Recommendations for Parents and Others to Protect Children

- Explain the dangers of communicating with strangers via the Net in the same terms that you discuss the dangers of talking to strangers anywhere else.
- Alert children to the questionable identity of anyone they meet exclusively through the Net or via e-mail. Discuss the possibility that people are not what they claim to be in their online persona.
- It is important that children feel confident of a supportive response from their parents when raising these issues. Establish a calm atmosphere so that children will not fear your reactions if they are troubled by what they encounter online. Worst of all would be to punish a child for reporting a disturbing incident.
- Tell children not to give their address to strangers they meet electronically.
- Children should not send pictures of themselves to strangers.
- Make a practice of discussing online relationships in a friendly and open way at home. Show interest in the new friends without expressing hostility or suspicion; ask to participate in some of the online chats and e-mail correspondence. Invite your children to sit in with you during your own online interactions.
- If a child feels that another child met online is becoming a good friend, parents should contact the child's parents by phone and, eventually, in person before allowing contacts.
- If a child wants to meet someone encountered on the Internet, be sure that a parent is involved at all stages. Never let a child meet anyone in the real world whom he or she has met only on the Net. Any attempt to induce a child to meet the correspondent alone or secretly should be reported to local police authorities for investigation.
- Make it clear that anyone who suggests hiding an online relationship from the child's parents is already doing something wrong.
- Make it clear to your children that no one has the right to send them age-inappropriate, sexually suggestive, or frankly pornographic materials, whether written or pictorial. Suggestions on the Internet that children engage in virtual sex play or sexual fantasies should be reported to parents right away. Making, transmitting, and storing child pornography is a felony; report such cases to local police authorities at once.
- Children receiving a request for anything unusual (e.g., a request for a piece of clothing or for nude pictures) should immediately report the incident to their parents. Teachers and other caregivers can adapt these principles for the specific circumstances of their relationship with the children they are taking care of.

33.23.3   Resources on Pedophilia

- "Child Pornography": *www.fbi.gov/contact/fo/detroit/crimes2.htm*

- Children's Protection and Advocacy Coalition: *www.thecpac.com/index3.html*

- "FBI Warns of Child Exploitation": *http://broadcast.webpoint.com/wphl/ cybersafe/cybersafe_fbi.htm*

- Guarding Our Children's Innocence against Pedophiles: *http://modena.intergate. ca/personal/ranubis*

- "Hunting Pedophiles on the Net: Is the Truth about Cybercrimes against Children Tamer than Fiction?" by J.R. Kincaid (2000): *www.salon.com/mwt/feature/ 2000/08/24/cyber_menace*

- "In Plain Site: Pedophiles Online, How to Protect Children": *www.thecpac.com/ protect.html*

- "Internet Rules for Children": *www.missingkids.org*

- "Internet Safety: Warning Signs": *www.fbi.gov/contact/fo/norfolk/intnet.htm*

- "Online Stalking and Pedophiles: Protect Yourself and Your Family," by L. Ratliff (1997): *www.carteret.com/children*

- "Parents Can Protect Their Children from Child Predators Roaming the Internet: Six Simple Guidelines": *www.yellodyno.com/html/inetpeds.html*

- "Pedophiles and Child Molesters: The Slaugher of Innocence," by M. Gado (2000): *www.crimelibrary.com/serial/pedophiles*

- "Pedophiles Flooding British Internet Chat Rooms," by J. Lovell (2001): *www. siliconvalley.com/docs/news/reuters_wire/1046323l.htm*

- "Protecting Children from Pedophiles," by M.A. Monahan: *www.afn.org/~monica*

- "When to Call the FBI": *http://broadcast.webpoint.com/zwphl/cybersafe/cybersafe_ fbi2.htm*

33.24   NOTES

1. Information on the Ponzi scheme is taken from *The People's Chronology,* copyright © 1995, 1996 by James Trager; published by Henry Holt & Co. and made available through the Microsoft Bookshelf CD. All rights reserved.

2. *Wall Street Journal,* May 5, 2000, as reported by NewsScan, edited by John Gehl and Susanne Douglas; see *www.newsscan.com.*

3. See, for example, "The Battle for the Heavenly Jukebox" by Charles Mann in the *Atlantic Monthly; www.theatlantic.com/issues/2000/09/mann.htm.*

4. For details, see P. Bates and M. Fain, "Cheating 101: Paper Mills and You," (1999, updated 2001): *www.coastal.edu/library/papermil.htm.*

5. Hamilton, A., 1998. "Arizona Lottery Pick 3 Random Number Bug." *RISKS Forum Digest* 19: 83, *catless.ncl.ac.uk/Risks/19.83.html#subj5.*

6. From the TrustWatch page at GeoTrust: *www.geotrust.com/building_trust/safe_market/ trustwatch.asp.*

7. From the TRUSTe Web site: *www.truste.org/about/truste/about_faqs.html#mission.*

8. From the WebTrust Web site: *www.cica.ca/cica/cicawebsite.nsf/public/SPWTe_ generalfaqs.*

9. Mark Potok, as quoted in *Network World,* July 24, 2000.

CHAPTER 34

WORKING WITH LAW ENFORCEMENT

Morgan Wright

CONTENTS

34.1   INTRODUCTION.   A criminal act, such as theft, may be committed in many different ways. That the crime occurred over the Internet, or at the local grocery, does not change the fact that a theft happened. However, it is much easier for law enforcement agents to investigate the local theft for a variety of reasons, including the physical presence of the perpetrator at the actual scene of the crime. Issues of conflicting jurisdiction are usually nonexistent, and investigating officers rarely need specialized skills to conduct a thorough investigation. But when the theft involves the use of computers, the complexity of the investigation increases exponentially. Add the elements of insider activity, the far-reaching Internet, and large distributed networks, and it is easy to arrive at a scenario where the cost of the solution far exceeds the value of the theft.

Until 1990, there were no standards or guidelines as to the seizure and handling of computer-generated evidence. During that time, there was little pressure to develop standards; both the prosecution and defense lacked understanding of the evidentiary implications. In addition, computer crime investigations or prosecutions were rarely carried out.

By the time of this writing in 2001, the situation has changed drastically. Computer crime investigations and prosecutions are taking place on a daily basis. The cases include possession and distribution of child pornography (one of the most prevalent forms of computer crimes), fraud, extortion, intrusions, denial of service, viruses and Trojan horses, espionage, theft and many more. The computer has become the tool, object, repository, and facilitator of criminal activity.

The proliferation of computer crime has far exceeded the ability of law enforcement to investigate adequately. Every enterprise may be called on to provide the needed expertise to assist law enforcement in detecting and investigating electronic crime. This chapter is intended to be a general guide in working with law enforcement; it is not, however, legal advice on how to handle criminal or civil issues in any particular jurisdiction. For detailed legal advice, readers should consult licensed practitioners of law in their jurisdictions.

34.2   GOALS OF LAW ENFORCEMENT.   The specific goals of any criminal investigation vary from agency to agency and from location to location. What is significant and newsworthy in one jurisdiction may not even warrant an investigation in another. Many agencies operate on the basis of preestablished thresholds promulgated by the office of the prosecutor. Some U.S. federal agencies require the approval of the United States Attorney before an active investigation can be authorized. The costly expenditure of personnel and equipment on an investigation must be weighed against the probability of success and the ultimate goals of the investigation. This process has caused conflict with the goals of the organization reporting the crime to law enforcement because victims do not understand that not all crimes will be investigated.

34.2.1   Identification and Prosecution.   Identifying the perpetrator(s) is usually the most intensive part of the investigation. Identification of specific people is necessary before the judicial process can proceed to prosecution. During this phase, law enforcement will look to the victimized enterprise for extensive cooperation in identifying potential suspects. Often during the investigation phase, employees will offer to assist the official investigation. Even though the offer is well intended, it creates potential problems with the admissibility of evidence. In the United States, the Fourth Amendment to the Constitution deals with search and seizure by the government. Usually, the Fourth Amendment does not restrain private citizens; for example, private citizens who believe that a next-door neighbor has robbed a bank might take it upon themselves to search for evidence. It is conceivable that a private citizen would enter the neighbor's house and discover very incriminating evidence of the crime. This evidence, if presented to law enforcement, could possibly be used in any subsequent judicial proceeding.

However, a law enforcement officer who is told by a private citizen that evidence exists cannot ask that citizen to retrieve evidence that would otherwise require a search warrant to obtain. Should the officer do so, the citizen would become an agent of the government at that point and would have the same constitutional constraints as the law enforcement officer. This same principle can be applied to a computer crime investigation.

Any actions taken by company personnel during an investigation need approval from corporate counsel. Hasty decisions made by company personnel without the prior advice of counsel will almost certainly reappear through the defense counsel in an evidentiary hearing or a trial. As a result, evidence that might prove guilt could be excluded, and impermissible actions might expose all involved to civil liability. One of the most compelling reasons to have legal advice is that in the rush to judgment inherent in very public and time-sensitive cases, misidentification of a suspect creates legal complexities and can cause incalculable grief for an innocent suspect. In addition, errors can obscure evidence that would identify the actual perpetrator.

When sufficient identification is made to warrant prosecution, whether through a criminal complaint or indictment, the prosecutor usually takes the case lead. During this phase the trial strategy is developed, based on the results of evidentiary hearings and other legal proceedings. During a jury trial, the prosecutor will call witnesses to establish the facts of the offense. Company personnel who assisted in collecting evidence, provided expert help, or otherwise contributed significantly in the investigation may be called to the stand to testify about their efforts months or years after the events occur. In civil cases, for example, the case may take years to come to trial. A well-documented investigation will help witnesses refresh their memory several months later.

34.2.2   Deterrence.   Prosecutors or law enforcement may authorize an investigation into an otherwise low-priority offense if they believe there is sufficient public interest in the event, and if there is a need to send a message of deterrence based on the potential seriousness of the crime. Newsworthy events such as denial of service, computer intrusions, theft of credit card information, or other similar acts may move law enforcement to demonstrate their commitment to fighting such crimes. Because of the high public visibility of such efforts, before an enterprise elects to report criminal activity in the heat of the moment, managers must understand that it is difficult to stop an investigation once it has begun.

Although legal deterrence is an admirable goal, it does not come without a price for the victims of the crime. In the case of computer crime, the victims may suffer from loss of public trust, loss of business, problems in long-term retention of customers, lack of new customers, and falling stock prices. The more media attention the case garners, the higher the price. Organizations about to report criminal activity need to thoroughly think through both the legal and public implications before making the call.

34.3   HISTORY OF LAW ENFORCEMENT AND COMPUTER CRIME.   Although computer-related crimes have not differed dramatically from traditional crime, the involvement of networks and computers has greatly increased the resources and expertise necessary to solve even the most basic felony and misdemeanor cases. Investigators and prosecutors struggle to define roles and responsibilities in the face of technological complexity.

34.3.1   Enforcement Rule.   Computer crime has led to new relationships among law enforcement agencies, including the military, as they cooperate in enforcing criminal statutes. Several multijurisdictional task forces have sprung up across the country in response to the overwhelming increase in criminal investigations, especially in combating fraud and crimes against children.

Because many computer investigations do not lend themselves to strict jurisdictional confinement, the need for broader authority has paved the way for task forces much as the same factors led to cooperation in drug enforcement. However, involvement in interagency task forces can cause crimes that might have been investigated by local authorities to be neglected. Cases that are addressed by a multijurisdictional task force may take precedence based on regional, rather than local, priorities. This shifting of priorities can cause some victims of computer crime to feel that their specific cases are being ignored.

34.3.2   Forensic Examinations.   A fundamental need in forensic examination is capturing data on long-term storage devices. The basic toolkit of forensic examiners during the early 1990s depended in large part on standard disk utilities that were never intended for investigative use. Norton Disk Editor, with its ability to recover deleted files, remains a staple of many forensic methodologies. To that utility have been added more sophisticated and automated tools for acquisition and analysis of very large storage devices.

A byproduct of computer forensics is the sharing of evidence examination and analysis between sworn and civilian personnel. Sworn law enforcement officers do not normally both collect and analyze evidence; civilian employees of the law enforcement agencies, however, often do both. Most agencies have a dedicated crime scene unit or technician whose duties involve collection of evidence in conventional crimes. With their advanced technical skills, such units would prove extremely useful if available on a wider basis.

34.3.3   Training.   The computer crime area has developed significantly since 1990, and so has the training of law enforcement personnel. Courses range from introduction and familiarization lasting two to three days, up to in-depth classes lasting two weeks or more. Many organizations dedicated to law enforcement have developed specific training courses; examples include the International Association of Computer Investigative Specialists (IACIS), National White Collar Crime (NWCC), the Federal Law Enforcement Training Center (FLETC), and others.

Even though there is a substantial amount of training available to law enforcement in computer crime and forensics, there is a substantial lack of training for corporate and private individuals. This gap has created an opportunity for many sworn and nonsworn enforcement individuals to move into the private sector with skills that are in demand and hard to come by for others. As a result, law enforcement agencies are forced to compete against the higher salaries found in the corporate world.

34.4 ANATOMY OF A CRIMINAL INVESTIGATION. Law enforcement must balance the need for openness with the need for secrecy. In many criminal investigations, victims believe that the authorities are less than forthcoming with information, in part because the victims are not familiar with the investigative process. Untrained people may not be able to distinguish between the need to know and the right to know; in addition, there are usually state and federal laws that prevent the disclosure of certain types of information.

To help the victims of crime through the process, many prosecutors have established victim and witness coordination units to help victims understand the many facets of the judicial process. Such units have led to better cooperation between authorities and crime victims.

34.4.1 Commission. The commission of a crime is the first step in the investigative route and establishes the important element of jurisdiction. Many states allow for the investigation of a crime when it originates or terminates in that state, even if it crosses state lines. The ability to pinpoint where the crime was committed can determine prosecution or rejection.

Hastily planned crimes usually leave enough evidence so that even less technically skilled investigators can solve the mysteries. On the other hand, careful planning can make a case nearly impossible to solve. For example, suppose a relatively unskilled criminal penetrates a military site using a dial-up connection to the Internet from his own house; investigating such a case will very likely be easy. So long as the offender takes but few steps to cover the electronic trail, it is a simple process to trace the perpetrator's Internet Protocol (IP) address back to an Internet service provider (ISP) and then to the subscriber.

In contrast, suppose an intruder attacks the same military site in the same way, with the same technique and leaves the same trail, but this time the attack originates from a compromised server in a country with no requirement to provide support to law enforcement in the United States. There is very little chance to solve a case such as this once an investigation is held up at the border of another nation state.

34.4.2 Discovery. As noted, the more planning that goes into a crime, the more difficult it becomes to solve. If the crime escapes detection, there will be no investigation at all. If, for example, a burglar were to break into an office building and remove a laptop computer, it is very likely that its theft will be noticed. In contrast, if that same burglar were merely to copy the data on the computer, the theft might never be discovered. Were the data theft to be discovered only months or years later, the statute of limitations could make investigation pointless.

Because time is of the essence in criminal investigations, the enterprise should implement real-time intrusion detection and other forms of due diligence that offer a reasonable chance of immediate discovery. Because criminals are constantly refining their reconnaissance and intrusion techniques to evade detection, the enterprise also must continuously update its defensive measures.

In intrusion cases, log files are usually the best evidence for documenting the activities leading to the break-in. It is also very important to document how the crime was discovered, so that detection processes can be developed and implemented. Unfortunately, many major investigations have resulted from luck rather than from established processes. Many attacks such as denial of service (DoS) are immediately obvious.

The discovery phase involves the most critical and volatile evidence needed for a successful resolution. It also contains the biggest chance for evidence destruction or contamination. Well-intentioned company personnel may discover evidence of a crime and inadvertently taint the evidence through destructive inquiries. For example, physical evidence can be damaged by manipulation; trace evidence such as fibers and fingerprints is fragile and can easily be contaminated or destroyed. In the case of electronic evidence, simply reading a file can alter the date/time stamp. To prevent such damage, proper precautions must be taken with potential criminal evidence; physical security and data security personnel must follow written procedures. All such personnel must be trained in how to protect the chain of custody.

Proper preservation of evidence through documentation of all actions during the discovery phase will largely determine the effectiveness of the ensuing investigation. How well evidence is preserved also will determine how well the victimized enterprise is treated by the media and the public when the discovery is made known.

34.4.3   Investigation.   The role of law enforcement in investigating computer crime is paradoxical to a certain extent. On the one hand, it is the responsibility of the investigating agency to take a lead role in the case and to direct the efforts of both sworn and nonsworn personnel in collecting, analyzing, interpreting, and reporting on the evidence. Yet in computer crime, law enforcement often lacks the capability to conduct an in-depth investigation and must rely on those with the technical knowledge to assist in almost all phases. At least in seizures of stand-alone computers running Windows, Mac OS, or Linux, the ability to conduct a forensic examination has greatly improved since 1990. Unfortunately, the improvement has not been as great for investigations of network-based or Internet crimes and investigations.

34.4.3.1   *Length and Control of the Investigation.*   Several factors influence the length of the investigation, including how much the victim is willing to cooperate. It may be necessary for the victim to provide constant support, especially if the offense is ongoing, as in DoS attacks or active intrusion.

Victims must understand that law enforcement agents are in control of the investigation. Although law enforcement usually will defer as much as possible to the wishes of the victim, most agencies will not yield operational control of the investigation. Once the investigation is in progress, victims may not be able to control decisions on releasing information to the media and to the public even when there is a potential for negative publicity or loss of public confidence. This point reinforces the importance of thinking carefully and using legal counsel before reporting the incident.

When there is an active investigation, most personnel involved in the process are reluctant to turn down requests from authorities for information or material. However, where valuable intellectual property and trade secrets are involved, it would be unwise to give blanket approval to such requests unless legal counsel or employees with the authority and experience to do so have sanctioned it. The value of an investigation is usually not comparable to the worth of the intellectual property being sought, and great care should be given before divulging this information.

34.4.3.2 Inadvertent Discovery of Malfeasance.

Although many victims would like to see an investigation concluded swiftly and the legal process move on, it is a fact that many cases never advance beyond this stage. Many of the reasons are beyond the control of law enforcement or the victim. For example, in the corporate environment, the investigation may have the potential for uncovering information that could be extremely damaging.

Imagine that an employee at a company has received a bomb threat against the enterprise that is delivered via internal e-mail from the account of one of the senior executives. Preliminary examination by internal security shows that the executive in question was not present when the message was sent. Rather, the individual neglected to log off or otherwise secure the computer. After law enforcement is called, one of the initial steps would be to copy all the data from the computers of the executive and the recipient. However, as the investigating officers track the initial inquiry, the general counsel advises law enforcement that the company no longer wishes to pursue the bomb threat and declines to assist further unless compelled by either a search warrant or court order.

The reason for the interruption is that the executive whose workstation was used is afraid that information of a personal and compromising nature will be revealed, possibly an illicit affair, pornography, or fraud. At this point, since no bomb was found, the authorities would most likely accede to the wishes of the company and terminate the investigation. The exact reasons for declining to proceed are known only to the general counsel and probably one or more of the senior executives.

However, one small change in the circumstances of the hypothetical case would prevent interruption of the investigation. If, in this new case, the message were a personal threat directed at a particular employee, then the general counsel would have little, if any, say in declining to pursue the investigation. This time the victim could go forward with the case, and the forensic examination would reveal the compromising information.

34.4.3.3 Interviews.

Another important part of the total investigative process is the interview. Interviews serve several functions, including

- Gathering information
- Eliminating unlikely suspects
- Identifying potential suspects
- Establishing the veracity of the witnesses
- Placing events and evidence in context

Good interviewers can significantly shorten investigations, especially with proper use of the behavioral analysis interview. Many cases have been solved through a good interview, followed by a thorough interrogation. The differences between the two are discussed in Section 34.4.3.4.

When dealing with what may be insider crime, the interview is used to screen multiple potential suspects in order to focus on those considered high risk by the investigator. A matrix of indicators often is used to assist in selecting those to be interviewed. This profile sheet looks at factors such as:

- Position?
- Tenure?
- Was subject present at the time?
- Did subject work in the area?
- Did subject have access?
- Any physical evidence linking the subject?
- Prior problems?
- Low salary?
- Changed demeanor?
- Disgruntled?
- Temper?
- Bad attendance?
- Stability?
- Did subject discover the crime? Many perpetrators believe there is inherent credibility in their interview if they discovered the offense.
- Personal problems?
- Does anyone suspect the subject to be guilty? The gossip mill may have a kernel of truth.

This matrix is tallied by a trusted individual within the organization in cooperation with law enforcement. After the evaluation is complete, the subjects usually are interviewed in order from least likely to most likely. Each preceding interview allows the investigator to refine the case facts and to develop more familiarity with the organization and its behavior. Finally, if the interviews go as planned, the primary suspect will be the last one questioned. If enough suspicion is raised during the interview, the investigator may proceed with the interrogation.

34.4.3.4 Interrogations.   The significant difference between the interview and the interrogation is that the interview is nonaccusatory whereas the interrogation *is* accusatory. During an interview, the investigator must be a good listener and must be highly attentive to detail. The interview often will present significant behavioral clues. In contrast, during the interrogation the investigator will do most of the talking, developing themes and deliberately attempting to make the subject anxious—especially the guilty subject. Eventually, the investigator hopes to elicit a confession from the suspect. This happens when the suspects has developed such a high level of anxiety that confession is the only way to alleviate the angst.

Regardless of the advance of technology, interview and interrogation techniques remain the most powerful weapons used by law enforcement. They stand as the only tool that can allow investigators to solve a crime in the absence of physical evidence or when the evidence is little more than circumstantial. Even when criminals commit the perfect crime, the perpetrators will still be imperfect—and that is the advantage law enforcement always will have.

34.4.4   Identification of the Perpetrator.   The goal of an investigation is to establish that a crime has been committed and then to determine who committed it. A law enforcement officer requires only probable cause to make an arrest. However, a higher standard is needed to obtain an indictment and a still higher standard to obtain a conviction.

Probable cause is generally defined as those facts and circumstances that would lead a reasonable person to believe that a particular crime is, has been, or will be committed and that a particular person is responsible for that particular crime. Many times a victim will lock onto a single fact that appears to be clear evidence of guilt. Based on this assumption, the victim may then wonder why law enforcement has not acted. Part of the investigation involves decisions that are made based on the totality of the circumstances, not merely on a single fact.

Before making an arrest in cases of physical crime (as distinct from computer-related crimes), law enforcement needs to address such issues as the following:

- Where was the suspect at the time the crime was committed? It would be virtually impossible to obtain a conviction if the suspect was in custody at the time of the offense.

- Did the suspect have legitimate access to the scene? Could the suspect have lived, worked, or been acquainted with previous residents of the location?

- Is there any connection between the victim and suspect?

- Was there evidence of forced entry?

- Does the suspect live nearby?

- Was the suspect spotted in the area before or after the assault?

- Is there other evidence that points to another suspect being involved?

- Is there any other evidence that points to the suspect being at the scene?

- What would have caused the suspect to bleed, and is the blood anywhere else at the scene?

- Was the DNA testing contaminated?

- Is it possible that the results were mixed up with another case?

- Does the laboratory that did the testing have any prior history of making critical errors in testing?

- What is the credibility of all involved? A sad but true fact is that alleged victims have falsified crimes for various reasons. Law enforcement also has been responsible for fabricating evidence.

This list of questions is by no means comprehensive, and will vary from case to case based on the unique circumstances of each investigation. However, failure to address these issues creates two problems initially. First, it makes identification of the assailant less authoritative for purposes of filing an affidavit for an arrest warrant. Second, it creates reasonable doubt if it does go to trial. A defense attorney will analyze the lack of other corroborative evidence in defending a client.

In investigating computer crime, it is crucial to gather as many facts as possible in an attempt to correctly identify the perpetrator. In the case of insider crime, physical evidence, such as access logs, could be a key element. However, it is also important to obtain other types of information; for example, it is not uncommon for employees to share user names and passwords, thus making the issue of who actually committed a particular offense more complicated. In the case of intrusions or denial of service attacks, many times the evidence will show only which IP address was responsible, not who was at the keyboard.

Once identification is made and law enforcement feels there is probable cause for an arrest, affidavits are prepared for prosecutorial review. An affidavit is a document that articulates the facts and circumstances of the case and establishes the elements of probable cause needed to meet the threshold for an arrest. This affidavit is not a rehash of the investigative report. Rather, it is the abridged version of the case that still gives the totality of the circumstances.

34.4.5   Decision to Prosecute.   Once the case has been investigated and the suspect has been identified, there is no guarantee that a prosecution will occur. Many factors have to be weighed before going forward. Within U.S. federal law enforcement, cases are not usually opened unless there has been an agreement beforehand that the United States Attorney will take the matter to trial. In state or local jurisdictions, such an arrangement may not be present.

At this stage in the process, law enforcement has very little to do with the decision to press on. The strength of the investigation may contribute to the decision, but this is not a call made by investigating agencies. The victim will have a significant voice in any decision, and almost all states have a victims' rights provision in the law.

If there is one area that is misunderstood more than any other, it is the knowledge of who is responsible for prosecution. Since law enforcement is arguably the most visible component of the criminal justice system, blame or dissatisfaction resulting from an unpopular decision in a criminal case may be pointed initially toward the investigating agency.

One alternative that is widely used in many types of cases to avoid prosecution is diversion; that is, shifting the perpetrator out of the criminal justice system into alternative systems that emphasize restitution and rehabilitation. Depending on the various state and federal laws, a suspect may be eligible to avoid prosecution by applying to the prosecutor for diversion in return for stipulating to the facts. Juveniles who have no prior record are prime candidates for consideration. However, adults with no record who commit low-level offenses also may be considered.

There are several reasons why prosecutors may choose not to go forward with a case. Defendants do not want to take the chance of getting convicted, and prosecutors do not want to take the chance of losing. A compromise is that the defendant stipulates to the facts of the case, agrees to restitution if appropriate, and promises not to engage in criminal activity for a specified period of time. In return, the prosecutor agrees to dismiss the case at the end of the stated period if all conditions are met. It is a win-win situation for both. The defendant avoids a criminal record, and the prosecution avoids an expensive trial.

There will be circumstances when an offer to plead might be rejected or a diversion application denied. Only the prosecuting attorney has the authority to make that initial determination, and it could be based on factors other than the case itself. Reality dictates that outside pressures, political and judicial, may influence some decisions to prosecute. The more significant the case in terms of exposure or publicity, the more likely it is to be seriously considered for further action.

Prosecutors also will consider whether going forward best serves the interests of justice. Many times the offense may be precipitated by unique circumstances that would otherwise not be present. For example, a father who hacks into a hospital system to provide expensive medicine for a terminally ill child because he cannot afford to buy it and has no insurance might benefit from the discretion of the prosecutor on an initial offense. Prosecutors would recognize how difficult it would be to drag the father before a jury and ask other parents to convict a man who was trying to save his dying child.

The prosecuting officials also must take into account many of the same factors listed in Section 34.4.4 on identification of the perpetrator. If the credibility of the victim or witness is lacking or nonexistent, the reliance on the physical evidence becomes extremely crucial. If the physical evidence is weak, prosecutors may refuse to take the case forward until additional witnesses or evidence is located.

34.4.6   Indictment.   Indictment is the formal accusation of a felony issued by a grand jury after considering evidence presented by a prosecutor. The formal charge is then issued by a grand jury upon finding that there is enough evidence to believe that the defendant committed the crime and therefore that a trial is justified. Indictment is used primarily for felonies. After the grand jury hands down the indictment (which is usually secret), the defendant is arrested pending further proceedings.

During this time, law enforcement usually provides the bulk of the testimony. Occasionally, the actual victim is called if the circumstances warrant. The goal of the prosecutor is to present enough evidence to the grand jury to obtain the indictment, but not so much that it causes confusion and jeopardizes the case. Normally, a thorough review by the lawyers produces the need for additional evidence or statements before going to the grand jury. If this happens, law enforcement will be directed to obtain the required information from the appropriate source. It is possible that this might take place several months after the commission of the crime and could include reinterviewing the victim.

In other states, the grand jury is not used in the same way. Instead, the investigating officer will prepare an affidavit for an arrest warrant that is sent to the prosecutors. If the prosecutors agree there is probable cause to charge the defendant, they will prepare a complaint that is sent to a judge. The judge will review the complaint for the elements of probable cause. If found, an arrest warrant will be issued. The first time a victim may have to testify would be at a preliminary hearing. If the prosecutors can establish a *prima facie* case (a case in which the evidence is sufficient to raise a presumption of fact or to establish the fact in question unless rebutted), then further proceedings are ordered.

For the victim, there is a significant obligation to appear and testify at the several different proceedings between arrest, indictment (or preliminary hearing), and trial. Some defense tactics call for having as many hearings as possible to cause the victim, the witnesses, and law enforcement to appear repeatedly. If any of the required persons are out of state, then timing and cost become considerations for the prosecution as to whether it is feasible to continue prosecuting the defendant. Quite often, victims are unaware of this burden when reporting the initial crime. It is not unusual to hear victims say that if they knew what was to follow, they would not have made a report.

34.4.7   Trial.   Once the investigation has made it to this stage, the cooperation of the victim is essential. As the prosecution opens the case, the first person to testify is usually the one who discovered the crime. The trial attorneys begin by laying a foundation upon which to build the case. The testimony of the victim underpins the groundwork, with law enforcement adding to the framework. At this juncture, the prosecutors are in full control of the case.

Law enforcement supports the prosecution through testimony, production of evidence, and analysis of evidence. At this time, the defense has an opportunity to cross-examine all witnesses, including the victim, and challenge the introduction of evidence. The judge will rule on the admissibility of the evidence. The jury will then deliberate and render a verdict. The majority of trials will end with a verdict, with a few declared as mistrials. A guilty verdict still leaves the door open for appeal, with a not-guilty verdict effectively ending any future proceedings because of legal restrictions on double jeopardy.

Apart from testimony and analysis of evidence, law enforcement has little control over the trial process and especially over the jury. Regardless of the strength of the evidence or the quality of the argument, the jury verdict is still the product of human understanding and negotiation. As such, it may not always follow popular thought about the case. In complex computer crime cases, jurors are exposed to technology they may not even use or understand. It has happened, and will continue to happen, that verdicts will be rendered not because of proof or the lack of proof but because of the gap between technology and understanding.

34.4.8   After the Verdict.   Depending on the verdict, there is little left for law enforcement to do. In the case of a not-guilty verdict, there may be issues related to evidence belonging to the victim that have to be addressed. Evidence that belongs to the defendant, such as computers and data files, probably will be returned, unless possession would be illegal. If a civil case is contemplated, the immediate assistance of competent legal counsel to address evidentiary issues is important.

If a guilty verdict is returned, there is the possibility of appeals and even a new trial. This can happen if there are procedural or other errors in the trial that are significant enough to warrant a reversal of the original verdict. Should this occur, it would be necessary for law enforcement or the court to retain the original evidence. It also means that the victim will have to repeat almost the entire process.

In the event of a not-guilty verdict, the prosecutors could decide not to try the case again and refuse to file new charges. Or they could direct law enforcement to conduct an additional investigation to uncover possible new evidence. The type of case, the probability of success in a new trial, the severity of the crime, the availability of witnesses and evidence, the economic loss (if applicable), and the desires of the victim will all be factors to be weighed before initiating new charges.

34.5   ESTABLISHING RELATIONSHIPS WITH LAW ENFORCEMENT.   The importance of a prior relationship with law enforcement and the local prosecutor cannot be overestimated. Whether it is simply knowing whom to call for timely advice or to initiate a full-scale investigation, the resultant effort is often directly proportional to the working association developed between the citizen and the investigating officer. That is not to say that cases are improperly investigated merely because there is no previous connection between the investigating agency and the victim. However, the more law enforcement understands about the victim beforehand, the easier it is to prioritize resources to achieve maximum investigative effort.

It is a fact of life that personalities and relationships affect, to some degree, the level of effort given to a case. An organization that previously had caustic relations with a law enforcement agency, especially if it was the target of a previous investigation, may find a tepid response to its circumstances. If investigating officers are constantly encountering barriers to cooperation, most supervisors will reallocate their thin investigative resources to cases that are more solvable.

Even though computer crimes are by their very nature technical, the human element cannot be ignored. Establishing a good working relationship with law enforcement is the first, and possibly the most important, step to successfully investigating computer crime.

34.5.1   Mutual Assistance Organizations.   Computer crime has offered one of the first chances for direct, ongoing cooperation between the private sector and law enforcement. Law enforcement has recognized that only through better cooperation can the complex arena of computer crime be investigated properly. Agency budgets do not expand as rapidly as the demand for investigations, and the lack of resources, training, and personnel makes it essential that law enforcement reach out to their private-sector counterparts to work together.

Several organizations and efforts are facilitating the achievement of common goals through public-private cooperation. Computer crime has served to overcome the feeling of isolation and suspicion that sometimes pervades law enforcement agencies; one reason for this improvement is that electronic offenses generally tend to be nonviolent and require more specific skills as compared to traditional street-level crime.

The following organizations support cooperation by all elements in the battle against computer-related crime.

34.5.1.1   *High Technology Crime Investigation Association.*   The High Technology Crime Investigation Association (HTCIA) has chapters worldwide. Its stated purpose is to "encourage, promote, aid and effect the voluntary interchange of data, information, experience, ideas and knowledge about methods, processes, and techniques relating to investigations and security in advanced technologies among its membership." HTCIA chapter meetings usually have federal, state, and local law enforcement officials mixing with corporate and data security personnel from all walks of business. HTCIA offers an excellent opportunity to network and create positive relationships beforehand. The HTCIA Web site (*www.htcia.org*) details the requirements for membership as follows:

> (a) Peace Officers, Investigators, and Prosecuting Attorneys engaged in the investigation and/or prosecution of criminal activity associated with computers and/or advanced technologies. Each member shall be regularly employed by the Federal Government, State Government, Counties, and/or Municipal subdivisions of any state, or:

> (b) Management level and senior staff security professionals in the regular employ of private business or industry, whose primary duties involve responsibility for security in computer or advanced technology environments. Also eligible are persons who, by virtue of their position or interests, have a need for, or can provide, information and training in the areas of computers or advanced technologies.

HTCIA also offers training opportunities in computer-crime investigation and forensics that is not restricted to law enforcement agents. This approach facilitates critical information sharing in technique, methodology, and investigative tools. It also presents the chance for counterparts to talk openly about sensitive matters or investigations without the need for formal procedures.

34.5.1.2   *National Infrastructure Protection Center and InfraGard.*   The National Infrastructure Protection Center (NIPC) sprang from Presidential Decision Directive 63 (PDD 63) and from the President's Commission on Critical Infrastructure Protection, which issued its report in 1997. NIPC was originally designed to be a cooperative effort among several federal agencies, with the center being housed at the FBI Headquarters in Washington, D.C. Charged with protecting the critical infrastructure of the United States, the NIPC is not limited to electronic threats. However, this has been the bulk of their activity since inception. A key component of the program is the collection, analysis, and dissemination of information.

One major drawback to success has been the reluctance of the private sector to share information with NIPC. Corporate America rarely likes to invite the government into their operations, and sharing sensitive or potentially embarrassing data usually is avoided. Sharing information with the NIPC has been compared with light going into a black hole—it never comes back again. In an effort to localize and personalize the outreach, InfraGard was established.

According to the NIPC Web site (*www.nipc.gov*), InfraGard provides "a mechanism for two-way information sharing about intrusion incidents and system vulnerabilities and provides a channel for the NIPC to disseminate analytical threat products to the private sector." InfraGard attempts to address the public and private sector information sharing needs at the local and national level. It is still too early to evaluate the effectiveness of InfraGard, as it will take a long time before the private sector fully trusts government involvement and commitment in such an area. However, at the time of this writing, several InfraGard chapters were in full operation and were successfully bringing security and business experts from government, utilities, and private industry together for regular information sharing. In addition, the relationships developed at InfraGard meetings were leading to increased out-of-band communication and cooperation among participants facing threats to their information infrastructure.

34.5.1.3   *Northwest Computer Technology and Crime Analysis Seminar.*   The Northwest Computer Technology and Crime Analysis Seminar (NCT) is a nonprofit organization founded in 1985 by members of the Salem, Oregon, Police Department, Oregon Department of Justice, and the Springfield, Oregon, Police Department, as a networking seminar for crime analysts and others in law enforcement to promote information and technology sharing. Since that time, NCT has evolved into an international organization comprised of members of law enforcement, government, and high-tech security.

NCT has formed many partnerships over the years with both private sector and government agencies to provide valuable resources to the attendees. Such organizations include Microsoft, Intel, Hewlett Packard, Nike, and many others. NCT also has formed partnerships with the Oregon Department of Justice, the Federal Bureau of Investigation, the Department of Justice's National Infrastructure Protection Center, and many other state and federal agencies. NCT attendees include organization and government agencies primarily in the western region of the United States and Canada, but include others from around the country. NCT's Web site is *www.crimes.org.*[1]

34.5.2   Prosecutors.   Although law enforcement may be the most visible aspect of the criminal justice system, it is the prosecutors who wield the most influence and power overall. From warrants to wiretaps, very little that law enforcement does is outside the authority of the attorneys who are charged with the responsibility of prosecuting criminal acts committed against the public.

Part of an overall company policy should be to have corporate counsel make contact with the prosecutors at the federal, state, and local level. It is important that a company appreciate what each office will and will not do if a potential criminal situation arises. The general public often misunderstands what authority each office has.

34.5.2.1   *Federal Prosecutors.* Federal prosecutors have authority to prosecute violations of federal law (i.e., violations of the United States Code). Local and state officials often cooperate with the federal prosecutors in critical areas such as organized crime, gangs, and, most recently, computer crime.

34.5.2.2   *State Prosecutors.* The attorney general of each state has broad authority for prosecuting violations of state law only. Their status usually allows them to appear in any state court to either directly prosecute or assist local authorities. High-profile cases and criminal cases that cross county lines are within the purview of this office.

There are also rare occasions when the attorney general may step in to prosecute a case that was rejected by the local county or district attorney. An assistant attorney general usually handles the matter after getting approval from the attorney general. While there are a number of reasons this might happen, it is often because the county and district attorney usually are elected whereas the assistant attorney general is not. Political considerations then may be excluded. Another clear reason a case may be referred to the attorney general is when it involves the local district or county attorney in some fashion. This is done to remove any appearance of impropriety in the decision-making process.

34.5.2.3   *Local Prosecutors.* County or district attorneys traditionally have the most impact in a community on a day-to-day basis. Their office works closely with state and local police on a variety of cases. Because of the demands of computer crime and the specific experience and skills needed to prosecute, many offices do not have a dedicated prosecutor for these issues. As a result, task forces have been created to address the need for prosecution, while at the same consolidating resources.

One advantage to making the acquaintance of local prosecutors is that they will understand the complexities of the local judicial system and can explain the considerations for accepting a case for prosecution. Except for intrusions and denial of service, most computer crime cases will be handled under state law and by the local prosecutor's office.

34.6   ORGANIZATIONAL POLICY. Clearly defined roles and responsibilities provide a framework to guide personnel and to prevent wasted time when criminal situations arise.

34.6.1   Use of Corporate Counsel. Corporate or external counsel must be involved in devising policies for responding to any type of criminal act. When dealing with sensitive matters, using attorneys provides additional legal protection in the form of attorney-client privilege. During a criminal investigation, the added layer of legal review makes it more likely that the interests of the enterprise will be safeguarded.

Lawyers can help management assess the risk posed by the existence, as well as by the lack, of specific policies and procedures. Although well-intentioned managers or system administrators may draft what they believe to be effective policies, only a properly trained attorney can determine the legal consequences of having and complying with such a policy.

34.6.2   Communicating with Law Enforcement. During the course of an active criminal investigation, there will be many times when interviews and background information on employees are necessary. Well-meaning employees who converse directly with law enforcement before getting clearance from management can cause irreparable harm to the investigation and may expose the company to criminal or civil liability.

There will be material and information that can be produced only after being compelled by some type of legal order, such as a search warrant or subpoena. Employees who feel that it is their civic duty to turn over information they feel is relevant without consulting corporate counsel may find that their actions have the opposite effect of the one they intended.

For example, an employee may be the target of a criminal investigation. The nature of the investigation might lead the investigating officers to ask for information deemed privileged by the attorney-client relationship. If another employee were to provide this information to law enforcement, outside the review of corporate counsel, it would taint any evidence discovered as a result of this disclosure—evidence that could be conclusive proof of the guilt of the employee being investigated. Such violations of policy and procedure could even subject the Good Samaritan employee to criminal charges.

It is therefore necessary to ensure that employees and management are given clear direction and guidance, backed up by written policy, to govern how communications with law enforcement should be conducted. Not only is it important for liability purposes, but also if the matter should ever end up at trial, any mistakes made will surely provide fodder for the defense to attack the motives of all parties involved. That could leave employees defending their own actions rather than testifying about the actions of the defendant.

34.6.3   Preservation of Computer Evidence.   Evidence of a crime comes in forms ranging from guns and bullets to microscopic fibers and DNA. How the evidence is found, documented, collected, transported, stored, and tested is all part of the chain of custody. Should any part of that chain be corrupted, the integrity of the evidence could be challenged successfully in court hearings.

Computer evidence is no different from other types of evidence. The same rules that apply to collecting trace evidence apply to electronic material. The method of collection differs from type to type, but not the overall process. As company policies are created, steps must be taken to safeguard the integrity of all investigations.

The presence of an approved policy instills confidence in the personnel responsible for handling evidence. It also serves to shield employees from charges of negligence or bias, to the extent that the written policies were followed. After review by counsel and management, checklists that outline how evidence is to be handled can improve the chances that collected evidence will be admissible in future proceedings.

34.6.4   Production of Evidence.   There are several scenarios in which evidence is produced to law enforcement or the court. One of the most frequent is the production of subscriber information held by various telephone and cellular companies. These companies have established processes for producing business records in response to subpoenas. The paper trail is easily documented and tracked in case future testimony is needed to corroborate the validity of the records.

What is not so well developed is the production of electronic evidence. Most scenarios involve the involuntary production of data due to the existence and service of a search warrant. In that case, law enforcement will most likely handle the imaging and collection of the data to preserve the chain of custody. However, if an internal investigation leads to the discovery of criminal offenses involving electronic data, but the collection process and chain of custody are contaminated, that alone may cause law enforcement or a prosecutor to reject the case. It is easier to collect evidence to a judicial standard than it is to defend against charges of incompetence.

34.7 DEVELOPING INTERNAL INVESTIGATIVE CAPABILITIES. One way for corporations to maintain control over potential criminal and civil liability is to establish an internal investigative capability. Depending on the size of the organization, the team may be part or full time. Potential members include physical and information security, corporate counsel, designated management, and trusted vendors or consultants.

These teams must have established communication channels, out-of-band contact procedures, clearly defined roles and responsibilities, and unambiguous lines of authority. If an incident arises, the last thing a company needs is to arbitrate a disagreement over who is in control. Shareholders have little tolerance for failure when a reasonable amount of prior preparation could have mitigated, or prevented, an adverse act.

Developing an internal capability means that the primary duties will be tactical in nature. The ability to respond quickly, to perform electronic triage, and to assess next steps is necessary first to contain the situation, then to take strides toward its resolution. Additional investigation can be handled internally if the skills exist, or outsourced to an appropriate consultant or vendor. Such examples might include fraud or embezzlement allegations or even espionage.

34.7.1 Incident Response. The nature of business today, and its dependence on computers, dictates that corporations large or small have some type of computer incident response capability. Sooner, rather than later, there is an excellent chance that there probably will be a need for an incident response team. The threat may come from a virus, Trojan horse, denial of service, insider crime, or extortion, but the need remains the same.

A designated response team that is properly trained is an invaluable asset in a criminal investigation. The collection and preservation of fragile and time-sensitive material is usually an opportunity that does not repeat itself. Successful cases are due to the quick work of well-trained personnel. And if there is to be publicity concerning the case, there is no doubt that shareholders, customers, vendors, and employees all prefer the positive kind. Negative publicity is rarely the product of prior training and preparation.

34.7.2 Computer Forensics. What was once the realm of law enforcement has now expanded to all facets of the corporate world. Software and training are becoming readily available to private-sector examiners, although there is still a significant gap. Computer forensics has emerged as an essential skill within many firms. The majority of the work for forensic examiners is internal in nature. Cases range from violations of acceptable use policy to criminal matters.

Former law enforcement officers or civilian employees of criminal justice agencies fill many of these positions. Previous training and experience in the field of forensic examination, and in the collection and preservation of evidence, make them ideal members of a security team. Having former law enforcement officers on board also serves another purpose. The close networking among current and former investigators extends worldwide and provides a vast pool of experience to draw upon. There are also closed e-mail lists where forensic information is shared among examiners in both the public and private sector.

34.8 INTERNAL INVESTIGATIONS.   There are several ways in which law enforcement is notified of criminal activity as it relates to an organization or an employee within it. One of the means is after an internal investigation. A potential civil situation also can call for internal efforts. Regardless of the nature of the inquiry, there should be no difference between how the matters are handled. By utilizing the same process for every type of investigation, should the case need to go to law enforcement, there will be a higher probability of its acceptance.

This process should be reviewed by corporate counsel and with law enforcement or the local prosecutor, if possible. Corporate investigators should attempt to conduct each case as if it would end up in criminal court. From the documentation and collection of evidence to the interviewing of victims and witnesses, the higher standards used in the criminal justice system ensure that the information gathered will be admissible in proceedings where a lower threshold is used, as, for example, civil cases and administrative and disciplinary hearings. Internal investigations should be handled on a "need-to-know" and "right-to-know" basis. More than one investigation has been compromised when the eventual suspect was found to be part of the incident response team or was given information that should not have been divulged. Corporate investigators can take several steps to make certain that delicate and confidential information remains undisclosed. Simple solutions include locking all doors and desk drawers, filing away all paperwork in secured cabinets, locked offices, the use of encryption, maintaining single points of contact between business units and investigators, verifying the claim for "need to know," printing and faxing to secure machines, and other practices.

For internal investigations involving military or economic espionage, the Federal Bureau of Investigation (FBI) has created the Awareness of National Security Issues and Response (ANSIR) program. Its Web site (*www.fbi.gov/programs/ansir/ansir.htm*) states the mission of ANSIR is to be the "public voice of the FBI for espionage, counterintelligence, counterterrorism, economic espionage, cyber and physical infrastructure protection and all national security issues." Any company engaged in a critical technology should have its security department make contact with the FBI's ANSIR representative.

34.8.1 Reportable versus Nonreportable.   Every corporate investigator should be aware of what is required to be reported to either law enforcement or a regulatory agency. As an example, the theft of $10,000 from a manufacturing company by an employee is far different from the same amount taken from a financial institution that is subject to federal regulation.

A good source of information is the audit or compliance department. These employees deal with various types of government regulation on a daily basis. When in doubt, check with local, state, or federal prosecutors. There may be specific requirements under state or local law that are not present in federal law. This information should be clearly spelled out in any policy manual that guides the efforts of the investigators.

34.8.2 Choice to Go Civil Instead of Criminal.   If there is no requirement to report suspected criminal activity to the authorities, many corporations have elected to use civil action rather than criminal prosecution. There also may be instances where the actions clearly do not constitute a violation of law and are instead completely civil in nature. This could include such charges as violation of noncompete or nonsolicitation agreements, contractual obligations, and other similar matters.

If there is evidence of a criminal violation, but no reporting requirement, a popular alternative has been to initiate civil action. This may be done for several reasons, including preventing unwanted publicity. Senior management, after consulting with corporate counsel, ultimately makes these decisions. Taking civil action does not preclude turning the matter over to law enforcement at a later date unless that restriction is part of the civil agreement.

In difficult cases, filing a civil case first can produce evidence and information that would not have been allowed in a criminal proceeding.

34.8.3   Acceptable-Use Policy Violations.   Companies with clearly defined acceptable use policies have a metric by which to measure compliance with company regulations. Corporate investigators are routinely asked to conduct inquiries into violations of these policies. Areas covered may include pornography (usually at the top of all lists), abuse of resources, harassment (sexual or otherwise), disclosure of confidential information, inappropriate postings to message boards, and a variety of others.

There is little law enforcement is able to do in assisting internal investigations such as these unless there is an accompanying criminal violation. Even with AUP violations, corporate investigators should take care to treat the situation as if it involved a criminal offense. The same standards should be used for the seizure and analysis of potential evidence, documentation of the events, interviews with potential witnesses, and thorough follow-up. Some of the most significant criminal cases of the twentieth century were discovered because of what appeared to be a small, insignificant anomaly. A stairway door that was previously checked by a security guard and found to be open a second time led to the discovery of the Watergate conspiracy and the downfall of U.S. President Richard Nixon. A discrepancy of 75 cents between two computer-resource accounting systems bothered astronomer Clifford Stoll enough to dig deeper. The resulting investigation, captured in *"The Cuckoo's Egg,"* led to one of the biggest investigations into the theft of sensitive military and security information, and to a best-selling novel penned by Stoll himself.

34.9   INTERNATIONAL INVESTIGATIONS.   Although international investigations might seem to be the stuff spy novels are made of, they are more common today due to the Internet. Although investigating any computer crime may be difficult, an international border complicates the investigation. The cases themselves need not be complicated or devious to be difficult to investigate. A denial-of-service attack launched from a Third World country could be easily traced back to the source. However, getting cooperation beyond that point is probably beyond the expertise of many corporations unless law enforcement is involved.

34.9.1   Coordinating Efforts.   Almost all multinational corporations have established procedures for handling corporate and legal affairs in the various countries in which they have a presence. Many do not realize that the FBI also has an established international presence.

The FBI's Legal Attaché Program represents the interests of America in 52 foreign countries. According to its Web site (*www.fbi.gov/contact/legat/legat.htm*), the program was created to "help foster good will and gain greater cooperation with international police partners in support of the FBI's domestic mission. The goal is to link law enforcement resources and other officials outside the U.S. with law enforcement in this country to better ensure the safety of the American public here and abroad."

This assistance is available for the investigation of criminal matters, but internal investigations and civil matters do not fall under the mandate for the FBI, here or abroad. This established program increases the chances of successfully investigating a case that has crossed international borders. Nevertheless, there still is a long way to go in the information age before there are no safe havens for criminal activity.

34.9.2   Criminal Process.   While there might appear to be similarities among the laws of many nations, from a criminal process standpoint, there is far less uniformity. Investigations that cross borders can have multiple sets of irreconcilable legal rules to deal with. When working with law enforcement, it is important to keep in mind that the laws of the United States cannot be applied to citizens of another country except under very limited circumstances.

It can be frustrating to know who the perpetrators are, and have them clearly identified, but be unable to take any kind of criminal or civil action. Even if there is recourse available, it may be that the remedies are so weak as to make filing a case cost-prohibitive. Generally, the FBI will have an excellent grasp on the realities of further action and the probabilities of success.

The most important principle determining whether suspects can be extradited from one jurisdiction to another is the doctrine of dual criminality; that is, a suspect may be extradited only if the offense is of equal severity (e.g., a felony) in both jurisdictions. This principle is illustrated by the case of the putative author of the Love Bug e-mail enabled worm that spread worldwide in May 2000. Although there was sufficient evidence to point to a specific resident of Manila as the author, Philippine law lacked any equivalent to the computer-crime laws of the United States, and so the suspect could neither be prosecuted in his home country nor extradited to the United States under federal computer fraud and abuse laws.

34.10   COMPUTER EVIDENCE.   Compared to traditional crime scenes, digital evidence has presented one of the greatest challenges to law enforcement. The difference between traditional crime and digital crime is the sheer volume of evidence to process and the technical difficulty in obtaining it. That has created a new market for training and tools in an attempt to come to terms with the magnitude of the problem.

34.10.1   Seizing and Preserving.   The most critical step in dealing with computer evidence is the initial seizure. Depending on the type of media, preserving the evidence could be as simple as making a duplicate copy of a hard drive, or as complicated as dealing with multiple servers with RAID (redundant array of independent disks) arrays. The evidence could be obvious, or it could be obscured using 256-bit Blowfish encryption. In any event, if the initial seizure is faulty, then all that follows is flawed also.

The International Association of Computer Investigative Specialists teaches a two-week course every year to law enforcement officers in the field of computer forensics. Because the seizure and preservation of evidence is so critical, a separate certification—Certified Electronic Evidence Collection Specialist (CEECS)—is required before proceeding to the main certification. Students must successfully complete a written test covering three days of training to receive the CEECS. The main certification is the Certified Forensic Computer Examiner (CFCE) and can take up to one year to complete.

The Computer Crime and Intellectual Property Section (CCIPS) of the Department of Justice most often provides the reference material law enforcement consults.

The guidelines can be found at *www.cybercrime.gov/searchmanual.htm.* Updated in 2001, the document is full of vital information for computer crime investigations. Although it is designed for law enforcement, corporate investigators and legal counsel can glean important procedural guidelines for their own internal investigations.

Several advances in tools and equipment have allowed law enforcement to do more data capture on-site. Unless the volume of information is enormous, or if the targeted computers are mission-critical machines, most electronic evidence will be collected on the scene. Some exceptions occur when the material includes child pornography; in those cases, the hard drives will likely be physically seized.

34.10.2   Chain of Custody.   Maintaining a proper chain of custody for evidence is the next priority that continues throughout the case. Even if the evidence is seized and collected properly, breaking the chain of custody can create insurmountable legal hurdles at any time during the investigation or trial.

The chain of custody does not have to be perfect. It just has to be reasonable. When any physical evidence is seized, documentary information such as measurements and photographs may be recorded at the same time. As a general rule, when an item is seized, enough information about it must be noted to enable the officer to testify at a later date. This could be several months or years down the line. Without proper foundation, the admissibility of the evidence could be challenged successfully. The same holds true for computer evidence; witnesses must be able to identify the evidence with confidence, and the court must be convinced that the risk of tampering has been kept to a minimum. Measures that support the reliability of computer evidence include:

- Copying to nonmodifiable media (e.g., CD-ROMs)
- Digital timestamps and signatures on all files
- Log files showing exactly who had access to the data and when
- Trustworthy custodians of the data

When conducting corporate investigations, enterprise personnel who follow the same rules of chain of custody as law enforcement should have no problem with the integrity of the evidence, even in a criminal trial. When in doubt, increase the detail of the documentation: Evidentiary problems are caused by too little documentation, not by having too much.

34.10.3   Reports and Documentation.   In any investigation, the amount of paperwork generated is usually directly proportional to the seriousness of the crime. One exception is computer crime, which often generates much more paperwork than other crimes that are just as severe. The technical nature of computer-related crime seems to require extensive explanations of the complex findings. Worse still, sometimes judges want to see a printout of a large computer file, and this demand can create a new set of problems.

One gigabyte of data printed in readable point size could generate over 100,000 pages—a stack of paper 33 feet high using 20-pound paper. Many personal computers now ship with drive sizes in excess of 30 gigabytes. This growth in disk size has lead to changes in the way investigations are handled and documented. Previously, a complete forensic examination and report was done on every piece of media that was seized and analyzed. However, because the amount of data to be searched and reported on has increased so much, law enforcement is moving toward more limited examinations and reports. In their online Forensic Procedure section (*www.cops.org/*

forensic_examination_procedures.htm), IACIS has attempted to deal with the overwhelming amount of media and evidence generated by the effort to do complete forensic examinations. These guidelines codify the essential steps and materials to be used in such examinations.

Prosecutors will have to decide how much is enough to secure a conviction, while at the same time being careful not to open the door to defense claims that exculpatory information still resides in the vast amount of data not examined.

34.11   DECISION TO REPORT COMPUTER CRIME.   The prevalence of computer crime, and the apparent ease with which it is committed, has caused many in the information security field to look for a modern day Code of Hamurabi. The code, 281 laws in all, provides for retribution that covers a variety of transgressions. Law 196 tells us "If a man put out the eye of another man, his eye shall be put out" while Law 200 provides that "If a man knock out the teeth of his equal, his teeth shall be knocked out." At the time, such laws represented an improvement in justice, since it was common to visit horrific punishments on people for even minor transgressions.

However, today, the desire for prosecution is sometimes the product of frustration for the increasing number of attacks against the computer systems so vital to commerce, security, and personal use. When a criminal offense is detected, some victims may rush to law enforcement looking for justice. Initially there are high hopes for identification of the perpetrator, believing that a trial will provide a measure of satisfaction when someone has paid for the crime.

In reality, not every case is investigated. Out of those that are, not every case makes it to trial. And out of those that make it to trial, not every case ends in a guilty verdict. And by the time the ordeal is over, the victim may have spent more time and money in pursuit of justice than the actual economic loss sustained. At this point, as at others previously discussed, it would be easy for victims to question the desirability of reporting the crime in the first place.

The evolution of computer crime investigation has just started. The capabilities and techniques are still immature and imperfect. However, the solution is not to ignore crime and give up reporting the offenses. The only way effective law and investigative techniques are developed is through frequent practice. Although the solutions may sometimes appear to be worse than the actual problems, they will get better with time and support.

34.11.1   Regulatory Requirements.   Government regulation requiring the reporting of certain offenses eliminates some judgment and discretion. Although no corporation welcomes additional governmental intrusion into business affairs, there have been some compromises. There are more voluntary efforts to address regulatory concerns and still meet the stated goals of improving safety and security in the electronic commerce arena. The formation of the Information Sharing Analysis Centers (ISAC) in response to Presidential Decision Directive 63 (PDD 63) has allowed certain business sectors to prevent additional, and unwelcome, oversight.

In time, as confidence and trust in the capabilities of law enforcement increases, corporations will grow comfortable reporting more than what is minimally required. This is a two-way street that requires efforts by both groups. Trust cannot be mandated in a policy, but it can be developed through cooperation and understanding. If this trust reaches an appropriate level, regulatory requirements for reporting certain offenses probably will ease. Corporate policy may eventually take this into account when agreeing to share sensitive information.

There is a fine line between reporting too much and reporting too little. The line is even finer in such rapidly developing areas as computer crime. As corporate policies mature, most of the content and guidance will be the result of actual and shared experiences. As a corporation seeks to define these guiding principles, partnering with law enforcement can help draft effective plans.

An effective policy will help guide difficult and complex decisions. But policies do not make decisions; people do. The people making decisions should have all the available facts before making a report to law enforcement. When the decision is made to report, there also should be the requisite support for the investigation from the victim.

Other factors to consider before making a report include:

- *Contacting* the appropriate local, state, or federal agency
- *Deciding* whether to conduct an internal investigation first
- *Seeking* the advice of corporate counsel
- *Determining* the nature of the act (ongoing versus completed),
- *Considering* employee involvement
- *Determining* the goals of the investigation, including recovery of loss, deterrence, publicity, liability, and cost

34.11.2   Ethical Considerations.   Regardless of regulatory requirements, policies, precedents, and other guidelines, there is almost certainly going to come a time when the nature of an offense had not been contemplated before. A scenario could include investigating a violation of the acceptable use policy as it relates to adult Web sites. A corporate investigator conducting the forensic examination finds some evidence of the violation, but discovers child pornography also.

The possible ramifications of reporting include adverse publicity. No corporation wants to be associated with child pornography. However, if the employee is fired for having downloaded and stored such materials (both actions are felonies) and the perpetrator is later arrested by law enforcement, it is quite possible the trail will lead back to the corporation. If it appears that the corporation knew about these criminal offenses but did not report them, there will be considerable adverse publicity of a kind that is far more damaging than if the transgressions had been reported initially.

And while sexual offenses may present a great ethical dilemma, there are still other issues, such as intellectual property, trade secret information, espionage, fraud, stalking, harassment, money laundering, stock manipulation, mergers and acquisitions, insider trading, and a whole host of other crimes. Statutory requirements may cover many situations and relieve a corporation of an ethical decision. However, due to advances in technology, there will be cases in the future that have not been contemplated now. Computer crime should not change the ethical considerations a corporation reviews before calling law enforcement. For a further discussion of ethics, see Chapter 30.

34.12   SUMMARY.   Working with law enforcement will be one of the few areas in the computer security arena that requires more people skills than technical skills. Computer crime is still a people problem, first and foremost. The commission, discovery, investigation, and adjudication of criminal acts are not technology problems. Technology was simply the instrument of choice.

It will be critical to forge cooperative working relationships between industry partners and all levels of law enforcement. Neither side can afford to go it alone, just as neither side can afford to be an island unto itself. In his book *The Seven Habits of Highly Effective People,* Steven Covey tells us in Habit 5 "Seek first to understand, then to be understood."[2] This is truly the cornerstone of future coalitions between the public and private sector.

34.13   NOTES

1. NCT can be contacted at the following address: Northwest Computer Technology and Crime Analysis Seminar, P.O. Box 619, Stayton, OR 97383-0619, USA.

2. Steven Covey, *The Seven Habits of Highly Successful People* (New York: Simon and Schuster, 1990).

CHAPTER 35

USING SOCIAL PSYCHOLOGY TO IMPLEMENT SECURITY POLICIES

M.E. Kabay

CONTENTS

35.1   INTRODUCTION.   Most security personnel have commiserated with colleagues about the difficulty of getting people to pay attention to security policies—to comply with what seems like good common sense. They shake their heads in disbelief as they recount tales of employees who hold secured doors open for their workmates—or for total strangers—thereby rendering million-dollar card-access systems useless. In large organizations, upper managers who decline to wear their identification badges discover that soon no one else will either. In trying to implement security policies, practitioners sometimes feel that they are involved in turf wars and personal vendettas rather than rational discourse.

These problems reflect the social nature of human beings; however, they also reflect the fact that although information systems security and network management personnel may have a wide variety of backgrounds, many lack any formal training in social psychology.

Security policies and procedures affect not only what people do but also how they see themselves, their colleagues, and their world. Despite these psychosocial issues, security personnel pay little or no attention to what is known about social psychology. The established principles of human social behavior have much to teach us in our attempts to improve corporate and institutional information security.

Information security (IS) specialists concur that security depends on people more than on technology. Another commonplace is that employees are a far greater threat to information security than outsiders.

It follows from these observations that improving security necessarily involves changing beliefs, attitudes, and behavior, both of individuals and of groups. Social psychology can help us understand how best to work with human predilections and predispositions to achieve our goals of improving security:

- Research on social cognition looks at how people form impressions about reality. Knowing these principles, we can better teach our colleagues and clients about effective security.

- Work on attitude formation and beliefs helps us present information effectively, and so convince employees and others to cooperate in improving security.

- Scientists studying persuasion and attitude change have learned how best to change people's minds about unpopular views, such as those regarding the security community.

- Studies of factors enhancing prosocial behavior provide insights on how to foster an environment where corporate information is willingly protected.

- Knowledge of the phenomena underlying conformity, compliance, and obedience can help us enhance security by encouraging compliance and by protecting staff against social pressure to breach security.

- Group psychology research provides warnings about group pathology and hints for working better with groups in establishing and maintaining IS in the face of ingrained resistance.

This chapter reviews well-established principles of social psychology that help security and network management personnel implement security policies more effectively. Any recent introductory college textbook in this field will provide references to the research that has led to the principles that are applied to security policy implementation. For this reason, academic references have been kept to a minimum.

35.2   RATIONALITY IS NOT ENOUGH.   Information security policies sometimes seem to evoke strong emotions. People can get very angry about what they perceive as interference with their way of getting the work done.

Sometimes people subvert IS by systematically getting around the rules. It is not uncommon for regularly scheduled outside delivery and maintenance persons to be given keys, or the door lock combination, for access into secured areas. These people are rarely subjected to security checks, yet their potential for intentional or inadvertent damage is great. A common response to new security rules or to attempts at enforcing existing policies and procedures is a charge of paranoia aimed at security personnel.

Other accusations include authoritarian behavior and undue interference with job functions. These responses usually indicate a conflict between accepted norms of behavior and the need to change behavior to conform to security principles.

35.2.1   The Schema.   Psychologists use the word "schema" to summarize the complex picture of reality upon which we base our judgments.

The schema is what social psychologists call the way people make sense of their social interactions. IS practitioners must change their colleagues' schemata.

Earlier we mentioned a case in which the manager's schema included supposedly trustworthy delivery people; an IS specialist's schema in the same circumstances includes all the potentially untrustworthy friends of those outsiders.

Schemata are self-consistent views of reality. They help us pay attention to what we expect to be important and to ignore irrelevant data. They also help us organize our behavior. For example, our schema for relations at the office includes polite greetings, civil discussions, written communications, and business-like clothes. The schema excludes obscene shrieks, abusive verbal attacks, spray-painted graffiti, and colleagues dressed in swim suits. It is the schema that lets people know what is inappropriate in a given situation.

Unfortunately, security policies and procedures conflict with most people's schemata. Office workers' schemata includes sharing office supplies ("Lend me your stapler, please?"), trusting their team members to share information ("Take a look at these figures, Sally"), and letting their papers stay openly visible when they have to leave their desks.

Sharing user IDs, showing sensitive information to someone who lacks the appropriate clearance, and leaving workstations logged on without protection are gross breaches of a different schema—that of the IS specialist. Think about access controls: Normal politeness dictates that when a colleague approaches the door we have just opened, we hold the door open for the person; when we see a visitor, we smile politely—after all, it might be a customer. In contrast, access-control policies require that we refuse to let even well-liked colleagues piggyback their way through an access-card system; security policies insist that unbadged strangers be challenged or reported to security personnel. Common sense tells us that when the chief executive officer (CEO) of the company wants something, we do not oppose it; yet good IS dictates that we train computer room operators to forbid entry to anyone without documented authorization—including the CEO.

If we persist in assuming that we can influence our colleagues to change their perception of IS simply by informing, cajoling, nagging, or browbeating them, we will continue to fail. Information security must be integrated into the corporate culture, a process that needs to use all of the techniques that social psychology can teach us.

35.2.2   Theories of Personality.   One of the most pervasive obstacles to cooperation in organizations is interpersonal conflict. Many conflicts are rooted in differences of *personality style*. For example, one widely used set of categories for describing people's personalities uses the following schemata:

- Extroversion
  - High: active, assertive, energetic, outgoing, talkative
  - Low: quiet, reserved, shy, silent, withdrawn
- Agreeableness
  - High: affectionate, appreciative, kind, soft-hearted, sympathetic

- ○ Low: cold, fault-finding, hard-hearted, quarrelsome, unfriendly
- Conscientiousness
    - ○ High: efficient, organized, planful, responsible, thorough
    - ○ Low: careless, disorderly, frivolous, irresponsible, slipshod
- Emotional stability
    - ○ High: calm, contented, stable, unemotional
    - ○ Low: anxious, moody, nervous, tense, worrying
- Openness or Culturedness
    - ○ High: imaginative, insightful, intelligent, original, wide interests
    - ○ Low: commonplace, shallow, simple, narrow interests, unintelligent

The adjectives used in this summary are positive for the "high" side of each trait and negative for the "low" side. However, the assumption that different personality types are easily characterized as superior and inferior seriously interferes with respectful communications among colleagues. For example, people with "low" characteristics might view the preceding summary in this way:

- Extroversion
    - ○ High: nervous, aggressive, excitable, pushy, chattering
    - ○ Low: dignified, respectful, unassuming, attentive, self-sufficient
- Agreeableness
    - ○ High: clinging, gushy, soft-headed, knee-jerk reactive, uncritical
    - ○ Low: stately, analytical, rational, principled, reserved
- Conscientiousness
    - ○ High: obsessive, compulsive, unspontaneous, pompous, slavish
    - ○ Low: free, spontaneous, creative, fun, youthful, having perspective
- Emotional stability
    - ○ High: frozen, ambitionless, boring, dead
    - ○ Low: vibrant, romantic, alive, strong, sensible
- Openness or Culturedness
    - ○ High: flaky, theoretical, complicated, off-the-wall, dilettante
    - ○ Low: earthy, smart, grounded, focused, practical

In discussing corporate culture change, leaders must be on guard to defuse conflicts based on the misperception that one particular response or view of an issue is necessarily good and another necessarily bad. The conflict may be rooted in personality styles rather than in problems of understanding. If the security working group proposes that all employees must challenge anyone in the secured areas who is not wearing a badge, some people—those who have low extroversion, for example—may have a great deal of difficulty with the concept that they should tell anyone else what to do, especially a manager of a higher rank than their own. Arguing over the reasons why such a policy would be useful would sidestep the fundamental problem: that the required behavior is in direct conflict with possibly lifelong and firmly held views on appropriate behavior.

Security personnel must remember that failure to comply with policy is not necessarily the result of a bad attitude.

When it becomes obvious that conflicts are rooted in personality, security personnel will have to try to arrive at a useful compromise. Instead of requiring that everyone confront the unbadged individual personally, the security policies could include a proviso allowing for individuals to choose simply to inform security personnel immediately.

Role-playing exercises sometimes can defuse a problem in accepting security policies by desensitizing resistant personnel. Going through the motions of what they fear or dislike sometimes can help them come to realize that the proposed change in behavior is not as bad as they originally thought. Returning to the example of confronting violations of security, many people have difficulty imagining that they could tell a superior in the management hierarchy not to piggyback. This term, like "hitchhiking" and "tailgating," describes entering through a secured door that has been opened by someone else using a valid access code or token. Going through exercises in which each person pretends in turn to be the upper manager and then the challenger seems to break down resistance to this particular security policy.

In general, leaders of the security team responsible for implementing security policies should be on the lookout for conflicts of style that interfere with the central task of making the enterprise more secure. If an individual likes short, direct instructions without chitchat about nonessentials, the security team member should adapt and stick to essentials; if an individual is known to like getting to know a stranger and wants to spend 10 minutes learning about family background, it should not be opposed. Communicating ideas in a way that is likely to be acceptable is more important than imposing one's own interpersonal style preferences on others.

Above all, security personnel—and management in general—ought to be doing a great deal more *listening* and a great deal less *commanding*.

35.2.3   Explanations of Behavior.   In practice, trying to change corporate culture can be a frustrating and long-drawn-out project. One aspect of this process that security group leaders should monitor closely is the interpretation of employee behavior by members of the security team. In general, people interpret (i.e., explain) other people's behavior according to two independent dimensions: internal or external and stable or unstable. Here are some explanations of why Betty has failed to log off her session for the fourth time this week before leaving the office:

- Internal, stable: "That's just the way she is—she never pays attention to these rules."
- Internal, unstable: "She's been under strain lately because her child is sick— that's why she's forgotten."
- External, stable: "The system doesn't respond properly to the logoff command."
- External, unstable: "This week, the system has not been responding properly to the logoff command."

This simple four-way classification is useful for leaders in understanding and avoiding classic errors of attribution. Such attribution errors can cause conflicts between the security staff and other employees or even among employees with different degrees of compliance to policy.

35.2.4   Errors of Attribution.   Some well-established misinterpretations of others' behavior can interfere with the acceptance of security policies. Such errors interfere with the ability of security personnel to communicate the value of security policies. Security group leaders should sensitize their staff to the consequences of these errors.

35.2.4.1   *Fundamental Attribution Error.*
The most important error people use when explaining other people's behavior is to assume that a person's actions are stable, internal features; a typical example of this error is the naïve belief that an actor's personality is essentially what that person portrays in performance. Anyone who has ever experienced surprise at the demeanor and speech of a favorite actor who is being interviewed has committed the *fundamental attribution error.* Some actors who play bad people have even been verbally and physically assaulted by viewers who cannot resist the fundamental attribution error and genuinely believe that the actors are as bad as the characters they portray.

In security work, being on guard against the fundamental attribution error helps to smooth relations with other employees. For example, if a security group member sees an employee, Jill, who is not wearing her badge, it is easy to assume that she never wears her badge and is refusing to wear it because of a character flaw. The security officer may act according to these assumptions by being harsh or unfriendly in correcting Jill's behavior. The harshness generates resentment, and Jill may come to associate security with unpleasant people, thus reducing the likelihood that she will comply with policy or encourage others to do so.

In fact, however, most people's behavior is far less stable and internal than unstable and externally based. For example, if the security officer simply asked about the lack of a badge instead of jumping to conclusions, he might discover that Jill's lack of a badge today was due simply to her having taken her jacket off just before an urgent call from the vice president, interrupting her normal procedure of moving the badge from jacket to shirt pocket. Thus, her lack of a badge would not be stable behavior at all—it would be a temporary aberration of no long-lasting significance. Similarly, just by asking, the security officer might learn that Jill normally does wear her badge, but today her four-year-old son took it off her jacket to play with it, without his mother's noticing the change. In this example, Jill's behavior is externally based and has nothing to do with character.

By being aware of the fundamental attribution error, security personnel can be trained to adopt a less judgmental, quick-draw mentality that can alienate other employees and damage security programs.

35.2.4.2   *Actor-Observer Effect.*
The *actor-observer effect* consists of interpreting one's own behavior as appropriate unstable, externally motivated responses to environmental conditions, whereas other people's behavior is viewed in the light of the fundamental attribution error as stable, internally motivated expressions of character traits. Becoming aware of this tendency helps security personnel resist the fundamental attribution error.

35.2.4.3   *Self-Serving Bias.*
The counterpart of the actor-observer effect is the *self-serving bias,* which fools people into believing that their own behavior is due to stable, internal aspects of their character. Security officers who are unaware of this dangerous error may come to feel that they are in some sense superior to other people who do not know as much about security as they do or who do not comply as fully as they do with security policy. The officers may have failed to integrate the fact that hours of training and coaching by their security group leaders are at least as responsible for their own knowledge of, and compliance with, security policies as any innate superiority.

By bringing this kind of erroneous thinking to light during training and supervision of security staff, managers can help reduce the conflicts that naturally result from an air of assumed superiority.

35.2.4.4   Salience and Prejudice.   When people are asked to guess which person in a group is the most influential (or least influential) person, social psychologists find that whichever person stands out the most, for whatever reason, is usually attributed with the special properties in question. Such effects apply to any characteristic that the psychologists ask about: most (or least) intelligent, aggressive, sympathetic, and so on. This phenomenon is known as the *salience effect.*

An application of the salience effect might occur if security officers see a group of employees who are violating security policies. A natural and counterproductive tendency is to leap to the conclusion that the tallest or shortest, the thinnest or fattest, the whitest or blackest person in the group must be to blame. This error can result in unfair treatment of perfectly innocent people.

This problem of misinterpreting salience is exacerbated by prejudice; for example, imagine there were an identifiable group called the "Ogunians" who traditionally wear, say, a seven-sided symbol of their identity. If an anti-Ogunian security officer sees a noncompliant group where one of the members is wearing the characteristic heptagon of Ogun, it may be hard for the officer to resist blaming the noncompliance on the Ogunian. Similarly, any minority—whether in terms of gender, gender orientation, religion, race, or disability—can be the focus of a prejudiced security officer's blame when a group disobeys policy. Security leaders should make their staff aware of the danger of applying this erroneous method of explaining group behavior.

Another factor in misinterpreting group behavior is that people can be strongly influenced by expectation—what social psychologists call the *schema*—a subject already introduced. Even observation itself can be biased by expectations; for example, a security officer may believe, erroneously, that (the imaginary) Ogunians are consistently noncompliant with security policies. Seeing a group of people passing through an open doorway into a secured area without using their badges, the officer may incorrectly report that it was the Ogunian's fault—when, in fact, the Ogunian was waiting to use a valid access card in full compliance with security policy. Such a mistaken report would not only infuriate the innocent Ogunian and possibly cause general Ogunian resentment or hostility toward "security," but it also could mislead the security group itself into trying to correct the behavior of the wrong person or people.

35.2.5   Intercultural Differences.   Many countries in the world are experiencing changes in their population due to immigration. Especially in areas where people have heretofore been largely homogenous, cultural, religious, and racial diversity can lead to interpersonal and intergroup conflicts. Such conflicts may be based in part on prejudice, but they also may be the result of differing values and assumptions.

Security personnel engaged in the process of corporate culture change should be sensitive to the possibility that people with different cultural backgrounds can respond differently to proposed security policies. For example, in 2001 the fundamentalist extremists of the Taliban in Afghanistan decreed that non-Muslim people would have to wear badges in public. One can imagine that a Hindu Afghan refugee in the United States who is told to wear a badge for security reasons might believe that its purpose was to mark him as a target—especially after the terrorist attacks of September 11, 2001. Before pressuring anyone who seems to be resisting a policy, it is valuable to inquire about the person's beliefs and attitudes and to explain the foundation for the policies in question. Especially where there are intercultural differences, such inquiry and discussion can forestall difficulties and dissension.

35.2.6   Framing Reality.

How can we make the corporate culture more supportive of information security?

Schemata influence what we perceive. For example, an employee refuses to take vacations, works late every night, is never late, and is never sick. A model employee? Perhaps, in one schema. From the security point of view, the employee's behavior is suspect. There have been cases where such people have been embezzlers unable to leave their employment: Even a day away might result in discovery of their crimes. Saint or sinner? Our expectations determine what we see.

To change the schema so that people take information security seriously, we should provide participants in training and security awareness with real-life examples of computer crime and security breaches, so that security policies make sense rather than seeming to be arbitrary.

Schemata influence what we remember. When information inconsistent with our preconceptions is mixed with details that fit our existing schemata, we selectively retain what fits and discard what conflicts. When we have been fed a diet of movies and television shows illustrating the premise that information is most at risk from brilliant hackers, why should we remember the truth—that carelessness and incompetence by authorized users of information systems cause far more harm than evil intentions and outsiders ever do.

Instructors should emphasize the practical side of information security by showing how policies protect all employees against false accusations, prevent damage to the organization's reputation and profits, and even play a role in national security. This is especially true where business touches the technical infrastructure on which we all depend.

Most important of all, teaching others about information security cannot be an occasional and haphazard affair. Before attempting to implement policies and procedures, we should ensure that we build up a consistent view of information security among our colleagues. In light of the complexity of social cognition, our usual attempts to implement security policies and procedures seem pathetically inept. A couple of hours of lectures followed by a video, a yearly ritual of signing a security policy that seems to have been written by Martians—these are not methods that will improve security. These efforts merely pay lip service to the idea of security.

According to research on counterintuitive information, people's judgment is influenced by the manner in which information is presented. For example, even information contrary to established schemata can be assimilated, if people have enough time to integrate the new knowledge into their worldviews. It follows that security policies should be introduced over a long time, not rushed into place.

An effective IS program includes frequent reminders of security. To change the corporate culture, practitioners should use methods such as a security corner in the corporate publication, security bulletins detailing the latest computer crime or security breach that has hit the news, contests for identifying the problems in realistic scenarios, and write-in columns to handle questions about policies. IS has to become part of the framework of reality, not just an imposition from management.

35.2.7   Practical Recommendations

- In every security course or awareness program, instructors and facilitators should explicitly address the question of corporate culture, expectations, and social schemata. Do not rely solely on intellectual discourse when addressing a question of complex perceptions and feelings. Use simulations, videos, and role-playing exercises to bridge the gap between intellect and emotion.

- Address the feelings and perceptions of all participants as they learn about the counterintuitive behaviors that improved security will demand. Encourage learners to think about how they might feel and respond in various situations that can arise during the transition to a more secure environment. For example, ask participants to imagine

  ○ Asking colleagues not to step through a secured entrance without passing through the access-control system with their own identity

  ○ Telling their boss that they will not copy software without a license to do so

  ○ Questioning a visitor or employee who is not wearing an identity badge

35.3   GETTING YOUR SECURITY POLICIES ACROSS.   What are some ways to change our colleagues' schemata so that they become more receptive to information security policies?

35.3.1   Initial Exposure.   Preliminary information may influence people's responses to information presented later. For example, merely exposing experimental subjects to words such as "reckless" or "adventurous" affects their judgment of risk-taking behavior in a later test.

It follows that when preparing to increase employee awareness of security issues, presenting case studies is likely to have a beneficial effect on participants' readiness to examine security requirements.

35.3.2   Counterexamples.   Preexisting schemata can be challenged by several counterexamples, each of which challenges a component of the schema. For example, prejudice about an ethnic group is more likely to be changed by contact with several people, each of whom contradicts a different aspect of the prejudiced schema.

It follows that security awareness programs should include many realistic examples of security requirements and breaches. In a counterexample, students in college information security (INFOSEC) courses have commented on the unrealistic scenario in a training video they were shown: a series of disastrous security breaches occuring in the same company. Based on the findings of cognitive social psychologists, the film would be more effective for training if the incidents were dramatized as occurring in different companies.

In practical terms, practitioners should stay current and update their materials. Many IS publications provide useful case studies that will help make awareness and training more effective.

35.3.3   Choice of Wording.   Perceptions of risks and benefits are profoundly influenced by the wording in which situations and options are presented. For example, experimental subjects responded far more positively to reports of a drug with "50 percent success" than to the same drug described as having "50 percent failure."

It follows that practitioners should choose their language carefully during security awareness campaigns. Instead of focusing on reducing failure rates (violations of policy), we should emphasize improvements in our success rates. Unfortunately, some rates cannot be expressed in positive terms; for example, it is not easy to measure the success rate of security measures designed to forestall attacks on systems.

Judgments are easily distorted by the tendency to rely on personal anecdotes, small samples, easily available information, and faulty interpretation of statistical information. Basically, we humans are not always rational processors of factual information. If security awareness programs rely strictly on presentation of factual information about risks and proposed policies and procedures, they are likely to run up against a stubborn refusal to act logically. Security program implementation must engage more than the rational mind. We must appeal to our colleagues' imagination and emotion as well. We must inspire a commitment to security rather than merely describing it.

35.4   BELIEFS AND ATTITUDES.   Psychologists distinguish between beliefs and attitudes. A *belief* refers to cognitive information that need not have an emotional component. An *attitude* refers to an evaluation or emotional response. Thus, a person may believe correctly that copying a large number of proprietary software packages without authorization is a felony while nonetheless having the attitude that it does not matter to him.

35.4.1   Beliefs.   Beliefs can change when contradictory information is presented, but some research suggests that it can take up to a week before significant shifts are measurable. Other studies suggest that when people hold contradictory beliefs, providing an opportunity to articulate and evaluate those beliefs may lead to changes that reduce inconsistency.

These findings imply that corporate security must explore the current structure of beliefs among employees and managers. Questionnaires, focus groups, and interviews may not only help the security practitioner, they actually may help move the corporate culture in the right direction.

35.4.2   Attitudes.   An attitude, in the classical definition, is a *learned evaluative response, directed at specific objects, which is relatively enduring and influences behavior in a generally motivating way.* The advertising industry spends over $50 billion yearly to influence public attitudes in the hope that these attitudes will lead to changes in spending habits—that is, in behavior.

Research on classical conditioning suggests that attitudes can be learned even through simple word association. If we wish to move our colleagues toward a more negative view of computer criminals, it is important not to portray computer crime using positive images and words. Movies that show criminal hackers as pleasant, smart, physically attractive, and likable people may do harm by minimizing the seriousness of industrial espionage and cybervandalism. When teaching security, we should avoid praising the criminals we describe in case studies.

Studies of how attitudes are learned consistently show that rewards and punishments are important motivators of behavior. Even apparently minor encouragement can influence attitudes. A supervisor or instructor should praise any comments that are critical of computer crime or that support the established security policies. Employees who dismiss security concerns or flout the regulations should be challenged on their attitudes, not ignored. Such challenges are best carried out in private to avoid causing embarrassment to the skeptics and possibly generating resistance due to pride or a misplaced sense of machismo.

35.4.3   Reward.   When enforcing security policies, too many organizations focus entirely on punishing those who break the rules. However, everything we know about modifying behavior teaches us to use reward rather than punishment. A security officer in a large corporation experimented with reward and punishment in implementing security policies. Employees were supposed to log off their terminals when leaving the office, but compliance rates were only around 40 percent. In one department, the security officer used the usual techniques: putting up nasty notes on terminals that were not logged off, reporting violators to their bosses, and changing the passwords on delinquent accounts. In a different department, she simply identified those users who had indeed logged off their terminals and left a Hershey's Chocolate Kiss on the keyboard. After one month, compliance rates in the department subject to punishment had climbed to around 50 percent. Compliance in the department getting chocolates had reached 80 percent.

35.4.4   Changing Attitudes toward Security.   Persuasion—changing someone's attitudes—has been described in terms of communications. The four areas of research include:

1. Communicator variables: Who is trying to persuade?
2. Message variables: What is being presented?
3. Channel variables: By what means is the attempt taking place?
4. Audience variables: At whom is the persuasion aimed?

35.4.4.1   Communicator Variables.   Attractiveness, credibility, and social status have strong effects immediately after the speaker or writer has communicated with the target audience; however, over a period of weeks to a month, the effects decline until the predominant issue is message content. We can use this phenomenon by identifying the senior executives most likely to succeed in setting a positive tone for subsequent security training. We should look for respected, likable people who understand the issues and sincerely believe in the policies they are advocating.

One personality style can be a threat to the success of security policies: the *authoritarian personality*. A body of research suggests that some people, raised by punitive parents highly concerned with social status, become rigidly devoted to conventional beliefs, submit to authority, exercise authority harshly themselves, and are hostile to groups they perceive as unpopular. The worst possible security officer would be an authoritarian person. Such an officer can derive more satisfaction from ordering people around and punishing them than from long-term success in implementing security policies.

35.4.4.2   Message Variables.   Fear can work to change attitudes only if judiciously applied. Excessive emphasis on the terrible results of poor security is likely to backfire, with participants in the awareness program rejecting the message altogether. Frightening consequences should be coupled immediately with effective and achievable security measures.

Some studies suggest that presenting a balanced argument helps convince those who initially disagree with a proposal. Presenting objections to a proposal and offering counterarguments is more effective than one-sided diatribes. The long-used Software Publishers' Association training video, *It's Just Not Worth the Risk,* uses this technique: It shows several members of a company arguing over copyright infringement and fairly presents the arguments of software copiers before rebutting them.

Modest repetition of a message can help generate a more positive response. Thus security awareness programs that include imaginative posters, mugs, special newsletters, audio and videotapes, and lectures are more likely to build and sustain support for security than occasional intense sessions of indoctrination. The use of multiple communications channels (discussed in the next section) also increases the effectiveness of the message.

35.4.4.3   *Channel Variables.*   The channel through which we communicate has a strong effect on attitudes and on the importance of superficial attributes of the communicator. In modern organizations, most people assume that a meeting is the ideal way to communicate new information. However, the most effective medium for convincing someone to pay attention to any topic is face-to-face persuasion. Security training should include more than tapes and books; a charismatic teacher or leader can help generate enthusiasm for—or at least reduce resistance to—better security.

In addition, security educators should not introduce new ideas to decision makers in a meeting. There is too much danger of confounding responses to policy with non-policy matters rooted in relationships among the participants. It is not uncommon for one executive to oppose a new policy simply because another has supported it. A good way to introduce security policies is to have individual meetings with one executive at a time in order to explain the issues and proposals and to ask for support.

Psychologists testing cognitive response theory have studied many subtle aspects of persuasion. Experiments have shown that rhetorical questions, such as "Are we to accept invasions of our computer systems?" are effective when the arguments are solid but counterproductive when arguments are weak.

Security officers should not ask rhetorical questions unless they are certain that almost everybody will inevitably have the same answer—the one the security officers are looking for.

Consideration of facts and logical arguments, as the central route to persuasion, has been found to lead to more lasting attitudes and attitude changes than the peripheral influences from logically unrelated factors, such as physical attractiveness of a speaker.

35.4.4.4   *Audience Variables.*   As mentioned, questionnaires and interviews may help cement a favorable change in attitude by leading to commitment. Once employees have publicly avowed support for better security, some will begin to change their perception of themselves. Specific employees should be encouraged to take on various areas of public responsibility for information security within their work group. These roles should periodically be rotated among the employees to give everyone the experience of public commitment to improved security.

To keep up interest in security, regular meetings of enthusiasts to discuss recent security news can keep the subject fresh and interesting. New cases can help security officers explain policies with up-to-date references that will interest their fellow employees and motivate managers to pay attention to security policies.

35.5   ENCOURAGING INITIATIVE.   The ideal situation would be for everyone actually to help enforce security policies. Actually, however, some people are cooperative and helpful whereas others—or even the same people in different circumstances—are reluctant and suspicious about new policies. What can be done to increase cooperation and reduce rejection?

35.5.1   Prosocial Behavior.   Studies of people who have come to the aid of others can help to encourage everyone in an organization to do the right thing. Some people intervene to stop crimes; others ignore crimes or watch passively. Social psychologists have devised a schema that describes the steps leading to prosocial behavior:

- People have to notice the emergency or the crime before they can act. Thus, security training has to include information on how to tell that someone may be engaging in computer crime.

- The situation has to be defined as an emergency—something requiring action. Security training that provides facts about the effects of computer crime on society and solid information about the need for security within the organization can help employees recognize security violations as emergencies.

- Everyone must take responsibility for acting, but the larger the number of people in a group confronted with an emergency, the slower the average response time. Larger groups seem to lead to a *diffusion of responsibility;* each person feels that someone else is more responsible for dealing with the emergency. Another possible factor is uncertainty about the social climate; people fear appearing foolish or overly emotional in the eyes of those present. To overcome this effect, a corporate culture must be established that rewards responsible individual behavior, such as reporting security violations.

- Once responsibility for solving a problem has been accepted, appropriate decisions and actions must be taken. Clearly written security policies and procedures will make it more likely that employees act to improve security. In contrast, contradictory policies, poorly documented procedures, and inconsistent support from management will interfere with the decision to act.

Another analysis proposes that people implicitly analyze costs of helping and of not helping when deciding whether to act prosocially. The combination of factors most conducive to prosociality is low cost for helping and high cost for not helping.

Security procedures should make it easy to act in accordance with security policy. There should be a hot line for reporting security violations, and anonymity should be respected if desired. Psychological counseling and follow-up should be available if people feel upset about their involvement. Conversely, failing to act responsibly should be a serious matter; personnel policies should document clear and meaningful sanctions for failing to act when a security violation is observed. Penalties would include critical remarks in employment reviews and, where appropriate, even dismissal.

One method that does *not* work to increase prosocial behavior is *exhortation;* merely lecturing people about what they ought to do has little or no positive effect.

Significantly, the general level of stress and pressure to focus on difficult tasks with seemingly impossible deadlines can greatly reduce the likelihood that people will act on their moral and ethical principles. Security is likely to flourish in an environment that provides sufficient time and support for employees to work professionally. Offices where everyone responds to a continuing series of apparent emergencies will not be likely to pay attention to security violations.

Some findings from research confirm common sense. For example, guilt motivates many people to act more prosocially. This effect works best when people are forced to assume responsibility. Thus, enforcing standards of security using reprimands and sanctions can indeed increase the likelihood that employees subsequently will act more cooperatively; however, as suggested earlier, punishment should not replace reward.

In addition, mood affects susceptibility to prosocial pressures. Bad moods make prosocial behavior less likely, whereas good moods increase prosociality. A working environment in which employees are respected is more conducive to good security than one that devalues and abuses them.

Even cursory acquaintance with other people makes it more likely that we will help them; it thus makes sense for security supervisors to get to know the staff from whom they need support. Encouraging social activities in an office (e.g., lunchtime discussion groups, occasional parties, and charitable projects) enhances interpersonal relationships and can improve the climate for effective security training.

35.5.2   Conformity, Compliance, and Obedience.   These days, many people react negatively to the words "conformity," "compliance," and "obedience," but ignoring social phenomena will not help security practitioners to attain their goals. Despite the unpopularity of this subject area, it is valuable to understand how people can work together in reinforcing security policies. The following sections look at how to increase conformity, compliance with security rules, and obedience to IS authorities.

35.5.2.1   *Social Pressure and Behavior Change.*   Turning a group into a community provides a framework in which social pressures can operate to improve an organization's information security. People respond to the opinions of others by shifting their own opinions, sometimes unconsciously, toward the mode—the most popular opinion. Security programs must aim to shift the normative values, the sense of what one should do, toward protecting confidentiality, possession or control, integrity, authenticity, availability, and utility of data.

35.5.2.2   *Changing Expectations.*   As has been evident in public campaigns aimed at eliminating drunken driving, it is possible to shift the mode. Thirty years ago, many people believed that driving while intoxicated was amusing; today, a drunken driver is a social pariah. High school children used to kill themselves in large numbers on the nights of their high school proms; today, many children spontaneously are arranging for safe rides home. In much the same way, we must move toward making computer crime as distasteful as public drunkenness.

The trend toward similar behavior increases when people within the group like or admire each other. In addition, the social status of an individual within a group influences that individual's willingness to conform to group standards. High-status people (those liked by most people in the group) and low-status people (those disliked by the group) both tend to be more autonomous and less compliant than people liked by some and disliked by others. Therefore, security officers should pay special attention to those outliers during instruction programs. Managers should monitor compliance more closely at both ends of the popularity range. If security practices are currently poor, and allies are needed to change the norm, working with the outliers to resist the majority's antisecurity bias may be the most effective approach.

35.5.2.3   *Norm of Reciprocity.*   According to social psychologists, the norm of reciprocity indicates that, in social relations, favors are usually returned. Even a small, unexpected, unsolicited, or even unwanted gift increases the likelihood that we will respond to requests. For example, members of various religious cults often hand out flowers or books at airports, knowing that the norm of reciprocity will increase the frequency and amount of donations from basically uninterested passersby.

A security awareness program that includes small gifts, such as an attractive mug labeled "SECURITY IS EVERYONE'S BUSINESS" or an inexpensive but useful booklet summarizing security policies, can help get people involved in security.

35.5.2.4   *Incremental Change.*   The foot-in-the-door technique suggests that a small initial request should be followed by an even larger second one. Political field workers, for example, know that they can start small by asking people to let them put candidate stickers in their window; then they ask to put a candidate's poster on their lawn; eventually they can ask for volunteer time or money. Every compliance with a request increases the likelihood that the person will agree to the next step in an escalating series. It is as if agreeing to one step helps to change the targets' sense of themselves. To reduce discomfort about their beliefs and their behavior (what psychologists call "cognitive dissonance"), people change their beliefs to conform with their behavior.

Employees can be asked personally to set a good example by blanking screens and locking terminals when leaving their desks. Later, once they have begun the process of redefining themselves ("I am a person who cares about computer security"), they can be asked for something more intense, such as participating in security training by asking others to blank their screens and lock their terminals. The same methods could be used to accomplish similar ends, and in this way the corporate culture would be changed so that a majority of people feel personally committed to good security practices.

35.6   GROUP BEHAVIOR.   Some groups of people are referred to as teams, while others are called gangs. Social psychological insights into group behavior can improve success rates for IS policies.

35.6.1   Social Arousal.   Studies on the behavioral effects of being in groups produced contradictory results; sometimes people did better at their tasks when there were other people around, and sometimes they did worse. Eventually, psychologists realized that the presence of other people is socially arousing; that is, people become more aware both of their own behavior and of social norms when they are in groups. Social arousal facilitates well-learned habits but it inhibits poorly learned habits. Thus, when trying to teach employees new habits to improve security, it is counterproductive to put them into large groups. Individualized learning (e.g., by means of computer-based training and videotapes) can overcome inhibitory effects of groups in the early stages of behavioral change.

35.6.2   Locus of Control.   Another factor that interferes with implementation of security policies is the *locus of control.* People do not like feeling that they have no control over their environment. For example, in a classic experiment reported in social psychology textbooks, two equivalent teams of people were both subjected to loud and disruptive noise coming through a loudspeaker in their work area. One group had no control whatever over the noise, whereas the other had a large button with which they could stop the noise at once. The group with the stop button did noticeably better at their complex task than the other group—yet in no case did anyone actually press the button. Simply feeling that they *could* exert control if they wanted to significantly altered the performance of the experimental subjects.

Similarly, in studies of healing among older patients, three groups were defined: (1) controls, (2) people given a plant in a pot, and (3) people given a plant in a pot plus instructions to water it regularly. The third group did significantly better than the second in their recovery. Once again, the sense of control over the environment appeared to influence outcomes.

In security policy implementation, experience confirms that those organizations with the most participation and involvement by all sectors do best at developing and implementing information protection plans. A common phrase that refers to this phenomenon is "buy-in," as in "The different departmental representatives felt that they could genuinely buy into the new policies because they had fully participated in framing them."

35.6.3 Group Polarization. Another branch of research in group psychology deals with group polarization. Groups tend to take more extreme decisions than would individuals in the group acting alone. In group discussions of the need for security, polarization can involve deciding to take more risks—by reducing or ignoring security concerns—than any individual would have judged reasonable. Again, one-on-one discussions of the need for security will generally be more effective in building a consensus that supports cost-effective security provisions than will large meetings.

35.6.4 Groupthink. In the extreme, a group can display groupthink, in which a consensus is reached because of strong desires for social cohesion. When groupthink prevails, evidence contrary to the received view is discounted; opposition is viewed as disloyal; dissenters are discredited. Especially worrisome for security professionals, those people in the grip of groupthink tend to ignore risks and contingencies. To prevent such aberrations, the leader must remain impartial and encourage open debate. Respected security consultants from the outside could be invited to address the group, bringing their own experiences to bear on the group's requirements. After a consensus—not the imposition of a dominant person's opinions—has been achieved, the group should meet again and focus on playing devil's advocate to try to come up with additional challenges and alternatives.

In short, security experts should pay attention to group dynamics and be prepared to counter possible dysfunctional responses that interfere with acceptance of information security policies.

35.7 SUMMARY. This chapter has reviewed the major findings of social psychology that can help to improve information security programs. These ideas can prove useful to readers who think about social psychology as they work to implement security policies:

- Recognize that information security policies often conflict with the schema for trusting, polite behavior in situations outside the work arena.
- Train information security personnel to recognize that failure to comply with security policies may be rooted in many other factors than simply bad attitude.
- Listen more than you command.
- Teach security personnel to avoid the classic errors of attribution when trying to understand their colleagues' motivations.
- Openly discuss and counter prejudice before it causes conflicts.
- Take intercultural differences into account when setting and implementing security policies.
- Before attempting to implement policies and procedures, ensure a consistent view of information security among colleagues.
- Security policies should be introduced over a long time, not rushed into place.
- Presenting case studies is likely to have a beneficial effect on participants' readiness to examine security requirements.
- Security awareness programs should include many realistic examples of security requirements and breaches.

- Attempt to inspire a commitment to security rather than merely describing it.
- Emphasize improvements rather than reduction of failure.
- Create a new concern for corporate security by exploring the current structure of beliefs among employees and managers.
- Never portray computer crime using positive images and words.
- Praise any comments that are critical of computer crime or that support the established security policies.
- Employees who dismiss security concerns or flout the regulations should be challenged on their attitudes, not ignored.
- Identify the senior executives most likely to succeed in setting a positive tone for subsequent security training and engage their cooperation to act as role models.
- Frightening consequences should be coupled immediately with effective and achievable security measures.
- Presenting objections to a proposal and offering counterarguments is more effective than one-sided diatribes.
- Security awareness programs should include many, frequent, and preferably novel and entertaining reminders of security issues.
- In addition to tapes and books, rely on a charismatic teacher or leader to help generate enthusiasm for better security.
- Encourage specific employees to take on public responsibility for information security within their work groups.
- Rotate security roles periodically.
- Security training should include information on how to tell that someone may be engaging in computer crime.
- Build a corporate culture that rewards responsible behavior, such as reporting security violations.
- Develop clearly written security policies and procedures.
- Security procedures should make it easy to act in accordance with security policy.
- Treat failures to act in accordance with security policies and procedures as very serious matters.
- Enforcing standards of security can increase the likelihood that employees will subsequently act more cooperatively.
- A working environment in which employees are respected is more conducive to good security than one that devalues and abuses them.
- Get to know the staff from whom you need support.
- Encourage social activities in the office.
- Pay special attention to social outliers during instruction programs.
- Monitor compliance more closely at both ends of the popularity range.
- Work with the outliers to resist the herd's antisecurity bias.
- Include small gifts in your security awareness program.
- Start improving security a little at a time, and work up to more intrusive procedures.
- Before discussing security at a meeting, have one-on-one discussions with the participants.

- Remain impartial and encourage open debate in security meetings.
- Bring in experts from the outside when faced with groupthink.
- Meet again after a consensus has been built and play devil's advocate.

35.8   FURTHER READING

Lippa, R.A. *Introduction to Social Psychology,* 2nd ed. Belmont, CA: Brooks/Cole Publishing Div. of Wadsworth, 1994.

Myers, D.G. *Social Psychology,* 4th ed. New York: McGraw-Hill, 1991–1993).

CHAPTER 36

AUDITING COMPUTER SECURITY

Diane E. Levine

CONTENTS

36.1 INTRODUCTION. Traditional auditing entails review of the financial records of an organization in order to validate the accuracy and integrity of financial statements and their supporting information. Internal controls represent the primary methodology used by management to assure protection of assets and reliability of information. The auditor serves as an independent appraiser of the internal controls in order to ensure management, regulatory authorities, and shareholders of the adequacy and validity of information.

The computer has had a pronounced impact on many different areas of business and many different professions. Auditors, for example, initially were accountants who reviewed the internal controls, control procedures, and audit procedures. Generally, the controls being reviewed related to accounting, taxes, and the audit procedure itself. These reviews involved large amounts of paperwork and research, often done manually, with time-consuming effort.

The advent of the computer has changed the entire process of control reviews or audits, especially electronic data processing (EDP) audits. As technology has evolved, the need for new, state-of-the-art skills has been created. Those skills are directly related to EDP technology, and a whole new specialty has developed. Even a certified public accountant (CPA) may not be qualified for an EDP audit. Instead, the job of an EDP auditor requires a significant amount of training and understanding of the EDP environment, the evolving technology, and the impact of the technology and environment on business. To that end, numerous undergraduate and graduate programs have been developed in universities and colleges around the world to train students in the discipline of EDP auditing.

36.1.1   Roles of External and Internal Auditors.   Many of the technical accounting requirements, and all of the professional ethics for internal and external auditors, including EDP auditors, are similar, if not the same, because of the relationship between various audit functions.

Expanded computer development since the 1960s caused auditing needs to become increasingly complicated. Accounting and operational data, previously calculated and stored manually, were more likely to be calculated and stored on computers. This change created the need for specially trained professionals who could effectively perform EDP reviews. Frequently, companies trained EDP auditors from within their ranks. In other instances, they hired suitably trained personnel from outside the company.

The EDP auditor function may be combined with either external or internal auditing. External auditing is an independent appraisal function to develop an opinion about the reliability of a firm's financial information. An external audit generally is conducted by an independent CPA or public accounting firm and includes a review of the firm's financial statements. Internal auditing is an independent appraisal function that exists within an organization under management's direction. Both internal and external auditors are concerned with the adequacy of existing controls and whether the procedures used are cost-effective. As defined by the American Institute of Certified Public Accountants (AICPA) committee on auditing procedures: "Internal control comprises the plans of organization and all of the coordinate methods and measures adopted within the business to safeguard assets, check the accuracy and reliability of its accounting data, promote operational efficiency and encourage adherents to prescribed managerial policy."

According to this definition, the internal auditor's primary function is to assist management in ensuring the following:

- Safeguarding company assets, both physical and data.
- Accuracy and reliability of data, as required for the health of the business, and compliance with legal and regulatory requirements.
- Promotion of operational efficiency through measurement and recommendations for improvement.
- Adherence to prescribed management policies, and compliance with regulatory and legal obligations for coordination and regulation of personnel in meeting business goals.

36.1.2 Role of the Electronic Data Processing Auditor. The EDP auditor brings highly technical, specialized skills to the audit, regardless of whether the audit is external or internal. Increasing complexity of the financial and operational environment creates an increased need for EDP expertise. The EDP auditor must test the more complex EDP controls and procedures in addition to developing and applying computerized audit techniques. This increased sophistication in the EDP environment, and the need to use technically advanced techniques, requires data-processing expertise.

36.1.3 Scope of Computer Security. Information is a critical organization resource. With the expanded availability of computers to users of all types throughout the world, more data are being processed in shorter periods of time. In addition, increasing amounts of data are stored in computers and computer media.

Understanding what computer security entails requires comprehension of the terms *vulnerability, exposure* and *computer risk.* A *vulnerability* is a weakness in the computer system or its surroundings that may become a threat or a risk. Actual *exposure* results from the threat of an event that has the potential of becoming a risk. A *computer risk* is the probability that an event could result in a loss. The impact of computer risks, exposures, and losses can include financial and personnel losses, loss of reputation and client base, inability to function in a timely and effective manner, inability to grow, and violation of government laws and regulations.

Management and auditors are concerned about the adequacy and effectiveness of computer security measures. Among their concerns are protection against such threats as:

- Inadequate data integrity
- Manipulation of financial, operating, and accounting records maintained on computers
- Unauthorized access to information by both employees and outsiders
- Industrial espionage
- Sabotage of programs, equipment, or facilities
- Loss, damage, or modification of data due to disasters
- Inefficient allocation of EDP resources
- Software copyright violations
- Infection and contamination of software or hardware or by malicious software
- Inadequate insurance coverage
- Obsolescence of equipment, programs, and data
- Computer abuse and misuse
- Theft of computer time
- Lack of a business continuity plan, backup facilities, or equipment
- Inadequate control of cost, availability, and security of remote computing and telecommunication processes

EDP auditors assess whether computer systems safeguard company assets, maintain data integrity, and achieve the organization's goals effectively while consuming resources efficiently. EDP auditors do this by recommending actions to eliminate or minimize losses; by identifying vulnerabilities, exposures, and risks; by determining if adequate controls are in place; by ensuring that audit trails and security measures are in place; and by ascertaining whether the controls, audit trails, and security measures are functioning in an effective manner.

The EDP audit function can be viewed as an effort that focuses on helping organizations attain the traditional audit objectives. To achieve this, EDP auditors should review systems under development (both preimplementation and enhancements), audit functioning data centers, and review application systems.

The Foreign Corrupt Practices Act (FCPA) of 1977 greatly affected auditing. The FCPA deals with illegal foreign payments, internal accounting control, and the regulation of disclosure of information. Its greatest impact was on internal accounting controls, since the FCPA requires that all publicly held corporations be properly controlled and adequate records be kept. The requirements amend the Securities Exchange Act of 1934 and primarily affect companies whose securities are traded either in the over-the-counter market or on the national stock exchanges. The FCPA was amended in August 1988 with clarification of what constitutes bribery, an increase in bribery penalties, and limits on the criminal penalties that relate to individuals who knowingly failed to comply with the FCPA internal control requirements.

36.2   ELECTRONIC DATA PROCESSING SYSTEM CONTROLS.   EDP system controls can be classified into two categories: overall EDP controls and individual application controls. Within each of these categories, three different types of controls are used. The types of controls include: (1) *preventive controls,* which stop undesirable events from occurring; (2) *detective* controls, which uncover undesirable offenses as they occur; and (3) *corrective* controls, which assist in restoring situations to normal after undesirable and unacceptable events have occurred. The implementation of these controls can be either discretionary or nondiscretionary. Discretionary controls are implemented and executed according to the implementer; for example, having everyone who enters a data center sign in and sign out is a discretionary control. Nondiscretionary controls are mandatory and generally automated. Requiring data center visitors to enter a code into a keypad, without which the door to the data center will not open, is a nondiscretionary control.

Overall EDP controls include a review of the management information systems (MIS) department's organizational structure, system development controls, monitoring procedures for change control to systems and programs, access controls, and hardware and systems software controls. Individual application controls include inputs, processing, data storage, telecommunications, and output controls.

36.2.1   Overall Electronic Data Processing Controls.   Overall controls encompass a range of activities common to most computer applications. Since users throughout a company generally share EDP resources, they usually share the same control strengths and weaknesses. Important overall controls include separation of duties, system development controls (implementation, maintenance, job setup, scheduling, and data control), computer operation controls (storage of data files, programs, and forms), production programming, quality assurance, telecommunications support, program library controls, and data library controls.

36.2.1.1   Separation of Duties.   A functioning system of checks and balances can help avoid the misappropriation of assets and damage or misuse of information. Among such checks and balances are:

- Staffing the data center adequately on each shift to support the users

- Restricting computer room access to only those individuals who have the need for access

- Providing supervision for computer room visitors and preventing any visitors from touching the computers

- Restricting access to various programs and files to those individuals who have a specific need, by the use of access control software

- Allowing funds to be paid or transferred only after two or more separate and disinterested individuals have checked the bills or invoices for validity and accuracy

- Permitting changes to be made to systems only by going through a formal procedure requiring specific sign-offs

- Permitting changes to systems only by authorized information systems personnel

- Dedicating an individual to security functions, and not permitting programmers and operators to bypass, modify, or eliminate the security controls in place

36.2.1.2 System Development Controls. Because retrofitting controls can be costly, difficult, and impracticable, an overall control design strategy should be adhered to for the development of systems. The control design process parallels the systems design process and specifies needs, designs, implementation, documentation, and testing. Ideally, the control design strategy should be incorporated into the systems design strategy, which may be called a system development methodology (SDM) or a system development life cycle (SDLC). These strategies use phased approaches, and require:

- Adopting, developing, or purchasing a formal SDM or SDLC

- Notifying staff and consultants that the SDM or SDLC will be used for systems development

- Requiring written approval of a project before development begins

- Maintaining documentation for all phases of the development

- Gaining written sign-off from both designers and users at the completion of each phase of design, before proceeding to the next phase

- Developing a test plan to ensure that program routines are operating correctly

- Developing a plan for reviewing, modifying, and maintaining the systems, as necessary

- Documenting a strategy for job setup and job scheduling that fits within the constraints of systems already in production

- Developing plans for data conversion and data control

- Documenting the system and consistently modifying the documentation as the system is modified

36.2.1.3 Computer Operation Controls. Computer operations controls ensure compliance with management policies. These include separation of duties, cost-effective and efficient operations, and effective security measures for ensuring that company assets (e.g., the underlying assets represented by the data, data files, equipment, software, and physical premises) are safe. Among the controls that can be implemented are:

- Documentation and written approval of system specifications by authorized systems and user management

- Maintaining an organizational structure to support sufficient separation of duties for system development in operational controls
- Verifying the presence and adequacy of approved standard operating instructions for every scheduled job
- Providing an audit trail of processing workloads by logging processor usage
- Examining the supervision of the computer usage log for accuracy and investigation of all abnormal endings, malfunctions, and reruns
- Auditing production programs to ascertain if all versions in use are tested and approved
- Participating in the regular testing, documentation, and enhancement of EDP contingency planning and disaster recovery programs, which ensure business continuity

Chapter 42 presents a methodology for business continuity planning, and Chapter 43 discusses disaster recovery.

36.2.1.4   *Program Revision Controls.*   Because business requirements are subject to change over time, programming changes are necessary. As opposed to systems development, with production programming controls the program already exists and is in use. It needs to be modified to meet the newer requirements, and the process of modification should be controlled in order to avoid unauthorized changes. Such controls apply to both application systems and operating systems and include:

- Written authorization, by both the user and programming management, to make additions or changes to production programs
- Maintenance of documentation authorizing program modifications
- Comprehensive production programming specifications, such as scope of activity, business objectives, proposed design and program details, layouts of data records or reports to be modified, testing procedures, and acceptance criteria

36.2.1.5   *Quality Assurance Controls.*   Quality assurance controls should be applied to every facet of data processing. The auditors should provide an independent review of the quality assurance function. Measures should include:

- Assigning specific individuals, preferably external to the information technology function, to take part in and to be responsible for quality assurance (QA)
- Reviewing the QA function organization, whether or not part of information technology, in regard to personnel and related policies, contracts, and written standards
- Reviewing the implementation and maintenance of systems for documentation; written approvals for system development, programs, and related modifications; testing of initial development and program modifications; and cataloging of new applications and program modifications
- Assessing job setup, scheduling, and data control in conjunction with QA objectives
- Ensuring that operating instructions and the update of production libraries conform with QA standards
- Reviewing system software programming for documentation, an approval methodology, testing the vendor-supplied systems enhancements, and acceptance of systems software

36.2.1.6   Telecommunications Security Controls.   The development and enforcement of telecommunications security controls, including policies, procedures, standards, and guidelines, should reduce the risk of unauthorized access to or misuse of data or destruction of network equipment and programs. Among the techniques used to attain control objectives are:

- Limiting system access, both local and remote, by employees, according to need
- Thorough testing of all telecommunication program updates and changes
- Establishing a centralized and separate network and control group
- Providing encryption for sensitive and confidential data and programs
- Utilizing authentication and identification hardware and software to prevent unauthorized access
- Properly administering a password and user ID program
- Using token access methods for identification purposes, where necessary
- Establishing recovery and restart guidelines for telecommunications systems and software
- Utilizing leased or dedicated lines for better security, when cost justifiable
- Monitoring telecommunication lines for abnormal conditions
- Utilizing a call-back system to identify remote users
- Utilizing a front-end communications controller for validation and authorization
- Advising employees of the copyright laws for software
- Physically preventing unauthorized access to equipment

36.2.1.7   Data Library Controls.   Accidental destruction or misuse of files can be avoided through the use of program security. Frequently, this is done by a data management system that records pertinent information on each file and can detect problems, such as mismounted tape reels or unavailable data. Among the controls employed to safeguard the data library are:

- *Accessing* data files only by authorized programs at authorized times
- *Maintaining* inventory records to ensure the issuing of needed files and their timely return
- *Using* passwords to control access to files and to limit activity concerning those files
- *Producing* and reviewing an audit trail of data file accesses. Deviations from the norm should be investigated

36.2.2   Individual Application Controls.   In instances where applications have vulnerable areas, specific controls may be required. However, the specific controls cannot be relied on unless the overall installation controls are functioning properly. Proper functioning can be ascertained via testing, competent supervision, and regular audits of the overall controls. From an audit standpoint, minimum considerations are:

- *Cost-effectiveness,* where the cost of controls is appropriate to the value of the data and the underlying assets
- *Early error detection* that permits early correction and fewer resulting programs

- *Correcting errors,* which provides an audit trail, especially after updating a master record

Individual application controls should be designed to protect against anticipated errors and irregularities such as erroneous or falsified data, misuse of data by authorized users, unauthorized system access, unproductive security procedures, MIS operations errors, storage media errors, programming errors, operating system errors, and communications systems failure. A classification of application controls includes input, processing, output, and additional controls. Following is an overview of common techniques used within this classification system.

36.2.2.1   Input Controls.   Input controls detect lost or duplicated data, ensure the accuracy of data, and identify transaction sources and the authorization of transactions. Techniques include:

- *Verification* by using check digits and preprocessing edit checks to verify key entry either by a second key entry or a visual review
- *Batch controls* that accumulate field totals and balances to source document totals in order to validate quantitative data
- *Master file reference* that facilitates both the extraction of data online from online master files in order to complete the transaction input, and direct verification of critical input data
- *Edit programs* that verify input by comparing fields against tables of expected values and by testing of logical relationships with other fields

36.2.2.2   Processing Controls.   *Processing controls* provide the foundation of system integrity. They protect against accessing or updating the wrong file or record. They detect incomplete processing, incorrect results, lost files or programs, and inappropriate or untimely transactions. Specific techniques include:

- *Test decks* that verify processing results by the use of prepared data for which totals and processing results have been established. The data should consist of a comprehensive set of transactions and a broad range of conditions that will be encountered under actual operations.
- *Batch or total controls* that provide for input validation and are automated to allow the system to be self-checking during the processing stage.
- *Cross-footing tests* that consist of logical tests for data consistency, usually between column totals and sum totals, that can be incorporated into the processing function.
- *Application reruns* that permit validation of processing consistency by comparison of reruns to the original run.

36.2.2.3   Output Controls.   *Output controls* include all procedures necessary to detect erroneous information, provide for error correction, ensure the proper distribution of output results, and protect against lost or late reports. These controls make sure that the data processing results are reliable and that no unauthorized modifications have been made to the transactions or records.

36.2.2.4   Additional Controls.   *Additional controls* permit proper monitoring of compliance with organizational policy. These include:

- *Item checking* to verify accuracy of detail
- *Batch total and file count reconciliation* to verify completeness of an input and update process
- *Sequence checking* for reporting of missing items
- *Matching transactions and master file data* to facilitate review of nonmatching items
- *Reasonableness checks* to bring attention to payments or pay rate increases, or any data item, over some established limit

36.3   RESPONSIBILITY FOR CONTROL OF ELECTRONIC DATA PROCESSING. It is essential to share certain responsibilities in order for each computer security concern of management and the auditors to be adequately addressed.

36.3.1   Senior Management.   Senior management must create a positive attitude toward adequate control and securing the environment. Specifically, management should establish and communicate security policies and goals. Management is also responsible for providing adequate funding. To achieve the goals and objectives, they should establish a formal security function and a steering committee to oversee that function. Management should approve and in some cases originate the controls. See Chapter 45 for more discussion of management responsibilities.

36.3.2   Data Processing Management and Staff.   The EDP security function should be headed by a specific individual known by any of the accepted titles, such as data security officer, information security officer, data security manager, systems security officer, or computer security manager or director. This individual and the requisite staff should be responsible for issuing computer security standards, procedures, and guidelines that include the design and modification of security features into new applications and systems software.

Additionally, this function should define systems and applications access rules and provide the appropriate physical and data security access controls. The security function should be responsible for:

- Classifying data and systems according to sensitivity and importance
- Providing consulting services, advice, and technical support on security matters
- Conducting regular risk assessments to analyze and reduce vulnerabilities
- Monitoring data security
- Conducting a security awareness program via regular bulletins, consultations, videos, and classes
- Working with developers to incorporate security within the system development methodology for both systems and software
- Investigating new security tools and techniques and advocating the use of the same, where appropriate
- Gathering time and cost accounting information to cost justify expenditures on security and, in specific instances, billing such costs to appropriate budgets

Security should be an ongoing function due to the changing technological environment, which necessitates changes in data security practices. Security projects should be managed according to standard project management guidelines, using either automated or manual project management tools and techniques. Use of such project management tools will help in accumulating relevant historical and statistical data for each data security project and will aid in producing more efficient and effective systems.

36.3.2.1   Data Originators.   Key operators may be given responsibility for such basic controls as:

- Item checking
- Key verification
- Total balancing

Adequate supervision of key operators will provide additional controls at the input source.

36.3.2.2   System Developers.   The design of adequate controls and automated systems should be a shared responsibility, including:

- System developers
- Data security function
- Auditors
- Senior management oversight

This responsibility should be shared because this activity requires:

- Sensitivity to goals and objectives by management
- Awareness of pitfalls by system developers and security specialists
- Knowledge of remedies by data processing management and security specialists

Controls should be built as the systems and software are designed and should parallel the systems development methodology or systems development life cycle used by the company

36.3.2.3   Computer Operators.   Operators should maintain logs of which jobs are run and which programs and data files are used provide basic information for both the operations staff and the supervisory operations personnel.

- The operations staff exercises basic control by the execution of scheduled workloads.
- Supervisory operations personnel extend control by verifying the usage of programs and data files in accordance with established and documented procedures.

36.3.2.4   Data Users Management and Staff.   End users also have responsibilities for control. These responsibilities include:

- Consulting with data processing management and staff regarding adequate protection for existing systems and those under development
- Fostering user awareness, which can be achieved by scheduling regular security training programs and encouraging respect for confidentiality of data
- Assigning, through management, accountability for primary and secondary system owners, and immediately notifying the security function when employees are terminated

- Reviewing program and data information for reasonableness, and supervising review, follow-up, and reentry

- Regularly reviewing detailed transaction logs for accuracy, completeness, and proper authorization, with follow-up on data errors and data omissions

- Investigating unauthorized entry, and ensuring reentry of corrections

- Understanding the importance of password confidentiality

- Cooperating with the auditing staff

- Identifying vital records in developing adequate records retention programs in a joint effort with data processing security, EDP and the internal auditors, and legal staff

- Actively participating in the development of data processing contingency and disaster recovery plans

- Participating in development and maintenance of business continuity plans covering the entire company and specific plans relating to the end user activities

36.3.3   Auditors.   Internal auditors are employees of the enterprise they audit; external auditors work for auditing firms and supply auditing services to their clients. However, these lines can become blurred; for example, internal auditors may report to corporate headquarters but audit the activities of divisions where they are not personally involved in day-to-day operations. Similarly, external auditors sometimes work so closely with specific clients that they come to be perceived as almost equivalent to internal auditors.

36.3.3.1   *Internal Auditors and Electronic Data Processing Auditors.* Internal auditors act as control advisors and consultants to management. Internal auditors or, if available, EDP auditors are involved with the following:

- Working with the data security function on risk analyses to identify vulnerabilities

- Performing regular security audits

- Helping select security systems software and hardware

- Participating in both the maintenance of existing systems and the development of new systems and software

- Evaluating the accomplishment of security goals and objectives

- Monitoring compliance with security policies, procedures, standards, and guidelines

- Notifying top management of absent or inadequate controls, and making recommendations for controls suitable for eliminating reducing vulnerabilities

36.3.3.2   *External Auditors.* Generally external auditors limit their scope to the fair presentation of published financial statements. Whenever those statements are either produced by, or dependent on, computer-based systems, external auditors may need:

- Special computer skills to ensure that the statements are accurately presented

- Evidence that correct accounting procedures are used consistently throughout the period covered by the statements

- Assessments of the adequacy of installed controls

36.4 AUDITING COMPUTER APPLICATIONS. In auditing computer or data processing security, it is useful to identify initially the overall controls and to test them to determine their current status as to the absence, presence, and adequacy of overall control. The quality of the overall control relates directly to the integrity of controls available to each application system.

To conduct an EDP audit, auditors must establish the audit scope and the approach to be used. To do this, auditors should:

1. Perform preliminary planning

2. Identify appropriate sources of computer security information

3. Gain an understanding of the computer security environment

4. Identify critical control points within the computer security environment

5. Develop a step-by-step audit work program

6. Conduct the actual security review and appropriate tests

7. Evaluate the results of the computer security reviewing tests

8. Prepare a report of audit findings that includes recommendations for eliminating or reducing any vulnerabilities that were uncovered

Regardless of controls and audit findings, data processing and users must meet certain objectives. Accuracy and completeness must be demonstrable through the various phases of authorization, preparation, conversion, editing, correction, reentry, and updating of data. Information must be available to authorize users on a timely and useful basis.

Additionally, data processing systems must rapidly identify the validity of input data using rigorous criteria. Although batch systems may survive brief delays, it is crucial that data validation for online systems be done efficiently in order to meet objectives for accuracy, authorization, timeliness, and completeness.

From a practical standpoint, the most cost-effective audit of the system is during the design phase, before it is programmed. Even though performance cannot be fully evaluated during the design phase, early disclosure of functional or control inadequacies can reduce the cost of redesign, redocumenting, reprogramming, and retesting. The analysis of auditability is an important part of preprogramming review. An auditable system is one that lends itself to an independent control appraisal.

Decentralization via microcomputers and client-server architecture has progressed rapidly in recent years. Fourth-generation tools have become the norm, supporting modularity and speed in the development process and changes to programmed routines. Frequently, decentralization shifts responsibility for control to the end user. In such environments, management must install alternative controls for any central system control that is bypassed. For instance, microcomputer media must be isolated and backed up for each area. In this way, security for a decentralized environment and its applications can be bolstered. If this is not done, reports produced by the microcomputers cannot be relied on for accuracy and integrity.

36.4.1 Audit Tools. Audit tools and techniques vary in cost, complexity, and applicability to specific systems and situations. One of the most important audit tools is the *audit work paper.*

36.4.2 Work Papers. Work papers represent the formal documentation of audit work, and they link staff work to the final audit report. Generally mandatory, audit work papers contain the following:

- A statement of the scope of activities
- Records of related meetings
- Exhibits
- Reports
- Documents
- Correspondence
- Checklists used
- Details of controls identified for testing
- Methods of testing
- Details of tests performed
- Results of tests
- Details surrounding a finding of missing controls or controls functioning unsatisfactorily
- A summary concluding statement about the overall adequacy of controls considered in the statement scope

In initial identification of internal controls, determining and documenting the absence or presence of numerous specific controls is crucial. Usually, auditors tailor the checklists or questionnaires they use to the types of controls that they are reviewing and testing. Such checklists should be revised and tested frequently to improve the understanding obtained about specific controls. Exhibit 36.1 presents an EDP auditing checklist.

An audit trail is used to ensure the accurate flow of transactions through a system. Each detail of a given input source document or transaction must be traceable to an output report or file, and vice versa. The tracing technique may be applied on a single-transaction basis for quick test to provide some indication of the presence of controls; however, to provide assurance that the control functions consistently, the test must be extended to cover large volumes of data over differing periods of time. Audit trails should be built into each production system as a normal part of the systems internal controls. Some systems can be purchased with an automated audit trail feature already in place.

Audit software consists of special sets of programs capable of auditing data stored on computer media. Generalized EDP audit software is an essential tool for all auditors to verify the validity of data and systems.

The sizable databases of large-scale computer systems and local area networks (LAN) and wide area network (WAN) servers would be extremely difficult to verify without such software. Additionally, because of the largely uncontrolled environments in which microcomputers operate, special audit approaches are needed for these systems. The special approaches should be applied to verify the integrity of important personal computer output, to ensure that sensitive data are properly protected, and to check whether vital data are backed up to prevent their loss.

Originally, auditing of each independent microcomputer was not recommended, but today, because of software piracy issues, every microcomputer within the company should be audited periodically to ensure that only approved programs and legitimate copies are on the computers. In addition, widespread abuse of Internet access has led to extensive downloading of pornography and other objectionable materials, including pirated music and video. Just as with larger mainframe computer systems, and because

Exhibit 36.1   Electronic Data Processing Auditing Checklist

---

1. Job Functions

   1.1   Who may enter the computer room?

   1.2   Under what circumstances may entry rules be overridden and by whose authority?

   1.3   How are entry rules enforced?

   1.4   Who may operate computer equipment?

   1.5   Under what circumstances may operation rules be overridden and by whose authority?

   1.6   How are operation rules enforced?

   1.7   Where and how are registers and records kept to control data being processed and stored?

   1.8   Who has access to the stored registers and records?

   1.9   How does the company ensure that only selected personnel have access to secure documents?

   1.10   Under whose authority and under what circumstances may access to records procedures be overridden?

   1.11   List and describe transactions of an accounting nature that can be initiated within the operations or systems development departments.

   1.12   In each case, who authorizes accounting transactions and how is this authorization evidenced?

   1.13   Who is responsible for the custody and issuance of

        1.13.1   Data files?

        1.13.2   Program and system files?

   1.14   Describe the functions of personnel responsible for data, program, and system files. What other duties do they have?

   1.15   Describe for questions 1 through 6 procedures for variations that occur

        1.15.1   During shifts outside the normal working day and weekends.

        1.15.2   During periods of nonproduction work (e.g., program testing).

   1.16   In each instance, who is responsible for reviewing and supervising the original procedures and the procedure variations?

   1.17   What evidence exists that this review and supervision are carried out?

2. Computer Operations

   2.1   What are the installation standards with respect to the preparation and use of operating instructions for each application? Attach copy of standard.

   2.2   Have such operating instructions, in accordance with the standards, been prepared for all applications?

   2.3   How are standards and operating instructions filed?

   2.4   Who approves operating instructions? How is this approval evidenced?

   2.5   Is a manual log of computer operations prepared? Attach sample copy.

        2.5.1   What information is included in the log?

        2.5.2   Does the log show details of how all computer time is spent?

        2.5.3   Does the log show all unusual situations (e.g., hardware malfunctions, reruns, abnormal endings)?

   2.6   Is a log of computer operations prepared by the computer in hard-copy form? Describe the software used to generate these logs.

Exhibit 36.1   Electronic Data Processing Auditing Checklist *(continued)*

2.7   Describe the information included on the systems console and in the system log.

2.8   Does the printed log and system log automatically record all system and operator interaction during the start of the job, file setup, processing, and end-of-job routines?

2.9   If the system log is being recorded, describe the software used to generate and print logs.

2.10   What standard options have been included and what nonstandard amendments have been made to software used to generate and print logs?

2.11   How does the company ensure that the logs are complete and that all pages are accounted for and seen by the reviewer?

2.12   Who reviews the logs?

2.13   Describe the procedures carried out by the reviewer. How does the reviewer evidence his or her review?

2.14   Is a processing schedule prepared? Is this processing schedule and all changes to its authorized? How is this authorization evidenced?

2.15   When, how often, by whom, and to what extent are the logs compared to the processing schedule?

2.16   Are all reruns and the reason for the reruns recorded? How does the company ensure that all reruns are recorded?

2.17   Who investigates and reviews the reasons for the reruns? How is this review evidenced?

2.18   How does the company ensure that the correct authorized programs are being called by each step in a job stream?

2.19   Provide a list and describe all standard and nonstandard utility programs that have the capability of making run-time amendments to data files and object programs.

    2.19.1   Describe the procedures for the access to and usage of the special utilities and name the personnel entitled to use them.

    2.19.2   Is each use of such a utility recorded?

    2.19.3   How does the company ensure that this record is complete and that all usages are accounted for?

    2.19.4   Who reviews and approves this record? How is this approval evidenced?

    2.19.5   In each case, who is responsible for reviewing and supervising the procedures described?

    2.19.6   What evidence exists that this supervision is carried out?

2.20   Who reviews the outstanding change forms to identify those that have been delayed? How is this review and the reason for the delay documented?

3. Software Testing

3.1   Describe the procedures for testing or reviewing output to ensure that all new facilities and capabilities are functioning properly.

    3.1.1   How are these procedures documented?

    3.1.2   Do the procedures equally apply for the selection of options and changes? If not, then list the differences.

(continued)

Exhibit 36.1   Electronic Data Processing Auditing Checklist *(continued)*

> 3.1.3   Who reviews and approves the results of the testing? How is this approval documented?
>
> 3.2   How, and under what circumstances, are urgent modifications made (e.g., by the use of utility programs) bypassing the normal testing procedures described above?
>
> 3.2.1   Who authorizes the waiver of the normal procedures? How is this authorization documented?
>
> 3.2.2   Describe the procedures for subsequently checking such modifications.
>
> 3.2.3   How does the organization ensure that all such modifications are subsequently checked?
>
> 3.3   Who is responsible for the final review and approval of all operating systems? How is this approval documented?
>
> 3.4   How does the organization ensure that all new operating systems and software are implemented as authorized and that no unauthorized amendments are made between the time of approval and when they are put into use?
>
> 3.5   Do the procedures apply equally to all selections of options and changes? If not, list the differences.
>
> 3.6   How does the company ensure that operating systems and software remain correct and up to date and that no unauthorized changes are made?
>
> **4. Systems Development: New Systems**
>
> 4.1   What are the installation standards with respect to the preparation and contents of online systems descriptions? Attach copy of standard.
>
> 4.1.1   Have such systems descriptions, in accordance with the standards, been prepared for all systems or applications? Attach a sample copy.
>
> 4.1.2   How are these documents filed?
>
> 4.1.3   Who in the user department has the authority to review and approve these outline systems descriptions? How is this approval evidenced?
>
> 4.1.4   Who in the data processing function has the authority? How is this approval evidenced?
>
> 4.2   What are the installation standards with respect to detailed systems descriptions? Attach copy of the standards.
>
> 4.2.1   Have such detailed systems descriptions been prepared for all systems or applications? Attach a sample copy
>
> 4.2.2   How are these documents filed?
>
> 4.2.3   Who in the user department has the authority to review and approve these detailed systems descriptions? How is this approval evidenced?
>
> 4.2.4   Who in the system development function has the authority? How is this approval evidenced?
>
> 4.2.5   Who in the computer operations function has the authority? How is this approval evidenced?
>
> **5. Application Program Modifications**
>
> 5.1   Describe the procedures for requesting changes to operational production systems or programs.

Exhibit 36.1   Electronic Data Processing Auditing Checklist *(continued)*

5.2   Are all changes documented on the standard change form? Attach copy.

5.3   Who reviews and approves the changes? How is this approval evidenced?

5.4   How are the change forms filed?

5.5   How does the company ensure that a change form is prepared in every case?

5.6   How does the company ensure that all changes are carried out?

5.7   How does the company ensure that all change forms are authorized?

5.8   Who reviews the outstanding change forms to identify those that have been delayed? How is this review and the reason for the delay documented?

6. **Testing**

6.1   For new systems, what are the installation standards (attach copy) with respect to

    6.1.1   Program testing?

    6.1.2   Systems testing?

    6.1.3   Testing of clerical and administrative procedures?

6.2   How does the company ensure that all testing is carried out in accordance with the standards?

6.3   Have all programs in systems been tested in accordance with the standards?

6.4   Describe the procedures for retaining and filing test data, test results, and other evidence of successful testing.

6.5   Do the procedures apply equally for all application program modifications? If not list the differences.

6.6   Do the standards require that systems testing be reperformed for every program change? If not, describe the extensive testing.

6.7   Who in the systems development function has the authority to review and approve the results of the testing? How is this approval evidenced?

6.8   Who in the computer operations function has this authority? How is this approval evidenced?

7. **Immediate Modifications**

7.1   How, and under what circumstances, are urgent modifications made (e.g., by the use of utility programs) bypassing the normal testing procedures described above?

7.2   Who authorizes the waiver of the normal procedures? How is this authorization documented?

7.3   Describe the procedures for subsequently checking such modifications.

7.4   How does the company ensure that all such modifications are subsequently checked by both the data processing function and the user department?

8. **Acceptance and Implementation**

8.1   As part of the final acceptance procedures, prior to implementation of the new system, who is responsible for ensuring that the following are prepared in accordance with the installation standards in each case, and how is this approval evidenced for:

    8.1.1   Program documentation?

    8.1.2   Systems documentation?

    8.1.3   Operating instructions?

(continued)

Exhibit 36.1   Electronic Data Processing Auditing Checklist *(continued)*

8.2	In the case of modifications to systems, do the procedures ensure that the documentation and instructions are amended so as to be up-to-date and in accordance with the company's standards?
8.3	Describe the procedures for using and controlling the program libraries including, where applicable, source statement libraries, object code libraries, executable libraries, procedure libraries, systems files, database definitions, and libraries. Name and describe any library and packages use.
8.4	Who is authorized to read and execute programs in these libraries?
8.5	Who is authorized to change these libraries?
8.6	How does the company ensure that all unauthorized use of the libraries is detected?
8.7	How does the company ensure that all programs are implemented as authorized and that no unauthorized amendments are made to approve systems between the time they are approved and when they are put into operation?
8.8	Who is responsible for ensuring that changes made to executable program libraries are also made to the source statement libraries and vice versa?
8.9	Who is responsible for reviewing and approving this work? How is this approval evidenced?
8.10	How does the company ensure that all program libraries remain correct and up-to-date and that all errors are detected?
8.11	Who in the data processing function is responsible for getting the final review and approval on systems for operational use? Does this review include an assurance that all necessary reviews and approval have been performed? How is the final review evidenced?
8.12	Are users notified in writing of the effective date when systems, and modifications to systems, become operational? Where is this notification filed?
8.13	Does this function ensure that all documentation and instructions remain correct and up-to-date?

of the critical functions of many personal computers (PCs), any microcomputer data that are used for management decisions, or as input to important information systems, should be audited to substantiate their correctness. This audit should verify the three following aspects:

1. Source data must be accurate and complete.
2. Computation procedures must be sound.
3. Source data and output should be identified with their creation dates so that users are aware of information currency.

Audit software was developed to facilitate verifying the integrity of computer databases. It also helps to improve auditor effectiveness by improving the quality and scope of audits, by allowing the auditor to be more independent of the data processing staff, and by allowing the auditor to utilize time more effectively. EDP audit software extends the auditor's technical skills and thereby provides better flexibility for using the computer to evaluate the automated data.

Two major types of programs used by auditors are data audit programs and source compare programs. The characteristics of these programs are described below.

36.4.3 Data Audit Programs. Data audit programs allow the auditor to sample the processing of transactions, and to validate processing. The auditor can examine computer files, establish tests for data validity, and produce reports. The audit program functions usually include data extraction, file handling, calculation of formulas, and cross-footing of values. Among the representative features that may be included are:

- *Interval sampling,* selecting items based on specific interval occurrences, such as the *n*th item.
- *Random sampling,* or random selection.
- *Statistical sampling,* based on population characteristics and statistical rules.
- *Monetary value samples,* based on set monetary values, such as balances over $10,000.
- *Data calculations,* reperforming critical calculations such as earned interest, payroll amounts, unearned income, discounts, and expense distribution amounts.
- *Data summarization,* which allows independent aggregation of numeric values for proof of controls.
- *Data resequencing,* which helps to verify data values or to isolate abnormalities by listing in sequence by date, serial number, time, amounts, account number, or any desired field.
- *Rule violation,* which checks for violations of rules that apply to changes and inputs, such as authorization for privileged transactions or overrides of special conditions.
- *Analysis and reporting,* which is oriented toward such applications as aging of receivables, overdue payables, payroll, or general ledger irregularities.
- *Creating special files* for audit use, which allows the creation and maintenance of separate automated files for use by the auditor. This permits all further processing such as the calculations, resequencing, and recording to take place without changing the original data.
- *Confirmation preparation,* which provides the ability to prepare confirmations or other documents necessary for direct verification of financial records. Selective confirmation capabilities and the creation of independent follow-up files are desirable.
- *Reporting of sampling results,* including diagrams, histograms, and other graphic formats, which sometimes are provided for the summarization and reporting of sampling results. These features can aid in reducing large masses of raw data to understandable information.
- *Database support,* such as data dictionaries and the ability to accommodate a variety of data structures, file structures, and access methods (offered by some systems).

36.4.4 Source Code and Other File Comparison Programs. Source code and other file comparison programs allow the auditor to track changes made to programs. The source code for two different versions of the program can be compared and the differences identified. This is an investigative aid to verify that only authorized changes have been implemented. It is helpful if programs are capable of comparing data files as well as source code on different types of media. Useful comparisons for audit purposes can be made between:

- Different data storage formats and media
- Program source code files
- Program object code files
- Input transaction files
- Output transaction files
- Output reports, on tape or disk

Flexibility for source program comparison is enhanced if the comparison program can ignore line numbering between source program versions or even allow comparison of restructured programs. Other useful features are those that permit comparison of entire program libraries to prior versions, identifying differences between the versions.

36.4.5 Computer-Assisted Audit Techniques. Within the two major types of audit software discussed, there are several different categories of computer-assisted audit techniques (CAATs). These categories include generalized audit software, application audit software, customized audit software, embedded audit data collection, query functions and report writers, system utility software, microcomputer-based audit software, time-sharing programs, and public databases and bulletin boards.

- *Generalized audit software* is readily adapted to similar tasks in different computing environments. The most adequate software is easy to use, requires limited programming skills, is self-documenting, and easily translates audit objectives into program code.
- *Application audit software* has predefined functions that often save software development costs and audit time. It should be efficient for testing numerous locations with the same system and capable of being utilized to achieve common audit objectives.
- *Customized audit software* generally is developed when system requirements make the use of prepackaged software difficult or impossible. Development is usually more expensive and requires that the auditor have greater technical skills and knowledge of computer languages.
- *Embedded audit data collection* requires that the auditor have advanced technical skills and be involved in the system design. Such tools provide continuous monitoring and often are used in cases where the size of the files, or their 24-hour online availability, makes it impractical to use other techniques.
- *Query functions and report writers* have become increasingly popular because of their flexibility and ease of use. They normally are limited to information retrieval and presentation in user-defined formats. Because the contents of reports can be changed at will, the auditor must be especially alert to misuse.
- *System utility software* can efficiently perform useful tasks and diagnoses on systems and is often powerful although not always easy to use. The auditor must have good technical knowledge, since the software produces reports that may be difficult to read, and there is often little or no audit trail.

- *Microcomputer-based software* can be used on PC or microcomputer, which requires that a unit be available to the auditor. In addition to its direct use for audit software, it is usually a good investment to enhance audit documentation productivity. In today's environment, such software is widely used and encompasses spreadsheets, electronic mail, hard-coded automated work paper programs, and software for downloading programs and files. Some packages also assist in risk assessment and in budget and performance evaluation.

- *Time-sharing or outsourced programs* provide an efficient way to make use of audit software for analytical reviews and generally provide quick turnaround. One drawback is that the auditor frequently cannot obtain all required programs from one vendor, and confidentiality may be breached.

- Public databases and bulletin boards contain information on various industries and provide the opportunity to share that information. However, in addition to the fact that the data may not be timely or reliable, it is difficult to integrate the data received with already automated data.

36.4.6 Special Microcomputer Techniques. Auditors should make sure that adequate measures are taken to confirm that important, sensitive data cannot accidentally or deliberately fall into the wrong hands. Because of the ease and speed with which microcomputer data can be copied, their systems are particularly vulnerable. Auditors should check to see that sensitive data are identified and that the responsibility and methods for their protection are clearly defined. Protective methods can take a number of forms, such as:

- Physically locking the computer and its data storage media
- Locking the microcomputer's functions with access control software
- Encryption
- Key controls that safeguard the encryption and decryption keys
- Library custodial controls that prevent access and modification to software libraries

36.4.7 Backup and Recovery. Backup and recovery methods for all computers should be audited to make certain that vital data are less vulnerable to loss due to catastrophe, physical damage, sabotage, mechanical failure, accident, or erroneous operation. Such procedures should be incorporated into contingency and disaster recovery plans, and these plans should be tested regularly. Auditors must be involved in the construction and testing of these plans.

Auditors should verify that backup methods are defined for each system and each program on every computer. This verification should include how often and on what type of media backups are made, how many generations of backups exist, whether the backups are located on or off site, frequency of backup rotation, and how the data can be reconstructed from the backup media.

Additionally, auditors should check contingency plans to see that adequate computer systems, electrical and telecommunication lines, and workspace facilities have been provided for, either at an alternate company site or through a lease arrangement with an external vendor.

In all instances, auditors should conduct their audits to verify compliance with the organization's policies on information security and to ensure that such policies are written and enforced.

See Chapter 41 for a more extensive discussion of data backup and recovery.

36.5 SUMMARY. The physical controls an auditor looks for in the EDP environment usually are found in the fabric of well-organized companies and well-planned, well-designed systems. EDP auditors have a responsibility to identify both an organization's strengths and its weaknesses in the computer environment and then to follow up and reevaluate periodically. Strengths should be tested for consistency, while weaknesses must be examined to determine whether any material losses have or could result. Strong prevention and detection controls should be recommended as appropriate to prevent the potential losses inherent in weak systems. Corrective measures should be recommended to repair and correct environments if they undergo loss or damage. These measures should be authorized in written documentation and should be tested regularly. Auditors should monitor progress in implementing recommended controls. Most important, a cooperative approach among auditor, data processing functions, and user departments can benefit each of them individually and their organization collectively.

36.6 FURTHER READING

In this volume:

- Chapter 25 discusses software development and quality assurance.
- Chapters 28, 35, and 46 are about security policies.
- Chapter 32 reviews operations and production controls.
- Chapter 38 reviews monitoring and control systems.
- Chapter 39 provides further information about formal methodology for controls.
- Chapters 40 through 43 focus on disaster prevention, mitigation, and recovery.

AuditNet: *www.auditnet.org*

Auerbach Information Management Service (AIMS) "EDP Auditing": *www.auerbach-publications.com/aims*

COBRA Policy Compliance Analyst: *www.security.kirion.net/securitypolicy/solution.htm*

Information Systems Audit and Control Association (ISACA): *www.isaca.org/isacafx.htm*

Information Systems Audit and Control Association (ISACA). "Standards & Guidelines for IS Auditing," 2001: *www.isaca.org/standard/stand2.htm*

IT Governance Institute: *www.itgovernance.org/index2.htm*

Risk Associates. "Resources for Security Risk Analysis, ISO 17799/BS7799, Security Policies & Security Audit," 2001: *www.securityauditor.net*

Sioma, L. "A Generalized Application Security Audit Program for Any Computing Platform with Comments," 2000: *www.sans.org/infosecFAQ/securitybasics/gen_app.htm*

U.S. General Accounting Office Special Publications: "Evaluation Research and Methodology," 2001: *www.gao.gov/special.pubs/erm.html*

U.S. General Accounting Office, 2001. "Information Security": *www.gao.gov/new.items/ai00295.*

Weber, R. *EDP Auditing: Conceptual Foundations and Practice,* 2nd ed. New York: McGraw-Hill College Division, 1988.

DETECTION

CHAPTER 37

VULNERABILITY ASSESSMENT AND INTRUSION DETECTION SYSTEMS

Rebecca Gurley Bace

CONTENTS

37.1   SECURITY BEHIND THE FIREWALL.   When asked how they would go about securing a computer network, most people mention firewalls. Indeed, firewalls were one of the first widely accepted network security products, and many commercial installations include firewalls as integral parts of their operational networks.

Despite their strengths, firewalls are not a complete security solution. Although they can restrict network traffic to what network managers wish to allow into the enterprise, they are incapable of preventing those attacks that occur once the traffic has been granted entry. Furthermore, firewalls cannot deal with security problems in the traffic that travels between hosts on internal networks. In order to deal with such internal security problems, many security architects include intrusion detection as a standard part of network security infrastructure.

Intrusion detection systems (IDSs) are software or hardware systems that automate the monitoring of events occurring within a computer system or network. IDSs not only collect and synchronize records of these events, they also analyze them for signs of security violations. Vulnerability assessment systems (VASs) are a special class of IDSs in which the system relies on static inspection and attack reenactment to gauge a target system's exposure to specific security vulnerabilities. As system attacks have become more numerous and inflicted more damage over the past few years, the demand for intrusion detection and vulnerability analysis systems has increased, making them a common addition to the security infrastructure.

37.1.1   What Is Intrusion Detection?   Intrusion detection is the process of collecting information about events occurring in a computer system or network and analyzing them for signs of *intrusions*. *Intrusions* are defined as violations of security policy, usually characterized as attempts to affect the confidentiality, integrity, or availability of a computer or network. These violations can come from attackers accessing systems from the Internet, or from authorized users of the systems who attempt to overstep their legitimate authorization levels or use their legitimate access to the system to conduct unauthorized activity.

Intrusion detection systems are software or hardware products that automate this monitoring and analysis process.

37.1.2   What Is Vulnerability Assessment?   Vulnerability assessment is the analysis of the security state of a system on the basis of system information collected at intervals. The four-step strategy for vulnerability assessment is as follows:

1. A predetermined set of target system attributes (e.g., specific parameters for particular firewalls) is sampled.

2. The sampled information is placed in a data store.

3. The data store is organized and compared to a reference set of attributes.

4. The differences between the data store and the reference set are documented and reported.

37.1.3   Where Do Intrusion Detection and Vulnerability Assessment Fit in Security Management?   Intrusion detection is a necessary function in most system security strategies. It is the primary security technology that supports the goal of *auditability*. Auditability is defined as the ability to independently review and examine system records and activities to:

- Determine the adequacy of system controls
- Ensure compliance with established security policy and operational procedures
- Detect breaches in security
- Recommend any indicated changes[1]

The presence of a strong audit function in turn enables and supports several vital security management functions, such as incident handling and system recovery. Intrusion detection also allows security managers a flexible means to accommodate user needs while retaining the ability to protect systems from certain types of threats.

Although intrusion detection and vulnerability assessment are necessary as system security functions, they are not sufficient to protect systems from all security threats. Both measures should be included in a more comprehensive security strategy that includes security policy and procedural controls (see Chapters 28 and 46), network firewalls (Chapter 20), strong identification and authentication mechanisms (Chapter 16), access control mechanisms (Chapter 17), file and link encryption (Chapter 23 and Tutorial 4), file integrity checking (Chapter 32), physical security measures (Chapter 15), and security training (Chapter 29).

37.1.4   Brief History of Intrusion Detection.   Intrusion detection is the automation of manual processes that originated in the earliest days of data processing. Joseph Wassermann of the Bell Telephone Company documented the origin of system and security audit as early as the mid-1950s, when the first computerized business system was being designed and implemented.[2]

Auditability was a key security feature from the earliest days of computer security, as proposed in J. P. Anderson's 1973 research study chartered by the U.S. Air Force.[3] Anderson proposed a scheme for automating the review of security audit trails in 1980, in a research report considered by many to be the seminal work in intrusion detection.[4] Dorothy Denning and Peter Neumann led a study of intrusion detection, conducted from 1984 to 1986, producing another seminal work in intrusion detection in 1986, in which Denning proposed a model for intrusion detection.[5]

An instantiation of Denning's intrusion detection model was prototyped as the Intrusion Detection Expert System (IDES) by a team at SRI International. IDES was a hybrid system that constructed statistical profiles of user behaviors as derived from operating system kernel audit logs and other system data sources. IDES also provided a rules-based expert system that allowed users to specify patterns of events to be flagged as intrusions.[6] IDES and the Next Generation IDES (NIDES) system that followed it marked an era in which numerous intrusion detection research projects and prototype systems were developed, including Haystack (Haystack Labs and U.S. Air Force), NADIR (Los Alamos National Laboratory), Wisdom and Sense (Los

Alamos National Laboratory and Oak Ridge National Laboratory), ISOA (PRC, Inc), TIM (Digital Equipment Corporation), ComputerWatch (AT&T), and Discovery (TRW, Inc).[7]

In the late 1980s, researchers at the University of California, Davis, designed the first network-based intrusion detection system (initially called the Network Security Monitor, but later renamed NID), which functioned much the same as many current commercial network-based intrusion detection products.[8] A subsequent U.S. Air Force–funded research product, called the Distributed Intrusion Detection System (DIDS), explored coordinating network-based and host-based intrusion detection systems. DIDS was prototyped by teams at the University of California, Davis, Haystack Laboratories, and Lawrence Livermore National Laboratory.[9]

Early VASs include the COPS system, developed in the late 1980s by Eugene H. Spafford and Daniel Farmer at Purdue University.[10] COPS was a Unix-targeted credentialed vulnerability assessment product that gained wide acceptance in security circles. The initial freeware version of the Internet Security Scanner (ISS) was also released in the early 1990s, as was Farmer's and Wietse Venema's vulnerability assessment product, SATAN.[11]

37.2   MAIN CONCEPTS.   Several strategies used in performing intrusion detection serve to describe and distinguish specific intrusion detection systems. These affect the threats addressed by each system and often prescribe the environments in which specific systems should be used.

37.2.1   Process Structure.   Intrusion detection is defined as a monitoring and alarm generation process, and, as such, it can be described using a simple process model. This model is outlined here and will be used to illustrate the fundamental concepts of intrusion detection.

37.2.1.1   Information Sources.   The first stage of the intrusion detection process comprises one or more information sources, also known as an event generator. Information sources for intrusion detection may be categorized by location: network, host, or application.

37.2.1.2   Analysis Engine.   Once event information is collected, it is passed to the next stage of the intrusion detection process, in which it is analyzed for symptoms of attack or other security problems.

37.2.1.3   Response.   When the analysis engine diagnoses attacks or security problems, information about these results is revealed via the response stage of the intrusion detection process. Responses span a wide spectrum of possibilities, ranging from simple reports or logs to automated responses that disrupt attacks in progress.

37.2.2   Monitoring Approach.   The first major classifier used to distinguish intrusion detection systems is the monitoring approach of the system. Monitoring is the action of collecting event data from an information source and then conveying that data to the analysis engine.

The monitoring approach describes the perspective from which intrusion detection monitoring is performed. The primary monitoring approaches found in intrusion detection systems today are *network-based, host-based,* and *application-based.*

37.2.3 Intrusion Detection Architecture. Even in the early days of manual security audit, researchers noted that in order for audit information to be trusted, it should be stored and processed in an environment separate from the one monitored. This requirement has evolved to include most intrusion detection approaches, for three reasons:

1. To keep an intruder from blocking or nullifying the intrusion detection system by deleting information sources
2. To keep an intruder from corrupting the operation of the intrusion detector in order to mask the presence of the intruder
3. To manage the performance and storage load that might result from running intrusion detection tasks on an operational system

In this architecture, the system running the intrusion detection system is called the *host.* The system or network being monitored is called the *target.*

37.2.4 Monitoring Frequency. Another common descriptor for intrusion detection approaches is the timing of the collection and analysis of event data. This is usually divided between *batch-mode* (also known as *interval-based*) and *continuous* (also known as *real-time*) approaches.

In batch-mode analysis, the event data from the information source is conveyed to the analysis engine in a file or other block form. As the name suggests, the events corresponding to a particular interval of time are processed (and results provided to the user) after the intrusion has taken place. This model was the most common for early intrusion detection because system resources did not allow real-time monitoring or analysis.

In real-time analysis, event data from the information source are conveyed to the analysis engine as the information is gathered. The information is analyzed immediately, providing the user with the opportunity to respond to detected problems quickly enough to affect the outcome of the intrusion.

37.2.5 Analysis Strategy. In intrusion detection, there are two prevalent analysis strategies, *misuse detection* and *anomaly detection.*

In misuse detection, the analysis engine filters event streams, matching patterns of activity that characterize a known attack or security violation. In anomaly detection, the analysis engine uses statistical or other analytical techniques to spot patterns corresponding to abnormal system use. Anomaly detection is based on the premise that intrusions significantly differ from normal system activity.

37.3 VULNERABILITY ASSESSMENT. Vulnerability assessment is a special case of intrusion detection that is of considerable value to security managers. Vulnerability assessment products snapshot the security state of systems, diagnosing problems that indicate that the system is vulnerable to specific attacks.

37.3.1 Relationship between Vulnerability Assessment and Intrusion Detection. Vulnerability assessment performs an examination of key indicators within systems that are known to correspond to security vulnerabilities. As such, it is a special case of a host-based, interval-based intrusion detection process and can be described in terms of the intrusion detection process model outlined earlier.

One can understand the difference between vulnerability assessment and intrusion detection by analogy: For example, when monitoring a critical location, one could use a still camera or a surveillance camera with guards watching monitors. Vulnerability assessment corresponds to the camera that takes snapshots that have to be developed and studied later; intrusion detection corresponds to the continuous, real-time surveillance by the guards.

37.3.2   Assessment Strategies.   As in intrusion detection systems, vulnerability assessment systems (VASs) have features that allow differentiation between them. The primary features of VASs describe the information sources and how those information sources are generated.

37.3.2.1   *Credentialed Monitoring.*   Credentialed monitoring approaches for vulnerability assessments are those that utilize system data sources such as file contents, configuration information, and status information. This information is gained from nonintrusive sources; that is, it is gained by performing standard system status queries and inspection of system attributes. These sources are accessible only when the entity gathering them has legitimate access to the system (i.e., the entity possesses access credentials). In Unix systems, this information is gathered at the host or device level; therefore, *credentialed approaches* are also *host-based* approaches. Windows NT and Windows 2000 systems handle status information differently, often providing it in the form of Application Programming Interfaces (APIs), so the "credentialed = host-based" equivalence does not always apply in those environment.

37.3.2.2   *Noncredentialed Monitors.*   Noncredentialed monitoring approaches are those approaches that stage system attacks and record target system responses to the attacks. These approaches are much more intrusive than credentialed attacks and do not assume (nor do they require) any legitimate access to the target system; they are launched from an attacker's perspective. Noncredentialed approaches are often called *active* approaches and have detection and monitoring features that complement those of credentialed approaches. In particular, noncredentialed approaches are usually superior for diagnosing vulnerabilities associated with network services. As noted, in Unix systems, noncredentialed assessments are usually considered *network-based* assessments; again, the equivalence relationship does not necessarily apply in Windows NT and 2000 environments.

37.3.3   Strengths and Weaknesses.   Knowing that security point products (e.g., firewalls and access-control systems) that defend particular features of a security perimeter cannot be perfect in the face of evolving knowledge of vulnerabilities and changing attack strategies, VASs serve an important function in the overall strategy for protecting information assets.

The benefits associated with vulnerability analysis are as follows:

- VASs conserve time and resources, as they allow even nonexpert personnel to check systems automatically for literally hundreds of problems, any one of each might result in an intrusion.

- VASs can be extremely helpful in training security novices to make systems more secure.

- VASs can be updated to reflect new knowledge of vulnerabilities found by vendors and researchers.

- VASs are systematic and therefore consistent. These attributes allow them to be used as quality assurance measures for network or security managers. Many security professionals routinely recommend that operational security policies include provisions for using VASs to check systems for problems after major changes have occurred (as might be the case whenever software is updated or system recovery is required).

Weaknesses in vulnerability assessment include the following:

- Although vulnerability assessment is necessary for system security, it is not in and of itself sufficient to secure a system.

- Many VASs serve only to diagnose problems, not to correct them. User follow-through is still required.

- If the VASs are not kept up to date, they may mislead users into underestimating the risk of penetration.

- As in many other knowledge-based security tools, vulnerability assessment can be used for either productive or malicious purposes. In the hands of a security manager, vulnerability assessment is a valuable diagnostic technique. In the hands of an attacker, vulnerability assessment may optimize efforts to identify targets of attack and provide insight as to exactly how those targets might be compromised.

37.3.4   Roles for Vulnerability Assessment in System Security Management. Vulnerability assessment products can be used at several points in the system security management life cycle.

First, when a new program is put into place, a vulnerability assessment can baseline the security state of the system. This application is particularly valuable in establishing the case for a security program, as it provides hard evidence that security problems exist.

Next, whenever significant changes occur in an operational system (as might be the case when software changes are fielded or new equipment is added), a vulnerability assessment can recognize specific security vulnerabilities that occur as side effects of these changes.

Finally, when security incidents occur or are suspected, vulnerability assessment results can assist investigators in diagnosing possible paths of entry for attackers, locating artifacts of attacks (such as back doors or Trojan horses), and identifying the system resources affected by an attack so that they may be restored to their original states.

37.4   INFORMATION SOURCES.   Information sources represent the first stage of the intrusion detection process. They provide event information from monitored systems upon which the intrusion detection process bases its decisions. Information sources encompass both *raw* event data (e.g., data collected directly from system audit and logging mechanisms) as well as data output by system management utilities (e.g., file integrity checkers, vulnerability assessment tools, network management systems, and even other intrusion detection systems). In this section, information sources for intrusion detection are classified by location: network, host, or application.

37.4.1   Network Monitoring.   The most common monitoring approach utilized in intrusion detection systems is *network-based*. In this approach, information is gathered in the form of network packets, often using network interface devices set to promiscuous mode. (Such a device operating in promiscuous mode captures all network traffic accessible to it—usually on the same network segment—not just traffic addressed to it). Other approaches for performing network-based monitoring include the use of *spanning ports* (specialized monitoring ports that allow capture of network traffic from all ports on a switch) on network switches or specialized Ethernet network taps (e.g., sniffers) to capture network traffic.

37.4.2   Operating System Monitoring.   Some approaches for monitoring collect data from sources internal to a computer. These differ from network-based monitoring in the level of abstraction at which the data is collected. *Host-based* monitoring collects information from the operating system (OS) level of a computer. The most common sources of operating system–level data are operating system audit trails, which are usually generated within the OS kernel, and system logs, which are generated by OS utilities.

37.4.3   Application Monitoring.   *Application-based* monitoring collects information from running software applications. Information sources utilized in application-based approaches include application event logs and application configuration information.

Application-based information sources are steadily increasing in importance as systems complexity increases. The advent of object-oriented programming techniques introduces data object naming conventions that nullify much of an analyst's ability to make sense of file access logs. In this situation, the application level is the only place in the system in which one can "see" the data accesses at an appropriate level of abstraction likely to reveal security violations.

37.4.4   Other Types of Monitoring.   As noted before, intrusion detection information sources are not limited to raw event data. In fact, allowing intrusion detection systems to operate on data output from other systems often optimizes the quality of the intrusion detection system's results. When the data are provided by other parts of the system security infrastructure (e.g., network firewalls, file integrity checkers, virus scanners, or other intrusion detection systems), the sensitivity and reliability of the intrusion detection system's results can increase significantly.

37.4.5   Issues in Information Sources.   There are several issues involving information sources for intrusion detection. The following are the major ones that have persisted over the history of intrusion detection:

- In host-based systems, there must be a balance between collecting enough information to accurately portray security violations and collecting so much information that the collection process cripples the monitored system.
- The fidelity of the intrusion detection process is dependent not only on collecting the appropriate information but on collecting it from appropriate vantage points within the monitored system or network.
- If the IDS is expected to produce event records that will be used to support legal processes, the system must collect and handle event information in a way that complies with legal rules of evidence.
- The information collected by IDSs often includes information of a sensitive nature. This information must be secured and handled in a way that complies with legal and ethical standards.

37.5   ANALYSIS SCHEMES.   Once information sources and sensors are defined and placed, the information so gathered must be analyzed for signs of attack. The *analysis engine* serves this purpose in intrusion detection, accepting event data from the information source and examining it for symptoms of security problems. As mentioned earlier, intrusion detection systems typically provide analysis features that fall into two categories, *misuse detection* and *anomaly detection.*

37.5.1 Misuse Detection. *Misuse detection* is the filtering of event streams for patterns of activity that reflect known attacks or other violations of security policy. Misuse detectors use various pattern-matching algorithms, operating on large databases of attack patterns or *signatures.* Most current commercial intrusion detection systems support misuse detection.

Misuse detection presumes that there is a clear understanding of the security policy for the system, which can be expressed in patterns corresponding to desirable activity and undesirable activity. Therefore, signatures can be described in terms of "this should never happen" as well as "Only this should ever happen." Signatures also can range from simplistic *atomic* (one-part) checks to rather complex *composite* (multipart) checks. An example of an atomic check is a buffer overflow signature, in which one looks for a particular command, followed by a string exceeding a particular length. An example of a composite check is a race condition signature, in which a series of carefully timed commands occur. Signatures are gathered and structured in some way to optimize the filtering of event data against them.

The next requirement for misuse detection is that the event data collected from information sources be encoded in a fashion that allows it to be matched against the signature data. There are various ways of doing this, ranging from regular expression matching (sometimes called "dirty word" matching) to complex coding schemes involving state diagrams and Colored Petri Nets. State diagrams are a graphical scheme for modeling intrusions. They express intrusions in terms of *states,* represented by nodes or circles, and *transitions,* represented by lines or arcs. Colored Petri Nets are an extension of the state diagram technique that add colored *tokens,* which occupy state nodes and whose color expresses information about the context of the state.

In some network-based systems, significant resources are devoted to identifying malformed packets, especially those in which the format of the content of the packet does not match the format of the service (e.g., SMTP) or associated port number of the packet.

37.5.2 Anomaly Detection. *Anomaly detection* is the analysis of system event streams, characterizing them using statistical and other classification techniques in order to find patterns of activity that appear to deviate from normal system operation. This approach is based on the premise that attacks and other security policy violations are a subset of abnormal system events.

Several common techniques are used in anomaly detection:

- *Quantitative analysis*—Most modern systems that use anomaly detection provide quantitative analysis, in which rules and attributes are expressed in numeric form. The most common forms of quantitative analysis are triggers and thresholds, in which system attributes are expressed as counts occurring during some time interval, with some level defined as permissible. Triggers and thresholds can be simple, in which the permissible level is constant, or heuristic, in which the permissible level is adapted to observed levels.

- *Statistical analysis*—Most early anomaly detection systems used statistical techniques to identify abnormal data. In statistical analysis, profiles are built for each user and system resource, and statistics are calculated for a variety of user and resource attributes for a particular interval of time (usually a "session," defined as the time elapsed between login and logout).

- *Learning techniques*—There has been a great deal of research interest in using various learning techniques, such as neural networks and fuzzy logic, in performing anomaly detection. Despite encouraging results, there remain many practical impediments to using these techniques in production environments.

- *Advanced techniques*—Anomaly detection as applied to intrusion detection remains an active research area. Recent research efforts include the application of such advanced analytic techniques as genetic algorithms, data mining, autonomous agents, and immune system approaches to the problem of recognizing new attacks and security violations. Again, these techniques have not yet been fielded in commercial IDSs.

37.5.3   Hybrid Approaches.   Although there are significant issues associated with both misuse detection and anomaly detection approaches to event analysis for intrusion detection, the combination of both approaches provides considerable benefit. The anomaly detection engine can allow the IDS to detect new or unknown attacks or policy violations. This is especially valuable when the target system protected by the IDS is highly visible on the Internet or other high-risk network.

The misuse detection engine, in turn, protects the integrity of the anomaly detection engine by assuring that a patient adversary cannot gradually change behavior patterns over time in order to retrain the anomaly detector to accept attack behavior as normal. Thus the misuse detector mitigates a significant deficiency of anomaly detection for security purposes.

37.5.4   Issues in Analysis.   Here are a few of the many issues in intrusion detection analysis:

- Misuse detection systems, although very effective at detecting those scenarios for which detection signatures have been defined, cannot detect new attacks.

- Anomaly detection systems are capable of detecting new attacks but have false positive rates that are so high that users often ignore the alarms they generate.

- Anomaly detection systems that rely on artificial intelligence (AI) techniques often suffer from a lack of adequate training data. (Data are used to define the detector's logic for distinguishing "normal" from "abnormal" events.)

- Malefactors with access privileges to the system while anomaly-detection systems are being trained, can covertly teach the system to accept specific patterns of unauthorized activities as normal. Later, the anomaly-detection systems will ignore the actual misuse.

37.6   RESPONSE.   The final stage of intrusion detection, response, consists of the actions taken in response to the security violations detected by the IDS. Responses are divided into *passive* and *active* options. The difference between passive and active responses is whether the user of the system or the system itself is responsible for reacting to the detected violations.

37.6.1   Passive Responses.   When passive responses are selected, the IDS simply communicates the results of the detection process to the user, who must then act on these results, independent of the IDS. In this option, the user has total control over the response to the detected problem. In some IDSs, the information provided to the user regarding detection results can be divided into *alarms* and *reports.*

37.6.1.1   *Alarms.* Alarms are messages that are communicated immediately to users. Commercial IDSs use a variety of channels for conveying these alarms to security personnel. The most common is a message screen or icon written to the IDS control console. Other alarm channels include pagers, e-mail, wireless messaging, and network management system traps.

37.6.1.2   *Reports.* Reports are messages or groups of messages that are generated on a periodic basis. They typically document events that have happened in the past and often include aggregate figures and trends information. Many commercial IDS products support extensive reporting features, allowing a user to set up automatic report generation with several versions, each targeting a different level of management.

37.6.2   Active Responses. When an IDS provides active response options, these usually fall into two categories. The first requires the IDS to take action, but with the active involvement of an interactive user. (This option is sometimes called a man-in-the-loop mechanism). The other provides for preprogrammed actions taken automatically by the system with no human involvement. The former option allows an operator to track an attacker or intervene in a sensitive situation in a flexible, exacting way. The automated response option is of value, even required, when dealing with certain sorts of automated attack tools or denial-of-service attacks. These attacks proceed at machine speed and therefore are outside the reach of a human-controlled manual intervention.

37.6.3   Automated Responses. Automated responses support three categories of response goals:

1. Collecting more information about the intrusion or intruder
2. Amending the environment
3. Taking action against the intruder

It is important to remember that although the last of these groups, sometimes labeled *strike back* or *hack back,* occasionally is discussed in security circles, the other options are far more productive in most situations. At this time, taking action against the intruder is considered inappropriate in almost all situations and should be undertaken only with the advice and counsel of a legal authority.

Amending the environment and collecting more information can occur in either stand-alone or integrated fashions.

37.6.3.1   *Stand-alone Responses.* Some automated responses are designed to use features that fall entirely within the intrusion detection system. For instance, an intrusion detection system may have special detection rules, more sensitive or detailed than those provided in normal modes of operation. In a stand-alone adaptive response, the IDS would use the more sensitive rules when evidence of the preamble of an attack is detected. This allows the IDS to turn sensitivity levels up only when the additional detection capabilities are needed, so that false alarm rates are reduced.

37.6.3.2   *Integrated Responses.* The response option often considered the most productive is that of using integrated measures that change the system settings to block the attacker's actions. Such responses can affect the configuration of the target system, the IDS host, or the network on which both reside. In the first case, the IDS might change the settings of the logging mechanisms on the target host to increase the amount or type of information collected. The IDS also might change its analysis engine so that more subtle signs of attack are recognized. In another response option that has engendered a great deal of research interest, the IDS responds to an observed attack signature by querying the target system to determine whether it is vulnerable to that specific attack. Should the vulnerability be present, the IDS directs the target system to correct that vulnerability. In effect, this process provides the target system with an immune function and permits it to "heal" itself, either blocking an attack outright or else repairing any damage done in the course of the attack. Finally, some systems may use special-purpose decoy systems (also called *honey pots* or *padded cells*) as diversions for attackers. When these systems are provided, the IDS may be configured to divert attackers into the decoy environments.

37.6.4   Investigative Support. Although the primary design objective of intrusion detection systems is detecting attacks and other possibly problematic system events, information collected and archived by IDSs also can support those charged with investigating security incidents. This functional requirement may levy additional technical requirements on IDSs. For instance, if investigators plan to use IDS monitoring features to perform a targeted surveillance of an attack in progress, it is critical that the information sources be "silent," so that adversaries are not aware that they are being monitored. Furthermore, the IDS monitors must be able to convey information to the investigators through a trustworthy, secure channel. Finally, the IDS itself must be under the control of the investigators or other trusted parties; otherwise, the adversaries may mask their activities by selectively spoofing information sources. Perhaps the most important thing for investigators to remember about IDSs is that the information provided should be corroborated by other information sources (e.g., network infrastructure device logs), not necessarily accepted at face value.

37.6.5   Issues in Responses. As in information sources and analysis strategies, certain issues associated with IDS response features have endured over the history of intrusion detection. The principal issues are as follows:

- Users' needs for IDS response capabilities are as varied as the users themselves. In some systems environments, the IDS response messages are monitored around the clock, with real-time action taken by system administrators based on IDS alarms. In other environments, users may use IDS responses (in the form of reports) as a metric to indicate the threat environment in which a particular system resides. It is important to consider the specific needs of the user when selecting an IDS.

- Given false-positive error rates for IDSs, response options must be tunable by users. Otherwise, users will simply tune out the IDS responses. This nullifies the value of the IDS.

- When the IDS provides automated responses to detected problems, there is a risk of the IDS itself launching an effective denial-of-service attack against the system it is protecting. For instance, suppose an IDS is configured with rules that tell it "upon detecting an attack from a given IP address, direct the firewall to block subsequent access from that IP address." An attacker, knowing this IDS is so configured, can launch an attack with a forged IP source address that appears to come from a major customer or partner of the organization. The IDS will recognize the attack and then block access from that organization for some period of time, effecting a denial of service.

37.7 NEEDS ASSESSMENT AND PRODUCT SELECTION. The value of intrusion detection products within an organization's security strategy is optimized by thorough needs assessment. These needs and security goals can be used to guide the selection of products that will enhance the security stance of the organization.

37.7.1 Matching Needs to Features. The needs most often addressed by intrusion detection systems include:

- Prevention of problem behaviors by increasing the risk of discovery and punishment for system attackers
- Detection of security violations not prevented (or even, in some cases, not preventable) by other security measures
- Documentation of the existing level of threat to an organization's computer systems and networks
- Detection and, where possible, mitigation of attack preambles (these include activities such as network probes, port scans, and other such "doorknob rattling")
- Diagnosis of problems in other elements of the security infrastructure (e.g., malfunctions or faulty configurations)
- Granting system security personnel the ability to test the security effects of maintenance and upgrade activities on the organizational networks
- Providing information about those violations that do take place, enabling investigators to determine and correct the root causes

Regardless of which of these specific needs are relevant to the user, it is important to consider the ability of the intrusion detection system to satisfy the needs for the specific environment in which it is installed. A critical part of this determination is considering whether the intrusion detection system has the ability to monitor the specific information sources available in the target environment. What is even more important is whether the organizational security policy translates into a monitoring and detection policy that can be used to configure the IDS.

37.7.2 Specific Scenarios. There is no universally applicable description for computer networks or the IDSs that protect them. There are, however, some common scenarios given current trends in networking and system usage.

A popular justification for using IDSs early in an organization's security life cycle is to establish the threat level for a given network enclave. Network-based IDSs often are used for this purpose, with monitors placed outside the organizational firewall. Those who are responsible for winning management support for security efforts often find this use of IDSs to be quite helpful.

Many organizations use IDSs to protect Web servers. In this case, the nature of the interactions that the Web server has with users will affect the selection and configuration of the IDS. Most Web servers serve two types of functions: (1) informational (e.g., Web servers that support simple HTTP and FTP queries from users) and (2) transactional (e.g., Web servers that allow user interaction beyond simple HTTP or FTP traffic). Transactional Web servers are usually more difficult to monitor than informational servers, as the range of interactions between users and servers is wider. For critical transactional Web servers, security managers may wish to consider multiple IDSs, monitoring the servers at multiple levels of abstraction (i.e., application, host, and network).

The third scenario involves organizations that wish to use IDSs as additional protection for specific portions of their networked systems. An example of this is the medical organization that wishes to protect the patient record database systems from privacy breaches. In this situation, as in the Web server example just given, it may be advisable to use multiple IDSs, monitoring interactions at multiple levels of abstraction. The output of these multiple systems can be synchronized and inconsistencies noted for a reliable indication of threat levels.

37.7.3   Integrating IDS Products with Your Security Infrastructure.   As mentioned before, an IDS is not a substitute for a firewall, virtual private network, identification and authentication package, or any other security point product. However, an IDS can improve the quality of protection afforded by the other point products by monitoring their operation, noting signs of malfunction or circumvention. Furthermore, an IDS with automated response capabilities can interact with the rest of the point products so that they can block access to an attack in progress.

37.7.4   Deployment of IDS Products.   The first generation of IDS installations has yielded some insights associated with deployment of IDSs. The key points include the location of sensors, scheduling the integration of IDSs, and adjusting alarm settings.

37.7.4.1   *Location of Sensors.* There are four general locations for IDS sensors:

1. Outside the main organizational firewall
2. In the network DMZ (inside the main firewall, but outside the internal firewalls)
3. Behind internal firewalls
4. In critical subnets (where critical systems and data reside)

As mentioned above, IDS sensors placed outside the main organizational firewall are useful for establishing the level of threat for a given network. Sensors placed within the DMZ[12] can monitor for penetration attempts targeting Web servers. IDSs monitoring for internal attacks are placed on internal network segments, behind internal firewalls. And for critical subnets, IDS sensors usually are placed at the choke points at which the subnets are connected to the rest of the corporate network.

37.7.4.2   *IDS Integration Scheduling.* Perhaps the most important thing learned in the first generation of intrusion detection products is that integration processes must not be rushed. IDSs still rely on operator interactions to screen out false alarms and to act on legitimate alarms. Hence, it is critical that the processes provide adequate time for operational personnel to learn the behavior of the IDS on target systems, developing a sense of how the IDS interoperates with particular system components in different situations.

37.7.4.3   *Alarm Settings.* IDSs have significant false alarm rates, with false positive rates as high as 80 percent in some situations. Many knowledgeable IDS integrators advise that alarms be suspended for a period of weeks, even months, as operators gain familiarity with the IDS and target systems. It is especially wise to delay activation of automated responses to attacks until operators and system administrators are familiar with the IDS and have tuned it to the target environment.

37.8 CONCLUSION. Intrusion detection is a valuable addition to system security suites, allowing security managers to spot those security violations that inevitably occur despite the placement of preventive security measures. Although current commercial IDSs are imperfect, they serve to recognize many common intrusion types, in many cases quickly enough to allow security personnel to block damage to systems and data. Furthermore, as research and development in intrusion detection continues, the quality and capabilities of available IDSs will steadily improve.

37.9 REFERENCES

Amoroso, E. *Intrusion Detection: An Introduction to Internet Surveillance, Correlation, Traps, TraceBack, and Response.* Sparta, NJ: Intrusion Net Books, 1999.

Anderson, James P., "Computer Security Technology Planning Study." ESD-TR-73-51, Vol. II, Electronic Systems Division, Air Force Systems Command, Hanscom Field, Bedford, MA 01730 (October 1972).

Anderson, James P., "Computer Security Threat Monitoring and Surveillance." James P. Anderson Co., Fort Washington, PA, April, 1980.

Bace, R.G. *Intrusion Detection.* Indianapolis, IN: Macmillan Technical Publishing, 2000.

Denning, Dorothy. "An Intrusion Detection Model," *Proceedings of the 1986 IEEE Symposium on Security and Privacy,* April 1986.

Escamilla, T. *Intrusion Detection: Network Security Beyond the Firewall.* New York: John Wiley & Sons, 1998.

Northcutt, S. *Network Intrusion Detection: An Analyst's Handbook.* Indianapolis, IN: New Riders Publishing, 1999.

Wassermann, Joseph J. "The Vanishing Trail," *Bell Telephone Magazine,* Vol. 47, No. 4, July/August 1968.

37.10 FURTHER READING

Crosbie, Mark, and E.H. Spafford. "Defending a Computer System Using Autonomous Agents," *Proceedings of the 18th National Information Systems Security Conference,* Baltimore, MD, October 1995.

ICSA Labs. "Intrusion Detection Systems Buyer's Guide," 1999. *www.icsa.net.*

Jackson, Kathleen A., D. DuBois, and C. Stallings. "An Expert System Application for Network Intrusion Detection." *Proceedings of the 14th National Computer Security Conference,* Washington, DC, October 1991.

Kumar, Sandeep, and E. Spafford. "A Pattern Matching Model for Misuse Intrusion Detection." Baltimore, MD, *Proceedings of the 17th National Computer Security Conference,* October 1994.

Lunt, Teresa, et al.. "A Real-Time Intrusion Detection Expert System (IDES)." Computer Science Lab, SRI International, Menlo Park, CA, May 1990.

Mukherjee, Biswanath, L.T. Heberlein, and K.N. Levitt. "Network Intrusion Detection." *IEEE Network,* Vol. 8, No. 3, May–June 1994.

Paxson, Vern. "BRO: A System for Detecting Network Intruders in Real Time." Seventh USENIX Security Symposium, San Antonio, TX, January 1998.

Porras, Phillip, and Peter Neumann. "EMERALD: Event Monitoring Enabling Responses to Anomalous Live Disturbances." *Proceedings of 20th National Information System Security Conference,* Baltimore, MD, October 1997.

Schaefer, Marvin, et al. "Auditing: A Relevant Contribution to Trusted Database Management Systems." *Proceedings of the Fifth Annual Computer Security Applications Conference,* Tucson, AZ, December 1989.

Shostack, Adam, and Scott Blake. "Towards a Taxonomy of Network Security Assessment Techniques." *Proceedings of 1999 Black Hat Briefings,* Las Vegas, NV, July 1999.

37.11   NOTES

1. See the Telecom Glossary 2000 from the American National Standards Institute, Inc. *www.its.bldrdoc.gov/projects/telecomglossary2000.*

2. Joseph J. Wassermann, "The Vanishing Trail," *Bell Telephone Magazine,* Vol. 47, No. 4, July/August 1968.

3. James P. Anderson, "Computer Security Technology Planning Study Volume II," ESD-TR-73-51, Electronic Systems Division, Air Force Systems Command, Hanscom Field, Bedford, MA 01730 (October 1972).

4. Anderson, James P., "Computer Security Threat Monitoring and Surveillance," James P. Anderson Co., Fort Washington, PA, April, 1980.

5. Dorothy Denning, "An Intrusion Detection Model," *Proceedings of the 1986 IEEE Symposium on Security and Privacy,* April 1986.

6. Teresa Lunt et al., "A Real-Time Intrusion Detection Expert System (IDES)," Computer Science Lab, SRI International, May 1990.

7. Biswanath Mukherjee, L.T. Heberlein, and K.N. Levitt, "Network Intrusion Detection," *IEEE Network,* Vol. 8, No. 3, May–June 1994.

8. Heberlein, L.T., K.N. Levitt, and B. Mukherjee, "A Network Security Monitor," *Proceedings of the 1990 IEEE Symposium on Research in Security and Privacy,* Oakland, California, May 1990.

9. S. Snapp et al., "DIDS (Distributed Intrusion Detection System) Motivation, Architecture, and an Early Prototype," *Proceedings of the 14th National Computer Security Conference,* Washington, D.C., October 1991.

10. Farmer, Dan and E.H. Spafford, "The COPS Security Checker System," *Proceedings of the Summer USENIX Conference,* pp. 165–170, Anaheim, California, June 1990.

11. Farmer, Dan and Wietse Venema, "Improving the Security of Your Site by Breaking into It," Internet white paper, 1993, *www.fish.com.*

12. A reserved area in some network architectures, in which Web servers are often placed, separated from the Internet by one firewall system, and separated from the internal corporate network by another firewall.

CHAPTER 38

MONITORING AND CONTROL SYSTEMS

Diane E. Levine

CONTENTS

38.1   INTRODUCTION.   Monitoring and control systems provide a crucial method of detecting problems or attacks in the operational environment. In addition, such systems can provide a wealth of information that enhances the performance as well as the security of any system. Every operating system is different, but having a regular surveillance program to monitor and audit activities on the system is key to a proactive security program. The most important items are system logging, which provides information in log files that can be printed out and analyzed, and data reduction, which enables an administrator to aggregate data into comprehensible formats for easier interpretation and detection of anomalies.

38.2   TERMINOLOGY.   *Monitoring* consists of periodically checking different aspects of the operational environment. Monitoring encourages constant awareness and vigilance over the state of the environment; the goal is to ensure that no system problems currently exist and to notice trends or anomalies that may signal trouble ahead. All operating systems have some type of monitoring, and many additional products (e.g., firewalls, intrusion detection, content filtering) provide additional information on the environment.

Control is also sometimes referred to as auditing. Control involves the systematic examination of all aspects of an operational environment in order to check for, and achieve compliance with, previously stated policies and operational requirements for the environment. The purpose of control and audit is to ascertain the state of performance within an operational environment. Audits can include whatever management deems necessary to ascertain the state of performance. Audits can take place whenever management decides they are necessary, although for control purposes it is preferable to have some predefined audit times assigned and published. Audits can take place at different levels, depending on the information that management decides they need and when they need it (see Chapters 36 and 38).

38.3   PURPOSE OF MONITORING AND CONTROL SYSTEMS.   Monitoring and control systems are designed to record who is doing what on the system and when the actions are taking place. Monitoring, especially in an Internet-savvy society, can introduce a self-regulation phenomenon that causes a significant decrease in non-business actions and increases management's level of comfort regarding the use of the system. Control systems, in addition to maintaining a record or log, also achieve the goal of limiting access to the system or specific activities by individuals. The result is that control systems act both as a preventive security measure and also as a reactive measure when an incident does take place and the perpetrators need to be pursued.

38.4   TYPES OF LOG FILE RECORDS.   A *log file* (sometimes known as an *audit trail*) traditionally contains records about transactions that have updated online files or otherwise represent events of interest (e.g., logging on to the system or initiating a process). Some database or application log files also may contain copies of records that were affected before or after the logged transaction. There are a number of different types of log file records, and each contains a specific kind of information. Typically, all the operating system log records are stored in a file with a maximum configured size and identified by a monotonically increasing file number. When the file fills up, the operating system opens another one with the next number in sequence as its identifier. Because log file records of different types have different sizes, on some operating systems the log file is defined with a variable record length.

38.4.1 System Boot.   The system boot log contains information on booting up, or starting, the machine. Since this is related to a specific activity and generally to a specific area of the hardware or media, information on the boot can prove helpful when the boot fails and analysis needs to take place.

38.4.2 System Shutdown.   The system shutdown log contains information on when the system was shut down and by whom. This information can be invaluable when attempting to analyze a problem or find a saboteur. On systems that include emergency shutdowns (e.g., by calling routines such as *suddendeath* when system parameters fall outside the range of allowable values), the shutdown record may contain specific information about the cause of the emergency shutdown.

From a security standpoint, trustworthy system boot and system shutdown records can prevent a malefactor from concealing a shutdown followed by unauthorized boot to a diagnostic subsystem that would allow file manipulations without log files to record the operations. The boot records would show an unexplained gap between shutdown and boot.

38.4.3 Process Initiation.   A *process* begins when a specific program is loaded and run by a particular user at a particular time. Log files for process initiation show when the various processes were initiated and who initiated them. These files provide a method of tracking employee activity as well as monitoring events that occur. In addition, such records allow cost recovery using chargeback at different rates for different programs or for program launches at different times of day. More important, the record of which programs were executed by whom at which times can be invaluable in forensic research.

38.4.4 Process Termination.   When reviewing the process termination log file, an administrator will be able to tell when each process completed or terminated for some other reason. Some systems may provide more information, such as why an unscheduled or abrupt termination occurred, but not all process termination log files provide that information. Process termination records typically include valuable statistical information such as:

- Which process spawned or forked the process in question
- Identification of any processes spawned by the processes
- Number of milliseconds of central processing unit (CPU) used
- Number of files opened and closed by the process
- Total number of input/output (I/O) operations completed by the process
- Total size of the memory partitions allocated to the process
- Maximum size of the data stack
- Number and maximum size of extra data segments in memory
- How many swaps to virtual memory were needed during the existence of the process
- Maximum priority assigned to the process for scheduling by the task manager

38.4.5   Session Initiation.   A *session* consists of the communication between a particular user and a particular server during a particular time interval. Whenever a user logs on to a system and initiates a session, a record of that event can be found in the session initiation log file. Review of these files frequently provides important information to alert administrators that an intruder is in the system. For instance, if an administrator knows that an authorized user is on vacation and the session initiation log file shows that a session was initiated for that particular user's ID, chances are significant that an unauthorized party used the system via a borrowed or stolen user ID. These records are particularly valuable during forensic work.

38.4.6   Session Termination.   When a session terminates, for whatever reason, a copy of the time and which session terminated is generally stored in the session termination log file. Much like the process termination record, the session termination record can include a great deal of aggregated information about the activities carried out during the session, such as total I/O, total number of processes launched and terminated, total number of files opened and closed, and so forth.

38.4.7   Invalid Log-On Attempts.   The invalid log-on attempt file can prove invaluable in cases where log-on attempts do not succeed. In some instances, the file can tell if the user attempted to log on with an incorrect password, if the user exceeded the allowed number of failed attempts, or if the user was attempting to log on at a seemingly unusual time. These log files can provide important information in cases where an administrator is attempting to track specific actions to a user or to ascertain if the log-on failure was due to a simple error or to an attempted impersonation by an unwanted outsider. In hardwired networks, where every device has a unique identifier, the records usually include a specific identifier that allows administrators to track down the physical device used for the attempted log-ons.

38.4.8   File Open.   The file open log file provides information on when each specific file was opened and by which process; in addition, the record generally records the mode in which the file was opened: for example, exclusive read and write, exclusive read, exclusive write with concurrent read, append only, or concurrent read and write.

38.4.9   File Close.   The file close log file gives an administrator information regarding when the file was closed, by which process, and by what means. The file usually captures information on whether the user specifically closed the file or whether some other type of interruption occurred. The records usually include details of total read and write operations, including how many physical blocks were transferred to accomplish the total number of logical I/O operations.

38.4.10   Invalid File Access Attempts.   An important log file record in the monitoring and control effort, the invalid file access attempt shows the administrator when and to which files there were invalid file access attempts. The records generally show which process attempted the I/O and why it was refused by the file system (e.g., attempted write to a file opened for read-only access, violation of access control list, or violation of file-access barriers).

38.4.11   File Input/Output.   Whenever information is placed into, read out of, or deleted from a file (input/output), the information regarding those changes is captured in the File I/O log. As mentioned earlier, the log includes images of a record before and after it was accessed. The I/O log can be used in file recovery after system or application crashes. Coupled with transaction-initiation and termination records, such data can be used for automatic roll-back or roll-forward recovery systems.

The activities recorded here can prove especially helpful when trying to validate actions that were taken and attribute them to specific individuals. Detailed logs are typical for databases, where a subsystem provides optional logging of all I/O. Application log files, designed and programmed by application developers, also typically allow administrators to enable such detailed logging.

38.4.12   System Console Activity.   The system console activity file provides information on any actions that originate from or are viewed at the system console. Typically, the system console includes not only log-on and log-off records but also special requests, such as printer form mounts, specific tape or cartridge mounts, comments sent to the console by batch jobs, and free-form communications from users. The console file records all such activity as well as every command from the system operator, and the system responses to those commands. These records provide an excellent tool for investigators tracking down the specific events in a computer incident.

38.4.13   Network Activity.   Network activity files provide valuable information on activity taking place on the network. Depending on the sophistication and settings of the system an administrator is using, the information derived can be plentiful or scant. Specific devices may generate their own records on network activity; for example, routers, gateways, and firewalls may all keep their own log files. However, typically these are circular files in which records to be entered after the file is full are shifted to the start of the file, where they overwrite the oldest records. In forensic work, it is essential to capture such data before the information of interest is obliterated. Unfortunately, in many systems, the volume of network activity is so high that log files contain only the most recent minutes of traffic.

38.4.14   Resource Utilization.   A review of the resource utilization log file will show all of the system's resources and the level of utilization for each. By monitoring this file, administrators frequently make important decisions regarding modifying system configuration or expanding the system.

38.4.15   Central Processing Unit.   The CPU file shows the capacity and usage of the central processing unit for whichever system is being used and monitored. Based on this information, administrators can monitor when usage is heaviest and the CPU is most stressed, and decide on utilization rules and requirements as well as possible CPU upgrades. As in all log-file analysis, any outliers (unusual values) and any unexpected change in usage can be investigated. Global CPU utilization records can be compared with the sum of CPU usage collected from process termination records; discrepancies may indicate stealth operation of unauthorized processes such as malicious software.

38.4.16   Disk Space.   The log files for disk space show the amount of disk space originally available on a system, the amount of disk space used (and generally what type of files it is being used for), and the amount of disk space that remains free and available. Comparison of total disk space utilization with the total space allocated to all files can reveal problems such as *lost disk space* (i.e., space allocated to files that were never closed properly; such space is unusable by the file system because there are no pointers indicating that the disk sectors are actually supposed to be free). Such unallocated sectors or clusters also may be where malefactors hide data they have stored without authorization by bypassing the file system.

38.4.17 Memory Consumption.

Important information on the amount of memory in a system and the amount actually being used can be obtained from the memory consumption log files. Such records typically also include information on virtual memory usage and therefore can provide warning of *thrashing* conditions, where memory segments are being copied to disk and read back from disk too often. Details of memory consumption may be useful in tracking down unauthorized processes such as worms.

38.4.18 System Level versus Job Level.

Different levels of monitoring, logging, and auditing may take place. Some of this may be preprogrammed, but in most environments it's possible to select the log files and related reports that are desired. For instance, a regular system level audit log may be produced just to provide information that the system is up and running without any extraordinary problems. But an in-depth job level audit may take place more frequently, in order to monitor the specific job and ensure that it is running correctly and providing the information needed.

38.5   ANALYZING LOG FILES.

Log files can be valuable to the system administrator, but only if they are put to use. Properly using a log file requires monitoring and reviewing its records and then taking actions based on the findings. Such analysis typically uses utilities provided by the supplier of the operating system or by third parties, such as commercial software companies or freeware distributors.

38.5.1   Volume Considerations.

Someone must make a decision regarding how big log files should be. Such a decision is generally made by the system administrator and is based on what is considered useful and manageable. If money is involved—for instance, if additional storage capacity is needed—the chief technology officer (CTO), chief information officer (CIO), chief operating officer (COO), system auditor, and a variety of other staff members might be called upon to review the activities and volumes of the logs and participate in any decisions regarding expenditures for new equipment. However, in the decades preceding this writing, disk space costs have fallen from about $5 per megabyte to less than $0.10 per megabyte in constant dollars, so disk space is not much of an issue anymore. More important is that log files, like any file, may be left in an inconsistent state if the system crashes; closing a log file and opening a new one in the series is a prophylactic measure that ensures that less information will be lost if there is a system crash.

38.5.2   Archiving Log Files.

Archiving is a very important part of making and using log files. Every company needs to decide how long to keep their log files and where to keep them. Decisions of this nature are sometimes made based on space considerations but more frequently are made based on legal requirements within specific industries. Some companies may decide to keep materials for a year or two, while others may be mandated by law to retain archived log files for seven or eight years.

The decisions regarding the archiving of log files should never be made arbitrarily; in every instance a careful review and check of company, legal, and industry requirements should be conducted. Based on the findings of that review, a written policy and procedures should be produced. Every company needs to tell its employees what these policies and procedures are, so they can be aware of what materials are being kept, where they can be found, and how they can be accessed.

38.5.3 Platform-Specific Programs for Log-File Analysis.
There are many operating systems in existence, and although there are certain similarities in how they function, there are also differences. Special training on each specific operating system may be necessary in order to do a correct analysis of the platform-specific log files it generates.

38.5.4 Exception Reports.
The volume of log file records can be overwhelming. For example, a large automated banking application with 10,000 users per day could generate millions of records of the log-ons, log-offs, file openings, file closings, and record changes alone. Exception reports allow the analyst to focus on specific characteristics (e.g., withdrawals of more than $200 from ATMs at a specific branch between 2:00 A.M. and 3:00 A.M. on last Tuesday night) or on statistical characteristics, such as the largest withdrawals in the network at any time. Such tools greatly simplify detection and analysis of anomalies and are particularly helpful in tracking down criminal behavior or other unauthorized activities.

38.5.5 Artificial Intelligence.
In our current advanced electronic society, artificial intelligence (AI) programs have been developed that actually can check user profiles for unusual and suspicious activities and generate an alert and a report whenever these types of activities are noticed. Because of the preprogrammed artificial intelligence and the parameters set, instead of having to launch the program and monitor it, the system launches the program on a regular basis and collects the data. Anything of an unusual nature causes an alert to be generated.

38.5.6 Chargeback Systems.
Chargeback systems, such as internal billing services and those used by external service bureaus, prove valuable in monitoring and tracing system activities through their logs. In some states and cities, legislation requires that these types of services keep accurate logs for audit purposes. The original records are used not only for tracking but also in court cases as evidence. In most situations, both internal and external services are the secondary "proof" of transactions, while the initial system logs provide the primary proof.

The log file records provide the basis for sophisticated billing algorithms that encourage rational use of resources. In addition, because unexpected changes in expenses can stimulate interest by accounting staff and managers, billing systems sometimes can help identify unauthorized usage such as online gambling, excessive downloads from the Internet, and installation of unauthorized code for processing using idle time on a computer.

38.6   PROTECTING LOG FILES AGAINST ALTERATION

38.6.1 Checksums.
Checksum programs work by performing computations based on the content of a record. The algorithm is run both at the time the record originates and when it is read; any discrepancy indicates that the record has been modified (by accident or through malfeasance) and that the checksum algorithm was not used for the modification. The most powerful application of checksums for log files creates a chain of verifiable information by incorporating the checksum from the preceding

record into the data used to generate the current record's checksum. Such chaining makes it very difficult for anyone to alter records within the file without knowing the checksum algorithm, and it requires a perpetrator to re-create an entirely new version of the modified log file, starting at the changed record and going on to the end of file.

38.6.2   Digital Signatures.   Another approach to marking log files so they cannot be altered after they have been generated is to append a digital signature (a cryptographically sound checksum) based on the entire content of the file. Any change without regenerating the digital signature would indicate corruption or unauthorized modification of the file, although it would not indicate which specific records had been tampered with. With a Public Key Infrastructure (PKI) system, a secret key would be used to generate the encrypted hash of the file, while the validation program would use the corresponding public key to test the validity of the digital signature (see Chapter 23).

38.6.3   Encryption.   Encryption is a method of camouflaging the information in a message so that it is not recognizable without a special key used for deciphering the message. Log files that are encrypted are safe so long as the key for decrypting the message can be accessed only by trusted personnel. In their encrypted state, log files also can be transmitted safely without fear of message exposure or loss of data. In addition, because the encryption algorithms typically used for such applications chain all the records together to create a stream of ciphertext, it is difficult (or impossible in practice) to change encrypted log file records so that the decrypted form is meaningful. Any change to the ciphertext generally results in invalid cleartext (see Chapter 50, and Tutorial 4 in this *Handbook*'s online Tutorials).

38.6.4   Physically Sequestering Log File Tapes and Cartridges.   In instances where a user wants to protect log file tapes or cartridges from being tampered with, it is possible to physically lock up the media in a secure facility. Generally these cartridges or tapes will be backup copies, but in instances where the material is not needed daily, the originals can also be taken off-site and sequestered.

38.7   MEMORY DUMPS.   Memory dumps are representations of the data in memory. Memory dumps are used most typically after a system failure, but they are also useful in forensic research when investigators want the maximum amount of information possible from the system. There are two approaches to obtaining copies of memory: online, using diagnostic utilities while the system is running, and offline, from magnetic storage media to which memory regions are copied.

38.7.1   Diagnostic Utilities.   Diagnostic utilities are system software routines that that can be used for debugging purposes. Also known as *debug* utilities, these programs run at maximum privilege (*root* or *supervisor* level, or their equivalents) and allow the privileged user to see or modify any portion of memory. The utilities usually print or display the contents of memory regions in a variety of formats such as binary, octal (base 8), or hexadecimal (base 16), with conversion to ASCII for easier readability. The utilities generally can provide immediate access to memory structures such as terminal buffers that allow the analyst to see what specific users are typing or seeing on their screens, file buffers that contain data in transit to or from specific open files, spoolers (print buffers), and program-specific regions such as data stacks. Because debug utilities also allow modification of memory regions, they are to be used with the utmost circumspection; for security reasons, it is wise to formulate a policy that no debug utility with root access can be run without having two people present. In high-security operations, the output of debug utilities should be logged to paper files for proof that there were no unauthorized operations carried out using these programs. Access to privileged debug programs should be tightly controlled, such as by strict access-control lists or even by encryption using restricted keys.

38.7.2   Output to Magnetic Media or Paper.   One method of doing a memory dump and follow-up analysis is by copying the data from memory onto magnetic media such as tape, removable disks, or rewriteable CDs. Although it was once practical to print the entire contents of memory to paper, the explosive growth of memory sizes makes such printing impractical in today's systems. In 1980, for example, a large multi-user minicomputer might have 1 megabyte of RAM available, so that the printout was a quite manageable half-inch thick. At the time of writing, however, it is common to see PCs with 256 megabytes of RAM; a printout of the entire contents of memory could be several feet thick.

Copying memory to a static storage medium is preferred for memory dumps following system crashes.

38.7.3   Navigating the Dump Using Exploratory Utilities.   On production systems using reliable operating systems, crashes are rare and are generally explored thoroughly to identify the causes of the anomaly. Generally after creating a dump it is necessary to study it looking for the problem and then correcting it. For large-memory systems, exploratory utilities are used to speed the search for problems in the dump by allowing the analyst to find and represent any named system table or other memory region.

38.7.4   Understanding System Tables.   System tables are directories of system data where each datum is identified by an assigned label, by its position in the table, or by pointers from other tables. An understanding of system tables is essential in analyzing system problems.

Regardless of the details of the operating system and the system-specific names of tables, some of the important system tables are as follows:

- **Process control table**—Pointers to the process tables for each process that is running on the system or that was running when the copy of memory was obtained
- **Process tables**—Detailed information about each process, with pointers to all the tables for that particular process
- **Data stacks**—All the variables used by specific processes
- **Buffers**—Data in transit to or from files and devices, such as disks and terminals
- **Memory management tables**—Lists of available memory blocks
- **Inter-process communications tables**—For example, information about resources locking or any logical flags used by multiple processes

Working with someone who understands the detailed structure of the operating system tables can be critically important for security work in which investigators must determine exactly what happened during an intrusion or other unauthorized use of a system.

38.7.5   Security Considerations for Dump Data.   Memory dumps must be secured while in use and destroyed when appropriate. The dump contains the totality of a system's information in memory, including such data as:

- Passwords that had just been typed into terminal buffers for use in changing log-ons or for accessing restricted subsystems and applications

- Encryption keys
- Confidential data obtained from restricted files and not authorized for visualization by operations staff (e.g., medical data from personnel files)
- Financial data that could be used in frauds
- National security information restricted to higher levels of clearance than the system administration

38.8   SUMMARY.   Monitoring, control, and auditing can be used to track systems, to document system problems, and to provide a means of correcting system and security problems. Every operating system keeps at least some log files that relate what is happening on the system, and some environments allow a great deal of flexibility in precisely which data will be recorded. The data in log files allow detailed analysis of who was doing what, with which data, at any given time; such information can be invaluable in system administration and security investigations. Historical data from log files can be used for internal billing purposes and to project system utilization and plan for future resource needs. They also can help spot anomalies, such as unauthorized use of the system. Special utilities allow investigators to focus on any desired region of memory, where system tables can be examined to see exactly what was happening in any given process on the computer. Log files should be secured and archived in accordance with policy.

38.9   BIBLIOGRAPHY

Information Systems Audit and Control Association. *Control Objectives for Net Centric Technology* Chicago, IL: ISACA, 2000.

Murphy, Michael A., and Xenia Ley Parker, eds. *Handbook of EDP Auditing,* 2nd Edition. New York: Warren, Gorham & Lamont, 1989.

NIST SPEC PUB 500-165. *Software Verification and Validation: Its Role in Computer Assurance and Its Relationship with Software Project Management Standards,* Dolores R. Wallace and Roger U. Fujii, National Bureau of Standards, September 1989.

Piper, Fred, Simon Blake-Wilson, and John Mitchell. *Digital Signatures.* Chicago, Il: Information Systems Audit and Control Association, 2000.

Raval, Vasant. "Today's IS Audits: Opportunities & Challenges." *www.isaca.org/articles/html.*

CHAPTER 39

APPLICATION CONTROLS

Myles Walsh

CONTENTS

39.1 PROTECTION IN DEVELOPMENT. In computer installations where systems development takes place, there are technologies that tend to enhance security. These technologies, together with mandatory organizational procedures and standards, force analysts and programmers to adhere to guidelines when they are developing in-house applications. This chapter reviews some of the methods programmers use to prevent and identify problems involving data corruption or unavailability.

One of the underpinnings of modern programming is the technology known as relational database management systems (DBMSs). Many applications are developed using this technology. Contemporary DBMSs support relational databases (RDBMSs). Relational databases themselves are based on an underlying technology developed in the 1960s and implemented through the remainder of the twentieth century. Relational database technology will continue to be used for the foreseeable future. Relational DBMSs are sets of programs that provide users with the tools to perform the following tasks:

- Create database structures (file or table layouts and screens or forms).
- Enter information into the structures.

- Establish cross-references among the files or tables.

- Manipulate (sort, index, and summarize) the information in the structures.

- Import information from nonrelational database structures and export information to nondatabase structures. This must allow for interfaces between applications using relational database management systems and applications using conventional files structures.

- Provide for the security and the integrity of the database.

Many DBMS also include the tools to create a data repository. Data repositories, expanded versions of data dictionaries that store information about databases, are documentation databases that include descriptive information about all the resources included in an information systems environment. Data dictionaries are often integrated with RDBMS, and if used as intended, force documentation standards in information systems environments. Common file or table structures, common program modules, and common field definitions contribute significantly to the reduction of confusion and communication breakdowns in an enterprise.

There are two primary methods of organizing files and databases for access and processing: batch and online. Protection of online files and databases requires additional planning when the systems using them are being designed, and special precautions when they are being used. Protection of batch files is more straightforward because the creation of backup copies is an inherent part of the batch process.

For related topics, see Chapter 25 on quality assurance and Chapter 32 on operations security and production controls.

39.2   PROTECTING ONLINE FILES

39.2.1   Types of Data Corruption.   Data corruption implies incorrect data. Corruption can occur because of physical factors or logical errors in programs.

Physical corruption occurs through breakdown or other failures of hardware such as computers and network equipment, especially of mass-storage devices such as magnetic disks, tapes and cartridges, or optical drives. Data corruption during transmission can occur through electromagnetic perturbations of communications cables or radio-frequency noise that affects wireless transmission. Fiber-optic cables are susceptible to cross-talk and to disruption caused by physical bends or kinks in the cables; CD-ROM (compact-disk read-only memory), CD-WORM (write-once, read-many), and CD-RW (read-write) disks are susceptible to dirt and abrasion. In addition to problems in the transmission or storage media, improper settings, or the effects of wear in the equipment, can cause errors. Examples include misalignment of magnetic heads on disks and tapes, bad contacts in wireless transmission equipment, causing noise, and improper positioning of lasers in optical media. See Chapters 14 and 15 for extensive discussion of physical factors that can cause data corruption.

Logical corruption occurs through programming errors such as incorrect sums, bad arithmetic formulas, incorrect logical conditions, bad data in look-up tables, out-of-bounds conditions allowing reading and writing in the wrong areas of memory, and the effects of malicious software.

It is sometimes possible to identify the source of errors by examining their characteristics. For example, physical corruption characteristically shows data written inappropriately across blocks, rather than in single fields defined by software applications. Such physical corruption usually has no relationship with the damaged records other than physical proximity on the disk; therefore, a cardinal sign of physical corruption is damage to files from completely different applications—a block of database records next to a block of text files, for example.

In contrast, logical corruption characteristically shows the same field in multiple records with errors. Another class of logical errors shows bad values for boundary conditions (e.g., the smallest or largest possible value) but correct data within the range. Such errors rarely cross application boundaries unless there is a logical relationship among the damaged files; for example, an error in a spreadsheet (almost always due to input or programming errors by the user) may propagate to text files if object linking and embedding (OLE) is used to insert the spreadsheet results into the document. Other documents will remain unaffected by such logical errors. For more extensive discussion of logical errors, see Chapter 25.

39.2.2   Database Management Systems.   In the 1960s, representing complex systems such as accounting records forced programmers to define their own file structures to represent relationships among the data; for example, an order header file would be linked to the corresponding order detail records through hard-coded relationships in the application programs. Each programmer or programming team had to define their own data access paths and code them explicitly. Coordinating access to multiple individually named files caused headaches for programmers. For example, it was easy to make errors such as forgetting to increment counters representing how many detail records corresponded to a master (index) record (e.g., line counts in order headers disagreeing with the actual number of detail lines). Because there was no particular protection for the files in such systems, it was easy to replace or delete individual files by mistake, leading to massive logical corruption. Deletion of header records could leave a fragment of inaccessible details in associated files. Programs had to keep pointers up-to-date for forward and backward chaining. Backups sometimes failed through operator error when not all related files were included. Furthermore, every system had its own unique methods for managing the data, causing maintenance and learning headaches.

The late 1960s saw many large programming shops defining their data access methods by using library routines that all programmers could share, but there was still a heavy investment in learning the new rules whenever a programmer changed jobs. In the early 1970s, the programming field saw explosive growth and implementation of database management systems (DBMSs), where the interface to the database controlled utility functions such as indexing, pointing, and chaining. A typical DBMS would protect all files, now called *datasets,* against accidental erasure, and would force all reads, writes, appends, and locks to be mediated by the DBMS routines. Such interfaces usually provide for identification and authorization codes to control access to the data. In addition to these barriers to accidental or uncontrolled access, DBMS also typically provide backup utilities to ensure that all datasets are copied together and to prevent accidental restoration of the wrong version of a dataset. DBMS also often provide *ad hoc* query tools that can substitute for specially written programs to accomplish simple requests; some also have more powerful report functions for formatting output with headers, footers, and calculations. Finally, DBMS usually provide logging facilities to keep records of different types of access to the database.

The most important rules enforced by a DBMS are referential integrity to prevent common logical data corruption, automatic uniqueness constraints to preclude duplicate and conflicting records, and *locking* for safe concurrent access.

39.2.2.1   Referential Integrity.   Referential integrity in DBMS design ensures that every dependent record has a primary key value that matches an existing primary key in the master file. In an order database, for example, order numbers in a header file (often called the order master) are the primary keys. Each order header record contains unique information about an order such as customer number, date placed, total price of materials, taxes, and shipping costs. The order detail file contains the dependent records, each of which can be located using its order number as the primary key. Each detail record contains information about a specific part of the corresponding order such as an item number, quantity ordered, price, extended price, and special charges or discounts. If an order header record is to be deleted, all the order detail records must first be deleted; otherwise, the detail records would be left with no way to locate them through their primary key value. Similarly, no detail record can be added unless the master record with the same primary key already exists.

39.2.2.2   Uniqueness Constraints.   Modern DBMSs allow configuration of non-repeating keys; for example, in an order database, the order number would typically be a nonrepeating or unique key because there should never be two orders with the same identifying number. Setting the uniqueness property would preclude adding a second header record with the same value in the order number field as another order.

39.2.3   Lock on Update.   When more than one user accesses a database, it is possible to experience conflicts over the use of specific records. A classic example occurs in an inventory database, where there are 15 units of part no. 1 in the inventory. User A needs to take five units of part no. 1 out of inventory, leaving a total of 10. The inventory program reads the inventory record for part no. 1 and modifies record no. 1 to show only 10 units of part no. 1. However, if while this is going on, user B needs three units of part no. 1, the inventory record still shows 15 units available because user A has not yet updated that record. After user A's program completes its update, the record shows 10 units available, but after user B's program overwrites that record to show 12 available units for part no. 1, the inventory total is off by five units.

   To avoid this kind of logical corruption, DBMSs provide facilities for *locking* parts of the database. In the inventory example, user A's program would lock the inventory record for part no. 1 (or the entire inventory dataset) until the update is completed. That way, user B's program would have to wait for user A's program to *unlock* the data before being able to act upon the inventory record.

   The obvious symptom of a bad locking strategy is a discrepancy between the database value and the real-world value. However, such a discrepancy is not by itself proof of logical corruption, because the same divergence could arise from events in the real world not reflected in the database. In the inventory example, the actual inventory may have been reduced by theft, or increased by an unrecorded addition of materials.

39.2.3.1   Unconditional Versus Conditional Locking.   There are two types of locking strategy: *conditional* locking and *unconditional* locking. Conditional locking attempts to obtain a lock, but if the required record or the entire dataset is already locked, the DBMS returns control to the calling program with a status indicator of this condition. The application program can then be written to loop until the lock is obtained. The unconditional lock request hangs the program until the lock is granted. The DBMS or the operating system provides automatic queuing using a first-in, first-out (FIFO) queue.

39.2.3.2   Deadlocks.   Unconditional locking carries risks if multiple resources are locked by programs. For example, if program A unconditionally locks resource no. 1 and program B locks resource no. 2, trouble will occur when program A then attempts to lock resource no. 2 while program B tries to lock resource no. 1. Neither program will release the resource it has locked until it is released, and so both will wait forever or until one of the programs is forcibly terminated. Such a situation is known as a *deadlock* or more colorfully as a *deadly embrace*. If the programmers insists on using unconditional locking, the deadlock prevention strategy is to ensure that all programs accessing the database must lock resources in the same order (e.g., lock no. 1, then lock no. 2) and must unlock in the reverse order (unlock no. 2, then unlock no. 1).

Other strategies are to keep transactions as short as possible, and to avoid the necessity for operator interactions that would keep the records locked for long periods of time.

39.2.4   Two-Phase Commit.   Sometimes many records or datasets must be locked for complex transactions to be completed. For example, in a hospital's clinical systems database, discharging a patient could require modifications in datasets such as the patient-master, treatment-detail, nursing assignment master and details, doctor assignment master and details, and datasets for the financial functions. Locking everything that might be needed and waiting for a human being to enter all the appropriate data could take seconds to minutes, during which all the affected records would be locked and unavailable to everyone else on the system. In the extreme, if an operator were to leave in the middle of a transaction, other users could be blocked out of large parts of the database for an indeterminate length of time, even for hours. The delays resulting from such locking around human intervention led to the principle that no transaction can be allowed to lock around a human intervention.

Another problem with locking around human intervention is that a system failure could terminate processing while the database was in an inconsistent state. For example, in the inventory case, the DBMS might have updated the order detail by adding an item but not yet updated the order header to show the new total cost of the order. To reduce the likelihood of such an occurrence, DBMSs can support the two-phase commit as an aid to making changes as fast as possible and thus reducing the window of vulnerability for interruption. In the two-phase commit, the DBMS obtains copies of all the records needed when the operator begins a transaction. Once the operator has taken all necessary steps for completing the transaction, the DBMS locks and reads all the changed records again and compares the current values with the initial values; if there are no differences, the DBMS makes all the required changes and immediately unlocks all the records. However, if the current values have been modified since the operator requested the initial copies, then some other process has been active and so the DBMS reports that verification is needed. The operator is typically given the choice of how to proceed; for example, if there are no items left in inventory, the order may have to be delayed or canceled, whereas if there are enough items, the operator need merely reinitiate the transaction with the new initial values.

39.2.5   Backup Files and System Logs.   When information in an online file or database is updated, the old information, that is, the information that was in the record before the change was made, is overlaid; unless steps are taken, it disappears without a trace. For this reason, many DBMS allow an image of the original record to be copied to the transaction log file. In other cases where the exact history of a particular group of records must be preserved, as with insurance and medical data, an application may append new records but not delete old ones.

If online files and databases were never damaged or lost, data loss would be of no concern. However, in an imperfect world, steps must be taken so that damaged or lost online files and databases can be recovered.

In order to recover online files and databases, it is first necessary to make periodic backup copies, and also to make log copies of records that have been updated in the time between the making of the backups. How often a backup copy is made depends on how dynamic the files or databases are In most enterprises, a significant number of total or partial files and databases are copied daily. It is not uncommon for computer operations departments to spend several hours each day doing backups. Whenever a backup copy of a file or database is created, there are two correct copies at that point in time. To explain how online file and database backup and system logging work, think of a single on-line file. The file is taken offline, and is no longer accessible to online transactions, at 4 A.M. and a copy is made. Both copies of this file are identical at that time. At 6 A.M. the original file is put back online and transactions recorded during that interval are run to update that file. From that point on, with each update transaction, the differences between that file and its backup increase.

At 2 P.M., if for some reason the file is no longer usable, the backup file is then eight hours behind. At this point, the log file becomes critical in the restoration process. The log file is in sequence by time and contains copies of the updated records both before and after update was performed. It also contains copies of the transaction record.

39.2.6 Recovery and Restart.   After it has been determined that an on-line file or database has been corrupted or destroyed, a procedure known as recovery and restart is initiated. The first step in this procedure is to copy the backup to create a new original. The next step uses the log file to reapply, in time sequence, all the transactions that had been executed since the backup copy was made. A schematic of this process appears in Exhibit 39.1.

Contemporary database systems have files that cannot be taken offline. They are online 24 hours a day, seven days a week. In order to make backup copies, parts of the database are copied periodically (dynamic backup). Conceptually, a database can be broken up into parts. Each part can be backed up separately at different time periods. A number of schemes can be devised to back up some of the records. For example, copy to a backup file every fifth record of the database in one time period, say records 5, 10, 15, 20, etc. A little later, copy to another backup file records 1, 6, 11, 16, 21, and so forth. If a conflict occurs between copying the record for backup and a transaction attempting to update the record, have an appropriate procedure established to let one or the other take place first. Recovery and restart, as well as back-out procedures, work the same way, with the additional complexity of establishing priorities for which gets done first when conflicts occur. Even though these conflicts increase complexity, they are resolved when the procedures for recovery, restart, and back-out are created.

39.2.7 Back-Out.   The log file is also used in a process known as *back-out*. This process is initiated when online update transactions fail to complete after making incomplete or partial updates to files or databases. For example, an update transaction in which there are additions to three fields in three separate files is supposed to take place. After making two out of the three updates, the transaction terminates abnormally because of a program malfunction. Eventually the program gets corrected, but something has to be done to undo the two partial updates. Otherwise, when the program is fixed and the transaction is rerun, those two updates would be reapplied, which would

Exhibit 39.1 Recovery of Damaged Online Files

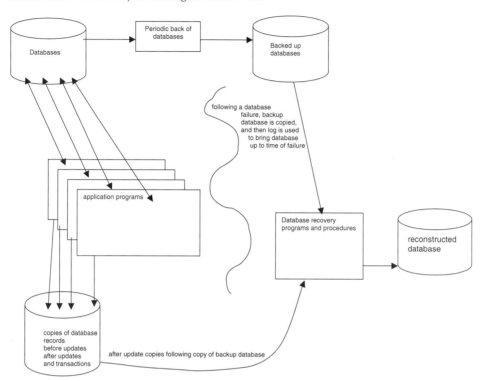

result in erroneous duplication. The back-out procedure is initiated for those transactions which have not been completed properly and would generate errors.

Recovery, using log files, requires marking the start and end of every transaction; if the log file records show a transaction start without the corresponding transaction end, recovery processes can recognize the transaction as incomplete. Such markers correspond to what are called *checkpoints* in the program design.

39.2.8 Roll-Forward Recovery. Another approach to recovery is to start from a known good state and redo all transactions that are known to have been accomplished correctly. This *roll-forward* recovery requires a database backup and a transaction log file to be synchronized so that the first record in the transaction log file represents the first transaction immediately following a database backup. With these data in hand, it is possible to reconstruct all the modifications up to and including the last complete transaction. All incomplete transactions are discarded, although the recovery program typically prints out all the details available for transactions that were not completed.

39.2.9 Distributed Databases. A *distributed* database is one that is stored in different databases on different computer platforms. Databases can be distributed over many sites, using several different architectures.

The simplest and most susceptible to failure is the single database server that houses the database and shares its contents among several local area networks. Whenever the server or the database is offline, or during a crash, all clients lose access to the database. The backup and recovery of a single server database follows the procedures described earlier.

A second architecture is the *replicated* database server, in which there are duplicate copies of the database on multiple servers. This type of system allows clients to access information from any of several copies of the database. With a replicated server environment, clients can still have access to the database, when one of the servers is offline. Such replicated systems usually have an additional benefit of being able to balance transaction traffic so as to keep any one server from being overwhelmed. The trade-off is the database synchronization process that increases the complexity of the replicated server architecture. Although the backup and recovery of a distributed database can also follow the procedures described earlier, it is complicated by the synchronization requirement.

A third architecture is known as a *partitioned* database server, in which specific subsets of a database are on two or more database servers. There could be a marketing database on one server, an accounting and finance database on a second server, and an inventory database on a third server. Because it is generally not possible to have mutually exclusive subsets of databases, synchronization must still be part of this architecture. Backup and recovery of partitioned databases requires application of the procedures described above for each of the subsets.

There is another distributed architecture known as *federated* database servers. This architecture is used in support of databases on two or more servers made up of ordinarily incompatible storage models such as hierarchical and relational models, supported by different DBMS. With the federated architecture, a single unified database definition, or schema, is created and stored on a combined database server. That server acts as an interface between application programs and the databases residing on the other servers. Queries and other transactions are sent to the combined database server, which translates these into queries and transactions to the underlying databases. Responses then return from the underlying databases to the unified schema to formulate a response to the user. Backup and recovery procedures such as those described above are used for the underlying databases.

Although federated database architecture can be complex and expensive to maintain, it can be less complex and less expensive than the process of supporting application programs for each of the underlying DBMS. Federated architecture is often used in the implementation of data warehouses, which are used to extract information from multiple internal databases, as well as external databases, to support management decision making.

39.3   PROTECTING BATCH FILES

39.3.1   Backup File Creation.   The protection of files that are updated by batch processing programs is automatic, because the file is completely recopied and the original is left in the form it was in before the program executed. Therefore, each processing cycle leaves its own backup. The name *batch processing* comes from the idea of sequentially processing transactions in a group. There are always two or more files involved. There is the master file that is being updated, and one or more transaction files that contain the information used to update the master. The process copies master file records that have no update activity into a new master file, updates the master records that do have activity and copies them into the new master file, and does not copy those master records that are flagged as deletions in the activity file. When the process completes, there are at least three files: the original master, the activity file(s), and the new master. Backups are the original master and the activity file(s). In the next processing cycle, the new master becomes input, together with that cycle's activity file(s). If a

problem is encountered with the master file, the prior cycle's master file and all subsequent activity files can be used to generate an updated master. Keeping two or three
generations of master and activity files is a common practice. The term *generation*
is often applied to the batch processing cycles as—generation 0, generation 1, generation 2, and so forth, or as grandfather, father, and son. This process is illustrated in
Exhibit 39.2.

39.3.2 Audit Controls. Another security measure applied when working with
batch files involves using control totals to assure that the batch process has executed
with accuracy. Specific controls may include counts of records. There also may be
control totals of the values in specific fields of the input records to compare with totals
in the output, after processing additions and subtractions. For example, in a payroll
system, information from time cards is submitted to a computer for processing. Along
with the time cards is a transmittal that contains a count of the time cards, and totals of
all the straight time and overtime hours compiled by the department that originated the
time cards. A procedure is run in which the control totals on the transmittal are checked
against the totals actually input from the time cards, to assure correctness before initiating the payroll process. If discrepancies are encountered, they need to be investigated
and corrected before taking the next step in processing the payroll.

39.4 ASSURING THAT INFORMATION IN THE SYSTEM IS VALID. The following sections present a brief overview of validation; however, for more extensive
coverage of this topic, see Chapter 32.

39.4.1 Validation Controls. Whether an application updates its files by means of
batch or online processing, or in some combination of both, validation of input is paramount. The term *GIGO* (garbage in, garbage out) is not heard as often as it used to

Exhibit 39.2 Backup in Batch Processing

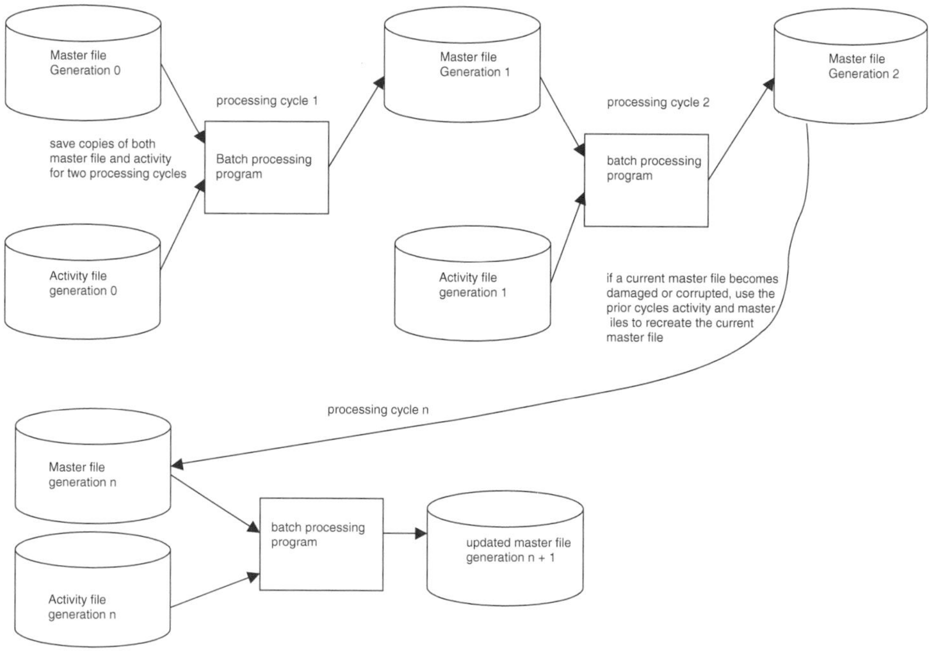

be, yet it is as true as ever. Most contemporary systems use online files and databases, with information entered interactively, allowing for validation at the source. There are several specific validation techniques that have been applied to reduce the amount of incorrect information input into files and databases.

39.4.1.1 Methods for Identifying Input Errors and Unauthorized Modifications.
Data input errors are common. Fours and nines, ones and sevens, and sixes, and zeros can easily be mistaken for one another. Operators can leave out a digit or insert an extraneous one. Transposition is another type of mistake that is made from time to time. For example, an order entry operator may key in 3286 instead of 3826 (a transposition error), or perhaps 7790 instead of 7796 (a transcription error). Such errors would be reported when the check digit calculation produces a number that differs from the input check digit. A check digit is an extra digit that is added to a generated variable as a suffix. For example, a five-digit stock number could have an extra digit; the sixth digit or check digit, as it is called, is calculated by applying an algorithm (performing some arithmetic) on the first five digits, resulting in a single-digit result. To minimize input errors, check digits can be used on any variables that are program generated; for example, part numbers, employee numbers, and codes of various types.

A single check digit can sometimes conceal the existence of double or multiple input errors in an input string because of the relatively simple arithmetic schemes. More complex versions of the check digit generate a sequence of digits called a *check sum* which provides greater power to help identify input errors or fraud; credit card numbers typically include a four-digit check sum.

An extension of the check sum, the hash total, is a common tool for identifying logical or physical data corruption. A hash total is simply the meaningless sum of numerical values, such as part numbers, rather than the meaningful sum of quantities. Recalculation of a hash total can usually indicate if the data have been corrupted since the last time the hash total was computed.

A digital signature is a cryptographically generated value based on an encryption key. Applying the same digital signature process to the data should generate an identical signature. In addition, as described in Chapter 23 and in Tutorial 4 available on the *Handbook* Web site at *www.wiley.com/go/securityhandbook,* using the public key cryptosystem allows one to verify the authenticity as well as the integrity of signed data.

39.4.1.2 Range Checks. Range checks offer another way of validating information at its source. In situations where quantities and currency values are being entered, lower and upper limits can be established. For example, a range check could be used on quantity ordered to ensure that the value entered is within specific bounds, such as no less than 10 or no more than 60 of a certain item. Although not completely error proof, such limits can at least eliminate obvious errors and reduce those not so blatant. Range checking with values of 10 and 60 will eliminate the extra 0 error, where an operator enters 100 or 600, or 1 or 4.

39.4.1.3 Validity Checks Using Tables. Using tables of values or valid codes is one of the best ways to ensure that only correct information is entered into files and databases. In contemporary files and databases, data type is specified as a property of the field during the design phase, and these properties can be used to make sure that text information is not entered into numeric fields and vice versa. Properties are also used to filter out invalid data configurations. Although impossible to filter out misspelled last names and other open-ended types of information, it is possible to filter out invalid state codes. A table containing the 51 (DC is the 51st) valid state codes can be used to assure that none but those 51 can be entered. Other such entities (e.g., department codes, product codes or types, and price classes) are primary candidates for table validation.

With tables, it is also possible to make combination tables. For example, if a certain product code fell within a specific range, then only four price classes would be allowable. To be concrete, when a product code falls within the 600 to 699 range, then the price class could only be R, PR, OC, and CD. Such tables are used to validate information as it is initially entered into files and databases. Entry of invalid information, whether intentional or inadvertent, is inhibited.

Tables should generally be used only for information that is relatively static, because of the need for maintenance. Frequent table maintenance can lead to errors that have a cascading effect. If a table is incorrect, then all the information supposedly validated by that table could be incorrect throughout the files and databases.

39.4.2   Diagnostic Utilities.   Production programs need to operate on verifiably correct data. Every production program should include diagnostic utilities to scan databases for logically impossible values or deviations from reality. For example, a diagnostic routine might check to be sure that every header total matches the total computed from the linked line item values. Because older data may have been accepted under older range-validation rules, all records should be checked to ensure that they conform to the current range constraints. Similarly, any other logical constraints in an application system should be explicitly addressed in the diagnostic program. The output from the program should give all the details appropriate for identifying and correcting the incorrect data. For example, instead of simply indicating "BAD VALUE IN PRICE FIELD, RECORD NO. 1234," the output should explain something like, "PRICE FOR ITEM NO. 234 = $45.67 WHICH EXCEEDS CONFIGURED LIMIT OF $40.00 SHOWN IN INVENTORY MASTER RECORD NO. 78999."

39.5   CONCLUSION.   In another application of the 80/20 rule, 20 percent of the design and development work is expended in handling 80 percent of the data (the normal and the correct) going through a system, whereas 80 percent of the design and development work is expended for handling 20 percent of the data (the errors, the exceptions, and the unusual situations) going through the system. It is safe to say that more effort should be expended on validation, and on back up and recovery procedures, than is spent on those processes that handle validated data and the routine tasks of application processing.

Every attempt should be made to assure that data are entered and validated expeditiously. Failure to get data into a system quickly delays the creation and display of the information, the very purpose of the system. When improper attention is directed to validation of the data as it enters the system, incorrect information is created by the system. The acronym *GIGO* has become part of the national lexicon of everyday language. Unfortunately, there are some techniques, such as prototyping, joint application development (JAD), and rapid application development (RAD), that contribute to the creation of incorrect information when improperly used. By definition, a prototype is a model that is put together to demonstrate that the concept of a proposed system is valid. Basically, prevalidated test data are used to test the concept. However, too often a successfully tested prototype system is put into production without adequate validation procedures. The same situation can arise with RAD efforts. JAD projects can be implemented without considering their impact on other systems within an organization.

Failure to include adequate backup and recovery procedures will jeopardize the operational integrity of an entire organization. The reliability of contemporary computer hardware together with built-in redundancy make outages due to equipment failure less likely. Unfortunately, the same cannot be said for software and procedures. In any case, operational systems do fail, albeit rarely. Adequate backup and recovery processes and procedures have to be put in place to handle system failures. These processes and procedures range from disaster recovery to single system or application recovery. To ensure that sites, enterprises, or applications can be brought back after failures requires that processes and procedures be put in place during the design and development process and kept up to date as the situation requires. For more details of software development and quality assurance, see Chapter 25.

39.6   FURTHER READING

Shelley, G.B., T.J. Cashman, and H.J. Rosenblatt. *Systems Analysis and Design,* 4th ed. Boston, MA: Course Technology, 2001. See, in particular, pp. 8.37, 9.29–9.31.

Stair, R.M., and G.W. Reynolds. *Principles of Information Systems,* 5th ed. Boston, MA: Course Technology, 2001. See, in particular, pp. 340, 510–512.

REMEDIATION

CHAPTER 40

COMPUTER EMERGENCY QUICK-RESPONSE TEAMS

Bernard Cowens and Michael Miora

CONTENTS

40.1 OVERVIEW.   An essential element of any effective information security program today is the ability to respond to computer emergencies. Although many organizations have some form of intrusion detection in place, far too few take full advantage of the capabilities those systems offer. Fewer still consistently monitor the data available to them from automated intrusion detection systems, let alone respond to what they see.

The key is to make use of the knowledge that something has happened, that something is about to happen, or that something is perhaps amiss. Intrusion detection systems can be costly to implement and maintain. It therefore makes little business sense to go to the trouble of implementing an intrusion detection capability if one does not, at the same time, have any way of making use of the data produced by these systems.

Computer emergency quick-response teams are generally called simply computer emergency response teams (CERTs, the abbreviation used in this chapter) or sometimes computer incident response teams (CIRTs) and computer security incident response teams (CSIRTs).

CERTs can provide organizations with a measurable return on their investment in computer security mechanisms and intrusion detection systems. Intrusion detection can indicate that something occurred; CERTs can do something about that occurrence. Often, their value to an organization can be felt in more subtle ways as well. Many times, computer emergencies and incidents cast an organization in an unfavorable light and can erode confidence in that organization. Efficient handling of computer emergencies can lessen the erosion of confidence, can help speed the organization's recovery, and in some cases can help restore its image.

When an incident occurs, the intrusion detection system makes us aware of the incident in one manner or another. We make use of this knowledge by responding to the situation appropriately. Appropriately can mean something different in different situations. Therefore, a well-trained, confident, authoritative CERT is essential.

Intrusion detection systems are not the only means by which we learn about incidents. In a sense, every component of a system and every person who interacts with the system form a part of the overall defense and detection system. End users are often the first to notice that something is different. They may not recognize a particular difference as an "incident"; however, proper awareness and training will encourage them to report such situations to those who can make a determination and act on the information.

40.1.1   Description.   CERTs are multifaceted, multitalented groups of individuals who are specially trained and equipped to respond quickly and effectively to computer emergencies.

CERTs come in a variety of forms and compositions. For example, while some teams are static, established groups, others are assembled dynamically to fit a specific mission or to deal with specific emergencies. Often the most effective teams are characterized as a mixture of these two approaches. These teams generally have a standing core membership made up of both technical and nontechnical members. When a situation arises that must be addressed by the CERT, additional members with specific skills are added to meet the requirements of handling the incident in progress. Once the incident is resolved, the team reverts to its core membership status.

40.1.2   Purpose.   CERTs provide the first reaction to an incident. Their immediate goal should be to take control of a situation in order to contain the scope of a potential compromise, to conduct damage control, and to prevent the possible spread of a compromise to adjacent systems. Containing the scope of compromise is also synonymous with preventing or reducing loss.

Maintaining a dedicated CERT at the ready, 24 hours a day, is a costly proposition from many perspectives. Virtually any organization today, no matter its mission, will be hard pressed to justify funding such a team only to have the team stand by awaiting an emergency. The cost of maintaining a team of highly trained resources, with only emergency response roles, is a most difficult issue to overcome. Therefore, it is important to make use of team members and their skills during nonemergency periods. In many organizations, the teams have important security and awareness roles as integral parts of their charters. Carefully selected, these additional roles can benefit team readiness while at the same time providing tangible and often visible value to the organization.

For example, some CERTs spend their nonemergency days and nights monitoring security issues and developments for the latest trends, threats, and countermeasures.

They analyze threat data and prepare reports for various levels of the organization on such topics as virus protection, password security, and emerging technology. Members of the team spend a significant amount of time and effort developing and maintaining leading-edge technical skills. They hone their response skills and procedures through continuous training. Training often is conducted in the classroom and through dry runs using a variety of response scenarios.

Often, response teams provide and maintain awareness programs for the organization. This serves several purposes. First, awareness programs benefit an organization by pointing out risks and ways to avoid them. Next, delivering awareness programs makes the team members more visible. As a result, should something unusual or out of the ordinary occur, members of the organization are not only more likely to notice it, they are also more likely to report the information, so that it winds up in the hands of the response team.

The teams respond to emergencies or incidents. Such incidents might be characterized as any unwanted or, in some cases, unexplained behavior. An incident does not always indicate something unwanted; it also can be something that is merely unexplained or out of the ordinary. Response not only acts to defend, or to fight back, or prevent further damage, but also to discover more information or to verify facts—in essence, it is part investigation and part education. To keep in step with the rapid pace of change in technology, quick response teams must be learning constantly. These teams should strive to remain abreast of each new development and technology that impacts or has the potential to impact the systems under their care. Therefore, responding to incidents, whether actual attacks or benign anomalies, should be seen as opportunities to sharpen the CERT's skills. This need is also served by the additional responsibilities the team holds in nonemergency times, typically including ongoing security research and evaluation.

If locks and other preventive measures were foolproof, intrusion detection and incident response would be unnecessary. Banks put huge vault doors, time locks, and other seemingly impenetrable defenses into their buildings. But they recognize that these measures are insufficient to prevent completely any loss of their money or other valuables. So they also install alarm systems. Alarm systems detect when one of the defensive barriers has been breached. But that knowledge is of little value if no one hears the alarm or, if having heard it, does not act on the information. Therefore, organizations also put into place guards, night watchers, and others, including law enforcement, to monitor systems and to respond. CERTs are the response part of the secure + monitor + detect + respond equation. Because connected systems are under constant passive and active attack virtually 24 hours a day, emergency response teams are a necessary part of the security equation.

40.1.3 History and Background. Organizations have been responding to incidents in various forms for just about as long as there have been organizations. While this is also true for computer incidents, the concept of emergency quick response teams dedicated to computer emergencies can be traced back to one of the more notorious computer incidents of all time.

In November 1988, the infamous Internet Worm was unleashed, and it wreaked havoc by disabling a significant portion, by some estimates as much as 10 percent, of the Internet. As organization after organization attempted to deal with the worm, it quickly became apparent that a coordinated response to such incidents would have helped to lessen the impact and speed recovery. There was no central place to report or disseminate information about the attack. Internally, few organizations were equipped with teams dedicated to responding to such attacks. As a result, they wasted time and resources duplicating efforts to identify the source of the attack, to formulate countermeasures, and finally to eradicate the worm.

At that time, the most common response was simply to disconnect from the Internet. That same response would carry unacceptable losses of revenues, confidence, and performance for today's commercial enterprises. As more commercial organizations, government agencies, and individuals became dependent on Internet-connected systems, the criticality of the need for teams capable of responding to emergencies quickly and effectively increased.

The Internet Worm incident served to highlight the need for a coordinated response to widespread computer emergencies. As a result, the Software Engineering Institute, a federally funded research organization located at Pittsburgh's Carnegie Mellon University, established the CERT Coordination Center (CERT/CC) under the direction of the Defense Advanced Research Projects Agency. The role of the CERT/CC was to coordinate communication among organizations during computer emergencies. Their role has since expanded dramatically to include, among other things, assisting with the establishment of other CERT teams, acting as a clearinghouse for threat and vulnerability data, and providing training and education programs relating to security incident handling. Many entities, both public and private, have since that time adopted CERT's incident-handling procedures.

Although coordinating and sharing information provides immeasurable benefits, many organizations also have come to realize that they require dedicated internal response capabilities to deal with specific emergencies, threats, attacks, and similar situations.

40.1.4   Types of Teams.   The exact composition of a CERT depends on a number of factors, such as the size, type, complexity, budget, and location of its founder. Some organizations might be able to justify and support a full-time, dedicated, in-house CERT with the very latest technology and training. Others might improvise teams once an incident occurs, or they might even hire outside expertise to handle computer emergencies on their behalf. Still others might use a combination of these approaches by having a core emergency quick response staff that can be augmented by other people as needed to manage incidents.

One viable alternative to developing in-house quick response teams is to take advantage of outsourced services in this area. Outsourced incident handling services are becoming increasingly popular, and many security companies offer them to their customers. In some cases, this might be the most practical option for companies that lack the resources or desire to develop in-house response capabilities. Outsourcing computer emergency quick response efforts can be an effective, albeit somewhat costly, alternative to developing in-house response teams, for both short- and long-term incident handling.

However, for many organizations, establishing their own incident response capabilities can provide significant advantages. Internal teams generally know the organization and understand its goals, issues, and requirements. Outsourced responses are often mechanical and standardized. Vendors can take longer to respond since they are normally located off site and might even be a considerable distance away. Vendors may undergo frequent staff turnover, which can mean that those assigned to respond to incidents at an organization might be unfamiliar with that organization or its mission. As a result, outsiders might require precious time to "ramp up" before effectively dealing with the current incident or situation. The connected nature of today's organizations and modern monitoring technologies may make up for distance in some ways, but there is no substitute for an expert on site.

Some organizations are fortunate enough to have implemented formal, standing CERTs whose members are dedicated primarily to monitoring systems, preventing intrusions, and responding to computer emergency incidents. These teams are superior to ad hoc or outsourced teams in their ability to respond quickly with customized procedures acting from a deep and current knowledge base.

40.2   PLANNING THE TEAM.   Establishing a CERT is a complex process that must be given careful thought and be based on comprehensive planning. Before establishing a CERT, the organization needs to plan exactly what it expects to accomplish. From this, the organization can decide on specific goals for the team, and perhaps most important, it can decide on policies that apply to the team. The team should be conceived and defined in terms of the organization to which it belongs. That is, the team should be tailored to achieving a specific mission. Clarity, vision, and focus are vital planning elements that ultimately will determine the success or failure of the CERT. Skimping during the planning stage will ensure failure. Devoting some extra effort to planning in this stage will help assure success.

40.2.1   Mission and Charter.   A clear, written mission and charter establishing the CERT is essential to its success. These documents should establish why the team exists and what the organization expects from the team at a high level. Although the current security landscape provides compelling reasons for establishing an incident response capability, identifying organization-specific goals and expectations for the team remains an essential task.

Effective policies are essential for any organization. The CERT's mission and charter should be based on organizational policies, especially information security policies. Establishing a team without having appropriate policies in place is ineffective and can put the team at odds with its own organization. Without formal policies upon which to base computer emergency response activities, the team can have no legitimate basis for deciding on courses of action that support the organization. During an incident, CERT decisions can be unpopular. Disconnecting systems from the Internet could prevent some, or perhaps all, of the organization from carrying out its mission. Without established policies both to define and to defend those decisions, often the team is viewed as an adversary.

Without this clear definition of mission and an idea of what can be expected from the CERT, internal cooperation and support for the team will be difficult to obtain and even more difficult to sustain. Without internal cooperation, the team's effectiveness will be diminished, which could exacerbate the impact of an incident or prevent the team from handling an incident in a timely manner.

The overarching goal of responding to an incident should always be to prevent further damage and to restore systems and operations to normal as expeditiously as possible, consistent with organizational policies. Without a clear idea of what the organization expects the team to accomplish, the team is likely to waste the limited time and resources it has available.

40.2.2   Interaction with Outside Agencies/Others.   No CERT can operate in a vacuum in an interconnected world. At some point, teams and their sponsors will require interaction with outside agencies and even with other emergency quick response teams. Rather than wait until an emergency is under way, the team should establish and document contacts such as:

- Internal
  - *Management.* The team should establish and maintain management contacts who hold sufficient authority to make the inevitably tough business decisions that will arise during an emergency situation.
  - *Systems.* The CIRT should have a working relationship with those responsible for operating and maintaining the organizations information systems. These contacts will be necessary to allow CIRT members appropriate system access during an emergency response situation.
  - *Applications.* As with systems personnel, the CIRT should have pre-established contact with those who manage and maintain applications. These individuals will be able to provide CIRT members with access to application logs, documentation, and access accounts during an emergency.
  - *Business units.* CIRT members should be familiar with and have established contacts with the various organizational business units they support. Having such contacts ahead of time will facilitate decision making and will avoid delays in gaining access to appropriate business personnel during an emergency.
- External
  - *CERT/CC.* The CERT/CC can provide valuable advice and assistance to the reponse team during an attack. Knowing who to contact and how to reach them before an emergency will speed the process.
  - *Consultants.* Often, organizations will rely on various outside consultants to augment technical skills and knowledge. Therefore, it is important that the organization be able to contact these consultants during an emergency in the event their expertise is required to resolve or respond to a situation. Planning for such emergency contact ahead of time will avoid delays in responding to an emergency.
  - *Vendors.* Responding to an emergency may require specialized information about hardware or software features and specifications that might only be available from a vendor. Additionally, backup systems or software may need to be acquired in order to return systems to operational status during or after an incident.
  - *Law enforcement.* Law enforcement agencies today frequently have specialized units capable of assisting an organization in tracing and identifying the perpetrator of an attack. However, it is important that law enforcement contacts be made in advance so that the organization can make sound decisions about who to notify and how best to use such assistance.
  - *Utilities.* Electrical power and similar infrastructure services are essential to any organization. Power outages and similar emergencies can have a devastating effect on operations. Maintaining contact with local utilities will help the organization plan for and mitigate impact from power outages. In the event of an outage, team members will know who to contact and can gather information about the cause and duration of an outage more quickly.
  - *Internet service providers (ISPs).* Typically, vital connectivity is provided to the organization by one or more Internet service providers. In many cases, Internet

service provides are the first line of defense against some types of Internet-originated attacks such as distributed denial of service attacks. In addition, if an organization is attempting to track a suspected intruder, the Internet service provider will be pivotal. It is therefore vitally important that the CIRT have pre-established contacts within the organization's Internet service provider in order to avoid wasting precious response time trying to get assistance during an emergency.

○ *Other incident response teams.* With few exceptions, there is little doubt that other incident response teams have faced the situation or emergency your team might be facing at any given time. Other incident response teams can provide advice and assistance, and some may even share resources and expertise to help an organization respond to an emergency. There is also an opportunity to share knowledge and conduct joint training with other teams.

40.2.3   Establish Baselines.   In order to be able to effectively spot that which is out of the ordinary, the CERT must determine what "normal" looks like. False incidents have occurred because the observer did not have adequate knowledge to realize that the event was actually normal. Emergency response teams called into action without well-documented baselines or detailed activity logs must work very hard to determine whether the event is normal.

In either case, whether the triggering event turns out to be false or genuine, resources and time will have been wasted by this identification effort. A good baseline can reduce the resources expended on false positives and hasten the response to real events.

40.3   SELECTING AND BUILDING THE TEAM.   An effective CERT is characterized by the following elements, dictated by the incident at hand:

- People
- Skills
- Knowledge
- Equipment
- Access
- Authority

The makeup of the team has everything to do with how effective and responsive it will be in an emergency. Careful selection of team members at the outset will provide for an effective, cohesive group with the right skills, authority, and knowledge to properly deal with a range of known and unknown incidents.

The first inclination, frequently, is to select the most technically knowledgeable individuals available as members of the team. While technical ability is essential to a CERT, this should not be the overriding characteristic. Given aptitude and motivation, appropriate technical skills can be learned. Indeed, during the course of an incident handling situation, an adept handler can draw on the technical expertise of people, either internal or outside, to augment his or her skills and knowledge.

Maturity and the ability to work long hours under stress and intense pressure are crucial characteristics. Integrity in the response team members must be absolute, since these people will have access and authority exceeding that given them in normal operations.

Exceptional communications skills are required because, in an emergency, quick and accurate communications are needed. Inaccurate communications can cause the emergency to appear more serious than it is and therefore escalate a minor event into a crisis.

40.4   TRAINING.   Teams that have no experience responding to incidents are of little value to an organization. Predictably, computer emergency responses by untrained or inexperienced teams result in loss or destruction of evidence, legal exposure by failing to properly protect individual rights, and failure to properly document and learn from the experience. To be most effective, training must be iterative (learn, exercise, review, analyze, repeat) and should involve as many realistic scenarios as possible so that the CERT becomes exposed to a wide variety of potential emergency situations.

40.4.1   Involve Legal Staff.   As with any crisis event, every action carries with it a potential legal implication. This is especially true in a situation were an evidentiary chain may be required. Even if evidence is not a primary concern, due diligence requires that accurate records be kept of the incident costs, including response team costs, and of the scope of compromise and effect.

The corporate legal staff must play an important role in developing response team procedures, in training the response team, and in crisis resolution.

40.4.2   Rehearse Often.   Experience can be gained only by responding to incidents or through training with simulated attacks. While the time and resources required to practice responding to incidents might be costly, more costly still is the potential damage resulting from an uncontained or poorly handled breach of the system.

An excellent opportunity to practice response procedures and to develop response teams occurs during periodic security assessments, including penetration testing. Penetration tests simulate external and internal attacks on a system and offer a real, yet controlled, environment in which to exercise, train, and evaluate a CERT. The simulation is especially effective when an outside, independent team is engaged to conduct the penetration test and security assessment. With proper coordination, the test can provide an opportunity for the team to observe and react to many different types of incidents.

40.4.3   Perform Training Reviews.   At the conclusion of any training exercise, it is important to reassemble the team as soon as possible not only to review management's view of their performance but to reveal their own perspectives as well. Each of the participants should be asked what went right and what went wrong. Were necessary resources (information, decision makers, tools, software, equipment) unavailable when the team needed them? Did the team have, or was it able to obtain in a timely manner, the physical and system access it needed? Did it have the right documentation and access to other company personnel? Were systems for communicating among the team and with other company or external personnel adequate and efficient?

Video cameras are a useful tool for recording events during the training sessions; many employees will have such equipment available and can make inexpensive recordings that can be analyzed during the training reviews.

40.5   RESPONDING TO COMPUTER EMERGENCIES.   While a complete treatment of incident response procedures is beyond the scope of this chapter, some general response steps and considerations are applicable to all incident-handling teams.

(See Chapters 42 and 43 for more on the topic of planning for and recovering from disasters.)

The primary consideration in responding to any emergency situation must be given to preventing loss of human life. Following that, a comprehensive information security program will have included the identification and classification of the most sensitive data and systems. This classification should provide a clear prioritization of what should be protected first in the event of an emergency. For example, a business's survival might depend on the confidentiality and integrity of some intellectual property, such as engineering diagrams. After the safety of personnel, those drawings and the systems on which they are stored would be the obvious first priority for protection. Keeping that in mind, a network intrusion that threatened an e-mail server located on a separate network segment would likely not immediately warrant disconnecting the entire network from the Internet. On the other hand, if the particular server containing the company's engineering drawings, or the network segment on which it sits, were under direct attack, an appropriate first response might well be to disconnect from the Internet.

In any case, there must be an unambiguous sense among the CERT that those responsible for taking actions in good faith will not suffer reprisals as a result of taking those actions. For example, based on facts in evidence at one time or another, a member of the team might decide to disconnect an operational system from the Internet because it appears to be under attack or to have been compromised. Should this turn out to be a false alarm of some sort, the individual authorizing the action should suffer no reprisal or sanction by taking what he or she believed was a legitimate action to stop or to respond to an attack.

40.5.1 Tailored Responses.   With appropriate plans in place before incidents happen, recovery can be effected much more quickly and with less residual damage.

Appropriate responses depend on the particular systems involved, and should be documented and agreed to before those systems are connected to the Internet. If a router or firewall protecting the outer perimeter of the network becomes compromised, it may be necessary to disconnect the entire system in order to contain the situation.

On the other hand, if a Web server in an isolated part of the network becomes compromised, disconnecting only that system should be sufficient. However, any business-related activities carried out using that server might no longer be available. A loss of revenue or image might result from disconnecting the server. Business units and others that depend on these systems must be made aware of, and must agree to accept, the impact of proposed responses the CERT might take during an incident.

Planned responses, combined with the authority and confidence to execute them, can save the organization both time and money. As an example, if every incident requires the presence of senior business managers or executives, those leaders must be taken away from their normal duties during rehearsals and during actual events. On the other hand, if the CERT leader on duty or on call finds the incident to be routine, and if the incident has been well planned for, a simple notification of the facts can be sent to appropriate senior-level personnel, leaving them free to attend to their normal duties and to participate only in a major event at their appropriate level of management.

Planned, preapproved responses can speed reaction times, enhance security, and lessen impact of a given breach or incident. In most cases, the CERT leader will follow a series of common-sense steps to handle an incident from identification through resolution. As the leader progresses through each step, he or she may choose from one of the pre-approved responses to handle the incident, or the situation may require the involvement of other people and resources for resolution. In either case, the basic flow of events should be similar to the following.

40.5.1.1   Step 1: Observe and Evaluate.   A response team leader must assess the situation as quickly as possible, based on available information. The leader should make a preliminary estimate of the type of incident, its scope, the people involved, the data or systems affected, and then begin formulating first responses. This is the point at which the team leader or other responsible person orders a move from a state of standby monitoring to one of active monitoring, focused on the particular event or events. It is important to maintain standby and baseline monitoring activities during an actual incident because the obvious event might well be a ruse designed to divert attention from a more serious attack.

If proper planning has taken place, the team leader usually will be able to direct a specific course of action in response to a particular incident. The leader can choose from a menu of planned responses while drawing on only those resources necessary to execute that particular response. Doing this minimizes the impact on staff at all levels and allows the incident to be dealt with efficiently and effectively. However, the more unique or complex the situation, the more likely it is that a complete team response may be required.

Responses, the players involved, and the audience are obviously different when considering a data-center type situation as opposed to a user-reported situation. Often, formal handling procedures are preestablished for data centers that generally are staffed by more technical personnel. The CERT can expect a higher level of response from data center personnel and will likely be able to communicate instructions more concisely and with more assured compliance.

Dealing with individual users, on the other hand, requires a greater degree of sensitivity and understanding. In most cases, the CERT will be moving quickly and enthusiastically when handling an incident, since this is what the team has trained so long and hard to do. Individual users often are stressed or bewildered when confronted by a computer emergency incident serious enough to warrant a response team. In these situations, users tend to be nervous rather than excited or confident. This can cause communication problems, especially when a team member converses with them over a phone. Instructions become garbled or may not be carried out exactly as desired.

Team members must be trained to communicate clearly and calmly when dealing with individual users who may not have exceptionally well-developed technical skills. This is especially important when giving end users instructions over the phone or via some remote means. A calm, careful conversation will lessen the amount of stress the individual feels, while helping to ensure that the CERT member's instructions are carried out properly. Proper compliance with instructions can make or break an incident investigation, especially when forensic issues are to be considered, as in the case of known or suspected criminal activity. Failure to properly maintain the state of an attacked system can thwart any subsequent attempt at a successful prosecution.

40.5.1.2   Step 2: Begin Notification.   Once the team leader establishes that an incident is in fact in progress, notification must begin to appropriate individuals within the organization, consistent with the type of situation. Notification and timing should be carried out, whenever possible, according to existing plans.

In some cases, the CERT leader might be able to identify the incident as one calling for a prearranged response. The leader, having the authority and confidence to carry out such a pre-approved response, will notify those appropriate to the incident and carry out the contemplated actions. In other cases, the situation might not be so clear, and the notification process might include additional personnel with authority to decide on various courses of action.

40.5.1.3   Step 3: Set Up Communications.   Team members, especially when dealing with remote or multiple sites, must be able to communicate easily and securely with one another as well as with management representatives. Team members need to be able to communicate data, status updates, actions, responses, and similar events. Communications should flow securely to the designated CERT leader for coordination. The team leader must be able to direct and advise other team members, but the potentially sensitive nature of an incident may require that these communications be handled out of band and through secure means. Out of band in this case refers to communication methods that are neither part of nor connected to the system believed to be under attack. For example, in communications regarding an attack, the use of unencrypted e-mail means that might be intercepted by an attacker, or by other unauthorized parties, should be avoided whenever possible.

40.5.1.4   Step 4: Contain.   The CERT's next course of action is to contain the incident. The goal is to limit the scope of any compromise as much as possible, by isolating the system under attack from other systems to prevent the problem, attack, or intrusion from spreading. Containment might involve steps such as disconnecting systems from the Internet. However, doing so might limit the organization's ability to catch an intruder who is currently active on the system. The priority level assigned to intruder identification and prosecution is a part of the mission and charter of the team, modified by the specific action plans in use for a particular incident.

40.5.1.5   Step 5: Identify.   Once the team has taken steps to contain the incident as much as possible, it should focus on identifying exactly what happened, why it happened, how it happened, and then identifying steps that can be taken to prevent a recurrence. This effort also might involve identifying who, if anyone, was or still is involved in the incident or attack.

40.5.1.6   Step 6: Record.   All CERTs should be trained to document everything during an incident. No event or detail is too small to record when responding to computer emergencies. Always try to answer "Who? What? Where? How? When? Why?" This is especially true when dealing with criminal activity when there is an expectation that the intruder will be prosecuted. Keeping accurate records of what happened and the team's actions can prove pivotal in the organization's ability to positively identify the cause or source of an incident and prevent similar incidents in the future.

In the case of criminal activity with an expectation of prosecution, a legal representative should be kept informed so that appropriate forensic measures may be ordered at appropriate times.

40.5.1.7   Step 7: Return to Operations.   For most business managers and executives, restoring operations is of paramount importance. Frequently they will pressure the EDP people and the CERT to put off all other activities and to direct all resources to that end. Except in extreme cases, that pressure should be resisted, and the orderly carrying out of all preceding steps must be assured. As soon as possible, the CERT should assist operations personnel with bringing systems back online and returning them to full operating capacity. In some cases, hard drives, logs, and even entire systems may need to remain off-line until detailed forensics examinations may be completed. In these situations, backup systems should be used to bring systems and operating capabilities back online.

40.5.1.8 *Step 8: Document and Review.*   While all CERT members should keep careful notes at all times, it is important to remember that formal procedures to document incidents and resulting actions is vital to the overall success of the incident response effort. This documentation can form the basis for new approaches, procedures, policies, awareness programs, and similar changes. Documenting successes and failures can provide the organization with a realistic view of its security posture and of its capability to respond to emergencies, and in some cases can justify the expenditure of additional funds on training or technology. This effort also ensures that the data captured can be used by the CERT to learn and to sharpen their skills.

40.5.2 Involving Law Enforcement.   The decision to involve law enforcement, or even when to involve law enforcement, in an incident response is one that must be given careful consideration. While most organizations recognize the benefit of a close relationship with law enforcement, involving such agencies when responding to a computer emergency can have consequences beyond those that are immediately evident.

Clearly, local and national law enforcement agencies have a great deal to offer when establishing CERTs and developing incident handling capabilities. It is not uncommon these days to find that many law enforcement agencies have specialized units dedicated to computer crimes and issues. They can be a valuable resource, likely to have a wealth of threat data on hand. For this reason, it is important to partner with appropriate agencies to take advantage of their experience and to establish relationships. Knowing whom to contact in an emergency not only will save time and frustration but may mean the difference between merely repelling an attack or catching and successfully prosecuting the perpetrator, which could help prevent future attacks.

Obviously, local laws and statutes may dictate specific notification requirements that an organization is obliged to follow in the event an actual or suspected incident occurs. Careful review of local laws, statutes, and ordinances should be undertaken to ensure the organization complies with notification requirements and other legal requirements.

When there is a choice to be made, the organization must weigh carefully the decision to involve law enforcement, and especially the question of when to do so. In most cases, formally involving law enforcement means that the organization may have to turn control of the incident and subsequent investigation over to the agency whose jurisdiction it is to investigate the crime.

While most professional law enforcement agencies will work with an organization to minimize any adverse impact on normal operations, this may not always be feasible. Because the goals of law enforcement often are different from those of others, especially of commercial enterprises, law enforcement agencies may not consider the impact of their response on the organization under attack.

Since law enforcement's mission is to investigate criminal activity, its focus will naturally be on identifying, tracking, and locating the intruder. This can, in some cases, result in seizure and removal for forensic purposes of systems and data, even systems that may be critical to the continued operation of the organization. In the case of a business, this might well mean loss of necessary servers or workstations while an investigation is under way, with a possibly devastating effect.

Indeed, decisions about a preferred response may be taken out of the hands of managers and executives when law enforcement enters into an incident response situation. A commercial business might focus on identifying the vulnerability that made the attack possible, protecting against that vulnerability, and restoring systems to full operating capability. If, during the course of these efforts, the perpetrator can be identified, law enforcement will be informed, but such identification is rarely the overriding objective of the business. On the other hand, for law enforcement, identification and prosecution of the perpetrator is the primary objective. Establishing contact with appropriate law enforcement agencies before the organization is forced to respond to an incident will help the CERT plan when to notify law enforcement and how most effectively to align both sets of objectives when dealing with an incident.

40.5.3 Need to Know. Protecting information about an incident in progress is essential, not only to a successful response but because it can have serious legal, privacy, and other ramifications as well. Those charged with handling an incident must use out-of-band communications, such as cellular telephones, pagers, and encrypted e-mail systems not connected to the system under attack to ensure that knowledge of the incident is restricted to those who need to know about it. Attackers could intercept team communications, if passed through in-band or normal channels, and use that information to cover their tracks or even to prolong an incident.

Responding to incidents always involves gathering information about systems, users, activities, and events. In most cases, sensitive system and even personal information may be collected. Members of the team frequently make assumptions about the identities of those responsible for the incident, during the course of their response and investigation. These assumptions are based on data that is continually being collected, refined, modified, and frequently changed during the course of an emergency response. Should an unproven or interim assumption that a particular individual was involved in the incident be made public, that individual's reputation might become needlessly tarnished, and the organization might well find itself facing legal proceedings as a result.

It is therefore essential that the CERT disseminate information about the incident according to a strict need-to-know policy. Limiting knowledge about an incident will help ensure that sensitive information remains in the hands of those who need it to perform their duties.

40.5.4 Management Role. Management plays a key role in the formation, operation, and support of a CERT. Ideally teams should be composed not only of technical personnel but of managers with sufficient authority to assist the team in taking actions that contain an incident and protect data and systems from further compromise. Outside of incident handling, management support for planning, establishing and enforcing policies, and preauthorizing responses is essential. More important, perhaps, is management support of the CERT. Without solid backing from the highest levels of management, the CERT will be frustrated in its attempts to carry out its mission.

40.5.5 Public Affairs. The nature of interconnected systems today all but guarantees that any incident will become obvious to partners, customers, clients, and others. In many cases, the organization will be compelled to advise its constituents continuously of the status of any outage or degradation of services resulting from an incident and the reasons behind it. Therefore, it is crucial that information released for general consumption be properly screened and cleared prior to release. It is equally important that such information be released through a single source, such as the public affairs office. Restricting release of incident-related information through the public affairs office or other designated point will help ensure that frequent, straightforward communication with stakeholders can take place while at the same time controlling rumors and misinformation. This simple step can do much to lessen anxiety about an incident and to reassure members, partners, and customers that the situation is well in hand and will be resolved.

40.5.6   Forensic Awareness.   Depending on the specific incident, the organization may desire not only to control the incident but to trace and prosecute the perpetrators in the case of known or suspected criminal activity. It is therefore highly advisable that members of the CERT receive thorough training in procedures for collecting and preserving evidence. Mishandling of evidence can result in an inability to take successful legal action against an attacker or to recover damages following an incident. Computer forensics and evidence handling should be high on the CERT's list of training topics. Chapters 2 and 34 of this volume contain additional material on computer forensics and working with law enforcement.

40.6   POSTINCIDENT ACTIVITIES.   The CERT's efforts do not end once the incident is resolved. Instead, the team should take a reasonable period to rest and recover. Then, while the details are still fresh in the team members' minds, they should examine the incident from start to finish, both formally and informally, asking questions such as "What happened? What went right? What went wrong?" This way, the team will learn from each incident and become more efficient and confident when handling new incidents in the future.

At the conclusion of each incident, the team should be assembled and a formal debriefing and review of the incident should be carried out. This debriefing should include a complete review of the team and its handling of the incident, including its adherence to policy and its technical performance. Each team member should be individually debriefed following the incident. Their recollections, thoughts, ideas, and reactions as to how the incident was handled and how the team performed should be documented and preserved. A management team might debrief members, team members might debrief each other, or they might even debrief themselves using a checklist or form. Regardless of the method, the CERT members themselves are the best source of data about the weaknesses and strengths of the team, and that data must be captured if the team is to improve and grow in skills and confidence.

Once individual impressions are captured, it is often effective to assemble the team as a group for an incident postmortem session. Starting from the beginning of the incident, the team should examine whether it had adequate, workable policies upon which to base its actions and decisions. The group should jointly evaluate each aspect of the team, its composition, skills, authority, and step-by-step handling of the incident. A list of lessons learned and action items for improvements should result from this review.

Data collected during this review process should form the basis for improving the team. This information provides input to what should be a continuous cycle involving planning, preparation, training, responding, and evaluating. Shortfalls in training, skills, equipment, access, policies, and authority will become evident through this process. These shortfalls can be corrected to improve the team's ability to respond effectively to incidents in the future.

CERTs are an effective organizational tool for responding to computer emergencies. However, to be effective, these teams must be carefully planned, built, trained, and supported. Proper planning and the establishment of a clear set of organizational objectives for the CERT are key to ensuring success. Teams that are well planned, well trained, confident, and that possess the authority and training to execute their stated mission ultimately can provide a real return on investment for an organization. This return often can be measured in terms of limiting the impact and cost, both tangible and intangible, of a computer emergency.

40.7   FURTHER READING

Brownlee, N., and E. Guttman. "Expectations for Computer Security Incident Response." RFC 2350 (1998): *www.cis.ohio-state.edu/htbin/rfc/rfc2350.html.*

CERT/CC. "Resources for Creating, Managing and Improving Your CSIRT" (2001): *www.cert.org/csirts,* included the following links (February 2002):

- "Avoiding the Trial-by-Fire Approach to Security Incidents": *http://interactive.sei.cmu.edu/Columns/Security_Matters/1999/March/Security.mar99.htm*
- "Computer Security Incident Handling: Step by Step": *www.sans.org/newlook/publications/incident_handling.htm*
- "The CSIRT Handbook": *www.sei.cmu.edu/publications/documents/98.reports/98hb001/98hb001abstract.html*
- "Expectations for Computer Security Incident Response" (RFC 2350): *www.ietf.org/rfc/rfc2350.txt*
- "Forming an Incident Response Team": *www.auscert.org.au/Information/Auscert_info/Papers/Forming_an_Incident_Response_Team.html*
- Forum of Incident Response and Security Teams: *www.first.org*
- "Incident Handling & Forensics": *www.sans.org/infosecFAQ/incident/incident_list.htm*
- "Model Security Policies": *www.sans.org/newlook/resources/policies/policies.htm*
- NIST Incident Handling Information and Publications: *csrc.nist.gov/topics/inchand.html*
- TERENA CSIRT Coordination Task Force (Europe): *www.terena.nl/task-forces/tf-csirt*
- "Site Security Handbook" (RFC 2196): *www.ietf.org/rfc/rfc2196.txt*

Stephenson, P. *Investigating Computer-Related Crime: A Handbook for Corporate Investigators.* Boca Raton, FL: Auerbach Publications, 1999.

CHAPTER 41

DATA BACKUPS AND ARCHIVES

M.E. Kabay

CONTENTS

41.1 INTRODUCTION. Nothing is perfect. Equipment breaks, people make mistakes, and data files become corrupted or disappear. Everyone, and every system, needs a well-thought-out backup policy. In addition to making backups, data processing personnel also must consider requirements for archival storage and retrieval of data copies. Backups also apply to personnel, equipment, and electrical power, but this chapter deals exclusively with data backups; for other applications of redundancy, see Chapters 15 and 31.

41.1.1   Definitions.   *Backups* are copies of data files or records. Normally, backups are stored on a different medium from the original data. In particular, a copy of a file on the same disk as the original is an acceptable backup only for a short time; the *.bak, *.bk!, *.wbk, and *.sav files created by programs such as word processors are examples of limited-use backups. However, even a copy on a separate disk loses value as a backup once the original file is modified, unless incremental or differential backups also are made. These terms are described in Section 41.3.2. Typically, backups are made on a schedule that balances the costs and inconvenience of the process with the probable cost of reconstituting data that were modified after each backup.

Deletion of an original working file converts the backup into an original. Those who do not understand this relationship mistakenly believe that once they have a backup, they can safely delete the original file. However, before original files are deleted, as when a disk volume is to be formatted, there must be double backups of all required data. Double backups will ensure continued operations should there be a storage or retrieval problem on any one backup medium.

This chapter uses the following abbreviations to denote data storage capacities:

- KB = kilobyte = 1,024 bytes (characters)
- MB = megabyte = 1,024 KB = 1,048,576 bytes
- GB = gigabyte = 1,024 MB = 1,073,741,824 bytes
- TB = terabyte = 1,024 GB = 1,099,511,627,776 bytes.

According to a 1998 proposal from the International Electrotechnical Commission (IEC), the preferred prefixes should be KiB for kibibytes, MiB for mebibytes, GiB for gibibytes, and TiB for tebibytes to distinguish them from the powers-of-10 notations using kilo (10^3), mega (10^6), giga (10^9), and tera (10^{12}), but this suggestion has not yet been widely accepted by the technical community.[1]

41.1.2   Need.   Backups are used for many purposes:

- First and foremost, to provide valid information in case of data corruption or data loss on the original media
- To satisfy legal requirements for access to storable data, as for audit purposes
- In forensic examination of data to recognize and characterize a crime, and to identify suspects
- For statistical purposes in research
- To satisfy requirements of due care and diligence in safeguarding corporate assets
- To meet unforeseen requirements

41.2   MAKING BACKUPS.   Because data change at different rates in different applications, backups may be useful when made at frequencies ranging from milliseconds to years.

41.2.1   Parallel Processing.   The ultimate backup strategy is to do everything twice at the same time. Computer systems such as Tandem and Stratus use redundant components at every level of processing; for example, they use arrays of processors, dual input/output (I/O) buses, multiple banks of random-access memory, and duplicate disk storage devices to permit immediate recovery should anything go awry. Redundant systems use sophisticated communications between processors to ensure identical results. If any computational components fail, processing can continue uninterrupted while the defective components are replaced.

41.2.2   Hierarchical Storage Systems.   Large computer systems with terabytes of data typically use a *hierarchical storage system* to place often-used data on fast, relatively expensive disks while migrating less-used data to less expensive, somewhat slower storage media such as magnetic tape. However, users need have no knowledge of, or involvement in, such migration; all files are listed by the file system and can be accessed without special commands. Because the tape cartridges are stored in dense cylindrical arrays, usually called *silos,* they may have total capacities in the hundreds of TB per silo, with fast-moving robotic arms that can locate and load the right tape within seconds. Users may experience a brief delay of a few seconds as data are copied from tape cartridges back onto hard disks, but otherwise there is no problem for the users. This system provides a degree of backup simply because data are not erased from tape when they are copied to disk, nor are data removed from disk when they are appended to tape; this data remanence provides a degree of temporary backup because of the duplication of data.

41.2.3   Disk Mirroring.   There are several methods for duplicating disk operations so that disk failures cause limited or no damage to critical data.

41.2.3.1   RAID.   Redundant arrays of inexpensive (or independent) disks (RAID) were described in the late 1980s and have become a practical approach to providing fault-tolerant mass storage. The falling price of disk storage (1 MB of hard disk cost about \$200 in 1980 versus about \$0.02 in 2001) has allowed inexpensive disks to be combined into highly reliable units that contain different levels of redundancy among the components, for applications with increasing requirements for full-time availability. The disk architecture involves special measures for ensuring that every sector of the disk can be checked for validity at every input and output operation. If the primary copy of a file shows data corruption, the secondary file is used and the system automatically makes corrections to resynchronize the primary file. From the user's point of view, there is no interruption in I/O and no error.

41.2.3.2   Workstation and Personal Computer Mirroring.   Software solutions also can provide automatic copying of data onto separate disks.

- SureSync software can mirror files on Windows NT and Windows 2000.
- UnixWare Optional Services include Disk Mirroring software for SCO Unix.
- McAfee's Safe & Sound product, among others, allows personal computer (PC) users to duplicate specific files, folders, and volumes onto separate disks in real time.

Early users of software-based disk mirroring suffered from slower responses when updating their primary files because the system had to complete output operations to the mirror file before releasing the application for further activity. However, today's software uses part of system memory as a buffer to prevent performance degradation. Secondary (mirror) files are nonetheless rarely more than a few milliseconds behind the current status of the primary file.

41.2.4   Logging.   If real-time access to perfect data is not essential, a well-established approach to high-availability backups is to keep a log file of all changes to critical files. *Roll-forward* recovery requires:

- Backups that are synchronized with log files to provide an agreed-upon starting point
- Markers in the log files to indicate completed sequences of operations (called *transactions*) that can be recovered
- Recovery software that can read the log files and re-do all the changes to the data, leaving out incomplete transactions.

An alternative to roll-forward recovery is *roll-backward* recovery, in which diagnostic software scans log files and identifies only the incomplete transactions and then returns the data files to a *consistent state*.

For a detailed discussion of logging, see Chapter 38.

41.2.5   Backup Software.   All operating systems have utilities for making backups. However, sometimes the utilities that are included with the installation sets are limited in functionality; for example, they may not provide the full flexibility required to produce backups on different kinds of removable media. Generally, manufacturers of removable media include specialized backup software suitable for use with their own products.

When evaluating backup software, users will want to check for the following minimum requirements:

- The software should allow complete control over which files are backed up. Users should be able to obtain a report on exactly which files were successfully backed up and detailed explanations of why certain files could not be backed up.
- Data compression should be available.
- Backups must be able to span multiple volumes of removable media; a backup must not be limited to the space available on a single volume.
- If free space is available, it should be possible to put more than one backup on a single volume.
- The backup software must be able to verify the readability of all backups as part of the backup process.
- It should not be easy to create backup volumes that have the same name.
- The *restore* function should allow selective retrieval of individual files and folders or directories.
- The destination of restored data should be controllable by the user.
- During the restore process, the user should be able to determine whether to overwrite files that are currently in place; the overwriting should be controllable both with file-by-file confirmation dialogs and globally, *without* further dialog.
- Restore operations should be configurable to respect the read-only attribute on files or to override that attribute globally or selectively.

41.2.6   Removable Media.   The density of data storage on removable media has increased thousands of times in the last quarter century. For example, in the 1970s, an eight-inch word-processing diskette could store up to 128 KB. In contrast, at the time of writing (January 2002), a removable disk cartridge three inches in diameter stored 20 GB, provided data transfer rates of 15 MB per second, and cost around $100. Moore's Law states that computer equipment power and capacity doubles every 12 to 18 months for a given cost; this relationship definitely applies to mass storage and backup media.

41.2.6.1   Diskettes.   Because of the growing size of application files (e.g., an empty document created with MS-Word 2000 can take 24 KB or 1.6 percent of a 1.44 MB 3.5-inch diskette), old-style diskettes are no longer practical for any but the simplest manual backups. In addition, floppy disk drives are so slow that users revolt against requirements to do backups using this medium.

The modern equivalents of floppy disks are in fact hard disks, but they are almost the same size as 3.5-inch floppy disks despite carrying hundreds or thousands of times more data. For example, IOMEGA Corporation[2] is the leading provider of the widely used ZIP diskette-like storage media with 100 MB and 250 MB capacities. Many PCs and servers include ZIP drives as well as or instead of 3.5-inch floppy drives. In addition, add-on drives are available as portable or in-system units with a variety of interfaces: SCSI, parallel port, and USB.

41.2.6.2   Large-Capacity Hard Disk Cartridges.   IOMEGA also makes JAZ drives in 1 GB and 2 GB capacities. Its Peerless units provide cartridges of 10 GB or 20 GB and drives with a high-speed Firewire interface. Its DataSafe product, intended for servers, has capacities of 160 GB or 320 GB per unit.

41.2.6.3   Optical Storage.   Many systems now use optical storage for backups. Compact-Disk Read-Write (CD-RW) disks are the most widely used format; each disk can hold approximately 700 MB of data and costs only a few dollars. Internal read/write drives cost about one hundred dollars in 2002. In addition, large numbers of CDs are easily handled using "jukeboxes" that apply robotics to access specific disks, from collections of hundreds or thousands, on demand.

41.2.6.4   Tape Cartridge Systems.   The old nine-track, reel-to-reel 6,250 bytes-per-inch (bpi) systems used in the 1970s and 1980s held several hundred MB. Today's pocket-size tape cartridges hold gigabytes. For example, the industry leader in this field, StorageTek,[3] makes individual tape drives with uncompressed capacities of 20 GB, 60 GB, and 110 GB; compression typically doubles, triples, or quadruples these capacities, depending on the nature of the data. Data seek can take 40 seconds; data transfer rates for such systems are typically in the range of 10 to 15 MB per second. Cartridges have mean-time-between-failure (MTBF) of 250,000 hours with 100 percent duty cycles and can tolerate 1 million tape passes. All such systems have streaming I/O using about 10 MB of random-access memory (RAM) buffer to prevent interruption of the read/write operations from and to the tapes and thus keep the tape moving smoothly to maximize data transfer rates.

In conjunction with automated tape library systems holding many cartridges and capable of switching automatically to the next cartridge, tape cartridge systems are ideal for backing up servers and mainframes with TB of data. Small library systems keep 10 to 20 cartridges in position for immediate access, taking approximately nine seconds for an exchange. These libraries have approximately 2 million mean exchanges between failures, with MTBF of around 360,000 hours at 100 percent duty cycle.

The largest library systems—for example, the StorageTek L700—can have up to 678 cartridges loaded at once, up to 20 drives for concurrent access, and total capacities of up to 149 TB with compression. Total throughput can exceed 2 TB per hour.

41.2.7   Labeling.   Regardless of the size of a backup, every storage device, from diskettes to tape cartridges, should be clearly and unambiguously tagged, both electronically and with adhesive labels. Diskettes or removable hard disks used on Windows systems, for example, can be labeled electronically with up to 11 letters, numbers, or the underscore character. Larger-capacity media, such as cartridges used for Unix and mainframe systems, have extensive electronic labeling available. On some systems, it is possible to request specific storage media and have the system automatically refuse the wrong media if they are mounted in error. Tape library systems typically use optical bar codes that are generated automatically by the backup software and then affixed to each cartridge for unique identification. Magnetic tapes and cartridges have electronic labels written onto the start of each unit, with specifics that are particular to the operating system and tape-handling software.

An unlabeled storage medium or one with a flimsily attached label is evidence of a bad practice that will lead to confusion and error. Sticky notes, for example, are not a good way to label diskettes and removable disks. If the notes are taken off, they can get lost; if they are left on, they can jam the disk drives. There are many types of labels for storage media, including printable sheets suitable for laser or inkjet printers and using adhesive that allows removal of the labels without leaving a sticky residue. At the very least, an exterior label should include the following information:

- Date the volume was created (e.g., "2001–09–08")

- Originator (e.g., "Bob R. Jones, Accounting Dept")

- Description of the contents (e.g., "Engineering Accounting Data for 2000")

- Application program (e.g., "Quicken v2002")

- Operating system (e.g., Windows 98)

Storing files with *canonical names* (names with a fixed structure) on the media themselves is also useful. An example of a canonical file much used on installation disks is "READ.ME." An organization can mandate the following files as minimum standards for its storage media:

- ORIGIN.mmm (where *mmm* represents a sequence number for unique identification of the storage set) indicating the originating system (e.g., "Accounting Workstation number 3875-3")

- DATE.mmm showing the date (preferably in year-month-day sequence) on which the storage volume was created; e.g., "2001 – 09 – 08"

- SET.mmm to describe exactly which volumes are part of a particular set; contents could include "SET 123; VOL 444, VOL 445, VOL 446"

- INDEX.mmm, an index file listing all the files on all the volumes of that particular storage set; e.g., "SET 123; VOL 444 FIL F1, F2; VOL 445 FIL F3, F4; VOL 446 FIL F5"

- VOLUME.nnn (where *nnn* represents a sequence number for unique identification of the medium) that contains an explanation such as "VOL 444 SET 123 NUMBER 1 OF 3"

- FILES.nnn, which lists all the files on that particular volume of that particular storage set; for example, contents could include "SET 123, VOL 444, Files F1, F2, F3"

Such labeling is best handled by an application program; many backup programs automatically generate similar files.

41.2.8 Indexing. As implied earlier, backup volumes need a mechanism for identifying the data stored on each medium. Equally important is the capacity to locate the storage media where particular files are stored; otherwise, one would have to search serially through multiple media to locate specific data. Although not all backup products for personal computers include such functionality, many do; server and mainframe utilities routinely include automatic indexing and retrieval. These systems allow the user to specify file names and dates, using wild-card characters to signify ranges and also to display a menu of options from which the user can select the appropriate files for recovery.

41.3 BACKUP STRATEGIES. There are different approaches to backing up data. This section looks at what kinds of data can be backed up and then reviews appropriate ways of choosing and managing backups for different kinds of computer systems.

41.3.1 Exclusive Access. All backup systems have trouble with files that are currently in use by processes that have opened them with write access (i.e., which may be adding or changing data within the files). The danger in copying such files is that they may be in an *inconsistent state* when the backup software copies their data. For example, a multiphase transaction may have updated some records in a detail file, but the corresponding master records may not yet have been posted to disk. Copying the data before the transaction completes will store a corrupt version of the files and lead to problems when they are later restored to disk.

Backup software usually generates a list of everything backed up and of all the files *not* backed up; for the latter, there is usually an explanation or a code showing the reason for the failure. Operators always must verify that all required files have been backed up and must take corrective action if files have been omitted.

Some high-speed, high-capacity backup software packages provide a buffer mechanism to allow high-availability systems to continue processing while backups are in progress. In these systems, files are frozen in a consistent state so that backup can proceed, and all changes are stored in buffers on disk for later entry into the production databases. However, even this approach cannot obviate the need for a minimum period of quiescence so that the databases can reach a consistent state. In addition, it is impossible for full functionality to continue if changes are being held back from the databases until a backup is complete; all *dependent* transactions (those depending on the previously changed values of records) also must be held up until the files are unlocked.

41.3.2 Types of Backups. Backups can include different amounts and kinds of data:

- *Full* backups store a copy of everything that resides on the mass storage of a specific system. To restore a group of files from a full backup, the operator mounts the appropriate volume of the backup set and restores the files in a single operation.

- *Differential* backups store all the data that have changed since a specific date or event; typically, a differential backup stores everything that has changed since the last full backup. The number of volumes of differential backups can increase with each additional backup. To restore a group of files from a differential backup, the operator needs to locate the latest differential set and also the full backup upon which it is based to ensure that all files are restored.

- *Incremental* backups are a more limited type of differential backup that typically store everything that has changed since the previous full or incremental backup. As long as multiple backup sets can be put on a single volume, the incremental backup requires fewer volumes than a normal differential backup for a given period. To restore a set of files from incremental backups, the operator may have to mount volumes from all the incremental sets plus the full backup upon which they are based.

- *Delta* backups store only the portions of files that have been modified since the last full or delta backup; delta backups are a rarely used type, more akin to logging than to normal backups. Delta backups use the fewest backup volumes of all the methods listed; however, to restore data using delta backups, the operator must use special-purpose application programs and mount volumes from all the delta sets plus the full backup upon which they are based.

Another aspect of backups is whether they include all the data on a system or only the data particular to specific application programs or groups of users:

- *System* backups copy everything on a system.
- *Application* backups copy the data needed to restore operations for particular software systems.

In addition to these terms, operators and users often refer to *daily* and *partial* backups. These terms are ambiguous and should be defined in writing when setting up procedures.

41.3.3   Computer Systems.   Systems with different characteristics and purposes can require different backup strategies. This section looks at large production systems (mainframes), smaller computers used for distributed processing (servers), individual computers used primarily by one user (workstations), and portable or handheld computers (*laptops* and *personal digital assistants,* often called *PDAs*).

41.3.3.1   Mainframes.   Large production systems using mainframes or networks of servers routinely do full system backups every day because of the importance of rapid recovery in case of data loss (see Chapters 42 and 43). Using high-capacity tape libraries with multiple drives and immediate access to tape cartridges, these systems are capable of data throughput of up to 2 TB per hour. Typically, all backups are performed automatically during the period of lowest system utilization. Because of the problems caused by concurrent access, mainframe operations usually reserve a time every day during which users are not permitted to access production applications. A typical approach sends a series of real-time messages to all open sessions announcing "Full Backup in xx minutes; please log off now." Operations staff sometimes phone offending users who are still logged on to the network when backups are supposed to start. To prevent unattended sessions from interfering with backups (as well as to reduce risks from unauthorized use of open sessions), most systems configure a time-out after a certain period of inactivity (typically 10 minutes). If users have left their sessions online despite the automatic logoff, mechanisms such as forced logoffs can be implemented to prevent user processes from continuing to hold production files open.

In addition to system backups, mainframe operations may be instructed to take more frequent backups of high-utilization application systems. Mission-critical transaction-processing systems, for example, may have several incremental or delta backups performed throughout the day. Transaction log files may be considered so important that they are also copied to backup media as soon as the files are closed. Typically, a log file is closed when it reaches its maximum size, and a new log file is initiated for the application programs.

41.3.3.2   Servers.   Managers of networks with many servers have the same options as mainframe operations staff, but they also have increased flexibility because of the decentralized, distributed nature of the computing environment. Many network architectures allocate specific application systems or groups of users to specific servers; therefore, it is easy to schedule system backups at times convenient for the various groups. In addition to flexible system backups, the distributed aspect of such networks facilitates application backups.

41.3.3.3   Workstations.   Individual workstations pose special challenges for backup. Although software and backup media are readily available for all operating systems, the human factor interferes with reliable backup. Users typically are not focused on their computing infrastructure; taking care of backups is not a high priority for busy professionals. Even technically trained users, who are aware of the dangers, sometimes skip their daily backups; many novice or technically unskilled workers do not even understand the concept of backups.

If the workstations are connected to a network, automated, centralized backup software utilities can protect all the users' files. However, with user disk drives containing as many as 80 GB of storage and with the popularity of large files such as pictures and videos, storing the new data, let alone the full system, hundreds of workstations can consume TB of backup media and saturate limited bandwidths. It takes a minimum of 291 hours to transfer 1 TB over a communications channel running at 1 MB per second. There are also privacy issues in such centralized backup if users fail to encrypt their hard disk files.

41.3.3.4   Portable Computers.   A portable or laptop computer is sometimes the only computer a user owns or is assigned; in other cases, the portable computer is an adjunct to a desktop computer. Laptop computers that are the primary system must be treated like workstations. Portables that are used as adjuncts—for example, when traveling—can be backed up separately, or they can be synchronized with the corresponding desktop system.

Synchronization software, such as LapLink, offers a number of options to meet user needs:

- A variety of hardwired connection methods, including cables between serial ports, parallel ports, SCSI ports, and USB ports.

- Remote access protocols allowing users to reach their computer workstations via modem or through TCP/IP connections via the Internet to ensure synchronization or file access.

- Cloning, which duplicates the selected file structure of a source computer onto the target computer; cloning deletes files from the target that are not found on the source.

- Filtering, which prevents specific files or types of files from being transferred between computers.

- Synchronization, in which all changes on the source computer(s) are replicated onto the target computer(s). One-way synchronization updates the target only; two-way synchronization makes changes to both the target and the source computers.

- Compression and decompression routines to increase throughput during transfers and synchronizations.

- Data comparison functions to update only those portions of files that are different on source and target; for large files, this feature raises effective throughput by orders of magnitude.

- Security provisions to prevent unauthorized remote access to users' computers.

- Log files to record events during file transfers and synchronization.

In addition to making it easier to leave the office with all the right files on one's hard disk, synchronization of portable computers has the additional benefit of creating a backup of the source computer's files. For more complete assurance, the desktop system may be backed up daily onto one or two removable drives, at the same time that the portable computer's files are synchronized. If the portable is worked on overnight, all files should be synchronized again in the morning.

41.3.3.5   Handheld Computers.   Another area that is often overlooked is handheld computers, or Personal Digital Assistants, including Palm, Psion, Handspring Visor, RIM Blackberry, daVinci, Helio, HP200LX, Newton/eMate, Rex, Zaurus, Smart Phones, Smart Pagers, and PocketMail. These PDAs often contain critically important information for their users, but not everyone realizes the value of making regular backups. Actually, synchronizing a PDA with a workstation has the added benefit of creating a backup on the workstation's disk. Security managers would do well to circulate an occasional reminder for users to synchronize or back up their PDAs to prevent data loss should they lose or damage their valuable tool. Some PDA docking cradles have a prominent button that activates instant synchronization, which is completed in only a minute or two.

41.3.4   Testing.   Modern backup software automatically verifies the readability of backups; this function must not be turned off. As mentioned in earlier, when preparing for any operation that destroys or may destroy the original data, two independent backups of critical data should be made, one of which may serve as the new original; it is unlikely that exactly the same error will occur in both copies of the backup. Dangerous activities include partitioning disk drives, physical repair of systems, moving disk drives from one slot or system to another, and installation of new versions of the operating system.

41.4   BACKUP ARCHIVES, MAINTENANCE, AND RETENTION.   Having created a backup set, what should one do with it? And how long should the backups be kept? This section looks at issues of archive management and retention from a policy perspective. Section 41.5 looks at the issues of physical storage of backup media, and Section 41.6 reviews policies and techniques for disposing of discarded backup media.

41.4.1   Retention Policies.   One obvious reason to make backup copies is to recover from damage to files; however, there are also legal and business requirements for data storage and retention. For example, certain jurisdictions require seven years of business data to be available for audits by regulatory or taxation agencies. The corporate legal staff may advise retention of certain data for even longer periods as support for claims of patent rights, or if litigation is envisaged. In all cases, the combination of business and legal requirements necessitates consultation outside the data processing department; decisions on data retention policies must involve more than technical resources.

The probability that a backup will be useful declines with time. The backup from yesterday is more likely to be needed than the same kind of backup from last week or last month. On the other hand, each backup contains copies of files that were changed in the period covered by that backup but that may have been deleted since the backup was made. Data center policies on retention vary because of perceived needs and experience as well as in response to the business and legal demands mentioned above. The following sample policy illustrates some of the possibilities in creating retention policies:

- Keep daily backups for one month.
- Keep the end-of-week backups for three months.
- Keep the end-of-month backups for five years.
- Keep the end-of-year backups for 10 years.

With such a policy in place, after one year there will be 55 backups in the system. After five years, there will be 108, and after 10 years, 113 backups will be circulating. Proper labeling, adequate storage space, and stringent controls are necessary to ensure the availability of any required backups.

41.4.2   Rotation.   Reusing backup volumes makes economic and functional sense. In general, when planning a backup strategy, different types of backups may be kept for different lengths of time., To ensure even wear on media, volumes should be labeled with the date on which they are returned to a storage area of available media and used in order of recovery, first in, first out. Backup volumes destined for longer retention should use newer media. An expiry date should be stamped on all tapes when they are acquired so that operations staff will know when to discard outdated media.

41.4.3   Media Longevity and Technology Changes.   For short-term storage, there is no problem ensuring that stored information will be usable. Even if a software upgrade changes file formats, the previous versions are usually readable. In one year, technological changes such as new storage formats will not make older formats unreadable.

Over the medium term, up to five years, difficulties of compatibility do increase, although not catastrophically. There are certainly plenty of five-year old systems still in use, and it is unlikely that this level of technological inertia will be seriously reduced in the future.

Over the longer term, however, there are serious problems to overcome in maintaining the availability of electronic records. During the last 10 to 20 years, certain forms of storage have become essentially unusable. As an example, the AES company was a powerful force in the dedicated word-processor market in the 1970s; eight-inch disks held dozens or hundreds of pages of text and could be read in almost any office in North America. By the late 1980s, AES had succumbed to word-processing packages running on general-purpose computers; by 1990, the last company supporting AES equipment closed its doors. Today, it would be extremely difficult to find the equipment for reading AES diskettes.

The problems of obsolescence include data degradation, software incompatibilities, and hardware incompatibilities.

41.4.3.1   Media Degradation.   Magnetic media degrade over time. Over a period of a few years, thermal disruption of magnetic domains gradually blurs the boundaries of the magnetized areas, making it harder for input/output (I/O) devices to distinguish between the domains representing ones and those representing zeros. These problems affect tapes, diskettes, and magnetic disks and cause increasing parity errors. Specialized equipment and software can compensate for these errors and recover most of the data on such old media.

Tape media suffer from an additional source of degradation: The metal oxide becomes friable and begins to flake off the Mylar backing. Such losses are unrecoverable. They occur within a few years in media stored under inadequate environmental controls and within five to 10 years for properly maintained media. Regular regeneration by copying the data before the underlying medium disintegrates prevents data loss.

Optical disks, which use laser beams to etch bubbles in the substrate, are much more stable than magnetic media. Current estimates are that CD-ROMs and CD-RW and DVD disks will remain readable for at least a decade and probably longer. However, they will remain readable if, and only if, future optical-storage systems include backward compatibility.

41.4.3.2   Software Changes.   Software incompatibilities include the application software and the operating system.

The data may be readable, but will they be usable? Manufacturers provide backward compatibility, but there are limits. For example, MS-Word 2000 can convert files from earlier versions of Word—but only back to version 4 for Windows. Over time, application programs evolve and drop support of the earliest data formats. Database programs, e-mail, spreadsheets—all of tomorrow's versions may have trouble interpreting today's data files correctly.

In any case, all conversions raise the possibility of data loss since new formats are not necessarily supersets of old formats. For example, in 1972, RUNOFF text files on mainframe systems included instructions to pause a daisy-wheel impact printer so the operator could change daisy wheels—but there was no requirement to document the desired daisy wheel. The operator made the choice. What would document conversion programs do with that instruction?

Even operating systems evolve. Programs intended for Windows 3.11 of the early 1990s do not necessarily function on Windows XP in the year 2002. Many older operating systems are no longer supported and do not even run on today's hardware.

Finally, even hardware eventually becomes impossible to maintain. As mentioned, it would be extremely difficult to retrieve and interpret data from word-processing equipment from even 20 years ago. No one outside museums or hobbyists can read an 800 bpi nine-track $\frac{3}{4}$-inch magnetic tape from the very popular 1980 HP3000 Series III minicomputer. Over time, even such parameters as data encoding standards (e.g., BCD, EBCDIC, ASCII) may change, making obsolete equipment difficult to use even if they can be located.

The most robust method developed to date for long-term storage of data is COM (Computer Output to Microfilm). Documents are printed to microfilm, appearing exactly as if they had been printed on paper, and then microphotographed. Storage densities are high, storage costs are low, and, if necessary, the images can be read with a source of light and a simple lens.

41.5   BACKUP STORAGE.   Where and how backup volumes are stored affects their longevity, accessibility, and usability for legal purposes.

41.5.1   Environmental Protection.   Magnetic and optical media can be damaged by dust, mold, condensation, freezing, and excessive heat. All locations considered for storage of backup media should conform to the media manufacturer's environmental tolerances; typical values are 40 to 60 percent humidity and temperatures of about 50 to 75° F (about 10 to 25° C). In addition, magnetic media should not be stacked horizontally in piles; the housings of these devices are not built to withstand much pressure, so large stacks can cause damaging contact between the protective shell and the data storage surface. Electromagnetic pulses and magnetic fields are also harmful to magnetic backup media; mobile phones, both wireless and cellular, should be kept away from magnetic media. If degaussers are used to render data more difficult to read before discarding media (see Section 41.6), these devices should never be allowed into an area where magnetic disks or tapes are in use or stored.

41.5.2   Onsite Protection.   It is obviously unwise to keep backups in a place where they are subject to the same risks of destruction as the computer systems they are intended to protect. However, unless backups are made through telecommunications channels to a remote facility, they must spend at least some time in the same location as the systems on which they were made.

At a minimum, backup policies should stipulate that backups are to be removed to a secure, relatively distant location as soon as possible after completion. Temporary on-site storage areas that may be suitable for holding backups until they can be moved off-site include specialized fire-resistant media storage cabinets or safes, secure media storage rooms in the data center, a location on a different floor of a multifloor building, or an appropriate location in a different building of a campus. What is *not* acceptable is to store backup volumes in a cabinet right next to the computer that was backed up. Even worse is the unfortunate habit of leaving backup volumes in a disorganized heap on top of the computer from which the data were copied.

In a small office, backups should be kept in a fire-resistant safe, if possible, while waiting to take the media somewhere else.

41.5.3   Offsite Protection.   As mentioned, it is desirable to store backups away from the computers and buildings where the primary copies of the backed-up data reside.

41.5.3.1   Care during Transport.   When sending backup media out for storage, operations staff should use lockable carrying cases designed for specific media. If external firms specializing in data storage pick up media, their staff usually supply such cases as part of the contract. If media are being transported by corporate staff, it is essential to explain the dangers of leaving such materials in a car: In the summer cars can get so hot that they melt the media, whereas in winter they can get so cold that the media instantly attract harmful water condensation when they are brought inside. In any case, leaving valuable data in an automobile exposes it to theft.

41.5.3.2   Homes.   The obvious but dangerous choice for people in small offices is to send backup media to the homes of trusted employees. There are a number of problems with this storage choice.

- Although the employee may be trustworthy, members of that person's family may not be so. Especially where teenage and younger children are present, keeping an organization's backups in a private home poses serious security risks.

- Environmental conditions in homes may be incompatible with safe long-term storage of media. For example, depending on the cleaning practices of the household, storing backups in a cardboard box under the bed may expose the media to dust, insects, cats, dogs, rodents, and damage from vacuum cleaners. In addition, temperature and humidity controls may be inadequate for safe storage of magnetic media.

- Homeowner's insurance policies are unlikely to cover loss of an employer's property and surely will not cover consequential losses resulting from damage to crucial backup volumes.

- Legal requirements for a demonstrable chain of custody for corporate documentation on backup volumes will not be met if the media are left in a private home where unknown persons may have access to them.

41.5.3.3   Safes.   There are no fireproof safes, only fire-resistant safes. Safes are available with different degrees of guaranteed resistance to specific temperatures commonly found in ordinary fires (those not involving arson and flame accelerants). Sturdy, small safes of one or two cubic feet are available for use in small offices or homes; they can withstand the heat during the relatively short time required to burn a house or small building down. They can withstand a fall through one or two floors without breaking open. However, for use in taller buildings, only more expensive and better-built safes are appropriate to protect valuable data.

41.5.3.4   Banks.   Banks have facilities for secured, environmentally controlled storage of valuables. Aside from the cost of renting and accessing such boxes, the main problem for backup storage in banks is that banks are open only part of the day; it is almost impossible to access backups in a safe deposit box after normal banking hours. In any case, it is impossible to rent such boxes with enough room for more than a few dozen small backup media. Banks are not a practical solution for any but the smallest organizations.

41.5.3.5   Data Vaults.   Most enterprises will benefit from contracting with professional, full-time operations specializing in maintaining archives of backup media. Some of the key features to look for in evaluating such facilities include:

- Storage areas made of concrete and steel to reduce risk of fire
- No storage of paper documents in the same building as magnetic or optical media storage
- Full air-conditioning including humidity, temperature, and dust controls throughout the storage vaults
- Fire sensors and fire-retardant technology, preferably without the use of water
- Full-time security monitoring including motion detectors, guards, and tightly controlled access

- Uniformed, bonded personnel
- Full time, 24/7/365 data pickup and delivery services
- Efficient communications, with procedures for authenticating requests for changes in the lists of client personnel authorized to access archives
- Evidence of sound business planning and stability

References from customers similar in size and complexity to the enquiring enterprise will help a manager make a wise choice among alternative suppliers.

41.5.3.6   *Online Backups.* An alternative to making on-site backup copies is to pay a third party to make automatic backups via high-speed telecommunications channels and to store the data in a secure facility. Some of the firms involved in these services move data to magnetic or optical backup volumes, but others use RAID (see Section 41.2.3.1) for instant access to the latest backups. Additional features to look for when evaluating online backup facilities:

- Compatibility of backup software with the computing platform, operating system, and application programs
- Availability of different backup options—full, differential, incremental, and delta
- Handling of files that are held in an *open* state by application programs
- Availability and costs of sufficient bandwidth to support desired data backup rates
- Encryption of data during transmission and when stored at the service facility
- Strong access controls to limit access to stored data to authorized personnel
- Physical security at the storage site and other criteria similar to those listed in Section 41.5.3.5
- Methods for restoring files from these backups, and the speed with which it can be accomplished

41.6   DISPOSAL. Before throwing out backup media containing unencrypted sensitive information, operations and security staff should ensure that the media are unreadable. This section looks at the problem of data scavenging and then recommends methods for preventing such unauthorized data recovery.

41.6.1   Scavenging. Computer crime specialists have described unauthorized access to information left on discarded media as scavenging, browsing, and dumpster-diving (from the trademarked name of metal bins often used to collect trash outside office buildings).

Scavenging can take place within an enterprise; for example, there have been documented cases of criminals who arranged to read *scratch tapes,* used for temporary storage of data, before they were reused or erased. Often they found valuable data left by previous users. Operations policies should not allow scratch tapes or other media containing confidential data to be circulated; all scratch media, including backup media that are being returned to the free list, should be erased before they are put on the media rack.

Before deciding to toss potentially valuable documents or backup media into the trash can, managers should realize that in the United States, according to a U.S. Supreme Court ruling, discarded waste is not considered private property under the law. Anything that is thrown out is fair game for warrantless searches or inspection by anyone who can gain access to it, without violating laws against physical trespass. Readers in other jurisdictions should obtain legal advice on the applicable statutes.

Under these circumstances, the only reasonable protection against data theft is to make the trash unreadable.

41.6.2   Data and Media Destruction.   Most users know that when a file is erased or purged from a magnetic disk, most operating systems leave the information entirely or largely intact, only removing the pointers from the directory. For example, DOS and Windows obliterate the first character of an erased file and remove its entries from the file allocation table (FAT). *Unerase* utilities search the disk or diskette and reconstruct the chain of *extents* (areas of contiguous storage), usually with human intervention to verify that the data are still good.

Multiuser operating systems remove pointers from the disk directory and return all sectors in a purged file to a disk's free-space map, but the data in the original extents (sections of contiguous disk space) persist until overwritten, unless specific measures are taken to obliterate them.

Formatting a disk is generally believed to destroy all of its data; however, even formatting and overwriting files on magnetic media may not make them unreadable to sophisticated equipment. Since information on magnetic tapes and disks resides in the difference in intensity between highly magnetized areas (1s) and less-magnetized areas (0s), writing the same 0s or 1s in all areas to be obliterated merely reduces the signal-to-noise ratio. That is, the residual magnetic fields still vary in more or less the original pattern—they are just less easily distinguished. Using highly sensitive readers, a magnetic tape or disk that has been zeroed will yield much of the original information.

One way of destroying data on magnetic media is to overwrite several passes of random patterns. The random patterns make it far more difficult to extract useful information from the discarded disks and tapes. Military-grade erasure programs use seven passes to obliterate data remanence.

Another solution is physical destruction of magnetic or optical backup media before they are discarded. For end-user departments, operations and security can provide identifiable secure collection receptacles (typically black) throughout the enterprise. Discarded media can be erased or destroyed by appropriate staff on a regular schedule.

Hard disks, tapes, optical disks, and floppy disks can be cut into pieces, melted with oxyacetylene torches, crushed in large compactors, and incinerated, although proper incineration requires specialized equipment to prevent atmospheric release of toxic by-products. Some commercial companies specialize in secure destruction of sensitive records and can provide bonded pickup services, or mobile destruction units, that move from enterprise to enterprise on a regular schedule and handle paper as well as magnetic and optical media.

41.7   COSTS.   All data center managers should be able to answer questions about the costs of the backups being made on their systems. Exhibit 41.1 presents the factors that should be included in a simple spreadsheet when calculating costs of backups, with tapes as an example of backup media.

41.8   OPTIMIZING FREQUENCY OF BACKUPS.   Suppose a manager asks the security and operations staff the following questions:

- "If backups are so important that you do a daily full backup, why don't you do a full backup twice a day?"

Exhibit 41.1   Calculating Costs of Backup Media

Tape Costs, Variable

   a. Tapes/Backup   _____

   b. Purchase Cost/Tape   _____

   c. Tape Cost/Backup (a*b)   _____

Time Costs, Variable

   d. Hours/Backup Tape   _____

   e. Total Tapes/Backup   _____

   f. Total Hours/Backup (d∗e)   _____

   g. Operator Cost/Hour (Salary + Benefits)   _____

   h. Time Cost/Backup (e∗f)   _____

Total Variable Costs/Backup (c + g)   _____

Fixed Costs

   i. Monthly costs of storage space, racks, insurance, transportation, hardware rental and maintenance, software rental and maintenance, cost of time to combine daily backups into weekly, weekly into monthly, etc.   _____

   j. Number of Backups/Month   _____

   k. Fixed Cost/Backup (h/i)   _____

Total Variable and Fixed Costs/Backup (c + g + j)   _____

Annualized Costs

   l. Backups/Year   _____

   m. Total Variable and Fixed Costs/Backup (c + g + j)   _____

   n. Total Cost/Year (k∗l)   _____

- "If taking a daily full backup is good enough for you, why don't you save money by doing a full backup only every other day?"

To answer such questions, managers must be able to adjust the frequency of backups to the perceived risk. One of the ways of approaching a rational allocation of resources when faced with random threats is to calculate the *expected value* of a strategy. The expected value is the average gain (if it is a positive quantity) or loss (if it is negative) that participants will incur in a process that involves random events. When this technique applies to losses over an entire year, it is called the *annualized loss expectancy.* Insurance companies use this approach to balance the costs of premiums against the disbursements to customers.

For backups, the principle is summarized by the following equation:

$$E(x) = P(u)*C(u) - P(n)*C(n)$$

where

- x is some particular strategy, such as doing a daily full backup.
- $E(x)$ is the expected value or cost of the strategy.
- $P(u)$ is the probability of having to use the backup within a single day; e.g., 1 chance in a 1,000 or 0.001.

- $C(u)$ is the money saved by not having to redo all the work that would otherwise be lost if there were no backup; e.g., the cost of paying for reconstruction of the previous day's data (e.g., $9,000) + avoidance of lost business, wasted salary, and other expenses during 3 hours of downtime during reconstruction (e.g., $30,000) for a savings of $39,000 per incident when the backups are available.

- $P(n)$ is the probability of not having to use the backups at all in a given day $= 1 - P(\mu) = 0.999$.

- $C(n)$ is the cost of making and storing a daily backup that will not be used (e.g., $50).

The expected value of doing a single daily full backup using the figures used in the examples above is

$$E(x) = (0.001*\$39,000) - (0.990*\$50) = \$39 - \$49.95 = -\$10.95$$

In other words, the daily full backup has an average cost of about $11 per day when the likelihood of its use is factored into the calculations. This is equivalent to a self-insurance strategy to prevent larger disasters by investing money in preventive mechanisms and measures for rapid and less expensive recovery than possible without the backups.

If one adjusts the frequency of backups, the calculated loss expectancy can be forced to zero or even to a positive number; however, no self-insurer can make a profit from loss-avoidance measures. Nonetheless, adjusting the frequency and costs of backup strategies using the suggested factors and calculation of loss expectancies can help a data center manager to answer questions from management about backup strategies in a rational manner. Since no one can estimate precisely how much a disaster costs, nor compute precise probabilities of having to use backups for recovery, these figures can serve only as rough guidelines.

In many organizations, the volume of changes follows a seasonal pattern. For example, 80 percent of all orders taken might come in two two-month periods spaced half a year apart. Registration for colleges occurs mostly in the autumn, with another bulge in January. Boat sales and ski sales follow seasonal variations. Despite this obvious variability, many organizations follow the same backup schedule regardless of date. It makes sense to adjust the frequency of backups to the volatility of data: operations can schedule more frequent backups when there are lots of changes and fewer when the data are relatively stable.

41.9   SUMMARY.   Backups are an essential component of operational security, and they play a crucial role in business resumption and disaster recovery. Backup policies should be developed rationally as a function of the specific requirements of each application and each computer system. Because conditions change, backup policies should be adjusted as needed to reflect changing requirements. Decisions on keeping archival copies of data should include consideration of legal requirements. Backup policies should include provisions for the full life cycle of the backup media, including acquisition, rotation, storage, and destruction.

41.10   FURTHER READING

Desai, A. *SQL Server 2000 Backup & Recovery.* New York: McGraw-Hill Professional Publishing, 2000.

Farkas, D.F. "Backups for Beginners" (2000). *PCWorld.com: www.pcworld.com/resource/printable/article/0,aid,15593,00.asp.*

Indiana University. "Unix System Administration Independent Learning (USAIL) Backups" (2000): *http://uwsg.iu.edu/usail/library/backups.html.*

Kozierok, C.M. ("The PC Guide: Backups and Disaster Recovery" (2001): *www.pcguide.com/care/bu.*

McMains, J.R. *Windows NT Backup & Recovery.* New York: Osborne McGraw-Hill, 1998.

Molina, Joe. "The RAB Guide to Non-Stop Data Access" (2001): *www.raid-advisory.com/rabguide.html.*

Preston, W.C., and G. Estabrook. *UNIX Backup and Recovery.* Sebastopol, CA: O'Reilly & Associates, 1999.

Velpuri, R., and A. Adkoli. *Oracle8 Backup and Recovery Handbook.* New York: McGraw-Hill Professional Publishing, 1998.

Winegarden, J. "Linux Backups HOWTO" (2000): *www-jerry.oit.duke.edu/linux/bluedevil/HOWTO/backups_howto.html.*

41.11   NOTES

1. *physics.nist.gov/cuu/Units/binary.html.*
2. *www.iomega.com.*
3. *www.storagetek.com.*

CHAPTER 42

BUSINESS CONTINUITY PLANNING

Michael Miora

CONTENTS

42.1 INTRODUCTION. We are in the Information Super Age, where businesses are turning in increasing numbers to high-technology systems and to the Internet to gain and maintain their competitive advantage. Businesses of all types are relying on high-technology products to build, promote, sell, and deliver their wares and services—and the same applies to government, educational, and non-for-profit enterprises. All of these enterprises are dependent on technology to maintain their income, image, and profitability. Business Continuity Planning (BCP) is the process of protecting organizations from the deleterious effects on their missions that can result from outages in information systems.

The goal of BCP is to protect the operations of the enterprise, not just the computing systems. Prudent planning is not restricted to computer or telecommunications systems but is enterprise-wide. There lies the key difference between the traditional hot sites and service providers and the newer, self-contained and supported backup and recovery capabilities. Without the people, procedures, and connectivity to keep the enterprise going, there is little point in restoring systems.

The enterprise has evolved to this dependency through the continual redefining of the word "fast" and the growing expectation of having access to information anywhere and at any time. In the 1960s and 1970s, fast turnaround meant a week or, with luck, a few days. In the 1980s, fast was redefined to mean today—the 1980s brought lower-cost computing and the beginning of high-speed communications. For the 1990s, fast meant now. The 1990s brought the Internet, intranets and extranets, with distributed systems, sophisticated client/server architectures, and high-speed communications.

Today, information is predominantly collected and sent electronically, often without human intervention. Analyses have been automated and streamlined, strengthened by user-friendly tools and by expert systems. Data are requested, sent, and analyzed in minutes; reports are generated automatically; and presentations can be created, edited, and delivered in near-real time. Moreover, access to information is provided almost equally fast to internal corporate personnel, business partners and allies, and customers and consumers.

42.1.1 Enterprise Risks and Costs.

The overall risk is to the continued survival of the enterprise. A company weakened by a disaster, and without adequate preparation, may be unable to recover before failure or a hostile takeover. In the 1970s, formal Business Continuity Plans did not exist; only data backup and recovery procedures with some disaster recovery planning for large systems was considered. Today, companies without active and tested enterprise contingency plans are likely to fail in the event of a disaster. Such failures may have dire consequences for the board and corporate officers, whose lack of due diligence is demonstrated by the absence of planning. By some estimates, no more than 30 percent of businesses are protected with comprehensive plans in place. The need for planning may be well recognized, but protected companies are still in the minority.

There is abundant evidence that unprotected companies suffer greatly during major outages. In investment trading, time is crucial, yet many investment firms did not have a plan in place until late 1993, when a major hot site provider first built a contingency trading facility in New York. Companies protected by disaster recovery plans can control their losses, holding them down to reasonable levels. Experts in the field believe that companies without such plans are likely to suffer significantly greater losses with consequences so critical that almost 50 percent of firms that do not recover within 10 days never will recover.

R.A. Elbra, the author of "Contingency Planning," a technical report published in 1989 for the National Computing Center (London), demonstrated that if a critical system was inoperable without suitable backup for as few as six days, the cumulative loss could amount to 200 percent of the net daily income produced by that system. After 12 days, the cumulative loss could be 800 percent of the net daily income, as shown in Exhibit 42.1. In the decade since that report was published, the reliance by large and small enterprises on their systems has grown significantly. As greater portions of corporate revenues are closely tied to systems and connectivity, these numbers take on even greater significance.

Even today, few industries have strict disaster recovery or business continuity planning regulations. The banking industry is subject to such regulations for portions of their systems only. Healthcare regulations, designed by the Joint Commission on

Exhibit 42.1   Fiscal Losses Caused By Disasters

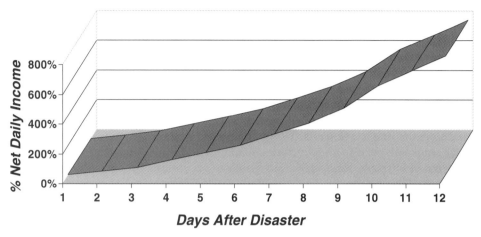

Accreditation of Healthcare Organizations (JCAHO), are only now beginning to address disaster recovery planning. The Health Insurance Portability and Accountability Act (HIPAA) has been delayed and diluted several times, but is now taking effect in stages over the years 2000 through approximately 2005. The security and privacy elements of HIPAA will have the effect of making Business Continuity Plans even more important than before. (See Chapter 49 for more information about HIPAA.)

There are many examples of serious downtime, including one instance of a construction crew repairing a nearby roadway and mistakenly damaging the power lines feeding a nearby set of buildings. Repairs required parts that delayed completion of repairs for almost 48 hours. One of the affected companies was an electrical supply company with revenues of approximately $50 million annually. The company felt safe because it had a plan that included reciprocal agreements to share spare computer time with other companies using similar equipment. Unfortunately, the company was unable to secure as much time as it expected because some of the other companies had changed equipment since the agreements were made, some were too busy with their own processing, and some simply did not abide by their agreements. To the chagrin of management, the replacement capability was limited to 30 percent of normal processing. Management reported that this outage cost the company over $250,000 in lost and unrecoverable sales. Although managers were unsure of their market share losses, they did know that two major customers subsequently split their orders between the affected company and another supplier. While this is not a headline-grabbing disaster, it did significantly affect this financially healthy company.

A less healthy company might have been bankrupted by such a loss. Even surviving businesses experience significantly lower profits for the two-year period following a disaster. Reconstruction costs usually exceed insurance allowances and typically involve uninsured costs for modernization. Insurance premiums usually rise, and advertising budgets increase, to repair the corporate image. The largest problems, however, are due to productivity declines and inefficient operations caused by production restarts, debugging efforts, and the need to retrain newly hired staff to replace employees who departed in fear of corporate collapse or layoffs.

Sunkist Growers, Inc., proved its disaster recovery plan by restoring its computer network at its Sherman Oaks, California, headquarters within 14 hours after the January 17, 1994, Northridge, California, earthquake. The plan was developed in the mid-1980s and was meticulously maintained through annual plan updates and tests. By using this plan, company executives were able to set up the company's sales department in Sunkist premises more distant from the epicenter as they worked to clear $3.5 million to $4 million of damage at Sunkist headquarters. An uninterruptible power supply had allowed the fruit grower's IBM AS/400 minicomputers to shut down in an orderly manner. Only five or six of the company's 200 microcomputers at the headquarters building were destroyed, and no data were lost. Within three days, the company's sales personnel returned to the headquarters building.

Just as Sunkist recovered from a major earthquake, Kemper Securities Inc. recovered from the first attack on the World Trade Center on February 26, 1993. The thick black smoke that rose from New York's World Trade Center did not put Kemper Securities out of business. Kemper, a Chicago-based securities firm, had a backup plan to protect the vital data processed by its World Trade Center office. Every night, Kemper automatically transfers copies of data stored by the New York office's three midrange computers to one of two mainframes in Milwaukee. When Kemper's 60 World Trade Center workers entered temporary quarters the following Monday, their customers' vital securities records were safe and work resumed with little interruption.

Cantor Fitzgerald, a bond company with a major office in the World Trade Center, lost 733 workers in the North Tower on September 11, 2001. Their disaster recovery plans and mirroring sites enabled them to be back in action and taking orders just 47 hours after that loss. This was especially noteworthy because of the range of the disaster and the fact that the loss of life included approximately 150 information technology workers.

Management's voice is needed to address another key issue. During natural disasters, employees at all levels of the corporate structure will make family and home their top priority. The successful recovery plan considers the need for employees with recovery responsibilities to first ascertain the condition of their own homes and families. Corporate management can make it clear to all employees that people come first. Recovery plans must provide participants with the time and the means to reach their loved ones. Once people are satisfied that families and homes are safe, then they can turn their full attention to corporate recovery.

42.1.2   Types of Disasters.   Many different threats can lead to disasters; see Chapter 14 for a discussion of physical threats to the information infrastructure. Exhibit 42.2 lists a small sampling of these potential threats. It is neither feasible nor desirable to design a strategy for each of these disasters. It is more important to consider the effects of each applicable potential threat. For example, a bomb threat may deny access to the building or to the local area for a time. A small fire may deny access to an entire building for a day and to a small portion of the building for a few months. All threats can then be grouped by their levels of impact. Exhibit 42.3 lists one hierarchical structure that maps the levels of impact to predefined duration of threats. These groupings are disaster types.

Identifying disaster threats and grouping them into disaster types fulfills a planning need. Each disaster type is associated with an outage duration, which is the length of downtime expected, and with a set of predefined outage durations, such as indicated in Exhibit 42.3. Therefore, each disaster type can be mapped to specific corporate functions that will be affected.

For example, a bomb threat may affect an entire building, but only for a fraction of a day. If this is so, then protecting against a bomb threat requires protecting only those corporate functions performed in that building whose survival time is one day or less. A

Exhibit 42.2   Disaster Threats

◆ Accidents	◆ Equipment Problems
◆ Airports	◆ Fire
◆ Arson	◆ Flood
◆ Blackout	◆ Forced Evacuation
◆ Bomb Threat	◆ Hurricane
◆ Building/Facility Inaccessibility	◆ Ice Storms
◆ Chemical Spills	◆ Key Resource Loss
◆ Civil Disorders	◆ Labor Disputes
◆ Civil Disturbances	◆ Malicious Damage
◆ Computer Compromise	◆ Municipal Services Stoppages
◆ Computer Virus	◆ Postal Service Disruption
◆ Construction Damage	◆ Power Loss or Fluctuation
◆ Construction Obstruction	◆ Riot
◆ Data Diddling	◆ Security Breach
◆ Data Loss	◆ Strike
◆ Disgruntled Employee	◆ Terrorism
◆ Drug Abuse	◆ Tornado
◆ Earthquake	◆ Toxic Spills
◆ Elevator Failure	◆ Vandalism
◆ Embezzlement	◆ Volcano
◆ Environmental Control Failure	◆ Water

toxic spill caused by a nearby train derailment may disrupt an entire facility, or campus of buildings, for several days. Protecting against a toxic spill requires protecting all functions whose survival time is less than several days. A regional disaster such as an earthquake, flood, or hurricane, however, disrupts operations for a longer period and may prevent quick recovery anywhere within the affected area.

Business Continuity Plans need to developed in a modular fashion so that modules can be activated depending on the disaster type. Assessing the expected duration of a disaster provides a means of determining which functions should be scheduled for recovery initiation; assessing the level of impact provides a mechanism for determining what type of recovery should be performed on each function. These are the two major factors that need to be identified promptly after a disaster: estimated duration and expected level of impact.

In 1988, First Interstate Bank's high-rise corporate headquarters building in downtown Los Angeles was severely damaged by fire. Major high-rise fires are very rare, as is clear by the age of this example, but rarity does not decrease the significance of the event. First Interstate Bank (now merged with Wells Fargo Bank) was prepared with a detailed recovery plan and was able to recover critical functions within the required timeline. The First Interstate fire story is a success story: It recovered with no discernible impact to its client base.

Exhibit 42.3   Levels of Impact and Durations

Area Affected	Duration of Outage
Partial Building	Less than 1 Day
	1–3 Days
	4–7 Days
	Week to Month
	More than Month
Full Building	Less than 1 Day
	1–3 Days
	4–7 Days
	Week to Month
	More than Month
Multi-Building (Campus Facility)	Less than 1 Day
	1–3 Days
	4–7 Days
	Week to Month
	More than Month
Local Area (Immediate)	Less than 1 Day
	1–3 Days
	4–7 Days
	Week to Month
	More than Month
Region	Less than 1 Day
	1–3 Days
	4–7 Days
	Week to Month
	More than Month

The key point is that planning for specific threats is not necessary. Planning for types of outages is more efficient and more effective. It may not matter whether the building is damaged by fire or water, but the extent of damage and the duration of the outage are important, for those factors determine the types of recoveries to make. Traditionally, enterprise risks were calculated on a per-threat basis. Each threat was analyzed to determine the percentage probability of that threat occurring within a period. Those probabilities were then summed over all possible threats. The resulting figure was a representation of probability of some disaster having a significant impact on business operations over a period such as a year. The disadvantage of this method is that it misleads management into believing that the probabilities are so small as to be insignificant. A different and more streamlined analysis is more useful for the disaster recovery process. It is called the Generalized Cost Consequence Model (GCC) and was developed by this author. It is described in Section 42.4.

Exhibit 42.4   Recovery Phases

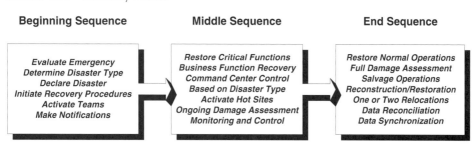

Beginning Sequence

> Evaluate Emergency
> Determine Disaster Type
> Declare Disaster
> Initiate Recovery Procedures
> Activate Teams
> Make Notifications

Middle Sequence

> Restore Critical Functions
> Business Function Recovery
> Command Center Control
> Based on Disaster Type
> Activate Hot Sites
> Ongoing Damage Assessment
> Monitoring and Control

End Sequence

> Restore Normal Operations
> Full Damage Assessment
> Salvage Operations
> Reconstruction/Restoration
> One or Two Relocations
> Data Reconciliation
> Data Synchronization

42.1.3   Recovery Scenarios.   Recovery scenarios are the planned steps to be followed when disaster strikes. These scenarios are designed based on the various threat levels of impact and durations. All recovery scenarios are built in three phases, or sequences, of activities as shown in Exhibit 42.4.

The beginning sequence evaluates the emergency to determine the effect of the event on the enterprise. This can be an unhurried, deliberate activity when there is sufficient notice of a problem under way. An example of this is the Los Angeles civil disturbances. Downtown Los Angeles businesses were able to watch carefully, evaluating information as it became available. In contrast, the pace is highly fast and frenetic during an evacuation due to fire, weather, or earthquake. Achieving a safe position is always the first consideration; following that are the other steps: determining the disaster type and declaring a disaster; activating the disaster recovery and other teams; making legal, regulatory, and other notifications; and establishing command and control centers. This beginning sequence often involves top corporate management.

The middle sequence includes most of the major recovery activities. Whereas the beginning sequence determines the type of disaster in progress, this sequence provides procedures to the various functional groups based on the type of disaster in progress. One key element of the middle sequence is to perform ongoing damage assessments and maintain contact with salvage operations. Knowledgeable information technology personnel should be available to review salvage and rebuilding plans for information equipment.

The end sequence restores normal operating conditions. This phase of recovery is the least predictable of all and is linked to disaster type and to specific threats. Therefore, this phase is planned in more general terms than the two preceding sequences. In the end sequence, detailed damage assessment is performed. Salvage operations for vital records, information equipment, data, and general facility equipment take place. Reconstruction or relocation activities are specified and executed. Finally, normal operations are restored. Often, the end sequence includes two facility relocations. The first relocation moves operations from the emergency operations centers, including the command center, hot sites, work area recovery centers, and other off-site workplaces, to a longer-term interim operating area. This longer-term operating area may be a cold site or other temporary work area. The second relocation is from the interim facility back to the reconstructed or to a newly constructed permanent home.

Completion of the recovery plan occurs when normal operations are restored. Ending the formalized recovery procedures before then may introduce errors and compromise integrity in the final move to the permanent facility. In this final move, large processing equipment is torn down and moved, just as it was during the initial disaster declaration, only in a more deliberate manner. Temporary operations may require use of the reserve systems as backup in case the move encounters problems. Often, much of the equipment at the interim site is required at the permanent site. Finally, data reconciliation, the merging of data from different operating environments, and data synchronization require planning and careful implementation to prevent the destruction and replacement of good data with erroneous information.

The traditional disaster recovery strategies include hot sites for data centers and emergency services for employees. These sites have been effective and continue to be necessary, but not sufficient. New strategies are needed to consider the new ways of doing business: mobile computing, real-time sales and service support, client/server architectures, extensive telecommunications, real-time process controls, and online customer service support. Preplanned recovery capabilities can resurrect functions that depend on huge databases and large systems in hours rather than days. Connectivity can be restored in minutes, and the client base need never know that a disaster has occurred. Business can continue, no matter what has happened, so long as proper recovery precautions have been taken.

42.2   DEFINING THE GOALS.   Defining the specific goals of a Business Continuity Plan is a multistep process that correlates what is important to the enterprise with what the enterprise does and is tempered by what is possible. A general goal for a plan may be stated as follows: Protect critical business functions so they will continue meeting minimum corporate objectives cost effectively during times of crises and disasters. This general statement describes BCP goals for many companies. Before building a plan, however, specific goals must be conjectured by the planner, evaluated by the planning team or steering committee, and validated by corporate management.

This section describes the specific elements and steps of defining the goal of the recovery and continuity plan and identifying the specific objectives required to meet that goal. Succeeding sections describe how to determine the criticality and time sensitivity of various corporate business functions, how to gain and keep commitments from management, and how to define what protections are needed for each business function.

A Business Continuity Plan may have many specific goals. For example, a central order entry and production scheduling system may reside at corporate headquarters or at the corporate sales office, while manufacturing may be dispersed geographically and by product across many facilities. A possible objective of the plan for such an enterprise is to maintain production levels at some fraction of normal levels even if the corporate center is damaged or destroyed.

A California manufacturer of custom filters devised exactly such an objective. For the vast majority of the firm's products, normal operating procedures were for a five-day cycle from order to shipment. Order entry was performed at corporate headquarters. Full Material Requirements Planning (MRP) of all North American manufacturing sites, including purchasing, control, scheduling, and shipping, was performed on the same system. Corporate management determined that the company could not survive for more than a short time unless overall plant production capacity was maintained at 50 percent of normal levels. Production of less than 50 percent would make it infeasible for the company to survive more than two weeks. Production of more than 50 percent but less than 100 percent of normal levels would severely reduce or eliminate profits but would not cause corporate failure. The clear goal of this plan was to protect the functions required to meet the objective of achieving a minimum of 50 percent of normal levels.

The firm performed an analysis of products and revenues. It considered the quantity and cost of the various filters it made, the resulting manufacturing load, and its customer base. Although the overall requirement was to maintain a manufacturing load of at least 50 percent of normal, the firm also wanted to make certain that major customers were served and that large contract commitments were met. All of these requirements were incorporated into the final Business Continuity Plan.

In another case, a major electronics manufacturer provided free, seven day, 24-hour customer service and technical support to all customers. Two facilities in the United States provided support to customers worldwide. This support was a major competitive advantage and was believed to be a major contributing factor to the reputation and exceptional customer loyalty enjoyed by the manufacturer. During normal operations, the call center guidelines were:

1. All incoming calls must be answered by the third ring.
2. Average waiting times must be less than two minutes.
3. Maximum waiting times would not exceed six minutes without operator intervention. Moreover, busy signals should not exceed one caller in 500. Communications systems linked technical support personnel with technical databases.

These were strict criteria for the company's service level objectives, and traffic engineering studies carefully monitored busy signals and queuing delays to prevent violations of call center guidelines. Trunk lines were added or removed, and staff members were rescheduled to maintain this level of support, which far exceeded industry standards. The major goal for the call center Business Continuity Plan was to maintain service-level objectives at a predefined minimum degradation level. The allowable queuing delay was increased significantly, and the busy signal allowance was increased slightly. A special message would play apologizing for any inconvenience, but all customers still would be served. The planning project identified what capabilities were needed to meet these requirements. The goal of this plan was to provide the backup capabilities needed to meet the reduced service level objectives using a combination of the preexisting surviving call center and some emergency capability for the damaged or destroyed call center.

Corporate goals are independent of means and systems; they are stated in business terms. Top management must make decisions about what needs to be protected and how protected it needs to be. Often, though, this is an iterative process in which management designs some preliminary decisions and instructs analysts to confirm or refine those thoughts. The disaster recovery planning process includes steps to do just that during the Business Impact Analysis (BIA) phase.

The goals of the plan are associated with the products and services that the enterprise or operating unit provides. In cases where the facility to be protected is a support facility, such as the corporate headquarters of a manufacturing conglomerate, the services provided are in support of the overall corporate operations, perhaps including banking and other support activities. In these cases, although the services are somewhat removed from actual production, they are still imperative to continuing production. Building the plan requires goals that are more specific in nature than those in the examples above. In this methodology, these lower-level goals are referred to as the plan objectives.

The BCP objectives are closely coupled with specific business functions and are not adequately defined until the conclusion of the Business Impact Analysis. In order to begin this definition process, however, first the recovery problem must be constrained. This is accomplished by defining the scope of the disaster recovery plan.

42.2.1 Scope. The scope of the plan is the definition of the environment to be protected. Before performing detailed analyses and interviewing management, decisions must be made regarding who and what is to be included in the plan. Specifying the systems, equipment, procedures, locations, and support capabilities that require protection identifies the scope. The corporate environment consists of people, information, facilities, and equipment. The plan focuses on a subset of the people, some of the information, selected facilities, and specific equipment. That constitutes the scope of the Business Continuity Plan. Stated more simply, no matter what the size or complexity of the enterprise, planning is performed on one part of the enterprise at a time.

The scope must be established in order to define the goals of the plan. However, during the planning process, the scope will be refined and redefined as the analysis progresses. Which facility is involved? Is part of a building being protected, such as the data center or the shop floor? Is it the entire facility, including a campus of buildings that fall into the scope of the plan? To perform a BIA, users must focus on the business elements that reside or utilize the people, information, facilities, and equipment that are in scope. However, sometimes it becomes clear during the analysis that the scope must be broadened or can be restrained to protect business functions adequately.

In a world of tight budgets, compressed schedules, and phased implementations, Business Continuity Planning usually is performed in stages. Perhaps the computer and telecommunications systems are protected first, followed later by other office support equipment such as copiers and hard copy files. No matter which elements are chosen for implementation, the scope must be clearly documented. For computer systems, the current systems in use must be identified. Hardware and software must be described in detail. Special equipment must be identified.

In the planning process, it sometimes becomes clear that important items have been excluded from the plan. Where those newly uncovered requirements prove to be critical, they must be included, but for all others, a well-defined scope will prevent creeping requirements that increase cost and lengthen implementation schedules. Requirements identified as desirable but not absolutely necessary can be recorded in an ongoing project log and scheduled for implementation in a later phase. It is better to put into place a plan that leaves out some capabilities while meeting basic objectives rather than to allow the planning scope to expand, thereby risking long delays or project abandonment. A clearly defined scope enables the planning team to communicate to management precisely what is and what is not protected or included in the planning process.

Major scope issues and disagreements sometimes can be resolved in this early phase of the planning project. If not, resolution of these issues is best delayed until the conclusion of the BIA, since that process reveals hidden functional interdependencies. For example, research and development (R&D) functions usually are longer-term projects that can be delayed without major impact on the enterprise. In many plans, R&D functions are relegated to low priority. Consider, however, the case of a customer service technical representative discussing the status of a custom-manufactured product with a key customer who is unhappy with the delivered prototype. If R&D technical personnel are required to resolve such issues, and resolution has an impact on production schedules, then R&D may be elevated to a higher priority. The BIA process usually reveals and prioritizes such hidden interdependencies.

42.2.2   Correlating Objectives to Corporate Missions and Functions.   It usually falls on the Information Systems and Technology department to build the BCP. Naturally, then, most plans focus first on computers and telecommunications. While there is nothing intrinsically wrong with starting that way, it must be just the first step of the analysis. The danger is the potential for myopic views of corporate functions; corporate computer and telecommunications systems may be required for the successful execution of critical business functions, but usually they are only part of many needed capabilities. Desktop paper files, telephones, personal phone directories, and copying machines may be just as important as access to the corporate database or to some tailored vertical application. The list of functions and equipment to be investigated must be complete or the resulting plan will be inadequate.

The Business Impact Analysis provides a formal methodology for ranking business functions by criticality and time sensitivity. The process includes interviews with key personnel from each business function included in the scope of the planning project. There are two dangers inherent to an information technology-based approach to disaster recovery planning.

1. Business functions that do not use information systems may be inadvertently overlooked.

2. Noncomputer support structures and systems may not be recognized and, therefore, not brought into the protection definition process.

When the information systems department leads the disaster recovery project, it will naturally base the plan on a systems-based knowledge of the enterprise. The accounting department, a traditional heavy user of computer systems, will naturally be included among the functions that potentially need protection. Similarly, all other functions that use computers in their normal activities will likely be included in any list of functions requiring analysis. All organizational elements that use computer systems will be recognized and included precisely because they use computers and therefore are known to the systems department. However, there are many important functions that may not regularly use computers or may use them in ways that are only minimally visible to the systems people.

Mail room operations are frequently omitted because often they are not computer users. Planning personnel are clearly well aware that mail operations exist; they just forget to include them in the planning process even though mail operations are important to every organization. Planning mail room recovery and continuation is simple before a disaster but very difficult after the fact.

Facilities management, maintenance and plant engineering organizations are seldom intensive computer users in their daily activities. Nevertheless, in normal circumstances, operations in a large facility would deteriorate quickly without these functions. During a disaster, these are the people who can rapidly determine the nature and breadth of facility damage. They are the people who need to be instantly available to evaluate damage, hasten repairs, and estimate duration of outages. They are also the individuals who are often left off the disaster recovery team lists and phone rosters. Similarly, security forces are needed when building damage leaves valuable equipment and other assets vulnerable to theft or vandalism. They may be needed to protect employees who are working during civil disturbances or other such incidents. Corporate communications and public relations departments are also frequently computer systems users who are not very visible to the systems department as unique functions, yet their contributions to a successful recovery are often essential.

The safest way to compile a list of business functions is to work from three documents: an organization chart, a corporate phone directory, and a list of corporate operations budget line items (see Exhibit 42.5). Using these three lists, the planner can develop a comprehensive list of business functions and can identify the manager or supervisor of each function. That comprehensive list should include every function performed, regardless of the perceived importance of that function. Criticality and time

Exhibit 42.5 Building and Filtering the List of Functions

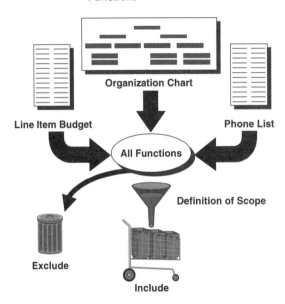

sensitivity will be determined during the BIA; leaving off any functions can lead to inaccurate BIA results.

Working from that comprehensive list, a second list should be compiled that includes or excludes each business function based on the defined scope of the BIA. When doubt exists, the function should be included. The BIA will be the final filter for out-of-scope functions. Therefore, for each function in the list, the planner must determine which of the included elements are relevant to the function under evaluation. While this may seem to be a complicated process, it is usually straightforward. The golden rule is: When in doubt, include the function. It can always be excluded later if analysis shows that the function is really out of scope.

42.2.3 Validating Goals. A full disaster recovery plan must consider the contribution of each element of the organization to the overall corporate goals. Clearly, no single area is dispensable, for if it were, it would have been discarded already. Properly defined goals are independent of specific functions as they are stated in global terms. Validating the goals requires examining each function to determine how it contributes to the corporate objectives. It is important to distinguish between the importance of a function toward meeting specific disaster recovery goals and the overall importance of a function to an enterprise.

Even functions that are not relevant to any specific disaster recovery goals may be crucial to the overall operation of the enterprise. The BCP focuses on protecting selected corporate functions for a specified period of time, but it is a mistake to assume that a function whose importance to recovery goals is low is not important to the enterprise in the longer run. For example, during a crisis, the corporate tax accounting function often can cease operations with little impact to the enterprise. If this is true, then the continuation requirements for that department are minimal, and the recovery timeline can be extended. Clearly this does not mean that the corporate tax accounting function is unimportant. Other examples of longer-term requirements include fulfilling regulatory and legal requirements.

The goals of the BCP are associated with the products and services of the enterprise and are expressed in business terms. Validating those goals requires presenting management with options for levels of protection and their associated costs. Gross estimates are possible at the outset; refined presentations require a complete BIA. The goals should be clearly defined and presented to management. Although these goals are not addressed specifically by each procedure in the ultimate BCP, they drive the entire recovery strategy development. A clear and concise description of the goals must be presented to management and approved by them. After this approval, the disaster recovery planners can attempt to attain those goals. During the strategy development, other alternatives may appear and be added for ultimate management consideration, but the initial goals become the operational baseline against which strategies and costs can be measured.

42.2.4   Mapping Goals to Recovery Phases.   There are three phases to the recovery process:

1. *Continuation* activities
2. *Resumption* activities
3. *Restoration* activities

The continuation activities are those specific tasks and procedures that enable a very limited set of functions to continue operating with little or no interruption. The resumption activities provide for resuming a full, or almost full, range of business functions, even if that resumption means using backup methods and temporary operating procedures. The restoration activities are those that bring back a normal operating environment in a permanent facility.

The continuation and resumption activities occur during the middle sequence of activities and are the activities that must meet the short-term recovery goals that are within the domain of the recovery plan. The restoration activities occur during the end sequence and may include some long-term goals. The long-term goals may include decisions about rebuilding versus relocating and other major decisions that are beyond the province of BCP construction.

Each goal should be assigned to one of these three sets of activities. This assignment is based primarily on timeline considerations: what must be quickly continued versus what can wait a short while and what can be delayed for the longer term. In the call center example, the number of rings, the allowable queuing delays, and the busy signal allowance were measurements of service levels. They constituted the goals for the recovery plan. After an interruption, the levels of service can be restored to normalcy gradually, as a function of time since the disaster. Stated differently, with each passing day, the level of service should improve. Therefore, the goal of the continuation activities may be for service within some stated parameters, and the goal of the resumption activities would be for improved levels of service. Normal levels may await the restoration activities.

Clearly, the same level of service can be attained at lower cost if the timing requirements are loosened. That is the reason it is important to assign each goal to a particular set of activities. Exhibit 42.6 illustrates a potential mapping of service levels to activity sets. In the first hours following a disaster, the continuation activities maintain a minimum required level of functionality, with some increases over time. The resumption activities dramatically increase functionality immediately and then bring functionality back, over time, to an almost normal condition. The restoration function,

Exhibit 42.6

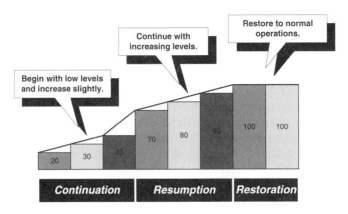

shown as two bars to represent temporary and permanent facilities, achieves full levels of service.

42.2.5   Emergency Issues.   A good plan includes provisions for ensuring the *safety* of all employees potentially affected by a disaster. This is especially true for employees working on site when a disaster occurs. Life safety issues include health and safety preparedness, shelter and care of employees caught in the enterprise facilities during a disaster, and search and rescue teams for employees in imminent danger. Some of these protections are required by various local, state, and federal regulatory agencies. Others are not mandated but are nonetheless important to the survival of the employees and the business.

Public relations is an important issue during any disaster. More than one enterprise has realized too late that neglecting the media can induce a second, even greater disaster than the original one to which the media was responding. Even a small fire can make major news in the local community. The public relations aspect includes recovery actions. For example, one chemical company suffered a minor fire but refused to inform the media on the status of cleanup operations. The result was predictable: The media reported that a fire had potentially released toxic chemicals into the local environment and that the company had refused to comment. That report did more to damage the reputation of this chemical company than did the fire that caused the spill, which was not in fact toxic and was brought under control within hours of the fire.

42.3   PERFORMING A BUSINESS IMPACT ANALYSIS.   The Business Impact Analysis comprises the heart of the planning process. It is here that the recovery planner determines what is important for inclusion into the BCP and what is not relevant to that effort. The BIA determines how far to go in protecting the people, information, and equipment that constitute the organization and its functions so that all survive to flourish another day.

The BIA assesses how unavailability of each system would affect the enterprise. The BIA is a multistep process that may be performed over a period of weeks or months, depending on the availability of various corporate personnel. Often, the BIA may be a first effort to determine the total cost and schedule required for a full plan. In all cases, the BIA should precede any other planning activities since it will help determine the direction and strategies for prevention, mitigation, and recovery.

42.3.1   Establishing the Scope of the Business Impact Analysis.   To succeed, a project must be well defined in terms of work effort and work product. Just as the BIA helps bound the recovery problem in precise recovery terms so that the project may be successful, the BIA subproject also must be understood in terms of the work required and the product of the analysis. This requires establishing the scope of the BIA by deciding what equipment the BIA will investigate and what people to interview.

The BIA begins with an inventory process to catalog the various equipment and capabilities to be protected. As systems evolve to meet ever-increasing customer demands, equipment changes and management responsibility changes along with it. For example, a mainframe shop and large local area networks (LANs) and wide area networks (WANs) may be managed by the information technology department, whereas smaller LANs may be managed by individual departments such as accounting or engineering.

Without a comprehensive and constantly updated list of systems across departments and functional areas, systems can evolve quickly with little or no overall corporate knowledge. For the recovery planner, this means the plan will be incorrect at its outset or will grow obsolete quickly.

The inventory should describe in detail the general hardware and software used in each included system, paying particular attention to special-purpose equipment, such as imaging equipment, custom equipment, and uncommon equipment.

The inventory must include communications links and equipment. A connectivity map showing LAN and WAN equipment and connections is useful; a cabling diagram with gateways, routers, bridges, firewalls, proxy servers, and other communication equipment is also important. General telephony diagrams and summaries of lines and capacities are required to bring voice communications systems into the recovery process.

The inventory provides an opportunity to decide what level of office equipment and supplies (e.g., paper, writing implements, staplers, note pads) should be protected by the recovery plan. Although staplers seldom will be critical, certain printed business forms might well require off-site storage for quick recovery. Boxes of corporate checks, for example, should be stored securely off site.

Security access controls and special alarm systems should be included in the inventory, along with current procedures for maintaining them. There have been instances of a recovery hampered by inaccessibility to the building caused by active alarm and access control systems. Inclusion of such systems into the inventory helps ensure that they will help rather than hinder the recovery process.

42.3.2   Interview Process.   The best source of information about the work performed by the enterprise is the enterprise's own labor force. Corporate executives understand and control corporate goals; managers understand and control operations. Front-line supervisors and workers perform the daily tasks that bring revenue to the enterprise, and these are the people who have the knowledge needed for the BIA. The recovery planner must collect that information, understand it, and translate it into terms meaningful for disaster recovery planning. Exhibit 42.7 shows the three steps of interviewing.

The first step is to compile a list of all the departments that fall within the scope of the BIA. The term *department* is used here to describe an organizational entity that may not correspond with a specific organization chart position or with the use of the term within the enterprise. The term is meant to convey a functionally complete unit performing a task or series of related tasks. It might well be that people from different

Exhibit 42.7   The Three Steps of Interviewing

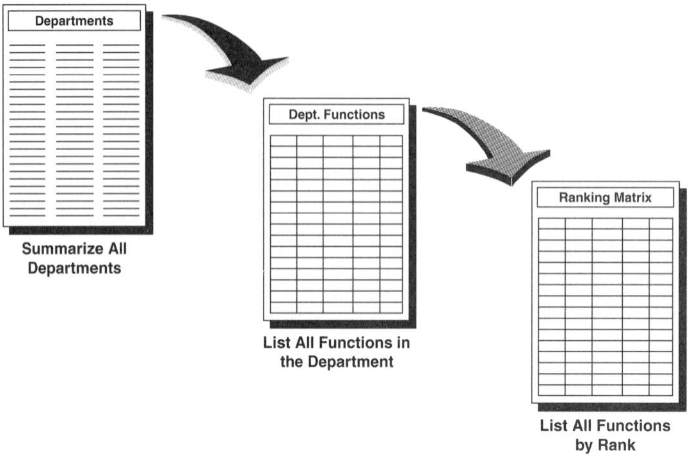

organization chart departments work more closely with one another than they do with people in their own departments.

For example, the accounting department of an organization may handle all corporate accounting functions, including Accounts Receivable (A/R), Accounts Payable (A/P), General Ledger (G/L), and Payroll. However, for the purpose of the planning project, the planner may choose to group Accounting into two departments: Accounting and Payroll. In this way, Payroll can be separated from its organizational component and combined with other portions of the enterprise that provide the payroll data, and with which the payroll department interacts daily.

Once the list of departments is complete, the next step is to choose an individual in each department to be the primary interview candidate. Because the primary interviewee from each department will perform two functions—first, identify all of the high-level functions performed within that department, and second, describe in detail many of those functions—that person should be an experienced and knowledgeable member of that department. It is neither necessary nor desirable to assign this interview position to a senior manager. Management interviews should be scheduled for a later phase that requires management insight. The first interviews should focus on daily task structures and purposes.

The recovery planner guides the interview. The first step of the interview is to describe the department in terms of its overall function and to list all the high-level functions performed. For example, in the accounting department, the high-level functions usually include Accounts Payable, Accounts Receivable, General Ledger, and Payroll. It may include corporate tax preparation, or that may be a completely separate function. It may include financial reporting for the Securities and Exchange Commission (SEC) and other filings, or a different department may perform those functions.

A corporate human resources department may include employee records, benefits management, payroll distribution, time sheet processing, and other common functions. For the planning project, the payroll distribution and time sheet processing functions may be more closely allied with the accounting department than with the human resources department.

During the interview process, the department expert will likely want to describe functions at a detailed level. For example, in the financial reporting area, the expert may want to list each and every report produced. While it may be useful for the planner to learn about the production of these reports, the BIA should categorize all related reporting functions into one function. Therefore, there is no function called 10K Reports, but there may be an overall SEC Reporting function. It is not possible to list all functions or potential functions here, but Exhibit 42.8 lists some examples. Each department should include several to a dozen functions. If a department contains only one function, it may be combined with another department, or it may be divided into lower-levels functions. If a department includes too many functions, then either the functions should be combined into a higher level, or that department can be divided into two departments.

The primary purpose of these interviews is to provide the information necessary to perform a matrix analysis that ranks all enterprise functions for recovery capabilities and timelines. An important secondary purpose is to raise corporate awareness of the recovery planning goals and preparations. During this interview process, the planner can explain that the overall purpose of the planning project is to protect employees and

Exhibit 42.8   Examples of High-Level Functions

Common Functions
◆ Accounts Payable
◆ Accounts Receivable
◆ Cash Accounting
◆ Customer Service
◆ Financial Analysis
◆ Financial Consolidation
◆ Financial Reporting
◆ General Ledger
◆ Inventory
◆ Invoicing
◆ Marketing Support
◆ Order Entry
◆ Parts Inventory
◆ Payroll
◆ POS, ATM & Related
◆ Process Control
◆ Purchase Order Generation
◆ SEC Reporting
◆ Tax
◆ Vital Records
◆ Work-In-Progress

the business functions they perform. This is the opportunity to promulgate disaster preparedness as a normal and necessary part of the corporate business posture.

42.3.3   Describing the Functions.   Once the functions have been listed, the interviewer must collect summary information about each function. This functional summary will be included in the BIA document so that it will be clear to the reader precisely what the function entails. The description of no more than one or two paragraphs prevents misunderstandings and helps focus discussions during the interview. Along with the summary description, the interviewer can further describe the function by identifying the key and alternate individuals responsible for performing that function. These are not the managers of the functional areas; these are the people who do the work on a daily basis, enter the data, and perform the function. Each function should be associated with those individuals and with the functional area manager, and the information should be recorded in a matrix format.

This matrix format provides a single place to record all the nonnarrative information about the function. The matrix, which also will include quantitative data, will be combined with the narrative descriptions and some analysis to become the BIA document. The descriptions of each function identify the function clearly, assess the survivability factors of the function, and associate the function with the various existing corporate capabilities. The following sections describe the information to be collected about each function and suggest ways to encourage objectivity, even when collecting subjective quantification information. Exhibit 42.9 shows a blank, sample matrix.

42.3.4   Definition of Departments and Functions.   The first column is titled *Department,* such as Financial Reporting, Central Distribution Center, A/P, Merchandising, Planning, Distribution, and Purchasing. Although these are not necessarily equal in number or scope, they are units that need to be analyzed as groups. When unsure of organizational entities, the planner can use the organization chart as a starting point. The department title can always be modified and the functions expanded as the need arises during the development of the BIA.

The second column is the *Functions* list. The functions are the high-level groups of activities performed within the department. Each function is a group of activities related to a single purpose. In the accounting department, for example, there is an accounts payable function that may include activities such as receiving invoices, requesting payment approval, scheduling payment, and printing checks. Although these detailed tasks

Exhibit 42.9   A Blank, Sample BIA Matrix

Department	Functions	Key Person	Key Alternate	Survival Days	Criticality	Ops Impact	Ranking Factor	No. Users	Category	Department Head	System Elements							

Exhibit 42.10

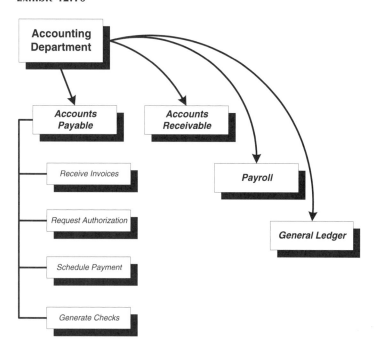

are very important, they need not be described individually since they all follow a single thread and timeline. The aim of the BIA is to establish the time and processing needs; therefore, any series of tasks that occur in a closely connected chain can be addressed together. Exhibit 42.10 pictorially depicts the relationship between departments and functions.

Another example of a department is the distribution center of a warehousing operation. This may include functions commonly known as receiving, processing, shipping, quality control, and inventory control. Some of these are aggregates of lower-level tasks. Processing is a function that includes "pulls," "moves," and "put-aways." If shipping, receiving, and processing are performed using the same resources according to a similar timeline, then they can be grouped as one function. Often, the BIA calls this the Shipping & Receiving function. If inventory control is an outcome or natural by-product of the Shipping & Receiving function, then it need not be addressed individually. On the other hand, if inventory control includes special functions apart from the Shipping & Receiving function, then it can be addressed separately.

One example of inventory as a separate function is regulated inventories. For example, alcohol storage requires careful scrutiny according to regulations of the Bureau of Alcohol, Tobacco and Firearms. Inventories must be documented according to length of storage time, source, destination, and quantities. In this case, inventory control is a special function with its own resource and timeline requirements. Another example of inventory control as a separate function is the isolated customs areas in import and export centers where inventory must be controlled according to source, arrival time, destination, departure time, and shipper.

If functions are defined too tightly, which means at too low a level of detail, then there will be a great many functions, thereby hiding the true set of functions requiring analysis. This will result in a large set of functions that are so interrelated that they cannot reasonably be separated for individual analysis. If the functions are defined too loosely, which means at too high a level, then there will be too few functions, thereby hiding the timelines and forcing all function to be rated as time critical. During the interview process, it is likely that the definition of functions will be refined and redefined several times. The functional area experts should guide the definitions, with the recovery specialist helping formulate the ideas.

42.3.4.1   *Key Person, Key Alternate, and Department Head.*   The third column identifies the *Key Person* for each function. The Key Person is typically neither a manager nor a supervisor. Rather, the Key Person normally performs the task at hand. For example, in the Accounting department's time-keeping function, the Key Person is the individual who collects and enters or validates the time-keeping information. For the Treasury department, bank transfer function, this is the individual who calls or connects to the banking system to perform the transfers and manage accounts. In other words, the person who will be responsible for performing the function during a crisis when little supervision, help, or direction is available. The manager may not know the phone numbers to dial, the people to talk to, or the keystrokes required to perform the function, but the key person must know these things, for that person may be working in virtual isolation immediately following a disaster.

The Key Person becomes an important member of the recovery team when that function is identified as a time critical, or Category I, function. In those cases, the Key Person receives training, special backup and communications equipment, and extra responsibilities. The Key Person is the enterprise's first line of defense against disasters.

The *Key Alternate Person,* identified in the fourth column, is the backup to the key person. When possible, the Key Alternate should be as well equipped and well trained as the Key Person. In practice, however, this is seldom feasible. The Key Alternate should be an employee who is as familiar with the tasks to be performed as the Key Person.

The eleventh column identifies the *Department Head.* This is the one individual who is held accountable for performance of all the functions listed for the department. The Department Heads for the various departments recorded in the matrix may report at different levels on the organization chart; this is an acceptable situation so long as each Department Head has direct management control of all functions listed for the department.

42.3.4.2   *Survival Time.*   The fifth column records the *Survival Days* as reported by the interviewee and discussed with the disaster recovery planner. The survival days is the length of time the enterprise can withstand the lack of a function with minimal impact. This length of time is measured in whatever units are appropriate to the enterprise, which may be minutes, hours, or months. This length of time is the maximum allowable downtime for the function, after which the enterprise begins to suffer serious repercussions. This measure does not determine the importance of the function to the enterprise; it only measures the time sensitivity of the function. Payroll, for example, is most often very time sensitive, affecting operations after only one or two days.

It may be possible to postpone tax accounting functions because there are alternative actions possible. Missing a filing deadline is avoidable by using past data and making reasonable, informal estimates of changes. Overpayments have few or no consequences. Underpayments may result in modest penalties and interest. Typically, payroll checks are generated close to the distribution date; there is, therefore, little spare time. However, most organizations can develop backup payroll procedures that can compress payroll processing into one or two days so that there is no delay in payroll distribution. Obtaining this information may require exploring past instances when the function had been postponed. The delay may have been due to illness, vacation, system downtime, or management direction. Inquiring about the effect of the delay may help refine the estimate of allowable downtime for the BIA.

42.3.4.3   Criticality.   The *Criticality* of a function, recorded in the sixth column, measures the magnitude of the immediate effect on the enterprise of function loss beyond the survival time. If payroll processing has been determined to have a one-day survival time, then criticality is the effect on the enterprise of payroll processing delays beginning on the second day and continuing from there. If tax accounting has been assigned an allowable downtime of 30 days, then its criticality is the affect on the enterprise after 30 days.

Criticality is a measure of time-phased impacts. The criticality of a function is loosely based on fiscal impact to the enterprise. It is not identical with fiscal loss because indirect impacts are also important. A corporate image of reliability and strength may be lost forever if functional capabilities are not restored. NASA's *Challenger* disaster had an effect far beyond any fiscal estimate. The space program suffered a setback and a long delay. Some believe that NASA's loss of funding in subsequent years was attributable to this disaster. The loss of life in the disaster is, of course, immeasurable.

A major telephone common carrier once lost a major switching station, thereby causing all of its customers to be without long distance phone capability for a significant time in the middle of a business day. Although the company lost only a relatively modest amount of money due to lost calls, the damage to its reputation lives on. Its loss of business is irreparable: Many of its dedicated customers decided to double-source their long distance providers and now split their services between this company and its major competitor. This event constituted a permanent, unrecoverable loss of market share.

The Criticality column records an estimate of the impact of loss once the survival period has been exceeded. It is an estimate because it is not the result of a detailed analysis but is rather an estimation by the interviewee based on heuristic analyses and experience. The interviewee is asked to rank each function on a scale of 1 to 10, where 1 is the least critical and 10 is the most critical. Exhibit 42.11 summarizes these level criticality ratings and provides brief descriptions. The recovery planner provides this information to the interviewee and solicits a response. These criticality ratings are subjective, so the planner and the expert must work together to attempt to smooth out individual prejudices and opinions as much as possible. However, the ratings are designed to work with the operational impact measure (described below) to minimize this problem.

On the rating scale, a value of 10 is the highest level of criticality possible. This value should be accepted only if it is clear that virtually all corporate functions will

Exhibit 42.11   Criticality Ratings and Descriptions

Range	Description
1 to 2	"Nobody would notice." Very minor inconvenience.
3 to 4	Minor inconvenience, virtually no fiscal impact.
5 to 7	Greater inconvenience, monetary impact.
8 to 9	Major problems, significant monetary impact.
10	"Out of business."

come to a standstill. Frequently, the payroll function for hourly employees fits this criterion. Hourly, unionized employees may be specifically barred from working by union rules if the enterprise cannot provide a paycheck within some number of hours after the checks are due. In the case of a manufacturing company, this could mean that all production, receiving, shipping, and related functions cease. This is tantamount to a company shutdown. The phrase "Out of business" from the summary table (Exhibit 42.11) fits this scenario. This phrase does not mean that the company ceases to exist; it means only that company operations cease until this function is restored.

The criticality range 8 to 9 often is used to signify that loss of a function will not drive an enterprise to close its doors but will cause severe damage or loss of confidence. Missed deliveries, loss of customer service functions, lower quality, and similar effects warrant a rating in this range. Functions such as corporate communications (e.g., press releases, customer relations, and shareholder notices), banking functions, some accounting filings, and order entry are examples of functions in this range.

The range of 5 to 7 is probably the criticality rating used most often. This range indicates considerable fiscal effect and significant inconvenience. If such a function were not recovered in time, the effect would be felt but would not be a major corporate event. Perhaps the significant difference between the range of 5 to 7 and the range of 8 to 9 can be summarized as follows: The former is an internal event that would be an internal problem. The latter would be reportable in annual reports and may require media involvement or public advertisements to explain the outage. The higher range has significance beyond corporate walls. Some functions that often meet the lower criteria are accounts payable, various reporting functions, and low-priority government regulatory requirements.

The criticality range of 3 to 4 identifies loss of a function as a minor inconvenience, with little or no monetary impact. Various filings, audits, and internal support functions often can be delayed, with no impact other than the need to perform the work later when functional capability is restored. These are not unimportant functions, but they are functions that can be delayed for a fixed interval with minimal impact on corporate operations. Examples of such functions are certifications, some SEC filings, electronic data processing (EDP) audit, financial audit, internal consulting, corporate directories, and ongoing training programs. Although these are important functions, sometimes significant to overall corporate survival, often they can be delayed without major problems.

The 1 to 2 criticality level indicates that loss of the function would be barely noticeable for the short term and would cause minimal inconvenience. Although these may be important, often regulated, functions, often they are fairly time independent. Examples include former employee tracking functions, claims management, charitable contributions, and equal employment opportunity/affirmative action plans. Although these are not necessarily level 1 to 2 functions in all companies, often they are functions that can be delayed for a significant time without jeopardizing the corporate mission.

42.3.4.4   Operational Impact, Ranking Factor, and Number of Users.   The *Operational Impact*, recorded in the seventh column, is an automated result that is a function of the criticality. Individuals within the enterprise will express their biases in the criticality ratings they assign to various functions. One employee may say that a function has a criticality rating of 7 and another may say 6 or 8. The operational impact measure lowers the granularity of the estimates by transforming a scale of 10 levels to a scale of 4 levels. In this way, individual biases can be normalized and the estimates adjusted to achieve a four-level assessment of functional criticalities and impacts.

Exhibit 42.12   Transformation of Criticality to Operational Impact

Criticality	Impact	Description
10–9	1	Critical operational impact or fiscal loss
8–7–6	2	Significant operational impact or fiscal loss
5–4–3	3	Some operational impact or fiscal loss
2–1	4	No short term impacts or fiscal losses

Operational Impact is derived through a many-to-one mapping that transforms criticality to operational impact as shown in Exhibit 42.12. This transformation achieves a data smoothing function that removes discontinuities caused by individual or organizational biases. It also reverses the order of importance, making 1 the highest impact and 4 the lowest impact. This transposes the Criticality measurements; where earlier a higher number meant higher criticality to a system, now a lower number means greater impact and higher priority. This provides a mathematical convenience for combining survival time and criticality into a single measure.

The eighth column is the *Ranking Factor,* which is the combination of survival time and operational impact, and hence criticality. The ranking factor is the product of the survival time in days and the operational impact. A function with short survival time and high operational impact receives the highest priority (lowest number) ranking factor. For example, a function with a one-day survival time and level 1 operational impact receives a ranking factor of 1. Another function with a seven-day survival time and operational impact of 3 earns a ranking factor of 21.

The purpose of the ranking factor is to provide a single measure that ranks all corporate functions from highest priority to lowest priority for recovery planning purposes. The compilation of all functions listed in ascending order of ranking factor will show functions in their order of priority for disaster recovery and restoration.

The ninth column of the matrix shown in Exhibit 42.9 is the *Number of Users.* This column simply records the number of employees involved in each function. Note that in most cases, individual employees perform multiple functions and, therefore, will be counted as users in several functional areas. As a result, the sum of users in this column may exceed the total employees of the enterprise. This duplication is acceptable and accounted for in the detailed plans.

42.3.4.5   *Category.* The tenth column is used to record the *Category* of the function. This column summarizes the analysis achieved through the assessment of survival time, identification of criticality, and computation of ranking factors. The category is simply a way of grouping functions with similar recovery periods. Once sorted by ranking factor in ascending order, the functions are then classified into several categories based on natural groupings.

Using heuristic techniques or more formal graphical ones, the survival times of the functions can be traced or mapped as they proceed from highest priority to lowest priority. The functions will naturally fall into groups or clusters. Often one category consists of functions requiring recovery within one to three days, which can be assigned Category I, and which form the foundation of functions requiring quick recovery. Another group, which can be assigned Category II, often consists of functions requiring recovery or resumption in one to two weeks. These are the highest-priority recovery functions once all of the Category I items have resumed. Other categories are similarly assigned.

Exhibit 42.13

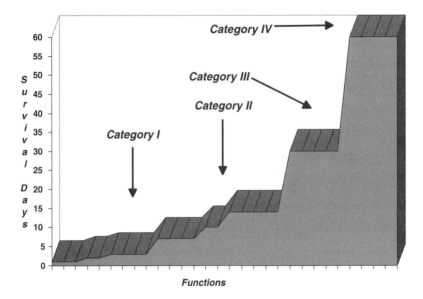

Exhibit 42.13 shows a sample translation of functions to a graph and the subsequent assignment of categories. Each function is represented by one "tick" mark on the horizontal axis, the X-axis. The corresponding survival time is the height, graphed on the Y-axis. In the exhibit, there are four categories: Category I functions have survival periods of from one to three days. Category II functions have survival times of seven to 14 days. Category III functions have survival times of 30 days, and Category IV have survival times of 60 days. Although there are usually more functions than those shown on the exhibit, the process is the same.

42.3.4.6 System Elements.   The twelfth and final column is really a series of columns each representing a system element. The system elements consist of hardware, software, communications systems, and operating units. The purpose of these columns is to record which functions make use of which system elements. For each function, the disaster recovery planner marks the appropriate system element used in performing that function.

Columns may correspond to hardware devices or to a functional hardware description, such as "imaging system." Major software systems may be column headings, especially for custom-built or custom-tailored software systems such as material requirements planning (MRP) or accounting systems. Office software systems such as word processors, spreadsheets, presentation software, databases, communication software, and many other software packages may each form column headings as well. Software packages that are always installed as a group may be described that way in the column. Several system elements may constitute one functional system. For example, the time-keeping and recording function may use electronic punch clocks, communication links between the clocks and a computer, and software to translate the electronic punch clock data into timesheets. This entire system may be labeled as the time-keeping system and be consolidated into one column.

This column also functions as a check and balance against the defined scope of the recovery plan. If columns are necessary for systems that are out of scope, then either the scope must be changed or important statements must be made regarding the limited recovery posture for those system elements not included in the plan.

42.4   BUSINESS IMPACT ANALYSIS MATRIX ANALYSIS.   The BIA matrix forms the heart of the Business Impact Analysis. The matrix provides the basic information needed to establish recovery requirements and timelines and to estimate costs of outages. The matrix can be manipulated to help the recovery planner perform the analyses required for translating the business objectives defined earlier in the process into the Business Continuity Plan objectives.

42.4.1   Listing the Functions Organizationally.   The major matrix manipulations that the planner will perform are a special set of sorts. Exhibit 42.14 shows a sample

Exhibit 42.14   A Sample BIA Matrix

Department	Functions	Survive Days	Criticality	Ops Impact	Ranking Factor	No. of Users	Category
Corp. Accounting	Cash Management	1	10	1	1	2	
Corp. Accounting	Benefits	1	5	3	3	1	
Corp. Accounting	Payroll (Mgt.)	2	9	1	2	2	
Corp. Accounting	A/P	2	6	2	4	3	
Corp. Accounting	Financial Planning	30	7	2	60	4	
Corp. Accounting	Income Tax	30	7	2	60	2	
Corp. Accounting	A/R	30	6	2	60	3	
Corp. Accounting	G/L	30	5	3	90	2	
Corporate Services	Auto Fleet Mgt.	30	6	2	60	1	
Corporate Services	Travel Administration	30	2	4	120	2	
Corporate Services	Facilities	1	10	1	1	2	
Customer Service	Order Entry	1	8	2	2	1	
Customer Service	Production Scheduling	2	9	1	2	1	
Human Resources	Payroll (Union)	1	10	1	1	2	
Human Resources	Workers Comp.	10	8	2	20	1	
Human Resources	Benefits	15	3	3	45	1	
Human Resources	OSHA Compliance Programs	90	N/A	N/A	N/A	1	
Human Resources	Rideshare Program	90	1	4	360	1	
Marketing	Pricing Strategies	2	10	1	2	3	
Marketing	Strategic Product Development	14	9	1	14	5	
Marketing	Account Targeting	30	6	2	60	3	
Marketing	Advertising	90	3	3	270	2	
Materials	Production Scheduling	1	8	2	2	2	
Materials	Purchasing	1	8	2	2	3	
Materials	Bill & Materials	3	6	2	6	1	
Materials	Materials Planning	7	4	3	21	2	
Materials	Invoice I/F	14	8	2	28	2	
QA	Inspection Records	7	3	3	21	1	
QA	Project Tracking	14	4	3	42	4	
QA	Reporting	30	3	3	90	1	
R&D	CAE	1	7	2	2	4	
R&D	General Research	14	4	3	42	2	

BIA matrix. This sample BIA matrix is representative of a corporate headquarters facility with some production and warehousing capabilities. The matrix shown is for illustrative purposes only and therefore is composed of only a selected subset of the columns found in an operational matrix. It also shows only a few of the many corporate functions that would normally comprise a full matrix.

This matrix is sorted alphabetically by department. Within departments, it is sorted first by survival time of functions starting with shortest survival. When the survival time of functions is equal, functions are sorted by criticality so that the most critical functions are listed first. This matrix sort, called the organizational sort because it follows corporate structures, frequently is the first one used and is most useful for summarizing interviews and results. This sort is also the one that is most useful when meeting with the department managers, for their concerns center on their own departments.

42.4.2   Finding Cross-Department Functions.   A second useful view emphasizes similar functions across departmental boundaries. In this view, shown in Exhibit 42.15, functions that cross departments are grouped together. This matrix, which for simplicity is a subset of the matrix shown in Exhibit 42.14, provides facility for uncovering functions with similar titles performed by different departments. In the exhibit, there are three sets of functions with similar names but different departments.

The Corporate Accounting and Human Resources departments both perform functions named *Benefits*. However, the two departments describe the survival time and criticality of these functions very differently. Human Resources considers this function a minor inconvenience with virtually no fiscal impact and an allowable downtime of more than two weeks. The Accounting Department tags this function with a downtime of only one day and a greater inconvenience with fiscal impact. The ranking factors of these two functions, both called Benefits, are widely different in value, showing at a glance that there is a discrepancy here. The planner must determine whether this discrepancy is the result of inconsistent descriptions, and therefore a problem, or the result of different functions with a similar name.

Exhibit 42.15   Emphasizing Cross-Departmental Functions

Department	Functions	Survive Days	Criticality	Ops Impact	Ranking Factor	No. of Users	Category
Corporate Services	Auto Fleet Mgt.	30	6	2	60	1	
Corp. Accounting	Benefits	1	5	3	3	1	
Human Resources	Benefits	15	3	3	45	1	
Customer Service	Order Entry	1	8	2	2	1	
Human Resources	OSHA Compliance Programs	90	N/A	N/A	N/A	1	
Corp. Accounting	Payroll (Mgt.)	2	9	1	2	2	
Human Resources	Payroll (Union)	1	10	1	1	2	
Marketing	Pricing Strategies	2	10	1	2	3	
Materials	Production Scheduling	1	8	2	2	2	
Customer Service	Production Scheduling	2	9	1	2	1	
QA	Project Tracking	14	4	3	42	4	

The other two sets of cross functions are the *Payroll* function, another overlap between the Corporate Accounting and Human Resources departments, and *Production Scheduling,* which is performed by both the Materials Department and Customer Service. In both cases, the survival time and criticality measures were assessed to be similar by both departments, with ranking factors that are close or the same.

The matrix makes apparent the existing overlaps, but the planner must determine whether the overlaps are similar, overlapping functions or different functions with similar names. In the first example, the function named Benefits is quite different. The Human Resources Department views this function as a regular record-keeping function with occasional changes, and it includes tracking and managing employee health plan choices, usually offered annually. Short processing delays are usually inconsequential to the enterprise and its employees. For the Corporate Accounting department, however, the same named function includes making matching funds payments, exercising stock options, and calculating other financial disbursements based on existing benefits packages and agreements. The functions are similarly named but different in meaning.

The other two examples are similar functions with the same meanings but performed from different perspectives. Payroll for management and union personnel is performed differently due to union rules and regulations. Therefore, Corporate Accounting can calculate regular salaries and benefits for management employees and produce payroll checks. However, the Human Resources department must be involved in calculating pay for unionized, hourly employees to make certain that all rules and regulations are followed precisely.

Production Scheduling, performed by Customer Service and by Materials, is a similar function with a different perspective. For Customer Service, production scheduling means setting requirements for customer deliveries and, thereby, determining production schedules. Materials finalizes the schedules to reconcile possibly conflicting production requirements for different customers by advancing or delaying schedules within corporate policy constraints.

The planner must understand the meaning of each function and recognize the differences between similarly named functions so that all recovery capabilities meet the true needs of the corporate users and customers.

42.4.3   Using the Ranking Factor.   A third view, which is the most important part of the matrix analysis, is the ranking factor view. In this sort, shown in Exhibit 42.16, functions are listed in ascending numerical order according to their ranking factor first and then in ascending numerical sequence according to survival days. The purpose of this view is to assign *Category* designations to all functions and to establish specific timelines for the categories. These timelines become the disaster recovery plan *technical* objectives. Exhibit 42.16 consists of the same data as the previous exhibits but sorted differently.

A useful function of the ranking factor is to list functions in a reasonable priority order for recovery timeline planning. The primary purpose of the Category designation is to group functions by recovery requirement or timeline, as a function of short-term importance to the enterprise. Therefore, the ranking factor sort is ideal for determining functional categorizations. All Category I functions for this organization must be recovered in less than three days. For most of these functions, the criticality is high and the survival time is low. Category II functions begin when the survival time jumps to 14 days.

This type of orderly grouping is not exceptional; it occurs in most organizations. The natural organizational activity is to perform functions, which generally must be

Exhibit 42.16   The Ranking Factor View

Department	Functions	Survive Days	Criticality	Ops Impact	Ranking Factor	No. of Users	Category
Human Resources	Payroll (Union)	1	10	1	1	2	I
Corporate Services	Facilities	1	10	1	1	2	I
Corp. Accounting	Cash Management	1	10	1	1	2	I
R&D	CAE	1	7	2	2	4	I
Materials	Production Scheduling	1	8	2	2	2	I
Materials	Purchasing	1	8	2	2	3	I
Customer Service	Order Entry	1	8	2	2	1	I
Marketing	Pricing Strategies	2	10	1	2	3	I
Customer Service	Production Scheduling	2	9	1	2	1	I
Corp. Accounting	Payroll (Mgt.)	2	9	1	2	2	I
Corp. Accounting	Benefits	1	5	3	3	1	I
Corp. Accounting	A/P	2	6	2	4	3	I
Materials	Bill & Materials	3	6	2	6	1	I
Marketing	Strategic Product Development	14	9	1	14	5	II
Human Resources	Workers Comp.	10	8	2	20	1	II
QA	Inspection Records	7	3	3	21	1	II
Materials	Materials Planning	7	4	3	21	2	II
Materials	Invoice I/F	14	8	2	28	2	II
R&D	General Research	14	4	3	42	2	II
QA	Project Tracking	14	4	3	42	4	II
Human Resources	Benefits	15	3	3	45	1	II
Marketing	Account Targeting	30	6	2	60	3	III
Corporate Services	Auto Fleet Mgt.	30	6	2	60	1	III
Corp. Accounting	Financial Planning	30	7	2	60	4	III
Corp. Accounting	Income Tax	30	7	2	60	2	III
Corp. Accounting	A/R	30	6	2	60	3	III
QA	Reporting	30	3	3	90	1	III
Corp. Accounting	G/L	30	5	3	90	2	III
Corporate Services	Travel Administration	30	2	4	120	2	III
Marketing	Advertising	90	3	3	270	2	III
Human Resources	Rideshare Program	90	1	4	360	1	III
Human Resources	OSHA Compliance Programs	90	N/A	N/A	N/A	1	III

performed in a regular, repeating pattern. Many functions are critical and performed almost daily. Other functions are performed weekly, monthly, quarterly, or annually. The ranking factor is a good tool for viewing functions according to their natural cycle. It works because this factor measures both cycles and relative importance. Either measure alone would be insufficient. Exhibit 42.17 graphs three basic measures: survival days, operational impact, and ranking factor. This graphical representation is based on the data contained in Exhibit 42.16.

Exhibit 42.17   Survival Days, Operational Impact, and Ranking Factor

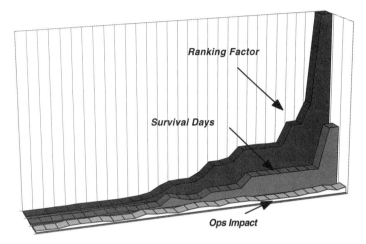

Each item on the horizontal (*X*) axis represents one function from the matrix. The height of each of the three curves represents their numerical values. The ranking is an increasing curve because the data are presented according to the ranking factor view. The survival days is "mostly" increasing but does drop near the middle of the graph and then rises again. This dip corresponds to the two functions with seven-day survival times. The operational impact curve begins at fairly low values, corresponding to high levels of effects, and ends with fairly high values, corresponding to lower levels of effects. This curve rises and falls but follows a generally increasing pattern.

Sorting this information according to operational impact would not yield sufficient information upon which to base recovery timelines. Some functions with great detrimental effects only begin to have an effect after a longer time. Similarly, a simple sort of survival time may erroneously include functions as high priority whose operational impacts are too low to merit the quick recovery and expense associated with Category I functions. In both cases, the timeline would not be accurate because the sorting criteria exclude either levels of impact or time. Only the ranking factor is reliable since it reflects both time and effect simultaneously.

42.5   JUSTIFYING THE COSTS.   One of the most difficult aspects of the planning process is justifying the costs of the planning process, the reserve equipment, and the contract services. The cost justification is performed best and most efficiently using the Generalized Cost Consequence Model rather than the Quantitative Risk Model. Both models are described in the following sections.

42.5.1   Quantitative Risk Model.   The Quantitative Risk Model is a formal and rigorous methodology for analyzing expected losses that will be incurred over a predetermined time period. This procedure requires a significant amount of analysis and research. The Quantitative Risk Model consists of three main factors: probability of loss, cost of loss, and annual loss expectancy (ALE). The probability of loss is really a sum of the probabilities of different catastrophic events that range from partial outages to severe interruptions. The cost of loss depends on the level of interruption. For example, a partial building loss affecting computer systems but leaving phone systems in operating condition has a much lower cost than a complete building destruction. Therefore, the cost of loss is dependent on the type of disaster.

A simplified risk model considers the probability of loss and the cost of the loss. The annual loss expectancy is the product of the probability and the cost. For example, assume there is a 5 percent probability (annual) of a major power failure. Stated differently, this means that the facility will experience a major power failure once in 20 years. Let us further assume that the power failure will cause a 72-hour outage, which will cost the enterprise $1,250,000. The ALE is calculated as 5% ¥ $1,250,000, or $62,500. This number is compared to the baseline cost of the recovery plan and the cost of capital. For example, say the cost of the recovery plan is $2,000 per month and the cost of capital is $25,000. Then the baseline cost or comparison figure is (12 ¥ $2,000) + $25,000, or $49,000. Since the comparison figure is lower than the ALE, recovery planning is justified.

There are some serious shortcomings in this simplified approach. First, the cost of the outage depends on the level of loss. A 72-hour power outage is significantly costlier than a 24-hour outage. Therefore, the ALE must reflect the difference in probabilities of different levels of impact. Another problem is defining the probability of occurrence for an aggregation of events.

The more acceptable risk model must consider the different levels of loss and sum the probabilities of all disasters that can cause that level of loss to define the true probability of loss for that loss level. This is accomplished for each loss level. First, a series of disaster events is defined. Each event is then refined into levels. For example, office buildings are susceptible to loss due to fire. Data on numbers of fires and amount of destruction (in predefined ranges) are available from various fire protection services. For a given facility, consider the total number of such buildings in the geographical vicinity. Then calculate the frequency or probability of a fire causing a range of damage. Perform this calculation for each defined range of damage. Assess the level of loss for each range of damage. Then calculate the ALE for each range of damage by multiplying the probability of a fire causing that range of damage with cost of the loss if there is such a fire. Sum all the ALE values to calculate the total fire ALE. This calculation must be performed for all types of disasters that can affect the facility to determine the grand total ALE. For each level of impact for all disasters, the baseline costs also must be calculated. These figures are also summed to form a total Baseline Cost. The grand total ALE is then compared with this baseline cost figure.

This analysis is a complex process that requires great effort to generate and even greater patience to explain. However, there are two more important problems with the Quantitative Risk Model.

1. Calculating all the outage costs is very difficult and subject to debate. Moreover, once the cost figures are finalized, they are subject to constant change due to the changing business climate and practices.

2. Calculating the probabilities is also very difficult and often requires many subjective conclusions. For example, what is the effect of modernizing the sprinkler system on the level of damage experienced by a particular type of fire? Each countermeasure can significantly alter both the cost and the probability. Moreover, the probability of any particular event tends to be quite small, often less than 1 percent.

While the Quantitative Risk Model is an interesting actuarial exercise, it is of marginal use in modern Business Continuity Planning.

42.5.2 Generalized Cost Consequence Model. The Generalized Cost Consequence (GCC) Model (developed by this author between 1990 and 1995) does not consider probabilities of specific disaster events. Instead, it estimates the total cost of outages as a function of time after an event. This model is significantly simpler than the Quantitative Risk Model: It is easier to build and simpler to explain. The GCC estimates the cost of an outage for each function and applies that cost to the total disaster cost after the maximum allowable down time has been exceeded.

For instance, assume the cost of delaying the Treasury Department's bank management function is $25,000 per day after the first day. Let us also assume that the cost of delaying the law department's general contract review is $5,000 per day after seven days. For the bank management function, we calculate the cost to the enterprise as $25,000 per day beginning on the first day. For the contract review function, we calculate the cost as $5,000 per day beginning on the eighth day. Therefore, the contract review function does not contribute to loss during the first seven days. We perform this calculation for each function, then collect the costs by category. This category cost summary is used to develop and present a graph that shows the total cost losses for each category level once they are activated and the total for all categories over time.

A sample graph of the contribution of functions aggregated by Category level is shown in Exhibit 42.18. In this example, Category I functions cause slightly more than $120,000 of loss on a daily basis once the maximum allowable downtime has been exceeded. Category II functions contribute slightly under $60,000 in this example. It is likely that different functions will commence their loss contribution at various times after the disaster event. Therefore, the true Category I loss contribution may begin at a lower level and increase to its full level. That distribution of effect will occur beginning on the first day any function exceeds its allowable downtime and continues to grow until the last day any function exceeds its downtime, at which point the effect will have achieved its full loss contribution. Since categorizations cluster functions with similar downtimes, the loss can be presented as a single, or point, value rather than as a value that varies over time.

The bars indicate that Category I has a higher value than Categories II and III. Category IV is also high. The U-shape is characteristic of this graph. No matter how many categories are used, the Category I functions tend to be quite high in their contributions. The next one or two categories are lower, but increasing in values until the lowest-priority category, which tends to be quite high. This shape results from the

Exhibit 42.18

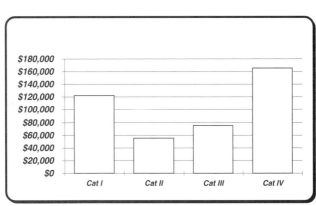

manner of the categorizations. The Category I functions are highly critical with great effects on corporate operations. Category I functions tend to be few in number, with each function contributing significantly. The middle categories tend to be larger in number than Category I, with the number increasing with each succeeding category, although still small compared to the overall set of organizational functions. The final category tends to contain the largest number of functions, each of which contributes less on a daily basis than the Category I functions, but the sheer magnitude of this set often causes it to be the largest overall contributor to loss. Of course, Category I functions begin their effects quickly, while loss of Category IV functions may be insignificant for weeks.

Exhibit 42.19 presents a sample graph showing the accumulation of losses from all categories following a disaster. This exhibit uses the same values as Exhibit 42.18 but presents them in a different format and represents the losses accumulated after 45 days. Neither this nor the previous exhibit measures physical losses such as real property, capital equipment, and the like. Physical losses are not issues that affect the planning process; they affect the cost to recover and are independent of continuation measures. The horizontal (X) axis represents the number of days since the disaster event caused damage and cessation of corporate functions. The vertical (Y) axis represents the total losses the enterprise will have sustained on the corresponding day represented on the x-axis.

At the time of the disaster occurrence, no losses will have accumulated. Thereafter, the accumulated loss is increased each day by the cost contribution of the category whose earliest start time has already been surpassed. Assume that Category I functions begin to contribute to corporate losses of $120,000 on the first day, that Category II functions begin to contribute losses of $60,000 on the seventh day, and that Category III functions contribute $80,000 daily beginning on the fourteenth day. In this case, the cumulative loss begins at zero and grows by $120,000 per day for the first six days. On the seventh day, the Category II functions begin to contribute $60,000 per day along with the ongoing contribution of the Category I functions. Therefore, beginning on the seventh day, the cumulative loss grows by the sum of $120,000 and $60,000, which is $180,000 daily. On the fourteenth day, the daily loss increases by another $80,000,

Exhibit 42.19   Cumulative Loss Summary

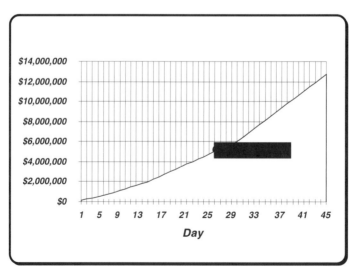

representing the Category III contribution. This brings the total daily loss to $240,000, which is the sum of the contributions of Categories I, II, and III.

The cumulative loss summary shows at a glance the loss that an enterprise will experience over time following the disaster, if no recovery planning is performed. The active simplifications of this model are the grouping of functions by category and the subsequent representation of each category as a single value beginning at a fixed point in time. This may render the estimate slightly inaccurate at some local points, but the overall values are as accurate as the underlying estimates.

The Generalized Cost Consequence Model summarizes at a glance the effects of loss of functions. These loss figures can be affected by insurance reimbursements, legal liabilities, and overall management objectives.

A second model can be developed if the recovery planning is in place, showing the residual loss proposed. That model would be developed in a similar manner, but with the assumption that certain functions are restored within established time parameters. There would be residual loss only if the restoration occurs later than the allowable downtime, which will almost certainly be the case for some functions. Exhibit 42.20 presents a graph that shows cumulative losses with and without a disaster recovery plan in place. The *Without Plan* curve is similar to the previous exhibit. The *With Plan* curve reflects the residual loss that would occur even if a plan were in place. This loss is normally dramatically lower but is seldom zero. Typically, a reduction to zero residual loss would require extraordinary and prohibitively expensive measures. Most organizations can benefit more from a substantial lowering of residual losses than from a full reduction to zero losses.

The estimation process itself is much simpler than for the Quantitative Risk Model. For each function, the loss estimate is based on three criteria, or types of losses. These are:

1. Tangible and direct losses
2. Tangible and indirect losses
3. Intangible losses

The tangible and direct losses are the easiest to calculate. These losses can be traced to specific revenue-producing functions. The results are direct because the loss occurs as a first-order effect, meaning that revenue stops because the function cannot be performed. The results are tangible because they can be measured easily. An example of

Exhibit 42.20   Cumulative Loss Summary With and Without Planning

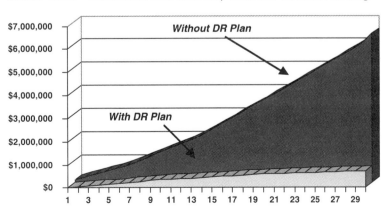

such a function is automated production control of an assembly line. If the systems exceed their allowable downtime, then production will cease. The cost is the resultant loss of sales after inventory is depleted. Another example is loss of order entry functions. In this case, the result is similarly calculable: lost sales after in-stock items are depleted and existing orders are produced. Tangible, direct losses include lost sales, lost manufacturing, lost deliveries, and other lost opportunities.

The tangible and indirect losses are the most common although slightly more difficult to estimate. Support functions generally produce tangible results whose deprivation would cause a financial loss indirectly. For example, a public corporation issues quarterly earnings reports that, if late, could have significant consequences on the company's stock value. Although this is not a direct loss resulting from cessation of sales or other production, the loss can be calculated using accounting standard practices. The internal accounting personnel are in the best position to provide this estimate to the disaster recovery planner. Tangible, indirect losses include penalties, fees, fines, market share, and other issues that can be directly calculated, or at least estimated with some degree of confidence.

Intangible losses are the most difficult to calculate. These intangible effects include reduced public confidence, compromised customer satisfaction, promises not kept, damaged reputation, and other losses that are general in nature and not easily calculable. Sometimes, these losses are not translated into specific financial losses and are, therefore, not represented in the cost graphs. In such cases, prominent notations should be made explaining the additional but not quantified losses.

According to a study by Contingency Planning Research, hourly losses by major companies can range from a low of $12,000 for service-oriented organizations to over $7 million for a major brokerage firm. There are no strict rules for estimating losses. The timeline can be specified in increments of days, as shown in the preceding examples. It also can be as fine as hours or minutes. Some industries, such as hospitals and other acute care facilities, must measure loss in finer increments.

The Generalized Cost Consequence Model can solve the problem of cost justification. This model shows the potential, possibly catastrophic, losses without engaging in the analysis paralysis that can stem from a detailed Quantitative Risk Model development effort.

42.6 FURTHER READING

Arnold, R. *Disaster Recovery Plan.* New York: John Wiley & Sons, 1993.

Barnes, J.C., and P.J. Rothstein. *A Guide to Business Continuity Planning.* New York: John Wiley & Sons, 2001.

Butler, J.G., and P. Badura. *Contingency Planning and Disaster Recovery: Protecting Your Organization's Resources.* Computer Technology Research Corp., 1997.

Fulmer, K.L. *Business Continuity Planning, 2000 Edition: A Step-by-Step Guide with Planning Forms on CD-ROM.* Brookfield: Rothstein Associates, 2000.

Hiatt, C.J. *A Primer for Disaster Recovery Planning in an IT Environment.* Hershey, PA: Idea Group Publishing, 2000.

Myers, K.N. *Manager's Guide to Contingency Planning for Disasters: Protecting Vital Facilities and Critical Operations,* 2nd ed. New York: John Wiley & Sons, 1999.

Schreider, T. *Encyclopedia of Disaster Recovery, Security & Risk Management.* Crucible Publishing Works, 1998.

Toigo, J.W. *Disaster Recovery Planning: For Computers and Communication Resources.* New York: John Wiley & Sons, 1995.

Toigo, J.W., and M.R. Toigo. *Disaster Recovery Planning: Strategies for Protecting Critical Information Assets,* 2nd ed. Englewood Cliffs, NJ: Prentice-Hall, 1999.

CHAPTER **43**

DISASTER RECOVERY

Michael Miora

CONTENTS

43.1 INTRODUCTION. In Chapter 42, the importance of a business impact analysis (BIA) and the method of preparing one were described. Once the preliminary groundwork is finished and the BIA analysis is complete, the next step is to design specific strategies for recovery and the tasks for applying those strategies. In this chapter we will discuss the specific strategies to recover the Category I functions, the most time-critical functions identified during the BIA, as well as the remaining lower priority functions. We will examine the traditional strategies of hot sites, warm sites, and cold sites, as well as a more modern technique we call reserve systems. We will describe how to make good use of Internet and client/server technologies, and of high-speed connections for data backup, for making electronic journals, and for data vaulting. We will develop the recovery tasks representing the specific activities that must take place to continue functioning and to resume full operations. These tasks begin with the realization that there is, or may be, a disaster in progress, continue through to full business resumption, and end with normalization. We examine a set of tasks taken from a real-world disaster recovery plan to illustrate how each task fits into an overall plan, accounting for anticipated contingencies while providing flexibility to handle unforeseen circumstances.

43.2   IDENTIFYING THREATS AND DISASTER SCENARIOS.   Threat assessment is the foundation for discovery of threats, and their possible levels of impact. Threat assessments can vary from rigorous analyses of natural events and the probabilities associated with them, to informal surveys of recent disasters and their regional characteristics. The rigorous analysis will yield detailed results, but will require significant effort to perform the required research and to interpret the results. The informal survey can yield sufficient information for the disaster recovery planner, and it requires significantly less effort.

43.2.1   Threats.   Local fire, police, and other emergency response services can provide the data needed for an informal survey. Flood district management agencies can provide data regarding floods of all types, whether caused by storms, draining, or other factors. Police departments can provide information about building or neighborhood closures due to man-made catastrophes, whereas city and county governments can provide information about emergency declarations over a period of years.

Compiling this list of threats accomplishes two objectives. First, it helps define the different levels of impact, and second, it helps to develop a risk mitigation plan. The mitigation techniques outlined in the plan are intended to lower the damage caused by the likeliest disasters. For example, an area prone to seasonal flooding can reduce the risk of computer outages by placing computer installations and important equipment above the flood level. Facilities located in areas prone to power failures can install uninterruptible power supply (UPS) equipment with higher capacities than usual for the type of equipment being protected.

There are many threats that can have important consequences to information-processing systems. Physical security risks stand out among them as the highest profile disasters. These are also the most highly dependent on geography and include events such as fire, flood, and earthquake, risks that are discussed more fully in Chapter 14.

Exhibit 43.1 lists a large number of threats to help the disaster recovery planner begin the process of listing threats that apply to specific facilities.

43.2.2   Disaster Recovery Scenarios.   Each of the threats described in Chapter 14 and Exhibit 43.1 causes specific damage, with the scope of damage and damage characteristics well known and predefined. Once the characteristics of specific threats are known, then mitigation measures can be applied. One of the important mitigation techniques is the application of survivable technologies to mission-critical functions. Survivable technologies applied to the most critical of the functions (Category I) can prevent outages, or at least significantly lower the probability and duration of the outage. For example, client/server and distributed architectures can be implemented with geographic data distribution, so that the loss of a single data center will not disrupt operations, but may only degrade them. One such strategy is the remote placement of two computers operating on a single main network with functionality shared between them. If backup data are regularly logged from one machine to another, then both systems maintain current databases. If one system is disrupted, then the other can assume full functions; the response times may degrade, but the functionality will not be lost. Replicated architectures are an even better alternative. The desirability of such measures was amply demonstrated by the catastrophe of September 11, 2001.

Escalation scenarios are mechanisms that map the expected duration of failures against the requirements for operational continuity. With well-known threats as described above, and the ensuing and defined outage durations that can be characterized, disaster declaration and escalation points can be calculated and presented. Timelines must be

Exhibit 43.1 List of Threats

List of Threats		
Accidents	Denial of Service Attacks	Kidnapping/Hostages
Acts of God	Disgruntled Employees	Labor Disputes
Aircraft Accident	Drug Abuse	Local Area Disaster
Alcohol Abuse	Dust Storms	Malicious Damage
Area Evacuation	Earthquakes	Mass Illness
Arson	Elevator Failure	Municipal Service Failure
Asbestos	Embezzlement	Nuclear Accident
Boiler Explosion	Environmental Controls Fail	Postal Strike
Bomb Threat	Evacuation	Power Failure
Brownout	Falling Object	Regional Disaster
Building Inaccessible	Fire	Sabotage
Chemical Spill	Flood	Sanctions
Civil Unrest/Riots	Fraud	Sand Storm
Cold Weather	Hacker Attack	Snow Storm
Communications Failure	Hardware Failures	Strike
Computer Virus	Heat	Terrorism
Construction Disturbance	Humidity	Tornado
Crime	Hurricane	Utility Failure
Data Diddling	Ice Storms	Volcano
Delivery Interruptions	Industrial Espionage	Water Damage
Demonstrations	Information Compromise	Water Supply Failure

carefully constructed to leave little room for doubt. Exhibit 43.2 provides an example of an escalation timeline. In this exhibit, the vertical row of boxes correspond to recovery time estimates. For each row, specific initiation parameters are established. The operators and engineers can, at a glance, determine whether this particular situation requires a disaster declaration. The key factors are that the operations personnel must be trained in the use of the procedures and have ready access to contact information for disaster recovery declaration authorities.

Disaster recovery scenarios and activities are dependent on the scope of the damage. Therefore, it is necessary to group specific events according to a classification of the damage they inflict on a facility. Once this is accomplished, the disaster recovery planner can identify declaration, escalation, and recovery activities based on the specific threats and their resulting disaster scenarios. Classifications of damage include the duration of an outage and the scope of its effects.

Exhibit 43.3 summarizes some threat durations and provides some sample classifications of damage. The first column of the exhibit lists a sampling of threats and the second column classifies each of the samples according to the possible scope of its effect. The set of possibilities contains systems only, partial or full building, local area, and regional area.

**Exhibit 43.2   Escalation
Timeline**

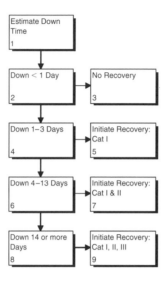

A systems-only disaster leaves the facility unaffected, but partially or fully disables the system's operations. Breaches of logical security usually affect only systems, as do hardware failures. The table does not attempt to differentiate between types of systems and number of systems affected, but the disaster recovery planner must do that classification for each facility and for the interactions of facilities. A characteristic of systems-only disasters is that they can sometimes travel across physical boundaries, such as when the incident involves a security breach, a connectivity disruption, or a software failure.

Partial- or full-building disasters consist of events that cause physical damage to a building. Fires usually affect only one building at a time. Even detection of asbestos, which most often occurs during building maintenance or improvement, is seldom a multi-building affair. Local and regional area disasters are difficult to distinguish from each other. Generally, a disaster that affects a single geographic area such as a city or neighborhood is a local-area disaster, whereas a disaster affecting more than one geographic entity is a regional disaster. The importance of this demarcation is that local area disasters at a company site may affect some of the employees personally, although most of them will be unaffected, except as it relates to company business. A regional disaster usually affects most employees' homes and families, as well as the organizations that employ them. A municipal services failure clearly affects a single geographic entity, and employees living outside of that municipality are unlikely to be affected. Conversely, a major storm resulting in floods, or a large earthquake, will affect residents and businesses over a wide area, probably leaving employees at work concerned with the health and safety of their families and homes. The availability of employees to handle a disaster is much greater when the disaster is local, or of smaller scope, than during a regional disaster.

The third column estimates the duration of the effect, ranging from hours to days to weeks. These are inexact and somewhat vague guidelines only. Although fire is listed as having a duration ranging from days to weeks, a very small fire may be managed and the building reoccupied in only a few hours. Similarly, an earthquake is listed as having a duration of days to weeks, yet a major earthquake may have large impacts

Exhibit 43.3   Sample Classifications of Damage

Sample Classifications of Damage		
Event Description	*Possible Scope of Effect*	*Potential Duration of Effect*
Aircraft Accident	Building to Local Area	Hours to Days
Asbestos	Partial to Full Building	Days to Weeks
Bomb Threat	Building to Local Area	Hours to Days
Chemical Spill	Building to Local Area	Hours to Days
Civil Unrest/Riots	Local to Regional	Days to Weeks
Cold Weather	Local to Regional	Days
Communications Failure	Building to Regional	Hours to Days
Computer Virus	Systems	Hours to Days
Data Diddling	Systems	Hours to Days
Earthquakes	Local to Regional	Days to Weeks
Environmental Controls Fail	Partial to Full Building	Hours to Days
Fire	Partial to Full Building	Days to Weeks
Flood	Local to Regional Area	Days to Weeks
Hardware Failures	Systems	Hours to Days
Hurricane	Local to Regional Area	Days to Weeks
Ice Storms	Local to Regional Area	Days to Weeks
Municipal Service Failure	Local	Hours to Days
Nuclear Accident	Regional Area	Days to Weeks
Snow Storm	Local to Regional Area	Days to Weeks
Volcano	Regional Area	Weeks
Water Damage	Building to Local Area	Hours to Days

lasting many months. After the 1994 Northridge earthquake in Southern California, major highway arteries were closed for many months, requiring employees to telecommute or spend hours per day traveling. This affected the operations of many companies, forcing them to redesign their workflows. The Seattle earthquake of February 2001, however, had no such long-term effects. Many initiated disaster recovery procedures to handle the commuting problem, even when there had been no physical damage to the corporate facilities. The terrorist destruction of the World Trade Center Twin Towers in New York on September 11, 2001, is perhaps the most obvious example of how the destruction or closure of major road and other transportation centers affected operations of companies not otherwise affected by the terrorist act itself.

The disaster recovery planner must analyze enough specific threats against the corporate operations and physical plant to build a series of disaster scenarios, which become the guiding forces of the recovery activity definitions. Some planners design disaster recovery scenarios to suit each disaster threat. Floods call for one set of activities; fires another. This can result in an extensive set of scenarios, each requiring training, testing, and maintenance. This technique may be too complex, and another similar approach uses active scenarios chosen from a set of only five possible levels of disasters: systems only, partial-building, full-building, local, and regional. Each organization should try to reduce the number of disaster scenarios, generally to no more than three, and many can handle emergencies adequately using only two scenarios. For most organizations, a systems-only disaster is not restricted to computer systems, but may include phone systems and telecommunications systems. Systems-only cases must be defined in the context of the organization's unique structure.

For example, a manufacturing facility may require three scenarios: systems only, partial building, and full building. Perhaps for the manufacturer, a loss of systems can be handled with a hot site for computers and a fast, high-bandwidth connection to the shop floor. A partial building disaster, affecting only office space, can be handled similarly, but with additional office space for support functions. A full-building disaster that damages or destroys manufacturing capability requires a completely different set of continuation and recovery procedures. As another example, a corporate office facility may require just two scenarios—systems-only and building disaster—where the building disaster is a combined building, local, and regional scenario. The systems hot site can handle the systems-only disaster. The building disaster scenario will require that all functions be restored at a hot site that provides full office functions from phone to fax to desks and copiers.

The planner defines the sets of disasters and develops recovery scenarios for those sets. This defines the number of scenarios required, and then the disaster recovery activities can be designed.

43.3   DEVELOPING RECOVERY STRATEGIES.   The BIA defines the timeline for recovery for each category of functions. The recovery strategies depend on factors such as: the complexity of the functions, the amount of information required to carry them out, the number of people involved in performing the function, and the amount of interaction between this function and other functions. The strategy of choice for each function is based on the timeline and the specific factors relating to it. The tasks required to activate the function, immediately following a disaster, follow directly from the BIA timeline and from the various factors that have been described.

Recovery strategies are defined differently from continuation strategies. The recovery strategy is the overall plan for resuming a function, or set of functions, in a near-normal work mode. The continuation strategy is the plan for immediate or nearly immediate operations of a key function, even if it results in significantly degraded performance, or limited capability. The continuation strategy is most often applied to a small set of functions rather than to a more complete set, and it is often only temporary. Although the recovery strategy may be used for several weeks or longer, the continuation strategy typically survives for hours or days.

Traditional recovery strategies include hot sites, warm sites, and cold sites. The most common recovery strategy uses a commercial service provider to maintain an on-demand operating capability for well-defined systems. There are a variety of such companies, some of which provide a standby mainframe or midrange system, along with selected peripherals, on a first-come, first-served basis. Others guarantee availability by providing a dedicated facility.

The operating capability required is defined at the outset. Processor type is specified down to the model level. Required disk space, hard drives, tape drives, ports, connectivity, and all other required elements must be explicitly specified. Timeline requirements must be stated precisely, with rehearsal, practice, and drill times negotiated in advance. Geographic location of the backup systems is often determined at the time of disaster declaration, and connectivity is usually provided to corporate fixed facilities. The obvious advantage of this strategy is ready access to maintained systems and environments. The principal disadvantage is cost.

A continuation strategy usually depends on internal resources rather than on commercially available providers. Continuation strategy requires that equipment be available instantly, with current data. Instant availability means that the systems must be local, or at least connected, yet survivable. The continuation strategy is becoming more common as microcomputer-based systems assume greater roles in corporate computing structures. The continuation strategy often relies on reserve systems, a concept pioneered over the past five years. This strategy, described in section 43.3.2.8, uses high-performance microcomputers residing offsite at homes, branch offices, and other locations easily accessible to employees.

The reserve system provides immediate, but limited, functionality so that operations can be continued after a disaster, while awaiting full restoration or recovery.

43.3.1   Recovery Phases.   Orderly recovery requires organized processes and procedures. The BIA uncovers the time sensitivity and criticality of functions, so that continuation and recovery strategies can be designed. Activation of these strategies is performed systematically in time-phased increments.

Exhibit 43.4 shows an example of such phasing. The figure illustrates a common schema that consists of three scenarios. Each scenario represents a collection of disasters according to their effects on the company. The first is labeled a systems disaster and represents an effect that has interrupted computer and related systems, but has left basic services such as heating and air conditioning, water, power, and life safety intact. The second scenario is the building or local disaster. In this case, a major portion of the building, the entire building, or even several surrounding buildings, are rendered unfit for occupancy. This may be due to a problem with the building or with the local area, including fire, toxic spills, minor flooding of surrounding areas, terrorist action, and other such events. The third scenario is the regional disaster, in which some calamitous event affects a wider geographic area. Examples of such catastrophes are earthquakes, hurricanes, floods, large fires or firestorms, and heavy ice and snowstorms.

Each of these scenarios requires different recovery strategies and tasks. However, the overall recovery phases remain similar. The figure shows that there are three basic phases: continuation of critical (Category I) functions, recovery of critical functions,

Exhibit 43.4   Strategy Overview

Strategy	Activation	Cost	Testability	Availability	Reliability
The "Ideal Strategy"	**Fast**	**Low**	**Excellent**	**High**	**Excellent**
Reserve Systems	Fast	Low	Excellent	High	Excellent
Internal Redundancy	Fast	Medium	Poor	Medium	Good
Commercial Providers	Fast	Varies	Excellent	High	Excellent
Hot Site	Fast	High	Excellent	High	Excellent
Mobile Data Centers	Medium	Low	Medium	High	Good
Reciprocal Agreements	Slow	Low	Poor	Low	Poor
Priority Replacement	Slow	Low	Poor	Low	Poor
Cold Site	Slow	High	Poor	High	Poor

and recovery of other functions. These are labeled near the bottom of the figure as "Continuation," "Recovery I," and "Recovery II."

The Continuation phase begins at the time of the disaster. For each scenario, the goal of the continuation phase is to support the Category I functions as best as possible, and within the time frames defined by the BIA. In this example, the BIA timeline for Category I functions is one to three days. For the systems disaster and the building or local disaster scenarios, the continuation phase depends on the local or on-site reserve systems. For the regional disaster, where local functioning may be impossible, the Category I functions must be supported by remote sites.

The Recovery phase is further divided into two subphases. The Recovery I phase restores full or nearly full functionality to the Category I functions that were partially supported by the reserve systems. In the example, the Recovery I phase begins after all continuation functions have been stabilized. In practice, it is more common for the Recovery I phase to begin shortly after the disaster event in order to minimize the duration during which the Category I functions must operate in a degraded fashion. The Recovery II phase is used to recover other functions in the order they are needed, as defined by the BIA. Exhibit 43.5 shows the typical spread of functions across categories. Typically, Category I functions constitute approximately 10 to 15 percent of the functions performed in a facility or campus. The Category II functions consist of functions that are very important and time critical, but which can be delayed for a short time. These significantly outnumber the Category I functions, sometimes reaching 20 to 35 percent of facility functions. Category III and, if applicable, Category IV functions are much greater in number, often comprising more than half of the facility functions performed.

The BIA process assessed the cost contribution of each category of functions to the total losses the company would sustain after a disaster without a plan. Exhibit 43.6 compares the number of functions per category to the total impact of the functions in each category on operations in a typical organization. Although Category I functions number the fewest of all categories, their impact is the greatest. The Category III functions typically rank second in contributions to losses, with Category II third in rank.

Exhibit 43.5   Spread of Functions Across Categories

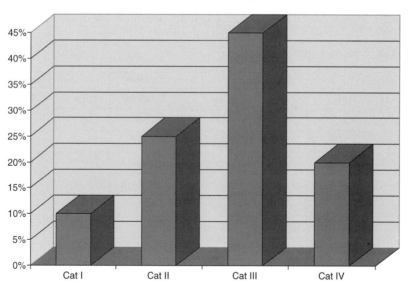

Exhibit 43.6   Number versus Impact of Functions

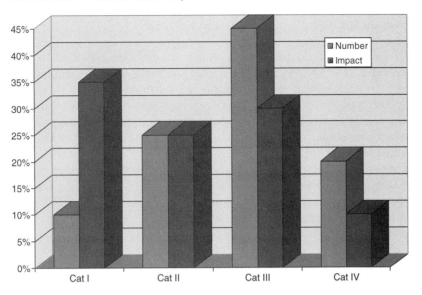

The critical functions that constitute Category I are ranked first precisely because of their high impact and time criticality. Category III is typically the largest group, so that even though the impact of each function may be small, the large number of functions increases the total effect of that group. Category IV tends to be a fairly small set of functions, so typically it is small in number and last in impact.

In the example, the systems disaster phases reflect certain assumptions. The continuation phase begins at the time of the disaster and continues for up to three days. The recovery phase is scheduled to begin no later than the fourth day, with full recovery by the seventh day, at which time a return to normal operations is expected. The underlying assumption is that the offsite reserve systems have been replicated on site. This is shown by the caption, Activate On-Site Reserve Systems. An additional assumption in this example is that the system can be recovered in less than seven days. Some analysis would have been performed to show that new equipment or equipment repairs could be obtained fairly early during the first seven days, leaving enough time for service restoration, including data recovery, to be completed by the seventh day. In this example, it is also clear that the Category II functions are required beginning on the seventh day. This is illustrated by the building or system disaster Recovery II phase, which begins on the seventh day and is labeled as restoring Category II, III, and other functions.

43.3.2   Range of Strategies.   There are three general areas of traditional recovery strategies that address the needs of mainframes, midrange systems, and PC LAN systems. There is a rich history and many years of experience in providing recovery for large, mainframe systems, with strategies that include hot sites, cold sites, reciprocal or mutual aid agreements, and commercial recovery facilities, as described below.

Strategies for recovery of midrange systems, including distributed systems, minicomputers, and workstations, include all the same strategies as those used for mainframe systems, along with mobile data centers, internal redundancy arrangements, and agreements with manufacturers for priority shipping of replacement equipment.

PC LAN system recovery strategies are the newest of the three areas. They typically make use of combinations of capabilities, including quick replacement, off-site equipment storage (equipment sparing), and hot sites.

43.3.2.1   Cold Sites.

A cold site is a room or set of rooms in a "ready-conditioned" environment. It is a fully functional computer room with all of the required facilities, including electrical power, air conditioning, raised floors, and telecommunications, all in operating condition and ready for occupancy. Missing from this fully functional room, because of high costs, is the computer equipment, including the processors and all required peripherals. Cold sites can be owned by one company or shared by several companies.

The major advantage of a dedicated cold site, somewhat diminished in the shared case, is simply that for a relatively low acquisition or leasing cost, the site is guaranteed to be available over the long term to the owner or lessee of the site. To be effective, a cold site must be distant enough from the main facility so that a disaster that makes the primary facility unusable will likely not affect the cold site.

There are several disadvantages to cold sites. First and foremost is that ordering, receiving, installing, and powering up the computer system can take many days. Once the system is functional, the cold site becomes a dedicated facility ready to perform all functions in a controlled environment, but the time required to achieve this state can stretch into a week or more. Few organizations can rely on a cold site as their primary vehicle for disaster recovery. A secondary disadvantage of cold sites is the inherent inability to test the recovery plan. An untested plan is an unreliable plan—testing a cold site would require obtaining all of the requisite equipment, installing the equipment, and performing operations on the new equipment. Few organizations can afford the costs associated with such testing. There are also hidden pitfalls with this strategy. Key equipment may be unavailable for immediate delivery. Communication lines may be untested and unreliable. This strategy is generally not a desirable first line of defense. It can, however, be a part of a larger overall strategy that includes other types of sites.

43.3.2.2   Hot Sites.

A hot site is a facility ready to assume processing responsibility immediately. The term usually refers to a site that contains equipment ready to assume all hardware functions, but requiring massive restoration of data, and an influx of personnel to operate the equipment. The hot site cannot, therefore, begin total processing instantaneously. In actuality, the site is only warm, with an ability to get hot fast. A hot site can be dedicated to one organization, shared by several organizations, or leased from a specialty company, called a commercial recovery service provider. The provider option is described in a later section.

The primary advantage of a hot site is the speed of recovery. The time to resume processing is defined as the time to reach the facility with people and backup media, plus the time to restore data and programs from the backup media, to test the operations, and to go live with a fully functional system. For larger systems, this period can range from less than two days to almost a week.

The primary disadvantage of a hot site is the cost associated with acquiring and maintaining the fully equipped site. For this reason, most organizations choose to share the cost of a hot site with other organizations, who may be sister companies or only neighbors. In any event, there is a large cost associated with maintaining the site, and ensuring that it is updated with every change to each of the participant's requirements, while still maintaining compatibility with all of them. One of the most common solutions to this problem is to use a service provider.

43.3.2.3   Reciprocal Agreements.   Reciprocal agreements were often used in the earlier decades of disaster recovery planning, but are uncommon today. A reciprocal agreement is an arrangement between two or more companies in which each agrees to make excess capacity available to the others in case of a disaster. The major advantage is the apparent low cost of this solution. The major disadvantage is that these arrangements rarely provide the needed computing power. A major issue with these arrangements is maintaining compatible systems. If one company changes a processor, it may find that its partners' systems cannot perform adequately, even in degraded mode. If the host company faces a crisis or deadline of its own, a reciprocal company may find itself with no computer power at all. These arrangements are seldom testable, because it is the rare company willing to shut down operations to help a partner perform a disaster recovery test.

43.3.2.4   Internal Redundancy.   A strategy of internal redundancy requires that a business have multiple facilities, geographically dispersed, with similar equipment in each site. If there are data centers at several sites, then the alternate data centers may be designed with excess capacity to support a potential failure at another site.

The major advantage of internal redundancy is that the organization maintains complete control of all equipment and data, without relying on any outside company to come to its aid. The excess capacity at the various alternate sites must be carefully protected, and management must exercise diligence in budgeting and operations. Careful intracompany agreements must be crafted to ensure that all parties are aware of, and agree to, the backup arrangements. Internal redundancy can be an effective solution in cases where temporarily degraded processing can still provide sufficient support to meet timeline requirements. If degraded performance is not an acceptable option, then the cost of the excess capacity will probably be too high. If reasonable degradation is acceptable, then those costs can be manageable.

Internal redundancy can also be difficult to test. Testing requires that processing be shifted to a recovery mode. Unlike external, separate computers, all of these redundant systems would be operational. Testing one disaster recovery plan requires affecting a minimum of two corporate locations. A failed test that causes a system crash or other problem can have damaging consequences.

43.3.2.5   Mobile Data Centers.   Mobile data centers are transportable units such as trailers outfitted with replacement equipment, air conditioning, electrical connections, and all other computer requirements. Mobile data centers are most often used for recovery of midrange and PC LAN systems. The primary advantage of the mobile data center is that it can be activated quickly at reasonably low cost. The primary disadvantages are the expense of testing such a facility, and the possibility that a local or regional disaster will prevent successful activation. Deploying a mobile data center requires careful planning. Land must be available to accommodate the transportable units, with outside parking lots as the most common resource. Local government and municipal regulations must be researched in advance to ensure that such units do not violate ordinances and can arrive as certified for immediate occupancy. External power and communications hookups also must be available.

43.3.2.6   Priority Replacement Agreements.   Some computer vendors support priority equipment replacement agreements. These are arrangements in which the vendor promises to ship replacement equipment on a priority basis. For midrange systems, this is often an agreement to send the "next off the line" system to the priority customer.

The major advantage of this strategy is its low cost. However, if the vendor is not currently manufacturing the required system, or if the assembly line is down for any reason, and if equipment stocks are depleted, there may still be a significant delay in receiving the equipment. This is the major disadvantage. This strategy also assumes the disaster recovery plan makes an alternate facility available in case the primary facility is damaged along with the equipment being replaced.

43.3.2.7   Commercial Recovery Services.   Commercial recovery service providers can support a combination of the strategies discussed above. These companies generally provide three major benefits: cost sharing, reduced management needs, and diminished risk of obsolescence. First, they spread facility costs across multiple subscribers so that each subscriber saves as compared with building and maintaining a comparable, privately held capability. Because all subscribers share the same physical space, each pays less than would be needed to maintain such a site independently.

The second major benefit of using a commercial provider is that these companies eliminate the need for the subscriber to manage backup resources. Management and maintenance of such a site by an individual business could be a heavy burden, but the provider's primary focus is on managing, maintaining, and upgrading the equipment and sites. The subscriber company can be assured that the equipment is exercised and serviced regularly, and that peripheral equipment, power systems, and facility support structures are properly maintained. A properly run site will also provide security, safety, compliance with evolving rules and regulations, and competent staffing. The provider assumes full responsibility for these functions during normal operations, and continues support during times of crisis. The subscriber brings its technical personnel, while the provider leaves its facilities staff in place.

The third major benefit centers around today's fast pace of hardware evolution. A subscriber company will typically lease a hot site or other service for a five-year period. During that time, hardware platforms will evolve. The subscribing company can protect its lease investment by ensuring that system upgrades are reflected in the leased equipment configuration for reasonable extra charges. A business that provides its own hot site must upgrade the hot site whenever hardware, and sometimes software, changes are made to the operational systems.

The disadvantage of commercial recovery services is in the obvious risk that the hot site may not be available in an emergency. Indeed, if there is a local or regional disaster that affects numerous subscribers, there could be significant contention for the provider's resources. To address this issue, providers typically maintain hot sites in geographically dispersed areas. Although it is likely that in the case of a local or regional disaster a subscriber would need to use a hot site further away than planned, it is unlikely that the subscriber would be left completely without the prearranged resources.

43.3.2.8   Reserve Systems.   The newest of strategies is the reserve system, which is a small replica of a portion of an operational system meant for use during the first few days following a disaster. The reserve system provides continuation of key functions for short durations, although in degraded mode. The reserve system usually resides off site at an employee's home or at another corporate office. Another version of the reserve system is also kept on site. A reserve site may be equipped with a microcomputer or a minicomputer ready to assume functioning in case the primary system becomes unavailable. This meets the important criteria of a reserve system, which must be fast and easy to activate, simple to move, low in cost, testable, available, and highly reliable.

Exhibit 43.7   Strategy Overview

Strategy	Activation	Cost	Testability	Availability	Reliability
The "Ideal Strategy"	**Fast**	**Low**	**Excellent**	**High**	**Excellent**
Reserve Systems	Fast	Low	Excellent	High	Excellent
Internal Redundancy	Fast	Medium	Poor	Medium	Good
Commercial Providers	Fast	Varies	Excellent	High	Excellent
Hot Site	Fast	High	Excellent	High	Excellent
Mobile Data Centers	Medium	Low	Medium	High	Good
Reciprocal Agreements	Slow	Low	Poor	Low	Poor
Priority Replacement	Slow	Low	Poor	Low	Poor
Cold Site	Slow	High	Poor	High	Poor

The reserve system concept was not feasible until client/server technology emerged, and Internet telecommuting with high-speed communications became accepted and readily available. Web-centric processing and remote application server technologies can provide powerful reserve systems for disaster recovery.

Proper security precautions must be taken to protect proprietary, confidential, and critical information stored on these reserve systems. Strong encryption safely protects against theft while redundant systems protect against other losses. The reserve system is a quick-response, short-term solution intended to solve the problem of immediate continuation even in the case where employees may be unable to travel outside their immediate residence areas.

43.3.3   Data Backup Scenarios and their Meanings.   Data backup is a key function in all system installations. The best recovery strategy, chosen to meet recovery timelines according to the BIA, is useless without a backup from which to restore and resume operations. Data backup is perhaps the single most critical element of a disaster recovery plan, yet only 31 percent of U.S. companies have backup plans and equipment. See Chapter 41 for details of backup scenarios.

43.4   DESIGNING RECOVERY TASKS.   The disaster recovery plan becomes an operating document when the strategies and reserve capabilities are translated into specific actions to be performed during the disaster recovery process. These are the actions required to protect assets, mitigate damage, continue partial operations, and resume full operations. Most tasks begin with actions to evaluate the disaster and then to initiate recovery procedures. The example recovery task flow (Exhibit 43.8) lists a series of steps to evaluate the situation. These steps, numbered 1 through 5, determine whether or not to declare a disaster. The second set of steps, numbered 6 through 10, is used to initiate recovery procedures. These first two sets of steps are called the beginning sequence.

The beginning sequence leads to full activation of a disaster recovery effort. The next set of activities is called the middle sequence, and institutes the actions necessary to perform business continuation and recovery. There are usually multiple choices for the middle sequence that correspond to the disaster scenarios developed. Each path in the middle sequence is executed for a particular scenario. At the end of the middle sequence, full operations are resumed as specified in the disaster recovery plan. In the

Exhibit 43.8   Recovery Task Flow

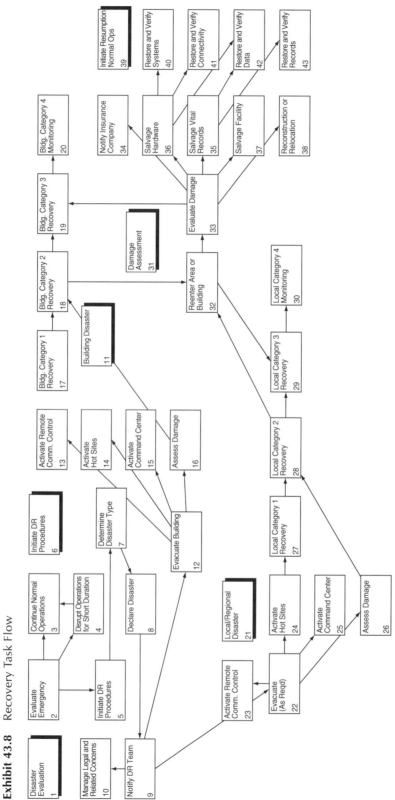

exhibit, the middle sequence includes two distinct paths. The first path includes steps numbered 11 through 20, and the second path includes steps numbered 21 through 30.

The end sequence begins with damage assessments and continues through resumption of normal operations in the original facility, a semi-permanent facility, or a new facility. The end sequence may begin while the middle sequence is still unfolding. The timing is dependent on the requirements specific in the BIA. The end sequence consists of two sets of activities performed in sequence. The first set consists of Steps 31 through 38, and the second set consists of Steps 39 through 43.

43.4.1   Beginning Sequence.   The beginning sequence (shown in Exhibit 43.9) helps the disaster recovery team in its first two major actions: evaluation of the emergency and initiation of the recovery procedures. Box 1, labeled "Disaster Evaluation," begins the process with a set of actions whose end goal determines what actions to take to meet the upcoming emergency. In Step 2, the disaster recovery team determines which course of action to take: continue normal operations, disrupt operations for a short while and then resume normal operations, or initiate a full- or partial-scale disaster recovery. The decision is based on a set of predetermined criteria.

Box 2 is labeled "Evaluate Emergency." This is the step in which the disaster recovery team assesses the expected duration and extent of the upcoming or existing outage. Using a set of criteria developed as part of the BIA, and based on the assessment of the outage, the team determines which course of action to take. For example, if the emergency is a power outage, the disaster recovery team will likely call the power utility to determine the cause. If the outage is expected to last less time than the shortest recovery requirement, then it may make the most sense to simply disrupt operations for a short time without initiating recovery procedures. The comprehensive disaster recovery procedures provide sufficient guidance in a simple form to support the team's decision-making process while leaving room for real-time evaluation and decision making.

If the decision is to initiate disaster recovery procedures, then the flow proceeds through Box 4, "Initiate DR Procedures," to the initiation phase labeled Box 6 and represented by the actions in Boxes 7 through 10. In Step 7, the disaster recovery team determines which of the disaster scenarios applies, formally declares that type of disaster in Step 8, and notifies the disaster recovery team and others, as required, of the decisions made and the next steps to take. All members of the team are pretrained and equipped with written procedures that anticipate each of these potential decisions. The only remaining step in the beginning sequence is Box 10, "Manage Legal and Related Concerns." From the moment a disaster situation is considered, the team must document its decisions. In some industries this is required by regulatory agencies; in public companies, it may be required for reporting to a board of directors committee meeting. For all companies it is important to maintain a clear record of the diligence used in planning and implementing recovery.

Exhibit 43.9   The Beginning Sequence

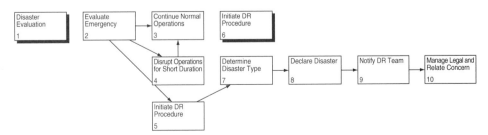

In addition to legal concerns, there are insurance concerns. Typically, money spent during the recovery process is reimbursable by insurance policies. This includes out-of-pocket expenditures by staff, the cost of travel, food and lodging vouchers, and other allowed expenditures for meeting disaster recovery needs. In its haste to restore damage systems, the team may neglect to document specific damages; once repaired, it is difficult to submit an insurance claim unless the damage is documented properly. Box 10 represents a step that begins early and continues throughout the disaster recovery process.

43.4.2 Middle Sequence.   The middle sequence represents the activities that begin once the disaster recovery procedures are underway. In our example there are two possible paths for the middle sequence to follow. The steps are labeled similarly, but the specific actions taken are quite different. There is an advantage to using a schematic representation of the steps and their relationships: the overall structure or shape can show at a glance the complexity or simplicity of the plan. It is best to be as uncomplicated as possible, even if the form and structure require larger content. Exhibit 43.10 describes the middle sequence, Building Scenario.

The first step listed in the middle sequence, Building Scenario, is evacuate the building. Although this is clearly performed as early as possible, perhaps even early in the beginning sequence, it is presented here for completeness. Human safety is the primary concern of any recovery plan—no employee should ever be allowed to delay evacuation or reenter a building except in the case of a qualified individual who is helping others evacuate or attempting a rescue attempt. The next four activities occur in parallel. They are represented by Boxes 3 through 6, and include activation functions for remote communications, the hot sites, and the command center. These four steps also include a first effort at damage assessment.

Box 3 is labeled "Activate Remote Communications Control." This is the activity that reroutes digital and analog communications from their normal patterns to their emergency routes. This may include telecommunications lines, call center toll-free lines, normal business lines, data lines, and other communications media. Typically, arrangements are made in advance with the various telecommunications carriers so that a series of short phone calls can initiate the rerouting. If arrangements were not made in advance, then the rerouting will not meet timeline requirements, and may significantly impair the efficiency of the disaster recovery team members.

Box 4, "Activate Hot Sites," represents the sets of actions required to inform the hot site provider that a disaster is in progress. Hot site activation must be performed at the earliest moment, so that the hot site can be available as soon as possible, and so that in cases of contention, the preferred hot site will be available.

Exhibit 43.10   The Middle Sequence, Building Scenario

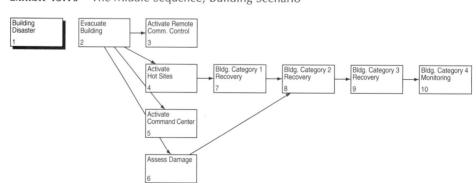

Hot site activation usually obligates the company to pay certain activation costs and occasionally a minimum usage cost. If the disaster requires the hot site, then insurance often reimburses the company for related expenses, but if the declaration was erroneous, the company will suffer a financial loss.

The major hot site providers' services are quite reliable. There are few instances of hot site providers failing to meet their obligations, and many stories of near-heroic feats performed to meet customer needs. One provider even abandoned its own operations so that a client suffering from a regional disaster could occupy the provider's corporate space to continue its own operations. Hot site contracts usually include a proviso that in cases of contention, where more than one company is seeking the same disaster recovery space, the provider can send the late declarer to another, equivalent site. This means that the disaster recovery plan must include instructions for multiple hot sites. All maps, directions, instructions, and delivery requirements must be consistent with the assigned hot site location. Clearly, it is in the company's best interest to declare early so that the hot site of choice is obtained. It would be prudent to err on the side of early declaration rather than late declaration, especially in cases of regional disasters.

Boxes 7 through 10 represent recovery of the various categories of functions. It is seldom possible or desirable to recover all functions simultaneously. The BIA determined and documented the timelines for all functions needing recovery. The procedures must reflect that analysis so that functions are in fact recovered "just in time." These four boxes are labeled Building Category Recovery I to IV. Each box represents the full set of procedures required to bring all the functions in each category into operational mode. For example, if there are seven functions in the Category I group, then there will be seven sets of procedures required to implement Box 7. Category I functions usually require special efforts, such as reserve systems. Therefore, each Category I function may require two sets of activation procedures: the first for the reserve system and the second for the hot site.

At the conclusion of the middle sequence, all required functions would have been recovered. It may be that during the beginning sequence a determination was made that the disaster would only require recovery of a subset of functions. A small-scale power failure, for example, may only require Category I functions to be recovered. A weather disaster with no lasting effects may require Category I and Category II functions. This decision is made during the early phases of the recovery and reevaluated continually throughout the recovery process.

43.4.3 End Sequence. The end sequence represented in Exhibit 43.11 is the long path back to normal operations. The end sequence consists of two major phases. The damage assessment set of activities comprises the first phase and includes Boxes 2 through 8. The initiate resumption of normal operations set of activities constitutes the second phase and includes Boxes 10 through 13. Although there is an assess damage activity at the beginning of the middle sequence, that activity is a quick assessment of damage for the purpose of determining what recovery options need to be activated. This damage assessment activity is a comprehensive evaluation of damage to equipment, facilities, and records.

Box 2 is labeled "Reenter Area or Building." This activity needs supporting procedures to guide disaster recovery team members on what regulatory, municipal, state, and federal authorities control access into damaged facilities. Often, access is restricted for long periods of time even when there is little or no apparent damage. For example, following an earthquake, structural engineers may tag a building as uninhabitable pending further analysis. As another example, after a fire, the fire marshal may prohibit entry pending analysis by chemical engineers to determine whether the fire produced

Exhibit 43.11   The End Sequence

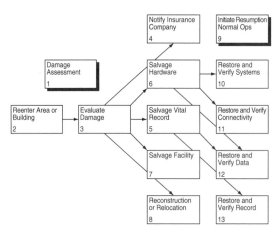

hazardous materials. Fires often cause chemical reactions that transform normal, benign office materials into toxic chemicals. The procedures for Box 2 should provide contact information for each major agency that may control the facility after a disaster.

Box 3 leads to five parallel activities. The first, "Notify Insurance Company," is related to the "Manage Legal and Other Concerns" activity in the beginning sequence. In this case, the various insurance carriers will need to send their own adjusters and engineers to help assess the damage.

The procedures for Box 4 should provide the disaster recovery team with specific contact information for all insurance carriers with which the company has policies in force. The insurance company must be given the opportunity to investigate the premises before any salvage, repair, or cleanup operations begin. Unlike the period immediately following a disaster, when some cleanup may be required for safety and health reasons, the insurance company will look very unfavorably at any attempt to disturb the scene prior to their inspections. This does not mean that facility repairs must await a leisurely investigation and inspection by the insurance company; there are immediate steps to take to make preparations for salvage and repair. The procedure for Box 4 will aid the disaster recovery team in deciding what they can do immediately, how they can document status prior to repairs, and what must await the approval of the insurance company and others.

Boxes 5 through 7 are the control procedures for salvaging hardware, records, and the facility. The procedures for "Salvage Hardware" must contain all the contact information for hardware vendors, including computer, communications, reproduction, and others. Each type of equipment requires different salvage operations; the best procedure for a computer may, for example, be the worst procedure for a magnetic tape drive. The salvage procedures should provide general guidelines and contact information for quick access to salvage experts. The same is true for facility salvage procedures.

Salvaging vital records is a complex and unpredictable process. For some records, drying is the top priority; for others, getting them into oxygen-free containers is far more important. The procedures supporting the "Salvage Vital Records" activity must provide contact points, general instructions, and guidance for making decisions about salvage possibilities. Unlike hardware, where the salvage decision is usually driven by cost considerations alone, vital records and legacy materials may be driven by other factors such as corporate legacy and history considerations or legal issues. The salvage decision is often much more subjective in this area.

Box 8 is labeled "Reconstruction or Relocation." This task differs from the other tasks in three important ways. First, it is likely that the members of the disaster recovery team will not have the required authority to make this decision, but will play an important role in presenting analyses to the decision-making top management people. Second, there are no specific company-external contacts to be made by the disaster recovery team as a part of this process. Although a real estate agent may be contacted for information, it is not likely that the disaster recovery team will undertake that task. The third difference is that the result of this activity is not some specific observable process, but a set of recommendations made to top management. The procedures built to support this activity should provide guidance to the disaster recovery team so that they can develop the analyses and present the results in a timely fashion.

Box 9 represents the last phase of the disaster recovery process, initiating the process that returns operations to a normal operating environment. At the time the plan is written, there is no way to predict whether by following this step the company will be relocating to a new facility, or making minor repairs or none, and returning to the existing facility. The importance of these last steps is that they confirm the operability of the newly restored and operational systems. Each of these activities needs to be supported by a set of procedures that guide qualified personnel in their tasks of restoring and verifying systems, networks, data, and records.

43.5   IMPLEMENTATION AND READINESS.   The final steps in preparing the disaster recovery plan are proving the plan works and ensuring that the people understand their roles. This is performed through rehearsals, walk-throughs, and testing. Once the plan is completed, and all of the reserve systems and capabilities have been installed, it is time to test whether these backup systems work as planned. There are a variety of testing phases, starting with extremely limited tests performed separately from ongoing operations, and proceeding through full tests using live data.

The first set of tests are intended to prove that specific functions and capabilities are in place and available for use. These are the on-site and off-site limited tests, whose goal is to segregate tasks into small groups of related functions. With only a few functions per tests, there can be many tests that, in the aggregate, prove that each required function is successfully represented in the suite of recovery capabilities. The on-site portion of these tests will disconnect the users from normal operating capabilities such as LAN, WAN, and support staff.

This is best accomplished by setting up a testing room within the facility, but away from operations. Users are given the tools and instructions they would receive during a real disaster and they attempt to perform their designated disaster recovery functions. An example of such a function is emergency payroll operations, where the outsource company is notified that this is only a test, or the backup company facility is put on notice that a test is in progress. The tests would determine whether offline systems were able to process and transfer data as expected. It also may demonstrate that manual procedures work as written. In this testing, the keys are to set test objectives in advance, monitor test progress, ensure that users have only the expected disaster recovery tools at their disposal and no others, and document the results. After the on-site tests prove satisfactory, these same basic, limited procedures should be followed off site as they would be during an actual emergency. This requires some employees to stay away from the office, so the tests should be planned to avoid periods of expected high activity.

Once the functions have been tested, the next set of tests are intended to prove that the technical systems can be made operational in the planned time frame and can support users as expected. Two types of tests accomplish this: off-site network tests and hot-site tests. These are discussed together because they are often overlapping capabilities performed at the same time. The off-site network and large-system hot-site tests demonstrate that the systems and networks can each be restored within the time allotted, and that the interface between them survives the transition to hot-site operations. One of the primary advantages of performing the off-site network and hot site tests concurrently is that connectivity and intersystem functionality can be demonstrated.

The last test is a full operations test that attempts to show that all of these elements will work together. Just as in a real emergency, the test will focus on a subset of normal operations. Critical functions are tested first, and other functions are added according to the recovery timeline. For these operations, a test disaster is declared and employees are notified that this is a test and that they are to cease normal operations and immediately implement their recovery procedures.

Most disaster recovery tests use simulated data or backup data that are real, but are not the operational data. Changes made and transactions recorded during such tests are never brought back into the operational environment. Processing performed during the test is based on simulated business operations, with "representative" transactions rather than real ones. In the past decade, there has been a trend toward making final full operations tests online, using actual backup sites, systems, and procedures for processing real transactions. This makes the test process significantly more exciting, with a corresponding increase in stress, for employees and management. Mistakes made in this type of testing can cost the company dearly, but success can assure the company of a recovery plan that is much more likely to succeed during a real crisis.

Employees participating in full operations tests, using real data, are going to be much more serious, but employee rewards are also greater. There is more of a feeling of accomplishment if the test processed live data rather than simulated data. After the test, employees can return to work without needing to catch up on missed work. Management is also more likely to be directly involved in a live test than in a simulated test—because in a real test, management will be called on to make real decisions. They are more likely to be present, just as they would be during a real emergency. Not all organizations are structured in such a way as to make live tests possible. When they can be used, they are the most valid test of the recovery plan. However, they should never be attempted until the plan has been proven using multiple instances of the full complement of tests that should precede the live test.

43.6 SUMMARY.   Over the past three decades, the nature of the threats we have considered and the preparations we made have changed dramatically. In the early days, major fears included equipment failures and minor geographic events such as storms and small floods. In the event of a major catastrophe, we felt confident that our plans would unfold as well as those of our neighboring companies; perhaps there would even be some cooperation between companies.

In the decade of the 1990s, however, the criticality of systems combined with an upsurge in human-made disasters forced us to rethink our practices, scenarios and procedures. The first bombing of the New York World Trade Center in 1993, the bombing of the Murrah Federal Building in Oklahoma City in 1995, and the damage to the Pentagon and the heinous destruction of the World Trade Center Twin Towers in 2001, have finally led us to the point where we must include "artificial" disasters in our planning as well as natural ones. The disaster recovery planner must now consider disasters and recovery scenarios that include terrorism as well as tornados. The task is difficult, but the techniques and technologies are the same as before.

CHAPTER 44

INSURANCE RELIEF

Robert A. Parisi, Jr.

CONTENTS

44.1 INTRODUCTION. This chapter presents an overview of traditional insurance products and how they may or may not provide coverage for the risks associated with computer and network security. It also addresses the new types of coverage that have been developed expressly for those risks. The process of how insurance companies analyze or "underwrite" the risk is examined, with particular attention paid to the role played by security assessments and ongoing managed security.

Network security is not a product, a software application, or a corporate edict. It is a process—a living entity that must evolve and adapt to meet the increasing and ever-changing threats. There is no substitute for the combination of a comprehensive security policy and the employment of best-of-breed technology applications.

What has become painfully apparent, to both board members and chief information officers, is that the only network that can be maintained inviolate is a network of one user on one computer. If business can be done across a network, then so too can malicious business be done across that network. This awareness is critical to an entity's network security awareness and maturity. This awareness also should lead the entity to look beyond its technology to the more traditional ways that businesses have employed to manage the risks of simply doing business. A company does not decline to buy fire insurance because it relies on its new sprinkler system; a bank does not refrain from purchasing crime coverage because it has the best locks and guards.

Changes in accounting rules over the past decade have served to bring computer and network security to the fore, as more and more companies now have an increasing percentage of the assets on their balance sheet represented by intangible assets that exist only in the ether of the database. Companies traditionally have bought insurance to protect against damage or loss of their principal assets—their plant, their fleet of vehicles, and so on. Where do they turn now that these "principal assets" are the data and information stored in their networks?

What this all leads up to is recognition that traditional insurance policies often fall short of providing the coverage necessary for companies operating in a networked environment.

Businesses traditionally have managed the risks they face through the purchase of insurance, principally commercial general liability (CGL) and property policies. The additional risks faced by financial institutions and professional services firms usually were addressed through a mix of fidelity/surety bonds and specialty insurance products, for example, errors and omissions insurance. What they have in common, however, is the fact that all these lines of coverage were created before the widespread, commercial use of the computers and networks, including the Internet. Not surprisingly, these policies often fall short of addressing the complex computer and network security exposures that companies face in the New Economy.

The CGL policy is the most fundamental component of a corporation's insurance portfolio and, not surprisingly, the coverage that receives the most attention upon the prospect of an Internet loss. Originally called "comprehensive general liability," CGL policies provide a wide range of coverage for the liability of an insured because of bodily injury or property damage suffered by a third party as a result of the insured's action or inaction. This coverage, which is explored later in greater detail, is the situs of coverage for intellectual property infringement claims—an issue of critical importance today when so much of a company's worth, even its existence, is due to its rights under patents, copyrights, or trademarks.

The basic CGL policy provides coverage for all sums the insured is legally obligated to pay as a result of "bodily injury," "property damage," or "personal and advertising injury." For obvious reasons, the potential "bodily injury" associated with information technology is limited.

44.2   INTELLECTUAL PROPERTY COVERAGE.   Of critical importance to a company dealing with new technologies is the potential that its new innovation is a variation on existing and protected intellectual property. In such cases, the "innovator" may be forced to cease production, to obtain a license from the entity that owns the intellectual property at issue, or to seek to have the legal protections of the applicable area of intellectual property invalidated through the courts. Alternatively, the company in possession of protected technology created through the expenditure of millions of research and development (R&D) dollars suddenly may find that such technology has been incorporated in new product of a competitor. The "victimized" company is faced with loss of market share and possibly with a threat to its very existence. It must enforce its legal property rights—either through a license to the offender or by seeking to preclude the use of the technology. In both situations, all parties will be subject to significant legal fees to resolve the issue. Chapter 12 examines intellectual property law in detail.

In CGL policies, coverage generally exists (on a defensive basis) for the infringement of a third party's intellectual property. However, the coverage is neither a broad grant nor a particularly effective one. In order to trigger coverage, the infringement must be deemed an "offense" under the policy's Personal and Advertising Injury section. Even then, coverage is limited by the applicable definitions, exclusions, and the restrictive insuring agreement.

The most current International Organization for Standardization (ISO) language for the ISO CGL form CG 00 01 (July 1998) provides:

COVERAGE B. PERSONAL AND ADVERTISING INJURY LIABILITY

1. Insuring Agreement.

    a. We will pay those sums that the insured becomes legally obligated to pay as damages because of "personal injury" or "advertising injury" to which this insurance applies. We will have the right and duty to defend the insured against any "suit" seeking those damages . . .

By virtue of the use of the defined term—"advertisement"—the form is clear that advertising injury liability coverage is applicable solely to offenses committed in the course of advertising the insured's business.

This grant of coverage is conditioned by caveats that are restrictive in the old economy of brick-and-mortar commerce and all the more troublesome when viewed in context of the Internet. In order to fully comprehend which coverage provisions may or may not exist, it is first necessary to understand how the policy defines the operative terms.

The current CGL policy includes the following key term:

"Personal and Advertising Injury" means injury arising out of one or more of the following offenses:

1. The use of another's advertising items in your "advertisement"; or

2. Infringement upon another's copyright, trade dress or slogan in your advertisement.

As identified herewith, the grant of coverage is limited. There is no coverage for an infringement if it does not satisfy the three-pronged test outlined in *New Hampshire Insurance Co. v. Foxfire:*[1]

1. Advertising activity of the policyholder

2. A claim that falls within one or more of the enumerated advertising injury offenses

3. Causal nexus between the offense and the advertising activity

This test is merely one of several threshold requirements that must be satisfied before coverage will apply. The policy requires that the advertising injury arise out of the covered offense and that the claim seeks damages recoverable under the policy. The question of coverage is further limited by several exclusions that serve to drive home the limited scope of coverage.

Ambiguity in the language of the CGL has created some confusion in the marketplace. The situation worsens when applied to the Internet. More specifically, the exclusion regarding ". . . an offense committed by an insured whose business is advertising, broadcasting, publishing or telecasting" makes the coverage particularly problematic.

If the policyholder specifically operates in the media business, the exclusion's applicability is clear and unequivocal. However, what happens in the more likely scenario where the policyholder is not a multimedia service provider but merely an e-tailer or someone who maintains an informational Web site? Not surprisingly, there are two schools of thought.

One group, championed by the plaintiff's bar, argues that, unless the policyholder is actively engaged in the business of advertising, broadcasting, publishing, or telecasting as those industries have been traditionally defined, the exclusion is not applicable. This logic rests on the argument that computers and the Internet do not alter the fundamentals of how the world does business.

The second school of thought looks to the way that computers and the Internet have blurred the line between traditional media activities and a company's online presence. By maintaining any presence online, the policyholder's activities now fall within the parameters defined by the exclusion. This position is not readily understood and bears further exploration.

It is rare for a Web site not to contain a banner advertisement, hyperlink to a third party's site, or material imported from sources other than policyholder's cache of copyrights and trademarks. The presence of such content clearly places the policyholder in the shoes of an advertiser, broadcaster, or publisher. Even the most literal policy interpreter is hard-pressed to differentiate between the newspaper or television network that accepts advertisements and the e-tailer that carriers a banner ad.

The applicability of the exclusion becomes less clear when a business carries no banner ads or hyperlinks and contains no material beyond that which has sprung from the corporate mind of the policyholder. The question then becomes one not involving misuse of a third party's content. Does the simple maintenance of a Web site presume a business of advertising, broadcasting, publishing, or telecasting? The logic behind that position argues that the insured, by maintaining a Web site, is effectively side-stepping the services of publishers and broadcasters and doing the job itself.

Finally, another argument considers the manner, speed, and magnitude with which business is conducted via the Internet. The medium of the Internet was never contemplated when the insurance industry drafted the CGL policy. Similarly, premiums charged for CGL policies do not reflect any actuarial data related to the Internet. In fact, the very nature of the Internet lies in direct opposition to most assumptions an insurance underwriter formulates when calculating a premium.

For instance, when a business contemplates launching an advertising campaign, a concept traditionally goes through some preliminary review or in-house analysis. That concept is then taken to an advertising agency, where, among other things, it would be reviewed for general propriety (whether it infringed another's copyright, trademark, etc.). The final product then would be marketed to either the print or broadcasting media, where the publisher would review the advertisement. In granting advertising injury/personal injury coverage, the insurance underwriter assumes the content has gone through similar independent reviews. On the World Wide Web, however, such levels of scrutiny are typically nonexistent.

It is unlikely that this coverage ambiguity will be resolved definitively until more cases reach the courts. Even then, there will be issues surrounding the applicability of boilerplate policy. Several carriers have either clarified the intent of the policy by expressly excluding Internet activity or simplified it by not offering such coverage to those entities that have an Internet exposure. Finally, several companies have addressed the issue by creating a policy that affirmatively covers the risks associated with a company presenting information, be it substantive content or just a banner advertisement.

44.2.1 Loss/Damage to Intangible Assets. Property damage is generally defined as "physical injury to tangible property including all resulting loss of use of that property" and "loss of use of tangible property that is not physically injured."

Several cases have looked at the nexus between the virtual world and property damage. In a recent case, a large assembler of personal computers purchased disk drives from a manufacturer and subsequently alleged that the disk drives were defective. It did not, however, allege that the defective drives caused any harm to the other components, nor did it claim any loss of use. The manufacturer presented the claim to its CGL carrier, which later denied the claim. In the resultant coverage litigation, the court ruled the claim did not involve property damage because "physical incorporation of a defective product into another does not constitute property damage unless there is a physical harm to the whole."[2] The implication is clear; the mere fact that a piece of hardware or application is defective will not trigger coverage based on an argument of property damage. The importance of this distinction cannot be underestimated. This issue will be emphasized further when first-party coverage is explored as a result of similar direct loss.

The more critical and interesting issue is whether damage to or loss of computer data is property damage. Generally, courts that have looked at the issue have held that loss of data in isolation does not constitute damage to tangible property.[3] This position is under attack.

44.2.2 Intellectual Property Policies. As a result of the emerging importance of technology and the increased financial recognition of intangible assets, various insurance products have been developed to fill the void.

These policies fall within three general types:

1. Third-party liability

2. Prosecution or abatement

3. First-party liability/loss

The most common forms of insurance coverage available for intellectual property are third-party liability policies, including policies offering errors and omissions or professional liability coverage. In these policies, coverage can be found for an insured's liability to a third party for infringing on that party's intellectual property rights. There is a limitation on this coverage, though. Coverage usually is conditioned on the infringement being part and parcel of the insured rendering the service that is the basis (or trigger) of the coverage. Additionally, coverage usually is restricted to claims for copyright or trademark infringement and generally carries express exclusions for trade secrets and patents.

This sort of coverage is written either on a claims-made or occurrence basis. Traditionally, firms that provide content (e.g., advertising agencies, media firms, and publishing companies) have found coverage copyright and/or trademark infringement in multimedia liability policies that are written on an occurrence basis. The policy covers an insured for claims arising out of wrongful acts that occur during the policy period. In contrast, most other errors and omission/professional liability policies are written on a claims-made basis. They provide coverage for claims made and reported to the carrier during the policy period. The two types of polices can be distinguished further by the fact that claims-made policies may provide coverage for wrongful acts of the insured that occurred prior to the policy period, often dating back several years.

Firms looking for more explicit coverage for intellectual property infringement claims, including coverage for trade secrets and patents, must look to policies with the sole purpose of providing such coverage.

44.2.3   Claims Made versus Occurrence Coverages.   Insurance policies generally fall into one of two types: claims-made or occurrence based. The differences in such policies is relatively simple to grasp.

An occurrence insurance policy provides coverage for claims that are made at any time so long as the wrongful acts that form the basis of the claim occurred during the policy period. As such, a one-year occurrence policy that was effective January 1, 1999, would respond to any claim relating to otherwise covered wrongful acts that occurred after January 1, 1999, and before January 1, 2000.

It generally does not matter if the claim is made long after the policy has expired. Traditionally, some CGL and most media liability policies have been written on an occurrence basis; this group of policies is often the first line of defense for claims of copyright and trademark infringement.

A claims-made insurance policy provides coverage for claims made during the policy period, regardless of when the wrongful acts giving rise to the claim occurred. Using the 1999–2000 example from above, a claims-made policy would respond to a claim made against the policyholder only during the policy period, even if the wrongful acts complained of occurred several years prior to the inception of the policy. Nearly all professional liability/errors and omissions policies and some CGL policies are written on a claims-made basis. Nearly all policies that offer express and specialized coverage for intellectual property infringement liability are written on a claims-made basis.

How the occurrence/claims-made distinctions apply to the exposures created by the Internet is generally of interest only to insurance brokers and underwriters. Some insurance companies have taken the approach that the Internet is entirely a media risk and, as such, should be addressed by occurrence-based coverage. In contrast, other carriers view the exposure as entirely based in the services a Web site provides, even if those services are media related, and offer only claims-made coverage to Internet businesses. Still another, smaller group of insurance carriers has taken the approach that the Internet presents risks that are best served by both types of coverage and have offered blended policies.

The benefits of occurrence versus claims-made policies really depends on whether the claimant is likely to discover and assert its claim soon after the wrongful act and whether the policyholder has any existing insurance coverage that will respond to potential claims from its prior actions.

44.2.4   Duty to Defund versus Indemnity.   Those policies providing express coverage for intellectual property are written on both a duty-to-defend and an indemnity basis. The differences between the two types of coverage are less subtle than the claims-made/occurrence distinction, although the two share some of the same history.

Generally, most third-party liability policies written by domestic insurance companies today obligate the insurance company to defend the policyholder so long as the asserted claim alleges facts that might reasonably be expected to result in coverage under the policy. Different jurisdictions take different views on how to interpret that duty and its trigger. The question is the subject of no small amount of case law and legal analysis. For the purposes of this discussion, it need merely be noted that the general duty to defend under the law is broader than the insurer's duty to indemnify the policyholder for damages. So long as a claim alleges arguably covered damages, the carrier will owe a defense.

Some older policies, as well as those offered through Lloyds' of London, are written on an indemnity basis. The practical effect of this is that the policyholder must incur the cost of defending itself and paying damages for which it is held liable. The insured then must seek indemnity or reimbursement, subject to any retention or deductible, from the carrier.

Whether a policyholder is better served by an indemnity or a duty-to-defend policy depends not only on its ability to fund a defense but also on its desire to maintain complete control over that defense. In a duty-to-defend policy, the carrier, subject to the deductible or retention, provides a defense for covered claims from day 1, including designating and appointing defense counsel.

Duty-to-defend policies usually are associated with a pay-on-behalf-of component. This element of coverage obligates the carrier to pay on behalf of the policyholder any covered damages for which the policyholder is held liable, subject only to the applicable deductible or retention.

In the case of an infringement liability policy, the duty to defend is triggered when a claim alleges that an insured has violated or infringed on the intellectual property rights of another in the course of its business or, if more narrowly underwritten, in the course of the expressly designated covered activity. It is important to note that the validity of the claim is often irrelevant to the duty of the carrier to provide a defense.

44.2.5 Who Is Insured?   The typical policy generally provides coverage to the principal or named insured and subsidiaries of the named insured; the named insured usually is the entity that applied for the insurance and completed the application. Subsidiary coverage traditionally has been limited to actions taken while a subsidiary of the named insured. Coverage also would be provided to any present or former partner, officer, director, or employee of the named insured or subsidiary, but only while acting in his or her capacity as such. Generally it includes the estates, heirs, legal representatives, or assigns of deceased persons who were insureds at the time that the intellectual property infringement was alleged to have been committed and the legal representatives or assigns of insureds in the event of the insured's incompetence, insolvency, or bankruptcy.

As can be seen, persons qualifying as insureds under the policy are a potentially large and diverse group. Traditionally, intellectual property infringement liability policies have focused not so much on the who but on the what of coverage. In this case, the what is the scope of the policyholder's business activity for which the insurance carrier has agreed to provide coverage. This can be anything from a single product or service to the entire breadth of the policyholder's operations.

44.2.6 Definitions of Covered Claims.   The value of intellectual property coverage can best be viewed by how it defines a claim. As can be seen by current cases, more often than not the first salvo fired by a plaintiff is not one seeking damages but rather one seeking to enjoin the infringer from further infringement. Unfortunately, many policies require that the claimant seek monetary damages before coverage attaches. For coverage to be truly effective, a company should make sure that it would respond to actions seeking:

- A demand for money, services, nonmonetary, or injunctive relief or
- A suit, including a civil, criminal or arbitration proceeding, for monetary or nonmonetary relief

Integral to a covered claim is how the policy defines claims expenses. Simply offering coverage for those expenses incurred in defense of an infringement action often gets to only half of an effective defense. To paraphrase the cliché, often the best defense is a strong offense. In order for defensive coverage to be effective, it needs to incorporate coverage for expenses incurred in seeking to challenge the validity of the patent that a company's product or service is allegedly infringing.

44.2.7   Prior Acts Coverage.   The question of prior acts coverage can be a crucial one when the coverage is written on a claims-made basis. A company must consider how long it has been doing what it is seeking to protect. Ideally, coverage should go back to the inception of the company; unfortunately, such broad coverage is not always available. Carriers often limit coverage to a discrete number of years prior to policy inception—the time when the policyholder instituted certain internal intellectual property controls and/or when it began the activities for which coverage is sought.

Prior acts coverage is not an issue for policies written on an occurrence basis, since, by definition, they provide coverage only for acts that occur within the policy period.

44.2.8   Extensions of Coverage.   Most intellectual property insurance policies currently available are written to cover only a specific type of intellectual property infringement, chief among them the patent infringement policy. The typical company, assuming that such an entity even exists, does not have the luxury of being sued only for an isolated activity. It is more probable that a company, by its very existence, will create potential exposures across the entire spectrum of intellectual property. As such, companies need coverage that will respond to an allegation of more than just patent infringement.

Several insurance carriers offer coverage options that address this range of intellectual property (IP) risks in a single policy form. Other carriers have addressed this issue by endorsing only that coverage that the company specifically requests. The most common coverage extensions available are for copyright and/or trademark infringement.

44.2.9   Common Exclusions.   The most common exclusions in third-party liability coverages generally relate to intentional and/or criminal activities. Several policies contain absolute exclusions when the infringement is willful or intentional. Other carriers soften the impact by providing a defense until the prohibited conduct is proven. Even then it is possible that coverage will apply to those insureds under the policy that did not know of or participate in the willful conduct.

Along similar lines is the exclusion for punitive or exemplary damages. Historically, such damages have been excluded as a matter of course. Recently, however, some carriers have offered coverage for awards of such damages to the extent that to do so is not against public policy or otherwise against the law.

Other common exclusions track with the principle that liability insurance is meant to cover fortuitous risks. They include claims arising out of breach of contract, antitrust activities, and infringements that existed prior to the inception of the policy. The policies are meant to cover unforeseen risks, not known claims or the cost of doing business.

44.2.10   Optional Endorsements and Other Key Provisions.   One breed of coverage differs by its very nature. This first-party coverage reimburses the policyholder for the loss of the value of its intellectual property after it is declared invalid (patents) or misappropriated (trade secrets). In addition, coverage is available in the market for a policyholder's loss of a trade secret resulting from a computer attack.

At the moment the number of carriers offering such coverage is very limited, and the underwriting is, in a word, intense. The first coverage is called patent validity coverage, which indemnifies buyers and/or sellers of patent rights for loss related to the patents subsequently being declared invalid or held unenforceable. Such coverage can be tailored to the premium that the company wants to pay. The basic coverage pays up to the purchase price of the patent rights. Expanded coverage pays for the loss of expected royalty income. This coverage is limited to patent only.

Another recent innovation provides first-party coverage for loss of a company's trade secrets. At least two Internet-focused policies also provide first-party coverage to a policyholder for the loss of its trade secrets. These policies provide coverage for the assets a policyholder has decided to treat as a trade secret. The policies generally require that the trade secrets be misappropriated through some deficiency in the security of the policyholder's computer system.

44.2.11   Property Coverage.   Of particular importance to any commercial entity that values its information is the protection, or lack thereof, afforded under existing property policy forms. Traditionally, such policies provide coverage for the direct financial loss suffered by the policyholder for "damage to or loss of use of" an entity's physical or tangible property as a result of such brick-and mortar-perils as fire, windstorm, theft, and the like. This form of property policy is referred to in the insurance industry as "all-risk"; while broader in the scope of the perils it covers, it is still subject to the brick-and-mortar restraint that what is damaged be of a tangible nature.

The realities of the how things work today and the shift away from a company's worth being largely comprised of physical assets suggests that such "tangible property" coverage is no longer adequate or sufficient, in and of itself. In today's economy, the lifeblood of an organization is generally not its buildings and equipment, although the events of September 11 demonstrate how vital such coverage may be. In fact, a fairly standard business model is for a company to have equipment provided to it only virtually, by its Web hosting company or any number of application service providers. The latter often replace many of the systems that a company would have leased or purchased outright, only a few short years ago.

Such relationships create further problems for the traditional property policy. The typical policy provides coverage for tangible property at the physical locations of a business. As such, even if one overcomes the hurdle of whether intangible assets are or are not covered under the policy, it is more likely than not that such "property" is not resident at the locations covered under the policy.

Often purchased in conjunction with the standard property policy is coverage for loss of income due to a business interruption. This coverage has the same "damage to or loss of use of" trigger, but whereas the basic property policy seeks to indemnify the policyholder for the actual lost or damaged property, business interruption coverage reimburses a policyholder for loss in the form of:

1. Loss of net income plus normal operating expenses that continue during the covered interruption; and

2. Necessary extra expense incurred in the effort to continue normal business operations.

In addition, coverage often is extended to include "contingent" or "dependent" business interruption. This provides coverage for a policyholder if a business that the policyholder depends on is interrupted by a peril covered under the policy and subsequently causes the policyholder to suspend business a result.

In today's world, most if not all business rely on third parties to maintain some element of their network or computer systems, from the obvious application service provider (ASP) or hosting company (ISP), to the less obvious but equally vital outsourcing of network security. The concept of weakest link applies not only to those allowed within a firewall—such as supply-chain elements and extranet members—but also to the backbone and infrastructure suppliers. The network or site will be just as inoperative, whether the distributed denial-of-service attacks the business directly or brings down its hosting company or ASP, backup and business continuity plans notwithstanding.

A recent case in Arizona threw into question much of what the insurance industry felt was well settled on the issue of tangible versus intangible. In *American Guarantee & Liability Ins. Co. v. Ingram Micro, Inc.,*[4] a policyholder sought coverage under a property policy for "loss of functionality" of its computer systems resulting from the loss of programming information in random access memory due to a power outage. The judge, in finding for the policyholder, based his decision largely on federal computer crime law and his own stated belief that the continued distinction between "tangible" and "intangible" property in this day and age was pointless.

Not surprisingly, the Ingram Micro case has had a galvanizing effect on the legal and insurance community. The policyholder bar has hailed it as a commonsense decision; whereas the carriers and the legal community at large has pointed at the holes in the logic, personal opinion, and leaps of faith in the decision. What all can agree on, however, is that it has created an increasing awareness and sensitivity by companies as to their insurance portfolios

The logical extension of increased interaction and dependencies between not just service providers and clients but between coventures and simple conversants is that, increasingly, businesses will come to hold or touch more and more information assets besides their own in their computer system. Such property, like its electronic brethren, will not, tortured judicial logic notwithstanding, rise to the level of "covered property," which generally is limited to tangible property located in or on the policyholder's premises.

It has been suggested that coverage might be found under the property policy pursuant to the "valuable papers and records" extension. The only problem with this argument is that absent express endorsement to the contrary, "valuable papers and records" are defined as manuscripts and the like, not electronic data or the media used to store or record such data.

There also have been attempts to resurrect the notion that coverage might be found under the "sue and labor" aspect of coverage. This would afford coverage not for the loss itself but for the costs associated with fixing the problem. Much was made of this in numerous cases seeking coverage for Y2K remediation efforts; these cases have begun to die quiet deaths due in large part to the "known" element of Y2K (the technological equivalent of a burning building in that programmers were well aware of the problem) and the nonevent that Y2K eventually proved to be. The analogy in network and computer security would be to look to one's insurance company to pay for the company's firewall and intrusion detection system. Chapter 48 analyzes the Y2K event in detail.

44.3   CRIME/FIDELITY COVERAGE.   Traditional crime and fraud policies have and do provide a certain level of coverage for direct financial loss due to computer fraud.

These policies have, however, usually been limited to indemnifying a policyholder for loss of "money, securities, and other property." The policies also can contain limitations as to coverage involving both the intent and the identity of the "thief," that is, whether an employee of the policyholder or a third party). However, these policies fall short in the protection or indemnification for the theft or misappropriation of information and intangible assets such as trade secrets, data, and technology—the essential stuff of e-commerce.

The policies that do afford express coverage for the loss suffered by a policyholder as a result of a computer crime generally focus the coverage to the loss of intangible property or information assets. They also can include loss that is other than the deprivation of the information asset, such as situations where the crime involves the copying of data. In today's economy, a company can effectively suffer as great a loss where its information assets are copied—for example the disclosure of a client list, business plan, vendor relationship details, and the like.

44.4   E-COMMERCE POLICIES.   Recently, a legion of new policies purporting to provide the definitive coverage for information technology, e-commerce, and/or network security have popped up. What is important to note is that all of these forms must and will continue to change with time as the technology to which they are tied changes and evolves. One need only look back to the early 1990s to find policies that spoke of the infinite channels of the Internet and information security as part and parcel of the general content–related risks faced by publishers and broadcasters.

These e-commerce policies generally fall into two categories: (1) those that cover damage caused to others by the actions or failures of the policyholder's computer systems and (2) those that cover direct financial loss of the policyholder from certain specified cyber perils.

The most common e-commerce policy is that which would defend and indemnify a policyholder for claims made against it by others for damages allegedly suffered by those third parties. In addition to filling the gaps in traditional polices, such as the CGL policy, such policies also extend new coverage that is peculiar to the needs and exposures of information technology and computer system security.

Typical third-party exposures include the infringement of another's intellectual property, violation of privacy rights, content-based liability such as libel and slander, and professional malpractice. Claims alleging such suffered wrongs are more often than not attributable to acts of negligence by an insured. They also do not differ dramatically from their old economy cousins, with the exception of the myriad of privacy issues that recently have come to the fore in the form of general privacy, healthcare, and financial information.

The new exposures or risks that these policies respond to include the damage caused by the transmission of malicious code, the unwitting participation in a distributed denial of service attack as a zombie,[5] and others. These perils also are the triggers for coverage for the direct loss suffered by the policyholder itself in the form of stolen information assets, corrupted data, network interruption, cyberextortion, and so on.

The more robust e-commerce policies must and will adapt to the inherent differences between the Old and the New Economy. Policyholders risk finding themselves bare at worst or at best succeeding in forcing a settlement after protracted litigation when they seek to shoehorn coverage for the unique risks of the Internet into hoary old policies from the days of black-and-white television and the Cold War. Just as new coverages developed around the new exposures of employment practices, so too have new coverages arisen to address the new exposures of a company Web-enabling its business practices.

Just as these new e-commerce policies cover new risks, so too must the due diligence performed by the insurance carrier in underwriting the risk break new ground. The few carriers that have taken the time to educate themselves about the risks inherent in computer and network security have turned to computer security professionals to assist in their due diligence. This due diligence generally takes the form of remote penetration testing, an online network security assessment, a full-blown on-site security audit, or some combination. What is important to note is that these activities basically are unrelated to insurance and focus exclusively on the computer and network security issues; as such, they represent a true value added to the applicant in the form of an additional set of eyes taking a critical look at its security without the applicant having to pay for it.

In addition, companies recently have begun to develop and market coverage that would allow individuals to cover the damages and costs associated with the loss and repair of their financial or credit identity. Such coverage also has been available to individuals under traditional personal lines policies, such as homeowner's insurance, although that capacity seems to be disappearing as the risks associated with such loss become more widespread and publicized.

Recent events, and like as not future events, will continue to highlight the vulnerability of even the most robust computer and network security. Apart from simply shutting down a business, the only way for a business to operate with the confidence that it will survive a successful computer attack and to instill that same confidence in its trading partners, be they customers or suppliers, is to have that traditional old risk-transfer vehicle, the insurance policy, sitting behind all that good technology.

The issue of computer and network security is itself changing as well. Accounting changes, shifts in asset composition, and the leveraging of intangible assets have caused network and computer security to evolve from a technology issue into a management liability issue. That evolution requires that companies address both the efficacy of their technology and the completeness of their insurance portfolio.

44.5   FURTHER READING

Dionne, G. *Handbook of Insurance,* vol. 22. Huebner International Series on Risk, Insurance and Economic Security. Dordrecht: Kluwer Academic Publishers, 2000.

Ostrager. B.R., and T.R. Newman. *Handbook on Insurance Coverage Disputes,* 9th ed. Aspen Law & Business, division of Aspen Publishers Inc., 1998.

Sutcliffe, G.S. *E-Commerce Insurance and Risk Management,* 2nd ed. Shelby Publishing Corp., 2001.

44.6   NOTES

1. 820 F. Supp. 489 (N.D. Cal. 1993).

2. *Seagate Technology, Inc. v. St. Paul Fire & Marine Ins. Co.,* 11 F. Supp 2d 1150 (N.D. Cal. 1998).

3. *Rockford Pharmacy, Inc. v. Digital Simlistic, Inc.,* 53 F. 3d 195 (8th Cir. 1995).

4. D. Ariz. 2000.

5. Zombies are computers that have been taken over by an attacker, and used to transmit large volumes of traffic. See Chapter 11 for details of Denial of Service attacks.

MANAGEMENT'S ROLE

CHAPTER 45

MANAGEMENT RESPONSIBILITIES AND LIABILITIES

Carl Hallberg, Arthur E. Hutt, and M.E. Kabay

CONTENTS

45.1 INTRODUCTION. This chapter reviews the critical roles of management in establishing, implementing, and maintaining information security policies in the modern enterprise. It also reviews some of the risks to management personnel in failing to ensure adequate standards of information security.

Management provides the essential framework for accomplishing technical work. Whether it is drawing up a security policy, enforcing such policies, training the individuals who will implement and enforce those policies, or proposing a budget to get all this done, management plays an essential role. Information technology (IT) managers ensure the consistent functioning of the organizational computing environment. Ideally, they also provide insights and guidance to upper management in strategic planning to take advantage of new opportunities.

Many organizations, regardless of size and history, have heterogeneous networks with many different operating systems running different applications and serving many purposes and clients. Web servers sit next to e-mail servers, which connect to outside networks, which then rely on connections to more than one third-party corporate networks. The rapid pace of technological change impedes the IT manager's ability to keep the enterprise IT infrastructure running smoothly.

A key function of IT managers is loss avoidance, by managing risk intelligently (see Chapters 42, 47, and 48) to reduce the likelihood of trouble in the IT sector and to reduce the costs of coping with such trouble.

IT managers must focus constantly on enabling business functions. Given that most enterprises do not consider security as their main task, IT managers must ensure that information security policies and technology support rather than hinder the principal business of the enterprise.

In recent years, information security has been growing in visibility as a major business concern. IT managers are now being joined by information security managers. For example, a major bank responded to infiltration of its systems in the 1990s by naming a CISO: a Chief Information Security Officer reporting at the same level as officers such as the CIO (Chief Information Officer), CFO (Chief Financial Officer), COO (Chief Operations Officer), CTO (Chief Technology Officer) and CEO (Chief Executive Officer). Together, the CIO and the CISO face complex responsibilities and are increasingly visible in the corporate infrastructure.

One of the factors in this increased visibility is the rapid growth in the popular press of technology issues coverage and of information security breaches in particular. For example, in February of 2000, several well-publicized distributed denial-of-service attacks served to focus a media spotlight on the arena of information security (see Chapter 11). Since that time, the media have not hesitated to report on any type of information security threat, including the I Love You and Anna Kournikova viruses, privacy policy issues, credit card number thefts, Web site defacements, and other forms of unauthorized access to systems and networks.

In some sense, publicity has helped the IT world because some IT managers now have increased ammunition with which to argue for management support of the security function. On the other hand, publicity has increased visibility, so that even a minor breach of security may spark an overreaction in the upper echelons of the enterprise.

IT security managers are now able to help their businesses achieve strategic goals and to further their responsibilities by showing that security involves more than just protecting assets; it is also potentially a business enabler. In the absence of a secure IT infrastructure, businesses may be slow to enter a given market for fear of losses and liabilities resulting from security breaches. However, with security integrated into the corporate culture, these enterprises can confidently enter new arenas and convince their potential clients that their data will be safe.

In an article by Karen Worstell, Mike Gerdes, and M.E. Kabay, the three described this proactive stance as the "Net Present Value (NVP)" of information security:

> As a key strategic enabler of new trusted e-business processes, information security becomes a generator of NPV for the organization. Information security protects business reputation, consumer confidence and market valuations, and it delivers a competitive edge by allowing new distribution channels, revenue streams and even business models in an otherwise diluted and overly compromised marketplace. In other words, instead of being viewed solely as a risk-avoidance measure (like a kind of insurance policy that never pays anything back), information security is required both to support and enable e-business.
>
> In today's e-commerce environment, effective information security can serve to increase business and profits, not merely to reduce risk. To assure success, therefore, e-businesses need to bring information security to the forefront of strategic thinking. They no longer can view security as an add-on feature relegated to the end of the design process or as a cost center, or as solely the purview of the technical staff in an organization. Instead, they must realize that information security is a process that is essential in meeting the legitimate needs of the public. They must also realize that their marketing and public relations departments

need to be well versed in the principles of information security so that they can communicate effectively with an anxious public about the measures that safeguard customer privacy and money.[1]

In this framework, information security becomes not an afterthought, preventing loss, but as part of the design strategy, which will help realize gain. This is a much more powerful, and positive, view of information security's role in the business world than is the traditional one. Using information security principles in the design of a product or service generally helps to create a more robust product or service, one that will be less prone to risk.

45.2   RESPONSIBILITIES.   Managers are responsible for specific tasks or functions to the extent that they make decisions about business processes and suffer the consequences or reap the benefits of those decisions.

45.2.1   Policy Management.   Managers spend more time on people issues than on technical issues. The right people must be hired for each position (see Chapter 31 for more on employment practices and policies). Employees who do not work responsibly and competently must either be brought up to the proper standard or let go. Employees who do their jobs properly must be kept satisfied, lest they move to a job with another organization. Management in the IT world must ensure compliance with corporate policies. Policy issues are discussed in detail in Chapters 28, 29, 35, and 46 of this book. Compliance with policies includes motivation, supervision, judgment, and adaptation.

45.2.2   Motivation.   Employees need motivation to pay attention to information security policies, which often are perceived as a nuisance, interfering with the fundamental goals of the enterprise. Upper management, in particular, must set an example by following enterprise policies; when top managers are seen to ignore policies, the people reporting to them quickly imitate their behavior, and the problem spreads throughout the organization. For example, if the CEO refuses to wear a picture badge, the vice-presidents (VPs) will quickly follow suit because they will associate *not* wearing badges with high status. Similarly, the directors reporting to VPs will start dropping their badges, and so within a few months the entire hierarchy will be convinced that no one but stock clerks should wear badges. Sometime later, the stock clerks will be resisting badges too.

Some managers think that punishment is the only motivation that can change behavior, but everything known about human psychology shows that reward is more powerful. (See Chapter 35 for more information about using social psychology to motivate compliance with security policies.) Reward is not limited to salary increases and bonuses; sometimes the most effective way to keep IT employees satisfied and productive is to provide training. The IT world is evolving, and the demand for competent staff has never been higher. Most employees want to feel that their employers value their services and that they are worth an investment to improve staff competence. Training employees and providing challenging opportunities for the exercise of intelligence serves the interests of both employer and employee.

Unfortunately, some managers fear that after they provide training, their employees will leave and use their new skills to benefit some other organization—perhaps even a competitor. In reality, some employees are more likely to walk out if the investment is *not* made. Numerous studies have shown that if employees feel valued, they will be more willing to stay.

Training need not be expensive or excessively time consuming. Online security training can be taken anytime and is self-paced. Training videos are also an excellent tool for stimulating employee knowledge and interest. The simplest way to locate such resources is to search on the World Wide Web with a good search engine such as Google (*www.google.com*) and to use keywords such as "security training."

Another alternative is to have the employer use obsolete equipment for training, equipment that would otherwise lie idle in a storage area. Even small departments are bound to have old PCs lying around dormant as well as hubs and possibly router/switches. These can be used to create a network for testing and learning at little cost. Companies that do not have spare equipment can buy used equipment for less than the cost of a one-week intensive course. For an employee who wants to learn the basics of firewalls, Linux is a cheap (and even free) operating system that has just recently started supporting firewalls. Setting up a Linux firewall requires no expensive software or appliances. It can provide an effective way of encouraging employees to learn the practical details of configuring firewalls—a valuable skill set in any security department—while rewarding loyal employees by showing confidence in their commitment to learning and to their continued employment in the enterprise.

Once the firewall is set up, other employees can use the testing and training network to learn about penetration testing, intrusion detection, and other security elements. Different operating systems can be installed, with various applications, all for a minimal investment. As technology, techniques, and tools change, this training network will be valuable in keeping skills up to date.

Challenging employees in other ways can be highly motivating. For example, managers can encourage staff to prepare and deliver presentations at internal meetings and at security conferences. Motivated employees can lead special interest group discussions at conferences and so develop a web of relationships that promote sharing of knowledge and enhance their self-image. There are also security contests to take part in, such as the Honeynet forensics contest, to test their skills.

The Honeynet Forensics Challenge (*www.project.honeynet.org/challenge*) was an open contest (held on February 19, 2001) that allowed security staff to challenge their forensics skills as well as learn and teach new tricks of the trade. The Honeynet Project posted an image of a hacked system, and tasked would-be contestants to unravel what the hack was and how it was performed. Along with finding out what had happened, judging also was based on how much information was uncovered and how this information was communicated.

Many journals and Web-based magazines are ready to accept articles written by professionals in the field. Not only does writing solidify employees' knowledge and build their own confidence, but it also instills confidence in the entire team. Writing and teaching help the enterprise, as well as its clients and partners, to view the security team as a real benefit, at the same time that the organization develops a strong reputation for excellence in security.

Another way for management to make the security team more cohesive is to build camaraderie. A monthly pizza party or an occasional outing to a sports event can do a lot to ease stress and to help everyone get to know each other. Having good friends at work can reduce turnover and motivate employees to do their best, not only for the rather abstract goal of doing good for the enterprise but also because of their commitment to their colleagues.

To help encourage a higher level of expertise and to establish a feeling of belonging, periodic "brown bag" lunch sessions can be effective. At each session, a different team member can be designated to present an informed talk or to lead a discussion on a topic of general interest. There could even be an informal call for papers, giving team members an opportunity to present valuable information in a professional manner.

At the same time, a little friendly competition can help as well. For example, if the enterprise has a training network that can be subdivided into several subnets, managers can organize a "tiger-team challenge." Each team will be responsible for securing a subnet or host and then given the opportunity to break into the subnet or host of another team. The winners would get both a reward and a responsibility. The reward can be as simple as pizza for the team or a modest trophy. The responsibility would be to present the exploits used and the ways to secure against them to the rest of the teams.

Another way to build the team is to support staff in choosing the areas in which they want to excel. There may be some overlap, but overlap can be good. Clearly, if there are two firewall experts, the enterprise is less vulnerable should one of them be absent. Furthermore, the firewall experts can provide better quality assurance by discussing alternatives when planning a change and better quality control by checking each other's work. It can also help to have the security team members switch roles periodically, both to ensure that no one gets into a rut and to contribute to the challenges presented when a change is made.

Last, almost nothing is more infuriating than being expected to accomplish a task without the necessary resources. Adequate time to get a task done is always an important issue, as many people have several tasks to do, and each of them may be seen as critical by someone. A manager should be willing to give the team all of the resources it needs to complete a task in the allotted time or should make clear to other departments or to higher management what the realistic expectations are for the completion of such tasks, if required resources are lacking. If expectations are properly managed, there should be less conflict and fewer problems.

It is useful to view management not as separate from the IT security team but as an integral part of it. Doing this allows management to contribute directly toward the employees' enthusiasm as well as to detect early warning signals of impending trouble. A manager who does not spend time listening to the team members or who does not understand what their jobs involve at a technical level will not be respected by the team. Lack of respect will block communication and keep the department from becoming a solid, effectively functioning unit.

45.2.3 Supervision. What little we know about damage to computer systems (see Chapter 4) indicates that errors and omissions are a major source of harm. Poorly trained employees make mistakes, but so do trained employees who have become careless. Managers should examine performance records as a normal part of their supervision of the security team. In particular, every incident that damages production systems (see Chapter 32) should be analyzed to identify the reasons for the event. Careful technical support records and log files (see Chapters 38 and 39) can help the team spot the crucial weaknesses, whether technical or human, that allowed compromise of the damaged systems.

Analysis of security breaches of all kinds may reveal that certain employees are associated with unusually high or unusually low frequencies of particular problems. Careful analysis of both types of extremes can be helpful in spotting weaknesses for remediation and strengths from which to learn, so that the knowledge can be spread across the entire unit. However, managers must not assume that disproportionate numbers of problems are necessarily caused by the employees involved; for example, low rates of penetration during the day shift may be associated with lower rates of attack from hackers, who often work in the evenings or nights. Similarly, higher rates of security breaches may, after detailed study, be found to have been caused by factors entirely outside the control of a particular employee.

In addition to monitoring performance, managers must ensure that all employees know that they are being monitored. Warning notices, preemployment agreements, and yearly policy reviews can ensure that staff develops no unwarranted expectation of privacy about their work (see Chapters 28, 29, 31, and 53).

One of the most effective supervisory practices an information security team leader, or any other manager, can use is managing by walking around. Managers should set aside time every week to observe the conditions and to absorb the atmosphere of the working areas. Visiting team members and hearing about their specific job experiences, both positive and negative, can only improve communications and motivation within the security team.

45.2.4   Judgment and Adaptation.   Management must not permit policies and procedures to keep the work from getting done. The comic strip *Dilbert* has become popular largely because it caricatures managers who apply policy unintelligently; for example, in one company, managers decided to give the marketing department new laptops because of all the traveling they had to do. The managers then decided that to prevent theft, the laptops should be so securely fastened to the employees' desks that they could not be moved at all.

When security policies interfere with productivity, the correct solution is rarely black and white. Usually, neither dropping the policy nor enforcing it without change is appropriate. A hospital security administrator, for example, might note that a workstation in the emergency room is always logged on for the entire day using the ID and password of the first person who logged on. Clearly, this violates the principle that everyone using the system must be positively identified and authenticated. Piggybacking on the first user's session damages the credibility of log files and makes it impossible to ascertain exactly which person is retrieving and modifying data at any time during the day. However, cracking down insensitively on the emergency room staff is a bad idea; chances are that the harried medical and support personnel are simply racing to get their work done saving lives. Logging off and on repeatedly is not a good method of identification and authentication in that environment. A reasonable security manager would listen to the employees and understand their point of view and their functional needs, and then explore technical alternatives to the usual ID-password technique. For example, the security manager might find that proximity cards or smart cards (see Chapter 16) could meet the requirements at reasonable cost.

45.3   LIABILITIES.   Security managers focus on minimizing liability by a practice generally known as risk management (see Chapters 47 and 48). Risk management is the traditional model for information security; ideally, one determines risk by identifying the threats and vulnerabilities (see Chapter 37) and then evaluating the associated costs and probabilities of each type of incident. As discussed in Chapters 4, 47, and 48, the probabilities are difficult to define, and as a result, much of risk management is, in practice, an intuitive, nonquantitative process.

Security managers face many liabilities. (See Chapter 2 for further information about legal aspects of information security.) Some of the possible negative consequences of inadequate security include:

- Loss of revenue
- Loss of reputation

- Loss of business partner confidence
- Loss of consumer confidence
- Loss of enterprise valuation
- Failure of the entire enterprise

Each of these types of loss also involves a loss of trust. Trust is easy to lose, especially in uncertain economic climates, and it is, unfortunately, harder to regain trust than to establish and maintain it. It is necessary for managers to understand that security and privacy are integral to the services and products offered by the enterprise. Security and privacy must apply to data from customers, business partners, employees, and every other individual or entity with whom the enterprise comes into contact.

45.3.1   Case Study.   At the beginning of the year 2001, the issue of trust was much discussed in the news media when Verisign, a leader in digital certificate technology (see Chapter 23), issued two certificates to someone posing as a Microsoft employee. As a result, the imposter could have signed Internet software as if it had been developed by Microsoft. Were such deceptively signed software to have malicious content, the results could have been disastrous.

Despite the error, Verisign's stock price was not adversely affected. Although, like most high-technology stocks in the early part of 2001, its stock price was generally falling, just days after the announcement of the two erroneously issued certificates, Verisign's stock price was up 8 percent. Investors, at least, continued to trust Verisign, perhaps because the company announced immediately that it realized its mistake, made known what the consequences might be, and worked openly to resolve the problem. (See Chapter 40 for more information on managing computer emergency response teams.) Openness and frankness are an effective strategy for keeping consumer confidence high. Had Verisign tried to deny the error or to downplay the consequences, consumer confidence might well have dropped.

In this case, Verisign seems to have responded well once the security breach was discovered, but waiting for problems to surface is a poor second to ensuring that the problems never happen. In many organizations, security is viewed as an add-on—something to be taken care of at the end of development—rather than as an integral part of the overall process. As many practitioners have been preaching for years, security is a continuing process, not a product or a stable state. Security, like quality, is an outcome of thinking about security at all stages of the business cycle.

45.3.2   Stakeholders.   It is easy to think of only stockholders and customers when evaluating the potential costs of security breaches. However, it is useful to enumerate all of the people and other entities that are potentially affected by information security breaches. Such *stakeholders* can include:

- *Stockholders:* people and organizations owning stock in a privately held or publicly traded enterprise.
- *Employees:* managers and workers depending on an enterprise for their livelihood.
- *Customers:* people and organizations depending on fulfillment of contractual obligations by the enterprise.
- *Potential customers:* those who might want to do business with the enterprise.
- *Suppliers:* those depending on the enterprise for acceptance of materials and services followed by payment as per contract.

- *Data subjects:* people or other entities about whom an enterprise stores, manipulates, and reports data.

- *Regulatory agencies and law enforcement:* people and organizations devoted to enforcing statutory regulations and laws.

- *Users of other systems victimized by means of a compromised system:* innocent bystanders who may be harmed through no fault of their own when a compromised system is used as an intermediary to launch attacks on an ultimate target.

When thinking about liability, managers should explore the potential consequences of specific types of security incident with respect to all of the stakeholders. This wider analysis contributes significantly to effective risk management.

45.3.3   Due Diligence of Care.   Due diligence of care in information security refers to the research and analysis carried out in establishing that risks have been minimized to an extent consistent with industry standards. Due diligence investigations typically are crucial in mergers and acquisitions; no one wants to acquire unanticipated liabilities resulting from inadequate governance.

Unfortunately, just as there is no sound basis for assertions about computer crime rates, there is not even the most rudimentary basis for asserting that any given level of security represents adequate care for information. What, precisely, is the right length for the asymmetric encryption key used in protecting confidential e-mail sent across the Internet? Does failing to update antivirus signatures daily constitute a violation of due diligence, or is once a week good enough? Does due diligence in securing a manufacturing system require installation of an intrusion detection system (IDS)? What about lacking an IDS in a hospital or a bank? Is a computer emergency response team a requirement to demonstrate due care in protecting information assets—or not?

Attempts at defining security standards (see Chapter 27) have not yet convinced more than a few enterprises to conform to their recommendations; the information security field is not yet at the point where quality assurance was a decade ago, when ISO 9000 certification became widely used in manufacturing plants around the world.

Sensitivity to due diligence of care should, at a minimum, begin with consideration of legal and regulatory requirements on the protection of information. Contractual obligations with any and all stakeholders will determine the required degree of responsiveness to intrusion and may help determine whether to cooperate with law enforcement authorities to investigate any breach of security (see Chapters 2 and 34).

45.3.4   Downstream Liability.   In recent years, a growing number of security experts and attorneys have predicted that the doctrine of downstream liability would become a significant factor in pushing management toward better security. Downstream liability is an application of the legal theory of contributory negligence, as it applies to information security. In turn, contributory negligence refers to reckless endangerment of others, reckless meaning without consideration of the consequences and endangerment resulting from putting others at risk of harm. The term "downstream" refers to the conventional model in which the source of data is viewed as being upstream of the recipient of those data; thus if someone compromises a university computer system and then launches an attack on a bank, the bank is viewed as downstream from the university.

Keeping in mind that neither author is an attorney and that the information being discussed here is in no sense legal advice (for legal advice, consult an attorney), examples of what might be construed in a court of law as downstream liability include:

- Distributing virus-infected documents through e-mail because all antivirus mechanisms have deliberately been turned off

- Allowing a malefactor to install *zombie* software on a poorly configured system and involving that compromised system in a distributed denial-of-service attack (see Chapter 11)

- Failing to install patches for a well-known and years-old vulnerability, thus allowing a criminal hacker to attack a third party via a root compromise of the poorly secured system (see Chapter 8)

- Allowing private information such as credit card numbers belonging to thousands of people to be stolen and distributed on the Internet for use in credit card fraud

- Providing an unsecured e-mail server that provides an open spam-relay point for junk e-mail, with a forged REPLY-TO address, to flood millions of mailboxes with unwanted messages, thereby causing thousands of bounce messages and angry accusations to clog the mail system of the innocent owner of the forged REPLY-TO address

- Having an employee who sends out thousands of fraudulent notices using the employer's e-mail system to libel a competitor, causing depression of that competitor's sales and stock price

- Configuring a *honey-pot* system on the enterprise network to attract the attention of criminal hackers—who then turn around and use the honey pot to attack a third party

It is important to note that "honey pots," while used as security measures in that they are used to attract a hacker to a specific server for the purpose of gathering data on an attack, do in fact introduce security holes. The honey pot is a live server, with intentional vulnerabilities built in, connected to a company's network. Once penetrated, an attacker may use it as a platform from which to launch future attacks. Special safeguards must be designed to prevent this.

As of this writing, there appear to have been no cases in which a plaintiff has successfully sued an enterprise for damages on the basis of downstream liability linked to inadequate security. However, in December 2000, FirstNet Online (Management) Limited filed a lawsuit in the Court of Sessions in Edinburgh, Scotland, against Nike, Inc., apparently an innocent victim. The incident began in June 2000, when someone hacked the DNS (Domain Name System) by filing incorrect data for resolution of the nike.com domain with Network Solutions, Inc., which is charged with the responsibility of managing acquisition and retention of certain classes of domain names. All subsequent attempts to reach nike.com were redirected to the s11.org domain, an activist site devoted to fighting globalization. The redirection allegedly caused serious harm to the Web-hosting service for s11.org; according to the plaintiffs (see *www.nikesucks. org*), FirstNET Online "experienced an 1800% increase of traffic over the 46 hours it took to correct the problem completely." Blaming Nike administrators for failing to protect the password required for updating the DNS records at Network Solutions, the plaintiffs demanded compensation for the expenses incurred. Nike officials rejected such accusations and blamed Network Solutions for allowing the redirection of Internet traffic to the s11.org site. Readers will want to search the Web for later developments in this interesting case.

45.3.5   Audits.   As managers attempt to manage security according to nebulous principles of due care, they must remember that in many enterprises, IT and information security departments are seen as being equivalent to the police. Many people in these departments have privileged access to other people's secrets; for example, they can read all e-mail and can often tell exactly what Web sites employees have been visiting. In some environments, network monitors allow administrators and security personnel to activate keystroke monitoring and to view in real time the appearance of any given terminal or workstation on the network. Because of the enormous power of such personnel, managers must ensure that such levels of access are not abused.

Information systems auditors are responsible for keeping the technical and security staff honest. In some larger enterprises, there is a department of internal audit whose director reports to the same level as other officers, such as the CEO and CFO. In other cases, third-party auditors monitor adherence to policy, standards, and procedures (see Chapter 36).

Security audits are often feared, and with good reason. In general, many audits are performed with the focus of finding fault. This approach is counterproductive and unnecessarily stressful. The point of an audit should not be to find the maximum number of offenses but rather to assess the level of compliance. The most important outcome of an audit is finding areas of potential improvement. A nonadversarial style facilitates positive results; thus an auditing team should provide constructive suggestions for improvement wherever possible.

An auditing team also needs to listen to those being audited. Although a particular network may not be configured to full compliance with security policy, there may be reasons for this apparent failure. For example, suppose a specific patch was required by security policy to have been installed on a Solaris server, but a particular Solaris server did not comply. An auditor might report a failure without further investigation even though, in reality, the patch might have been installed but found to be incompatible with a critical application. Just like managers, audit teams need to see the big picture, not just the rules and procedures. The main point is that all audits must be done with the needs of the business in mind. It does no good to have a process that gets in the way of the business at hand. Instead, to enable the business, alternative measures must be found. That is the job of the auditor—to help ensure compliance and to provide another set of eyes that can see to it that all needs are taken care of.

To prove due diligence, auditing is a must. Generally, third-party audits create more trust, as a third party has no bias about the findings. However, it is important to ensure that a third-party audit firm maintains its independence. It can be risky to use a small firm that bases more than a modest fraction of its revenue on income from any one client. On the other hand, it may be undesirable to have the same large firm perform accounting or auditing functions while also serving as security consultants.

45.4   SUMMARY.   Information security managers have many responsibilities, not all of them technical. An IS manager is in a position to help his or her company realize not only its current goals but, by being able to offer secure means of new service and product offerings, also may help the company realize new areas of business. Designing security from the beginning, rather than as an afterthought, will help build more robust services and products. This is a new role for information security, more powerful than the traditional model of simple loss avoidance.

Some of the responsibilities of management are psychological, as managers spend a great deal of time managing people, not machines. Managers must keep their employees trained on current tools and procedures, and keep them motivated to use these. They also should try to build not simply a security department but a security *team* of colleagues who are committed to each other as strongly as they are to their jobs and their company. Managers who can accomplish this go a long way toward their goal of keeping their enterprise secure.

Managers also must ensure that a business's security policies make sense and that they do not interfere with accomplishing the task at hand. A policy that blocks work needs to be reviewed and modified. Security managers must help to strike a balance between security and productivity.

Managers also face numerous liabilities as well, from loss of data and consumer confidence, to the complete failure of the entire enterprise. When evaluating the potential costs of security breaches and their countermeasures, managers must account for everyone these may affect, not just the enterprise's stockholders. Employees, customers, potential customers, suppliers, even users of other systems victimized by means of a compromised system must be taken into account when thinking of liabilities. All of these people and entities have a stake in the security of an enterprise.

Due diligence is one way of alleviating possible security exposures and legal exposures as well. Managers must take steps to ensure that all reasonable steps are taken to secure an enterprise's systems and data, to avoid both legal and perceptual suffering in the event of a security breach. At a minimum, due diligence must take into consideration of legal and regulatory requirements, and contractual obligations.

A number of security experts and attorneys predict that an enterprise also may be deemed responsible for the breach of a separate entity if that breach originates from the enterprise itself. IS managers must look for ways to prevent such downstream liabilities from tarnishing the image of their company in addition to avoiding damages and legal action. Such breaches may include propagation of viruses, failure to install patches, attacks originating from a compromised system, and so on.

To ensure that security for an enterprise is at an optimum level, managers will want to schedule periodic audits of their systems and procedures. These audits may be performed both by the security staff and by third party security services. Auditing should be performed with an eye toward compliance with security policies and procedures, not toward finding faults. Audits also should not be done in a vacuum. Auditors must listen to the personnel who are being audited, in order to understand the environment they are in.

45.5 NOTE

1. Karen Worstell, Mike Gerdes, and M.E. Kabay, "Net Present Value of Information Security," November 1, 2000.

CHAPTER 46

DEVELOPING SECURITY POLICIES

M.E. Kabay

CONTENTS

46.1   INTRODUCTION.   This chapter reviews methods for developing security policies. Some of the other chapters of this *Handbook* that bear on policy content, development, and implementation are as follows:

- Chapter 15 provides an extensive overview of physical security policies.
- Chapter 18 discusses local area network security issues and policies.
- Chapter 25 reviews software development policies and quality assurance policies.
- Chapter 28 presents principles, topics, and resources for creating effective security policy guidelines.
- Chapter 29 looks at methods for enhancing security awareness.
- Chapter 31 provides guidance on employment policies from a security standpoint.
- Chapter 32 makes explicit recommendations about operations management policies.
- Chapter 33 reviews specific recommendations for e-mail and Internet usage.
- Chapter 35 presents concepts and techniques from social psychology to make security policy implementation more effective.
- Chapter 39 discusses the policies that apply to application design.
- Chapter 51 looks at censorship and content filtering on the Internet.

46.2   COLLABORATING IN BUILDING SECURITY POLICIES.   Policies are the foundation of effective information security, but the task of policy creation is complicated by human and organizational resistance. Technology alone does not work. In changing human behavior, rationality and substance are not enough: The *process* of development affects how people feel about policies and whether they see these rules as needless imposition of power or an expression of their own values.

Security is always described as being everyone's business; however, in practice, security *interferes* with everyone's business. For example, network managers work hard to make networks user-friendly. They do everything they can to make life easier for users; they provide network access routines with a graphical user interface, client-server systems with hot links between local spreadsheets and corporate databases, and a gateway to the Internet for the engineering users. Superficially, one might think that implementing network security would simply involve defining access controls, applying encryption, and providing people with hand-held password generators. Unfortunately, as discussed in Chapter 35, security policies offend deep-seated self-conceptions. People form close-knit work groups in which people trust each other; they do not lock their desks when they leave them for a few minutes, so why should they obey the network security policy that dictates locking their sessions? They even lend people car keys in an emergency; why should it be such a terrible breach of security to lend access codes and passwords to trusted colleagues in an emergency?

Security policies challenge users to change the way they think about their own responsibility for protecting corporate information. Attempting to impose security policies on unwilling people results in resistance both because more stringent security procedures make people's jobs harder, and because people do not like being told what to do—especially by security officials perceived as being outside the chain of command.

The only approach that works in the long run is to present security to everyone in the organization in a way that causes them to recognize that they, personally and professionally, have a stake in information protection. Security managers, to be successful, must involve employees from throughout the enterprise in developing security policies. Users must justifiably feel that they own their security procedures; employees with true involvement in the policy development process become partners rather than opponents of effective security.

46.3   PHASE 1: PRELIMINARY EVALUATION.   Studies of the extent to which information security policies are in place consistently show that relatively few of the respondents have adequate policies in place. For example, the 2000 Global Security Survey run by *InformationWeek* and PricewaterhouseCoopers (see *www.informationweek.com/ 794/security.htm*) interviewed 4,900 executives, security professionals, and technology managers about their organization's security policies. According to the report, "only 38% of the respondents say their security policies are very well aligned with their business goals. Forty-five percent say their security policies are somewhat aligned with business goals, and 17% say the two don't mesh at all."[1] In other words, almost two-thirds of the organizations represented had inadequate security policies.

In what follows, it is assumed that a specific officer or manager (or group of officers or managers) in the enterprise have taken on the task of developing security policies. The group will be called the *policy development group.*

Before attempting to formulate policies, the policy development group needs formal authorization to use corporate resources in such a project. It should not be too difficult to obtain a short memorandum from top management to everyone in the organization that lays out the reasons for asking for their time and energy in gathering information about the current state of security. Such authorization and continuing top-level support are essential tools in convincing people to cooperate with the policy development group.

In the absence of existing or adequate security policies, a preliminary inventory is the first step in providing upper management with the baseline information that will justify developing a corporate information security policy. The preliminary evaluation should be quick and inexpensive—perhaps days of work by a few people. There is no point in wasting time in expensive detail work before getting approval, support, and budget from upper management.

The goal of the preliminary evaluation is to ask the people who work with information resources what they believe are their most important security needs. Even though they may not be conscious of security as a distinct need, in practice employees and managers do have valuable insights that transcend theory and generalizations. Data entry clerks may tell the security staff about security violations that no one else has observed or even thought about; for example, they may observe that a bug in a particular program makes the previous operator's data entry screen available for unauthorized entries when the shift changes and a new operator sits at the same terminal.

The policy development group should work closely with the human resources (HR) personnel in developing the research instruments for interviewing staff. The HR staff members are likely to know the key managers to contact in each department. The managers have to be convinced to support the effort so researchers can interview willing staff. Some of the HR people are likely to have the professional skills and experience required to provide accurate and cost-effective evaluations of beliefs, attitudes, and behavior affecting security. They may be able to help construct unbiased questionnaires, organize focus groups, and guide interviews.

However, if the security staff and the HR staff are not confident about being able to handle this preliminary data collection, the policy development group should see if it can obtain authorization to hire a consultant with proven expertise in collecting and analyzing social attitudes. The policy development group might want to discuss such a study with a firm specializing in security audits and organizational analysis. If no one knows where to start looking for such resources, the policy development group can contact information security associations, security magazines, security Web sites, and local universities and colleges to ask for suggestions.

The following key issues should be part of the preliminary study:

- Introduction to the study
- State of current policy
- Data classification
- Sensitive systems
- Critical systems
- Authenticity
- Exposure
- Human resources, management, and employee security awareness
- Physical security
- Software development security
- Computer operations security
- Data access controls
- Network and communications security
- Anti-malware measures
- Backups, archives, and data destruction
- Business resumption planning and disaster recovery

The following sections suggest some typical questions that would be helpful in gathering baseline data about the current state of security. All these questions (and more site-specific topics) should be asked of all the respondents in the preliminary evaluation. Applicable questions are not necessarily repeated in each section; instead, questions in the earlier parts of this list may be adapted for use in later sections. These suggestions are not intended to limit creativity but rather to stimulate development of more questions that would be particularly useful for a specific enterprise.

46.3.1   Introduction to the Study.   Employees may perceive many of the following questions as threatening. The preamble or introduction to the study, whether it is by survey or by interviews, should make it clear that this is not an audit or an attempt to punish people. The information should be anonymized so that no person will be targeted for reprisal if the study discovers problems. Every effort should be made to reassure employees that the study is designed to learn about the facts of security with a view to improvement rather than a search for culprits who will be punished.

46.3.2   State of Current Policy.   The questions that follow not only gather baseline information about security policies but also determine whether employees have any idea about who is responsible for formulation of those policies.

- Does the enterprise have any security policies at all?
- Who developed them? An individual? A group?
- Where and how are the security policies available (paper, electronic)?

- When were the policies last updated? Last disseminated?
- Who, if anyone, has explicit responsibility for maintaining security policies?
- Who implements security policy at the enterprise level?
- To whom does the chief information security officer report within the enterprise?
- Who monitors compliance with security policies, standards, and compliance?

46.3.3 Data Classification. Questions to ask include:

- Are there levels of security classification that apply to your work? If so, what are they called?
- Are there rules for determining whether information you handle should be classified at a particular level of confidentiality?
- Are documents or files labeled to show their security classification?
- What is your opinion about the value of such classification?
- Do people in your group pay attention to security classifications?
- Do you have any suggestions for improvement of how data are classified?

46.3.4   Sensitive Systems.   The questions in this section focus on information that ought to be controlled against unauthorized disclosure and dissemination.

- In your work, are there any kinds of information, documents, or systems that you feel should be protected against unauthorized disclosure? If so, name them.
- How do you personally protect sensitive information that you handle?
- How do others in your department deal with sensitive information? No names, please.
- To your knowledge, have there been any problems with release of sensitive information in your department?
- Do you have any suggestions for improving the handling of sensitive data in your area?

46.3.5   Critical Systems.   The questions in this section focus on information that requires special attention to availability and correctness.

- In your work, are there any kinds of information, documents, or systems that you feel are so critical that they *must* be protected against unauthorized modification or destruction? If so, name them.
- Are there any special precautions you use or know of to safeguard critical data in your area?

46.3.6   Authenticity.   Questions to ask include:

- Do you know of any cases in which anyone has used someone else's identity in sending out messages such as letters, faxes, or e-mail? If so, were there any consequences?
- Does anyone in your group use digital signatures on electronic documents?
- Does anyone in your group make or use unauthorized copies of proprietary software? If so, do you think there is any problem with that?

46.3.7   Exposure.   Questions to ask include:

- What are the worst consequences you can realistically imagine that might result from publication of the most sensitive information you control in the newspapers?
- What might happen, in your opinion, if key competitors obtained specific confidential information that you use or control in your area?
- Can you estimate monetary costs associated with the scenarios you have described above?
- What would be the worst consequences you can foresee if critical information you work with were altered without authorization or through accidental modification?
- What might happen if you could not access critical information quickly enough for your work?
- Can you estimate the costs of such breaches of data integrity and data availability?
- Could there be trouble if someone forged documents in your name or in the enterprise's name? Can you sketch out some scenarios and associated costs resulting from such breaches of authenticity?

46.3.8   Human Resources, Management, and Employee Security Awareness.   For additional ideas in framing questions about security awareness, see Chapter 29. For ideas on appropriate questions dealing with employment practices and policies, see Chapter 31.

- As far as you know, who is responsible for developing security policies?
- Do you know where to find the security policies that apply to your work?
- When, if ever, did you last sign any documents dealing with your agreement to security policies?
- Who is responsible for monitoring compliance with security policy in your work group? In the enterprise as a whole?
- Have you ever received any training in security policies? If so, when was the last time?
- Have you ever seen any written materials circulating in your work group that discuss information security?
- Do you think of protecting corporate information as one of your official responsibilities?

46.3.9   Physical Security.   For more details about physical security and additional ideas on appropriate questions, see Chapters 14 and 15.

- Does anyone check your identity when you enter the building where you work?
- Are there any electronic access-control systems limiting access to your work area? What are they?
- Do people hold a secured door open to let each other into your work area? Do you let people in after you open a secured door?
- Have you ever seen a secured door into your area that has been blocked open (e.g., for deliveries)?
- Do people leave your work area unlocked when everyone leaves?

- Do staff members wear identity badges at work? Are they supposed to? Do you wear your badge at work?
- Do visitors wear badges?
- Have you ever seen strangers in your area who are not wearing visitor badges?
- What would you do if you saw a stranger in your area who was not wearing a visitor's badge?
- Do you lock any parts of your desk when you leave your workspace?
- What would you do if you heard the fire alarm ring?
- Where is the nearest fire extinguisher?
- Who is the fire marshal for your floor?
- What would you do if someone needed emergency medical attention?
- Is there an emergency medical station in your area or on your floor?
- Do you know who is qualified in cardiopulmonary resuscitation (CPR) in your group or on your floor? Do such people wear identifying pins?
- Have you had recent training in what to do in the event of an emergency? Have you been trained in how to evacuate the building?
- Is there anything that comes to mind that you would like to see to improve physical security and safety in your work area?

46.3.10   Software Development Security.   The following questions would be asked only of the software development team. For much more information suitable for devising questions about development security, see Chapter 25.

- Are there any security policies that apply to your work? What are they?
- Have you ever discussed security policies in your group?
- Is security viewed positively, neutrally, or negatively in your group? And by yourself?
- Do you and your colleagues discuss security during the requirements analysis and specification phases when developing software?
- How do you see quality assurance as part of the development process?
- Do you use automated software testing tools?
- Tell us about version control in your group. Do you use automated version control software?
- How do you document your systems?
- Do you think that your source code is adequately protected against unauthorized disclosure and modification?
- What is your opinion about Easter eggs (unauthorized code for an amusing picture or game)?
- Could anyone plant an Easter egg or a logic bomb (unauthorized, harmful functions) in code being developed in your group?
- Have you ever seen an Easter egg or a logic bomb in code from your group? Did it get through to production?
- Can you think of ways you would like to see better security in your work?

46.3.11   Computer Operations Security.   The following questions would be asked only of the computer operations team. For more information suitable for devising questions about operations security, see Chapter 32.

- How long do you wait after initial release before installing new operating system versions on your production machines?
- How do you put new software into production?
- Can development personnel access production software? Production data?
- How do you handle problem reports? Do you have an automated trouble-ticket system?
- Can people from outside the operations group enter the operations center?
- Are contractors, including repair technicians, allowed to circulate in operations without being accompanied?
- Do cleaning staff ever circulate within the secured areas of operations without operations staff present?
- Are system components labeled?
- Is there an emergency cutoff switch for main power to the entire data center? Does it include air conditioning?
- Are there uninterruptible power supplies for critical components of your systems?
- Do you keep records of system downtime? What is your downtime over the last three months? The last year?
- What accounts for most of the downtime?
- Who monitors system resource utilization? Are there automated reports showing trends in disk space usage? CPU utilization? Network bandwidth usage?
- What improvements in security would you like to see in operations?

46.3.12   Data Access Controls.   For additional ideas on looking at identification and authentication, see Chapter 16.

- Do you have to identify yourself to the computers and networks you work with?
- Do you have a user name (ID) that no one else shares?
- Are you required to use a password, passphrase, or personal identification number (PIN) as part of your routine when starting to use your computer?
- Have you ever shared your unique user ID and password or PIN with someone else? Or have you borrowed someone else's user ID and password to get some work done? If so, how often does this happen?
- Do you use a token, such as a physical key or a smart card, to prove who you are to the computer system? If so, have you ever lent or borrowed such tokens? What for? How often?
- In your work, are there any limitations on the data you are allowed to work with?
- Are there data you can see but not change?
- Do you use encryption on any of the data you work with?
- Do you or members of your group use laptop computers? If so, do you encrypt sensitive data on the disks of those portable systems?

- Do you or anyone in your group take work home? If so, do you put corporate data on your own, personal (noncompany) computers? Does anyone else have access to those computers? Are there any controls on accessing corporate data on the home computers?

46.3.13   Network and Communications Security.   Most of the following questions would be appropriate only for network managers, administrators, and technicians. However, some of the questions are suitable for everyone. For more ideas to help in developing detailed technical questions, see Chapters 8, 17, 18, 19, 20, 21, and 22.

- As a user, do you know what the rules are about using your employer's e-mail system and Internet access?
- Do you know anyone who regularly violates system usage restrictions? No names, please.
- Have you ever seen pornography on corporate systems? Child pornography? Racist and other objectionable materials? If so, did you know what to do? And what did you do?
- Has anyone ever discussed rules for secure e-mail with you? Do you know how to encrypt sensitive messages? Do you ever encrypt messages?
- As a network manager, do you have up-to-date network diagrams, or can you produce them on demand?
- Do you know which services are running on your Internet-connected systems? Are all of the running services needed?
- How do you determine which patches are appropriate for installation on your systems? How often do you check? Who is responsible for managing patches? How long does it take between notification of a vulnerability and installation of an appropriate patch?
- Does your security architecture include firewalls? If so, what determines the security policies you instantiate in the filtering rules?
- Do you have egress filtering enabled on your firewalls?
- Do you have intrusion detection systems? If so, who responds to apprehended intrusions? How are the responsible people notified of an intrusion?
- What are the procedures for responding to an intrusion?
- If your organization uses passwords, how do you handle requests for new passwords?
- Do you have centralized remote-access controls?
- Do remote users use virtual private networks (VPNs) to access corporate systems from outside the firewalls?
- Are your users supposed to use encryption for sensitive e-mail that traverses the Internet? Do they? How do you know?
- Do your users apply digital signatures to all communications?
- Are your Web servers protected against intrusion and vandalism?
- Have you kept sensitive information off your Web servers?
- Do you encrypt all sensitive information stored on your Web servers?

- How long would it take you to recover a valid version of the Web site if it were destroyed or vandalized?

- Do your telephone voice-mail boxes have unique, nonstandard passwords? How do you know?

- How do you find out if an employee is being fired or has resigned? How long does it take between termination of employment of such an employee and deactivation of all system and network access?

46.3.14   Anti-Malware Measures.   See Chapter 24 for more ideas on checking for appropriate levels of anti-malware precautions.

- Do you and all of your users have anti-malware products installed on every workstation?

- How often are anti-malware products updated? How are they updated?

- How long does it take for all vulnerable systems to be brought up-to-date?

- Do you or your users open unexpected, unsolicited e-mail attachments?

46.3.15   Backups, Archives, and Data Destruction.   For additional suggestions to help in framing questions about data backups, see Chapter 41.

- How often do you do backups of your electronic data?

- Where do you store backup media? Are current copies retained off-site as well as on? How do you know which media to use to restore a specific file?

- How long do you keep different types of backups? Why?

- How do you prevent unauthorized access to backup media?

- If you keep data backups for several years, how do you ensure that the old media will be readable and that the data developed for old applications will be usable?

- How do you dispose of magnetic and optical storage media after their useful life is over? Are the discarded media readable?

- Do you make backup copies of paper documents? Where are these copies kept? How would you locate a specific document you needed?

- How long do you keep various types of papers? Why?

- When you dispose of paper documents, does their content influence how they are destroyed? How do you dispose of sensitive paper documents?

46.3.16   Business Resumption Planning and Disaster Recovery.   For more ideas on questions that are appropriate in quickly evaluating the state of business resumption planning and disaster recovery, see Chapters 42 and 43.

- Do you have business resumption planning (BRP) or disaster recovery plans (DRP)? If so, where are they kept?

- Who is responsible for keeping BRP and DRP up to date?

- Have you ever participated in a BRP or DRP testing? If so, how long ago was the last one? When is the next scheduled test?

- During BRP and DRP tests, does anyone use movie cameras or tape recorders to keep track of critical steps in the recovery?

- After a test, have you participated in analyzing the results of the tests to improve the plans?

46.4   PHASE 2: MANAGEMENT SENSITIZATION.   Support from upper management is essential for further progress. The goal in this phase is to get approval for an organization-wide audit and policy formulation project. In conjunction with the rest of the information security project team, the responsible managers should plan on a meeting that lasts no more than one or two hours. The meeting should start with a short statement from a senior executive about the crucial role of information in the organization's business.

Professional aids such as management-oriented training videos are helpful to sensitize the managers to the consequences of poor information security. For an up-to-date list of such videos, enter the keywords "information security training video" into a search engine such as Google.[2] After the video film, the team can present its findings from the preliminary evaluation. The immediate goal is to constitute an *information protection working group* to set priorities, determine an action plan, define a timetable and milestones, and formulate policies and procedures to protect corporate information resources. The presenters should name the people you want to see on your working group; all of these people should be contacted before the meeting to be sure that they have agreed in advance to participate in the working group.

The presenters should provide estimates of the time involved and the costs of in-house, and consulting, services and software. To end the briefing, it is useful to offer upper managers a range of background reading about security; Appendix 2 on the Internet at *www.wiley.com/go/securityhandbook* has suggestions for such readings. Some managers may be intrigued by this field; the more they learn, the more they will support security efforts.

46.5   PHASE 3: NEEDS ANALYSIS.   The information protection working group should include representatives from every sector of the enterprise. As the group investigates security requirements, the participants' wide experience and perspective will be crucial in deciding which areas to protect most strongly. More important, their involvement is a concrete expression of corporate commitment to a fundamental attitude change in the corporate culture: Security is to be an integral part of the corporate mission.

For example, in a manufacturing firm, the team would include managers and staff from the factory floor, the unions, engineering, equipment maintenance, shipping and receiving, facilities management (including those responsible for physical security), administrative support, sales, marketing, accounting, personnel, the legal department, and information systems. Each of these members of the working group will help improve enterprise security.

If the organization is very large, the group may have to set up subcommittees to deal with specific sectors. Each subcommittee evaluates to what degree the systems and networks are vulnerable to breaches of security. For example, one group could focus on local and campus communications, another on wide area enterprise networks, and a third on electronic data interchange with clients and suppliers.

A typical audit covers the facilities, personnel policies, existing security, application systems, and legal responsibility to stakeholders (owners, shareholders, employees, clients, and the surrounding community). Based on the findings, the subcommittees formulate proposals for improving security. This is where the specialized knowledge obtained from information security specialists and information security courses will prove especially useful.

Chapters 36, 45, and 47 have information that will help the information protection working group develop an evaluation plan. In addition, the National Institute of Standards and Technology has published the *Guide for Selecting Automated Risk Analysis Tools* (*http://csrc.nist.gov/publications/nistpubs/500-174/sp174.txt*); risk analysis tools can help practitioners speed up the evaluation process in this phase of the policy development process.

46.6   PHASE 4: POLICIES AND PROCEDURES.   Once the information protection working group have built a solid floor of understanding of enterprise information security needs, they are ready to construct the policies and procedures that meet those needs. Chapter 28 contains many suggestions and resources for the content and style of security policies. The process should start from existing templates and normally takes weeks to months to complete a workable draft.

Genuine participation by all the representatives from every sector of the enterprise is a critical element of success; without a thoroughgoing sense of ownership of the policies, working group members will fail to internalize the new policies. All the members of the working group must become enthusiasts for their collective efforts; in some sense, these people become missionaries engaged in the long-term conversion efforts of phase 5, the implementation of the policies.

46.7   PHASE 5: IMPLEMENTATION.   Once the working group members have defined the new or improved security policies, they are about halfway to their goal. The hardest part is ahead: explaining the need for security and the value of the new policies to fellow employees and convincing them to change. Even if they agree intellectually, there is a good chance that their ingrained social habits will override the new rules for at least months and possibly years. The challenge is to overcome these habits.

Chapter 35 shows in detail how to use the insights of social psychology to change corporate culture by working on beliefs, attitudes, and behavior. In addition to the suggestions in that chapter, the information protection working group should organize and deliver awareness and training sessions for all levels of the enterprise:

- Upper management
- Technical support
- Lower-level staff
- Other technical staff

The following sections offer some simple agendas for such preliminary sessions.

46.7.1   Upper Management.   Security policies and procedures require management support and sanctions. The transformation of corporate culture should begin at the top. Although it is difficult to coordinate the presence of top executives, the working group should try to organize a half-day executive briefing session on enterprise security. In practice, the group may be able to convince upper management to attend for one or two hours. The focus should be intensely practical and show executives how to protect themselves and the enterprise against common dangers. Suggested topics:

- A review of the business case for improving security: industrial espionage, natural and man-made disasters, vandalism
- Network security: protection against eavesdropping and tampering
- Access controls: tokens, biometrics, passwords

- Encryption: e-mail, laptops, provision for emergency data recovery
- Backup policies for PCs, networks, and mainframes
- Security agreements: summaries of the policies and procedures to be read and signed annually
- Need for total support to convince other staff to comply with security policies

46.7.2   Technical Support.   The next target is the technical support group, the people who help explain security policies to users. In a one-day training session, the presentations can cover

- Everything covered in the executive briefing
- Operating system security provisions
- Security software features
- Changes in operations to comply with new procedures

46.7.3   Lower-Level Staff.   Lower-level staff need a half-day session that answers the following questions in terms that apply directly to their own work:

- Why should I care about information security?
- What are my obligations as an employee?
- How do I protect the PC I am responsible for against viruses?
- How do I back up my data?
- How do I manage my passwords?
- What must I do if I see someone violating our security policies?

The class ends with participants signing the security agreement.

46.7.4   Other Technical Staff.   More intensive training and education are needed for technical staff, such as members of the software development, operations, and network administration groups. More in-depth, specific material will have to be incorporated into their training; however, such training can be spread over a longer time than that for the groups already discussed because of the rhythm of work and the crucial importance of technical competence for implementation of the policies. Most enterprises rely on outside trainers, specialized off-site or online courses, and certification programs to raise their staff to the appropriate levels of competence. Appendixces A1 (Professional and Trade Associations) and A3 (Online Sources of Security Information) on the Internet at *www.wiley.com/go/securityhandbook* provide leads to such sources of knowledge.

46.8   PHASE 6: MAINTENANCE.   Once the enterprise has begun to integrate a concern for security into every aspect of its work, the issue must be kept fresh and interesting. As described in Chapter 29, successful security awareness programs include amusing posters, interesting videos, occasional seminars on stimulating security topics such as recent frauds or computer crimes, and regular newsletters with up-to-date information. Finally, every employee should regularly reread and sign the annual security agreement. This practice ensures that no one can argue that the organization's commitment to security is a superficial charade.

46.9 CONCLUSION. For a secure installation, three things are essential:

1. Sound policies that have been developed with the cooperation of everyone concerned and that are updated periodically
2. Widespread dissemination of those policies, with ongoing observation of their implementation, and with frequent training and continual reinforcement
3. Commitment to security on the part of everyone, from top management on down

When these essential elements are in place, the entire organization will function at a more productive level, one at which the possibilities of disruption and damage will have been reduced to a minimum. Nothing less is acceptable.

46.3 NOTES

1. *See www.informationweek.com/794/security.htm.*
2. *www.google.com.*

CHAPTER 47

RISK ASSESSMENT AND RISK MANAGEMENT

Robert V. Jacobson

CONTENTS

47.1 AN INTRODUCTION TO RISK MANAGEMENT

47.1.1 What Is Risk? *Webster's New College Dictionary,* 1995, defines risk as the possibility of suffering harm or loss. The definition shows that there are two parts to risk: the possibility that a risk event will occur, and the harm or loss that results from occurrences of risk events.

Exhibit 47.1 Four Risk Management Activities

Risk is important to the design and management of information technology (IT) systems because IT systems are increasingly an essential part of the operation of organizations. As a result, both the size of the potential harm or loss, and the possibility of a risk event keep increasing. If an organization's risk management program is deficient, the organization may suffer excessive harm or loss, and at the same time may be wasting resources on ineffective or misdirected mitigation measures. In extreme cases, a risk loss may be large enough to destroy an organization.

47.1.2 What Is Risk Management? This chapter discusses risk management with special emphasis on two aspects of risk management: risk assessment and risk mitigation. Exhibit 47.1 shows how risk assessment relates to risk management. As this exhibit suggests, risk management can be thought of as a four-step process. The first step in managing the risks to an IT system is to assess them. The second step is to use the product of the risk assessment to identify the optimum set of mitigation measures.[1] The third step, security management, is to provide the ongoing actions necessary for the effective functioning of the mitigation measures. Finally, security auditing is used to detect conditions that require a reassessment of risks, the implementation of new mitigation measures, or modifications to the security management program. Security management and security auditing are discussed elsewhere in this *Handbook,* and so this chapter will confine itself to risk assessment and risk mitigation.

47.2 OBJECTIVE OF A RISK ASSESSMENT. This *Handbook* describes the pros and cons of a wide range of security measures that can be applied to an IT system. Because no organization has unlimited resources, it is necessary to decide which measures should be implemented.[2] It would be convenient if there were a set of security standards that applied equally to all IT systems, but this is not the case for two basic reasons:

1. Each IT system has its own particular risk environment.
2. Each IT system has a unique workload. Although two or more IT systems may perform the same list of functions, it is highly unlikely that the systems will have exactly the same level of activity for each of the functions, and so the cost of lost data and service interruptions will not be the same.

Because of these differences, each IT system will have a unique security requirement.[3] These two factors correspond to the two elements in the definition of risk: the risk environment determines the possibility of experiencing harm or loss, whereas the system workload and the associated IT system assets determine the magnitude of the harm or loss.

The objective of a risk assessment is to generate the information about risk exposures needed to optimize risk mitigation decisions. In this context, *optimize* means to allocate the organization's resources to those actions that will yield the best overall performance. It would be suboptimum to spend $10,000 to avert $1,000 in expected losses, but to avoid such wasteful expenditures, one must be able to estimate expected losses and the effect of proposed mitigation measures quantitatively. For this reason, in all but the simplest situations a risk assessment must produce a quantitative, monetary measure of risk so that:

1. Risks can be compared with one another on a common basis, and

2. The cost of risk mitigation measures can be related to the risks they are meant to address.

Assessing a risk as "high," "unacceptable," or in other qualitative terms does not provide the information needed to support the decision to implement risk mitigation measures, which will always have quantitative implementation costs.

47.3   LIMITS OF QUESTIONNAIRES IN ASSESSING RISKS.   One may be tempted to think of a security questionnaire as a risk assessment, but this is not the case. At best, a questionnaire can only compare the target of the questionnaire with a security standard implicit in the individual questions. Questionnaires do not meet the objective of a risk assessment, because the answers to a questionnaire will not support optimized selection of risk mitigation measures. A well-designed questionnaire will identify potential risk areas, and so can be of help in scoping and focusing a quantitative risk assessment.

Questionnaires suffer from several other shortcomings:

- The author of the questionnaire, and the person who is answering the questions may have different understandings of the meanings of key words. As a result, an answer may not apply to the intended question.

- Questionnaires are inherently binary, but some answers are inherently quantitative. For example, consider the question "Do users comply with password construction policy?" Although the anticipated answer is yes or no, the correct answer is much more complicated because each user will have a unique pattern of compliance. Some users will make every effort to be 100% compliant, some will make every effort to circumvent the policy, and the remaining users will comply to a greater or lesser extent.

- Because questionnaires are inherently "open loop," and because of the binary answer issue discussed above, questionnaires tend to miss important information that would be elicited by a person who interacts directly with the sources.

Questionnaires are appealing because they relieve the risk assessor of the need to probe into the IT system being assessed, but something better is needed. The following sections of this chapter build a model of risk and then show how to apply quantitative parameters to the model. Although greater effort is required, far superior results are achieved. Exhibit 47.2 illustrates a highly simplified model, which helps to show the "business case" for the proposed risk mitigation strategy.

Exhibit 47.2   "Jacobson's Window," a Simple
Risk Model

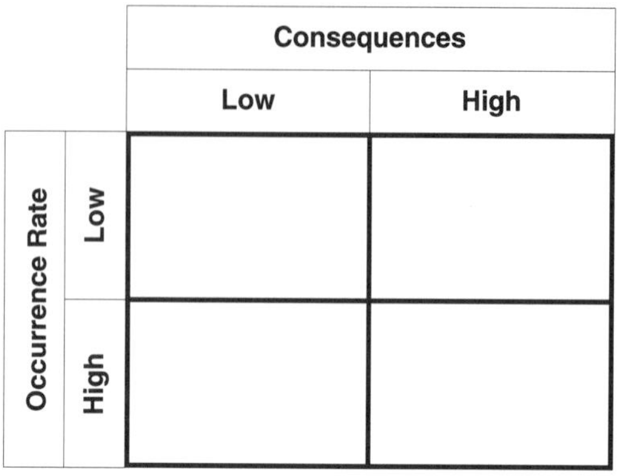

47.4   A MODEL OF RISK.   Exhibit 47.2, a simplified model of threats and consequences devised by the author of this chapter, takes the first steps toward quantification of risks. In this simple model, all risk events are assumed to have either a low or high rate of occurrence, and all consequences of risk event impacts are assumed to be either low or high. William H. Murray, an Executive Consultant at Deloitte and Touche, has referred to this risk model as "Jacobson's Window." Let us now consider the implications of the model.

47.4.1   The Two Inconsequential Risk Classes.   The two-by-two matrix model implies that there are four classes of risk: low-low, high-low, low-high, and high-high. Exhibit 47.3 suggests that two of the classes can be ignored. The low-low class can be ignored because it does not matter. It is obvious that a risk event that occurs at about 10,000 year intervals and that causes a $1 loss can safely be ignored. Experience suggests that the high-high class can be assumed not to exist in the real world. If 50-ton meteorites crashed through the roofs of computer rooms every day, there would be no attempt to use computers. In practice, high-probability, high-loss risks just do not exist.

47.4.2   The Two Significant Risk Classes.   This analysis suggests that there are only two significant risk classes: high-low and low-high. Keystroke errors are an example

Exhibit 47.3   The Two Inconsequential
Risk Classes

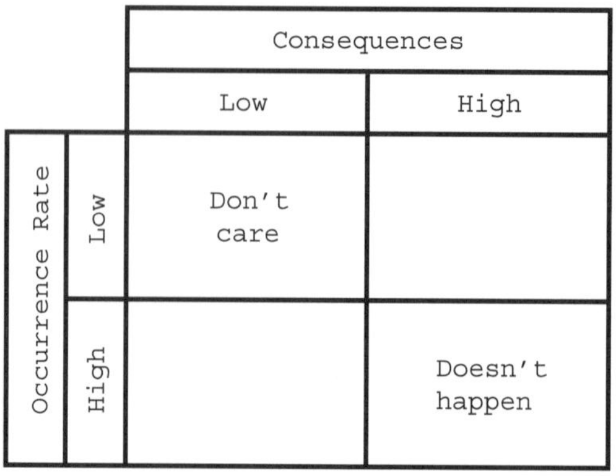

Exhibit 47.4   The Spectrum of Real-World Risks

		Consequences	
		Low	**High**
Occurrence Rate	**Low**		"low-high" major fire flooding cash fraud
	High	power failure software bug key error "high-low"	

of a high-low risk: a high probability of occurring, and usually a low resulting loss. A major fire that destroys the building housing an IT system is an example of a low-high risk: a low probability of occurrence, and a high consequential loss. However, we know that real world risks do not fall into these two classes, but that instead there is a spectrum of risks from high-low to low-high.

47.4.3   Spectrum of Real-World Risks.   Exhibit 47.4 illustrates their distribution from high-low (key stroke errors) to low-high (major fires). Conceptually, there is no difference between the high-low, and low-high threats: both cause losses. Experience suggests that averaged over the long term the high-low and low-high threats will cause losses of similar magnitude to an organization. This concept is quantified by the notion of annualized loss expectancy (ALE). The ALE of a risk is simply the product of its rate of occurrence, expressed as occurrences per year, and the loss resulting from a single occurrence expressed in monetary terms, for example, dollars.

Here is a simple example of ALE. If 100 terminal operators each worked 2,000 hours per year, the occurrence rate of keystroke errors might be 20,000,000 per year (100/hour/operator), a high occurrence rate risk. If 99.9% are immediately detected and corrected at no cost, then 20,000 errors slip by and must be corrected later at a cost of $1 each, a low consequence for each occurrence. Thus, the ALE of the high-low risk: keystroke error is estimated to be 20,000 occurrences per year X $1 per occurrence, or $20,000/year.

If the probability of a major fire in any one year is 1/10,000 (the probability of occurrence of a major fire is estimated to be 0.0001), and if the loss resulting from a major fire would be $100 million, then major fire is a low-high risk. These assumptions lead to an estimate of $10,000 for the ALE of major fires.

Thus, the two risks from opposite ends of the risk spectrum are seen to have ALEs of about the same magnitude. Of course, we have manipulated the two sets of assumptions to yield similar ALEs, but the results are typical of the real world.

47.5   RISK MITIGATION.   The preceding discussion shows that the effect of risk exposures on IT systems can range from trivial to catastrophic, and it is not always immediately obvious which risk exposures are the most dangerous. For this reason, it is essential to base the selection of risk mitigation measures on a quantitative assessment of risks. In this section we consider the practical considerations in generating quantitative assessments, and applying them to risk mitigation decisions.

47.5.1   Difficulties Applying ALE Estimates.   The discussion above shows that ALE is a useful concept for comparing risks, but we recognize intuitively that ALE is not an entirely satisfactory basis for making risk mitigation decisions about the low-probability high-consequence risks. There are two reasons for this.

The first reason is the difficulty of generating a credible estimate of rate of occurrence for low-probability risks. As a rule, one can generate credible estimates of the consequences of even a low-probability risk, but the same is not true of its occurrence rate. Risks that flow from human actions such as fraud, theft, and sabotage are particularly difficult to quantify. See Chapter 4 for further discussion of such problems.

The second reason stems from what appears to be a common human trait that this writer has postulated as Jacobson's 30 Year Law:

People (including risk managers) tend to dismiss risks that they have not experienced themselves within the last 30 years.

Why 30 years? It is not clear, but it may be related genetically to human life expectancy, which until just a few generations ago was about 30 years. Possibly, people who were able to suppress anxiety about rare events were more successful than those who worried too much. Numerous instances of Jacobson's 30 Year Law can be found. For example, the United States government has had a major fire at about 28-year intervals beginning in 1790, most recently at the Military Records Center. Presumably, each new generation of federal property managers must relearn the lessons of fire safety by direct experience. Similarly, it is common for senior managers, particularly public officials, in responding to a calamity, to say, "Who could have imagined that such a thing would happen? However, we have taken steps to see that it never happens again."

47.5.2   What a Risk Manager Tries to Do.   On the other hand, this is exactly what an organization's risk manager should be trying to do: to imagine every possible risk the organization faces, even those not personally experienced, and to develop estimates of the impact of the risks. Next, the risk manager should strive to identify the optimum response to each risk by identifying security measures that have a positive return on investment (ROI).

For example, the ALE for keystroke errors has been estimated as $20,000 per year, or $200 per operator. This is credible because there is ample past experience with both the occurrence rate and impact cost of the risk.

The risk manager considers how to treat this risk. Evidence might suggest that spending $100 each year on keyboard skills training for each operator would reduce the undetected error rate by 30%. Because the $100 per operator expense would yield a benefit of $60 in reduced ALE (30% of $200, the per-operator ALE), the training would not be worthwhile. However, if the error rate could be reduced by 90% instead of 30%, the training would appear to be a good investment; spending $100 each to train operators, would produce a return of $180 each. The goal of the risk manager is to find the package of mitigation measures, which yields the greatest overall ROI.[4]

47.5.2.1   The Three Risk Management Regions.   It will help Risk Managers to understand that the universe of risk events to which an organization is exposed, can be divided into the three regions, as shown in Exhibit 47.5, that define appropriate risk management actions. The regions are defined by two senior management decisions. The first decision is to define the minimum significant threat event occurrence rate. The concept is that it is reasonable to simply ignore the risk of threat events for which we

Exhibit 47.5   Three Risk Management Regions

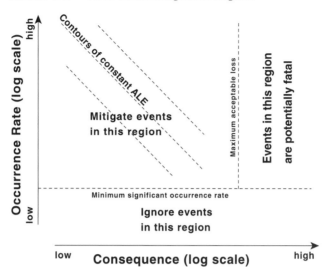

© Copyright 2001 International Security Technology, Inc.

have estimated occurrence rate less than the minimum rate. For example, senior management may decide to ignore risks with occurrence rates less than once in 100,000 years.

Senior management may also identify a loss level (consequence) that is intolerably high. Risk events of this type will appear in the upper right-hand corner of Exhibit 47.5. The occurrence rate of these events is immaterial. If we estimate that the loss caused by an occurrence of a threat event (commonly referred to as the Single Occurrence Loss) exceeds the loss threshold *and* the occurrence rate exceeds the minimum material occurrence rate, then we *must* take steps to reduce the loss, perhaps by transferring the risk with an insurance policy, or by reducing the estimated occurrence rate to a value below the minimum material occurrence rate. The remaining portion of the Exhibit 47.5 graph, the upper left-hand side, is where we can attempt to find cost/beneficial mitigation measures. It is instructive to consider where to plot a risk event like the attack on the World Trade Center on September 11, 2001. It is likely that many organizations have facilities that would generate losses in excess of their maximum tolerable loss if totally destroyed by a similar terrorist attack. This implies that such organizations should take steps to protect these facilities against terrorist attacks. Note, however, that we must also take the estimated rate of occurrence into account before making a decision. How can we make a credible estimate? We can begin by estimating how many such events will occur next year in the United States. For example, we might assume that there will be two such attacks. Second, we must estimate the likelihood that, of all the facilities in the United States, our facility would be selected for attack. This will depend on the "attractiveness" of our facility to a terrorist group compared with all other potential targets in the United States. For example, assume that there are one hundred buildings that are as widely recognized and as vulnerable as the WTC. If our facility is one of the hundred, then we might estimate the occurrence rate as $1/100 \times 2$, or a probable occurrence rate of 0.02/year. If our building is *not* one of the one hundred high-profile buildings, then we might estimate that if there are 200,000 similar buildings in the United States, our occurrence rate is $1/200,000 \times 2$ or an occurrence rate of 1/100,000. In this case, our senior management might choose to ignore the risk.

This brief discussion is intended to show that risk managers can address risks as nebulous as the WTC attack quantitatively, and provide useful guidance to senior management for risk exposures to the right of the intolerable loss threshold.

47.5.2.2   *Where ROI-Based Risk Mitigation Is Effective.* ROI-based mitigation works well for high-probability, low-consequence risk exposures for two reasons: the manager who approves the expenditure believes that the risk exists and should be addressed, and believes further that the parameters used to generate estimates of ALE and the reduction in ALE are reasonable and credible.

The technique does not work for the low-probability, high-consequence risks because both factors—the credibility of risk estimates and management's concern about the risk—are negative. End-users commonly have a higher level of concern about risks than IT system managers, but it is the IT system managers who make the decisions about security measures. An IT system manager generally has no difficulty choosing between buying a faster computer, and a safer computer. Thus, although a risk manager may identify a significant low-occurrence, high-cost risk before it occurred, an organization's senior managers probably would be unaware of these low-high risks, and would be genuinely surprised were a major loss to occur. Hence the "Who could have imagined" press releases. In other words, simply identifying an exposure is enough to justify adoption of a mitigation measure to address the exposure. This line of reasoning suggests that the risk manager needs additional criteria for selecting risk mitigation measures. The next section presents an overview of mitigation measures, which clarifies the selection criteria.

47.5.2.3   *Four Reasons for Adopting a Mitigation Measure.* It appears that ROI-based mitigation measures can be identified and implemented for the high-low risks, but not for the low-high risks. This suggests the use of using a spectrum of risk mitigation techniques to manage the spectrum of risks. There are four tests of the utility of a mitigation measure:

1. The mitigation measure is required by law or regulation. In effect, a governing body has determined (one hopes) that the mitigation measure makes good public policy because it will always meet one of the remaining three tests.

2. The cost of the mitigation measure is trivial, but its benefit is material. For example, the lock on a little-used door, which compromises physical access controls, is not being used. One can institute a procedure to keep the door locked at very low cost.

3. The mitigation measure addresses a low-high risk that has an intolerable single occurrence loss (SOL). For example, it would be intolerable for a corporation to experience an SOL that exceeded owner equity or net worth. The failure several years ago of a prominent British merchant bank following unwise speculation by a staff member is a tragic example of an organization that failed to address an intolerable SOL exposure.

4. The cost of the mitigation measure will be more than offset by the reduction in future losses (ALE) that it will yield. In other words, the mitigation measure has a positive ROI. This reason is commonly used to justify protection against the high-low risks. Operator keyboard training is an example.

Treatment of low-high risks requires the participation of senior management, because judgment rather than an ROI analysis is required to decide how safe is safe enough. A brief outline of a procedure for managing low-high risks follows.

47.5.3 How to Mitigate Infrequent Risks. After the high-low threats have been addressed using an ROI analysis, the risk manager considers all imaginable low-high risks, one by one, and makes an estimate of the SOL, and the rate of occurrence for each. The report of this analysis should describe the confidence level of each estimate of SOL, and of its occurrence rate. These are arranged in descending order of SOL, and the list is presented to senior management, who draws a line somewhere on the list and says, "The risks above the line are intolerably high. Do something about them." The risk manager then considers each of the unacceptable risks in two ways.

47.5.3.1 Reduce the Magnitude of High Single-Occurrence Losses. Sometimes the magnitude of an SOL can be reduced. There are several possibilities:

- *Transfer the risk by obtaining insurance against it.* The premium will depend in part on the amount of the loss that is deductible. For example, one might obtain insurance against a $100 million SOL with a $10 million deductibility. The intolerable $100 million SOL has been reduced to a tolerable $10 million SOL at the cost of the insurance policy premium.
- *Disburse the risk exposure.* For example, replace a single IT center with an intolerable SOL of $500 million of catastrophic physical damage, and service interruption losses, with three centers having SOLs of $167 million each. The centers should be sufficiently isolated from one another to rule out shared disasters. The cost will be the incremental cost of the less efficient operation of three facilities.
- *Reduce the vulnerability of the IT system to the risk.* For example, implementing an enhanced business resumption plan, at some additional cost, can speed up recovery offsite. This will reduce the SOL associated with catastrophic service interruption losses.

The risk manager also may strive to reduce the occurrence rate of a high SOL. Because of the uncertainty of the estimates of low occurrence rates, this is less satisfactory. Nonetheless, even the uncertain occurrence rate estimates can be useful. If two risk exposures have the same SOL, but differ by a factor of two in estimated occurrence rate, it is reasonable to assume that the risk with the lower occurrence rate represents a lesser danger to the organization.

47.5.3.2 Mitigation Selection Process. Assume that the risk manager has presented a risk assessment/risk mitigation report to senior management as described above. The report lists the low-high risks with one or more strategies for treating each risk. The senior manager is responsible for selecting the mitigation measures for implementation.

1. If the risk manager is able to identify a relatively low-cost mitigation measure that reduces the rate of occurrence of a risk to a low enough value, senior management may elect to adopt the mitigation measure.
2. There is some rate of occurrence below which the senior manager is willing to ignore a risk, even if the estimate is low confidence. Typically this applies to very low occurrence rate events, for example a nuclear detonation or a crashing meteorite.
3. Risk transfer by insurance, or one of the other techniques listed above, reduces the SOL to a tolerable level, and the senior manager is willing to accept the cost.

Exhibit 47.6   A Quantitative Risk Mitigation Model

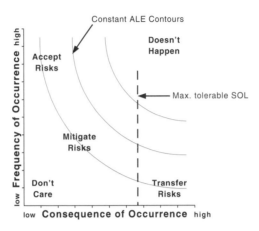

A complete tabulation of occurrence rates, and the costs of mitigating actions for all the high-SOL risk exposures, will help senior management to prioritize the implementation of the mitigation measures.

47.5.4   Summary of Risk Mitigation Strategies.   Exhibit 47.6 superimposes these risk mitigation concepts on the model of risk shown in Exhibit 47.4. (The Frequency and Consequence scales have been flipped to conform to conventional graphing practice.)

The upper-left or high-low region is labeled "Accept Risks." This is because experience shows that in most cases of high-low risk exposures, there is no mitigation measure available that has a positive ROI. The reason is simply that because the risk event is very common, the IT operating staff is familiar with the risk and has already taken all cost-effective steps to mitigate it. The point along the Consequence scale labeled "Max. tolerable SOL" is the point at which the SOL value exceeds the capacity of the organization to accept the loss, however infrequent a risk event might be. The determination of this value is a senior management policy question. The implication is that some risk mitigation action must be taken with respect to all events that lie to the right of the maximum tolerable SOL, in order to preserve the organization against potentially fatal events. The low-high region in the lower-right is labeled "Transfer Risks" because this is the most common risk mitigation strategy for low-high risk events.

The central region is labeled "Mitigate Risks" because in general one can develop credible ALE estimates, and so can select risk mitigation measures using an ROI evaluation of alternate mitigation strategies.

For the reasons discussed in Section 47.4.1, "The Two Inconsequential Risk Classes," the low-low and high-high regions are labeled "Don't Care" and "Doesn't Happen," respectively.

47.5.4.1   Risk Assessment/Risk Mitigation Summary.   The risk model illustrated by "Jacobson's Window" leads to the following conclusions:

1. Risks can be broadly classified as ranging from high-probability, low-consequence to low-probability, high-consequence. In general, risk events in this range cause losses of the same order of magnitude when expressed at an annual rate or ALE.

2. Because of IT operating staff familiarity with the high-low risks, there may not be any cost-beneficial way to reduce the ALE of the high-low risks.

3. Midrange risks can be addressed by selecting mitigation measures with a positive ROI, based on the relationship between the cost to implement a mitigation measure and the reduction in ALE it is expected to yield.

4. Treatment of low-high risks requires the judgment of senior management, based on estimates of SOL, and, to a lesser extent, estimates of rate of occurrence. Mitigation measures may reduce SOLs to acceptable levels, or decrease occurrence rates to the level at which risks can be ignored.

5. To be effective the risk management function must be:

○ Performed by properly qualified persons,

○ Independent of IT management, and

○ Reporting to senior management to ensure that all risks are recognized and resource allocation is unbiased.

47.6 RISK ASSESSMENT TECHNIQUES.   The first step in performing a risk assessment is to define the scope and focus of the assessment. The scope will define the IT functions, the physical assets, intangible assets, and the liability exposures, which are to be included in the assessment. The focus means the kinds of risk events to be included in the analysis. Risk events may include failures of the IT hardware and software, software logical errors, deliberate destructive acts by both insiders and outsiders, and external events such as earthquakes, hurricanes, river floods, and so forth.

The ROI analysis of a risk mitigation measure will understate its benefit, if the risk assessment does not include all the risk events that the mitigation measure will affect.

47.6.1 Aggregating Threats and Loss Potentials.   Aggregation is a key concept of quantitative modeling, and refers to the practice of combining related items to keep the model at a manageable size. For example, one can define a single risk event ("IT Hardware Failure") or two risk events ("Server01 Failure and "Server02 Failure") and so on in ever-increasing detail. The more risk events defined for a risk assessment, the greater will be the effort required to establish the risk parameters. However, the individual risk events will not all have the same impact on the results of the assessment. Indeed, some risk events will be found to be completely immaterial, so the time expended to estimate the inconsequential parameters will have been wasted.

This suggests that one should begin an assessment using highly aggregated risks and loss potentials, perhaps, no more than 10 to 15 of each in a typical situation. This preliminary analysis will show which elements are important to the results. One can then add details to the important elements to improve the validity of the model, and thus concentrate the effort on the important issues.

47.6.2 Basic Risk Assessment Algorithms.   It is generally accepted that Annualized Loss Expectancy, in dollars per year, is calculated as follows:

Annualized Loss Expectancy = Threat Occurrence Rate (number/year) ¥ Vulnerability Factor (0.0 to 1.0) ¥ Loss Potential (monetary units)

- The term *threat occurrence rate* (TOR) is used to designate the estimate of the probability of occurrence of a threat event during a risk mitigation planning period, typically one year.

- The term *loss potential* is used to designate the worst-case loss of an organizational element.

- The term *vulnerability factor* is used to designate the relationship between a threat event and an organizational element. If the threat event has no impact on the element, the vulnerability factor will be zero. If the threat event triggers the worst-case loss, the vulnerability factor will be 1.0. The vulnerability factor will range between zero and 1.0 for all threats.

The Single Occurrence Loss, in dollars per event with respect to a given threat event, is calculated as follows:

Single Occurrence Loss = Vulnerability Factor (0.0 to 1.0) ¥ Loss Potential (monetary units)

- The terms *loss potential* and *vulnerability factor* are as defined above.

The sections that follow discuss these two equations in more detail and describe techniques for estimating values for TOR, loss potential, and vulnerability factor.

47.6.3   Loss Potential.   There are three basic kinds of IT system losses:

1. *Property damage losses.* Property damage losses occur when a threat event impacts an asset of the organization. The asset may be physical property damaged, for example, by a fire or flood, or the asset may be an intangible asset such as a trade secret or a proprietary database, the improper disclosure, modification, or destruction of which causes a loss to the organization.

2. *Liability losses.* The operation of an IT system may expose the organization to liability for damage or injury. For example, improper operation of an IT-controlled process might release a toxic gas. Improper disclosure of personal information may cause the individual to sue the organization for damages. If third parties place reliance on data generated or maintained by an IT system, there may be an exposure to damage suits if the data are incorrect as a result of flaws in the IT system.

3. *Service interruption losses.* Service interruption losses occur when IT system services are interrupted, or are not initiated in a timely manner. In general, the longer the duration of an interruption, the greater will be the amount of the loss. This means that service interruption losses should be presented in the form of a table of values, appropriate to the expected range of interruption durations.

Loss potentials, as described in the two following subsections, should include estimates of the worst-case losses in the list of risk events.

47.6.3.1   *Property Damage and Liability Losses.*   These losses are treated the same way, so they can be discussed together. It is advisable to begin consideration of property damage losses by making an aggregated list of possible sources. For example, the initial list might consider together all the hardware in an IT facility, and similarly all of the databases needed to operate each of the principal IT applications. For each such asset, an estimate should be made of the worst-case loss that the organization could experience with respect to that asset. For example, the worst-case loss for a set of databases would be the cost to reconstruct the database from back-up resources, and the cost to recover any lost or corrupted data. There will be other losses resulting from interruptions to IT services that require the availability of the database, but these losses are described separately in the next subsection.

Liability loss potentials should be estimated in the same way. The first step is to determine which liabilities should be included in the risk assessment. The organization may already have a mechanism for addressing liability exposure, possibly through a risk transfer mechanism. However, the liability exposures that are unique to the IT operations should be included, and the worst-case loss potential estimated as described above.

47.6.3.2 Service Interruption Losses. Service interruption losses apply to services supplied by IT systems to end users. The first step in estimating service interruption losses is to construct a list of the IT services for which there is a significant loss potential. Examination of a wide range of functions suggests that there are six different causes of service interruption losses. Reviewing the causes with the persons most familiar with each service, typically end users, will determine which ones apply. By tabulating the losses associated with each of the causes, one can generate an overall loss potential for a suitable range of service interruption durations.

- *Reduced productivity.* Would people be idled if there were a service interruption? If yes, how many and how soon? What is their total pay in rough figures, including benefits? (If substantial production facilities would be idled, what is the approximate hourly cost of ownership, computed as the total life-cycle cost of ownership divided by the total remaining operating life in hours.

- *Delayed collection of funds.* Does the application trigger collection of funds for the organization by a billing system, or by a loan-notes-due collection system? If yes, determine the average amount collected each business day, which would be affected by a service interruption. Because in most cases it will be possible to do some manual processing of the high-value items, the affected amount may be less than the full daily processing dollar volume. Determine a suitable cost-of-money percentage for use in present-value calculations by consulting the organization's treasurer or controller. Alternatively, the current commercial bank prime rate plus one or two percentage points can be used.

- *Reduced income.* Will an interruption of the application impact sales revenue or other income receipts? If yes, estimate the amount of income lost both immediately, and over the long term, for a range of service interruption durations appropriate to the risk events included in the risk assessment. It may be difficult for the end-user to make an estimate, unless it is possible to remember the last major service interruption, and to describe what happened. What would the user do if a major competitor had a service outage? How would this fact become known, and how would it be exploited to increase income? These questions may help to determine the amount of reduced income to be expected.

  Along with reduced income, there would probably be a reduction in operating expenses, such as cost of sales, caused by the decreased activity. When the reduction in operating costs is subtracted from the reduced revenues, the result is the net loss. Estimates should be made for the shortest service interruption duration that the user believes would cause significant lost business; in addition, planning should include provisions for one or more service interruptions of greater duration.

- *Extra expense.* How would the user respond to an outage. Would it be necessary to hire temporary help, or to work overtime? Could an outside service be used? Would there be an increased error rate, which would increase error research and correction expenses? Might there be increased fraud loss? The cost to catch up, after the outage ends, is often a major extra expense factor. Beginning with the shortest significant duration, several estimates should be made, including a worst-case scenario.

- *Lateness penalties.* If the user is aware of any lateness penalties, contractual, regulatory, or legal, associated with the application, estimates should be made of the amount of penalties that would be triggered by an outage.

- *Intangible losses.* If there is a significant service interruption, it will most likely have negative effects not listed above. Staff morale and customer attitudes may be affected negatively by the impression that the organization's risks are not being effectively managed. The value of publicly traded stock may be adversely affected, and pending mergers or stock offerings may be derailed.

This procedure does not involve asking end-users to estimate the maximum "tolerable" service interruption duration. This is not meaningful. An attempt by end-users to establish the value of "tolerable" is simply a subjective judgment call. The basic risk assessment will establish the expected annualized loss expectancy. Then an evaluation of alternative risk mitigation measures, to reduce the number and duration of service interruptions, will identify the optimum IT system configuration.

47.6.4   Risk Event Parameters.   As noted in the prior section, during the determination of loss potential, a list of significant risk events can be constructed. The list should be critically examined to determine if additional event types should be added to the list, bearing in mind the aggregation considerations discussed above.

Once the risk events list has been completed, two parameters can be estimated for each event as follows:

1. *Occurrence rate.* There are several ways to estimate occurrence rates. If the event has had a relatively high occurrence rate in the past, typically more than once in 10 years, the organization is likely to have records of those events, from which the occurrence rate can be inferred. However, there are two cautions. First, consideration must be given to any changes in the environment that would affect the occurrence rate. For example, the root cause of some system crashes may have been corrected, so that one would expect the future rate to be lower than in the past. Second, it is important to avoid double counting. For example, a system outage log may lump electric power failures into a catch-all category: hardware failure. If electric power failure is included in the risk assessment as a separate risk event, its occurrences will be counted twice.

   If the risk event is external to the IT facility, for example, river flooding and earthquake, one can usually find external sources of information about past occurrences. For example, one could use the Web page (*www.nhc.noaa.gov/pastint. html*) to determine if a given U.S. location has ever been impacted by a high-intensity hurricane. There are numerous Web sites that can support a risk assessment. One also may find that past copies of local publications can help to determine the past local history.

   In some cases, there will be no meaningful past history for a risk event, particularly if the event is of recent origin, for example, e-business fraud. In these cases, it may be possible to reason by analogy with other similar risk events, to develop a reasonable estimate.

2. *Outage duration.* The average outage duration for each risk event must be estimated in order to be able to forecast service interruption losses. If the outage

duration is not the same for all the IT systems that the risk event impacts, one may either use an average value or define a separate risk event for each of the systems, keeping in mind the aggregation considerations discussed above.

47.6.5   Vulnerability Factors, ALE, and SOL Estimates.   From the basic risk assessment algorithms, it is possible to determine the risk event/loss potential pairs for which the vulnerability factor is greater than zero (see section 47.6.2), and having done so to estimate the value of the factor. It is then possible to use the risk data discussed above, and the algorithms, to calculate an estimate of the ALE and SOL for each of the pairs, and then to tabulate the individual ALE and SOL estimates to obtain a complete risk assessment for the IT organization. This is useful as a baseline because it provides an assessment against which to evaluate potential risk mitigation measures.

In order to validate the assessment, it is necessary to identify the risk event/loss potential pairs that account for the majority of the expected losses, typically 80 percent of the total. Reviewing the details of each input item, these questions should be asked: Were source data transcribed correctly? Are the assumptions made reasonable? Were calculations made correctly? Does any risk event/loss potential account for so much of the expected losses that it should be disaggregated from other data items? Once the validation process is complete, and indicated changes have been made, it is feasible to consider risk mitigation.

47.6.6   Sensitivity Testing.   The preceding discussion implies that a single value is to be estimated for each of the risk parameters included in the risk assessment. However, it may not be desirable for a parameter to be limited to a single value, and a Monte Carlo technique could be used to generate a set of ALE and SOL estimates. There are two obstacles to using this approach. Apart from the big increase in the complexity of the calculations, there is still a requirement to select a single risk mitigation strategy based on the set of ALE and SOL estimates. As described previously, cost-beneficial risk mitigation measures are selected by calculating the baseline ALE, and then recalculating the ALE assuming that the proposed mitigation measure has been installed. The difference between the two ALE estimates is the return in the ROI calculation. Assuming two sets of 1,000 ALE estimates, which were generated by a Monte Carlo simulation, calculating all possible differences produces a set of 1,000,000 returns. Which one should be selected to calculate ROI?

Using the most likely value for each risk parameter, and generating only two ALE estimates, we use the difference between the two to calculate ROI. Because the ROI flows from a relatively large number of parameters, the overall result will average out the individual departures from the average values used, and so will be a fair representation of the actual risk losses that will occur.

However, if confidence in the accuracy of an estimate is extremely low, estimates using low, median, and high values of the parameters should be used to evaluate the effect on the overall results. Whenever a risk assessment includes a material low-confidence parameter, full disclosure should be made to the managers who review and act on the results. Almost all other decisions about resource allocations, which senior managers make, are based on uncertain estimates of future events. There is nothing unique about the uncertainties surrounding risk mitigation decisions.

47.6.7   Selecting Risk Mitigation Measures.   The objective of the risk mitigation process is to identify the optimum set of mitigation measures. The first step is to address the intolerable SOL exposures as discussed in Section 47.5.3.4. The risk assessment and the evaluation of potential risk mitigation measures provide the raw material on which to base an implementation strategy for the risk exposures in the midrange. Considerations include:

1. The mitigation measures with negative ROIs can be discarded.
2. The remaining mitigation measures can be tabulated in three ways:
   - In descending order of net benefit: ALE reduction—implementation cost
   - In descending order of implementation cost
   - In descending order of ROI.
3. Based on other considerations, senior management selects mitigation measures from the three lists. Other considerations include the following:
   - The availability of resources for risk mitigation may be limited, in which case some mitigation actions must be deferred until the next budgeting period; in extreme cases, the lowest cost measures may be selected.
   - Mitigation of risk exposures that have a particularly undesirable effect on marketing considerations.
   - Selecting mitigation measures with the highest net benefit.

47.7   SUMMARY.   This chapter has shown the tremendous advantage of having a detailed, quantitative assessment of the risk exposures, and a quantitative evaluation of prospective mitigation measures. Senior managers will appreciate the advantage of using business judgment in place of seat-of-the-pants guesswork.

47.8   BIBLIOGRAPHY

Berg, Anna, and Sofia Smedshammer. *Cost of Risk: A Performance Vehicle for the Risk Manager.* Linköpings, Sweden: Linköpings University, 1994.

Hamilton, Gustaf. *This Is Risk Management.* Studentlitteratur Chartwell-Bratt, 1988.

Jacobson, Robert V. "What Is a Rational Goal for Security?" *Security Management,* December 2000.

Lalley, Edward P. *Corporate Uncertainty & Risk Management.* Risk Management Society Publishing, 1982.

Murray, William Hugh. "Security Should Pay: It Should Not Cost." In *Proceedings of the IFIP/Sec '95.* Chapman & Hall, 1995.

National Institute of Standards and Technology. *Guideline for the Analysis of Local Area Network Security.* Federal IT Standard Publication 191, November 1994.

47.9   NOTES

1. The term *mitigation measure* is used here broadly to refer to all actions taken to manage risks, and may include logical controls over access to data, physical controls over access to IT hardware, facilities to monitor operations, selection and supervision of IT personnel, policy and procedures to guide operations, and so forth. In short, all of the security techniques described in this *Computer Security Handbook.*

2. Another way of expressing this concept is as follows: Perfect security is infinitely expensive, and so it is not a rational goal of a risk management program.

3. As a practical matter, it may become obvious that in some situations the differences between the members of a group of IT systems are too small to be significant, and that a single set of security measures can be adopted for all of the systems.

4. Return on investment is the ratio of the return received from an investment to the investment itself. If a bank pays back $1.05 one year after $1.00 has been deposited in the bank, the ROI is roughly 5%. To determine ROI precisely, one must take the ratio of the present value of the return to the present value of the investment.

CHAPTER 48

Y2K: LESSONS LEARNED FOR COMPUTER SECURITY

Timothy Braithwaite

CONTENTS

48.1 LOOKING BACK. The most important lesson that architects of successful computer security programs can draw from the year 2000 (Y2K) problem may well be that they find themselves accused of fraudulent misrepresentation.

Put simply, because there was no Y2K disaster, it has been alleged that the possibility of a disaster never really existed.

Readers will recall that the use of two digits to represent dates, originally designed as a memory-saving measure when both live memory and mass storage were relatively expensive, led to a flurry of remediation in the 1990s, with a peak of public alarm in the months before the end of 1999. There were however, few reports of catastrophic failures and certainly no widespread breakdown of infrastructure or of law and order anywhere in the world due to date errors. In the aftermath of this nonevent, voices arose accusing the entire information technology (IT) industry, and Y2K remediation experts in particular, of having whipped up hysteria as a mechanism for tricking management into spending billions of dollars on unnecessary modifications to computer programs.

The fundamental problem underlying this kind of allegation is the difficulty of justifying non–revenue-generating Y2K activities after the fact to observers who never understood the nature and seriousness of a problem that someone else was trying to prevent. The difficulty also stems from the impossibility of proving a negative. For example, one cannot prove to the uninvolved or unimpressed observer that the time, money, and human resources spent on Y2K remediation were well spent simply because a disaster was averted. Such an observer will take the fact that a disaster did not occur as evidence that the possibility of disaster never really existed or that the problem was exaggerated in the media. In the same way, a skeptical observer may take the absence of security breaches as evidence that no such threat existed or that it was never as bad as claimed. The problem is exacerbated after spending time and effort on establishing security policies, security controls, and enforcement mechanisms

In both cases, the money, time, and effort expended to prevent adverse computing consequences from harming an organization are viewed with suspicion. But such suspicions are not new in the world of information processing. Throughout the history of IT, this attitude has existed regarding problem-prevention activities such as quality assurance, quality control testing, documentation, configuration management, and other system-management controls designed to improve quality, reliability, and system maintainability.

48.2   Y2K: THE ACCUSATION AND A DETAILED REBUTTAL.   The following analysis is based in part on material from *Y2K Lessons Learned: A Guide to Better Information Technology Management.*[1]

48.2.1   The Allegation.   First, the accusation has been made that Y2K was a scam foisted on the unsuspecting community of IT users. It has been suggested that unscrupulous IT vendors and consultants created a hypothetical problem and hyped it beyond its true importance in order to create work and wealth for themselves. To give credence to such accusations is to, by inference, accuse sophisticated executive management at such corporations as Citibank and AT&T of incompetence, or worse. No corporation spends $900 million (Citibank) and $500 million (AT&T) on a hyped hypothetical problem. To be sure, some of the monies associated with Y2K were probably misdirected, exaggerated, wasted, or even spent on non-Y2K activities, but not $100 billion.

An early argument advanced to support the accusation of scam centered on the apparent fact that countries and businesses that spent little or nothing on Y2K appear to be doing as well as those that spent heavily and were experiencing no greater number of date-related problems. To aid in making some sense of this seemingly powerful proof, four categories of IT systems and related business settings likely to be operating in any given country or company need to be identified. The following system categories, based on their intrinsic technical vulnerability to the Y2K problem, were cataloged by the Institute of Electrical and Electronics Engineers (IEEE):

1. Physical control systems

2. Primary production systems

3. Support systems

4. Administrative and accounting systems

Physical control systems are those that control physical things and processes, such as power generation and distribution, water treatment and distribution, phones, airplanes, elevators, traffic lights, and the like. These are the systems where the dreaded embedded chip failures were most anticipated. These systems, however, are well engineered and thoroughly understood, well tested under stress, and often designed with redundancy built-in. Such systems always have had a good degree of management attention and investment because in many cases these systems actually constitute the business.

Primary production systems of an Online Transaction Processing (OLTP) System such as banking and e-commerce processing systems were on the vulnerability list because of the highly integrated and frequently customized nature of hardware and software components and their convergence. Also, OLTP systems often are not engineered with sufficient redundancy and are not adequately tested.

Support systems are those that monitor and detect faults, schedule maintenance, automatically order parts, and to some extent manage primary production systems (OLTPs) for efficiency and safety. Such systems are not overly complex and are generally well understood. They are not as well engineered as OLTP systems, are not stress tested, and have limited redundancy. Note that Y2K problems with support systems would not appear immediately but would surface only after a preprogrammed time interval has elapsed. In other words, these categories of systems can be deemed safe only after all time intervals with 1999-initiated start times have been successfully compared to a post-2000 stop time and all computations and resulting programmed actions have been carried out. Also note that a combination of category 1, 2, and 3 systems, operating at different companies, constitutes and supports the just-in-time (JIT) business model on which many corporations depend.

Administrative and accounting (A&A) systems are heavily date dependent and support the general economic activities of organizations, such as purchasing, order processing, invoicing, accounting, human resources, payroll, benefit calculations, and tax reporting. These systems are virtually all software, and after years of modifications and extensions they are extremely complex. A&A systems run on daily, weekly, monthly, quarterly, semiannual, and annual cycles, meaning that an entire software portfolio did not execute under actual year 2000 conditions until after year end processing in January 2001. These systems typically provide the data against which "what-if" queries are run and are also used for "data warehousing" activities. A&A systems are often very large and highly interconnected with many shared data sources, and often are composed of heterogeneous technologies of diverse vendors, models, and age. As a whole, such systems are not generally well understood due to a lack of documentation. These systems present virtually the worst-case scenario for all Y2K-related risk factors. Because they have historically been reviewed as a cost center, they have received relatively little management attention and investment.

But A&A problems due to Y2K may have caused unexpected internal problems as systems progressed through their calendar year 2000 processing cycles. Although failures with A&A systems may be difficult to link to Y2K date-processing problems, this does not lessen the impact. An increase in unexplained processing problems during year 2000 would have been a telltale sign.

The existence of these four categories of systems, with their intrinsic Y2K vulnerabilities, provides a partial answer to the accusation that nonspenders are faring as well as heavy spenders. It seems likely that there are two possibilities with regard to physical control systems, primary production systems, and their support systems. First, since these are highly visible and liability-prone systems providing the basic infrastructures of a nation and corporations, they were in fact rigorously remediated and tested. Due diligence would have demanded nothing less. Second, such systems in developing nations and less IT-intensive businesses do not even exist, at least to the degree of sophistication that they do in developed nations and large corporations. Thus, there were no reported problems simply because there was nothing to fail that could not be handled manually. Only in more advanced and sophisticated systems has the progressive elimination of the human override element become a desired cost-cutting design goal. Such systems had to be fixed, whereas less sophisticated systems in developing nations or less IT-intensive businesses retained the luxury of the human override and workaround.

Those addressing perceived system vulnerabilities have been accused of spending too much money on Y2K. In response, it can only be pointed out that reasonable men and women, upon analysis, practiced responsible risk management and perhaps erred on the side of caution. Again, it is a fact that developed nations and highly IT-intensive businesses had more at risk because of their great dependence on systems built to reduce the labor-intensive nature of the work processes.

48.2.2   The Allegation and the Human Element.   In an editorial, Tim Wilson of *Internet Week* wrote the following: "Sometimes I wonder why anybody works in the IT Department. If computers fail, you get yelled at. If Internet or dial-up connections fail, you get yelled at. And now, if everything works well, you really get yelled at." [2]

It is clear, looking at this not uncommon reaction to Y2K, that dealing successfully with future IT problems—perhaps an Internet security crisis—will become a complex social as well as technical undertaking. The apparent fact that many users perceive the IT industry and IT workers with such suspicion and antipathy means that much work lies ahead to develop mutual respect.

This essential work can begin by identifying and exploring the IT management lessons to be learned from the Y2K experience. This is so because Y2K, as a discrete event in the history of IT, presents a unique opportunity to examine past practices and then use what can be observed to positively influence the future evolutionary path of IT. At the same time, if poor IT management practices of the past, which contributed to the Y2K problem and the extreme expense of its resolution, are allowed to continue, Y2K can be viewed as just a minor harbinger of things to come.

Such self-examination is absolutely essential for those striving to improve the state of computer security. Now is the time to challenge and change those systems development and IT management practices that led to Y2K. If the same inadequate practices are left unchanged in the face of increasing cyberthreats, they will only continue contributing to the insecure systems of tomorrow just as they have contributed to the insecure systems of today. Chapter 25 provides details of software development security; Chapter 32 examines operations security.

48.3   LOOKING AHEAD.   Stated differently, the major problem associated with Y2K was not that a six-digit date field needed to be changed to somehow accommodate an eight-digit date, or even that the issue had been ignored until it became a crisis. The real problem was that most organizations had such a difficult time managing and executing what was essentially a simple "code" change. Because of a general lack of basic IT organizational discipline and adherence to fundamental software and systems development and maintenance principles, most code remediation efforts were excessively expensive, with a collective price tag of over $100 billion in the United States alone.

Thus the primary concern of the computer security practitioner must be the correction of these same basic and fundamental IT management defects; otherwise effective security can never be attained or maintained. Why? Because you can't secure what you aren't managing!

48.3.1 Y2K Was Really a Computer Security Issue. At its core, the threat posed by Y2K made it a computer and communications security issue. It was primarily a threat to systems availability and data integrity. It had the potential to be the greatest of all denial-of-service (DOS) events and to put at extreme risk the continuity of business and government services.

For many in the security community, Y2K was seen as a dress rehearsal that would, hopefully, prepare an IT-dependent society to address the technology and business management practices that had contributed to the crises.

Y2K, as a business threat, was seen to be serious enough to force worldwide continuity of operations (COOP) planning. It was also seen as serious enough, along with the increasing threat of cyber-terrorism, to prompt the creation of the President's Commission on Critical Infrastructure Protection (CIP) to examine the growing issue of national infrastructure interdependencies and especially the growing dependencies of business and government on information and communications technology.

Y2K, seen as a security threat to the global information infrastructure, created high awareness, in all industrialized nations, to their great dependency on information and communications technology. In fact, the Y2K experience and the events of 11 September 2001 are now causing many leaders to inquire about other ways in which business and governments are threatened by their growing dependence on IT and other forms of technology.

This increased awareness has created for the computer security practitioner an opportunity that never before existed, to take computer security out of the merely technical realm and establish it as a business issue. Doing this will elevate computer security to the level of top management, even to oversight by the board of directors.

48.3.2 Critical Infrastructure Protection. As previously mentioned, the Clinton administration, in 1998, convened a Presidential Commission on Critical Infrastructure Protection. As a result of the commission's findings, the administration issued a Presidential Decision Directive (PDD-63), which created the Critical Infrastructure Assurance Office (CIAO) within the Department of Commerce. The CIAO, and lead federal agencies, were tasked to work with the private sector to implement the directive which named certain industry sectors as critical to the national infrastructure. The critical sectors were: National Defense, Energy, Financial Services, Transportation, Communications and Information Services, Health Care, and Vital Government and Human Services. Many member companies from these industry sectors joined together as the Partnership for Critical Infrastructure Security (PCIS), which is jointly sponsored by the U.S. Chamber of Commerce and the CIAO for the purpose of implementing the directive.

Following the events of September 11, 2001, the Bush administration issued an Executive Order, "Critical Infrastructure Protection in the Information Age," which created the President's Critical Infrastructure Protection Board. Twenty-seven federal agencies and organizations are represented on the board. In addition to being advised by the board, the president will be consulting panels of senior experts from outside government on the best way to protect the nation's critical infrastructure.

The IT industry's principle venue for addressing the critical information infrastructure issue is the Information Technology Association of America (ITAA). ITAA is functioning as the IT industry sector focal point for coordination, cooperation, and information sharing between and across government- and private-sector cyberprotection activities.

Any IT company would be well advised to participate in the ITAA's effort to represent the information technology industry to each of the other industry sectors that have been identified as "critical." This is especially true if an IT organization supports any of the critical sectors either in-house or through outsource agreements. Beyond demonstrating a sense of responsibility, a reason for this involvement would likely be self-defense, since all critical industry sectors now appreciate that their major, non-natural and nonterrorist vulnerabilities come from their dependence on information and communications technology. It will not be long before failures in one or another critical sector industry will be laid at the doorstep of the IT industry.

It is imperative, therefore, that IT companies and in-house IT support organizations become active in the CIP search for solutions. Soon it will become essential to be perceived as part of the security solution, not part of the security problem.

At a personal level, each computer security professional must be well versed in the activities of the PCIS and other CIP organizations and should lobby for his or her corporation's participation in these programs. Being able to report on CIP issues and activities will open executive doors for the security professional and provide opportunities to seek high-level support for internal security program initiatives. Chapters 14 and 15 examine many aspects of CIP.

48.3.3   Y2K Lessons Learned.   The overarching lesson learned from the recent Y2K experience is that no organization is an island. Computers and communications have linked organizations together at a technological level, and globalization has linked them at a business and economic level. Those who feared a downside to such linkage were vindicated when the potential impacts of an uncorrected Y2K problem were uncovered. It is now clear that the same linkages and interdependencies are at risk from cyberattacks against the computer and communications infrastructure of any nation or business.

What lessons from Y2K can the computer security practitioner, and managers of other departments, use in improving the security of their corporate computing infrastructure?

48.3.3.1   Lesson 1: Information and Process Integrity Are Now Believed by Management to be Important to the Business.   Before Y2K, executive management of most organizations gave little thought to the importance of the integrity of their corporate information assets and their computer processing capabilities. These were issues for the chief information officer and the technical people who ran the computers and networks.

A vague awareness of the vulnerability surrounding increased computer dependencies has grown gradually until Y2K brought it to full maturity. In earlier days, the information from computerized operations generally was seen as byproducts of a manual, paper-driven business process and was historic in nature. Such computerized information, it was felt, could always be replaced, in the event of problems, by going back to the original manual transaction processing, and business would go on as usual. People conducted business, and computers were used merely as calculating, recording, storage, and reporting tools.

All this changed during the last decade with the advent of the Internet and the revolutionary impact of data communications on the way business is conducted. Today, in many cases, there is no predecessor "manual" paper-based process for the Web-based business, and so dependence on the reliability and security of the automated system is nearly total. For an increasing number of organizations, distributed information processes, implemented via the World Wide Web and other networked environments, have become the critical operating element of their business. In some cases, the information processing system is the business. Not only must the processing system work when needed, but the information processed must retain its integrity so that it can be "trusted" in use. If trust is lost, the system won't be used.

Because of the impact assessments that were done for Y2K, it is now fully understood that when a networked environment fails because of a software defect, electrical failure, DOS attack instigated by a hacker, or any other interruptive activity, the business suffers.

And, because Y2K threatened to destroy the integrity of date-related processing and many databases, it is now better appreciated that breaches of security controls resulting in unauthorized or accidental modification or compromise of corporate or private information can lead to a public relations and legal nightmare.

48.3.3.2   Lesson 2: "Supply Chain" Collaboration for Achieving Mutually Assured Information and Process Integrity Is Now Better Appreciated.
Y2K demonstrated to industry sector companies how interdependent they had become, on information and communications technology. This new awareness is focusing attention on the responsibility of a company to its business partners and to everyone else in a supply chain who is dependent on the firm's capability to continuing conducting business without interruption.

As a result, reliable and secure systems and processes are now beginning to be mutually expected of all businesses that are members of a supply chain. For example, Visa recently published security guidelines for its Internet-enabled business partners. Visa partners must:

- Install and maintain a working network firewall to protect data accessible via the Internet.
- Keep security patches to software up to date.
- Encrypt stored data.
- Encrypt data sent across networks.
- Use and regularly update antivirus software.
- Restrict access to a "need-to-know" basis.
- Assign unique identifiers to those with access to data.
- Not use vendor-supplied defaults for passwords and other security parameters.
- Track data access by unique identifier.
- Regularly test security systems and and computing support processes.[3]

These requirements recognize the harsh reality that a lack of systems security with any single company in a supply chain can adversely affect everyone else in the chain. No company wants to become known as a weak link and be threatened with possible breach-of-contract actions and related economic and reputation loss.

48.3.3.3   Lesson 3: Information and Computer Processes Are Important Corporate Assets that Need to Be Rigorously Managed.
Y2K demonstrated that information and supporting computer and communications technology assets are the critically important glue that holds the modern enterprise together. Yet, historically, no other corporate assets are as poorly managed as these. This fact has been documented repeatedly by independent audit groups, not the least of which is the U.S. General Accounting Office (GAO). The GAO reviews not only government agencies but,

at the request of Congress, private-sector companies doing business with the federal government or receiving federal funding. GAO IT Management Audit Reports present a reasonably accurate picture of IT management across both the government and the private sectors.

From a high-level IT management perspective, the GAO and other agencies have consistently identified the following problems as fundamentally contributing to IT project and IT management failures:

- Lack of executive management commitment
- Inadequate IT planning and execution
- Abandonment of the project plan
- Inexperienced project managers
- Flawed technical approaches
- Failure to anticipate advances in technology
- Failure to satisfy user needs
- Inadequate documentation of systems and system-related decisions
- Acquisition problems

Although each of these problems appears to be a separate area of difficulty, they all impact and directly affect, the IT manager and the security practitioner who must somehow cope with these, and a myriad other issues, to deliver a successful information system and a secured processing environment.

Since the vast majority of computer security problems are symptoms of poorly managed applications of IT to the business, until the overall management problems cited by the GAO are corrected, it will be virtually impossible to adequately secure the systems that support the enterprise. Unless these underlying business and system management problems are solved, treating the "lack of security" symptoms will at best be a hit-or-miss proposition.

48.3.3.4   *Lesson 4: Y2K Demonstrated that Existing Technical Infrastructure Management Was Poor.*   For most organizations, Y2K, a rather simple technical problem to correct, became a far too expensive undertaking when it was discovered that most software and systems, were generally not being managed according to acknowledged best practices of the IT industry.

Y2K was a wake-up call for improving management of systems and software. Major improvements in quality assurance, configuration management, software testing, documentation, intrusion detection, and continuity planning activities will be required if computer security is ever to be fully achieved.

48.3.3.5   *Lesson 5: Risk Management Must Become a Way of Life.*   Unlike the time-dependent nature of the Y2K threat, the computer security challenge will always be present and will constantly take on new forms as technologies and business processes evolve. While Y2K was a one-time event, computer security is forever, and the only way to manage it effectively is to integrate the practice of assessing security risks into each and every systems decision.

The type of risk assessment that is needed goes far beyond the replacement cost approach of superficial risk analysis models. The degree of dependence that most organizations now place on automation requires a much broader and constant evaluation of potential damages than just estimating the cost of replacing hardware and software assets.

Effective management, of the contemporary risks faced by most organizations, must begin by placing a value on the following information categories:

- Corporate proprietary information
- Intellectual property
- Client and customer data
- Business partner information

Additionally, critical business processes must have a value associated with them, and the adverse consequences of an inability to process must be determined. From this analysis, revenue losses due to system outages can be estimated, based on appropriate threat scenarios.

Further extension of the risk assessment analytic process should take into account such nonquantifiable items as:

- Potential for liability exposure if business partners are harmed due to a system's insecurity or unavailability
- Loss of business opportunity revenue, because system insecurities do not allow exploitation of new business opportunities
- Potential for liability exposure, should confidentiality of sensitive information be compromised
- Loss of reputation with consumers and with the capital markets of the world, due to publicized security exposures

And finally, there is the important perception of acting responsibly. Whether a company measures up to that challenge will likely be determined by its participation in the critical infrastructure protection and computer security initiatives of their industry sector and whether they can demonstrate "due diligence" in their handling of security threats.

48.3.3.6   *Lesson 6: Automated Business Environments Must Be Monitored Continually for New Vulnerabilities, and Their Protection Improved.*   Unlike Y2K, the nature of the computer security challenge is that of dynamically changing vulnerabilities and threats, based on rapidly changing technologies, used in increasingly complex business applications. Organizations need to build their computer security programs around the idea of a continuous improvement model as popularized by the total quality movement. For purposes of quality improvement, this model was viewed as a cycle of plan-do-check-and-act. For computer security it can be thought of as a cycle of plan-fix-monitor-and-assess. A security management process to execute this model must be established and integrated into the day-to-day operations of the business. Integration means that the computer security initiative does not stand alone as a watchdog or act merely as an audit function. It must be considered an essential part of all other systems development and management activities, including requirements definition, systems design, programming, package integration, testing, systems documentation, training, configuration management, operations, and maintenance.

A security management process must be designed in such a way that the activities of planning, fixing, monitoring, and assessing are accomplished in an iterative fashion for systems under definition, design, and implementation, and for systems that are executing the day-to-day applications of the business.

While many organizations were being diverted by the Y2K problem, networked business environments were being built with little or no attention to security concerns. Subsequently, many of these e-business and Internet-based applications were placed into full production. Because such systems are already operating, the only way realistically to identify and assess their security risks is to begin aggressively monitoring for intrusions and then to design and implement corrective security policies and controls based upon what is discovered The effective sequence of security activities for systems already in operational status then will be to monitor current operations, assess suspicious activity, plan a corrective policy and technology control, implement the control on the system, and then monitor for continuing effectiveness.

48.3.3.7   *Lesson 7: Y2K Became a Due Diligence Issue for the Board and So Will Computer Security.*   To address the computer security issue effectively, it must become an issue for the board of directors just as Y2K demanded board attention.

The Y2K experience introduced business executives and IT managers to the concept of due diligence as applied to the uses of information technology. Because of the potential for legal fallout, it became necessary to view Y2K-related actions through the definitions of due diligence and reasonable care. It became imperative to document all Y2K deliberations, decisions, and actions in order to be able to defend against possible charges of lax Y2K preparations. This same focus now influences computer security deliberations, decisions, and actions.

The significance of the concepts of due diligence and reasonable care is that they allow for an evolving metric against which an organization's computer security deliberations, decisions, and actions can be compared. The comparison is usually against a similar company, in like circumstances of vulnerability and threat, and with similar predictable adverse impacts on customers, partners, shareholders, employees, and the public.

For example, if one company employs a security control and does not experience any security breaches that the technique was suppose to prevent, that fact could be used to establish a baseline against which other similar companies could be compared. If enough similar companies employ the same technique, the security control may become categorized as a best practice for that industry.

If, on the other hand, another company in the same industry did not employ the security control and did experience security breaches of the type the technique was suppose to prevent, it might clearly indicate a lack of due diligence or reasonable care. Computer security decisions and implementations are not a one-time event but need to be under a continuous process of risk evaluation, management, and improvement.

It is therefore imperative, in order to demonstrate an ability to exercise continual due diligence to the board, to establish a documented computer security risk management program and integrate it into the overall management processes of the business. Nothing less will demonstrate that a company, and its board, is capable of assessing computer security threats and of acting in a reasonable manner.

Due diligence guidelines include:

- The U.S. National Institute for Standards and Technology's (NIST) *Generally Accepted Systems Security Principles* (GSSPs) (*ftp.ru.xemacs.org/pub/security/ csir/nist/nistpubs/gssp.pdf*).

- ISO 17799, the *Code of Practice for Information Security Management,* based on the British Standards Institute BS 7799 documents. The International Organization for Standardization (ISO) (*www.iso.ch/iso/en/ISOOnline.frontpage*) began the process of defining BS7799 as an international standard; ISO 17799 was published in 1999.

- The COBIT™ (Control Objectives for Information and Related Technology), a business-oriented set of standards for guiding management in the sound use of information technology. COBIT was developed by volunteers working under the aegis of the IT Governance Institute® (*www.itgovernance.org/index2.htm*), which was itself founded by the Information Systems Audit and Control Association (ISACA).

- The *Common Criteria* (CC), a project that developed out of the 1985 *Trusted Computer System Evaluation Criteria* (TCSEC; also known as the *Orange Book*) developed by the National Computer Security Center of the National Security Agency of the United States. An overview of the CC can be found at *www.commoncriteria.org/faq/faq.html* for an overview of the CC, which says, "The Common Criteria for Information Technology Security Evaluation (CC) defines general concepts and principles of IT security evaluation and presents a general model of evaluation. It presents constructs for expressing IT security objectives, for selecting and defining IT security requirements, and for writing high-level specifications for products and systems."

In the Y2K postmortem, it was generally agreed that the involvement of the board of directors was essential to solving the problem. Success in solving the computer challenge will also require intervention by the board. Representing the security challenge and possible solutions to a board of directors will require considerable preparation. The next section outlines the essential steps. Chapter 28 reviews the standards described above. Chapter 45 examines management responsibilities.

48.4   MAKING COMPUTER SECURITY AN ISSUE FOR THE BOARD OF DIRECTORS.   To present the issue of computer security successfully to a board of directors, the following activities need to be undertaken. It is important that these tasks be accomplished using the various staff disciplines of the corporation, to include the chief executive officer, chief financial officer, chief information officer, Human Resources Department, the affected business unit managers, general counsel, the Public Relations Department, and the corporate Risk Management Office.

A critical guiding principle for such an undertaking is that it must include the non-quantifiable items of the risk management program, with which members of a board should be able to identify. Another issue to impress upon the board is the need for continuous support and funding to counter the reality of a continuously evolving threat.

48.5   THIRTEEN STEPS FOR BOARD OVERSIGHT

1. Conduct a thorough inventory of all IT "hard" assets and identify replacement costs.

2. Identify information assets to include intellectual property, proprietary information, client data, customer data, and business partner data. For each category, determine a dollar value or weight as a form of information valuation.

3. Identify critical business processes, and determine a value for each process by estimating lost revenues should the process be disrupted. Do this also for each process in which a business partner has a direct business interest.

4. Perform a security vulnerability and threat assessment of the cyberenvironment in which the business is operating. This may include attempts, by an independent third party, to penetrate the system defenses. For each confirmed vulnerability, estimate a probability of occurrence based on various threat scenarios and identify potential losses both quantitative (e.g., replacement costs, business exposure,) and nonquantitative (e.g., loss of corporate reputation, competitive edge, and standing in financial markets). Since quantification will be difficult to calculate and defend, concentration might well be on the nonquantifiable, but highly visceral, issues of loss of reputation and trust with customers, business partners, the business community in general, and investors.

5. Examine inter-dependence vulnerabilities that exist with regard to business partners and ask for evidence of their commitment to security. In certain critical instances, a company may want to issue security guidelines for business partners as part of agreement renewal requirements.

6. Join the industry sector's Critical Infrastructure Protection (CIP) Group.

7. Determine the corporation's legal exposure to customers, business partners, shareholders, other investors, employees, and third parties. Include the general counsel in all security deliberations.

8. Based on a program of continuous technology and business risk assessments, fund, design, implement, test, manage, and monitor computer and business process security controls and business recovery plans.

9. Formulate a crisis communications plan for computer security incidents.

10. Monitor the computer and business process security practices of the business partners and competitors in the industry sector. This is important to stay current with industry best practices so that due diligence can be demonstrated.

11. Stay active. Make computer security a periodic agenda item for the board. Practice due diligence and create a documentation trail of computer security actions, deliberations, and decisions.

12. Maximize legal defenses.

13. Review corporate indemnification and investigate the purchase of specialized insurance.

48.6   CHALLENGES TO BE OVERCOME.   Any organization's long-term ability to contain and manage the computer security problem will depend on several premeditated changes in the way IT systems and computer security are currently managed. Until senior executives and the board of directors meet the following challenges, little true progress will be made:

- *Challenge 1:* Executives must require that system activities be managed according to best practices of the IT industry and their own industry sector with special emphasis on those practices that ensure the integrity, availability, and confidentiality of information, of processing assets, and of business processes. This is imperative in mounting a due diligence defense and in establishing a defensible foundation for computer security.

- *Challenge 2:* Convincing business unit managers and the board of directors that computer security requires a program of continuous measurement and investment to counter a continually evolving threat of increased sophistication.

- *Challenge 3:* Organizations must demand better security in the products they buy and/or lease from IT vendors. This is best accomplished by bringing pressure to bear through the special interest groups (SIGs) that represent the users of vendor products and by making security an agenda item of great importance in all enterprise acquisitions of hardware, software, and services.

48.7   CRITICAL INFRASTRUCTURE PROTECTION ISSUES THAT NEED RESOLUTION.   From the broadest perspective, that of the nation's critical information infrastructure, three issues need resolution before effective protection can be realized.

1. An industry's interdependencies that are technologically vulnerable need to be reidentified in the post-Y2K Internet environment and continuously evaluated for changes and additions. Protection of the technical infrastructures supporting these interdependencies is the purpose of the CIP movement. However, this movement cannot be effective unless mechanisms are devised to monitor changes to these infrastructures, within and between interdependent industry sectors. These mechanisms need to be developed and are within the province of PCIS activities.

2. Mechanisms for the effective sharing of security incident information need to be refined and expanded. Currently, there are several Information Sharing and Analysis Centers (ISACs) for the collection, distillation, analysis, and dissemination of data about computer security vulnerabilities and system attacks such as those from hackers and viruses. Some of these are government sponsored and some are private. The various ISACs, functioning as separate entities, need to be integrated so that the interdependent nature of business and government is reflected. It was envisioned that the PCIS would perform this function, but given the new direction of the Bush administration it is not clear how it will now be accomplished. Whatever is proposed there are inhibitors such as the next issue that need to be resolved first.

3. For an ISAC information-sharing mechanism to work, there must be legislative relief from the Freedom of Information Act (FOIA) and from antitrust laws. At present, any security incident or product weakness information made available to a government-sponsored ISAC, from an industry ISAC, may be obtained through a FOIA request. Because of this, IT vendors and corporations are hesitant to make such information available to the government because it is then possible for competitors to obtain it.

And, without relief from antitrust laws, IT vendors working together to solve a joint security problem could be accused of collusion that would give them a future monopolistic advantage.

These are issues of great importance to the players in the security arena, and they must be solved before effective information sharing can occur among interdependent industries.

48.8   CONCLUSION

> *Those who cannot remember the past are condemned to repeat it.*
> —George Santayana

The Y2K episode offered many lessons concerning the effectiveness of IT management as it had been practiced prior to the year 2000. Organizations were generally found wanting, and what should have been a routinely handled problem became huge, and cost the United States in excess of $100 billion.

It is extremely important for the computer security practitioner and for top-level managers to understand that the same IT management deficiencies, left unchanged, will sabotage efforts to establish and sustain effective computer security programs.

48.9   NOTES

1. Timothy Braithwaite, *Y2K Lessons Learned: A Guide to Better Information Technology Management* (New York: John Wiley & Sons, 2000).

2. Tim Wilson, "Editorial," *Internet Week,* January 10, 2000.

3. Reported in *Computerworld,* October 2, 2000.

PART EIGHT

OTHER CONSIDERATIONS

CHAPTER **49**

MEDICAL RECORDS SECURITY

Paul J. Brusil and David Harley

CONTENTS

49.1 INTRODUCTION. This chapter identifies and examines the issues pertaining to privacy and security within the healthcare industry. The role of information and technology in healthcare, and the needs and challenges of privacy and security, are considered in opening sections. The drivers for privacy and security in healthcare are then detailed and contrasted from the perspectives of primarily two countries—the United States and the United Kingdom—in both of which healthcare expenditures represent large fractions of their national economies. The chapter ends with a brief discussion of difficulties in implementing security countermeasures in the medical context.

49.1.1 Information Is Key to Healthcare. Information often is described as the lifeblood of a healthcare resource: patient data, research data, human resources and other administrative data, financial data—in fact, all of the details that keep the machine ticking and that are the basis of further development. Infrastructure, hardware, and software matter, but they are the framework and tools that allow the service to process the information that justifies its existence.

A healthcare resource needs information to meet its obligations to its customers. Information supports the timely, cost-effective supply of all the deliverables that are normally thought of as coming under the healthcare umbrella. Information, in the form of medical records, is used to match each patient profile to a given course of treatment and is also a deliverable in its own right. Information is required to map present and future needs to resources throughout the organization and to map individual profiles to global (e.g., epidemiological) concerns, to take a somewhat very narrow view of medical research.

Patients benefit when healthcare providers and facilities have rapid access to accurate information. Researchers, and ultimately patients, benefit from analyses of treatment efficacies as well as from identification of long-term public health trends and population statistics. Healthcare delivery is improved when healthcare oversight bodies have access to diagnoses and treatment plans.

But with the benefits of electronic medical records, there also come the risks of health information exposure and misuse.

49.1.2 Why Security and Privacy Are Important to Healthcare Information. Security is important in the healthcare industry for two major reasons. It enables the business side of healthcare to conduct electronic commerce, and to reap its benefits, while minimizing the business costs of dealing with electronic attacks, such as falsifying billing claims—prosecutable under false-claims laws.

From the patient side, security is important to improve the reliability of data used in medical decisions, while protecting the privacy of healthcare information. There is also an issue of personal safety—and even of population safety—that is tied to the security of healthcare information.

In these days of growing violence, it is not inconceivable that cyberterrorists would make deadly changes to electronic medical records and treatment orders.

There has never before been as urgent a need to protect medical information; hackers, crackers, pranksters, and busybodies are now showing why this is so important. Some examples of problems arising from inadequate privacy and security for healthcare information have been reported in the consumer advocacy media. One emergency room patient attempted suicide after being called by a prankster who stole patient contact information and wrongfully informed the patient of pregnancy and HIV infection. While not as life threatening, it was reported that over 100 hospital employees pried into the medical records of a renowned athlete receiving treatment. In another incident, a governor's health records—as well as nearly all the records associated with a list of registered voters in a large city—were retrieved from a database of state employee health insurance claims, using birth date and ZIP code data obtained from a voters' database. Cross-referencing and merging snippets of semisensitive data can create highly sensitive, cradle-to-grave medical histories subject to abusive commercial data-mining, while making targeted healthcare consumers feel violated.

The need for security within a healthcare organization is not restricted to medical information. Inventory records, human resources data, and financial reports, for instance, might be tempting targets. All are subject to data protection legislation, but medical records, with their vital characteristics, also require unique controls.

Medical records may be accessed by the state, by a private hospital at which the subject is an inpatient or outpatient, or by a neighborhood physician or dentist. In conjunction with other records, possibly anonymized, they might be used in bulk by health authority administrators for cost analysis, prediction, and other valid purposes. They may be seen by a partner organization, such as a social work department or a law enforcement agency, in a case conference. Medical records contribute, usually in anonymized or semianonymized form, to a multitude of research projects. There is evidently a need for a wide range of legal and quasi-legal restraints, reflecting the intra- and extraorganizational uses to which they may be put.

Medical records may be defined as those that are used for medical purposes, which can including preventive and curative treatments, diagnosis, research, and administration. All of these functions require stringent security measures, but even nonmedical documentation can have security implications, as a basis for social engineering attacks, for instance.

49.1.3   Impacts of Information Technology.   The healthcare sector has been slower than other industries to embrace business-sector–specific automation technology. Many in the sector have been late adopters of information technology (IT) and e-business principles as means of improving their organization, increasing its efficiency, differentiating its services, and cutting its costs of doing business. Now technology is increasingly becoming a priority for the healthcare industry, especially to help deal with the dramatic changes being brought about by decreasing revenues and increasing costs. More and more, the healthcare industry is relying on networked information systems to conduct its essential, day-to-day business, but these new technologies tend to bring new risks and vulnerabilities.

As the healthcare industry gets increasingly networked, medical data distribution among multiple parties becomes more widespread. Data collected by healthcare providers is increasingly reported electronically to numerous government and institutional agencies for applications such as state and federal disease control; research project analyses; government and private health insurance premiums and claims; medical claims clearinghouse operations; hospital discharge records; outpatient encounter tracking; registries of births, deaths, immunizations; and so on. Healthcare data also can be obtained from commercial databases such as those maintained by pharmacies, rehabilitation facilities, and medical supply stores, as well as from databases where consumers might least expect personal, medically relevant, healthcare information to be extracted, such as information derived from catalog orders, warranty registrations, consumer questionnaires, and the like. As more and more sensitive healthcare information is accumulated and made accessible, there is a greater chance that it can be exposed to abuse, that the potential for breakdowns of medical services increases, and that catastrophic economic loss becomes more feasible.

With each new information technology introduced into the healthcare field, there come increased risks and vulnerabilities. For example, new decision-support technologies to help combat fraud and abuse and to identify patterns of potentially fraudulent behavior provide tempting targets to those who would perpetrate fraud.

Furthermore, the advent of sophisticated IT capabilities, such as data warehousing and data mining, that support information fusion, information convergence, and information analysis also brings new privacy and security problems. Information merger across private and public databases can lead to the creation of confidential personal medical information from distributed pieces of less sensitive data. The possibilities loom large to link the disparate medical records databases with other personal information databases that house shopping and credit card information to create data warehouses that aggregate disturbing amounts of personal and medical information.

Use of the attack-prone Internet and Internet-related technologies to communicate and process healthcare transactions escalates the risks of security breeches. For example, the pervasiveness of Web technology now allows competitive, online healthcare companies to set up personal electronic medical records that can be accessed via the Internet, and managed, amended, and corrected online, both through portals for health-care providers and portals for healthcare consumers. Not only does file sharing and transaction processing on the Internet escalate risks of security breeches to medical records, but also the vast number of individuals who have access to the Internet greatly escalates system vulnerabilities.

As new Internet technology features and protocols are adopted, more vendor implementations of such new technologies need to be trusted both for their ability to be implemented correctly and for assurance that they can prevent new risks and exposures. Trust must be established that there are no vendor implementation flaws that allow unauthorized information to be entered into or extracted from medical records. Matters pertaining to trust, with respect to healthcare IT products and systems, are the focus of attention of the Forum of Privacy and Security in Healthcare, described later.

As networking, IT processing and storage capabilities, and online transactions take an increasingly more essential role in the delivery of healthcare and in the success of the healthcare enterprise, the consequences are that privacy and security become vital to the success and stability of the enterprise. However, given the industry's slowness to accept IT, it can be expected that healthcare industry attention to IT security also may be slow.

49.1.4   Information and IT Security Challenges.   Many security challenges are somewhat unique to healthcare information. Some of the more significant ones include:

- Wireless communication of orders and patient information to and from the bed-side can be prone to disclosure, modification, and eavesdropping by roaming medical information thieves.

- Because the healthcare industry is such a fragmented industry, with a multitude of different players and stakeholders, it literally takes an act of Congress to coordinate the industry in matters such as IT and IT security.

- As the healthcare industry is a relative latecomer to using IT, it tends to lack experience in concepts such as IT security, strategies, and procedures, such as security help desks, Public Key Encryption (PKI), and cryptography.

- Electronic commerce among supply-chain trading partners provides potential points of entry to medical systems. Trading partners must establish trust in the security provided by parties that they may never have met or spoken with.

- The Gartner Group consulting house has indicated that by the year 2004, healthcare providers will be submitting 40 percent of all claims directly to healthcare payers via the Internet, with enormous increases in the associated risk of security incidents.

- The proliferation of government, institutional, and commercial databases that house medical information, coupled with factors such as the large number of people involved in settling a health insurance claim and the possibility of unauthorized access to records, as well as the number of people, authorized and unauthorized, who can access a person's medical information, all act to increase the likelihood that medical information will be used improperly.

In addition to the unique challenges, many issues facing healthcare are entirely like those facing any other market sector. For example:

- Unauthorized modem access to an enterprise's central data stores from remote locations raises the need to prevent unauthorized access to the data network side of an enterprise from the telephony network side of an enterprise.

- Multiple data replications and multiple data users accessing the data elevate the risks of data exploitation.

- Mischievous access to information pertaining to the business operations of an enterprise is as serious a problem as access to data associated with products and services.

- Reliance on a single IT, or networking vendor's, product line can be deleterious since if hackers can get through into one part of the enterprise, they may be able to hack an enterprise's entire security architecture.

It is believed that the costs associated with deliberate and accidental security breaches in the healthcare industry are large. Hard costs of losses are difficult to determine. However, they can be inferred to be much over $100 billion per year since, according to a report in *Information Week,* all businesses worldwide were estimated to have lost $1.6 trillion in 1999 because of security breaches, virus attacks, and related downtime.[1] This $100 billion figure is reasonable because the healthcare industry represents a large fraction of many national economies.

Soft costs attributed to security losses are even harder to estimate. They are mainly caused by the decrease in revenues that follow a loss of consumer confidence in the privacy and appropriate use of their healthcare information after reports of data being stolen or otherwise inappropriately used.

49.1.5   Core Security Model in the Healthcare Context.   The classic model of information security is built on availability, confidentiality, and integrity:

- *Availability*—information has to be available to those who are entitled to see it or to process it, at the time when they need it. Conversely, those who do not need the information, in the performance of their duties, must not be able to access it. Threats to availability arise from denial of service (DoS) attacks and from deliberate or accidental infrastructural damage to networks, hardware, and software.

- *Integrity*—information needs to be defended against accidental or deliberate corruption and modification. Threats include viruses, nonreplicating malware (e.g., Trojan horses), unauthorized or accidental modification, errors in structural integrity, logical corruption, and fraudulent misuse.

- *Confidentiality*—information should not be available to those who are not entitled to see or otherwise process it. Threats include unauthorized access and disclosure by hackers or by careless disregard for the rights of privacy. Solutions include access management, passwords, and encryption. To some extent, this is the glamour area of security: The problem is implementing it without compromising availability and integrity.

Often, a fourth leg is added: accountability. This is not just a matter of assigning blame, although that may be necessary. It is also a safeguard against anyone's denial of some specific action; in security parlance it is called nonrepudiation. It is not possible to establish a viable security architecture without determining who is responsible for what. A security incident may be nobody's fault, but it could be a major problem if prevention is nobody's *job*. Only when individual responsibility is a matter of record can appropriate action be taken including the assignment of blame and additional training.

This model is not the only favored view of security: The Parkerian Hexad (see Chapter 5) adds possession, authenticity, and utility to integrity, availability, and confidentiality. In the aggregate, these qualities form the essential underpinnings for ensuring trust in medical information during its storage, processing, and transmission.

Information security is primarily and literally about keeping information safe, not only from intrusion but from corruption and from becoming inaccessible to those who should be able to process it. Here are some typical attacks and other security issues, all of which have implications for the entry and maintenance of medical records:

- Unauthorized access may result in inadvertent errors by untrained personnel or in deliberate alteration of such records as drug dispensing or billing charges. Password stealing and piggybacking are two means of gaining unauthorized access. The results may be loss of confidentiality and integrity, with damage to any and all medical records.

- Unauthorized modification destroys the integrity and authenticity of any affected record and impairs its utility. Even one instance can introduce doubt as to the integrity of the entire database.

- *Malware* is software introduced for the specific purpose of damaging or destroying a database or particular medical functions. Malware may be used to affect adversely any of the characteristics of the security model.

- Denial of service is a malicious effort to bring all of an organization's data communications or computer operations to a complete halt by making the services unavailable.

- User error can inadvertently affect the integrity and authenticity of medical records. In an extreme case, administrator error can bring down an entire system.

- Programming errors can be trivial, or, like malware, they may damage or destroy any of the security model's desired characteristics.

There are always tradeoffs: Emphasizing one aspect of the security model often has negative implications for other aspects. Emphasis on confidentiality usually impacts adversely on availability, if only because physical and electronic access controls tend to complicate legitimate access. In combination with other factors—for instance, human error, or hardware or software failure—efforts at preserving confidentiality may result in data becoming less accessible. Medical information security measures need to be tailored to each specific healthcare environment.

49.2   EXTERNAL DRIVERS.   Security is not primarily a technical issue, which is why technological solutions frequently disappoint. How security is perceived, with its positive benefits and negative constraints, may be as important as how technically effective it is. Information security in healthcare is usually subject to social, administrative, and regulatory pressures both outside and inside the care provider infrastructure.

49.2.1   Political Pressure.   Healthcare, especially national healthcare, is from time to time a core political issue. Some administrations will be more aggressive in cost-cutting than others, but all will maintain that healthcare services should be expanded. Mistakes in treatment, money wasted on ineffectual research, difficulties with health maintenance organizations (HMOs), and similar issues will always be attributed, at least in part, to the current political administration. Politicians, therefore, have a vested interest in stressing security, and the confidentiality of medical records as well as the shortcomings of previous governments. On the other hand, promises to cut back on red tape and bureaucracy, and to pass on savings to the patient, to family members providing care, to professional care providers, and to taxpayers are almost always used as vote-getters.

In the United Kingdom, healthcare is primarily the responsibility of the National Health Service, and security management is formally addressed in the NHS IM&T Security Manual and the more recent resource pack "Ensuring Security and Confidentiality in NHS Organisations." It is not coincidental that both these resources include an incident classification table with an "Acute" scenario involving the resignation of a minister from the government and a No Confidence motion against the government.

In the United States, a major part of healthcare services is the responsibility of state or federal governments. Politicians are currently focusing on how to extend coverage to different population groups, what coverage to add, and how to provide sufficient public funds to maintain the viability of government-sponsored healthcare. Issues surrounding the privacy and security of medical information have not yet surfaced widely as a discriminator among the interests of different political parties.

In many other countries, such as Canada, total healthcare spending is quite a bit lower than in the United States. For such countries, healthcare security is low on the national priority list, as compared to the introduction of new healthcare equipment.

49.2.2 Media Pressure. Between the political administration and the public, and "interpreting" for both, are the media. Almost every medium has its own political or socioeconomic agenda, but all are interested in good stories. Bureaucratic incompetence is newsworthy, as are medical or computer malefactors.

Reports of the removal of the wrong organ, surgical evidence of misdiagnosis or previous mistakes in surgery, are assured of a wide audience. In the United Kingdom, especially as it relates to patient data, privacy infringement is of widespread concern, unlike in the United States where, until now, the media has paid little attention to patient privacy issues.

49.2.3 Public Pressure. Politicians and the media shape public opinion, but also represent it, so in a way these first three drivers are different aspects of the same input.

In a recent article about the public's interest in the privacy and security of their medical information, the conclusion was that the public did not know what it wanted, beyond simplistic slogans such as "Patients should control their own data."[2] Furthermore, it was not clear how significant a priority medical information privacy should be during the heat of a medical emergency.

The public sensitivity about medical records is related to the possible embarrassment that would be caused if the sufferer's maladies were known.

Some conditions, like cancer, epilepsy, AIDS, and depression, carry their own emotional baggage and taboos. In addition, such information may have significant effects on a person's everyday life, as it relates to:

- Job and promotion prospects
- Assessment of fitness as parents

- Eligibility for insurance

- The right to healthcare based on earlier decisions about eligibility, quality of life, and other criteria

- Creditworthiness or financial status

To this may be added the all-too-real risk of being targeted by commercial organizations for intrusive sales efforts on the basis of specific medical data. Such tactics are rightly viewed as constituting an invasion of privacy.

49.2.4   Patient Expectations.   Patients, and the public in general, have a perception that information about them is confidential and an expectation that anyone who works with those data has a "duty of confidence."

49.2.4.1   *Expectation in the United States.*   In the United States, numerous polls have shown that many people feel protective about their personal health information. For example, in one national poll of 1,000 individuals across the country in 1999, researchers found that:

- Computerization was seen as the greatest threat to privacy: 54 percent of respondents said the shift from paper record-keeping to computer-based systems made it more difficult to protect their medical information from unauthorized disclosure.

- Most people were reluctant to divulge their medical records to anyone other than their care providers: 60 percent of the respondents preferred not to grant access to a prospective employer, and 70 percent did not want drug companies to have access to their medical records for marketing drugs and other health-related products to specific individuals whose personal data appear within pharmaceutical databases.

- Most respondents did not trust private and government health insurers to maintain confidentiality; only 35 percent said they trusted private health insurance plans and only 33 percent trusted Medicare to maintain confidentiality "all or most of the time."

- Many individuals appear increasingly worried that the privacy of their medical information will be violated. About 15 percent of the sample had even taken such steps as withholding information when asked for medical history, providing false information, paying medical fees personally even when insured, changing doctors, asking doctors not to keep a record of the patient's condition, or avoiding medical care altogether.[3]

Nonetheless, while individuals feel that aspects of their personal medical information should be private, no widespread or grassroots outcries have surfaced. Nor have any significant movements been started to raise the priority of medical information privacy or to increase the security needed to establish and maintain privacy. In fact, in another survey, the majority of respondents who were asked whether they thought IT security would be a significant problem indicated that they did not see it as a major problem; instead, they felt that vendors and companies relying on IT would take care of security on their own. Such opinions seem to exist despite widely reported and continuing high-profile financial losses and financial information thefts from large commercial Web merchants and service providers.

49.2.4.2 Expectations in the United Kingdom. Within the United Kingdom's National Health Service (NHS-), there is a formally recognized expectation that the following have a duty of confidence:

- All NHS bodies and those carrying out functions on behalf of the NHS
- Everyone working with or for NHS who works with information
- Health professionals
- Other individuals and agencies to whom information is passed legitimately

Patients, and the public in general, also expect that their data will be:

- Used only for legitimate purposes
- Acquired, kept, and processed in accordance with data protection principles
- Relevant to the intended purpose of the record
- Accessible to them as of right under the Data Protection Act
- Accurate and up-to-date[4]

49.2.5 Legal Pressure. Like many other organizations, a healthcare provider needs to conform with a wide range of legislation, some specific to the healthcare industry, some more general.

49.2.5.1 Protection Legislation. Protection legislation is, in itself, wide-ranging in scope, and varies between countries and jurisdictions.

49.2.5.2 Laws and Regulations in the United States. In the United States, several laws and regulations are now in place. As detailed below, these include:

- The Privacy Act of 1974
- The Health Insurance Portability and Accountability Act of 1996 (HIPAA)
- State-specific privacy and security laws
- The Electronic Signature Act of 2000
- The False Claims Act

In addition, several legislative activities are under way. New laws and regulations are likely to emerge.

Given the significant attention being paid to HIPAA, more material is presented here than on any other relevant U.S. laws and regulations.

49.2.5.2.1 Privacy Act of 1974. One of the earliest laws covering medical databases in the United States is the federal Privacy Act of 1974. This law forbids disclosure of the personally identifiable health information collected by the U.S. government, such as Medicare treatment records. It is not clear what impact this law will have on other government-collected healthcare data such as the data that will appear in new computerized patient record systems from military hospital upgrade programs such as the Composite Health Care System program.

49.2.5.2.2 Health Insurance Portability and Accountability Act. The Health Insurance Portability and Accountability Act of 1996 (HIPAA) is a massive and comprehensive law pertaining to several areas of healthcare.[5] It has become Part C of Title

11 of the Social Security Act. HIPAA includes a section on Administrative Simplification (hereafter referred to as just "HIPAA") which includes provisions for security and privacy for healthcare information.

Given the pervasive and serious nature of HIPAA, material presented below includes:

1. The intent and goals of HIPAA

2. The HIPAA approach

3. Penalties associated with disregard of HIPAA

4. The expectations and impacts of HIPAA

5. HIPAA's strategy for developing the security and privacy regulations to be embodied within the HIPAA law

6. The HIPAA security and electronic signature standards

7. The proposed HIPAA privacy rules

8. The pragmatic linking of HIPAA-relevant liabilities and penalties to other industries supporting healthcare

49.2.5.2.2.1   Health Insurance Portability and Accountability Act Intent and Goals.   In part, the intent of Administrative Simplification is to:

- Use standards to substantially reduce the estimated 17 to 30 cents-per-healthcare dollar being wasted in administrative transactions

- Use standards to help ensure that all electronic patient information is protected from improper access, alteration, or loss, and kept confidential

- Help minimize abuse and fraud (estimated at about 10 percent of the total cost of healthcare)
  - By securing transactions between healthcare systems and
  - By securing information that, by its nature of being stored electronically, is at risk to fraud and abuse, via electronically perpetrated attacks

More specifically, the goal of HIPAA is to improve the efficacy and reliability of the healthcare system by standardizing the electronic exchange of standardized, HIPAA-specified, administrative and financial data among healthcare payers and providers and others in the system. Another goal is to provide security against deliberate or inadvertent misuse or disclosure of such transmitted information. HIPAA also provides for the privacy of personally identifiable information via appropriate security measures during the storage, processing, and transmission of such information. The scope of personally identifiable information is amplified within HIPAA.

In particular, HIPAA stipulates the use of a specific set of EDI (Electronic Data Interchange) transactions with certain content standards. The HIPAA-specified transactions pertain to health claims, claims attachments, claims status, encounters, first report of injury, health plan eligibility, enrollment, disenrollment, care payments, remittance advice, plan premium payments, referral certification, authorization, and so on.[6] HIPAA also stipulates that industry-acceptable security standards, as well as specified administrative requirements, that are reasonable and appropriate to each situation, be used to protect healthcare information. (HIPAA also allows for the national adoption of other standards as long as such standards improve the healthcare system, especially its efficiency.)

49.2.5.2.2.2   Health Insurance Portability and Accountability Act Approach.
The HIPAA approach for security standards is to minimize bureaucratic burdens on the
healthcare industry by focusing on requirements that need to be met by the security
technology deployed by a healthcare entity. While every healthcare entity that electronically receives, maintains, or transmits patient information must comply with HIPAA's
security requirements, some healthcare enterprises may need to implement more sophisticated security solutions than others. HIPAA is not looking to specify a one-size-fits-
all technological security solution, applicable to all situations. Instead, it is seeks to
provide flexibility, scalability, and technology-neutrality, so that different healthcare
entities can meet HIPAA-stipulated security requirements by whatever security technology is appropriate to each situation. More specifically, the security requirements
stipulated by HIPAA were chosen so as to be:

- *Scalable,* so that they would work for both the small office and large healthcare
  enterprise, at reasonable cost
- *Technology-neutral,* so that as technology changes, the efficiencies of new technologies could be leveraged without having to change the security standards specified in HIPAA
- *Flexible,* so that different healthcare entities and partners can use security technologies appropriate to their situations—as long as these technologies meet
  HIPAA's security requirements

These three factors together act to increase the longevity of the HIPAA law by allowing
ever-newer, emerging security technologies to be used.

49.2.5.2.2.3   Noncompliance and Disclosure Penalties.   The HIPAA law specifies relatively small penalties on the officers and/or employees of healthcare-relevant
organizations that fail to use the specified standards. Additionally, there are larger, criminal penalties including fines and imprisonment for those who wrongfully disclose confidential information. Organizations can be penalized $100 per violation, up to $25,000
per year for not complying with and using HIPAA standards. Furthermore, any person who knowingly obtains, uses, causes to use, intends malicious harm, tries to sell or
transfer or gain from, or discloses patient information inappropriately faces penalties
of $50,000 to $250,000 and/or up to 10 years imprisonment, depending on the seriousness of the offense. The law also provides safe harbors for whistle blowers.

While penalties are stiff, it may be that the real dangers arise not from these penalties but from loss of public confidence and possible litigation under contract law.

*49.2.5.2.2.4   Impacts of the Health Insurance Portability and Accountability
Act.*   HIPAA is a serious topic. It is the subject of many discussions, conferences, and
articles.[7] It is said to be the most sweeping change to the American healthcare industry since the introduction of Medicare, a change that will dramatically alter the use of
technology and information in the healthcare industry. It may even necessitate the
replacement or revision of older IT systems that cannot meet all HIPAA requirements;
for example, the ability of older IT systems to maintain transaction logs with detailed
information about each data exchange is severely restricted and may not meet HIPAA
requirements.

The government expects that HIPAA will:

- Tie the healthcare industry together
- Save money

- Increase productivity and efficiency
- Lower the costs of products based on implementing a more limited number of standards
- Lower administrative and back-office costs by lowering error rates, creating cleaner claims, speeding payments
- Lower the costs of maintaining and managing the healthcare IT infrastructure, introduce modern e-business principles into healthcare, so that,for example, today's six- to 12-month delays for patients to get paper reports from a hospital as to what may or may not be covered by an insurance company can be reduced to an operation taking but a few seconds
- Streamline healthcare operations
- Reduce fraudulent activities
- Protect patient privacy
- Pave the way for cost-effective, uniform, and confidential healthcare information practices
- Pave the way for uniform, confidential, electronic medical records that have the potential to increase the quality and efficiency of healthcare while lowering cost

While promising to save billions in annual operations costs, the initial implementation costs associated with HIPAA are expected to be large. Briefings by senior officials of the U.S. Department of Health and Human Services to several healthcare groups across the United States have indicated that the financial impact from implementing the required changes are expected to rival and perhaps exceed the $8 billion cost of fixing the Year 2000 problem across the healthcare industry.

The government hopes that strategic cost-savings and competitive pressures will be strong motivators for HIPAA to be promulgated throughout the U.S. healthcare industry. Furthermore, healthcare accrediting organizations are seriously considering adopting HIPAA regulations as accrediting criteria for healthcare stakeholders. Also, in an attempt to lower/mitigate their HIPAA-imposed liabilities, payment clearinghouses will likely put pressure on healthcare providers to comply with HIPAA regulations.

49.2.5.2.2.5   Strategy for Developing Security and Privacy Regulations.   According to the provisions of HIPAA, since the U.S. Congress did not enact security and privacy laws by stipulated dates, the U.S. Department of Health and Human Services (DHHS) became responsible for developing and adopting such rules. DHHS released proposed rules for security[8] in 1998 and for privacy[9] in 1999. The proposed rules stimulated much community interest: Over 2,000 comments were received about security, and over 150,000 comments were received about privacy. Some U.S. government apolitical factions believe that privacy standards need to be in place in short order because the public may not be comfortable with personal information more easily accessible via new Web and Internet technologies.

Final security and privacy rules that address the comments are scheduled for timely release by DHHS.[10] Decisions about the contents of the final security and privacy rules are being made at the highest levels of the White House. These rules will become effective as federal regulations 60 days after being published. Thereafter, large healthcare enterprises covered by the regulations will have 24 months to comply, and small healthcare organizations with 50 or fewer employees will have 36 months to comply. Given expected timetables for publication of the final security and privacy rules, large enterprises will likely need to be compliant to HIPAA security and privacy regulations sometime in 2003 whereas small organizations will have until about 2004 to be compliant.

An idea of what the final rules are likely to cover can be gotten by considering the summaries below of the proposed security and privacy rules. Any questions concerning interpretations of the HIPAA regulations can be submitted via e-mail to *http://HIPAA-question@list.nih.gov,* where an interpretations committee within the DHHS will develop a generalized answer and electronically post it to the DHHS HIPAA Web site.

49.2.5.2.2.6   Health Insurance Portability and Accountability Act Security and Electronic Signature Standards.   New security and electronic signature standards (SESS) are being proposed to protect the confidentiality, integrity, and availability of all individually identifiable healthcare information as well as healthcare financial information, and proprietary information.

The SESS rules apply to any healthcare entity that transmits HIPAA-standard transactions over telecommunications systems and networks or that electronically houses healthcare information pertaining to an individual.

Information to be protected and kept private—either while in electronic storage or during electronic transmission—includes information including demographic information, whether oral or recorded in any form or medium, that (a) is created or received by a healthcare provider, health plan, public health authority, employer, life insurer, school or university, or healthcare clearinghouse; and (b) relates to the past, present, or future physical or mental health or condition of an individual, the provision of healthcare to an individual, or the past, present, or future payment for the provision of healthcare to an individual. HIPAA requires that every healthcare entity that maintains or conveys health information shall maintain reasonable and appropriate administrative, technical, and physical safeguards to:

- Ensure the integrity and confidentiality of information to be protected
- Protect against any reasonably anticipated threats or hazards to the information and any unauthorized uses or disclosures of information
- Ensure compliance to these rules by officers and employees of the healthcare entity

The electronic signature portion of the SESS rules requires a reliable method for assuring specified message integrity, nonrepudiation, and user authentication for HIPAA-specified transactions. An HIPAA-specified digital signature on an HIPAA standard transaction will verify the identity of the person signing the transactions and the authenticity of the enclosed electronic healthcare information. None of the current HIPAA-standard electronic transactions is required to be electronically signed. However, whenever an electronic signature is employed by a healthcare entity in the transmission of any HIPAA standard transaction, the healthcare entity must comply with the new HIPAA electronic signature standard. The electronic signature standard applies only to the transactions adopted under HIPAA.

The SESS rules also require all healthcare entities to:

- Assess risks and vulnerabilities
- Implement overlapping administrative safeguards, physical safeguards, technical security services, and technical security mechanisms
- Document implementation of such protection measures with appropriate policies and procedures

Specifically, it is recommended that each healthcare entity, regardless of size, begin with a risk analysis that identifies threats and vulnerabilities as well as the value of each healthcare datum, and from this analysis to develop a security plan. Such risk analyses and plans should focus especially on the categories of safeguards and associated security requirements stipulated in the SESS rules.

The four categories of safeguards for which security requirements are delineated are:

1. Administrative procedures safeguards
2. Physical safeguards
3. Technical security services
4. Technical security mechanisms

Administrative procedures safeguards (Exhibit 49.1) are specified to ensure that security-relevant plans, policies, procedures, training, and contractual agreements exist. These requirements are used to define what specific items of information must be protected, who is to have access to such information, and how well such information must be protected. For security technology to work, behavioral safeguards must be established and enforced. Security technology and safeguards are worthless without administrative commitment and responsibilities. The administrative procedures requirements are the largest set of requirements in the proposed security rules. Over time it may be possible that some of these requirements will be addressed by automated systems that will themselves require HIPAA safeguards.

Exhibit 49.1   Proposed Administrative Safeguards

Administrative Safeguard Category	Further Details
Certification	Computer and network systems must be certified to comply with security requirements.
Chain of Trust	Chain-of-trust agreements must be established between business partners for the purpose of passing (and legally binding) trust for protecting conveyed information to the next party, in a chain of parties through which the information is to pass.
Contingency Plans	Contingency plans must be established for dealing with system emergencies, including: (1) assessment of the sensitivity, vulnerabilities, and security of an entity's information; (2) a data backup plan; (3) a disaster recovery plan; (4) an emergency operation plan; (5) testing and revision procedures.
Access Policies	Policies and procedures must be established regarding access to information including (1) rules and policies for establishing a right to access; (2) rules and policies for modifying rights of access.
Formal Records Processing	A formal records processing mechanism must be established.

Exhibit 49.1   Proposed Administrative Safeguards *(continued)*

Access Auditing	An internal auditing of access mechanisms must be established.
Personnel Security	Provisions must be established regarding: (1) supervision of maintenance personnel by authorized individuals; (2) recording grants of access; (3) authorizing operations and maintenance personnel with proper access; (4) personnel clearance procedures; (5) personnel security procedures; and (6) security awareness training.
Security Configuration Management	Provisions must be established to create a coherent system of security, including: (1) documentation of security plans; (2) security hardware and software installation; (3) reviews of maintenance and testing; (4) hardware and software inventory reviews; (5) security testing; and (6) virus reporting.
Security Incident Reporting	Reporting procedures must be established to document security incidents.
Security Management	Provisions must be established to include: (1) risk analysis; (2) risk management; (3) a security policy; and (4) employee sanction policies.
Employee Termination	Procedures must be established regarding: (1) changing locks; (2) removals from access lists; (3) removals from user accounts; and (4) collection of keys and other forms of access.
Training	Training must be established to include (1) security awareness training; (2) periodic security reminders; (3) education regarding virus protection; (4) education regarding the importance of monitoring and reporting login success/failure; and (5) education regarding maintenance of password confidentiality.

Physical safeguards (Exhibit 49.2) are specified to protect computer systems and facilities from hazards such as fire, natural disasters, and environmental hazards, and to prevent unauthorized physical access or intrusion to computer systems. Means for protection and prevention include locks, keys, and administrative measures, with associated policies and procedures such as employee badges and termination practices. Requirements are provided in the areas of assignment of security responsibilities, media controls, physical access controls, workstation security, and security awareness training.

Technical security services (Exhibit 49.3) are specified regarding system and user access controls, authorization controls, authentication controls, and audit controls to support the integrity, confidentiality, and availability of information electronically stored within electronic healthcare systems. Strong authentication requirements are stipulated so that healthcare information can be better protected. Automatic logging of accesses to healthcare information or to administrative and financial transactions will tend to make fraud more difficult to perpetrate.

Exhibit 49.2   Proposed Physical Safeguards

Physical Safeguard Category	Further Details
Media Controls	Safeguards must be established regarding the receipt and removal of hardware and software from a facility including access control, accountability for tracing removed property, data backup systems, data storage systems, and data disposal systems.
Security Responsibilities	Pertains to the assignment of security responsibilities.
Physical Access Controls	Controls must be established to include: (1) disaster data recovery plans; (2) emergency mode operation plans; (3) equipment control into and out of a facility; (4) facility security plans to prevent unauthorized physical access; (5) procedures for verifying access authorization before granting physical access; (6) documentation of maintenance to hardware and to the facility; (7) need-to-know procedures limiting access to only necessary data; (8) visitor sign-in procedures; and (9) restrictions of testing and revision to authorized personnel.
Workstations	Safeguards must be established regarding the creation of a secure workstation location and policies on workstation use.
Training	Pertains to security awareness training.

Exhibit 49.3   Proposed Technical Security Services

Technical Security Services Category	Further Details
Access Control	Access controls must be established to include: (1) procedures for emergency access; (2) the optional use of encryption; and (3) context-based access, role-based access, or user-based access.
Authorization Controls	Authorization controls must be established for obtaining consent for use and disclosure through either role-based access or user-based access technologies.
Data Authentication	Data authentication must be established to ensure integrity of information via appropriate technology approaches.
Entity Authentication	Entity authentication must be established: (1) to identify users, including (a) unique user identifiers, or (b) biometric identification, password, personal identification number, telephone callback procedure, or token; and (2) to maintain authentication using concepts such as automatic logoff.
Audit Controls	Audit controls must be established to examine system activities and accesses.

Technical security mechanisms (Exhibit 49.4) are specified to establish communication and network controls to protect healthcare information, to avoid the risk of interception, and to avoid the risk of alteration as information is in transit over a network.

SESS rules provide a compendium of security requirements that must be met. These rules state the objectives that security standards must achieve (e.g., Personnel Security in Exhibit 49.1) and how the security objectives should be achieved (e.g., assure supervision of maintenance personnel by authorized knowledgeable individuals, and other items listed in Exhibit 49.1). The SESS rules do not select specific security practices and security technologies to be used; to do so might bind the healthcare industry to security solutions that might soon be superseded by other rapidly developing technologies. Rather, the SESS rules allow adoption of the latest and most promising security solutions that meet the needs of healthcare entities of different size and complexity. Healthcare entities must each assess their own potential risks to the healthcare information they handle and then develop, implement, and maintain appropriate security measures. Particular security solutions may vary from situation to situation; but each solution must meet the requirements stipulated in the SESS.

49.2.5.2.2.7   Proposed Health Insurance Portability and Accountability Act Privacy Rules.   As the first standards intended to protect patients' personal medical information, the U.S. DHHS proposed the privacy rules to be promulgated as mandatory by HIPAA. The intent of the privacy rules is to strike a balance between providing patients with greater peace of mind versus the public responsibility to support such national medical priorities as protecting public health (e.g., from outbreaks of infectious diseases), identifying public health trends, conducting medical research, improving the quality of care available for the nation, and fighting healthcare fraud and abuse.

Exhibit 49.4   Proposed Technical Security Mechanisms

Technical Security Mechanism Category	Further Details
Integrity	Mechanisms must be established to ensure the validity of data being transmitted or stored.
Message Authentication	Mechanisms must be established to confirm that a message received is in fact the message sent.
Access Capabilities	Access controls or encryption must be established to limit access.
Entity Authentication Capabilities	Controls must be established to identify authorized and unauthorized users.
Alarm Capabilities	Mechanisms must be established to detect abnormal system conditions.
Event Reporting Capabilities	Mechanisms must be established to report abnormal system conditions, irregularities in the physical elements of all systems, and the completion of significant tasks.
Auditing Capabilities	Mechanisms must be established to create and maintain an audit trail for use in a security audit.

The proposed privacy rules include the following nine exemplar provisions:

1. A healthcare organization cannot disclose individually identifiable healthcare information that it electronically maintains or transmits—even to business partners, contractors, and other parties (as stipulated in the proposed HIPAA privacy rule)—except as authorized by the informed consent of the individual whose data is involved.

2. Under an assumed regulatory authorization, such information may be disclosed without patient authorization when it is required to carry out certain healthcare activities, such as treatment, payment, medical teaching and training, healthcare business operations, healthcare oversight to improve quality, judicial or certain law enforcement procedures, national priorities such as research, and certain public health considerations, and others as stipulated by the HIPAA privacy rule.

3. No more than the minimum data necessary for each intended purpose can be disclosed.

4. As the use of an individual's healthcare information should be for healthcare purposes only, employers who also function as healthcare providers are barred from using healthcare information for nonhealth purposes such as hiring, firing, or determining promotions. Similarly, insurers cannot use such information to underwrite products such as life insurance.

5. Data anonymized by mechanisms stipulated in the HIPAA rule may be disclosed.

6. Individuals have the rights to inspect, obtain, account, amend, and correct healthcare information about themselves and to obtain documentation of disclosures of their health information.

7. Clear procedures must be established to protect patient's information privacy, including posting notices of privacy policies and designating officials to monitor privacy procedures and to notify patients about privacy practices.

8. Healthcare enterprises must have administrative, training, technical, and physical safeguards as stipulated in the HIPAA Security and Electronic Signature Rule to protect the privacy of healthcare information.

9. These candidate privacy standards are proposed to apply to the electronic information—or printouts thereof—pertaining to individuals who are privately insured, uninsured, or participants in public programs such as Medicare or Medicaid. The candidate privacy standards do not apply to records that are maintained in paper form only. The standards apply to healthcare information created by healthcare providers, hospitals, health plans, healthcare clearinghouses, and others. The standards do not apply to information maintained by other insurers or maintained by employers for workers' compensation purposes.

49.2.5.2.2.8   Linked Liability.   In a recent workshop on privacy and security in the telecommunications industry, computer intrusion crime attorneys warned attendees that legislation and attendant litigation risks are now turning from the tobacco industry to focus on matters of privacy and security in IT-powered industries such as healthcare, telecommunications, and power.[11] The language and severe penalties in the HIPAA law pertaining to breaches of electronic privacy and security may cause organizations forced into litigation to try passing the blame to others in associated fields, such as telecommunications service providers. Executives in associated fields are warned that like those in the healthcare industry, they too must be able to show three things:

1. They exercised due diligence with regard to providing security and privacy.

2. Their privacy and security solutions

   - are in line with normal and customary, best industry practices regarding privacy and security,
   - are in line with provisions of HIPAA, and
   - as required in HIPAA, can anticipate and address new threats.

3. Correct decisions were made with regard to deployment of those IT security services in their enterprises that support healthcare in some overt or indirect way.

49.2.5.2.3   State Privacy and Security Laws.   Several states have applicable laws. While HIPAA will provide for the first national standards for electronic signatures on specified healthcare transactions and for security and privacy of electronic healthcare information, the HIPAA standards do not preempt those state laws that deal with these issues in a more stringent fashion. HIPAA provides a national floor for the protection of electronic healthcare information; and states may provide even stronger protections. In circumstances where the federal and state laws are in conflict, the stronger privacy protection prevails. As such, HIPAA does enhance and preempt the protections afforded by many states that have weaker privacy protections than those afforded by HIPAA.

HIPAA will also preempt, in part, state laws that require the maintenance or conveyance of written rather than electronic forms of medical information. HIPAA does not preempt state laws that are necessary to prevent fraud and abuse, that ensure appropriate state regulation of insurance or health plans, that address controlled substances, or for other purposes as deemed by the secretary of the Department of Health and Human Services.

49.2.5.2.4   Electronic Signature Act of 2000.   Complicating matters even more is the new federal law—the Electronic Signatures in Global and National Commerce (E-Sign) Act—that provides for an e-signature to have the same legally binding weight as a written signature. The relationships and presidencies between such laws and HIPAA are not clear.

49.2.5.2.5   False Claims Act.   The federal government can punish fraudulent healthcare providers with triple damages, penalties of $5,000 to $10,000 per wrongful billing, and the ultimate threat: exclusion from government insurance programs. Many of the accused settle out of court because it is often more expensive to win such legal cases and much more costly if they lose.[12] Without adequate security, electronic billing can open the doors to malicious attacks on healthcare claims so that they appear to be wrongful, prosecutable, billing claims.

49.2.5.2.6   Emerging Legislation.   The HIPAA law appears to have started a chain reaction of new legislation related to privacy and security associated with the use of IT. According to officials from the White House Office of Science and Technology Policy, as reported to a recent workshop on privacy and security in another vertical industry, 70 pieces of privacy and security legislation are in the works and more are to be expected over the coming years.[13]

For example, legislation is being developed that pertains to privacy on wireless transmissions. Such legislation is likely to have an impact on the use of Personal Digital Assistants (PDAs) and other bedside devices or portable ambulatory care devices used for medical record information capture and retrieval as well as for medical order entry. Another piece of legislation being developed pertains to the nondisclosure of Social Security numbers as well as any other personal identifying and personally identifiable information. The "Privacy Commission Act" legislation is looking to establish a government commission to investigate privacy issues in the United States. Other legislation being drafted include "The Internet Integrity and Critical Infrastructure Protection Act" and an amendment to financial security laws regarding "Restricting the Use of Healthcare Information in Making Credit and Other Financial Decisions." While not all of these pieces of legislation under development are specifically targeted toward the healthcare industry, nonetheless their impacts will be felt in the healthcare industry.

It appears that the development of such legislation in the United States will only intensify, especially if industry-led, self-regulatory efforts continue to sputter. The applicability of emerging legislation is spreading into other IT-powered national infrastructure industries, such as telecommunications, energy, and power, which support the healthcare industry. Prominent attorneys in the computer crime field believe that legislative development and actions pertinent to IT privacy and security will be occurring for several years. The strong language and penalties of the HIPAA are serving as a model and being incorporated into emerging legislation. HIPAA's strong language regarding the need to maintain and evolve security solutions to protect against any reasonably expected threats, as well as the stiff penalties to be imposed, are seen as harbingers of things to come. HIPPA appears to be setting the stage for a dramatic expansion in the number and scope of new and more pervasive laws and regulations impacting healthcare information privacy and security.

49.2.5.3 *Laws and Regulations in the United Kingdom.*   Legislation such as the 1998 Data Protection Act does not deal exclusively with electronic data, since not all medical records exist electronically. If data processing in general is to be defined as "lawful," at least one of a number of conditions must be met, in accordance with the eight Principles listed in Exhibit 49.5. The subject must have consented to the processing, or:

- Processing must be necessary in order to enter into or execute a contract to which the party is subject.
- The data controller is under a legal obligation, other than contractual, entailing a need for the processing.
- The processing is necessary to protect the vital interests, or to save the life, of the data subject.
- The processing is necessary for the administration of justice, for the exercise of functions necessary for administrative functions within the public sector, or by government, or other functions necessary in the public interest.
- The processing is necessary for the data controller's legitimate interests without being detrimental to the legitimate interests of the data subject.

Lawful processing in terms of sensitive data is subject to additional conditions. Sensitive data is defined as data relating to the following:

- The subject's racial or ethnic origin
- The subject's political opinions
- The subject's religious beliefs

- The subject's trade union membership or nonmembership
- The subject's physical or mental health
- The subject's sexual life
- The subject's criminal record or being subject to criminal proceedings

One or more of the following conditions must be met:

- The subject's explicit and informed consent to processing has been obtained.
- The controller is legally bound to undertake processing.
- Processing is in the vital interests of the subject or of another in an emergency situation.
- Processing is in pursuit of legitimate nonprofit activities.
- The data subject has deliberately made the data public
- Processing is necessary in relation to legal rights such as obtaining legal advice; establishing, exercising, or defending legal rights; or in the conduct of ongoing or prospective legal proceedings.
- Processing is necessary for the administration of justice, public sector interests, or the public interests.
- Processing is necessary for medical purposes, including, but not confined to, preventive medicine, medical diagnosis, medical research, provision and care of treatment, and the management of healthcare services. The inclusion of "medical research" is specific to the United Kingdom's Data Protection legislation; it does not appear in the European Data Protection Directive (see Section 49.2.5.4.1).
- Processing is necessary to trace equality of opportunity between peoples of different racial or ethnic backgrounds.
- Other conditions specifically listed by the Secretary of State. The European Directive requires such conditions to be in the public interest and suitably safeguarded, but this requirement is not included in the U.K. legislation.

Exhibit 49.5 Data Protection Principles (U.K. Data Protection Act 1998)

1st Principle: Personal data shall be processed fairly and lawfully (must satisfy schedule 2 and, in the case of sensitive data, schedule 3).
2nd Principle: Personal data shall be obtained only for one or more specified and lawful purposes, and shall not be further processed in any manner incompatible with that purpose or those purposes.
3rd Principle: Shall be adequate, relevant, and not excessive in relation to their purpose.
4th Principle: Shall be accurate and, where necessary, kept up to date.
5th Principle: Shall not be kept for longer than is necessary . . .
6th Principle: Shall be processed with the rights of the data subject to this act.
7th Principle: Appropriate technical and organizational measures shall be taken against unauthorized or unlawful processing of personal data and against accidental loss or destruction of, or damage to, personal data.
8th Principle: Shall not be transferred . . . outside the European Economic Area unless an adequate level of protection assured by the target country or territory.

In addition to the general Data Protection Act, there is a significant body of legislation specific to medical issues and privacy:

- The Access to Health Records Act controls the individual's statutory right of access to his or her own medical records.
- The Access to Personal Files Act deals with files held by Social Services departments. This becomes relevant in cases of joint care.
- The Access to Medical Reports Act deals with medical reports for employers and insurance companies.

There is also a considerable body of other legislation, not specific to healthcare provision.

The Copyright, Designs, Patents Act deals with software piracy primarily in this context: thus, it primarily addresses an internal problem. It may not be immediately obvious how this affects medical records. In a standardized environment using in-house or bespoke software ("custom-made," in the United States), such as a Patient Administration System (PAS), it may have no particular relevance, depending on the source and licensing terms. In other contexts, however, it can be entirely pertinent. Patient records may be standardized, but they may be used as source data for other protected records, such as mailing lists. Word-processed documents used for notification of appointments, for instance, may use mail-merged data lists consisting purely of names and addresses (which in principle are likely to constitute protected but not necessarily sensitive data). However, lists held, for instance, by a cancer or HIV clinic may be not only protected but sensitive, purely because of their context.

The Computer Misuse Act is also relevant to medical information security:

- Section 1 of the Computer Misuse Act is aimed at outlawing unauthorized access to programs or data if the offenders know at the time of access that they do not have the right to do so.
- Section 2 expands this concept into the area of "ulterior intent": that is, it identifies instances where unauthorized access is gained with intent to commit or facilitate further offences (e.g., blackmail or extortion).
- Section 3 deals with the offense of intentionally causing "an unauthorized modification of the contents of any computer." There is a known instance of a nurse who was convicted of changing patient prescription data under this section.

Many countries have equivalent legislation dealing with the key concepts of unauthorized access and unauthorized modification. Legislation addressing criminal damage, incitement, and interference with telecommunications equipment also may be relevant.

49.2.5.4   Laws and Regulations in Other Countries.   This chapter does not purport to examine the healthcare security and privacy climates across all other countries. For many countries, expansion in the quality of basic healthcare and procurement of newer healthcare equipment easily take precedence over the needs to address privacy and security. Even very highly advanced countries, such as Canada, are just in the early stages of taking note of healthcare privacy and security matters. For example, Canada does have Canadian Privacy legislation and the Canadian Medical Association's Privacy Code of Ethics. The Canadian Security Establishment, somewhat akin to the National Security Agency in the United States, has indicated that certification of the security features of products for the Canadian healthcare sector is a high priority. But neither the Canadian government nor Health Canada (the Canadian equivalent of the U.S. Department of Health and Human Services) has any efforts under way regarding the establishment of national laws and regulations akin to HIPAA in the United States. The criteria against which healthcare products should be certified simply do not yet exist.

Data protection legislation in the European Union has a family resemblance, being based (like the U.K.'s Data Protection Act) on the European Data Protection Directive 95/46/EC. Member states may make additional conditions in the public interest, as long as suitable safeguards are incorporated. In general, there is far less agreement on other relevant legislation between member states. Some specific divergences in the U.K. legislation from the Directive are noted above.

49.2.5.4.1 European Data Protection Principles.   The European Data Protection Directive (95/46/EC), on which the United Kingdom's Data Protection Act is based, aims to protect the individual's privacy relative to the processing of personal data and the harmonization of data protection legislation across all member states of the European Union. Article 6 defines a number of fundamental principles (compare Exhibit 49.5, the Eight Principles of the 1998 Data Protection Act).

Data processing requires the consent of the data subject, except when:

- Processing is necessary to execute a contract to which the subject is party.
- Processing is necessary to fulfill a legal obligation.
- Processing is necessary in the vital interests of the data subject (for vital, read something close to life-critical).
- Processing is necessary in the public interest or in the exercise of official authority.
- Processing is necessary if the data controller is to pursue legitimate interests (but only if those interests are compatible with the interests, rights, and freedoms of the subject).

Categories of data are defined that correspond to the categories defined in Exhibit 49.5 as "sensitive" and that can be processed only under strict conditions, including the explicit consent of the data subject.

The data subject has the right to know the identity of the data controller and the purpose for which the data are collected, from the subject or from a third party. The data subject also has the right of reasonable access to the data ("reasonable" apparently meaning not too often but without undue delay or expense) and the right to have inaccurate data corrected or deleted. The subject has right to object to and even block the processing of data, the right to object to their use for direct marketing, and the right not to be subject to a legally binding decision based solely on the automatic processing of data.

There is also a requirement corresponding fairly closely to the 7th Principle of the 1998 Act. Personal data must be protected against accidental or unlawful destruction or loss, unauthorized alteration, disclosure, or access, the level of security being appropriate to the risk, the nature of the data, and the cost and availability of remedial technology.

49.2.6   Government Policies

49.2.6.1   Government Policies in the United Kingdom.   It is not clear that either of the main political parties in the United Kingdom have clear intentions toward healthcare in general and the National Health Service in particular, other than the reduction of costs and the imposition of high service levels relative to patient and public expectations, in which security generally plays only a minor role. Governmental thinking is more likely to be expressed through the National Health Service (and, in particular, the National Health Service Information Authority) than at Prime Minister's Question Time.

49.2.6.2   *Government Policies in the United States.*   Policy directives have been issued in the United States regarding the need to protect critical national infrastructures including healthcare. Policy has also been established that requires the U.S. Defense Department, and that strongly recommends that government civil-sector agencies, purchase and use IT products whose security features and properties have been evaluated according to the Common Criteria paradigm. The U.S. Department of Health and Human Services also has issued policies regarding requisite security measures needed when transmitting certain types of healthcare information on the Internet.

49.2.6.2.1   Presidential Decision Directive 63.   In 1998, the U.S. President issued Presidential Decision Directive 63 (PDD 63) as an executive order directing the elimination of vulnerabilities to cyberattacks on critical national infrastructures and to assure the continuity and viability of such infrastructures upon which the nation and its economy depend.[14] Healthcare was specifically cited as one of the most critical infrastructures needing protection from cyberterrorism. More information about PDD 63 is available in Chapter 27.

49.2.6.2.2   National Security Telecommunications and Information Systems Security Committee Policy 11.   In 2000, the representatives of over 20 major agencies in the U.S. federal government jointly issued a government policy directive pertaining to the purchase and use of IT products by these agencies (and by inference to the civil sectors related to these agencies).[15] Acquisition of products evaluated according to the Common Criteria paradigm was either mandated or strongly recommended (depending on the agency) for all U.S. federal departments and agencies, because of the increased trust that the security features of such products have been implemented correctly and that they have been appropriately designed, developed, tested, and delivered. More information about the National Security Telecommunications and Information Systems Security Committee (NSTISSC) Policy 11 is available in Chapter 27.

49.2.6.2.3   Health Care Financing Agency Internet Security Policy.   The Department of Health and Human Services' Health Care Financing Administration (HCFA) issued a policy providing guidelines for the security and appropriate use of the Internet to transmit information that is protected by the HCFA Privacy Act and other sensitive HCFA information.[16] The policy requires that healthcare IT and network systems or processes that transmit or receive sensitive HCFA data via the Internet, or that interface with the Internet for the purpose of conveying sensitive HCFA information, must incorporate security functionality that complies to this policy. Such products or systems include, for example, a hospital's Medicare/Medicaid eligibility and benefits inquiry system, a Medicare/Medicaid claims billing system, or an e-mail system conveying HCFA-sensitive data.

49.2.7   Consortia and Standards Organizations.   Many consortia and standards bodies worldwide are involved in the generation and promotion of standards specifically pertaining to security in the healthcare IT sector. Still others focus on general-purpose IT and networking security standards that can apply across several vertical industry sectors.

49.2.7.1   *Forum on Privacy and Security in Healthcare.* The Forum on Privacy and Security in Healthcare (FPSH) is the premier organization (*www.healthcaresecurity. org*) in the United States focused on promoting and helping to establish industry-wide privacy and security solutions. It provides an environment for the many efforts in healthcare IT security to share technology progress and developments. It also provides a coherent voice on the technology issues of privacy, confidentiality, and security to the industry and to the public.

The FPSH is taking the forefront in identifying and promoting the use of standardized, quantitative measures to establish or to assess the degree of compliance to security laws and regulations such as HIPAA. The FPSH strategy is to bring together healthcare IT vendors, general-purpose IT and networking vendors, healthcare IT consumers, healthcare accrediting bodies, and other pertinent stakeholders, so that emerging IT and networking products will better meet healthcare consumers' needs and comply with HIPAA.

The FPSH is promoting the use of Common Criteria (CC) standards[17] and the Common Criteria Evaluation and Validation Scheme[18] for use in the U.S. healthcare industry. The FPSH sees the CC paradigm (see Chapter 27) as a powerful mechanism for:

- Increasing trust and confidence that IT products comply with HIPAA
- Establishing the healthcare industry's "best practice" to verify and to validate compliance to security laws and regulations
- Providing due diligence evidence about healthcare entities' security solutions

Healthcare industry influencers like the Gartner Group corroborate FPSH views. They, too, recommend using the Common Criteria paradigm as a standard way to document security requirements and as a standard way to specify and undergo third-party testing of security implementations.[19] In particular, as an internationally recognized standard, the CC tends to reduce security costs and legal liabilities that typically are amplified by the haphazard initiatives of a confused marketplace, fractured into responding to the opinions *du jour* of what constitutes adequate security. Also, Gartner indicates that CC-based testing and evaluation of products "is a substantial improvement over the testing practices used by many vendors today [that result in] seriously undertested software."

The FPSH is participating in projects to demonstrate the application of the CC paradigm as a way of mapping healthcare IT security policy to technology requirements, measurement, and compliance. In particular, the FPSH is supporting efforts to specify users' IT security requirements as well as IT product and system security claims, according to the Common Criteria's language and specification formats. It has contributed to efforts to prototype the development of standard healthcare security requirements in terms of CC-based Protection Profiles (PPs).

In one such effort in conjunction with the U.S. Department of Commerce's National Institute of Standards and Technology, the FPSH has supported the development of CC-based, federal regulation–specific, security requirements packages. Any of these packages could be imported as a whole into other more detailed and comprehensive security requirements profiles for healthcare products and systems.

For example, a core package of CC-articulated, security requirements[20] was developed to correspond to DHHS's Health Care Financing Administration Internet security policy.[21] According to the CC paradigm (see Chapter 27) developers who want to claim compliance with the HCFA Internet Security Policy can specify and implement security measures in their products or systems that address the security requirements in the

CC HCFA security functional package.[22] Such product-specific security features are documented in a product-specific CC profile called a Security Target (ST). The developer also can specify, in the ST, the level of confidence (or assurance) that the security features have been designed, developed, implemented, and delivered correctly, completely, according to specifications, and with quality. A commercial security testing laboratory accredited in its knowledge and use of the Common Criteria can then verify that the developer's implementation is in accord both with the CC security functional package and with the developer's level of assurance claims. The security testing laboratory thereby can confirm that the developer's implementation complies—with a specific level of confidence—to the originating HCFA policy. Government oversight bodies, such as the National Information Assurance Partnership (NIAP; *http://niap.nist.gov*) in the United States, can validate the testing efforts of the commercial security testing laboratory and issue CC certificates to products and systems whose security testing has been independently validated by the oversight body. Such CC certificates are yet another independent piece of evidence to enhance trust in tested products even further.

Healthcare accreditation and certification bodies can rely on these CC certificates. The Common Criteria certificates provide a means of gaining assurance that a system developed by a particular vendor for a specific purpose (e.g., use of the Internet for uploading and downloading information protected by the HCFA Privacy Act) does indeed comply with the applicable security regulation or policy (e.g., HCFA Internet Security Policy).

Similar security requirements packages have been prototyped to correspond to the security regulations of HIPAA[23] and have been incorporated into product and system-specific security requirements Protection Profiles, such as that for Admission, Discharge and Transfer (ADT).[24]

Vendors are beginning to embrace CC-specified HIPAA requirements packages and are beginning to show in their product specifications—for example, in their product-specific STs—how such requirements are addressed. Even vendors based outside the United States, who have products that implement solutions to HIPAA requirements profiles, are contemplating security testing of their products by accredited, CC-knowledgeable, testing laboratories. Many see such independent security testing, and the associated issuance of CC certificates, as an enabler for access into the U.S. healthcare market and as one that subsequently can enable sales to other countries.

In conjunction with the National Association of Chain Drug Stores, the FPSH also is exploring how to evaluate the chain pharmacy industry's assessment of risks and levels of security. It is also exploring how to use the Common Criteria paradigm to evaluate the technical security solutions as provided by independent third parties and used by chain pharmacies.

More recently, the FPSH has been investigating the potential use of PKI (Public Key Infrastructure) technologies and concepts by the healthcare industry. PKI has the ability to:

- Provide digital signatures and other associated infrastructure elements such as Certificate Issuing and Management Components.
- Address many of the other HIPAA requirements to protect and authenticate healthcare information exchanges over networks.

PKI often is considered as a primary way to protect and authenticate data exchanged via the Internet, especially as it pertains to the legalities of electronic dealings (see Chapter 23).

The FPSH is looking to examine the various existing PKI issues as they apply to the healthcare industry, and, if appropriate, to stimulate healthcare industry uptake of the PKI Protection Profile (PP) (*csrc.nist.gov/pki/documents/CIMC_PP_20000929-final.pdf*) developed by a consortium of U.S. federal agencies. The PKI PP contains the functional and assurance security requirements for general-purpose PKI with Certificate Issuing and Management Components. These include a Certification Authority component and potentially a Registration Authority component, and others. This PP does not specify the requirements for the client of a PKI, that is, one with general user access.

A Canadian CC security testing laboratory is exploring strategies as to how to test healthcare systems integrating: (1) solutions that address PKI requirements such as specified in the PKI PP, and (2) PKI enabling solutions, such as smart card or biometric devices, that address authentication requirements.

The FPSH also provides an electronic newsletter, which is one of the more widely circulated periodicals pertaining to healthcare security and privacy. The FPSH is a leader in this field, especially with regard to establishing trust about product and system compliance to HIPAA. All healthcare stakeholders should stay abreast of FPSH activities.

49.2.7.2   Other Consortia.   In the United States, many other organizations, such as the North Carolina Healthcare Information and Communications Alliance Inc. (*www.nchica.org*) and the Workgroup for Electronic Data Interchange (*www.wedi.org*) are providing leadership and advocacy in helping the healthcare industry capitalize on the business improvements HIPAA can bring. The Strategic National Implementation Process (SNIP) is looking to stimulate a nationally coordinated industry solution to the practical issues surrounding the implementation of the HIPAA standards. SNIP is being fostered by the association of Blue Cross and Blue Shield insurance providers, with the participation of the government's Medicare and Medicaid programs.

Other, more technology-specific, consortia such as the Smart Card Forum (*www.smartcardforum.org/aboutscf/wglist.htm*) also have working groups that focus on applications and solutions of their technology to specific healthcare security challenges.

Many industry events, workshops and conferences continue to help educate healthcare community about HIPAA and its ramifications.[25]

49.2.7.3   Nonmandatory (External) Imperatives—BS7799/ISO 17799.   BS7799, "Code of Practice for Information Security Management Systems," on whose objectives the *Information Management and Technology (IM&T) Manual* was based, has replaced that document as the basis of healthcare security in the U.K. National Health Service. BS7799 has been taken up by the International Standards Organization (ISO) and is the basis for the ISO 17799 standard.

The 1995 version of BS7799 includes 10 key controls:

1. A written policy document universally available
2. Explicit definition of responsibilities for protecting assets and implementing security measures
3. Precautions against computer viruses
4. Protection of organizational records from loss, destruction, and falsification
5. Data protection compliance
6. Business continuity

7. User education

8. Establishment of channels to report security incidents

9. Respect of copyright

10. Regular review of compliance with organizational security policy and standards

The 1998 revision of BS7799 differs in two main respects from the earlier version. First, it addresses the issue of compliance certification, and stresses the importance of independent certification. It also places less importance on the idea of key controls, although the controls described within the document are essentially the same. The National Health Service is now committed to BS7799 compliance, but not to independent certification.

49.3   INTERNAL DRIVERS.   The preceding imperatives drive the internal policies, procedures, and protocols to be considered next.

In the United Kingdom, the National Health Service's *IM&T Security Manual,* and the more recent *Executive Security and Data Protection Programme's Resource Pack,* address issues such as:

- The assessment of NHS systems for security
- Conformance with the tripartite security model described previously
- Awareness of all staff of their security roles and responsibilities
- Communicating security awareness

This is done in the context of a security architecture that relies on the cooperation of national management, local management, security professionals (IM&T Security Officers at the same organizational level as local managers), and a network of organizational guardians. These last are known as Caldicott Guardians (after the committee that proposed them), and are concerned with the use of patient-identifiable information according to the principles summarized in Exhibit 49.6.

Documents such as the NHS Code of Connection, the NHS-wide Networking Security Policy, and the Data networking security policy identify specific technical issues.

49.4   DIFFICULTIES IN IMPLEMENTING COUNTERMEASURES.   All of the normal countermeasures that are described elsewhere in this handbook should be considered in the medical context. However, specific issues affect security in the medical context. M.E. Kabay notes a number of problems to some extent unique to healthcare:

Exhibit 49.6   The Caldicott Principles

1. Justify the purpose(s). The use and transfer of data must be clearly defined, scrutinized, and periodically reviewed by the guardian.
2. Do not use patient-identifiable data unless absolutely necessary.
3. Use the minimum necessary patient-identifiable information—each item to be justified to reduce identifiability.
4. Access to patient-identifiable information should be on a strict need-to-know basis.
5. Everyone should be aware of their responsibilities.
6. Understand and comply with the law.

- Failure of access control procedures. The need for urgent data retrieval results in a reluctance to log on and off every time information is accessed.

- The reluctance to log out permits everyone to use the same account, that of the first person to access the terminal. This in turn results in a total inability to follow audit trails, since there is no way to distinguish between individuals using the same account. Kabay suggests a number of alternative identification/authentication strategies that might ease this problem: smart cards and biometrics, for example.

- Psychological resistance to restricted access measures in academic or team-motivated environments.

- Increased vulnerability to interception and removal of data.

- Lack of resources to meet information security requirements.[26]

49.5   U.K. RESOURCES

Anderson, R.J. "Security in Clinical Information Systems" (1996): *www.cl.cam.ac.uk/ users/rja14/policy11/policy11.html* and in PDF at *www.cl.cam.ac.uk/ftp/users/rja14/ policy11.pdf.*

Anderson, R.J. "An Update on the BMA Security Policy" (1996): *www.cl.cam.ac.uk/users/ rja14/bmaupdate/bmaupdate.html* and in PDF at *www.cl.cam.ac.uk/ftp/users/rja14/ bmaupdate.pdf.*

Anderson, R.J. "Information Technology in Medical Practice: Safety and Privacy Lessons from the United Kingdom" (1998): *www.cl.cam.ac.uk/users/rja14/austmedjour/austmedjour.html.*

Data Protection Act 1998 (came into force March 1, 2000): *www.hmso.gov.uk/acts/acts1998/ 19980029.htm.*

"The Data Protection Act 1998: An Introduction": *www.dataprotection.gov.uk/eurotalk.htm.*

Department of Health Circulars: *www.doh.gov.uk/coinh.htm.*

Department of Trade and Industry, Medical Systems Industry page: *www.dti.gov.uk/sectors/ healthcare.htm.*

"Ensuring Security and Confidentiality in NHS Organisations." Information Security Resource Pack: *www.standards.nhsia.nhs.uk/sdp/resource/index.htm.*

For the Protection of Individuals with Regard to the Processing of Personal Data and the Free Movement of Such Data. EU Directive, July 24, 1995.

"Guide to the Practical Implementation of the Data Protection Act 1998" (DISC PD 0012 1999): *www.bsi.org.uk/pd12*

"The Guidelines: The Data Protection Act 1984": *www.dataprotection.gov.uk/dpr/guide.htm.*

Handbook of Information Security: Information Security within General Practice: www.secu-rity.nhsia.nhs.uk/library/cards/c0000360.htm

Health Service Guideline: The Protection and Use of Patient Information: *www.doh.gov.uk/ nhsexipu/confiden/protect/hsg9618.htm*

National Health Service Executive: *www.doh.gov.uk/nhs.htm.*

Play IT Safe: A Practical Guide to IT Security for Everyone Working in General Practice: www.security.nhsia.nhs.uk/resource/pk1/safe/home.htm and *www.security.nhsia.nhs.uk/ resource/pk1/safe/safe.zip.*

"The Protection and Use of Patient Information—Guidance from the Department of Health": *www.doh.gov.uk/nhsexipu/confiden/protect/pguide.htm.*

The NHS Executive Information Management Group has produced a range of documents on the NHSnet, including the following:

- Next Steps towards NHS-wide networking (ref. E5120)
- A strategy for NHS-wide Networking (ref. E5155)
- NHS-wide Networking Programme (ref. E5216)

- Data Network Security Policy (ref. E5221)
- Code of Connection for NHS Organisations (ref. E5222)
- Code of Connection for non-NHS Organisations (ref. E5223)

You can order any of these documents, or find out the full range, by contacting:

Department of Health, PO Box 410, Wetherby, West Yorkshire LS23 7LN, UK. *Tel:* +(44)(0)1937-840-250; *Fax:* 01937-845-381

49.6   U.S. RESOURCES

AHIMA (American Health Information Management Association) *Information Security Resource Page: www.ahima.org/hot.topics/info.security.html.*

California Healthcare Foundation eHealth Reports: *http://ehealth.chcf.org.*

Dick, R.S., E.B. Steen, and D.E. Detmer , eds. *The Computer-Based Patient Record: An Essential Technology for Health Care, Revised Edition.* Washington, DC: National Academy Press, 1996.

Donaldson, M.S., and K.N. Lohr , eds. *Health Data in the Information Age: Use, Disclosure, and Privacy.* Committee on Regional Health Data Networks, Institute of Medicine. Washington, DC: National Academy Press, 1994.

Field, M.J., ed. *Telemedicine: A Guide to Assessing Telecommunications for Health Care.* Committee on Evaluating Clinical Applications of Telemedicine, Institute of Medicine. Washington, DC: National Academy Press, 1996.

Forum on Privacy and Security in Healthcare: *www.healthcaresecurity.org.*

Health Privacy Project of the Institute for Health Care Research and Policy, Georgetown University: *www.healthprivacy.org.*

JCAHO (Joint Commission on Accreditation of Healthcare Organizations) Standards Page: *www.jcaho.org/standards_frm.html.*

Winker, MA., et al. "Guidelines for Medical and Health Information Sites on the Internet." *Journal of the American Medical Association* 283, no. 12 (2000); *http://jama.ama-assn. org/issues/v283n12/ffull/jsc00054.html.*

49.7   NOTES

1. *informationweek.com/794/security.htm.*

2. L. Lorton, "When Is the Patient's Desire for Privacy, Not?" *www.hipaadvisory. com/views/pinion/index.htm;* The HIPAAdvisory Web Site: *www.hipaadvisory.com,* Phoenix Health Systems, October 2000.

3. Confidentiality of Medical Records: National Survey. Princeton Survey Associates for the California Health Care Foundation: *http://admin.chcf.org/documents/ehealth/survey.pdf.*

4. "The Protection and Use of Patient Information—Guidance from the Department of Health," *www.doh.gov.uk/nhsexipu/confiden/protect/pguide.htm.*

5. Health Insurance Portability and Accountability Act of 1996, P.L. 104-191, 104th Congress, August 21, 1996: *http://thomas.loc.gov/cgi-bin/bdquery/z?d104:HR03103:|TOM:/bs.*

6. Mary Beth Johnston, "HIPAA Privacy and Security Standards." Memorandum from Wimble, Carlyle, Sandbridge & Rice, Durham, NC, January 2000: *www.nchica.org/activities/ HIPAA/HIPAA%20for%20NCHICA.doc.*

7. For a partial bibliography, see *www.smed.com/hipaa/news.php, www.nchica.org/ activities/HIPAA/HIPAA_links.html,* and *www.aha.org/hipaa/links.asp.*

8. Department of Health and Human Services, Office of the Secretary, "Security and Electronic Signature Standards, Proposed Rule," 45 CFR (Code of Federal Regulation) Part 142, [HCFA-0049-P], RIN 0938-AI57, *The Federal Register,* Vol. 63, No. 155, August 12, 1998, pp. 43242–43280: *http://erm.aspe.hhs.gov/ora_web/plsql/erm_rule.rule?user_id = &rule_id = 62.*

9. Ibid., Parts 160 through 164, RIN 0991-AB08, *The Federal Register,* Vol. 64, No. 212, November 3, 1999, pp. 59918–60065; *http://erm.aspe.hhs.gov/ora_web/plsql/erm_rule.rule?*

user_id = &*rule_id* = *228;* as modified by technical amendments posted in *The Federal Register,* Vol. 65, No. 3, January 5, 2000, pp. 427–429; *http://spe.os.dhhs.gov/admnsimp/nprm/000105fr.htm.*

10. Check *http://aspe.hhs.gov/admnsimp* for the contents of the final rules or to sign up for a list-serve through which to be notified when significant HIPAA regulations are published.

11. *www.cis.utulsa.edu/tisw2000.*

12. *www.healthcarebusiness.com/archives/healthcarebusiness/0599/60.html.*

13. Paul Brusil, Don Marks, and Helen Shaw, "Critical Telecommunications Infrastructures Demand Security—A Report of the Telecommunications and Information Security Workshop (TISW), *Journal of Network and Systems Management,* Vol. 9, No. 1, March 2001, pp. 113–120.

14. Bill Clinton, "The Clinton Administration's Policy on Critical Infrastructure Protection," Presidential Decision Directive/NSC-63, PDD 63, The White House, Washington, DC, May 22, 1998; *www.ciao.gov/CIAO_Document_Library/paper598.html.*

15. National Security Telecommunications and Information Systems Security Committee (NSTISSC), "National Security Telecommunications and Information Systems Security Policy (NSTISSP) No. 11; National Information Assurance Acquisition Policy," NSTISSC Secretariat, National Security Agency, 9800 Savage Road STE 6716, Ft. Meade, MD, January 2000; *www.nstissc.gov/Assets/pdf/nstissp11.pdf.*

16. "Internet Communications Security and Appropriate Use Policy and Guidelines for HCFA Privacy Act-Protected and Other Sensitive HCFA Information," U.S. Department of Health and Human Services, Office of Information Services, HCFA, Division of HCFA Enterprise Standards—Internet, 7500 Security Blvd., Baltimore, MD., November 24, 1998; *www.hcfa.gov/security/isecplcy.htm.*

17. "Common Criteria for Information Technology Security Evaluation," Version 2, ISO/IEC International Standard (IS) 15408-1 through 15408-3, ISO/IEC JTC1 SC27 WG3, 1999; *http://csrc.nist.gov/cc/ccv20/ccv2list.htm.*

18. "Common Criteria Evaluation and Validation Scheme for Information Technology Security—Organization, Management and Concept of Operations (Draft)," Version 1, NIAP (a joint NIST NSA initiative), *http://niap.nist.gov,* Department of Commerce, National Institute of Standards and Technology, Computer Security Division, Room 426, NN, 100 Bureau Drive, Mail Stop 8930, Gaithersburg, MD 20899-8930, August 1998 (or succeeding versions). Available at *http://niap.nist.gov/schemeCC.html.*

19. W. Rishel, "ISO 15408 for Healthcare Security and Privacy Standards," Research Note, Technology T-10-4415, Gartner Group, Inc., March 2, 2000; and W. Rishel, "ISO 15408 for Security and Privacy in Healthcare," Research Note, Technology T-10-5507, Gartner Group, Inc., March 2, 2000.

20. Ramaswamy Chandramouli, "Security Functional Package for Systems Transmitting Sensitive HCFA Data (STS-HCFA)," Version 1.0, National Institute of Standards and Technology, 100 Bureau Drive, Gaithersburg, MD, August 3, 1999; *www.healthcaresecurity.org/documents/iso_iec_15408_fp_hcfa.doc.*

21. "Internet Communications Security and Appropriate Use Policy and Guidelines for HCFA Privacy Act-Protected and other Sensitive HCFA Information." U.S. Department of Health and Human Services, Office of Information Services, HCFA, Division of HCFA Enterprise Standards–Internet, 7500 Security Blvd., Baltimore, MD, November 24, 1998: *www.hcfa.gov/security/isecplcy.htm.*

22. "Protection Profile for Healthcare Provider Intranet with Limited Internet Exposure." ATR: 99043. Version 1.0, Claire Barrett, Diann Carpenter, Lisa Gallagher, and Noelle Hardy; Arca Systems, September 7, 1999; *www.healthcaresecurity.org/documents/system_level_protection_profile.doc.*

23. Ibid.

24. Ramaswamy Chandramouli, "ADT PP," National Institute of Standards and Technology, 100 Bureau Drive, Gaithersburg, MD.

25. Partial listings of other organizations and events involved with HIPAA and its implementation can be found at *www.smed.com/hipaa/news.php, www.nchica.org/activities/ HIPAA/HIPAA_links.html,* and *www.aha.org/hipaa/links.asp.*

26. M.E. Kabay, "Educating the Medical Community about Medical Information Security." ICSA White Paper, 1998; see *www.trusecure.com/html/whitepaper_index.shtml* for current URL.

CHAPTER 50

USING ENCRYPTION INTERNATIONALLY

Diane E. Levine

CONTENTS

50.1 INTRODUCTION. Because cryptography can be used not only to protect information from criminals and spies but also to protect criminals' and spies' information from lawful government and law enforcement authorities, it is a controversial technology in many countries around the world. Government restrictions generally are imposed to protect the country and its citizens from perceived threats to their security. Many governments control the development and use of encryption and cryptography products internally and limit the export of such products. Totalitarian regimes, in particular, fear the consequences of private communications among their people; such governments are particularly keen to limit the use of cryptography.

With the widespread use of the Internet, the growing popularity of e-commerce, and the revenues that are at stake, encryption has taken on a new and enhanced significance throughout the world.

This chapter reviews some of the national standards and legislation on the use and export of encryption software, hardware, and technology and provides guidelines for the use of this technology across national borders.

50.2   TERMINOLOGY.   Encryption is a science with specific terminology. *Plaintext* refers to the unaltered, easily readable text that is used to relay messages. A *cipher* is a system where symbols or groups of symbols representing plaintext are scrambled or rearranged so that the message becomes difficult to interpret. *Ciphertext* refers to encrypted plaintext. *Encryption* is the process of converting plaintext into ciphertext using an *encryption algorithm*. *Decryption* converts ciphertext back into plaintext. *Algorithms* are sets of mathematical rules that are used during the process of encryption and decryption. Encryption and decryption confer security through one or more unique, controlled or secret sets of data called *keys*. The number of possible keys of a particular length is the *keyspace*. Encryption can be implemented through software and by hardware. Systems that use the same key to decrypt and encrypt are called *symmetric cryptosystems*. Systems that use one key to encrypt and a separate key to decrypt are called *asymmetric systems*. The most important asymmetric encryption system is the *Public Key Cryptosystem* in which two keys are generated at the same time for any given user; one is kept secret (the *private* key) and the other is made known to anyone who needs it (the *public* key). The Public Key Cryptosystem can be used to generate unique *digital signatures* that assure the origin and integrity of signed messages.

Refer to Tutorial 4 for a more in-depth discussion of encryption.

50.3   USE OF ENCRYPTION INTERNATIONALLY.   Anyone planning to use encryption should know the local regulations that control such technology. In some parts of the world, failing to heed national laws on using or exporting cryptographic tools may land a company in legal difficulties or a traveler in prison. One of the most important influences on international regulation of cryptography is the Wassenaar Arrangement, described later in this chapter.

50.3.1   United States.   It has never been illegal to use any cryptography within the United States, nor for transmission or reception of encrypted messages out of or into the this country. However, there have been attempts to control some aspects of domestic cryptography usage to help law enforcement agencies interpret encrypted communications during wiretaps.

Key escrow involves storing either entire keys or portions of keys with one or more *escrow agents*. Under judicial compulsion (warrants), the escrow agent would surrender the decryption key only for use by law enforcement or other judicially mandated function. In the business world, it is useful to have extra keys to unlock encrypted information when the employee, or former employee, who has the normal decryption key is unavailable; such commercial applications of the key escrow principle generally are known as *key recovery* systems.

By the early 1990s, encryption no longer required expensive special hardware; anyone with a personal computer could encrypt e-mail using free software such as Pretty Good Privacy (PGP). Law enforcement agencies expressed concern about the impossibility of decrypting such encrypted communications among lawbreakers, such as organized crime and pedophile rings.

In April 1993, the Clinton administration floated a proposal for key escrow that became known as the *Clipper Chip Initiative*. The theory was that the government would require all government employees transmitting sensitive, but not classified, communications to use specially equipped telecommunications equipment. This proposed new technology for phones, fax machines, and modems would use SKIPJACK, a secret algorithm developed by the National Security Agency (NSA). Cryptographers generally frown on secret algorithms because it is more difficult to be sure of how strongly resistant to cryptanalysis they are. SKIPJACK would be implemented in a special microchip called the Clipper Chip; the important feature was that Clipper would automatically encrypt communications using the Law Enforcement Access Field (LEAF), a unique key for each chip that would be stored in two pieces by two unspecified agencies of the U.S. government.

Under warrant, law enforcement or other authorized agencies could request that the two parts of the LEAF be extracted from escrow and recombined to allow decryption of specific encrypted communications among suspects.

Public reaction was not favorable. Technical objections from the cryptography community criticized the secret algorithms and demonstrated weaknesses; other analysts complained about the practical difficulties of secure key escrow. Many commentators predicted that if the Clipper Initiative were implemented, the government would press for universal installation of the Clipper Chip in all consumer communications electronics.

Although in 1996 Vice President Al Gore was enthusiastic about establishing a key-recovery policy to enable Americans to use stronger encryption products both in the United States and abroad, there were significant concerns about the complexity, scalability, and legality of implementing this technology. Similar concerns arose regarding the key-escrow legislation policy advocated by William Reinsch, then Undersecretary for Export Administration at the U.S. Department of Commerce.

Reinsch envisioned a worldwide standard for key escrow, theorizing that if the use of key escrow became pervasive in international commerce, criminals, including terrorists, would be forced to use cryptography that included key recovery systems. At the time he suggested this policy, stringent export regulations were still in place in the United States and there was a fear that U.S. companies would relocate overseas in order to avoid the U.S. escrow requirements. Eventually the Reinsch proposals were abandoned.

As business requirements changed and use of the Internet and e-commerce expanded, the regulations in place proved to be limiting and prohibitive in regard to permitting U.S. companies to be competitive. Recognizing that change was needed, Representative Robert Goodlatte (R-VA) introduced the Security and Freedom Through Encryption (SAFE) Act, or H.R. 850, in February 1997. SAFE was geared to relax export regulations on selected encryption products. More important, SAFE would permit U.S. citizens to use encryption of any strength, anywhere in the world, and prohibited the U.S. government from creating any back doors or mandatory key escrow in U.S. citizens' computer systems. While it created criminal penalties for the use of cryptography in the crimes, it also prohibited all federal government agencies from mandating access codes that could be used to decipher encrypted data. In March 1997, the SAFE Act, with more than 250 cosponsors, passed without amendments through the U.S. House of Representatives Judiciary Subcommittee on Courts and Intellectual Property.

With the movement to relax encryption export regulations gaining momentum and increased Internet usage and e-commerce becoming a way of life, in April 1999 the Promote Reliable On-Line Transactions to Encourage Commerce and Trade (PRO-TECT) Act was introduced. As stated in the act, its purposes were to promote the widespread use of encryption and electronic growth that would foster e-commerce, create consumer confidence in e-commerce, meet the needs of individuals and businesses using electronic networks, prevent crime, and improve national security. By doing this, the act was geared to assisting the U.S. government and its agencies in developing technical capabilities that could be used to respond to new technological challenges. In June, 1999, in the U.S. Senate, the Committee on Commerce, Science, and Transportation passed S.798, the PROTECT Act, a bill to promote electronic commerce. The bill would do the following:

1. Direct the National Institute of Standards and Technology (NIST) to complete the establishment of an advanced encryption standard by January 1, 2002.

2. Allow for immediate exportation of encryption of key lengths up to 64 bits.

3. Permit the exportation of non-defense encryption, above 64 bits, to responsible entities and governments of North Atlantic Treaty Organization (NATO), Association of Southeast Asian Nations (ASEAN), and Organization for Economic Cooperation and Development (OECD).

4. Allow for liberalization of export controls for encryption by creating an Encryption Export Advisory Board to review applications for exemption of encryption of over 64 bits, and to give recommendations to the Secretary of Commerce.

The bill was then passed by the full Commerce Committee.

In June 1999, the House Subcommittee on Telecommunications voted against an amendment to the SAFE Act that would guarantee the federal government access to the plaintext version of any encrypted communications or computer file. This amendment, which would have imposed restrictions on encryption within the United States for the first time in history, did not go over well with the public or the government.

In September 1999, President Clinton issued a public letter addressed to the Congress, pushing for passage of the Cyberspace Electronic Security Act of 1999 (CESA), which simultaneously deregulates most encryption software exports and provides for key escrow accessible to law enforcement agencies under warrant. In mid-November, the Clinton administration began circulating its revised proposal for new cryptographic export controls. However, according to critics and proponents of unregulated crypto exports, the actual proposals were far less liberal than original indications back in September. In particular, the export regulations continued to enforce license reviews for sales of cryptographic software and hardware to governments overseas.

In January 2000, the Clinton administration finally gave up on the U.S. government's futile attempts to restrict exports of strong encryption. Henceforth, only crypto sales to foreign governments or military would require U.S. government authorization. What the State Department terms "rogue nations" would still be on the forbidden list: Iran, Iraq, Libya, Syria, Sudan, North Korea, and Cuba.

In an about-face in February 2000, the U.S. government said it would allow computer scientist Daniel Bernstein to post the source code for his Snuffle encryption software on his Web site. This reversal of years of legal action followed a ruling by a federal district court that in light of the new, liberalized encryption software export restrictions implemented in January, Bernstein should be able to post his code.

In April 2000, a federal appeals court in Ohio ruled that encryption software code is protected by the First Amendment. The court decided that encryption algorithms and programs are a means of communication between computer programmers and therefore protected as free speech.

50.3.2   Canada.   Canada currently has no domestic regulations or restrictions on cryptography and follows export regulations dating to the pre-1998 Wassenaar Arrangement. The Wassenaar Arrangement received final approval in July 1996 from the 33 founding countries. It was designed to prevent the acquisition of armaments and sensitive dual-use (civilian and military) items for military end use, in the event that the situation in any region, or the actions of any state, become a serious cause of concern to its member states. The members maintain an agreed list of items over which they undertake to exercise effective export controls. Cryptographic technology and related products are generally considered to be included on the Export Control List.

During a 12-month trial period begun in December 1996, Canada granted export of 56-bit cryptography to most countries and then extended the trial period. Excluded from export controls are mass-market and public domain software.

Although the United States and Canada freely transport cryptography across their border, any cryptography imported from the United States and not included on the Export Control List remains under U.S. export rules and regulations. Even though public domain and mass-market software can be freely exported, any dual-use products that contain U.S.- origin restricted products must be accompanied by qualifying paperwork.

In October 1998, Industry Minister John Manley reaffirmed the Canadian government's commitment to the Wassenaar Agreement but stated that in its new cryptography policy, the Canadian government would consider the export practices of other countries. Additionally, the new policy streamlined the export-permit process and included the issuing of multiuser permits for many products, users, or destinations, after a one-time review.

Canada is advancing quickly in the use of a Public Key Infrastructure (PKI) throughout its federal agencies and departments. The PKI regulates certification and distribution of cryptographic keys used for encryption and for digital signatures. To accomplish this, the government set definite goals and dates by which PKI must be implemented in various sectors, such as the health agencies; the various agencies and departments have worked hard to keep to the schedule.

50.3.3   United Kingdom.   Within the United Kingdom (UK), export is controlled jointly with the European Union's (EU) dual-use regulation (SI 1996/2721) and the Wassenaar Arrangement preceding 1998. These controls include the export of crypto software to other EU member states. However, crypto export over the Internet, referred to as "by intangible means," is free of controls because the export regulations do not cover it. The requirement for this free export is that it not be sent to any embargoed countries and that it conform to the Official Secrets Act. To be on the safe side, most companies, at the urging of the Department of Trade and Industry (DTI) consult a lawyer and apply for an export license. A paper released by the DTI entitled "Strategic Export Controls" proposes an extension of the current export controls to the Internet and any other intangible transfers.[1] These regulations would also affect exports by e-mail and fax.

A personal-use exemption exists for "anyone who wishes to export cryptographic systems for use with personal computers or laptop computers for their own use to do so. The goods must accompany the user." This exemption is available through the

Open General Export License of January 20, 1998, but does not include the export of crypto products for online voice communication.

There has been a long-time movement within the United Kingdom and the DTI to remove or lift export controls for approved products. Alternatively, the government may keep the export controls in place but simplify the export process. The DTI has further committed itself to working on updating and streamlining export controls internationally.

The Regulation of Investigatory Powers Act 2000 (RIPA) contains the power to order disclosure in cases where encrypted data is involved. The power can be assigned or given under very specific circumstances. Accompanying the power is a prison term of up to two years for anyone who deliberately fails to comply with the order. Part III of RIPA also provides additional punishments for specific acts in violation of the regulations; it also provides safeguards to be invoked and considered by government officials who order disclosure.

In 1999, the United Kingdom rejected all key recovery solutions presented to the government and various committees. The UK appears diametrically opposed to the solution proposed by the United States.

50.3.4   France.   With the exception of the General Software Note, France signed the Wassenaar Arrangement for export controls. The law of July 26, 1996, and the decrees of 1998 and 1999 regulate imports and exports of cryptography from countries outside the European Union and the European Economic Area (EEA). Import within the EU/EEA is free.

The 1999 decrees define exactly which categories of cryptography do and do not require prior declaration. Arrangements have been made to permit a user declaration to serve as an export declaration in the case where cryptography is used solely for an individual's personal use.

France has always had extremely strict laws regulating the domestic use and supply of cryptography. Although slightly liberalized in 1996 when a law was passed mandating key deposits with Trusted Third Parties (TTPs), true liberalization did not occur until 1999. During this liberalization, the use of cryptography of up to 128 bits was allowed, raised from 40 bits. The mandatory nature of key deposits with TTPs was abolished, and legislation is being enacted requiring people to hand over the plaintext of encrypted documents when requested by the judiciary. It would appear that turning over purported cleartext without decryption from ciphertext could not ensure an accurate version.

The French government and all related organizations dealing in cryptography have maintained their aversion to key recovery as a bona fide cryptography restraint or solution. As recently as 1999, the French government turned down the plan proposed by the United States.

50.3.5   Germany.   There are no domestic laws and regulations regarding cryptography in Germany. Export is regulated within the constraints of the EU regulation and the Wassenaar Agreement as amended by the General License Number 16, in effect since September 1999.

In June 1999, the German government announced "Eckpunkte der deutschen Kryptopolitik" elaborating five cornerstones of the German crypto policy. The cornerstones state that:

1. The German government will not restrict the availability of cryptography and will support the spread of secure encryption within the nation.

2. The government is actively involved in establishing a framework for trust for secure encryption, and values the developers and manufacturers of secure crypto products.

3. The German government intends to closely monitor crypto developments and issue a report in two years, while encouraging and assisting law enforcement and security agencies within the country to accept and use secure encryption.

4. The German government announced it would advocate market-driven, open standards and interoperable systems.

While maintaining control over the export of encryption via the EU regulation and the Wassenaar Arrangement, the Germans have remained steadfast in their opposition to all proposed key recovery schemes including those suggested by the U.S. government.

50.3.6   Other European Union Countries.   The EU countries have a regulation in force since July 1995 that regulates the export of dual-use goods, including cryptography. Judgements of October 1995 by the European Court of Justice have reinforced the fact that the European Community has exclusive jurisdiction in these matters.

Generally speaking, countries within the EU make their own decision regarding whether a product falls within the mass-market crypto category that only requires a general license. Although not required to declare anything specifically, exporters must be able to justify and document their exports when requested.

In some very specific instances where military applications are involved, the government must approve the export of any crypto products. Without that approval, the products cannot be exported.

According to the regulation, a license is required for the export of crypto software outside of the EU, excluding all mass-market and public domain software. Friendly countries such as Australia, Canada, Japan, New Zealand, Norway, Switzerland, and the United States require fewer license procedures than other countries, and there is a license procedure for intra-EU trade of all encryption products.

Due to the EU's Dual-Use Regulation, which leaves room for individual national implementation of encryption licensing, a number of individual domestic licensing schemes and procedures exist. The European Council decided to accept the December 1998 amendments to the Wassenaar Arrangement in March 1999, and those amendments have been in effect since April 1999. The result of this adoption is that mass-market crypto can now be exported within the EU on a general license, without restrictions on key length.

50.3.7   People's Republic of China.   Import and export of encryption products require a license from the State Encryption Management Commission according to State Council Order No. 273, "Commercial Use Password Management Regulations." In effect since October 9, 1999, according to the government, this State Council Order applies only to hardware and software that have encryption and decryption as core functions. The regulations do not entail key escrow and exempt all cryptography products where the cryptography is built in.

In January 2000, the Chinese government tried to get all foreign companies to register the type of encryption they were using. New rules also forbade Chinese companies from using foreign cryptographic software. Interpreted narrowly, such rules would hamper further development of Internet commerce in that country, but only a handful of people showed up to register.

50.3.8   Myanmar (Burma).   In Myanmar, the totalitarian regime (SLORC, the State Law and Order Restoration Committee) can restrict import and export of cryptography based on the Computer Science Development Law (SLORC Law No. 10/96) from September 1996. This law allows the Myanmar Computer Science Development Council to proscribe software and information that are not permitted for import or export. Penalties for violation of this law may include a jail sentence of five to 10 years.

As of the current time, crypto import and export appear to be unrestricted because the SLORC has not promulgated either a permission or a prohibition.

50.3.9   Gulf States.   Disclosure of any information from the Gulf States is difficult to obtain. Sources report that in Saudi Arabia there are no import or export controls on crypto products; it is also reported, but not verified, that internally, the use of encryption is prohibited.

50.3.10   Turkey.   Turkey regulates its import and export of cryptographic software according to the Wassenaar Arrangement and controls, including the General Software Note. If there are restrictions, the Turkish government is not openly declaring them. While restrictions may certainly exist, their nature is generally unknown until they are actually encountered.

50.3.11   Former Soviet Union.   The former Soviet Union is now broken into separate nations that have their own individual governments and policies. In order to understand what is happening in the former Soviet Union, it is necessary to look at each country individually.

Russia imposes the restriction of a license in order to import encryption facilities manufactured abroad. Export of cryptography is done under tight state control. Although it signed the Wassenaar Arrangement, Russia uses regulations that are much more stringent.

When he was in office, President Boris Yeltsin issued a decree prohibiting unauthorized encryption. Encryption used by state organizations and enterprises requires a license for both transmission and storage. Businesses that use uncertified cryptography do not receive state orders. All required licenses are issued by a former KGB department now known as the Federal Bureau for Government Information (FAPSI) and are issued based on internal regulations.

The Ukraine signed the Wassenaar Arrangement, and export controls are regulated according to the pre-December 1998 regulations and General Software Note.

50.3.12   Israel.   Israel is noted for the development of many security products, including encryption products and antivirus software. Export of crypto products and technology require a license from the director-general of the Ministry of Defense. Licenses are granted on an individual basis, and there is no specific limit on key size. Strong encryption is widely used within Israel, and licenses appear to be easily obtained. A number of laws pertain to the regulation of cryptography internally, but there is no history of any prosecution for using unlicensed crypto products.

50.3.13   Japan.   Decisions for export licenses are made on an individual basis, and export controls have been tightened. This restriction is due to a change in attitude on the part of the government, which is in the process of deciding whether it considers encryption to be a threat to law enforcement or national security. In its wiretapping law, law enforcement is permitted to record all communications, including any encryption that makes eavesdropping difficult.

50.3.14   The Netherlands.   Although the Netherlands follows the pre-December 1998 Wassenaar rules, they do not apply to export through electronic means or export to Belgium or Luxembourg. Internally, if, during a house search, a home computer is found to contain encrypted material, the police can order anyone with encryption knowledge, including the suspect, to decrypt the information.

The Dutch have consistently attempted to restrict having, using, or trading strong cryptography, and this has resulted in demonstrations and protests, causing proposed legislation to be withdrawn. It is acknowledged that the judicial authorities fear the dissemination of strong cryptography and favor a key-escrow scheme. The Computer Crime Act II of 1999 gives new power to law enforcement by establishing that if the police encounter encryption in a wiretap, they can actually order the conversants to assist in decrypting the recording. The government is currently working on a policy for Trusted Third Parties (TTPs), which it expects to implement through a government project called TTP.NL, a joint venture between government and industry.

50.4   EXPORT REGULATIONS

50.4.1   United States.   Since the days of Julius Caesar, cryptography has been used to encipher and decipher military messages. Because the primary market for encryption products was for diplomatic, military, and intelligence use, the National Security Agency had primary responsibility for regulating cryptography until the 1970s. Most of the regulatory controls were derived from two major items of legislation: the Arms Export Control Act (AECA) of 1949 and the Export Administration Act (EAA). Categorizing cryptography with "munitions," the U.S. government heavily regulated the export of the technology and related products through the International Traffic in Arms Regulations (ITAR). These controls were a controversial mainstay of the national cryptography policy of the United States.

Until the signing of the relaxed restrictions regarding the export of strong encryption products, although the United States had signed the Wassenaar Arrangement, it generally imposed stricter controls. The recent relaxation came about, in part, because of public outcry that the United States could not remain competitive in the field without permitting the export of strong encryption software with 128-bit keys. The United States has always held tight control of encryption.

50.4.1.1   International Traffic in Arms Regulations.   The ITAR were administered by the Department of State. The ITAR allowed unrestricted export of "strong" encryption (encryption using a key length of more than 40 bits) to Canada but required government approval for exports to other countries. Certain countries were not permitted to receive U.S. encryption products at all: Cuba, Iran, Iraq, Libya, North Korea, Sudan, and Syria. For relatively strong encryption products, ITAR generally issued a license only to foreign branches of American enterprises or financial institutions. Weak cryptography that had a limited maximum key length also could be exported.

U.S. users and makers of cryptography products complained that the ITAR was an unnecessary impediment to trade and to secure business communications. Getting permission for export was a cumbersome process with secret rules and apparently arbitrary decisions. Competitors overseas produced and sold strong encryption products to the detriment of U.S. market share.

In February 1996, the ITAR rules were amended in regard to personal use of cryptography, exempting the temporary personal use of products from requiring a license, based on the exporter taking precautions to ensure the security of the product and maintaining records for five years.

50.4.1.2   *Export Administration Regulations.*

In 1996, responsibility for cryptographic export controls passed from the Department of State to the Department of Commerce. Under the Export Administration Regulations (EAR), restrictions on cryptography exports were eased, especially for transborder data flows in multinational corporations.

Also in 1996, 33 countries agreed to limit the arms trade, including most cryptography. This Wassenaar Arrangement, of which the United States is a founding member, was used in 1998 by the Department of Commerce in its revised export regulations. Further details are presented elsewhere in this chapter.

The Export Administration Regulations have undergone considerable changes and modifications since they became responsible for the export of cryptography. The EAR was already responsible for the export of cryptography that served only authentication or integrity purposes.

In October 1996, Vice President Gore announced the relaxation of the cryptography export policy to favor the export of data-recovery cryptography. The Commerce Department issued the Export Administrative Regulations draft in December 1996. Crypto export decisions including those of the Department of Justice and the Department of Commerce began to borrow crypto and export control specialists from the Federal Bureau of Investigation and NSA in order to process license applications in a more timely manner.

Export rules under EAR distinguish between five categories including mass-market encryption software, data-recovery crypto, 56-bit cryptography, "other" encryption items that may be eligible for licensing arrangements, and encryption technology that may be licensed on an individual case basis. During January 1998, the Bureau of Export Administration (BXA) published an interim rule that revised the Commerce Control List and imposed new reporting restrictions on exports to non-Wassenaar countries.

Under the new EAR, the ITAR personal use exemption was replaced by license exceptions TMP[2] and BAG,[3] with an announcement by the Department of Commerce in 1997 that it intended to clarify the personal exemption for laptop computers.

After two major reviews of the export controls in 1998, an interim rule introduced a licensing policy specific to banking and financial institutions. This was followed in September 1998 by a major relaxation of export controls that was implemented in December of that year. By September 1999, the President's Export Council Subcommittee on Encryption advised a further easing of controls and the government announced the Cyberspace Electronic Security Act (CESA). New regulations were finally published in January 2000 after extensive testimony on the part of cryptography developers and manufacturers to the government.

50.4.2   Organization for Economic Cooperation and Development.

In process is a proposal for Cryptography Policy Guidelines for the Organization for Economic Cooperation and Development (OECD). The premise behind these guidelines is to help countries formulate national policies.[4]

The OECD has a history of involvement in setting policy for an information security policy for its member countries since 1992, when it initially issued a set of guidelines. Stating that it wanted to protect its members from failures of the major security functions of availability, confidentiality, and integrity, the OECD guidelines are also defined by accountability, awareness, ethics, integration, timeliness, reassessment, and democracy. The general information security policy was expanded in March 1997 to encompass an international cryptography policy.

While its guidelines are logical and admirable, members are not bound by the guidelines. The result is that members consider the guidelines but are free to develop and follow their own policies. The OECD guidelines emphasize:

- Trustworthiness of cryptographic methods
- Choice of method
- Market-driven development of cryptographic methods
- Development of technical standards, criteria, and protocols
- The right of individuals to privacy, protection of personal data, and secrecy of communications
- Lawful access under national policies
- Liability of cryptographic service providers and key holders
- The coordination and cooperation of governments in the production of viable policies

The OECD's principles have proved controversial because while they do not condone key recovery, they do not prohibit it either. While some nations object to the broadness of the principles that allow a range of interpretations, other nations consider it to be a repudiation of U.S. key recovery considerations. Although the guidelines explicitly speak of the cooperation and joint efforts of members to reach an acceptable policy, thus far the various members have not been able to agree and the responsibilities and decisions have fallen mainly on individual national governments.

50.4.3 Wassenaar Arrangement. The Wassenaar Arrangement on Export Controls for Conventional Arms and Dual-Use Goods and Technologies was established in 1995 by 28 countries, as a follow-up to the Coordinating Committee for Multilateral Export Controls (COCOM).[5] The original international organization of COCOM consisted of 17 member nations and dealt with the mutual control of the export of any product deemed strategic, plus technical data, from participating country members to proscribed destinations. COCOM maintained the International Industrial List and the International Munitions List. In 1991, COCOM decided to permit the export of mass-market cryptographic software, and although most of its members followed the COCOM regulations, the United States decided to maintain separate regulations.

COCOM's main goal was to prevent cryptography from being exported to any country deemed "dangerous." The term "dangerous" was generally applied to nations that maintained friendly ties with terrorist organizations, including Libya, Iraq, Iran, and North Korea. Following the dissolution of COCOM in 1994, most of its member nations agreed to maintain the status quo and maintain cryptography products on export control lists.

By the time the negotiations over the Wassenaar Arrangement were completed in 1996, final approval was given by 33 founding countries, including the United States. The Wassenaar Arrangement is broader in scope than the COCOM regulations. It was designed to prevent the acquisition of armaments and sensitive dual-use (civilian and military) items for military end use, in the event that the situation in any region, or the actions of any state, become a serious cause of concern to its member states. The members maintain an agreed list of items over which they undertake to exercise effective export controls. Cryptographic technology and related products are generally considered to be included on the Export Control List.

The General Software Note (GSN) that was applicable until December 1998 excepted mass-market and public domain crypto software from the controls. Deviations to the GSN were applied by the United States, Australia, France, New Zealand, and Russia. The Wassenaar Arrangement does not appear to apply to export via the Internet. And, for personal use, there is an exemption that permits "export of products accompanying their user for the user's personal use," such as when traveling with a laptop and encryption software. Negotiations in Vienna, Austria, in September 1998 did not result in any changes to the crypto controls.

Finally, when the Wassenaar Arrangement was formally revised in December 1998, the results were some restrictions on the General Software Note and some relaxations on crypto product export. Since there was no change in the provisions on public domain crypto, all the public domain software is still free for export. The Wassenaar provisions are actually the responsibility of each member state or nation to implement as each sees fit.

50.5   OUTLOOK FOR THE FUTURE.   Many different policies and restrictions are in place regarding the export and use of cryptography throughout the world. As e-commerce grows, the use of cryptography takes on added importance, and yet there seems to be no way to get a consensus of opinion regarding the best or even an acceptable method or technique that should be used by everyone and every country.

The inability of nations and individuals to reach agreement on one unified acceptable cryptography policy is due both to national security and safety concerns and to the commercial needs of international trade. It appears inevitable that, while various committees and organizations can and will recommend the policy and methods they want to use, limiting it to one overall standard or policy will be a practical impossibility.

It seems equally certain that the widely divergent views of cryptography's place in military affairs are not likely ever to be resolved. For the foreseeable future, business will continue to be conducted in a world filled with a variety of standards, practices, policies, and products, with each transaction between parties required to be in compliance with the regulations decreed by the parties and by the countries involved in that particular transaction.

50.6   SUMMARY AND RECOMMENDATIONS

50.6.1   For Crypto Products Producers.   The relaxation of U.S. controls over the export of cryptography will work to level the playing field and to permit American producers of such products to compete around the world. However, in the face of growing antagonism to American influence and power, technical superiority alone may not be sufficient to assure marketing dominance. Equally important will be the suppliers' conformance to all applicable laws and the degree to which they meet the needs of their customers, within the customers' perception of service, reliability, and responsiveness.

50.6.2   For Crypto Users Engages in International Commerce.   Businesses using cryptography must understand, and conform to, the regulations and laws of the country exporting the products and of the individual countries importing them.

Regulations and laws change frequently, as governments and organizations attempt to do what they deem best for their countries. Prior experience in the export of crypto products or in the use of cryptography for secure commercial information or transactions does not assure later success. The rules may have changed.

Wherever possible, a knowledgeable person should be made responsible for monitoring changes in applicable regulations and for checking to see that all transactions are in compliance.

50.6.3 For Travelers. In most countries, the personal use of encryption, including its importation on laptops for strictly personal use, is generally but not always permitted. Because of the differences between countries, every traveler must be certain to know the requirements for the home country as well as the policy for each country to be visited. Even if just passing through, visitors are subject to all of the local laws and regulations. If these are not observed, and if required special permissions and licenses are not obtained, the result may be confiscation, fines, or in certain countries even jail.

50.7 FURTHER READING. Additional materials relating to this chapter can be found at the following URLs:

www.answersleuth.com/words/e/encryption.chtml
www.cwis.kub.nl/frw/people/koops/cls2.htm#co
www.efa.org.au/issues/crypto/wass98.html
www.epic.org/crypto/legislation/cesa
www.epic.org/crypto/legislation/protect_act.html
www.freedom.house.gov/contract/
www.nvca.org/la92199.html
www.oecd.org/dsti/sti/it/secur/index.htm
www.privada.com/news/releases/19990.304.html

50.8 NOTES

1. *www.dti.uk.*
2. Federal Register 66FR42108, § 740.9, August 10, 2001.
3. Federal Register 66FR42108, § 740.14, August 10, 2001.
4. For the complete guidelines, see *www.oecd.org/dsti/sti/it/secur/prod/e-crypto.htm.*
5. Full information is available from *www.wassenaar.org.*

CHAPTER 51

CENSORSHIP AND CONTENT FILTERING

Lee Tien and Seth Finkelstein

CONTENTS

51.1 INTRODUCTION. "Everyone has the right to freedom of opinion and expression; this right includes freedom to hold opinions without interference and to seek, receive, and impart information and ideas through any media and regardless of frontiers."[1]

One might think that the Internet will make this ringing proclamation a reality. Like no other technology, the Internet transcends national borders and eliminates barriers to the free flow of information. Governments, however, are trying to control speech on the Internet.

51.1.1   Scope of This Chapter: Government Intervention.   Many nations protect rights of free speech and free expression. The First Amendment to the U.S. Constitution provides that "Congress shall make no law . . . abridging the freedom of speech or of the press." The Canadian Charter of Rights and Freedoms protects freedom of speech and press in article 2 as fundamental rights. While Great Britain has no formal constitution, freedom of speech is protected by the Magna Carta of 1215, the 1512 Privilege of Parliament Act, the 1689 Bill of Rights, and the 1911 Parliament Act.[2]

Despite such constitutional protections, speech is regulated everywhere. Article 1 of the Canadian Charter of Rights and Freedoms permits "demonstrably reasonable" limitations on freedom of expression. Great Britain and Canada have promulgated legislation regulating racially defamatory speech, group defamation, or speech that incites racial hatred. While American law is far more protective of speech, some expression is deemed "unprotected" by the First Amendment, and even protected speech can be regulated in a variety of circumstances.

Accordingly, some governments have enacted laws prohibiting certain content on the Internet and have sought to prosecute users and service providers. Others have tried to control access by insisting on the installation of national "proxy servers" and requiring the blocking of targeted Web sites. Governments also have encouraged "self-regulation" intended to enlist service providers to control customer behavior.

51.1.2   Whose Laws, Whose Standards?   It is often thought that governments cannot successfully censor the Internet. After all, one nation's laws may be unenforceable elsewhere. But national laws can be applied to communication intermediaries like Internet service providers (ISPs), blocking access by people in that country.

Moreover, just as speech originating in one nation can reach a worldwide audience, one nation's laws can have powerful effects in other nations. As commentators have put it, "[t]he reach of the Internet multiplies both the number of laws and the number of jurisdictions applicable to speech transmitted on-line."[3] Indeed, "[b]ecause content posted on the Internet is instantaneously transmitted worldwide, Internet users and providers almost automatically face potential liability in any country to which the Internet is connected—not just the nation where the speech was created or where the author lives."[4]

The most prominent example is a recent case in which a French court ordered the U.S.-based Yahoo to "take all necessary measures to dissuade and make impossible any access via Yahoo.com to the auction service for Nazi merchandise as well as to any other site or service that may be construed as an apology for Nazism or contesting the reality of Nazi crimes."[5] The French court held that "the simple act of displaying [Nazi artifacts] in France violates Article R645-1 of the Penal Code and therefore [is] a threat to internal public order."[6] It described the mere availability of such information to be "a connecting link with France, which renders our jurisdiction perfectly competent to rule in this matter."[7] After the French order was handed down, Yahoo filed suit in the United States seeking a judgment that it need not comply with the French order.[8] The French parties moved to dismiss the U.S. case for lack of personal jurisdiction, but the U.S. district court denied the motion, allowing Yahoo to proceed.[9]

Resolving international jurisdiction in cyberspace is one of the most difficult and important issues for the Internet, but it is beyond the scope of this chapter. Moreover, the ways in which the laws of one nation may affect Internet speech in another extend beyond the topic of this chapter, state-backed censorship. Even when governments do not themselves target particular kinds of speech, their laws may give private parties legal rights against expression originating overseas, as in the area of defamation.[10]

Laws relating to commerce also may raise free speech concerns, as in the areas of intellectual property[11] and privacy regulation. For instance, the 1995 European Union Data Protection Directive generally restricts all "processing" of "personal data," giving data subjects legal rights quite different from those found in the United States.[12]

51.1.3 Defining Objectional Material: International Differences.

For most countries, the major concerns stem from the increased availability of "objectionable" content over the Internet. This section focuses on how the meaning of "objectionable" differs from country to country.

51.1.3.1 Sex. A common type of objectionable material is speech about sex. In the United States, a series of attempts have been made to regulate the availability of sexually oriented speech over the Internet, although with little success. Several Middle Eastern nations also block pornographic sites.

In 1995, the Bavarian Justice Ministry informed CompuServe that senior company officials could face prison terms for violation of German antipornography laws. German police provided CompuServe a list of the discussion groups that contained potentially objectionable material.[13] In February 1997, Germany indicted Felix Somm, head of CompuServe's German subsidiary, for failure to prevent the dissemination of illegal material on its online service, becoming the first Western democracy to prosecute an official of an online service for illegal Internet content.[14] German prosecutors argued that because CompuServe had access to screening software, the company had the opportunity to block the offending material but failed to do so. Soon thereafter, Germany enacted its Information and Communications Services Act of 1997 (ICSA). The ICSA, however, has been sharply criticized for failing to resolve the uncertainties faced by ISPs.[15]

51.1.3.2 Hate. Another major category of objectionable speech is what might loosely be called "hate speech."[16] American hate sites include sites promoting white supremacy, Nazi or neo-Nazi views, "skinheads," and the Christian Identity Movement.[17] Internet content that promotes Nazi views and Holocaust denial has attracted considerable international attention.

For instance, the German constitution, known as the Basic Law, incorporates freedom of expression as a fundamental individual right. But Article 5, the main provision concerning free speech, expressly provides that the government may limit an individual's expressive right if it conflicts with other people's rights, public order, or criminal laws. Thus, under Germany's general laws and the laws protecting youths, publishing or distributing neo-Nazi or Holocaust denial literature is a criminal offense.[18]

In February 1996, German prosecutors in Mannheim investigated several ISPs, including America Online, regarding alleged distribution of neo-Nazi material on the Internet in violation of anti-Nazi laws.[19] More recently, German-born Frederick Toben, who uses the Web site of his Australian-based Adelaide Institute to advocate Holocaust denial, was found guilty of offending the memory of the dead.[20] The lower court had ruled "that German law against inciting racial hatred could not be applied to content on a foreign Web site."[21] Germany's Federal Court of Justice, the Bundesgerichtshof, overturned the lower court ruling and found that German law applies to Internet content that originates outside the country's borders, so long as people inside of Germany can access that content.[22]

Canadian law directs courts to balance an individual's free speech rights with societal equality interests. Thus, Canadian courts have upheld hate speech convictions under laws that criminalize the willful promotion of hatred.[23] The Canadian Supreme Court held the statute constitutional.[24] The Court defined hate speech as including a requirement that "the accused 'promote' hatred against an identifiable group, indicating more than simple encouragement or advancement and rather required that the hate monger intend or foresee as substantially certain a direct and active stimulation of hatred against an identifiable group."[25]

The Internet has raised new issues in Canada regarding hate speech. Bernard Klatt runs the Fairview Technology Center out of his home in British Columbia, and about a dozen neo-Nazi, white supremacist, and skinhead clients have used his server to publish material against immigration and homosexuality while celebrating Hitler's accomplishments and "Euro-Christianity." The Canadian government has attempted to shut down Klatt, but he and his clients have insisted that they had not broken any laws.[26]

The Zundelsite, a multilingual archive and news service, may be the most prominent Holocaust-denial Web site run by an individual. Its administrator, German-Canadian Ernst Zundel, became one of the denial movement's martyrs when he was convicted in Canada for his Holocaust-denial pamphlets.[27] The Canadian Supreme Court later overturned his conviction.[28] Zundel's U.S.-based Web page then became the target of an official inquiry by the Canadian Human Rights Commission.[29]

51.1.3.3   Politics and Culture.   Various countries also regulate Internet content that generally threatens the government or political, social, and cultural values.

51.1.3.3.1   China.   As of February 2001, there were approximately 22 million Internet users in China, an increase from 8.6 million users in January 2000.[30] The Chinese government, although eager to capitalize on the Internet, feels that the "Internet is a very real threat to the hold their dictatorial regime has over the country."[31] Accordingly, China severely restricts communication via the Internet, including much dissent and the free reporting of news. The so-called Measures for Managing Internet Information Services prohibit private Web sites from publishing "news" without prior approval from communist officials.[32]

A major obstacle for would-be Chinese Internet users is the registration process required to get online. One must pick an ISP and provide identification. One must also fill out a Police File Report Form that will be sent to the ISP, the local Public Security Bureau (PSB), and the provincial-level PSB Computer Security and Supervision Office. In addition, users must complete a Net Access Responsibility Agreement, pledging "not to use the Internet to threaten state security or reveal state secrets [or] . . . to read, reproduce, or transmit material that endangers the state, obstructs public safety, or is obscene or pornographic."[33] The ISP application itself requests information such as employer's address, home address, and profession; home, office, cell phone, and pager numbers; as well as details about the computer, the modem type, and permit number, which is assigned by the PSB.[34]

In January 2000, the Chinese newspaper the *People's Daily* published new Internet regulations issued by China's State Secrecy Bureau. These new laws "ban the release, discussion, or transfer" of "state secret information" on bulletin board systems, chat rooms, or Internet news groups. E-mail users were banned from sending or forwarding state secrets by e-mail. In addition, all Web sites are required to undergo a security check. A provision requiring that anyone using encryption technology register with the government was later rescinded.[35]

In May 2000, after the China Finance Information Network, a financial Web site, republished a Hong Kong newspaper about corruption by a provincial official, Chinese public security officials suspended the site for 15 days and fined the site 15,000 yuan (US $1,800).[36] On August 3, 2000, state security officials forced a Chinese ISP to shut down the Xinwenming (New Culture Forum) site run by a group of dissidents in Shandong Province for posting "reactionary content."[37]

The following month, China's State Council passed Internet laws that limited foreign investment and imposed strict surveillance requirements on Internet content by mandating that Internet content providers monitor both the material they publish and the people who access that material, including the times users log onto the Internet, their account numbers, their Internet addresses, and the phone numbers they are dialing in from.[38]

On November 7, 2000, the Ministry of Information Industry and the Information Office of the State Council released new laws banning commercial media organizations from setting up independent news sites; prohibiting commercial portals from carrying news items based on their own sources; and requiring China-based Web sites to obtain permission from the State Council Information Office before linking to overseas news sites or carrying news from overseas news media. The new Internet laws also restrict the content of online chat rooms and bulletin boards.[39]

In December 2000, the National People's Congress passed a new law to foster Internet safety. This law criminalizes several forms of online political activity, including using the Internet to "incite the overthrow of state power, topple the socialist system, or . . . destroy national unity," promote "cults," or support the independence of Taiwan.[40]

The Ministry of Public Security announced on February 27, 2001, that it released Internet filtering software called Internet Police 110 on February 26. The software comes in three versions for households, Internet cafés, and schools that can monitor Web traffic and delete or block messages from sources deemed "offensive." According to a news report published in the China Securities News, it can send text or voice warnings to network administrators about any unauthorized Internet surfing.[41]

On March 20, 2001, official Chinese media reported that China is developing a surveillance system to monitor activities on the Internet, which will be similar to the data-recording "black box" installed in commercial airplanes. According to Hong Kong *iMail*, it will be able to record all communications through the Internet.[42]

Most recently, in April 2001, the official Chinese news agency Xinhua reported that China would impose a three-month ban on the opening of new Internet cafés. This is part of "a major offensive against unchecked use of the Internet. Xinhua said authorities are to conduct a massive probe into existing Internet outlets, which it views as potential hotbeds of dissent and vice."[43]

In addition, since January 2000 the Chinese government has been arresting individuals who use the Internet in a manner they deem dangerous, often for online political or religious activity. Qi Yanchen, sentenced to four years in prison on September 19, 2000, is the first Chinese convicted of subversion for material he wrote that was published on the Internet. Qi was officially charged for writing articles in the May 6, 1999, and May 17, 1999, U.S.-based Chinese dissident e-mail publication *Dacankao* (*V.I.P. Reference*).[44] Guo Qinghai, a freelance writer, was arrested in September 2000 for "subverting state power." Guo published articles on the Internet that discussed Qi Yanchen's case. He also posted, on overseas online bulletin boards, essays promoting political reforms in China. He was sentenced to four years in prison.[45]

Zhang Haitao, creator of the only China-based Web site on the outlawed Falun Gong, was charged with subversion on October 11, 2000, and is accused of establishing a site promoting Falun Gong and of posting an online petition urging followers to protest the government ban on the group.[46] Zhang Ji, a college student in Heilongjiang

Province, was charged on November 8, 2000, with "disseminating reactionary documents via the Internet." Authorities say Zhang had e-mailed information to U.S. and Canada-based Web sites of the Falun Gong religious group as well as downloaded news about the group and shared it with others in China.[47]

51.1.3.3.2   The Middle East.   According to Human Rights Watch, the United Arab Emirates (UAE) is "the regional leader in advocating censorship of the Web through the use of high-tech means."[48] Dial-up users in the UAE do not access the Internet directly; they dial into a proxy server maintained by Etisalat, the state telecommunications company, in collaboration with a U.S. firm that is contracted to maintain and update the software. While UAE officials have insisted that the proxy server's sole purpose is to block pornographic sites, at least one nonpornographic site, that of the Gay and Lesbian Arabic Society (*www.glas.org*) is blocked. When asked about the site, an Information and Culture Ministry official explained that there had been complaints about it.

Saudi Arabia bans publishing or even accessing various types of online expression, including "[a]nything contrary to the state or its system"; "[n]ews damaging to the Saudi Arabian armed forces"; "[a]nything damaging to the dignity of heads of states"; "[a]ny false information ascribed to state officials"; "[s]ubversive ideas"; and "[s]landerous or libelous material."[49]

All 30 of the country's ISPs are linked to a ground-floor room at the Riyadh Internet entranceway, where all of the country's Web activity is stored in massive cache files and screened for offensive or sacrilegious material before it is released to individual users. The central servers are configured to block access to "sensitive" sites that might violate "the social, cultural, political, media, economic, and religious values of the Kingdom."[50]

According to Human Rights Watch, while official Saudi explanations of Internet censorship focus on materials deemed offensive to conservative Muslim sensibilities, Saudi blocking apparently extends to political sites. In early 1999, the site of at least one exiled dissident group, the Committee against Corruption in Saudi Arabia (*www.saudhouse.com*) was reportedly blocked.

Yemen's telecommunications service provider, Teleyemen, told Human Rights Watch that there is a "general requirement . . . to limit information which is considered to be undesirable in terms of causing offenses against social, religious, or cultural standards," and that Teleyemen uses the Surfwatch censorware program in conjunction with a proxy server.

51.1.3.3.3   Myanmar/Burma.   In 1988 a new military clique called the State Law and Order Restoration Council (SLORC) took power in the country formerly known as Burma, now known as Myanmar. They have managed to achieve cease-fires with 15 armed organizations, but they refuse to step down, asserting that only "the military can ensure national unity and solidarity,"[51] even after the National League for Democracy's overwhelming victory in the 1990 election.

SLORC maintains power partly by controlling access to information. In January 2000, the Myanmar Post and Telecommunication (MPT), the only ISP in Myanmar, passed a measure that forbids Internet users from posting political speech on the Web, such as writings "detrimental to the interests of the Union of Myanmar" or "directly or indirectly detrimental to the current policies and secret security affairs of the government of the Union of Burma."[52] Only the person granted an Internet account may use it, and the account holder is held responsible for all use of that account. Web pages may not be created without government permission, and violation of any regulation is subject to legal action.[53]

Public access to the Internet is nonexistent in Myanmar; the nation's lone Internet café in Yangon does not even provide Internet service. The Burmese military has been effective at "warding off any Internet revolution by limiting the rights of its citizens."[54]

51.2   THE U.S. CONTEXT: FIRST AMENDMENT RIGHTS.   The First Amendment of the U.S. Constitution strongly protects freedom of speech in the United States. In several ways, the right to speak is the most powerful of all U.S. constitutional rights. First Amendment scrutiny can be much stricter than in other areas of constitutional law. It is usually easier to get in front of a court when "speech" is at issue, and to win, because many technical legal requirements are relaxed.

Thus, while the right to speak is not constitutionally absolute, and may be restricted by government, several basic principles limit governmental authority to restrict freedom of speech, more than it is limited from restricting other activities. These principles have been articulated through a variety of legal doctrines.

51.2.1   What Does the First Amendment Protect?   Today, the First Amendment generally protects all forms of communicative or expressive activity[55] from "state action" or governmental interference.[56] Courts generally presume that linguistic acts or visual depictions are covered by the First Amendment but require litigants to show that nonlinguistic acts are speech unless the law has already so held.[57]

Nevertheless, the coverage of the First Amendment is quite broad. It includes not only the right to speak but also the right *not* to speak, or against "compelled" speech,[58] the right to speak or associate anonymously,[59] and the right to read or to receive information.[60] Often, activity that is not necessarily communicative is protected because it enables or facilitates expression. Highly discretionary city licensing of newsracks was found to be an invalid scheme of licensing that affected liberty of circulation.[61] Money is not speech, but election campaign contributions and expenditures are protected as speech.[62]

In addition, the First Amendment requires that the government observe some degree of neutrality in its treatment of speakers[63] and speech media[64]; it cannot arbitrarily prefer one speaker or one medium over another.

51.2.2   Basic First Amendment Principles.   There is no consensus or accepted theory underlying U.S. protection of free speech. The different rationales for freedom of speech can be categorized as more or less "positive" or "negative." Positive justifications identify speech as related to some special moral, social, or political value. For example, the "marketplace of ideas" theory is based on the notion that "the best test of truth is the power of the thought to get itself accepted in the competition of the market."[65] Courts also have defended the right to free expression as embodying the value of "speaker autonomy,"[66] thus "putting the decision as to what views shall be voiced largely into the hands of each of us, in the hope that use of such freedom will ultimately produce a more capable citizenry and more perfect polity, *and in the belief that no other approach would comport with the premise of individual dignity and choice upon which our political system rests.*"[67]

Negative theories presume the value of speech and focus instead on the dangers of government regulation of speech. The main idea here is that speech is as vulnerable to threats of punishment as to punishment itself. "It is characteristic of freedoms of expression in general that they are vulnerable to gravely damaging yet barely visible encroachments."[68] This fear of "chilling effects" on speech sometimes is associated with the possibility that juries may not treat unpopular speakers or unorthodox ideas fairly, but it also reflects a concern that individuals may censor themselves. Such self-censorship can harm public debate while being almost invisible to the courts because it occurs through many small individual choices.[69]

51.2.2.1 Harm/Causation. Perhaps the most important First Amendment principle is that the government has the burden to show that the speech it wishes to regulate truly causes significant harm. This principle was not accepted for many years; in the early days of First Amendment law, speech could be punished as an "attempt" if the natural and reasonable tendency of what was said would be to bring about a forbidden effect. Thus, for instance, individuals who had mailed circulars to draftees arguing that conscription was unconstitutional and urging them to assert their rights were convicted for conspiring to attempt to obstruct the draft.[70]

Today, courts are far more skeptical about government claims of harm. If speech could be restricted merely because the mathematical expectation of harm were significant, speech would be easier to restrict as it were more widely disseminated. Such a result is inconsistent with the First Amendment's protection of open, public discourse. As a classic opinion stated, "no danger flowing from speech can be deemed clear and present, unless the incidence of the evil apprehended is so imminent that it may befall before there is opportunity for full discussion. If there be time to expose the evil by the processes of education, the remedy to be applied is more speech, not enforced silence."[71]

The concern here is not only for the speech itself; it includes a concern that the speaker can properly be held responsible for harm. The modern approach is exemplified by a case where a speaker was convicted for advocating violence. The Supreme Court reversed the conviction because the law did not require the government to show both that the speaker intended to produce "imminent lawless action" and that the speech was "likely to incite or produce such action."[72] The requirement of intent helps protect speakers from being held responsible for the acts of others. As one court put it, "Much speech is dangerous. Chemists whose work might help someone build a bomb, political theorists whose papers might start political movements that lead to riots, speakers whose ideas attract violent protesters, all these and more leave loss in their wake."[73] Without careful attention to harm and causation, the right to speak would mean little.[74]

51.2.2.2 Neutrality. Not all reasons that government might use to restrict speech are valid. Thus, a second basic First Amendment principle is governmental neutrality as to speech content. Government is likely to have illegitimate reasons for wishing to restrict speech, such as the desire to suppress political criticism, but it may be able to disguise such hostility by claiming that less selfish interests, such as "public order" or the civility of discourse, are truly at stake.[75] Also, because public officials may have a strong self-interest in stifling dissent, they are likely to ignore or undervalue the social interest in free speech. Such motivations may lead to regulation that skews or distorts public debate. In general, then, government may not regulate speech based on its substantive content or the message it conveys.[76]

51.2.2.3 Precision. Third, all speech regulation must be precise. "Because First Amendment freedoms need breathing space to survive, government may regulate in the area only with narrow specificity."[77] Much of the First Amendment's force stems from this principle. Imprecise regulation not only chills speech but gives officials too much discretion to discriminate on the basis of content. Without clearly stated standards, courts cannot easily ferret out content-based discrimination.[78] Insisting on precision also allows courts to avoid assessing the importance of the legislature's goals; they need only say that the means are too blunt.

51.2.2.4 Background Doubt-Resolution Principles.

Adding to the strength of First Amendment protection for speech are several principles for resolving uncertainty. Speech regulation generally requires knowledge or intent on the speaker's part, which protects bookstores and others that "carry" others' speech.[79] Moreover, the factual burden of proof is usually on the person or entity seeking to restrict speech.[80] Finally, speech that in itself might be disfavored receives "strategic" protection in order to protect undue chill to public discourse; for instance, while false statements of fact may be considered of little First Amendment value, permitting the punishment of mere falsehood would overly burden speakers.[81] Put simply, doubts generally are called in favor of speech.

51.2.3   Limitations on Government Interference with Speech

51.2.3.1 Distinction between Substantive Tests and Procedural Safeguards: Example of Prior Restraints.

A critical distinction in First Amendment (and other) law is between substantive and procedural review. The difference is best explained by reference to "prior restraints," which are presumed unconstitutional.

Most people are familiar with prior restraints as judicial orders preventing speech or publication. In such cases, government "carries a heavy burden of showing justification for the imposition of such a restraint."[82] For instance, the Supreme Court required the government to demonstrate that publication of the *Pentagon Papers* "will surely result in direct, immediate, and irreparable damage to our Nation or its people."[83] Judicial "gag orders" on press publication are subject to similarly searching scrutiny.[84] In these cases, courts are concerned with whether the particular restraint on speech is sufficiently justified.

A second line of prior restraint doctrine illustrates procedural scrutiny. American hostility to prior restraints is a reaction to English press licensing systems under which nothing could be printed without the prior approval of government or church authority. The fear is that discretionary permit schemes make freedom of speech "contingent upon the uncontrolled will of an official."[85] Thus, the law authorizing such a licensing scheme must provide "narrowly drawn, reasonable and definite standards for the [administering] officials to follow."[86] Thus, licensing schemes, such as for screening obscene movies, are constitutional only if accompanied by procedural safeguards necessary "to obviate the dangers of a censorship system."[87] There must be a "prompt final judicial decision" reviewing any "interim and possibly erroneous denial of a license." Moreover, "because only a judicial determination in an adversary proceeding ensures the necessary sensitivity to freedom of expression," the censor must, "within a specified brief period, either issue a license or go to court."[88] In such cases, the particular restraint is relatively unimportant: The issue is whether the statute itself contains sufficient procedural safeguards.

51.2.3.2 Levels of Substantive Scrutiny and the Issue of Content Neutrality.

First Amendment cases typically feature three levels of substantive scrutiny, turning mainly on how the statute regulates the meaning of speech: by subject, by viewpoint, or without reference to meaning at all. In general, strict scrutiny applies to laws that attempt to stifle "speech on account of its message."[89] In such situations, the government must demonstrate both that there is a compelling interest in restricting the speech and that it has chosen the least restrictive means of furthering that compelling interest.

When the government targets not subject matter but particular views taken by speakers on a subject, the violation of the First Amendment is all the more blatant.[90] Viewpoint discrimination is thus an egregious form of content discrimination. The government must abstain from regulating speech when the specific motivating ideology or the opinion or perspective of the speaker is the rationale for the restriction.[91] Such scrutiny is so stringent that it applies to otherwise "unprotected" speech.[92]

On the other hand, the government often regulates speech without reference to its meaning or communicative impact. So-called content-neutral speech regulation is subject to intermediate rather than strict scrutiny "because in most cases they pose a less substantial risk of excising certain ideas or viewpoints from the public dialogue."[93] Such laws "do not pose such inherent dangers to free expression, or present such potential for censorship or manipulation, as to justify application of the most exacting level of First Amendment scrutiny."[94]

Intermediate scrutiny comes in two main flavors. Content-neutral regulation of the time, place, or manner of speech must be narrowly tailored to serve a significant government interest and leave open ample alternative channels for communication.[95] Content-neutral regulation in other contexts must further a substantial government interest and not burden substantially more speech than necessary to further that interest.[96]

A third type of intermediate scrutiny is the "secondary effects" doctrine, which operates as an exception to the general rule that content-based speech regulation is subject to strict scrutiny. The doctrine asks whether the harm is attributable to the communicative aspects of the speech; if not, the regulation is said to be aimed not at speech but rather at its "secondary effects," and the regulation is deemed content-neutral.[97] Thus, city zoning ordinances have been upheld even though they only applied to theaters that showed adult films because their purposes of preventing crime and protecting property values and the quality of urban life were deemed unrelated to speech content. This doctrine has been criticized for permitting speech suppression "whenever censors can concoct 'secondary' rationalizations for regulating the content of political speech."[98] The main limit on the doctrine is the rule that "listeners' reaction to speech is not a content-neutral basis for regulation."[99]

51.2.3.3 Types of Procedural Scrutiny: Vagueness and Overbreadth.
Laws generally may not "set a net large enough to catch all possible offenders, and leave it to the courts to step inside and say who could be rightfully detained, and who should be set at large."[100] This hostility to vague laws is greater when speech is concerned; courts will assume that ambiguous legal language will be used against speech.[101] The void-for-vagueness doctrine emphasizes both fair notice to citizens of what conduct is prohibited and clear standards for law enforcement to follow.[102]

A closely related doctrine is that of overbreadth. A law is overbroad when it "does not aim specifically at evils within the allowable area of [government] control, but . . . sweeps within its ambit other activities that constitute an exercise" of First Amendment rights.[103] The danger is "not merely the sporadic abuse of power by the censor" but the "continuous and pervasive restraint on all freedom of discussion that might be reasonably regarded as within its purview."[104] Accordingly, the overbreadth doctrine permits facial[105] invalidation of laws that inhibit speech if impermissible applications of the law are substantial, when "judged in relation to the statute's plainly legitimate sweep."[106] Both doctrines exemplify the basic precision principle.

51.2.4 Exceptions Where Speech Can Legally Be Limited. The government can restrict speech both directly and indirectly. Roughly speaking, the government is more limited in direct regulation of speech than in indirect regulation. First Amendment law also contains many subdomains with their own special rules, such as over-the-air broadcasting,[107] government enterprises,[108] and government subsidies.[109]

51.2.4.1 Neutral Laws of General Applicability. Many laws, in some sense, restrict speech to an extent. Absent special circumstances, "generally applicable" laws can be applied to speech without triggering First Amendment scrutiny. Classic example are laws against speeding applied to a news reporter hurrying to file a story or taxes that apply to books and newspapers as well as other goods.

The "generally applicable" doctrine contains its own limits. Courts will look to see whether the law appears to be a pretext for targeting speech and whether it was based on perceived secondary effects.[110] If so, then there will be some level of First Amendment scrutiny.

51.2.4.2 Constitutionalization of Crimes and Torts: Advocacy of Illegality, Threats, and Defamation. Another major category of First Amendment doctrines relates to crimes and torts directed at speech. In general, the First Amendment does not prevent the application of criminal law to speech simply because it is speech. While agreeing to participate or assist in doing an unlawful act is usually accomplished through "speech," the larger course of conduct in which that speech is integrated overrides any potential First Amendment applicability.[111] Even so, there can be concern for speech-suppressive effects.

Criminal laws that are likely to involve speech "must be interpreted with the commands of the First Amendment clearly in mind."[112] As discussed in Section 51.2.2.1, laws that criminalize incitement to unlawful action must require proof of both intent and harm. Similarly, threatening may be criminally punished if the law is carefully defined and applied to "true threats" but not "political hyperbole."[113] Recently, the Supreme Court held that federal law prohibiting the disclosure of unlawfully intercepted communications could not be applied to those who had innocently acquired the information of public concern.[114]

Tort laws that target speech also must be construed and applied in light of First Amendment concerns. The prime example is libel or defamation law. For many years, the First Amendment simply did not apply to libel suits. In 1967, however, the Supreme Court held that libel suits were a form of government action because courts must enforce libel judgments, and thus imposed First Amendment restrictions on such lawsuits.[115]

51.2.4.3 "Fighting Words," Obscenity, and Child Pornography (So-Called "Unprotected Speech"). Certain categories of speech, such as obscenity, child pornography, "fighting words," and so on, are considered "unprotected" even though they are linguistic or pictorial. Here the issue is not that the speech is not communicative but that its value is low; "fighting words," for instance, are deemed "utterances [that] are no essential part of any exposition of ideas, and are of such slight social value as a step to truth that any benefit that may be derived from them is clearly outweighed by the social interest in order and morality."[116]

Even so, the definition of "fighting words" is closely limited. First, the words must "by their very utterance inflict injury or tend to incite an immediate breach of the peace."[117] Second, they must be "directed to the person of the hearer."[118]

The Supreme Court defines obscenity as works that, (1) taken as a whole, appeal to the prurient interest of the average person in sex, (2) portray sexual conduct in a patently offensive way, and (3) taken as a whole, lack serious literary, artistic, political, or scientific value.[119] This definition illustrates how the Supreme Court has sought to ensure that even laws that target unprotected speech do not reach too far. In particular, the first prong of the obscenity test is evaluated with reference to "contemporary community standards." As the Supreme Court observed, "It is neither realistic nor constitutionally sound to read the First Amendment as requiring that the people of Maine or Mississippi accept public depiction of conduct found tolerable in Las Vegas, or New York City."[120] Moreover, any statute regulating obscenity must define the "sexual conduct" at issue.

Child pornography is defined generally as works that visually depict sexually explicit conduct by children below a specified age.[121] As with obscenity, the statute must clearly define the conduct that may not be depicted[122] and must require some element of knowledge or intent. Unlike obscenity, however, legally regulable child pornography need not appeal to the prurient interest of the average person, need not portray sexual conduct in a patently offensive manner, and need not be considered as a whole.[123] Child pornography is the least protected type of speech.

But even "unprotected" speech is not entirely invisible to the First Amendment. Regulations that target such speech must be based on the reason why the speech is categorized as unprotected; thus, even though "fighting words" may be regulated because of their potential to generate violence, regulating only "fighting words" that relate to race, color, creed, religion, or gender would "impose special prohibitions on those speakers who express views on disfavored subjects," amounting to unconstitutional viewpoint discrimination.[124]

51.2.4.4 Less-Protected Speech, Media, and Recipients.

Other categories of speech are protected by the First Amendment but may be regulated more easily. The main examples are commercial speech, broadcast speech, and speech that is "indecent" or "harmful to minors."[125]

Commercial speech is defined as speech that proposes a commercial transaction; the main example is advertising. Originally, such speech was considered unprotected, but today its regulation is subject to a form of intermediate scrutiny.[126]

Broadcast speech is also subject to a form of intermediate scrutiny.[127] The Supreme Court has long adhered to the view that different media of expression may require different First Amendment analyses. The standard for regulating the speech of cablecasters is not entirely clear.[128]

With regard to sexual content, there are three forms of less-protected speech. First, while nonobscene sexual expression is in a sense "fully" protected, cities may rely on "secondary effects" analysis to regulate the location of bookstores and theaters that sell "adult" material or offer "adult" entertainment like nude dancing.[129]

Second, the Supreme Court has permitted substantial regulation of "indecent" speech over the airwaves[130] and on cable TV.[131] Indecency regulation is closely tied to the interest of preventing minors' access to sexual material. As that interest varies, so does the latitude for regulation. For example, the regulation of indecent speech delivered telephonically was not permitted.[132] Thus, indecency is an odd speech category that is regulated primarily with respect to the audience: The government has a strong interest in regulating minors' access to indecency, but it has no such interest in regulating adults' access.

Closely related to the category of "indecency" is "harmful to minors" (HTM) material. Roughly speaking, this category is like obscenity, but geared to those under the age of 17.[133] This category has become increasingly important in the censorware context given the "full" protection accorded to speech over the Internet. Courts have narrowly tailored HTM-based access restrictions to its constitutional boundaries. This point was made clear in *Reno v. ACLU,* where the Supreme Court held unconstitutional a general prohibition of indecent speech on the Internet. The Court found:

1. Parents may disseminate HTM speech to their children.[134]

2. The HTM concept applies only to commercial transactions.[135]

3. The government may not simply ban minors' exposure to a full category of speech, such as nudity, when only a subset of that category can plausibly be deemed HTM.[136]

4. The government interest is not equally strong throughout the HTM age range.[137]

51.2.5 Legislation and Legislative Initiatives in the United States. Since the advent of the Internet, there have been many attempts to regulate access to Internet speech. Such legislation can be divided into two basic categories. In the first category, the law imposes liability for communicating certain kinds of material over the Internet. Such laws did not require the use of software to block Internet sites or to filter their content (censorware) because they focused on the conduct of the speaker or publisher. In the second category, the law requires or encourages the use of censorware by those who make Internet speech available.

In 1996, Congress enacted the Communications Decency Act (CDA), which sought to regulate the communication of "indecent" material over the Internet. The CDA prohibited Internet users from using the Internet to communicate material that, under contemporary community standards, would be deemed patently offensive to minors under the age of 18. In holding that the CDA violated the First Amendment, the Supreme Court explained that without defining key terms, the statute was unconstitutionally vague. Moreover, the Court noted that the breadth of the CDA was "wholly unprecedented" in that, for example, it was "not limited to commercial speech or commercial entities" but rather embraced "all nonprofit entities and individuals posting indecent messages or displaying them on their own computers."

In response to the Supreme Court's invalidation of the CDA, Congress in 1998 enacted the Child Online Protection Act[138] (COPA). The COPA scaled down the restrictions of the CDA by using the "harmful to minors" category of speech. The COPA was found unconstitutional by a district court because it failed the strict scrutiny test for content-based regulation of speech.[139] That holding was affirmed on appeal although on a different rationale—that because "harmful to minors," like obscenity, must be defined by reference to discrete, diverse, geographically defined communities, COPA's attempt to promulgate a national "harmful to minors" standard was necessarily unconstitutional.[140] States also have attempted to control access to Internet speech by using the "harmful to minors" concept, but these attempts have proven similarly unsuccessful.[141]

The second category is exemplified by the recent Child Internet Protection Act (CHIPA),[142] which, roughly speaking, requires all schools and libraries that receive certain types of federal funding to adopt and implement an Internet safety policy and to use "technology protection measures" on all computers that offer Internet access. Such measures must block or filter Internet access to visual depictions that are obscene, child pornography, or harmful to minors. Libraries must also regulate access by minors to "inappropriate material." Thus, the CHIPA effectively requires the use of censorware.

51.2.6   Attempts to Control Access: Case Law.   The American Library Association has taken a firm stance against censorware in libraries[143] and has committed itself to challenging federal censorware requirements. To date, the use of censorware to control access to speech on the Internet has been litigated in only two pre-CHIPA cases (discussed below), both involving libraries. As of this writing, a third case—directly challenging the CHIPA—is scheduled for trial in late March 2002.[144] The plaintiffs in these cases are library and librarian associations, including the American Library Association, library patrons and users, and entities and individuals whose Web sites are likely to be blocked by censorware.

51.2.6.1   Public Libraries.   The two cases discussed below illustrate two sides of the libraries' situation with respect to Internet access. On one hand, public libraries must be concerned that, by implementing censorware, they violate patrons' First Amendment right to receive information. On the other hand, public libraries also have been concerned that they might face liability for not implementing censorware on their Internet terminals.

As to the first concern, libraries almost certainly may not censor adults' access to constitutionally protected material on the Internet. In the only published case to date evaluating the First Amendment status of censorware in libraries, *Mainstream Loudoun v. Bd. of Trustees of the Loudoun County Library,* a federal district court found the library's policy unconstitutional.[145] The challenged policy required that "site-blocking software . . . be installed on all library computers" so as to block child pornography, obscene material, and harmful-to-minors material.[146] The defendants implemented the policy by installing the commercial filtering software X-Stop on all public library terminals in the county.

The court first concluded that the public libraries were limited public forums and then subjected the defendants' indisputably content-based filtering policy to strict constitutional scrutiny.[147] Assuming that the library's interests were compelling, the court found that its policy was not the least restrictive means of furthering those interests. First, the court held that the library had not even considered less restrictive means, including privacy screens, library staff monitoring of Internet use (which had been used to enforce other library policies), and filtering software installed only on Internet terminals used by minors or only when minors are using them.

More important, the court found that the censorware-based policy violated the First Amendment because censorware is both overbroad and overinclusive. On one hand, the X-Stop censorware blocked more speech than that targeted by the policy.[148] On the other hand, even if censorware could somehow be tailored to exclude only restricted materials, it unconstitutionally "limit[s] the access of all patrons, adult and juvenile, to material deemed fit for juveniles."[149]

Finally, the court found that the library policy violated the doctrine barring prior restraints. Mandatory filtering policies that rely on commercial blocking software arguably constitute prior restraints because, as in *Mainstream Loudoun,* they "entrust all . . . blocking decisions . . . to a private vendor" whose standards and practices cannot be monitored by the filtering library.[150]

As to the second concern, libraries are unlikely to face liability from patrons for failing to use censorware. For example, in *Kathleen R. v. City of Livermore,*[151] a woman sued a public library, complaining that her 12-year-old son was able to view and download pornography at a public library in Livermore, California. The plaintiff sought an injunction that would prohibit the library "from maintaining any computer system on which it allows people to access . . . obscene material or on which it allows minors to access . . . sexual material harmful to minors." The plaintiff also claimed that the library had a constitutional duty to "protect" library patrons from unwanted and "harmful" sexually explicit materials. The California court of appeals rejected all of the plaintiff's claims.

A different concern here is library liability to employees for failing to use censorware under sexual harassment "hostile work environment" theories. Federal civil rights laws and many states' parallel civil rights laws afford employees the "right to work in an environment free from discriminatory intimidation, ridicule and insult."[152] Arguably, access to materials over the Internet that are offensive due to their sexually explicit nature or messages regarding race, religion, or ethnicity may subject a library to liability for a hostile environment under these laws. To date, no published judicial opinion addresses such a hostile environment claim brought by a library employee on this basis.[153]

51.2.6.2 *Public Schools.*

There are no cases involving the use of censorware in public schools. Schools traditionally have been considered places where the government has a strong interest in regulating speech,[154] particularly with respect to curricular materials.[155] Prevailing cases emphasize the importance of inculcating values and maintaining civility in schools, along with the risk that the viewpoints expressed by student speech would be attributed to the school. Moreover, most public school students are too young to enjoy the same constitutional rights as adults.

Nevertheless, the First Amendment should place significant limits on public schools' use of censorware. In general, students do not "shed their constitutional rights to freedom of speech or expression at the schoolhouse gate."[156] Thus, while schools have maximum authority over curriculum and school-sponsored activities and substantial authority to regulate student speech, they have less authority to regulate students' right to receive information. Despite schools' "comprehensive authority" to prescribe and control student conduct, "students may not be regarded as closed-circuit recipients of only that which the State chooses to communicate."[157]

Moreover, the extent of governmental power to regulate conduct of minors not constitutionally regulable when committed by adults is a "vexing" question, "perhaps not susceptible of precise answer."[158] While the government has a general interest in regulating schools, the interest in regulating students' access to "objectionable" extracurricular information is of uncertain pedigree. For instance, the Supreme Court has characterized the government interest in protecting children against "harmful to minors" material as derivative of or secondary to parents' interests.[159] Thus, "[s]peech that is neither obscene as to youths nor subject to some other legitimate proscription cannot be suppressed solely to protect the young from ideas or images that a legislative body thinks unsuitable for them."[160] This characterization suggests that the state has no interest in blocking a minor's access to HTM material to which parents do not object.[161]

Moreover, the state's interest is not uniformly strong across all minors. In general, minors' fundamental rights, including the right to receive information, strengthen as they grow older; "constitutional rights do not mature and come into being magically only when one attains the state-defined age of majority."[162] Moreover, some high school students are 18 or 19 and thus not minors for HTM purposes.

51.3   FILTERING TECHNOLOGY

51.3.1   Underlying Principles.   The fundamental technology used by censorware programs is the matching of strings against a database of forbidden items. To retrieve any material, first it must be specified in some manner. Comparing these specifications against a list of items to be prohibited is the most common method of operation. For example, the Uniform Resource Locator (URL) is extensively used to identify and retrieve material.[163] Consider the URL

> *http://www.eff.org/awards/20010305_pioneer_press_release.html*

This URL specifies a protocol (*http*), a host server (*www.eff.org*), a path to the document (*awards/20010305_pioneer_press_release*), and a standard for formatting text (*.html*). All of these elements can be compared against an internal database in order to determine if a request to read this document should be permitted or denied.

The very simplest comparison, keyword-matching, just looks for prohibited patterns in the text of the URL string itself. The first inkling of difficulty arises from the issue of how exactly to perform that pattern-matching. Testing for "sex" as a word will fail on "/sexy" or "/sexstuff." But performing even a prefix test will then match on "/sextet" and "/sexton."

The checking of the host server against the list of prohibited items can be done in two different ways. It can either be tested "by-name" (*www.eff.org*) or "by-address," which uses the result of resolving the domain name to a corresponding Internet Protocol (IP) address (here, *204.253.162.3*). This is a critical difference in operation. Some hosts have several different names that resolve to the same address (*www.eff.org, www.eff.com,* and *www.eff.net* are all different names for the same host). However, in the case of the http protocol, a large number of different hosts with very different names can all share the same IP address. This name-sharing is called "virtual hosting." Moreover, a host name may resolve at various times to one of several different addresses, in order to distribute the workload among several machines.

The string form of an IP address is merely one textual representation of the address. That is, "204.253.162.3" is one way of representing the IP address that corresponds also to "www.eff.org." It is a very common way of representing an address but by no means the only method. Censorware programs that compare on a by-name basis often contain some text representations of addresses for common sites. But this is not actual by-address functionality. It is much closer to being just another variant name of the site. A name that is different from the names on the list will not match in terms of string comparison yet still map to the correct IP address and permit access that the program would have otherwise denied.

The list of prohibited items can be stored either locally on the target machine (client-based) or remotely in another location (server-based). As the databases of forbidden items increase in size, tracking the overall growth of the Internet and World Wide Web, the trend is to store the lists on a remote machine. All information requests are then funneled through this choke-point.

Although (at least in the United States) the most frequent topic of prohibition is sex, the idea of string comparison against an index of prohibited sites is quite general. Many censorware companies offer approximately 30 different lists, ranging from "hate" sites to those that provide unrestricted news feeds. Internally, ordinarily this is implemented as various flags in a large database of forbidden sites rather than in physically separate lists. Although a few small client-based programs do have physically separate lists, this is typically unwieldy and inefficient.

51.3.2   Legal Aspects of Censorware Investigation.   Critically, the database of prohibited sites is almost always encrypted and kept secret. Some enterprising programmers have decrypted such lists and publicized the results. This situation has resulted in legal threats and a lawsuit against one set of programmers.[164]

The basis for legal action against such programmers typically involves various legal theories of copyright, trade secret, license contracts, and a new "paracopyright" offense called "circumvention."[165] Under the new offense of circumvention, one may not circumvent technological measures like encryption that limit access to the content of a copyrighted work.[166] Thus, if a program's database of censored sites was encrypted, it would be illegal to bypass the encryption in order to learn what sites were on the list.

In October 2000, however, the Library of Congress issued a three-year exemption to the circumvention provision of the DMCA for such blacklists, stating:

> It appears that the prohibition on circumvention of technological measures that control access to these lists of blocked sites will cause an adverse effect on noninfringing users since persons who wish to criticize and comment on them cannot ascertain which sites are contained in the lists unless they circumvent. The case has been made for an exemption for compilations consisting of lists of Web sites blocked by filtering software applications.[167]

However, the scope of all other legal issues (copyright, trade secret, license contracts) still remains problematic.

51.3.3   Vulnerabilities and Exploits.   The fundamental problem for censorware is the existence of Web sites that provide privacy and anonymity for reading material over the Internet. This is an intrinsic difficulty. The goal of such services is to mask from outside observers what persons might want to see and to hide from interested authorities their identities. This information—what is being read and who wants to read it—is exactly the data critical to controlling the authorization to permit or deny the request.

In terms of censorware's requirements, privacy and anonymity sites are security holes. The typical response of vendors has been either to regard such sites as forbidden in all possible categories[168] or to have a special category collecting such sites (a category where all such sites must certainly be prohibited, otherwise the effectiveness of the product will be near nil). The program BESS calls the category "LOOPHOLE."[169] WebSense writes of "Proxy Avoidance Systems."[170]

Language-translation Web sites present a similar vulnerability. While not specifically designed to hide information about what is being read (and who is reading it), they often have such an effect in practice. A typical language translation site has a form where a person can type the address of a Web page, set the source and target languages, and then view the translated result. Functionally, this can act as a method of retrieving the material through the translation site (as translating an English-language site from, say, Chinese into English is typically highly accurate). These sites commonly are treated the same way as the privacy and anonymity services.[171]

Caching services present a different control problem. A caching service keeps copies of Web pages and then delivers those copies itself. The reasons for using caching range from increasing speed and lowering bandwidth usage, to archiving of material. To a censorware program, however, the information often is regarded as being sent from the Internet address of the cache machine, not the address of the original site. The URL of the Web page also may be encoded or at least transformed beyond recognition in terms of the censorware's string-matching. This creates a dilemma for censorware vendors. They can either ban the cache entirely or hope that its use as an alternate means of access does not become widely known.

The most well-publicized example of such a cache exploit was the discovery by Peacefire's Bennett Haselton[172] that the "Akamai" commercial high-speed routing network could be used to retrieve arbitrary Web pages. There was no authentication or encryption in requests to their caching/routing servers, and the format for creating a request was very simple. As a result, the page would appear to originate from Akamai. Vendors were not willing to ban the IP addresses in Akamai's network, as that would have affected many large corporate sites. Akamai subsequently improved the checking of the validity of its requests and implemented access controls so that only Web pages of Akamai customers could be requested through its network.

One very popular search engine, Google, maintains an extensive quasi-archival cache of Web pages. Although Google only caches text, there is no restriction on the content. Google also has recently acquired and made available the multiyear archive of netnews messages from the company DejaNews. The DejaNews archive at times has been considered an exploit with regard to censorware, in that the archive supplies a vast amount of material (ranging from the very technical to extremely sexual) on a single site.[173]

It remains to be seen if these resources, the page cache and netnews archives, will be considered too dangerous as a possible way to avoid content controls. If so, they probably will have to be completely banned by censorware programs.

The growth of peer-to-peer file-sharing protocols has been viewed as a serious threat to the effectiveness of censorware. Although these systems became well known for sharing music (Napster), any other type of file can readily be shared. To some developers, this is a feature, a desirable extension of anonymity and privacy.[174] But no less than a U.S. House Committee has considered such file sharing to be a serious problem for enforcement of content controls.[175]

Programs installed on local machines (i.e., client- or home-based software) often can be disabled by renaming certain system files or by editing configuration files. Peacefire has made available a program that automates this process for several common programs.

The string-matching functions in censorware are usually extremely simple. Producing a variant of a hostname that passes the string-matching check at times can be as simple as adding a dot to the end of the hostname.[176]

51.3.4   Performance.   It has been difficult to devise metrics to measure the accuracy of censorware. The encryption of the database, along with the concomitant legal risk,[177] hinders such research.

Moreover, devising a meaningful method of assessment is extremely complex, even though it is not difficult to collect a very large list of sexuality oriented sites by searching various directories.[178] If the database is examined in a naïve manner, the ease of collection of a large list of commercial sex sites can lead to a type of statistical masking. This problem is amplified by aspects of both by-name and by-address lists. For example, in a by-name list, should *www.eff.org, www.eff.com,* and *www.eff.net* be considered as three items or one? In a by-address list, virtual hosting makes counting Web sites all the more difficult. Where a list consists only of Internet addresses, it can be hard to determine whether an address represents only one site or virtually hosts many Web sites.

Some companies provide a free hosting service that allows members to set up their own Web pages. Popular examples are Yahoo/Geocities and America Online. If everything on these services is banned, it would be inaccurate to count that as just one Web site.

A promising approach has been to examine server log files of activity and to attempt to estimate how often a rejected request has been denied for prohibited content (as opposed to being rejected because of a shared IP address or being on a free service). One study put the error rate here as one in 20.[179] No detailed examination of server log files has been done to see how many connections to sex sites are not detected by censorware.

Several grassroots investigations have made detailed examination of performance. Some of the most technically astute can be found on sites like Peacefire,[180] Censorware Project,[181] and Seth Finkelstein's Anticensorware Investigations.[182] While these sites may be dismissed as activist and partisan, the reports are based on a level of technical sophistication that is not readily found elsewhere.

Well-regarded consumer organizations also have conducted evaluations. The most recent consumer study appeared in the March 2001 issue of *Consumer Reports.* It stated that "Most of the products we tested failed to block one objectionable site in five."[183] This finding is consistent with a similar 1998 *Consumer Reports* study.[184] The Consumer's Association (United Kingdom) reached a similar conclusion in May 2000, reporting that "All seven [products] allowed access to at least six of the 23 offensive sites."[185] Many instances of innocuous Web sites being banned are given in these reports.

Perhaps the most interesting statements are the self-assessment of the vendors in company documents filed with the Securities and Exchange Commission. Because fraudulent filings are illegal, such filings reflect a standard more serious than claims that can be made in a company press release.

As the company N2H2 states (emphasis in original):

OUR FILTERING CATEGORIZATIONS ARE SUBJECTIVE, AND WE MAY FAIL TO FILTER ALL POTENTIALLY OBJECTIONABLE CONTENT.

We may not succeed in sufficiently filtering internet content to meet our customers' expectations. We rely upon a combination of automated filtering technology and human review to categorize Web site content through our Bess filtering services and on Searchopolis, our filtered Web portal. The total number of Web sites and partial Web sites is growing rapidly. . . .[186]

Similarly, Websense also disclaims (again, emphasis in original)

OUR DATABASE CATEGORIES AND OUR PROCESS FOR CLASSIFYING WEB SITES WITHIN THOSE CATEGORIES ARE SUBJECTIVE, AND WE MAY NOT BE ABLE TO CATEGORIZE WEB SITES IN ACCORDANCE WITH OUR CUSTOMERS' EXPECTATIONS.[187]

51.3.5 Parental Involvement/Responsibility.
While the technical issues of censorware are identical regardless of whether it is being applied by government, employers, or parents, the parent-child case generates much of the political discussion. Two conflicting mental models are at work in the debate.

The primary impetus for censorware arises out of an idea that might be called the "toxic material" theory, under which viewing certain information has a toxic effect, akin to a harmful drug or a poison. As stated in a lawsuit seeking an injunction against a library with unrestricted Internet access: "Children such as Brandon P. who view obscenity and pornography on the library's computers can and have sustained emotional and psychological damage in addition to damage to their nervous systems. It is highly likely that such damage will occur given the library's policy."[188]

The outcome of the toxic material threat model has been legislation such as the CHIPA. In contrast, theoretical discussion typically takes place in a model that can be termed the "control-rights" theory. This is concerned primarily with authority relationships within some framework. One paper submitted to a government commission stated:

> [T]he decision by a third party that a person may not use a computer to access certain content from the Internet demands some sort of justification. The burden should be on the filterer to justify the denial of another person's access. The most plausible justifications for restricting access are that the third party owns the computer or that the third party has a relation of legitimate authority over the user.[189]

However, the control-rights discussion does not address the assumptions and threat model inherent in the toxic material theory. A belief in harmful information logically requires restrictions to be as extensive and widespread as possible. In fact, this is an instance of typical security practices, where the potential attack is viewed along the lines of dangerous contamination. All possible environments where the subject may be located then need to be secured to the greatest extent possible. This social need is similar to the technical requirement discussed earlier regarding banning privacy, anonymity, and even language-translation Web sites. It is all a matter of security holes.

51.4 SUMMARY. Although the Internet has the technological potential to create a global forum for free expression, one must not underestimate the political and technological barriers at work.

- *Internet-specific laws:* Some governments have criminalized certain types of Internet speech. Such criminal penalties may come in the form of laws intended to protect minors from "harmful" material. Under U.S. law, however, requiring Internet speakers to shield certain populations from their speech has been found to effect a ban on that speech.[190]

- *Application of existing laws:* Governments need not specifically enact laws targeting Internet-based speech. For example, the German government action against CompuServe for providing access to illegal material merely applied existing laws to the Internet.

- *Content-based license terms applied to Internet users and service providers:* Some countries have established licensing systems that require Internet users and/or service providers to agree to refrain from certain kinds of speech or that block access to speech as a condition of having, or using, or providing access to the Internet. For instance, China has issued rules requiring anyone with Internet access to refrain from proscribed speech.

- *Compelled use of computerized censorship, rating, or content labeling tools:* Various techniques can:

  ○ Prevent individuals from using the Internet to exchange information on topics that may be controversial or unpopular

  ○ Enable the development of country profiles to facilitate a global rating system desired by some governments

  ○ Block access to content on entire domains

  ○ Block access to Internet content available at any domain or page that contains a specific keyword or character string in the address

  ○ Override self-rating labels provided by content creators and providers

51.5 FURTHER READING

Electronic Privacy Information Center, *Filters and Freedom* 2.0 (2001): *http://epic.org/book-store/filters2.0/default.html.*

Lessig, Lawrence. *Code and Other Laws of Cyberspace.* New York: Basic Books, 1999.

Semitsu, Junichi P. "Note, Burning Cyberbooks in Public Libraries: Internet Filtering Software vs. the First Amendment," 52 *Stan. L. Rev.* 509 (2000).

Sullivan, Kathleen M. "First Amendment Intermediaries in the Age of Cyberspace," 45 *UCLA L. Rev.* 1653 (1998).

Weinberg, Jonathan. "Rating the Net," 19 *Hastings Comm. & Ent. L.J.* 453 (1997).

51.6 NOTES

1. Universal Declaration of Human Rights, art. 19, G.A. Res 217A, U.N. GAOR, 3d Sess., U.N. Doc. A/810 (1948).

2. Thomas D. Jones, "Human Rights: Freedom of Expression and Group Defamation Under British, Canadian, Indian, Nigerian and United States Law—A Comparative Analysis," 18 *Suffolk Transnat'l L. Rev.* 427, 428 (1995) (footnotes omitted).

3. Samuel Fifer and Michael Sachs, "The Price of International Free Speech: Nations Deal With Defamation on the Internet," 8 *DePaul-LCA J. Art & Ent. L.* 1, 2 (1997).

4. Ibid.

5. Order of the County Court of Paris, at 2, in *La Ligue Contre Le Racisme Et L'Antisemitisme v. Yahoo! Inc.,* No. RG: 00/05308 (Nov. 20, 2000) (translated).

6. Ibid., p. 4.

7. Ibid.

8. Although the merits of this case have not yet been reached, the district court on June 7, 2001, rejected the French parties' motion to dismiss the case: *www.cdt.org/jurisdiction/010607yahoo.pdf.*

9. *Yahoo! Inc. v. La Ligue Contre le Racisme et L'Antisemitisme, et al.,* 145 F. Supp. 2d 1168 (N.D. Cal. 2001).

10. See generally Fifer and Sachs, supra.

11. See, e.g., Jane Ginsburg, "Copyright Without Borders? Choice of Forum and Choice of Law for Copyright Infringement in Cyberspace," 15 *Cardozo Arts & Ent. L.J.* 153 (1997).

12. Peter Swire, "Of Elephants, Mice, And Privacy: International Choice of Law and the Internet," 32 *Int'l Law.* 991 (1998).

13. See John T. Delacourt, "Recent Development: The International Impact of Internet Regulation," 38 *Harv. Int'l L. J.* 207, 212 (1997).

14. Kim Rappaport, Note, "In the Wake of Reno v. ACLU: The Continued Struggle in Western Constitutional Democracies with Internet Censorship and Freedom of Speech Online," 13 *Am. U. Int'l L. Rev.* 765, 791 (1998).

15. Ibid., pp. 795–799.

16. Some observers reported that the Internet seems to foster "hate" sites. Laura Leets, "Responses to Internet Hate Sites: Is Speech Too Free in Cyberspace? 6 *Comm. L. & Pol'y* 287, 288 (2001) (noting that watchdog groups have documented about 2800 hate sites).

17. Ibid., pp. 291–294.

18. Rappaport, supra, at 785–786 (footnotes omitted).

19. Ibid., p. 789 (footnotes omitted).

20. Steve Kettmann, "German Hate Law: No Denying It" (December 15, 2000): *www.wired.com/news/politics/0,1283,40669,00.html.*

21. Ibid.

22. Ibid.

23. Canadian Criminal Code § 319(2), R.S.C. 1985, c. C-46 (willful promotion of hatred against an identifiable group); see ibid., § 181 (willful publication of false statements likely to injure a public interest).

24. *R. v. Keegstra,* 3 S.C.R. 697 (1990).

25. *Keegstra,* supra.

26. Robert Cribb, "Canadian Net Hate Debate Flares" (March 25, 1998): *www.wired.com/news/news/politics/story/11195.html* ("Cribb").

27. Zundel was charged with spreading "false news" in violation of § 181 of the Canadian Criminal Code.

28. *R. v. Zundel* (1992) 2 S.C.R. (Can.) 731.

29. Credence Fogo-Schensul, "More Than a River in Egypt: Holocaust Denial, the Internet, and International Freedom of Expression Norms," 33 *Gonz. L. Rev.* 271, 245 n.32 (1997–1998) (citation omitted).

30. Digital Freedom Network (February 27, 2001): *www.escribe.com/internet/proxy-methods/m2557.html.*

31. China again seeks to control the Internet (December 6, 2000): *www.bizasia.com/gen/articles/stand_art.htm?ac = EKBGN-Y.*

32. Managing Internet Information-Release Services, P.R.C. Ministry of Information Industry Regulation, Nov. 7, 2000; see also "China Issues Regulations on Managing Internet Information-Release Services," China Online, November 13, 2000: *www.chinaonline.com/issues/internet_policy/NewsArchive/Secure/2000/November/C00110604.asp.* Other restrictions target a variety of disfavored groups, particularly supporters of the Falun Gong spiritual movement. See "China Passes Internet Security Law," China Online, December 29, 2000: *www.chinaonline.com/issues/internet_policy/NewsArchive/Secure/2000/December/C00122805.asp.*

33. Geremie R. Barme and Sang Ye, "The Great Firewall of China" (June 1997): *www.wired.com/wired/archive/5.06/china.html?person = bill_gates&topic_set = wiredpeople.*

34. Ibid.

35. Digital Freedom Network, "Attacks on the Internet in China" (April 30, 2001): *www.dfn.org/focus/china/netattack.htm.*

36. Ibid.

37. Ibid.

38. Ibid.

39. Ibid.

40. Ibid.

41. Ibid.

42. Ibid.

43. Ibid.

44. Ibid.

45. Ibid.

46. Ibid.

47. Ibid.

48. Human Rights Watch, "The Internet in the Middle East and North Africa: Free Expression and Censorship": *www.hrw.org.*

49. Saudi Internet regulations, Saudi Arabia Council of Ministers Resolution (February 12, 2001): *www.al-bab.com/media/docs/saudi.htm.*

50. Human Rights Watch World Report 1999, "Freedom of Expression on the Internet": *www.hrw.org/hrw/worldreport99/special/internet.html.*

51. Christina Fink, Burma: "Constructive Engagement in Cyberspace?" (1997): *www.burmafund.org.*

52. Digital Freedom Network, "The New Net Regulations in Burma" (January 31, 2000): *www.dfn.org/voices/burma/webregulations.htm.*

53. Ibid.

54. Digital Freedom Network, "Burma Wards Off the Internet Revolution (January 31, 2000): *www.dfn.org/focus/burma/Web-crackdown.htm.*

55. The notion of "unprotected" speech is discussed in Section 2.4.3.

56. In the context of the right to speak, the requirement of state action is somewhat relaxed compared to other constitutional rights. For example, when private persons—not the government—use the courts against another private person's speech, "state action" is usually found.

See *New York Times Co. v. Sullivan,* 376 U.S. 254 (1964) (defamation); *Hustler Magazine, Inc. v. Falwell,* 485 U.S. 46 (1988) (intentional infliction of emotional distress).

57. *Texas v. Johnson,* 491 U.S. 397, 403 (1989).

58. *W. Va Bd. of Educ. v. Barnette,* 319 U.S. 624, 632 (1943).

59. *McIntyre v. Ohio Elections Comm'n,* 514 U.S. 334 (1995).

60. *Lamont v. Postmaster General,* 381 U.S. 301, 307 (1965) (invalidating law requiring willing recipient to request that certain, state-defined materials be sent to him); *Virginia Pharmacy Bd. v. Virginia Consumer Council,* 425 U.S. 748, 756 (1974).

61. *City of Lakewood v. Plain Dealer Publishing Co.,* 486 U.S. 750 (1988).

62. *Buckley v. Valeo,* 424 U.S. 1, 19 (1976).

63. *Simon & Schuster, Inc. v. Members of N.Y. State Crime Victims Bd.,* 502 U.S. 105, 117 (1991).

64. *City of Ladue v. Gilleo,* 512 U.S. 43 (1994).

65. *Abrams v. United States,* 250 U.S. 616, 630 (1919) (Holmes, J., dissenting).

66. *Hurley v. GLIB,* 515 U.S. 557 (1995).

67. *Cohen v. California,* 403 U.S. 15, 24 (1971) (emphasis added).

68. *Bantam Books, Inc. v. Sullivan,* 372 U.S. 58, 66 (1963).

69. *Thornhill v. Alabama,* 310 U.S. 88, 97 (1940). ("It is not merely the sporadic abuse of power by the censor but the pervasive threat inherent in its very existence that constitutes the danger to freedom of discussion.")

70. *Schenck v. United States,* 249 U.S. 47, 52 (1919).

71. *Whitney v. California,* 274 U.S. 357, 377 (1926) (Brandeis, J., concurring).

72. *Brandenburg v. Ohio,* 395 U.S. 444, 447 (1969).

73. *American Booksellers Assn., Inc. v. Hudnut,* 771 F.2d 323, 333 (7th Cir. 1985), aff'd mem. 475 U.S. 1001 (1986).

74. See also *Planned Parenthood v. American Coalition of Life,* 244 F.3d 1007 (9th Cir. 2001).

75. *New York Times Co. v. Sullivan,* 376 U.S. 254, 292 (1964).

76. *Police Dept. of Chicago v. Mosley,* 408 U. S. 92, 96 (1972).

77. *NAACP v. Button,* 371 U.S. 415, 433 (1963).

78. *Lakewood, supra.*

79. *Smith v. California,* 361 U.S. 147 (1959).

80. *Speiser v. Randall,* 357 U.S. 513 (1958).

81. *Gertz v. Robert Welch, Inc.,* 418 U.S. 323 (1974).

82. *Organization for a Better Austin v. Keefe,* 402 U.S. 415, 419 (1971).

83. *New York Times Co. v. United States,* 403 U.S. 713, 729 (1971) (Stewart, J., concurring).

84. *Nebraska Press Ass'n v. Stuart,* 427 U.S. 539 (1976).

85. *Staub v. Baxley,* 355 U.S. 313, 322 (1958).

86. *Niemotko v. Maryland,* 340 U.S. 268, 271 (1951).

87. *Freedman v. Maryland,* 380 U.S. 51, 58 (1965).

88. Ibid. at 58–59.

89. See, e.g., *United States v. Playboy Entertainment Group, Inc.,* 120 S. Ct. 1878, 1880 (2000); *Reno v. ACLU,* 521 U.S. 844 (1997).

90. See *R.A.V. v. St. Paul,* 505 U. S. 377, 391 (1992).

91. See *Perry Ed. Assn. v. Perry Local Educators' Assn.,* 460 U. S. 37, 46 (1983).

92. *R.A.V.,* supra (government may not regulate otherwise unprotected "fighting words" based on viewpoint).

93. *Turner Broadcasting System, Inc. v. FCC,* 512 U.S. 622, 642 (1994) (citations omitted).

94. Ibid. at 661.

95. *Clark v. Community for Creative Non-Violence,* 468 U.S. 288, 293 (1984).

96. *United States v. O'Brien,* 391 U.S. 367, 376–77 (1968).

97. *City of Renton v. Playtime Theatres, Inc.,* 475 U.S. 41, 47 (1986).

98. *Boos v. Barry,* 485 U.S. 312, 335 (1988) (Brennan, J., concurring).

99. *Forsyth County v. Nationalist Movement,* 505 U.S. 123, 135 (1992).

100. *United States v. Reese,* 92 U. S. 214, 221 (1876).

101. *NAACP v. Button,* 371 U.S. at 337.

102. *Kolender v. Lawson,* 461 U.S. 352, 357–358 (1983).

103. *Thornhill v. Alabama,* 310 U.S. 88, 97 (1940).

104. Ibid., pp. 97–98.

105. Often, laws are struck down only "as applied," that is, the particular application of the law to a particular person is found to violate the Constitution. Facial invalidation, on the other hand, is not limited to the particular application but to the entire law, roughly speaking. See, e.g., Richard H. Fallon, Jr., "As-Applied and Facial Challenges and Third-Party Standing," 113 *Harv. L. Rev.* 1321 (2000).

106. *Broadrick v. Oklahoma,* 413 U. S. 601, 612–615 (1973).

107. *Red Lion Broadcasting Co. v. FCC,* 395 U.S. 367 (1969).

108. *Int'l Soc'y for Krishna Consciousness, Inc. v. Lee,* 505 U.S. 672, 678 (1992).

109. *Legal Services Corporation v. Velazquez,* 531 U.S. 533, (2001).

110. *Arcara v. Cloud Books, Inc.,* 478 U.S. 697, 707 n.4 (1986).

111. *Giboney v. Empire Storage & Ice Co.,* 336 U.S. 490, 502 (1949).

112. *Watts v. United States,* 394 U.S. 705, 707 (1969).

113. Ibid., pp. 707-708.

114. *Bartnicki v. Vopper,* 121 S.Ct. 1753, 1765 (2001).

115. *New York Times Co. v. Sullivan,* 376 U.S. 254 (1964).

116. *Chaplinsky v. New Hampshire,* 315 U.S. 568, 571 (1942).

117. Ibid., p. 572.

118. *Cohen v. California,* 403 U.S. 15, 20 (1971).

119. *Miller v. California,* 413 U.S. 15, 24 (1973).

120. Ibid. at 32.

121. *New York v. Ferber,* 458 U.S. 747, 764 (1982).

122. The federal child pornography statute reaches "any visual depiction" of a minor under 18 years old engaging in "sexually explicit conduct," which includes "actual or simulated" sexual intercourse, bestiality, masturbation, sadistic or masochistic abuse, or "lascivious exhibition of the genitals or pubic area." 18 U.S.C. § 2256.

123. *Ferber,* 458 U.S. at 764–765. Notably, the rationale for regulating child pornography is not content-based. Instead, it is based on the harm to children from being subjects of sexual performances, as well as the harm from the distribution of such photographs.

124. *R.A.V. v. City of St. Paul,* 505 U.S. 377, 391 (1992).

125. *Ginsberg v. New York,* 390 U.S. 629 (1968).

126. *44 Liquormart, Inc. v. Rhode Island,* 517 U.S. 484 (1996).

127. *Red Lion Broadcasting Co. v. FCC,* 395 U.S. 367 (1969).

128. Speech on the Internet, however, is entitled to "full" First Amendment protection.

129. *City of Erie v. Pap's A.M.,* 120 S.Ct. 1382 (2000).

130. *FCC v. Pacifica,* 438 U.S. 726 (1978).

131. *Denver Area Educ. Telecom. Consortium v. FCC,* 518 U.S. 727 (1996); but see *Playboy,* supra.

132. *Sable Communications v. FCC,* 492 U.S. 115 (1989).

133. Speech is "harmful to minors" if it (i) is "patently offensive to prevailing standards in the adult community as a whole with respect to what is suitable . . . for minors"; (ii) appeals to the prurient interest of minors; and (iii) is "utterly without redeeming social importance for minors." *Ginsberg v. New York,* 390 U.S. 629, 633 (1968) (upholding conviction of magazine vendor for selling adult magazine to 16-year-old).

134. *Reno,* 521 U.S. at 865.

135. Ibid.

136. *Erznoznik v. City of Jacksonville,* 422 U.S. 205, 212–214 (1975).

137. *Reno,* 521 U.S. at 878. Lower courts have held that "if a work is found to have serious literary, artistic, political or scientific value for a legitimate minority of normal, older adolescents, then it cannot be said to lack such value for the entire class of juveniles taken

as a whole." *American Booksellers Ass'n v. Webb*, 919 F.2d 1493, 1504–5 (11th Cir. 1990) (quoting *American Booksellers Ass'n v. Virginia*, 882 F.2d 125, 127 (4th Cir. 1989) (other citations omitted).

138. Pub. L. No. 105-277, 112 Stat. 2681 (1998) (codified at 47 U.S.C. § 231).

139. *ACLU v. Reno*, 31 F. Supp. 2d 473 (E.D. Pa. 1999).

140. *ACLU v. Reno*, 217 F.3d 162, 177 (3d Cir. 2000), cert. granted sub. nom. *Ashcroft v. ACLU*, (121 S.Ct. 1997) (2001), argued Nov. 28, 2001.

141. See, for example, *ACLU v. Johnson*, 194 F.3d 1149 (10th Cir. 1999) (affirming injunction against enforcement of New Mexico statute criminalizing dissemination by computer of material harmful to minors); *American Libraries Ass'n v. Pataki*, 969 F. Supp. 160 (S.D. N.Y. 1997) (enjoining a New York statute similar to the CDA that criminalized the use of a computer to disseminate sexually explicit materials to minors).

142. Codified at 47 U.S.C. § 254(h) and 20 U.S.C. § 9134.

143. The ALA's Resolution on the Use of Filtering Software in Libraries is available from the ALA Office for Intellectual Freedom.

144. *Multnomah County Public Library v. United States*, 01-CV-1322 (E.D. Pa.); and *American Library Ass'n. v. United States*, 01-CV-1303 (E.D. Pa.). These two cases were consolidated into one.

145. *Mainstream Loudoun v. Bd. of Trustees of the Loudoun County Library*, 2 F. Supp. 2d 783 (E.D. Va.1998) (*Mainstream Loudoun I*); *Mainstream Loudoun v. Bd. of Trustees of the Loudoun County Library*, 24 F. Supp. 2d 552 (E.D. Va. 1998) (*Mainstream Loudoun II*).

146. *Mainstream Loudoun I*, 2 F. Supp. 2d at 787.

147. *Mainstream Loudoun II*, 24 F. Supp. 2d at 564–565.

148. Ibid., p. 556 ("undisputed" that "sites that do not contain any material that is prohibited by the Policy" were blocked).

149. *Mainstream Loudoun II*, 24 F. Supp. 2d at 567.

150. *Mainstream Loudoun II*, 24 F. Supp. 2d at 569.

151. 87 Cal. App. 4th 684 (1st Dist. 2001).

152. *Meritor Savings Bank FSB v. Vinson*, 477 U.S. 57, 65 (1986).

153. The issue was raised indirectly in *Mainstream Loudoun*, where the library offered fear of "hostile work environment" liability as one justification for using censorware. The court rejected that argument. *Mainstream Loudoun II*, 24 F. Supp. 2d at 566–568.

154. *Bethel School District No. 403 v. Fraser*, 478 U.S. 675 (1986) (upholding suspension of high school student for making sexually suggestive speech at school assembly).

155. *Hazelwood Sch. Dist. v. Kuhlmeier*, 484 U.S. 260 (1988) (upholding teacher's censorship of articles destined for newspaper prepared by journalism class).

156. *Tinker v. Des Moines Indep. Community School Dist.*, 393 U.S. 503, 506 (1969).

157. Ibid., p. 511. Schools may, however, regulate students' First Amendment rights if the prohibited speech would "materially and substantially interfere with the requirements of appropriate discipline in the operation of the school." Ibid., p. 509. This burden cannot be satisfied by "undifferentiated fear or apprehension of disturbance"; the school must show "something more than a mere desire to avoid the discomfort and unpleasantness that always accompany an unpopular viewpoint." Ibid., p. 508.

158. *Carey v. Population Servs. Int'l*, 431 U.S. 678, 692 (plurality opinion) (1977).

159. *Reno v. ACLU*, 521 U.S. 844 (1997); *Ginsberg v. New York*, 390 U.S. 629 (1968); *Prince v. Massachusetts*, 321 U.S. 158, 166 (1944).

160. *Erznoznik*, 422 U.S. at 213–214.

161. In other contexts, schools often accommodate or try to accommodate parental wishes as to the exposure of their children in school to undesired material, even when the material is part of the school's chosen curriculum. Catherine J. Ross, "An Emerging Right for Mature Minors to Receive Information," 2 *U. Pa. J. Const. L.* 223, 247 n. 119 (1999) ("nearly every school district in the country allows parents 'to opt their own children out of sexuality and AIDS education, as well as out of specific activities or assignments that conflict with their religious beliefs.'"), *quoting* People for the American Way, *A Right Wing and a Prayer: The Religious*

Right and Your Public Schools 60 (1997). In some states, such accommodation with respect to all or specified categories of curricular materials is required. *Minn. Stat. Ann.* § 126.699 (West 1994) (schools must allow parents to review curricular materials and must provide alternative materials to replace those that parents find objectionable for any reason); *Mass. Gen. Laws Ann.* ch. LXXI 32A (West 1998) (requiring that school districts notify parents of the content of any curriculum primarily involving "human sexual education or human sexuality" and afford parents a flexible way of exempting their children from such curricula upon written notice to the school); *Va. Code Ann.* § 22.1-207-2 (Michie 1998) (giving public school parents the right to review "the complete family life curricula [sic], including all supplemental materials").

162. *Planned Parenthood of Cent. Mo. v. Danforth,* 428 U.S. 52, 74 (1976) (minors' right to abortion).

163. *www.w3.org/Addressing.*

164. *Microsystems Software, Inc. v. Scandinavia Online,* 98 F. Supp. 2d 74 (D. Mass 2000), aff'd, 226 F.3d 35 (1st Cir. 2000).

165. Digital Millennium Copyright Act (DMCA), 17 U.S.C. § 1201–1204.

166. 17 U.S.C. § 1201(a)(1)(A).

167. *www.loc.gov/copyright/fedreg/65fr64555.html.*

168. Seth Finkelstein, "SmartFilter's Greatest Evils" (censorware vs. privacy and anonymity): *http://sethf.com/anticensorware/smartfilter/greatestevils.php.*

169. *http://sethf.com/anticensorware/bess/loophole.php.*

170. *www.websense.com/products/about/database/version4.cfm.*

171. See "SmartFilter's Greatest Evils," supra, and "BabelFish Blocked by Censorware": *www.peacefire.org/babelfish.*

172. *http://peacefire.org.*

173. *www.spectacle.org/cs/cypa.html.*

174. See SafeWeb's "Triangle Boy": *http://fugu.safeweb.com/sjws/solutions/triangle_boy.html.*

175. *www.house.gov/reform/min/porn.html.*

176. *http://slashdot.org/features/00/07/15/0327239.shtml.*

177. See *http://ansuz.sooke.bc.ca/cpbfaq.html.*

178. For instance, *http://dir.yahoo.com/Business_and_Economy/Shopping_and_Services/Sex* would be a simple starting point, and would easily yield many thousands of items.

179. *http://censorware.net/reports/utah/followup.*

180. *http://peacefire.org.*

181. *http://censorware.net.*

182. *http://sethf.com/anticensorware.*

183. *Consumer Reports,* "Digital Chaperones for Kids": *www.consumerreports.org/Special/ConsumerInterest/Reports/0103fil0.html.*

184. *Consumer Reports,* "When Online Becomes Off-Limits for Kids": *www.consumersunion.org/other/onlineny1198.htm.*

185. Consumer's Association (UK), "Internet Filters Don't Safeguard Children against Pornography and Other Net Nasties": *www.which.net/whatsnew/pr/may00/which/netnannies.html.*

186. *www.sec.gov/Archives/edgar/data/1077301/0000891020-99-001215.txt.*

187. *www.sec.gov/Archives/edgar/data/1098277/0000936392-00-000148.txt.*

188. First Amended Complaint in *Kathleen R. v. City of Livermore,* supra, *www.techlawjournal.com/courts/kathleenr/19981103.htm.*

189. "Filtering the Internet: A Best Practices Model," by members of the Information Society Project at Yale Law School: *www.copacommission.org/papers/yale-isp.pdf.*

190. *Reno v. ACLU,* 521 U.S. 844 (1997).

CHAPTER 52

PRIVACY IN CYBERSPACE

Benjamin S. Hayes, Henry L. Judy, and Jeffrey B. Ritter*

CONTENTS

*Messrs. Hayes, Judy, and Ritter practice law in the Washington, D.C., office of the U.S. law firm of Kirkpatrick & Lockhart LLP (*www.kl.com*). The firm represents financial services firms, international manufacturers, and emerging businesses in privacy law matters. This publication is for informational purposes and does not contain or convey legal advice. The information herein should not be used or relied upon in regard to any particular facts or circumstances without first consulting with a lawyer. Furthermore, any opinions expressed herein are the views of the individual authors and do not necessarily represent the opinion of Kirkpatrick & Lockhart LLP. The final version of this chapter was prepared in November 2001 and does not reflect events occurring after that date.

52.1   INTRODUCTION: WORLDWIDE TRENDS.   As information technology continues to develop, increased opportunities and incentives are created to collect information about individuals and to use that personal information for diverse and lucrative purposes. Some believe that, in a global information economy, the most economically valuable electronic asset will be aggregations of information on individuals. For over two decades, concerns regarding the privacy of the individual have been reflected in significant European legal governance on the collection and cross-border movement of personal information. In recent years, these concerns have escalated in Europe and in other economies, particularly due to the rapid commercialization of the Internet and the development of new and more powerful information technologies. These concerns have motivated a growing accumulation of privacy law, with recent enactments in the United States, Europe, and other areas of the world.[1]

52.1.1   Laws, Regulations, and Agreements.   Across the emerging body of global privacy law, which varies substantially from jurisdiction to jurisdiction, general patterns are beginning to emerge. Virtually any piece of information related to an individual is being defined as "personal information" and, therefore, potentially subject to regulation with respect to its collection, storage, use, and transfer. Different types of personal information, and different uses of personal information, are subject to different levels of regulation. Typically, the collection and use of medical and other highly sensitive data, such as data revealing the subject's race, religion, political affiliation, or sexual orientation, or data relating to children, is most highly regulated.

What conduct is regulated? Privacy laws are structured on the essential principle that the individual person—a "data subject"—should retain some control over the information about himself or herself that is collected or used by a person or organization, whether a business, a nonprofit organization, or a government Privacy laws impose obligations that are intended to prevent the collection or use of information in any manner that is inconsistent with the expectations of the data subject. In effect, the data subjects' control of their own personal information cannot be circumvented or denied except with their consent. Essentially, each time personal information is collected, a contract is established with the data subject that governs the use of that personal information from that time onward. Privacy laws empower the data subject and the state to enforce the data subject's rights under that agreement.

In addition, across different legal systems and, particularly in the United States, across different regulatory schemes governing different industries, privacy laws embrace comparable core principles, also referred to as "fair information practices."[2] These practices include the concept of control by the data subject but also may embrace rules that prohibit or limit certain data practices regardless of the consent of, or other involvement by, the data subject.

For chief information officers, security officers, risk managers, general counsels, systems designers, and consultants of any company charged with assuring compliance with privacy laws, the rules of the game are changing. Regulatory controls that target information assets such as personal information are transforming how information systems are designed and managed. Technology executives are required to assume increased responsibility for legal compliance across divergent legal regimes; business executives and legal officers are required to acquire significant new understandings of the technologies deployed in information management and the business relationships through which personal information is collected, used, and transferred in support of the execution of business relationships. Ironically, the power of information technology is both a source, and a means of addressing, privacy issues.

What makes privacy law important to all of these participants is not the imposition of yet another set of regulations requiring compliance. Instead, privacy law tests companies in their ability to truly integrate business, law, and technology into the coherent planning and execution of their information systems. Few question the value of the Y2K exercise in advancing companies and their business partners to a new level of inter-dependent collaboration; privacy presents the next threshold. As the world's economy continues its remarkable transformation into a global environment in which information in electronic form is a significant measure of economic wealth, those companies that master privacy as a competitive opportunity, rather than as a regulatory cost without economic benefit, will be best positioned to remain competitive.

However, although attention is increasingly paid to overcoming inadequate protection of personal privacy, there is a corresponding increase in the attention paid to the policy issues raised by, arguably excessive, protection of personal privacy. A few examples will suffice. Law enforcement and national security agencies are concerned about how increased privacy protection, including encryption and anonymizer techniques, will weaken their ability to detect crime and terrorism. Medical researchers are concerned about their ability to conduct statistically valid medical research. Globally, societies are groping with the task of finding new balance points among conflicting rights in a new technological environment.

A point to remember when considering privacy laws is that such laws frequently have little to do with "privacy" in the traditional sense of the word. Instead, these laws primarily are concerned with the rules by which personal information is collected, stored, used, transferred, and destroyed.

52.1.2 Sources of Privacy Law. The legal structures governing personal information use have developed along different lines concerning public and private entities. Typically, governments and other public sector entities are restrained from undue intrusion into citizens' private lives by constitutional mechanisms.[3] Citizens typically are provided access to government-held personal information by statutes, although there has been an increase in constitutionally mandated access rights to personal information as formerly oppressive regimes give way worldwide to more democratic governments.[4]

By contrast, restraints and obligations placed on private uses of personal information derive almost exclusively from statutory law. However, the recent adoption of the European Charter of Fundamental Rights requires that nation-states treat personal data protection as a basic human right. Such a requirement will stand as a prerequisite for any new potential member of the European Union.[5]

This development suggests a new trend: that data protection may be enshrined into constitutions or supranational law. Indeed, certain developing nations that have recently enacted new constitutions have created bases for their private-sector data protection laws in them. Examples include Hungary,[6] South Africa,[7] and Lithuania.[8] As a result, any attempt to master what privacy law is all about will demand, regrettably perhaps, complex legal analysis.

52.2 EUROPEAN APPROACHES TO PRIVACY

52.2.1 History and Organization for Economic Cooperation and Development Principles. Interest in the right of privacy increased in the 1960s and 1970s with the advent of information technology. The surveillance potential of computers prompted public demands for specific rules governing the collection and handling of personal information. The genesis of legislation in this area usually is traced to the first modern data protection law, enacted in the Land of Hesse in Germany in 1970. That enactment was followed by national laws with differing objectives and scope in Sweden (1973), the United States (1974), Germany (1977), and France (1978). [9]

Two highly influential international instruments emerged following these enactments. The Council of Europe (COE) passed the Convention for the Protection of Individuals with regard to the Automatic Processing of Personal information[10] (COE Convention) in 1981. In the same year, the Organization for Economic Cooperation and Development (OECD) issued Guidelines Governing the Protection of Privacy and Transborder Data Flows of Personal Information (OECD Guidelines).[11] Both instruments articulate specific rules regarding the handling of personal information. Both present a comparable set of principles for fair information use that have since become the framework for the data protection laws of dozens of countries. These principles recognize personal information as data to be afforded legal protection at every step of their "life cycle" of collection, processing, storage, use, transfer, and destruction.

To date, over 20 countries have adopted the COE Convention, and another six have signed it but not adopted it into law. In addition to being relied upon by OECD nations to create data protection laws, the OECD Guidelines have been relied on by other nations that are not OECD members.[12] The OECD has continued to be involved in privacy issues and, indeed, makes available a privacy policy statement generator on the privacy page of its Web site.[13]

52.2.2 European Union Data Protection Directive 95/46/EC. In 1990, to both (1) ensure that Member States protected "fundamental" privacy rights when processing personal information, regardless of the national citizenship of the data subjects, and (2) prevent Member States from restricting the free flow of personal information within the European Union (E.U.), the European Commission proposed the E.U. Directive on Data Protection. On October 24, 1995, following years of discussion and debate, the Council and Parliament of the E.U. adopted the final version of Directive 95/46/EC (the "E.U. Directive" or the "Directive").[14] The Directive became effective on October 25, 1998.

The Directive is not self-executing. Instead, it requires E.U. Member States to pass national legislation enacting its terms. It is important to realize that the national laws that have been enacted in each of the E.U. Member States are not identical. Indeed, there are fairly significant differences among these laws. Thus, having an understanding of the Directive by no means guarantees that a business understands all of the steps it must take to comply with each national law.

52.2.2.1 European Union Directive Requirements. The E.U. Directive applies to all commercial uses of personal information. The Directive establishes limitations and obligations on "controllers" (entities directing the collection, use, or transfer of personal information) and "processors" (those utilizing personal information at another party's direction) with respect to the "processing" (virtually any collection, use, transfer, or destruction of personal information) of "personal information" (any information that is readily traceable to a particular individual). The Directive, like other privacy laws, is organized around certain key principles of information use. These can be summarized as follows:

> **Notice**—Data subjects, individuals to whom personal information relates, must be informed of:
>
> > • The identity of the collector of the information;

- The uses or purposes for which it is collected;
- How they may exercise any available choices regarding its use;
- Where and to whom it may be transferred; and
- How data subjects may access information relating to themselves by an organization.

Consent—Data subjects have the right, except under certain exceptions, not to have their personal information used without their consent, the right to opt out of having personal information used for direct marketing purposes, and the right not to have any "sensitive information" collected or used without express permission. Sensitive information includes information relating to race, religion, health, union membership, beliefs, and sex life.

Consistency—Organizations may use personal information only in strict accordance with the terms of the notice given to the data subjects and any choices with respect to its use exercised by them.

Access—Organizations must give data subjects access to the personal information held about them and must allow them to propose corrections to inaccurate information.

Security—Organizations must provide adequate security, using both technical and other means, to protect the integrity and confidentiality of personal information. The sufficiency of such means is measured with respect to the state of the art.

Onward Transfer—Personal information may not be transferred to a third party unless that third party has been contractually bound to use the data consistently with the notice given to data subjects, any choices they have exercised, and applicable law.

Enforcement—The Directive grants a private right of action to data subjects where organizations do not follow the law. In addition, each E.U. country has established a Data Protection Authority—a regulatory enforcement agency—that has the power to investigate complaints, levy fines, initiate criminal actions, and demand changes in businesses' information-handling practices.

52.2.2.2   *International Data Transfer Restrictions.* While the Directive governs much of the interaction between a business and its data subjects (i.e., its customers and employees), it also regulates how companies operating in multiple jurisdictions worldwide may move personal information within themselves and among their various affiliates or subsidiaries.

Transfers of personal information relating to E.U.-based data subjects to non-E.U. countries are *prohibited* unless the country of destination has "adequate" legal protections for privacy. Many countries, including the United States, are not considered by the EU to have adequate legal protection. Transfers to such countries may take place only with the consent of the data subject, or where other guarantees exist that personal information will be treated according to the E.U. standard. E.U. regulators have the legal authority to prohibit transfers of personal information where such guarantees cannot be demonstrated. This requirement is very problematic for many businesses and may require significant technological, organizational, and/or contractual changes.

One possible solution to the Directive's transfer restrictions is the U.S./E.U. "Safe Harbor." This arrangement is discussed in Section 52.3.3.5.

52.2.2.3   State of Implementation.   As of the publication deadline of this volume, Austria, Belgium, Denmark, Finland, Germany, Ireland, Italy, Greece, the Netherlands, Portugal, Spain, Sweden, and the United Kingdom had passed legislation fully implementing the Directive. France and Luxembourg have not yet passed such legislation and have been sued by the European Commission before the European Court of Justice for noncompliance with the Directive. However, all of these countries are expected to fully enact implementing legislation during 2002.

52.2.3   Harmonization of non–EU European Countries to the EU Directive.   Largely due to the EU Directive's prohibition on the transfer of personal information to countries with lesser degrees of legal protection, and the fear in many countries of the potential adverse economic impact that could result from the interruption of data flows from EU countries, a number of other countries have passed essentially identical national legislation so as to assure "adequate" levels of legal protection. These countries can be roughly divided into two categories: E.U. trading partners that wish to ensure that data flows will not be interrupted[15] and countries actively conforming their national legislation to the E.U. model in hopes of gaining membership to the EU.[16]

52.2.4   European Union Telecommunications Directive.   In addition to the general Data Protection Directive, the EU has enacted a second Directive, imposing specific privacy-protective obligations on communications service providers. The Telecommunications Directive[17] obliges carriers and service providers to ensure technologically the privacy of the communications carried on their systems, including e-mail and other Internet communications. This Directive also restricts access to billing information, places limitations on marketing, allows for per-line blocking of caller ID, and requires that information gathered during a communication be deleted upon the termination of the communication.[18] A draft proposal being prepared by the European Commission would replace the Telecommunications Directive with a broader version affecting all "electronic communications" in the European Union.[19]

52.3   UNITED STATES

52.3.1   History of Common-Law Torts.   The concept of privacy as a tort is a twentieth-century phenomenon. The framers of the U.S. Constitution did not recognize an explicit right to privacy, perhaps because privacy was intrinsic to an agrarian society. But the necessity for privacy protection under law gradually became apparent with urbanization and industrialization in the late nineteenth and early twentieth centuries. The concept of a "right to be left alone" was posited by Charles Warren and Louis Brandeis in a seminal 1890 article in the *Harvard Law Review.*[20] Today, virtually every state recognizes a common law or statutory right of privacy.[21]

Like most common-law torts, privacy law matured in a piecemeal fashion at the state level because there was no federal law on point. In 1960, the *Restatement of Torts* defined four "subtorts" that are generally held to comprise the common law of privacy. These are:

1. *Intrusion*—the unreasonable intrusion, by physical or other means, upon the seclusion of another, if the intrusion is substantial and would be highly offensive to a reasonable person.

2. *Revelation of private facts*—the unauthorized and unreasonable publicity of facts about a person's private life, if the matter publicized is of a kind that would

be highly offensive to a reasonable person, and which is not of legitimate concern to the public. These facts must be communicated to more than a single person or a small group in order to trigger this tort.

3. *"False Light"* — publicity that unreasonably places the other in a false light before the public. Essentially, a photo or story cannot be used if that photo or story conveys a false impression of someone. Note that this tort can be used if the person is cast in either a negative or *positive* false light.

4. *Misappropriation* — the unauthorized appropriation of another's name or likeness for benefit or gain. Misappropriation actions are most commonly brought by celebrities whose image is used without authorization in connection with advertising or promotion.[22]

52.3.2   Public Sector.   In the United States, government traditionally has been restrained from undue intrusion into the private lives of citizens by various provisions of the U.S. Constitution and similar provisions in the constitutions of many of the states of the Union. The Fourth Amendment to the U.S. Constitution, for instance, prohibits "unreasonable search and seizure" by the government. The Fourth Amendment protection is also made applicable to the states by operation of the Fourteenth Amendment to the U.S. Constitution, which provides that "No state shall make or enforce any law which shall abridge the privileges or immunities of citizens of the United States. . . . " Yet, except in certain state constitutions, there is no explicit right of privacy. Thus, many of the rules regarding how government may collect, maintain, and use personal information relating to citizens has been defined by case law and statutes. In the public sector, state governments may have greater privacy protection obligations to their employees than private sector businesses in the same states have to their employees.

52.3.2.1   *Privacy Act of 1974 (Including the Freedom of Information Act).*
The first piece of sweeping privacy legislation in the United States, the Privacy Act of 1974,[23] placed limitations on how the federal government may use and transfer personal information, and gave individuals a right, subject to certain exceptions, to know what information is held about them by the federal government. The Privacy Act incorporates the Freedom of Information Act (FOIA), which allows access to federal government records, except in certain situations.
The act is intended to:

1. Permit individuals to determine what records pertaining to them are collected, maintained, used, or disseminated by federal agencies

2. Permit individuals to forbid records that are obtained by an agency for one purpose to be used for another purpose without consent

3. Permit individuals to obtain access to agency records pertaining to them and to correct or amend such records as appropriate

4. Ensure that agencies collect, maintain and use personal information in a manner that ensures that the information is current, adequate, relevant, and not excessive for its intended use

5. Create a private right of action for individuals whose personal information is not used in accordance with the act[24]

All provisions of the act are subject to certain exceptions, such as criminal investigations or national security concerns. In addition, the act protects each individual, so access to certain information can be limited where providing such information would compromise another individual's privacy.

52.3.2.2   Electronic Communications Privacy Act of 1986.   The Electronic Communications Privacy Act (ECPA)[25] generally prohibits unauthorized and intentional "interception" of wire, oral, and electronic communications during the transmission phase, and unauthorized "accessing" of electronically stored wire or electronic communications. It is applicable in many connections. For example, it establishes standards for capturing telephone numbers through the use of pen registers and trap-and-trace devices. Pen registers record telephone numbers of outgoing calls; trap-and-trace devices record telephone numbers from which incoming calls originate, much like common caller-ID systems. Although telephone numbers are not protected by the Fourth Amendment,[26] ECPA requires law enforcement agencies to obtain court orders to install and use these devices. Rather than the strict probable cause showing necessary for wiretaps, pen register orders require only certification from a law enforcement officer that "the information likely to be obtained is relevant to an ongoing criminal investigation."[27] It is also relevant to workplace invasions of privacy by electronic means (see Section 52.3.3.6).

52.3.2.3   Right to Financial Privacy Act of 1978.   Under the Right to Financial Privacy Act,[28] the federal government is prohibited from obtaining the financial records of an individual, or information contained therein, from a financial institution without giving notice to the individual. Where the disclosure is sought via a subpoena, the required disclosure normally must be made within 90 days after the subpoena is served on the financial institution. Where the disclosure is sought by all other means, the required notice normally must be given prior to, or contemporaneously with, the disclosure request.

52.3.2.4   Driver's Privacy Protection Act.   The Driver's Privacy Protection Act[29] marked the first time the U.S. Congress passed a law limiting how state governments may use personal information. Specifically, the act prohibits disclosures of personal information obtained in connection with a motor vehicle record by state governments, except in order to facilitate legitimate government activities, facilitate recalls, and the like. This act provides civil and criminal penalties as well as a private right of action. The act survived a challenge to its constitutionality, brought by the state of South Carolina, by a nine to zero vote in the U.S. Supreme Court.[30]

52.3.2.5   Law Enforcement and National Security Surveillance.   As technology has developed, crime and criminal activities have become increasingly sophisticated. Yet the same developments of technology have greatly facilitated information gathering and surveillance by law enforcement and national security organizations.

Law enforcement agencies have used technology to investigate crimes such as money laundering, narcotics trafficking, insider trading, and fraud. The technology used can be divided roughly into two categories: monitoring and surveillance. Monitoring technology is used to search for indicia of criminal behavior, without focusing on the activities of particular individuals. Examples of monitoring technologies used to detect crime online include:

- Packet sniffers—programs that monitor all traffic flowing through a network, looking for keywords, phrases, e-mail addresses, and the like. When a packet sniffer finds the type of data it is looking for, it saves the communication for later review.

- "Black boxes"—hardware installed by law enforcement agencies at Internet service providers (ISPs) in order to monitor communications or Web traffic. Typically, but not always, black boxes use packet-sniffing technology. In the United States, the Federal Bureau of Investigation (FBI) is currently promoting the use of its "Carnivore" system, a black box that it wishes to install at all ISPs and whose name has been described in the press as a colossal public relations blunder. At least one ISP has refused to install Carnivore[31]; currently the program is under review. In February 2001, the FBI renamed its software DCS1000.

Surveillance technology, by contrast, is used to eavesdrop on the communications or transactions of particular individuals. Monitoring technologies often are used or usable for this purpose. In addition, audio listening devices (bugs), and closed-circuit television (CCTV) are increasingly in use.[32]

National security agencies worldwide conduct monitoring and surveillance of communications, to varying degrees. The United States, United Kingdom, New Zealand, Australia, and Canada are reputed to have an integrated global surveillance system known as Echelon. While details of the Echelon system's capabilities are closely guarded state secrets, some credible reports indicate that the system is able to intercept virtually any electronic communication on earth.[33] Telecommunications operators in the United States should be aware that the Communications Assistance for Law Enforcement Act of 1994 (CALEA)[34] mandates certain technical standards for telecommunications networks in order to facilitate law enforcement interception of communications. Recent court decisions may, however, ultimately limit CALEA's application.[35]

Currently, the Council of Europe is developing, in consultation with the U.S. Department of Justice, an international Convention on Cyber-Crime.[36] Privacy advocates have criticized the draft versions of this convention for being unduly intrusive.[37]

52.3.3   Private Sector.

Compared to other nations, the United States has been fairly slow to pass privacy laws affecting the private sector, preferring instead to rely on industry self-regulation (see Section 52.4.1). Nonetheless, the development of the Internet and electronic commerce, the integration of the financial services industries, and the integration of healthcare services have all spawned new private sector legislation. Thus far, this legislation has concentrated on particular business sectors rather than regulating uses of personal information generally and has generally emphasized online business practices.

52.3.3.1   *Financial Services Sector (The Gramm-Leach-Bliley Act).*

The Gramm-Leach-Bliley Act (GLB), enacted in 1999, requires every "financial institution" to protect the security and confidentiality of its customers' nonpublic personal information, disclose its privacy policies to consumers, and provide consumers with an opportunity to direct that the institution not share their nonpublic personal information with unaffiliated third parties.[38] Violations of the privacy provisions of GLB are subject to enforcement by various federal regulators; the specific sanctions that may be imposed vary according to the regulatory agency that has jurisdiction in a particular case.

Eight federal agencies have issued regulations enacting the privacy provisions of GLB.[39] The Federal Trade Commission (FTC), among others, has acted aggressively to apply GLB as broadly as possible. Specifically, the FTC defines "financial institution" by reference to a variety of other regulations. This has the effect of causing a number of businesses not traditionally thought of as "financial institutions," such as career counselors,[40] real estate settlement services, and property appraisers,[41] to be subject to GLB's privacy regulations.

Another example of the broad application of these regulations is how "nonpublic personal information" is defined: In the case of certain agencies, it is defined as *any* personal information given by a consumer to an institution, whether or not the information is otherwise publicly available.

The regulations went into effect on July 1, 2001. All affected companies were required to have systems in place to comply with the regulations by that date. The following are the critical aspects of the GLB regulations:

- "Customers,"[42] and in some instances "consumers,"[43] must receive initial and annual notices of how their personal information will be used by the financial institution and to which nonaffiliated third parties, other than service providers, it may be transferred.

- Where personal information is to be shared with nonaffiliated third parties other than service providers, the "customer" or "consumer" must be given an opportunity to opt out of having the personal information transferred.

- Appropriate security controls must be maintained, and specified procedures must be followed, for the adoption and testing of information security protocols.

- Sharing of personal information among affiliates remains unaffected.

The following are some of the effects of GLB that businesses should be aware of:

- Systems must be created to capture a reliable record of a customer's opt-out (where applicable) at any time and to adopt controls to prevent that customer's personal information from being transmitted outside of a company or its affiliates.

- Systems must be created to deliver the appropriate notices to customers.

- Credit bureaus will no longer be legally able to sell "credit header" information.

- Banks and other financial institutions may become limited in their ability to sell or transmit lists of customers.

- Banks and other financial institutions must draft and execute, in most cases, detailed written information security policies.[44]

- Contract provisions governing the security of information transferred from financial institutions to other entities should be reviewed and may need to be amended.

- Where a particular company may be subject to GLB regulation by more than one federal agency, particular care should be used to establish any differences in the different agencies' regulations, and any provisions that may defer to a different agency's rules in such a situation.

52.3.3.2 *Children's Online Privacy Protection Act.*   The Children's Online Privacy Protection Act of 1998 (COPPA) prohibits the collection, use, or disclosure of personally identifiable information from and about children under the age of 13 on the Internet without prior "verifiable parental consent."[45] Obtaining "verifiable parental consent" has proven technologically challenging for some organizations. Violations of

COPPA are enforced as "unfair or deceptive" trade practices by the Federal Trade Commission.[46] Web site operators should refer to the FTC's informational Web site[47] for more information. See also Chapter 52 of this *Handbook*.

52.3.3.3 *Health Insurance Portability and Accountability Act.*   The Health Insurance Portability and Accountability Act of 1996 (HIPAA) mandated the establishment of standards to protect the privacy and confidentiality of individually identifiable health information.[48] Under HIPAA, the Department of Health and Human Services has adopted rules to implement the legislative mandate.[49] Both civil and criminal penalties can be assessed for violations.

The HIPAA regulations present significant challenges to "covered entities." A number of the key concepts embodied in the regulations are not clearly defined. The obligations created by the regulations will require significant changes in the system's infrastructure and business processes of many affected entities. HIPAA is likely to dramatically affect any business dealing with personal information gathered in a health-care setting. Compliance with the HIPAA privacy rules becomes mandatory for covered entities in April 2003, although the compliance deadline for small health plans is April 2004.

The Bush administration surprised many by first indicating that it would delay or substantially alter the HIPAA regulations and then reversing course and allowing them to become effective on schedule in April 2001. However, in so doing, Health and Human Services (HHS) secretary Tommy G. Thompson indicated that the regulations would be modified and interpreted by guidance from his office. The first such interpretive guidance has now been published by HHS.[50] Additional interpretations are expected.

The following are key features of the HIPAA privacy regulations:

- Providers and health plans are required to give patients a clear written explanation of how they will use, keep, and disclose information.

- Covered entities must provide patients with access to their health records.

- Permitted uses and disclosures of personally identifiable health information must, subject to certain exceptions, be limited to the "minimum amount necessary to accomplish the purpose for which the information is used or disclosed."[51]

- Disclosure logs must be kept that record each entity to which personally identifiable health information has been disclosed, and individuals must have a right to access these logs.

- A provider or payer generally is not able to condition treatment, payment, or coverage on a patient's agreement to the disclosure of health information for other purposes.

- Federal criminal penalties will apply to obtaining health information under false pretenses, and knowing and improper disclosures of health information, with penalties set higher if the violation is done for "monetary gain."

- States are not preempted from further regulation of health information, so long as an affected entity could comply with both the federal and the state requirements.

- Violations of the regulations will be subject to substantial fines.

The HIPAA regulations are complex with respect to privacy and electronic data transactions.[52] In addition, HHS is expected to issue information security regulations during 2002 that are likely to establish detailed requirements for ensuring the security and integrity of health-related information. See Chapter 49 for details of HIPAA.

52.3.3.4   Cable and Video Acts.   Although the United States has been very hesitant to pass private sector legislation regulating how businesses use personal information, it has not altogether shied away from doing so. Two important exceptions to that general policy stance are in the form of federal legislation: the Cable Communications Policy Act[53] and the Video Privacy Protection Act.[54]

The Cable Communications Policy Act, section 551, governs the "protection of subscriber privacy." This section requires that cable television companies give their customers initial and annual notice of what personal information the companies collect, to whom it is distributed, how customers may access it, and what other limitations the act places on the companies. Cable companies are prohibited from using their cable systems to collect personal information without prior consent of customers. Companies are also prohibited from re-transferring any personal information without customers' prior consent. Companies may re-transfer names, addresses, and telephone numbers to other companies, but only after offering customers the chance to opt out of such disclosures. Law enforcement may obtain personal information from cable companies by court order. The act creates a private right of action for customers, which includes the ability to recover punitive damages and attorneys' fees from companies that violate it.

The Video Privacy Protection Act prohibits the transfer of videotape rental and sales records except by permission of the customer. Transfers of such records may be made to law enforcement agencies enforcing a warrant. Customers may bring civil suits against violators of this act.

52.3.3.5   United States/European Union Safe Harbor.   The E.U. Directive restricts the export of personal information to only those nations with laws offering "adequate" privacy protection.[55] Since, as of 1998, no official body in the E.U. had determined U.S. law to be "adequate," ongoing data transfers from Europe to the United States across a wide number of significant industries (airlines, entertainment, credit cards, retailing) were in jeopardy of disruption.

In April 1998, U.S. and European Commission officials entered into negotiations to create a "Safe Harbor" for American companies desiring to import from Europe personal information relating to European citizens, by which American companies (and their trading counterparts) would not be required to prove the "adequacy" of American law as a condition to the execution of data transfers. Difficult negotiations ultimately produced, in July 2000, an arrangement under which transfers of personal information from the European Union to the United States will be allowed for those companies willing to comply with the "Safe Harbor" principles (the "Principles").[56] In substance, the Principles are similar to the requirements of the Directive. Under those Principles, in the absence of committing to the jurisdiction of European officials, an American company importing personal information on European citizens must:

- Comply with the Safe Harbor principles, according to the guidance offered in the FAQs (see *www.export.gov/safeharbor* for more details).

- Self-certify, on a voluntary basis, with the U.S. Department of Commerce its adherence to principles for the protection of personal information that are consistent with European legal principles, which adherence must be publicly announced.

- Provide for independent third-party verification that the company adheres to the Safe Harbor principles. This step can be accomplished by joining a self-regulatory privacy program that adheres to the Safe Harbor. Joining such an organization can, by itself, also qualify the company for the Safe Harbor. Examples such as

TRUSTe or BBBOnline have been cited as representative of the types of programs contemplated; in effect, the U.S. and E.U. governments are encouraging self-regulation by deferring to nongovernment programs to enforce suitable standards on participating companies.[57]

Companies subject to explicit federal regulations regarding the privacy of personal information (e.g., HIPAA)[58] may in the future be eligible to self-certify their compliance with the applicable laws and gain the "Safe Harbor" recognition that would permit their transactions with European data to occur.[59] In the meantime, companies must be subject to the jurisdiction of the Federal Trade Commission for unfair or deceptive trade practices, under the U.S. Federal Trade Commission Act, or subject to the jurisdiction of the U.S. Department of Transportation in order to be eligible to join the Safe Harbor.[60] Failure of a company that has joined the Safe Harbor to abide by its stated privacy policy is actionable under the FTC act as an unfair or deceptive trade practice.[61] In addition, companies would be subject to sanctions under other applicable laws.[62]

Currently, European officials in those nations that have enacted laws responsive to the EU Directive are authorized to enforce those laws against American companies, or their trading partners, involved in exporting personal information. To date, few conspicuous actions have been taken (largely as a result of an informal "stand-still" agreed upon during the pendency of the Safe Harbor negotiations).[63] As of August 7, 2001, only 84 U.S. companies had elected to use the Safe Harbor mechanism, although the pace of new certifications had seemed to increase over the prior few months.

52.3.3.6 *Workplace Privacy.*   Software has been developed, and is increasingly used, to monitor employee e-mail, voicemail, and Web usage. Some software can record every keystroke made by an employee,[64] or allow an employer to see what Web page the employee has on the screen in real time.

The area of workplace privacy presents an especially difficult Hobson's choice for employers. Monitoring gives rise to assertions of invasion of privacy, and the failure to monitor gives rise to claims of negligence in failing to detect and act on claims of maintaining a discriminatory work environment.

In the United States, the common law is fairly well established that because employers own the computer equipment and networks used by their employees, and particularly where employees have been given explicit notice that their Web usage or e-mail may be subject to monitoring, employers may monitor such computer usage.[65]

The Electronic Communications Privacy Act (ECPA) (see Section 52.3.2.2) is the only federal statute relevant to claims of workplace invasions of privacy by electronic means. ECPA prohibits unauthorized and intentional "interception" of wire, oral, and electronic communications during the transmission phase and unauthorized "accessing" of electronically stored wire or electronic communications. An e-mail is an "electronic communication."[66]

ECPA contains two important exceptions. The first is the "system provider" exception. There is considerable debate whether an employer who provides a company system for e-mail and/or Internet access is covered by this exception. The second is the "consent" exception. Under this exception, an employer may intercept electronic communications if the prior consent of *one* of the parties to the communication has been obtained.[67] Hence, an employer needs the implied or express consent of *only* the employee. An employee probably will be considered to have given consent if he or she continues to use a communications system after having been advised of the employer's monitoring policy, although evidence of explicit consent through a signed writing, a returned e-mail, or other technique is clearly preferable. For this reason, many companies require that employees agree to the company monitoring policy in writing as a condition of employment.

While voicemail is subject to employer monitoring by the same rules that apply to e-mail, live employee telephone calls, even when made from company phones on company time, are subject to different rules. ECPA's prohibition on the "interception" of telephone calls during the transmission phase requires that employers not monitor employees' *non–work-related* telephone calls. Although it is awkward, the rule requires employers to cease monitoring of employees' telephone calls upon the first indication that the call is made for personal purposes.[68]

In Florida and Maryland, state law requires that *both* parties to a communication consent to the monitoring of that communication.[69] Obtaining only an employee's consent therefore is unlikely to be legally sufficient to allow such monitoring in these states. In addition, other state laws governing the monitoring and interception of communications may apply. As of the publication deadline date of this chapter, however, there were no laws at either the state or the federal level prohibiting workplace e-mail or Web usage monitoring in the United States.

In the European Union, all workplace monitoring is considered to be the collection of personal information and is subject to the terms of the Data Protection Directive, discussed earlier.

52.3.3.7 Anonymity of Internet Postings and "Cybersmearing."   Internet
chat rooms, forums, and message boards have been used increasingly by disgruntled employees, customers, competitors, and others to attempt to damage or artificially elevate the stature of companies in the marketplace. Postings may include personal attacks; assertions about a company's business practices, the quality of its goods and services, or the worth of its stock. Such postings may be highly offensive to particular individuals, may result in intangible changes of perception about a company in the marketplace, or may result in a very real and measurable impact on the company's stock price. Understandably, companies that find themselves subject to such postings may wish to take action.

The following are options that a company may wish to consider when faced with negative or harmful Internet postings:

- *Do nothing.* Posters of negative messages may feed on the attention created by a public response. If ignored, they may become disinterested in pursuing the activity.

- *Utilize investigators to identify the poster.* If the poster's identity is known and the person is contacted by the company's counsel, the poster may cease the offending activity.

- *Contact law enforcement.* This option is appropriate where postings seem to have been intended to manipulate stock prices, or where messages threaten or suggest harm to individuals or property.

- *File suit against "John Doe" and subpoena the relevant ISP to discover the identity of the poster.* This option is not as straightforward as it may seem. Many "John Doe" defendants have vigorously challenged such subpoenas,[70] and a recent court decision ruled that an ISP did not have to reveal the poster's identity.[71] However, that case was premised on the judge's determination that no law had been broken. Where libel, fraud, manipulation of securities, or another crime can be clearly demonstrated from the content of the postings, the poster's identity will likely be discoverable.

Companies should also consider the potential public relations impact of a public response to negative online postings. What might have started as an obscure posting on a message board with poor exposure can be turned into a media event by the ill-considered reaction of the company.

For a more detailed review of anonymity in cyberspace, see Chapter 53.

52.3.3.8   Online Monitoring Technology.   Much of the public concern surrounding privacy has derived from the use of various technologies to, often without clear notice to consumers, monitor Internet usage and compile information about users. This section gives a brief description of the most prevalent technologies currently in use for online information gathering.

"Cookies" are small text files that are placed by a Web server onto the hard drive of an Internet user when that user visits a Web site. Cookies allow Web servers to "recognize" computers bearing their cookies when users revisit Web sites. Web sites can use cookies to monitor what pages users view, what sites they come from to the Web site, and where they go when they leave the site; cookies also can be used to trigger stored user settings and preferences at the Web site. The use of cookies is almost ubiquitous on commercial Web sites. Users have the ability, through browser software, to view and delete cookies or to set their browsers to reject them or warn them each time a cookie is placed.

"Web beacons," also called "Web bugs," "single-pixel Graphics Interface Formats (GIFs)," or "clear GIFs," are extremely small graphics files, invisible to the naked eye, that are used by online advertisers to gather marketing data. Web beacons function by recognizing cookies. When a user visits a Web site bearing a company's Web beacon, that company can now learn that this is the same user who visited that company's own site earlier. Or, if the cookie was placed by an advertising company, the company can identify each site that the user visits that bears the company's Web beacons. This allows the company to know more about users' exact Internet usage and surfing patterns than were possible using only cookies. Unlike the case with cookies, browsers do not readily detect the presence of Web beacons, nor do Web site privacy policies typically disclose the use of Web beacons.[72] Their use has provoked increasing consumer uneasiness; therefore, companies should proceed with care when electing to use or host Web beacons.

52.3.3.9   Location Privacy.   An explosion in the use of wireless devices, many of which are equipped with Global Positioning System (GPS) devices that allow for the identification or monitoring of the location of the device, has spurred corresponding public concern over how to protect the privacy of location information. Great marketing opportunities are envisioned, such as being able to extend special offers to consumers who are in the physical vicinity of a store or restaurant, but many people also have identified the potential for abuses. Great concern has been expressed by privacy advocates that information about individuals' every move will become available before any clear rules are established concerning the protection or use of that information.

One case that has already caught media attention was that of a Connecticut rental car company that installed GPS chips in its cars in order to monitor their speed. The company disclosed in its rental agreement that speed limit violations above a certain threshold would result in financial penalties. The company's rationale for this practice was that by providing a disincentive to speeders, it would reduce the number of accidents involving its cars and thus lower its insurance and damage payments. After a customer discovered that his bank card had been charged $450 for three instances of speeding while using one of the company's cars, he sued the company. The Connecticut

Department of Consumer Protection agreed with the customer's position and declared the fines illegal. This case is likely to be the first in a rapidly developing area of privacy law.

Because the technology that allows for the collection and use of this information is so new, industry best practices have not yet developed, and little legal guidance is available. It is expected, however, that location privacy will be the subject of intense policy and legislative debate over the next two to four years. Because of consumer and media sensitivity to issues of location privacy, companies should carefully consider the legal and public relations aspects of collecting, using, or transferring such information.

52.3.4 State Legislation. As noted in other sections, most federal privacy laws and regulations in the United States do not preempt state action. Most often, federal statutes set a kind of "floor" upon which states may create stricter rules. The problem with this situation is that the uniformity provided by federal law can be disrupted by a patchwork of state laws. Lack of uniformity imposes increased operating costs, especially on businesses seeking to operate over wider geographic areas. Paradoxically, the increased cost often falls most heavily on smaller businesses, since the Internet enables them to operate over a wider area but they do not have the larger revenue base to absorb the increased compliance costs.

U.S. states have acted aggressively to pass new legislation regarding personal information. New proposals number in the hundreds, making it all but impossible to chart all such proposals and enactments. The following chart[73] details the state-level privacy enactments, by affected business sector, in 1998 alone:

Industry Sector	Number of Laws
Healthcare	179
Direct Marketing/Telecommunications	65
Financial Services	59
Insurance	39
Online/Internet	14

The important point regarding state privacy laws is that such laws are numerous and often organized by industry or commercial sector. A company always should research the laws of the state(s) in which it operates to determine whether there are state-level laws that affect its use of personal information.

States already have passed legislation affecting the same industries that the U.S. federal government has recently acted to regulate—for example, healthcare and financial services. But, as noted earlier, recent federal laws have allowed for the passage of more restrictive state laws and have not invalidated preexisting stricter state laws. The following are examples of state laws that impose additional burdens on companies that already must comply with federal privacy laws or regulations.

- The Illinois Banking Act[74] requires that banks obtain opt-in customer consent prior to disclosure of personal financial information to nonaffiliated businesses. By contrast, GLB (see Section 52.3.3.1) only requires that the customer be offered an opt-out prior to such disclosures.

- In Vermont, banks may not share personal information even with *affiliated* institutions, unless under one of a few exceptions in the law or unless the customer opts in.[75] By contrast, GLB allows affiliated institutions to share personal information freely.

- In Maine[76] and Maryland,[77] banks may not share customer information among affiliates without express consent to any greater degree than is permissible under federal or state fair credit reporting acts. By contrast, GLB allows affiliated institutions to share personal information freely.

- In Pennsylvania, health records relating to a patient HIV+ status may be released only by court order.[78] A second law prohibits records created in drug and alcohol treatment from being disclosed except with a patient's consent, or by court order (but never in a criminal case).[79] HIPAA (see Section 52.3.3.3) does not contain such provisions.

52.4 COMPLIANCE MODELS.   Responding to the challenges presented by rapidly developing privacy laws and the threats posed by hackers requires the confrontation of complex new issues. A number of different paradigms are emerging. Each is interrelated, but for purposes of explanation it may be best to consider each individually. Real-world solutions to privacy issues will, in almost every case, involve the use of multiple overlapping compliance models. This section illustrates, by providing a broad overview, the various models that are emerging as themes of privacy law compliance.

52.4.1 Self-Regulatory Regimes and Codes of Conduct.   Self-regulatory regimes, including industry codes of conduct, are emerging as a means for achieving compliance with fair information practices among businesses. Self-regulation has two appealing aspects: (1) it minimizes the need for government to devote resources to enforcement, and (2) it allows the greatest degree of flexibility of business practices—important to those who stress that overregulation will stunt the growth of electronic commerce. In July 1997, President Bill Clinton announced a *Framework for Global Electronic Commerce* that committed his administration toward a policy of self-regulation.[80]

TRUSTe and BBBOnline[81] are the self-regulatory programs of two nonprofit organizations. TRUSTe was launched by the Electronic Frontier Foundation; the second program by the Better Business Bureau. Each program offers companies conducting business on the Internet the opportunity to register their compliance with described privacy practices and to agree to certain investigation and enforcement processes.

There are two important characteristics to these self-regulatory programs:

1. Qualifying registered companies are permitted to display on their Web sites the logo or icon of the program. This logo is intended to communicate to consumers a "seal of approval" of that company's privacy practices that is intended to increase trust in the Web site's operations.

2. Enforcement of the privacy standards occurs through organizational sanctions only. There is no recourse to traditional venues, such as the courts, in the event of noncompliance, although serious violations will be referred to the Federal Trade Commission.

The TRUSTe program has been influential in causing the Safe Harbor principles to identify and endorse self-regulatory programs as a compliance strategy. However, practical success has been mixed. TRUSTe has faced public criticism for failing to take action against certain of its members who appeared to violate the terms of the program.

In July 2000, a group representing 90 percent of U.S.-based Internet advertising companies formed the Network Advertising Initiative (NAI).[82] The NAI is a self-regulatory initiative for the Internet advertising industry that establishes basic rules of conduct, including that non-personally identifiable information may be merged with personally identifiable information only with the express consent ("opt-in") of the data subject.

Codes of conduct are explicitly contemplated by the E.U. Data Protection Directive as one means of compliance. The Directive encourages E.U. Member States to foster codes of conduct within self-policing industries as a means of ensuring compliance with data protection laws across entire business sectors.[83]

52.4.2   Contract Infrastructure.   Many privacy laws, including GLB, the E.U. Directive and HIPAA, contemplate the use of contracts to define how personal information will be collected, used, and/or transferred. While the specific uses of contracts varies from law to law, an underlying trend is emerging: The rules governing the entire "life cycle" of personal information will be supplemented and maintained by a network of contracts.

Personal information, under most privacy laws, is collected from an individual subject to the terms of a notice of how that information will be used and to whom it may be transferred. This notice can be viewed as essentially a contract with the individual, the agreed-to terms by which that individual furnishes his or her personal information to a company.

The rules for how personal information may be used are defined by the notice given to the data subject. Once a company has collected personal information, it must process and use the data pursuant to the rules. Since personal information often passes from the collecting company to its affiliates, service providers, and others, additional contracts must be executed among and between all of these entities to ensure that the rules originally defined in the notice are followed.

Companies should begin to think about a "chain of contracts" that starts with the notice to the data subject—essentially a contract between the company and the individual. The terms of that contract are then enforced, by means of other contractual relationships, as personal information moves to different business entities, across national boundaries, and to third-party businesses.

52.4.3   Synthesis of Contracts, Technology, and Law.   Contracts alone are not a complete solution to privacy issues. While indemnity provisions and contractual warranties may, on paper, ensure that personal information has been properly collected, used, and transferred, the practical realities of the situation may be otherwise. Some points to consider:

- Policing such contracts may be beyond the means or the inclinations of many businesses.
- Most businesses are not likely to sue their trading partners to enforce these contracts, except in the most grievous cases.
- Most consumers do not perceive themselves as having enough at stake to bring actions on an individual level, but the possibility of class-action lawsuits may exist.
- The security of personal data, once compromised, is difficult to resecure—it is hard to unring the bell.
- Finally, given the massiveness of the data files typically involved, the speed with which data can be moved, and the multiplicity of jurisdictions into which it

can be sent, governmental enforcement may face a larger challenge than governments will be willing to pay for.

Accordingly, technological controls on the collection, processing, access, storage, and transfer of personal information become a key element in the management of personal information.

Technology can be used to enforce the contract infrastructure (see Section 52.4.2). For instance, when a customer makes a choice not to be included on a mailing list, it is technology that will segregate that person's information and ensure that the choice is honored. It is technology that will ensure that information relating to all the people who opted out of a proposed use of their data is not transferred to a third party for marketing uses. And it is, therefore, technology that ensures that the third party receiving personal information for marketing uses can use the information in those ways without incurring regulatory or public relations damage. Even simple policing techniques, such as the use of dummy names to detect unauthorized uses by onward transferees, can be administered more effectively using modern information technology. In this example, contracts and technology combine to add value: Contracts set terms of use for personal information that eliminate legal risk, technology ensures that the terms are followed. The end product is a valuable asset—usable personal information, the currency of the new economy.

It is vital that technological infrastructures embody both the specific legal rules that a company must observe with respect to personal information and the contracts created to manage that compliance process. Likewise, it is vital that the contracts themselves embody the legal requirements, the needs of the business, and the limitations of available technology. Business processes must adapt to the realities of the law but must utilize technology and contractual relationships in order to maximize profits. To manage personal information assets effectively, technologists and businesspeople must begin to think about law, while lawyers must become familiar with technology and business.

52.4.4 Getting Started: A Practical Checklist. The following is an outline of some of the practical steps that must be taken for an organization to begin to implement effective personal information management practices. This checklist is not all-inclusive but is designed to illustrate how the core privacy principles and different compliance models begin to interact in the management process:

- Achieve buy-in at the highest level of the organization to the idea that personal information management must be part of an organization's critical infrastructure.

- Perform due diligence to identify *all* types of personal information collected and the routes by which the data travel in and out of the organization.

- Identify all of the uses to which the information is put during its life cycle through collection, processing, use, transfer, storage, and destruction.

- Identify each law affecting the collection, use, and transfer of personal information to which the company is subject.

- Create an institutional privacy policy that accurately balances both a commitment to abide by various legal requirements and the legitimate business activities of the organization.

- Create supporting materials that educate employees and instruct on policy implementation.

- Implement consistent data transfer agreements with all data-trading partners, vendors, service providers, and others with whom personal information is acquired or transferred.

- Build privacy management into the organization's strategic planning, providing sufficient resources for personnel, training, technology, and compliance auditing.

- Hold employees accountable for implementation and compliance with the privacy policy and contract requirements.

- Periodically audit compliance.

52.5   FURTHER READING

52.5.1   Books

Bamford, James. *Body of Secrets: Anatomy of the Ultra-Secret National Security Agency—From the Cold War Through the Dawn of a New Century.* New York: Doubleday, 2001.

Garfinkel, Simson. *Database Nation: The Death of Privacy in the 21st Century.* Sebastopol: O'Reilly, 2000.

Rotenberg, Marc. *Privacy and Human Rights 2001.* Washington: Electronic Privacy Information Center and Privacy International, 2001.

Rotenberg, Marc. *The Privacy Law Sourcebook 2001.* Washington: Electronic Privacy Information Center, 2001.

Smith, Robert Ellis. "Ben Franklin's Web Site: From Plymouth Rock to the Internet," Providence: *Privacy Journal* (2000).

Swire, Peter, and Robert Litan. *None of Your Business.* Washington: Brookings Institution Press, 1998.

52.5.2   Web Sites

- *www.epic.org*
- *www.pandab.org*
- *www.privacyexchange.org*
- *www.privacyfoundation.org*
- *www.privacyinternational.org*
- *www.the-dma.org/library/privacy/index.shtml*

52.6   NOTES

1. In this context, various non-U.S. legal systems, especially European law, tend to use the term "data protection," while the law in the United States tends to use the term "privacy." This chapter uses the terms interchangeably, although readers should be aware that "privacy" often is considered to be a broader concept than "data protection."

2. An excellent summary of these emerging principles is found in "National Principles for the Fair Handling of Personal Information," issued by the Office of the Privacy Commissioner, Australia (revised ed., January 1999), available at: *www.privacy.gov.au/private/index.html#4.1.*

3. E.g., the Fourth Amendment to the U.S. Constitution.

4. The U.S. Freedom of Information Act typifies the former trend; the constitutions of Argentina and South Africa typify the latter.

5. See Draft Charter of Fundamental Rights of the European Union, Charter 4487/00, Brussels, September 28, 2000: Article 7 ("Respect for Private and Family Life") of the charter states: "Everyone has the right to respect for his or her private and family life, home and communications." Article 8 ("Protection of Personal Data") states: "1. Everyone has the right to the protection of personal data concerning him or her. 2. Such data must be processed fairly

for specified purposes and on the basis of the consent of the person concerned or some other legitimate basis laid down by law. Everyone has the right of access to data which has been collected concerning him or her, and the right to have it rectified. 3. Compliance with these rules shall be subject to control by an independent authority."

6. Constitution of the Republic of Hungary, available at: *http://centraleurope.com/ceo/country/hungary/constit/hucons01.html.*

7. The Constitution of the Republic of South Africa, Act 108 of 1996, available at: *www.parliament.gov.za/legislation/1996/saconst.html.*

8. The Constitution of the Republic of Lithuania, available at: *www.litlex.lt/Litlex/Eng/Frames/Laws/Documents/CONSTITU.HTM.*

9. Sweden: The Data Act of 1973, found in *Svensk Författningssamling (SFS;* Swedish Code of Statutes) 1973: 289, amended at *SFS* 1982: 446; United States: The Privacy Act of 1974, P.L. 93-579, 5 U.S.C. § 552a; Germany: The Federal Data Protection Act (BDSG), available in English in Ulrich Dammann, Otto Mallmann, and Spiros Simitis, eds., *Data Protection Legislation: An International Documentation* (Frankfurt am Main: [West] Germany, 1977); France: Loi No. 78-17 du 6 janvier 1978 relative à l'informatique, aux fichiers et aux libertés, *Journal Officiel de la République Française,* January 7, 1978.

10. ETS No. 108, Strasbourg, 1981. Available at *www.coe.fr/eng/legaltxt/108e.htm.*

11. Paris, 1981. An important distinction in the activities of the OECD (as opposed to the activities of the COE) is the involvement and support of the United States government. The OECD is supported by nearly 30 governments. For more information, see *www.oecd.org.*

12. For example, Hong Kong, Estonia, and Lithuania seem to have based their privacy laws, in part, on the OECD Guidelines. Brazil and Malaysia are currently considering passage of privacy laws based on the OECD Guidelines.

13. See *www.oecd.org/privacy.htm.*

14. Directive 95/46/EC of the European Parliament and of the Council of October 24, 1995, on the protection of individuals with regard to the processing of personal information and on the free movement of such data, text available at: *http://europa.eu.int/eur-lex/en/lif/dat/1995/en_395L0046.html.*

15. Hong Kong, New Zealand, Chile, Argentina, and Canada have passed such laws; Japan, India, Brazil, and Australia, among others, have proposed new conforming legislation.

16. The Czech Republic, Hungary, Poland, Latvia, and Estonia have already passed national legislation that mimics the E.U. model. Romania, Turkey, and Russia, among others, have proposed such legislation.

17. Directive Concerning the Processing of Personal Data and the Protection of Privacy in the Telecommunications Sector (Directive 97/66/EC of the European Parliament and of the Council of December 15, 1997), available at: *www.ispo.cec.be/legal/en/dataprot/protection.html.*

18. See David Banisar, *Privacy & Human Rights 2000,* EPIC and Privacy International; available at: *www.privacyinternational.org/survey/phr2000/threats.html.*

19. European Commission, "Proposal for a Directive of the European Parliament and of the Council Concerning the Processing of Personal Data and the Protection of Privacy in the Electronic Communications Sector," available at: *http://europa.eu.institutionalize/comm/information_society/policy/framework/pdf/com2000385_en.pdf.*

20. Charles Warren and Louis Brandeis, "The Right of Privacy," 4 *Harv L Rev* 193 (1890).

21. See, e.g., *Cox Broadcasting v. Cohn,* 420 U.S. 469 (1975); *Time, Inc. v. Hill,* 385 U.S. 374 (1967).

22. See Restatement (2d), Torts, § 652.

23. 5 U.S.C. § 552a. 5 U.S.C. § 552 incorporates the Freedom of Information Act (originally passed in 1966).

24. P.L. 93-579, congressional finding and statement of purpose, paragraph (b).

25. 18 U.S.C. § 3121 et seq.

26. See *Smith v. Maryland,* 442 U.S. 735, 742-45 (1979).

27. 18 U.S.C. § 3122(b)(2).

28. See 12 U.S.C. §§ 3401–22.

29. 18 U.S.C. § 2721 (1994).

30. See *Reno v. Condon,* 528 U.S. 141 (2000).

31. "Earthlink Says It Refuses to Install FBI's Carnivore Surveillance Device," *Wall Street Journal,* July 14, 2000.

32. For more details on monitoring and surveillance, see Banisar, "Privacy & Human Rights."

33. See "Interception Capabilities 2000" (Part 2/5: "The State of the Art in Communications Intelligence [COMINT] of the Automated Processing for Intelligence Purposes of Intercepted Broadband Multi-language Leased or Common Carrier Systems, and Its Applicability to COMINT Targeting and Selection, Including Speech Recognition"), European Parliament, PE 168. 184 Vol 2/5.

34. 47 U.S.C. § 1001 et seq.

35. See *United States Telecom Ass'n v. FCC,* 227 F.3d 450 (D.C. Cir. 2000).

36. See *http://conventions.coe.int/treaty/EN/projets/projets.htm.*

37. See, e.g., *www.cdt.org/international/cybercrime/001211cdt.shtml.*

38. Signed into law on November 12, 1999; to be codified at 15 U.S.C. § 6801 et seq.

39. The Federal Deposit Insurance Corporation (FDIC), the Office of the Comptroller of the Currency (OCC), the Office of Thrift Supervision (OTS), and the Federal Reserve Board issued joint regulations. The Securities and Exchange Commission (SEC), the National Credit Union Administration (NCUA), the Commodity Futures Trading Commission (CFTC), and the Federal Trade Commission (FTC) have each issued separate sets of regulations.

40. See 47248 *Federal Register,* Vol. 61, No. 174, Friday, September 6, 1996.

41. See 12 CFR Ch. 11 § 211.5(d).

42. Individuals with whom a "financial institution" has an ongoing relationship.

43. All individuals who seek financial products or services for personal, family, or household purposes, whether or not those products or services are ever actually obtained.

44. A degree of variation has emerged concerning required information security standards under GLB. The SEC and CFTC regulations set forth very general requirements; the OTS, OCC, FDIC and Federal Reserve Board jointly issued detailed information security guidelines (66 *Federal Register.* 8615, February 1, 2001); the NCUA also issued guidelines paralleling those issued by the banking agencies (66 *Federal Register* 8152, January 29, 2001); the FTC issued a proposed regulation that represents a significant simplification of the banking agencies' guidelines (66 *Federal Register* 46112, August 7, 2001).

45. 15 U.S.C. § 6501 et seq.

46. 16 CFR § 312.9.

47. *www.ftc.gov/bcp/conline/pubs/buspubs/coppa.htm.*

48. Public Law 104-191, August 21, 1996.

49. The final rule was published December 28, 2000, at 65 *Federal Register* 82,461 (2000).

50. Available at: *www.hhs.gov/ocr/hipaa/finalmaster.html.*

51. See 45 CFR § 164.506

52. More information about HIPAA's privacy regulations can be obtained at: *www.hhs.gov/ocr/hipaa,* or at *hipaadvisory.com.*

53. 47 U.S.C. § 551 (1984).

54. 18 U.S.C. § 2710 (1988).

55. See Section 52.2.1.2.2 for more details.

56. The full text of the Safe Harbor Principles is available at *www.ita.doc.gov/td/ecom/menu.html.*

57. Additional information on TRUSTe and BBBOnline can be obtained at *www.truste.org* and *www.bbbonline.org.* Note that neither organization offers certification of offline privacy practices and is therefore not available as a complete solution to any company that engages in any type of offline collection or use of the personal information of EU residents.

58. The European Commission has deferred a review of whether the privacy provisions of GLB are "adequate" pending implementation and possible further legislative action in the United States.

59. Although the Safe Harbor principles allow for "adequacy" determinations for U.S. business sectors that are subject to particular sectoral privacy laws, no determination has yet been made of the adequacy of any particular law.

60. See Introduction and Annex to Safe Harbor Principles; 15 U.S.C. § 45. Note that banks, savings and loans, and entities such as stockyards and meat packers are excluded from the scope of the FTC act and are therefore not eligible for Safe Harbor membership.

61. See draft Safe Harbor FAQ No. 11: Dispute Resolution and Enforcement, available at: *www.ita.doc.gov/td/ecom/RedlinedFAQ11Enforc300.htm.* Note that entities that are eligible for Safe Harbor membership because they are subject to the jurisdiction of the Department of Transportation may be subject to enforcement actions brought by the department.

62. Ibid.

63. The "Safe Harbor" came into effect in early November 2000. The informal stay of enforcement by EU Data Protection Authorities against U.S. companies was due to end in June 2001. Some enforcement actions have been brought against U.S. companies already; for instance, American Airlines was forced to change its practices with respect to passenger information by the Swedish authority, Microsoft was fined $60,000 in Spain.

64. Such keystroke monitoring has, during 2001, been the subject of increasing controversy. In the first case testing the use of such technology for law enforcement purposes, a federal judge in New Jersey recently ordered the U.S. government to reveal how it had performed keystroke monitoring of an alleged criminal. See Opinion and Order, August 7, 2001, *United States v. Nicodemo Scarfo et al.,* available at: *www2.epic.org/crypto/scarfo/order_8_7_01.pdf.* In another recent incident, judges of the Ninth U.S. Circuit Court, based in San Francisco, ordered their information technology personnel to remove keystroke monitoring software that had been installed on their computers by order of the Judicial Conference of the United States. See Neil Lewis, "Rebels in Black Robes Recoil at Surveillance of Computers," *New York Times,* August 8, 2001.

65. See, e.g., *Smyth v. Pillsbury Co.,* 914 F. Supp. 97 (E.D. Pa. 1996).

66. 18 U.S.C. § 2510.

67. 18 U.S.C. § 2511(2)(d).

68. See *Watkins v. L.M. Berry & Company,* 704 F.2d 577 (11th Cir. 1983); *Ali v. Douglas Cable Communications,* 929 F. Supp. 1362 (D. Kan. 1996); *U.S. v. Murdock,* 63 F.3d 1391 (6th Cir. 1995); *Deal v. Spears,* 980 F.2d 1153 (8th Cir. 1992).

69. Fla. Stat. 934.03-934.09; Md. Cts. & Jud. Proc. Code Ann. Sec. 10-402 (1980). The Maryland law was the basis for the criminal investigation into Linda Tripp's recording of her conversations with Monica Lewinsky regarding then-president Clinton.

70. See *www.johndoes.org* for more information.

71. See *Dendrite International, Inc. v. John Does 1-14, et al.,* New Jersey Superior Court (Morris/Sussex Vicinage), November 28, 2000, docket no. MRSC-129-00.

72. Free software that allows users to identify Web beacons on Web sites is available at: *www.bugnosis.com.*

73. Data from Statenet, except Online/Internet figures, which were published by the staff of *Privacy & American Business,* Vol. 6, No. 5 (September/October 1999).

74. See 205 ILCS 5/48.1.

75. See Vt. Stat. Ann. tit. 8, §§ 10201 *et seq.*

76. See Me. Rev. Stat. tit. 9-B, § 131.

77. See Md. Fin. Inst. Code Ann. §§ 1-301 *et seq.*

78. See 35 P.S. § 7608.

79. See 71 P.S. § 1690.108.

80. Text available at: *www.iitf.nist.gov/eleccomm/ecomm.htm.*

81. See *www.truste.org* or *www.bbbonline.org.*

82. For more information, see *www.networkadvertising.org.*

83. Directive 95/46/EC, Article 27. The International Commercial Exchange provides an example of such an industry initiative. See *www.icx.org* for more information.

CHAPTER 53

ANONYMITY AND IDENTITY IN CYBERSPACE

M.E. Kabay*

CONTENTS

53.1 INTRODUCTION. As electronic communications technology becomes widespread among increasingly international populations of computer users, one of the most hotly debated questions is how to maintain the benefits of free discourse while simultaneously restricting antisocial communications and behavior on the Net. The debate is complicated by the international and intercultural dimensions of communications

---

*This chapter is a revised and updated version of a paper delivered in March 1998 at the annual conference of the European Institute for Computer Antivirus Research (EICAR) in Munich, Germany.

today; what is viewed as freedom in some parts of the world is perceived as license in other communities. Conversely, what are conceived by some as attempts to impose civility on international discourse are sometimes rejected as gross interference in freedom of speech by others.

At the heart of much of the debate over the advisability and possibility of imposing limits on behavior in cyberspace is the question of identity. Some of the most egregious abuse of cyberspace seems reasonably to be attributable in part to the ease of concealing identity; using no names or false names, malefactors can often escape almost all of the consequences of their actions.

Corporations and individuals can suffer serious damage to their interests from abuse of anonymous communications. For example, denial-of-service (DoS) attacks depend on concealing the origins of the streams of spurious data. The availability of anonymous, highly critical postings to discussion groups about specific companies has resulted in problems in hiring new staff and depression of stock prices.[1] Anonymous abuse of individuals can cause great personal distress; in 1997, for example, an Annapolis, Maryland, woman was mail bombed after she warned other writers about extortionate fees from an author's agency; her name, phone number, and address were posted on alt.sex groups on the Usenet and resulted in floods of offensive phone calls.[2] A woman in Atlanta was appalled when someone posted a photograph of an unknown anonymous woman with the victim's name and contact information; she received calls from men who told her the announcement claimed she was offering free sex. A victim of such anonymous harassment founded WHOA (Women Halting Online Abuse) to help victims fight this oppression. The CyberAngels, an offshoot of the Guardian Angels vigilante group, claim to be willing and able to help victims.

In Florida, two students posted a picture of one of their high school classmates on a Web site. The boy was pictured dancing with his prom date—but the girl's head was replaced by the picture of one of their male teachers. An electronic voice on the site announced that the teacher "must die." The student was profoundly disturbed by the intimations of homosexuality, as were the teacher and his colleagues. However, the state attorney's office reluctantly concluded that there is no valid state statute making it illegal for someone to publish libelous information anonymously on the Net. Although Florida does have a law forbidding "anonymous publication of material that holds a person up to ridicule or contempt," legal experts concluded that such a limitation on speech is unconstitutional.

An innocent Florida businessman, Bruce Hovland, was harassed by thousands of phone calls from angry strangers who complained about junk e-mail that threatened to bill their credit cards for almost $200 in return for nonexistent pornographic videos they had never ordered and did not want. Hovland was the victim of a deliberate smear campaign, probably by a malefactor who had refused to pay rent at Hovland's marina and who had lost his boat in a seizure as a result. The malefactor spammed the net in Hovland's name and suggested that people call his business number collect. Hovland guesses that he lost about two weeks of business because his phones were ringing off the hook. Hovland points out that his case was relatively minor; he imagines the mayhem if an emergency number were posted on the Net in such a fraud. The case illustrates the difficulty for victims in finding an agency willing to receive and follow up on complaints about such outrageous and dangerous attacks.

Anonymity is fundamental to the abuse of the Net practiced by many spammers. Almost all spam contains forged headers in an attempt to escape retribution; in some cases the forgeries name real domains. One of the most significant cases in the last year began in May 1997, when Craig Nowak, a college student, chose flowers.com at random as the fraudulent return address for his first attempt at junk e-mail.[3] In so doing, he was merely following the suggestions of the unscrupulous purveyors of spam-distribution programs, who usually advise their naive users to forge the headers of their junk e-mail. Unfortunately for his victim, flowers.com is a legitimate business whose owner received 5,000 bounced messages and plenty of abuse for supposedly spam-ming the world. The enraged owner of flowers.com, Tracy LaQuey Parker, launched a lawsuit for damages and was supported by the Electronic Frontier Foundation (Austin chapter) and the Texas Internet Service Providers Association. In late September 1997, the plaintiffs won a temporary injunction against Nowak and his company, prevent-ing him from further use of the appropriated domain name. In November 1997, Judge Suzanne Covington imposed a fine of over $18,000 on the defendants and added a par-ticularly significant passage in her judgment that clearly enunciates the damages caused by forgery of return addresses:

> The Court additionally finds that the Plaintiffs have suffered, and will continue to suffer if [the defendant is] not enjoined, irreparable harm in the form of diminution in value of Plain-tiffs' domain name; the possibility that Plaintiffs' reputation will be damaged forever by unauthorized use of a domain name associated with them in the controversial and hated practice of Internet spamming; and service disruptions. The potential harm to the Plaintiffs cannot be adequately valued in damages, and therefore the Plaintiffs have no adequate remedy at law. . . . The Court further finds that Plaintiffs . . . suffered actual damages from the unauthorized actions of the Defendants, including lost time, lost income, lost business opportunities and lost use of their respective computer systems.[4]

In light of the seriousness of these abuses of inadequate identification in cyberspace, system managers and others concerned with the continued success of the Internet as an effective communications medium should consider the reasons for abusive behavior of anonymous individuals. Is such abuse an aberration particular to cyberspace, or are there precedents in history and in other areas of life that can provide insights to shape public and corporate policy toward identification in cyberspace?

This chapter reviews some of the findings of social psychology that show how anonymity has generally been associated with antisocial behavior. It appears that anonymity on the Net will inevitably continue to spawn antisocial behavior in cyber-space and that we must somehow integrate this kind of abuse into plans for the further development of the Internet. The chapter then presents some practical ways system managers can encourage employees in their own organizations to use the Net respon-sibly. Some practical suggestions on how different degrees of tolerance for anonymity can be integrated into a cyberspace polity are discussed.

53.2 DEFINITIONS. Before exploring anonymity in cyberspace, it is helpful to establish some common vocabulary. What is cyberspace? What is identity and its absence? What is pseudonymity?

53.2.1 Cyberspace. In this chapter, "cyberspace" means the totality of electronic data storage and transmission; this chapter focuses on communications using the Inter-net. On the Internet, there are users of specific domains defined in the Domain Naming System (DNS), such as companies (those using addresses ending in ".com"), univer-sities and other educational institutions (".edu" addresses), U.S. government agencies and departments (".gov"), the U.S. military (".mil"), and network service providers (".net"). There are many geographical domain names, such as those ending in ".de" (Germany) or ".uk" (United Kingdom), which include users from commercial, educa-tional, government, and military organizations. In addition, there are many ISPs in the

.net and .com domains in the United States, and others throughout the world in geographical domains, whose members communicate through the Internet. Customers of ValueAdded Networks (VANs) such as America Online (AOL) and CompuServe (CS) communicate through the Internet as well as having restricted areas within their VANs where only members can post messages and files. All Internet users can post messages in public discussion lists on the Usenet or through remailing lists, which broadcast all inbound e-mail to participants. Henceforth, for convenience, "the Internet" or "the Net" will include any of these users. Users of direct-dial bulletin board systems and modem-to-modem direct links are explicitly excluded from this discussion.

53.2.2   The Real World.   As used here, "the real world" refers to the material, physical, atomic, and molecular world of everyday human interactions. Using "real world" in this way is not intended to imply that cyberspace is less significant, useful, or even "real" than the planetary level on which we interact; it is merely a convenient reference to distinguish the physical from the electronic.

53.2.3   Identity in the Real World.   The key meanings of the noun "identity" for our purposes are defined as follows:

- The collective aspect of the set of characteristics by which a thing is definitively recognizable or known
- The set of behavioral or personal characteristics by which an individual is recognizable as a member of a group
- The distinct personality of an individual regarded as a persisting entity; individuality

53.2.3   Anonymity and Pseudonymity in the Real World.   Clarke summarizes the importance of personal identification as follows:

> The purposes of the interchange of identification include
> - to provide a gesture of goodwill,
> - to develop mutual confidence, and
> - to reduce the scope for dishonesty;
> - to enable either person to initiate the next round of communications; and
> - to enable either person to associate transactions and information with the other person.[5]

Anonymity can be defined simply as being without a name or with an unknown name. Pseudonymity is the use of a false name. These terms are imbued in English with a negative connotation; nonetheless, anonymity has an honorable history in world philosophy and politics. In the United States, for example, the seminal *Federalist Papers,* which appeared in 1787 under the pen name "Publius," is a publication held up as an outstanding example of anonymous contribution to political thought.[6]

Clarke explores the concepts and history of human identity in a section of his paper on management and policy issues relating to human identification. Individuality has been a central concept in Western civilization since the Renaissance, says Clarke.[7] However, individuals can adopt more than one identity; for example, some women use their husband's surname in private life but maintain their original family name in their professions. Some people have several identities; for example, novelists with different styles sometimes use various pen-names. The Danish philosopher Sørren Kierkegaard wrote under 16 pseudonyms; Charles Dodgson wrote as Lewis Carroll; Eric Blair wrote as George Orwell. As the work of these writers illustrates, anonymity and pseudonymity are not inherently linked to antisocial behavior.

53.3   SOCIAL PSYCHOLOGY OF ANONYMITY.   Technological change can have profound consequences on social behavior. For example, the development of mass-produced automobiles made possible the development of suburban shopping malls in the United States, which in turn have led to an adolescent mall culture unimaginable in the 1920s.[8] Most of us have observed that driving an automobile can alter a person's behavior from civility to incivility; in some cases, otherwise normal people become violent when they are behind the wheel of a car.[9]

It seems quite likely that the pervasive spread of the Internet will have equally profound effects on social organization and interactions. We should study what is already known about the effects of anonymity as we analyze anonymity in cyberspace. The following sections review some well-established information on anonymity and social behavior from the social psychology literature. The implications of these principles for individuals, corporate policy makers, ISPs, and governments are discussed in the final section.

53.3.1   Deindividuation Theory.   What do scientists know about the behavior of anonymous people? In general, the findings are not encouraging for the future of cyberspace unless we can somehow avoid the known association of antisocial behavior and anonymity.

Early work on people in groups focused on anonymity as a root of the perceived frequency of antisocial behavior.[10] The anonymous members of a crowd show reduced inhibition of antisocial and reckless, impulsive behavior. They are subject to increased irritability and suggestibility. One wonders if the well-known incidence of flaming (rude and largely ad hominem communications through e-mail and postings on the Usenet and other public areas) may be traceable to the same factors that influence crowd behavior.

Later social psychologists formulated a theory of deindividuation[11] in which they proposed that one's personal sense of identity can be overwhelmed by the sense of belonging to a group. Zimbardo (1970) suggested that anonymity, diffusion of responsibility, and arousal contributed to deindividuation and antisociality.[12] He noted that deindividuated people display reduced inhibitions, reduced reliance on internal standards that normally qualify their behavior, and little self-awareness.

53.3.1.1   Deindividuation and Technology.   As mentioned briefly above, there is some reason to suppose that technology can contribute to the deindividuation of its users.

Anonymity has been postulated to account in part for the strong contrast between normal behavior and the behavior of those who become aggressive and hostile when driving cars.[13] It seems intuitively plausible that being isolated in a tight personal space, a cocoon of glass and metal, gives some drivers a feeling of power precisely because of their (possibly temporary) anonymity. In addition, the anonymity of the other drivers may lead to a kind of dehumanization of the other. It would be interesting to study how many angry drivers refer to "that car" instead of "that driver" when they rail against some random act of road rudeness. Similarly, it may be that the isolation of an Internet user also may contribute to aggressivity; the object of wrath may, much like the driver of another car, be dehumanized. Sometimes it seems that e-mail flamers are engaged in their version of a video game; they give the impression of losing sight of the real human beings on the other end of their verbal aggression.

Writers of computer viruses and others in the criminal computer underground may also focus so intensely on the challenge of defeating machines that they lose sight of their human victims. Criminal hackers have expressed themselves as attacking systems, not people. At a hacker conference, comments were heard such as "Oh, I would never steal anything from a person, but if I found a radio in an office and it were labeled with a company sticker I wouldn't think twice about taking it." A commonplace informal interpretation of the insouciance of hackers and virus writers is that they are subject to what is laughingly called the "video-game syndrome": They seem to focus on their actions as if they were part of a game with only computers on the receiving end.

Chapter 6 of this *Handbook* provides more detail on deindividuation theory.

53.3.1.2 *Anonymity and Aggression.*

Sometimes, anonymous people go beyond verbal abuse and seem willing to inflict harm on others. Experimental work by Zimbardo suggested that anonymity can significantly increase aggression.[14] For example, when women were asked to deliver electric shocks to victims, those who agreed to wear white lab coats and hoods administered what they thought were longer shocks to the supposed victims compared with women who wore their own clothes and name tags.

In a cross-cultural study, Watson analyzed the correlations between the ritual, anonymizing costumes and war paint of warriors and their style of battle and their post-battle treatment of prisoners.[15] He found a strong positive relationship between anonymity and brutality.

Violent soccer fans seem to be disinhibited in part because of the anonymity of the crowd.[16] In a personal undercover investigation, a journalist found that anonymity and pseudonymity are integral components of the antisocial behavior of soccer hooligans.[17] These findings suggest that so-called dark-side hackers may be influenced significantly in their willingness to cause damage to computer systems and networks precisely because their very anonymity influences them to cross normal behavioral boundaries. These people may not be the permanently, irremediably damaged human beings they sometimes seem; they may, instead, be relatively normal people responding in predictable ways to the absence of stable identification and identity.

53.3.1.3 *Anonymity and Dishonesty.*

Does anonymity increase the likelihood that people will transgress rules and laws? Apparently yes.

In an experiment involving children, young trick-or-treaters were asked to take only one candy from a bowl and then left alone or in groups, supposedly unobserved. Those children who had given their names to adults were observed to be far less likely to take extra candy or to steal coins than those who had remained anonymous, even when the adults were apparently away.[18] (If these effects of anonymity on youngsters are consistent and widespread, they may contribute to the problems of system administrators who are under siege by underage hackers.

53.3.1.4 *Deindividuation and Self-Awareness.*

Why does anonymity change people's normal inhibitions and influence them to behave abnormally? It seems that the deindividuation of anonymous people lowers their self-reflective propensities.

Exploration of the inner world of deindividuated people suggests that they are less aware of themselves and may even enter a state of altered consciousness.[19] Prentice-Dunn and Rogers studied the behavior of college men who, as in the work of Zimbardo cited earlier, were asked to administer what they thought were electric shocks to confederates of the experimenters who were masquerading as victims. Some subjects were subjected to dim lighting and loud background noise; their names were not used; and they were told that the levels of the shocks they gave would not be recorded. These subjects were thought to be deindividuated. Other subjects experienced bright lights in quiet rooms; they were called by name; and they were told that the shock levels they delivered would be monitored. The deindividuated subjects administered more severe shocks to their victims than did the individuated students.

These observations may tie into the work on autotelic experiences.[20] Autotelic experiences are deeply satisfying activities that result in a temporary loss of self-awareness; they typically occur in repetitive, challenging, feedback-rich activities such as programming (or perhaps virus-writing) and criminal computer hacking. Csikszentmihalyi studied people in a variety of work environments and in their home life and hobbies. The subjects reported on their attainment of a state of timelessness, where the passage of time was insensible. Many who have programmed know how easy it is to forget to eat or to go home when deeply involved in work; similarly, writers and musicians can lose track of time. The research suggested that some of the key attributes of an activity that leads to this autotelic experience are rapidity of feedback (e.g., seeing an article grow as one writes or running an increasingly complex program under development) and being at the limits of one's abilities. In contrast, challenges that are too easy or too hard tend not to result in the loss of self-awareness that defines the autotelic state.

Several recent popular books dealing with criminal hackers have mentioned the ability of legendary hackers to stick to their hacking for hours on end as if they were entranced. Combine the autotelic nature of hacking with the deindividuation associated with anonymity, and we have a prescription for trouble.

53.3.1.5 *Anonymity and Prosocial Behavior.*   The picture is not necessarily all bad, however. Sometimes a different environment actually can liberate anonymous subjects from their counterproductive inhibitions. For example, in some cases, it can be shown that anonymity has an unusual effect: It increases prosocial behavior instead of increasing antisocial behavior.[21] Gergen, Gergen, and Barton put people into brightly lit chambers or in totally dark chambers and monitored the behavior of the strangers they had put together; in the dark room, there was much more uninhibited and positive expression of physical contact such as hugs and of emotional openness such as discussions of personal matters.[22] However, directionality of these effects may be affected by the demand characteristics of the situation. That is, the way the experimental objectives were described could cause significant differences in the subjects' behavior.

The constructive, supportive communications often seen in discussion groups dealing with substance abuse, abusive relationships, and other personal and interpersonal problems illustrate the possible benefits of anonymity in a positive context.

53.3.2 Identity in Cyberspace.   What exactly is meant by identity when using electronic communications? Is one's e-mail address an identity? Could a made-up name be an identity?

Identity on the Internet is primarily the e-mail address.[23] The e-mail address sometimes provides crude and unreliable information about affiliation (e.g., domain names .gov, .mil, .edu) and geographic location (e.g., .ca, .uk, .fr).[24] Roger Clarke, a scholar with a long professional interest in questions of identity, identification, and privacy in cyberspace, has written an excellent introduction to these questions.[25] For discussions of information technology, Clarke defines "identification" as "the association of data with a particular human being."[26]

53.3.2.1   Theory of "Nymity."   There has been considerable discussion on the Net about the kinds of identity (sometimes called "nymity" in these discussions) that people assume in cyberspace. One of the best-known writers on this subject was "L. Detweiler." It is still not known whether this is a real name. Detweiler suggested that identity on the Internet is amorphous and unstable because there is no one-to-one relationship between a person and an e-mail address. One person may use multiple e-mail addresses and many people may share a single address.[27]

Detweiler conducted a vigorous battle against what he perceived as a sinister and deceptive practice he called pseudospoofing. Pseudospoofing, in Detweiler's conception, is the use of multiple aliases by an individual or a conspiracy; these aliases allow the perpetrators to deceive observers into misjudging the number of people agreeing or disagreeing over specific positions.[28] One of the literary sources for such a practice is the science-fiction book *Enders Game* by Orson Scott Card.[29] Card posits a galactic political debate in which two individuals distort political debate by engaging in erudite polemics using pseudonyms; but they also invent subsidiary personae who agree or disagree with the main pseudonyms. These subsidiary personae lend credibility to the desired winning side by offering support for their chosen position or by deliberately posting poor arguments and attitudes to discredit the opposing side. The spurious numbers of these constructed personalities convinces politicians to pay attention to the debates.

A current illustration of the problems of pseudospoofing is the widespread difficulties experienced in online voting. The ease with which identity can be created, coupled with the ease of automatically scripting multiple votes, leads to thoroughly unreliable tallies in almost all online polls. The only way to avoid such abuses is to enforce some tight coupling of real-world identity with the electronic identity registered for voting. Eventually, biometric identification may be the only acceptable form of authentication for voting online.

53.3.2.2   Types of Anonymity and Pseudonymity.   To understand the problem of anonymity and pseudonymity, it is useful to define varying degrees of the behavior. Froomkin distinguishes among four forms of imprecise or absent identification:

1. *Traceable anonymity:* Any anonymous remailer that keeps a record of the relation between the original message and the anonymized message allows tracing.

2. *Untraceable anonymity:* No record is kept or available showing the origin of an anonymized message.

3. *Untraceable pseudonymity:* A continuous identity or persona allows communication with a correspondent but there is no way to link the pseudonym to the correspondent's real-world identity.

4. *Traceable pseudonymity:* Someone, somewhere has the information required to complete the link between a pseudonym and a real-world identity.[30]

The "anonymizing" remailer anon.penet.fi was actually a traceable pseudonym remailer. When a message was received by the server, its headers were stripped and it was assigned a fixed random pseudonym. In order to allow replies to the pseudonym to be forwarded to the original sender, every pseudonymous identity was linked in a table to the original e-mail address. When Finnish police ordered Johan Helsingius in 1995 to identify the pseudonymous poster of copyrighted Scientology texts on the Usenet, Helsingius felt obliged to reveal the link.[31] Traceable online anonymity allows people to maintain their privacy by using screen identities, but many ISPs will furnish the real-world identity to law enforcement officials with a warrant or to tort lawyers with a subpoena. AOL, for example, furnished subscriber details to the lawyers for a Caribbean resort considering a lawsuit for defamation based on postings by "Jenny TRR."[32] All ISPs that charge money for access inherently provide traceable pseudonymity even when they permit false screen names.

Larry Lessig, David Post, and Eugene Volokh also distinguish between anonymity, pseudonymity and traceability in their Internet course on cyberspace law.[33] They emphasize that private organizations, such as Internet service providers, can freely set terms of service that allow or forbid anonymity, but they may be required in the United States to provide traceability if the courts require it for individuals.[34] In general, it is difficult to see how the rule of law can apply to cyberspace without some form of traceability. Whether civil law or the criminal law is involved, the defendant must be found for court proceedings to have any effect. Untraceable anonymity and untraceable pseudonymity preclude justice for the aggrieved parties. Clarke points out that privacy interests are always to be balanced with other interests such as the public good, commercial interests, and the interests of other individuals.[35] For example, the desire to post anonymous libel (construed as privacy of personal behavior) conflicts with the desire of the victim to be free from libel; anonymity makes it impossible to use the civil law for redress.

53.3.2.3 *Why Anonymity and Pseudonymity Are Commonplace in Cyberspace.*
Surely anonymity and pseudonymity are possible using older means of communication: People have thrown rocks through windows, sent anonymous vituperation through the mail, and harassed people with anonymous phone calls for millennia, centuries, and decades respectively. Historically, such behavior has been of relatively minor importance. How is it that anonymity and pseudonymity seem so important in cyberspace?

One factor is the ease with which one can be untraceably anonymous in cyberspace. Many ISPs allow users to define screen names or aliases; some ISPs, such as AOL, have distributed millions of trial subscription disks that allow one to create an identity and then dispose of it after 50 hours online.

Anonymous remailers permit users to send e-mail to a central address where all identifying information is stripped, and the original text is then retransmitted to the desired destination. In the wake of the tragic events of September 11, 2001, when terrorists killed thousands of people in attacks on the World Trade Center in New York City and on the Pentagon in Washington, D.C., commentators expressed doubts about the future of anonymizing services. "Using anonymizers at all raises all sorts of red flags," said John Young, operator of the Cryptome Web site (*www.cryptome.org*) that covers intelligence matters. Even before the terrorist attacks, the well-respected Freedom Network operated by Zero-Knowledge Systems had experienced financial difficulties; that service shut down on October 22, 2001.[36]

Some moderated Usenet groups and e-mail–based mailing lists require a "real" name, but there is little effort or even possibility, as things currently stand, for authentication of such names. Unmoderated groups, by definition, do not require real names at all; such groups allow postings by anyone. Almost all contributions to countercultural or frankly criminal Usenet groups and distribution lists are anonymous or at best pseudonymous.

In addition, some people systematically forge the headers of their e-mail, often introducing completely false addresses for their origin but occasionally picking real addresses, whether by accident or design.[37] Forging e-mail headers can conceal the true origin of a message.[38] Junk e-mail almost always includes false return addresses.

Another way to generate false header information is to compromise someone's e-mail account. If security on an e-mail address is compromised, messages can be forged with a false ID.

The other factor that makes anonymity and pseudonymity especially significant in cyberspace is the ease of replication of messages. An anonymous communicator could hope to reach at best a few dozen or hundred people in a day with the phone system or by mail; in most areas, each phone call or letter would cost something to send. In contrast, outbound electronic mail and postings to Usenet groups generally cost the originator nothing.

53.4   BALANCING RIGHTS AND DUTIES.   Is there a basis for evaluating the ethics of using anonymous and pseudonymous communications? Are these modes of communications protected by principles of privacy, for example?

53.4.1   Benefits of Anonymity and Pseudonymity.   In discussions of whether society ought to restrict anonymity and pseudonymity, a common argument is that these modes of communication are necessary to fight tyrannical corporate and political institutions. Anonymity and pseudonymity are, in this view, expressions of the right to privacy. Abuses are the price society has to pay to preserve the benefits of these tools of expression. The following sections examine the concepts of privacy and the resulting benefits of anonymity and pseudonymity.

53.4.1.1   Privacy in Cyberspace.   If privacy rights are claimed to protect anonymous and pseudonymous communications, it is important to understand the concepts of privacy.

Clarke defines privacy as "the interest that individuals have in sustaining a 'personal space,' free from interference by other people and organizations." He analyzes the concept further, naming four dimensions of privacy:

1. *Privacy of the person:* Freedom from compulsory tampering with one's body.
2. *Privacy of personal behavior:* Freedom in such matters as sexual preferences, religion, and politics.
3. *Privacy of personal communications:* Freedom from routine monitoring of interpersonal communications.
4. *Privacy of personal data:* Control over who can obtain and what can be done with personal information.[39]

Political discussion groups, resistance to totalitarian regimes, and discussions of socially embarrassing or traumatic problems are made easier for many people by the use of pseudonyms or of anonymity. Anonymity permits unrestricted political speech, whistle-blowing with reduced likelihood of retaliation, and public or private discussions of potentially embarrassing personal problems.[40] Ubois writes:

> Anonymous communications are helpful in many ways. They've long been a tool of suicide prevention hotlines, suggestion boxes, and personal ads. Anonymity assures privacy, confidentiality and security for individuals, but it also highlights the clash of interests between the individual and the community. Under a repressive government, it is a vital tool for keeping discourse alive. Just consider that Tom Paine would have landed in prison shortly after the publication of Common Sense if his identity hadn't been kept a secret.[41]

In chat rooms and multiuser dungeons, anonymity permits a flowering of imaginative departures from the strictures of a participant's real-world identity, social status, personality, gender and gender preferences, political affiliation, national origin, and religion. Multimedia environments such as WorldsAway (*www.worldsaway.com/home.shtml*) provide an imaginative pseudonymity by allowing players to select a name and a pictorial representation of themselves (an avatar) with amusing and fanciful features, such as various imaginary animal heads, skin colors, body shapes, and so on. Players adopt personae that can be quite different from their real-world identities, yet there is a consistent identity within the virtual world. Because of this consistency, social mechanisms have arisen in these worlds; for example, avatars can be invited to join parties if they are perceived as friendly or excluded and shunned if they have violated the norms of the imaginary world.

Anonymous, invisible electronic personalities can escape some of the damaging effects of intolerance and prejudice.[42] Everyone probably knows of a famous cartoon showing two dogs at a terminal, one of whom is saying "On the Internet no one knows you're a dog." For example, some professors may spend more time and effort in discussions with undergraduate students if they do not realize with whom they are corresponding.[43] At an intellectual level, stripping the authors of published materials of all details of their age, sex, race, national origin, and other attributes can reduce the effects of prejudice and focus discussion on substance. Absent such details, correspondents must perforce focus on the texts rather than on personalities.[44]

In electronic commerce, anonymity is a prerequisite for successful implementation of some trading systems.[45] All electronic or digital cash schemes (e-cash) emphasize the value of anonymous transactions for safeguarding consumer privacy.

In a legal sense, anonymity and pseudonymity are analogous to limited liability—a concept familiar from the business world. In business, people pool their assets into a limited liability partnership or other form of collectivity to prevent seizure of all their private assets if their collective entity becomes liable for debts or penalties.[46] Perhaps cyberspace anonymity and pseudonymity can encourage collective publications in an analogous way; for example, Post and others have formed the Cyberspace Law Institute. Some members would be reluctant to participate if their real-world identities were known to the public.

Thus, anonymity and pseudonymity cannot reasonably be forbidden without the loss of important benefits to individuals, corporations, and society at large.

53.4.1.2 Defeating Dataveillance.   Another area where anonymity and pseudonymity have marked benefits is in preventing intrusive monitoring of individual behavior in cyberspace. Clarke has defined dataveillance as surveillance using electronically compiled information about a person.[47] The growth of some kinds of electronic commerce will increase pressures for strong identification and authentication[48]; anonymity serves to protect privacy in a world of electronic commerce. For example, without anonymous digital cash, it would be easy to accumulate detailed records of every electronic purchase made by an individual. Complete knowledge of purchasers' interests can be unfair for customers; for example, knowing that a user is addicted to fantasy simulation games, a retailer may neglect to offer that person a discount—or may even increase the price of the next game.[49] Froomkin summarizes the issues well in his magisterial review of the challenges of anonymity in cyberspace:

> Anonymity lies at the heart of three interrelated problems arising from computer-aided communications over distributed networks (which I will call "the Internet" for short). First, communicative anonymity is an issue in itself: the Internet makes anonymous communication easy, and this has both good and bad consequences. . . .
>   Second, the availability of anonymous electronic communication directly affects the ability of governments to regulate electronic transactions over the Internet (both licit and illicit).

Third, anonymity may be the primary tool available to citizens to combat the compilation and analysis of personal profile data, although data protection laws also may have some effect. The existence of profiling databases, whether in corporate or public hands, may severely constrict the economic and possibly even the political freedoms of the persons profiled; although profiling may not necessarily change the amount of actual data in existence about a person, organizing the data into easily searchable form reduces her effective privacy by permitting "data mining" and correlations that were previously impossible.[50]

Froomkin discusses digital cash as an application of electronic anonymity and emphasizes the potential for abuse by "the Argus State" if anonymity is not guaranteed for readers. For example, he points out, in the absence of anonymous digital cash, reading texts on the Internet using micropayments for each access could provide a traceable record of a person's interests. Such records would be a gold mine for repressive regimes worldwide.

Again, trying to ban anonymity and pseudonymity would have serious disadvantages for everyone, not just the benefits of impeding abuse by a minority of antisocial users.

53.4.2   Disadvantages of Anonymity and Pseudonymity.   Several commentators have reviewed the abuses of anonymous and pseudonymous modes of communication.

In considering the benefits of having a professor communicate with an anonymous student, misrepresentation of identity by such an undergraduate in one sense manipulates a professor into a decision based on a falsehood.[51] Contrary to the beliefs of many supporters of anonymity, social interactions are not necessarily equivalent to isolated streams of data interchange; conversing with a student can be enriched by having a sense of previous conversations, a picture of shared knowledge based on a relationship. Anonymity strips interactions of the deeper communication that is enhanced by such relationships.

Widespread use of untraceable e-cash may lead to increased fraud, tax evasion, money laundering, extortion, blackmail, and kidnapping.[52] Some crimes where solicitation leads to potential blackmail—for example, hiring a murderer—may become easier with anonymity and untraceable e-cash. Industrial sabotage by anonymous publication of trade secrets can damage organizations; e.g., the publication of RC4 encryption algorithms from the respected company RSADSI has lowered the monetary value of the algorithm. Froomkin writes, "[The] inability to redress legitimate claims is, I believe, the strongest moral objection to the increase in anonymous interaction."

Jurisprudence in the United States has generally supported claims to a right of anonymity in political speech. However, there have been several precedents where anonymity used to cloak socially harmful acts has been stripped from the perpetrators. Perfect (untraceable) anonymity prevents society from bringing sanctions to bear on malefactors.[53] Detweiler suggested "that Internet anonymity is a bad thing [and] that all user accounts should lead back to real users in the hopes of improving online behavior, especially in chat systems and the like." He responded to critics who claimed that "anonymity is an important part of life and ought to be part of the Internet as well" by pointing out that in real life, anonymous people cannot engage in such activities as opening a bank account, getting a driver's license, getting telephone service, or buying insurance coverage. He concluded, "So grow up and accept responsibility for what you do on the Internet."[54]

Rose, well-known in cyberspace law circles, writes scathingly of the seamier applications of online anonymity:

People can anonymously transmit all sorts of illegal and injurious materials into public areas: copyright infringements, obscenity, stolen credit information, lies and slander, and so on.

Individuals with a bone to pick against anyone else can get their licks in without fear of reprisal. Anonymous remailers are great for cowards. People who want to spread messages of hate and misunderstanding, but are unwilling to stand behind their views in public, can operate behind a wall of complete anonymity and inject a strong dose of thought pollution into the public arena.[55]

Another argument supporting disclosure of the origins of speech is quoted by Froomkin, ironically from an anonymous author: "'Disclosure advances the search for truth,' because when propaganda is anonymous it 'makes it more difficult to identify the self interest or bias underlying an argument.'"[56] Libel on the Internet is particularly pernicious, since once anything has been circulated via the Net, it becomes impossible in practice to destroy all, or even many, of the copies that may reside on numberless computers around the world.

The imaginary Good Times virus supposedly destroys hard disks as soon as the victim reads an e-mail message; Craig Shergold was once a sick child in England who asked for postcards—and is now heartily sick of the bagsful of cards he receives daily; and the "Jessica Mydek" hoax claims to be an appeal on behalf of an unfortunate girl, but she never existed.

The resurgence of hoaxes and rumors such as the Good Times virus and the pathetic stories of Craig Shergold and Jessica Mydek illustrate the persistence of undated, unsigned and untrue messages in Cyberspace. These unfounded, exaggerated or obsolete stories, threats and appeals circulate endlessly among the gullible on the Net. There is no reason to suppose they will ever stop.

One of the significant lessons from e-mail hoaxes and chain letters is that unsigned, undated correspondence is always to be treated with skepticism. This principle of devaluing anonymous or pseudonymous communications will be used later in this chapter in a model for categorizing and sequestering communications as a function of their traceability.

53.5   SYSTEMS ANALYSIS OF ANONYMITY.   Why can the usual protections of the criminal and civil law not deal with anonymous and pseudonymous communications? This problem is addressed by David Post and David Johnson.

Post and Johnson argue that geographically-defined nation-states cannot reasonably cope with a virtual, boundaryless communications medium.[57] In the real world, geographical clustering combines with basic concepts of consent of the governed through some form of representation to legitimize the exercise of state power. Without the consent of the governed, state power fades insensibly into state tyranny. In their requirements analysis of possible systems of governance of cyberspace, they add that wherever possible, those affected by the conduct to be regulated have some say in framing the regulations.

However, in cyberspace, argue Post and Johnson, there is no geographical clustering. There is no "here" or "there" in cyberspace. "Location is indeterminate because there is no necessary relationship between electronic addressing . . . and the location of the addressee (machine or user) in physical space."

Post and Johnson applied the work of the scientist Stuart Kauffman on self-organizing systems to study the nature of rule-making in a complex system that can model the interactions among users in cyberspace.[58] Research on self-organization of complex systems suggests that optimum configurations of constraints (regulations) can evolve when there is some degree of aggregation (they refer to "patches") in the population. These aggregates represent groups where individuals sacrifice some of their preferences in return for overall improvement in the way the whole society works. Members of a patch share responsibility for governing their behavior.

One of the most striking findings of Post and Johnson's research is that systems where most of the effects of an individual's actions are felt by others, outside its decision-making unit, lead to chaos or to suboptimal configurations of rules. Contrariwise, a balance between bringing consequences to bear on individuals in a "patch" and allowing effects to propagate through the larger population leads to more optimal results in the system.

As a result of the experiments, Post and Johnson suggest that one of the most powerful tools for rebuilding comity in cyberspace is grouping users by their Internet Service Providers. Each ISP can develop its own rules governing the behavior of members; sanctions for transgression of these local rules would include banishment from the ISP.

The authors examine the case of unsolicited commercial e-mail ("spam"). As long as each ISP enforces technical measures against allowing fraudulent origination addresses, everyone in cyberspace can decide whether or not to filter out messages from any given ISP. ISPs that allow behavior judged harmful by others will limit the range of communication of their members.

Those that are viewed as restrictive will self-select their own members accordingly. Thus without any global legislation, simply allowing individuals to choose ISPs that have published rules they like could lead to an effective self-regulation of communications. In essence, loud-mouthed rumor mongers would end up talking only to each other; junk e-mail could be identified simply from its provenance; and even copyright violations could be punished by collective banning of communications from the offending ISPs.

Such a model is an instance of the ideal "market of ideas" in that objectionable ideas are not forbidden, they are just ignored. Of course, admirable and desirable ideas may also be ignored, but at least there is a choice involved. Access for communication becomes a form of currency in such a model—perhaps appropriate for the governance of cyberspace, the realm of electronic communications.

53.6   IMPLICATIONS AND DISCUSSION.   Any attempt to restrict anonymity on the Internet would inevitably affect pseudonymity as well.[59] Anonymity and pseudonymity make law enforcement difficult enough, but these difficulties are exacerbated by the jurisdictional problems caused by a thoroughly decentralized communications medium like the Internet; "[W]ho should be setting the rules that apply to this new global medium?"[60] What, then, are some of the practical measures we can individually and collectively take to preserve the benefits of anonymity and pseudonymity without suffering the consequences of abuse?

53.6.1   Individuals, Families, and Schools.   Absorbing and applying normative behavior begins in earliest childhood and continues throughout the development of the child's capacity for rationality and ethical judgement. Children should be taught that anonymity and pseudonymity are not acceptable under normal circumstances. The same methods that parents, teachers, and other adults use to teach children a visceral dislike of antisocial behaviors such as lying, cheating, stealing and bullying should be applied to behavior in cyberspace. As this author has written elsewhere:

> It takes time to integrate morality into our technological universe. Twenty years ago, many
> drivers felt that driving under the influence of alcohol was adventurous. Today most people

feel that it's stupid and irresponsible. Smoking in public is becoming rare. Many of us in northern cities have witnessed exiled smokers huddled together in the cold outside buildings where they once lit up with impunity.

Similarly, we need a consensus on good behavior in cyberspace.

Criminal hackers who break into computer systems and roam through users' private files should be viewed as Peeping Toms. Criminals using computers to steal services should be recognized as thieves. Those who destroy records, leave logic bombs, and write viruses should be viewed as vandals. Hackers who smear obscenities in source code should be seen as twisted personalities in need of punishment and therapy. Government agencies proposing to interfere in electronic communications should be subject to scrutiny and intense lobbying.

Beyond such prohibitions and inhibitions of taboos, cyberspace needs the electronic equivalent of Emily Post. We need to discuss the immorality of virus writing, the ethical implications of logic bombs, and the criminality of electronic trespassing. We should teach children how to be good citizens of cyberspace, and not just in schools. We should sit down with computer-using youngsters and follow them through their adventures in cyberspace. Parents should ask their teenage whiz-kids about hacking, viruses, software theft and telephone fraud. We must bring the perspective and guidance of adult generations to bear on a world that is evolving faster than most of us can imagine.

The adolescent confraternity of criminal hackers and virus writers have already begun developing totems: the personae of Dark Avenger and Acid Phreak loom over youngsters much as Robin Hood once did for another generation.

What we need now are taboos to match the totems.[61]

53.6.2 Ethical Principles.

How do people make judgements about a course of action when there are no explicit guidelines? There are several kinds of principles that people use in reasoning about a new situation (see Chapter 30 of this *Handbook* for a more extensive discussion of ethical decision-making).

53.6.2.1 *Rights and Duties (Deontology).*

The concepts of rights ("something that is due to a person or governmental body by law, tradition, or nature. . . .") and duties ("an act or a course of action that is required of one by position, social custom, law, or religion," according to the 1992 edition of the *American Heritage Dictionary*) should influence one's decisions.

Are any rights abridged by anonymity? For example, the right to know the source of a warning so that we may judge the motives and credibility of the statement are infringed when such a message is posted anonymously or pseudonymously.

Personal duties at issue in a decision on posting anonymous warnings about a competitor's product include notions of trust, integrity, and truthfulness, all of which are violated by such an act. We lower the trust of technical advice when we use anonymous postings; we damage the integrity of an entire profession; and we implicitly betray truthfulness by failing to identify the source of such information.

Professional duties or responsibilities also apply. We are expected to maintain appropriate professional relationships, but anonymous posting does not further a web of trust among colleagues. Posting anonymous messages casts doubt on the goodwill of all the innocent people who are perceived as possibly being the author of such messages. In terms of maintaining efficacy, anonymous postings reduce the flow of information among professionals by aborting the possibility of private communication with the authors of the anonymous messages.

53.6.2.2 *Consequentialism (Teleology).*

One approach to evaluating the ethical dimensions of a proposed act is to look at the possible consequences of the act. Does the action minimize actual and potential harm? Egoism looks at what is good for me or does the least harm to me. Anonymous posting of critical information about a competitor's product offers the potential of benefits to one's employer with minimal direct consequences. On the other hand, such behavior opens up the organization to less obvious consequences, such as the risk of blackmail, degradation of trust within the group, lowered morale, and departure of employees whose moral sensibilities are outraged by what they see as unethical behavior.

Utilitarianism views decisions in terms of what is good for the group or does the least harm for the group. The question here is the inclusivity of the "group." If the group includes all users and potential users of the defective product, then posting the information serves a good purpose; the decision on whether to post anonymously resolves to the same questions as those raised in discussions of the consequences for an organization of having an employee post messages anonymously. The climate of trust, the credibility of warnings in general, and respect for the entire industry can be harmed by anonymous postings of warnings.

An altruistic approach to decisions accepts that what is good for all may be worth doing even if there is some harm to one's self. By this yardstick, posting a warning with full attribution is definitely the preferred way of communicating information about a problem. Another altruistic approach, however, would be to inform the competitor of the flaw in its product via private communications. The hope here is that such altruism will be reciprocated and that the industry as a whole can benefit from improvement in all products.

53.6.2.3   *Kant's Categorical Imperative.*   At a different level, Immanuel Kant's principles for judging the ethical dimensions of an act are immensely useful in all aspects of life. The principle of consistency asks, "What if everyone acted this way?" In our example, if everyone posted anonymous warnings, the credibility of all warnings would be damaged. In the absence of a mechanism of redress, unscrupulous people would contaminate the alerts with false information, making it difficult to trust any warning. Since some people would retaliate for fraudulent postings about their products by posting equally fraudulent attacks on their competitors, the system of alerts would collapse, causing harm to users and to producers.

Another principle Kant enunciated was that of respect: Are people treated as ends rather than means? The author of an anonymous message may not be thinking about the people affected by that message; they remain ciphers—amorphous, unknown entities of no importance. In contrast, an empathic and ethical person remembers that every group consists of individual human beings with pretty much the same range of feelings as anyone else. Using them as a means of increasing market share is not respectful.

53.6.3   Corporations and Other Organizations.   How can organizations contribute to the reduction of harmful anonymous or pseudonymous communications?

Every corporation, government department, nonprofit organization, educational institution, healthcare facility, banking or financial services organization, and so on should explicitly address the question of anonymity and forgery on the Net. The following are some practical guidelines to consider in setting organizational policy:

- No user of a corporate user ID should ever forge headers or use pseudonyms when communicating using corporate resources.

- Corporate firewalls should be configured to prevent all TCP/IP packets from passing outward through the firewall with forged IP addresses.

- SMTP servers should be configured to prevent any e-mail from leaving a site with forged headers.

- All corporate e-mail outbound from a site should be signed digitally by its author(s) to provide a basis, when necessary, for repudiation of unsigned and fraudulent e-mail.

In addition, discussions of the ethical framework for making decisions about the use of technology should be integrated into employee training at all levels. Managers, in particular, ought to be cognizant of the principles of ethical decision making so that they can fluently guide their staff in practical problem-solving.

53.6.4   Internet Service Providers.   Because many users send e-mail or post to Usenet groups, through accounts with ISPs, these services have an obligation to become involved in preventing abuses of anonymity and pseudonymity. Except for some free services that are independently funded or that derive revenue from advertising rather than from user fees, ISPs must establish a relationship with their users in order to be paid; most use credit card accounts for this purpose. This method of billing inherently provides a link to the real-world identity of a user through the credit card issuers. Thus for most ISPs, it is possible to enforce traceable anonymity and pseudonymity. Faced with a subpoena, for example, most ISPs will be able to provide authorities with all the information needed to track down the person whose account was used to send a message. Whether the owner of the account is the author of a particular message depends on the security of identification and authentication mechanisms in use. Passwords, for example, are unlikely to be considered strong authentication because there are too many ways passwords can be compromised. Biometric authentication, on the other hand, may provide for strong authentication if error rates are considered sufficiently low to warrant the imputation of authorship based on biometrics.

One of the most interesting suggestions about the role of ISPs in governing anonymity and pseudonymity—and behavior in general—in cyberspace comes from Lewis.[62] Lewis suggested that those interested in banning anonymity online could support ISPs requiring traceable identity for all their customers. Let individuals choose what kind of ISP they want to use, but control access to their communications according to the degree of strong identification and authentication in use by the ISP. This suggestion is remarkably close to Post and Johnson's work on model systems in that ISPs can play a pivotal role in determining the future of the Internet without having to involve governments.[63]

Some practical suggestions for ISPs:

- ISPs could automatically sign every outbound message using their Public Key Cryptosystem secret key.[64] With today's fast parallel processors, it should be possible to sign outbound traffic without inordinate interference with transmission speed and at acceptable cost.

- Every e-mail message could be verified instantly as authentically coming from the specified ISP; forgeries would be practically impossible as long as the security of the ISPs secret keys was maintained.

- The next step would be publication of every ISP's terms of service in a public forum, signed by its secret key; these summaries would allow ISPs to sort themselves out immediately according to how restrictive their policies on anonymity and pseudonymity were.

- The SMTP would have to be modified to provide for verification of digital signatures, but given such changes, any ISP could automatically block incoming mail from ISPs whose policies were unacceptable.

For example, suppose the Truthful ISP insisted on maintaining records of exactly who was registered for any given ID and blocked outbound forged e-mail and unsolicited commercial e-mail. Truthful ISP might want to block mail from the CyberSleaze ISP, where forgeries and floods of spam were commonplace.

53.6.5   A Free Market Model for Identity in Cyberspace.   What might happen over time as a result of allowing communications only with selected ISPs, depending on their terms of service? Eventually there would likely be an equilibrium in which those users who wished to send and receive anonymous, untraceable e-mail could subscribe to those ISPs supporting that kind of communication. Others could automatically block e-mail from unwanted ISPs. Furthermore, individuals who wished to use anonymity or pseudonymity sometimes could subscribe to more than one ISP and take advantage of their different policies. Computer systems managers who wanted to deal only with other professionals at work could use a restrictive ISP; however, they also could use a different ISP to post and read messages in a highly charged, free-wheeling discussion group about the politics of gun control, without having to reveal their real names or fear that they could ultimately be traced through a pseudonym.

As the forces of the marketplace continued to work on ISPs, there might be further evolution toward different degrees and types of communication. ISPs with a reputation for harboring miscreants who libel and defame others without cause could find themselves being shut out of an increasing number of reputable communities of users. Those whose users exercised moderation and responsibility might find themselves being received by a widening circle of ISPs.

The advantage of this model is that individuals could exert power over their electronic environment by voting with their subscriptions, but no one would be censored by bureaucrats or tyrants. Just as Hyde Park in England allows both geniuses and crackpots to speak yet forces no one to listen, the electronic Hyde Park would provide a mechanism for shutting out the lunatics while letting the loonies talk to each other as they wish.

What this model would not permit is the imposition of unwanted communications on powerless victims. This model would spell the end of unsolicited commercial e-mail. If digital signatures indicating the source ISP from which executable code was first distributed became commonplace, the same mechanism could seriously interfere with the distribution of viruses and other harmful programs. ISPs that became known for harboring virus-writers or distributors would see their credibility as communications partners eroded. This model does not require individuals to sign their product or messages; the only constraint is that the ISP do so.

What about individuals who own their own domain on the Net? The same principles would apply. The modified SMTP software would automatically sign all output from their sites. Any site that refused to provide digital signatures could be excluded by any ISP that chose to apply such an exclusionary rule.

53.6.6   Governments.   The role of governments in cyberspace is complex. On one hand, several governments—notably that of the United States—have contributed to the development of the Internet through legislation and funding. On the other hand, many governments, especially totalitarian regimes, are intolerant of unfettered communications. Under the Communist regimes, most countries in the Soviet Union and its satellites made ownership of unregistered spirit duplicators, photocopiers, fax machines, and modems illegal. Today, Burma, in the grip of the tyrannical State Law and Order Restoration Committee, still does. See Chapters 51 and 52 for more details of government constraints on speech in cyberspace.

No matter how carefully crafted they are, attempts to apply legal constraints on anonymity in cyberspace will be undermined by inconsistent government regimes throughout the globe. The least restrictive geographical entities will subvert more restrictive jurisdictions.[65] If, say, Restrictopolis were to impose strictures on anonymous Internet use, its anonymity-seeking citizens might be able to use the ISPs in Liberalopolis, where the rules would be much more free.

On a less practical, more philosophic level, there are profound objections to any government regulation of the Internet. As Lewis has written:

> We do not outlaw wig shops or Halloween masks just because some people use them for illegal or immoral purposes. We do not require caller-ID services for everyone just because some people make obscene or harassing phone calls. Nor should we strip the cloak of online anonymity from everyone, including those who legitimately need privacy, just to prevent sickos from abusing it.[66]

In the United States, the government would likely run up against strong constitutional guarantees of speech, especially political speech—and including anonymous political speech—if it tried to ban anonymity outright.[67] A particularly significant setback for government attempts to control anonymity in the United States came in June 1997. The case began in January 1997.[68] As Declan McCullagh described the judgment:

> In Georgia, Judge Marvin Shoob ruled that a state law forbidding anonymity online is unconstitutional since it violates free speech and free association rights. The law is so broadly written, the judge indicated, that even America Online screen names could be considered illegal. Judge Shoob "understood clearly the very strong need for our plaintiffs to communicate anonymously," the ACLU's Ann Beeson says. Both judges [in Georgia and in a similar case in New York] issued preliminary injunctions barring the state attorneys general from enforcing the laws. . . .
>
> Georgia's Judge Shoob, in a 21-page opinion, ruled that the law—that the Democrat-controlled legislature passed in haste last year to muzzle a dissident Republican representative—violated the First Amendment.
>
> This echoes a recent Supreme Court case, McIntyre v. Ohio, in which the justices ruled that the right to anonymity extends beyond political speech; that requiring the author's name on a leaflet is unconstitutional; that writing can be more effective if the speaker's identity is unknown.[69]

Democratic governments worldwide would do better to stay out of cyberspace and allow users to develop their own transnational solutions for governing behavior, including the use of anonymity and pseudonymity.

53.7 CONCLUSION. Readers of this brief review of anonymity and pseudonymity are urged to consider these key observations and recommendations:

- Anonymous and pseudonymous communications are inherently associated with an increased incidence of antisocial behavior through deindividuation.

- There are circumstances where anonymity and pseudonymity are useful tools in the defense of liberty and justice.

- Anonymous and pseudonymous electronic communications have already been used to harass victims, damage commercial interests, and launch hoaxes and rumors into cyberspace.

- The major problems of anonymity and pseudonymity in cyberspace can be avoided by the use of traceable identification.

- Making ISPs responsible for enforcing their chosen level of strong identification and authentication will allow a nongovernmental, nonlegalistic approach to reducing abuse by anonymous and pseudonymous Internet users.

- All electronic communications ought to be tagged with unforgeable authenticators of identity.

- Individuals, families, and schools have a role to play in integrating cyberspace into the moral universe of children.

- Corporations and other organizations ought to integrate ethical decision making into their management procedures.

- Governments will continue to fail in their efforts to govern cyberspace because electronic communications networks are inherently divorced from geographical jurisdictions.

53.8   SUMMARY.   The growth of the Internet has increased the use of anonymity and pseudonymity in electronic communications. Internet users must be able to preserve the benefits of privacy while fighting the abuses of anonymous and pseudonymous people. In the real world, identity resides in the ways that individuals are recognized and held responsible for their actions; in cyberspace, identity is potentially just a user ID. Social psychologists have found that anonymity can contribute to deindividuation—a state of loss of self-awareness, lowered social inhibitions, and increased impulsivity.

This chapter suggests practical applications of these insights from social psychology for managers concerned with reducing abusive behavior by their own employees. In addition, the chapter addresses the wider problem that, given the social psychology of anonymity, abuses of the Internet are certain to continue. There must develop a collective response to incivility and irresponsibility, without falling into authoritarian strictures on speech. This chapter further suggests that a free market approach using accessibility to communications as a kind of currency may help the Net evolve toward a more civil society. By blocking e-mail from ISPs that fail to enforce acceptable standards for a given community of users, Net users can sort themselves into groups that tolerate or welcome different levels of anonymity and pseudonymity. No government intervention would be required under such a system.

In addition, this chapter suggests a framework for reaching into the early years of the educational system to help integrate cyberspace into the moral universe of children worldwide. In addition to being a moral imperative to support educational efforts on computer ethics, such programs are in the best economic interests of industry, academia, and government systems managers.

53.9   NOTES   An asterisk (*) marks a secondary reference drawn from D.G. Myers, *Social Psychology,* 4th ed. (New York: McGraw-Hill, 1993); R.A. Lippa, *Introduction to Social Psychology,* 2nd ed. (Pacific Grove, CA: Brooks/Cole Publishing, 1994); or D.O. Sears, L.A. Peplau, and S.E. Taylor, *Social Psychology,* 7th ed. (Englewood Cliffs, NJ: Prentice-Hall, 1991).

1. R. Abelson, "By the Water Cooler in Cyberspace, the Talk Turns Ugly," *New York Times;* see: *www.nytimes.com/2001/04/29/technology/29HARA.html.*

2. M.E. Kabay, "The INFOSEC Year in Review 1997"; see: *www2.norwich.edu/mkabay/ iyir/1997.pdf.*

3. J. Kornblum, "Antispam Efforts Heat Up"; see: *http://news.cnet.com/news/0,10000,0-1005-200-324044,00.html.*

4. S. Covington, No. 97-06273 of the District Court of Travis County, Texas, 345th Judicial District; see: *www.mids.org/nospam/judgment.html.*

5. R. Clarke, "Human Identification in Information Systems: Management Challenges and Public Policy Issues," *Information Technology & People,* Vol. 7, No. 4 (1997): 6–37; online at: *www.anu.edu.au/people/Roger.Clarke/DV/HumanID.html.*

6. A.M. Froomkin, "Anonymity and Its Enmities," *Journal of Online Law,* 1995, article 4; see: *www.law.cornell.edu/jol/froomkin.htm.*

7. Clarke, "Human Identification in Information Systems."

8. Froomkin, "Anonymity and Its Enmities."

9. C. Free, "Make Their Day: Fury at the Wheel Turns Frustrated Drivers into Outlaw Dirty Harrys with a Rage for Revenge," *People Weekly,* Vol. 48, No. 9 (1997): 59.

10. G. Le Bon, *The Crowd: A Study of the Popular Mind.* New York: Macmillan, 1896.*

11. L. Festinger, A. Pepitone, and T. Newcomb, "Some Consequences of Deindividuation in a Group," *Journal of Abnormal and Social Psychology,* Vol. 47 (1952): 382–389.*

12. P. G. Zimbardo, "The Human Choice: Individuation, Reason and Order versus Deindividuation, Impulse, and Chaos," in W.J. Arnold and D. Levine, eds., *Nebraska Symposium on Motivation* (Lincoln: University of Nebraska Press, 1970).*

13. Free, "Make Their Day"; J.J. Russell, "The New Menace on the Road," *Good Housekeeping,* Vol. 224, No. 4 (1997): 100–110.

14. Zimbardo, "The Human Choice."

15. R.I. Watson, Jr., "Investigation into Deindividuation Using a Cross-Cultural Survey Technique," *Journal of Personality and Social Psychology,* Vol. 25 (1973): 342–345.*

16. J. H. Kerr, *Understanding Soccer Hooliganism.* Buckingham: Open University Press, 1994.*

17. B. Buford, *Among the Thugs* (London: Mandarin Paperbacks, 1991).

18. E. Diener, S.C. Fraser, A.L. Beaman, and R.T. Kelem, "Effects of Deindividuating Variables on Stealing by Halloween Trick-or-Treaters," *Journal of Personality and Social Psychology,* Vol. 33 (1976): 178–183.*

19. S. Prentice-Dunn and R.W. Rogers, "Effects of Deindividuating Situation Cues and Aggressive Models on Subjective Deindividuation and Aggression," *Journal of Personality and Social Psychology,* Vol. 39 (1980): 104–113*; E. Diener, "Deindividualtion, Self-Awareness, and Disinhibition," *Journal of Personality and Social Psychology,* Vol. 37 (1979): 1160–1171.*

20. M. Csikszentmihalyi, *Flow: The Psychology of Optimal Experience* (New York: Harper & Row, 1990).

21. C.B. Spivey and S. Prentice-Dunn, "Assessing the Directionality of Deindividuation: Effects of Deindividuation, Modeling, and Private Self-Consciousness on Aggressive and Prosocial Responses," *Basic and Applied Social Psychology,* Vol. 11 (1990): 387–403.*

22. K.J. Gergen, M.M. Gergen, and W.H. Barton, "Deviance in the Dark," *Psychology Today* (October 1973): 129–130.*

23. L. Detweiler, "Anonymity on the Internet FAQ" (1993); online at: *www.webster.edu/~bumbaugh/net/anonfaq.html;* L. Detweiler, "The Joy of Pseudospoofing" (1993); online at: *cypherpunks.venona.com/date/1993/10/msg01172.html.*

24. Detweiler, "Anonymity on the Internet FAQ."

25. R. Clarke, "Introduction to Dataveillance and Information Privacy, and Definitions of Terms"; online at: *www.anu.edu.au/people/Roger.Clarke/DV/Intro.html.*

26. Clarke, "Human Identification in Information Systems."

27. Detweiler, "Joy of Pseudospoofing."

28. Ibid.

29. O.S. Card, *Ender's Game* (New York: Tor Books, 1985).

30. Froomkin, "Anonymity and Its Enmities."

31. Ibid.

32. C. Johnson, "Anonymity On-line? It Depends on Who's Asking," *Wall Street Journal,* November 24, 1995, p. B1.

33. L. Lessig, D. Post, and E. Volokh, *Cyberspace Law for Non-Lawyers.* Lesson 23—Privacy 11: Privacy: Self-Help: Anonymity, Part 1. 1997; online at: *www.ssrn.com/update/lsn/cyberspace/lessons/priv11.html.*

34. L. Lessig, D. Post, and E. Volokh, *Cyberspace Law for Non-Lawyers.* Lesson 24—Privacy 12: Privacy: Self-Help: Anonymity, Part 2. 1997; online at: *www.ssrn.com/update/lsn/cyberspace/lessons/priv12.html.*

35. Clarke, "Introduction to Dataveillance and Information Privacy."

36. W. Rodger, "Zero-Knowledge to Close Anonymity Service" 2001; online at: *www.securityfocus.com/news/262.*

37. C. Pappas, "The A to Z of Internet Sleaze," *Home Office Computing,* Vol. 15, No. 8 (1997): 70.

38. Detweiler, "Anonymity on the Internet FAQ."

39. Clarke, "Introduction to Dataveillance and Information Privacy."

40. Froomkin, "Anonymity and Its Enmities"; A.M. Froomkin, "Flood Control on the Information Ocean: Living with Anonymity, Digital Cash and Distributed Databases," *University of Pittsburgh Journal of Law and Commerce,* Vol. 15 (1996): 395; online at: *www.law.miami.edu/~froomkin/articles/ocean1.htm.*

41. J. Ubois, "Anonymity Has Its Place," *MIDRANGE Systems,* Vol. 8, 8 (1995): 28.

42. Detweiler, "Anonymity on the Internet FAQ."

43. Ibid.

44. Froomkin, "Flood Control on the Information Ocean."

45. Ibid.

46. D. Post, "Knock Knock, Who's There? Anonymity and Pseudonymity in Cyberspace." 1995; online at: *www.cli.org/DPost/X0012_KNOCK.html.*

47. Clarke, "Introduction to Dataveillance and Information Privacy."

48. Detweiler, "Anonymity on the Internet FAQ."

49. Froomkin, "Anonymity and Its Enmities."

50. Froomkin, "Flood Control on the Information Ocean."

51. Detweiler, "Anonymity on the Internet FAQ."

52. Froomkin, "Anonymity and Its Enmities."

53. Post, "Knock Knock, Who's There?"

54. Detweiler, "Anonymity on the Internet FAQ."

55. L.J. Rose, *NetLaw: Your Rights in the Online World.* New York: Osborne/McGraw-Hill, 1994, pp. 183–184.

56. Froomkin, "Flood Control in the Information Ocean."

57. D. Post and D. R. Johnson, "The New Civic Virtue of the Net: Lessons from Models of Complex Systems," 1997; online at: *www.cli.org/paper4.htm.*

58. Ibid.; S.A. Kauffman, *The Origins of Order: Self-Organization and Selection in Evolution.* Oxford: Oxford University Press, 1993.

59. Post, "Knock Knock, Who's There?"

60. Post and Johnson, "New Civic Virtue of the Net."

61. M.E. Kabay, "Totem and Taboo: Civility and Vandalism in Cyberspace." Proceedings of the 17th National Computer Security Symposium, Baltimore, Maryland, October 11–14, 1994. Reprinted in *NCSA News* (June 1995): 4; online at: *www2.norwich.edu/mkabay/ethics/totem_taboo_cyber.pdf.*

62. P. Lewis, "Cloaks and Daggers: Online Anonymity Is a Blessing and a Curse," *Home Office Computing,* Vol. 14, No. 7 (1996): 133.

63. Post and Johnson, "New Civic Virtue of the Net."

64. VeriSign, "Introduction to Cryptography," 2000; online at: *www.verisign.com/docs/pk_intro.html;* RSADSI, "Frequently Asked Questions: Cryptography—The Latest from RSA Labs." 2001; online at: *www.rsasecurity.com/rsalabs/faq.*

65. Froomkin, "Anonymity and Its Enmities."

66. Lewis, "Cloaks and Daggers."

67. Lessig et al., *Cyberspace Law for Non-Lawyers,* Lesson 24.

68. D. McCullagh, (1997a). "Brick by Brick," The Netly News (Editorial), 1997; online at: *http://cgi.pathfinder.com/netly/editorial/0,1012,590,00.html.*

69. D. McCullagh, "Courts Strike Down New York and Georgia Net-Censorship Laws," sent Friday, June, 1997, 13:49:06 -0700 (PDT) on *www.fight-censorship-announce@vorlon. mit.edu* mailing list.

CHAPTER 54

THE FUTURE OF INFORMATION SECURITY

Peter Tippett

CONTENTS

54.1 RISK EQUATION. Many of the past and present criteria for evaluating and implementing computer security have proven to be only marginally effective, at best. This chapter presents the risk equation as another way to view the major elements of a sound computer security approach. The risk equation is useful to network administrators and security managers because it, better than anything else known, can clarify thinking and help to maintain a well-directed, effective security course well into the future.

There are many ways to look at risk and many subtle and substantial differences in the use of risk-related terms. In the following simple approach, developed at TruSecure—ICSA Labs, just four risk-related terms are tied together as a simple equation:

$$Risk = Threat \times Vulnerability \times Cost$$

54.1.1   Threat.   Threat is the frequency, or occurrence rate, of potentially adverse events. Since threat by this definition is always a frequency, it may be measured or estimated. Because the events are only potentially adverse, threat per se is not dangerous, detrimental, or even necessarily worth worrying about.

The threat of earthquakes greater than Richter 4 in Southern California is dozens per month. The threat rate of hurricanes that impact Florida averages 1.4 per year. The rate at which insiders use others' logged-in personal computers (PCs) to access restricted information is about 4 per 1,000 users per day. The rate of virus encounters by a 1,000 PC organization is about 88 per month. The frequency that Web sites are compromised worldwide is about 450 per day. The threat of "attack-related scans" against a single Internet provider (IP) address is about 12 per day, and so on.[1]

Threats for all major categories of security breaches—electronic, malicious code, privacy, downtime, physical and human factors—are increasing each year. However, two categories—electronic, with external hacking, and malware (malicious code), with its viruses, worms, and Trojans—are increasing at between two- and 20-fold per year whereas other threat rates are growing at a more modest 15 to 25 percent per year.[2] Exhibit 54.1 shows increases in the rates of Web defacements and of vulnerability *pings* over various short periods of time. Simple extrapolation can provide estimates of the vast increases to be expected in the near future.

Threats come in global and local occurrence rates. Local rates are considered since an organization, because of geography, status, political stance, or other reasons, may be exposed to more or fewer occurrences than the global rate for any given security event.

Many threats, particularly those driven by humans, change constantly. The rate of "attack-related scans" was up more than 20-fold in 2001, while the rate of virus encounters has about doubled each of the past five years. Furthermore, since much of the threat milieu is intentional and human-driven, there needs to be a way to predict the rate of

Exhibit 54.1   Examples of Changes
in Threat Rates

Web Defacements	Threat Rate
May 1999	15 per day
October 2000	61 per day
March 2001	180 per day
May 2001	580 per day

Vulnerability Pings	Threat Rate
September 1999	1 per 6 days
January 2000	1 per day
October 2000	5.5 per day

change of threat in the future as well as the natural rate of change of a particular threat through its life cycle.

The *ballistic threat model* describes the progression of threat from its smallest potential quantum, in which a particular vulnerability exists, through roughly order-of-magnitude jumps in the threat index, defined as the predictive *threat pressure*. For example, one such progression is shown in Exhibit 54.2. In this tabulation, the basic threat index is to be modified by an estimated value of the modifiers:

Exhibit 54.2   Ballistic Threat Model, Electronic Threat Category, Hacker-Related

Base Threat Index	Description
1	Vulnerability exists, but no one knows of it.
10	Someone knows, at least the developer.
100	Someone outside discovers or knows of it.
1,000	It has been published to many people.
10,000	A tool, with average availability, has been produced to exploit the vulnerability.
Vulnerability Knowledge Modifier	D—few people N—100s–1,000s A—very widely known
Anonymity Modifier	D—easy to identify the attacker N—some anonymity A—strong, and easy-to-get, anonymity
Ease-of-Use Modifier	D—source code must be modified N—compilation required A—"click here" to attack
Attack Vogue Modifier	D—copy cat, old technology N—average A—new, novel, by a popular author
Tool Availability Modifier	D—limited white-hat trust circle N—limited black-hat trust circle A—broad availability

Threat can then be quantified according to its current rate and its likely growth trend according to a ballistic model. The key to thinking about ballistic threat is either to estimate or determine the rate of the occurrence one is considering mitigating and to predict its future trend.

54.1.2   Vulnerability.   Vulnerability is the likelihood of success of a particular threat category against a particular organization. If this were the likelihood of success of a particular attack like the ping of death (a denial-of-service attack using malformed packets) against a particular machine, the likelihood would be either 0 or 1 (no possibility of success or entirely likely to succeed). But binary terms do not work when determining vulnerability to an entire class of threat at an organizational level, with perhaps 1,000 PCs and 50 servers configured and architected in a particular way. Instead, vulnerability is the probability of success, expressed as a percent.

The likelihood of success is not easy to measure, but a related term, *vulnerability prevalence,* is more so. Vulnerability prevalence is the number of organizations with machines of a particular type, say NT-based Web servers running IIS that are exposed to the Internet, and that exhibit the particular vulnerability in their current environment.

Many factors work together to make some machines vulnerable in their current environment and others not, even though the software, hardware, and data might be identical between machines. For example, router rules, firewall configuration, proxy settings, network address translation, location on a subnet, coexistence of other running processes, existence of data of certain types, secondary connections of certain types, and more all may change the likelihood of success of a particular threat.

Besides the modifiers of Exhibit 52.1, for hacking-related threats there are six primary drivers for the visibility of a particular vulnerability to an attacker:

1. Where the vulnerable machine is virtually located, relative to the attacker
2. Whether a particular service, or file, exists, is installed, or is running
3. Operating system, application, and service software versions, and their service pack levels
4. Whether or not particular patches or hot fixes have been applied
5. How the operating system and applications are configured
6. What other services and connections are also running

54.1.3   Cost and Economic Impact.   Event cost is the total cost in both *real* and *soft* dollars related to the total ramifications of a particular exploit experienced by a vulnerable target company or system. It includes not just the actual costs of overtime, food, and lodging that might be required to recover and harden a system after an attack, but also any hard dollars for equipment, software, technicians' time, and the like. Included *semihard* dollars consist of costs associated with transaction time increases, delays in producing reports, and so on. Softer costs include productivity losses caused by users' inability to work with a downed or altered system, public relations damage, user confidence damage, lost sales opportunity, lost business, and lost promotional opportunities.

54.1.4   Risk.   It is risk, not threat, vulnerability, or cost alone, that must be of concern. From the risk equation *Risk = Threat × Vulnerability × Cost,* it can be seen that for there to be any risk, there must be at least *some* threat *and* vulnerability *and* cost. Because anything multiplied by zero is zero, if any of the three components of risk is zero, then risk is also zero. This concept should be applied to evaluating any suggestion that some particular risk must be addressed and also to evaluating any proposed mitigation for the purported risk.

The question to be asked of any security proposal is "What is the risk here?" Most people suboptimize by worrying about threat, vulnerability, or cost instead of risk. Each component of risk should be either estimated or measured, but mainly in order to determine total risk. By studying each component, very often it will be concluded that there is no risk or at least no imminent risk because some component of risk is zero or negligibly low. Frequently, it will be concluded that there are very many things that are far more risky and that ought to be addressed first.

When it has been decided that there is real risk worth mitigating, the cost and value of the mitigation also should be estimated. Anything that mitigates risk must mitigate at least one of the three risk components; it must reduce threat, vulnerability, or cost.

Reducing vulnerability is the usual approach; indeed, it is the element where, generally, most control can be exercised. There are always places, other than the obvious, where vulnerability can be reduced at least partially, and where often it can be done easily and inexpensively. These partial solutions, called "synergistic controls," usually are overlooked, but they are exceedingly useful, especially together with other serially related, partial controls.

For example, suppose a particular control is very cheap and noninfringing (i.e., not interfering significantly with normal productivity) but is effective at mitigating only four out of five attacks in a particular category. The single control would be 80 percent effective, and most security practitioners might balk at utilizing such a control. On the other hand, if there were two controls, each of which was similarly effective and which acted independently of each other, then adding the second control would change the control failure rate from one in five to one in 25. So two synergistic controls would together be 96 percent effective. Three would fail at a rate of one in 125 or would demonstrate 99.2 percent effectiveness. This concept has been called "defense in depth." It is a much-confused concept primarily because some controls are independent of each other and some are not. Some act in parallel and some in series. Reducing the cost impact of a security event means either discovering a problem earlier or responding and recovering faster. Early discovery is the major function of intrusion detection systems, hashing strategies, log reviews, and alarms of various sorts. Rapid discovery and response relates to good fail-over, backups, disaster recovery plans, and an efficient, fully functioning Computer Incident Response Team.

Security managers should focus on real, relevant, present and near-term future risks by looking at their components. This total approach to security can be more effective, less expensive, and less intrusive than other methods.

54.2   SEVEN MACROTRENDS IN INTERNET SECURITY.   Seven important trends are changing the nature of information security today and are certain to be even more prominent in the future:

1. Increasing complexity drives accelerating growth in vulnerability.

2. Rapidly changing environment drives rapidly changing risks.

3. Greater all-to-all connectivity drives greater malicious connectivity.

4. Growth in Internet users drives growth in Internet abusers.

5. Internet anonymity drives the tendency toward abuse.

6. "E-democratization" provides greater power and access for abusers.

7. Lack of accepted security processes drives pursuit of dogma.

Unless these trends can be reversed, the future of Internet security will be even more problematic than it is today.

54.2.1   Increasing Complexity Drives Accelerating Growth in Vulnerability.   One of the earliest tenets of computer security relates to simplicity. No system can be proven to be secure unless all of its actions and interactions can be understood completely. In practical terms, the early security philosophers thought that software with no more than a few hundred lines of code, and without electronic interactions with other systems, might, with sufficient study, be understood well enough to permit a full description of the system's security.

Simplicity should be a driving force in security fundamentals. It provides the underpinnings for such basic concepts as least privilege, default deny, default disable, and secure architecture, among others.

The converse of the principle of simplicity suggests that the more complex a system, the more vulnerable it is and that a system's vulnerability is proportional to its complexity. However, it is more likely that the proportionality curve is upwardly curvilinear, that is, that vulnerability grows faster with complexity than would a straight-line function

The complexity of systems today is mind-boggling, especially when compared with the systems of more than 40 years ago. Where secure or semisecure systems then had no notion of networks, and had only a few hundred lines of well-understood code, usually from a single author or team, the typical system today is multinetworked, with tens of millions of lines of code—just to power the underlying operating system. Today's systems run applications created with millions more lines of code, utilizing collateral services, with numerous, often undocumented application program interfaces (APIs), multiple entry points, and parallel and multithreaded processing, often with very complex object dependencies. To make matters worse, portions of these incredibly complex systems are upgraded, patched, and changed by other applications, services, utilities, and many different manufacturers, all without anything like comprehensive regression testing.

The complexity and range of configurations possible with modern systems is immense, and growing rapidly. Identical systems with identical programming code behave differently, according to configuration options driven by multi-megabytes of configuration data. For example, in the Windows environment, the Registry, Metabase, start-up batches and folders, .INI files, and many other elements together typically constitute many thousands of individual settings. Therefore, the possible permutations are probably more than 21,000.

Of course, the complexity of networked systems does not stop there. Each of these incredibly complex systems is connected to other systems from the same, similar, and totally different code bases. Each is managed by people with the same, similar, and totally different goals, principles, motivations, time, knowledge, and experience.

Even if vulnerability is only linearly proportional to complexity, then we have very vulnerable systems, with no way reliably to achieve a secure stand-alone system, let alone a secure network. This analysis further suggests that the hundreds of vulnerabilities that are eventually discovered in a given system pale, probably by several orders of magnitude, in comparison to the total vulnerabilities that must actually be there, but that will never be discovered.

This line of reasoning also suggests that "security by obscurity" reflects the reality that probably millions of vulnerabilities exist in a given system but will never be discovered. Obscurity is the major mitigator to a large proportion of these vulnerabilities, but not to all. Every day new vulnerabilities are plucked out of obscurity into the glare of actual attacks.

The trend, of course, is for complexity to continue to increase and therefore for vulnerabilities to continue to grow.

54.2.2   Rapidly Changing Environment Drives Rapidly Changing Risks.   Systems are changing at an increasingly rapid rate, so vulnerabilities that arise out of failures to keep up with the changes will be more and more common.

Not only will this rate of change of security management failures grow and continue to worsen, but many security experts still do not fully understand the problem. Yet understanding this problem is central to achieving actual, meaningful, consistent, and continuous risk reduction. Worse still, some current security "best practices" and security management strategies—as evidenced by the actual practices, day-to-day recommendations, and activities of many security experts—are static, ineffective, and dogma-based. We cannot simply apply our current know-how and just do it faster.

We are not currently well-equipped to manage security dynamically in a rapidly changing world, and even our static focus often misses the point. Instead of addressing the easily mitigated, frequent, and costly risk, we commonly focus on low-likelihood threats against systems with low vulnerability and with low value of assets. Any analysis of real security breaches and losses almost always points to systems where numerous different mitigations were possible, most of which were well understood beforehand. Unfortunately, the mitigations were not even attempted, or were attempted but not working, or were not modified to keep pace with known changes in the risk landscape.

Not only does the rate of change of our systems provide new vulnerability, as demonstrated by the increased rate of security management failures, but the rate of change of threat is also increasing. Examples of these threats include increases in the types of attacks; the numbers of explicit attack vehicles, such as tools, scripts, and scams; and the number and diversity of those perpetrating the attacks. In addition, even the types of motivations for attacking may be increasing, as ideologues turn to information warfare to accomplish their ends. (See Chapter 7 for more details on information warfare.)

The value of information assets at risk is also accelerating in most environments. Therefore, all components of risk—vulnerability, threat, and cost or asset value—are each individually growing and changing rapidly.

54.2.3 Greater All-to-All Connectivity Drives Greater Malicious Connectivity. This might be the connectivity corollary to the system complexity trend discussed above. The more pathways between malicious people and vulnerable targets, the more malice-driven attacks there will be. The more accessible a given system is to larger numbers of other systems, the more vulnerable that system will be. The more protocols over old pathways, and the more pseudopathways, the more opportunity for malice.

Most people would agree that vulnerability is somehow proportional to connectivity. Many would even suggest that risk increases as something like the square of the number of independent connections. If either of these relationships is true, then risk certainly will rise based solely on connectivity.

When there were only mainframes, generally they were not connected to any other computers, except possibly to a very few similar systems in the same company, managed by the same people. When PCs began to proliferate, they too generally were not connected to other computing devices. As Local Area Networks (LANs) developed, initially they were not connected to other LANs; even when Wide Area Networks (WANs) began to interconnect LANs, there were few connections within the same company. With the initial movement to the Internet, computing resources were generally connected to a single, or at most a small number of, devices such as proxy servers, firewalls, and mail gateways, which were then connected to the Internet. The Internet, therefore, was originally composed of universities, laboratories, and companies connected to it, not of individual computing devices independently connected.

Today, not only are more users connected, but more pathways for connection exist among small devices, hand-held computers, beepers, wireless devices, beverage machines, traffic cameras, and the like. There are more and more protocols including streaming audio and video, management protocols, and instant messaging, to name a few. There is a trend for peer-to-peer connectivity, usually tunneling through ports such as http port 80, which are not individually fire-walled. This situation effectively means that the single-perimeter, guarded connections of corporate networks to the Internet are rapidly subverted to the equivalent of many-to-any, independent PCs-to-"direct" connections over pseudopathways.

The trend is toward more and more connectivity to more and more kinds of systems. Therefore, risk attributable to this trend is likely to grow at an accelerating pace.

54.2.4   Growth in Internet Users Drives Growth in Internet Abusers.   Most information risk involves human perpetrators. Some proportion of all people are, by nature or nurture, bad. As more and more people use the Internet, there will obviously be more and more bad people using the Internet. Therefore, as the total number of users of the common network grows, the trend is toward more and more malicious people performing more and more security exploits.

54.2.5   Internet Anonymity Drives Tendency toward Abuse.   Two distinct kinds of anonymity are embedded in the Internet or its culture: (1) "handles" or pseudonyms for people and machines, and (2) the inherent anonymity allowed in the communications protocols.

Multiple e-mail addresses are one kind of personal handle, as are handles or pseudonyms frequently used for chat, message boards, newsgroups, or even direct mail attribution. For access to data that requires "registration," it is usually possible to log in as Mickey Mouse with a sham address in Orlando, Florida. If access is available only to those over 21 years of age, it is no problem to claim to be 22. Without the physical presence, voice characteristics, community knowledge, and other attributes of the physical world, Internet users can, and routinely do, hide behind pseudonyms.

Those who are intentionally malicious, tend to be more aggressive at hiding behind handles and are more and more careful not to mix their handles with real, personally identifying information.

The basic protocols of the Internet support electronic anonymity. User Datagram Protocol (UDP) is connectionless, so source addresses are almost irrelevant. Transmission Control Protocol (TCP), which is used for many types of traffic, can be spoofed, meaning that the perpetrator can replace the return TCP address in the traffic header with a different one. In cases where spoofing does not allow for successful communication, it is easy to change the headers in e-mail messages. Anonymous remailers and anonymizing browsers provide the ability to subvert one system, then use that system to subvert another, and so on, all without revealing the true identity of the originator.

Attribution keeps honest people honest, but anonymity makes borderline people more likely to behave with malice. A 12-year-old standing in a candy store is more likely to steal a candy bar if there is no-one anywhere in the store than if the storekeeper is nearby. The youngster is even less likely to shoplift if his aunt, school principal, or another person who knows him is nearby.

This is the only trend of the seven in this section where there is any chance of improvement. Handle anonymity probably will continue for many practical social reasons, but it is unlikely to grow significantly. Without electronic protocol anonymity to support it, handles themselves will have less and less value to criminals and malicious perpetrators. To deny nonauthenticated connections, the following measures should be considered:

- Good authentication and cryptographic authentication procedures
- Moving the Internet to IPv6, which includes source address authentication

- Utilizing more and more Virtual Private Networks (VPNs) with cryptographic authentication

- Achieving critical mass using client-side certificates in, for example, Secure Sockets Layer (SSL)

- Implementing Robert Moskowitz's Host Identity Payload (HIP) to allow for good, lightweight authentication at lower Open Systems Interconnect (OSI) layers, even with low-power, mobile devices[3]

If these measures are implemented, then more and more computing platforms will be able to deny all nonauthenticated connections. When this day arrives, remote abuse will decrease markedly because it will be too easy to get caught.

The trend, however, is for continued worsening of the anonymity problem, and therefore risk, over the next two or three years, followed by the beginnings of a turnaround.

54.2.6 "E-Democritization" Drives Greater Power and Access for Abusers.   In the 1950s and 1960s, when computers were mainframes and users were forced to hand in their card decks to technicians in a computer room so they could receive output an hour later, using computers was more like praying to a deity than like using a utility. The total number of people with direct access to computers was in the thousands at most.

In the 1970s and 1980s, as networking allowed increasing numbers of employees to use remote computers, the total number of computer users rose into the hundreds of thousands. Access originally was limited to authorized users of internal networks requiring direct physical connections to the computers. Later, the use of modems opened up such access to millions, as PCs began to spread outside the corporate environment.

Underlying the increasing number of computers is Moore's law, which in one form states that the cost of any given level of processing power declines by half roughly every 12 to 18 months. For example, a single megabyte of random access memory (RAM) cost $64,000 in 1980 but only $0.31 in 2001. Also in 2001, a computer running a 2.0 gigahertz processor cost less than half the price of a computer running at a 4 megahertz clockspeed in 1983. As a result of this astonishing decline in cost, personal ownership of computers in the United States rose from 1 percent of the population in 1980 to around 66 percent in 2001.

When the Internet opened up in a major way to users in the .com domain in the early 1990s, the number of networked users exploded. As of January 2001, there were more than 109 million hosts registered on the Domain Name System.[4] The total number of Internet users was estimated to be 513 million as of August 2001.[5] Anyone who can access the Internet can attempt to access every single host connected to the Internet. The difficulties of the defensive role in information technology have thus grown by orders of magnitude within a single human life span, with much more to come.

Another aspect of the democratization of information technology is that an increasing number of tools are available to automate attacks. In the early days of modem use, attackers might spend hours manually dialing numbers to locate other modems; that problem was quickly resolved by war dialers—programs to dial all the numbers in an exchange automatically and to record which numbers had modem tones. The limitations of human speed and attention were overcome by automation. Today, automated attack scripts allow even untrained children to scan thousands of systems per hour, effortlessly, in order to locate vulnerable computers susceptible to hosting distributed denial-of-service clients. Unless these unwanted tools can be controlled, the future will be even more chaotic than it is now.

54.2.7   Lack of Accepted Security Processes Drives the Pursuit of Dogma.   Security dogma fixes on the wrong issues and will continue to do so.

We spend significant money and human capital on some things that not only have minimal security value but actually cost far more than any possible gain. That is, they wind up being on the wrong side of the cost-benefit equation. This section illustrates the dangers of security dogma by analyzing password policies and applications.

54.2.7.1   Password Policies.   For typical office end users, so called *strong* passwords, such as those with seven, eight, or more characters composed of numbers, letters, and special characters, may have had merit at one time, but they no longer do.

It is not that strong passwords do not work, so we should go to something stronger like tokens; instead, we should seriously consider recognizing the fact that passwords are usually ineffectual and paradoxically that going with something easier, such as simple passwords for the majority of our users, will suffice.

Passwords typically are not stored in their native form, and they are not really encrypted either. Instead, passwords are "hashed." The password file typically contains a user ID and the hash of the user's password. Names like SHA or MD5 (or even CRC or Checksum) all refer to different hashing algorithms, although the first two are cryptographically far superior to the latter two. It is possible to hash the entire Bible and represent it as eight bytes of gibberish. Obviously there is no way to go from the eight bytes with any algorithm and ever get the Bible back. So hashes are truly one-way functions; there is no reversing them.

What are the actual risks that strong passwords are purported to mitigate? Actually there are only two: someone might (1) steal the password file or (2) listen in, or sniff, on the wire while someone is logging in, and capture the user ID and password hash pairs, then run one of the many tools generically called Crack. Since you cannot decrypt a hash back to a password, what Crack does is to guess a password—say helloworld. It then runs the hash function against it, checking to see if the result is the same as one of the hashed entries in the password file. If it is, then that password hash represents the password "helloworld," if not, then Crack takes another guess. Crack programmatically tries all the words in a dictionary and all the names in a phone book, mixes in names of football teams, and for good measure throws in a few numbers and special characters to each of these. If any of the passwords in the password file contain any of the guesses, then Crack gives the attacker the real password to use when logging in. Strong passwords with mixed numbers, special characters, and perhaps both upper- and lowercase letters were promulgated to solve this so-called dictionary attack.

There are three related problems:

1. Strong password policies work only for very small groups of people. In real companies they fail miserably.

2. With modern processing power, even strong passwords are no match for modern versions of Crack.

3. Strong passwords are incredibly expensive to maintain and manage in an organization.

Strong password policies can work only in small companies, with few computer users and tight supervision . On the other hand, with a typical strong password policy in a 1,000-user organization, just over 50 percent, or only about 500 users, actually will succeed at creating a password that meets the policy. With subliminal messages on piped-in sound, mouse pads promoting the value of strong passwords, and full management buy-in, good companies only get up to 80 percent compliance. Even with software that will not accept "bad" passwords, it is rare that a company can run such software on most devices. If a company is beyond good, and gets to 90 percent compliance, an attacker who gets a password file and runs Crack will get about 100 user ID—password pairs to log in with. For the company, 100 is not significantly better than 500; either way, the attacker can log in.

The combination of common desktop processors, good hash dictionaries, and algorithms to deal with numbers, special characters, and capitalization means that, even if 100 percent of users had passwords that meet the policy, the cracking tools would still win; it is just a matter of time. Typical cracking tools against a 1,000-password file will get 15 percent, or 150 passwords, in a few hours, even if they are all "strong" passwords. This is because, if the dictionary attack fails, the tools generally use an algorithmic attack. That is, they are quite good at putting numbers before and after each dictionary item and generating a hash for each, then putting special characters through different positions in a dictionary item and capitalizing most likely places in the guessed passwords.

If the dictionary attack and the algorithmic attacks both fail, which is rather unlikely, then all modern cracking programs simply do an "exhaustive" attack that is neither difficult nor time-consuming. For example, if the network in question has any Windows 95, 98, or ME devices, the password system must support the LanManager password hash mechanism. Although that mechanism tried for 14-byte hashes, it really is two different seven-byte hashes that are solved independently by the cracking brute-force program. This means that no matter how long a password, the cryptographic problem generally is solved by a seven-byte, brute-force attack. Also, a seven-byte password actually is derived from far less than a seven-byte keyspace. Since passwords must be typed by a user at a real keyboard, all come from the "lower half" of the ASCII character set. That leaves out significantly more than half of the possible keyspace. For all of these reasons, brute force is normally not needed, but if it is, it is relatively easy with modern processing power.

Real money is spent in both dollars of salary and in human resources trying to support strong passwords. The second or third most expensive aspect of most help desks is directly related to resetting forgotten passwords, which would not be as likely to be forgotten if they were not so convoluted. Many companies have whole permanent sections of the help desk dedicated to just resetting passwords for users. In addition to the costs for help desk password resets, real productivity is lost when users struggle for minutes or hours before calling the help desk. Real costs and political capital costs also are incurred in training personnel as well as in promulgating, administering, and reinforcing the policy.

Here, then, is an expensive policy that drains valuable resources, that never achieves 100 percent compliance (anything less than 100 percent is about the same as no compliance at all), and even if it achieves 100 percent compliance, there is password-cracking software available to any malefactor. A lot of expense and little security gain.

So what is the solution? In the old days, it was conceptually possible to beat password cracking with strong passwords. Nowadays it is not even worth thinking about. If the mitigation has little value and lots of cost, then it might well be abandoned.

We could make passwords truly strong, say with two-factor authentication using tokens or pins, plus biometrics, for every single person in an organization. Or we could recognize that 95 percent of users could do with simple passwords—good enough to keep a person from guessing it using a keyboard within five attempts. Four or five characters, without names, initials, or sports teams, and changed once or twice a year, probably has security equivalent to our current strong passwords but would be remarkably easier to train and maintain, and would yield more user productivity and less support costs—all at no measurable security degradation.

Under this scenario, the super-strong passwords or tokens would be reserved for the 5 percent of system administrators who really yield a large span of control over many accounts or devices or for users who authorize a money transfer, or large purchases, or who can access credit card information. Everyone else could use simple passwords as described above. This simpler system would be remarkably easier to implement and maintain, and would yield more user productivity with much lower support costs— all at no measurable security degradation.

This simple system requires that the password file be made extremely difficult to steal. For added security, that system could be combined with measures to mitigate sniffing—for example, network segmentation, or desktop automated inventory for sniffers as well as for other electronic malice tools such as keystroke capture programs or spyware. A stronger step would be encrypting all network traffic, with IPSec on every desktop and server—a solution that for many applications is both impractical and impracticable.

It *is* possible to cut costs and disruption for both users and management and to get a real budget for solving real security problems with practical, effective controls. To do so, however, it is necessary to think clearly about the vulnerability, threat, and cost of each risk, compared with the cost of its mitigation, and then to find a solution with greater security impact, at even less cost.

54.2.7.2 *Encryption.*   Encryption is one more security measure that seems like the right thing to do but clearly demonstrates a lack of focus on the prevalent, pressing security issues.

Probably the biggest failure in implementing good corporate security is misdirected focus. Of course, when fires are raging, the focus is on extinguishing those fires, and these reactive processes take precedence over proactive, preventive activities. But even when attention is paid to *preventing* problems, the resulting actions often are misdirected toward what peers, security experts, auditors, regulators, and common sense tell us is important or effective. Unfortunately, what seems the right thing to do often is not.

For example, there is a prevailing belief that encryption is valuable in protecting sensitive information, such as credit card numbers, in transit across the Internet. For more than 15 years there has been a growing movement toward Internet encryption. The argument: Because the Internet uses packet switching rather than circuit switching, all traffic is part of giant party lines—easily sniffed, eavesdropped, snooped, or wiretapped by almost anyone with a packet sniffer and a little ambition. There are incessant reminders to make sure that all browsers are in secure mode, with the lock icon closed, whenever sensitive information like addresses and credit card numbers are submitted to Web sites.

There have been constant reminders that 40-bit encryption in default browsers can easily be broken with an old desktop PC in a day. Therefore, it is said, 56-, 64-, or 128-bit encryption should be used. It has been estimated that it would take a week for 1,000 desktop computers, using brute-force methods, to break a 56-bit encoded message, or a century for all the computers on the planet to break a 128-bit encryption. Some security people even recommend 256-bit encryption for 10,000 + years of protection.

Application of the risk equation *Risk = Threat × Vulnerability × Cost* can help to clarify the encryption issue. The risk that is mitigated by encrypting e-commerce transactions is the risk of someone's gaining useful information by eavesdropping on traffic somewhere between its origin and the destination—that is, by sniffing across the Internet—and then by decrypting the data. In order to determine the risk, it is only necessary to measure or estimate

- The *vulnerability,* as the likelihood of success or vulnerability prevalence
- The *threat* as the frequency of successes
- The *cost* of a successful security breach

So what is the *vulnerability* of Internet sniffing? The likelihood of successful sniffing somewhere between a home or office and an e-commerce Web server appears to be incredibly low, perhaps as low as 10^{-7}. A few years ago, at an ISP Backbone Security Consortium meeting (ISPsec Consortium), one discussion centered on a problem that MCI and other Internet service providers (ISPs) were having in fulfilling a wiretap request from the FBI. The court ordered the ISP to write to disk a week's worth of data from an OC3 Internet pipe that it maintained, for later analysis. After many months of technical work with the fastest processors and disk arrays obtainable, and with the development of a (now-public) tool called OC3mon, the team was able to sniff the *headers only* from the wire and provide it to law enforcement.

In the three years that have passed since that meeting, Moore's law shows that processors are perhaps three times faster, and disk drives perhaps two times faster, but today an OC3 pipe would be a rare, slow vestige. Today, much of the Internet moves at OC192, more than 60 times faster. That means that sniffing, even for a backbone ISP, just got many times harder.

There is also the problem of which optical fiber to sniff. In an underground location there may be many cables, with some 100,000 fibers in each. Locating a particular strand is nearly impossible, as is isolating and bending it in such a way as to record the light pulses, without breaking the strand. To do so at any of the switching points is virtually impossible as well, due to their very good physical security. To further complicate the problem for sniffers, the packets into which every message is broken may travel over several different fibers. The only alternative to sniffing somewhere in the middle is to sniff at the end points. But at the end points, especially for something like Secure Sockets Layers, the encryption also ends. Therefore, the protection that encryption might provide ends, as well.

It is obvious, then, that the *vulnerability* for sniffing Internet traffic is low whether encrypted or not. But the risk equation, since it involves multiplication, shows that something small times something big might still yield a significant risk, so the *threat* also must be considered.

The best measure of *threat* in this context comes from risk-group research, carried out over five years, in which the following groups were repeatedly queried for data, statistics, or case studies of credit card theft by sniffing the public Internet: law enforcement including the National Infrastructure Protection Center (NIPC), the FBI, Scotland Yard, and the Royal Canadian Mounted Police; credit card companies including Visa, MasterCard, American Express, and Discover; financial regulators including the Federal Deposit Insurance Corporation (FDIC) and the Federal Reserve; hundreds of banks, merchants, and ISPs large and small; security and fraud professionals; and even some in the malicious hacker community.

In over five years, not one of these groups has come up with even a single case of credit card fraud by sniffing the public Internet. This cannot be considered evidence of successful encryption, because informed sources estimate that even in the year 2000, less than half of the credit card numbers traveling across the Internet were encrypted by any means. For the remaining half, more than 70 percent of browsers in the Western world only support 40-bit encryption. Business-to-business (B2B) sites still largely use private, unencrypted lines, or the 56-bit Data Encryption Standard (DES). So, the *threat* at least by the measure of successful attacks, or knowledge of attempts, appears to be no more than zero.

The third factor is *cost.* For consumers, the loss of credit card information recently has been reduced to a minor inconvenience. Any discovered fraudulent use of a card results in a new one arriving in the mail in a few days. Some credit cards go beyond the common waiver of a maximum potential $50 loss, to include things like a guaranteed refund, even if the Web-based merchant goes out of business between the time a purchase is billed and its attempted return. Merchants, banks, and credit card providers accrue a significant cost due to credit card fraud, with merchants shouldering the greatest burden. For consumers, the direct cost of credit card fraud is not zero, but it is usually very low.

The *risk* of credit card fraud by sniffing the public Internet, then, has a very low *vulnerability index,* times an *occurrence rate* approaching zero, times a small *cost.* The product of these three very small numbers equals an extremely small number indeed.

For the same reasons that credit card sniffing across the public Internet is not a real risk worth worrying about, neither is sniffing other sensitive information. This has not always been true, but even as the sniffing technology improves, the security of the public Internet improves even more rapidly. Sniffing is still a real risk on slow segments, on wireless links, and inside an organization's perimeter, but not on the public Internet.

Of course, credit cards are stolen frequently. Only in the last 24 months has the e-theft rate approximated the physical theft rate. Even for credit cards stolen in electronic form, until about two years ago, the primary method required people to be physically present, with local access to systems containing credit card information. Since then, e-credit cards have been stolen mostly by malicious hacking into Web sites.

The recent "million credit card theft" from more than 40 e-commerce sites, along with other exploits, demonstrates that the number-one e-credit card problem is focusing on the wrong protective measures. Instead of addressing the top four well-known and easily fixed server vulnerabilities, or setting up enforceable schedules to make sure Internet-facing machines are patched and updated for security fixes at least every three months, money and resources are spent on pervasive and unprovable Internet security myths. Internet sniffing is no part of the credit card theft problem, and no amount of transit encryption has any real value, despite "common sense" and expert opinion.

54.2.8   Five Microtrends in Internet Security.   In addition to the broad Internet-related trends discussed above, there are five security-specific trends that will determine future security strategies:

1. Threat rates will continue to increase.

2. Unchecked corporate vulnerabilities will increase.

3. Costs will increase.

    a. The cost of electronic assets protected will continue to rise.

    b. Spending on security mitigation will increase.

    c. The cost and impact of adverse security events will increase.

4. Therefore, corporate electronic risk will continue to increase across the board.

    a. The malicious code problem will worsen.

    b. Outside malicious hacking will worsen.

    c. Intentional insider abuse will worsen.

5. The solution: A dynamic, holistic, security process, focused on real risk, will be recognized as the sensible approach to security management.

54.3 DYNAMIC, HOLISTIC SECURITY PROCESS. We need to focus on demonstrably important, practicable risk management measures, not on prophylaxis for theoretically interesting but rare or nonexistent risks.

54.3.1 Strongest Security: Fix Simple Things, and Repeat Often. Virtually all successful Internet attacks succeed by exploiting easy things, yet top priority continues to be assigned to fixing the hard things.

A study of the attack vector used in 2,100 Web site defacements during March 2001 showed that 88 percent were due to an old vulnerability where the system manufacturer had issued an alert or advisory and had provided a patch or other mitigation at least six months prior to the attack. In addition, 94 percent of the attacks exploited vulnerabilities that were known and published more than three months prior to the attacks. It follows that an organization adhering to a simple, semiannual maintenance schedule for its Web servers would experience a nearly 10-fold risk reduction compared with an organization that did not. A quarterly, simple maintenance schedule would lead to more than a 16-fold risk reduction for electronic attacks against Internet-facing Web sites.

Any organization should be able to spare a half day, four times per year, for someone to check with vendors or security partners to make sure that software versions, essential configurations, and relevant security patches are all up-to-date. Observing this practice is probably stronger than any other mitigations against Web site hacking. In fact, it may be stronger than all others combined, but most organizations do not have such a simple mechanism in place.

54.3.2 It Takes Three Mistakes to Kill You. Pilots often say that it almost always takes three mistakes to kill you; any interruption in the chain of errors may save the day. The same is largely true for network security losses.

Consider 53 very public malicious Web site attacks in 2000 where credit card information was stolen: Western Union lost 17,000, American Israel Public Affairs Committee lost hundreds, and CD Universe lost over 100,000 credit cards, when their Web sites were breached. In addition, in early 2001, the FBI reported a Russia-based group had successfully stolen credit card information from 50 commerce Web sites. TruSecure analysis showed that all of these attacks were successful because at least three different, simple security "mistakes" were all required for the attacks to succeed:

1. All sites had unnecessary services running, or configuration errors, on the Web server that were part of the exploit.

2. All lacked important security patches that had been known for at least six months.

3. All kept credit card numbers in a database, in a "temporary" file on the Internet-exposed Web server, or on a drive shared with that Web server.

Had any of these sites not had all three mistakes, they would not have lost credit card information to the attacker.

During mid-2001, the Code Red worm and its variants successfully breached over 500,000 Windows computers running the IIS Web server, although the patch for the explicit vulnerability was released by Microsoft about a month before the attacks began. Several other well-known security practices also would have been effective, but they were not in general use. The Microsoft IIS Security checklist, along with other more proprietary security configuration guides, provided at least two other configuration suggestions that, if followed, would have been at least as effective as the month-old security patch. These recommendations were known and published at least two years before the specific vulnerability was discovered, yet they were largely unutilized.

During 2000 and early 2001, over 80 percent of attacks on NT-based Web servers were apparently exploited through the Remote Data Services (RDS) vulnerability. Over 70 percent of the successful attacks on Unix-based Web servers were due to WU File Transfer Protocol (WU-FTP) or unused remote services, although these were well known to be the number-one vulnerabilities for both NT and Unix environments. By early 2001, the RDS vulnerability was over two years old. It was well understood and its mitigations were widely published in 1998 and again in 1999. It became the number-one Web site attack in October 1999 and held that position for well over a year afterward. In October 1999, when the attacks began, and for a full year and a half after the first security bulletins became public, about 44 percent of Internet-facing NT-based Web sites were vulnerable. A year later, about 28 percent were still vulnerable. There were at least three fixes, all easy: (1) delete a file, (2) turn off the RDS service through a registry key or (3) use third-party tools.

The Unix issues are almost identical. The most exploited vectors were directed against services the user did not use and usually did not even know were installed and running. Most Web sites were attacked through Sysadmin-d, r-services, or WU-FTP. In almost every case, the service could be blocked from access to the Internet or completely turned off, since these attacked services are almost never in actual use by the site. If they *are* used, patches must be installed to eliminate the vulnerabilities, or it might be preferable to turn off FTP and deal with any complaints that might arise.

In summary, the top three fixes for hacking are very simple:

1. Turn off all unneeded services on boxes exposed to the Internet
2. Patch Internet-exposed boxes on a schedule of at least every three months.
3. Do not use Web servers for anything else—no DNS, no database, no mail, nothing.

54.3.3 Coping with Malicious Code. The Melissa virus was a .DOC macrovirus that invoked a local mail client to mail itself to the top 50 people on local address books. Some 20 percent of North American companies experienced Melissa somehow, and 15 percent of them had a "disaster" from it. A disaster is defined as an incident where more than 25 computers have the same virus at the same time. Likewise, the Lovebug worm, contained in e-mail with a .SCR attachment that used the Windows scripting facility to similarly mail itself to others, was encountered by 61 percent of North American companies and caused a disaster at about 42 percent. More than a year passed between these viruses. The most persistent remailer virus, Happy 99, has caused probably as much damage as Melissa, but over a much longer time period. And in the past few months, Win32 viruses (almost all .EXE or .SCR file attachments) are gaining ground.

In the virus prevalence survey cited earlier, it was found that less than half of companies used perimeter antivirus products, and less than 10 percent used generic virus protection, such as file filtering, at the perimeter. If e-mail attachments with a dozen file types, including .EXE, and .SCR, were filtered out, there would be no problem from these "surprise" viruses, even without up-to-date antivirus software.

These defenses are quick, easy, and inexpensive to install. They require almost no maintenance, and they work, without installing or maintaining Public Key Infrastructure (PKI) for everyone, call-back modems, intrusion detection systems (IDS), complex passwords, or anything else of marginal value.

54.3.4   Insider Threats.   The same simple approach that can be effective against outside attacks will work as well within an organization. Probably the most prevalent inside exploit occurs when one person uses another's already logged-in PC to gain entry to that person's data and access privileges. There is no hacking involved. Hardening the database server would not help, nor would IDS or most other security measures in place. The easiest, most certain way to stop the number-one inside attack vector is to use the screen saver provided with every desktop operating system. It need not be a secure screen saver, and users can choose any password at all. The password need not be eight characters of three different data types; even an easily remembered word will do, and changing the password once a year is probably enough. This will not prevent a brute-force, tool-oriented attack, but it will prevent a person physically present at the keyboard from trying to find a usable password before getting caught. The Windows screen saver on Windows 95 or 98 is easily circumvented by rebooting, but rebooting requires logging in to the server, which the average inside attacker does not attempt to do. If the system does log in to the server, there will often be a record in the audit trail—a fact that may deter abusers.

54.3.5   Effective Risk Management.   The approaches just described will reduce risk from malicious code and from hackers in most organizations by more than 10-fold and by more than 25-fold in some. None is particularly intrusive, expensive, or maintenance-demanding. Together they are stronger than any new technology, replacement firewall, new architecture, intrusion detection, or almost anything else now available.

To avoid a future beset with the same security ills as the past, these simple fixes must be implemented and tested repeatedly. The recent penetration of Microsoft's source code for their new operating system came from at least three vulnerabilities: (1) no firewall at a remote office, (2) no (or a very old) anti-virus program in a developers' environment, and (3) a wide-open pipe from the remote office to the innards of Microsoft.

No other security measures should be undertaken until these easy remedies have been applied and proved to be working.

54.4   ENVISIONING THE FUTURE.   There is an old Chinese curse: May you live in interesting times. How much better would our world be if wars, terrorism, famine, disease, and other such "interesting" events were not to occur.

However, for the foreseeable future, both in the computer world and in the wider one beyond, there will continue to be many interesting events, some predictable, others unimaginable. There is no more important task for computer security personnel than to ensure a future in which computer systems, and the people who operate and are affected by them, live in circumstances that are predictably routine.

It is the goal of this *Handbook* to equip information technology practitioners and functional managers with the theory and practical knowledge of techniques for minimizing or eliminating the threats, vulnerabilities, and costs that might otherwise be overwhelming.

The ends are of critical importance, while the means are almost entirely within the grasp of competent personnel. With determination, with the commitment of all concerned, and with the financial and organizational support of top management, the term "interesting" may revert to a more desirable meaning—holding the attention with pleasant and rewarding events or concepts. This was always the promise of computers and computer systems. With appropriate emphasis on computer security, the promise actually may be fulfilled.

54.5   NOTES

1. All mid-2000 data from ICSA Labs.
2. ICSA Labs quarterly threat data, June 2001.
3. See *http://homebase.htt-consult.com/~hip.*
4. Internet Domain Survey, January 2001: *www.isc.org/ds.*
5. "How Many Online?" NUA Surveys: *www.nua.ie/surveys/how_many_online.*

INDEX